9-29 (a) LIFO, $24,300; weighted average, $26,100
9-30 (a) $90,000
9-31 (b) Weighted average
9-32 (a)(1) $28,770
9-33 (a) Cost-to-retail percentage, 69%
9-34 (a) $42,000
9-35 No key figure
9-36 No key figure
9-37 (a) Apr. 29 inventory balance, $5,665
9-29A (a) FIFO, $56,600
9-30A (a) $88,000
9-32A (a)(2) $42,350
9-33A (a) Cost-to-retail percentage, 62%
9-36A No key figure
9-37A (b) June 29 inventory balance, $2,740
Business Decision Problem No key figure

10-29 Building, $2,804,200
10-30 (a) $87,900 allocated to Land
10-31 (b) Year 2, $18,000; (c) year 2, $16,000
10-32 No key figure
10-33 19X3 depreciation, $2,070
10-34 (a) 19X3 depreciation, $6,000
10-35 No key figure
10-29A Land, $244,600
10-30A (a) $79,500 allocated to Trucks
10-31A (b) 19X3, $31,200; (c) 19X3, $27,000
10-33A 19X5 depreciation, $2,380
10-34A (b) $27,700
Business Decision Problem No key figure

11-29 (d) Loss of sale of plant assets, $8,000
11-30 No key figure
11-31 (b) $30,000
11-32 No key figure
11-33 (b) Depreciation, $115
11-34 Total assets, $810,000
11-29A (f) Theft loss, $5,100
11-30A No key figure
11-31A (c) $91,800
11-33A No key figure
11-34A Total assets, $1,780,000
Business Decision Problem No key figure

12-24 (a) $4,500
12-25 (a) Payroll payable, $65,880
12-26 Sales tax liability, $6,400
12-27 (a) Payroll payable, $70,720
12-28 (a) Total net earnings, $1,513.92
12-24A (a) $3,300
12-25A (a) Payroll payable, $54,300
12-26A Sales tax liability, $11,520
12-27A (a) Payroll payable, $48,640
12-28A (a) Total net earnings, $1,585.41
Business Decision Problem No key figure

13-28 No key figure
13-29 (a) May, $2,700 loss
13-30 (b)(2) 19X8, $45,360
13-31 (b)(2) 19X2, $4,200,000
13-32 No key figure
13-33 (a) Total assets, $2,114,000
13-34 (a) Net income, $17,000
13-28A No key figure
13-30A (b)(2) 19X[illegible]
13-31A (b)(2) [illegible]
13-33A (b) 19X[illegible]
13-34A (a) Net [illegible]
Business Decision Problem 19X1 revenue, $140,000

14-26 (a)(3) Credits to capital: Martin, $9,000; Johnson, $7,000
14-27 (a)(3) Credits to capital: Read, $7,500; Kell, $7,500; Turner, $15,000
14-28 (c) Credits to capital: Barton, $1,000; Kelly, $1,000; Dorn, $14,000
14-29 (c) Debits to capital: Perry, $60,000; Gibbs, $2,000; Lane, $2,000
14-30 (b) Capital balances: Bell, $30,000; Harms, $27,000
14-31 Ending capital balance for Lewis, $74,000
14-32 (a) Cash distribution: Ray, $20,000; Mack, $74,000; Clark, $36,000
14-33 (b)(4) Cash distribution: Burt, $40,000; Dawes, $12,000
14-26A (a)(3) Credits to capital: Holt, $11,000; Wilson, $7,000
14-27A (a)(3) Credits to capital: Brady, $15,360; Flood, $13,440; Gann, $19,200
14-28A (c) Credits to capital: Casey, $4,000; Dobson, $4,000; Gordon, $23,000
14-29A (c) Debits to capital: Nunn, $60,000; Archer, $6,000; Kyle, $6,000
14-32A (a) Cash distribution: Barr, $5,000; Steele, $19,000; Timm, $36,000
14-33A (b)(4) Cash distribution: Upton, $94,000; Wild, $46,000
Business Decision Problem No key figure

15-27 (b) Total stockholders' equity, $1,917,500
15-28 (b) Dividends: preferred, $320,000; common, $128,000
15-29 (c) Total stockholders' equity, $1,647,000
15-30 (b) $19 per share
15-31 (a) Preferred stock, $104; common stock, $39.60
15-32 (c) Total stockholders' equity, $1,575,800
15-33 No key figure
15-27A (b) Total stockholders' equity, $1,565,000
15-28A (b) Dividends: preferred, $81,000; common, $99,000
15-29A (c) Total stockholders' equity, $2,034,000
15-31A (a) Preferred stock, $77; common stock, $21.88
15-32A (c) Total stockholders' equity, $2,033,300
Business Decision Problem (a) Total assets, $352,300

16-27 (a) Net income, $59,500
16-28 (a) $3.90
16-29 Net income, $71,400
16-30 (b) $213,000
16-31 (b) Total year-end retained earnings, $348,000
16-32 (b) Total year-end retained earnings, $608,210
16-33 (c) Total stockholders' equity, $1,894,300
16-27A (a) Net income, $162,000
16-28A (a) $5.20

FOURTH EDITION

PRINCIPLES OF ACCOUNTING

PAUL H. WALGENBACH
The University of Wisconsin

ERNEST I. HANSON
The University of Wisconsin

NORMAN E. DITTRICH
The University of Tennessee

HBJ

HARCOURT BRACE JOVANOVICH, PUBLISHERS

SAN DIEGO NEW YORK CHICAGO AUSTIN
LONDON SYDNEY TOKYO TORONTO

ISBN: 0-15-571375-2
Library of Congress Catalog Card Number: 85-82649
Printed in the United States of America

Illustrations by Evanelle Towne.

PREFACE

Like its earlier editions, the Fourth Edition of *Principles of Accounting* provides a comprehensive first course in accounting for students planning a career in the field as well as for students desiring a general understanding of the subject. We present a balance of conceptual and procedural material for both financial and managerial accounting, using carefully designed examples and illustrations, a variety of interesting problems, and a complete program of study aids integrated with the textbook.

New features in this edition include the following:

- Chapter objectives appear at the beginning of each chapter. These objectives also serve as an outline in the instructor's manual; all questions, exercises, and problems are keyed to these objectives in the manual.

- Self-test questions have been added at the end of each chapter to assist students in reviewing the key ideas in the chapter. Answers are provided with the end-of-chapter material.

- Comprehensive problems are provided at the end of the six major divisions of the text. Each problem is based on real-life data, generally taken from annual reports of actual companies. The sixth comprehensive problem covers the latest available annual report data of Whirlpool Corporation.

- New material on segment and department performance analysis has been introduced in Chapter 25, "Special Analysis for Management."

- New exhibits have been added to help students with difficult material. Examples include the relationship between plant asset control accounts and the related subsidiary ledger in Chapter 11 and the relationship between multiple inventory accounts, manufacturing cost categories, the manufacturing process, and the selling process in Chapter 21.

- Increased emphasis has been given to the application of managerial accounting concepts to service industries in the form of boxed inserts on hospital accounting

(Chapter 22) and restaurant accounting (Chapter 24) and a comprehensive problem on accounting firms (Part 5).

- An appendix on international accounting has been included in this edition in response to the requests of users who wish to introduce this subject in a fairly nontechnical fashion.

- Brief descriptions of all exercises and problems have been placed in the margins beside end-of-chapter material to aid instructors in selecting assignment material and students in identifying the focus of the material.

- Completely up-to-date discussions of FASB pronouncements are incorporated in the Fourth Edition, including the new statement of cash flows.

- The chapter on accounting principles has been extensively revised to include a comprehensive treatment of financial statement disclosures.

- More than half of the boxed inserts (enrichment pieces) are new to this edition. These items furnish students with either additional background, extended coverage, or real-world examples of the accounting and business topics discussed in the chapter. They treat a range of subjects, such as accounting careers, reports to stockholders, fraudulent source documents, in-house theft, microcomputers, short-term financing, the social security system, and hospital cost accounting.

- Selected exercises and problems throughout the text are identified by a computer logo, to indicate that they can be solved using the methods and programs of the *Computer Resource Guide*.

A number of successful features have been carried forward from previous editions, including the following:

- *Demonstration Problems for Review* in selected chapters aid students in understanding significant processes or ideas.

- A *Business Decision Problem* in each chapter applies accounting concepts to typical business decision situations.

- Alternate problems for the key ideas of each chapter permit greater depth in the study of particular concepts and more flexibility for instructors in assigning material.

- *Key Points to Remember* at the end of each chapter give students an inventory of the main ideas contained in the chapter.

- A *Glossary* at the end of the text makes it easy for students to locate the definition for any particular term at any point in their study.

- A *Checklist of Key Figures* on the endpapers of the text provides detail and summary figures to enable students to check their work without having the complete solution.

HIGHLIGHTS OF CHANGES AND ADDITIONS IN THE FOURTH EDITION

Chapter 13 ("Accounting Principles and Financial Statement Disclosures") contains a completely new discussion of financial statement disclosures, designed to enhance the students' appreciation for the variety and extent of information available in annual reports. The material on inflation accounting has been simplified and is presented as one example of a supplemental financial statement disclosure.

In Chapter 17 ("Long-term Liabilities and Bond Investments"), we have added a basic introduction to the important topic of accounting for pension plans. Chapter 18 ("Long-term Stock Investments and Consolidated Financial Statements") now includes a discussion and illustration of consolidating majority-held subsidiaries after date of acquisition.

Appendix C on International Accounting is new to this edition. This appendix gives instructors the opportunity to include an international dimension in the basic accounting course.

Chapter 19 is completely rewritten to provide thorough coverage of the newly-required statement of cash flows (which replaces the statement of changes in financial position). Both the direct and indirect methods of determining cash flow from operations are discussed. Worksheet formats for both methods are presented, as well as illustrative financial statements for each method. Ample problem material is also provided for each method.

A new section on internal reporting of segment operations and departmental operations has been added to Chapter 25. In Chapter 26, the discussion of budgeting now precedes the material on standard costs. This sequence permits a more logical flow of the chapter's material.

In light of the recent shifts in tax structure, Chapter 28 has been altered to reflect the latest U.S. tax reforms of 1986.

PROGRAM OF SUPPLEMENTARY AIDS

SOLUTIONS MANUAL The solutions manual describes all the problem material and requirements and offers probable difficulty and estimated time for solution of each problem. Answers are given for all questions, exercises, and problems at the end of each chapter and appendix. Answers are also provided for all comprehensive problems.

TEST BOOKLET A class-tested test booklet is a part of the instructional package. For this edition, we have revised and expanded the 50 objective questions for each chapter, and we continue to provide five or six short exercises for each chapter. The new booklet contains more than 1,500 items.

ACHIEVEMENT TESTS A AND B Each version contains 16 achievement tests—14 two-chapter tests suitable for 50-minute class periods, and two comprehensive tests, each covering 14 chapters. Both versions are available to adopters of the book. A *Key to the Achievement Tests* is also provided.

STUDY GUIDE Prepared by Imogene A. Posey of the University of Tennessee, the Study Guide provides a comprehensive chapter review, a check-your-knowledge section, and a set of exercises for each chapter and appendix. Answers to questions and solutions to exercises appear the end of each study guide chapter.

WORKING PAPERS Working papers (in two sets) are available for all problems, alternate problems, business decision problems, and comprehensive problems. The working papers are identified by problem number and name, and contain headings, columns, and other necessary aids to assist students in organizing answers and solutions. When appropriate, given problem data have been entered to save the student's time. Working papers related to the two corporation chapters (15 and 16) are included in each set, so that this material may be covered in either the first or second semester.

TRANSPARENCIES Transparencies of problem solutions are available to departments adopting the text. Each transparency carries the problem number and heading as it appears in the *Solutions Manual*. Two-color *Teaching Transparencies* of text material are also available from the publisher on request.

PRACTICE SETS Four practice sets have been prepared for use with the text. Both *Practice Set A* and *Practice Set A with Business Papers* deal with a single proprietorship. *Practice Set B* deals with a corporation, and *Practice Set C* uses a manufacturing company. Practice sets A and B were prepared by Ronald Burnette of Macomb Community College, and Practice Set C has been revised by James C. Hamre of Informax Corporation.

INSTRUCTOR'S MANUAL The instructor's manual contains learning objectives and an outline of lecture points for each chapter and analyzes end-of-chapter problems in terms of the learning objectives covered. The solutions to the practice sets are also included in the instructor's manual.

COMPUTER RESOURCE GUIDE Prepared by John W. Wanlass of De Anza College, this new guide is divided into two parts. Part 1 adapts selected end-of-chapter problems to a real-world computer system. The manual accounting cycle is compared with a computer accounting system, allowing the user to design the system structure and to process business transactions. Part 2 uses an electronic spreadsheet approach in setting up and solving selected end-of-chapter problems; the user will learn declarative programming principles, which can then be applied to a wide variety of business problems. A separate *Instructor's Manual* contains solutions.

We are indebted to many people for the success of the first three editions of *Principles of Accounting* and for their contributions to the Fourth Edition. Special acknowledgment is due to Dr. James C. Hamre of Informax Corporation, for his significant contributions to the revision of the managerial accounting chapters and to Ron Burnette of Macomb County Community College for his work on *Practice Set A* and *Practice Set B*. We are also grateful to Jed Ashley (*Grossmont College*), Duane E. Baldwin (*University of Nevada*), Thomas E. Balke (*University of Nebraska–Lincoln*), John Blahnik (*Lorain Community College*), James Bower (*University of Wisconsin*), Ken M. Boze (*University of Alaska–Fairbanks*), Bruce Bublitz (*University of Kansas*), F. Eugene Butts (*Appalachian State University*), Charles Chanter (*Grand Rapids Junior College*), Kenneth L. Coffey (*Johnson County Community College*), Edward Corcoran (*Community College of Philadelphia*), Rosalind Cranor (*Virginia Polytech Institute and State University*), Anthony P. Curatola (*Louisiana State University*), Dennis C. Daley (*University of Minnesota*), Troy E. Daniel (*Mississippi State University*), Susan Downs (*University of Utah*), Dean Edmiston (*Emporia State University*), Keith B. Ehrenreich (*California State Polytechnic University–Pomona*), Kenneth O. Elvik (*Iowa State University*), Edwin H. Fankhauser (*University of Utah*), Sharron M. Graves (*Stephen F. Austin State University*), Olen L. Greer (*Southwest Missouri State University*), Marcia Halvorsen (*University of Cincinnati*), Gordon Heslop (*University of Southern Mississippi*), Irene M. Herremans (*University of Wisconsin–Parkside*), Linda Herrington (*Community College of Allegheny County*), George C. Holdren (*University of Nebraska–Lincoln*), Jean Marie Hudson (*Lamar University*), James F. Jones (*Appalachian State University*), William C. Kilpatrick (*Colorado State University*), Harry Knight (*South Oregon State College*), Alvin Koslofsky (*San Jose City College*), Marcella Y. Lecky (*University of Southwestern Louisiana*), Gerard Ludwig (*West Los Angeles College*), John B. MacArthur (*University of Northern Iowa*), John McGrath (*Champlain College*), Richard W. Metcalf (*University of Nebraska–Lincoln*), Jerold J. Morgan (*University of Southern Mississippi*), Paula Morris (*Kennesaw College*), Mark D. Moss (*Utah Technical College at Salt Lake*), Lee H. Nicholas (*University of Northern Iowa*), Jon Norem (*University of Northern Iowa*), John T. O'Brien (*City University of New York, Staten Island*), Fred Petro (*Pepperdine University*), Theresa M. Porter (*Western Illinois University*), David Ravetch (*University of California, Los Angeles*), Jewel M. Riddle (*California State Polytechnic University–Pomona*), Ronald N. Savey (*Western Washington University*), Suzanne Sevalstad (*University of Nevada, Las Vegas*), Gail Shaw (*West Virginia University*), Leon J. Singleton (*Santa Monica College*), Sammie L. Smith (*Stephen F. Austin State University*), Charles Snow (*Temple University*), Kirk Lee Tennant (*Southern Methodist University*), Ralph B. Tower (*Wake Forest University*), Gerald Unruh (*Arapahoe Community College*), Russell Vermillion (*Prince George's Community College*), Maxine K. Wilson (*Los Angeles City College*), Emogene Wind (*Stephen F. Austin State University*), Steven W. Wong (*Merritt College*, and William Zahurak (*Community College of Allegheny County*) for their many valuable comments and suggestions. We also thank Don Stuart and Ralph Kapalczynski of Whirlpool Corporation for their kind assistance in furnishing their firm's annual report and for answering related questions.

We also wish to thank editors Kenneth Rethmeier and Johanna Schmid, who greatly assisted us in planning and executing this revision. Finally, we extend our grateful thanks to the Harcourt Brace Jovanovich staff who contributed their efforts and expertise to prepare this edition and keep it on schedule: Audrey Thompson, manuscript editor; Bruce Daniels, production editor; Schamber Richardson, production manager; Merilyn Britt, designer; and Eleanor Garner, permissions editor.

PAUL H. WALGENBACH
ERNEST I. HANSON
NORMAN E. DITTRICH

CONTENTS

The Let There Be Light or the Travis Apparel Shop Practice Set may be used after Chapter 6.

16 Corporations: Earnings Disclosure, Dividends, and Retained Earnings 571

The "In" Frequencies, Inc., Practice Set may be used after Chapter 16.

17 Long-term Liabilities and Bond Investments 607

Appendix A: Present Values and Effective Interest Amortization 640

18 Long-term Stock Investments and Consolidated Financial Statements 647

The Excell Manufacturing, Inc., Practice Set may be used after Chapter 22.

27 Capital Budgeting 1041

28 Income Taxes and Their Effect on Business Decisions 1075

Part One

The Basic Framework of Accounting

1

Accounting: An Information System

Chapter Objectives

- Provide a basis for understanding the accounting process and the role played by accountants in this process.
- Present an overview of the basic financial reports and their underlying concepts.
- Explain and illustrate the effect of transactions on the balance sheet.
- Describe and illustrate the relationship of the balance sheet to the income statement and statement of owner's equity.

The right information at the right time is nine-tenths of any battle.

NAPOLEON

Modern accounting is widely recognized as a basic component of business management. Accounting is the means by which managers are informed of the financial status and progress of their companies, thus contributing to the continuing processes of planning, control of operations, and decision making. Accounting provides a method of systematically recording and evaluating business activities. This is, perhaps, the fundamental reason for business managers and business students to familiarize themselves with the accounting discipline.

A large portion of the information that a business manager requires is derived from accounting data. The ability to analyze and use these data helps managers accomplish their objectives. Through your study of accounting, you will discover the types of business activities that can be accounted for usefully, the methods used to collect accounting data, and the implications of the resulting information. Furthermore—and often just as important—you will become aware of the limitations of accounting reports.

ACCOUNTING AS AN INFORMATION SYSTEM

Virtually all profit-seeking organizations and most nonprofit organizations maintain extensive accounting records. One reason is that these records are often required by law. A more basic reason is that, even in a very small organization, a manager is confronted with a multitude of complex variables. Not even the most brilliant manager can be sufficiently informed just by observing daily operations. Instead, he or she must depend on the accounting process to convert business transactions into useful statistical data that can be abstracted and summarized in accounting reports. In every sense, this process is essential to the coordinated and rational management of most organizations—regardless of their size. Thus, accounting is an *information system* necessitated by the great complexity of modern business.

In today's society, many persons and agencies outside of management are involved in the economic life of an organization. These persons frequently require financial data. For example, stockholders must have financial information in order to measure management's performance and to evaluate their own holdings. Potential investors need financial data in order to compare prospective investments. Creditors must consider the financial strength of an organization before permitting it to borrow funds. Also, labor unions, financial analysts, and economists often expect a considerable amount of reliable financial data. Finally, many laws require that extensive financial information be reported to the various levels of government. As an information system, the accounting process serves persons both inside and outside an organization.

THE ACCOUNTING PROCESS

Accounting can be defined as the process of (1) *recording,* (2) *classifying,* and (3) *reporting and interpreting* the financial data of an organization. Once an accounting system has been designed and installed, recording and classifying data may become somewhat routine and repetitive. While it is important for accountants to have a sound knowledge of this phase of the accounting process, it is often a relatively minor part of their total responsibility. Accountants direct most of their attention to the reporting and interpretation of the meaningful implications of the data.

Except in small businesses, much routine accounting work has become highly mechanized and automatic. Thus, many persons not acquainted with current accounting trends think that the profession is becoming progressively narrower. Quite the contrary is true. The emergence of electronic data processing has freed accountants from the routine aspects of recording and classifying data, enabling them to concentrate more on the analytical and interpretive aspects of the accounting function. These are the areas most affected by the new demands for accounting information. Indeed, the number of licensed accountants in the United States has grown from about 60,000 in the early 1960s to an estimated 300,000 today. The demand for better educated and more experienced accountants will undoubtedly continue to rise in the future.

Whether the accounting records for a given organization should be maintained manually or electronically will depend on several things, such as the size of the organization, the amount of data to be processed, the amount of information required, and the need for prompt access to stored data. The recent introduction of inexpensive microcomputers and related software programs (see Chapter 6) has enabled even small firms to process accounting data electronically.

Regardless of the method used, the underlying accounting concepts are essentially the same. Because a manually maintained system is most easily handled in the classroom and in problem situations, we use this type of system throughout this book. Where appropriate, however, we include comments relating to electronic systems. Also, certain of the exercises and problems in the text, identified by a computer logo, may be worked using the Computer Resource Guide (see Preface).

THE REPORTING PROCESS

The reporting process, comprising four main channels of information flow, is graphically represented in Exhibit 1–1.

Channel (1): Managerial Data and Reports

A major function of accounting is to provide management with the data needed for decision making and for efficient operation of the firm. Although management people routinely receive the financial reports, tax returns, and special reports prepared for outsiders, they also require various other information, such as the

EXHIBIT 1–1
Typical Flows of Accounting Information

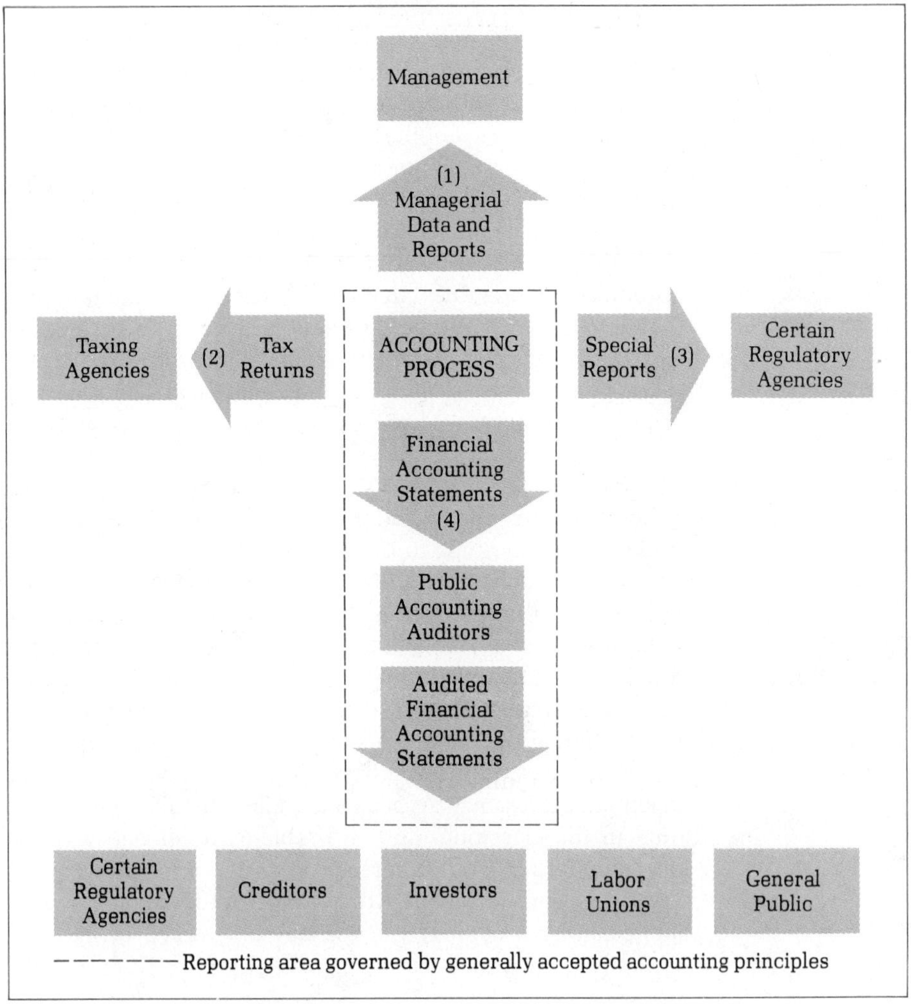

unit cost of a product, estimates of the profit earned from a specific sales campaign, cost comparisons of alternative courses of action, and long-range budgets. Because of the strategic nature of some of this information, it may be available only to the firm's high-level management. The process of generating and analyzing such data is often referred to as **managerial accounting.** Emphasis on this area of accounting has increased in recent years as a result of the implementation of computers and sophisticated quantitative tools.

Channel (2): Tax Returns

Most businesses are required to file many kinds of tax returns—for example, federal, state, and municipal income taxes, excise taxes, and payroll taxes. The preparation of these returns is governed by the rulings and special reporting requirements of the taxing agencies involved. Proper compliance is generally a matter of law and can be quite complicated. Consequently, many firms, especially when preparing income tax returns, retain certified public accountants or attorneys specializing in taxation.

Channel (3): Special Reports

Some companies, by the nature of their activities, are required to report periodically to certain regulatory agencies. For example, certain banks must report to the Comptroller of the Currency, and most public utility companies must report to a public utility commission. The regulatory agency may use the reported information to monitor solvency (as in the case of the banks) or the rate of income to be earned (as in the case of public utilities). Although these reports are based primarily on accounting data, often they must be prepared in accordance with additional conditions, rules, and definitions. Some agencies, such as stock exchanges and the Securities and Exchange Commission, do require reports prepared in accordance with the generally accepted accounting principles that we shall discuss later. We have therefore shown certain regulatory agencies in both channels (3) and (4) of Exhibit 1–1.

Channel (4): Financial Accounting Statements

One of the most important functions of the accounting process is to accumulate and report accounting information that shows an organization's financial position and the results of its operations. Many businesses publish such financial statements at least annually. The subdivision of the accounting process that produces these general-purpose reports is referred to as **financial accounting.** Financial accounting is essentially retrospective, because it deals primarily with historical information, or events that have already happened. Its focus is on income determination and financial position as an aggregate financial picture of an enterprise.

Although financial accounting data are primarily historical, they are also useful for planning and control. Indeed, a considerable amount of planning must be based on what has happened in the recent past. In addition, historical financial information is inherently a control mechanism, since it can be used to measure the success of past planning. We should also emphasize that, although financial accounting is primarily historical, it is not merely a process of "filling in the numbers." As you study further, you will discover that determining the financial position and profitability of an enterprise is an exceedingly complex job that requires professional judgment.

Financial accounting statements are the main source of information for parties—other than governmental agencies—outside the business firm. Because these reports will often be used to evaluate management, their objectivity could be subject to question. To establish the validity of their financial statements, most firms have them audited by independent public accountants. The independent auditor examines the statements and suggests any changes that may be warranted. He or she then expresses a professional opinion that the financial statements are fairly stated "in accordance with generally accepted accounting principles" or indicates any reservations about the statements. Usually, outside parties have greater faith in financial statements that have been audited. Both the role of the professional public accountant and the nature of "generally accepted accounting principles" are complex. Therefore, each is treated separately in later sections of this chapter.

ACCOUNTING PRINCIPLES

To be useful, financial accounting information must be assembled and reported objectively. Those who must rely on such information have a right to be assured that the data are free from bias and inconsistency, whether deliberate or not. For this reason, financial accounting relies on certain standards or guides that have proved useful over the years in imparting economic data. These standards are called **generally accepted accounting principles.** Because accounting is more an art than a science, these principles are not immutable laws like those in the physical sciences. Instead, they are *guides to action* and may change over time. Sometimes specific principles must be altered or new principles must be formulated to fit changed economic circumstances or changes in business practices.

Because accounting principles are based on a combination of theory and practice, there has always been, and probably always will be, some controversy about their propriety. A number of organizations are concerned with the formulation of accounting principles. The most prominent among these is the Financial Accounting Standards Board (FASB). The FASB, organized in 1973, is a nongovernmental body whose pronouncements have the force of setting authoritative rules for the general practice of financial accounting. Before the creation of the FASB, the Accounting Principles Board (APB) of the American Institute of Certified Public Accountants (AICPA) fulfilled the function of formulating accounting principles. If the *attest* function (auditing and independent reporting) of the independent certified public accountant is to be meaningful, the business enterprises of this country must generally observe substantially comparable accounting principles.

Various regulatory bodies—such as the Securities and Exchange Commission and the Internal Revenue Service—also prescribe rules to be used in financial reporting. Because these rules often touch upon accounting principles and may conflict with the rules and practices specified by other agencies, compromises sometimes have to be made in financial reporting. This has been especially true when the rules of a regulatory body have conflicted with those considered "generally accepted" by accounting practitioners.

Often, income determined by tax regulations differs from that determined by generally accepted accounting principles. When rules or methods prescribed by the Internal Revenue Service for the determination of taxable income conflict with those acceptable for business reporting, an enterprise may keep more than one set of records to satisfy both reporting requirements. Uninformed people may think that this practice is illegal or unethical; actually, there is nothing sinister or illegal about keeping separate records to fulfill separate needs, as long as all the records are subject to examination by the appropriate parties.

As Exhibit 1–1 indicates, generally accepted accounting principles are primarily relevant to financial accounting. In managerial accounting, the main objective is to assist management in making decisions and in operating effectively, and in such cases it is frequently useful to depart from concepts utilized in financial accounting. On many occasions, financial accounting data must be reassembled or altered to be most useful in solving internal business problems.

FIELDS OF ACCOUNTING ACTIVITY

Accountants perform many diverse services and are engaged in various types of employment. The three major fields of accounting activity are private accounting, public accounting, and governmental accounting. Because each of these may comprise many aspects of accounting activity, it is possible to give only a broad description for each type of accounting employment.

Private Accounting

More accountants are employed in private accounting than in any other field. Private employers of accountants include manufacturers, wholesalers, retailers, and service firms. Depending on the size and complexity of the business, the private accountant's duties may vary from routine reporting to the design and implementation of electronic accounting systems. The major objective of the private accountant, however, is to assist management in planning and controlling the firm's operations. In many large business firms, the head of the accounting department is called the **controller** and is a key executive who works closely with other management personnel.

Frequently, a large company will have an **internal auditing** staff that reports to a high-ranking management officer or to an audit committee of the board of directors. Internal auditing is an appraisal activity conducted within the business firm to determine if management's financial and operating controls are effective and are being properly utilized. An internal auditor investigates policies and procedures designed to safeguard assets, promote operational efficiency, and provide reliable information.

Public Accounting

The field of public accounting is composed of firms that render independent, expert reports on financial statements of business enterprises. Public accounting

THE MODERN ACCOUNTANT—IMAGE AND PROSPECTS

A little over 25 years ago, two social scientists who conducted a government survey of attitudes among 1,000 students at five unnamed but "highly selective" universities found that in the students' eyes, "the accountant is the anti-hero of the occupational world. . . . The accountant is a conformist, with a minimum of social skills. . . . He is rated as passive, weak, soft, shallow, and cold."*

This stereotyped image has been dramatically erased in the past two decades and replaced by that of a dynamic, sophisticated, professional person. Recently, a prominent business magazine quoted the chairman of the accounting department of a major university as saying, "Suddenly students see accounting as glamorous, sexy. Many of our best students who would have gone to law school a couple of years ago, are now going into public accounting." Today's young men and women know that the field can be a lot more challenging and rewarding than merely balancing debits and credits. In a recent newspaper article, James R. MacNeill of the American Institute of Certified Public Accountants was quoted as saying, "Thanks to the computer, a lot of the pencil-pushing has been done away with. The emphasis is on people who are sophisticated in business, finance, and communications."

An estimated 60,000 college graduates with bachelor's degrees and 8,500 with advanced degrees entered the accounting field in 1985—more than three times the number entering the field fifteen years before. Not only are there plenty of job openings with increasingly attractive salaries, but the positions available also have more dimension and challenge than ever before. In fact, the immediate and long-term prospects for accounting graduates are better than for most other professions, such as law. The U.S. Bureau of Labor Statistics indicates that employment of accountants and auditors is expected to grow faster than average through the 1990s.

Slightly more than one-fourth of current accounting graduates enter public accounting (described in this chapter); the remainder may become management accountants or internal auditors, working in industry, in government, for financial institutions, or for not-for-profit organizations. Many graduates who enter the public accounting field may "opt out" after several years of experience in this field to take high-level positions with clients. For example, many chief financial officers, treasurers, and controllers have prior CPA firm experience.

Both industry and government offer a broad spectrum of opportunities for accounting graduates. A graduate with good grades and course work in another specialty, such as hospital administration or information systems, will fare well in private accounting.† Students interested in auditing for the private sector will find that the field of internal auditing has expanded dramatically just during the last decade. For most companies, the present-day focus of internal auditing is operational auditing—auditing for efficiency, economy, and profits. Internal auditors are therefore in a good position to learn about all facets of a firm's operations, and subsequently can often work their way into top management positions within their firms.

Government positions also offer a wide variety of opportunities with outstanding fringe benefits. For example, the Federal Bureau of Investigation, in recent years, has been hiring more accountants than lawyers, and the Internal Revenue Service recruits accountants at most colleges and universities with an accounting program. Overall, government and industry offer better job security than CPA firms, and job security rates high among job criteria by many accounting graduates.

Women and minority accounting graduates are in particular demand by all accounting fields. In 1985, roughly 40 per cent of the accounting graduates hired by public accounting firms were women—up from 24 per cent ten years before. The major difficulty in recruiting minority graduates is that not many go into accounting as undergraduates, so there is a limited pool from which to draw. The minority student who enters a good accounting program and achieves high grades is in an enviable competitive position.

*Steve Lohr, "Good-bye to the Ink-stained Wretch," *Atlantic Monthly*, August, 1980, p. 68.

†Robert E. Jensen and John D. Rice, "The Times Are Changing," *New Accountant*, September, 1985, p. 8.

firms also perform a wide variety of accounting and managerial services, acting as consultants to their clients. Most accountants in public accounting firms are certified public accountants (CPAs), holding certificates from the particular states in which they work.[1] These certificates declare that the CPA has passed a rigorous examination and has met the requirements for education and experience set by the state to ensure high standards of performance. The CPA profession, like the older professions of law and medicine, has a comprehensive code of ethics—a set of rules of professional conduct—that governs the behavior of its practitioners in the performance of their work.

The professional responsibility of the certified public accountant is unique. While the attorney and the physician are responsible only to their clients and patients, the certified public accountant may be professionally responsible to third parties who rely on the financial statements the CPA has audited. This is true even though the third party in no way contributes to the fee paid for the audit and has no contractual relationship whatsoever with the accountant.

Governmental Accounting

A large number of accountants are employed by federal, state, and local governmental agencies. The services performed by these accountants parallel those of private and public accountants and may cover the entire spectrum of financial and managerial accounting. For example, the General Accounting Office of the federal government and the Department of Audit in the various state governments engage in auditing activities similar to those of public accountants. Audits may be conducted not only of governmental agencies but also of private firms doing business with a governmental unit. Accounting personnel of the Internal Revenue Service and the corresponding state agencies conduct accounting investigations of firms and individuals in connection with their tax liabilities. Among the many other governmental agencies and regulatory bodies that employ accountants are the Securities and Exchange Commission, the Department of Defense, the Federal Power Commission, the Interstate Commerce Commission, and state utility commissions and agencies.

BASIC FINANCIAL REPORTS

As we mentioned earlier, one of the major functions of accounting is to provide periodic reports to management, owners, and outsiders. The two principal reports resulting from the process of financial accounting are the balance sheet and the income statement. Although the form of these financial statements may vary among different business firms or other economic units, their basic purpose is the same. The **balance sheet** portrays the financial position of the organization at a particular point in time. The **income statement** portrays the operating results for a period of time. These financial statements are prepared at least yearly, but quarterly or monthly reports are also customary.

[1]Most states still allow certain accountants who are not "certified" to practice public accounting.

Another basic statement, called the **statement of cash flows,** is generally required in reporting to outsiders. This statement will be discussed in Chapter 19.

Although the balance sheet and income statement are the end result of the process of financial accounting, we shall introduce them in simplified form here, early in our study. Having some knowledge of the ultimate objective of financial accounting will help you understand the various steps in the accounting process.

THE BALANCE SHEET

The balance sheet, sometimes called the **statement of financial position,** is a listing of a firm's assets, liabilities, and owners' equity on a given date (these terms are explained below). Exhibit 1–2 is a balance sheet prepared for Art Graphics, a single-owner business, showing its financial position at December 31, 19XX.

The proper heading of a balance sheet consists of (1) the name of the organization, (2) the title of the statement, and (3) the date for which the statement was prepared.

The body of the statement in Exhibit 1–2 contains three major sections: assets, liabilities, and owner's equity. With this presentation, the reader can tell at a glance that the resources of this firm total $120,000 and that these assets are being financed by two sources—$40,000 by the creditors (liabilities) and $80,000 by the owner (owner's equity). Occasionally, the right-hand portion of this statement is called *Equities*, with subdivisions called *Creditors' Equity* and *Owners'*

EXHIBIT 1–2

Art Graphics
Balance Sheet
December 31, 19XX

Assets		**Liabilities**		
Cash	$ 6,000	Accounts Payable	$ 5,000	
Accounts Receivable	8,000	Mortgage Payable	35,000	
Supplies on Hand	4,000			
Land	10,000	Total Liabilities		$ 40,000
Building (Less Accumulated Depreciation)	32,000	**Owner's Equity**		
		George Taylor, Capital		80,000
Equipment (Less Accumulated Depreciation)	60,000			
Total Assets	$120,000	Total Liabilities and Owner's Equity		$120,000

Equity. The total assets always equal the sum of the creditors' and owners' equities. This balancing is sometimes described as the **accounting equation**, which dictates that all of the listed resources are attributed to claims of creditors and owners. Conversely, the claims of both creditors and owners must be balanced by total listed resources. These relationships can be diagramed as follows:

Technical terms:	**Assets**	=	**Liabilities**	+	**Owners' Equity**
Basic meanings:	Business resources	=	Outsiders' claims	+	Owners' claims
Amounts (Exhibit 1–2):	$120,000	=	$40,000	+	$80,000

We now briefly explain each of the three elements in the accounting equation.

Assets

Assets are the economic resources of the business that can usefully be expressed in monetary terms. Assets may take many forms. Some assets—such as land, buildings, and equipment—may have readily identifiable physical characteristics. Others may simply represent claims for payment or services, such as amounts due from customers (accounts receivable), or prepayments for future services (for example, prepaid insurance). As a convenience to the reader of the balance sheet, the assets are usually listed in an established order, with the most liquid assets (cash, receivables, supplies, and so on) preceding the more permanent assets (land, buildings, and equipment).

Assets are usually recorded at their acquisition price, or cost. The recorded costs of assets may be reduced for a variety of reasons. Supplies are used up, and assets such as buildings and equipment depreciate. For example, in Exhibit 1–2, Art Graphics' buildings and equipment have both been reduced by accumulated depreciation over the years. We shall develop the concept of depreciation in Chapter 3 and discuss it fully in Chapter 10.

Accounting principles do not permit upward valuation of assets, simply because it is often difficult or impossible to determine the *actual value* of an asset at regular intervals in a completely *objective* way. Assume, for example, that 10 years ago a firm purchased some real estate for $20,000. Today the property may well be worth considerably more. Assigning a current market value to the real estate may be helpful, but it would be difficult to accomplish unless the property were offered for sale. However, most business firms plan to use their long-term operating assets, not to sell them. Therefore, the accounting convention of reflecting assets in financial statements at acquisition cost has persisted, although criticism is frequently leveled at this practice.

Liabilities

Liabilities, or creditors' equity, are the obligations, or debts, that the firm must pay in money or services at some time in the future. They therefore represent creditors' claims on the firm's assets. Liabilities are listed on the balance sheet in the order that they will come due. Short-term liabilities—such as notes payable given for money borrowed for relatively short periods, accounts payable to creditors, and salaries owed employees—are shown first. Below the short-term liabilities, the long-term debt is presented. Long-term debt—for example, mortgages and bonds payable—will normally not be repaid in full for several years.

Although most liabilities are payable in cash, some may involve the performance of services. A magazine publisher, for example, may receive advance payments for three- or five-year subscriptions. These payments constitute a liability that the publishing company will reduce periodically by supplying the publication during the subscription period. Should the publisher be unable to fulfill this commitment, the unexpired portion of the subscription amount must be refunded.

Owners' Equity

The owners' equity in the resources, or assets, of the firm is shown below the liabilities. The owners' interest is equal to the **net assets** of the business, which is defined as the difference between the assets and the liabilities. Thus, owners' equity is a *residual claim*—a claim to the assets remaining after the debts to creditors have been discharged. Formerly, the term *net worth* was frequently used to describe owners' equity. This expression is no longer considered good terminology, because it conveys an impression of value, and as we have seen, the value, or current worth, of assets may not be portrayed in the balance sheet. We also often employ the term **capital** to describe owners' interest in a firm. (This practice is derived from legal usage of the term.) Sometimes in economic literature the assets of a business are referred to as the firm's "capital." This use of the term is avoided in accounting literature.

The owner's equity in Art Graphics amounts to $80,000. It consists of the amounts invested in the organization and the net earnings of the organization that have not been withdrawn by the owner.

UNDERLYING ACCOUNTING CONCEPTS

Certain fundamental concepts provide a framework for recording and reporting business transactions. These concepts have been developed over time to provide general guides to making financial reports as objective and as useful as possible. Although various terms—such as **principles, standards, assumptions,** and **conventions**—are often used to describe such guides, a distinction among these terms is not essential to an understanding of the guides. At this point, a brief discussion of certain of these guides may be helpful in understanding the structure of the accounting process. A more thorough discussion is given in Chapter 13.

The Accounting Entity

Any business enterprise—whether a sole proprietorship, a partnership, or a corporation—is an individual accounting unit separate and distinct from the other economic activities and the personal affairs of the owners. Thus, if sole proprietor George Taylor owned other businesses or participated in other economic ventures, these activities would be accounted for separately and would not affect the accounting for the sole proprietorship art graphics business. A separate set of accounting records would be maintained, and a separate set of financial statements would be prepared for each enterprise.

Historical Cost

We have mentioned that assets are recorded and subsequently reported at their acquisition price, or **historical cost.** Although other measurements, such as appraised values or market prices, might be used for reporting in subsequent periods, accountants have long recognized that historical cost is probably the most objective and verifiable basis for reporting assets. As you will learn, reported asset costs are often *reduced* over time to reflect expiration, and in some cases, they may be reduced to market values; upward revaluations, however, are not permitted in conventional financial statements. We explain later how certain reported *supplemental* information departs from the cost principle.

Objectivity

Because accounting data are most useful when they are objective and verifiable, the recording of transactions should be based on actual invoices, physical counts, and other relatively bias-free evidence whenever possible. Undocumented opinions of management or others do not provide a good basis for accounting determinations. Even when a certain amount of subjectivity cannot be avoided—as in estimating the useful lives of plant assets, collectibility of accounts receivable, or possible liability for product warranties—it is important that such estimates be supported by some sort of objective analysis.

Going Concern

The **going concern** concept is based on the presumption that a business will continue indefinitely and will not be sold or liquidated. This assumption permits the accountant to carry certain incurred costs such as plant assets and supplies into future periods and to reflect them as costs of operation when the items are used in operations. The concept also supports the cost principle, because it assumes that such assets will be *used* in operating the business rather than sold; hence, it is considered rational to use cost, rather than market price or liquidation value, as the basis for measurement.

The Measuring Unit

Accounting transactions and their results appearing in financial statements are expressed in terms of a monetary unit (the dollar in the United States). Unfortunately, the U.S. dollar (as well as the currencies of other countries) is not a stable unit of measure. Inflation causes a currency's purchasing power to decline through time. As a result, use of the cost principle may distort the financial statements of business firms, because the amounts appearing in the statements are expressed in dollars of different vintages. Over the years, there have been many proposals to adjust the amounts in financial statements by the use of price indexes or to substitute some current value such as replacement cost or appraisal value. Currently, conventional financial statements prepared in this country are still unadjusted, cost-based statements. However, the Financial Accounting Standards Board does require certain large publicly held firms to make supplementary disclosures concerning the effects of inflation on their operations. A more detailed discussion of the problem will be given in Chapter 13.

EFFECT OF TRANSACTIONS ON THE BALANCE SHEET

An **accounting transaction** is a business activity or event that requires accounting recognition. Therefore, an event that affects any of the elements in the accounting equation (assets, liabilities, or owners' equity) must be recorded. Some activities—for example, ordering supplies, bidding for an engagement or contract, and negotiating for the acquisition of assets—may represent business activities, but an accounting transaction does not occur until such activities result in a change in the firm's assets, liabilities, or owners' equity.

Earlier, we observed that the balance sheet of a business indicates the firm's financial position at a particular point in time. We emphasized that the total assets should always equal the sum of the creditors' and owners' equities. If a balance sheet were prepared after each accounting transaction was completed, this equality of assets and equities would always hold true. Obviously, no one would care to do this, since the statements are required only periodically. However, keep in mind that although each transaction changes the complexion of the balance sheet, equality of assets and equities is always maintained.

Transactions Not Affecting Owners' Equity

Certain transactions may change the character and amounts of assets or liabilities, or both, but have no effect on owners' equity. For example, if George Taylor of Art Graphics (see Exhibit 1–2) purchases additional equipment for $1,000 cash, the asset Equipment will increase by $1,000, but the asset Cash will decrease by $1,000. Obviously, this transaction causes only a shift in assets on the balance sheet. In the same way, collection of accounts receivable causes a shift of assets. Collection of $500 of Accounts Receivable would result in a decrease in this asset and an increase in Cash of $500.

If the $1,000 worth of equipment had been purchased on credit rather than for cash, the result would have been a $1,000 increase in Equipment and an equal increase in the liability Accounts Payable. On the other hand, payment of liabilities reduces both assets and liabilities. If Taylor paid $500 to his creditors, both Cash and Accounts Payable would decrease by $500.

Transactions Affecting Owners' Equity

The following four types of transactions change the amount of owners' equity:

	Effect on Owners' Equity
(1) Owner contributions	Increase
(2) Owner withdrawals	Decrease
(3) Revenue	Increase
(4) Expenses	Decrease

When an owner contributes cash or other assets to a business firm, the firm's balance sheet shows an increase in assets and an increase in owners' equity. Conversely, when an owner withdraws assets from the firm, both assets and owners' equity decrease. The primary goal of any business, however, is to increase the owners' equity by earning profits, or **net income.** The net income of a firm is determined by subtracting *expenses incurred* from *revenue earned*. Owners' equity is increased by revenue and decreased by expenses. Let us examine the nature of revenue and expenses.

Revenue

Revenue is the increase in owners' equity a firm earns by providing goods or services for its customers. The revenue earned is measured by the *assets received* in exchange, usually in the form of cash or an account receivable. It is important to recognize that *revenue is earned and reflected in the accounting process at the time that goods or services are provided*. Receipt of cash by a business does not necessarily indicate that revenue has been earned. In a cash sale, revenue is earned at the time that cash is received. Revenue is also reflected when services are rendered on *credit*; assets are increased when Accounts Receivable is increased. Subsequent collection of an account does not increase revenue—it merely results in a shift in assets from Accounts Receivable to Cash. Neither is revenue earned when a business borrows money or when the owners contribute assets. Such increases in assets are not earned, because the business firm has provided no goods or services.

Expenses

Expenses are costs incurred by the firm in the process of earning revenue. Generally, expenses are measured by the costs of *assets consumed* or *services used* during an accounting period. Depreciation on equipment, rent, employees' salaries, and costs of heat, light, and other utilities are examples of expenses incurred in producing revenue.

Because expenses are deducted from revenue to determine net income, the accounting process must relate expenses in a period to the revenue of that same period. For example, January rent—no matter when it is paid—should be related to January revenue in determining that month's net income. If an annual rent of \$6,000 is prepaid on January 1, only $\frac{1}{12}$ of the \$6,000, or \$500, is considered expense for January. At the end of January, the remaining prepayment of \$5,500 constitutes an asset (called Prepaid Rent) to be apportioned over the remaining 11 months. Other examples of assets that are used up over a period of time are Prepaid Insurance and Prepaid Advertising.

Cash expenditures made to acquire assets do not represent expenses and do not affect owners' equity. Cash expenditures made to pay liabilities, such as the payment of an account payable, also do not represent expenses and do not affect owners' equity. Similarly, owners' withdrawals, although they reduce owners' equity, do not represent expenses. Expenses are directly related to the earning of revenue. They are determined by measuring the amount of assets or services consumed (or expired) during an accounting period.

Accrual Basis

The foregoing concepts of revenue and expenses apply to firms that employ an **accrual basis** accounting system. In accrual accounting, expenses incurred are matched with related revenue earned to determine a meaningful net income figure for a particular period. As we mentioned earlier, the revenue and expenses for determining net income do not depend on when cash is actually received or expended.

Certain businesses, principally service enterprises (such as law, architecture, or hairdressing) often use a **cash basis** mode of accounting. In contrast to accrual basis accounting, the cash basis system recognizes revenue when money is received and expenses when money is paid. Cash basis accounting is used primarily because it can provide certain income tax benefits and because it is simple. Cash basis financial statements, however, may distort the portrayal of financial position and operating results of a business. Consequently, most business firms use accrual basis accounting.

TRANSACTIONS AND THE BALANCE SHEET: AN ILLUSTRATION

Now that we have described the basic concepts underlying the preparation of financial statements, let us illustrate their application with an example.

Experienced driver education instructor John King established a private driving school called Westgate Driving School. King intends to buy a lot for vehicle storage and driver instruction, but to lease training vehicles. The transactions for June, the first month of operations, are analyzed below. A balance sheet is presented after each transaction so that the effect on the balance sheet may be examined.[2]

Initial Investment in Firm

TRANSACTION (1): On June 1, King invested $60,000 of his personal funds in the school. This first business transaction increased the asset Cash and increased King's equity (Capital) on the school's balance sheet.

Balance Sheet

Assets		**Liabilities**	
Cash	$60,000	(none)	
		Owner's Equity	
		J. King, Capital	$60,000
		Total Liabilities and	
Total Assets	$60,000	Owner's Equity	$60,000

Purchase of Land

TRANSACTION (2): On June 2, King paid $24,000 cash for a lot to be used for storing vehicles and for some driving instruction. This transaction reduced the asset Cash and created another asset, Land, for an equivalent amount. This transaction was merely the conversion of one asset to another.

[2]Note that the totals in the various financial statements shown in this chapter have been double ruled. Accountants do this principally to signify that all necessary calculations have been performed and to emphasize final amounts for the benefit of readers. We shall also employ double rulings in various other accounting records and forms illustrated in this text for these reasons and also to separate certain recorded data by time periods.

Balance Sheet

Assets		Liabilities	
Cash	$36,000	(none)	
Land	24,000		
		Owner's Equity	
		J. King, Capital	$60,000
Total Assets	$60,000	Total Liabilities and Owner's Equity	$60,000

Payment of Rent

TRANSACTION (3): On June 3, King paid $800 to rent a furnished office near the parking lot for June, and $5,000 to lease training vehicles. These items are June expenses, the cost of services received (use of office and vehicles) for the month. The transaction reduced assets (Cash) and owner's equity (J. King, Capital) by $5,800.

Balance Sheet

Assets		Liabilities	
Cash	$30,200	(none)	
Land	24,000		
		Owner's Equity	
		J. King, Capital	$54,200
Total Assets	$54,200	Total Liabilities and Owner's Equity	$54,200

Prepayment of Insurance

TRANSACTION (4): On June 4, King paid vehicle insurance premiums of $7,200 for three years. This payment for future coverage created a new asset, Prepaid Insurance, and reduced Cash. As each month passes, $\frac{1}{36}$ of the amount, or $200, will appear on the income statement as Insurance Expense, the cost of that month's insurance coverage.

Balance Sheet

Assets		Liabilities	
Cash	$23,000	(none)	
Prepaid Insurance	7,200		
Land	24,000		
		Owner's Equity	
		J. King, Capital	$54,200
Total Assets	$54,200	Total Liabilities and Owner's Equity	$54,200

Purchase of Supplies on Account

TRANSACTION (5): On June 5, King purchased fuel and other supplies on account for $3,600. This transaction increased assets (Supplies on Hand) by $3,600 and resulted in a liability (Accounts Payable) of $3,600. The increase in assets did not change owner's equity; it merely created a liability on the balance sheet. Because King could not anticipate the amount of supplies that would be used (become expense) in June, he classified the entire $3,600 as an asset. Later, when the amount of supplies *used* is determined, an expense will be reflected.

Balance Sheet

Assets		**Liabilities**	
Cash	$23,000	Accounts Payable	$ 3,600
Prepaid Insurance	7,200		
Supplies on Hand	3,600	**Owner's Equity**	
Land	24,000	J. King, Capital	54,200
		Total Liabilities and	
Total Assets	$57,800	Owner's Equity	$57,800

Billing for Fee Revenue

TRANSACTION (6): On June 26, students were billed $21,500 for June instructional fees. Providing instruction during the month generated an asset, Accounts Receivable, and revenue, which increased owner's equity (J. King, Capital), even though payment may not be received until a later period.

Balance Sheet

Assets		**Liabilities**	
Cash	$23,000	Accounts Payable	$ 3,600
Accounts Receivable	21,500		
Prepaid Insurance	7,200	**Owner's Equity**	
Supplies on Hand	3,600		
Land	24,000	J. King, Capital	75,700
		Total Liabilities and	
Total Assets	$79,300	Owner's Equity	$79,300

Payment of Salaries

TRANSACTION (7): On June 30, King paid instructors' salaries of $9,000 for June. This amount was June expense, because it represented the cost of employees' services used during June. Therefore, the Cash account and J. King, Capital were both reduced by $9,000.

Balance Sheet

Assets		**Liabilities**	
Cash	$14,000	Accounts Payable	$ 3,600
Accounts Receivable	21,500		
Prepaid Insurance	7,200	**Owner's Equity**	
Supplies on Hand	3,600		
Land	24,000	J. King, Capital	66,700
		Total Liabilities and	
Total Assets	$70,300	Owner's Equity	$70,300

Collection of Accounts Receivable

TRANSACTION (8): On June 30, the school collected $18,000 on account from students billed in transaction (6). This transaction increased Cash and decreased Accounts Receivable—merely a shift in assets. Note that the revenue, which increased owner's equity, had already been reflected when the month's billings were made on June 26.

Balance Sheet

Assets		Liabilities	
Cash	$32,000	Accounts Payable	$ 3,600
Accounts Receivable	3,500		
Prepaid Insurance	7,200	**Owner's Equity**	
Supplies on Hand	3,600		
Land	24,000	J. King, Capital	66,700
		Total Liabilities and	
Total Assets	$70,300	Owner's Equity	$70,300

Payment on Accounts Payable

TRANSACTION (9): On June 30, the school paid $1,600 on account for the fuel and supplies purchased in transaction (5). Paying $1,600 of the $3,600 owed reduced both Cash and Accounts Payable, therefore reducing both assets and liabilities. This payment was the partial settlement of a previously recorded obligation—*not* an expense.

Balance Sheet

Assets		Liabilities	
Cash	$30,400	Accounts Payable	$ 2,000
Accounts Receivable	3,500		
Prepaid Insurance	7,200	**Owner's Equity**	
Supplies on Hand	3,600		
Land	24,000	J. King, Capital	66,700
		Total Liabilities and	
Total Assets	$68,700	Owner's Equity	$68,700

Payment of Utilities

TRANSACTION (10): On June 30, King paid $250 for office utilities (electricity and telephone). This amount was a June expense decreasing both assets and owner's equity because the amount represented the cost of utility services used during the month. Cash and J. King, Capital were reduced by $250.

Balance Sheet

Assets		Liabilities	
Cash	$30,150	Accounts Payable	$ 2,000
Accounts Receivable	3,500		
Prepaid Insurance	7,200	**Owner's Equity**	
Supplies on Hand	3,600		
Land	24,000	J. King, Capital	66,450
		Total Liabilities and	
Total Assets	$68,450	Owner's Equity	$68,450

Withdrawal by Owner

TRANSACTION (11): On June 30, King withdrew $2,000 from the firm for personal use. This withdrawal reduced Cash and J. King, Capital by $2,000. Note that the effect of this transaction was the reverse of transaction (1), in which King invested personal funds in the school.

Balance Sheet

Assets		Liabilities	
Cash	$28,150	Accounts Payable	$ 2,000
Accounts Receivable	3,500		
Prepaid Insurance	7,200	**Owner's Equity**	
Supplies on Hand	3,600		
Land	24,000	J. King, Capital	64,450
Total Assets	$66,450	Total Liabilities and Owner's Equity	$66,450

Recording Insurance Expense

TRANSACTION (12): On June 30, $\frac{1}{36}$ (one month) of the prepaid insurance, or $200, had expired and no longer represented an asset; it became insurance expense for June. [Recall that in transaction (4) on June 4, the firm paid $7,200 for a 36-month policy.] Therefore, both the asset, Prepaid Insurance, and J. King, Capital were reduced by $200.

Balance Sheet

Assets		Liabilities	
Cash	$28,150	Accounts Payable	$ 2,000
Accounts Receivable	3,500		
Prepaid Insurance	7,000	**Owner's Equity**	
Supplies on Hand	3,600		
Land	24,000	J. King, Capital	64,250
Total Assets	$66,250	Total Liabilities and Owner's Equity	$66,250

Recording Supplies Expense

TRANSACTION (13): On June 30, supplies were counted, and only $1,350 worth of supplies remained on hand. Because supplies purchased for $3,600 in transaction (5) on June 5 were reflected as an asset, that portion of the purchase no longer on hand, $2,250, represented supplies used, or the supplies expense for the month. The result was a $2,250 decrease in both Supplies on Hand and J. King, Capital.

Balance Sheet

Assets		Liabilities	
Cash	$28,150	Accounts Payable	$ 2,000
Accounts Receivable	3,500		
Prepaid Insurance	7,000	**Owner's Equity**	
Supplies on Hand	1,350		
Land	24,000	J. King, Capital	62,000
Total Assets	$64,000	Total Liabilities and Owner's Equity	$64,000

EXHIBIT 1–3
Summary of June Activities
and Their Effect on the Balance Sheet Equation

	Assets					= Liabilities +	Owner's Equity
Transactions	**Cash**	**+ Accounts Receivable**	**+ Prepaid Insurance**	**+ Supplies on Hand**	**+ Land**	**= Accounts Payable**	**+ J. King, Capital**
(1)	+ $60,000						+ $60,000
(2)	− 24,000				+ $24,000		
(3)	− 5,800						− 5,800
(4)	− 7,200		+ $7,200				
(5)				+ $3,600		+ $3,600	
(6)		+ $21,500					+ 21,500
(7)	− 9,000						− 9,000
(8)	+ 18,000	− 18,000					
(9)	− 1,600					− 1,600	
(10)	− 250						− 250
(11)	− 2,000						− 2,000
(12)			− 200				− 200
(13)				− 2,250			− 2,250
	$28,150	+ $ 3,500	+ $7,000	+ $1,350	+ $24,000	= $2,000	+ $62,000
	$64,000					$64,000	

Transactions (12) and (13) are reflected on the balance sheet to ensure that the items on that statement reflect the current end-of-period amounts. Because $200 of prepaid insurance has expired and $2,250 of supplies on hand are used during June, the related assets are reduced, and the amounts, representing June expenses, must be subtracted from the owner's capital account. These transactions are referred to as *adjustments*. A thorough discussion of adjustments is given in Chapter 3.

Exhibit 1–3 summarizes the June activities of the Westgate Driving School and shows their effect on the balance sheet equation. The final results are, of course, identical with those given on the balance sheet prepared after transaction (13). The June 30 balance sheet is the only one that the Westgate Driving School would actually prepare, because June 30 is the end of the accounting period.

As a result of the driving school's June activities, John King's capital increased from his original investment of $60,000 to $62,000, an increase of $2,000. Had King not withdrawn $2,000 for personal use, the increase would have been $4,000, which represents the net income, or net earnings, for June.

THE INCOME STATEMENT

Although it is important to know the amount of net income, it is equally important to know how it was earned. To show the results of operations for a period, we prepare an income statement, which lists the revenue and expenses. When total revenue exceeds total expenses, the resulting amount is net income; when expenses exceed revenue, the resulting amount is a net loss. To prepare a June income statement for the Westgate Driving School, we must identify the revenue and expenses by analyzing the changes in owner's equity for the period. The changes in John King's capital, taken from Exhibit 1–3, are shown below, with an explanation of each change:

(1)	Capital contribution	+	$60,000
(3)	Rent expense	−	5,800
(6)	Billings to students	+	21,500
(7)	Salaries expense	−	9,000
(10)	Utilities expense	−	250
(11)	Withdrawal by King	−	2,000
(12)	Insurance expense	−	200
(13)	Supplies expense	−	2,250
	Ending Capital Balance		$62,000

From this list of transactions and adjustments, we see that revenue, or instructional fees, equals $21,500, the June billings to students in transaction (6). The expenses are derived from transactions (3), (7), (10), (12), and (13) for rent, salaries, utilities, insurance, and supplies. Items (1) and (11), representing contributions and withdrawals by King, are ignored in preparing the income statement.

Westgate Driving School's formal income statement for the month of June, which would be prepared to accompany the June 30 balance sheet, appears in Exhibit 1–4.

EXHIBIT 1–4

Westgate Driving School
Income Statement
For the Month of June, 19XX

Revenue		
Instructional Fees		$21,500
Expenses		
Rent Expense	$5,800	
Salaries Expense	9,000	
Utilities Expense	250	
Insurance Expense	200	
Supplies Expense	2,250	
Total Expenses		17,500
Net Income		$ 4,000

RELATIONSHIP OF BALANCE SHEET AND INCOME STATEMENT

We have seen that the balance sheet and the income statement complement each other. The income statement summarizes a firm's operating results for the accounting period, and these results are reflected in the owners' equity on the balance sheet. For yearly statements, this complementary relationship might be shown graphically as follows:

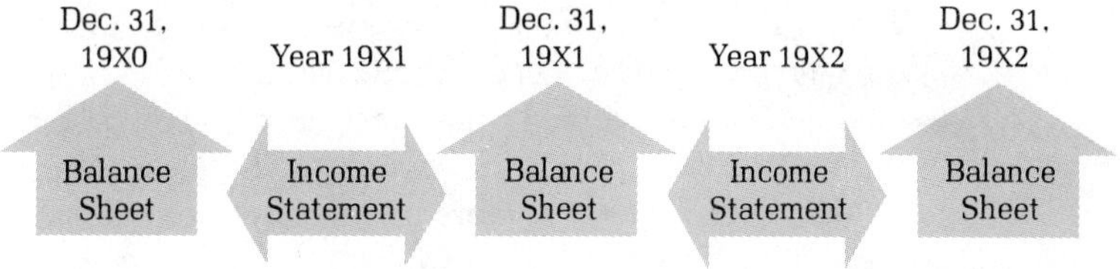

STATEMENT OF OWNER'S EQUITY

Frequently at the end of an accounting period, a statement of owner's equity is prepared to accompany the balance sheet and income statement. This is simply a summary of the changes in the owner's capital balance during the period. Exhibit 1–5 shows this type of statement for the Westgate Driving School. Note that the ending balance on this statement agrees with the owner's capital balance on the balance sheet at June 30, 19XX.

This statement further demonstrates the relationship between the income statement and the balance sheet. The net income (or net loss) for a period is an input into the statement of owner's equity, while the ending owner's equity bal-

EXHIBIT 1–5

Westgate Driving School
Statement of Owner's Equity
For the Month of June, 19XX

J. King, Capital, June 1, 19XX	$ –0–
Add: Capital Contributed in June	60,000
Net Income for June	4,000
	$64,000
Less: Capital Withdrawn in June	2,000
J. King, Capital, June 30, 19XX	$62,000

ance on the statement is an input into the balance sheet at the end of the period. When financial statements are prepared, the sequence suggested by this relationship is customarily followed; that is, the income statement is prepared first, then the statement of owner's equity (when such a statement is prepared to accompany the income statement and balance sheet), and then the balance sheet.

FORMS OF BUSINESS ORGANIZATION

The principal forms of business organization are the **sole proprietorship,** the **partnership,** and the **corporation.** Although sole proprietorships, or single-owner businesses, are probably the most numerous, the corporate form of business is the most important in our economy. The partnership form is often used when two or more sole proprietorships merge into one business. For many years, professional people such as physicians, attorneys, and public accountants operated as partnerships because their codes of ethics or state laws prohibited incorporation. Most states now permit a special type of incorporation or association, and professional organizations have changed their codes of ethics to accommodate this change. Most professional firms, however, still operate as partnerships. For large-scale operations, the corporate form of organization has many advantages. These will be discussed in Chapter 15.

The principal differences in the balance sheets for the three types of business organizations just described appear in the owners' equity section. State corporation laws require that corporations segregate, in their balance sheets, the owners' investment (the amount paid for their stock) and any accumulated earnings. Because there are no comparable legal restrictions on sole proprietorships and partnerships, these types of businesses do not have to distinguish between amounts invested by owners and undistributed earnings.

The following illustrations demonstrate the variations in the balance sheet presentation of owners' equity for the three forms of business organization. In Chapters 14–18, we will consider in more detail the distinctive features of corporation and partnership accounting.

CASE I: SOLE PROPRIETORSHIP George Taylor originally invested $50,000 in a graphics business. Subsequent earnings left in the business amounted to $30,000. The owner's equity section of the firm's balance sheet would appear as follows:

Owner's Equity	
George Taylor, Capital	$80,000

CASE II: PARTNERSHIP George Taylor, Eva Williams, and John Young invested $25,000, $15,000, and $10,000, respectively, in a graphics business. Each partner's share of subsequent earnings not withdrawn from the business was $10,000. The owners' equity section of this firm's balance sheet would appear as follows:

Owners' Equity	
George Taylor, Capital	$35,000
Eva Williams, Capital	25,000
John Young, Capital	20,000
Total Owners' Equity	$80,000

CASE III: CORPORATION George Taylor, Eva Williams, and John Young began a corporation investing $25,000, $15,000, and $10,000, respectively, and receiving shares of stock for those amounts, totalling $50,000. This amount, called Capital Stock, is not available for distribution to the owners (stockholders). Unlike sole proprietorships and partnerships, in which owners are personally liable for the firm's debts, corporate stockholders' liability is usually limited to their investment. Therefore, the capital stock amount is kept intact to protect the firm's creditors. Because there may be many shareholders and because the shares of stock are freely transferable, the identity of the stockholders cannot be shown. Corporate earnings that have not been distributed are identified as *retained earnings* in the corporate balance sheet. Ordinarily, this is the maximum amount that can be distributed to the shareholders. The stockholders' equity section of the firm's balance sheet would appear as follows:

Stockholders' Equity	
Capital Stock	$50,000
Retained Earnings	30,000
	$80,000

In sole proprietorships and partnerships the owners may make withdrawals quite informally, at their own discretion. A withdrawal results in a decrease in cash and a decrease in the owner's capital account. In a corporation, a formal procedure is needed. The board of directors, elected by the stockholders, must meet and "declare a dividend" before the distribution can be made to the stockholders. If the firm in our illustration declared and paid a dividend of $5,000, both cash and retained earnings would be reduced by that amount, and the retained earnings balance would be $25,000.

DEMONSTRATION PROBLEM FOR REVIEW

L. D. Ford operates the Ford Courier Service, a single proprietorship. The firm utilizes leased vehicles, and specializes in delivery services to banks, computer centers, film dealers, pharmacies, and various small businesses. On January 1 of the current year, the assets and liabilities of the business were as follows: Cash, $8,000; Accounts Receivable, $4,200; Supplies on Hand, $1,200; Prepaid Insurance, $1,800; and Accounts Payable, $1,400. The January business activities were as follows:

(1) Paid $600 on Accounts Payable.
(2) Paid January rent, $3,600.
(3) Received $2,000 on account from customers.
(4) Purchased supplies on account, $500.
(5) Billed customers for delivery services performed on account, $11,500.
(6) Paid employees' wages, $2,400.
(7) Received $2,000 for delivery services performed for cash customers.
(8) Paid utilities expense, $180.
(9) Withdrew $900 cash for Ford's personal use.
(10) Counted supplies on hand at the end of January, $980.
(11) Determined that $150 insurance premiums had expired during January.

REQUIRED

(a) From the data in the first paragraph, prepare a balance sheet equation for Ford Courier Service as of January 1 of the current year. Use the horizontal form illustrated in Exhibit 1–3 and place the amounts on the first line of the form.

(b) Following the form of Exhibit 1–3, show how transactions (1)–(11) affect the beginning balance sheet amounts, and total the columns to prove that total assets equal liabilities plus owner's equity at January 31.

(c) Prepare an income statement for January.

SOLUTION TO DEMONSTRATION PROBLEM

	Cash	+ Accounts Receivable	+ Supplies on Hand	+ Prepaid Insurance	=	Accounts Payable	+ L. D. Ford, Capital
(a)	$8,000	+ $ 4,200	+ $1,200	+ $1,800	=	$1,400	+ $13,800
(b) (1)	− 600					− 600	
(2)	− 3,600						− 3,600
(3)	+ 2,000	− 2,000					
(4)			+ 500			+ 500	
(5)		+ 11,500					+ 11,500
(6)	− 2,400						− 2,400
(7)	+ 2,000						+ 2,000
(8)	− 180						− 180
(9)	− 900						− 900
(10)			− 720				− 720
(11)				− 150			− 150
	$4,320	+ $13,700	+ $ 980	+ $1,650	=	$1,300	+ $19,350

$20,650 (total assets) = $20,650 (liabilities plus owner's equity)

(c)

Ford Courier Service
Income Statement
For the Month of January, 19XX

Revenue		
Delivery Fees		$13,500
Expenses		
Rent Expense	$3,600	
Wages Expense	2,400	
Utilities Expense	180	
Supplies Expense	720	
Insurance Expense	150	
Total Expenses		7,050
Net Income		$ 6,450

KEY POINTS TO REMEMBER

(1) Although a balance sheet and an income statement are usually prepared at the same time, a balance sheet presents financial position at a *point in time*, while the income statement presents operating results for a *period of time*.

(2) The accounting equation, Assets = Liabilities + Owners' Equity, represents the basic structure of the balance sheet and holds true after each accounting transaction.

(3) In determining net income (Revenue − Expenses) on the *accrual* basis, *revenue* is recognized *when earned* rather than when cash is collected, and *expenses* are recognized when goods and services are *used* rather than when they are paid for.

(4) Owners' equity can be increased by contributions from owners and by revenue. It can be decreased by withdrawals and expenses. Only revenue and expenses are used in determining net income.

(5) Certain fundamental concepts underlying the accounting process include the following:

Accounting entity—each business venture is a separate unit, accounted for separately.

Historical cost—assets are reported at acquisition price and are not adjusted upward.

Objectivity—where possible, recording of transactions should be supported by verifiable evidence.

Going concern—the assumption is made in accounting that a business will continue indefinitely.

Measuring unit—conventional accounting statements are expressed in money amounts, unadjusted for changes in the value of the dollar.

SELF-TEST QUESTIONS
(Answers are at the end of this chapter.)

1. Which of the following types of accountants should be completely independent of the firm or organization whose financial data is being examined?
   (a) Controller
   (b) Certified Public Accountant
   (c) Internal Auditor
   (d) Firm's Budget Director
2. A sole proprietor decided to use the same bank account for his personal affairs as for his business. Which of the following accounting concepts is violated?
   (a) Going Concern
   (b) Accounting Entity
   (c) Measuring Unit
   (d) Objectivity
3. Which of the following transactions does not affect the balance sheet totals?
   (a) Purchasing $500 supplies on account.
   (b) Paying a $3,000 note payable.
   (c) Collecting $4,000 from customers on account.
   (d) Withdrawal of $800 by the firm's owner.
4. The ending balance of owner's equity is $21,000. During the year, the owner contributed $6,000 and withdrew $4,000. If the firm had $8,000 net income for the year, what was the beginning owner's equity?
   (a) $19,000 (b) $11,000 (c) $21,000 (d) $23,000
5. Beginning and ending total assets were $25,000 and $32,000, respectively, for the current year. At year-end, owner's equity was $20,000 and liabilities were $4,000 larger than at the beginning of the year. If owner's withdrawals exceeded contributions by $2,000, what was the net income or net loss for the year?
   (a) $5,000 net loss
   (b) $13,000 net income
   (c) $9,000 net income
   (d) $5,000 net income

QUESTIONS

1–1 Distinguish between *financial* and *managerial* accounting.

1–2 Name some outside groups that may be interested in a company's financial data and state their particular interests.

1–3 What factors are important in determining a firm's need for electronic data processing?

1–4 Since financial accounting data are primarily historical, how are they useful for control purposes?

1–5 What are *generally accepted accounting principles*, and by whom are they established?

1–6 Why do business firms frequently keep more than one set of records on certain aspects of their financial activities?

1–7 How do the functions of private accountants and public accountants differ?

1–8 What is the purpose of a balance sheet? An income statement?

1–9 Define *assets*, *liabilities*, and *owners' equity*.

1–10 Explain how the presentation of owners' equity in the balance sheet of a corporation differs from that of a single proprietorship.

1–11 State the effect on a corporation's balance sheet of
(a) The declaration of a dividend.
(b) The payment of a dividend.

1–12 What is meant by the *accounting entity*?

1–13 Explain the concepts of *historical cost, objectivity,* and *going concern*. How are they related?

1–14 When the owners of a business withdraw cash, do the withdrawals appear as expenses on the income statement? Explain.

1–15 The owner's capital on a particular balance sheet is $30,000. Without seeing the rest of this financial statement, can you say that the owner should be able to withdraw $30,000 cash from the business? Justify your answer.

1–16 How do the accrual basis and the cash basis of accounting differ?

1–17 Describe a transaction that would
(a) Increase one asset but not change the amount of total assets.
(b) Decrease an asset and a liability.
(c) Decrease an asset and owners' equity.
(d) Increase an asset and a liability.

1–18 Indicate whether each of the following would increase, decrease, or have no effect on owners' equity:
(a) Purchased supplies for cash.
(b) Withdrew supplies for personal use.
(c) Paid salaries.
(d) Purchased equipment for cash.
(e) Invested cash in business.
(f) Rendered service to customers, on account.
(g) Rendered service to customers, for cash.

1–19 On December 31 of the current year, the Kirby Company had $500,000 in total assets and owed $220,000 to creditors. If this corporation's capital stock amounted to $200,000, what amount of retained earnings should appear on a December 31 balance sheet?

1–20 During 19XX, the owners' equity of the Briggs Sport Shop increased from $70,000 to $85,000 even though the owners withdrew $10,000 for personal use. What was the net income (or loss) during 19XX if capital contributions were $8,000?

1–21 A business had total liabilities of $50,000 at the beginning of the year and $30,000 at year-end. At year-end, net assets were $70,000 and total assets were $10,000 greater than at the beginning of the year. If capital contributed exceeded capital withdrawn by $16,000, what was the net income for the year?

EXERCISES

Transaction analysis

1–22 Following the example shown in (a) below, indicate the effects of the listed transactions on the assets, liabilities, and owner's equity of the balance sheet of Victoria Webb, certified public accountant, a sole proprietorship.
(a) Purchased, for cash, a typewriter for use in office.
ANSWER: Increase assets (Office Equipment)
Decrease assets (Cash)

(b) Rendered accounting services and billed customer.
(c) Paid rent for month.
(d) Rendered tax services to customer for cash.
(e) Received amount due from customer in (b).
(f) Purchased, on account, supplies estimated to last two years.
(g) Paid employees' salaries for month.
(h) Paid for supplies purchased in (f).
(i) Withdrew cash for personal use.

Balance sheet and net income determination

1–23 At the beginning of the current year, Ross Decorators had the following balance sheet:

Assets		Liabilities	
Cash	$ 8,600	Accounts Payable	$ 9,000
Accounts Receivable	6,400		
Equipment (Less Accumulated Depreciation)	18,000	**Owner's Equity**	
		Ross, Capital	24,000
Total Assets	$33,000	Total Liabilities and Owner's Equity	$33,000

(a) At the end of the current year, Ross had the following assets and liabilities: Cash, $11,500; Accounts Receivable, $9,000; Equipment (less Accumulated Depreciation), $17,500; and Accounts Payable, $1,500. Prepare a year-end balance sheet for Ross Decorators.
(b) Assuming that Ross did not invest any money in the business during the year, but withdrew $8,000 for personal use, what was the net income or net loss for the current year?
(c) Assuming that Ross invested an additional $6,000 early in the year, but withdrew $10,000 before the end of the year, what was the net income or net loss for the current year?

Transaction analysis and net income determination

1–24 The balance sheet of R. Yates, attorney, at the beginning of an accounting period is given in equation form below, followed by seven transactions whose effects on the equation are shown.
(a) For each numbered item, describe the transaction that occurred. Of all the transactions affecting R. Yates, Capital, only transaction (5) had no effect on net income for the period.
(b) What is the amount of net income for the period?

	Cash	+ Accounts Receivable	+ Supplies on Hand	+ Prepaid Rent	=	Accounts Payable	+ R. Yates, Capital
Balance	$6,000	+ $8,000	+ $600	+ $2,400	=	$500	+ $16,500
(1)	+ 3,600	− 3,600					
(2)			+ 300			+ 300	
(3)		+ 5,200					+ 5,200
(4)	− 400					− 400	
(5)	− 1,500						− 1,500
(6)			− 450				− 450
(7)				− 400			− 400
	$7,700	+ $9,600	+ $450	+ $2,000	=	$400	+ $19,350

Determination of net income and ending capital

1–25 The following income statement and balance sheet information is available for Mallory Appraisers at the end of the current month:

Supplies on Hand	$ 2,400	Cash	$ 9,500
Accounts Receivable	12,600	Accounts Payable	4,000
Utilities Expense	500	Salaries Expense	15,000
Supplies Expense	700	Appraisal Service Fees	24,000
Rent Expense	1,800	D. Mallory, Capital (at beginning of month)	16,000

(a) Without preparing a formal income statement, calculate the net income or net loss for the month.

(b) If D. Mallory made no additional investment during the month, but withdrew $1,500, what is the amount of her capital at the end of the month?

Determination of omitted financial statement data

1–26 For the four unrelated situations below, compute the unknown amounts indicated by the letters appearing in each column.

	A	B	C	D
Beginning:				
Assets	$7,000	$10,000	$22,000	$ (d)
Liabilities	2,800	3,000	8,000	9,000
Ending:				
Assets	9,000	15,000	28,000	31,000
Liabilities	2,000	(b)	10,000	9,000
During year:				
Capital Contributed	2,000	1,800	(c)	1,500
Revenue	(a)	8,500	9,000	18,000
Capital Withdrawn	1,000	800	1,600	2,500
Expenses	6,200	6,000	5,800	12,000

Determination of retained earnings and net income

1–27 The following information appears in the records of Martin Corporation at the end of the current year:

Accounts Receivable	$ 34,000	Retained Earnings	$?
Accounts Payable	16,000	Supplies on Hand	6,000
Cash	15,000	Equipment	
Capital Stock	100,000	(Less Accumulated Depreciation)	95,000

(a) Without preparing a formal balance sheet, calculate the amount of retained earnings at the end of the current year.

(b) If the amount of the retained earnings at the beginning of the current year was $20,000, and $5,000 in dividends were declared and paid this year, what was the net income for the year?

PROBLEMS

Transaction analysis, income statement, and owner's equity statement

1–28 L. D. Cutler Appraisal Service is a sole proprietorship providing commercial and industrial appraisals and feasibility studies. On January 1 of the current year, the assets and liabilities of the business were the following: Cash, $4,500; Accounts Receivable, $5,200; Supplies on Hand, $800; and Accounts Payable, $1,500. The following business transactions occurred during January:

(1) Paid rent for three months, $1,200.
(2) Received $3,600 on customers' accounts.
(3) Paid $650 on accounts payable.
(4) Received $1,800 for services performed for cash customers.
(5) Purchased $300 worth of supplies on account.
(6) Billed the city for a feasibility study performed, $4,800, and various other credit customers, $3,700.
(7) Paid salary of assistant, $2,200.
(8) Paid utilities expense, $250.
(9) Withdrew $1,000 cash for personal use of L. D. Cutler.
(10) Supplies on hand at the end of January amounted to $520.
(11) Determined that rent expense for the month was $400 [see transaction (1)].

REQUIRED

(a) From the data in the first paragraph, prepare a balance sheet equation for L. D. Cutler Appraisal Service as of January 1 of the current year. Use the horizontal form illustrated in Exhibit 1–3 and place the amounts on the first line of the form. The headings should be as follows: Cash, Accounts Receivable, Supplies on Hand, Prepaid Rent, Accounts Payable, and L. D. Cutler, Capital.
(b) Following the form of Exhibit 1–3, show the effects of transactions (1)–(11) on the beginning balance sheet amounts, and total the columns to prove that assets equal liabilities plus owner's equity at January 31.
(c) Prepare an income statement for January.
(d) Prepare a statement of owner's equity for January.

Transaction analysis

1–29 An analysis (similar to Exhibit 1–3) of the transactions of Barton Detective Agency for the month of May appears below. Line (1) summarizes Barton's balance sheet data on May 1; lines (2)–(10) represent the business transactions for May.

	Cash	+ Accounts Receivable	+ Supplies on Hand	+ Prepaid Insurance	=	Notes Payable	+ Accounts Payable	+ Barton, Capital
(1)	$3,600	+ $9,000	+ $630	+ $360	=	$2,000	+ $650	+ $10,940
(2)	+ 1,500					+ 1,500		
(3)	+ 3,600	− 3,600						
(4)			+ 350				+ 350	
(5)		+ 8,200						+ 8,200
(6)	− 750							− 750
(7)	+ 1,800							+ 1,800
(8)			− 480					− 480
(9)				− 30				− 30
(10)	− 2,000					− 2,000		

REQUIRED
(a) Prove that assets equal liabilities plus owner's equity at May 1.
(b) Describe the apparent transaction indicated by each line. [For example, line (2): Borrowed $1,500, giving a note payable.] If any line could reasonably represent more than one type of transaction, describe each type of transaction.

Income statement, owner's equity statement, and balance sheet

1–30 On March 1, Amy Harris began the Bluebird Delivery Service, which provides delivery of bulk mailings to the post office, neighborhood delivery of weekly papers, data delivery to computer service centers, and various other delivery services via leased vans. On March 1, Harris invested $20,000 of her own funds in the firm and borrowed $10,000 from her father on a six-month, non-interest-bearing note payable. The following information is available at March 31:

Accounts Receivable	$19,300	Delivery Fees	$26,400
Rent Expense	2,200	Cash	20,200
Advertising Expense	600	Supplies on Hand, March 31	6,500
Supplies Expense	2,700	Notes Payable	10,000
Accounts Payable	5,400	Prepaid Insurance, March 31	2,200
Salaries Expense	10,600	Insurance Expense	200
Miscellaneous Expense	300	A. Harris, Capital, March 1	20,000

Harris made a $5,000 additional investment during March, but withdrew $2,000 during the month.

REQUIRED
(a) Prepare an income statement for the month of March.
(b) Prepare a statement of owner's equity for the month of March.
(c) Prepare a balance sheet at March 31.

Balance sheets for a corporation

1–31 The following balance sheet data is given for the Normandy Catering Service, a corporation, at May 31 of the current year:

Accounts Receivable	$ 9,600	Accounts Payable	$ 4,800
Notes Payable	9,000	Cash	15,300
Equipment (Less Accumulated Depreciation)	41,500	Capital Stock	50,000
Supplies on Hand	10,100	Retained Earnings	?

Assume that, during the next two days, only the following transactions occurred:

June 1 Purchased additional equipment costing $5,000, giving $3,000 cash and a $2,000 note payable.
2 Declared and paid a dividend, $2,500.

REQUIRED
(a) Prepare a balance sheet at May 31 of the current year.
(b) Prepare a balance sheet at June 2 of the current year.

Transaction analysis and income statement for a corporation

1–32 On June 1 of the current year, a group of bush pilots in Fort Frances, Ontario, formed the Rainy Lake Fly-In Service, Inc., by selling $50,000 capital stock for cash. The group then leased several amphibious aircraft and docking facilities, equipping them to transport fishermen and hunters to outpost camps owned by various resorts. The following transactions occurred during June of the current year:

(1) Sold capital stock for cash, $50,000.
(2) Paid June rent for aircraft, dockage, and dockside office, $4,500.
(3) Purchased fuel and other supplies on account, $2,150.
(4) Paid bill for June advertising in various sport magazines, $720.
(5) Paid insurance premiums for six months in advance, $4,800.
(6) Rendered fly-in services for various groups for cash, $18,000.
(7) Billed the Ministry of Natural Resources for transporting mapping personnel, $5,250, and also billed various firms for fly-in services, $6,150.
(8) Paid $350 on accounts payable.
(9) Received $3,250 on account from clients.
(10) Paid June wages, $9,400.
(11) Declared and paid a dividend, $3,000.
(12) Determined that supplies and fuel on hand at June 30 amounted to $460.
(13) Determined that $800 insurance premiums expired during June.

REQUIRED

(a) Using the horizontal form of the balance sheet equation illustrated in Exhibit 1–3, designate the following column headings: Cash, Accounts Receivable, Supplies on Hand, Prepaid Insurance, Accounts Payable, Capital Stock, and Retained Earnings.
(b) Following the form of Exhibit 1–3, show how the June transactions affect the balance sheet amounts, and total all columns to prove that assets equal liabilities plus stockholders' equity.
(c) Prepare an income statement for June.

Balance sheets and income determination

1–33 Balance sheet information for the Sawyer Packaging Service at the end of the last two years is given below.

	December 31, This Year	December 31, Last Year
Accounts Receivable	$48,000	$36,000
Accounts Payable	18,000	17,000
Cash	21,000	16,000
Equipment (Less Accumulated Depreciation)	22,000	25,000
Prepaid Insurance	800	600
Supplies on Hand	3,200	2,800
Land	12,000	12,000
Building (Less Accumulated Depreciation)	30,000	31,000
Mortgage Payable	34,000	37,000
Sawyer, Capital	?	?

REQUIRED

(a) Prepare balance sheets for December 31 of each year.
(b) Sawyer contributed $5,000 to the business early this year but withdrew $8,000 in December of this year. Calculate the net income for this year.

ALTERNATE PROBLEMS

Transaction analysis, income statement, and owner's equity statement

1–28A Susan Russell began the Russell Answering Service, a sole proprietorship, during December of last year. The firm provides services for professional people and is currently operating with leased equipment. On January 1 of this year, the assets and liabilities of the business were: Cash, $4,100; Accounts Receivable, $5,600; Supplies on Hand, $720; and Accounts Payable, $450. The following transactions occurred during January.

(1) Paid rent on office and equipment for January through March, $1,500.
(2) Collected $3,250 on account from clients.
(3) Purchased supplies on account, $230.
(4) Billed clients for work performed on account, $8,600.
(5) Paid $200 on accounts payable.
(6) Paid advertising expense, $160.
(7) Paid salaries expense, $2,400.
(8) Paid utilities expense, $140.
(9) Withdrew $600 for Susan Russell's personal use.
(10) Supplies on hand at the end of January amounted to $680.
(11) Determined that $500 of prepaid rent had expired [see transaction (1)].

REQUIRED

(a) From the information in the first paragraph, prepare a balance sheet equation for Russell Answering Service. Use the horizontal form illustrated in Exhibit 1–3 and place the balance sheet amounts at January 1 on the first line of the form. Column headings should include: Cash, Accounts Receivable, Supplies on Hand, Prepaid Rent, Accounts Payable, and S. Russell, Capital.
(b) Following the form of Exhibit 1–3, show the effects of the January transactions on the balance sheet amounts, and total all columns to prove that assets equal liabilities plus owner's equity.
(c) Prepare an income statement for January.
(d) Prepare a statement of owner's equity for January.

Transaction analysis

1–29A Appearing below is an analysis (similar to Exhibit 1–3) of the June transactions for Robert Clayton, consulting engineer. Line (1) summarizes Clayton's balance sheet data on June 1; lines (2)–(10) are the business transactions for June.

	Cash +	Accounts Receivable	+ Supplies on Hand +	Prepaid Rent	=	Accounts Payable	+ Notes Payable +	R. Clayton, Capital
(1)	$2,300 +	$6,100	+ $550 +	$840	=	$640	+ 0 +	$9,150
(2)			+ 360			+ 360		
(3)	+ 3,000						+ $3,000	
(4)	+ 4,800	− 4,800						
(5)		+ 3,500						+ 3,500
(6)	− 160							− 160
(7)	− 520					− 520		
(8)	− 3,000						− 3,000	
(9)			− 480					− 480
(10)				− 420				− 420

REQUIRED
(a) Prove that assets equal liabilities plus owner's equity on June 1.
(b) Describe the apparent transactions indicated by each line. For example, line (2): Purchased supplies on account, $360. If any line could reasonably represent more than one type of transaction, describe each type of transaction.

Income statement, owner's equity statement, and balance sheet

1–30A After all transactions and adjustments have been reflected for the current year, the records of L. Norwood, interior decorator, show the following information:

Notes Payable	$ 1,800	Supplies on Hand, December 31	$ 1,700
Prepaid Insurance, December 31	450	Cash	2,800
Decorating Fees	31,500	Accounts Receivable	21,500
Supplies Expense	1,900	Advertising Expense	460
Insurance Expense	150	Salaries Expense	8,400
Miscellaneous Expense	140	Rent Expense	4,800
L. Norwood, Capital, January 1	9,850	Accounts Payable	850

Norwood made an additional investment of $2,000 in the business during the year and withdrew $3,700 near the end of the year.

REQUIRED
(a) Prepare an income statement for the current year.
(b) Prepare a statement of owner's equity for the current year.
(c) Prepare a balance sheet at December 31 of the current year.

Balance sheets for a corporation

1–31A The following balance sheet data is given for Ward Plumbing Contractors, Inc., at June 30 of the current year:

Accounts Payable	$ 5,100	Capital Stock	$100,000
Cash	22,400	Retained Earnings	?
Supplies on Hand	7,600	Notes Payable	5,000
Equipment (Less Accumulated Depreciation)	84,000	Accounts Receivable	18,000
		Prepaid Insurance	800

Assume that, during the next two days, only the following transactions occurred:

July 1 Paid non-interest-bearing note due today, $5,000.
2 Purchased equipment for $7,000, paying $5,000 cash and giving a note payable for the balance.
2 Declared and paid a dividend, $3,000.

REQUIRED
(a) Prepare a balance sheet at June 30 of the current year.
(b) Prepare a balance sheet at July 2 of the current year.

BUSINESS DECISION PROBLEM

Rodney Dunn, a friend of yours, is negotiating the purchase of a firm called Cascade Car Wash, which operates two car washes in the city. Dunn has managed a car wash in another city and knows the technical side of the business. However, he knows little about accounting, so he asks for your assistance. The sole owner of the firm, M. Klein, has provided Dunn with income statements for the past three years, which show an average net income of $45,000 per year. The latest balance sheet shows total assets of $150,000 and liabilities of $25,000. Included among the assets are buildings listed at $35,000 after accumulated depreciation and equipment listed at $75,000 after accumulated depreciation. Dunn brings the following matters to your attention:

(1) Klein is asking $150,000 for the firm. He has told Dunn that, because the firm has been earning 36% on the owner's investment, the price should be higher than the net assets on the balance sheet.

(2) Dunn has noticed no salary for Klein on the income statements, even though he worked half-time in the business. Klein explained that because he had other income, he withdrew only $8,000 each year from the firm for personal use. If he purchases the firm, Dunn will hire a full-time manager for the firm at an annual salary of $20,000.

(3) Dunn wonders whether the buildings and equipment are really worth $110,000, the net amount shown on the balance sheet.

(4) Klein's tax returns for the past three years report a lower net income for the firm than the amounts shown in the financial statements. Dunn is skeptical about the accounting principles used in preparing the financial statements.

REQUIRED

(a) How did Klein arrive at the 36% return figure given in (1)? If Dunn accepts Klein's average annual income figure of $45,000, what would Dunn's percentage return be, assuming that the net income remained at the same level and that the firm was purchased for $150,000?

(b) Should Klein's withdrawals affect the net income reported in the financial statements? What will Dunn's percentage return be if he takes into consideration the $20,000 salary he plans to pay a full-time manager?

(c) What explanation would you give Dunn with respect to the value of the buildings and equipment?

(d) Could there be legitimate reasons for the difference between net income shown in the financial statements and net income reported on the tax returns, as mentioned in (4)? How might Dunn obtain additional assurance about the propriety of the financial statements?

ANSWERS TO SELF-TEST QUESTIONS

1. (b) 2. (b) 3. (c) 4. (b) 5. (d)

2

The Double-entry Accounting System

Chapter Objectives

- Review transaction analysis.
- Explain nature and format of an account.
- Describe the system of debits and credits.
- Illustrate debit and credit analysis of transactions.
- Explain nature and format of a trial balance.
- Discuss common types of errors in transaction analysis.

When the book lies open in front of you and you look at the book (not the book at you) then the side where you have your heart is the left or Debit side. The side away from your heart is the right side and is called Credit.

MATHÄUS SCHWARTZ, 1518

The format for analyzing and recording transactions illustrated in Chapter 1 was useful in conveying a basic understanding of how transactions affect financial statements. This approach is not effective, however, in meeting management's needs for timely financial information. The transactions of most business firms are numerous and complex, affecting many different items appearing on the financial statements. Therefore, a formal system of classification and recording is required so that data may be gathered for day-to-day management requirements and timely accounting reports. In this chapter, we will examine the classification and recording system commonly called double-entry accounting. At the same time, we will expand several of the basic ideas introduced in Chapter 1.

CATEGORIES OF DATA NEEDED

Exhibit 2–1 shows the balance sheet and the income statement forms explained in Chapter 1. To prepare both the balance sheet and the income statement, we need five categories of information from the accounting system: **assets, liabilities,**

EXHIBIT 2–1
The Basic Financial Statements

ABC Company
Balance Sheet
December 31, 19XX

(List of assets)	$ XX	(List of liabilities)	$ XX
	XX		XX
	XX		
	XX	Total Liabilities	$ XX
		Owners' Equity	XX
Total Assets	$XXX	Total Liabilities and Owners' Equity	$XXX

ABC Company
Income Statement
For the Month of December, 19XX

Revenue		$XXX
Expenses:	$XX	
	XX	
	XX	
	XX	
Total Expenses		XX
Net Income		$ XX

owners' equity, revenue and **expenses.** The first three relate to the balance sheet and the last two relate to the income statement.

In Chapter 1 we analyzed the effects of transactions on the balance sheet equation by starting with the three major categories: assets, liabilities, and owners' equity. When we used the basic accounting equation (Assets = Liabilities + Owners' Equity), we noted that owners' equity included increases from revenue and decreases from expenses. Specifically, owners' equity at the balance sheet date consisted of (1) the beginning balance, (2) net capital contributions (additional contributions less withdrawals), and (3) net income for the period (revenue less expenses). In preparing an income statement, we analyzed changes in owners' equity to obtain the necessary revenue and expense data.

Since in a typical business, most transactions relate to revenue and expense, it is more efficient to keep track of revenue and expense as a separate part of owners' equity. The following expanded form of the accounting equation is useful:[1]

ASSETS = LIABILITIES + ——OWNERS' EQUITY——

$$\left[\textbf{Beginning Capital} + \textbf{Contributions} - \textbf{Withdrawals}\right] + \left[\textbf{Revenue} - \textbf{Expenses}\right]$$

If we had used this expanded equation in summarizing the June transactions of the Westgate Driving School (see Exhibit 1–3, page 23), the changes in owner's equity would have been shown in three columns, as follows:

	J. King, Capital + Contributions − Withdrawals	**+ Revenue**	**− Expenses**
(1) Capital contribution	+ $60,000		
(3) Rent expense			− $ 5,800
(6) Billings to students		+ $21,500	
(7) Salaries expense			− 9,000
(10) Utilities expense			− 250
(11) Withdrawal by King	− 2,000		
(12) Insurance expense			− 200
(13) Supplies expense			− 2,250
	$58,000	+ $21,500	− $17,500
		$62,000	

Observe that the column totals in the above illustration, when added together, amount to $62,000, exactly the amount of the ending owner's equity shown in Exhibit 1–3. Segregating revenue and expense amounts, however, permits us to prepare an income statement without first having to analyze all changes in the owner's capital for the period. The desirability of doing this is apparent even in a situation as simple as our Westgate Driving School example. In more complex

[1]In a corporation, beginning capital consists of both capital stock and retained earnings. Contributions would equal additional capital stock sold, whereas withdrawals would be the amount of dividends declared during the period.

business situations—with many sources of revenue and possibly hundreds of different types of expenses—separate recording of revenue and expenses is imperative.

So far, our discussion of transaction analysis has been conceptual; we have tried to convey an understanding of how transactions affect the financial statements. Obviously, the system of transaction recording we have illustrated would be entirely inadequate for even relatively simple businesses, since even they will usually have a substantial number of transactions involving a variety of data to be reported in financial statements. In practice, the necessary data are accumulated in a set of records called *accounts*.

THE ACCOUNT

The basic component of the formal accounting system is the **account**, which is an individual record of increases and decreases in specific assets, liabilities, owner capital, revenue, and expenses. The Cash account for the Westgate Driving School might appear as shown in Exhibit 2–2.

The amounts in the Westgate Driving School Cash account consist of the additions and deductions in the cash column of Exhibit 1–3. Increases in the Cash account have been placed on the left side and the decreases on the right side. A formal system of placement for increases and decreases in various accounts is explained later in this chapter. In our example, there was no beginning amount (balance), because June was the first month of business. A beginning amount would have appeared with the increases, above the entry for $60,000.

The form illustrated in Exhibit 2–2, called a *two-column* account, is often used in a manually maintained record-keeping system. Another popular form, called a *running balance*, or *three-column* account, is illustrated later in this chapter. Most account forms facilitate recording the following information:

(1) The account title and number.

(2) Amounts reflecting increases and decreases.

(3) Cross-references to other accounting records.

(4) Dates and descriptive notations.

Each account has a short account title that describes the data being recorded in that account. Some common account titles are Cash, Accounts Receivable, Notes Payable, Professional Fees, and Rent Expense. In manually maintained records, increases and decreases are recorded in ruled columns under headings that indicate the meaning of the amounts appearing there. These amounts are referred to as **entries**. In other words, making an entry in an account consists of recording an amount in a particular place to represent either an increase or a decrease in the account. The normal balance of any account is simply the excess of increases over decreases that have been recorded to date. In Exhibit 2–2, we have indicated this balance, $28,150, on the left side of the account beside the

EXHIBIT 2–2
Cash Account for the Westgate Driving School

Cash Account No. ______

Date	Description	Post. Ref.	Amount	Date	Description	Post. Ref.	Amount
19XX				19XX			
June 1			60,000	June 2			24,000
30	28,150		18,000	3			5,800
			78,000	4			7,200
				30			9,000
				30			1,600
				30			250
				30			2,000
							49,850

last entry for an increase. This is the difference between the sum of the increases, $78,000, and the sum of the decreases, $49,850, both of which are written in pencil to provide temporary totals. Finally, most accounts contain space for presentation of other types of information—for example, the date of any entry, possibly some memoranda explaining a particular entry, and a posting reference column (indicated by Post. Ref.). The posting reference column is used for noting the records from which entries into this account may have been taken. This practice will be explained more fully in the next chapter.

The account is an extremely simple record that can be summarized in terms of four money elements:

(1) Beginning balance.

(2) Additions.

(3) Deductions.

(4) Ending balance.

Obviously, if any three elements are known, the fourth can easily be computed. Normally, after transactions have been recorded, only the ending balance needs to be computed. Accountants, however, are sometimes confronted with situations in which available data are incomplete and reconstruction of accounts is necessary. Let us demonstrate such an analysis with the following example:

	A	B	C	D
Beginning balance	$10	$70	$ 40	$ (?)
Additions	40	30	(?)	100
Deductions	20	(?)	160	120
Ending balance	(?)	10	0	40

In column A, the ending balance must be $20 greater than the beginning balance, because the additions exceed the deductions by $20. The ending balance is therefore $30. In B, the account balance decreased by $60, so the deductions must exceed the additions by $60. Therefore, total deductions are $90. Show that the unknown variable in C is $120 and in D is $60.

A simplified form often used to represent the account in accounting textbooks and in the classroom is referred to as the **T account** (because it resembles the letter T). This is merely a skeleton version of the account illustrated for actual record keeping. A T-account form with the June changes in Cash entered for the Westgate Driving School follows:

Cash

(1)	60,000	(2)	24,000
(8)	18,000	(3)	5,800
	78,000	(4)	7,200
		(7)	9,000
		(9)	1,600
		(10)	250
		(11)	2,000
			49,850

Because dates and other related data are usually omitted in T accounts, it is customary to "key" the entries with a number or a letter to identify the transactions or entry. This permits a systematic review of the entries in the event that an error has been made. It also enables anyone to review a set of such accounts and match related entries. The numbers in this T account are the ones used to identify the June transactions for the Westgate Driving School in our Chapter 1 example.

The printed account form in Exhibit 2–2 is appropriate for classifying accounting data in manual record-keeping systems. In accounting systems employing computers, the account form may not be obvious because the actual data might be stored on media such as magnetic tapes or discs. Every accounting system, however, whether manual or automated, must provide for the retrieval and printing out of the types of information shown in the manual form.

THE SYSTEM OF DEBITS AND CREDITS

One basic characteristic of all account forms is that entries recording increases and decreases are separated. In some accounts, such as the Cash account illustrated in Exhibit 2–2, increases are recorded on the left-hand side of the account and decreases on the right-hand side; in other accounts the reverse is true. The method used in different types of accounts is a matter of convention; that is, a simple set of rules is followed. The remainder of this chapter is devoted to the discussion and illustration of such rules.

The terms **debit** and **credit** are used to describe the left-hand and the right-hand sides of an account, as shown below.

(Any type of account)

Debit	**Credit**
Always the left side	Always the right side

Regardless of what is recorded in an account, an entry made on the left-hand side is a debit to the account, while an entry recorded on the right-hand side is a credit to the account. Sometimes the abbreviations dr. and cr. are used.

THE ORIGINS OF RECORD KEEPING

Double-entry bookkeeping is simply a specialized form of keeping accounts. It is neither a discovery of science nor the inspiration of a happy moment, but the outcome of continued efforts to meet the changing necessities of trade.*

The origin of keeping accounts has been traced as far back as 8500 B.C., the date archaeologists have established for certain clay tokens—cones, disks, spheres, and pellets—found in Mesopotamia (modern Iraq). These tokens represented such commodities as sheep, jugs of oil, bread, or clothing and were used in the Middle East to keep records. The tokens were often sealed in clay balls, called *bullae*, which were broken on delivery so the shipment could be checked against the invoice; *bullae*, in effect, were the first bills of lading. Later, symbols impressed on wet clay tablets replaced the tokens. Some experts consider this stage of record keeping the beginning of the art of writing, which spread rapidly along the trade routes and took hold throughout the known civilized world.†

Development of more formal account keeping methods is attributed to the merchants and bankers of Florence, Venice, and Genoa during the thirteenth to fifteenth centuries. The earliest of these methods consisted of accounts kept by a Florentine banker in 1211 A.D. The system was fairly primitive; accounts were not related in any special way (in terms of equality for entries), and balancing of the accounts was lacking. Systematic bookkeeping evolved from these methods, however, and double-entry records first appeared in Genoa in 1340 A.D.‡

The first treatise on the art of systematic bookkeeping appeared in 1494, in Venice. "Everything About Arithmetic, Geometry, and Proportion" (*Summa de Arithmetica, Geometria, Proportioni et Proportionalita*) was written by the Franciscan monk, Fra Luca Paciolo, one of the most celebrated mathematicians of his day. The work was not, in fact, intended to give instruction in bookkeeping, but to summarize the existing knowledge of mathematics. The treatise on bookkeeping appeared in the arithmetical part of the work. Although Paciolo made no claim to developing the art of bookkeeping, he has been regarded as the father of double-entry accounting. In "An Historical Defense of Bookkeeping," eminent accountant Henry Rand Hatfield referred to the system as one "sired four hundred years ago by a monk, and today damned by thousands of university students."§

*Richard Brown, ed., *A History of Accounting and Accountants* (New York: Augustus M. Kelly Publishers, 1968), page 93.

†"The Roots of Writing," *Time*, August 1, 1977, page 76.

‡Richard Brown, page 99.

§A paper read before the American Association of University Instructors in Accounting (now the American Accounting Association), December 29, 1923 and reprinted in *The Journal of Accountancy*, April 1924, page 247.

EXHIBIT 2–3
Pattern of Increases and Decreases, Debits and Credits, and Normal Balances

Five Major Categories of Accounts

	Assets		Liabilities		Owners' Equity		Revenue		Expenses	
(1) Always true	Debit	Credit	Debit	Credit	Debit	Credit	Debit	Credit	Debit	Credit
(2) Increases	+			+		+		+	+	
(3) Decreases		−	−		−		−			−
(4) Normal balance	★			★		★		★	★	

The terms *debit* and *credit* are not synonymous with the words *increase* and *decrease*. The system of debits and credits related to increases and decreases in each of the five categories of accounts—assets, liabilities, owners' equity, revenue, and expenses—is shown in Exhibit 2–3.

The system of debits and credits illustrated here is the standard **double-entry** system, so-called because at least two entries, a debit and a credit, are made for each transaction. The system of rules is analogous to the set of traffic rules whereby everyone in this country agrees to drive on the right-hand side of the road. Obviously, the system would work if we reversed everything; the important point is that we all follow the same rules.

Observe the following relationships in Exhibit 2–3:

(1) Debit always refers to the left side of any account, and credit refers to the right side.

(2) Increases in asset and expense accounts are debit entries, while increases in liability, owners' equity, and revenue accounts are credit entries.

(3) Decreases are logically recorded on the side opposite increases.

(4) The normal balance of any account is on the side on which increases are recorded—asset and expense accounts normally have debit balances, while the other three groups normally have credit balances. This result occurs because increases in an account are customarily greater than or equal to decreases.

Note that the pattern for assets is opposite that for liabilities and owners' equity. Also observe that the pattern for revenue is the same as for owners' equity. This is to be expected, because revenue increases owners' equity. Following the same logic, the pattern for expenses is opposite that of owners' equity, because expenses reduce owners' equity.

THE RUNNING BALANCE ACCOUNT

In manually maintained accounting records, the running balance, or three-column, ledger account is often used rather than the symmetrical two-column form illustrated in Exhibit 2–2. The Cash account for the Westgate Driving School in running balance form is shown in Exhibit 2–4. Notice that the account contains all the information shown in the two-column account but also provides a balance after each transaction.

The major advantage of this type of account over the two-column account is that the account balance is apparent for any date during the period. Use of the running balance account also avoids the monthly ruling of accounts, which is customarily done when the two-column account is used. A slight disadvantage is that one must be careful to note whether the account has a normal balance or not. An abnormal account balance should be placed in parentheses. For example, if we overdrew our bank balance, the Cash account balance would be abnormal (a credit balance).

We shall employ the running balance account in our formal illustrations throughout the succeeding chapters. To assist you in the earlier chapters, we have placed an asterisk (*) in the column of the account that designates its normal balance. In illustrations in which detail is not needed and concepts are emphasized, we will use T accounts.

EXHIBIT 2–4
Cash Account for the Westgate Driving School

Cash Account No. ______

Date		Description	Post. Ref.	Debit*	Credit	Balance
19XX						
June	1			60,000		60,000
	2				24,000	36,000
	3				5,800	30,200
	4				7,200	23,000
	30				9,000	14,000
	30			18,000		32,000
	30				1,600	30,400
	30				250	30,150
	30				2,000	28,150

ILLUSTRATION OF DEBIT AND CREDIT ANALYSIS

The following illustration of debit and credit analysis uses the transactions given in Chapter 1 for the first month's operations of the Westgate Driving School. Each transaction is stated, analyzed, and followed by an illustration of the appropriate debit and credit entries in the various accounts, using T accounts for simplicity. We have numbered each transaction for reference as in Chapter 1. In the transaction analysis and the resulting debits and credits, each entry resulting from a particular transaction is parenthetically keyed to the transaction number.

TRANSACTION (1): On June 1, John King deposited $60,000 of his personal funds in a special checking account for the Westgate Driving School.

Analysis: In the first transaction of Westgate Driving School, King's contribution of capital increases both the assets and the equities of the firm. Specifically, Cash increases by $60,000, and the owner's equity account, J. King, Capital, increases by the same amount. The entries are

Debit Cash $60,000 **Credit** J. King, Capital $60,000

The related accounts would appear as follows:

Cash			
(1)	60,000		

J. King, Capital			
		(1)	60,000

TRANSACTION (2): On June 2, King paid $24,000 for a lot to be used for storing vehicles and for some driving instruction.

Analysis: This transaction represents the conversion of one asset to another, resulting in an increase in the asset, Land, and a decrease in the asset, Cash. The entries are

Debit Land $24,000 **Credit** Cash $24,000

The related accounts would appear as follows:

Land			
(2)	24,000		

Cash			
(1)	60,000	(2)	24,000

TRANSACTION (3): On June 3, King paid $800 to rent a furnished office and $5,000 for leasing training vehicles for June.

Analysis: The cost of using the office and the training vehicles is a June operating expense. When financial statements are prepared at the end of June, the month's rent will appear on the income statement as an expense. The transaction reduces Cash and increases Rent Expense. The entries are

Debit Rent Expense $5,800 **Credit** Cash $5,800

The related accounts would appear as follows:

Rent Expense			
(3)	5,800		

Cash			
(1)	60,000	(2)	24,000
		(3)	5,800

TRANSACTION (4): On June 4, King paid vehicle insurance premiums of $7,200 for three years.

Analysis: This payment for future coverage creates an asset, Prepaid Insurance, and reduces the asset Cash. As each month passes, $\frac{1}{36}$ of the amount, or $200, will appear on the income statement as Insurance Expense, the cost of that month's coverage [see transaction (12)]. The entries are

Debit Prepaid Insurance $7,200 **Credit** Cash $7,200

The related accounts would appear as follows:

Prepaid Insurance			
(4)	7,200		

Cash			
(1)	60,000	(2)	24,000
		(3)	5,800
		(4)	7,200

TRANSACTION (5): On June 5, King purchased fuel and other supplies on account for $3,600.

Analysis: King has purchased the fuel and other supplies on credit terms rather than with cash. This transaction increases both an asset, Supplies on Hand, and a liability, Accounts Payable. At the end of the month, supplies will be counted to determine the amount used during the month. The asset will then be reduced and the related expense increased [see transaction (13)]. The entries are

Debit Supplies on Hand $3,600 **Credit** Accounts Payable $3,600

The related accounts would appear as follows:

Supplies on Hand			
(5)	3,600		

Accounts Payable			
		(5)	3,600

TRANSACTION (6): On June 26, the school's students were billed $21,500 for June instructional fees.

Analysis: Providing instruction during the month generates an asset, Accounts Receivable, and revenue, Instructional Fees. Note that the revenue is reflected in the month that instruction is given, even though the students may not pay the fees until a later period. The entries are

Debit Accounts Receivable $21,500 **Credit** Instructional Fees $21,500

The related accounts would appear as follows:

Accounts Receivable

(6)	21,500		

Instructional Fees

		(6)	21,500

TRANSACTION (7): On June 30, King paid instructors' salaries for June of $9,000.

Analysis: The services received from driving instructors during the month represent an expense that will be shown on the June income statement. Therefore, this transaction increases an expense, Salaries Expense, and decreases an asset, Cash. The entries are

Debit Salaries Expense $9,000 **Credit** Cash $9,000

The related accounts would appear as follows:

Salaries Expense

(7)	9,000		

Cash

(1)	60,000	(2)	24,000
		(3)	5,800
		(4)	7,200
		(7)	9,000

TRANSACTION (8): On June 30, the school collected $18,000 on account from students billed in transaction (6).

Analysis: Receipt of this amount represents the collection of students' accounts, not new revenue. Recall that the related revenue was recorded in transaction (6), when the claims against students were recognized as the asset Accounts Receivable. This transaction changes one asset form (Accounts Receivable) into another asset form (Cash). Cash increases by $18,000 and Accounts Receivable decreases by the same amount. The entries are

Debit Cash $18,000 **Credit** Accounts Receivable $18,000

The related accounts would appear as follows:

Cash

(1)	60,000	(2)	24,000
(8)	18,000	(3)	5,800
		(4)	7,200
		(7)	9,000

Accounts Receivable

(6)	21,500	(8)	18,000

TRANSACTION (9): On June 30, the school paid $1,600 on account for the supplies purchased in transaction (5).

Analysis: Paying $1,600 of the $3,600 owed reduces both Cash and Accounts Payable by $1,600, therefore reducing both assets and liabilities. This payment is the partial settlement of a previously recorded obligation, not an expense. The entries are

Debit Accounts Payable $1,600 **Credit** Cash $1,600

The related accounts would appear as follows:

Accounts Payable

(9)	1,600	(5)	3,600

Cash

(1)	60,000	(2)	24,000
(8)	18,000	(3)	5,800
		(4)	7,200
		(7)	9,000
		(9)	1,600

TRANSACTION (10): On June 30, King paid $250 for office utilities (electricity and telephone).

Analysis: Since the utility services have been used in June, this amount is a June expense and will be reflected in the income statement prepared at June 30. Utilities Expense increases and Cash decreases by $250. The entries are

Debit Utilities Expense $250 **Credit** Cash $250

The related accounts would appear as follows:

Utilities Expense

(10)	250		

Cash

(1)	60,000	(2)	24,000
(8)	18,000	(3)	5,800
		(4)	7,200
		(7)	9,000
		(9)	1,600
		(10)	250

TRANSACTION (11): On June 30, King withdrew $2,000 from the firm for personal use.

Analysis: King has withdrawn this amount for his personal living expenses. The transaction reduces Cash and decreases King's equity in the Westgate Driving School by $2,000.

Although the reduction in owner's equity may be entered as a debit to the J. King, Capital account, King prefers to show all his withdrawals in a separate account. A proprietor uses a separate account, called the **drawing** account, to determine quickly the total amount withdrawn during a period without having to analyze the capital account. Drawing accounts (sometimes called *personal* accounts) are commonly used in sole proprietorships and partnerships. The account, J. King, Drawing, is a **contra** account because its balance represents a reduction of its related account, J. King, Capital. Debiting the drawing account to reflect the reduction in owner's equity has the same effect as debiting the owner's capital account directly. At the end of the period, after the net income has been added to the owner's capital account, the debit balance in the drawing account is deducted to arrive at the ending amount of owner's capital. Thus, the entries for King's withdrawal are

Debit J. King, Drawing $2,000 **Credit** Cash $2,000

The related accounts would appear as follows:

J. King, Drawing

(11)	2,000		

Cash

(1)	60,000	(2)	24,000
(8)	18,000	(3)	5,800
		(4)	7,200
		(7)	9,000
		(9)	1,600
		(10)	250
		(11)	2,000

TRANSACTION (12): On June 30, $\frac{1}{36}$ (one month) of the prepaid insurance, or $200, had expired.

Analysis: In transaction (4), the firm paid $7,200 in insurance premiums for a 36-month policy. Because this amount represented payment for future coverage, the asset Prepaid Insurance was debited. At the end of June, $\frac{1}{36}$ of the premiums has expired and no longer represents an asset. It will appear as Insurance Expense on the income statement prepared on June 30. The entries are

Debit Insurance Expense $200 **Credit** Prepaid Insurance $200

The related accounts would appear as follows:

Insurance Expense

(12)	200		

Prepaid Insurance

(4)	7,200	(12)	200

TRANSACTION (13): On June 30, supplies were counted, and only $1,350 worth of supplies remained on hand.

Analysis: In transaction (5), supplies costing $3,600 were purchased and recorded as an asset. Supplies on hand now amount to only $1,350, and the $2,250 difference represents the supplies used during June. As we explained in the analysis of transaction (5), supplies used are a June expense. Therefore, an entry should be made to reduce Supplies on Hand by $2,250 and increase Supplies Expense by $2,250. The entries are

Debit Supplies Expense $2,250 **Credit** Supplies on Hand $2,250

The related accounts would appear as follows:

Supplies Expense

(13)	2,250		

Supplies on Hand

(5)	3,600	(13)	2,250

After the foregoing transactions have been entered properly, the account balances can be determined. The accounts of the Westgate Driving School are shown in Exhibit 2–5 (see pages 56–57), together with the financial statements that would eventually be prepared from the balances of these accounts. Observe the following:

(1) Accounts accumulate data, especially revenue and expense accounts, which provide data for the income statement.

(2) Keying transactions permits tracing any entry to both its originating transaction and its related change in some other account.

(3) John King's equity of $62,000 at the end of June results from

(a) His original capital contribution	$60,000
(b) Plus his earnings for June	4,000
	$64,000
(c) Minus his withdrawals	2,000
Ending balance in balance sheet	$62,000

(4) Using the contra account, J. King, Drawing, does not change the net amount of owner's equity shown on the financial statements.

EXHIBIT 2–5
The Accounts and Financial Statements of the Westgate Driving School

Assets = **Liabilities** + **Owner's Equity**

Assets

Cash

(1) 60,000	(2) 24,000
(8) 18,000	(3) 5,800
	(4) 7,200
	(7) 9,000
	(9) 1,600
	(10) 250
	(11) 2,000
Bal. 28,150	

Accounts Receivable

(6) 21,500	(8) 18,000
Bal. 3,500	

Prepaid Insurance

(4) 7,200	(12) 200
Bal. 7,000	

Supplies on Hand

(5) 3,600	(13) 2,250
Bal. 1,350	

Land

(2) 24,000	

Liabilities

Accounts Payable

(9) 1,600	(5) 3,600
	Bal. 2,000

Owner's Equity

J. King, Capital

	(1) 60,000

J. King, Drawing

(11) 2,000	

Instructional Fees

	(6) 21,500

Rent Expense

(3) 5,800	

Salaries Expense

(7) 9,000	

Utilities Expense

(10) 250	

Insurance Expense

(12) 200	

Supplies Expense

(13) 2,250	

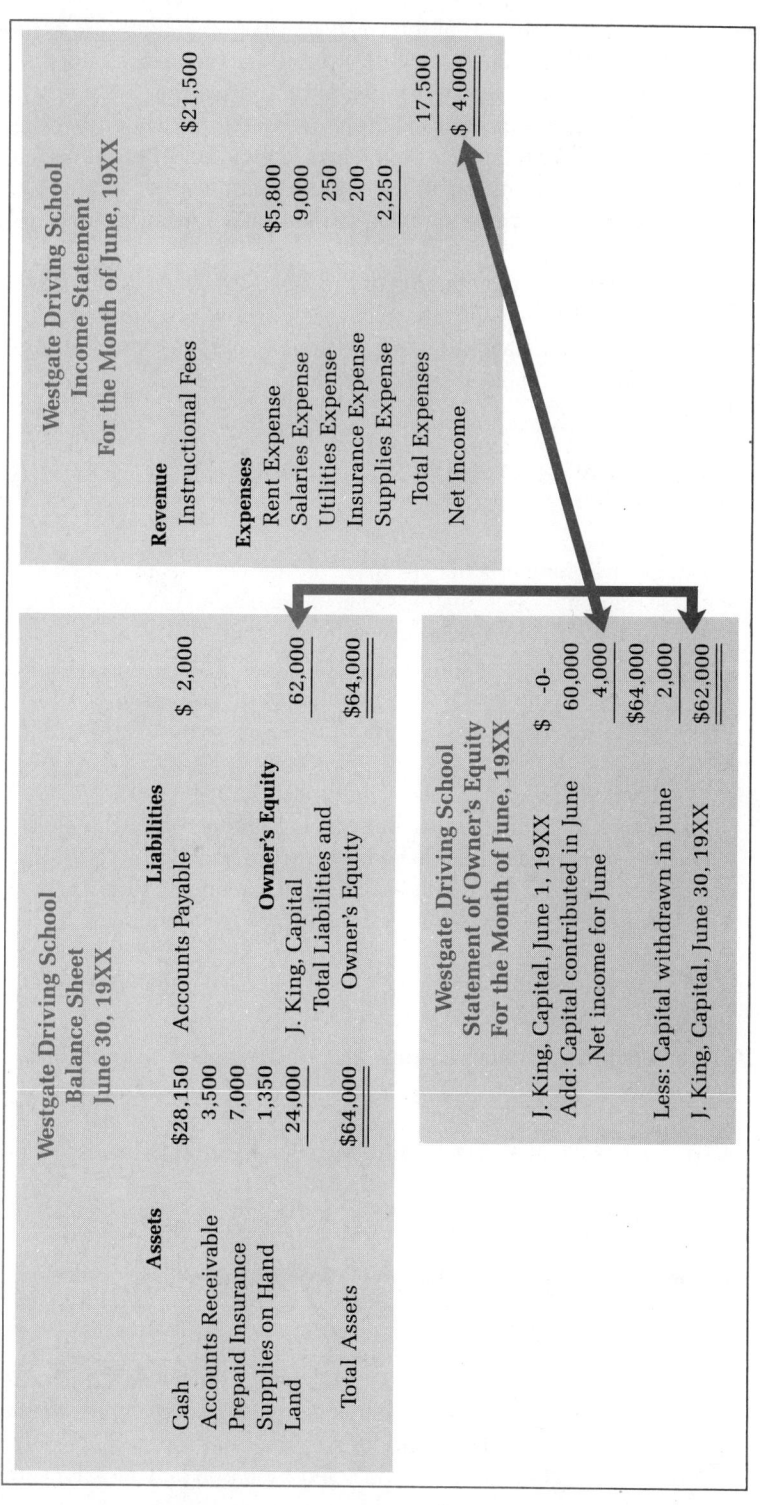

Westgate Driving School
Income Statement
For the Month of June, 19XX

Revenue		
Instructional Fees		$21,500
Expenses		
Rent Expense	$5,800	
Salaries Expense	9,000	
Utilities Expense	250	
Insurance Expense	200	
Supplies Expense	2,250	
Total Expenses		17,500
Net Income		$ 4,000

Westgate Driving School
Balance Sheet
June 30, 19XX

Assets		**Liabilities**	
Cash	$28,150	Accounts Payable	$ 2,000
Accounts Receivable	3,500		
Prepaid Insurance	7,000		
Supplies on Hand	1,350	**Owner's Equity**	
Land	24,000	J. King, Capital	62,000
		Total Liabilities and	
Total Assets	$64,000	Owner's Equity	$64,000

Westgate Driving School
Statement of Owner's Equity
For the Month of June, 19XX

J. King, Capital, June 1, 19XX	$ -0-
Add: Capital contributed in June	60,000
Net income for June	4,000
	$64,000
Less: Capital withdrawn in June	2,000
J. King, Capital, June 30, 19XX	$62,000

The June activities of the Westgate Driving School that we have just analyzed included both transactions with individuals, for which documents such as bills or checks are usually available, and activities that are sometimes described as internal transactions. For example, transactions (12) and (13)—reflecting insurance expense and supplies expense—are called internal because they represent account adjustments not initiated by documents. In Chapter 3 you will learn that entries for adjustments are usually made at a particular time and are a significant part of the accounting process.

The financial statements of the Westgate Driving School in Exhibit 2–5 are illustrated together with the accounts to show their relationship to the accounts. However, these statements would not be prepared until after a trial balance is taken, as explained in the next section.

THE GENERAL LEDGER AND THE TRIAL BALANCE

The **general ledger** is the grouping of the accounts that are used to prepare financial statements for a business. The 14 accounts that we used in our example for the Westgate Driving School would each constitute a page in the general ledger, which is usually maintained in a binder so that, when necessary, accounts may be added or removed. Usually, the accounts are grouped by category in the following order: (1) assets, (2) liabilities, (3) owners' equity, (4) revenue, and (5) expenses.

The **trial balance** is a list of the account titles in the general ledger with their respective debit or credit balances. It is prepared at the close of an accounting period after transactions have been recorded. Exhibit 2–6 illustrates a trial balance for the Westgate Driving School at the end of June.

The two main reasons for preparing a trial balance are

(1) To serve as an interim mechanical check to determine if the debits and credits in the general ledger are equal.

(2) To show all general ledger account balances on one concise record. This is often convenient when preparing financial statements.

Note that a trial balance should be dated; the trial balance of the Westgate Driving School was taken at June 30, 19XX.

ERRORS IN TRANSACTION ANALYSIS

It is always reassuring when a trial balance does balance. However, even when a trial balance is in balance, the accounting records may still contain errors. A balanced trial balance simply proves that, *as recorded*, debits equal credits. The following errors may not be detected by taking a trial balance:

EXHIBIT 2–6

Westgate Driving School
Trial Balance
June 30, 19XX

	Debit	Credit
Cash	$28,150	
Accounts Receivable	3,500	
Prepaid Insurance	7,000	
Supplies on Hand	1,350	
Land	24,000	
Accounts Payable		$ 2,000
J. King, Capital		60,000
J. King, Drawing	2,000	
Instructional Fees		21,500
Rent Expense	5,800	
Salaries Expense	9,000	
Utilities Expense	250	
Insurance Expense	200	
Supplies Expense	2,250	
	$83,500	$83,500

(1) Failing to record or enter a particular transaction.

(2) Entering a transaction more than once.

(3) Entering one or more amounts in the wrong accounts.

(4) Making an error that exactly offsets the effect of another error.

Several types of errors will cause a trial balance to be out of balance. If only one of these is present, it may be identified and located by one of the approaches suggested below. If several errors exist, however, often the only way to find them is to retrace each entry, check the arithmetic performed in balancing the accounts, and make certain that no error has occurred in transcribing amounts or in adding the trial balance. To search for errors, one should systematically follow certain procedures so that all steps are retraced only once and no steps are overlooked.

When there is a mistake in a trial balance, the first step is to determine the amount by which the total debits and credits disagree. Certain characteristics of this amount may provide a clue to identifying the type of error and finding where it was made.

DEBITS AND CREDITS INTERCHANGED When a debit is entered as a credit (or vice versa), the trial balance totals will differ by twice the amount involved. For example, if the credits exceed the debits by $246, one should look for a $123 debit that has been treated as a credit. With this type of error, the amount of the discrepancy in the trial balance totals is divisible by two. If this is not the case, either another type of error or a number of errors are involved.

ARITHMETIC ERRORS Single arithmetic errors frequently cause trial balance totals to differ by amounts such as $1,000, $100, $1, and so on. Multiple arithmetic errors may either combine or offset and result in discrepancies such as $990 (errors of $1,000 and $10 offsetting) and $101 (errors of $100 and $1 combining).

TRANSPOSITION OF NUMBERS Transposing numbers means simply reversing their order. For example, transposing the first two digits in $360 would result in $630. This type of error usually occurs when amounts are transcribed from one record to another. The resulting discrepancy is easily identified because it is always divisible by nine ($630 − $360 = $270, and $270/9 = $30). Therefore, if total debits exceeded total credits by $270, one would suspect a transposition error.

AMOUNTS OMITTED An amount can be omitted if one enters only part of an entry, fails to include an entry when balancing an account, or leaves out an account balance in a trial balance. The resulting discrepancy is equal in amount to the omitted item. Of course, the omission of a debit amount will cause an excess of credits by that amount, and vice versa.

KEY POINTS TO REMEMBER

(1) In recording changes in owners' equity, the primary reason for segregating revenue and expense items is to facilitate preparation of the income statement.

(2) The rules of debit and credit are
- (a) The left side of an account is always the debit side; the right side is always the credit side.
- (b) Increases in assets and expenses are debit entries; increases in liabilities, owners' equity, and revenue are credit entries.
- (c) The normal balance of any account appears on the side for recording increases.

(3) In transaction analysis
- (a) Each accounting transaction should be analyzed into equal debits and credits.
- (b) All accounting transactions are analyzed using one or more of the five basic account categories: (1) assets, (2) liabilities, (3) owners' equity, (4) revenue, and (5) expenses. Contra accounts, which offset related accounts in a basic category, may also be used.

SELF-TEST QUESTIONS
(Answers are at the end of this chapter.)

1. In recording transactions
   (a) The word "debit" means to increase and the word "credit" means to decrease.
   (b) Assets, expenses, and owners' drawing accounts are debited for increases.
   (c) Liabilities, revenue, and owners' drawing accounts are debited for increases.
   (d) Assets, expenses, and owners' capital accounts are debited for increases.
2. Which of the following combinations of trial balance totals does not indicate a transposition?
   (a) $65,470 debit and $64,570 credit
   (b) $32,540 debit and $35,420 credit
   (c) $25,670 debit and $26,670 credit
   (d) $14,517 debit and $15,471 credit
3. Todd had a beginning credit balance of $21,000 in his capital account. At the close of the period, Todd's drawing account had a debit balance of $2,200. On the end-of-period balance sheet, Todd's capital balance is $32,000. If Todd contributed an additional $2,000 to the firm during the period, the period's net income is
   (a) $12,400 (b) $11,200 (c) $9,000 (d) $10,800
4. The ending balance of the Accounts Receivable account was $12,000. Services billed to customers for the period were $21,500, and collections on account from customers were $23,600. The beginning balance of Accounts Receivable was
   (a) $33,500 (b) $14,100 (c) $9,900 (d) $33,100
5. Which of the following is not true of a general ledger trial balance?
   (a) It proves that the total debits equal total credits, if it balances.
   (b) It facilitates preparation of financial statements.
   (c) It proves that no errors have been made in recording transactions, if it balances.
   (d) It will not detect an error where the accounts debited and credited are reversed in recording a particular transaction.

QUESTIONS

2–1 Why is it useful to record revenue and expenses separately from the owner's capital account?

2–2 Name the five categories of information needed to prepare the balance sheet and the income statement. Which categories are identified with the balance sheet? Which are identified with the income statement?

2–3 What information is recorded in an account?

2–4 Explain the terms *general ledger* and *trial balance*. What are the reasons for preparing a trial balance?

2–5 What general statement can be made about the *normal* side of an account?

2–6 Present three common business transactions that would not affect the amount of owners' equity.

2–7 Identify the following as asset, liability, owner's equity, revenue, or expense accounts and indicate whether a debit entry or a credit entry increases the balance of the account.

Professional Fees	Adams, Capital
Accounts Receivable	Advertising Expense
Accounts Payable	Supplies on Hand
Cash	Adams, Drawing

2–8 Indicate the normal balance (debit or credit) of each account in Question 2–7.

2–9 What are the advantages and disadvantages of the running balance, or three-column, account form compared with the two-column form?

2–10 What is the justification for using a separate owner's drawing account?

2–11 "During the year, the total owner's equity of Carver Gift Shop increased from $48,000 to $62,000. Therefore, the annual earnings must have been $14,000." Is this statement necessarily true? Explain.

2–12 Explain why purchases of supplies are usually charged to an asset account rather than to an expense account.

2–13 Describe three distinct types of errors that may be present even when a trial balance is in balance.

2–14 "A trial balance is a list showing all account titles in the general ledger and the total of debits and credits in each account." Do you agree with this statement? Why or why not?

2–15 Discuss the types of errors that may be present in each of the following independent sets of trial balance totals:

	Trial Balance Totals	
Trial Balance	**Debit**	**Credit**
A	$62,400	$63,400
B	36,480	36,210
C	23,644	23,573
D	54,226	55,750
E	41,984	41,654

2–16 The assistant bookkeeper of Ace Sports prepared a trial balance that had total debits of $51,110 and total credits of $53,890. Compute the correct trial balance totals by assuming that only the following errors were involved:

(1) Accounts Payable of $3,560 was listed as a debit.

(2) During the current period, a $300 check for Salaries Expense was debited to Office Expense.

(3) Supplies on Hand of $4,500 had been omitted.

(4) Ace, Drawing of $2,700 was included as a credit.

EXERCISES

Transaction analysis and trial balance

2–17 Make T accounts for the following accounts that appear in the general ledger of J. R. Curtis, a veterinarian: Cash; Accounts Receivable; Supplies on Hand; Office Equipment; Accounts Payable; J. R. Curtis, Capital; J. R. Curtis, Drawing; Professional Fees; Salaries Expense; and Rent Expense. Record the following transactions in the T accounts and key all entries with the number identifying the transaction. Finally, prove equality of debits and credits by preparing a trial balance.

(1) Curtis opened a checking account on December 1 at the United Bank in the name of Animal Hospital and deposited $25,000.
(2) Paid rent for December, $600.
(3) Purchased office equipment on account, as follows: Desks, $900; typewriters, $1,450; filing cabinets, $750; and chairs, $600.
(4) Purchased supplies for cash, $800.
(5) Billed clients for services rendered, $5,600.
(6) Paid secretary's salary, $950.
(7) Paid $1,500 on account for the equipment purchased in transaction (3).
(8) Collected $3,800 from clients previously billed for services.
(9) Withdrew $1,600 for personal use.

Determination of omitted financial statement data

2–18 In the five independent situations below, replace the question marks with the amounts that should appear.

	A	B	C	D	E
Owner's Equity:					
Beginning Balance	$32,000	$56,000	$38,000	$ (?)	$66,000
Capital Contributions	10,000	16,000	(?)	10,000	6,000
Net Income (Loss)	(?)	12,000	9,000	(4,000)	(?)
Capital Withdrawals	7,000	(?)	5,000	3,000	8,000
Ending Balance	$43,000	$74,000	$45,000	$20,000	$56,000

Transaction analysis

2–19 Match each of the following transactions of B. Sanchez, Printer, with the appropriate letters, indicating the debits and credits to be made. The correct answer for transaction (1) is given.

	Answer
(1) The owner contributed cash to the business.	a, f
(2) Purchased equipment on account.	______
(3) Received and immediately paid advertising bill.	______
(4) Purchased supplies for cash.	______
(5) Borrowed money from bank, giving a note payable.	______
(6) Billed customers.	______
(7) Made partial payment on account for equipment.	______
(8) Paid employee's salary.	______
(9) Collected amounts due from customers billed in transaction (6).	______

Effect of Transaction

(a) Debit an asset	(f) Credit owner's capital
(b) Credit an asset	(g) Debit revenue
(c) Debit a liability	(h) Credit revenue
(d) Credit a liability	(i) Debit an expense
(e) Debit owner's capital	(j) Credit an expense

Transaction analysis

2–20 The accounts below are from the general ledger of a local accountant. For each letter given in the T accounts, describe the type of business transaction(s) or event(s) that would most probably be reflected by entries on that side of the account. For example, the answer to (a) is: The amounts of services performed for clients on account.

Accounts Receivable	
(a)	(b)

Supplies on Hand	
	(c)

Office Equipment	
(d)	

Prepaid Insurance	
(e)	

Professional Fees	
	(f)

Owner's Drawing	
(g)	

Owner's Capital	
	(h)

Salaries Expense	
(i)	

Accounts Payable	
(j)	(k)

Analysis of accounts

2–21 Compute the unknown amount required in each of the following five independent situations. The answer to situation (a) is given as an example.

Account	Beginning Balance	Ending Balance	Other Information
(a) Cash	$ 5,200	$ 4,450	Total cash disbursed, $5,600
(b) Accounts Receivable	4,900	3,700	Services on account, $6,000
(c) Supplies on Hand	750	680	Supplies used, $560
(d) Prepaid Insurance	150	400	Premiums paid in advance, $600
(e) Ames, Capital	22,000	33,000	Capital contributions, $3,000

Unknown Amounts Required

(a) Total cash received	$4,850
(b) Total amount received from credit customers	______
(c) Supplies purchased during the period	______
(d) Amount of insurance expense for the period	______
(e) Net income, if no withdrawals were made	______

Effect of errors on trial balance

2–22 Indicate how each of the following errors would affect the trial balance totals. For each error, specify whether the debit or credit totals would be overstated, understated, or whether both totals would be unaffected.

(a) The Accounts Receivable balance of $62,100 was listed in the trial balance as $61,200.
(b) A $480 payment for Utilities Expense was debited to Miscellaneous Expense during the accounting period.
(c) The Accounts Payable balance of $32,600 was omitted from the trial balance.
(d) Salaries Expense of $2,100 was listed in the trial balance as a credit.
(e) The Owner's Drawing account, with a debit balance of $7,500, was listed as a credit in the trial balance.

PROBLEMS

Transaction analysis and trial balance

2–23 Peter Ruiz, electrical contractor, began business on May 1 of the current year. The following transactions occurred during May:

(1) Ruiz invested $25,000 of his personal funds in the business.
(2) Purchased equipment on account, $2,400.
(3) Paid the premium for a one-year liability insurance policy, $720.
(4) Purchased supplies on account, $580.
(5) Purchased a truck for $8,500. Ruiz paid $2,500 cash and gave a note payable for the balance.
(6) Paid rent for May, $750.
(7) Paid fuel bill for truck, $70.
(8) Billed customers for services rendered, $9,200.
(9) Paid $1,000 on account for equipment purchased in transaction (2).
(10) Paid utilities expense for May, $120.
(11) Received invoice for May advertising expense, to be paid in June, $150.
(12) Paid employees' wages, $1,450.
(13) Collected $5,300 on accounts receivable.
(14) Withdrew $800 for personal expenses.
(15) Counted supplies on hand at May 31, $320 worth remained.
(16) Recorded the insurance expired at May 31, $60.

REQUIRED

(a) Record the above transactions in T accounts, and key entries with the numbers of the transactions. The following accounts will be needed to record the transactions for May: Cash; Accounts Receivable; Supplies on Hand; Prepaid Insurance; Equipment, Truck; Notes Payable; Accounts Payable; P. Ruiz, Capital; P. Ruiz, Drawing; Service Fees; Rent Expense; Wages Expense; Utilities Expense; Truck Expense; Advertising Expense; Supplies Expense; and Insurance Expense.
(b) Prepare a trial balance of the general ledger as of May 31.

Trial balance, income statement, and balance sheet

2–24 The following account balances, in alphabetical order, are from the general ledger of Norton's Waterproofing Service at January 31, 19XX. The firm's accounting year began on January 1. All accounts had normal balances.

Accounts Payable	$ 1,100	Norton, Drawing	$2,750
Accounts Receivable	10,400	Prepaid Insurance	880
Advertising Expense	150	Rent Expense	640
Cash	6,800	Salaries Expense	3,200
Service Fees	16,200	Supplies Expense	2,250
Insurance Expense	80	Supplies on Hand	8,420
Norton, Capital, January 1	18,500	Utilities Expense	230

REQUIRED

(a) Prepare a trial balance in good form from the given data.
(b) Prepare an income statement for the month of January.
(c) Prepare a balance sheet at January 31.

Transaction analysis and the effect of errors on trial balance

2–25 The following T accounts contain numbered entries for the May transactions of Erica Hanson, a market analyst, who opened her offices on May 1 of the current year:

Cash

(1)	25,000	(2)	6,000
(9)	2,800	(4)	750
		(6)	900
		(8)	1,200

E. Hanson, Capital

		(1)	25,000

Accounts Receivable

(5)	5,600	(9)	2,800

E. Hanson, Drawing

(8)	1,200		

Supplies on Hand

(3)	1,800	(7)	680

Professional Fees

		(5)	5,600

Office Equipment

(2)	6,000		

Rent Expense

(4)	750		

Accounts Payable

(6)	900	(3)	1,800

Supplies Expense

(7)	680		

REQUIRED

(a) Give a reasonable description of each of the nine numbered transactions entered in the above accounts. Example: (1) Erica Hanson invested $25,000 of her personal funds in her business.

(b) The following trial balance, taken for Hanson's firm on May 31, contains several errors. Itemize the errors and indicate the correct totals for the trial balance.

Erica Hanson, Market Analyst
Trial Balance
May 31, 19XX

	Debit	Credit
Cash	$19,850	
Accounts Receivable	5,600	
Supplies on Hand	1,120	
Office Equipment	6,000	
Accounts Payable		$ 900
E. Hanson, Capital		25,000
E. Hanson, Drawing		1,200
Professional Fees		5,600
Supplies Expense	680	
	$33,250	$32,700

Transaction analysis, trial balance, and financial statements

2–26 Janet King owns Nu-Art, a firm providing designs for advertisers, market analysts, and others. On July 1 of the current year, her general ledger showed the following account balances:

Cash	$ 8,600	Notes Payable	$ 4,500
Accounts Receivable	15,500	Accounts Payable	1,800
Prepaid Rent	900	J. King, Capital	24,100
Supplies on Hand	5,400		
	$30,400		$30,400

The following transactions occurred in July:

(1) Collected $8,300 on account from customers.
(2) Paid $1,500 installment due on the $3,000 non-interest-bearing note payable to a relative.
(3) Billed customers for design services rendered on account, $16,400.
(4) Rendered design services for cash customers, $800.
(5) Purchased various art supplies on account, $1,620.
(6) Paid $1,200 to creditors on account.
(7) Collected $8,100 on account from customers.
(8) Paid a delivery service for delivery of graphics to commercial firms, $170.
(9) Paid July salaries, $2,450.
(10) Received invoice for July advertising expense, to be paid in August, $480.
(11) Paid utilities expense for July, $220.
(12) Withdrew $750 for personal use.

(13) Recorded rent expense for July, $450. (Note that on July 1, two months' rent, $900, was prepaid.)
(14) Counted supplies on hand at July 31, $4,250 worth remained.

REQUIRED
(a) Set up the appropriate T accounts for the July 1 balance sheet and enter the beginning balances. Also provide the following T accounts: J. King, Drawing; Service Fees; Rent Expense; Salaries Expense; Delivery Expense; Advertising Expense; Utilities Expense; and Supplies Expense. Record the listed transactions in the T accounts, and key entries with transaction numbers.
(b) Prepare a trial balance at July 31.
(c) Prepare an income statement for July.
(d) Prepare a statement of owner's equity for July.
(e) Prepare a balance sheet at July 31.

Transaction analysis, trial balance, and financial statements

2–27 Rainy Lake Fly-In Service, Inc. (introduced in Problem 1–32) operates leased amphibious aircraft and docking facilities, equipping the firm to transport fishermen and hunters from Fort Frances, Ontario, to outpost camps owned by various resorts in Ontario. On August 1 of the current year, the firm's trial balance was as follows:

Rainy Lake Fly-In Service, Inc.
Trial Balance
August 1, 19XX

	Debit	Credit
Cash	$40,250	
Accounts Receivable	21,600	
Supplies on Hand	14,200	
Prepaid Insurance	2,400	
Notes Payable		$ 3,000
Accounts Payable		6,800
Capital Stock		50,000
Retained Earnings		18,650
	$78,450	$78,450

During August the following transactions occurred:

Aug. 1 Paid August rental cost for aircraft, dockage, and dockside office, $4,500.
3 Purchased fuel and other supplies on account, $5,100.
5 Paid bill for August advertising in various sports magazines, $750.
6 Rendered fly-in services for various groups for cash, $15,250.
8 Billed the Ministry of Natural Resources for services in transporting mapping personnel, $4,500.
13 Received $11,500 on account from clients.
16 Paid $4,800 on accounts payable.
18 Paid miscellaneous expenses, $260.
24 Billed various clients for services, $5,800.
31 Paid August wages, $8.400.
31 Declared and paid a dividend, $5,000 (debit Retained Earnings).

Aug. 31 Determined that $600 insurance premiums expired during August.
31 Determined that fuel and other supplies on hand at August 31 amounted to $14,600.

REQUIRED

(a) Set up running balance accounts for each item in the August 1 trial balance. Also provide similar accounts for the following items: Service Fees, Wages Expense, Advertising Expense, Rent Expense, Supplies Expense, Insurance Expense, and Miscellaneous Expense. Record the transactions for August in the accounts, using the dates given.
(b) Prepare a trial balance at August 31, 19XX.
(c) Prepare an income statement for August.
(d) Prepare a balance sheet at August 31.

Effect of errors on trial balance

2–28 The following trial balance for Lund Janitorial Service, prepared after its first month of operations on January 31 of the current year, does not balance because of a number of errors.

Lund Janitorial Service
Trial Balance
January 31, 19XX

	Debit	Credit
Cash	$ 5,910	
Accounts Receivable	7,800	
Supplies on Hand	4,520	
Prepaid Insurance	360	
Equipment	16,000	
Accounts Payable		$ 4,450
Lund, Capital		21,650
Lund, Drawing		1,500
Service Fees		17,500
Wages Expense	4,800	
Insurance Expense	120	
Advertising Expense	220	
Supplies Expense	2,350	
	$42,080	$45,100

(1) Utilities Expense, with a $180 balance, was omitted from the trial balance.
(2) Supplies on Hand, listed in the trial balance as $4,520, should be $4,250.
(3) During the period, a cash payment of $530 on accounts payable was recorded as a $350 credit to Cash.
(4) A debit of $120 to Accounts Payable was erroneously recorded as a credit.
(5) In determining the Accounts Receivable balance, a credit of $150 was overlooked.
(6) The $1,500 balance of the Lund, Drawing account is listed as a credit in the trial balance.
(7) The balance of the Service Fees account was overfooted (overadded) by $200.

REQUIRED

Prepare a corrected trial balance as of January 31 of the current year.

ALTERNATE PROBLEMS

Transaction analysis and trial balance

2–23A Jane Weston opened a tax practice on June 1 of the current year. The following accounts will be needed to record her transactions for June: Cash; Accounts Receivable; Office Supplies on Hand; Prepaid Insurance; Office Furniture and Fixtures; Notes Payable; Accounts Payable; J. Weston, Capital; J. Weston, Drawing; Professional Fees; Rent Expense; Salaries Expense; Supplies Expense; Utilities Expense; and Insurance Expense. The following transactions occurred in June:

(1) Weston opened a special checking account at the bank for the business, investing $10,000 in her practice.
(2) Purchased office furniture and fixtures for $2,400, paid $1,400 cash and gave a non-interest-bearing note payable for the balance.
(3) Paid the premium for a one-year liability insurance policy, $600.
(4) Purchased office supplies on account, $380.
(5) Paid rent for June, $650.
(6) Billed clients for professional services rendered, $5,400.
(7) Paid $200 on account to stationers for the office supplies purchased in transaction (4).
(8) Collected $3,200 on account from clients billed in transaction (6).
(9) Paid June salaries, $1,600.
(10) Withdrew $750 for personal use.
(11) Paid utilities for June, $140.
(12) Counted supplies on hand at June 30, $250 worth remained.
(13) One month's insurance premium expired during June.

REQUIRED
(a) Record the above transactions in T accounts, and key entries with the numbers of the transactions.
(b) Prepare a trial balance of the general ledger as of June 30.

Trial balance, income statement, and balance sheet

2–24A The following account balances were taken (out of order) from the general ledger of L. Ford, investment counselor, at January 31, 19XX. The firm's accounting year began on January 1. All accounts had normal balances.

Prepaid Insurance	$ 360	Rent Expense	$ 650
Insurance Expense	90	Supplies Expense	380
Supplies on Hand	520	Utilities Expense	160
Advertising Expense	260	Service Fees	10,680
L. Ford, Capital, January 1	22,000	Accounts Receivable	9,700
Cash	18,440	Salaries Expense	1,750
Accounts Payable	430	L. Ford, Drawing	800

REQUIRED
(a) Prepare a trial balance in good form from the given data.
(b) Prepare an income statement for the month of January.
(c) Prepare a balance sheet at January 31.

Transaction analysis and the effect of errors on trial balance

2–25A The following T accounts contain numbered entries for the May transactions of Arthur Doyle, attorney, who opened his offices on May 1 of the current year:

Cash			
(1)	15,000	(2)	4,500
(10)	3,100	(4)	825
		(6)	720
		(8)	1,000
		(9)	420

A. Doyle, Capital			
		(1)	15,000

Accounts Receivable			
(5)	4,800	(10)	3,100

A. Doyle, Drawing			
(8)	1,000		

Prepaid Insurance			
(6)	720	(11)	120

Professional Fees			
		(5)	4,800

Supplies on Hand			
(3)	675	(7)	380

Rent Expense			
(4)	825		

Office Equipment			
(2)	4,500		

Insurance Expense			
(11)	120		

Accounts Payable			
(9)	420	(3)	675

Supplies Expense			
(7)	380		

REQUIRED

(a) Give a reasonable description of each of the 11 numbered transactions entered in the above accounts. Example: (1) Arthur Doyle invested $15,000 of his personal funds in his law firm.

(b) The following trial balance, taken for Doyle's firm on May 31, contains several errors. Itemize the errors, and indicate the correct totals for the trial balance.

Arthur Doyle, Attorney
Trial Balance
May 31, 19XX

	Debit	Credit
Cash	$10,365	
Accounts Receivable	1,600	
Supplies on Hand	675	
Office Equipment	4,500	
Accounts Payable		$ 255
A. Doyle, Capital		15,000
A. Doyle, Drawing		1,000
Professional Fees		4,800
Rent Expense	825	
Insurance Expense	120	
Supplies Expense	380	
	$18,465	$21,055

Transaction analysis, trial balance, and financial statements

2–26A Lisa Howell operates the Howell Dance Studio. On June 1 of the current year, her general ledger contained the following information:

Cash	$ 8,500	Notes Payable	$ 2,500
Accounts Receivable	3,750	Accounts Payable	320
Prepaid Insurance	420	L. Howell, Capital	10,390
Supplies on Hand	540		
	$13,210		$13,210

The following transactions occurred in June:

(1) Paid June rent for practice and performance studio, $750.
(2) Paid June piano rental, $60 (Rent Expense).
(3) Collected $2,150 from students on account.
(4) Paid $500 installment on non-interest-bearing note owed to a relative.
(5) Billed students for June instructional fees, $4,200.
(6) Purchased supplies (tickets, brochures, sheet music, and so on) on account, $270.
(7) Paid $160 for advertising ballet performance.
(8) Paid costume rental, $340 (Rent Expense).
(9) Collected $2,750 from performances.
(10) Paid Kleen Towel Company for June services, $60 (Miscellaneous Expense).
(11) Paid utilities expense for June, $140.
(12) Withdrew $600 for personal expenses.
(13) Counted supplies on hand at June 30, $230 worth remained.
(14) Determined that $140 insurance premiums had expired in June.

REQUIRED

(a) Set up the appropriate T accounts, and enter the beginning balances shown in the June 1 balance sheet. Also provide the following accounts: L. Howell, Drawing; Instructional Fees; Performance Revenue; Rent Expense;

Supplies Expense; Insurance Expense; Utilities Expense; Advertising Expense; and Miscellaneous Expense. Record the listed transactions in the T accounts and key entries with transaction numbers.

(b) Prepare a trial balance at June 30.

(c) Prepare an income statement for June.

(d) Prepare a statement of owner's equity for June.

(e) Prepare a balance sheet as of June 30.

Transaction analysis, trial balance, and financial statements

2–27A On December 1 of the current year, a group of individuals formed a corporation to establish the Weekender, a neighborhood weekly newspaper featuring want ads of individuals and advertising of local firms. The paper will be mailed free to about 5,000 local residents; revenue will be generated from advertising and want ads. The December transactions are summarized below:

Dec. 1 Sold capital stock of Weekender, Inc., for cash, $30,000.
2 Paid December rent on office, $500.
4 Purchased office furniture and equipment for $8,000, paying $5,000 cash and giving a $3,000 note payable for the balance.
5 Purchased stationery and other office supplies on account, $760.
8 Collected want ad revenue in cash, $1,800.
12 Paid post office for bulk mailing expense, $420.
14 Billed for advertising in first two issues of the newspaper, $4,250.
15 Paid delivery expense to Acme Courier Service for transporting newspapers to post office, $45.
16 Paid printing expense, $1,950.
18 Collected $2,400 want ad revenue in cash from various individuals.
28 Paid utilities expenses, $120.
31 Paid printing expense, $1,950.
31 Paid salaries expense, $3,400.
31 Billed for advertising in last two issues of the newspaper, $5,850.
31 Paid post office for bulk mailing expense, $450.
31 Paid delivery expense to Acme Courier Service for transporting newspapers to post office, $45.
31 Collected $5,600 on accounts receivable.

REQUIRED

(a) Set up three-column running balance accounts for the following: Cash, Accounts Receivable, Supplies on Hand, Office Furniture and Equipment, Notes Payable, Accounts Payable, Capital Stock, Advertising Revenue, Want Ad Revenue, Printing Expense, Mailing Expense, Utilities Expense, Salaries Expense, Rent Expense, and Delivery Expense. Record the foregoing transactions in the accounts.

(b) Take a trial balance at December 31.

(c) Assuming that unrecorded expenses—such as supplies expense, and so on—amount to $600, calculate the net income for December.

(d) If the firm decides to declare and pay a dividend of $1,000 on January 1 of the following year, what would be the amount of stockholders' equity immediately after paying the dividend?

BUSINESS DECISION PROBLEM

Jean Francis operates the Wings Picture Gallery, selling original art and signed prints received on consignment (rather than purchased) from recognized wildlife artists throughout the country. The firm receives a 30% commission on all art sold and remits 70% of the sales price to the artists. Jean began business in January of this year, but has not yet arranged for a formal set of records. She has prepared cash receipts and disbursements statements for each of the first three months of the year, but she is uneasy about relying on them to determine how well she is doing. She asks you to prepare a proper set of financial statements for the month of March.

By reviewing bank statements, check stubs, invoice files, and other data, you derive a set of balance sheets at March 1 and March 31. These are shown below, followed by a statement of cash receipts and disbursements for March.

Wings Picture Gallery
Balance Sheets

Assets	**March 31, 19XX**	**March 1, 19XX**
Cash	$20,800	$12,400
Accounts Receivable	6,000	5,600
Supplies on Hand	1,300	1,200
Prepaid Insurance	800	1,000
	$28,900	$20,200
Liabilities and Owner's Equity		
Accounts Payable to Artists	$ 4,800	$ 5,200
J. Francis, Capital	24,100	15,000
	$28,900	$20,200

Wings Picture Gallery
Statement of Cash Receipts and Disbursements
For the Month of March, 19XX

Cash Receipts		
Received on account from customers	$33,600	
Cash sales	6,000	
Total cash receipts		$39,600
Cash Disbursements		
Supplies purchased for cash	$ 900	
Payments to artists on account	28,400	
Payment of salaries	1,000	
Payment for March rent	750	
Payment for utilities expense	150	
Total cash disbursements		31,200
Net increase in cash balance		$ 8,400

REQUIRED

(a) From the above information, prepare an accrual basis income statement for the month of March. To obtain the data needed, you may wish to use T accounts to reconstruct the accounts.

(b) Illustrate the apparent correctness of your net income amount by preparing a statement of owner's equity for March.

ANSWERS TO SELF-TEST QUESTIONS

1. (b) 2. (c) 3. (b) 4. (b) 5. (c)

3

The Accounting Cycle

Chapter Objectives

- Identify the steps in the accounting cycle.
- Explain the role of source documents in transaction analysis.
- Describe the general journal and the process of journalizing transactions.
- Explain the process of posting information from the general journal to the general ledger accounts.
- Describe the adjusting process and illustrate typical adjusting entries.

There is a right time for everything.

ECCLESIASTES 3:1

The double-entry accounting system provides a basic framework for the analysis of business activities. Now we wish to go into greater detail about the accounting procedures used to account for the operations of a business during a specific period. The accounting procedures of most businesses involve certain basic steps that are accomplished in a given order. This sequence of operations is known as the *accounting cycle*.

STEPS IN THE ACCOUNTING CYCLE

The **accounting cycle** can be divided into the following steps:

(1) Analyze transactions from source documents.

(2) Record transactions in journals.

(3) Post journal entries to general ledger accounts.

(4) Adjust the general ledger accounts.

(5) Prepare financial statements.

(6) Close temporary accounts.

The steps in the accounting cycle enable the accountant to combine and summarize the net results of many business activities into relatively concise financial reports. Even a medium-sized business has thousands of transactions annually, each evidenced by one or more source documents (step 1); these transactions are recorded and summarized (step 2) in possibly only five or six journals. Next, data from these journals might be posted (step 3) to one general ledger having, say, 100 accounts. After certain adjustments are made (step 4), these accounts provide the balances necessary to prepare the basic financial statements (step 5). Much of the analytical usefulness of the accounting process is a result of this ability to condense and summarize business data.

The various steps in the accounting cycle do not occur with equal frequency. Usually, analyzing, journalizing, and posting (steps 1–3) take place throughout each operating period, whereas accounts are adjusted and statements are prepared (steps 4 and 5) only when management requires financial statements, usually at monthly or quarterly intervals, but at least annually. Temporary accounts are customarily closed (step 6) only at the end of the accounting year.

EXHIBIT 3–1
Frequency of Accounting Cycle Steps
Required for Quarterly Financial Statements

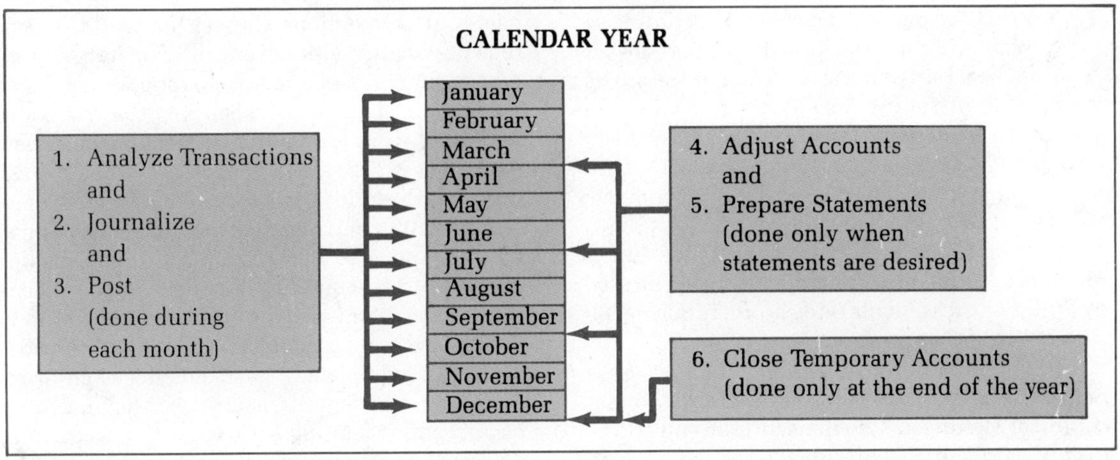

Business firms whose accounting year ends on December 31 are said to be on a **calendar-year** basis. Many firms prefer to have their accounting year coincide with their "natural" business year; that is, the year ends when business is slow and inventory quantities are small and easy to count. Year-end accounting procedures are most efficiently accomplished at this time. For example, most department stores choose a year ending on the last day of January or February, when their inventories are depleted from the normally heavy holiday sales and from post-holiday clearance sales. An accounting year ending with a month other than December is called a **fiscal year.**

Exhibit 3–1 illustrates the timing of steps in the accounting cycle during a calendar year for a business that prepares quarterly financial statements. In the remainder of this chapter and in Chapter 4, we shall explain the various steps in the accounting cycle. As an example, we use the first month's transactions of the Landen TV Service, a repair business begun by Mark Landen on December 1 of the current year.

TRANSACTION ANALYSIS AND SOURCE DOCUMENTS

Step 1: Analyze Transactions from Source Documents

Source documents are printed or written forms that are generated when the firm engages in business transactions. Even a brief source document usually specifies the dollar amounts involved, the date of the transaction, and possibly the party dealing with the firm. Some examples of source documents are (1) a sales invoice showing evidence of a purchase of supplies on account, (2) a bank check indicating payment of an obligation, (3) a deposit slip showing the amount of funds

ABOUT THOSE SOURCE DOCUMENTS . . . ?

Source documents underlie the recording of accounting transactions and, thus, are an integral part of the accounting process. The significance of source documents has not been overlooked by various embezzlers and swindlers who try to cover up their schemes with false accounting entries. Fictitious source documents are created to support the fake entries. A prominent example is the fraud perpetrated upon McKesson & Robbins, a pharmaceutical company, by Philip Musica and his three brothers during the period 1927–1938.

Philip Musica, alias William Johnson alias Frank D. Costa alias Dr. F. Donald Coster, bought control of McKesson & Robbins in 1926 and immediately assumed the presidency. Although convicted twice in earlier years (on charges of bribery and embezzlement), Musica had successfully managed to hide his unsavory past by 1926. In 1927, Musica organized McKesson & Robbins, Ltd., a Canadian subsidiary that ostensibly would buy and sell crude drugs outside the United States—*ostensibly,* because the entire operation was fictitious.

Musica put himself in charge of the Canadian subsidiary's activities. Within McKesson & Robbins, he was aided by his brothers George (assistant treasurer) and Robert (shipping department head). Both brothers used aliases. Another brother, Arthur (alias George Vernard), headed up two fictitious outside firms—W. W. Smith & Co., a trading agent for the Canadian subsidiary, and Manning & Co., a private banking firm. With this arrangement, Musica was ready to siphon funds from the parent McKesson & Robbins company to pay for the "purchase" of crude drugs by the Canadian subsidiary and to pay fees to W. W. Smith & Co.

According to the accounting records and source documents, the Canadian subsidiary traded millions of dollars' worth of crude drugs throughout the world. Yet no crude drugs were actually traded. About all that really existed in the subsidiary's Montreal location were a rented office, five rented (and empty) warehouses, and a vacant lot.

An elaborate facade of false documents concealed the fraud. Musica hired a printer to print letterheads, invoices, and receipts bearing the names of corporations all over the world. A secretary working with seven different typewriters typed all correspondence, trading orders, and inventory statements (she believed she was doing important work for an international business network). The Montreal locations were essentially mail drops—secretaries there received large envelopes sent by Arthur and remailed the smaller envelopes they contained to W. W. Smith & Co. The smaller envelopes, of course, contained forged documents. W. W. Smith & Co. provided McKesson & Robbins with documentation showing sales made, deliveries completed, payments received from customers, and deposits made in the Manning bank. Each month Manning & Co. sent the accounting department a detailed statement showing bills paid, deposits received from sales, and itemized inventories of the crude drugs in the warehouses.

By the end of 1937, the Canadian subsidiary showed accounts receivable and inventories of crude drugs totaling $18,000,000—all fictitious. Through the years, McKesson & Robbins' auditors did not detect the fraud. They never visited the Canadian warehouses, relying instead on statements of drugs on hand provided by the warehouses and carefully checking these statements against the source documents in McKesson & Robbins' headquarters. These forged documents, however, did contain some strange data that went unnoticed by the auditors. Some drug quantities on hand, for example, would supply the entire United States for years, and some shipping orders moved drugs from South America to Australia by truck.

The fraud was finally uncovered in 1938 by a company officer who became suspicious when he noted that the Canadian crude drug inventories were not insured. This fraud had a significant impact on auditing procedures. Shortly after the fraud was detected, the physical observation of inventory counts and the direct confirmation of receivables with customers became standard audit techniques—techniques that continue to this day.*

*For a complete story of Philip Musica and the McKesson & Robbins fraud, see Charles Keats, *Magnificent Masquerade: The Strange Case of Dr. Coster and Mr. Musica* (New York: Funk & Wagnalls Company, Inc., 1964).

turned over to the bank, (4) a cash receipt indicating funds received from a customer, and (5) a cash register tape listing a day's over-the-counter sales to customers.

Exhibit 3–2 lists the December transactions of Landen TV Service, together with their related source documents. Ordinarily, source documents or business

EXHIBIT 3–2
December Transactions
Landen TV Service

Number	Date	Brief Description	Related Source Documents
(1)	Dec. 1	Mark Landen deposited $25,000 in the firm's bank account.	Bank deposit slip
(2)	1	Paid December rent, $600.	Bank check, lease contract
(3)	2	Purchased truck for $10,800 cash.	Seller's invoice, bank check
(4)	2	Purchased test equipment for $3,600; paid $2,000 down; remainder to be paid in 60 days.	Seller's invoice, bank check
(5)	2	Signed two service contracts to perform	
		(a) Service work for a local TV dealer for four months, December–March, at $250 per month. Received $1,000 in advance.	Contract, dealer's check
		(b) Service work for a local hotel at a rate of $16 per hour. Settlement to be made whenever 40 hours of service has been rendered.	Contract, periodic bills to hotel
(6)	3	Purchased supplies and parts on account, $950.	Seller's invoice
(7)	7	Performed TV service for various customers during first week of December and received $650 cash.	Duplicates of cash receipt forms
(8)	14	Billed various agencies and customers for TV service rendered on account, $900.	Bills to customers
(9)	14	Paid employee's wages for first two weeks of December, $540.	Bank check
(10)	14	Performed TV service for various customers during second week of December and received $680 cash.	Duplicates of cash receipt forms
(11)	17	Paid advertising bill, $80.	Seller's invoice, bank check
(12)	19	Received $500 on account from customers.	Customers' checks
(13)	21	Performed TV service for various customers during third week of December and received $520 cash.	Duplicates of cash receipt forms
(14)	28	Paid truck expenses (gas and oil), $160.	Seller's invoice, bank check
(15)	28	Billed various agencies and customers for TV service rendered on account, $2,400.	Bills to customers
(16)	28	Paid employee's wages for second two weeks of December, $540.	Bank check
(17)	28	Withdrew $800 for personal use.	Bank check
(18)	28	Performed TV service during fourth week in December and received $300 cash.	Duplicates of cash receipt forms

papers such as those listed in Exhibit 3–2 will alert the bookkeeper to the need for an entry in the records. Usually the bookkeeper is able to analyze the transaction by examining the documents to determine the appropriate accounts to be debited and credited. For example, in transaction (2), a scrutiny of the check stub from the rent payment would reveal the need for debiting Rent Expense and crediting Cash. In transaction (4), the seller's invoice or bill of sale would probably indicate both the cost of the equipment and the down payment. The check stub would further corroborate the amount paid, and the bookkeeper would debit Test Equipment for $3,600, credit Cash for $2,000, and credit Accounts Payable for $1,600, the amount still owing.

Some transactions can be analyzed only by making further inquiry or by referring to previously received documents and the accounting records themselves. For example, consider the two contracts signed by Mark Landen on December 2 [transaction (5)]. The mere signing of the contracts would not require bookkeeping entries, since the contracts are just agreements to provide services. In transaction (5a), however, Landen TV Service received $1,000 in advance, which requires a debit to Cash and a credit to Unearned Service Fees. In this case, the Unearned Service Fees of $1,000 represent an obligation (liability) to provide services for four months. At the end of each of these months, an entry must be made to reduce the obligation and to reflect an appropriate amount in the revenue account Service Fees. To ensure the proper entry, the bookkeeper can refer to the contract terms or review the entry made when the advance was received.

As a result of transaction (5b), the bookkeeper would record an account receivable from the hotel and credit the revenue account Service Fees at the end of each accounting period. To do this, the bookkeeper might check the contract terms to calculate the amounts of such entries. The periodic entries required to reflect properly the services rendered under these two contracts fall into the category of *adjusting entries;* we describe these in step 4 of the accounting cycle and show that such entries frequently require reference to previous accounting records.

JOURNALS

Step 2: Record Transactions in Journals

For simplicity, the entries used in Chapter 2 were made directly in the general ledger accounts. This method would not prove feasible, however, for even a modest-sized business. For instance, suppose an owner wished to investigate a $1,000 credit in the Cash account. If entries were actually recorded directly in the general ledger, the purpose of the $1,000 expenditure could be difficult to determine. The owner might be forced to search through the entire general ledger to discover the offsetting debit of $1,000. Consequently, accounting records include a set of **journals** or **records of original entry,** which show the total effect of a business transaction or adjustment in one location.

Journals are tabular records in which business activities are analyzed in terms of debits and credits and recorded in chronological order before they are entered in the general ledger. An accounting journal may be one of a group of special journals, or it may be a general journal. A special journal is designed to record a specific type of frequently occurring business transaction. For example, a business with 100 employees who are paid every two weeks would probably use a special journal for payrolls. Because two paydays would normally occur in a month, at least 200 payroll transactions would be recorded. Other types of transactions that are often kept in special journals are cash receipts, cash disbursements, merchandise sales, and merchandise purchases.

In contrast to the special journals, the general journal is a relatively simple record in which any type of business transaction or adjustment may be recorded. All adjustments are recorded in the general journal as are transactions that do not occur often enough to warrant entry in a special journal. All businesses, even those using many special journals, have a general journal. In this chapter, we shall illustrate only the use of a general journal; in Chapter 6, we will introduce the use of special journals.

Exhibit 3–3 shows the first four transactions from Exhibit 3–2 as they would be recorded in Landen's general journal. Most journal entries are based on information appearing on a source document resulting from a transaction between the

EXHIBIT 3–3

General Journal

Page 1

Date		Description	Post. Ref.	Debit	Credit
19XX					
Dec.	1	Cash		25,000	
		M. Landen, Capital			25,000
		Opened the TV Service's bank account using personal funds.			
	1	Rent Expense		600	
		Cash			600
		Paid rent for December.			
	2	Truck		10,800	
		Cash			10,800
		Purchased truck for cash.			
	2	Test Equipment		3,600	
		Cash			2,000
		Accounts Payable			1,600
		Purchased electronic test equipment for $3,600. Terms: $2,000 down, remainder due in 60 days.			

business and an outside party. The procedure for recording entries in the general journal is as follows:

(1) Indicate the year, month, and date of the entry. Usually the year and month are rewritten only at the top of each page of the journal or at the point where they change.

(2) Enter titles of the accounts affected in the description column. Accounts to receive debits are entered close to the left-hand margin and are traditionally recorded first. Accounts to receive credits are then recorded, indented slightly.

(3) Place the appropriate money amounts in the left-hand (debit) and right-hand (credit) money columns.

(4) Write an explanation of the transaction or adjustment below the account titles. The explanation should be as brief as possible, disclosing all the information necessary to understand the event being recorded.

Each transaction and adjustment entered in the journal should be stated in terms of equal debits and credits. The account titles cited in the description column should correspond to those used for the related general ledger accounts. To separate clearly the various entries, we leave a line blank between entries. We explain the use of the column headed "Post. Ref." (posting reference) later in step 3 of the accounting cycle.

COMPOUND JOURNAL ENTRIES A journal entry that involves more than just two accounts is called a **compound** journal entry. The last journal entry in Exhibit 3–3 is an example of a compound journal entry involving three accounts. The debit of $3,600 to Test Equipment is offset by credits of $2,000 to Cash and $1,600 to Accounts Payable. Any number of accounts may appear in a compound entry; but, regardless of how many accounts are used, the total of the debit amounts must always equal the total of the credit amounts.

CORRECTION OF JOURNAL ERRORS Certain procedures should be followed when errors are found in journal entries. Errors should not be erased, because erasures completely remove the original recording. As you might imagine, the acceptance of erasures might allow someone to falsify accounting records; consequently, other procedures are used.

If an erroneous journal entry has not been transferred to the general ledger, a single line is drawn through the erroneous amount or account title, and the correction is entered on the same line just above the error. Often the person correcting the entry must place his or her initials near the correction. This facilitates any subsequent inquiry about the nature of or reason for the correction. Once an erroneous journal entry has been transferred to the ledger accounts, both records contain the error. The recommended procedures for correcting this situation are discussed in step 3.

POSTING

Step 3: Post Journal Entries to General Ledger Accounts

After transactions have been journalized, the next step in the accounting cycle is to transcribe the debits and credits in each journal entry to the appropriate general ledger accounts. This transcribing process is called **posting** to the general ledger. Thus, data from a journal that stresses the total effect of particular transactions (such as the collection of accounts receivable) are transcribed to a ledger that stresses the total effect of many business transactions on a particular business variable (such as cash, accounts receivable, and so on). This latter type of data is specifically needed for the preparation of financial statements.

When records are kept by hand, posting from the general journal may be done daily, every few days, or at the end of each month. Journalizing and posting often occur simultaneously when the record-keeping process is automated. The posting of special journals is discussed in Chapter 6.

POSTING REFERENCES It is important to be able to trace any entry appearing in a ledger account to the journal from which it was posted. Consequently, accounting records use a system of references. Both journals and accounts have posting reference columns. Entries in the posting reference columns of journals indicate the account to which the related debit or credit has been posted. Posting references appearing in ledger accounts identify the journal from which the related entry was posted. The posting references in the journals and ledger accounts are entered when the journal entries are posted to the ledger accounts.

To keep accounting records uncluttered, we make posting references simple. For example, the posting reference of the general journal might be GJ or simply J. Similarly, special journals such as Cash Receipts and Payroll might be indicated by posting references of CR and PR, respectively. Because both general and special journals usually involve many pages of entries, journal pages are numbered in sequence. Thus, a posting reference of J9 appearing on the line with a $1,000 debit entry in the Cash account means that the ninth page of the general journal contains the entire entry in which the $1,000 debit to Cash appears. Because all entries should be posted from some journal, every entry appearing in a ledger account should have a related posting reference. Posting references appearing in journals are usually the numbers that have been assigned to the general ledger accounts.

CHART OF ACCOUNTS In all but the simplest accounting systems, a number is assigned to each general ledger account. Such a numbering system permits easy reference to accounts even if the account title contains several words. For example, the account Depreciation Expense—Test Equipment might be referred to simply as account No. 57.

A **chart of accounts** is usually prepared in order to facilitate the analysis of activities and the formulation of journal entries. The chart of accounts is a list of

EXHIBIT 3–4
Landen TV Service
Chart of Accounts

Assets
11. Cash
12. Accounts Receivable
14. Supplies and Parts on Hand
16. Test Equipment
17. Accumulated Depreciation—Test Equipment
18. Truck
19. Accumulated Depreciation—Truck

Liabilities
21. Accounts Payable
22. Utilities Payable
23. Wages Payable
24. Unearned Service Fees

Owner's Equity
31. M. Landen, Capital
32. M. Landen, Drawing
33. Income Summary

Revenue
41. Service Fees

Expenses
51. Rent Expense
52. Wages Expense
53. Advertising Expense
54. Supplies and Parts Expense
55. Utilities Expense
56. Truck Expense
57. Depreciation Expense—Test Equipment
58. Depreciation Expense—Truck

the titles and numbers of all accounts found in the general ledger. The account titles should be grouped by, and in order of, the five major sections of the general ledger (assets, liabilities, owners' equity, revenue, and expenses). Exhibit 3–4 shows a chart of accounts for the Landen TV Service, indicating the account numbers that will now be used.

The method of assigning account numbers usually ensures that the numbers of all the accounts in a major section of the general ledger start with the same digit. In Exhibit 3–4, all asset accounts begin with 1, liabilities with 2, and so on. Complicated accounting systems may use three- or four-digit account numbers and may even employ suffixes to designate various branches, departments, or divisions.

Exhibit 3–5 diagrams the posting of Landen TV Service's first transaction from the general journal to the ledger accounts. Each debit entry and each credit entry is posted as follows:

(1) The date (year, month, and day) is entered in the appropriate account. Note that this is the date of the journal entry, not necessarily the date of the actual posting. As with journals, the year and month are restated only at the top of a new account page or at the point where they change.

(2) The amount is entered in the account as a debit or a credit, as indicated in the journal's money columns, and the new balance is calculated.

EXHIBIT 3–5
Diagrams of Posting to Ledger Accounts

General Journal

Page 1

Date		Description	Post. Ref.	Debit	Credit
19XX Dec.	1	Cash	11	25,000	
		M. Landen, Capital	31		25,000
		Opened the TV Service's bank account using personal funds.			

General Ledger
Cash

Account No. 11

Date		Description	Post. Ref.	Debit*	Credit	Balance
19XX Dec.	1		J1	25,000		25,000

General Journal

Page 1

Date		Description	Post. Ref.	Debit	Credit
19XX Dec.	1	Cash	11	25,000	
		M. Landen, Capital	31		25,000
		Opened the TV Service's bank account using personal funds.			

General Ledger
M. Landen, Capital

Account No. 31

Date		Description	Post. Ref.	Debit	Credit*	Balance
19XX Dec.	1		J1		25,000	25,000

*Throughout this chapter, the asterisk indicates the column that designates the normal balance.

(3) The posting reference from the journal (both symbol and page number) is placed in the posting reference column of the ledger account.

(4) The account number is placed in the posting reference column of the journal.

Regardless of the types of journals or the number of entries involved, the total debits posted should equal the total credits posted. Exhibit 3–6 (see pages 89–94) is a comprehensive illustration of the journalizing and posting of the December transactions of Landen TV Service. You should review each transaction in the illustration for (1) the nature of the transaction, (2) the related journal entry, and (3) the subsequent postings. Bear in mind that the account numbers in the posting reference column of the journal are not entered when the journal entry is recorded; they are inserted when the entry is posted.

TAKING A TRIAL BALANCE After the journal entries have been posted to the ledger accounts, a trial balance of all the accounts is prepared. The trial balance of the Landen TV Service at December 31 is shown in Exhibit 3–7.

CORRECTING ERRONEOUS POSTINGS Even the most carefully kept accounts will occasionally contain posting errors. An error involving only the wrong amount being posted may be corrected by drawing a line through the incorrect amount, entering the correct amount above, and initialing the correction. When an amount

EXHIBIT 3–7

Landen TV Service
Trial Balance
December 31, 19XX

	Debit	Credit
Cash	$13,130	
Accounts Receivable	2,800	
Supplies and Parts on Hand	950	
Test Equipment	3,600	
Truck	10,800	
Accounts Payable		$ 2,550
Unearned Service Fees		1,000
M. Landen, Capital		25,000
M. Landen, Drawing	800	
Service Fees		5,450
Rent Expense	600	
Wages Expense	1,080	
Advertising Expense	80	
Truck Expense	160	
	$34,000	$34,000

EXHIBIT 3–6
Journalizing and Posting for Landen TV Service

General Journal Page 1

Date		Description	Post. Ref.	Debit	Credit
19XX					
Dec.	1	Cash	11	25,000	
		M. Landen, Capital	31		25,000
		Opened the TV Service's bank account using personal funds.			
	1	Rent Expense	51	600	
		Cash	11		600
		Paid rent for December.			
	2	Truck	18	10,800	
		Cash	11		10,800
		Purchased truck for cash.			
	2	Test Equipment	16	3,600	
		Cash	11		2,000
		Accounts Payable	21		1,600
		Purchased electronic test equipment for $3,600. Terms: $2,000 down, remainder due in 60 days.			
	2	Cash	11	1,000	
		Unearned Service Fees	24		1,000
		Received advance on four-month contract at $250 per month.			
	3	Supplies and Parts on Hand	14	950	
		Accounts Payable	21		950
		Purchased supplies and parts on account; 60-day terms.			
	7	Cash	11	650	
		Service Fees	41		650
		Services for cash, December 1–7.			
	14	Accounts Receivable	12	900	
		Service Fees	41		900
		Services rendered on account.			
	14	Wages Expense	52	540	
		Cash	11		540
		Paid wages for first two weeks of December.			

EXHIBIT 3–6 (continued)

General Journal Page 2

Date		Description	Post. Ref.	Debit	Credit
19XX					
Dec.	14	Cash	11	680	
		Service Fees	41		680
		Services for cash, December 8–14.			
	17	Advertising Expense	53	80	
		Cash	11		80
		Paid *Daily News* for December advertising.			
	19	Cash	11	500	
		Accounts Receivable	12		500
		Received $500 on account from credit customers.			
	21	Cash	11	520	
		Service Fees	41		520
		Services for cash, December 15–21.			
	28	Truck Expense	56	160	
		Cash	11		160
		Gas and oil for December.			
	28	Accounts Receivable	12	2,400	
		Service Fees	41		2,400
		Services rendered on account.			
	28	Wages Expense	52	540	
		Cash	11		540
		Paid wages for second two weeks of December.			
	28	M. Landen, Drawing	32	800	
		Cash	11		800
		Withdrew $800 for personal use.			
	28	Cash	11	300	
		Service Fees	41		300
		Services for cash, December 22–28.			

General Ledger

Cash

Account No. 11

Date		Description	Post. Ref.	Debit*	Credit	Balance
19XX						
Dec.	1		J1	25,000		25,000
	1		J1		600	24,400
	2		J1		10,800	13,600
	2		J1		2,000	11,600
	2		J1	1,000		12,600
	7		J1	650		13,250
	14		J1		540	12,710
	14		J2	680		13,390
	17		J2		80	13,310
	19		J2	500		13,810
	21		J2	520		14,330
	28		J2		160	14,170
	28		J2		540	13,630
	28		J2		800	12,830
	28		J2	300		13,130

Accounts Receivable

Account No. 12

Date		Description	Post. Ref.	Debit*	Credit	Balance
19XX						
Dec.	14		J1	900		900
	19		J2		500	400
	28		J2	2,400		2,800

Supplies and Parts on Hand

Account No. 14

Date		Description	Post. Ref.	Debit*	Credit	Balance
19XX						
Dec.	3		J1	950		950

EXHIBIT 3–6 (continued)

Test Equipment Account No. 16

Date		Description	Post. Ref.	Debit*	Credit	Balance
19XX Dec.	2		J1	3,600		3,600

Truck Account No. 18

Date		Description	Post. Ref.	Debit*	Credit	Balance
19XX Dec.	2		J1	10,800		10,800

Accounts Payable Account No. 21

Date		Description	Post. Ref.	Debit	Credit*	Balance
19XX Dec.	2		J1		1,600	1,600
	3		J1		950	2,550

Unearned Service Fees Account No. 24

Date		Description	Post. Ref.	Debit	Credit*	Balance
19XX Dec.	2		J1		1,000	1,000

M. Landen, Capital Account No. 31

Date		Description	Post. Ref.	Debit	Credit*	Balance
19XX Dec.	1		J1		25,000	25,000

M. Landen, Drawing Account No. 32

Date		Description	Post. Ref.	Debit*	Credit	Balance
19XX Dec.	28		J2	800		800

Service Fees Account No. 41

Date		Description	Post. Ref.	Debit	Credit*	Balance
19XX Dec.	7		J1		650	650
	14		J1		900	1,550
	14		J2		680	2,230
	21		J2		520	2,750
	28		J2		2,400	5,150
	28		J2		300	5,450

Rent Expense Account No. 51

Date		Description	Post. Ref.	Debit*	Credit	Balance
19XX Dec.	1		J1	600		600

Wages Expense Account No. 52

Date		Description	Post. Ref.	Debit*	Credit	Balance
19XX Dec.	14		J1	540		540
	28		J2	540		1,080

EXHIBIT 3–6 (continued)

Advertising Expense Account No. 53

Date		Description	Post. Ref.	Debit*	Credit	Balance
19XX Dec.	17		J2	80		80

Truck Expense Account No. 56

Date		Description	Post. Ref.	Debit*	Credit	Balance
19XX Dec.	28		J2	160		160

has been posted to the wrong account, however, the correction should be made with a journal entry. Let us assume that Landen TV Service purchased test equipment for $100 cash and that the bookkeeper erroneously debited the amount to Supplies and Parts on Hand instead of to Test Equipment. The following entry in the journal corrects the error by transferring the debit to the correct account:

Test Equipment	100	
Supplies and Parts on Hand		100
To correct entry for purchase of test equipment.		

ADJUSTMENTS

Step 4: Adjust the General Ledger Accounts

It is important that accounts appearing in financial statements at the end of an accounting period be properly stated. Clearly, if the income statement is to portray a realistic net income figure based on accrual accounting, all revenues *earned* during the period and all expenses *incurred* must be shown. Therefore, revenues and costs must be properly aligned for the reporting period in question. This process of aligning costs and expenses with related revenue is the **matching** concept frequently mentioned in accounting literature.

Many of the transactions reflected in the accounting records through the first three steps in the accounting cycle affect the net income of more than one period. Therefore, to achieve a proper matching of costs and expenses with revenue, we must adjust the account balances at the end of each accounting period. The **adjusting** step of the accounting cycle occurs after the journals have been posted, but before financial statements are prepared.

Four general types of adjustments are made at the end of an accounting period:

(1) Aligning *recorded costs* with the appropriate accounting periods.

(2) Aligning *recorded revenue* with the appropriate accounting periods.

(3) Reflecting *unrecorded expenses* incurred during the accounting period.

(4) Reflecting *unrecorded revenue* earned during the accounting period.

Adjustments in the first two categories—aligning recorded costs and revenue with the appropriate periods—are often referred to as **deferrals.** Adjustments in the last two categories—reflecting unrecorded expenses and revenue—are often referred to as **accruals.**

ALIGNING RECORDED COSTS Many business outlays may benefit a number of accounting periods. Some common examples are purchases of buildings, equipment, supplies, and payments of insurance premiums covering a period of years. Ordinarily, these outlays are debited to an asset account at the time of expenditure. Then, at the end of each accounting period, the estimated portion of the outlay that has expired during the period or that has benefited the period is transferred to an expense account.

The preceding chapters included two examples of adjustments aligning recorded costs with the appropriate accounting period. One example allocated part of the cost of three years' insurance coverage to insurance expense for the current month. The total cost of the insurance premium had been debited initially to the asset account Prepaid Insurance. The adjustment then allocated the cost of one month's coverage ($\frac{1}{36}$ of the premium) to insurance expense. The other example dealt with the cost of supplies. The adjustment transferred the cost of supplies used during the current month from the asset account Supplies on Hand to the expense account Supplies Expense. We shall consider another example involving supplies and parts in this chapter.

Under most circumstances, we can discover when adjustments of this type are needed by inspecting the monthly trial balance for costs that benefit several periods. By looking at the December 31 trial balance of Landen TV Service (Exhibit 3–7), for example, we would find that adjustments are required to apportion the costs of the supplies and parts, the test equipment, and the truck between December and subsequent periods.

Supplies and parts During December, Landen TV Service purchased supplies and parts and recorded the outlay in an asset account, Supplies and Parts on Hand, as follows:

Dec. 3	Supplies and Parts on Hand	950	
	Accounts Payable		950
	Purchased supplies and parts on account; 60-day terms.		

The firm could not conveniently keep a daily count of parts and supplies used in service work. Instead, at the end of December, it would count the items still on hand. Suppose the count shows $510 worth of supplies and parts on hand at the end of the month, indicating that $440 worth of supplies and parts have been used in service work during the month. Therefore, at the end of the period, an adjusting entry will transfer this amount to an expense account, Supplies and Parts Expense, as follows:

Dec. 31	Supplies and Parts Expense	440	
	Supplies and Parts on Hand		440
	To record expense of supplies and parts used in December.		

When this adjusting entry is posted, it will properly reflect the December expense for supplies and parts and will reduce the asset account Supplies and Parts on Hand to $510, the actual amount of the asset remaining at December 31. After the entry is posted, the related ledger accounts appear as follows:

Supplies and Parts on Hand Account No. 14

Date		Description	Post. Ref.	Debit*	Credit	Balance
19XX						
Dec.	3		J1	950		950
	31		J3		440	510

Supplies and Parts Expense Account No. 54

Date		Description	Post. Ref.	Debit*	Credit	Balance
19XX						
Dec.	31		J3	440		440

Obviously, if financial statements were prepared without this adjustment, the December income statement would omit an important expense and would overstate net income by $440. Similarly, the balance sheet would overstate assets by $440, because the Supplies and Parts on Hand balance would remain at $950. As a result of overstating net income, owner's equity in the balance sheet would also be overstated by $440.

Depreciation The process of allocating the costs of a firm's equipment, vehicles, and buildings to the periods benefiting from their use is called **depreciation** accounting. Because these long-lived assets help generate revenue in a company's operations, each accounting period in which the assets are used should reflect a portion of their cost as expense. This periodic expense is known as depreciation expense.

Periodic depreciation expense must be estimated by accountants. The procedure we use here estimates the annual amount of depreciation expense by dividing the cost of the asset by its estimated useful life in years. This method is called *straight-line* depreciation. (We will explore other methods in Chapter 10.)

When recording depreciation expense, the asset amount is not reduced directly. Instead, the reduction is recorded in a contra account called Accumulated Depreciation. *Contra* accounts are so named because they are used to record reductions in or offsets against a related account. The Accumulated Depreciation account will normally have a credit balance and will appear in the balance sheet as a deduction from the related asset amount. Use of the contra account Accumulated Depreciation allows the original cost of the related asset to be shown in the balance sheet, followed by the accumulated amount of depreciation.

Let us assume that the test equipment purchased by Landen TV Service for $3,600 has an estimated life of five years and that the truck costing $10,800 is expected to last six years. Straight-line depreciation recorded on the test equipment is therefore $720 per year, or $60 per month. Similarly, the depreciation on the truck is $1,800 per year, or $150 per month. At the end of December, we would make the following adjusting entries:

Dec. 31	Depreciation Expense—Test Equipment	60	
	Accumulated Depreciation—Test Equipment		60
	To record December depreciation on test equipment.		
Dec. 31	Depreciation Expense—Truck	150	
	Accumulated Depreciation—Truck		150
	To record December depreciation on truck.		

When the preceding entries are posted, they will properly reflect the cost of using these assets during December, and the correct expense will appear in the December income statement. After the adjusting entries have been posted, the asset accounts, accumulated depreciation accounts, and depreciation expense accounts appear as follows:

Test Equipment Account No. 16

Date		Description	Post. Ref.	Debit*	Credit	Balance
19XX						
Dec.	2		J1	3,600		3,600

Accumulated Depreciation—Test Equipment Account No. 17

Date		Description	Post. Ref.	Debit	Credit*	Balance
19XX Dec.	31		J3		60	60

Depreciation Expense—Test Equipment Account No. 57

Date		Description	Post. Ref.	Debit*	Credit	Balance
19XX Dec.	31		J3	60		60

Truck Account No. 18

Date		Description	Post. Ref.	Debit*	Credit	Balance
19XX Dec.	2		J1	10,800		10,800

Accumulated Depreciation—Truck Account No. 19

Date		Description	Post. Ref.	Debit	Credit*	Balance
19XX Dec.	31		J3		150	150

Depreciation Expense—Truck Account No. 58

Date		Description	Post. Ref.	Debit*	Credit	Balance
19XX Dec.	31		J3	150		150

If the firm failed to record the adjusting entries for depreciation, expenses would be omitted from the income statement. In the above situation, such an omission would result in an overstatement of net income by $210. Furthermore, assets and owner's equity would be overstated by the same amount on the balance sheet.

On the balance sheet, the accumulated depreciation amounts are subtracted from the related asset amounts. The resulting balances (cost less accumulated depreciation), which are the assets' **book values,** represent the unexpired asset costs to be applied as expenses against future operating periods. For example, the December 31, 19XX, balance sheet would show test equipment with a book value of $3,540, presented as follows:

Test Equipment	$3,600	
Less: Accumulated Depreciation	60	$3,540

ALIGNING RECORDED REVENUE Sometimes a business receives fees for services before service is rendered. Such transactions are ordinarily recorded by debiting Cash and crediting a liability account. The liability account in this situation, sometimes called a **deferred credit,** shows the obligation for performing future service. For example, a monthly magazine publisher receiving $72 for a three-year subscription would debit Cash and credit Unearned Subscription Revenue for $72. Each month that magazines are supplied to the subscriber, $\frac{1}{36}$ of the publisher's obligation is fulfilled. At the end of each month, the bookkeeper would transfer $2 from the liability account Unearned Subscription Revenue to a revenue account, Subscription Revenue. This procedure reflects revenue when service is performed rather than when it is paid for.

During December, Landen TV Service entered one transaction that requires an end-of-month adjustment to recorded revenue. On December 2, the firm signed a four-month contract to perform service for a local TV dealer at $250 per month, with the entire contract price of $1,000 received in advance. The entry made on December 2 was as follows:

Dec. 2	Cash	1,000	
	Unearned Service Fees		1,000
	Received advance on four-month contract at $250 per month.		

On December 31, the following adjusting entry would be made to transfer $250, the revenue earned in December, to Service Fees and reduce the liability Unearned Service Fees by the same amount:

Dec. 31	Unearned Service Fees	250	
	Service Fees		250
	To record portion of advance earned in December.		

After this entry is posted, the liability account will show a balance of $750, the amount of future services still owing, and the Service Fees account will reflect the $250 earned in December.

Unearned Service Fees Account No. 24

Date		Description	Post. Ref.	Debit	Credit*	Balance
19XX						
Dec.	2		J1		1,000	1,000
	31		J3	250		750

Service Fees Account No. 41

Date		Description	Post. Ref.	Debit	Credit*	Balance
19XX						
Dec.	7		J1		650	650
	14		J1		900	1,550
	14		J2		680	2,230
	21		J2		520	2,750
	28		J2		2,400	5,150
	28		J2		300	5,450
	31		J3		250	5,700

A similar entry would be repeated at the end of each month of the contract period; $250 in revenue would be included in Service Fees in the income statement, and the liability account in the balance sheet would be reduced by $250.

We emphasize here that if the adjusting entries are ignored, the revenue is never reflected in any income statement and the liability remains on the balance sheet after the obligation has been discharged. Therefore, it is important to make these adjustments carefully.

REFLECTING UNRECORDED EXPENSES Often a business will use certain services before paying for them. Obligations to pay for services such as salaries, utilities, and taxes may build up, or accrue, over a period of time. Most businesses make adjusting entries for such **accrued expenses** in order to reflect the proper cost in the period when the benefit was received. The bookkeeper must realize that services received have not yet been reflected in the accounts and make appropriate adjustments. If source documents are not available, amounts may be estimated.

Accrued utilities During December, Landen TV Service used telephone service and utility service for heat and light. Bills from the telephone and power companies will not arrive until January. Let us assume, however, that based on inquiries to the landlord and knowledge of local rates, the firm estimates that it received $120 worth of services during the month. On December 31, the bookkeeper makes the following adjusting entry:

Dec. 31	Utilities Expense	120	
	Utilities Payable		120
	To record estimated amount of December utilities expense.		

This adjustment reflects both the cost of services received during the period and the estimated amount owed for such services to be included on the balance sheet. If this adjustment were not made, net income would be overstated by $120 in the December income statement; on the December 31 balance sheet, liabilities would be understated and owner's equity overstated by $120.

Note that the credit in the adjusting entry above could have been made to Accounts Payable. Because the amount is an estimate, however, many businesses prefer to credit a separate account such as Utilities Payable.

After the bookkeeper posts the adjusting entry for estimated utilities expense, the expense and liability accounts would appear as follows:

Utilities Expense Account No. 55

Date		Description	Post. Ref.	Debit*	Credit	Balance
19XX Dec.	31		J3	120		120

Utilities Payable Account No. 22

Date		Description	Post. Ref.	Debit	Credit*	Balance
19XX Dec.	31		J3		120	120

Suppose the utility bill that arrives in early January is for $124, indicating that the firm has underestimated the December expense by $4. Obviously, $124 will be credited to Cash since the full amount of the bill must be paid. But what would be debited to balance the $124 credit? The firm might remove the liability by debiting $120 to Utilities Payable and debiting the remaining $4 to Utilities Expense for January. This tactic places some of December's utilities expense in January. Such a small discrepancy as $4 is not material, however, and most persons would not be disturbed about the minor inaccuracy. Another method of handling the accrual in the subsequent period, involving reversing entries, will be explained in Chapter 4.

Accrued wages A Landen TV Service employee is paid every two weeks at the rate of $270 for each six-day workweek. The employee was paid $540 on December 14 and December 28. Let us assume that both these dates fell on Saturday and that Sunday in the employee's day off. If financial statements are prepared at the close of business on Tuesday, December 31, the employee will have worked two days (Monday and Tuesday) during December for which he will not be paid until January. Because the employee's wages are $45 per day ($270 ÷ 6 days), additional wages expense of $90 should be reflected in the income statement for December. The adjusting entry at the end of December would be as follows:

Dec. 31	Wages Expense	90	
	Wages Payable		90
	To record accrued wages for December 30 and 31.		

After posting, the Wages Expense and Wages Payable accounts would appear as follows:

Wages Expense Account No. 52

Date		Description	Post. Ref.	Debit*	Credit	Balance
19XX						
Dec.	14		J1	540		540
	28		J2	540		1,080
	31		J3	90		1,170

Wages Payable Account No. 23

Date		Description	Post. Ref.	Debit	Credit*	Balance
19XX						
Dec.	31		J3		90	90

This adjustment enables the firm to reflect as December expense all wages *earned* by the employee during the period rather than just the wages *paid*. In addition, the balance sheet will show the liability for unpaid wages at the end of the period. Omitting this adjustment would cause a $90 overstatement of net income in the December income statement, with a concurrent $90 overstatement of owner's equity and a $90 understatement of liabilities in the December 31 balance sheet.

When the employee is paid on the next regular payday in January, the bookkeeper must make sure that the two days' pay accrued at the end of December is not again charged to expense. If we assume that the employee is paid $540 on Saturday, January 11, the following entry can be made:

Jan. 11	Wages Payable	90	
	Wages Expense	450	
	Cash		540
	To record wages paid.		

This entry eliminates the liability recorded in Wages Payable at the end of December and debits January Wages Expense for only those wages earned by the employee in January. Another method of avoiding dual charges, that of reversing entries, will be explained in Chapter 4.

REFLECTING UNRECORDED REVENUE A company may provide services during a period that are neither billed nor paid for by the end of the period. Yet the value of these services represents revenue earned by the firm and should be reflected in the firm's income statement. Such accumulated revenue is often called **accrued revenue.** For example, a firm may have loaned money on which interest has been earned that is not collected by the end of the period. The amount of the interest should be reflected in the net income of the period in which it is earned. In this situation, an adjusting entry would be made debiting Interest Receivable and crediting Interest Income for the amount of interest earned.

In the case of Landen TV Service, the service contract with the local hotel negotiated on December 2 could result in accrued revenue. Under the terms of the contract, Landen TV Service will bill the hotel for work at $16 per hour whenever 40 hours of work have been completed. Suppose that by December 31, Landen has performed 15 hours of work for the hotel. Unbilled revenue of $240 (15 hours × $16) has accrued during the month and should be reflected in the accounts by the following adjusting entry:

Dec. 31	Accounts Receivable	240	
	Service Fees		240
	To record unbilled revenue earned during December.		

This entry includes in the December accounts the revenue earned by performing service but not yet billed to the hotel. It also enters the amount owed by the hotel as a receivable on the balance sheet. After the entry is posted, the related accounts would appear as follows:

Accounts Receivable Account No. 12

Date		Description	Post. Ref.	Debit*	Credit	Balance
19XX						
Dec.	14		J1	900		900
	19		J2		500	400
	28		J2	2,400		2,800
	31		J3	240		3,040

Service Fees Account No. 41

Date		Description	Post. Ref.	Debit	Credit*	Balance
19XX						
Dec.	7		J1		650	650
	14		J1		900	1,550
	14		J2		680	2,230
	21		J2		520	2,750
	28		J2		2,400	5,150
	28		J2		300	5,450
	31		J3		250	5,700
	31		J3		240	5,940

The bookkeeper must be careful when the regular 40-hour billing is sent to the hotel in January. Let us assume that 40 hours of work has accumulated by January 21. Because the revenue from 15 hours of work ($240) was recorded in the December 31 adjusting entry, the billing made on January 21 contains only $400 (25 hours × $16) of revenue earned during January. The following entry could be made when the hotel is billed for $640 (40 hours × $16):

Jan. 21	Accounts Receivable	400	
	Service Fees		400
	To record revenue earned during January; Customer billed $640 for work performed in December and January.		

An alternative way of handling this situation, using reversing entries, is discussed in Chapter 4.

If we did not make the adjustment for accrued revenue, the December net income for Landen TV Service would be understated by $240, and the January net income would be overstated by the same amount. On the December 31 balance sheet, assets and owner's equity would also be understated.

PREPAYMENTS RECORDED IN EXPENSE AND REVENUE ACCOUNTS Expenditures made to benefit future periods and amounts received for services yet to be performed should be recorded initially in balance sheet accounts. Then the adjusting procedure consists of transferring the expired portion of prepaid expenses to expense accounts and transferring the earned portion of unearned revenue to revenue accounts. We have essentially just described these procedures.

Occasionally, an outlay benefiting future periods may be debited to an expense account rather than to prepaid expense, or an amount received for future services may be credited to a revenue account rather than to unearned revenue. In such situations, the adjusting procedure consists of transferring the unexpired or unearned portion of the recorded amount to the appropriate balance sheet account. For example, suppose that a one-year insurance premium of $1,200 was initially debited to Insurance Expense. At the end of the first month after the outlay, the following adjusting entry is appropriate:

Prepaid Insurance	1,100	
Insurance Expense		1,100
To transfer unexpired insurance cost to asset account.		

This entry sets up an asset of $1,100 and leaves $100 in the expense account.

Suppose also that the firm received a six-month prepayment of rent totaling $1,800 from a tenant and credited the entire amount to Rental Income (a revenue account). After the first month has elapsed, the appropriate adjusting entry is:

Rental Income	1,500	
Unearned Rental Income		1,500
To transfer unearned rental income to liability account.		

This adjustment records $1,500 as a liability and leaves a $300 balance in the revenue account.

It is important to note that the nature of the adjusting entry depends on how the transaction was recorded initially (a prepayment debited to either an asset or expense account and an advance receipt credited to either a liability or revenue account). *After* the adjusting entry has been made and posted, however, the balances in the affected accounts will be the same regardless of how the transaction was initially recorded.

Exhibit 3–8 summarizes our discussion about the various types of adjustments.

EXHIBIT 3–8
Summary of Adjustments

Adjustment Category	Nature of Adjusting Entry	Examples			
		Text Page	Entry		
1. Aligning Recorded Costs					
a. Initially recorded as an asset	Increase expense	96	Supplies and Parts Expense	440	
	Decrease asset		Supplies and Parts on Hand		440
For depreciation	Increase expense	97	Depreciation Expense—Test Equipment	60	
	Increase contra asset (which decreases asset's book value)		Accumulated Depreciation—Test Equipment		60
		97	Depreciation Expense—Truck	150	
			Accumulated Depreciation—Truck		150
b. Initially recorded as an expense	Increase asset	105	Prepaid Insurance	1,100	
	Decrease expense		Insurance Expense		1,100
2. Aligning Recorded Revenue					
a. Initially recorded as a liability	Decrease liability	99	Unearned Service Fees	250	
	Increase revenue		Service Fees		250
b. Initially recorded as revenue	Decrease revenue	105	Rental Income	1,500	
	Increase liability		Unearned Rental Income		1,500
3. Reflecting Unrecorded Expenses	Increase expense	101	Utilities Expense	120	
	Increase liability		Utilities Payable		120
		102	Wages Expense	90	
			Wages Payable		90
4. Reflecting Unrecorded Revenue	Increase asset	103	Accounts Receivable	240	
	Increase revenue		Service Fees		240

KEY POINTS TO REMEMBER

(1) Six major steps are in the accounting cycle:

Steps	When Normally Done
1. Analyze transactions 2. Record in journals 3. Post to ledger	Throughout every period
4. Adjust accounts 5. Prepare statements	When statements are required
6. Close temporary accounts	At the end of the year

(2) Source documents usually provide the basis for analyzing business transactions.

(3) Accounting entries are initially recorded in a journal; the entries are in chronological order, and the journal shows the total effect of each transaction or adjustment.

(4) After journal entries are posted to the accounts, a trial balance is taken to ensure that the general ledger is in balance.

(5) Adjusting entries made to achieve the appropriate matching of expenses and revenue consist of the following four types:
- (a) Aligning recorded costs with periods benefited.
- (b) Aligning recorded revenue with periods in which it is earned.
- (c) Reflecting unrecorded expenses incurred during the period.
- (d) Reflecting unrecorded revenue earned during the period.

SELF-TEST QUESTIONS
(Answers are at the end of this chapter.)

1. The first step in the accounting cycle is to
   - (a) Record transactions in journals.
   - (b) Analyze transactions from source documents.
   - (c) Post journal entries to general ledger accounts.
   - (d) Adjust the general ledger accounts.
2. A journal entry that contains more than just two accounts is called
   - (a) A posted journal entry.
   - (b) An adjusting journal entry.
   - (c) An erroneous journal entry.
   - (d) A compound journal entry.
3. Posting refers to the process of transferring information from
   - (a) Journals to general ledger accounts.
   - (b) General ledger accounts to journals.
   - (c) Source documents to journals.
   - (d) Journals to source documents.

4. Which of the following is an example of an adjusting entry?
(a) Recording the purchase of supplies on account.
(b) Recording depreciation expense on a truck.
(c) Recording the billing of customers for services rendered.
(d) Recording the payment of wages to employees.

5. An adjusting entry to accrue wages earned but not yet paid is an example of
(a) Aligning recorded costs with the appropriate accounting periods.
(b) Aligning recorded revenue with the appropriate accounting periods.
(c) Reflecting unrecorded expenses incurred during the accounting period.
(d) Reflecting unrecorded revenue earned during the accounting period.

QUESTIONS

3–1 List in their proper order the steps in the accounting cycle.

3–2 If we assume that a business prepares quarterly financial statements, at what time(s) during the year is each step in the accounting cycle accomplished?

3–3 Give three examples of source documents that underlie business transactions.

3–4 Explain the nature and purpose of a general journal.

3–5 What is a compound journal entry?

3–6 What is the appropriate procedure for correcting an erroneous general journal entry (a) before it has been posted and (b) after it has been posted?

3–7 Explain the technique of posting references. What is the justification for their use?

3–8 Describe a chart of accounts, and give an example of a coding system for identifying different types of accounts.

3–9 Why is the adjusting step of the accounting cycle necessary?

3–10 What four different types of adjustments are frequently necessary at the close of an accounting period? Give examples of each type.

3–11 On January 1, Prepaid Insurance was debited with the cost of a one-year premium, $648. What adjusting entry should be made on January 31?

3–12 Referring to Question 3–11, suppose the bookkeeper had charged the entire $648 premium to Insurance Expense when it was paid on January 1. What adjusting entry should be made on January 31 before financial statements are prepared for the month?

3–13 At the beginning of January, the first month of the accounting year, the Supplies on Hand account had a debit balance of $400. During January, purchases of $900 worth of supplies were debited to the account. Although only $500 worth of supplies were on hand at the end of January, the necessary adjusting entry was omitted. How will the omission affect (a) the income statement for January and (b) the balance sheet prepared at January 31?

3–14 *International Focus*, a monthly magazine, received two-year subscriptions totaling $9,600 on January 1. (a) What entry should be made to record the receipt of the $9,600? (b) What entry should be made at the end of January before financial statements are prepared for the month?

3–15 Farley Travel Agency pays an employee $350 in wages each Friday for the five-day workweek ended on that day. The last Friday of January falls on January 26. What adjusting entry should be made on January 31?

3–16 Juan Salazar earns interest amounting to $162 per month on some of his investments. He receives the interest every six months, on December 31 and June 30. What adjusting entry should be made on January 31?

EXERCISES

Transaction analysis

3–17 Creative Services, a firm providing art services for advertisers, has the following accounts in its general ledger: Cash; Accounts Receivable; Supplies on Hand; Office Equipment; Accounts Payable; G. Lorens, Capital; G. Lorens, Drawing; Service Fees; Rent Expense; Utilities Expense; and Salaries Expense. Record the following transactions for June in a two-column general journal:

June	1	Gail Lorens invested $19,000 cash to begin the business.
	2	Paid rent for June, $800.
	3	Purchased office equipment on account, $5,600.
	6	Purchased art materials and other supplies costing $2,200; paid $1,000 down with the remainder due within 30 days.
	11	Billed clients for services, $3,800.
	17	Collected $2,750 from clients.
	19	Paid $2,800 on account to office equipment firm (see June 3).
	25	Gail Lorens withdrew $700 for personal use.
	30	Paid utilities bill for June, $210.
	30	Paid salaries for June, $1,800.

Source documents

3–18 For each transaction in Exercise 3–17, indicate the related source document or documents that evidence the transaction.

Error corrections

3–19 The following erroneous journal entries have been posted to the general ledger. Prepare the journal entries to correct the errors.

(a) A $400 cash collection of an account receivable was recorded as a debit to Cash and as a credit to Service Fees.

(b) A $700 purchase of supplies on account was recorded as a debit to Supplies on Hand and as a credit to Cash.

(c) A $600 billing of customers for services rendered was recorded as a debit to Accounts Payable and as a credit to Service Fees.

(d) A $250 cash payment for the current month's newspaper advertising was recorded as a debit to Rent Expense and as a credit to Cash.

(e) A $900 cash payment for office equipment was recorded as a debit to Cash and as a credit to Office Equipment.

Adjusting entries

3–20 Selected accounts of Super Properties, Inc., a real estate management firm, are shown below as of January 31 of the current year, before any adjusting entries have been made.

	Debit	Credit
Prepaid Insurance	$5,040	
Supplies on Hand	1,950	
Office Equipment	6,240	
Unearned Rental Fees		$ 5,600
Salaries Expense	2,300	
Rental Fees		12,000

Using the following information, record in a general journal the adjusting entries necessary on January 31:

(a) Prepaid Insurance represents a three-year premium paid on January 1.
(b) Supplies of $800 were on hand January 31.
(c) Office equipment is expected to last eight years.
(d) On January 1, the firm collected eight months' rent in advance from a tenant renting space for $700 per month.
(e) Accrued salaries not recorded as of January 31 are $320.

Adjusting entries

3–21 Judy Busse began the Furniture Refinishing Service on July 1 of the current year. Selected accounts are shown below as of July 31, before any adjusting entries have been made.

	Debit	Credit
Prepaid Rent	$3,300	
Prepaid Advertising	270	
Supplies on Hand	1,000	
Unearned Refinishing Fees		$ 600
Refinishing Fees		1,500

Using the following information, record in a general journal the adjusting entries necessary on July 31:

(a) On July 1, Busse paid one year's rent of $3,300.
(b) On July 1, $270 was paid to the local newspaper for an advertisement to run daily for the months of July, August, and September.
(c) Supplies on hand at July 31 total $650.
(d) At July 31, refinishing services of $400 have been performed but not yet billed to customers.
(e) One customer paid $600 in advance for a refinishing project. At July 31, the project is one-half complete.

Adjusting entries

3–22 For each of the following unrelated situations, prepare the necessary adjusting entry in general journal form.

(a) Unrecorded depreciation expense on equipment is $750.
(b) The Supplies on Hand account has a balance of $920. Supplies on hand at the end of the period total $490.
(c) On the date for preparing financial statements, an estimated utilities expense of $120 has been incurred, but no utility bill has yet been received.
(d) On the first day of the current month, rent for four months was paid and recorded as a $2,000 debit to Rent Expense and a $2,000 credit to Cash. Monthly statements are now being prepared.
(e) Nine months ago, Stable Insurance Company sold a one-year policy to a customer and recorded the receipt of the premium by debiting Cash for $720 and crediting Premium Revenue for $720. No adjusting entries have been prepared during the nine-month period. Annual statements are now being prepared.
(f) At the end of the accounting period, wages expense of $815 has been incurred but not paid.
(g) At the end of the accounting period, $300 of repair services have been rendered to customers who have not yet been billed.

Transaction analysis and adjusting entries

3–23 Top Building Maintenance Service offers janitorial services on both a contract basis and an hourly basis. On January 1 of the current year, Top collected $10,800 in advance on six-month contracts for work to be performed evenly during the next six months.

(a) Give the general journal entry to record the receipt of $10,800 for contract work.

(b) Give the adjusting entry to be made on January 31 for the contract work done during January.

(c) At January 31, a total of 24 hours of hourly rate janitor work was unbilled. The billing rate is $10 per hour. Give the adjusting entry needed on January 31.

Analysis of adjusted data

3–24 Selected T-account balances for the Taylor Company are shown below as of January 31 of the current year; adjusting entries have already been posted. The firm operates on a calendar year.

Supplies on Hand	
Jan. 31 Bal. 300	

Supplies Expense	
Jan. 31 Bal. 540	

Prepaid Insurance	
Jan. 31 Bal. 600	

Insurance Expense	
Jan. 31 Bal. 75	

Wages Payable	
	Jan. 31 Bal. 400

Wages Expense	
Jan. 31 Bal. 3,800	

Truck	
Jan. 31 Bal. 9,000	

Accumulated Depreciation—Truck	
	Jan. 31 Bal. 2,125

(a) If the amount in Supplies Expense represents the January 31 adjustment for the supplies used in January, and $500 worth of supplies were purchased during January, what was the January 1 balance of Supplies on Hand?

(b) The amount in the Insurance Expense account represents the adjustment made at January 31 for January insurance expense. If the original premium was for one year, what was the amount of the premium and on what date did the insurance policy start?

(c) If we assume no balance existed in Wages Payable or Wages Expense on January 1, how much was paid in wages during January?

(d) If the truck has a useful life of six years, what is the monthly amount of depreciation expense and how many months has Taylor owned the truck?

Analysis of the impact of adjustments on net income

3–25 The Wyland Repair Service shows the following trial balance at the end of its first month of operations:

	Debit	Credit
Cash	$ 3,000	
Supplies on Hand	1,800	
Equipment	14,000	
Accounts Payable		$ 1,400
Wyland, Capital		15,000
Service Revenue		5,500
Wages Expense	2,300	
Utilities Expense	380	
Advertising Expense	420	
	$21,900	$21,900

The firm's bookkeeper prepared an income statement for the month showing a net income of $2,400. She obtained this sum by deducting the $3,100 total of Wages Expense, Utilities Expense, and Advertising Expense from the Service Revenue of $5,500. However, she did not consider the following:

(a) Depreciation for the month should have been $150.
(b) Supplies on hand at the end of the month were $1,300.
(c) Accrued wages payable at the end of the month were $240.
(d) Unbilled service revenue at the end of the month was $500.

Using the preceding information, calculate the correct net income for the month.

PROBLEMS

Transaction analysis, posting, trial balance, and adjusting entries

3–26 John Ladd opened the Ladd Roofing Service on April 1 of the current year. Transactions for April are as follows:

Apr.	1	Ladd contributed $10,000 of his personal funds to begin the business.
	2	Purchased a used truck for $5,000 cash.
	2	Purchased ladders and other equipment for a total of $2,600; paid $1,500 cash, with the balance due in 30 days. (Classify this outlay as Equipment.)
	3	Paid two-year premium on liability insurance, $960.
	5	Purchased supplies on account, $1,200.
	5	Received an advance payment of $800 from a customer for roof repair work to be done during April and May.
	12	Billed customers for roofing services, $2,000.
	18	Collected $1,600 on account from customers.
	29	Paid bill for truck fuel used in April, $50.
	30	Paid April newspaper advertising, $80.
	30	Paid assistants' wages, $1,300.
	30	Billed customers for roofing services, $1,900.

REQUIRED

(a) Record these transactions in general journal form.
(b) Devise a chart of accounts for the firm and set up the general ledger. Allow

for accounts that may be needed when adjusting entries are made at the close of the accounting period [see part (e)].

(c) Post journal entries to the ledger accounts.

(d) Take a trial balance.

(e) Make the journal entries to adjust the books for insurance expense, supplies expense, depreciation expense on the truck, depreciation expense on the equipment, and roofing fees earned. Supplies on hand on April 30 amounted to $300. Depreciation for April was $125 on the truck and $50 on the equipment. One-half of the roofing fee received in advance was earned by April 30. Post the adjusting entries.

Adjusting entries

3–27 Coyle Carpet Cleaners ended its first month of operations on June 30 of the current year. The unadjusted account balances are as follows:

Coyle Carpet Cleaners
Trial Balance
June 30, 19XX

	Debit	Credit
Cash	$ 800	
Accounts Receivable	400	
Prepaid Rent	1,200	
Supplies on Hand	900	
Equipment	5,400	
Accounts Payable		$ 500
Coyle, Capital		6,000
Coyle, Drawing	300	
Service Fees		3,200
Wages Expense	700	
	$9,700	$9,700

The following information is also available:

(1) The balance in Prepaid Rent was the amount paid on June 1 for the first three months' rent.

(2) Supplies on hand at June 30 were $540.

(3) The equipment, purchased June 1, has an estimated life of six years.

(4) Unpaid wages at June 30 were $200.

(5) Utility services used during June were estimated at $165. A bill is expected early in July.

(6) Fees earned for services performed but not yet billed on June 30 were $300.

REQUIRED

In general journal form, make the adjusting entries needed at June 30.

Trial balance and adjusting entries

3–28 The Studio, Inc., a commercial photography studio, has just completed its first full year of operations on December 31 of the current year. The general ledger account balances before year-end adjustments follow. No adjusting entries have been made to the accounts at any time during the year. Assume that all balances are normal.

Cash	$1,400	Unearned Photography Fees	$ 1,150
Accounts Receivable	2,200	Capital Stock	10,000
Prepaid Rent	7,740	Photography Fees	20,900
Supplies on Hand	3,650	Wages Expense	6,000
Equipment	8,640	Insurance Expense	1,930
Accounts Payable	1,820	Utilities Expense	2,310

An analysis of the firm's records discloses the following items:

(1) Photography services of $600 have been rendered, but customers have not yet been billed.
(2) The equipment, purchased January 1, has an estimated life of nine years.
(3) Utilities expense for December is estimated to be $260, but the bill will not arrive until January of next year.
(4) The balance in Prepaid Rent represents the amount paid on January 1 for a three-year lease on the studio.
(5) In November, customers paid $1,150 in advance for pictures to be taken for the holiday season. When received, these fees were credited to Unearned Photography Fees. By December 31, all these fees are earned.
(6) A two-year insurance premium paid on January 1 was debited to Insurance Expense.
(7) Supplies on hand at December 31 are $1,200.
(8) At December 31, wages expense of $120 has been incurred but not paid.

REQUIRED

(a) Prove that debits equal credits for the unadjusted account balances shown above by preparing a trial balance.
(b) Record adjusting entries in general journal form.

Determination of adjustments from account balances

3–29 For the *unrelated* accounts given below, the current balances and the balances they should have after adjusting entries have been posted are indicated.

Account Title	Current Balance	Adjusted Balance
(1) Supplies on Hand	$940	$410
(2) Depreciation Expense—Building	600	800
(3) Utilities Payable	—	325
(4) Insurance Expense	560	640
(5) Wages Payable	—	750
(6) Unearned Service Fees	850	400
(7) Accumulated Depreciation—Equipment	770	825
(8) Prepaid Rent	900	600
(9) Unearned Commissions Revenue	480	200
(10) Prepaid Advertising	—	500
(11) Interest Receivable	—	100

REQUIRED

For each item listed, prepare the *most probable* general journal entry (including an explanation) for each adjustment.

Transaction analysis, posting, trial balance, and adjusting entries

3–30 The Nutritious Catering Service had the following transactions in July, its first month of operations:

July	1	Julia Mead contributed $11,000 of personal funds to the business.
	1	Purchased the following items for cash from a catering firm that was going out of business (make a compound entry): delivery van, $3,600; equipment, $1,800; and supplies, $1,400.
	2	Paid premium on a one-year liability insurance policy, $780.
	2	Entered into a contract with a local business to cater weekly luncheon meetings for one year at a fee of $400 per month. Received six months' fees in advance.
	3	Paid rent for July, August, and September, $1,500.
	12	Paid employee's two weeks' wages (five-day week), $1,000.
	15	Billed customers for services rendered, $2,800.
	18	Purchased supplies on account, $1,700.
	26	Paid employee's two weeks' wages, $1,000.
	30	Paid July bill for gas, oil, and repairs on delivery van, $350.
	30	Collected $2,200 from customers on account.
	31	Billed customers for services rendered, $3,000.
	31	Mead withdrew $900 for personal use.

REQUIRED

(a) Set up a general ledger that includes the following accounts, using the account numbers shown: Cash (11); Accounts Receivable (12); Supplies on Hand (13); Prepaid Rent (14); Prepaid Insurance (15); Delivery Van (16); Accumulated Depreciation—Delivery Van (17); Equipment (18); Accumulated Depreciation—Equipment (19); Accounts Payable (21); Wages Payable (22); Unearned Catering Fees (23); J. Mead, Capital (31); J. Mead, Drawing (32); Catering Fees (41); Wages Expense (51); Rent Expense (52); Supplies Expense (53); Insurance Expense (54); Delivery Van Expense (55); Depreciation Expense—Delivery Van (56); and Depreciation Expense—Equipment (57).

(b) Record July transactions in general journal form and post to the ledger accounts.

(c) Take a trial balance at July 31.

(d) Record adjusting journal entries in the general journal and post to the ledger accounts. The following information is available on July 31:

Supplies on hand, $1,300
Accrued wages, $300
Estimated life of delivery van, four years
Estimated life of equipment, six years

Also, make any necessary adjusting entries for insurance, rent, and catering fees indicated by the July transactions.

Adjusting entries

3–31 The following information relates to December 31 adjustments for Fine Print, a printing company:

(1) Weekly salaries for a five-day week total $900, payable on Fridays. December 31 of the current year is a Wednesday.

(2) Fine Print received $1,000 during December for printing services to be performed during the following year. When received, this amount was credited to Printing Fees.
(3) During December, Fine Print provided $400 of printing services to clients who will be billed on January 2.
(4) All maintenance work on Fine Print's equipment is handled by Prompt Repair Company under an agreement whereby Fine Print pays a fixed monthly charge of $125. Fine Print paid four months' service charge in advance on December 1, debiting Prepaid Maintenance for $500.
(5) The firm paid $800 on December 5 for a series of radio commercials to run during December and January. One-half of the commercials have aired by December 31. The $800 payment was debited to Advertising Expense.
(6) Starting December 16, Fine Print rented 200 square feet of storage space from a neighboring business. The monthly rent of $1.60 per square foot is due in advance on the first of each month. Nothing was paid in December, however, because the neighbor agreed to add the rent for one-half of December to the January 1 payment.
(7) Fine Print invested $4,000 in securities on December 1 and earned interest of $35 on these securities by December 31. No interest will be received until January.
(8) The monthly depreciation on the firm's equipment is $180.

REQUIRED
Prepare the required December 31 adjusting entries in general journal form.

Alternative adjusting entries

3–32 Every summer the Classical Music Society sponsors a series of six classical music concerts. For 19X3, two concerts monthly are scheduled for June, July, and August.

Season tickets are on sale June 1–16, 19X3 (the first concert is June 16) and cost $48 for the six concerts. Tickets for individual concerts cost $10 each and go on sale June 15, 19X3. The Society sold 600 season tickets during June 1–16 and credited the $28,800 proceeds to the Unearned Ticket Revenue account.

The concerts are given in a pavilion located in a city park. The Society rents the facility from the city for $500 per concert. The city requires advance payment for all concerts by June 5. On June 3, 19X3, the Society mailed a $3,000 check to the city and debited the amount to the Prepaid Rent account. The Society incurs no other rent costs.

The two concerts for June were presented as scheduled. Individual tickets sold for the June concerts totaled $6,000 and were credited to the Ticket Revenue account. Other than the season tickets sold during June 1–16, no advance tickets have been sold by June 30 for the July and August concerts.

REQUIRED
(a) Prepare the necessary adjusting entries at June 30, 19X3, for rent expense and ticket revenue.
(b) After the adjustments made in (a) have been posted, what are the June 30, 19X3, balances in the following accounts: Prepaid Rent, Unearned Ticket Revenue, Ticket Revenue, and Rent Expense?

(c) Assume the Society credited the $28,800 season ticket sales amount to the Ticket Revenue account rather than to the Unearned Ticket Revenue account. Also assume the Society debited Rent Expense rather than Prepaid Rent for the $3,000 payment on June 3, 19X3. Given these assumptions, prepare the necessary adjusting entries at June 30, 19X3, for rent expense and ticket revenue.

(d) After the adjustments made in (c) have been posted, what are the June 30, 19X3, balances in the following accounts: Prepaid Rent, Unearned Ticket Revenue, Ticket Revenue, and Rent Expense?

ALTERNATE PROBLEMS

Transaction analysis, posting, trial balance, and adjusting entries

3–26A The Chin Karate School began business on June 1 of the current year. Transactions for June were as follows:

June 1 Po Chin contributed $6,500 of his personal funds to begin business.
2 Purchased equipment for $1,680, paying $500 cash, with the balance due in 30 days.
2 Paid six months' rent, $2,100
3 Paid one-year premium on liability insurance, $792.
8 Paid June newspaper advertising, $100.
15 Billed participants for karate lessons to date, $1,500.
20 Received $450 from a local company to conduct a special three-session class on self-defense for its employees. The three sessions will be held on June 29, July 6, and July 13, at $150 per session.
21 Collected $1,300 on account from participants.
25 Paid $250 to repair damage to wall caused by an errant kick.
30 Billed participants for karate lessons to date, $1,600.
30 Paid assistant's wages, $550.

REQUIRED

(a) Record the given transaction in a general journal.
(b) Devise a chart of accounts for the firm and set up the general ledger. Allow for accounts that may be needed when adjusting entries are made at the close of the accounting period [see part (e)].
(c) Post journal entries to the ledger accounts.
(d) Take a trial balance.
(e) Make the adjusting entries for rent expense, insurance expense, depreciation expense, utilities expense, and karate fees earned. Depreciation expense for June is $20; estimated utilities expense for June is $120. Post the adjusting entries.

Adjusting entries

3–27A The Wheel Place, Inc., began operations on March 1 of the current year to provide automotive wheel alignment and balancing services. On March 31, the unadjusted balances of the firm's accounts are as follows:

The Wheel Place, Inc.
Trial Balance
March 31, 19XX

	Debit	Credit
Cash	$ 2,900	
Accounts Receivable	4,350	
Prepaid Rent	3,200	
Supplies on Hand	2,800	
Equipment	23,100	
Accounts Payable		$ 1,600
Unearned Service Revenue		700
Capital Stock		27,000
Service Revenue		10,550
Wages Expense	3,500	
	$39,850	$39,850

The following information is also available:

(1) The balance in Prepaid Rent was the amount paid on March 1 to cover the first four months' rent.
(2) Supplies on hand on March 31 amounted to $1,200.
(3) The equipment has an estimated life of seven years.
(4) Unpaid wages at March 31 were $425.
(5) Utility services used during March were estimated at $380. A bill is expected early in April.
(6) The balance in Unearned Service Revenue was the amount received on March 1 from a new car dealer to cover alignment and balancing services on all new cars sold by the dealer in March and April. Wheel Place agreed to provide the services at a fixed fee of $350 each month.

REQUIRED
In general journal form, make the adjusting entries needed at March 31.

Trial balance and adjusting entries

3–28A Sure Delivery, a mailing service, has just completed its first full year of operations on December 31 of the current year. The firm's general ledger account balances before year-end adjustments are given below. No adjusting entries have been made to the accounts at any time during the year. Assume that all balances are normal.

Cash	$ 3,540	Fahey, Drawing	$ 6,000
Accounts Receivable	6,300	Mailing Fees	68,000
Prepaid Advertising	1,020	Wages Expense	33,100
Equipment	38,000	Rent Expense	5,400
Accounts Payable	1,910	Utilities Expense	2,900
Fahey, Capital	30,000	Supplies Expense	3,650

An analysis of the firm's records reveals the following:

(1) The balance in Prepaid Advertising represents the amount paid for newspaper advertising for one year. The agreement, which calls for the same amount of space each month, covers the period from February 1 of the

current year to January 31 next year. Sure Delivery did not advertise during its first month of operations.
(2) The equipment, purchased January 1, has an estimated life of 10 years.
(3) Utilities expense does not include expense for December, estimated at $310. The bill will not arrive until January of next year.
(4) At year-end, employees have earned $700 in wages that will not be paid until January.
(5) All supplies purchased during the year were debited to Supplies Expense. Supplies on hand at year-end amounted to $1,000.
(6) Mailing services amounting to $3,000 were rendered to customers who have not yet been billed for the services.
(7) The firm's lease calls for rent of $450 per month payable on the first of each month, plus an amount equal to $\frac{1}{2}$% of annual mailing fees earned. The rental percentage is payable within 15 days after the end of the year.

REQUIRED
(a) Prove that debits equal credits for the unadjusted account balances shown above by preparing a trial balance.
(b) Record adjusting entries in general journal form.

Transaction analysis, posting, trial balance, and adjusting entries

3–30A Market-View, a market research firm, had the following transactions in June, its first month of operations.

June 1 J. Bryant invested $20,000 of personal funds in the firm.
1 The firm purchased the following from an office supply company: office equipment, $10,800; office supplies, $1,500. Terms called for a cash payment of $3,500, with the remainder due in 60 days. (Make a compound entry.)
2 Paid June rent, $750.
2 Contracted for three months' advertising in a local newspaper at $200 per month and paid for the advertising in advance.
2 Signed a six-month contract with an electronics firm to provide research consulting services at a rate of $2,000 per month. Received two months' fees in advance.
10 Billed various customers for services rendered, $3,100.
12 Paid two weeks' salaries (five-day week) to employees, $2,400.
15 Paid J. Bryant's travel expenses to business conference, $800.
18 Paid post office for bulk mailing of survey research questionnaire, $380 (postage expense).
22 Billed various customers for services rendered, $4,200.
26 Paid two weeks' salaries to employees, $2,400.
30 Collected $5,000 from customers on account.
30 J. Bryant withdrew $950 for personal use.

REQUIRED
(a) Set up a general ledger that includes the following accounts, using the account numbers shown: Cash (11); Accounts Receivable (12); Office Supplies on Hand (14); Prepaid Advertising (15); Office Equipment (16); Accumulated Depreciation—Office Equipment (17); Accounts Payable (21); Sal-

aries Payable (22); Unearned Service Fees (23); J. Bryant, Capital (31); J. Bryant, Drawing (32); Service Fees (41); Salaries Expense (51); Advertising Expense (52); Supplies Expense (53); Rent Expense (54); Travel Expense (55); Depreciation Expense—Office Equipment (56); and Postage Expense (57).

(b) Record June transactions in general journal form and post to the ledger accounts.

(c) Take a trial balance at June 30.

(d) Record adjusting journal entries in general journal form, and post to the ledger accounts. The following information is available on June 30:

Supplies on hand, $850
Accrued salaries, $480
Estimated life of office equipment, nine years
Unbilled services rendered, $1,600

Also, make any necessary adjusting entries for advertising and for service fees indicated by the June transactions.

Adjusting entries

3–31A The following information relates to the December 31 adjustments for Water Shield, a firm providing waterproofing services for commercial and residential customers.

(1) The firm paid a $3,240 premium for a three-year insurance policy, coverage to begin September 1 of the current year. The entire amount of the premium was debited to Insurance Expense; no other entry concerning this premium has been recorded.

(2) Weekly wages for a five-day workweek total $1,200, payable on Fridays. December 31 of the current year is a Thursday.

(3) Water Shield received $1,300 during December for services to be performed during the following year. When received, this amount was credited to Service Fees.

(4) During December, Water Shield provided $650 worth of services to clients who will not be billed until early January.

(5) During December, fuel oil costs of $475 were incurred to heat the firm's buildings. Because the monthly bill from the oil company has not yet arrived, no entry has been made for this amount (fuel oil costs are charged to Utilities Expense).

(6) The Supplies on Hand account has a balance of $7,400 on December 31. However, the December purchases of supplies, totaling $600, were inadvertently debited to the Supplies Expense account, which now has a balance of $600. A count of supplies on December 31 indicates that $500 worth of supplies are still on hand.

(7) On December 1, Water Shield borrowed $7,000 from the bank, giving an interest-bearing note payable. Interest is not payable until the note is due near the end of January. However, the interest expense for December is $70. No entries have been made for the interest expense or interest payable.

REQUIRED

Prepare the necessary December 31 adjusting entries in general journal form.

BUSINESS DECISION PROBLEM

Kinney Analytic Services, a firm started several years ago by Matt Kinney, offers consulting services for material handling and plant layout. The balance sheet prepared by the firm's bookkeeper at the close of the current year is shown below:

Kinney Analytic Services
Balance Sheet
December 31, 19XX

Assets			**Liabilities**		
Cash		$ 4,700	Accounts Payable	$ 3,400	
Accounts Receivable		17,000	Notes Payable—Bank	20,000	
Supplies on Hand		9,300	Unearned Consulting Fees	6,600	
Equipment	$40,000		Total Liabilities		$30,000
Less: Accumulated			**Owner's Equity**		
Depreciation	14,000	26,000	M. Kinney, Capital		27,000
			Total Liabilities and		
Total Assets		$57,000	Owner's Equity		$57,000

Earlier in the year, Kinney obtained a bank loan of $20,000 for the firm. One of the provisions of the loan is that the year-end ratio of total liabilities to total owner's equity shall not exceed 1:1. Based on the above balance sheet, the ratio at the end of the current year is 1.11:1.

Kinney is concerned about being in violation of the loan agreement and asks your assistance in reviewing the situation. Kinney believes that his rather inexperienced bookkeeper may have overlooked some items at year-end.

In discussions with Kinney and the bookkeeper, you learn the following:

(1) On January 1, 19XX, the firm paid a $4,500 insurance premium for three years of coverage. The full amount was debited to Insurance Expense.
(2) Depreciation on the equipment should be 10% of cost per year. The bookkeeper has recorded only one-half this amount for the current year.
(3) Interest on the bank loan has been paid through the end of the current year.
(4) The firm concluded a major consulting engagement in December, doing a plant layout analysis for a new factory. The $4,000 fee has not been billed or recorded in the accounts.
(5) On December 1, 19XX, the firm received a $6,600 advance payment from Endres Corporation for consulting services to be rendered over a three-month period. This payment was credited to the Unearned Consulting Fees account. One-third of this fee was earned by December 31, 19XX.
(6) Supplies costing $3,200 were on hand on December 31. The bookkeeper filed the record of the count but made no entry in the accounts.

REQUIRED

What is the correct ratio of total liabilities to total owner's equity at December 31, 19XX? Is the firm in violation of the loan agreement? Prepare a schedule to support your computation of the correct total liabilities and total owner's equity at December 31, 19XX.

ANSWERS TO SELF-TEST QUESTIONS

1. (b) 2. (d) 3. (a) 4. (b) 5. (c)

4

The Accounting Cycle Concluded

Chapter Objectives

- Identify the role of a worksheet in compiling information for the preparation of financial statements.
- Explain the procedures for preparing a worksheet.
- Describe the process of closing the temporary accounts of a sole proprietorship and a corporation.
- Discuss the purpose of reversing entries.

Everything ends that has a beginning.

QUINTILIAN

The first four major steps in the accounting cycle—analyzing and recording transactions, posting to accounts, and adjusting the accounts—are essential to the process of classifying financial data and, where necessary, aligning the data with appropriate periods. The goal of these procedures is to prepare the data so that they can be summarized in a set of meaningful financial statements.

In this chapter, we shall explain the two remaining principal steps in the accounting cycle: preparation of financial statements (other than the statement of cash flows) and closing procedures. Our discussion is based on the December financial data given in Chapter 3 for Landen TV Service. We will discuss the preparation of the statement of cash flows in Chapter 19.

PREPARING FINANCIAL STATEMENTS

Step 5: Prepare Financial Statements

Once the appropriate adjusting entries have been made and posted to the ledger accounts, another trial balance is taken to ensure that the general ledger still balances. This **adjusted trial balance** lists the proper balances for all accounts. An income statement and a balance sheet may be prepared directly from these account balances.

In practice, however, many accountants utilize a **worksheet** in compiling the information necessary for the preparation of financial statements. The worksheet is a tool of the accountant, not part of a company's formal accounting records. The accountant prepares a worksheet at that stage of the accounting cycle when it is time to make adjustments and prepare financial statements.

The basic structure of the worksheet is presented in Exhibit 4–1, which includes an explanation of the format being used. A completed worksheet for Landen TV Service appears in Exhibit 4–2. A careful study of these two illustrations shows the following advantages of the worksheet:

(1) The balances of all general ledger accounts appear in one location and may be easily reviewed to determine whether any of them need adjusting.

(2) The total effect of any adjustment—whether contemplated or actually made on the worksheet—can be readily determined. Because these adjustments are reviewed before adjusting entries are journalized and posted, the likelihood of incorrect adjustments appearing in the formal accounting records is reduced.

EXHIBIT 4–1
Basic Structure of Worksheet

❶
(Heading for worksheet)

Description	Trial Balance		Adjustments		Adjusted Trial Balance		Income Statement		Balance Sheet	
	Debit	Credit	Debit	Credit	Debit	Credit	Debit	Credit	Debit	Credit
❷ (The unadjusted trial balance)			❸ (Amounts of adjustments)		❹ (Amounts of adjusted account balances)			❺ (Extension of adjusted account balances)		
							(Income statement accounts)		(Balance sheet accounts)	
(Titles of accounts not in unadjusted trial balance, added as needed)								❻ (Balancing of columns for each statement)		

EXHIBIT 4–2

Landen TV Service
Worksheet
For the Month Ended December 31, 19XX

Description	Trial Balance Debit	Trial Balance Credit	Adjustments Debit	Adjustments Credit	Adjusted Trial Balance Debit	Adjusted Trial Balance Credit	Income Statement Debit	Income Statement Credit	Balance Sheet Debit	Balance Sheet Credit
Cash	13,130				13,130				13,130	
Accounts Receivable	2,800		(7) 240		3,040				3,040	
Supplies and Parts on Hand	950			(1) 440	510				510	
Test Equipment	3,600				3,600				3,600	
Truck	10,800				10,800				10,800	
Accounts Payable		2,550				2,550				2,550
Unearned Service Fees		1,000	(4) 250			750				750
M. Landen, Capital		25,000				25,000				25,000
M. Landen, Drawing	800				800				800	
Service Fees		5,450		(4) 250 (7) 240		5,940		5,940		
Rent Expense	600				600		600			
Wages Expense	1,080		(6) 90		1,170		1,170			
Advertising Expense	80				80		80			
Truck Expense	160				160		160			
	34,000	34,000								
Supplies and Parts Expense			(1) 440		440		440			
Depreciation Expense—Test Equipment			(2) 60		60		60			
Accumulated Depreciation—Test Equipment				(2) 60		60				60
Depreciation Expense—Truck			(3) 150		150		150			
Accumulated Depreciation—Truck				(3) 150		150				150
Utilities Expense			(5) 120		120		120			
Utilities Payable				(5) 120		120				120
Wages Payable				(6) 90		90				90
			1,350	1,350	34,660	34,660	2,780	5,940	31,880	28,720
Net Income							3,160			3,160
							5,940	5,940	31,880	31,880

(3) Once all the adjustments have been made, the adjusted account balances can be determined and separated into a group for the income statement and a group for the balance sheet, simplifying the preparation of these statements.

The worksheet is prepared in the order indicated by the circled numbers in Exhibit 4–1. Refer to Exhibits 4–1 and 4–2 when reading through the following procedures for preparing a worksheet.

(1) HEADING The worksheet heading should include (a) the name of the accounting entity involved, (b) the term "Worksheet" to indicate the type of analysis performed, and (c) a date describing the period covered. The worksheet includes both income statement data (for the period described) and balance sheet data (for the end of the period described).

The worksheet form we have illustrated has a description column and 10 amount (money) columns. A set of debit and credit columns is provided for each of the five headings, "Trial Balance," "Adjustments," "Adjusted Trial Balance," "Income Statement," and "Balance Sheet."

(2) UNADJUSTED TRIAL BALANCE The trial balance, taken in step 3 of the accounting cycle, is entered in the description column and the first pair of money columns. Because this trial balance reflects the account balances before adjustment, it is often designated the **unadjusted trial balance.** Once the trial balance is placed on the worksheet and double ruled, it reflects the state of the general ledger at the time the worksheet is prepared.

(3) ADJUSTMENTS When a worksheet is used, all adjustments are first entered on the worksheet. This procedure permits the adjustment to be reviewed for completeness and accuracy. To adjust accounts already appearing in the unadjusted trial balance, we simply enter the amounts in the appropriate side (debit or credit) of the adjustments columns on the lines containing the accounts. When accounts not appearing in the unadjusted trial balance require adjustment, their titles are listed as needed in the description column below the accounts already listed.

The adjustments recorded on the worksheet in Exhibit 4–2 are identical with those recorded in general journal form in step 4 of the accounting cycle (see Chapter 3). It is common practice to "key" the amounts of each adjusting entry with the same letter or number. Note that the numbers (1) through (7) are used in Exhibit 4–2. This procedure makes it easy to check the equality of debits and credits in each entry and to identify all the amounts related to a particular adjustment.

We repeat the adjusting entries made at the end of December for Landen TV Service and explain their placement on the worksheet (Exhibit 4–2). Remember, because we are preparing a worksheet, these adjustments are entered on the worksheet; they are not yet recorded in the general journal.

(1)	Supplies and Parts Expense	440	
	Supplies and Parts on Hand		440

Because $510 worth of supplies were on hand at December 31, we needed to reduce the asset Supplies and Parts on Hand from $950 to $510 and to record the $440 difference as expense. Note that the expense account, Supplies and Parts Expense, does not appear in the unadjusted trial balance and must be added below the accounts already listed.

(2)	Depreciation Expense—Test Equipment	60	
	Accumulated Depreciation—Test Equipment		60
(3)	Depreciation Expense—Truck	150	
	Accumulated Depreciation—Truck		150

These entries recorded the expiration of the test equipment and truck costs for December. The entries to record depreciation expense and reduce the asset accounts (via accumulated depreciation contra accounts) require accounts that do not appear in the unadjusted trial balance. Therefore, the four accounts in entries (2) and (3) must be listed in the description column below the accounts in the trial balance.

(4)	Unearned Service Fees	250	
	Service Fees		250

This adjustment was made to reflect the portion of a $1,000 advance earned in December. The liability account Unearned Service Fees, originally credited for the $1,000 advance, was reduced by a $250 debit, and a corresponding credit was made to the revenue account Service Fees. Since both accounts appear in the unadjusted trial balance, we record this adjustment on the lines already provided for these accounts.

(5)	Utilities Expense	120	
	Utilities Payable		120
(6)	Wages Expense	90	
	Wages Payable		90

These adjusting entries reflected expenses incurred in December but not paid until January. The utilities expense was the estimated cost of services consumed in December. Wages were accrued for the last two days in December. Because no utilities expense was paid in December, the expense account does not appear in the unadjusted trial balance. Both the expense account and the liability Utilities Payable must be added below the accounts already listed. Since wages were paid during December, Wages Expense appears in the trial balance, but Wages Payable must be added.

(7)	Accounts Receivable	240	
	Service Fees		240

This entry was made to reflect unbilled service fees earned in December. Since both accounts appear in the unadjusted trial balance, we record this adjustment on the lines already provided for these accounts.

After recording all the adjusting entries on the worksheet, we total the adjustments columns to prove that debits equal credits.

(4) ADJUSTED TRIAL BALANCE The numbers in the adjusted trial balance are the account balances reflecting the impact of adjustments. These figures are determined by combining horizontally, line by line, the amounts in the first four money columns—that is, the unadjusted trial balance and the adjustments.

We review the calculations for the first three lines of Exhibit 4–2 to illustrate this process. The first line shows Cash with a debit of $13,130 in the trial balance. Because Cash is not affected by any adjustments, the $13,130 appears in the debit column of the adjusted trial balance. The second line shows a debit of $2,800 for Accounts Receivable in the trial balance and a debit of $240 in the adjustments columns. These two debit amounts are added, and the sum of $3,040 is shown in the debit column of the adjusted trial balance. On the third line, Supplies and Parts on Hand begins with a debit of $950 in the trial balance and then shows a credit of $440 in the adjustments columns. The $440 credit is subtracted from the $950 debit, and the remaining $510 is shown as a debit in the adjusted trial balance.

After computing the adjusted trial balance amounts for all the accounts on the worksheet, we total the two columns of the adjusted trial balance to confirm that they are equal and that our worksheet, therefore, still balances.

(5) EXTENSION OF ADJUSTED BALANCES The amounts in the adjusted trial balance columns are extended into the two remaining pairs of columns as follows:

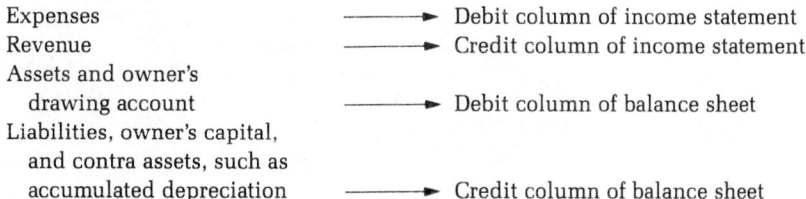

Expenses	→	Debit column of income statement
Revenue	→	Credit column of income statement
Assets and owner's drawing account	→	Debit column of balance sheet
Liabilities, owner's capital, and contra assets, such as accumulated depreciation	→	Credit column of balance sheet

Note that the positions of the adjusted balances in the worksheet correspond to the normal balances of the accounts. That is, expenses and assets are debits on the income statement and balance sheet, respectively; revenue is a credit on the income statement, and liabilities and owner's capital are credits on the balance sheet. The owner's drawing account is a debit in the balance sheet columns because it is a contra owner's equity account. The accumulated depreciation accounts are credits on the balance sheet because they are contra asset accounts. Once the proper extensions are made, the worksheet is complete except for the balancing of the two pairs of statement columns containing the adjusted balances.

(6) BALANCING THE WORKSHEET The first step in balancing is to add each of the income statement and balance sheet columns and record their respective totals on the same line as the totals of the adjusted trial balance columns. The difference between the total debits and total credits in the income statement columns will be the difference between total revenue and total expenses—that is, the net income for the period. The net income should also be the amount by which the debit and credit columns for the balance sheet differ. This is true because the capital account balance, as extended, does not yet reflect the net income for the current period.

When revenue exceeds expenses, we balance the two pairs of statement columns by adding the net income figure to both the debit column of the income statement and the credit column of the balance sheet. If expenses exceed revenue, we add the amount of net loss to the credit column of the income statement and to the debit column of the balance sheet. After we have added the net income (or loss) to the proper columns, we total and double rule the four columns. The worksheet is now complete and contains the account data necessary to prepare an income statement and a balance sheet. Note that Mark Landen's equity at this point is indicated by three amounts appearing on the worksheet:

Credit balance of capital account	$25,000
Debit balance of drawing account	(800)
Credit amount of net income to balance the balance sheet columns	3,160
Mark Landen's equity at end of period	$27,360

Exhibits 4–3 and 4–4 illustrate an income statement and a balance sheet, respectively, for the Landen TV Service, prepared from the worksheet.

EXHIBIT 4–3

Landen TV Service
Income Statement
For the Month of December, 19XX

Revenue		
Service Fees		$5,940
Expenses		
Rent Expense	$ 600	
Wages Expense	1,170	
Advertising Expense	80	
Truck Expense	160	
Supplies and Parts Expense	440	
Depreciation Expense—Test Equipment	60	
Depreciation Expense—Truck	150	
Utilities Expense	120	
Total Expenses		2,780
Net Income		$3,160

EXHIBIT 4–4

Landen TV Service
Balance Sheet
December 31, 19XX

Assets			**Liabilities**		
Cash		$13,130	Accounts Payable	$2,550	
Accounts Receivable		3,040	Utilities Payable	120	
Supplies and Parts on Hand		510	Wages Payable	90	
Test Equipment	$ 3,600		Unearned Service Fees	750	
Less: Accumulated Depreciation	60	3,540	Total Liabilities		$ 3,510
Truck	$10,800		**Owner's Equity**		
Less: Accumulated Depreciation	150	10,650	M. Landen, Capital		27,360
Total Assets		$30,870	Total Liabilities and Owner's Equity		$30,870

A formal set of financial statements frequently includes a **statement of owner's equity.** This statement simply lists the beginning balance, additions, deductions, and ending balance of owner's equity for the accounting period. Exhibit 4–5 illustrates such a statement for Landen TV Service for the month of December.

When capital contributions have been made during the accounting period, we cannot determine from the worksheet alone the beginning balance of owner's capital and amounts of capital contributions during a period. Consequently, in preparing a statement of owner's equity, we must examine the owner's capital account in the general ledger.

RECORDING AND POSTING WORKSHEET ADJUSTING ENTRIES At the close of the calendar or fiscal year, the adjusting entries on the worksheet must be recorded in the general journal and posted to the general ledger accounts in order

EXHIBIT 4–5

Landen TV Service
Statement of Owner's Equity
For the Month of December, 19XX

Mark Landen, Capital, December 1, 19XX		$ -0-
Add: Capital Contributed in December	$25,000	
Net Income for December	3,160	28,160
		$28,160
Less: Capital Withdrawn in December		800
Mark Landen, Capital, December 31, 19XX		$27,360

EXHIBIT 4–6
Adjusting Entries

General Journal

Page 3

Date		Description	Post. Ref.	Debit	Credit
19XX					
Dec.	31	Supplies and Parts Expense	54	440	
		Supplies and Parts on Hand	14		440
		To record expense of supplies and parts used in December.			
	31	Depreciation Expense—Test Equipment	57	60	
		Accumulated Depreciation—Test Equipment	17		60
		To record December depreciation on test equipment.			
	31	Depreciation Expense—Truck	58	150	
		Accumulated Depreciation—Truck	19		150
		To record December depreciation on truck.			
	31	Unearned Service Fees	24	250	
		Service Fees	41		250
		To record portion of advance earned in December.			
	31	Utilities Expense	55	120	
		Utilities Payable	22		120
		To record estimated amount of December utilities expense.			
	31	Wages Expense	52	90	
		Wages Payable	23		90
		To record accrued wages for December 30 and 31.			
	31	Accounts Receivable	12	240	
		Service Fees	41		240
		To record unbilled revenue earned during December.			

to accomplish the proper closing procedures described in the next section. Although Landen TV Service has been in business only for December, its accounting year ends on December 31. Therefore, the adjusting entries are entered in the records and closing procedures are followed. The adjusting entries appear in the general journal as shown in Exhibit 4–6.

These journal entries are posted to the general ledger accounts of Landen TV Service shown in Exhibit 4–9 (pages 137–42). The entries are identified by the parenthetical notation "(adjusting)."

Interim Financial Statements

Financial statements covering periods within a company's calendar or fiscal year—such as monthly or quarterly statements—are called **interim financial statements.** Most companies prepare interim financial statements from worksheet data because they prefer to journalize and post adjusting entries only at year-end. Interim adjustments, then, are reflected only on the worksheet. When making interim adjusting entries on the worksheet, the bookkeeper must consider the period for which the adjustments are made. Some adjustment amounts will accu-

REPORTS TO STOCKHOLDERS

Corporations include their financial statements in periodic reports to stockholders. The annual report to stockholders for large corporations may be quite extensive, often running 20–50 pages or more. In addition to financial statements, the annual report may include a message from the chairman of the board of directors and the chief executive officer, a review of the year's operations, a financial review, the accountants' report, and selected financial statistics for several years. Supplementing these items may be a variety of charts, graphs, and photographs of the company's products and facilities.

Reports to stockholders covering less than one year (interim reports) are much less extensive. They are intended to provide owners and potential investors with timely information on the corporation's progress and may include summarized financial information rather than a complete set of financial statements.

Comprehensive annual reports to stockholders are a relatively recent development in the United States. Before the 1900s, corporate management generally disclosed little, if any, financial information to stockholders. The first corporations were usually small and obtained much of their funding through short-term bank loans rather than from the public sale of stocks. Bankers who needed to assess the borrower's ability to repay short-term loans considered the balance sheet the primary financial statement because it revealed the total short-term obligations and the assets that would likely be converted to cash in the near future. By the late 1920s, however, corporate expansion led to increased financing through stock issuances and long-term debt. Owners and creditors used the income statement to judge earning power. Corporate reporting, then, evolved from providing balance sheets for bankers to providing income statements and balance sheets for stockholders and creditors.*

The first modern annual report was issued in 1902 by U.S. Steel Corporation. The report was lengthy and detailed, revealing so much about the corporation's operations that the directors were practically scandalized.† The extensive disclosures broke with tradition, and most corporations did not follow U.S. Steel's lead for many years.

Considerable variety exists in the length and detail of reports to stockholders. Remarks by the president of Diamond Match Company used 100 pages of the company's 1942 annual report.‡ In contrast, a 1972 semiannual report from North American Publishing of Philadelphia was more to the point. The report was poster size (3 feet long) and featured letters 8 inches high and 6 inches wide that stated: "We Had a BIG IMPROVEMENT for the First Six Months."§

Many corporations view the annual report, in part, as a public relations document. Imagine the chagrin, then, at Citizens Valley Bank in Albany, Oregon, several years ago. Half of the copies of the bank's 1973 annual report had been mailed before a particular omission was noted—the bank's name had been dropped from the report's cover and did not appear anywhere in the report.‖

*A.C. Littleton and V.K. Zimmerman, *Accounting Theory: Continuity and Change* (Englewood Cliffs, NJ: Prentice-Hall, Inc. 1962), pages 92–97.

†"Annual Reports—No Longer Dry," *Fortune*, February 1944, page 62.

‡*Ibid.*

§"The Numbers Game: A Few (Fairly) Kind Words," *Forbes*, May 1, 1973, page 36.

‖"Business Bulletin," *The Wall Street Journal*, February 14, 1974, page 1.

mulate, while others will not. For example, in writing off a $1,200 one-year prepaid insurance premium paid on January 1 and debited to the asset account, the bookkeeper would debit Insurance Expense and credit Prepaid Insurance for $100 on the worksheet at January 31. The amount of the adjustment would be $200 at the end of February, $300 at the end of March, and so on. Similarly, the amount of the worksheet adjusting entry for depreciation will increase each month. On the other hand, an adjusting entry to accrue salaries at the end of any month will consist only of unpaid salaries at the date of adjustment, because salaries accrued at the end of each month are ordinarily paid during the ensuing month.

When the year-end worksheet is prepared, the adjusting data will pertain to the entire year. Therefore, the adjusting entries to be journalized and posted to the ledger accounts can be taken directly from this worksheet.

CLOSING PROCEDURES

Step 6: Close Temporary Accounts

Revenue, expense, and drawing accounts are temporary accounts that accumulate data related to a specific accounting year. These temporary accounts facilitate preparation of the income statement and provide additional information. At the end of each accounting year, the balances of these temporary accounts are transferred to the capital account (the Retained Earnings account for corporations). Therefore, the balance of the owner's capital account includes on a cumulative basis the net result of all revenue, expense, and drawing transactions. This final phase in the accounting cycle is referred to as **closing procedures.**

A temporary account is said to be *closed* when an entry is made that changes its balance to zero—that is, an entry that is equal in amount to the account's balance but is opposite to the balance as a debit or credit. An account that is closed is said to be closed *to* the account that receives the offsetting debit or credit. Thus, a closing entry simply transfers the balance of one account to another account. In this manner, closing procedures transfer the balances of temporary accounts to the capital account.

A summary account is traditionally used to close the temporary revenue and expense accounts. For our illustration, we shall use an account titled "Income Summary," although a variety of titles are found in practice (Revenue and Expense Summary, Income and Expense Summary, or Profit and Loss Summary, for example). The entries for opening and closing Income Summary are quite simple and occur only during the closing procedures. The entries that close the temporary accounts are as follows:

(1) Debit each revenue account in an amount equal to its balance, and credit Income Summary for the total revenue involved.

(2) Credit each expense account in an amount equal to its balance, and debit Income Summary for the total expense involved.

After these temporary accounts have been closed, the balance of the Income Summary account is equal to the net income for the period—hence the title "Income Summary." The remaining closing steps are as follows:

(3) Debit Income Summary for its balance, and credit the capital account (Retained Earnings for a corporation) for the same amount. In the case of a net loss, debit the capital account and credit Income Summary.

(4) For noncorporate businesses, credit the drawing account in an amount equal to its balance and debit the capital account for the same amount.

In Exhibit 4–7, we illustrate the entries for closing the revenue and expense accounts to the Income Summary account of Landen TV Service as they would be recorded in the general journal. The effect of these two entries is shown using T accounts.

At this point, the balance of the Income Summary is a credit equal to the net income of $3,160. The closing procedure is completed by closing the Income Summary and M. Landen, Drawing accounts to the M. Landen, Capital account. These two entries are recorded in the general journal as shown in Exhibit 4–8. The effect of these entries on the general ledger is also diagramed.

It is probably most convenient to take the data necessary for formulating the closing entries from the worksheet, although the information can also be derived from the ledger. After the closing entries for Landen TV Service have been recorded and posted to the firm's general ledger, all temporary accounts have zero balances and the capital account has a balance equal to the amount shown on Landen TV Service's balance sheet (see Exhibit 4–4). Exhibit 4–9 illustrates the general ledger of Landen TV Service after all the closing procedures have been followed. Closing entries are identified by the parenthetical notation "(closing)."

CORPORATION ACCOUNTING The entries involving owners' equity are different if Landen TV Service is organized as a corporation. The persons forming the corporation receive capital stock in exchange for the $25,000 cash contribution. The transaction is recorded as a debit to Cash and a credit to Capital Stock. The $800 cash withdrawal is considered a cash dividend and is recorded as a debit to Retained Earnings and a credit to Cash.

The revenue and expense accounts of a corporation are closed to the Income Summary account exactly as they are closed in a proprietorship. Because a corporation is subject to an income tax, however, it must close an additional expense account, Income Tax Expense. Disregarding income taxes, the revenue and expense accounts are closed as shown in Exhibit 4–7. Once the revenue and expense accounts are closed to Income Summary, the closing procedures for a corporation are completed by closing the Income Summary account to Retained Earnings. We show this in the T accounts below.

Capital Stock		Retained Earnings		Income Summary	
	25,000	800	3,160	2,780	5,940
				3,160	

After closing entries are posted, the Retained Earnings account reflects the $2,360 earned and retained in the business. Combined with the Capital Stock of $25,000, total stockholders' equity is $27,360.

EXHIBIT 4–7
Closing Revenue and Expense Accounts

General Journal Page 4

Date		Description	Post. Ref.	Debit	Credit
19XX					
Dec.	31	Service Fees	41	5,940	
		Income Summary	33		5,940
		To close the revenue account.			
	31	Income Summary	33	2,780	
		Rent Expense	51		600
		Wages Expense	52		1,170
		Advertising Expense	53		80
		Truck Expense	56		160
		Supplies and Parts Expense	54		440
		Depreciation Expense—Test Equipment	57		60
		Depreciation Expense—Truck	58		150
		Utilities Expense	55		120
		To close the expense accounts.			

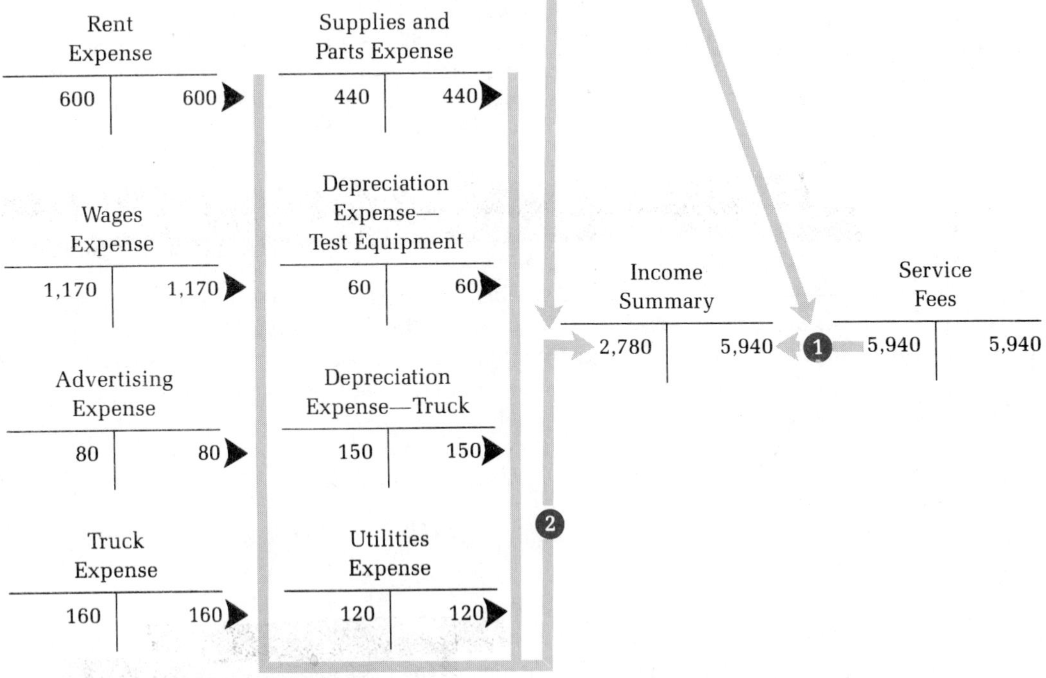

EXHIBIT 4–8
Closing the Income Summary and Drawing Accounts

General Journal Page 4

Date		Description	Post. Ref.	Debit	Credit
19XX					
Dec.	31	Income Summary	33	3,160	
		M. Landen, Capital ③	31		3,160
		To close the Income Summary account.			
	31	M. Landen, Capital	31	800	
		M. Landen, Drawing ④	32		800
		To close the drawing account.			

M. Landen, Drawing	
800	800 ④ →

M. Landen, Capital	
800	25,000
	3,160

Income Summary	
2,780	5,940
③ 3,160	

EXHIBIT 4–9
Landen TV Service General Ledger

Cash Account No. 11

Date		Description	Post. Ref.	Debit*	Credit	Balance
19XX						
Dec.	1		J1	25,000		25,000
	1		J1		600	24,400
	2		J1		10,800	13,600
	2		J1		2,000	11,600
	2		J1	1,000		12,600
	7		J1	650		13,250
	14		J1		540	12,710
	14		J2	680		13,390
	17		J2		80	13,310
	19		J2	500		13,810
	21		J2	520		14,330
	28		J2		160	14,170
	28		J2		540	13,630
	28		J2		800	12,830
	28		J2	300		13,130

EXHIBIT 4–9 (continued)

Accounts Receivable Account No. 12

Date		Description	Post. Ref.	Debit*	Credit	Balance
19XX						
Dec.	14		J1	900		900
	19		J2		500	400
	28		J2	2,400		2,800
	31	(adjusting)	J3	240		3,040

Supplies and Parts on Hand Account No. 14

Date		Description	Post. Ref.	Debit*	Credit	Balance
19XX						
Dec.	3		J1	950		950
	31	(adjusting)	J3		440	510

Test Equipment Account No. 16

Date		Description	Post. Ref.	Debit*	Credit	Balance
19XX						
Dec.	2		J1	3,600		3,600

Accumulated Depreciation—Test Equipment Account No. 17

Date		Description	Post. Ref.	Debit	Credit*	Balance
19XX						
Dec.	31	(adjusting)	J3		60	60

Truck Account No. 18

Date		Description	Post. Ref.	Debit*	Credit	Balance
19XX						
Dec.	2		J1	10,800		10,800

EXHIBIT 4–9 (continued)

Accumulated Depreciation—Truck

Account No. 19

Date		Description	Post. Ref.	Debit	Credit*	Balance
19XX Dec.	31	(adjusting)	J3		150	150

Accounts Payable

Account No. 21

Date		Description	Post. Ref.	Debit	Credit*	Balance
19XX Dec.	2		J1		1,600	1,600
	3		J1		950	2,550

Utilities Payable

Account No. 22

Date		Description	Post. Ref.	Debit	Credit*	Balance
19XX Dec.	31	(adjusting)	J3		120	120

Wages Payable

Account No. 23

Date		Description	Post. Ref.	Debit	Credit*	Balance
19XX Dec.	31	(adjusting)	J3		90	90

Unearned Service Fees

Account No. 24

Date		Description	Post. Ref.	Debit	Credit*	Balance
19XX Dec.	2		J1		1,000	1,000
	31	(adjusting)	J3	250		750

EXHIBIT 4–9 (continued)

M. Landen, Capital Account No. 31

Date		Description	Post. Ref.	Debit	Credit*	Balance
19XX						
Dec.	1		J1		25,000	25,000
	31	(closing)	J4		3,160	28,160
	31	(closing)	J4	800		27,360

M. Landen, Drawing Account No. 32

Date		Description	Post. Ref.	Debit*	Credit	Balance
19XX						
Dec.	28		J2	800		800
	31	(closing)	J4		800	–0–

Income Summary Account No. 33

Date		Description	Post. Ref.	Debit	Credit*	Balance
19XX						
Dec.	31	(closing)	J4		5,940	5,940
	31	(closing)	J4	2,780		3,160
	31	(closing)	J4	3,160		–0–

Service Fees Account No. 41

Date		Description	Post. Ref.	Debit	Credit*	Balance
19XX						
Dec.	7		J1		650	650
	14		J1		900	1,550
	14		J2		680	2,230
	21		J2		520	2,750
	28		J2		2,400	5,150
	28		J2		300	5,450
	31	(adjusting)	J3		250	5,700
	31	(adjusting)	J3		240	5,940
	31	(closing)	J4	5,940		–0–

EXHIBIT 4–9 (continued)

Rent Expense Account No. 51

Date		Description	Post. Ref.	Debit*	Credit	Balance
19XX						
Dec.	1		J1	600		600
	31	(closing)	J4		600	–0–

Wages Expense Account No. 52

Date		Description	Post. Ref.	Debit*	Credit	Balance
19XX						
Dec.	14		J1	540		540
	28		J2	540		1,080
	31	(adjusting)	J3	90		1,170
	31	(closing)	J4		1,170	–0–

Advertising Expense Account No. 53

Date		Description	Post. Ref.	Debit*	Credit	Balance
19XX						
Dec.	17		J2	80		80
	31	(closing)	J4		80	–0–

Supplies and Parts Expense Account No. 54

Date		Description	Post. Ref.	Debit*	Credit	Balance
19XX						
Dec.	31	(adjusting)	J3	440		440
	31	(closing)	J4		440	–0–

EXHIBIT 4–9 (continued)

Utilities Expense

Account No. 55

Date		Description	Post. Ref.	Debit*	Credit	Balance
19XX						
Dec.	31	(adjusting)	J3	120		120
	31	(closing)	J4		120	–0–

Truck Expense

Account No. 56

Date		Description	Post. Ref.	Debit*	Credit	Balance
19XX						
Dec.	28		J2	160		160
	31	(closing)	J4		160	–0–

Depreciation Expense—Test Equipment

Account No. 57

Date		Description	Post. Ref.	Debit*	Credit	Balance
19XX						
Dec.	31	(adjusting)	J3	60		60
	31	(closing)	J4		60	–0–

Depreciation Expense—Truck

Account No. 58

Date		Description	Post. Ref.	Debit*	Credit	Balance
19XX						
Dec.	31	(adjusting)	J3	150		150
	31	(closing)	J4		150	–0–

EXHIBIT 4–10

Landen TV Service
Post-closing Trial Balance
December 31, 19XX

	Debit	Credit
Cash	$13,130	
Accounts Receivable	3,040	
Supplies and Parts on Hand	510	
Test Equipment	3,600	
Accumulated Depreciation—Test Equipment		$ 60
Truck	10,800	
Accumulated Depreciation—Truck		150
Accounts Payable		2,550
Utilities Payable		120
Wages Payable		90
Unearned Service Fees		750
M. Landen, Capital		27,360
	$31,080	$31,080

POST-CLOSING TRIAL BALANCE A post-closing trial balance is usually taken after the closing process. This procedure ensures that an equality of debits and credits has been maintained throughout the adjusting and closing procedures. Obviously, since the temporary accounts have been closed, only balance sheet accounts appear in this trial balance. Exhibit 4–10 presents the post-closing trial balance for Landen TV Service.

REVERSING ENTRIES

In our discussion of adjusting entries for accrued items in Chapter 3, we pointed out that certain precautions are necessary to avoid reflecting the same expense or revenue in two successive periods. We now review two alternative procedures for recording the settlement of accrued items in the period after their accrual. We illustrate these procedures using wages expense for Landen TV Service.

Wages Expense in December

Recall from Chapter 3 that the Landen TV Service employee received wages of $270 for each six-day workweek ($45 per day) and that the employee was paid every other Saturday. We assumed that the two paydays in December fell on December 14 and 28. Wages expense of $90 was accrued for December 30 and 31. We made the following adjusting entry to reflect the proper expense for December:

Dec. 31	Wages Expense	90	
	Wages Payable		90
	To record accrued wages for December 30 and 31.		

After this adjusting entry was posted, the Wages Expense account had a debit balance of $1,170. This consisted of two debits of $540 made on December 14 and 28 and the $90 accrual on December 31. Along with other expenses, the Wages Expense account was closed to Income Summary on December 31. After the closing procedures, the Wages Expense and Wages Payable accounts appeared in the ledger as follows:

Wages Expense Account No. 52

Date		Description	Post. Ref.	Debit*	Credit	Balance
19XX						
Dec.	14		J1	540		540
	28		J2	540		1,080
	31	(adjusting)	J3	90		1,170
	31	(closing)	J4		1,170	–0–

Wages Payable Account No. 23

Date		Description	Post. Ref.	Debit	Credit*	Balance
19XX						
Dec.	31	(adjusting)	J3		90	90

January Accounting Without Using Reversals

On January 11, the employee will receive another $540 wage payment. Of this amount, only $450 should be reflected as January expense since only 10 days were worked in January (the other two days were worked in December and accrued as December wages expense). We may record the wage payment and the correct January wages expense by making the entry we presented in Chapter 3, as follows:

Jan. 11	Wages Payable	90	
	Wages Expense	450	
	Cash		540
	To record wages paid.		

This procedure, however, requires extreme vigilance in recording routine transactions on the part of the bookkeeper, who must keep in mind previously made accruals in order to record subsequent payments correctly. Many bookkeepers find this a nuisance and avoid the problem by reversing adjustments made for accruals.

January Accounting Using Reversals

As an alternative to the preceding procedure, then, a bookkeeper may use **reversing entries.** Reversing entries are made after all closing procedures have been completed, and they are dated the first day of the following period. A reversing entry is so named because the entry exactly reverses the debits and credits of an adjusting entry. For example, the reversing entry for the accrual of wages would be

Jan. 1	Wages Payable	90	
	Wages Expense		90
	To reverse accrual made December 31.		

This entry reduces the liability Wages Payable to zero and results in a $90 abnormal credit balance in the Wages Expense account at the start of the new accounting period. On the next payday, however, the wage payment of $540 is recorded as all wage payments are recorded, as follows:

Jan. 11	Wages Expense	540	
	Cash		540
	Paid wages for two weeks ended January 11.		

When this entry is posted to the Wages Expense account, the $540 debit is combined with the $90 credit balance created by the reversing entry. As a result, the account balance is the proper wages expense for January 1–11 ($450). After the January 1 reversing entry and the January 11 payment have been posted, the Wages Expense and Wages Payable accounts appear as shown below. Note that the $90 abnormal balance is placed in parentheses.

Wages Expense Account No. 52

Date		Description	Post. Ref.	Debit*	Credit	Balance
19XX						
Dec.	14		J1	540		540
	28		J2	540		1,080
	31	(adjusting)	J3	90		1,170
	31	(closing)	J4		1,170	–0–
19X1						
Jan.	1	(reversing)	J5		90	(90)
	11		J6	540		450

Wages Payable Account No. 23

Date		Description	Post. Ref.	Debit	Credit*	Balance
19XX						
Dec.	31	(adjusting)	J3		90	90
19X1						
Jan.	1	(reversing)	J5	90		–0–

Both of the alternative procedures for handling the December accrued wages in January give the same result—the elimination of the $90 wages payable and the portrayal of $450 of wages expense for the first 11 days in January. By using reversals, however, the bookkeeper can record the first January payroll without having to consider the amount of wages accrued at December 31.

Other Reversals

A reversing entry may simplify the recording of a transaction that relates to an earlier adjusting entry. No hard and fast rule determines which adjusting entries should be reversed. Generally, though, *accruals* of revenue and expenses that relate to routine, repetitive transactions are the most appropriate adjustments to reverse. Of the adjustments made by Landen TV Service (in addition to the accrual of wages), reversing entries would be employed for the two other accruals—the $120 estimated utilities expense and the $240 unbilled service fees. The bookkeeper would therefore make two additional reversing entries after the books are closed:

Jan. 1	Utilities Payable	120	
	Utilities Expense		120
	To reverse accrual made December 31.		
Jan. 1	Service Fees	240	
	Accounts Receivable		240
	To reverse accrual made December 31.		

These entries eliminate the accrued amounts from the liability and asset accounts and create an abnormal credit balance of $120 in Utilities Expense and an abnormal debit balance of $240 in Service Fees.

The credit balance in Utilities Expense will be eliminated when the utility bills are received and paid in January. If we assume that bills amounting to $124 arrived and were paid on January 6, the entry would be:

Jan. 6	Utilities Expense	124	
	Cash		124
	To record payment of December utilities.		

After the entry for payment is posted, Utilities Expense will have a $4 debit balance to be absorbed in January. As we mentioned in Chapter 3, charging a small amount of one period's expense in another period must be tolerated when estimates are used.

The debit balance in Service Fees is eliminated when Landen TV Service bills the local hotel after the completion of 40 hours of work (per its contract with the hotel). This billing, made on January 21, is recorded as follows:

Jan. 21	Accounts Receivable	640	
	Service Fees		640
	To record billing for 40 hours of work at $16 per hour.		

This entry leaves a credit balance of $400 in the Service Fees revenue account, reflecting the proper amount of revenue for work performed in January (25 hours × $16). The $640 debit to Accounts Receivable represents the amount of cash to be collected from the hotel.

Although the use of reversing entries is optional, it does permit us to analyze routine, repetitive transactions the same way all the time. For example, if reversals are used, a bookkeeper may be instructed (or a computer programmed) to debit Wages Expense and credit Cash every time wages are paid. Similarly, every utility payment may be analyzed as a debit to Utilities Expense and a credit to Cash, and every billing of service fees may be recorded as a debit to Accounts Receivable and a credit to Service Fees. Reversals eliminate the need to remember the effects of previous accruals and, therefore, contribute to the more efficient processing of data.

Reversals normally are not appropriate for adjustments involving prepayments of expense or advance receipts of revenues. Only if a company's policy is to record expense prepayments in expense accounts and advance revenue receipts in revenue accounts might adjustments involving these items be reversed. In these cases, the reversals reestablish the remaining expense prepayments and advance revenue receipts in the appropriate expense and revenue accounts. These types of situations, however, are not common and will not be illustrated here.

KEY POINTS TO REMEMBER

(1) The worksheet facilitates the preparation of financial statements.

(2) The unadjusted trial balance is recorded directly on the worksheet; adjustments usually are made only on the worksheet when interim financial statements are being prepared.

(3) Adjusted balances, which are extended into the income statement and balance sheet columns of the worksheet, provide the data for formal financial statements.

(4) Adjusting and closing entries are recorded in the general journal and general ledger at the end of the accounting year.

(5) *Closing the books* means closing the revenue, expense, and other temporary accounts. Revenue and expense account balances are transferred to the Income Summary account. The balances of the Income Summary account and the owners' drawing accounts are closed to the owners' capital accounts. For corporations, the Income Summary account is closed to Retained Earnings.

(6) The method of reversing adjustments made for *accrued* items permits normal recording of subsequent transactions. It safeguards against reflecting the same revenue or expense in successive periods.

SELF-TEST QUESTIONS
(Answers are at the end of this chapter.)

1. Which two steps in the accounting cycle are aided by the preparation of a worksheet?
   (a) Analyzing source documents and preparing financial statements.
   (b) Posting journal entries and adjusting the accounts.
   (c) Adjusting the accounts and preparing financial statements.
   (d) Journalizing transactions and closing the accounts.
2. In preparing a worksheet, you have just extended the adjusted account balances to the income statement and balance sheet columns and totaled these columns. If the company is profitable this period, the total of the income statement credit column will be
   (a) Larger than the balance sheet debit column total.
   (b) Larger than the income statement debit column total.
   (c) Smaller than the income statement debit column total.
   (d) Larger than the balance sheet credit column total.
3. Closing entries
   (a) Are an optional step in the accounting cycle.
   (b) Affect only balance sheet accounts.
   (c) Permit a company to analyze routine, repetitive transactions the same way all the time.
   (d) Remove the balances from a firm's temporary accounts.
4. Which of the following closing procedures is unique to a corporation?
   (a) Close each revenue account to the Income Summary account.
   (b) Close each expense account to the Income Summary account.
   (c) Close the Income Summary account to the Retained Earnings account.
   (d) Close the owner's drawing account to the owner's capital account.
5. Assume Zee Company initially records prepayments in balance sheet accounts and makes reversing entries when appropriate. Which of the following year-end adjusting entries by Zee Company should be reversed?
   (a) The entry to record depreciation expense for the period.
   (b) The entry to record the portion of service fees received in advance that is earned by year-end.
   (c) The entry to record supplies used during the period.
   (d) The entry to record service fees earned by year-end but not yet billed.

QUESTIONS

4–1 Assume that a company does not use a worksheet to help prepare financial statements. On December 31, the close of the accounting year, all transactions have been analyzed, recorded, and posted, and adjusting entries have been recorded and posted to the accounts. What two major steps of the accounting cycle remain?

4–2 Assume that a company uses a worksheet to help prepare financial statements. After the worksheet is completed at the end of the accounting year, what steps remain to complete the accounting cycle?

4–3 What are the advantages of preparing a worksheet?

4–4 Identify each of the 10 amount columns of the worksheet and indicate to which columns the adjusted balances of the following accounts would be extended:

(a) Accounts Receivable
(b) Accumulated Depreciation
(c) Barker, Drawing
(d) Wages Payable
(e) Depreciation Expense
(f) Rent Receivable
(g) Prepaid Insurance
(h) Service Fees
(i) Capital Stock
(j) Retained Earnings

4–5 Suppose the total adjusted revenue of a business is $95,000 and total adjusted expense is $75,000. (a) When the worksheet is completed, in which columns would the $20,000 difference appear? (b) If total adjusted expense amounted to $105,000, in which columns of the computed worksheet would the $10,000 difference appear?

4–6 What information is presented in a statement of owner's equity?

4–7 What is the reason why the totals of the balance sheet columns of the worksheet may differ from the total asset amount on the formal balance sheet?

4–8 When adjusted balances are extended on the worksheet, Unearned Fees of $1,000 is extended as a credit in the income statement columns and Accounts Receivable of $800 is extended as a debit in the income statement columns. All other extensions are properly made. (a) Does the worksheet balance? (b) How do these incorrect extensions affect the calculation of net income shown on the worksheet?

4–9 Define *interim financial statements.* Give an example of an interim financial statement.

4–10 When would adjusting entries be entered only on a worksheet and not in the accounts? Why?

4–11 A firm on a calendar-year basis prepares cumulative statements monthly, using a worksheet. Adjusting and closing entries are entered in journals and posted only on December 31. On January 1, the firm paid $936 for a two-year insurance policy. What worksheet adjustments for insurance should be made on (a) January 31, (b) February 28, and (c) May 31?

4–12 Which groups of accounts are closed at the end of the accounting year?

4–13 How is the Income Summary account used in closing procedures?

4–14 How do closing entries for a corporation differ from closing entries for a proprietorship?

4–15 What is the purpose of a post-closing trial balance? Which of the following accounts should not appear in the post-closing trial balance: Cash; Unearned Revenue; Jensen, Drawing; Depreciation Expense; Utilities Payable; Supplies Expense; and Retained Earnings?

4–16 Why are reversing entries made? If reversals are made, which entries would normally be reversed?

4–17 A firm accrued wages of $1,200 on December 31. On January 8, the next payday, the firm paid $3,000 in wages. The company does not make reversing entries. On January 8, the company debited Wages Expense and credited Cash for $3,000. How will this procedure affect January net income?

4–18 Since the firm in Question 4–17 did not make a reversing entry, what entry should it have made to record the January 8 payment of wages?

4–19 Assume that the firm in Question 4–17 did use reversing entry procedures. What reversing entry should the firm have made on January 1? How should the company have recorded the January 8 payment if a reversing entry had been made?

EXERCISES

Worksheet

4–20 The adjusted trial balance columns of a worksheet for L. Boyer, consultant, are shown below. The worksheet is prepared for the year ended December 31, 19XX.

	Adjusted Trial Balance	
	Debit	**Credit**
Cash	3,000	
Supplies on Hand	5,500	
Equipment	60,000	
Accumulated Depreciation		15,000
Accounts Payable		2,300
L. Boyer, Capital		40,600
L. Boyer, Drawing	10,000	
Service Fees		45,700
Rent Expense	12,000	
Supplies Expense	7,100	
Depreciation Expense	6,000	
	103,600	103,600

Complete the worksheet by (a) extending these amounts to the income statement and balance sheet columns and (b) balancing the worksheet.

Income statement and balance sheet

4–21 The income statement and balance sheet columns of a worksheet for Hillstrom Corporation are shown below. The worksheet is prepared on December 31, 19X4, for the year ended on that date.

	Income Statement		Balance Sheet	
	Debit	Credit	Debit	Credit
Cash			3,400	
Accounts Receivable			8,200	
Office Equipment			36,000	
Accumulated Depreciation				9,000
Accounts Payable				4,100
Wages Payable				500
Capital Stock				10,000
Retained Earnings				11,200
Service Fees		37,000		
Wages Expense	9,800			
Rent Expense	6,600			
Depreciation Expense	3,000			
Advertising Expense	2,600			
Income Tax Expense	2,200			
	24,200	37,000	47,600	34,800
Net Income	12,800			12,800
	37,000	37,000	47,600	47,600

Prepare an income statement and a balance sheet for Hillstrom Corporation.

Statement of owner's equity

4–22 On January 1, 19X2, the credit balance of the Tara Lamon, Capital account was $12,000, and on December 31, 19X2, the credit balance before closing was $15,000. The Tara Lamon, Drawing account had a debit balance of $6,800 on December 31, 19X2. After revenue and expense accounts were closed, the Income Summary account had a credit balance of $9,400. Prepare a 19X2 statement of owner's equity for Tara Lamon, architect.

Closing entries

4–23 The income statement columns of a worksheet prepared December 31 contain only the following accounts:

	Debit	Credit
Service Fees		31,200
Rent Expense	7,800	
Salaries Expense	20,800	
Supplies Expense	2,500	
Depreciation Expense	4,600	

Included among the accounts in the balance sheet columns of the worksheet are Flynn, Capital, $42,000 (credit), and Flynn, Drawing, $2,700 (debit). Prepare entries to close the accounts, including the owner's drawing account. After these entries are made, what is the balance of the Flynn, Capital account?

Closing entries

4–24 In the midst of closing procedures, Byden Corporation's bookkeeper became ill and was hospitalized. You have volunteered to complete the closing of the books, and you find that all revenue and expense accounts have zero balances and that the Income Summary account has a single debit entry for $92,300 and a single credit entry for $126,900. The only entry in Retained Earnings this year is a debit of $8,000 for dividends, which reduced the balance to $85,000. Capital Stock has a normal balance of $160,000 and shows no entries for the year. Give the journal entry (or entries) to complete the closing procedures and calculate the balance of the stockholders' equity.

Closing entries

4–25 Use the information in Exercise 4–20 to prepare the closing entries for L. Boyer, consultant, on December 31, 19XX.

Closing entries

4–26 Use the information in Exercise 4–21 to prepare the closing entries for Hillstrom Corporation on December 31, 19X4.

Reversing entries

4–27 The following selected accounts appear in a firm's unadjusted trial balance at December 31, the end of the accounting year (all accounts have normal balances):

Prepaid Advertising	$ 750	Unearned Service Fees	$ 2,700
Wages Expense	28,500	Service Fees	69,000
Prepaid Insurance	1,920	Rental Income	3,400

(a) Make the necessary adjusting entries in general journal form at December 31, assuming the following:
  (1) Prepaid advertising at December 31 is $500.
  (2) Unpaid wages earned by employees in December are $660.
  (3) Prepaid insurance at December 31 is $1,280.
  (4) Unearned service fees at December 31 are $1,000.
  (5) Rental income of $400 owed by a tenant is not recorded at December 31.

(b) Assume the company makes reversing entries. Which of the adjustments in part (a) should be reversed? Make the proper reversing entries on January 1.

(c) Assume reversing entries have been made. Prepare the journal entries on January 4 to record (1) the payment of $1,100 in wages and (2) the receipt from the tenant of the $400 rental income.

(d) Assume reversing entries have not been made. Prepare the journal entries on January 4 to record (1) the payment of $1,100 in wages and (2) the receipt from the tenant of the $400 rental income.

PROBLEMS

Worksheet and closing entries

4–28 Klay Cleaning Service will prepare financial statements on December 31, 19X1. The trial balance and adjustments columns of the firm's worksheet at December 31 follow.

	Trial Balance Debit	Trial Balance Credit	Adjustments Debit		Adjustments Credit	
Cash	4,500					
Accounts Receivable	5,800					
Supplies on Hand	7,500				(1)	6,100
Prepaid Insurance	1,080				(2)	360
Equipment	30,000					
Accumulated Depreciation		5,000			(3)	2,000
Accounts Payable		2,300				
B. Klay, Capital		16,900				
B. Klay, Drawing	1,200					
Cleaning Fees		38,700				
Salaries Expense	9,800		(4)	300		
Rent Expense	2,400					
Miscellaneous Expense	620					
	62,900	62,900				
Supplies Expense			(1)	6,100		
Insurance Expense			(2)	360		
Depreciation Expense			(3)	2,000		
Salaries Payable					(4)	300
				8,760		8,760

REQUIRED
(a) Complete the worksheet.
(b) Prepare the closing entries at December 31 in general journal form.

Worksheet and financial statements

4–29 The following unadjusted trial balance was taken at March 31 of the current year:

Bell Travel Agency
Trial Balance
March 31, 19XX

	Debit	Credit
Cash	$ 1,900	
Accounts Receivable	2,000	
Supplies on Hand	980	
Prepaid Insurance	840	
Equipment	10,400	
Accumulated Depreciation		$ 2,080
Accounts Payable		350
Unearned Commissions		600
G. Bell, Capital		6,100
G. Bell, Drawing	900	
Commissions Earned		13,610
Salaries Expense	3,200	
Rent Expense	1,350	
Advertising Expense	790	
Utilities Expense	380	
	$22,740	$22,740

The trial balance data are cumulative for the first three months of 19XX. No adjusting entries have been made in the accounts during this period. The following additional information is available:

(1) Depreciation for the first quarter is $260.
(2) Supplies on hand at March 31 amount to $530.
(3) During the quarter, $400 of the unearned commissions were earned.
(4) Insurance expense for the quarter is $210.
(5) Accrued salaries payable total $550 at March 31.
(6) Commissions earned but not billed at March 31 are $320.

REQUIRED

(a) Enter the trial balance on a worksheet and complete the worksheet using the adjustment data given above.
(b) Prepare an income statement for the first quarter of the year and a balance sheet at March 31.

Adjusting entries and account classification

4–30 The first six columns of a worksheet for Total Upholstery Service, Inc., are given below. However, only the totals of the adjustments columns are given.

Total Upholstery Service, Inc.
Worksheet
For the Year Ended December 31, 19XX

	Trial Balance		Adjustments		Adjusted Trial Balance	
	Debit	**Credit**	**Debit**	**Credit**	**Debit**	**Credit**
Cash	2,600				2,600	
Accounts Receivable	3,920				3,920	
Prepaid Rent	1,280				960	
Supplies on Hand	9,240				5,140	
Equipment	18,000				18,000	
Accumulated Depreciation		3,600				5,400
Accounts Payable		1,000				1,000
Unearned Service Fees		900				400
Capital Stock		10,000				10,000
Retained Earnings		7,470				7,470
Service Fees		24,330				24,830
Wages Expense	7,500				7,950	
Utilities Expense	1,240				1,400	
Rent Expense	3,520				3,840	
	47,300	47,300				
Supplies Expense					4,100	
Depreciation Expense					1,800	
Wages Payable						450
Utilities Payable						160
			7,330	7,330	49,710	49,710

REQUIRED

(a) Determine the adjusting entries for Total Upholstery Service, Inc., and prepare these entries in general journal form.

(b) For each account in the adjusted trial balance, indicate whether it will appear in an income statement or in a balance sheet.

Worksheet, financial statements and closing entries

4–31 The unadjusted trial balance shown below is for Howell Freight Service at December 31, 19X1. The following data for adjustments are also available at December 31:

(1) Supplies on hand amount to $810.
(2) Prepaid insurance is $500.
(3) Depreciation for the year is as follows: Equipment, $550; Trucks, $2,350.
(4) Accrued wages payable are $650.
(5) Estimated December utilities expense is $320; the bill has not arrived.
(6) Howell has completed, but not yet billed, work amounting to $800.

	Debit	Credit
Cash	$ 2,100	
Accounts Receivable	3,470	
Supplies on Hand	1,760	
Prepaid Insurance	2,000	
Equipment	4,400	
Accumulated Depreciation—Equipment		$ 825
Trucks	18,800	
Accumulated Depreciation—Trucks		3,525
Notes Payable		5,000
Accounts Payable		400
B. Howell, Capital		8,750
B. Howell, Drawing	6,000	
Service Fees		77,270
Rent Expense	7,200	
Salaries and Wages Expense	38,400	
Fuel Expense	8,000	
Utilities Expense	3,190	
Interest Expense	450	
	$95,770	$95,770

REQUIRED

(a) Prepare a 10-column worksheet for the year ended December 31, 19X1. Set up any additional accounts needed.
(b) Prepare an income statement for the year and a balance sheet at December 31, 19X1.
(c) Prepare closing entries in general journal form.

Complete accounting cycle

4–32 R. Hasset, tax consultant, began business on December 1 of the current year. December transactions were as follows:

Dec. 1 R. Hasset invested $13,000 in the business.
2 Paid rent for two months to Star Realty, $900.
2 Purchased various supplies on account, $770.
3 Purchased $6,000 of office equipment, paying $2,400 down with the balance due in 30 days.
8 Paid $770 on account for supplies purchased December 2.
13 Paid assistant's wages for two weeks, $625.

Dec. 20 Performed consulting services for cash, $1,800.
27 Paid assistant's wages for two weeks, $625.
30 Billed customers for December consulting services, $3,200.
31 Hasset withdrew $1,000 from the business.

REQUIRED

(a) Open the following general ledger accounts, using the account numbers shown: Cash (11); Accounts Receivable (12); Prepaid Rent (13); Supplies on Hand (14); Office Equipment (15); Accumulated Depreciation (16); Accounts Payable (21); Wages Payable (22); R. Hasset, Capital (31); R. Hasset, Drawing (32); Income Summary (33); Consulting Fees (41); Supplies Expense (51); Wages Expense (52); Rent Expense (53); and Depreciation Expense (54).
(b) Journalize the December transactions, and post to the ledger.
(c) Prepare a trial balance directly on a worksheet, and complete the worksheet using the following information:
 (1) Supplies on hand at December 31 are $410.
 (2) Accrued wages payable at December 31 are $170.
 (3) Depreciation for December is $75.
 (4) Hasset has spent 16 hours on an involved tax fraud case during December. When completed in January, his work will be billed at $40 per hour.
 (5) Prepaid rent at December 31 is $450.
(d) Prepare a December income statement and a December 31 balance sheet.
(e) Journalize and post adjusting and closing entries.
(f) Prepare a post-closing trial balance.
(g) Journalize and post the appropriate reversing entries.

Closing entries and corporation accounts

4–33 The last four columns of a 10-column worksheet prepared at December 31, 19XX, for Technic, Inc., are reproduced below.

	Income Statement		Balance Sheet	
	Debit	Credit	Debit	Credit
Cash			5,200	
Accounts Receivable			8,000	
Prepaid Insurance			1,800	
Equipment			54,000	
Accumulated Depreciation				8,200
Accounts Payable				1,600
Capital Stock				24,000
Retained Earnings				12,600
Service Fees		55,800		
Miscellaneous Income		2,800		
Salaries Expense	21,400			
Rent Expense	7,000			
Insurance Expense	800			
Salaries Payable				600
Depreciation Expense	3,000			
Income Tax Expense	4,400			
	36,600	58,600	69,000	47,000
Net Income	22,000			22,000
	58,600	58,600	69,000	69,000

REQUIRED
(a) From the given information, prepare closing entries in general journal form.
(b) After the closing entries are posted, what is the balance in the Retained Earnings account?
(c) Which accounts in the worksheet would not appear if the company were organized as a sole proprietorship rather than as a corporation?

Worksheet and financial statements

4–34 Midwest Engineering Services prepares a year-to-date income statement and a year-to-date statement of owner's equity each month. Also, a balance sheet is prepared at the end of each month. The firm makes adjusting and closing entries in its accounts only at December 31 each year. The firm, owned by Mark Field, is a sole proprietorship. The firm's unadjusted trial balance at April 30, 19X5, is given below.

Midwest Engineering Services
Trial Balance
April 30, 19X5

	Debit	Credit
Cash	$ 12,100	
Prepaid Insurance	2,040	
Supplies on Hand	9,200	
Equipment	156,000	
Accumulated Depreciation		$ 35,100
Accounts Payable		2,300
M. Field, Capital		100,600
M. Field, Drawing	3,700	
Service Fees		87,500
Salaries Expense	28,000	
Advertising Expense	4,400	
Rent Expense	3,600	
Utilities Expense	1,960	
Legal Fees Expense	4,500	
	$225,500	$225,500

The following data for adjustments are available at April 30, 19X5:
(1) Two years of insurance coverage was purchased January 1, 19X5.
(2) Supplies on hand at April 30 are $6,300.
(3) Monthly depreciation on equipment is $1,300.
(4) Accrued salaries at April 30 are $750.
(5) The firm is involved in a lawsuit with a former client. Legal fees incurred in April but not yet billed are estimated at $1,500 (credit Legal Fees Payable).

REQUIRED
(a) Record the April 30 trial balance on a 10-column worksheet. Enter the necessary adjusting entries and complete the worksheet for the four months ended April 30, 19X5.

(b) Prepare an income statement for the four months ended April 30, 19X5.
(c) Prepare a statement of owner's equity for the four months ended April 30, 19X5. Field has made no capital contributions during 19X5.
(d) Prepare a balance sheet at April 30, 19X5.

ALTERNATE PROBLEMS

Worksheet and closing entries

4–28A The trial balance and adjustments columns of the worksheet for Gentle Moving Service at December 31 of the current year are shown below.

	Trial Balance		Adjustments	
	Debit	Credit	Debit	Credit
Cash	4,100			
Accounts Receivable	5,820			
Supplies on Hand	3,700			(1) 1,900
Prepaid Insurance	3,000			(2) 1,000
Trucks	24,500			
Accumulated Depreciation—Trucks		6,300		(3) 2,100
Equipment	8,600			
Accumulated Depreciation—Equipment		2,400		(4) 800
Accounts Payable		1,580		
Unearned Service Fees		1,900	(5) 1,300	
F. Pike, Capital		20,920		
F. Pike, Drawing	5,000			
Service Fees		52,000		(5) 1,300
Wages Expense	22,800			
Rent Expense	6,500			
Advertising Expense	1,080			
	85,100	85,100		
Supplies Expense			(1) 1,900	
Insurance Expense			(2) 1,000	
Depreciation Expense—Trucks			(3) 2,100	
Depreciation Expense—Equipment			(4) 800	
			7,100	7,100

REQUIRED
(a) Complete the worksheet.
(b) Prepare the closing entries at December 31 in general journal form.

Worksheet and financial statements

4–29A The July 31 unadjusted trial balance of Wahtur Outfitters, a firm renting various types of equipment to canoeists and fishermen, is shown below.

Wahtur Outfitters
Trial Balance
July 31, 19XX

	Debit	Credit
Cash	$ 3,800	
Supplies on Hand	5,100	
Prepaid Insurance	2,200	
Equipment	98,000	
Accumulated Depreciation		$ 18,200
Accounts Payable		2,700
Unearned Rental Fees		4,200
C. Wahtur, Capital		48,950
C. Wahtur, Drawing	1,500	
Rental Fees		67,850
Wages Expense	25,300	
Rent Expense	1,800	
Advertising Expense	3,480	
Travel Expense	720	
	$141,900	$141,900

The trial balance data are cumulative for the first three months of the firm's fiscal year, which begins May 1. No adjusting entries have been made in the accounts during the quarter. The following additional information is available:

(1) Supplies on hand at July 31 amount to $3,400.
(2) Insurance expense for the first quarter is $550.
(3) Depreciation for the first quarter is $2,275.
(4) The unearned rental fees consist of deposits received from customers in advance when reservations are made. During the quarter, $2,650 of the unearned rental fees were earned.
(5) At July 31, unbilled revenue from rental services earned for outfitting several church groups during July amounts to $3,100.
(6) Accrued wages payable for equipment handlers and guides amounts to $900 at July 31.

REQUIRED

(a) Enter the trial balance in a worksheet and complete the worksheet using the adjustment data given above.
(b) Prepare an income statement for the first quarter and a balance sheet at July 31.

Worksheet error corrections

4–30A Brenda Gould, owner of the Gould Refinishing Service, has completed a worksheet for her business at the end of its first year of operations. She is unsure of her accounting skills, however, and asks you to review the worksheet before she prepares financial statements from it. You have reviewed the unadjusted trial balance, the adjustments, and the compilation of the adjusted trial balance columns and have found no errors. The last six columns of the worksheet are shown below (as noted, the adjusted trial balance columns are correct).

Gould Refinishing Service
Worksheet
For the Year Ended December 31, 19XX

	Adjusted Trial Balance		Income Statement		Balance Sheet	
	Debit	Credit	Debit	Credit	Debit	Credit
Cash	560				560	
Accounts Receivable	950				950	
Prepaid Rent	380				380	
Supplies on Hand	590				950	
Equipment	4,000					4,000
Accounts Payable		270				270
B. Gould, Capital		4,800				4,800
B. Gould, Drawing	1,500				5,100	
Service Fees		8,750		8,570		
Wages Expense	3,600		3,600			
Utilities Expense	720		720			
Rent Expense	1,140		1,140			
Supplies Expense	630		630			
Depreciation Expense	400		400			
Accumulated Depreciation		400	400			
Wages Payable		170				170
Utilities Payable		80				80
	14,470	14,470	7,190	8,570	7,940	9,320
Net Income			1,380		1,380	
			8,570	8,570	9,320	9,320

REQUIRED
(a) Identify the errors contained in this partial worksheet.
(b) Prepare a correct partial worksheet (the last six columns).

Worksheet, financial statements, and closing entries

4–31A Bike and Hike, Inc., publishes magazines for cyclists and hikers. The firm has the following unadjusted trial balance at December 31 of its second year of operations.

Bike and Hike, Inc.
Trial Balance
December 31, 19X2

	Debit	Credit
Cash	$ 8,200	
Accounts Receivable	12,400	
Supplies on Hand	7,500	
Prepaid Insurance	3,120	
Office Equipment	45,000	
Accumulated Depreciation—Office Equipment		$ 4,500
Building	250,000	
Accumulated Depreciation—Building		10,000
Land	64,000	
Accounts Payable		2,400
Unearned Subscription Revenue		6,200
Capital Stock		150,000
Retained Earnings		92,870
Subscription Revenue		305,200
Advertising Revenue		92,600
Salaries Expense	126,250	
Printing and Mailing Expense	80,600	
Advertising Expense	8,320	
Utilities Expense	3,180	
Income Tax Expense	55,200	
	$663,770	$663,770

The following information for adjusting the accounts is available at December 31:

(1) Supplies on hand amount to $2,900.
(2) Prepaid insurance at December 31 is $1,560.
(3) Accrued salaries at December 31 are $1,600.
(4) Of the unearned subscription revenue shown in the trial balance, $4,100 was earned during the year. The remainder will be earned next year.
(5) Advertising revenue earned during the period but unbilled at December 31 is $3,300.
(6) Depreciation on office equipment for the year is $4,500.
(7) Depreciation on the building for the year is $10,000.

REQUIRED

(a) Prepare a 10-column worksheet for the year ended December 31, 19X2. Set up any additional accounts needed.
(b) Prepare an income statement for the year and a balance sheet at December 31.
(c) Prepare closing entries in general journal form.

Complete accounting cycle

4–32A E. Aubey, attorney, opened her practice on December 1 of the current year. December transactions were as follows:

Dec. 1 E. Aubey invested $11,000 in the firm.
2 Paid rent for six months to Beyer Realty, $3,300.
2 Purchased various supplies for cash, $780.
3 Purchased office furniture and fixtures on account, $4,800.
8 Paid $1,600 on account for furniture and fixtures purchased December 3.
12 Paid assistant's salary for two weeks, $700.
20 Performed legal services for cash, $800.
26 Paid assistant's salary for two weeks, $700.
30 Billed clients for legal work completed during the month, $3,800.
31 Aubey withdrew $500 from the business.

REQUIRED

(a) Open the following general ledger accounts, using the account numbers shown: Cash (11); Accounts Receivable (12); Prepaid Rent (13); Supplies on Hand (14); Furniture and Fixtures (15); Accumulated Depreciation (16); Accounts Payable (21); Salary Payable (22); E. Aubey, Capital (31); E. Aubey, Drawing (32); Income Summary (33); Professional Fees (41); Supplies Expense (51); Salary Expense (52); Rent Expense (53); and Depreciation Expense (54).
(b) Journalize the December transactions, and post to the ledger.
(c) Prepare a trial balance directly on a worksheet, and complete the worksheet using the following information:
 (1) Supplies on hand at December 31 are $620.
 (2) Accrued salary payable at December 31 is $210.
 (3) Depreciation for December is $70.
 (4) Aubey has spent 25 hours on an involved estate planning case during December. When completed in January, her work will be billed at $50 per hour.
 (5) Prepaid rent at December 31 is $2,750.
(d) Prepare a December income statement and a December 31 balance sheet.
(e) Journalize and post adjusting and closing entries.
(f) Prepare a post-closing trial balance.
(g) Journalize and post the appropriate reversing entries.

BUSINESS DECISION PROBLEM

As an alternative to a summer job paying $5 per hour between her junior and senior years in college, Jean Rohlik accepted an opportunity to lease and operate the tennis court concession in a local city recreational complex during June, July, and August. Although she kept no accounting records, Jean was careful to handle all funds related to the tennis concession through a special bank account opened for that purpose. An analysis of those deposit slips and check stubs for the three months is summarized on the next page.

Receipts:	
Rohlik's investment of personal funds	$ 1,500
Court rental fees	8,450
Tennis lesson fees	900
Proceeds of short-term loan from bank	1,000
Total receipts	$11,850
Disbursements:	
Purchase of ball-throwing machine	$ 140
Supplies purchased	945
Utilities	330
Lease payments to city	1,600
Wages to part-time assistant	1,200
Liability insurance premiums	165
Repayment of bank loan, including interest	1,025
Withdrawals of cash for personal expenses	650
Total disbursements	$ 6,055
Cash balance, August 31	$ 5,795

Jean confides in you, a personal friend who happens to be studying accounting, that she is pleased with her apparent profit of $5,795 for the summer. Eager to practice your newly acquired skills, you offer to review her records and prepare an income statement for the three months and a balance sheet at the end of August. In discussions with Jean, you learn that:

(1) Rental receipts include all revenue earned except for $600 due from a company that rented the entire set of courts for a weekend late in August.
(2) Some tennis lessons, paid for in advance, could not be scheduled during the summer. Jean plans to refund these fees, which total $110.
(3) A ball-throwing machine, purchased used, turned out to be quite temperamental. After a complete breakdown in July, it was junked.
(4) Supplies consisted of cans of tennis balls. Jean gave away a free can of tennis balls for each five hours of court time rented by an individual. Supplies amounting to $125 were on hand at August 31; these may be returned for a full refund. Jean estimates that each month during the summer, she took home $15 worth of supplies for personal use.
(5) The insurance premiums represent coverage for the months of June, July, and August.
(6) Repayment to the bank included $25 of interest expense on the loan.
(7) All lease payments due the city were paid except for the final amount of $320.
(8) Jean estimates that the utility bill for August, when received, will be $190.

REQUIRED
Prepare financial statements for Jean's tennis concession (a sole proprietorship). You should formulate general journal entries summarizing the cash receipts and the cash disbursements and incorporating the additional data. After posting these to T accounts, you will be able to prepare the financial statements.

In further talks with Jean, you learn that the amount she contributed had been in a savings account earning 8% interest and that she worked an average of 60 hours in each of the 13 weeks the tennis concession was operated. What observations might you offer Jean regarding the financial success of the summer venture? What nonfinancial considerations are involved?

ANSWERS TO SELF-TEST QUESTIONS

1. (c) 2. (b) 3. (d) 4. (c) 5. (d)

5

Merchandising Operations

Chapter Objectives

- Describe the nature of merchandising enterprises and the steps in merchandising transactions.
- Illustrate the accounting entries for types of merchandise transactions.
- Illustrate the treatment of merchandise accounts in the worksheet.
- Describe classified financial statements for a merchandising firm.
- Illustrate adjusting and closing entries for a merchandising firm.

Deliver all things in number and weight, and put all in writing, that thou givest out or receivest in.

ECCLESIASTICUS 13:5

Thus far in our discussion of the accounting cycle, we have used as examples firms providing services rather than those selling products. Revenue for small service enterprises such as the driving school and the television repair service consisted of fees earned for the services performed. In these firms, net income is determined simply by deducting total expenses incurred from total fees earned during a period.

Revenue for firms that sell products consists of the total amount for which the products are sold. To determine net income for such firms, we deduct from the revenue (called *sales*) for the period not only the operating expenses incurred, but also the costs of acquiring the products sold. In this chapter we shall discuss the procedures followed in accounting for the costs of acquiring and selling products.

THE NATURE OF MERCHANDISING OPERATIONS

The total business segment of society is often classified into three broad types of enterprises: (1) service, (2) manufacturing, and (3) merchandising. Commercial airlines, physicians, lawyers, insurance companies, and banks are examples of service enterprises. Manufacturing enterprises convert raw materials into finished products through the application of skilled labor and machine operations. Merchandising enterprises are characterized by the basic operations of buying and selling finished products and include both wholesalers and retailers. Exhibit 5–1 illustrates the position of merchandising enterprises in the manufacturing and distribution process.

The accounting records of a merchandising firm must accommodate many transactions for the purchase of products and payment of the related accounts. Moreover, the accounting reports should indicate whether the difference between the acquisition price and the sales price to customers covers the costs of storing, displaying, advertising, selling, delivering, and collecting for the merchandise. Finally, the accounting records must reflect not only cash sales but also individual accounts receivable for a large number of customers.

EXHIBIT 5–1
The Manufacturing and Distribution Process

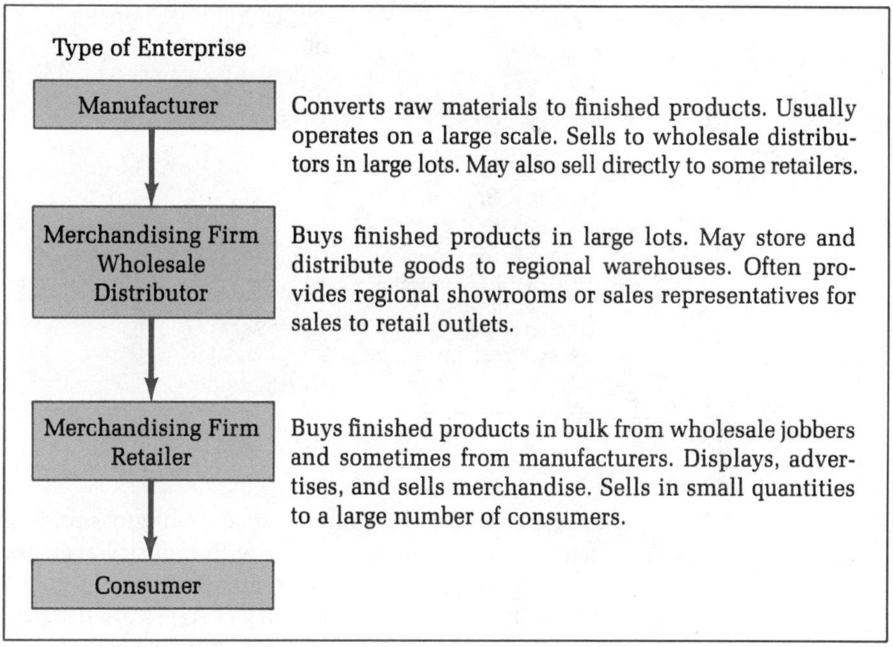
Type of Enterprise
Manufacturer
Converts raw materials to finished products. Usually operates on a large scale. Sells to wholesale distributors in large lots. May also sell directly to some retailers.
Merchandising Firm Wholesale Distributor
Buys finished products in large lots. May store and distribute goods to regional warehouses. Often provides regional showrooms or sales representatives for sales to retail outlets.
Merchandising Firm Retailer
Buys finished products in bulk from wholesale jobbers and sometimes from manufacturers. Displays, advertises, and sells merchandise. Sells in small quantities to a large number of consumers.
Consumer

INCOME STATEMENT FOR A MERCHANDISING FIRM

Exhibit 5–2 is an income statement for a merchandising firm, Madison Electronics Company. For simplicity, we have condensed the operating expenses into two amounts—selling expenses and administrative expenses. (These classifications are explained later in the chapter.)

The major difference between the income statement of a merchandising firm and that of a service business is the inclusion of an amount for the cost of goods sold to customers in the merchandising firm's statement. Ordinarily, this amount is deducted from the revenue figure (sales) to arrive at an intermediate amount called **gross profit on sales.** The operating expenses are then deducted from the gross profit on sales to obtain net income.

The gross profit on sales amount (sometimes called *gross margin*) is highly significant to management. When divided by the sales amount, it yields a gross profit percentage (sometimes called *average mark-up percentage on sales*), which is carefully monitored by the firm. In our illustration, the gross profit is 40% of sales ($170,000/$425,000 = 0.40 = 40%). This figure means that after 60 cents is deducted from each sales dollar to cover the cost of goods sold, 40 cents remains to cover operating expenses and provide a net income.

EXHIBIT 5–2

Madison Electronics Company
Income Statement
For the Year Ended December 31, 19XX

Sales		$425,000
Cost of Goods Sold		255,000
Gross Profit on Sales		$170,000
Operating Expenses:		
Selling Expenses	$96,200	
Administrative Expenses	48,300	
		144,500
Net Income		$ 25,500

Management usually compares its current gross profit percentage with similar calculations for prior periods or with industry averages. Such comparisons may alert management to a need to modify prices, purchasing policies or merchandise control procedures. Industry averages are usually available from such sources as trade associations or credit reporting agencies that compile statistics for various industries.

Cost of Goods Sold

To calculate the cost of goods sold to customers, we must consider data from a number of special merchandise accounts. We discuss the treatment of such accounts in detail later in this chapter. To provide a perspective, however, we show in condensed form in Exhibit 5–3 how cost of goods sold was calculated for the income statement in Exhibit 5–2.

At the beginning of the year, Madison Electronics had a supply of merchandise costing $115,000. During the year, the firm purchased additional merchandise with a net cost of $260,000. The sum of these two amounts is the total cost

EXHIBIT 5–3
Computation of Cost of Goods Sold

Beginning Inventory, January 1	$115,000
Add: Net Cost of Purchases	260,000
Cost of Goods Available for Sale	$375,000
Less: Ending Inventory, December 31	120,000
Cost of Goods Sold	$255,000

of all goods that were available for sale to customers during the year ($375,000). At the end of the year, merchandise costing $120,000 remained unsold, so we deduct this amount to arrive at the cost of goods sold, which is $255,000.

STEPS IN A MERCHANDISE TRANSACTION

Whenever a transaction for the purchase or sale of merchandise occurs, the buyer and the seller should agree on the price of the merchandise, the terms of payment, and the party to bear the cost of transportation. Owners or managers of small merchandising firms may settle the terms of the transaction informally by telephone or by discussion with the supplier's sales representative. Most large businesses, however, fill out a purchase order when ordering merchandise. A typical sequence of events for a large firm is as follows:

(1) When certain items are needed or when quantities of certain merchandise fall below established reorder points, a request for a purchase, called a **purchase requisition,** is sent to the purchasing department by the person in charge of merchandise stock records. These requisitions may also be initiated by other authorized personnel, such as department heads.

(2) The purchasing department then prepares a **purchase order** after consulting price lists, quotations, or suppliers' catalogs. The purchase order, addressed to the selected vendor, indicates the quantity, description, and price of the merchandise ordered. It may also indicate expected terms of payment and arrangements for transportation, including payment of freight costs.

(3) After receiving the purchase order, the seller forwards an **invoice** to the purchaser upon shipment of the merchandise. The invoice—called a **sales invoice** by the seller and a **purchase invoice** by the buyer—defines the terms of the transaction. A sample invoice is shown in Exhibit 5–4.

(4) Upon receiving the shipment of merchandise, the purchaser's receiving department counts and inspects the items in the shipment and makes out a **receiving report** detailing the quantities received.

(5) Before approving the invoice for payment, the accounts payable department compares copies of the purchase order, invoice, and receiving report to ensure that quantities, descriptions, and prices are in agreement.

Although all of the above papers—purchase requisition, purchase order, invoice, and receiving report—are source documents, only the invoice provides the basis for recording the purchase. The other three documents are merely supporting documents. The purchaser makes no entries in the accounts until the invoice is approved for payment. The seller enters the transaction in the records when the invoice is prepared, usually upon shipment of the merchandise.

EXHIBIT 5–4
Invoice

MADISON ELECTRONICS COMPANY
1400 South Park St.
Madison, Wisconsin 53705

Customer's Order No. & Date 1503
Requisition No.
Contract No.

Refer to Invoice No. 12015
Invoice Date Nov. 20, 19XX
Vendor's Nos.

SOLD TO ABC Company
120 Weston Street
Kenosha, Wisconsin

Shipped to and Destination Same
Date Shipped Nov. 20, 19XX From Madison Prepaid or Collect
Car Initials and No.
How Shipped and Route F.O.B. Kenosha Prepaid
Terms 2/10, n/30

FOR CUSTOMER'S USE ONLY
Register No. Voucher No.
F.O.B. Checked
Terms Approved | Price Approved L.N.D.
Calculations Checked R.S.D.
Transportation
Freight Bill No. Amount
Material Received
Date Signature Title
Satisfactory and Approved
Adjustments
Accounting Distribution
Audited | Final Approval

QUANTITY	DESCRIPTION	UNIT PRICE	AMOUNT
7	Model E Voicemaster Tape Recorders	$70	$490

TERMS OF TRANSACTIONS

Merchandise may be purchased and sold either on credit terms or for cash on delivery. Most merchandise transactions today are made on account rather than on cash (sometimes referred to as *net cash*) terms. When goods are sold on account, a period of time called the **credit period** is allowed for payment. The length of the credit period varies among business firms and may even vary within a firm, depending on the type of product. A typical credit period for wholesalers is 30 days. Payment is expected within 30 days of the invoice date, after which the purchaser is considered delinquent. The credit period is frequently described as the *net* credit period, or *net terms*, and the notation commonly used to designate this period is "n/" followed by the length of the period in days; for example, n/30 indicates that the credit period is 30 days.

Cash Discounts To encourage early payment of bills, many firms designate a **discount period** that is shorter than the credit period. Purchasers who remit payment during this period are entitled to deduct a **cash discount** from the total payment. Ostensibly, this discount is for prompt payment. The discount is designated by such notation as "2/10," which means that 2% may be deducted if payment is made within 10

IMPACT OF SALES TERMS ON PRICING

The concept of pricing is frequently confined to the identification of the price per unit charged to the customer on the sales invoice, or as listed on the company's price sheet or in its catalog. The terms and conditions of sale, often shown in fine print on the back of the invoice, are not always seen as having any direct bearing on price. In reality, they have a substantial impact on the actual price recovered, and in many instances serve to negate completely the effect of the pricing decision. Some of the sales terms are readily measurable as to the effect on price; others are not, being either hidden from view or misleading as to interpretation. In total they constitute an integral part of the pricing process, and the effects of each must be measured on a step-by-step basis to obtain the desired economic results.

One of the more obvious examples of pricing impact is the measurement of cash discounts allowed for early payment. Typical is the discount of "2% 10 days net 30." First, the discount is a direct reduction of 2% in the selling price, a reduction that will usually be taken by the customer, even beyond the 10-day period allowed. Second, the offer of a 2% reduction for payment 20 days early—in 10 days rather than 30—amounts to an annual interest rate of 36% per year, a payment for the use of money far in excess of the bank rate for funds even in times of double-digit inflation.

Taken together, these two points add up to the fact that cash discounts seldom work as intended, that in practice they routinely become nothing more than a price concession. Management is not deliberately offering 36% per annum for the use of money, but an alert customer will make the calculation properly and be quick to take advantage of it. Furthermore, the fact that many accounts take the discount well after the time allowed is evidence that customers regard it more as a price concession than a reward for early payment. Some companies attempt to charge back the unearned discount, a procedure that creates undesirable friction with their own customers, a situation the sales force would prefer to avoid.

Variations of the cash discount terms, such as "2% 10th prox," further complicate the picture by encouraging customers to bunch their orders around the first of the month to get the greatest leverage on the terms offered. This, obviously, can have the undesirable effect of creating peak work loads in order entry, shipping, and billing with consequent dry periods toward month-end.

In short, cash discounts make little economic sense as payment for the use of funds and in practice become nothing more than a reduction of price. In recent years, the great majority of companies have found it to be an awkward vehicle for price adjustment and have abandoned it in favor of net terms.

days. For example, if a November 10 invoice for $800 carries terms of 2/10, n/30, the purchaser may deduct 2% from the invoice price if the bill is paid by November 20. The cash discount would be $16 (2% of $800), and the amount of the remittance would be $784. The full amount of the invoice, $800, would be expected if the purchaser paid between November 20 and December 10. After December 10, the amount would be overdue.

Most business firms maintain a good cash position so they can take advantage of discounts. For example, assume that a firm purchased $800 worth of merchandise on terms of 2/10, n/30. The firm has a choice of paying $784 within 10 days of the invoice date or the full amount before the end of another 20 days. Passing up the discount is essentially the same as paying 2% interest for the use of $800 for 20 days, which is equivalent to a 36% annual interest rate (360 days/20 days × 2%). Clearly, the firm would be wiser to borrow from a bank at an annual interest rate of 12–15% rather than lose a discount that amounts to a much higher rate.

Trade Discounts Certain business firms furnish customers with price lists or catalogs showing suggested retail prices for their products. These firms, however, also include a schedule of **trade discounts** from the listed prices that enable a customer to determine the invoice price to be paid. Suppose that the Madison Electronics Company quoted a list price of $100 for each Model E tape recorder, less a discount of 30% if purchased in lots of 10 items or less and 40% if purchased in lots of more than 10. If the ABC Company ordered seven tape recorders, it would calculate its invoice cost as follows:

List Price ($100 × 7)	$700
Less 30%	210
Invoice Cost	$490

Trade discounts enable a supplier to vary prices for small and large purchasers and, by changing the discount schedule, to alter prices periodically without the inconvenience and expense of revising catalogs and price lists.

Trade discounts are simply a means of determining invoice prices and should not be confused with cash discounts. Trade discounts and list prices are not reflected in the accounts of either the purchaser or the seller of merchandise. In the foregoing example, both the purchaser and the seller would record only the $490 invoice amount.

RECORDING MERCHANDISE SALES

After a vendor has processed a customer's purchase order and prepared the goods for shipment, a sales invoice is prepared in several copies. The original copy is usually sent to the customer; duplicate copies are retained by the seller. The duplicates may be distributed to the shipping department to support its shipping records; to the sales department so it can analyze sales by product, territory, or sales representative; and to the accounting department so that the transaction will be recorded in the accounts.

Suppose the accounting department of Madison Electronics Company receives its copy of the November 20 invoice for the sale of the tape recorders described in the previous section. The general journal entry to record the sale would be

Nov. 20	Accounts Receivable	490	
	Sales		490
	To record the sale of seven Model E tape recorders to the ABC Company. Terms 2/10, n/30.		

The **Sales** account is used by almost all manufacturing and merchandising companies to record revenue transactions. It is the same type of account as the Instructional Fees (revenue) account used by the Westgate Driving School, our example in Chapter 2. The Sales account is credited whenever credit or cash sales are made, and invariably it has a credit balance at the end of the accounting period. Only sales of merchandise held for resale are recorded in the Sales account. If a merchandising firm sold one of its delivery trucks, the credit would be made to the Delivery Equipment account, not to the Sales account. At the end of the accounting period, the Sales account is closed to the Income Summary account in the same way that the Instructional Fees account is closed. Sales is debited and Income Summary is credited for the accumulated credit balance in the Sales account.

As we mentioned earlier, the sales invoice is the document used to record credit sales. For cash sales, however, the procedure is different. For a large volume of cash sales, as in a retail merchandising establishment, cash sales are recorded and accumulated on a cash register tape as they are made. At the end of each day, the amount of sales shown on the tape is recorded on a summary sheet or report. The totals on these reports are usually recorded in the Sales account for the week. Shorter or longer recording intervals may be used, depending on management's reporting needs. In general journal form, the entry to record a week's cash sales of $3,200 would be

Nov. 27	Cash	3,200	
	Sales		3,200
	To record cash sales for week of November 23–27.		

RECORDING MERCHANDISE PURCHASES

When a business purchases merchandise for resale to customers, the amount is debited to the **Purchases** account. The credit is made to Accounts Payable or to Cash, depending on whether the purchase was on credit or cash terms. Assume that on November 23, the ABC Company received its shipment of seven tape recorders from the Madison Electronics Company, along with the vendor's invoice for $490. To record the credit purchase, the ABC Company makes the following entry:

Nov. 23	Purchases	490	
	Accounts Payable		490
	To record the purchase of seven Model E tape recorders from Madison Electronics Company. Terms 2/10, n/30.		

Only merchandise purchased for resale is recorded in the Purchases account. Acquisitions of such things as equipment, supplies, and investments are entered in the corresponding asset accounts rather than in Purchases.

The Purchases account normally has a debit balance at the end of the accounting period. The account is treated as an income statement account and, like the other temporary accounts, is closed at the end of the accounting year. The closing of the Purchases account is explained later in this chapter.

RETURNS AND ALLOWANCES

Sometimes a customer returns merchandise to the seller because of defects, damage in transit, or because the wrong merchandise was shipped. Upon returning merchandise, the customer requests an appropriate reduction in the original amount billed. Similar requests are made when an invoicing error has occurred. Upon receiving notification that the buyer has returned goods or has requested an allowance, the seller usually issues the customer a **credit memorandum** such as the one illustrated in Exhibit 5–5.

The credit memorandum (sometimes called *credit memo*) is a formal acknowledgment that the seller has reduced the amount owed by the customer.

EXHIBIT 5–5
Credit Memorandum

MADISON ELECTRONICS COMPANY
1400 South Park St.
Madison, Wisconsin 53705

CREDIT MEMORANDUM
No. 23

TO: ABC Company
120 Weston Street
Kenosha, Wisconsin

Date Nov. 25, 19XX

We credit your account as follows:

Return of two Model E tape recorders,
our invoice No. 12015 . . . . $140.00

When the seller issues a credit memorandum, the accounting department retains a duplicate copy, which is the source document for an entry crediting the customer's account. For example, suppose two of the seven tape recorders sold to the ABC Company were returned for credit. Upon issuing a credit memo to the ABC Company, Madison Electronics Company would make the following entry:

Nov. 25	Sales Returns and Allowances	140	
	Accounts Receivable		140
	To record the issuance of credit memo No. 23 for two Model E tape recorders returned by the ABC Company.		

Upon receipt of the credit memo, the ABC Company would make the following entry:

Nov. 27	Accounts Payable	140	
	Purchases Returns and Allowances		140
	To record the receipt of credit memo No. 23 for two Model E tape recorders returned to Madison Electronics Company.		

In the first entry above, Madison Electronics Company could have debited the Sales account rather than Sales Returns and Allowances. If Sales were debited, however, the account balance at the end of the accounting period would not reveal total sales made but total sales less all returns and allowances. Most companies prefer to record sales returns and allowances in a separate contra account in order to determine the aggregate amount of such items. If the amount is abnormally large, an investigation should be made to determine the reason. Returns may be caused by defective products, faulty packing or shipping, or improper billing procedures. The additional handling of goods and the additional clerical work of making adjustments can be costly, and customers may be lost in the process.

For similar reasons, the purchaser ordinarily credits the Purchases Returns and Allowances account rather than the Purchases account when a credit memorandum is received. The separate accounting permits a company to determine whether its purchasing or requisitioning procedures should be reviewed. The company may discover, for instance, that not enough care is exercised in filling out requisitions and purchase orders or in selecting reliable suppliers.

The Sales Returns and Allowances account invariably has a debit balance at the end of the accounting period. On the income statement, the amount is a deduction from the Sales amount. The Purchases Returns and Allowances account has a credit balance at the end of the accounting period, and the balance is subtracted from the Purchases amount on the income statement. Both the Sales Returns and Allowances and the Purchases Returns and Allowances accounts are closed at the end of the accounting year in a manner we shall explain shortly.

Many companies record all credit memos in the returns and allowances accounts. When the memos are issued as a result of mere clerical or arithmetical errors, however, the adjustment is best recorded in the Sales or Purchases accounts.

RECORDING RECEIPTS AND PAYMENTS

A set of merchandise transactions concludes when the seller receives the proper remittance from the purchaser and each firm makes the appropriate entries for the settlement of accounts. To illustrate let us review the entries made thus far for Madison Electronics Company's sale of the tape recorders to the ABC Company.

Seller (Madison Electronics Company)

To Record Sale

Nov. 20	Accounts Receivable	490	
	Sales		490
	To record the sale of seven Model E tape recorders to the ABC Company. Terms 2/10, n/30.		

To Record Return of Merchandise

Nov. 25	Sales Returns and Allowances	140	
	Accounts Receivable		140
	To record the issuance of credit memo No. 23 for two Model E tape recorders returned by the ABC Company.		

Buyer (ABC Company)

To Record Purchase

Nov. 23	Purchases	490	
	Accounts Payable		490
	To record the purchase of seven Model E tape recorders from Madison Electronics Company. Terms 2/10, n/30.		

To Record Return of Merchandise

Nov. 27	Accounts Payable	140	
	Purchases Returns and Allowances		140
	To record the receipt of credit memo No. 23 for two Model E tape recorders returned to Madison Electronics Company.		

After these transactions have been posted, the seller's Accounts Receivable account and the buyer's Accounts Payable account appear as follows:

Seller (Madison Electronics Company)

Accounts Receivable

19XX		19XX	
Nov. 20	490	Nov. 25	140

Buyer (ABC Company)

Accounts Payable

19XX		19XX	
Nov. 27	140	Nov. 23	490

If the ABC Company takes advantage of the 2% discount, its remittance must be made within 10 days of the November 20 invoice date. Usually, the discount is granted if the remittance is postmarked on the last day of the discount period. The amount that the ABC Company should remit by November 30 is $343 ($350 balance owing less 2% discount of $7). Note that the discount is calculated only on the cost of the merchandise kept by the purchaser, not on the invoice price of the goods originally shipped. The entries made on the books of the seller and buyer are

	Seller (Madison Electronics Company)				**Buyer (ABC Company)**		
Dec. 2	Cash	343		Nov. 30	Accounts Payable	350	
	Sales Discounts	7			Purchases Discounts		7
	Accounts Receivable		350		Cash		343
	To record remittance in full of account.				To record payment of account.		

After this entry is posted, the seller's Accounts Receivable and the purchaser's Accounts Payable appear as follows:

Seller (Madison Electronics Company)

Accounts Receivable

19XX		19XX	
Nov. 20	490	Nov. 25	140
		Dec. 2	350

Buyer (ABC Company)

Accounts Payable

19XX		19XX	
Nov. 27	140	Nov. 23	490
30	350		

Note that the discount taken in this transaction is not revealed in either the seller's Accounts Receivable account or the buyer's Accounts Payable account. Discounts are accumulated in Sales Discounts on the seller's books and Purchases Discounts on the buyer's books.

The other accounts relevant to the set of transactions for the tape recorders are shown below in T-account form, after the appropriate postings have been made.

Seller (Madison Electronics Company)

Sales

		19XX	
		Nov. 20	490

Sales Returns and Allowances

19XX			
Nov. 25	140		

Sales Discounts

19XX			
Dec. 2	7		

Buyer (ABC Company)

Purchases

19XX			
Nov. 23	490		

Purchases Returns and Allowances

		19XX	
		Nov. 27	140

Purchases Discounts

		19XX	
		Nov. 30	7

From this illustration, we see that both Sales Returns and Allowances and Sales Discounts have debit balances, and the Sales account has a credit balance. This relationship always holds true, and at the close of the accounting period, the net sales for the period can be calculated by subtracting the balances of the Sales Returns and Allowances account and the Sales Discounts account from the Sales account. The revenue section of the income statement for the year will show this calculation as follows:

Revenue		
Sales		$433,000
Less: Sales Returns and Allowances	$2,500	
Sales Discounts	5,500	8,000
Net Sales		$425,000

Similarly, Purchases Returns and Allowances and Purchases Discounts have credit balances at the close of the accounting period. On the income statement for the period, the sum of these account balances is deducted from the Purchases account balance. However, because the concept of net cost of purchases is a net *delivered* cost, we usually add another amount, *Transportation In*, to arrive at net cost of purchases. (Transportation In will be explained later in this chapter.) The calculation of net cost of purchases for Madison Electronics Company for the year appears on its income statement as follows:

Net Cost of Purchases		
Purchases		$256,500
Less: Purchases Returns and Allowances	$1,800	
Purchases Discounts	4,400	6,200
		$250,300
Add: Transportation In		9,700
Net Cost of Purchases		$260,000

This calculation appears in the cost of goods sold section of the income statement, which we shall examine more closely later in this chapter.

NET PRICE METHOD OF RECORDING PURCHASES

Some firms anticipate the cash discounts they expect to take on merchandise purchases and initially record such purchases net of the discounts. For example, if a firm purchased merchandise for $500 on terms of 2/10, n/30, the 2% discount ($10) would be deducted from the invoice cost and the entry to record the transaction would debit Purchases and credit Accounts Payable for $490. When this amount is paid during the discount period, the debit to Accounts Payable and the credit to Cash would be for the net amount, $490. No purchase discount would be recorded. When the net price method is used, returns and allowances are also recorded net of the related discount.

If a firm delays payment beyond the discount period, the amount of the discount not taken is debited to an account called Discounts Lost when the remittance is made. If the firm in our example failed to remit within the discount period, it would record the payment as a $490 debit to Accounts Payable, $10 debit to Discounts Lost, and a $500 credit to Cash.

The Discounts Lost account balance is normally added to the cost of purchases in the cost of goods sold section of the income statement. However, some firms include it with operating expenses. The principal advantage of the net price method is that it focuses attention on discounts not taken, so that management can take immediate corrective action when the aggregate amount of lost discounts becomes significant.

Illustrations of the types of entries used in the net price method are given below:

Purchase of merchandise for $500 on terms of 2/10, n/30		
Purchases	490	
Accounts Payable		490
($500 purchase, less 2% discount)		
Return of $200 merchandise		
Accounts Payable	196	
Purchases Returns and Allowances		196
($200 return, less 2% discount)		
Payment within discount period		
Accounts Payable	294	
Cash		294
($300 merchandise, less 2% discount)		
Payment after discount period		
Accounts Payable	294	
Discounts Lost	6	
Cash		300
($300 merchandise, less 2% discount lost)		

TRANSPORTATION ACCOUNTS

DESTINATION FREIGHT PREPAID

SHIPPING POINT FREIGHT COLLECT

When merchandise is forwarded by a common carrier—a railroad, a trucking company, or an airline—the carrier prepares a *freight bill* in accordance with the instructions of the party making the transportation arrangements. (As mentioned earlier, such arrangements may be specified in the purchase order.) The freight bill designates which party bears the shipping costs and whether the shipment is *prepaid* or *collect*.

Freight bills usually show whether the shipping terms are F.O.B. shipping point or F.O.B. destination (F.O.B. is an abbreviation for "free on board"). When the freight terms are F.O.B. shipping point, the purchaser bears the shipping costs; when the terms are F.O.B. destination, the seller bears the shipping costs.

The shipping costs borne by a purchaser are debited to an account called **Transportation In**. On the firm's income statement, the balance in this account is included in the computation of net cost of purchases. Transportation costs incurred by a seller are debited to an account called **Transportation Out**. This account—sometimes called Delivery Expense—is listed with expenses on the income statement. The primary reason for such treatment is that the seller ordinarily has a number of different types of expenses directly associated with selling merchandise. Such expenses as advertising, salespersons' salaries, and insurance are frequently grouped in the income statement under the caption "Selling Expenses"; including Transportation Out with this group is logical.

Usually, the party assuming the freight cost pays the carrier. Thus, goods are shipped *freight collect* when the terms are F.O.B. shipping point and *freight prepaid* when the terms are F.O.B. destination. Sometimes, as a matter of convenience, the firm not assuming the freight cost pays the carrier. When this situation occurs, the seller and buyer simply adjust the amount of the payment for the merchandise. To illustrate, let us assume that Madison Electronics Company sells $600 worth of merchandise on account to Chicago Supply Company on terms F.O.B. shipping point, 2/10, n/30, and shipping costs of $60 are prepaid by the seller. Madison Electronics Company adds the $60 freight charge to the invoice amount, billing Chicago Supply Company for $660. On its records, Chicago Supply Company reflects the freight cost as Transportation In.

In this situation, the buyer is not entitled to a discount on the amount of the freight. Thus, if Chicago Supply Company pays the invoice during the discount period, the amount to be remitted is calculated as follows:

Invoice amount ($600 plus $60 prepaid freight)	$660
Less: Discount (2% of $600)	12
Amount to be remitted	$648

On the other hand, if freight terms are F.O.B. destination but the buyer pays the shipping charges (freight collect), the buyer deducts the freight charges in remitting to the seller. The buyer, however, is entitled to a discount calculated on the invoice price of the merchandise. Thus, if $600 worth of merchandise is purchased and freight is $60, a 2% discount of $12 would be taken and the remittance would be $528 ($600 worth of merchandise less the $12 discount less the $60 shipping charge paid by the buyer).

WORKSHEET FOR A MERCHANDISING FIRM

We pointed out in Chapter 4 that a worksheet is prepared at the close of an accounting period to facilitate preparation of the financial statements. The structure of a worksheet for a merchandising firm is the same 10-column form used in Chapter 4 for a service firm, with pairs of columns for the trial balance, adjustments, adjusted trial balance, income statement, and balance sheet. Madison Electronics Company's worksheet in Exhibit 5–6 (pages 182–83) is prepared after all transactions for the year are recorded and posted to the accounts. The first step in preparing the worksheet is to take a trial balance of the general ledger at December 31 and record the account balances in the first two columns of the worksheet.

Adjustments in the Worksheet

The second step in preparing the worksheet is to record the year-end adjusting entries in the adjustments columns. These entries, with explanations, are as follows:

(1)	Dec. 31	Insurance Expense	280	
		Prepaid Insurance		280
		To charge one year's premium to expense. (Three-year premium, $840, paid January 1.)		
(2)	31	Supplies Expense	1,200	
		Supplies on Hand		1,200
		To charge to expense the supplies used during year. (Inventory of supplies is $1,600 on December 31.)		
(3)	31	Depreciation Expense	6,000	
		Accumulated Depreciation		6,000
		To charge to expense one year's depreciation on delivery equipment.		
(4)	31	Sales Salaries Expense	500	
		Salaries Payable		500
		To reflect the salaries earned by salespersons but not paid at December 31.		

To reflect the adjusting entries, we add the accounts not included in the trial balance to the bottom of the worksheet. After making these entries, we total the adjustments columns to confirm that debits equal credits. The trial balance amounts are combined with the adjustments to obtain the adjusted trial balance amounts; these amounts are also summed to determine the equality of the totals. We then extend the adjusted trial balance amounts into the income statement and balance sheet columns. We can see in Exhibit 5–6 that Sales, Purchases, related returns and allowances, discounts, and expense accounts are extended into the income statement columns. Assets, liabilities, and owner's equity accounts are extended into the balance sheet columns.

Inventories in the Worksheet

The inventory of a merchandising firm consists of a stock of goods that are owned by the firm and are available for sale to customers. The dollar amount of this stock of goods is carried in an asset account called **Merchandise Inventory,** or simply **Inventory.** A firm that records the acquisition of merchandise during the period in a Purchases account is using a *periodic* inventory system.[1] This system

[1]Under the *perpetual* inventory system described in Chapter 9, the Inventory account is adjusted throughout the accounting period for the cost of goods purchased and sold.

EXHIBIT 5–6

Madison Electronics Company
Worksheet
For the Year Ended December 31, 19XX

Description	Trial Balance Debit	Trial Balance Credit	Adjustments Debit	Adjustments Credit	Adjusted Trial Balance Debit	Adjusted Trial Balance Credit	Income Statement Debit	Income Statement Credit	Balance Sheet Debit	Balance Sheet Credit
Cash	18,240				18,240				18,240	
Accounts Receivable	32,000				32,000				32,000	
Inventory, ~~January 1~~	115,000				115,000		115,000			
Prepaid Insurance	840			(1) 280	560				560	
Supplies on Hand	2,800			(2) 1,200	1,600				1,600	
Delivery Equipment	30,000				30,000				30,000	
Accumulated Depreciation		4,300		(3) 6,000		10,300				10,300
Accounts Payable		17,500				17,500				17,500
Long-term Notes Payable		20,000				20,000				20,000
J. Madison, Capital		134,000				134,000				134,000
J. Madison, Drawing	5,400				5,400				5,400	
Sales		433,000				433,000		433,000		
Sales Returns and Allowances	2,500				2,500		2,500			
Sales Discounts	5,500				5,500		5,500			
Purchases	256,500				256,500		256,500			

Purchases Returns and Allowances		1,800				1,800		1,800		
Purchases Discounts		4,400				4,400		4,400		
Transportation In	9,700				9,700		9,700			
Sales Salaries Expense	64,000		(4) 500		64,500		64,500			
Advertising Expense	6,170				6,170		6,170			
Delivery Expense	19,250				19,250		19,250			
Office Salaries Expense	27,500				27,500		27,500			
Rent Expense	16,500				16,500		16,500			
Utilities Expense	3,100				3,100		3,100			
	615,000	615,000								
Insurance Expense			(1) 280		280		280			
Supplies Expense			(2) 1,200		1,200		1,200			
Depreciation Expense			(3) 6,000		6,000		6,000			
Salaries Payable				(4) 500		500				500
			7,980	7,980	621,500	621,500				
~~Inventory, December 31~~								~~120,000~~	~~120,000~~	
							533,700	559,200	207,800	182,300
Net Income							25,500			25,500
							559,200	559,200	207,800	207,800

implies that the inventory account balance does not change during the period. Before the firm prepares year-end financial statements, it must determine the amount of unsold goods to be reported. The amount of this asset is usually calculated by counting and pricing individual items in stock, multiplying unit costs by number of items, then adding all amounts to obtain an aggregate measure.

In Exhibit 5–6, the inventory figure that appears in the unadjusted trial balance is the January 1 inventory. This amount still appears in the account because additions and deductions during the year have not been reflected in the account. The beginning inventory of $115,000 is extended as a debit in the income statement columns because it is combined with Purchases (less returns and allowances and discounts) and Transportation In to determine the cost of goods available for sale. The $120,000 ending inventory, recorded at the bottom of the worksheet, is a credit in the income statement columns because it is deducted from cost of goods available for sale in the calculation of cost of goods sold. In Exhibit 5–6, all the amounts comprising cost of goods sold appear in color to emphasize how cost of goods sold is reflected in the income statement columns of the worksheet. The ending inventory of $120,000 is also entered as a debit in the balance sheet columns because it is an asset at December 31.

The last step in completing the worksheet is to total the income statement and balance sheet columns and insert the balancing amount—the $25,500 net income for the year. A net income amount results in a debit in the income statement columns and a credit in the balance sheet columns. A net loss would result in a credit in the income statement columns and a debit in the balance sheet columns.

FINANCIAL STATEMENTS OF A MERCHANDISING FIRM

Once the worksheet is completed, preparing the formal financial statements for the period is a simple matter. Exhibits 5–7 and 5–8 present the income statement for the year and the balance sheet at the end of the year for Madison Electronics Company. Both were prepared from the worksheet in Exhibit 5–6. Note that these are **classified** financial statements, meaning that accounts are separated into various categories. The income statements in previous illustrations were not classified because only a few accounts were used. A business with many accounts and transactions, however, classifies the items on the statements to facilitate analysis and interpretation of the data.

The Income Statement

The major categories of the income statement are revenue, cost of goods sold, and operating expenses. For a merchandising firm, the major revenue source is sales of goods to customers. In the revenue section, sales returns and allowances and sales discounts are deducted from gross sales to yield net sales.

We stated earlier that the cost of goods sold amount is obtained by adding the beginning inventory and net cost of purchases and deducting the ending inventory. To calculate net cost of purchases, we deduct purchases returns and

EXHIBIT 5–7

Madison Electronics Company
Income Statement
For the Year Ended December 31, 19XX

Revenue				
Sales				$433,000
Less: Sales Returns and Allowances			$ 2,500	
Sales Discounts			5,500	8,000
Net Sales				$425,000
Cost of Goods Sold				
Inventory, January 1			$115,000	
Add: Net Cost of Purchases				
Purchases		$256,500		
Less: Purchases Returns and Allowances	$1,800			
Purchases Discounts	4,400	6,200		
		$250,300		
Add: Transportation In		9,700	260,000	
Cost of Goods Available for Sale			$375,000	
Less: Inventory, December 31			120,000	
Cost of Goods Sold				255,000
Gross Profit on Sales				$170,000
Operating Expenses				
Selling Expenses				
Sales Salaries Expense		$ 64,500		
Delivery Expense		19,250		
Advertising Expense		6,170		
Depreciation Expense		6,000		
Insurance Expense		280		
Total Selling Expenses			$ 96,200	
Administrative Expenses				
Rent Expense		$ 16,500		
Office Salaries Expense		27,500		
utilities Expense		3,100		
Supplies Expense		1,200		
Total Administrative Expenses			48,300	
Total Operating Expenses				144,500
Net Income				$ 25,500

allowances and purchases discounts from the purchases amount and add transportation costs of purchased goods.

A business firm's *operating expenses* relate to its primary function and appear with some regularity on the income statement. The operating expenses of a mer-

EXHIBIT 5–8

Madison Electronics Company
Balance Sheet
December 31, 19XX

ASSETS			LIABILITIES AND OWNER'S EQUITY		
Current Assets			**Current Liabilities**		
Cash	$ 18,240		Accounts Payable	$17,500	
Accounts Receivable	32,000		Salaries Payable	500	
Inventory	120,000		Total Current Liabilities		$ 18,000
Prepaid Insurance	560				
Supplies on Hand	1,600				
Total Current Assets		$172,400	**Long-term Liabilities**		
			Long-term Notes Payable		20,000
Long-term Assets			**Owner's Equity**		
Delivery Equipment	$ 30,000		J. Madison, Capital		154,100
Less: Accumulated Depreciation	10,300	19,700			
Total Assets		$192,100	Total Liabilities and Owner's Equity		$192,100

chandising business are typically classified as selling or administrative expenses. Therefore, in our illustration, expenses resulting from sales efforts—such as salespersons' salaries, advertising, and delivery costs—are classified separately from expenses of rent, utilities, and other administrative costs. Of course, certain types of expenses may appear under both categories. For example, the insurance expense in Exhibit 5–7 is apparently on merchandise or delivery equipment, because it appears as a selling expense. Insurance on a company-owned office building, on the other hand, would appear with the administrative expenses.

Some business items affecting the final net income amount may not relate to the primary operating activity of the business. Interest income and interest expense, for example, may relate more to financing and investing activities than to merchandising efforts. For this reason, such items are often shown in a separate category called "Other Income and Expense" at the bottom of the income statement. Likewise, any extraordinary items (explained in Chapter 16), such as catastrophic loss from an earthquake, are shown in a separate "Extraordinary Items" category before the final net income amount is figured. Madison Electronics Company had no such transactions or events to list on the income statement in Exhibit 5–7.

Because the income statement is divided into the major categories just discussed and expenses are classified into selling and administrative expenses, the reader of the statement may pick out key figures at a glance. The reader might first observe the net income figure, \$25,500, and perhaps relate it (as a percentage) to the net sales figure, \$425,000. This result, called **return on sales,** is 6% for Madison Electronics Company. Next, the reader might determine the gross margin percentage by performing the calculation

$$\frac{\$170{,}000\ (\text{gross profit})}{\$425{,}000\ (\text{net sales})} = 40\%$$

In a similar fashion, we can relate the total expenses, expense categories, or even individual expenses to net sales. We might also compare the results with those of prior periods or industry averages to determine whether the company's progress is satisfactory. A detailed treatment of such analysis appears in Chapter 20.

The Balance Sheet

The balance sheet for Madison Electronics Company at December 31 is shown in Exhibit 5–8. Note that the company's assets have been classified into *current assets* and *long-term assets.*

CURRENT ASSETS **Current assets** include cash and assets that will be converted into cash or used up during the normal operating cycle of the business or one year, whichever is longer. The *normal operating cycle* of a business is the average period required for merchandise to be bought and sold and the resulting accounts receivable to be collected. For many businesses, this period is one year or less, although certain industries—such as lumbering and distilling—may have an operating cycle of several years. Examples of current assets other than those shown in Exhibit 5–8 are notes receivable and marketable securities acquired as temporary investments. Current assets are usually listed in the order of their *liquidity,* that is, their convertibility into cash.

Prepaid expenses such as rent, insurance, and supplies are normally consumed during the operating cycle rather than converted into cash. These items are considered current assets, however, because the prepayments make cash outlays for services unnecessary during the current period.

LONG-TERM ASSETS **Long-term assets** are noncurrent, relatively long-lived assets used in operating a business. When its balance sheet was prepared, Madison Electronics Company had only one long-term asset, delivery equipment, but many firms own land, buildings, machinery, and equipment. The terms *plant assets* or *plant and equipment* are often used when such assets are extensive. Depreciable assets are normally shown at their original cost, and the accumulated depreciation to date is credited to a separate account. Other examples of long-term assets held by some firms include natural resources, intangible assets, and long-term investments. These assets are explained in later chapters.

CURRENT LIABILITIES **Current liabilities** are amounts due within the normal operating cycle or one year, whichever is longer. Examples of current liabilities are accounts payable, accrued wages and salaries payable, income or property taxes payable, and short-term notes payable. Any amounts a firm has received

EXHIBIT 5–9

Madison Electronics Company Statement of Owner's Equity For the Year Ended December 31, 19XX	
J. Madison, Capital, January 1	$134,000
Add: Net Income for 19XX	25,500
	$159,500
Less: Withdrawals for 19XX	5,400
J. Madison, Capital, December 31	$154,100

from customers but has not yet earned as revenue are also included in this category when they will be earned within the normal operating cycle or one year, whichever is longer. Examples include customers' deposits on future purchases and magazine subscriptions covering future periods.

LONG-TERM LIABILITIES After current liabilities, the balance sheet lists all **long-term liabilities**—amounts that are not due for a relatively long time, typically more than one year. Long-term notes, mortgages, and bonds payable are a few examples. Madison Electronics Company owed $20,000 on a long-term note when its balance sheet was compiled (Exhibit 5–8).

OWNER'S EQUITY The owner's interest in the assets of the firm appears in the owner's equity section of the balance sheet. J. Madison's capital balance at December 31 (Exhibit 5–8) is determined by adding the net income to the beginning capital balance and deducting withdrawals, as shown in Exhibit 5–9, the year-end Statement of Owner's Equity.

ADJUSTING AND CLOSING ENTRIES

As we explained in Chapter 4, a company often will prepare monthly or quarterly financial statements directly from worksheets and not record adjusting and closing entries in the general ledger until the end of the year. Let us examine year-end procedures for Madison Electronics Company.

Adjusting Entries

After financial statements have been prepared from the worksheet, the adjusting entries shown on the worksheet are recorded in the general journal and posted to the accounts. These entries, given in general journal form on page 181, will not be repeated here.

Closing Entries

The closing entries follow the adjusting entries in the general journal. The procedure consists of the following steps:

(1) Close the beginning inventory and all income statement accounts with *debit* balances, and debit the total to the Income Summary account.

(2) Record the ending inventory, close all income statement accounts with *credit* balances, and credit the total to the Income Summary account.

(3) Transfer the balance of the Income Summary account to the owner's capital account (the Retained Earnings account in a corporation).

(4) Transfer the balance of the owner's drawing account to the owner's capital account.

Closing entries for Madison Electronics Company are given below:

Dec. 31	Income Summary	533,700	
	Inventory (January 1)		115,000
	Sales Returns and Allowances		2,500
	Sales Discounts		5,500
	Purchases		256,500
	Transportation In		9,700
	Sales Salaries Expense		64,500
	Advertising Expense		6,170
	Delivery Expense		19,250
	Office Salaries Expense		27,500
	Rent Expense		16,500
	Utilities Expense		3,100
	Insurance Expense		280
	Supplies Expense		1,200
	Depreciation Expense		6,000
	To close the beginning inventory and income statement accounts with debit balances.		
31	Inventory (December 31)	120,000	
	Sales	433,000	
	Purchases Returns and Allowances	1,800	
	Purchases Discounts	4,400	
	Income Summary		559,200
	To record the ending inventory and to close income statement accounts with credit balances.		
31	Income Summary	25,500	
	J. Madison, Capital		25,500
	To close the Income Summary account and transfer net income to the owner's capital account.		
31	J. Madison, Capital	5,400	
	J. Madison, Drawing		5,400
	To close the owner's drawing account to the capital account.		

After the adjusting and closing entries have been recorded and posted, the Income Summary and J. Madison, Capital accounts appear as shown below. Although we have labeled these entries for illustrative purposes, they would ordinarily not be labeled in the actual accounts.

Income Summary

Beginning Inventory, Purchases, Expenses, and Other Debits	533,700	Ending Inventory, Sales, and Other Credits	559,200
Net Income	25,500		
	559,200		559,200

J. Madison, Capital

Withdrawals	5,400	Beginning Balance	134,000
Ending Balance	154,100	Net Income	25,500
	159,500		159,500
		Ending Balance	154,100

POST-CLOSING TRIAL BALANCE As we explained in Chapter 4, another trial balance of the ledger accounts is customarily taken after the books have been closed to ensure that the ledger balances and is ready for recording transactions in the next period. A December 31 post-closing trial balance for Madison Electronics Company is shown in Exhibit 5–10.

EXHIBIT 5–10

Madison Electronics Company
Post-closing Trial Balance
December 31, 19XX

	Debit	Credit
Cash	$ 18,240	
Accounts Receivable	32,000	
Inventory	120,000	
Prepaid Insurance	560	
Supplies on Hand	1,600	
Delivery Equipment	30,000	
Accumulated Depreciation		$ 10,300
Accounts Payable		17,500
Salaries Payable		500
Long-term Notes Payable		20,000
J. Madison, Capital		154,100
	$202,400	$202,400

REVERSING ENTRIES If Madison Electronics Company employs reversing entries in its accounting system (see Chapter 4), it would make only one reversing entry on January 1. The only accrual made by the firm at the end of December was for salespersons' salaries; therefore, the entry to reverse this accrual would be

Jan. 1	Salaries Payable	500	
	Sales Salaries Expense		500
	To reverse accrual of salespersons' salaries made on December 31.		

DEMONSTRATION PROBLEM FOR REVIEW

Sportcraft, a wholesaler of sporting goods, had the following trial balance at December 31 of the current year:

Sportcraft
Trial Balance
December 31, 19XX

	Debit	Credit
Cash	$ 6,200	
Accounts Receivable	28,000	
Inventory, January 1	45,000	
Office Supplies on Hand	800	
Prepaid Insurance	2,100	
Land	34,000	
Building	82,000	
Accumulated Depreciation—Building		$ 16,000
Office Equipment	21,300	
Accumulated Depreciation—Office Equipment		5,300
Accounts Payable		19,000
J. Moran, Capital		161,200
J. Moran, Drawing	10,000	
Sales		252,000
Sales Discounts	3,500	
Purchases	151,000	
Purchases Returns and Allowances		2,400
Transportation In	8,200	
Sales Salaries Expense	27,600	
Transportation Out	7,800	
Advertising Expense	6,100	
Office Salaries Expense	22,300	
	$455,900	$455,900

The following information is available at December 31:

(1) Office supplies on hand at December 31 are $250.

(2) Prepaid insurance at December 31 is $1,500.

(3) Depreciation for the year is building, $2,000; office equipment, $2,400.

(4) Salaries payable at December 31 are sales salaries, $300; office salaries, $200.

(5) Inventory at December 31 is $43,500.

REQUIRED

(a) Prepare a 10-column worksheet for the year.

(b) Prepare a classified income statement for the year. Of the insurance expense and depreciation expense on the building, 75% is treated as selling expense and 25% is treated as administrative expense.

(c) Prepare a classified balance sheet at December 31.

(d) Prepare adjusting entries in general journal form.

(e) Prepare closing entries in general journal form.

SOLUTION TO DEMONSTRATION PROBLEM

(a) See pages 194–195.

(b)

Sportcraft
Income Statement
For the Year Ended December 31, 19XX

Revenue			
Sales		$252,000	
Less: Sales Discounts		3,500	
Net Sales			$248,500
Cost of Goods Sold			
Inventory, January 1		$ 45,000	
Add: Net Cost of Purchases			
Purchases	$151,000		
Less: Purchases Returns and Allowances	2,400		
	$148,600		
Add: Transportation In	8,200	156,800	
Cost of Goods Available for Sale		$201,800	
Less: Inventory, December 31		43,500	
Cost of Goods Sold			158,300
Gross Profit on Sales			$ 90,200
Operating Expenses			
Selling Expenses			
Sales Salaries Expense	$ 27,900		
Transportation Out	7,800		
Advertising Expense	6,100		
Insurance Expense	450		
Depreciation Expense—Building	1,500		
Total Selling Expenses		$ 43,750	

Administrative Expenses			
Office Salaries Expense	$ 22,500		
Office Supplies Expense	550		
Insurance Expense	150		
Depreciation Expense—Building	500		
Depreciation Expense—Office Equipment	2,400		
Total Administrative Expenses		26,100	
Total Operating Expenses			69,850
Net Income			$ 20,350

(c)

Sportcraft
Balance Sheet
December 31, 19XX

ASSETS

Current Assets			
Cash		$ 6,200	
Accounts Receivable		28,000	
Inventory		43,500	
Office Supplies on Hand		250	
Prepaid Insurance		1,500	
Total Current Assets			$ 79,450
Long-term Assets			
Land		$34,000	
Building	$82,000		
Less: Accumulated Depreciation	18,000	64,000	
Office Equipment	$21,300		
Less: Accumulated Depreciation	7,700	13,600	
Total Long-term Assets			111,600
Total Assets			$191,050

LIABILITIES AND OWNER'S EQUITY

Current Liabilities		
Accounts Payable	$19,000	
Salaries Payable	500	
Total Current Liabilities		$ 19,500
Owner's Equity		
J. Moran, Capital*		171,550
Total Liabilities and Owner's Equity		$191,050

*$161,200 Beginning Balance + $20,350 Net Income − $10,000 Withdrawals = $171,550

(a)

Sportcraft
Worksheet
For the Year Ended December 31, 19XX

Description	Trial Balance Debit	Trial Balance Credit	Adjustments Debit	Adjustments Credit	Adjusted Trial Balance Debit	Adjusted Trial Balance Credit	Income Statement Debit	Income Statement Credit	Balance Sheet Debit	Balance Sheet Credit
Cash	6,200				6,200				6,200	
Accounts Receivable	28,000				28,000				28,000	
Inventory, January 1	45,000				45,000		45,000			
Office Supplies on Hand	800			(1) 550	250				250	
Prepaid Insurance	2,100			(2) 600	1,500				1,500	
Land	34,000				34,000				34,000	
Building	82,000				82,000				82,000	
Accumulated Depreciation—Building		16,000		(3) 2,000		18,000				18,000
Office Equipment	21,300				21,300				21,300	
Accumulated Depreciation—Office Equipment		5,300		(3) 2,400		7,700				7,700
Accounts Payable		19,000				19,000				19,000
J. Moran, Capital		161,200				161,200				161,200
J. Moran, Drawing	10,000				10,000				10,000	
Sales		252,000				252,000		252,000		

Sales Discounts	3,500				3,500		3,500			
Purchases	151,000				151,000		151,000			
Purchases Returns and Allowances		2,400				2,400		2,400		
Transportation In	8,200				8,200		8,200			
Sales Salaries Expense	27,600		(4) 300		27,900		27,900			
Transportation Out	7,800				7,800		7,800			
Advertising Expense	6,100				6,100		6,100			
Office Salaries Expense	22,300		(4) 200		22,500		22,500			
	455,900	455,900								
Office Supplies Expense			(1) 550		550		550			
Insurance Expense			(2) 600		600		600			
Depreciation Expense—Building			(3) 2,000		2,000		2,000			
Depreciation Expense—Office Equipment			(3) 2,400		2,400		2,400			
Salaries Payable				(4) 500		500				500
			6,050	6,050	460,800	460,800				
Inventory, December 31								43,500	43,500	
							277,550	297,900	226,750	206,400
Net Income							20,350			20,350
							297,900	297,900	226,750	226,750

(d) Adjusting entries:

Dec. 31	Office Supplies Expense	550	
	Office Supplies on Hand		550
	To reflect as expense supplies used during the year.		
31	Insurance Expense	600	
	Prepaid Insurance		600
	To reflect as expense insurance expired during the year.		
31	Depreciation Expense—Building	2,000	
	Depreciation Expense—Office Equipment	2,400	
	Accumulated Depreciation—Building		2,000
	Accumulated Depreciation—Office Equipment		2,400
	To record depreciation on building and office equipment.		
31	Sales Salaries Expense	300	
	Office Salaries Expense	200	
	Salaries Payable		500
	To reflect salaries earned by employees but unpaid at December 31.		

(e) Closing entries:

Dec. 31	Income Summary	277,550	
	Inventory (January 1)		45,000
	Sales Discounts		3,500
	Purchases		151,000
	Transportation In		8,200
	Sales Salaries Expense		27,900
	Transportation Out		7,800
	Advertising Expense		6,100
	Office Salaries Expense		22,500
	Office Supplies Expense		550
	Insurance Expense		600
	Depreciation Expense—Building		2,000
	Depreciation Expense—Office Equipment		2,400
	To close the beginning inventory and income statement accounts with debit balances.		

Dec. 31	Inventory (December 31)	43,500	
	Sales	252,000	
	Purchases Returns and Allowances	2,400	
	Income Summary		297,900
	To record the ending inventory and to close income statement accounts with credit balances.		
31	Income Summary	20,350	
	J. Moran, Capital		20,350
	To close the Income Summary account and transfer net income to the owner's capital account.		
31	J. Moran, Capital	10,000	
	J. Moran, Drawing		10,000
	To close the drawing account.		

KEY POINTS TO REMEMBER

(1) Purchase and sales invoices are the basic documents initiating entries for merchandise transactions.

(2) Cash discounts (for prompt payment during the discount period) are normally reflected in financial records, but trade discounts are not. Cash discounts are calculated on the billed price of merchandise retained in a purchase or sale—not on amounts representing returns and allowances or transportation costs.

(3) The terms prepaid and collect designate the party expected to remit to the freight company. The party who is to bear transportation costs is designated by the terms F.O.B. destination (seller) and F.O.B. shipping point (buyer).

(4) A major difference between the financial statements of service firms and merchandising firms is the inclusion of cost of goods sold in the income statement of merchandising firms. Cost of goods sold is deducted from net sales to obtain gross profit. Expenses are then deducted from gross profit to arrive at net income.

(5) A firm using a periodic inventory system determines its inventory only at the end of a period. In the closing procedures, the beginning inventory is closed to Income Summary, together with the income statement accounts having debit balances. The ending inventory is recorded in the entry to close the income statement accounts with credit balances to Income Summary.

(6) The final steps in the closing procedure are to close the Income Summary account—representing net income or net loss—to the owner's capital account (Retained Earnings in a corporation) and to close the owner's drawing account to the capital account.

SELF-TEST QUESTIONS

(Answers are at the end of this chapter.)

1. Which of the following documents does *not* initiate an entry to be made in the accounts?
   (a) Sales invoice.
   (b) Purchase invoice.
   (c) Purchase order.
   (d) Credit memorandum.

2. Troy, Inc., purchased merchandise from Athens, Inc., for $2,400 list price, subject to a trade discount of 25%. The goods were purchased on terms of 2/10, n/30, F.O.B. destination. Troy paid $50 transportation costs. Troy returned $200 of the merchandise to Athens and later paid the amount due Athens within the discount period. The amount paid is
   (a) $1,518 (b) $1,521 (c) $1,502 (d) $1,618

3. Bennett, Inc., which uses the net price method of recording purchases, bought merchandise for $900, terms 2/10, n/30. If Bennett returns $300 of the goods to the vendor, the entry to record the return should include a
   (a) Debit to Accounts Payable of $300.
   (b) Debit to Discounts Lost of $6.
   (c) Credit to Purchases Returns and Allowances of $294.
   (d) Debit to Purchases Returns and Allowances of $294.

4. A firm's gross profit on net sales is 35%. The firm had net sales of $400,000 and net cost of purchases of $280,000. If the beginning inventory was $40,000, the ending inventory was
   (a) $180,000 (b) $60,000 (c) $20,000 (d) $40,000

5. In preparing a ten-column worksheet for a merchandising firm
   (a) The beginning inventory is extended as a credit in the income statement columns.
   (b) The beginning inventory is extended as a credit in the balance sheet columns.
   (c) The ending inventory is shown as a debit in the income statement columns and as a credit in the balance sheet columns.
   (d) The ending inventory is shown as a credit in the income statement columns and as a debit in the balance sheet columns.

QUESTIONS

5–1 What is the most significant difference between the income statement of a service firm and that of a merchandising firm?

5–2 What is meant by *gross profit on sales*, and of what significance is this item to management?

5–3 Explain the nature, purpose, and key information appearing on each of the following forms:
(a) Purchase requisition.
(b) Purchase order.
(c) Sales invoice.
(d) Receiving report.
(e) Credit memorandum.

5–4 Differentiate between (a) credit period and discount period and (b) cash discounts and trade discounts.

5–5 For the accounts titled Sales Returns and Allowances and Purchases Returns and Allowances, indicate (a) the justification for their use; (b) their normal balances (debit or credit); and (c) their position in the financial statements.

5–6 Explain the appropriate treatment in the income statement of the accounts Transportation In and Transportation Out.

5–7 Under each of the following selling terms, who (buyer or seller) would *bear* the freight cost and who would *remit* to the freight company?
(a) F.O.B. shipping point, freight collect.
(b) F.O.B. destination, freight prepaid.
(c) F.O.B. shipping point, freight prepaid.
(d) F.O.B. destination, freight collect.

5–8 On April 2, Kelly Company purchased $950 worth of merchandise from Gard Company, F.O.B. shipping point, freight collect, terms 2/10, n/30. On April 4, Kelly Company returned $100 of the goods for credit. On April 5, Kelly paid $50 freight on the shipment. If Kelly settles its account with Gard Company on April 11, how much would the company remit?

5–9 How much does Kelly remit in Question 5–8 if the terms are F.O.B. destination rather than F.O.B. shipping point?

5–10 A wholesale firm's gross purchases during an accounting period totaled $50,000, and Transportation In was $3,000. If the firm returned goods amounting to $1,500 and took $500 in purchases discounts during the period, what was the net purchases cost for the period?

5–11 When an unadjusted trial balance of the general ledger is taken for a merchandising firm on a periodic inventory basis, does the beginning inventory or the ending inventory appear in the trial balance? Explain.

5–12 The beginning inventory for a merchandising firm was $64,000 and the ending inventory is $52,000. If the net cost of purchases was $80,000 and net sales was $142,000, what was the gross profit?

5–13 A portion of a worksheet for a merchandising firm follows. Identify the columns—A, B, C, or D—into which the balance of any of the listed accounts should be extended.

	Income Statement		Balance Sheet	
	Debit	Credit	Debit	Credit
	(A)	(B)	(C)	(D)
Inventory (Beginning)				
Sales				
Sales Returns and Allowances				
Purchases				
Purchases Returns and Allowances				
Purchases Discounts				
Transportation In				
Salaries Payable				
Inventory (Ending)				

5–14 Define (a) current assets and (b) current liabilities.

5–15 The Larson Company had net sales of $600,000, cost of goods sold of $408,000, and net income of $30,000. Compute (a) its gross profit percentage and (b) its return on sales.

5–16 A firm using the net price method of recording merchandise purchases bought goods with a price of $750, terms 2/10, n/30. What amount would be debited to the Purchases account?

EXERCISES

Trade and cash discount calculations

5–17 On April 1, Sims Company sold merchandise with a list price of $3,000. For each of the sales terms below, determine (a) the amount recorded as a sale and (b) the proper amount of cash received.

	Applicable Trade Discount (%)	Credit Terms	Date Paid
(1)	30	2/10, n/30	April 8
(2)	40	1/10, n/30	April 15
(3)	—	2/10, n/30	April 11
(4)	20	1/15, n/30	April 14
(5)	40	n/30	April 28

Cash discount and remittance calculations

5–18 For each of the following Baker Company purchases, assume that credit terms are 2/10, n/30 and that any credit memorandum was issued and known before Baker Company made the payments.

	Amount	Shipping Terms	Prepaid Freight (by seller)	Credit Memorandum
(1)	$ 800	F.O.B. shipping point	$ 50	$150
(2)	1,500	F.O.B. destination	120	100
(3)	1,000	F.O.B. shipping point	—	200
(4)	3,000	F.O.B. shipping point	150	—

In each case, determine (a) the appropriate cash discount available and (b) the cash remitted if the payment is made within the discount period.

Entries for sale, return, and remittance

5–19 On June 8, Witt Company sold merchandise listing for $900 to Troy Company, terms 2/10, n/30. On June 12, $150 worth of the merchandise was returned because it was the wrong color. On June 18, Witt Company received a check for the amount due.

Record the general journal entries made by Witt Company for the above transactions.

Entries for purchase, return, and remittance

5–20 On March 10, Ash Company purchased $3,000 worth of merchandise from Lloyd Company, terms 1/10, n/30, F.O.B. shipping point. On March 12, Ash paid $50 freight on the shipment. On March 15, Ash returned $200 worth of the merchandise for credit. Final payment was made to Lloyd on March 19. Ash Company records purchases at invoice price.

(a) Give the general journal entries that Ash should make on March 12, March 15, and March 19.

(b) Give the entries that Ash should make on these three dates if the terms are F.O.B. destination.

Entries for merchandise transactions on seller's and buyer's records

5–21 The following are selected transactions of Wilson, Inc.:

April 20 Sold and shipped on account to Ayres Stores merchandise listing for $600, terms 2/10, n/30.

27 Ayres Stores returned defective merchandise billed at $50 on April 20.

29 Received from Ayres Stores a check for full settlement of the April 20 transaction.

Record, in general journal form, the above transactions as they would appear on the books of (a) Wilson, Inc., and (b) Ayres Stores. Ayres Stores records purchases at invoice price.

Net price method of recording purchases

5–22 Brown, Inc., uses the net price method of recording purchases. On July 1, the firm purchased merchandise for $850, terms 2/10, n/30. On July 5, the firm returned $250 of the merchandise to the seller. Payment of the account occurred on July 8.

(a) Give the general journal entries for July 1, July 5, and July 8.

(b) Assuming that the account was settled on July 14, give the entry for payment on that date.

Determination of omitted income statement data

5–23 The box below contains portions of five unrelated income statements, each with certain data omitted. Fill in the lettered blanks with the appropriate amounts.

	(1)	(2)	(3)	(4)	(5)
Net Sales	$70,000	$ (d)	$85,000	$60,000	$150,000
Beginning Inventory	15,000	25,000	(g)	18,000	(m)
Net Cost of Purchases	45,000	(e)	50,000	42,000	120,000
Cost of Goods Available for Sale	(a)	(f)	80,000	(j)	(n)
Ending Inventory	10,000	15,000	(h)	(k)	60,000
Cost of Goods Sold	(b)	55,000	(i)	(l)	(o)
Gross Profit	(c)	25,000	15,000	10,000	24,000

Effects of inventory errors

5–24 A company's operating figures for four consecutive periods are given below.

	Period			
	(1)	(2)	(3)	(4)
Beginning Inventory	$20,000	$30,000	$25,000	$28,000
Net Cost of Purchases	60,000	40,000	55,000	62,000
Cost of Goods Available for Sale	$80,000	$70,000	$80,000	$90,000
Ending Inventory	30,000	25,000	28,000	35,000
Cost of Goods Sold	$50,000	$45,000	$52,000	$55,000

Assuming that the following errors were made, compute the correct cost of goods sold for each period:

Period	Error in Ending Inventory
1	Overstated $2,000
2	Understated $1,000
3	Overstated $3,000

Closing entries

5–25 A portion of the December 31 worksheet for King Distributors is shown below. For simplicity, all operating expenses have been combined.

	Income Statement		Balance Sheet	
	Debit	Credit	Debit	Credit
Inventory, January 1	40,000			
King, Capital				75,000
King, Drawing			4,000	
Sales		250,000		
Sales Returns and Allowances	2,500			
Sales Discounts	3,500			
Purchases	160,000			
Purchases Returns and Allowances		2,000		
Purchases Discounts		3,000		
Transportation In	4,000			
Operating Expenses	60,000			
Inventory, December 31		35,000	35,000	

Using the given information, prepare the general journal entries to close the books.

PROBLEMS

Entries for merchandise transactions on seller's and buyer's records

5–26 The following transactions occurred between the Burton Company and Cable Stores, Inc., during March of the current year.

Mar. 8 Burton sold $2,600 worth of merchandise to Cable Stores, terms 2/10, n/30, F.O.B. shipping point. Burton paid freight charges of $40 and added it to the amount of the invoice for the merchandise.

Mar. 12 Cable Stores returned $200 of the merchandise shipped on March 8. Burton issued a credit memorandum for this amount.
17 Burton received full payment for the net amount due from the March 8 sale.
20 Cable Stores returned goods that had been billed originally at $100. Burton issued a check.

REQUIRED
Record the above transactions in general journal form as they would appear on (a) the books of Burton Company and (b) the books of Cable Stores, Inc. Cable Stores, Inc., records purchases at invoice price.

Entries for merchandise transactions

5–27 Cardinal Corporation, which began business on August 1 of the current year, sells on terms of 2/10, n/30, F.O.B. shipping point. Credit terms and freight terms for its purchases vary with the supplier. Selected transactions for August are given below. Unless noted, all transactions are on account and involve merchandise held for resale. All purchases are recorded at invoice price.

Aug. 1 Purchased merchandise from Patton, Inc., $750, terms 2/10, n/30, F.O.B. shipping point, freight collect.
4 Purchased merchandise from Malone Company, $1,400, terms 2/10, n/30, F.O.B. destination. Freight charges of $60 were prepaid by Malone Company.
5 Paid freight on shipment from Patton, Inc., $60.
7 Sold merchandise to Steele Corporation, $800.
7 Paid freight on shipment to Steele Corporation, $45, and billed Steele for the charges.
9 Returned $50 worth of the merchandise purchased August 1 from Patton, Inc., because it was defective.
9 Issued a credit memorandum to Steele Corporation for $100 worth of merchandise returned by Steele.
10 Paid Patton, Inc., the amount due.
14 Purchased from Fletcher, Inc., goods with a list price of $1,600. Cardinal Corporation was entitled to a 25% trade discount; terms 1/10, n/30, F.O.B. shipping point, freight collect.
15 Paid freight on shipment from Fletcher, Inc., $60.
17 Received the amount due from Steele Corporation.
18 Sold merchandise to Walton, Inc., $2,200.
19 Paid Malone Company for the amount due on its August 4 invoice.
20 Paid freight on August 18 shipment to Walton, Inc., $70.
20 Received a credit memorandum of $200 from Fletcher, Inc., adjusting the price charged for merchandise purchased on August 14.
24 Paid Fletcher, Inc., the amount due.
28 Received the amount due from Walton, Inc.

REQUIRED
Record the transactions for Cardinal Corporation in general journal form.

Preparation of a worksheet

5–28 The unadjusted trial balance of Wales Distributors on December 31 of the current year is shown below:

Wales Distributors
Trial Balance
December 31, 19XX

	Debit	Credit
Cash	$ 8,100	
Accounts Receivable	38,500	
Inventory, January 1	65,000	
Prepaid Insurance	2,400	
Supplies on Hand	3,600	
Delivery Equipment	46,000	
Accumulated Depreciation		$ 10,500
Accounts Payable		32,500
Wales, Capital		87,000
Wales, Drawing	15,000	
Sales		415,000
Sales Returns and Allowances	5,200	
Sales Discounts	7,300	
Purchases	272,000	
Purchases Returns and Allowances		2,800
Purchases Discounts		5,200
Transportation In	5,800	
Salaries Expense	53,000	
Rent Expense	21,000	
Gas, Oil, and Repairs Expense	8,600	
Utilities Expense	1,500	
	$553,000	$553,000

① INS.EXP
② PRE INS

The following data are available at December 31:
(1) Prepaid insurance at December 31 is $1,600.
(2) Supplies on hand at December 31 amount to $2,300.
(3) Depreciation on the delivery equipment is 20% per year.
(4) At December 31, the company owes its employees $700 in salaries.
(5) At December 31, the company has not recorded a utility bill for $200.
(6) Inventory at December 31 is $56,000.

REQUIRED
Prepare a 10-column worksheet for Wales Distributors for 19XX.

Income statement and calculation of gross profit rate and return on sales

5–29 The following selected information is available for the Blackwood Wholesale Company for March of the current year.

Purchases	$45,500
Sales	94,500
Transportation In	3,200
Purchases Discounts	700
Inventory, March 1	38,500
Inventory, March 31	31,000
Purchases Returns and Allowances	800

Sales Returns and Allowances	1,400
Transportation Out	420
Rent Expense	1,450
Sales Salaries Expense	18,400
Sales Discounts	1,100
Depreciation Expense—Office Equipment	120
Office Supplies Expense	310
Office Salaries Expense	7,850
Advertising Expense	1,400
Insurance Expense (a selling expense)	150

REQUIRED

(a) Prepare the March income statement for Blackwood Wholesale Company.
(b) Calculate the ratio of gross profit to net sales and express it as a percentage.
(c) Calculate the ratio of net income to net sales and express it as a percentage.

Worksheet, financial statements, and adjusting, closing, and reversing entries

5–30 Seneca Trading Company, whose accounting year ends on December 31, had the following normal balances in its general ledger at December 31 of the current year:

Cash	$ 6,200	Sales	$275,000
Accounts Receivable	15,000	Sales Returns and Allowances	3,100
Inventory, January 1	49,000	Sales Discounts	2,900
Prepaid Insurance	2,400	Purchases	185,000
Office Supplies on Hand	1,800	Purchases Returns and Allowances	2,600
Furniture and Fixtures	12,500	Purchases Discounts	3,600
Accumulated Depreciation—Furniture and Fixtures	2,500	Transportation In	4,800
Delivery Equipment	40,000	Sales Salaries Expense	40,000
Accumulated Depreciation—Delivery Equipment	8,000	Delivery Expense	6,200
Accounts Payable	22,300	Advertising Expense	2,400
Notes Payable (Long-term)	20,000	Rent Expense	7,500
R. Seneca, Capital	72,000	Office Salaries Expense	22,000
R. Seneca, Drawing	4,000	Utilities Expense	1,200

Rent expense and utilities expense are administrative expenses. During the year, the accounting department prepared monthly statements using worksheets, but no adjusting entries were made in the journals and ledgers. Data for the year-end procedures are as follows:

(1) Prepaid insurance, December 31 (75% of insurance expense is classified as selling expense, and 25% is classified as administrative expense)	$ 400
(2) Office supplies on hand, December 31	1,200
(3) Depreciation expense on furniture and fixtures for the year (an administrative expense)	800
(4) Depreciation expense on delivery equipment for the year	5,000
(5) Salaries payable, December 31 ($600 sales salaries and $300 office salaries)	900
(6) Inventory, December 31	61,000

REQUIRED
(a) Prepare a worksheet for the current year.
(b) Prepare a classified income statement for the year.
(c) Prepare a classified balance sheet at December 31.
(d) Record the necessary adjusting entries in general journal form.
(e) Record the closing entries in general journal form.
(f) Record any necessary reversing entries in general journal form.

Preparation of income statement from incomplete data

5–31 While on her way to the bank to negotiate a loan, Martha Byer, the treasurer of Artcraft, Inc., realizes that the income statement for the current year is missing fom her papers. She has a December 31 balance sheet, however, and after searching through her papers, locates an unadjusted trial balance taken at December 31. She arrives at your office shortly before her appointment at the bank and asks your assistance in preparing an income statement for the year. The available data at December 31 are given below:

	Unadjusted Trial Balance Debit	Unadjusted Trial Balance Credit	Balance Sheet Data
Cash	$ 28,000		$ 28,000
Accounts Receivable	51,000		51,000
Inventory	77,000		75,000
Office Supplies on Hand	4,100		2,900
Prepaid Insurance	2,400		1,600
Delivery Equipment	48,000		48,000
Accumulated Depreciation		$ 14,500	(22,500)
			$184,000
Accounts Payable		34,000	$ 34,000
Salaries Payable			500
Capital Stock		100,000	100,000
Retained Earnings		30,000	49,500
Sales		240,000	
Purchases	155,000		
Rent Expense	7,500		
Salaries Expense	33,000		
Advertising Expense	5,100		
Delivery Expense	7,400		
	$418,500	$418,500	$184,000

REQUIRED
Use the given data to prepare the year's income statement for Artcraft, Inc., for Martha Byer.

Effect of worksheet errors

5–32 The first six columns of a 10-column worksheet prepared for the Turner Sport Shop are as follows:

	Trial Balance Debit	Trial Balance Credit	Adjustments Debit	Adjustments Credit	Adjusted Trial Balance Debit	Adjusted Trial Balance Credit
Cash	7,000				7,000	
Inventory, January 1	38,000				38,000	
Office Supplies on Hand	2,400			1,800	600	
Prepaid Insurance	1,600				1,600	
Equipment	40,000				40,000	
Accumulated Depreciation		8,000		4,000		12,000
Accounts Payable		10,000				10,000
R. Turner, Capital		45,000				45,000
R. Turner, Drawing	6,000				6,000	
Sales		140,000				140,000
Purchasės	75,000				75,000	
Transportation In	1,500				1,500	
Rent Expense	3,500				3,500	
Salaries Expense	28,000		500		28,500	
	203,000	203,000				
Depreciation Expense			4,000		4,000	
Salaries Payable				500		500
Office Supplies Expense			1,800		1,800	
			6,300	6,300	207,500	207,500
Inventory, December 31						
Net Income						

In completing the worksheet, Turner's accountant made the following errors:

(1) The adjustment for expired insurance was omitted; premiums amounting to $600 expired during the year.

(2) The $6,000 balance of Turner's drawing account was extended as a debit in the income statement columns.

(3) The $500 credit to Salaries Payable was extended as a credit in the income statement columns.

(4) The January 1 Inventory balance of $38,000 was extended as a credit in the income statement columns.

(5) The December 31 Inventory balance of $42,000 was recorded as a debit in the income statement columns and as a credit in the balance sheet columns.

REQUIRED

(a) Which of the errors would cause the worksheet not to balance?

(b) Without completing the worksheet, calculate the net income for the year. Assume that the accountant made no other errors and that the worksheet totals, before adding net income or net loss, were:

	Debit	Credit
Income Statement	$162,300	$178,500
Balance Sheet	49,200	109,000

ALTERNATE PROBLEMS

Entries for merchandise transactions on seller's and buyer's records

5–26A Warner Distributing Company had the following transactions with Sutherland, Inc.:

Nov. 10 Warner sold and shipped $2,000 worth of merchandise to Sutherland, terms 2/10, n/30, F.O.B. shipping point. Warner paid freight charges of $160 and added the amount to the invoice for the merchandise.

14 Warner issued a credit memo for $400 for merchandise returned by Sutherland.

19 Warner received payment in full for the net amount due on the November 10 sale.

24 Sutherland returned goods that had originally been billed at $150. Warner issued a check.

REQUIRED

Record the above transactions in general journal form as they would appear (a) on the books of Warner Distributing Company and (b) on the books of Sutherland, Inc. Sutherland, Inc., records purchases at invoice price.

Entries for merchandise transactions

5–27A The Tobin Company was established on July 1 of the current year. Its sales terms are 2/10, n/30, F.O.B. destination. Credit terms for its purchases vary with the supplier. Selected transactions for the first month of operations are given below. Unless noted, all transactions are on account and involve merchandise held for resale. All purchases are recorded at invoice price.

July 1 Purchased goods from Benson, Inc., $750; terms 1/10, n/30, F.O.B. shipping point, freight collect.

2 Purchased goods from Rowe Company, $1,800, terms 2/10, n/30, F.O.B. destination. Freight charges of $60 were prepaid by Rowe.

3 Paid freight on shipment from Benson, $30.

5 Sold merchandise to Gunn, Inc., $675.

5 Paid freight on shipment to Gunn, Inc., $40.

8 Returned $50 worth of the goods purchased July 1 from Benson, Inc., because some goods were damaged.

9 Issued credit memorandum to Gunn, Inc., for $75 worth of merchandise returned.

10 Paid Benson, Inc., the amount due.

10 Purchased goods from Hill Company with a list price of $900. Tobin was entitled to a $33\frac{1}{3}\%$ trade discount; terms 2/10, n/30, F.O.B. destination, freight collect.

11 Paid freight on shipment from Hill Company, $35.

15 Received the amount due from Gunn, Inc.

15 Sold merchandise to Morse Corporation, $1,800.

16 Mailed a check to Rowe Company for the net amount due on its July 2 invoice.

17 Received a notice from Morse Corporation stating that it had paid freight of $80 on the July 15 shipment.

18 Received a credit memorandum of $50 from Hill Company, as an allowance for defective merchandise purchased on July 10.

July 19 Paid Hill Company the amount due.
25 Received the amount due from Morse Corporation.

REQUIRED
Record the transactions for Tobin Company in general journal form.

Preparation of a worksheet

5–28A The unadjusted trial balance of Dover Corporation on December 31 of the current year is shown below:

Dover Corporation
Trial Balance
December 31, 19XX

	Debit	**Credit**
Cash	$ 22,800	
Accounts Receivable	28,500	
Inventory, January 1	46,000	
Prepaid Insurance	1,200	
Supplies on Hand	2,000	
Furniture and Fixtures	18,000	
Accumulated Depreciation—Furniture and Fixtures		$ 2,400
Delivery Equipment	38,000	
Accumulated Depreciation—Delivery Equipment		12,000
Accounts Payable		7,200
Capital Stock		100,000
Retained Earnings		28,000
Sales		190,000
Sales Returns and Allowances	2,500	
Sales Discounts	1,500	
Purchases	116,000	
Purchases Returns and Allowances		2,600
Purchases Discounts		1,600
Transportation In	4,800	
Salaries Expense	38,000	
Rent Expense	12,500	
Delivery Expense	7,200	
Utilities Expense	4,800	
	$343,800	$343,800

The following data are available at December 31:
(1) Prepaid insurance at December 31 is $700.
(2) Supplies on hand at December 31 amount to $1,400.
(3) Depreciation on the furniture and fixtures is 10% per year.
(4) Depreciation on the delivery equipment is 20% per year.
(5) At December 31, accrued salaries total $800.
(6) Inventory at December 31 is $59,000.

REQUIRED
Prepare a 10-column worksheet for Dover Corporation for 19XX.

Income statement and calculation of gross profit rate and return on sales

5–29A The following selected information is available for the Olympia Trading Company for February of the current year.

Purchases	$ 71,000
Sales	132,000
Transportation In	1,500
Purchases Discounts	1,200
Inventory, February 1	26,500
Inventory, February 28	22,000
Purchases Returns and Allowances	1,800
Sales Returns and Allowances	800
Transportation Out	3,600
Rent Expense	5,400
Salaries Expense	28,500
Sales Discounts	1,200
Depreciation Expense	3,200

REQUIRED

(a) Prepare a February income statement for Olympia Trading Company.
(b) Calculate the ratio of gross profit to net sales and express it as a percentage.
(c) Express the ratio of net profit to net sales as a percentage.

Worksheet, financial statements, and adjusting, closing, and reversing entries

5–30A Castle Distributors, whose accounting year ends on December 31, had the following normal balances in its ledger accounts at December 31 of the current year:

Cash	$19,500	Sales	$610,000
Accounts Receivable	28,700	Sales Returns and Allowances	5,000
Inventory, January 1	72,000	Sales Discounts	9,400
Prepaid Insurance	4,800	Purchases	420,000
Office Supplies on Hand	2,400	Purchases Returns and Allowances	2,400
Furniture and Fixtures	16,000	Purchases Discounts	5,400
Accumulated Depreciation—Furniture and Fixtures	5,200	Transportation In	16,200
Delivery Equipment	42,000	Sales Salaries Expense	52,000
Accumulated Depreciation—Delivery Equipment	14,000	Delivery Expense	16,500
Accounts Payable	38,500	Advertising Expense	11,800
Notes Payable (Long-term)	20,000	Rent Expense	15,000
J. Castle, Capital	80,000	Office Salaries Expense	34,000
J. Castle, Drawing	5,000	Utilities Expense	5,200

Rent expense and utilities expense are administrative expenses. During the year the accounting department prepared monthly statements using worksheets, but no adjusting entries were made in the journals and ledgers. Data for the year-end procedures are as follows:

(1) Prepaid insurance, December 31 (insurance expense is classified as a selling cost)	$ 3,600
(2) Office supplies on hand, December 31	1,100

(3) Depreciation expense on furniture and fixtures for the year (an administrative expense)	$ 1,600
(4) Depreciation expense on delivery equipment for the year	6,000
(5) Salaries payable, December 31 ($400 sales salaries and $200 office salaries)	600
(6) Inventory, December 31	69,000

REQUIRED
(a) Prepare a worksheet for the current year.
(b) Prepare a classified income statement for the current year.
(c) Prepare a classified balance sheet at December 31.
(d) Make the necessary adjusting entries in general journal form.
(e) Make the closing entries in general journal form.
(f) Make any necessary reversing entries in general journal form.

BUSINESS DECISION PROBLEM

This year's income statement for Royal Wholesalers is given below in condensed form.

Sales	$336,000
Cost of Goods Sold	240,000
Gross Profit	96,000
Operating Expenses	65,760
Net Income	$ 30,240

Royal allows its customers a trade discount of 30% of list price. To arrive at the list price, Royal adds a mark-up of 100% to its cost.

Royal's president asks you to evaluate a proposal she has received from the sales manager to improve the company's return on sales. The memo from the sales manager states, "I suggest we permit our customers a trade discount of 35% rather than 30%. My estimates show that with the higher trade discount, we will sell 20% more units next year than this year. We can achieve this increased volume with only a 10% increase in operating expenses."

REQUIRED
(a) Compute Royal's return on sales for this year.
(b) Compute what Royal's return on sales will be if the sales manager's proposal is accepted and his projections are correct. Support this computation with an income statement showing the effect of the sales manager's proposal.
(c) What is your recommendation with respect to the sales manager's proposal?

ANSWERS TO SELF-TEST QUESTIONS

1. (c) 2. (a) 3. (c) 4. (b) 5. (d)

6

Data Processing: Manual and Electronic Systems

Chapter Objectives

- **Describe the difference between control accounts and subsidiary ledger accounts.**
- **Provide an overview of the recording process using special journals.**
- **Describe and illustrate specific special journals.**
- **Describe the voucher system and illustrate the use of a voucher register and a check register.**
- **Introduce the use of electronic systems for processing accounting data.**

Man is a tool-using animal. . . . Without tools he is nothing, with tools he is all.

THOMAS CARLYLE

In the preceding chapters, we limited our discussion of the processing of accounting transactions to recording in a general journal and posting to a general ledger. Such a system is satisfactory for introducing basic accounting procedures. However, for two reasons, this method would be inadequate for a business having even a moderate number of transactions. First, recording all transactions in the general journal would seriously curtail the number of transactions that could be processed in a day, simply because only one person at a time could make entries. Second, transactions recorded in a general journal must be posted individually, resulting in a great deal of posting labor. Therefore, even small- and moderate-sized firms employ *special journals* to make their systems flexible and to reduce the amount of posting required. The use of special journals is one of the features we consider in this chapter.

Our previous illustrations were simple and contained a single Accounts Receivable account and a single Accounts Payable account. Business firms that keep accounts with individual customers and creditors find it quite burdensome to work with a general ledger containing a large number of customer and creditor accounts. Therefore, firms often use *control accounts* in the general ledger and keep separate *subsidiary ledgers* to record accounts of individual customers and creditors.

Finally, in large businesses, the sheer volume of transactions and the need for fast processing and retrieval of information call for electronic data-processing systems. In the last section of this chapter, we introduce the principal types of equipment used in such systems.

CONTROL ACCOUNTS AND SUBSIDIARY LEDGERS

In Chapter 3, we entered all the charges to and payments from customers of Landen TV Service in a single general ledger account. The following T account illustrates these transactions:

Accounts Receivable

Dec. 14	900	Dec. 19	500
28	2,400		

Landen TV Service cannot bill or mail statements to customers, answer inquiries about individual customer balances, or make any collection efforts if the firm has only a single record showing total claims against customers. The company needs to know each customer's name and address, transaction dates, amounts charged for services, and amounts received on account for each account receivable.

We could solve this problem by maintaining in the general ledger an individual Account Receivable for each customer. The trial balance of such a general ledger might appear as follows:

	Trial Balance	
	Debit	**Credit**
Cash	$13,130	
Accounts Receivable—Customer A	300	
Accounts Receivable—Customer B	700	
Accounts Receivable—Customer C	800	
Accounts Receivable—Customer D	1,000	
(All other assets)	15,350	
(All liabilities)		$ 3,550
Owner's Capital		25,000
Owner's Drawing	800	
Revenue		5,450
(All expenses)	1,920	
	$34,000	$34,000

We can easily see the limitations of this approach. The general ledger becomes unreasonably large when hundreds of customers' accounts are involved. With thousands of customers, it becomes absolutely unworkable. Alternatively, we might use one **control account** titled Accounts Receivable in the general ledger and maintain individual customer accounts in a **subsidiary ledger.** Under this approach, the general ledger is kept to a manageable size, and a detailed record of transactions with individual customers exists.

The accounts receivable subsidiary ledger, like the general ledger, may be simply a group of accounts in a binder, or it may be a file card arrangement.[1] In either case, the order is usually alphabetical by customer name. Exhibit 6–1 shows a typical form for an accounts receivable subsidiary ledger. When the three-column form is used, abnormal balances are enclosed in parentheses or shown in red. The information placed at the top of the account varies with the needs of the business and the type of customer. Often, such information concerns the granting of credit.

In the following diagram, we show the relationships between the Accounts Receivable control account in the general ledger and the accounts receivable subsidiary ledger.

[1] In electronic data-processing systems (discussed in the last section of this chapter), the customers' ledger might be in the form of a magnetic tape file or stored internally in a computer.

EXHIBIT 6–1
Customer Account Form in Subsidiary Ledger

Name ______________________

Address ______________________ Phone ______________

Employed at ______________________ Position ______________

Special terms ______________________ Maximum credit $ ______________

Date	Remarks	Debit		Balance

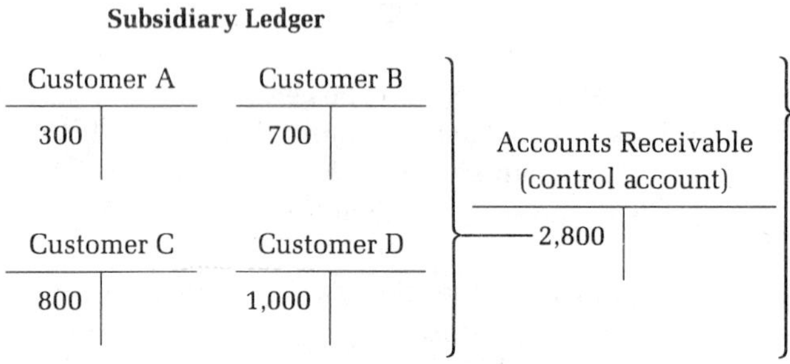

	General Ledger Trial Balance Debit	Credit
Cash	$13,130	
Accounts Receivable	2,800	
(All other assets)	15,350	
(All liabilities)		$ 3,550
Owner's Capital		25,000
Owner's Drawing	800	
Revenue		5,450
(All expenses)	1,920	
	$34,000	$34,000

Because the total of all the balances in the accounts receivable subsidiary ledger must equal the balance in the Accounts Receivable control account in the general ledger, it follows that for every amount posted to the Accounts Receivable control account, an equal amount must be posted to one or more of the customers' accounts in the accounts receivable subsidiary ledger. We shall consider the specific posting procedures later in this chapter.

The control account–subsidiary ledger technique can be used to yield a detailed breakdown of many general ledger accounts, not just Accounts Receivable. Subsidiary ledgers are often used for Accounts Payable, Inventory, Buildings, and Equipment.

SPECIAL JOURNALS

Journals specifically designed in a tabular fashion to accommodate the recording of one type of transaction are called **special journals**. In addition to a general journal, most firms use at least the following special journals:

Special Journal	**Specific Transactions Recorded**
Sales journal	Sales on credit terms
Cash receipts journal	Receipt of cash
Invoice register (purchases journal)	Purchase of merchandise and other items on credit terms
Cash disbursements journal	Payment of cash

Cash sales are usually recorded in the cash receipts journal rather than in the sales journal because cash is best controlled when *all* routine cash receipts are recorded in one journal. Similarly, a firm can increase control over cash disbursements by recording purchases of merchandise for cash in the cash disbursements journal rather than in the purchases journal.

Advantages of Special Journals

A major advantage of special journals is that their use permits a division of labor. When special journals are used, the recording step in the accounting cycle can be divided among several persons, each of whom is responsible for particular types of transactions. Persons making entries in special journals do not have to be highly skilled or have a thorough knowledge of the entire accounting system.

The use of special journals often reduces recording time. Special journal transactions of a given type need no routine explanations for each entry. Also, because special column headings are used, account titles need not be repeated as is necessary in the general journal.

Probably the most significant advantage of using special journals is the time saved in posting from the journals to the ledgers. When a general journal is used, each entry must be posted separately to the general ledger. The tabular arrangement of special journals, however, often permits all entries to a given account to be added and posted as a single aggregate posting. For instance, if we entered 1,000 sales transactions in a general journal, we would make 1,000 separate credit postings to the Sales account. If we use a sales journal, however, the amounts of the 1,000 sales will appear in one money column. Therefore, we may easily obtain a total and post it as one credit to the Sales account. The sales journal has saved us the time necessary for 999 postings to the Sales account. Clearly, as more transactions are involved, more posting time is saved.

The advantages of special journals will be apparent in the examples we use on the following pages.

SALES JOURNAL

The **sales journal** of the Excel Company, shown in Exhibit 6–2, lists all credit sales for June. The information for each sale comes from a copy of the related sales invoice. Note that the tabular form of the journal is specifically designed to record sales on account.

EXHIBIT 6–2

Sales Journal Page 1

Date		Invoice No.	Account	Post. Ref.	Amount
19XX					
June	1	101	J. Norton	✓	$ 200
	5	102	L. Ross	✓	100
	12	103	B. Travis	✓	1,000
	22	104	R. Douglas	✓	400
	29	105	M. Holton	✓	300
	30	106	E. Knight	✓	500
				12/40	$2,500

General Ledger

Accounts Receivable (12)

Debit		Credit
6/30	S1 2,500	

Sales (40)

Debit	Credit	
	6/30	S1 2,500

Accounts Receivable Subsidiary Ledger

R. Douglas

Debit			Credit
6/22	S1	400	

J. Norton

Debit			Credit
6/1	S1	200	

M. Holton

Debit			Credit
6/29	S1	300	

L. Ross

Debit			Credit
6/5	S1	100	

E. Knight

Debit			Credit
6/30	S1	500	

B. Travis

Debit			Credit
6/12	S1	1,000	

If the same credit terms are extended to all customers, we need not describe them in the sales journal. We assume this case in our illustration. When credit terms vary from customer to customer, a column can be added to the sales journal to explain the terms of each sale.

As we might expect, the posting of any journal to the general ledger must result in equal debits and credits. Also, for any posting to a control account in the general ledger, the same total amount must be posted to one or more related subsidiary ledger accounts. Exhibit 6–2 illustrates how to post the amounts in Excel Company's sales journal.

Usually, as entries are recorded in the sales journal throughout each month, they are also posted to the accounts receivable subsidiary ledger. A customer's account then reflects a transaction within a day or two of its occurrence. Consequently, the credit office can check a customer's account balance at times other than a billing date. Daily postings to the accounts receivable subsidiary ledger also allow for cycle billings (for example, billing customers whose names begin with different letters at different times of the month). The advantage of cycle billings is that statements of account can be mailed throughout the month rather than in one large group at the end of the month.

A check mark is placed in the posting reference column of the sales journal to indicate that the amount has been posted to the customer's account. At the end of the month, when all sales have been recorded and the sales journal has been totaled and ruled, the total sales figure is posted to the general ledger as a debit to the Accounts Receivable control account and as a credit to the Sales account. Note the double posting reference at the bottom of the posting reference column in the illustration; this indicates that Accounts Receivable is account No. 12 in the ledger and Sales is account No. 40. Posting of the sales journal is now complete.

Sales journals may accommodate additional information. For example, columns could be included for sales by department or by product, so that a breakdown of sales is available to management. Columns may also be provided for sales tax information, where necessary.

CASH RECEIPTS JOURNAL

Transactions involving cash receipts are recorded in a **cash receipts journal** similar to that shown in Exhibit 6–3. Because cash sales and collections from credit customers occur most often, this journal provides special columns for recording debits to Cash and to Sales Discounts and credits to Sales and Accounts Receivable. In addition, the columns on the right-hand side of the journal can be used for debits and credits to any other account.

Note that the entries on June 15 and June 30, debiting Cash and crediting Sales, record cash sales for a certain period. Actually, cash sales would be recorded daily rather than semimonthly, but we have recorded them only twice here for simplicity. The entry on June 8 records $196 received from J. Norton in payment of his June 1 purchase of $200, less the 2% cash discount taken. The entry debits

EXHIBIT 6–3

Cash Receipts Journal

Date		Description	Cash Debit	Sales Discounts Debit	Accounts Receivable Post. Ref.	Accounts Receivable Credit	Sales Credit	Other Accounts Account	Other Accounts Post. Ref.	Other Accounts Debit	Other Accounts Credit
19XX											
June	1	Sale of capital stock	$ 5,000					Capital Stock	(31)		$5,000
	8	J. Norton	196	$ 4	✓	$ 200					
	10	United Bank loan	3,000					Notes Payable	(23)		3,000
	15	Cash sales, June 1–15	2,000				$2,000				
	21	B. Travis	490	10	✓	1,000		Notes Receivable	(15)	$500	
	29	M. Holton	294	6	✓	300					
	30	Cash sales, June 16–30	2,500				2,500				
			$13,480	$20		$1,500	$4,500			$500	$8,000
			(10)	(42)		(12)	(40)			(X)	(X)

General Ledger

Cash (10)

Debit		Credit	
6/30 CR1	13,480		

Accounts Receivable (12)

Debit		Credit	
6/30 S1	2,500	6/30 CR1	1,500

Notes Receivable (15)

Debit		Credit	
6/21 CR1	500		

Sales Discounts (42)

Debit		Credit	
6/30 CR1	20		

Sales (40)

Debit		Credit	
		6/30 S1	2,500
		6/30 CR1	4,500

Capital Stock (31)

Debit		Credit	
		6/1 CR1	5,000

Notes Payable (23)

Debit		Credit	
		6/10 CR1	3,000

Accounts Receivable Subsidiary Ledger

R. Douglas

Debit		Credit	
6/22 S1	400		

M. Holton

Debit		Credit	
6/29 S1	300	6/29 CR1	300

E. Knight

Debit		Credit	
6/30 S1	500		

J. Norton

Debit		Credit	
6/1 S1	200	6/8 CR1	200

L. Ross

Debit		Credit	
6/5 S1	100		

B. Travis

Debit		Credit	
6/12 S1	1,000	6/21 CR1	1,000

Cash for $196, debits Sales Discounts for $4, and credits Accounts Receivable for $200. The entry for M. Holton on June 29 is similar. The June 21 entry illustrates the use of the Other Accounts debit column. Here, B. Travis settles her $1,000 billing of June 12 by giving a note for $500 of the debt and remitting $490 ($500 less the 2% discount) for the remainder. The debits are to Notes Receivable, $500, in the Other Accounts column; to Cash, $490; and to Sales Discounts, $10. The $1,000 credit to Accounts Receivable completes the entry. The entries on June 1 and June 10 represent cash received for the sale of capital stock and for a bank loan, respectively. In both cases, the Other Accounts credit column is used.

Before posting the cash receipts journal, we add each column and *balance* the journal to make sure that aggregate debits equal aggregate credits. (Note in our illustration, that $13,480 + $20 + $500 = $1,500 + $4,500 + $8,000.) The totals of the Cash, Sales Discounts, Accounts Receivable, and Sales columns are posted to the general ledger, as noted by the posting references below these columns. Also, the individual items in the Other Accounts columns are posted to the general ledger; the totals of the Other Accounts columns are used only to balance the journal and are not posted. Finally, the individual items in the Accounts Receivable column are posted to the customers' subsidiary ledger to keep this ledger in balance with the Accounts Receivable control account. The postings to the customers' accounts are indicated by a check mark (✓).

A **schedule** of the account balances in a subsidiary ledger is usually prepared at the end of each accounting period, to verify that the subsidiary ledger agrees with the related control account. The following schedule of Accounts Receivable for Excel Company indicates that the subsidiary ledger agrees with its control account in the general ledger.

Excel Company
Schedule of Accounts Receivable
June 30, 19XX

R. Douglas	$ 400
E. Knight	500
L. Ross	100
Total	$1,000

INVOICE REGISTER (PURCHASES JOURNAL)

To record purchases of merchandise on account, we can use a single-column journal similar to the sales journal considered earlier. (See Exhibit 6–2, page 218). Then, we would post each entry in the journal to the individual creditors' accounts in the accounts payable subsidiary ledger. At the end of the month, we would post the total of the amount column to the general ledger as a debit to the Purchases account and as a credit to the Accounts Payable control account.

Most businesses, however, keep a multicolumn journal to record all acquisitions on account, including such items as supplies and equipment, as well as merchandise. This journal may be called a **purchases journal**, but it is usually called an **invoice register**. Exhibit 6–4 illustrates an invoice register.

The illustration shows special columns for debits to Purchases, Office Supplies on Hand, and Store Supplies on Hand, as well as for credits to Accounts Payable. A column is also provided for debits to accounts for which no special column is available.

The amounts in the Accounts Payable column are posted to the accounts payable subsidiary ledger on a daily basis. A check mark in the posting reference column indicates that this has been done. At the end of the month, the columns of the register are totaled and the journal is balanced to ensure that total debits equal total credits. (In the example, $4,000 + $500 + $200 + $1,200 = $5,900.) The posting pattern for the invoice register is diagramed in Exhibit 6–4.

CASH DISBURSEMENTS JOURNAL

Exhibit 6–5 (page 224) shows the June **cash disbursements journal** for Excel Company after the related transactions have been recorded and the journal balanced and posted. Note the special columns for credits to Cash and Purchases Discounts, and for debits to Accounts Payable. Ordinarily these accounts will have the most entries. Also observe that, as in the cash receipts journal, the Other Accounts columns are available for recording debits or credits to any other accounts.

The June 2 entry in Exhibit 6–5 recorded a check for $2,800, which provided the cash needed to pay employees for the last part of May. The entries on June 12 and June 19 paid the accounts payable balances due Able, Inc., and Barr Company, less 2% and 1% cash discounts, respectively. Note that $1,000 of equipment was purchased on June 15 by giving $500 cash and a note payable for $500; the latter amount was recorded in the Other Accounts credit column. Also observe that the cash purchase of merchandise for $150 is recorded in the cash disbursements journal rather than in the purchases journal. The other entries in the journal are self-explanatory. Again, we have diagramed the posting format for the journal.

After both the invoice register and the cash disbursements journal have been posted, the Accounts Payable control account has a $3,300 balance ($5,900 − $2,600). This total agrees with the following schedule of creditors' accounts:

Excel Company
Schedule of Accounts Payable
June 30, 19XX

Echo Distributors	$ 400
Holt, Inc.	300
Stix Supply Company	1,200
Ward Company	1,400
	$3,300

EXHIBIT 6–4

Invoice Register

Page 1

Date		Account Credited	Post. Ref.	Accounts Payable Credit	Purchases Debit	Office Supplies on Hand Debit	Store Supplies on Hand Debit	Other Debits		
								Account	Post. Ref.	Amount
19XX										
June	2	Able, Inc.	✓	$ 700	$ 700					
	9	Barr Company	✓	1,900	1,900					
	14	Stix Supply Company	✓	1,200				Office Equipment	19	$1,200
	18	Ward Company	✓	1,400	1,400					
	25	Echo Distributors	✓	400		$400				
	30	Holt, Inc.	✓	300		100	$200			
				$5,900	$4,000	$500	$200			$1,200
				(21)	(50)	(16)	(17)			(X)

Accounts Payable Subsidiary Ledger

Able, Inc.

		6/2 IR1	700

Barr Company

		6/9 IR1	1,900

Echo Distributors

		6/25 IR1	400

Holt, Inc.

		6/30 IR1	300

Stix Supply Company

		6/14 IR1	1,200

Ward Company

		6/18 IR1	1,400

General Ledger

Purchases (50)

6/30 IR1	4,000		

Office Supplies on Hand (16)

6/30 IR1	500		

Store Supplies on Hand (17)

6/30 IR1	200		

Accounts Payable (21)

		6/30 IR1	5,900

Office Equipment (19)

6/14 IR1	1,200		

EXHIBIT 6–5

Cash Disbursements Journal

Page 1

Date		Ck. No.	Description	Cash Credit	Purchases Discounts Credit	Accounts Payable Post. Ref.	Accounts Payable Debit	Other Accounts Account	Other Accounts Post. Ref.	Other Accounts Debit	Other Accounts Credit
19XX											
June	2	101	Paid employees	$2,800				Wages Payable	27	$2,800	
	3	102	Paid June rent	600				Rent Expense	56	600	
	12	103	Able, Inc.	686	$14	✓	$ 700				
	15	104	Purchased equipment	500				Store Equipment	18	1,000	
								Notes Payable	23		$500
	19	105	Barr Company	1,881	19	✓	1,900				
	28	106	Purchased merchandise	150				Purchases	50	150	
	30	107	Insurance policy	120				Prepaid Insurance	14	120	
				$6,737	$33		$2,600			$4,670	$500
				(10)	(52)		(21)			(X)	(X)

General Ledger

Cash (10)

6/30 CR1	13,480	6/30 CD1	6,737

Accounts Payable (21)

6/30 CD1	2,600	6/30 IR1	5,900

Notes Payable (23)

		6/10 CR1	3,000
		6/15 CD1	500

Prepaid Insurance (14)

6/30 CD1	120		

Purchases (50)

6/28 CD1	150		
6/30 IR1	4,000		

Wages Payable (27)

6/2 CD1	2,800	5/31 Bal.	2,800

Store Equipment (18)

6/15 CD1	1,000		

Purchases Discounts (52)

		6/30 CD1	33

Rent Expense (56)

6/3 CD1	600		

Accounts Payable Subsidiary Ledger

Able, Inc.

6/12 CD1	700	6/2 IR1	700

Barr Company

6/19 CD1	1,900	6/9 IR1	1,900

Echo Distributors

		6/25 IR1	400

Holt, Inc.

		6/30 IR1	300

Stix Supply Company

		6/14 IR1	1,200

Ward Company

		6/18 IR1	1,400

USE OF THE GENERAL JOURNAL

When special journals are used, transactions that cannot be recorded appropriately in a special journal are recorded in the general journal. Examples include certain transactions involving notes receivable and notes payable, dispositions of plant assets, write-offs of uncollectible accounts, and merchandise returns. A special posting pattern is followed for posting to subsidiary ledgers. For example, Exhibit 6–6 demonstrates the treatment of purchases returns and allowances and sales returns and allowances. Note that whenever a posting is made to the Accounts Receivable control account or to the Accounts Payable control account from the general journal, a posting is also made to the related subsidiary ledger account. The latter posting is indicated by a check (✓) in the posting reference column.

THE VOUCHER SYSTEM

Many companies control expenditures with a method that is known as the **voucher system.** Under this system, a written authorization form, called a **voucher,** is initiated for every disbursement the firm makes. Before the designated responsible official approves the voucher for payment, different employees must perform several verification steps, including the following:

(1) Comparison of purchase requisition, purchase order, invoice, and receiving report for agreement of quantities, prices, types of goods, and credit terms.

(2) Verification of extensions and footings (additions) on invoice.

(3) Approval of account distribution (items to be debited).

EXHIBIT 6–6

General Journal

Page 1

Date		Description	Post. Ref.	Debit	Credit
19XX					
July	2	Sales Returns and Allowances	41	100	
		Accounts Receivable—R. Douglas	12/✓		100
		R. Douglas returned $100 merchandise for credit.			
	5	Accounts Payable—Ward Company	21/✓	70	
		Purchases Returns and Allowances	51		70
		Returned $70 merchandise to Ward Company for credit.			

Usually, each step in the verification process is listed on the face of the voucher, along with space for the signature or initials of the various employees responsible for accomplishing the procedures. The original copies of the purchase requisition, purchase order, invoice, and receiving report (if the item is merchandise) should be attached to the voucher. The voucher is then recorded in a book of original entry called the voucher register.

The Voucher Register

When a voucher system is used, the **voucher register** replaces the invoice register (or purchases journal) we discussed earlier. The voucher register provides columns for all items—merchandise, other assets, and services—for which payment must be made. Because all such items are recorded in the voucher register whether the transaction is for cash or on account, the voucher register also substitutes for part of the cash disbursements journal. Exhibit 6–7 shows one form of a simple voucher register.

Vouchers are entered in the voucher register in sequence. They should be prenumbered, of course, so they can be accounted for and referred to easily. All entries result in a credit to Vouchers Payable, which serves as the Accounts Payable control account for the company. The register has columns for those expense and asset accounts most frequently debited, such as Purchases, Transportation In, Office Supplies on Hand, and Delivery Expense. Debits to accounts for which columns are not provided are made in the Other Accounts section. A credit column also included in this section may be used for adjustments to vouchers and for recording purchases returns and allowances.

After vouchers have been entered in the voucher register, they are filed in an unpaid vouchers file in the order of required date of payment. In this way, the company will not miss discounts, and its credit standing will not be impaired. When a voucher is processed, the due date is usually written on the face of the voucher for filing convenience.

On the due date, the voucher is removed from the unpaid file and forwarded to the firm's disbursing officer for final approval of payment. After signing the voucher, the disbursing officer has a check drawn and mailed to the payee. The check number and payment date are recorded on the voucher, which is then returned to the accounting department. To safeguard against irregularities, the voucher should not be handled again by those who prepared it, and the underlying documents should be canceled or perforated by the disbursing officer before the voucher is returned to the accounting department.

After a voucher is paid, the check number and payment date are entered in the appropriate columns of the voucher register. The total unpaid ("open") vouchers at any time may be determined by adding the items in the Vouchers Payable column for which the date paid and check number columns contain no entries. This total should, of course, agree with the total of vouchers in the unpaid file and, at the end of the month, with the amount in the Vouchers Payable account.

After these procedures have been followed, the payment is recorded in a book of original entry called the check register. Finally, the vouchers are filed in numerical sequence in a paid vouchers file.

EXHIBIT 6–7

Voucher Register

Voucher No.	Date	Name	Date Paid	Check No.	Vouchers Payable Credit	Purchases Debit	Trans-portation In Debit	Office Supplies on Hand Debit	Delivery Expense Debit	Other Accounts			
										Account	Post. Ref.	Debit	Credit
121	12–1	Olson Company	12–9	528	$ 350	$ 350							
122	12–3	Tempo Freight	12–5	527	30		$ 30						
123	12–5	Horder, Inc.	12–15	531	120			$120					
•													
•													
•													
146	12–21	Jones Company	12–31	539	1,200					Office Equipment	15	$1,200	
147	12–27	Green Company			250	250							
148	12–30	Dee Delivery			25				$ 25				
					$18,500	$12,200	$850	$460	$320			$4,670	
					(32)	(55)	(56)	(16)	(68)			(X)	

The Check Register

In a voucher system, the **check register** replaces the cash disbursements journal. Because debits to asset, expense, and other accounts are made in the voucher register, only a few columns are required in the check register. We can see in Exhibit 6–8 that these consist of a debit column for vouchers payable and credit columns for purchases discounts and cash in bank. In addition, the check register has columns for the check number, date, and voucher number.

The check register is a company's chronological record of all check payments. Since checks are entered in the check register in numerical sequence, this record provides a convenient reference for payments when either the date or check number is known.

Under the voucher system, discounts may cause the amount of the check to differ from the gross amount of the voucher. For example, the entries for recording and paying the liability to the Olson Company for merchandise (voucher No. 121, dated December 1; see Exhibit 6–7) are summarized in general journal form as follows:

	Voucher Register				Check Register		
Dec. 1	Purchases	350		Dec. 9	Vouchers Payable	350	
	Vouchers Payable		350		Purchases Discounts		7
					Cash in Bank		343

Because both the gross and the net amounts of the liability are indicated on the voucher, this system should create no difficulty. Some companies, however, anticipate taking all discounts and prepare vouchers at the net amount. When this procedure is followed, only two money columns are needed in the check

EXHIBIT 6–8

Check Register

Check No.	Date	Payee	Voucher No.	Vouchers Payable Debit	Purchases Discounts Credit	Cash in Bank Credit
525	12–2	Able Corporation	120	$ 250		$ 250
526	12–4	Smith Company	119	500	$ 10	490
527	12–5	Tempo Freight	122	30		30
528	12–9	Olson Company	121	350	7	343
•						
•						
•						
539	12–31	Jones Company	146	1,200		1,200
				$16,700	$120	$16,580
				(32)	(57)	(11)

register—one for a debit to Vouchers Payable and one for a credit to Cash in Bank. If the company should miss a discount, an adjustment must be made in the voucher (or the original voucher must be canceled and a new one prepared). The bookkeeper must also record discounts lost in the general journal. (We explained the "net of discount" procedure and the Discounts Lost account in Chapter 5.) An alternative solution for handling lost discounts when the net price method is used is to provide a Discounts Lost column in the check register.

Recording Purchases Returns and Allowances

Companies usually handle purchases returns and allowances by canceling the original voucher and issuing a new one for the lower amount. Consider the following example.

Voucher No. 147 for $250, prepared for a merchandise purchase from the Green Company, is recorded in the voucher register on December 27. Assume that merchandise costing $50 is returned for credit and that a credit memo arrives on December 30. The original voucher for $250 is canceled and a reference made on it to a new voucher for $200. Furthermore, a note about the new voucher (No. 149) is made in the date paid column of the voucher register beside the entry for the original voucher. In recording the new voucher, the bookkeeper credits $200 in the Vouchers Payable column. In the Other Accounts columns, Vouchers Payable is debited for $250 and Purchases Returns and Allowances is credited for $50. The net effect of these recording procedures is a debit of $250 to Purchases, a credit of $200 to Vouchers Payable, and a credit of $50 to Purchases Returns and Allowances (see Exhibit 6–9).

Recording Partial Payments

When installment or other partial payments are made on invoices, a separate voucher is prepared for the amount of each check issued. If a single voucher has been prepared for an invoice and the firm later decides to pay in installments, the original voucher is canceled and new vouchers are prepared. The cancelation of the original voucher and the issuance of new vouchers can be recorded in the same way that purchases returns are recorded.

ELECTRONIC DATA PROCESSING (EDP)

We have described the manner in which data-processing functions are accomplished in a manual record-keeping system. Source documents are prepared and entered manually; classification and sorting are accomplished through columnar arrangements such as journals and ledgers; computations are often done manually; and storage is achieved by manual filing. Storage is in the form of ledger accounts, subsidiary ledgers, and various files. Retrieval and summarization are entirely manual. This type of record keeping is suitable for small firms with a limited number of transactions.

Computer Processing

Today, all large business firms—and even many small firms—employ computers in processing accounting data. Computers perform essentially the same record-

EXHIBIT 6–9

Voucher Register

Voucher No.	Date	Name	Date Paid	Check No.	Vouchers Payable Credit	Purchases … Debit	Other Accounts: Account	Other Accounts: Debit	Other Accounts: Credit
147	12–27	Green Company	Canceled, see # 149		$250	$250 …			
•									
•									
•									
149	12–30	Green Company			200		Vouchers Payable	$250	
							Purchases Returns and Allowances		$50

keeping functions as a manual system performs. Data from source documents—such as sales invoices, purchases invoices, and checks—are converted into an input mode that can be read by the computer. A set of instructions, called a **program**, processes this transaction data to prepare summaries (equivalent to journals), post to the general and subsidiary ledgers, determine balances, and prepare various reports, including financial statements.

The more expensive, high-capacity computers used by large firms are usually called **mainframe** computers. In recent years, advancing technology has reduced both the size and cost of computers, and small computers **(microcomputers)** are now used by many modest-sized firms. Both types of computers offer the advantages of speed in processing, fast retrieval of data, and less human intervention in processing. The basic difference between the two types of computers is that they are designed to handle information on differing scales. Mainframes are custom-designed to deal with large volumes of data and multi-user business applications (including almost simultaneous demands from many different users). Compared to microcomputers, mainframes can do more tasks faster, have better manufacturer support and service, and generally can accommodate a larger number of users at the same time. Microcomputers of today are really individual work stations. Their value is in their ability to stand alone and process and analyze data on a relatively low-volume scale. As discussed in the boxed insert (p. 232), however, both large and small firms can use microcomputers effectively.

Elements of an EDP System

An electronic data-processing system contains the following elements:

(1) A central processing unit (CPU), often called the computer, which performs arithmetic, logic, data storage while processing, and control.

(2) Associated peripheral equipment, including data-preparation, input, and output devices.

(3) Personnel and programs to provide instructions for the computer.

(4) Procedures that coordinate the preparation and processing of data and the reporting of results.

The computer and associated equipment are often referred to as the system's **hardware**, whereas the programs, written procedures, and other documentation for the system are called **software.** Exhibit 6–10 diagrams a typical system's hardware components, which are designed to perform input, processing, storage, and output functions.

INPUT Input devices transmit the instructions to the computer and the data on which the various steps will be carried out. The major input media are punched cards, magnetic tape, magnetic characters, disks, and terminals. The devices that transmit data include card readers, tape and disk drives, character recognition devices, and terminal keyboards.

In some cases, source document data are converted into machine-readable media by such data preparation devices as keypunch machines, key-to-tape devices, and key-to-disk devices. In other cases, source documents can be read directly.

MICROS IN ACCOUNTING

The computing and processing capabilities of a microcomputer approach those of the largest mainframe of only 20 years ago. Ever smaller, faster, cheaper, and easier to use, the microcomputer has enjoyed spectacular sales growth. Microcomputer sales are now running over two million units per year. And the business market—as opposed to the home or hobbyist market—is now accounting for the lion's share of sales.

The small business is an obviously large market. Long closed out from the advantages of computer processing by prohibitive cost, and the need for specially trained personnel, an increasing number of small businesses now find it feasible to use microcomputers to process their basic accounting transactions, to provide ready access to necessary operating data, and to handle correspondence.

But this use—essential as it is—is only the tip of the iceberg. Microcomputers expand the options available to businesses of all sizes. Using microcomputers, management can arrange data-processing facilities with much less concern for hardware costs. A micro might be used to automate activities that for reasons of cost or confidentiality are not suitable for processing on the company's mainframe. Typical business applications include the following:

(1) Forecasting, modeling, and financial statement consolidation are simplified by a microcomputer program known as an electronic spreadsheet. Once a model of relationships among a specific set of data has been established, an electronic spreadsheet program will automatically update all of the items affected by a change in one or more components. Some simple examples include the effect on the bottom line if sales double, if a division is sold, or if a union contract is settled at various possible levels.

(2) Data bases may be created for the use of individual executives or departments. Once a data base file has been created in a common format, the information can be retrieved, summarized, sorted, rearranged, or used to prepare special purpose reports. The publications department might use a microcomputer to keep its mailing list current. Personnel data, meeting calendars, information on contracts with potential customers, tickler files, almost any type of data an individual or department needs to file and find for later use could become the subject of a microcomputer application. Applications that may not be cost-effective on the company's mainframe computer might well be practicable on a micro.

(3) Graphics software available for microcomputers can reduce the time and cost associated with preparing illustrative charts for many types of presentations. The graphics capabilities of microcomputers are easily seen in the games run on home computers.

(4) Security portfolio analysis, trend analysis, and plotting are possible with specialized programs. Arrangements can be made to use the microcomputer as a terminal to access data bases of specialized information maintained by outsiders. The Source and CompuServe are such examples available in the United States. Prestel can be accessed in the United Kingdom, and so on.

Not so long ago corporate electronic data processing was highly centralized. The high cost of the computer carried with it the need to allocate service facilities principally to priority tasks. Relatively inexpensive machines with enough processing power were simply not available. That has changed—less expensive computers have put computer power into the hands of many individuals. The power of the computer is being dispersed throughout the business organization.

Microcomputers—ever smaller and less expensive machines—are accelerating this already widespread trend. Microcomputers will not replace the mainframe computer for large-scale applications, but microcomputers are becoming so inexpensive that it is quite reasonable to automate additional activities. Distributed data processing—the use of several different computers (and now including microcomputers) in different locations all connected by transmission facilities—is becoming more and more common.

From *Microcomputers: Their Use and Misuse in Your Business*, Price Waterhouse, 1983, pages 1–2.

EXHIBIT 6–10
Hardware Components of a Data-processing System

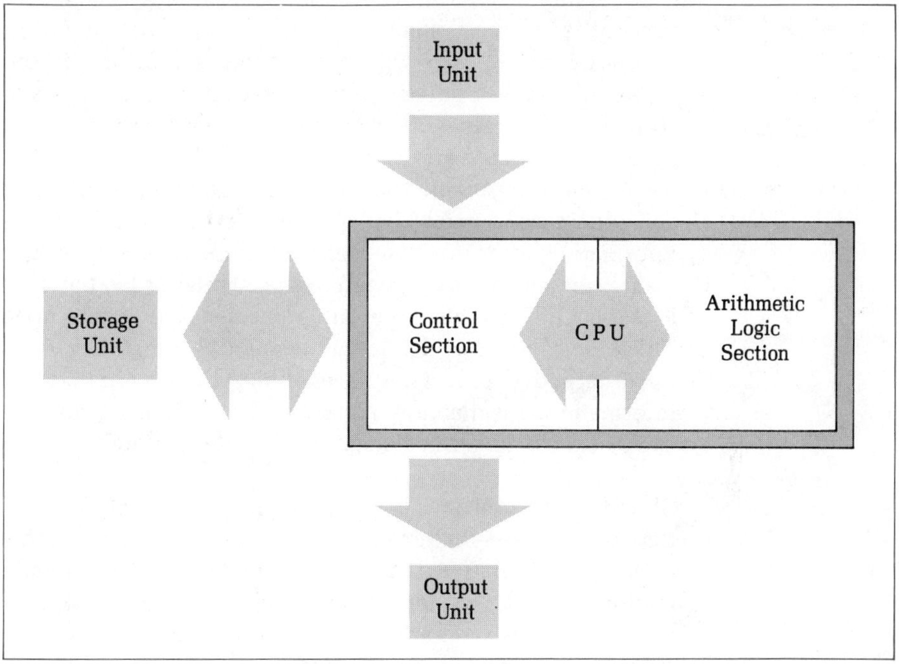

For example, in commercial banks, bank checks and deposit tickets with magnetic ink characters are processed directly by magnetic character readers. Data input by terminals is effected by a keyboard device. Terminal input, which is slow compared to other input devices, does not transmit large amounts of data. The use of terminals is expanding, however, because they permit direct interaction with the computer. Most terminals have a visual screen or printing capability for output. Thus, computer files can be interrogated and can print out answers in a short period of time. This aspect makes terminals useful in updating accounts when a transaction is occurring. Such processing is often referred to as **real time** processing.

PROCESSING AND STORAGE In an EDP system, practically all of the manipulative functions of record keeping—classifying, matching, calculating, and so on—are performed automatically by the central processing unit. These functions are directed by stored instructions—a program. The control unit interprets the instructions and directs the various processing operations. If required, fairly standardized programs may be obtained from equipment and software vendors. In other cases, special programs are written by programmers, who usually first work out a flowchart that shows the specific operations and decisions to be made by the computer and the sequence in which they should occur. The programmer then prepares the instructions in a special programming language, and the program is eventually stored in the computer to be called into use when needed.

All computers have temporary storage facilities that are used during processing. Permanent storage of files (such as accounts receivable master files) may be external, on media such as magnetic tapes or punched cards, when the storage capabilities of the system are limited. These files, in **off-line storage,** must be processed periodically with current transaction files in order to "update" the master files. When storage capacity within the system is adequate—most often, core or disk storage—direct access to master files is possible, and storage is **on-line.**

When storage is off-line, transaction data are usually accumulated for a period and processed in **batches** at specific intervals. Batch processing is useful when information needs do not demand the immediate processing of transactions. Data must be organized (sequenced) in a particular order, however, because all master files must be read when they are processed with a current batch of transactions. This type of processing is called **sequential** processing.

Interactive processing is possible with on-line storage. Here, master file information is available at random, and sequencing is not necessary. Transactions can be processed immediately, in any order, without batching.

OUTPUT Output devices provide either immediately usable information or results that can be stored for further processing and analysis. Because terminals perform both input and output, they are important in providing immediately usable information. Though less immediate, printers also provide useful output information that can be analyzed and interpreted. Output often is in the form of magnetic tapes or disks when further processing is contemplated. Punched cards create a storage problem and slow down processing, so they are falling into disuse as an output medium.

The various electronic data-processing systems can be quite detailed and complex, and an elaborate discussion of such systems is beyond the scope of this book. We hope, however, that this brief introduction will help you appreciate some of the basic concepts.

KEY POINTS TO REMEMBER

(1) A single *control* account for accounts receivable and another for accounts payable are used in the general ledger, while individual customer and creditor accounts are kept in separate *subsidiary* ledgers.

(2) When the journals have been posted at the end of the accounting period, subsidiary ledger balances are totaled. These totals should agree with control account balances.

(3) The use of special journals for credit sales and purchases (sales journal and invoice register, or purchases journal) and for cash transactions (cash receipts journal and cash disbursements journal) has the following advantages: (a) It permits a division of labor and often requires fewer skilled record keepers;

(b) it reduces the labor required to enter transactions; and (c) it requires fewer postings.

(4) Only sales of merchandise on account are recorded in the sales journal. Cash sales are recorded in the cash receipts journal.

(5) Purchases of any items on account are recorded in the invoice register (purchases journal). Acquisitions of any items for cash are recorded in the cash disbursements journal.

(6) Transactions that cannot be appropriately recorded in a special journal are recorded in the general journal.

(7) When master files (such as customer records) in an EDP system are stored off-line (outside the system), transactions are batched and processed *sequentially* to update records at specific time intervals.

(8) Master files that are stored on-line (within the system) can be updated at random without batching. This type of processing is sometimes called an *interactive* system.

SELF-TEST QUESTIONS

(Answers are at the end of this chapter.)

1. If a firm uses special journals, in which journal would the sale of merchandise for cash be recorded?
(a) Sales journal.
(b) Cash receipts journal.
(c) General journal.
(d) Cash disbursements journal.

2. A firm that uses special journals acquires merchandise for $500, giving a $500 note payable. In which journal would the transaction be recorded?
(a) Invoice register.
(b) Sales journal.
(c) Cash disbursements journal.
(d) General journal.

3. A special journal contains columns for Cash, Purchases Discounts, and Accounts Payable. This journal is a (an)
(a) Invoice register.
(b) Sales journal.
(c) Cash receipts journal.
(d) Cash disbursements journal.

4. Which of the following is true of a voucher system?
(a) All major expenditures, including cash transactions for payment of rent and utilities expense, would first be credited to Vouchers Payable before payment is made.
(b) Transactions are first entered in the check register, and later, when payment is made, in the voucher register.
(c) The check register replaces the cash receipts journal.
(d) The voucher register contains a debit column for Vouchers Payable.

5. In an EDP system, batch processing is a prevalent type of processing when
(a) Master file storage is off-line.

(b) Real time processing is desired.
(c) Interactive processing is used.
(d) Master files must be updated at the time a transaction occurs.

QUESTIONS

6–1 What is a control account? What is a subsidiary ledger?

6–2 Criticize the following statement: "When a debit entry is made to a control account, one or more credit entries of the same aggregate total must be posted to the related subsidiary ledger."

6–3 Compare the benefits of using special journals with using only a general journal.

6–4 Explain why transactions should be posted to the subsidiary ledgers more frequently than to the general ledger.

6–5 How would you prove that a special journal "balances"?

6–6 Identify the type of transactions that would be entered in the following:
(a) A sales journal.
(b) A (single-column) purchases journal.
(c) An invoice register.
(d) A cash receipts journal.
(e) A cash disbursements journal.

6–7 A sale made on account to James Rowe for $500 was recorded in a single-column sales journal on April 7. On April 9, Rowe returned $75 worth of merchandise for credit. Where should the seller record the entry for the sales return? What entry would be made and how would it be posted?

6–8 A $460 purchase of merchandise on account from R. Wood was properly recorded in the invoice register, but was posted as $480 to Wood's subsidiary ledger account. How might this error be discovered?

6–9 Indicate how the following errors might be discovered:
(a) The total of the Accounts Payable column of the invoice register was overstated by $40.
(b) The total of the single-column sales journal was understated by $70.

6–10 A retail merchandising firm recorded the sale of one of its delivery trucks in the sales journal. Why is this procedure incorrect?

6–11 Mark Ryan keeps an invoice register and employs the net method of recording merchandise purchases. Assume that he makes a $750 purchase from Lane Company, terms 2/10, n/30. Which journal columns would he use to record the purchase, and what debits and credits would be made?

6–12 Suppose that, in Question 6–11, Ryan made his remittance 20 days after the date of purchase. State the amounts involved, and describe how the payment would be recorded in a multicolumn cash disbursements journal.

6–13 What supporting documents are reviewed before a voucher for the purchase of merchandise is approved?

6–14 When a voucher system is used, what special journals are replaced by the voucher register and the check register?

6–15 What are the major differences between a mainframe computer and a microcomputer?

6–16 Compare the advantages of electronic accounting systems with manual data processing.

6–17 What are the major elements in an EDP system?

6–18 What is meant by *hardware* in an EDP system? What is meant by *software*?

6–19 What is meant by *real time* processing in a computer processing system?

6–20 Distinguish between *sequential processing* and *interactive processing* in EDP systems.

EXERCISES

Posting special journals and general journal

6–21 Listed below are headings for the columns into which dollar amounts are entered for four special journals and a general journal. (For the sales journal, the accounts to which the single column relates are shown.) For each column heading, show where the amounts in that column should be posted, using the space provided. Use the appropriate letter (or letters) from the following key.

Key

(a) Column total posted to general ledger
(b) Column detail posted to subsidiary ledger
(c) Column detail posted to general ledger

The correct answer for the first item is given.

Sales Journal

(1) Accounts Receivable ______a, b______
(2) Sales ____________

Invoice Register

(3) Accounts Payable ____________
(4) Purchases ____________
(5) Office Supplies on Hand ____________
(6) Store Supplies on Hand ____________
(7) Other Debits ____________

Cash Receipts Journal

(8) Cash ____________
(9) Sales Discounts ____________
(10) Accounts Receivable ____________
(11) Sales ____________
(12) Other Accounts—Debit ____________
(13) Other Accounts—Credit ____________

Cash Disbursements Journal

(14) Cash ____________
(15) Purchases Discounts ____________
(16) Accounts Payable ____________
(17) Other Accounts—Debit ____________
(18) Other Accounts—Credit ____________

General Journal

(19) Debit column ____________
(20) Credit column ____________

Recording transactions in journals

6–22 Weldon Suppliers uses the four special journals illustrated in this chapter and a general journal. In which journal(s) would each of the following kinds of transactions be recorded?

(a) Owner's cash investment in business.
(b) Sale of merchandise for cash.
(c) Sale of merchandise on account.
(d) Return of merchandise sold on account.
(e) Owner's withdrawal of cash.
(f) Owner's withdrawal of merchandise for personal use.
(g) Collections from customers on account.
(h) Purchase of merchandise for cash.
(i) Purchase of merchandise on account.
(j) Return of merchandise purchased on account.
(k) Purchase of office supplies on account.
(l) Purchase of equipment for cash and a note payable.

Designing sales and purchases journals

6–23 Tim Brown is a wholesaler of office supplies, vending equipment, and commercial cleaning supplies. His income statement shows sales, cost of goods sold, and gross profit amounts for each of his three product lines. He takes periodic inventories separately for each of these three departments. Design multicolumn sales and purchases journals to provide the information Brown wants.

Errors in recording and posting

6–24 In recording transactions and posting from various journals, the bookkeeper made the following errors. In each case, state how the error might be discovered or whether discovery is unlikely.
(a) In the single-column sales journal, this month's total was underfooted (underadded) by $200.
(b) The total of the purchases column in the multicolumn invoice (purchases) register, correctly footed as $8,590, was posted to the Purchases account as $8,950.
(c) In the single-column sales journal, a sale to L. Page was correctly recorded at $890, but posted to L. Pine's account as $980.
(d) A $500 remittance from B. Weeks was correctly recorded in the cash receipts journal, but the amount was inadvertently posted to B. Woods' account in the customers' ledger.
(e) A $380 payment to a creditor, R. Pike, was recorded in the cash disbursements journal as $280.

Recording transactions in journals

6–25 Describe how the following transactions would be recorded, indicating the journals used, the columns of each journal involved, and the way in which posting procedures are accomplished. Assume the four special journals illustrated in the chapter are available, together with a general journal.
(a) Purchased equipment for $3,000, giving $1,800 cash and a note payable for $1,200.
(b) Returned to a creditor merchandise purchased on account for $360.
(c) Owner contributed $600 cash and $8,000 in delivery equipment to the business.
(d) The business sold the delivery equipment in part (c) for $8,000 cash.
(e) Sent check for $70 to a customer, J. Kirby, who had overpaid his account by this amount.
(f) Paid $60 freight to Ideal Express Company on sale to a customer, B. Marsh. However, terms were F.O.B. shipping point, and customer was obligated to bear the freight cost.

PROBLEMS

Note: In the following problems, the journal forms used should correspond to those illustrated in the chapter.

Recording in the sales, cash receipts, and general journals

6–26 The Bennett Company makes all sales on terms of 2/10, n/30. Transactions for May involving sales, related returns and allowances, and cash receipts are shown below:

May 1 Sold merchandise on account to Mead, Inc., $600. Invoice No. 901.
2 Collected $600 from Bright, Inc., on account.
3 Sold merchandise for cash to R. Cameron, $70.
4 Issued credit memorandum to Mead, Inc., for return of $200 worth of merchandise purchased May 1.
7 Sold merchandise on account to Rollins Company, $750. Invoice No. 902.
8 Received remittance from Mead, Inc., for the amount owed, less discount.
11 Sold merchandise for cash to L. Weber, $140.
16 Sold merchandise to C. Murray, receiving a note receivable for $400. Invoice No. 903.
21 Collected a non-interest-bearing note receivable from T. Ash, $900.
22 Sold merchandise on account to Todd Company, $900. Invoice No. 904.
25 Owner C. Bennett contributed cash to the business, $4,000.
28 Rollins Company paid for merchandise purchased May 7.
29 Issued credit memorandum to Todd Company for $60 worth of merchandise purchased on May 22.
30 Sold merchandise on account to Link, Inc., $850. Invoice No. 905.

REQUIRED

(a) Record the given transactions in a single-column sales journal, a general journal, and a cash receipts journal.
(b) Open the following general ledger accounts and insert balances, when given: Cash (11) $8,000; Notes Receivable (15) $900; Accounts Receivable (16) $600; C. Bennett, Capital (31) $15,000; Sales (41); Sales Returns and Allowances (42); and Sales Discounts (43). Also open a subsidiary ledger with the following customer accounts: Bright, Inc., $600; Link, Inc.; Mead, Inc.; Rollins Company; and Todd Company. Only Bright's account had a beginning balance.
(c) Post all necessary amounts to the general and subsidiary ledger accounts.
(d) Prove that the Accounts Receivable control account agrees with the subsidiary ledger.

Recording in invoice register, cash disbursements journal, and general journal

6–27 Parker Company had the following transactions involving purchases, purchases returns and allowances, and cash payments during August. Parker records purchases at gross invoice price.

Aug. 1 Purchased merchandise on account from Webb Company, $900, terms 2/10, n/30, F.O.B. shipping point.
2 Paid Ace Trucking, Inc., freight bill for August 1 purchase, $60. Check No. 100.
5 Paid Gibson, Inc., on account, $400. Check No. 101.

Aug. 8 Purchased store supplies on account from Lake Supply Company, $320, terms n/30.
9 Owner M. Parker withdrew $700 cash from the business. Check No. 102.
11 Paid Webb Company for August 1 purchase. Check No. 103.
12 Returned $20 worth of the store supplies purchased from Lake Supply Company on August 8.
15 Purchased store supplies for cash from Shannon Wholesalers, $160. Check No. 104.
17 Purchased merchandise on account from Frost, Inc., $800, terms 2/10, n/30.
18 Paid Lake Supply Company in full of account. Check No. 105.
19 Returned $150 worth of merchandise to Frost, Inc., for credit.
22 Paid Frost, Inc., for August 17 purchase. Check No. 106.
24 Purchased office supplies on account from Gibson, Inc., $70, terms n/30.
26 Purchased delivery equipment from Keyes, Inc., $7,000, giving $2,000 cash and a note payable for $5,000. Check No. 107.
29 Purchased office equipment on account from Gibson, Inc., $450, terms n/30.
31 Purchased merchandise on account from Webb Company, $950, terms 2/10, n/30, F.O.B. shipping point.

REQUIRED

(a) Record these transactions in an invoice register (purchases journal), a cash disbursements journal, and a general journal.
(b) Open the following general ledger accounts and insert balances, when given: Cash (11) $9,000; Office Supplies on Hand (15) $650; Store Supplies on Hand (16) $300; Delivery Equipment (17) $8,000; Office Equipment (18) $3,500; Notes Payable (21); Accounts Payable (22) $400; M. Parker, Drawing (32); Purchases (51); Purchases Returns and Allowances (52); Purchases Discounts (53); and Transportation In (54). Also open a subsidiary ledger with the following creditor accounts: Frost, Inc.; Gibson, Inc., $400; Lake Supply Company; and Webb Company. Only the Gibson account had a beginning balance.
(c) Post all necessary amounts to the general and subsidiary ledger accounts.
(d) Prove that the Accounts Payable control account agrees with the subsidiary ledger.

Recording in cash receipts and cash disbursements journals

6–28 Brooks Company began business on April 1. The purchases and sales made on account during April have been recorded in the sales and purchases journals below. Purchases are recorded at gross invoice price.

Sales Journal Page 1

Date		Customer	Terms	Post. Ref.	Amount
19XX					
Apr.	5	Lund, Inc.	2/10, n/30		$600
	10	Allen Wholesalers	2/10, n/30		500
	18	Poole, Inc.	2/10, n/30		800
	21	Allen Wholesalers	2/10, n/30		400
	28	R. Hillyer	2/10, n/30		900

Purchases Journal Page 1

Date		Creditor	Terms	Post. Ref.	Amount
19XX					
Apr.	2	Forbes Company	2/15, n/30		$1,800
	4	Winter Corporation	n/30		850
	12	Sage, Inc.	2/10, n/30		400
	22	Forbes Company	2/15, n/30		750
	29	Sheridan, Inc.	1/10, n/30		300

The April transactions to be recorded in the cash receipts and cash disbursements journals are the following:

Apr. 1 Brooks invested $6,000 cash and $12,000 worth of office equipment in the firm, a sole proprietorship. (Use two lines for entry.)
2 Paid April rent, $820. Check No. 101.
5 Received rental income for space sublet to Lord Realty, $320.
7 Purchased office supplies for cash, $480. Check No. 102.
14 Paid Forbes Company for April 2 purchase. Check No. 103.
15 Received $588 from Lund, Inc., in payment of account.
18 Received $490 from Allen Wholesalers in payment of account.
21 Paid Sage, Inc., for April 12 purchase. Check No. 104.
30 Paid office clerk's salary, $1,500. Check No. 105.

REQUIRED
(a) Record the April transactions in cash receipts and cash disbursements journals.
(b) Total and balance the cash receipts and cash disbursements journals.

Recording in special journals, posting, and taking a trial balance

6–29 Trevor Distributors, which sells on terms of 2/10, n/30, had the following transactions during October, the first month of the current fiscal year.

Oct. 1 Paid October rent, $400. Check No. 200.
2 Paid Ryan, Inc., $833 for merchandise purchased September 28. A 2% discount was taken. Check No. 201.
3 Issued checks of $400 to Blake Company and $650 to Kidd Suppliers, both creditors. No discount was taken on these amounts. Checks No. 202 and No. 203.
7 Sold merchandise on account to Landon, Inc., $350. Invoice No. 470.
8 Received checks in payment of accounts as follows: Landon, Inc., $294; Tyson Company, $700; and Warden Company, $196. Discounts had been taken by Landon, Inc., and Warden Company.
9 Sold merchandise on account to Tyson Company, $600. Invoice No. 471.
10 Issued check for freight to West Freight, Inc., on Tyson Company shipment, $60, terms F.O.B. destination. Check No. 204.
11 Issued credit memorandum to Tyson Company for merchandise returned, $100.
14 Purchased merchandise on account from Blake Company, $900, terms 1/10, n/60.
15 Issued check for freight to Wade Transport on purchase from Blake Company, $45, terms F.O.B. shipping point. Check No. 205.

Oct. 15 Paid office salaries, $1,400. Checks No. 206 and No. 207 for $700 each for R. Mann and L. Riggs.

16 Received check in payment of Ferris Company account, $550.

17 Received check from Landon, Inc., in payment of October 7 shipment, $343.

18 Purchased store supplies, $80; equipment, $500; and office supplies, $60, on account from Kidd Suppliers, terms n/30.

21 Paid Blake Company for October 14 purchase, $891. Check No. 208.

22 Paid miscellaneous expenses, $35. Check No. 209.

24 Issued check to B. Trevor for a personal withdrawal, $650. Check No. 210.

28 Purchased merchandise on account from Ryan, Inc., $1,200, terms 2/15, n/60.

29 Returned $200 worth of merchandise to Ryan, Inc., for credit.

30 Sold merchandise on account to Warden Company, $475. Invoice No. 472.

31 Sold merchandise for cash to J. Malone, $150.

31 Collected miscellaneous income from Acme Advertising for use of billboard space, $250.

REQUIRED

(a) Open the following general ledger accounts, and enter the indicated October 1 balances. Number the accounts as shown.

Cash (11)	$ 4,500	Sales Discounts (43)
Accounts Receivable (12)	1,750	Miscellaneous Income (44)
Inventory (14)	16,000	Purchases (51)
Store Supplies on Hand (15)	500	Purchases Returns and Allowances (52)
Office Supplies on Hand (16)	250	Purchases Discounts (53)
Equipment (17)	22,000	Transportation In (54)
Accumulated Depreciation (18)	(5,000)	Rent Expense (61)
Accounts Payable (21)	(1,900)	Salaries Expense (62)
B. Trevor, Capital (31)	(38,100)	Transportation Out (63)
B. Trevor, Drawing (32)		Miscellaneous Expense (64)
Sales (41)		
Sales Returns and Allowances (42)		

(b) Open the following accounts in the subsidiary ledgers and enter the October 1 balances:

Customers		Creditors	
Ferris Company	$ 550	Blake Company	$ 400
Landon, Inc.	300	Kidd Suppliers	650
Tyson Company	700	Ryan, Inc.	850
Warden Company	200		
	$1,750		$1,900

(c) Record the October transactions in the four special journals (sales, invoice register, cash receipts, and cash disbursements) and in the general journal. Trevor records purchases at gross invoice price.

(d) Using the forms prepared in parts (a) and (b), post all necessary amounts to the general ledger and subsidiary ledgers from the journals. Postings should be made to the subsidiary ledgers throughout the month.

(e) Prepare a trial balance of the general ledger.
(f) Prepare a schedule of accounts receivable and a schedule of accounts payable to prove control account balances.

Posting special journals and preparing a trial balance

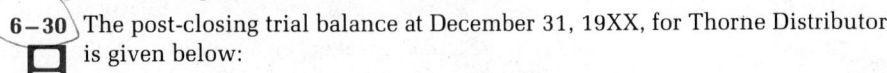

6–30 The post-closing trial balance at December 31, 19XX, for Thorne Distributors is given below:

Thorne Distributors
Post-closing Trial Balance
December 31, 19XX

	Debit	Credit
Cash	$ 9,500	
Accounts Receivable	17,600	
Inventory	53,500	
Office Supplies on Hand	580	
Store Supplies on Hand	320	
Office Equipment	10,000	
Accumulated Depreciation		$ 3,500
Accounts Payable		24,300
D. Thorne, Capital		63,700
	$91,500	$91,500

At the end of January, 19X1, the totals of the firm's special journals, before posting, are as follows:

Invoice Register:	
Accounts Payable	$67,450
Purchases	63,200
Office Supplies on Hand	400
Store Supplies on Hand	650
Other Accounts:	
Office Equipment (Dr.)	3,200

Sales Journal	$81,500
Cash Receipts Journal:	
Cash	80,290
Sales Discounts	1,140
Accounts Receivable	62,600
Sales	12,830
Other Accounts:	
D. Thorne, Capital (Cr.)	6,000

Cash Disbursements Journal:	
Cash	56,180
Purchases Discounts	840
Accounts Payable	52,360
Other Accounts:	
Rent Expense (Dr.)	1,500
Advertising Expense (Dr.)	760
Salaries Expense (Dr.)	2,400

REQUIRED
Prepare an unadjusted trial balance for Thorne Distributors at January 31. *Note*: A convenient method is to use a six-column worksheet, placing the post-closing trial balance in the first two columns and listing the account titles of the temporary accounts below. The next two columns are used to record the debits and credits from the special journals, while the last two columns are used for the unadjusted trial balance at January 31.

Recording in a voucher register and check register

6–31 Vanguard, Inc., controls its disbursements through a voucher system. The following transactions occurred during June of the current year. The firm records merchandise purchases at gross invoice price.

June 1 Recorded voucher No. 601 payable to White Realty for June rent, $950.
2 Recorded voucher No. 602 payable to Harmon Supply, Inc., for $850 worth of merchandise purchased, terms 2/10, n/30.
3 Issued check No. 702 in payment of voucher No. 601.
5 Recorded voucher No. 603 payable to Rockton Sales, Inc., for $620 worth of office supplies, terms n/30.
7 Recorded voucher No. 604 payable to Barton Freight Company for transportation in on merchandise purchased, $40, terms F.O.B. shipping point.
10 Issued check No. 703 in payment of voucher No. 602, less discount.
12 Issued check No. 704 in payment of voucher No. 603.
15 Recorded voucher No. 605 payable to Rowe, Inc., for equipment, $1,800, terms 2/20, n/60. (Make voucher for net amount.)
18 Issued check No. 705 in payment of voucher No. 604.
22 Recorded voucher No. 606 payable to Poole, Inc., for merchandise purchased, $760, terms 2/10, n/30.
26 Recorded voucher No. 607 payable to United Gas and Light Company for utilities expense, $216.
26 Issued check No. 706 in payment of voucher No. 607.
28 Received credit memo for $60 from Poole, Inc., for merchandise returned to it. Canceled original voucher (No. 606) and issued voucher No. 608.
28 Issued check No. 707 in payment of voucher No. 605.
30 Recorded voucher No. 609 payable to Stern, Inc., for merchandise purchased, $625, terms 2/10, n/30.

REQUIRED
(a) Record Vanguard's transactions in a voucher register and check register.
(b) Total the voucher register and the check register amount columns, and post the appropriate amounts to the following accounts:

Cash in Bank (11)	Purchases Returns and Allowances (52)
Office Supplies on Hand (17)	Purchases Discounts (53)
Equipment (18)	Transportation In (54)
Vouchers Payable (21)	Rent Expense (61)
Purchases (51)	Utilities Expense (62)

(c) List the unpaid vouchers, and compare the total with the balance of the Vouchers Payable account.

Recording in a voucher register and check register

6–32 The Conroy Company, which employs a voucher system, had the following transactions during July:

July 1 Recorded voucher No. 701 payable to J. West for $800 worth of merchandise purchased, terms 2/10, n/30.
2 Recorded voucher No. 702 payable to Walker Rentals for July rent, $725.
3 Issued check No. 803 in payment of voucher No. 702.

July 9 Recorded voucher No. 703 payable to Ross Express, Inc., for transportation in, $55, terms F.O.B. shipping point.
10 Issued check No. 804 in payment of voucher No. 701.
11 Issued check No. 805 in payment of voucher No. 703.
15 Recorded voucher No. 704 payable to Stewart Company for $675 worth of merchandise, terms n/30.
20 Received credit memo from Stewart Company for $250 worth of the merchandise recorded on voucher No. 704. Canceled voucher No. 704 and issued voucher No. 705.

REQUIRED
Prepare a voucher register and check register, and record the transactions for the Conroy Company. The firm records merchandise purchases at gross invoice price.

ALTERNATE PROBLEMS

Note: In the following problems, the journal forms used should correspond to those illustrated in the chapter.

Recording in the sales, cash receipts, and general journals

6–26A The Wilson Sales Company makes all sales on terms of 2/10, n/30. Transactions for May involving sales, related returns and allowances, and cash receipts are shown below:

May 1 Collected $700 from L. Wright on account.
1 Sold merchandise on account to Byrd, Inc., $450. Invoice No. 201.
4 Sold merchandise for cash to M. Diaz, $80.
5 Issued credit memorandum to Byrd, Inc., for return of $150 worth of merchandise purchased May 1.
8 Sold merchandise on account to Knight Company, $550. Invoice No. 202.
10 Received remittance from Byrd, Inc., for the amount owed, less discount.
12 Sold merchandise for cash to L. James, $65.
15 Sold merchandise to F. Sands, receiving a note receivable for $800. Invoice No. 203.
18 Collected a non-interest-bearing note receivable from S. Lowe, $500.
20 Owner T. Wilson contributed cash to the business, $2,500.
24 Sold merchandise on account to Gerard Company, $380. Invoice No. 204.
25 Knight Company paid for merchandise purchased on May 8.
26 Issued credit memorandum to Gerard Company for $60 merchandise purchased on May 24.
30 Sold merchandise on account to D. Racine, Inc., $560. Invoice No. 205.

REQUIRED
(a) Record the given transactions in a single-column sales journal, a general journal, and a cash receipts journal.
(b) Open the following general ledger accounts and insert balances, when given: Cash (11) $5,600; Notes Receivable (15) $500; Accounts Receivable (16) $700; T. Wilson, Capital (31) $16,500; Sales (41); Sales Returns and

Allowances (42); Sales Discounts (43). Also open a subsidiary ledger with the following customer accounts: Byrd, Inc.; Gerard Company; Knight Company; D. Racine, Inc.; and L. Wright, $700. Only L. Wright's account had a beginning balance.

(c) Post all necessary amounts to the general ledger and subsidiary ledger accounts.

(d) Prove that the Accounts Receivable control account agrees with the subsidiary ledger.

Recording in invoice register, cash disbursements journal, and general journal

6–27A Crown Distributors had the following transactions involving purchases, purchases returns and allowances, and cash payments during June. Crown records purchases at gross invoice price.

June 1 Paid Abbott, Inc., on account, $380. Check No. 100.
1 Purchased merchandise on account from Green Company, $550, terms 2/10, n/30, F.O.B. shipping point.
2 Paid freight bill to West Delivery for June 1 purchase, $30. Check No. 101.
5 Purchased store supplies on account from Burns Supply Company, $270, terms n/30.
7 Owner R. Crown withdrew cash from the business, $450. Check No. 102.
8 Purchased store supplies for cash from Dale Wholesalers, $90. Check No. 103.
10 Paid Green Company amount due for June 1 purchase. Check No. 104.
11 Returned $40 worth of the store supplies purchased from Burns Supply Company on June 5.
15 Purchased merchandise on account from Riley, Inc., $750, terms 1/10, n/30.
16 Paid Burns Supply Company in full of account. Check No. 105.
18 Returned $150 worth of merchandise to Riley, Inc., for credit.
20 Paid Riley, Inc., for June 15 purchase. Check No. 106.
21 Purchased office supplies on account from Abbott, Inc., $175, terms n/30.
25 Purchased delivery equipment from Rider, Inc., $5,000, giving $2,000 cash and a note payable for $3,000. Check No. 107.
30 Purchased office equipment on account from Abbott, Inc., $325, terms n/30.
30 Purchased merchandise on account from Green Company, $645, terms 2/10, n/30, F.O.B. shipping point.

REQUIRED

(a) Record these transactions in an invoice register (purchases journal), a cash disbursements journal, and a general journal.

(b) Open the following general ledger accounts and insert balances, when given: Cash (11) $6,500; Office Supplies on Hand (15) $280; Store Supplies on Hand (16) $320; Delivery Equipment (17) $7,000; Office Equipment (18) $2,400; Notes Payable (21); Accounts Payable (22) $380; R. Crown, Drawing (32); Purchases (51); Purchases Returns and Allowances (52); Purchases Discounts (53); and Transportation In (54). Also open a subsidiary ledger with the following creditor accounts: Abbott, Inc., $380; Burns Supply Company; Green Company; and Riley, Inc. Only the Abbott, Inc., account had a beginning balance.

(c) Post all necessary amounts to the general ledger and subsidiary ledger accounts.
(d) Prove that the Accounts Payable control account agrees with the subsidiary creditors' ledger.

Recording in cash receipts and cash disbursements journals

6–28A Douglas Wholesalers began business on May 1. The purchases and sales made on account during May have been recorded in the sales and purchases journals below. Purchases are recorded at gross invoice price.

Sales Journal Page 1

Date		Customer	Terms	Post. Ref.	Amount
19XX					
May	6	Ward, Inc.	2/10, n/30		$400
	9	Post and Company	2/10, n/30		550
	17	S. M. Cullen	2/10, n/30		850
	22	Post and Company	2/10, n/30		300
	25	M. B. Wagner	2/10, n/30		200

Purchases Journal Page 1

Date		Creditor	Terms	Post. Ref.	Amount
19XX					
May	3	G. Fowler	2/10, n/30		$900
	5	Bowen Corporation	n/30		350
	16	Fastline, Inc.	2/10, n/30		600
	25	G. Fowler	n/30		250
	30	M. Hale	1/10, n/30		500

The May transactions to be recorded in the cash receipts and cash disbursements journals are the following:

May 1 B. Douglas invested $20,000 cash and $8,000 worth of office equipment in the firm, a sole proprietorship. (Use two lines for entry.)
2 Paid May rent, $850. Check No. 101.
3 Received rental income for space sublet to Ideal Glass, Inc., $350.
4 Purchased office supplies for cash, $420. Check No. 102.
10 Paid G. Fowler for May 3 purchase. Check No. 103.
16 Received $392 from Ward, Inc., in payment of account.
19 Received $539 from Post and Company in payment of account.
26 Paid Fastline, Inc., for May 16 purchase. Check No. 104.
31 Paid office clerk's salary, $925. Check No. 105.
31 Cash sales were $384.

REQUIRED
(a) Record the May transactions in cash receipts and cash disbursements journals.
(b) Total and balance the cash receipts and cash disbursements journals.

Recording in special journals, posting, and taking a trial balance

6–29A Kirk Wholesalers, which sells on terms of 2/10, n/30, had the following transactions during January, the first month of the current accounting year.

Jan. 2 Paid Slater, Inc., for merchandise purchased December 28, $686. Check No. 125. Kirk took a 2% discount.

3 Paid January rent, $750. Check No. 126.

5 Issued checks of $240 to Boyd Company and $380 to Gorman Suppliers, both creditors. No discount was taken on these amounts. Checks No. 127 and No. 128.

5 Sold merchandise on account to Jason, Inc., $550. Invoice No. 251.

6 Received checks in payment of accounts as follows: Jason, Inc., $392; Martin Company, $520; and Richards Distributors, $294. Discounts had been taken by Jason, Inc., and Richards Distributors.

7 Sold merchandise on account to Martin Company, $260. Invoice No. 252.

8 Issued check for freight to Starline, Inc., on Martin Company shipment, $40, terms F.O.B. destination. Check No. 129.

9 Issued credit memorandum to Martin Company for merchandise returned, $60.

12 Purchased merchandise on account from Boyd Company, $800, terms 1/10, n/60.

13 Issued check for freight to Dorn Freightways on purchase from Boyd Company, $36, terms F.O.B. shipping point. Check No. 130.

14 Received check in payment of Busby Company account, $370.

15 Received check from Jason, Inc., in payment of January 5 shipment, $539.

15 Paid office salaries, $1,500. Checks No. 131 and No. 132 for $750 each for R. Fraser and S. Vitale.

19 Purchased store supplies, $375; equipment, $850; and office supplies, $120, on account from Gorman Suppliers, terms n/30.

20 Paid Boyd Company for January 12 purchase, $792. Check No. 133.

21 Paid miscellaneous expense, $85. Check No. 134.

22 Owner C. Kirk made a personal withdrawal, $600. Check No. 135.

26 Purchased merchandise on account from Slater, Inc., $490, terms 2/15, n/60.

27 Returned $70 worth of merchandise to Slater, Inc., for credit.

28 Sold merchandise on account to Richards Distributors, $675. Invoice No. 253.

30 Sold merchandise for cash to L. Best, $85.

30 Collected miscellaneous income from Ace Advertising for use of billboard space, $125.

REQUIRED

(a) Open the following general ledger accounts, and enter the indicated January 1 balances. Number the accounts as shown.

Cash (11)	$ 8,700	Sales Discounts (43)
Accounts Receivable (12)	1,590	Miscellaneous Income (44)
Inventory (14)	14,500	Purchases (51)
Store Supplies on Hand (15)	430	Purchases Returns and Allowances (52)
Office Supplies on Hand (16)	300	
Equipment (17)	20,000	Purchases Discounts (53)

Accumulated Depreciation (18)	(4,000)	Transportation In (54)
Accounts Payable (21)	(1,320)	Rent Expense (61)
C. Kirk, Capital (31)	(40,200)	Salaries Expense (62)
C. Kirk, Drawing (32)		Transportation Out (63)
Sales (41)		Miscellaneous Expense (64)
Sales Returns and Allowances (42)		

(b) Open the following accounts in the subsidiary ledgers and enter the January 1 balances:

Customers		Creditors	
Busby Company	$ 370	Boyd Company	$ 240
Jason, Inc.	400	Gorman Suppliers	380
Martin Company	520	Slater, Inc.	700
Richards Distributors	300		
	$1,590		$1,320

(c) Record the January transactions in the four special journals (sales, invoice register, cash receipts, and cash disbursements) and in the general journal. Kirk records purchases at gross invoice price.
(d) Using the forms prepared in parts (a) and (b), post all necessary amounts to the general ledger and subsidiary ledgers from the journals. Postings should be made to the subsidiary ledgers throughout the month.
(e) Prepare a trial balance of the general ledger.
(f) Prepare a schedule of accounts receivable and a schedule of accounts payable to prove control account balances.

Recording in a voucher register and check register

6–31A Vulcan, Inc., controls its disbursements through a voucher system. The following transactions occurred during April of the current year. The firm records merchandise purchases at gross invoice price.

Apr. 1 Recorded voucher No. 401 payable to Dalton Realty for April rent, $950.
2 Recorded voucher No. 402 payable to Sherman Service Corporation for $650 worth of merchandise purchased, terms 2/10, n/30.
2 Issued check No. 506 in payment of voucher No. 401.
5 Recorded voucher No. 403 payable to Prairie Sales, Inc., for $365 worth of office supplies, terms n/30.
7 Recorded voucher No. 404 payable to Pronto Freight Lines, Inc., for freight in on merchandise purchased, $65, terms F.O.B. shipping point.
10 Issued check No. 507 in payment of voucher No. 402, less discount.
12 Issued check No. 508 in payment of voucher No. 403.
14 Recorded voucher No. 405 payable to Elmore Equipment Sales, Inc., for equipment, $1,800, terms 2/15, n/60. (Make voucher for net amount.)
18 Issued check No. 509 in payment of voucher No. 404.
21 Recorded voucher No. 406 payable to Cross, Inc., for merchandise purchased, $475, terms 2/10, n/30.
25 Recorded voucher No. 407 payable to Citizen's Gas and Light Company for utilities expense, $132.
26 Issued check No. 510 in payment of voucher No. 407.

Apr. 28 Received credit memo for $75 from Cross, Inc., for merchandise returned to it. Canceled original voucher (No. 406) and issued voucher No. 408.

28 Issued check No. 511 in payment of voucher No. 405.

30 Recorded voucher No. 409 payable to Logan, Inc., for merchandise, $525, terms 2/10, n/30.

REQUIRED

(a) Record Vulcan's transactions in a voucher register and check register.

(b) Total the voucher register and the check register amount columns, and post the appropriate amounts to the following accounts:

Cash in Bank (11)	Purchases Returns and Allowances (52)
Office Supplies on Hand (17)	Purchases Discounts (53)
Equipment (18)	Transportation In (54)
Vouchers Payable (21)	Rent Expense (61)
Purchases (51)	Utilities Expense (62)

(c) List the unpaid vouchers and compare the total with the balance of the Vouchers Payable account.

BUSINESS DECISION PROBLEM

Heritage, Inc., sells carpeting, lighting fixtures, wall paneling, and related supplies to the retail market. Most sales are on account; however, there are some cash sales over the counter for do-it-yourself customers.

Manager R. Drummond asks you to provide special journals for the firm's accounting system. After discussing the matter with Drummond, you decide to design journals for four departments: Carpeting, Lighting, Paneling, and Supplies. Drummond wants the income statement to show sales, cost of goods sold, and gross profit for each of the four departments. Merchandise inventory for the four departments will be taken separately.

Practically all the firm's purchases are merchandise for resale. Most cash disbursements are payments on account to suppliers, freight on purchases (most purchases are made on terms F.O.B. shipping point), and for advertising expense. Spot advertising in local newspapers and television is paid when bills are received; no accounts payable are kept for these expenses. Employees are paid monthly.

REQUIRED

List the column headings (from left to right) that you would provide in the (a) sales journal, (b) invoice register, (c) cash receipts journal, and (d) cash disbursements journal for the four departments in Heritage, Inc.

ANSWERS TO SELF-TEST QUESTIONS

1. (b) 2. (d) 3. (d) 4. (a) 5. (a)

COMPREHENSIVE PROBLEM—PART 1

This comprehensive problem, which utilizes financial data of actual companies, consists of two parts. The first part focuses on balance sheet data while the second part utilizes income statement data. The two parts use data from different companies and are not related.

(I) BALANCE SHEET

Following is a list, in alphabetical order, of the items included in a recent balance sheet of an actual company. The balance sheet date is the company's fiscal year-end, February 2, 1985.

Item	Amount (in thousands)
Accounts Payable	$103,010
Accounts Receivable	45,912
Accrued Expenses (short-term)	47,719
Accumulated Depreciation	112,705
Cash and Equivalents	7,494
Common Stock	29,807
Income Taxes Payable	9,378
Inventories	190,014
Investment in Subsidiary Corporation (long-term)	23,672
Long-term Debt	60,139
Other Current Liabilities	29,109
Other Long-term Assets	19,476
Other Long-term Liabilities	42,394
Other Stockholders' Equity	22,466
Prepaid Expenses	13,056
Property and Equipment	380,233
Retained Earnings	223,130

REQUIRED

(a) Prepare a classified balance sheet for this company. (Omit the company's name from the heading.)

(b) Following is a brief description of three companies:

Emery Air Freight Corporation—A firm providing air courier and air cargo services to cities around the world.

The Limited, Inc.—A nationwide retail firm specializing in women's apparel.

Kelly Services, Inc.—A firm providing temporary help services to a diversified group of customers.

The balance sheet prepared in part (a) is the balance sheet for one of these three firms. Whose balance sheet is it? Briefly explain.

(II) INCOME STATEMENT

One of the most unusual and interesting companies listed on the New York Stock Exchange is Perry Drug Stores, Inc. The firm, which had about $150 million in total assets and about $370 million in sales in 1984, is headquartered in Pontiac, Michigan, and operates 146 drug stores and 110 auto parts outlets in eight midwestern states.

The firm's income statement data, taken from its annual reports for 1982, 1983, and 1984, are given below:

	1984	1983	1982
Sales			
Drugstore	$291,189,614*	$245,418,621	$215,865,078
Automotive	80,700,907	40,083,836	28,407,096
Total Sales	$371,890,521	$285,502,457	$244,272,174
Cost of Goods Sold	256,293,344	200,155,781	171,563,995
Gross Profit	$115,597,177	$ 85,346,676	$ 72,708,179
Operating Expenses	$101,255,916	$ 74,908,244	$ 65,469,314
Interest Expense	2,078,263	2,802,212	2,842,745
Total Expenses	$103,334,179	$ 77,710,456	$ 68,312,059
Income before Income Tax	$ 12,262,998	$ 7,636,220	$ 4,396,120
Income Tax Expense	4,613,000	3,091,000	1,528,000
Net Income	$ 7,649,998	$ 4,545,220	$ 2,868,120

*Includes $1,605,448 sales of health-care division, begun by the firm in 1984.

REQUIRED

(a) Calculate the firm's gross profit percentage for each of the three years and comment on the change in this percentage between 1982 and 1984.

(b) What percent of total sales each year consisted of drugstore sales? Automotive parts sales? Which division is apparently growing faster?

(c) Based on your answers to (a) and (b), which division, drugstore or automotive parts, has the higher average mark-up percentage on sales?

(d) For each year, calculate the following as a percent of total sales: operating expenses, interest expense, income before income tax, and net income. What effect have changes in operating expenses and interest expense had on the return on sales before taxes?

Part Two

Accounting for Assets and Current Liabilities

7

Internal Control, Cash, and Short-term Investments

Chapter Objectives

- Describe the internal control features of an accounting system.
- Explain the procedures for preparing a bank reconciliation.
- Discuss the accounting for a petty cash fund.
- Describe the accounting for short-term investments in stocks and bonds.

The use of money is all the advantage there is in having money.

BENJAMIN FRANKLIN

Most people agree that accounting is the most important part of any management information system. To assist management in planning and controlling operations, the accounting system should be dependable and efficient and provide a measure of security for the firm's resources. A system with these attributes provides an adequate measure of *internal control.*

The elements of control are important to all aspects of a firm's operations, but they are particularly critical in establishing methods of handling and accounting for monetary assets. We therefore consider first the general features that are desirable in an accounting control system and then examine certain procedures that are especially important in accounting for and controlling cash transactions. The latter procedures include bank reconciliations and petty cash procedures.[1] We conclude the chapter by examining accounting for short-term investments in stocks and bonds.

THE NATURE OF INTERNAL CONTROL

Internal control has been defined as

> the plan of organization and all of the coordinate methods and measures adopted within a business to safeguard its assets, check the accuracy and reliability of its accounting data, promote operational efficiency, and encourage adherence to prescribed managerial policies.[2]

The organization, planning, and procedures for safeguarding assets and the reliability of financial records are usually called *accounting controls*. The procedures and methods concerned mainly with operational efficiency and managerial policies are *administrative controls*. These controls include statistical analyses, time-and-motion studies, performance reports, and quality controls.

An accountant should be conversant with both accounting controls and administrative controls. Indeed, many controls within these two categories are interrelated. Naturally, an accountant is more directly concerned with accounting controls, which we now discuss.

[1]The voucher system discussed in Chapter 6 is a system of controls over cash disbursements.
[2]Auditing Standards Board, *Codification of Statements on Auditing Standards* (New York: American Institute of Certified Public Accountants, 1983), Auditing Section 320.09.

FEATURES OF AN ACCOUNTING CONTROL SYSTEM

Good internal accounting control includes the following requirements:

(1) Competent personnel.
(2) Assignment of responsibility.
(3) Division of work.
(4) Separation of accountability from custodianship.
(5) Adequate records and equipment.
(6) Rotation of personnel.
(7) Internal auditing.
(8) Physical protection of assets.

Competent Personnel

Employees should be carefully selected and their talents used intelligently in the operation of the accounting information system. Each individual should thoroughly understand his or her function and its relationship to other functions in the system. Above all, an employee must realize the importance of following the procedures prescribed by management and should be in sympathy with the system. A well-formulated system of internal control can be destroyed by employees' lack of confidence or cooperation.

Assignment of Responsibility

The plan of organization should fix responsibility for functions and confer the authority necessary to perform them. Responsibility and authority for a given function should not be shared, because this may result in duplication of effort and in jobs going undone if individuals think that another is performing the assignment. When one person is responsible for a function, praise or blame can be clearly assigned for specific results. Thus, if a plant foreman is responsible for staying within budgeted amounts for labor costs, he or she should be given the authority to assign personnel to jobs, control overtime, and so on.

Division of Work

Division of work is one of the most important facets of a good system of controls. The duties of individuals should be defined so that no single individual has complete control over a sequence of related transactions. That is, the person who authorizes a purchase order should not also confirm receipt of the merchandise or authorize payment for the merchandise. Likewise, the person handling bank deposits and the person keeping the cash books should not receive bank statements or make bank reconciliations. Improper segregation of duties increases the possibility of fraud, carelessness, and unreliable record keeping, whereas with a proper division of duties, the work of one person or group can act as a check on work performed by another person or group. For example, when purchase orders and receiving reports are processed by different individuals, a third person can compare the order, receiving report, and vendor's invoice before approving payment. This practice reduces the likelihood of errors from carelessness as well as the possibility of fictitious purchases or fraudulent conversion of goods.

Work division is valuable not only in preventing errors and fraud, but also in providing the advantages of specialization—better performance and easier employee training.

Separation of Accountability from Custodianship

Employees who are responsible for keeping records of a firm's assets should not have custody of the assets or access to them. Separating the custody of assets from the maintenance of records is another safeguard against fraud. An employee should not be able to convert assets for personal use and cover up the conversion by falsifying the records. When custody of assets is adequately separated from record keeping, collusion among employees is usually necessary to perpetrate fraud. If collusion does exist, embezzlement can go undetected for a long time.

The separation feature, which should be incorporated in the system to protect all assets, is especially important in handling cash and negotiable items. For example, cash remittances from customers should be listed by personnel who have no access to accounting records. These lists can then be forwarded to the accounts receivable department for posting to customer accounts in the subsidiary ledger, while the remittances themselves are sent to the cashier for deposit. A duplicate list of remittances should also be given to the person who makes the cash receipts journal entries. This method provides several cross-checks—bank deposits must agree with the recorded cash receipts, and the Accounts Receivable control account must agree with subsidiary ledger totals. Finally, the bank should send its statement to someone other than the cashier or those keeping cash-related records, so that an independent bank reconciliation can be made.

Adequate Records and Equipment

Adequate records are important not only in accounting for a company's resources but also in providing management with accurate and reliable information. One of the most important features in a satisfactory record-keeping system is a comprehensive chart of accounts that classifies information in a manner best suited to management's needs. Control accounts and subsidiary records should be used when appropriate, so that work can be subdivided, and cross-checks may be made when the two types of accounts are reconciled. Control and subsidiary accounts can be used for such areas as accounts and notes receivable, accounts and notes payable, plant assets, and the major expense classifications of selling expense and administrative expense.

The forms used with the accounting records should promote accuracy and efficiency. If possible, individual forms should be prenumbered so that the sequence of forms used can be accounted for. Moreover, prenumbering helps a firm trace its transactions and reduces the possibility of failing to record a transaction. For example, suppose a firm issues prenumbered sales slips for each sale. A check of the number sequence would disclose any diversion of sales proceeds accomplished by destruction of the sales slip. Likewise, accounting for the sequence of prenumbered checks can detect whether unrecorded checks have been issued for unauthorized purchases.

Various types of equipment can be used with the record-keeping system to provide helpful controls. The cash registers used in retail operations, for example, have several important control features—a bell or other sound signals that the register has been opened, and a receipt allows the customer to check the transaction. Furthermore, most cash registers have a locked-in tape that accumulates and classifies transactions that have been registered. A responsible employee controlling the key can reconcile amounts shown on the tape with daily cash counts. Some registers contain separate cash drawers so that several clerks can handle the same cash register and each be accountable for his or her own operation. Another device that protects cash is the autographic register, which produces a locked-in copy of a sales invoice when the original is prepared in an over-the-counter sale. Check protectors, which perforate checks with indelible ink, are another example of a protective device for cash transactions. Checks written with such a machine cannot be altered without the change being obvious.

An electronic cash register tied in to a computer may improve control over the extension of credit to a customer using a credit card. Quick point-of-sale credit verification is possible. In a few seconds, the computer can ensure that the customer has not exceeded his or her credit limit and has been prompt with payments. The computer can also determine if the card has been reported lost or stolen. The computer either authorizes or disapproves the use of the credit card, depending on the status of the customer's account.

Bookkeeping machines, punched-card equipment, and electronic data-processing equipment all permit certain procedural controls or have built-in controls to reduce the possibility of errors and unauthorized actions. The automatic features of such equipment produce records more error-free and legible than those resulting from a manual system.

Rotation of Personnel

Some companies rotate the positions of certain operating personnel. For example, accounts receivable clerks, each responsible for a certain alphabetical segment of the accounts, might be rotated periodically to other segments. This procedure may disclose errors and irregularities caused by carelessness or dishonesty. Requiring employees to take vacations may also reveal lapses, carelessness, and dishonesty on the part of employees. Misappropriations of funds—especially in financial institutions such as banks—have often been discovered during an employee's absence, when the perpetrator could no longer control or manipulate records.

Internal Auditing

An important feature of the internal control system of large companies is the internal audit function. The internal auditing department independently appraises the firm's financial and operational activities. In addition to reviewing activities for errors and irregularities, the internal audit staff determines whether prescribed policies and procedures are being followed and attempts to uncover wasteful and inefficient situations. Internal auditing is a *staff*, or advisory, function that consists of reviewing activities and making written recommendations to management. To be effective, the internal audit staff must be independent of operating (line) functions and should report to a high-ranking executive or to the firm's board of directors.

Physical Protection of Assets

Frequently, management initiates a number of physical controls to protect company property. Although some of these controls may not be closely related to the accounting system, they are almost invariably discussed in the context of internal control.

Only minimal amounts of cash or negotiable assets should be kept on the company premises, and these should be stored in a vault. A firm should keep its inventory in a secure area and maintain strict controls over issuances and physical counts of inventory. Security personnel are often engaged to protect inventories and other physical property. A company may employ outside protection services to safeguard against burglary and arson and might post gatekeepers at plant entrances and exits to observe employees and others entering and leaving the plant.

A business must be adequately insured against losses from fire, outside theft, and similar events. In addition to insuring its physical assets, a company should obtain fidelity insurance; employees having access to cash, securities, and other easily diverted assets should be bonded. For a fee, a bonding company guarantees to make good any loss from theft or embezzlement by the bonded person, up to some specified maximum amount. The bonding company investigates employees to be bonded, and anyone with a record of questionable integrity is not likely to qualify.

CASH AND CASH CONTROLS

In accounting, the term **cash** means paper money, coins, checks, and money orders—all items that are acceptable for deposit in a bank—as well as money already on deposit with a bank. IOUs, postdated checks (checks dated in the future), and uncollected customers' checks returned by the bank stamped "NSF" (not sufficient funds) are not considered cash but are normally classified as **receivables.** Notes sent to the bank for collection remain classified as **notes receivable** until notification of collection is received from the bank.

Cash in the Balance Sheet

Various ledger accounts are used to record cash transactions; some common examples are Cash on Hand, Petty Cash, and Cash in Bank. The Cash on Hand account reflects cash receipts not yet deposited in the bank, and Petty Cash represents a fund used for small disbursements. Cash in Bank usually refers to demand deposits in a checking account.

When a business firm has several checking accounts, a separate ledger account should be maintained for each account rather than one overall Cash in Bank account. Although a balance sheet prepared for management may show all individual cash accounts, a balance sheet prepared for outsiders normally shows the combined balances of all cash accounts under a single heading, *Cash*. Management is interested in the detail because it must establish policies on balances to be maintained in various bank accounts and on hand. Most outsiders, on the other hand, are interested only in the aggregated cash balance and its relationship to other items on the financial statements.

Cash amounts subject to use or withdrawal without restriction are current assets and are normally shown first in the balance sheet listing of assets. Sometimes the cash account may include an amount, called a **compensating balance**, that is not readily available for use. A compensating balance is a minimum amount

IN-HOUSE THIEVES

Few people, from corporate executives on down, realize how big employee theft is. The fact is, it's a crime that amounts to 1% of the Gross National Product, or some $40 billion a year, and just about every employee this side of sainthood will commit it some time during his or her working life. Moreover, employee theft accounts for 80% of all crime against corporations.

Security experts divide internal crime into three categories—the theft of things such as raw materials, finished products, cash, and tools; the theft of information; and fraud.

The theft of raw materials occurs primarily in the manufacturing and construction businesses. For a manufacturing firm, it most often occurs in the shipping and receiving or warehouse end of the operation, where controls are notoriously lax. With hundreds of shipments going in and out of a docking area each day, keeping an eye on materials is taxing, and the opportunity for theft astounding.

At construction sites, there are often hundreds of workers performing a wide variety of tasks and trucks coming and going with materials. It is relatively easy for an employee to slip off the job to nab some lumber, plasterboard, or insulating material and stash it in a pick-up truck, or to arrange for a commercial truck to pick up material and haul it away.

The illegal siphoning off of crude and refined oil plagues the oil industry. The measurement of how much oil goes into a tank is relatively imprecise, so employees are able, undetected, either to siphon oil from a storage tank or to pump only part of the oil in a tanker truck into a tank.

When it comes to the outright theft of money, banks are where the big action is. Wells Fargo Bank was the victim of one of the biggest recent rip-offs. An employee in the operations department fiddled with customer accounts entered in the bank computers and embezzled about $21 million in a two-year period before he was caught.

Theft of information, though less prevalent than the theft of objects or services, can be disastrous. The energy industry is a frequent target of such thefts. Seismic surveys and exploration data, which cost millions of dollars to collect, have been pilfered from major oil companies and sold to small independent drillers or to foreign concerns.

Fraudulent schemes are the most costly form of employee theft. "The creation of dummy or shell companies is on the upswing, and it is not especially difficult to arrange," says Errol M. Cook, a security expert at Arthur Young. He tells of one executive who formed an "offshore" insurance company. This executive had the authority to place insurance, so he bought a policy from the dummy company and pocketed the premiums. Cook notes that "where phony insurance companies are used, the type of insurance placed is usually where claims would not be occurring—officers' and directors' liability and bonding insurance, for example."

Employees in a payroll department can easily rip off a company. At a Baltimore hospital, one worker added the names of two friends to the payroll and managed to funnel $40,000 their way before she was caught.

The most distressing thing about employee theft, security experts say, is that companies make it so easy. They leave valuable items unlocked or do not check to see that supplies actually exist. "It is just astounding the number of the top 500 corporations in America that have woefully inadequate security systems. I should know, because many of them are my clients," says August Bequai, a lawyer, author, and consultant in the area of corporate security.

From Lynn Adkins, "The High Cost of Employee Theft." Reprinted with the special permission of *Dun's Business Month* (formerly *Dun's Review*), October 1982, pages 66–73, Dun & Bradstreet Publications Corporation.

that a financial institution requires a firm to maintain in its account as part of a borrowing arrangement. Compensating balances related to short-term borrowings are current assets but, if significant, should be reported separately from cash available for use without restriction. Compensating balances related to long-term borrowings should be classified among a firm's long-term assets.

Cash Control Procedures

A firm must control the handling and recording of cash because it is so susceptible to misappropriation. An adequate system of internal control over cash would include the following features:

(1) Cash is handled separately from the recording of cash transactions.

(2) The work and responsibilities of cash handling and recording are divided in such a way that errors are readily disclosed and the possibility of irregularities is reduced.

(3) All cash receipts are deposited intact in the bank each day.

(4) All major disbursements are made by check, and an imprest (fixed amount) fund is used for petty cash disbursements.

In our earlier discussion of internal control, we described and explained the desirability of the first two features. By observing the last two—depositing all receipts intact daily at the bank and making all disbursements by check—a company establishes a double record of cash transactions. One record is generated by the firm's record-keeping procedures, and another is furnished by the bank. Comparing the two records and accounting for any differences provides control. This important procedure is called *reconciling the bank statement with the book record of cash transactions* or, simply, making a *bank reconciliation*.

The Bank Account

When a firm opens a checking account at a bank, the members of the firm who are authorized to draw checks sign signature cards that the bank files. Occasionally, bank employees may check the signatures on these cards against the signatures on the checks.

The bank submits monthly statements to the depositor showing the beginning cash balance, all additions and deductions for the month, and the ending cash balance. In addition, the bank returns the paid (or canceled) checks for the month, together with "advice" slips indicating other charges and credits made to the account. The bank may also send copies of such advice slips individually during the month to the depositor.

To reduce handling costs, some banks do not return canceled checks to the depositor, but use a procedure called *check truncation*. The bank retains the canceled checks for a period of time (typically 90 days) and a microfilm copy of the checks for a longer period (at least one year). Should the depositor need to review a canceled check within these periods, the bank provides the check or a photocopy of it for a small fee. A bank's monthly statements to a depositor usually list paid checks in numerical sequence, so check truncation does not affect the preparation of a bank reconciliation. Further, businesses generally use a check preparation system that produces a copy of each check issued.

Exhibit 7–1 is an example of a bank statement. The left-hand section of the statement lists deposits and other credits in sequence by date. The middle section lists checks paid and other charges to the account. The checks are listed in numerical sequence, and the payment date for each check is shown in the date column.

EXHIBIT 7–1
Bank Statement

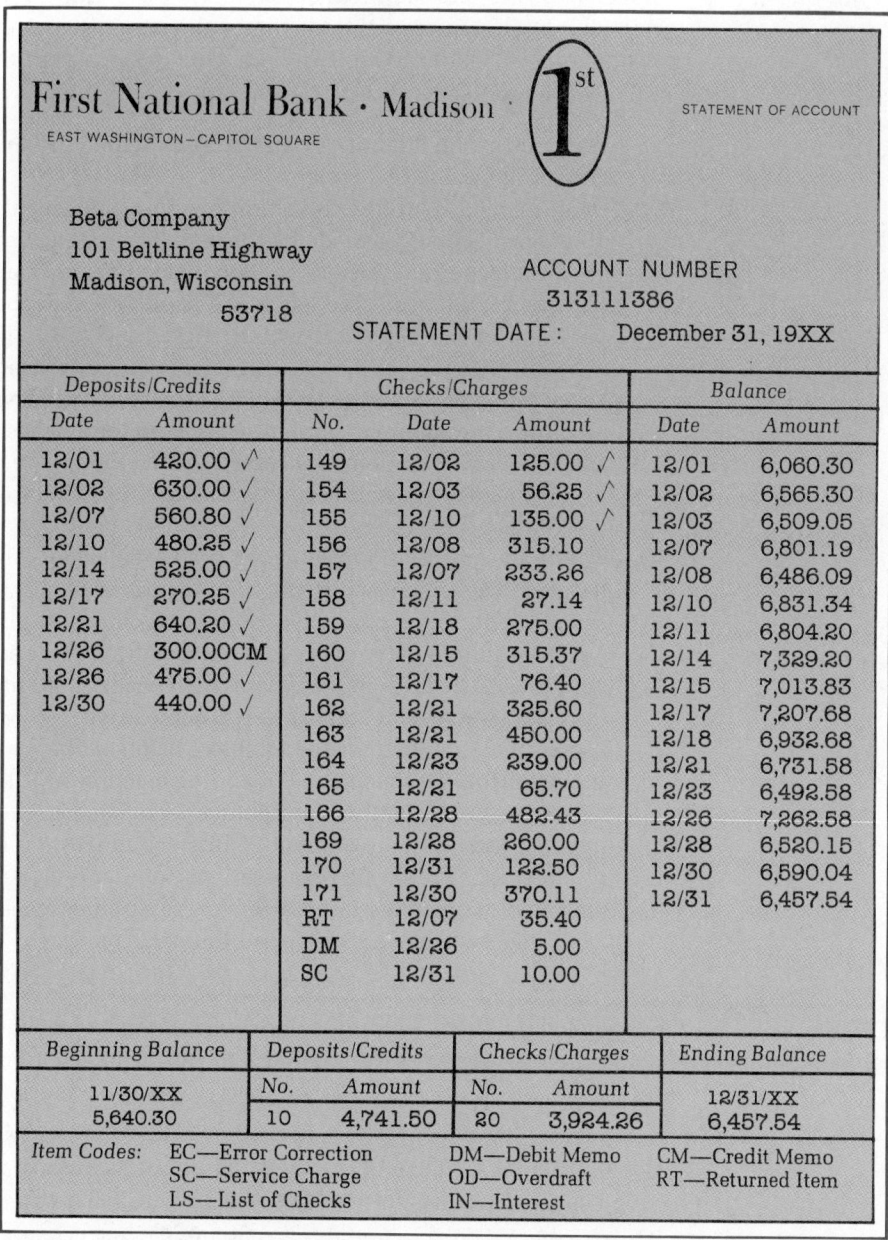

First National Bank · Madison 1st

EAST WASHINGTON–CAPITOL SQUARE

STATEMENT OF ACCOUNT

Beta Company
101 Beltline Highway
Madison, Wisconsin
53718

ACCOUNT NUMBER
313111386

STATEMENT DATE: December 31, 19XX

Deposits/Credits		*Checks/Charges*			*Balance*	
Date	*Amount*	*No.*	*Date*	*Amount*	*Date*	*Amount*
12/01	420.00 √	149	12/02	125.00 √	12/01	6,060.30
12/02	630.00 √	154	12/03	56.25 √	12/02	6,565.30
12/07	560.80 √	155	12/10	135.00 √	12/03	6,509.05
12/10	480.25 √	156	12/08	315.10	12/07	6,801.19
12/14	525.00 √	157	12/07	233.26	12/08	6,486.09
12/17	270.25 √	158	12/11	27.14	12/10	6,831.34
12/21	640.20 √	159	12/18	275.00	12/11	6,804.20
12/26	300.00CM	160	12/15	315.37	12/14	7,329.20
12/26	475.00 √	161	12/17	76.40	12/15	7,013.83
12/30	440.00 √	162	12/21	325.60	12/17	7,207.68
		163	12/21	450.00	12/18	6,932.68
		164	12/23	239.00	12/21	6,731.58
		165	12/21	65.70	12/23	6,492.58
		166	12/28	482.43	12/26	7,262.58
		169	12/28	260.00	12/28	6,520.15
		170	12/31	122.50	12/30	6,590.04
		171	12/30	370.11	12/31	6,457.54
		RT	12/07	35.40		
		DM	12/26	5.00		
		SC	12/31	10.00		

Beginning Balance	*Deposits/Credits*		*Checks/Charges*		*Ending Balance*
	No.	*Amount*	*No.*	*Amount*	
11/30/XX 5,640.30	10	4,741.50	20	3,924.26	12/31/XX 6,457.54

Item Codes:			
	EC—Error Correction	DM—Debit Memo	CM—Credit Memo
	SC—Service Charge	OD—Overdraft	RT—Returned Item
	LS—List of Checks	IN—Interest	

Listing checks in numerical sequence helps the depositor identify checks written but not yet paid by the bank. The right-hand section shows the checking account balance as of the date shown in the date column. Each time a receipt or a payment occurs, a new balance is shown.

Code letters on a bank statement identify charges and credits not related to paying checks or making deposits. A legend usually appears at the bottom of the statement explaining the code letters. Although such codes are not standard from bank to bank, they are easy to understand. As we mentioned before, the depositor also receives an advice slip from the bank explaining nonroutine entries. The statement illustrated in Exhibit 7–1 uses the following codes:

EC —Error correction. Identifies transcription, arithmetic, and similar errors and corrections made by the bank.

DM—Debit memo. Identifies collection charges, repayment of bank loans, and other special charges made by the bank against the depositor's account.

CM—Credit memo. Identifies amounts collected by the bank for the depositor, such as a note receivable left at the bank by the depositor, or a loan from the bank to the depositor which is credited to the depositor's checking account.

SC —Service charge. Identifies the amount charged by the bank for servicing the account. The amount is normally based on the average balance maintained and the number of items processed during the month. Service charges are usually made on small accounts that are not otherwise profitable for the bank to handle.

OD—Overdraft. Indicates a negative, or credit, balance in the account.

RT —Returned item. Indicates items such as postdated checks or checks without proper endorsement received from customers and deposited. Sometimes NSF (not sufficient funds) checks charged back to the account are identified with these letters in the statement. NSF checks may also be identified with the letters DM (debit memo), explained earlier.

LS —List of checks. Identifies the total of a batch of checks too numerous to list separately on the statement. An adding machine tape listing the individual check amounts usually accompanies each batch of checks listed.

IN —Interest. Indicates the amount of interest added to the account. Sole proprietorships, nonprofit organizations, and individuals may open NOW (negotiable order of withdrawal) checking accounts and earn interest monthly based on the balance maintained in the account.

The Bank Reconciliation

Almost invariably, the ending balance on the bank statement differs from the balance in the company's Cash in Bank account. Some reasons for the differences are:

(1) Outstanding checks—checks written and deducted in arriving at the book balance but not yet presented to the bank for payment.

(2) Deposits not yet credited by the bank—deposits made near the end of the month and processed by the bank *after* the monthly statement has been prepared. These deposits in transit will appear on next month's statement.

(3) Charges made by the bank but not yet reflected on the depositor's books—for example, service and collection charges, NSF checks, and repayments of the depositor's bank loans.

(4) Credits made by the bank but not yet reflected on the depositor's books—for example, collections of notes and drafts by the bank for the depositor and interest earned by the depositor on the checking account balance.

(5) Accounting errors—errors may be made either by the depositor or by the bank.

The bank reconciliation is a schedule that accounts for any of the above differences between the bank statement balance and the company's book balance. Although we could reconcile either of these figures to the other, it is more convenient to reconcile both figures to an **adjusted balance**, which is the cash balance that will appear on the balance sheet. This amount could be withdrawn from the bank after all outstanding items have cleared. A convenient reconciliation form is illustrated below.

Balance per bank statement		$XXX	Balance per books	$XXX
Add: Deposits not yet credited by bank		XXX	Add: Items credited by bank, not yet entered on books (i.e., notes collected)	XXX
		$XXX		$XXX
Less: Outstanding checks: (list)	$XXX		Less: Items charged by bank, not yet entered on books (i.e., service and collection charges, NSF checks)	
	XXX			
	XXX	XXX		XXX
Adjusted balance		$XXX	Adjusted balance	$XXX

These final amounts should agree

After the reconciliation is prepared, the adjusted balance per bank statement should agree with the adjusted book balance. If these amounts do not agree, we should look carefully for reconciling items omitted from the schedule or for possible errors in record keeping. The bank reconciliation may not only bring to light transactions that must be recorded, but may also detect errors or irregularities.

BANK RECONCILIATION PROCEDURE Assume that a December 31 bank reconciliation is to be prepared for the Beta Company, whose bank statement is illustrated in Exhibit 7–1. Exhibits 7–2 and 7–3 show the company's December cash receipts and cash disbursements journals, respectively, in abbreviated form. Cash receipts journals may have a column for bank deposits, as shown in Exhibit 7–2.

EXHIBIT 7–2
Beta Company
(Partial) Cash Receipts Journal
December 19XX

Date		Description	Cash Receipts	Bank Deposits
19XX				
Dec.	1	Hickman, Inc.	$ 230.00	
	2	Cash sales	400.00	$ 630.00 ✓
	4	Denton Company	410.80	
	7	Jewel and Son	150.00	560.80 ✓
	8	Benson Company (note)	300.00	
	10	Cash sales	180.25	480.25 ✓
	14	Taylor Brothers	525.00	525.00 ✓
	17	Cash sales	270.25	270.25 ✓
	18	Johnson Company	250.15	
	21	Bates Company	390.05	640.20 ✓
	26	Jordan Brothers	475.00	475.00 ✓
	30	Cash sales	440.00	440.00 ✓
	31	Johnson Company	225.00	225.00
			$4,246.50	$4,246.50

After the cash journals have been posted, the Cash in Bank account of the Beta Company appears as follows:

Cash in Bank (First National Bank) Account No. 11

Date		Description	Post. Ref.	Debit	Credit	Balance
19XX						
Nov.	30	Balance				5,744.05
Dec.	31		CR	4,246.50		9,990.55
	31		CD		4,699.27	5,291.28

The procedures for reconciling the December 31 bank statement balance of $6,457.54 with the $5,291.28 balance on the company's books are:

(1) Trace outstanding items on the previous (November) bank reconciliation to this period's statement. The November reconciliation for the Beta Company appears in Exhibit 7–4. The items identified with the ✓^ mark, which were outstanding at the end of November, were all processed in December; these amounts are identified by the same mark (✓^) on the bank statement in Exhibit

EXHIBIT 7–3
Beta Company
(Partial) Cash Disbursements Journal
December 19XX

Date		Description	Check No.	Cash Payments
19XX				
Dec.	1	Boynton Company	156	$ 315.10 ✓
	2	Meyer, Inc.	157	233.26 ✓
	4	Rapid Transit, Transportation In	158	27.14 ✓
	7	Acme Realty, December rent	159	275.00 ✓
	8	Stanton Company	160	315.37 ✓
	10	Horder, Inc., Office supplies	161	76.40 ✓
	14	A. L. Smith Company	162	325.60 ✓
	17	J. B. Adams, Office salary	163	450.00 ✓
	17	O. L. Holmes, Office salary	164	239.00 ✓
	18	Abbot Van Lines, Transportation In	165	65.70 ✓
	21	Millston, Inc.	166	482.43 ✓
	21	Odana Corporation	167	301.66
	22	R. W. Knight, Cash purchase	168	149.50
	26	W. A. Sutton	169	260.00 ✓
	29	Border and Son, Cash purchase	170	122.50 ✓
	30	R. L. Olson	171	370.11 ✓
	31	J. B. Adams, Office salary	172	450.00
	31	O. L. Holmes, Office salary	173	240.50
				$4,699.27

EXHIBIT 7–4
Beta Company
Bank Reconciliation
November 30, 19XX

Balance per bank statement		$5,640.30	Balance per books	$5,754.05
Add: Deposit not credited by bank		420.00 ✓		
		$6,060.30		
Less: Outstanding checks:			Less: Bank service charge	10.00
No. 149	$125.00 ✓			
No. 154	56.25 ✓			
No. 155	135.00 ✓	316.25		
Adjusted balance		$5,744.05	Adjusted balance	$5,744.05

7–1. Any checks that have still not cleared in December should appear again on the December reconciliation.

(2) Compare the record of deposits in the cash receipts journal (Exhibit 7–2) with the list of deposits on the bank statement. A check mark (✔) has been placed next to the amounts that appear in both records. Note that the $225.00 deposit made on December 31 does not appear on the bank statement. Enter this item in the December bank reconciliation as a deposit not yet credited by the bank.

(3) Arrange in numerical sequence the paid checks that have been returned by the bank. Compare the record of checks written from the cash disbursements journal (Exhibit 7–3) with the checks paid by the bank and returned with the bank statement. A check mark (✔) has been placed in the cash disbursements journal next to the amount of each check paid by the bank. Since checks numbered 167, 168, 172, and 173 have not cleared the bank, enter them in the December bank reconciliation as outstanding checks. (If paid checks are not returned with the bank statement, compare the record of checks written from the cash disbursements journal with the numerical listing of paid checks on the bank statement.)

(4) Scan the bank statement for charges and credits not yet reflected in the company's records. Note that the statement contains a charge of $35.40 for a returned item, a debit memo of $5.00, and a service charge of $10.00. Also, a credit for $300.00 appears in the deposits column on December 26. Bank advices indicate that an NSF check for $35.40 was charged against the company's account; that a $300.00 note receivable was collected on the company's behalf and a $5.00 collection charge was made; and that a $10.00 service charge was made for the month. Enter these items also in the December bank reconciliation.

EXHIBIT 7–5
Beta Company
Bank Reconciliation
December 31, 19XX

Balance per bank statement		$6,457.54	Balance per books		$5,291.28
Add: Deposits not credited			Add: Collection of note	$300.00	
by bank		225.00	Less: Collection charge	5.00	295.00
		$6,682.54			$5,586.28
Less: Outstanding checks:					
No. 167	$301.66				
No. 168	149.50				
No. 172	450.00		Less: NSF check	$35.40	
No. 173	240.50	1,141.66	Bank service charge	10.00	45.40
Adjusted balance		$5,540.88	Adjusted balance		$5,540.88

After the preceding procedures have been completed, the December bank reconciliation for the Beta Company appears as shown in Exhibit 7–5.

Before financial statements are prepared for the period ended December 31, journal entries should be made to bring the Cash account balance into agreement with the adjusted balance shown on the reconciliation. The entries for the Beta Company would reflect the collection of the note receivable and the related collection expense, reclassification of the NSF check as an account receivable, and the bank service charge for the month.

Cash	295.00	
Miscellaneous Expense	5.00	
Notes Receivable		300.00
To record note collected by bank, less service charge.		
Accounts Receivable	35.40	
Cash		35.40
To reclassify NSF check as an account receivable.		
Miscellaneous Expense	10.00	
Cash		10.00
To record bank service charge for December.		

Electronic Funds Transfer

Billions of paper checks are written each year by businesses and individuals. The costs of processing this large volume of checks have motivated financial institutions to develop systems for transferring funds among parties electronically, without the need for paper checks. The exchange of cash through such a system is called **electronic funds transfer (EFT).**

A typical example of EFT is the payment of a payroll. An employer firm obtains authorizations from its employees to deposit their payroll checks directly to their checking accounts. The firm then sends to the bank a magnetic tape coded with the appropriate payroll data. The bank's computer processes the magnetic tape, deducts the total payroll amount from the firm's checking account, and adds each employee's payroll amount to his or her checking account.

EFT may also be useful for retailers in situations where customers typically pay for goods with a check at the time of purchase. Some grocery stores, for example, now use EFT. At the check-out counter, the customer uses a plastic card to activate a computer terminal connected with the bank. Funds to pay for the groceries are immediately transferred from the customer's checking account to the grocery store's account at the bank. This procedure not only eliminates the cost of processing the paper checks for the bank, but also eliminates the risk of bad checks for the grocery store.

The use of EFT will increase with the development of expanded computer networks capable of handling electronic funds transfers. The specific controls over cash transactions handled through EFT, of course, may vary from the internal control procedures under a paper check system. However, adequate controls are no less important in an electronic funds transfer system.

THE PETTY CASH FUND

Most business firms find it inconvenient and expensive to write checks for small expenditures. Therefore, small amounts of cash needed for such items as postage, delivery service, and purchases of supplies and notions are most conveniently handled by establishing a **petty cash fund.**

The size of the petty cash fund depends on the number and the amounts of minor expenditures. Of course, it is unwise to have a large amount of cash on hand because of the risk of theft or misuse. Yet, too frequent replenishment can be a nuisance. Many firms maintain funds that will last three or four weeks. The size of expenditures made from the fund is also usually limited.

Although the use of a petty cash fund technically violates the control maxim of making all expenditures by check, control can be maintained by handling the fund on an **imprest** basis and by following certain well-established procedures. In accounting, an imprest fund contains a fixed amount of cash.

Although expenditures from an imprest petty cash fund are made in currency and coin, the fund is established by writing a check against the general bank account. Replenishments are also accomplished by issuing checks—after a review of expenditures. Therefore, in the final analysis, all expenditures are actually controlled by check.

Establishing the Fund

Assume that the Beta Company establishes a petty cash fund of $100. It draws a check payable to Cash and exchanges it at the bank for currency and coin in denominations that are convenient for small expenditures. The entry reflecting establishment of the fund is:

Petty Cash	100	
Cash in Bank		100
To establish imprest petty cash fund.		

As evidence of a disbursement from the fund, the person in charge should place a prenumbered petty cash receipt in the petty cash box. At any time, the total cash on hand plus the amounts on the receipts should equal $100. Each receipt should give the date, amount, and nature of the expenditure and should be signed by the recipient of the cash. Such documents as cash register tapes and copies of invoices should be attached to the receipts.

Replenishing the Fund

When the fund must be replenished, a check is drawn to Cash in an amount that will bring the cash value of the fund back to $100. Expenditures from the fund are analyzed according to expense or other account category and recorded in the books. For example, assume that the Beta Company's fund has been drawn down to $28 and that analysis of the $72 in receipts reveals the following expenditures: Office Expense, $40; Transportation In, $27; and Postage Expense, $5. The bookkeeper makes the following entry in the cash disbursements journal (shown in general journal form):

Office Expense	40	
Transportation In	27	
Postage Expense	5	
Cash in Bank		72
To replenish petty cash fund.		

The fund cashier cashes the replenishment check at the bank and places the cash in the petty cash box.

If the imprest amount is adequate, no further entries are made to the Petty Cash account itself. Notice that replenishment results in an entry to the Cash in Bank account. Only when the prescribed amount of the imprest fund is changed will entries be made to the Petty Cash account, increasing or decreasing the amount of the fund.

One person in the firm's office should be solely responsible for custody of the fund and expenditures made from it. The replenishment checks, however, should be written by another authorized person, after review of the petty cash receipts and the expense distribution. Furthermore, this person should stamp, perforate, or otherwise mutilate the supporting receipts and documents to prevent them from being used again as a basis for reimbursement.

Cash Short and Over

Errors in making change from cash funds result in less or more cash than can be accounted for. Usually, such shortages or overages are not material in amount. An account called **Cash Short and Over** is commonly used to record these discrepancies; shortages are debited to the account, and overages are credited. For example, suppose a $100 petty cash fund contains $80 in receipts for office expense and only $16 in currency and coins. The entry to replenish the fund and to record the $4 shortage would be:

Office Expense	80	
Cash Short and Over	4	
Cash in Bank		84
To replenish petty cash fund and record shortage.		

If the fund had contained $24 in cash together with the $80 in expense receipts, the $4 overage would be credited to the Cash Short and Over account. The credit to Cash in Bank for replenishment would be $76.

The Cash Short and Over account may also be used to record cash short or over from sales when cash register tape totals do not agree with the count of cash receipts. Large discrepancies, particularly recurring shortages, should always be investigated to determine appropriate corrective steps.

A Cash Short and Over account with a debit balance at the close of an accounting period is classified as Miscellaneous Expense on the income statement. A credit balance can be classified as Other Income.

INTERNAL CONTROL IN OTHER AREAS

While it is vitally important to establish effective controls over the handling of and accounting for cash, control should also be provided for a firm's other activities. As with cash, most controls separate the authorization of a transaction, accounting for the transaction, and the custody of any related assets. For example, the purchase and sale of securities normally require authorization by a company's board of directors, and officers who have access to the securities should not have access to the accounting records. Other personnel should record security transactions and keep a record of security certificates by certificate number and amount.

Similarly, clerks handling inventory items should not have access to inventory records, and their duties should be separated from the receiving department and the processing of accounts payable. Similar controls should be exercised over receivables, plant assets, payroll transactions, and every other facet of business activity.

The subject of internal control is quite complex. Both external and internal auditors devote a great deal of attention to internal control when analyzing an accounting system and preparing audits. The importance of internal control was underscored by the enactment of the Foreign Corrupt Practices Act in 1977. Among other provisions, this law requires all corporations registering with the Securities and Exchange Commission to devise and maintain an adequate system of internal accounting controls.

SHORT-TERM INVESTMENTS

Corporate stocks and bonds may be acquired by a variety of investors, including individuals, partnerships, corporations, mutual funds, pension funds, foundations, and trusts. Shares of stock, of course, represent ownership interests in a corporation. Some corporations have more than one type of stock (discussed in Chapter 15). Investors holding a corporation's *common stock* have the most basic ownership rights. *Bonds* are long-term debt securities issued by corporations and various governmental agencies. Our discussion here focuses on short-term investments in stocks and bonds made by corporations.

A firm issuing stocks or bonds may sell directly to investors, or the securities may be sold through an underwriter. Most investments, however, do not involve original issues. In the typical investment, one investor purchases from another investor who happens to be selling at that time. Stocks and bonds are bought and sold on organized exchanges—such as the New York Stock Exchange—and through a less formal *over-the-counter market*. Both the buyer and the seller of a security normally use the services of a broker to acquire or dispose of their investments.

Many firms make temporary investments in highly marketable securities using seasonal excesses of cash. Furthermore, some firms invest in high-quality stocks and bonds as "back-up cash." Management could convert these securities to cash, if needed, without interfering with the company's normal operations. In the meantime, the investments produce dividend and interest income for the company. Both of these types of investments (investments of seasonal excesses of cash and for "back-up cash") are considered **short-term investments** and are classified as current assets on the balance sheet. They may be identified as either short-term investments or **marketable securities** on the balance sheet.

Short-term Investments in Stocks

When stock is purchased as a short-term investment, the amount initially recorded in the investment account is the stock's cost; that is, its total purchase price. The purchase price may include charges for such items as broker's commissions and transfer taxes. Suppose 100 shares of United Pride common stock are acquired as a short-term investment on October 1 at a cost of $4,290, including commissions and taxes. The investment is recorded as follows:

Oct. 1	Investment in United Pride Stock	4,290	
	Cash		4,290
	To record purchase of 100 shares of common stock for $4,290.		

DIVIDENDS A corporation's board of directors may declare a **dividend**, which is a distribution of the corporation's assets. The asset distributed is usually cash. A corporation also may distribute a **stock dividend**—shares of its own stock. For example, if a board of directors declares a 5% stock dividend, then additional shares of stock equal to 5% of the corporation's outstanding stock are distributed to the current stockholders in proportion to their current stock holdings.

Cash dividends do not accrue on shares of stock. A corporation has no legal obligation to pay a dividend until it is declared by the board of directors. A company holding stock may record the cash dividend after it has been declared by debiting Dividends Receivable and crediting Dividend Income, but ordinarily no entry is made until the dividend is received. Assuming the United Pride board of directors declares a cash dividend of $1.00 per share and dividend income is recorded when received, the entry to record the receipt of the dividend on December 29 would be:

Dec. 29	Cash	100	
	Dividend Income		100
	To record receipt of $100 dividend on investment in United Pride stock.		

The receipt of a stock dividend does not constitute income, and requires no formal journal entry. A memorandum of the number of shares received, however, should be recorded in the investment account. The recipient of the stock dividend now holds more stock without further investment, so the average cost of each share held has been reduced. If United Pride declares a 10% common stock dividend, the company holding 100 shares of United Pride would make the following notation on receipt of 10 additional shares:

(Memorandum) Received 10 shares of United Pride common stock as stock dividend. Average cost per share of 110 shares held is now $39 ($4,290/110).

LOWER OF COST OR MARKET FOR PORTFOLIO A corporation's stock **portfolio** refers to its investment in several different stocks. At the end of an accounting period, short-term stock investments are reported on the balance sheet at the lower of the aggregate cost or market value of the portfolio. A portfolio valuation is used because firms typically view (and manage) their stock investments as collective assets (a portfolio). Should the aggregate market value drop below total cost, an unrealized loss[3] is recorded and a contra asset account (to offset short-term stock investments) is credited. To illustrate, let us assume a company has the following portfolio of short-term stock investments at the end of its first year of operations:

Stock	Cost	Market Value
United Pride Common	$ 4,290	$ 3,800
Bayou Oil Common	17,000	17,500
Swan, Inc., Common	16,500	15,200
Total	$37,790	$36,500

Because the total market value ($36,500) is less than total cost ($37,790), the following journal entry is made:

Dec. 31	Unrealized Loss on Short-term Investments	1,290	
	Allowance to Reduce Short-term Investments to Market		1,290
	To record unrealized loss on portfolio of short-term stock investments.		

The unrealized loss is reported in the current year's income statement. The credit to the contra asset account (1) permits original cost to remain in the various stock investment accounts and (2) reduces the total book value of the investments to market value on the balance sheet. The short-term stock investments would appear on the balance sheet as follows:

Short-term Stock Investments (cost)	$37,790	
Less: Allowance to Reduce Short-term Investments to Market	1,290	$36,500

Or, the investments may be reported in condensed form:

Short-term Stock Investments, at market (cost $37,790)	$36,500

Of course, if the portfolio's market value exceeds its total cost, the investments are reported at cost and no allowance account is created.

[3]Unrealized losses are losses on securities still owned by the firm. For details, see *Statement of Financial Accounting Standards No. 12*, "Accounting for Certain Marketable Securities" (Stamford, CT: Financial Accounting Standards Board, 1975).

SALE OF SHORT-TERM STOCK INVESTMENTS When a short-term stock investment is sold, a gain or loss is recorded equal to the difference between the proceeds of the sale and the stock's original cost (or the original cost adjusted for the effect of a stock dividend). For example, if all 110 shares of the United Pride stock discussed above were sold on February 1 of the next year for $3,800, the following entry would be made:

Feb. 1	Cash	3,800	
	Loss on Sale of Investments	490	
	Investment in United Pride Stock		4,290
	To record sale of stock for $3,800.		

The $490 loss is a realized loss because it relates to securities sold by the firm. Realized losses and realized gains from the sale of investments are included in the income statement in the year the securities are sold.

RECOVERY OF UNREALIZED LOSS The difference between the total cost and market value of a short-term stock portfolio will likely change from one year-end to the next because of changes in market values or in the portfolio's composition. Thus, the contra asset account will be increased or decreased each year-end to reflect the net unrealized portfolio loss at that time. If the net unrealized loss at year-end is smaller than it was the year before, the adjusting entry records a recovery of an unrealized loss. To illustrate, let us assume the company whose investments we have been analyzing has the following portfolio of short-term stock investments at the end of its second year of operations:

Stock	Cost	Market Value
Bayou Oil Common	$17,000	$17,600
Swan, Inc., Common	16,500	15,700
Total	$33,500	$33,300

The net unrealized loss is now $200 ($33,500 − $33,300); at the end of the preceding year, it had been $1,290. The following entry would adjust the allowance account:

Dec. 31	Allowance to Reduce Short-term Investments to Market	1,090	
	Recovery of Unrealized Loss on Short-term Investments		1,090
	To record decrease in net unrealized loss on short-term stock investments.		

The recovery of the unrealized loss is included in the current year's income statement. The $200 credit balance now in the allowance account offsets the cost of short-term investments in the year-end balance sheet.

Short-term Investments in Bonds

A short-term bond investment is initially recorded at its acquisition cost, which includes any broker's commissions and transfer taxes. Because a bond is a debt security, the bondholder receives periodic interest payments from the bond issuer. Interest accrues daily on a bond and usually is paid semiannually. On an interest payment date, a bondholder receives the full amount of interest accrued since the last payment date, regardless of when the bond was purchased. As a result, the purchase price of a bond that is sold between interest payment dates includes not only the current market price but also any interest accrued since the last interest payment date. The bond seller, therefore, receives the interest income earned up to the date of sale. The bond investor debits the accrued interest purchased to a Bond Interest Receivable account. Because the accrued interest is received with the first interest payment, it is not treated as part of the initial cost of the investment.

The **face value,** or **maturity value,** of a bond is the amount of principal to be repaid at the maturity date. The annual rate of interest payable on a bond—often called the *coupon* or *nominal* rate of interest—is stated in the bond agreement. To determine the amount of interest paid semiannually on such bonds, we multiply the face value by one-half the coupon rate of interest.

Purchasing a bond at **par** means paying an amount equal to its face value. A bond purchased at a **discount** costs less than its face value, and a bond purchased at a **premium** costs more than its face value. An investor discounts a bond when the current market rate of interest exceeds the bond's coupon interest rate; a bond sells at a premium when its coupon rate exceeds the current market interest rate. Bond prices are usually stated as a percentage of face value—for example, a bond selling at 98 costs 98% of its face value, and a bond quoted at 101 sells for 101% of its face value.

Let us assume that $10,000 face value of Anko Company 12% bonds are bought on May 1 at 97 plus accrued interest. The brokerage commission is $40. Semiannual interest is paid on January 1 and July 1. The accrued interest from January 1 to May 1 is $400 ($10,000 × 0.12 × $\frac{4}{12}$), which is recorded separately in a Bond Interest Receivable account. The cost entered in the bond investment account is $9,740, including the brokerage commission. The following entry records the acquisition:

May 1	Investment in Anko Company Bonds	9,740	
	Bond Interest Receivable	400	
	Cash		10,140
	To record purchase of bonds at 97 plus commission of $40 plus four months' accrued interest.		

The entry to record the receipt of the semiannual interest payment on July 1 would be:

July 1	Cash	600	
	Bond Interest Receivable		400
	Bond Interest Income		200
	To record receipt of semiannual interest on Anko Company bonds.		

The $200 credit to interest income reflects the interest earned for the two months the bonds have been held. The other $400 is the accrued interest purchased when the bonds were acquired.

Short-term bond investments are usually sold at a gain or loss. Such gain or loss is computed by comparing the proceeds of the sale, net of any accrued interest received, to the carrying value of the investment. If the proceeds from the sale of the Anko Company bonds on October 1 were $9,800 plus accrued interest of $300 for three months, the following entry would be made:

Oct. 1	Cash	10,100	
	Investment in Anko Company Bonds		9,740
	Bond Interest Income		300
	Gain on Sale of Investments		60
	To record sale of bond investment for $9,800 plus interest of $300.		

Certificates of Deposit

In addition to marketable stocks and bonds, a corporation may invest excess cash in another type of security—a **certificate of deposit (CD).** These certificates may be purchased at banks and other financial institutions. They offer fixed rates of return on investments for specified periods (such as 90 days, six months, or one year). Generally, the fixed interest rate increases with the amount or the duration of the investment. CDs are recorded at cost and reported on the balance sheet as a current asset immediately below cash. Interest income from CDs is recorded in the period in which it is earned. These accounting guidelines apply also to short-term investments in other forms of savings certificates: The investment is recorded at its cost, and interest income is recorded in the period in which it is earned.

DEMONSTRATION PROBLEM FOR REVIEW

At December 31 of the current year, the Cash account in Tyler Company's general ledger had a debit balance of $18,434.27. The December 31 bank statement showed a balance of $19,726.40. In reconciling the two amounts, you discover the following:

(1) Bank deposits made by Tyler on December 31 amounting to $2,145.40 do not appear on the bank statement.

(2) A non-interest-bearing note receivable for $2,000, left with the bank for collection, was collected by the bank near the end of December. The bank credited the proceeds, less a $5 collection charge, on the bank statement. Tyler Company has not recorded the collection.

(3) Accompanying the bank statement is a debit memorandum indicating that John Miller's check for $450 was charged against Tyler's bank account on December 30 because of insufficient funds.

(4) Check No. 586, written for advertising expense of $869.10, was recorded as $896.10 in Tyler Company's cash disbursements journal.

(5) A comparison of the paid checks returned by the bank with the cash disbursements journal revealed the following checks still outstanding at December 31:

No. 561	$306.63	No. 591	$190.00
No. 585	440.00	No. 592	282.50
No. 588	476.40	No. 593	243.00

(6) The bank mistakenly charged Tyler Company's account for check printing costs of $30.50, which should have been charged to Taylor Company.

(7) The bank charged Tyler Company's account $42.50 for rental of a safe deposit box. No entry has been made in Tyler's records for this expense.

REQUIRED

(a) Prepare a bank reconciliation at December 31.

(b) Prepare any necessary journal entries at December 31.

SOLUTION TO DEMONSTRATION PROBLEM

(a)

Tyler Company
Bank Reconciliation
December 31, 19XX

Balance per bank statement		$19,726.40	Balance per books		$18,434.27
Add: Deposits not credited by bank		2,145.40	Add: Collection of note	$2,000.00	
Error by bank (Check printing charge of Taylor Co.)		30.50	Less: Collection charge	5.00	1,995.00
		$21,902.30	Error in recording check No. 586		27.00
Less: Outstanding checks:					$20,456.27
No. 561	$306.63		Less:		
No. 585	440.00		NSF check	$450.00	
No. 588	476.40		Charge for safe deposit box	42.50	492.50
No. 591	190.00				
No. 592	282.50				
No. 593	243.00	1,938.53			
Adjusted balance		$19,963.77	Adjusted balance		$19,963.77

(b)

Dec. 31	Cash	1,995.00	
	Miscellaneous Expense	5.00	
	Notes Receivable		2,000.00
	To record collection of note by bank, less collection charge.		

Dec. 31	Cash	27.00	
	Advertising Expense		27.00
	To correct error in recording advertising expense.		
31	Accounts Receivable	450.00	
	Cash		450.00
	To reclassify NSF check as an account receivable.		
31	Miscellaneous Expense	42.50	
	Cash		42.50
	To record rental expense of safe deposit box.		

KEY POINTS TO REMEMBER

(1) *Internal control* consists of the measures to safeguard a firm's assets, check accuracy and reliability of accounting data, promote operational efficiency, and encourage adherence to managerial policies. *Accounting controls* are related to the protection of assets and the reliability of accounting data; *administrative controls* deal mainly with efficiency and management's policies.

(2) Depositing all receipts intact at the bank and making all cash disbursements by check are important cash controls. These procedures provide a double record of cash—the firm's record and the bank's record.

(3) Neither the book balance nor the bank statement balance of cash usually represents the cash balance shown on the balance sheet. Both amounts are reconciled to a third figure—the adjusted balance—which appears on the balance sheet and is the amount that could be withdrawn after all outstanding items have cleared.

(4) Petty Cash is debited when an imprest fund for small expenditures is established or increased. When the fund is replenished, the individual accounts for which expenditures have been made are debited.

(5) Short-term investments in stock are normally carried at the lower of cost or market value of the portfolio. Unrealized losses or recoveries of unrealized losses are included in the income statement, as are realized gains and losses from the sale of investments.

(6) Short-term investments in bonds are recorded at their acquisition cost. When sold, the difference between the sales proceeds (net of accrued interest) and the bond's carrying value is shown as a gain (when proceeds exceed carrying value) or as a loss (when carrying value exceeds proceeds).

SELF-TEST QUESTIONS
(Answers are at the end of this chapter.)

1. A system of good internal accounting controls includes
   (a) Sharing the responsibility and authority for a given function among competent employees.
   (b) Placing one person in complete control over a sequence of related transactions.
   (c) Using checks and sales invoices that are prenumbered.
   (d) Keeping large amounts of cash on the company premises.
2. A bank reconciliation is
   (a) A formal financial statement that lists all of a firm's bank account balances.
   (b) A merger of two banks that previously were competitors.
   (c) A statement sent monthly by a bank to a depositor that lists all deposits, checks paid, and other credits and charges to the depositor's account for the month.
   (d) A schedule that accounts for differences between a firm's cash balance as shown on its bank statement and the balance shown in its general ledger Cash account.
3. An entry to debit Petty Cash is made when
   (a) A petty cash fund is established.
   (b) A petty cash fund is replenished.
   (c) A petty cash fund is established *and* when it is replenished.
   (d) A shortage in the petty cash fund is recorded.
4. Which of the following is a contra asset account?
   (a) Recovery of Unrealized Loss on Short-term Investments.
   (b) Unrealized Loss on Short-term Investments.
   (c) Loss on Sale of Investments.
   (d) Allowance to Reduce Short-term Investments to Market.
5. Finn Corporation purchased bonds with a face value of $50,000 and a 10% coupon rate at 99 plus three months' accrued interest. The brokerage commission is $50. What amount should be debited to the bond investment account?
   (a) $50,000 (c) $49,500
   (b) $49,550 (d) $50,800

QUESTIONS

7–1 Define *internal control*. Name several specific features of a good system of internal control.

7–2 What is the difference between internal accounting controls and administrative controls?

7–3 Why is work division an important feature of good internal accounting controls?

7–4 What internal control procedures are especially important in handling cash transactions?

7–5 Indicate whether the following statements relating to internal control systems are true or false:

(a) Under the principle of separating accountability and physical custodianship, the accounts receivable bookkeeper should not make bank deposits.
(b) When possible, the general ledger bookkeeper should also keep subsidiary records.
(c) Rotation of personnel in record-keeping duties violates the rule that responsibility should not be shared.
(d) Even with careful attention to good internal controls, guarding against defalcations and irregularities involving collusion among employees is difficult.
(e) Internal auditing departments eliminate the need for audits by independent public accountants.

7–6 The owner of a medium-sized business asks you why she should be concerned with an internal control system for the firm, since all officers and employees who have access to cash and other liquid assets are bonded. How should you respond to this question?

7–7 What is the purpose of a bank reconciliation?

7–8 In preparing a bank reconciliation, how should you determine (a) deposits not recorded in the bank statement and (b) outstanding checks?

7–9 Indicate whether the following bank reconciliation items should be (1) added to the bank statement balance, (2) deducted from the bank statement balance, (3) added to the ledger account balance, or (4) deducted from the ledger account balance:

(a) Bank service charge.
(b) NSF check.
(c) Deposit in transit.
(d) Outstanding check.
(e) Bank error charging company's account with another company's check.
(f) Difference of $540 in amount of check written for $715 but recorded in the cash disbursements journal for $175.

7–10 Which of the items listed in Question 7–9 require a journal entry on the company's books?

7–11 What is an imprest petty cash fund? How is such a fund established and replenished? Describe the accounting entries involved.

7–12 In preparing to replenish the $200 petty cash fund, the cashier discovers that the fund contains $188 in petty cash vouchers for office expenses and $9 in currency and coins. (a) What should be the amount of the replenishment check? (b) How should the $3 discrepancy be recorded?

7–13 Why do corporations make short-term investments in securities? Where should short-term investments be classified in the balance sheet?

7–14 Interest on bond investments is accrued, but dividends on stock investments are not accrued. Why?

7–15 What entry, if any, should be made when a corporation receives a stock dividend on a short-term stock investment? What entry should be made when a cash dividend is received on a short-term stock investment?

7–16 At what amount are short-term stock investments reported in the balance sheet? Where are unrealized losses on the short-term stock investments portfolio reported?

7–17 Tylin Corporation purchased bonds with a face value of $40,000 and a 9% coupon rate at 103 plus four months' accrued interest. Calculate the total cash outlay for the bonds. What amount should be charged to the bond investment account?

7–18 What is a certificate of deposit? When should interest income on a certificate of deposit be recorded?

EXERCISES

Internal control

7–19 The following four situations occurred in the Gray Corporation:

(a) The mail opener converted a check payable to Gray Corporation to his personal use. The check was included in the list of remittances sent to the accounting department. He treated the missing amount as a deposit in transit while doing the bank reconciliation.

(b) The purchasing agent used the company's purchase order form to order building materials. Later, she instructed the building supply company by telephone to deliver the materials to her home and to charge Gray Corporation's account. At month-end, she approved the invoice for payment.

(c) A vendor was paid twice for the same shipment. One payment was made on receipt of the invoice and a second payment on receipt of the monthly statement—the first remittance had arrived too late to appear on the monthly statement.

(d) The cashier pocketed cash received over the counter from certain customers paying their accounts. He then wrote off the receivables as uncollectible.

For each situation, indicate any violations of good internal control procedures, and describe the steps you would take to safeguard the system against this type of occurrence.

Internal control

7–20 Explain how each of the following unrelated procedures strengthens internal control:

(a) After preparing a check for a cash disbursement, Western Lumber Company's treasurer cancels the supporting documentation (purchase requisition, receiving report, and invoice) with a perforator.

(b) The clerks of the Gorman Department Store give each customer a cash register receipt along with the proper change.

(c) The ticket-taker of the Palace movie theater tears each admission ticket in half and gives each patron a stub.

(d) The Gourmet Restaurant provides waiters and waitresses with prenumbered customer's checks. The servers are to void spoiled checks and issue new ones rather than make alterations or corrections on them. Voided checks must be given to the manager every day.

Bank reconciliation

7–21 Use the following information to prepare a bank reconciliation for the Lancer Company at June 30 of the current year.

(1) Balance per Cash account, June 30, $5,045.25.

(2) Balance per bank statement, June 30, $5,500.35.

(3) Deposits not reflected on bank statement, $554.

(4) Outstanding checks, June 30, $1,234.10.
(5) Service charge on bank statement not recorded in books, $15.
(6) Error by bank—Larson Company check charged on Lancer Company's bank statement, $300.
(7) Check for advertising expense, $340, incorrectly recorded in books as $430.

Petty cash

7–22 Record the following Meyer Corporation activities in general journal form:

Apr. 1 Established a $150 petty cash fund by writing a check on the First National Bank.

17 Replenished the petty cash fund by writing a check on the First National Bank. The fund contains the following:

Currency and coins	$ 19.00
Bills and receipts:	
Delivery Expense	66.00
Contributions Expense	25.00
Office Expense	40.00
	$150.00

30 Replenished the petty cash fund and increased it to $250 by writing a check on the First National Bank. The fund contains:

Currency and coins	$ 26.00
Bills and receipts:	
Transportation In	85.00
Delivery Expense	12.00
Office Expense	27.00
	$150.00

Stock investments

7–23 During its first year of operations, Vogel, Inc., made two purchases of common stock as short-term investments. On May 20, 19X1, the firm acquired 300 shares of A Company at $32 per share plus a $100 broker's fee, and on July 16, 19X1, it purchased 200 shares of X Company at $55 per share plus a $130 broker's fee. On December 27, Vogel, Inc., received a cash dividend of $1.20 per share from A Company (Vogel records dividend income when received). The December 31 quoted market prices per share for the stock were A Company, $34, and X Company, $50. On January 26, 19X2, Vogel sold the A Company stock for $36 per share. Present journal entries to reflect (a) the stock purchases, (b) the receipt of the A Company dividend, (c) the reduction of the stock portfolio to the lower of cost or market at December 31, and (d) the sale of the A Company stock.

Bond investment

7–24 As a short-term investment, Barnett Company purchased fifteen $1,000, 10% bonds at 98 plus three months' accrued interest on April 1, 19X2. The brokerage commission was $100. The bonds pay interest on June 30 and December 31. Present journal entries to reflect (a) the purchase of the bonds for cash on April 1, 19X2; (b) the receipt of the semiannual interest payment on June 30, 19X2; and (c) the receipt of the semiannual interest payment on December 31, 19X2.

Bond investment

7–25 Present a journal entry to record the sale of the bonds described in Exercise 7–24 at 101 plus accrued interest on March 1, 19X3.

PROBLEMS

Internal control

7–26 The western branch of Sports Distributors, Inc., handles a significant amount of credit sales, over-the-counter cash sales, and C.O.D. (cash on delivery) sales. The sales clerk prepares two copies of a sales ticket for all cash sales. One copy is given to the customer. The cashier keeps the other copy and stamps it "paid" when cash is received from an over-the-counter customer or from the delivery service. Because the sales tickets are not prenumbered, the cashier files them by the date of sale. At the end of each day, the cashier summarizes the over-the-counter cash sales and the amounts received from the delivery service for C.O.D. sales and sends the total to the bookkeeper for recording.

The branch does its own billings and collects receivables from credit customers. Mail remittances from credit customers are opened in the mailroom. Mailroom personnel make one copy of a list of remittances, which they forward to the bookkeeper together with the customers' checks. The bookkeeper verifies the cash discounts (credit sales are 2/10, n/30), records the remittances, and then sends the checks to the cashier. The cashier makes up the daily deposits for the bank, including both cash sales and remittances received on account. At the end of the month, the cashier receives the bank statement and makes the bank reconciliation. Also at month-end, the bookkeeper mails monthly statements of account to customers with outstanding balances.

REQUIRED

(a) List the irregularities that might occur with this system.

(b) Suggest improvements in the system of internal control.

(c) What feature of internal control in the current system would likely reveal that a mail clerk has converted checks received through the mail to personal use (that is, the mail clerk keeps the check and does not record it on the list of remittances)?

Internal control

7–27 Each of the following lettered paragraphs (a)–(d) briefly describes an independent situation involving some aspect of internal control.

REQUIRED

Answer the questions at the end of each paragraph.

(a) As the office manager of a small business, F. A. Miner opens all incoming mail, makes bank deposits, and keeps both the general ledger and the customers' subsidiary ledger. Two assistants write up the special journals (cash, purchases, and sales) and prepare the customers' monthly statements.

(1) If Miner pocketed Customer A's $100 remittance in full of account and made no effort to conceal his defalcation in the books, how would the misappropriation probably be discovered?

(2) What routine accounting procedure would disclose Miner's $100 defalcation in (1), even if he destroyed Customer A's subsidiary ledger card?

(3) What circumstances might disclose Miner's $100 defalcation if he marked Customer A's account "paid in full" and set up a $100 account for fictitious Customer B with a fictitious address?

(4) In (3) above, why might Miner be anxious to open the mail himself each morning?

(5) In (3) above, why might Miner want to have the authority to write off accounts considered uncollectible?

(b) A doughnut shop uses a cash register with a locked-in tape that accumulates registered transactions. A prominently displayed sign announces a free doughnut for every customer who is not given the cash register receipt with his or her purchase. How is this procedure an internal control device for the doughnut shop?

(c) Robin Steele, a swindler, sent several business firms invoices requesting payment for office supplies that had never been delivered to the firm. A 5% discount was offered for prompt payment. What internal control procedures should prevent this swindle from being successful?

(d) Customers of The Famous Cafeteria encounter the cashier at the end of the food line. At this point, the cashier rings up the food costs, and the customer pays the bill. The customer line frequently backs up while the person paying searches for the correct amount of cash. To speed things up, the cashier often collects money from the next customer or two who have the correct change without ringing up their food costs. After the first customer finally pays, the cashier rings up the costs for those customers who have already paid.

(1) What is the internal control weakness in this procedure?

(2) How might the internal control over the collection of cash from the cafeteria customers be strengthened?

Bank reconciliation

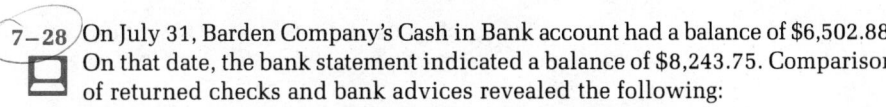

7–28 On July 31, Barden Company's Cash in Bank account had a balance of $6,502.88. On that date, the bank statement indicated a balance of $8,243.75. Comparison of returned checks and bank advices revealed the following:

(1) Deposits in transit July 31 amounted to $3,407.

(2) Outstanding checks July 31 totaled $2,140.37.

(3) The bank erroneously charged a $950 check of the Barkley Company against the Barden bank account.

(4) A $20 bank service charge has not yet been recorded on the books.

(5) Barden neglected to record $4,000 borrowed from the bank on a 10% six-month note. The bank statement shows the $4,000 as a deposit.

(6) Included with the returned checks is a memo indicating that J. Martin's check for $882 had been returned NSF. Martin, a customer, had sent the check to pay an account of $900 less a 2% discount.

(7) Barden Company recorded a $95.50 payment for repairs as $955.

REQUIRED

(a) Prepare a bank reconciliation for Barden Company at July 31.

(b) Prepare the general journal entry or entries necessary to bring the Cash in Bank account into agreement with the adjusted balance on the bank reconciliation.

Bank reconciliation

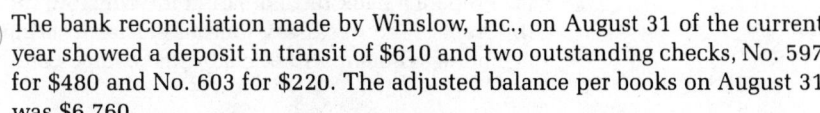

7–29 The bank reconciliation made by Winslow, Inc., on August 31 of the current year showed a deposit in transit of $610 and two outstanding checks, No. 597 for $480 and No. 603 for $220. The adjusted balance per books on August 31 was $6,760.

The following bank statement is available for September.

Bank Statement

TO Winslow, Inc.
St. Louis, MO

September 30, 19XX
STATE BANK

Date	Deposits	No.	Date	Charges	Date	Balance
					Aug. 31	$6,850
Sept. 1	$610	603	Sept. 1	$220	Sept. 1	7,240
2	450	607	5	850	2	7,690
5	520	608	5	320	5	7,040
9	273	609	9	292	8	6,782
15	580	610	8	258	9	6,763
17	604	611	17	435	15	7,101
25	465	612	15	242	17	7,270
30	256	614	25	158	25	7,577
		NSF	29	465	29	7,112
		SC	30	15	30	7,353

A list of deposits made and checks written during September, taken from the cash receipts journal and cash disbursements journal, respectively, is shown below:

Deposits Made		Checks Written	
Sept. 1	$ 450	No. 607	$ 850
4	520	608	320
8	273	609	292
12	580	610	258
16	604	611	453
24	465	612	242
29	256	613	315
30	530	614	158
	$3,678	615	377
		616	168
			$3,433

The Cash in Bank account balance on September 30 was $7,005. In reviewing checks returned by the bank, the bookkeeper discovered that check No. 611, written for $435 for advertising expense, was recorded in the cash disbursements journal as $453. The NSF check for $465, which Winslow deposited on September 24, was a payment on account from customer D. Davis.

REQUIRED

(a) Prepare a bank reconciliation for Winslow, Inc., at September 30.

(b) Prepare the necessary journal entries to bring the Cash in Bank account into agreement with the adjusted balance on the bank reconciliation.

Petty cash

7–30 Ranger, Inc., established an imprest petty cash fund on July 1 of the current year. The following transactions took place during July:

July 1 Wrote check against United Bank account to establish the petty cash fund, $250.

15 Replenished the fund by check against the United Bank account for $201.50. The following bills and receipts were on hand:

Freight on C.O.D. purchase of merchandise	$ 81.50
Postage	44.00
Typewriter repair	57.00
Lunch with client (entertainment expense)	19.00
	$201.50

29 Replenished the fund and increased it to $300 by writing a check against the United Bank account. On this date, the fund contained $15.80 in currency and coins. Bills and receipts on hand were for postage, $60; office supplies expense, $58.20; charitable contributions, $35; and freight on C.O.D. purchase of merchandise, $75.

REQUIRED

Record the July petty cash transactions for Ranger, Inc., in general journal form.

Short-term investments

7–31 The following selected transactions relate to the Hall Corporation during 19X1 and 19X2, its first two years of operations. The company closes its books on December 31.

19X1

Mar. 26 Purchased 2,000 common shares of Moyle, Inc., as a short-term investment at a total cost of $42,900.

July 1 Invested $10,000 in a one-year certificate of deposit at Local Bank. The annual interest rate on the certificate is 8.5%.

1 Purchased, as a short-term investment, thirty $1,000, 10% Hizer Company bonds at 102 plus $100 of commissions and taxes. The bonds pay interest on June 30 and December 31.

Sept. 7 Purchased 3,500 common shares of Breen, Inc., as a short-term investment at a total cost of $112,000.

Dec. 2 Breen, Inc., declared a cash dividend of 60 cents per common share, payable on December 29. Hall Corporation records dividend income when dividends are received.

3 Received 200 shares of Moyle, Inc., common stock as a 10% stock dividend. The stock's current market price per share was $20.

29 Received cash dividend, declared December 2, from Breen, Inc.

31 Received semiannual interest payment on Hizer Company bonds.

31 Accrued interest receivable for six months on certificate of deposit. (Hall Corporation does not use reversing entries.)

31 Adjusted portfolio of short-term stock investments to lower of cost or market. Current market prices per share were Moyle, Inc., $18.50, and Breen, Inc., $30.

19X2

June 30 Received $10,850 when the one-year certificate of deposit (purchased July 1, 19X1) was cashed in.

30 Received semiannual interest payment on Hizer Company bonds.

REQUIRED

(a) Record these transactions in general journal form.

(b) Assume that holdings of short-term stock investments did not change during 19X2. What entry would be made at December 31, 19X2, to adjust the portfolio to the lower of cost or market if the per share market prices at that date were Moyle, Inc., $19; and Breen, Inc., $31.25?

Short-term investments in stocks

7–32 The Thorn Corporation began operations on January 1, 19X1. The following transactions relate to Thorn Corporation's short-term investments in stocks during 19X1 and 19X2:

19X1

Feb. 15	Purchased 3,000 common shares of Holden, Inc., at a total cost of $69,000.
April 20	Purchased 1,200 common shares of Knox Corporation at a total cost of $30,240.
June 25	Received 60 shares of Knox Corporation common stock as a 5% stock dividend. The stock's current market price per share was $26.
Aug. 6	Purchased 2,000 common shares of Field, Inc., at a total cost of $41,000.
Sept. 3	Sold 460 Knox Corporation common shares at a price of $27 per share.
Dec. 15	Received a cash dividend of $1.25 per common share from Holden, Inc. Holden declared the dividend on November 20. Thorn Corporation records dividend income when dividends are received.
30	Received a cash dividend of $1.10 per common share from Field, Inc.
31	Adjusted portfolio of short-term stock investments to lower of cost or market. Current market prices per share were Holden, Inc., $24; Knox Corporation, $22.50; and Field, Inc., $18.25.

19X2

Mar. 11	Sold remaining 800 Knox Corporation common shares at a price of $21 per share.
Dec. 15	Received a cash dividend of $1.20 per common share from Holden, Inc.
30	Received a cash dividend of 70 cents per common share from Field, Inc.
31	Adjusted portfolio of short-term stock investments to lower of cost or market. Current market prices per share were Holden, Inc., $23.50; and Field, Inc., $19.25.

REQUIRED

Record these transactions in general journal form.

ALTERNATE PROBLEMS

Internal control

7–26A The Holland Company has three clerical employees who must perform the following functions:

(1) Maintain general ledger.
(2) Maintain accounts payable ledger.
(3) Maintain accounts receivable ledger.
(4) Prepare checks for signature.
(5) Maintain cash disbursements journal.

(6) Issue credits on returns and allowances.
(7) Reconcile the bank account.
(8) Handle and deposit cash receipts.

The office manager of the Holland Company wishes to assign the above functions to the three employees in the manner that achieves the highest degree of internal control.

REQUIRED

Distribute the functions among the employees in a manner compatible with good internal control.

Internal control

7–27A The Wild Ride amusement ride has the following system of internal control over its cash receipts. All persons pay the same price for a ride. An individual taking the ride pays the cashier and receives a ticket. The individual then walks to the ride site, hands the ticket to a ticket taker (who controls the number of people getting on each ride), and passes through a turnstile. All tickets are prenumbered. At the end of each day, the beginning ticket number is subtracted from the ending ticket number to determine the number of admissions sold. The cash is counted and compared with the number of tickets sold. The turnstile records each person that passes through it. At the end of each day, the beginning turnstile number is subtracted from the ending turnstile number to determine the number of riders that day. The number of riders is compared with the number of tickets sold.

REQUIRED

Which internal control feature would reveal each of the following irregularities?

(a) The ticket taker admits her friends without a ticket.
(b) The cashier gives his friends tickets without receiving any cash.
(c) The cashier gives too much change.
(d) The ticket taker returns the tickets she has collected to the cashier. The cashier then re-sells these tickets and splits the proceeds with the ticket taker.
(e) An individual sneaks into the ride line without paying the cashier.

Bank reconciliation

7–28A On May 31, the Cash in Bank account of the Rand Company, a sole proprietorship, had a balance of $6,851.21. On that date, the bank statement indicated a balance of $8,102.28. Comparison of returned checks and bank advices revealed the following:

(1) Deposits in transit May 31 totaled $1,618.
(2) Outstanding checks May 31 totaled $2,240.32.
(3) The bank added to the account $32.75 of interest income earned by Rand during May.
(4) The bank collected a $1,000 note receivable for Rand and charged a $5.00 collection fee. Both items appear on the bank statement.
(5) Bank service charges in addition to the collection fee, not yet recorded on the books, were $15.
(6) Included with the returned checks is a memo indicating that L. Pryor's check for $294 had been returned NSF. Pryor, a customer, had sent the check to pay an account of $300 less a 2% discount.
(7) Rand Company recorded the payment of an account payable as $127; the check was for $217.

REQUIRED
(a) Prepare a bank reconciliation for Rand Company at May 31.
(b) Prepare the general journal entry or entries necessary to bring the Cash in Bank account into agreement with the adjusted balance on the bank reconciliation.

Bank reconciliation

7–29A The bank reconciliation made by Geneva Company, a sole proprietorship, on March 31 of the current year showed a deposit in transit of $830 and two outstanding checks, No. 797 for $445 and No. 804 for $500. The adjusted balance per books on March 31 was $7,960.

The following bank statement is available for April:

Bank Statement

TO Geneva Company
Fairbanks, AK

April 30, 19XX
FAIRBANKS NATIONAL BANK

Date	Deposits	No.	Date	Charges	Date	Balance
					March 31	$8,075
Apr. 1	$830	797	Apr. 2	$445	Apr. 1	8,905
3	740	807	3	375	2	8,460
7	910	808	7	730	3	8,825
13	490	809	7	474	7	8,531
18	680	810	16	198	13	8,637
23	355	811	13	384	16	8,439
27	590	813	27	272	18	8,969
30	480	814	23	450	23	8,874
30	35 IN	NSF	18	150	27	9,192
		SC	30	25	30	9,682

A list of deposits made and checks written during April, taken from the cash receipts journal and cash disbursements journal, respectively, is shown below:

Deposits Made		Checks Written	
Apr. 2	$ 740	No. 807	$ 375
6	910	808	730
10	490	809	474
17	680	810	198
22	355	811	348
24	590	812	135
29	480	813	272
30	675	814	450
	$4,920	815	310
		816	578
			$3,870

The Cash in Bank account balance on April 30 was $9,010. In reviewing checks returned by the bank, the bookkeeper discovered that check No. 811, written for $384 for delivery expense, was recorded in the cash disbursements journal as $348. The NSF check for $150 was that of customer R. Jenson, deposited in April. Interest for April added to the account by the bank was $35.

REQUIRED

(a) Prepare a bank reconciliation for Geneva Company at April 30.

(b) Prepare the necessary journal entries to bring the Cash in Bank account into agreement with the adjusted balance on the bank reconciliation.

Petty cash

7–30A Delevan, Inc., established an imprest petty cash fund on May 1 of the current year. The following transactions took place during May:

May 1 Wrote check against American Bank account to establish the petty cash fund, $200.

12 Replenished the fund by check against the American Bank account for $171.65. The following bills and receipts were on hand:

Charge for rush delivery of package across town	$ 25.75
Postage	55.00
Calculator repairs	42.00
Flowers sent to customer opening new office (advertising expense)	48.90
	$171.65

25 Replenished the fund and increased it to $250 by writing a check against the American Bank account. On this date, the fund contained $9.50 in currency and coins. Bills and receipts on hand were for postage, $39; office supplies expense, $89.50; and instant printing charges (advertising expense), $65.

REQUIRED

Record the May petty cash transactions for Delevan, Inc., in general journal form.

Short-term investments

7–31A The following selected transactions relate to the Cardex Corporation during 19X1 and 19X2, its first two years of operations. The company closes its books on December 31.

19X1

Feb. 17 Purchased 1,600 common shares of Stemler, Inc., as a short-term investment at a total cost of $67,200.

May 31 Purchased, as a short-term investment, fifteen $1,000, 8% Mayo Company bonds at 98 plus five months' accrued interest. The brokerage commission was $75. The bonds pay interest on June 30 and December 31.

June 30 Received semiannual interest payment on Mayo Company bonds.

July 1 Invested $50,000 in a one-year certificate of deposit at Hilldale Bank. The annual interest rate on the certificate is 8.2%.

Aug. 10 Purchased 2,500 common shares of Ogden, Inc., as a short-term investment at a total cost of $43,050.

Dec. 1 Stemler, Inc., declared a cash dividend of $1.15 per common share, payable on December 28. Cardex Corporation records dividend income when dividends are received.

5 Received 125 shares of Ogden, Inc., common stock as a 5% stock dividend. The stock's current market price per share was $17.

Dec. 28 Received cash dividend, declared December 1, from Stemler, Inc.
31 Received semiannual interest payment on Mayo Company bonds.
31 Accrued interest receivable for six months on certificate of deposit. (Cardex Corporation does not use reversing entries.)
31 Adjusted portfolio of short-term stock investments to lower of cost or market. Current market prices per share were Stemler, Inc., $40.50; and Ogden, Inc., $15.

19X2

Feb. 1 Sold Mayo Company bonds for $14,900 plus accrued interest for one month.
June 30 Received $54,100 when the one-year certificate of deposit (purchased July 1, 19X1) was cashed in.

REQUIRED

(a) Record these transactions in general journal form.
(b) Assume that holdings of short-term stock investments did not change during 19X2. What entry would be made at December 31, 19X2, to adjust the portfolio to the lower of cost or market if the per share market prices at that date were Stemler, Inc., $41; and Ogden, Inc., $16?

Short-term investments

7–32A The following transactions relate to Haven Company's short-term investments in stocks and bonds during 19X5:

19X5

Jan. 10 Purchased 3,100 common shares of Berman Corporation at a total cost of $78,864.
Feb. 1 Purchased twelve $1,000, 13% Moore Company bonds at 104 plus one month's accrued interest. The brokerage commission was $60. The bonds pay interest on January 1 and July 1.
May 28 Purchased 1,400 common shares of Cook, Inc., at a total cost of $16,800.
June 30 Received a cash dividend of 40 cents per common share from Cook, Inc.
July 1 Received semiannual interest payment on Moore Company bonds.
1 Purchased nine $1,000, 10% Wolter Company bonds at 99 plus a $50 brokerage commission. The bonds pay interest on January 1 and July 1.
Sept. 30 Received 186 shares of Berman Corporation common stock as a 6% stock dividend. The stock's current market price was $26.
Nov. 1 Sold the Moore Company bonds for $12,100 plus accrued interest for four months.
17 Sold the Berman Corporation common stock for $26.50 per share.
Dec. 1 Sold the Wolter Company bonds for $9,200 plus accrued interest for five months.
14 Sold the Cook, Inc., common stock for $10.25 per share.

REQUIRED

Record these transactions in general journal form.

BUSINESS DECISION PROBLEM

On December 15 of the current year, Lyle Fifend, who owns the Fifend Drum Company, asks you to investigate the cash-handling activities in his firm. He thinks that an employee might be abstracting funds. "I have no proof," he says, "but I'm fairly certain that the November 30 undeposited receipts amounted to more than $7,000, although the November 30 bank reconciliation prepared by the cashier shows only $4,694.41. Also, the November bank reconciliation doesn't show several checks that have been outstanding for a long time. The cashier told me that these checks needn't appear on the reconciliation because he had notified the bank to stop payment on them and he had made the necessary adjustment on the books. Does that sound reasonable to you?"

At your request, Fifend shows you the following November 30 bank reconciliation prepared by the cashier:

Bank Reconciliation
November 30, 19XX

Balance per bank statement		$11,260.15	Balance per books		$16,456.85
Add: Deposits in transit		4,694.41			
		$16,964.56			
Less:			Less:		
Outstanding checks:			Bank service charge	$ 25	
			Unrecorded credit	500	525.00
No. 2351	$430.71				
No. 2353	266.80				
No. 2354	335.20	1,032.71			
Adjusted balance		$15,931.85	Adjusted Balance		$15,931.85

You discover that the $500 unrecorded bank credit represents a note collected by the bank on Fifend's behalf; it appears in the deposits column of the November bank statement. Your investigation also reveals that the October 31 bank reconciliation showed three checks that had been outstanding longer than 10 months: No. 1432 for $256; No. 1458 for $190.50; and No. 1512 for $183.50. You also discover that these items were never added back into the Cash account in the books. In confirming that the checks shown on the cashier's November 30 bank reconciliation were outstanding on that date, you discover that check No. 2353 was actually a payment of $626.80 and had been recorded on the books for that amount.

To confirm the amount of undeposited receipts at November 30, you request a bank statement for December 1–12 (called a "cut-off" bank statement). This indeed shows a December 1 deposit of $4,694.41.

REQUIRED

(a) Calculate the amount of funds abstracted by the cashier.
(b) Describe how the cashier concealed the abstraction.
(c) What sort of entry or entries should be made when a firm decides that checks outstanding for a long time should no longer be carried in the bank reconciliation?
(d) What suggestions would you make to Fifend about cash control procedures?

ANSWERS TO SELF-TEST QUESTIONS

1. (c) 2. (d) 3. (a) 4. (d) 5. (b)

8

Trade Accounts and Notes

Chapter Objectives

- **Define trade receivables and payables and explain a firm's credit policies.**
- **Describe the two methods that can be used to recognize losses from uncollectible accounts.**
- **Illustrate the procedures for estimating and recording credit losses.**
- **Describe and illustrate notes and interest calculations.**
- **Illustrate the discounting of notes receivable and payable.**

Creditors are a superstitious sect,
great observers of set days and time.

BENJAMIN FRANKLIN

Business practice today is governed by credit. Indeed, the vast daily sales of goods and services might not be made without it. In recent years, the use of credit has expanded immensely, particularly in the retail field. Millions of consumers possess and regularly use several credit cards.

The growth of credit has created a need for more elaborate and sophisticated systems for processing transactions and gathering credit information. However, the basic accounting problems of keeping track of payables and receivables have remained essentially the same.

TRADE RECEIVABLES AND PAYABLES

The terms **trade receivable** and **trade payable** usually refer to receivables and payables that arise in the regular course of a company's transactions with customers and suppliers. Payments normally are made within 30 to 60 days. Therefore, the amount of a sale of merchandise sold on account is debited to the appropriate customer's account in the subsidiary accounts receivable ledger; this amount is also debited to the Accounts Receivable control account when credit sales are posted periodically to it. The subsidiary record and the control account should reflect only trade accounts. Advances to company employees or officers should not be included here, nor should advances to affiliated companies, such as subsidiaries, be included. Such receivables should be recorded in separate accounts. In many instances, such receivables are not current, and as a result, they often appear in the balance sheet under a noncurrent heading, such as Other Assets. Advances to subsidiary companies are frequently semipermanent, and they may be found in the balance sheet under the Investments caption.

Likewise, trade accounts payable consist only of open amounts owing for the purchase of merchandise, materials, or the acquisition of services from outsiders. Separate current liability accounts contain amounts that a firm owes for salaries, wages, various types of taxes, sundry accruals, and so on.

The principal reason for separating trade accounts from other receivables and payables is to facilitate analyses by both management and outsiders. You will learn in Chapter 20 that certain techniques employed in studying a company's current accounts depend on such separation.

Occasionally, individual accounts within the accounts receivable or accounts payable subsidiary ledgers may show abnormal balances. A customer may have overpaid an account, paid an advance on goods not yet shipped, or returned goods already paid for. A substantial credit balance in a customer's account is reclassified as a current liability when a balance sheet is prepared. On the other hand, if the firm itself makes advances on purchases or overpays accounts, the resulting debit balances in accounts payable are reclassified as current assets in the balance sheet.

INSTALLMENT ACCOUNTS

Many business concerns—such as mail-order houses and appliance dealers—make many of their sales on the installment basis. Typically, a customer of such a firm purchases merchandise by signing an installment contract in which he or she agrees to a down payment plus installment payments of a fixed amount over a period such as 24 or 36 months. Normally, the total price of the merchandise sold includes an interest charge, and the contract allows the seller to repossess merchandise if the installment payments are not made. If the installment contract conforms to the firm's normal trade practices and terms, the installment receivable is classified as a current asset.

LOSSES FROM UNCOLLECTIBLE ACCOUNTS

Few firms that extend credit to customers are immune to credit losses. Indeed, most companies anticipate them. The magnitude of such losses is often directly related to the firm's credit policy. Sometimes a company deliberately liberalizes its credit policy to obtain increased sales, fully anticipating an increase in credit losses.

Most large companies have credit departments to administer management's established credit policies. Credit personnel may set credit limits, conduct investigations of credit ratings, and follow up on unpaid accounts. They may also decide, after following established collection procedures, when a debt is uncollectible.

Credit losses, considered operating expenses of the business, are debited to an appropriately titled account such as *Uncollectible Accounts Expense*. Other account titles frequently used are *Loss from Uncollectible Accounts, Loss from Doubtful Accounts*, or *Bad Debts Expense*. Normally, the expense is classified as a selling expense on the income statement, although some companies include it with administrative expenses.

Timing of Recognition

There are two methods for recognizing losses from uncollectible accounts. One is called the **direct write-off method**. The other method, which is preferable, is called the **allowance method.**

THE DIRECT WRITE-OFF METHOD Under the direct write-off method, uncollectible accounts are charged to expense in the period when they are discovered to be uncollectible. Suppose that in December of last year, J. B. Stone purchased merchandise billed at $125, and that, after repeated collection attempts, the credit department decided on July 15 of the current year that the amount will never be collected. The following entry would record the loss:

July 15	Uncollectible Accounts Expense	125	
	Accounts Receivable—J. B. Stone		125
	To write off J. B. Stone's account		

This entry charges the loss to the current year's expenses and reduces the asset Accounts Receivable by $125. Also, J. B. Stone's subsidiary ledger account no longer has a balance.

The major shortcoming of the direct write-off method is that credit losses are not matched with related sales. In our example, the revenue from the sale to J. B. Stone would be reflected in last year's income statement, but the loss would appear in the current year's income statement. The use of the direct write-off method also causes the consistent overstatement of Accounts Receivable on the balance sheet. Since generally accepted accounting principles prescribe that receivables be shown at the amount the firm expects to collect, most accountants disapprove of the direct write-off method.

This method would be obviously inappropriate in certain situations. Suppose a firm liberalized its credit policy in one year, realizing a large increase in sales revenue. Much of the related uncollectible accounts expense would not appear on the income statement until the next year, because collection efforts and follow-up procedures often extend over long periods of time. Most accountants and credit people believe that the credit loss occurs at the time of sale and therefore should be reflected in the same period.

THE ALLOWANCE METHOD Most businesses employ the matching concept to determine net income. Therefore, they prefer to estimate the amount of uncollectible accounts expense that will eventually result from a period's sales in order to reflect the expense during the same period. This procedure not only matches credit losses with related revenue, but also results in an estimated realizable amount for accounts receivable in the balance sheet at the end of the period. The estimate is introduced into the accounts by an adjusting entry.

Let us assume that a firm with accounts receivable of $100,000 at the end of its first business year estimates that $4,000 of these accounts will be uncollectible. The firm makes the following adjusting entry:

Dec. 31	Uncollectible Accounts Expense	4,000	
	Allowance for Uncollectible Accounts		4,000
	To record uncollectible accounts expense.		

Note that in the adjusting entry, the credit is made to an account called *Allowance for Uncollectible Accounts* rather than to Accounts Receivable. This is done for two reasons. First, when the firm makes the adjusting entry, it does not know which accounts in the subsidiary accounts receivable ledger will be uncollectible. If the Accounts Receivable control account is credited and no entries are made in the subsidiary ledger, then the two records no longer agree in total. Second, because the amount involved is only an estimate, it is preferable not to reduce Accounts Receivable directly.

The Allowance for Uncollectible Accounts is a *contra* asset account with a normal credit balance. To present the expected realizable amount of Accounts Receivable, we deduct the Allowance for Uncollectible Accounts from Accounts Receivable in the balance sheet as follows:

Current Assets		
Cash		$XXXXX
Accounts Receivable	$100,000	
Less: Allowance for Uncollectible Accounts	4,000	96,000
Inventory		XXXXX
Other Current Assets		XXXXX
Total Current Assets		$XXXXX

Writing Off Specific Accounts

The credit manager or other company official normally authorizes writing off a specific account. When the accounting department is notified of the action, it makes the following entry:

Jan. 5	Allowance for Uncollectible Accounts	250	
	Accounts Receivable—James Baker		250
	To write off James Baker's account.		

The credit in the above entry is made to James Baker's account in the subsidiary accounts receivable ledger as well as to the Accounts Receivable control account; therefore, these two records are still in agreement.

The entry to write off an account does not affect net income or total assets. By means of the adjusting entry, the expense is reflected in the period when the related revenue is recorded. Furthermore, because the Allowance for Uncollectible Accounts is deducted from Accounts Receivable in the balance sheet, the *net* realizable amount of accounts receivable is not changed by the write-off. After Baker's account has been written off, the Accounts Receivable and Allowance for Uncollectible Accounts ledger pages appear as follows:

Accounts Receivable Account No. 12

Date		Description	Post. Ref.	Debit	Credit	Balance
19XX						
Jan.	1	Balance				100,000
	5	Write-off, James Baker			250	99,750

Allowance for Uncollectible Accounts Account No. 13

Date		Description	Post. Ref.	Debit	Credit	Balance
19XX						
Jan.	1	Balance				4,000
	5	Write-off, James Baker		250		3,750

In these accounts, the net realizable amount of accounts receivable on January 1 is $96,000 ($100,000 − $4,000 allowance). After the January 5 write-off, the net realizable amount of accounts receivable is still $96,000 ($99,750 − $3,750 allowance). Thus, the write-off of an account does not affect the net asset balance.

Estimating Credit Losses

Estimates of credit losses are generally based on past experience, with consideration given to forecasts of sales activity, economic conditions, and planned changes in credit policy. The most commonly used calculations are related either to credit sales for the period or to the amount of accounts receivable at the close of the period.

ESTIMATES RELATED TO SALES Through experience, many companies can determine the approximate percentage of credit sales that will be uncollectible. At the end of an accounting period, the amount of the adjusting entry is determined by multiplying the total credit sales by this percentage. Suppose that credit sales for a period amount to $200,000 and that past experience indicates a loss of $1\frac{1}{2}$%. The adjusting entry for expected losses would be:

Dec. 31	Uncollectible Accounts Expense	3,000	
	Allowance for Uncollectible Accounts		3,000
	To record uncollectible accounts expense.		

Because the periodic estimates for uncollectibles under this procedure are related to sales, a firm should review its allowance account regularly to ensure a reasonable balance. Should the allowance account balance become too large or too small, the percentage used for the periodic estimates should be revised accordingly.

A company that estimates its credit losses from sales figures customarily uses credit sales only. In some cases, however, a percentage of both credit and cash sales may be calculated, as long as the proportions of the two types of sales remain relatively constant over time. Whether sales discounts or sales returns and allowances are deducted before applying a percentage to sales figures depends on how the percentage was developed; the exercises and problems in this text assume that percentages are applied to gross credit sales.

ESTIMATES RELATED TO ACCOUNTS RECEIVABLE A company's experience may show that a certain percentage of accounts receivable at the end of a period is likely to prove uncollectible. The credit balance in the allowance account should equal this amount. Therefore, the adjustment for uncollectibles is the amount needed to create the desired credit balance in the company's allowance account.

Suppose that a company estimates uncollectibles as 5% of accounts receivable and that the Accounts Receivable balance at the end of an accounting period is $50,000. Therefore, the desired credit balance in the allowance account is $2,500. If the allowance account already has a residual credit balance of $400, the amount of the adjustment is $2,100. The adjusting entry is a debit to Uncollectible Accounts Expense and a credit to Allowance for Uncollectible Accounts.

Instead of using a fixed percentage of the aggregate customers' balances, some companies determine the amount needed in the allowance account after analyzing the age structure of the account balances. These companies prepare an aging schedule similar to the one in Exhibit 8–1. An **aging schedule** is simply an analysis that shows how long customers' balances have remained unpaid. Assume that the firm whose aging schedule appears in Exhibit 8–1 sells on net terms of 30 days. Alton's account is current, which means that the $320 billing was made within the last 30 days. Bailey's account is 0–30 days *past due*, which means that the account is from 31 to 60 days old. Wall's balance consists of a $50 billing made from 91 to 150 days ago and a $100 billing made from 151 days to seven months ago, and so on.

Companies that analyze their bad accounts experience with the aged balances may develop percentages of each stratum that are likely to prove uncollectible. At the end of each period, these percentages are applied to the totals of each age group to determine the allowance account balance. For our example, these percentages are shown below. Applying the percentages to the totals in our aging schedule, we calculate an allowance requirement of $1,560.

EXHIBIT 8–1
Aging Schedule of Customer Balances, December 31, 19XX

			Past Due				
Customer	**Account Balance**	**Current**	**0–30 Days**	**31–60 Days**	**61–120 Days**	**121 Days –6 Mos.**	**Over 6 Mos.**
Alton, J.	$ 320	$ 320	$	$	$	$	$
Bailey, C.	400		400				
.							
.							
.							
Wall, M.	150				50	100	
Zorn, W.	210			210			
	$50,000	$42,000	$4,000	$2,000	$1,000	$800	$200

	Amount	Percent Doubtful	Allowance Required
Current	$42,000	2	$ 840
0–30 days past due	4,000	3	120
31–60 days past due	2,000	5	100
61–120 days past due	1,000	20	200
121 days–6 months past due	800	25	200
Over 6 months past due	200	50	100
Total Allowance Required			$1,560

Again, if the allowance account has a residual $400 credit balance, the adjustment is for $1,160. The entry would be:

Dec. 31	Uncollectible Accounts Expense	1,160	
	Allowance for Uncollectible Accounts		1,160
	To record uncollectible accounts expense.		

The adjustment brings the credit balance in the allowance account to the required amount—$1,560.

Recoveries of Accounts Written Off

Occasionally, accounts written off against the Allowance for Uncollectible Accounts later prove to be wholly or partly collectible. In such situations, a firm should reinstate the customer's account for the amount recovered before recording the collection, so that the payment is recorded in the customer's account. The entry made for the write-off is reversed to the extent of the recovery and the receipt is recorded in the usual manner. For example, assume that a company using the allowance method wrote off James Baker's $250 account on January 5 but received payment in full on April 20. The following entries (including write-off) illustrate the recovery procedure.

To write off the account

Jan. 5	Allowance for Uncollectible Accounts	250	
	Accounts Receivable—James Baker		250

To reinstate the account

Apr. 20	Accounts Receivable—James Baker	250	
	Allowance for Uncollectible Accounts		250

To record remittance

Apr. 20	Cash	250	
	Accounts Receivable—James Baker		250

These last two entries may be made even if the recovery occurs in a year after the write-off.

A business employing the direct write-off method that recovers a written-off account during the year of write-off simply reverses the entry made to write off the account to the extent of the recovery and records the remittance in the usual manner. Recoveries made in years after the write-off normally require two entries also. One entry reinstates the customer's account balance, with the credit made to an income statement account titled Recoveries of Accounts Written Off. The second entry records the remittance in the usual manner.

CREDIT CARD FEES

Many retailing businesses have their credit sales handled through banks and other financial institutions that issue credit cards such as VISA and MasterCard. The issuer incurs the costs of processing and collecting the amounts charged on its credit cards and absorbs any losses from uncollectible accounts. In exchange for these services, the retail firm is charged a fee, usually ranging from $\frac{1}{2}$–5% of the amount of the credit sale. The retailer makes the credit card sale and deposits the charge slip with the financial institution, which credits the retailer's account for the amount of the sale less the credit card fee. The retailer records the transaction by debiting Cash (for the amount of the sale less the fee), debiting a Credit Card Fee Expense account (for the amount of the fee), and crediting Sales.

Credit sales may also be made to customers who use other credit cards, such as American Express and Diner's Club cards. The retailer sends the charge slip to the credit card company, then receives a check from that company for the sales amount less the credit card fee. The retailer records these sales by establishing a receivable from the credit card company (for the amount of the sale less the fee), debiting Credit Card Fee Expense (for the amount of the fee), and crediting Sales. The receivable is credited when the check is received from the credit card company.

NOTES RECEIVABLE AND PAYABLE

Promissory notes are often used in transactions when the credit period is longer than the 30 or 60 days typical for open accounts. Although promissory notes are used frequently in sales of equipment and real property, a note is sometimes exchanged for merchandise. Occasionally, a note is substituted for an open account when an extension of the usual credit period is granted. In addition, promissory notes are normally executed when loans are obtained from banks and other parties.

A **promissory note** is a written promise to pay a certain sum of money on demand or at a fixed and determinable future time. The note is signed by the **maker** and made payable to the order of either a specific **payee** or to the **bearer.** The note may be *non-interest bearing* or *interest bearing* at an annual rate specified on the note. An interest-bearing promissory note is illustrated in Exhibit 8–2.

EXHIBIT 8–2
A Promissory Note

$2,000.00 Madison, Wisconsin May 3, 19XX

Sixty days after date I promise to pay to

the order of Robert Ward

Two Thousand and no/100---------------------------------dollars

for value received with interest at 9%.

payable at American Exchange Bank

James Stone

A note from a debtor is called a **note receivable** by the holder and a **note payable** by the debtor. A note is usually regarded as a stronger claim against a debtor than an open account because the terms of payment are specified in writing. Although open accounts can be sold (factored), a note can be converted to cash more easily by discounting it at a bank. (We treat the discounting of notes later in this chapter.)

Interest on Notes

Interest on notes is commonly paid on the maturity date of the obligation, except in certain discounting transactions. Interest incurred is debited to an Interest Expense account, and interest earned is credited to an Interest Income account. When business firms distinguish between operating and other items of income and expense in their income statements, they show interest expense and interest income under the heading Other Income and Expense.

INTEREST CALCULATION The formula for determining simple interest is:

$$\text{Principal} \times \text{Rate} \times \text{Time} = \text{Interest}$$

Unless otherwise specified, we shall assume that interest rates on notes are annual rates. For example, interest on a one-year note for $2,000 at 9% would be calculated as follows:

$$\$2{,}000 \times \frac{9}{100} \times 1 = \$180$$

When a note is for a certain number of months, the time is usually expressed in twelfths of a year. Thus, the interest on a six-month note for $2,000 at 9% would be calculated as follows:

$$\$2{,}000 \times \frac{9}{100} \times \frac{6}{12} = \$90$$

When the note's duration is given in days, we express the time as a fraction of a year; the number of days' duration is the numerator and 360 is the denominator. (It is general business practice to use 360 days here, although federal agencies and certain lenders may use 365 days.) Interest on a 60-day note for $2,000 at 9% would be calculated as follows:

$$\$2{,}000 \times \frac{9}{100} \times \frac{60}{360} = \$30$$

DETERMINING MATURITY DATE When a note's duration is expressed in days, we count the exact days in each calendar month to determine the maturity date. For example, a 90-day note dated July 21 would have an October 19 maturity date, which we determine as follows:

10 days in July (remainder of month—31 days minus 21 days)
31 days in August
30 days in September
19 days in October (number of days required to total 90)
90

If the duration of a note is expressed in months, we find the maturity date simply by counting the months from the date of issue. For example, a two-month note dated January 31 would mature on March 31, a three-month note of the same date would mature on April 30 (the last day of the month), and a four-month note would mature on May 31.

RECORDING NOTES AND INTEREST When a note is exchanged to settle an open trade account, an entry is made to reflect the note receivable or payable and to reduce the balance of the related account receivable or payable. For example, suppose Acme Company sold $4,000 of merchandise to Bowman Company. On October 1, after the regular credit period had elapsed, Bowman Company gave Acme Company a 60-day, 12% note for $4,000. The following entries would be made by each of the parties:

Acme Company

Oct. 1	Notes Receivable	4,000	
	Accounts Receivable—Bowman Company		4,000
	Received 60-day, 12% note in payment of account.		

Bowman Company

Oct. 1	Accounts Payable—Acme Company	4,000	
	Notes Payable		4,000
	Gave 60-day, 12% note in payment of account.		

If Bowman Company pays the note on the November 30 maturity date, the following entries would be made by the parties involved:

Acme Company

Nov. 30	Cash	4,080	
	Interest Income		80
	Notes Receivable		4,000
	Collected Bowman Company note.		

Bowman Company

Nov. 30	Notes Payable	4,000	
	Interest Expense	80	
	Cash		4,080
	Paid note to Acme Company.		

SPORTING ECONOMICS

As you proceed down life's highway, if you keep your eyes open, you'll find some curious types. As an example, no one can spend much time on this planet without meeting somebody who has an acute case of the frugals. It has been suggested that some people of the hunter/fisher persuasion fall into that category. It's almost inconceivable that a fisherman would be penurious when it comes to essential expenditures like a boat, motor, or boron/graphite rod. Likewise, a dedicated hunter seldom carries a shooting iron with a popple stock. Nevertheless, we have all met folks who enjoy camping, hunting and fishing and are quite snug with the buck in other ways.

Jerry Groler was an example. Jerry never married. He thought it was a dreadful waste of money. He rented his autos, too. He never loaned money to anyone because he claimed it gave them amnesia. But he owned quality guns and rifles. His fishing equipment was top shelf and he drank only the best Kentucky bourbons. He had two dogs of magnificent reputation and he loved to shoot over them. While he had an equal enjoyment for the accumulation of capital, he wouldn't think of parting with either of the animals—even at the terribly inflated amounts he had been offered.

Jerry's income was not within the nation's top twenty percent, but his expense ratios were low and that was the secret of his comfortable economic status. A conservative investor, he was dividend and interest conscious, but had the courage to sell and reinvest. So he had a nice volume of high interest securities working for him. He was also reported to keep a large amount of cash neatly tied in easy-to-count bundles stashed away in and around the leased ten acres that contained his home, a wood lot, and a stream reported to hold trout.

I always thought that story was a lot of hogwash. Jerry wouldn't keep cash when he could have it producing 10.8% for him. But the rumor persisted and, I'm sure, was accepted as gospel by many. Two of those 'many' were William Meyer and Thomas Thaves.

Meyer and Thaves were the presidents of two local competing banks. Either of them would have given an eye tooth to get Jerry's hidden cache securely reposing in his depository. Whenever either one of them met Jerry, sooner or later the conversation turned to the absolute safety of their institution, the interest rate on term deposits and such stuff like that there. But Jerry never got caught up in the spirit of the thing. He never opened an account in either bank. Until last fall, he had carefully followed the advise of Polonius and was neither a borrower nor a lender (at least as far as the local banking institutions were concerned).

Note that the interest for 60 days at 12% is reflected by the respective parties on the maturity date of the note. This would be true even if the maker defaulted on the note. If Bowman Company did not pay the note when due, Acme would debit the $4,080 to Accounts Receivable rather than to Cash. When a note receivable is dishonored at maturity, the combined principal and interest are converted to an open account. This procedure leaves only current, unmatured notes in the Notes Receivable account.

Discounting Customer Notes

Occasionally, a business may not wait until the maturity date of a note receivable to obtain cash from a customer transaction. Instead, it can endorse the note over to a bank, *discounting* the note and receiving an amount equal to the note's maturity value less the discount charged by the bank. By endorsing the note (unless it is endorsed *without recourse*), the business agrees to pay the note at

As a result of all this, it was a pleasant surprise when Tom looked up one morning last September and saw Jerry Groler standing in the bank lobby—nervous and ill at ease. Tom's pulse rate increased when he came into his office and sat down. Jerry wasn't carrying a little black box, but it was clear he was there for some special purpose. After an agonizing five minutes of small talk, Jerry finally got around to wondering what interest rate he might get on a savings account. Tom began to salivate and figured the potential was good enough to kick the rate up an eighth of a point, so he said: $5\frac{5}{8}$%. (He didn't know Bill Meyer had already quoted $5\frac{3}{4}$%.) Then Jerry went back to another five minutes of small talk while Tom managed to keep control of himself. Then he wondered what the interest rate would be if he borrowed two thousand dollars. Tom shaved the rate to 12%. (This was the right thing to do, because a half hour earlier Bill Meyer had said $12\frac{1}{2}$%.)

Jerry supposed a bank would want collateral for a loan like that, but Tom said absolutely no collateral would be required from a good, fine, upstanding, honest, well-respected, honorable citizen like Jerry Groler. This apparently was a mistake because the old conservative nature of Jerry's progenitors came to the forefront. He said he didn't want any special treatment and he wasn't sure he wanted to deal with a bank that didn't insist on proper security for a loan. It might not be safe. As he got up to leave, Tom blocked his way to the door, hastened to assure him the bank usually took security, in fact, almost always took security, would be willing to take security from Jerry and why didn't he sit down and we'll discuss the arrangements now.

Once the matter was fully out in the open, Jerry came straight to the point. He had a chance to take a trip. The opportunity had developed without notice and his money was tied up in investments which wouldn't come due for a month or so. He had a dismaying choice to make—cash in and lose interest—borrow short term from a bank—or stay home. The only security he could give was his two hunting dogs—known to be worth well over $5,000.00. Tom was understanding and agreed to the loan. Jerry insisted he take the dogs as hostage for the promise to pay. The deal was struck. Jerry got the money, delivered the dogs and after an almost tearful farewell to them, he left town.

Thirty days later, Jerry returned from a long fishing vacation in Alaska. He went to Bill's bank and withdrew the same $2,000.00 he had borrowed from Tom—plus a month's interest at $5\frac{3}{4}$% ($9.58). Then he went to Tom's bank and gave him the $2,009.58—plus $10.42 of his own money—in payment of the total loan principal and interest of $2,020.00

(And that wasn't so bad. Where else can you board two dogs for 30 days for $10.42?)

Galen Winter, "Sporting Economics," as it appeared in *Wisconsin Sportsman*, September/October 1985. Reprinted by permission.

the maturity date if the maker fails to pay it. Consequently, the note is the endorser's **contingent liability** (that is, the liability is contingent on the failure of the maker to pay). While the note is outstanding, the endorser discloses the contingent liability in its balance sheet. However, because a contingent liability is a potential liability rather than an actual liability, the amount is not included with the liabilities, but is disclosed in a footnote to the balance sheet. For example, the footnote may read "At December 31, 19XX, the Company was contingently liable for discounted notes receivable having a maturity value of $(amount)."

DISCOUNTING NON-INTEREST-BEARING NOTES RECEIVABLE Assume that the $4,000, 60-day note received on October 1 by Acme Company from Bowman Company is non-interest-bearing. Suppose that Acme Company discounts the note at the bank on October 31 and that the bank's discount rate is 12%.

The bank discount calculation is always based on the **maturity value** (Principal + Interest) of the note and the number of days that the bank must hold the note. Because the note in our example is non-interest-bearing, the maturity value equals the face value, $4,000. The bank must hold the note for 30 days—October 31 to November 30. (In calculating the discount period, we ignore the discount date and count the maturity date as a full day.) We calculate the proceeds as follows:

$$\text{Maturity Value} \times \text{Discount Rate} \times \text{Discount Period} = \text{Discount}$$
$$\$4{,}000 \times 12\% \times \frac{30}{360} = \$40$$

$$\text{Maturity Value} - \text{Discount} = \text{Proceeds}$$
$$\$4{,}000 - \$40 = \$3{,}960$$

To record the discounting transaction, Acme Company makes the following entry:

Oct. 31	Cash	3,960	
	Interest Expense	40	
	Notes Receivable		4,000
	Discounted Bowman's non-interest-bearing note.		

DISCOUNTING INTEREST-BEARING NOTES RECEIVABLE We also use the procedure just described for interest-bearing notes. In this case, however, maturity value includes interest for the full term of the note. The discount computation and calculation of proceeds for a $4,000, 60-day, 12% note dated October 1 and discounted at 12% on October 31 by Acme Company is as follows:

$$\text{Maturity Value} \times \text{Discount Rate} \times \text{Discount Period} = \text{Discount}$$
$$\$4{,}080 \times 12\% \times \frac{30}{360} = \$40.80$$

18,300 122

$$\text{Maturity Value} - \text{Discount} = \text{Proceeds}$$
$$\$4{,}080 - \$40.80 = \$4{,}039.20$$

Acme Company records the discounting transaction as follows:

Oct. 31	Cash	4,039.20	
	Interest Income		39.20
	Notes Receivable		4,000.00
	Discounted Bowman's 60-day, 12% note at 12%.		

Note that although Acme Company and the bank each hold a note 30 days, the bank exacts an additional amount of interest. The extra 80 cents is the interest for 30 days on $80 at the 12% bank discount rate. The bank considers the transaction a loan of $4,080, the amount that must be repaid at the end of the note's term.

Normally, a firm discounting a customer's interest-bearing note at the bank earns interest income, as shown in our illustration. However, the proceeds from discounting may be less than the note's face value when the firm's holding period is fairly short and the bank's discount rate exceeds the interest rate on the note.

Suppose that Acme Company discounts the $4,000 note after holding it only six days, and the discount rate is 16%. The discount would be $\$4{,}080 \times 16\% \times \frac{54}{360} = \$97.92$. Subtracting this amount from the $4,080 maturity value yields proceeds of $3,982.08. In this case, Acme Company would record the $17.92 difference between face value and proceeds as interest expense.

Oct. 7	Cash	3,982.08	
	Interest Expense	17.92	
	Notes Receivable		4,000
	Discounted Bowman's 60-day, 12% note at 16%.		

DISCOUNTED NOTES RECEIVABLE DISHONORED When the maker of a note receivable fails to pay it (dishonors it) at maturity, the bank notifies the endorsing party and charges the full amount owed, including interest, to the endorser's bank account. In addition, the bank may also charge a small protest fee. Suppose that Bowman Company's $4,000, 60-day, 12% note, which Acme discounted on October 31, was dishonored by Bowman Company at maturity. Assume also that the bank notified Acme Company on November 30 that the maturity value of the note, $4,080, plus a $5 protest fee, was charged against Acme Company's bank account. Acme Company's entry to record paying the maturity value of the note plus the protest fee and to charge the entire amount to Accounts Receivable—Bowman Company is as follows:

Nov. 30	Accounts Receivable—Bowman Company	4,085	
	Cash		4,085
	Paid Bowman Company's note and $5 protest fee.		

Acme Company would then endeavor to collect the $4,085 from Bowman Company. If Acme fails in its efforts, it writes off the account as uncollectible, using the procedures described earlier in this chapter.

Borrowing at a Discount

When a business borrows from a bank by giving its own note, the bank often deducts the interest in advance. With this type of transaction, a business is said to be "discounting its own note." Suppose that Acme Company discounts at 12% its own $8,000, 60-day note, dated December 16, at the bank. The calculation of discount and proceeds follows the pattern used for discounting notes receivable:

$$\text{Maturity Value} \times \text{Interest Rate} \times \text{Discount Period} = \text{Discount (Interest)}$$
$$\$8,000 \times 12\% \times \frac{60}{360} = \$160$$

$$\text{Maturity Value} - \text{Discount (Interest)} = \text{Proceeds}$$
$$\$8,000 - \$160 = \$7,840$$

Acme records this transaction as follows:

Dec. 16	Cash	7,840	
	Discount on Notes Payable	160	
	Notes Payable		8,000
	Discounted our 60-day note at 12%.		

Note that the $160 is charged to Discount on Notes Payable. This *contra* account balance is subtracted from the Notes Payable amount on the balance sheet. As the period for the note elapses, the discount is reduced and charged to Interest Expense. Thus, at December 31, after 15 days have elapsed, $40 would be charged to Interest Expense and credited to Discount on Notes Payable. A complete discussion of the adjustment procedure is offered in the next section.

Because the proceeds of this type of note are less than the maturity value of the note, the *effective interest rate* for the loan is greater than the stated interest rate. The effective interest rate may be calculated by the following formula:

$$\text{Effective Interest Rate} = \frac{\text{Maturity Value of Note} \times \text{Stated Interest Rate}}{\text{Cash Proceeds from Note}}$$

Therefore, the effective interest rate on the Acme Company note is computed as follows:

$$\frac{\$8,000 \times 12\%}{\$7,840} = 12.24\%$$

Adjusting Entries for Interest

When the term of an interest-bearing note extends beyond the end of an accounting period, adjusting entries are usually necessary to reflect interest in the proper period. When material amounts are involved, year-end adjustments are normally made to accrue interest income on notes receivable and interest expense on notes payable. Often, entries are also necessary to record interest expense on a company's own discounted notes.

ACCRUED INTEREST Assume that Acme Company received a $12,000, 60-day, 10% note from Cable Company on December 16 of the current year. By the close of the accounting period on December 31, Acme Company would have earned 15 days' interest, or $50, on the note, and Cable Company would have incurred an equal amount of interest expense. The adjusting entries made by each company on December 31 are shown below:

Acme Company

Dec. 31	Interest Receivable	50	
	Interest Income		50
	To accrue interest income on Cable Company note.		

Cable Company

Dec. 31	Interest Expense	50	
	Interest Payable		50
	To accrue interest expense on note to Acme Company.		

As a result of its adjusting entry, Acme Company would report the interest earned during December in its income statement for the current year and would show the interest receivable at December 31 among the current assets in its balance sheet. Likewise, Cable Company would report the interest expense incurred during December in its income statement for the current year and the interest payable as a current liability in its December 31 balance sheet.

In Chapter 4, we mentioned that some accountants prefer to make reversing entries for most accrual adjustments, after the books have been closed and statements have been prepared. If Acme Company followed this practice, the January 1 reversing entry (debit Interest Income and credit Interest Receivable for $50) would eliminate the Interest Receivable balance and reflect a debit balance of $50 in the Interest Income account (which had no balance after closing). Collection of the note and interest on the maturity date, February 14, would be recorded in the usual manner, as follows:

Feb. 14	Cash	12,200	
	Interest Income		200
	Notes Receivable		12,000
	Collected Cable Company note and interest.		

After this collection entry has been posted to the accounts, the Interest Income account would show a net credit balance of $150—the proper amount of income earned on the note during the new year. The Interest Income account would appear as follows:

Interest Income Account No. 42

Date		Description	Post. Ref.	Debit	Credit	Balance
19XX						
Jan.	1	(reversing)		50		(50)
Feb.	14	Collection of interest			200	150

Alternatively, if Acme Company had not reversed the accrual adjustment on January 1, it would record the collection of principal and interest as follows:

Feb. 14	Cash	12,200	
	Interest Receivable		50
	Interest Income		150
	Notes Receivable		12,000
	Collected Cable Company note and interest.		

When accrual adjustments are not reversed, we must analyze the subsequent related cash transaction as we did in the above entry. This procedure accomplishes the same result with fewer entries than reversing accruals, but we must be more circumspect in recording transactions during the period after adjustment.

Obviously, our remarks also apply to accrued interest on notes payable. For example, if Cable Company reversed its accruals, the entry for payment of the note and interest would be:

Feb. 14	Notes Payable	12,000	
	Interest Expense	200	
	Cash		12,200
	Paid note and interest to Acme Company.		

If Cable Company did not follow the practice of reversing accruals, the entry at maturity date would be:

Feb. 14	Notes Payable	12,000	
	Interest Payable	50	
	Interest Expense	150	
	Cash		12,200
	Paid note and interest to Acme Company.		

DISCOUNT ON NOTES PAYABLE We pointed out earlier that when a firm discounts its own note payable, the bank deducts the interest (discount) immediately from the note's face value to obtain the proceeds. In our example, Acme Company's $8,000, 60-day note payable was discounted at 12% at the bank on December 16. Acme Company's entry is repeated below:

Dec. 16	Cash	7,840	
	Discount on Notes Payable	160	
	Notes Payable		8,000
	Discounted our 60-day note at 12%.		

At the close of the accounting period on December 31, 15 of the 60 days had elapsed, and one-fourth, or $40, of the discount was recognized as interest. Acme Company would make the following adjusting entry on December 31:

Dec. 31	Interest Expense	40	
	Discount on Notes Payable		40
	To record interest expense on our discounted note.		

In its December 31 balance sheet, Acme Company would show the remaining $120 Discount on Notes Payable as a *contra* liability account, subtracted from the Notes Payable amount.

When the note is paid, Acme Company would make the following entry:

Feb. 14	Notes Payable	8,000	
	Interest Expense	120	
	Discount on Notes Payable		120
	Cash		8,000
	Payment of discounted note at maturity.		

Notes and Interest in Financial Statements

A business shows short-term trade notes receivable as current assets in the balance sheet; because they can normally be converted to cash fairly easily, these notes usually are placed above trade accounts receivable. As with accounts receivable, trade notes receivable are separated from notes from officers and employees and notes representing advances to affiliated companies. If such notes are not truly short-term, they should not be classified as current assets. Interest Receivable is normally shown with Notes Receivable.

Sometimes companies with a large volume of notes receivable must provide for possible losses on notes. Frequently, the provision for credit losses also covers losses on notes as well. In such cases, the Allowance for Uncollectible Accounts is deducted from the sum of Accounts Receivable and Notes Receivable in the balance sheet.

Trade notes payable and notes payable to banks are usually shown separately in the current liabilities section of the balance sheet. Interest Payable is normally shown with Notes Payable—often as an addition, as presented in Exhibit 8–3. Discount on Notes Payable is deducted from the related Notes Payable amount. The order in which current payables appear is less important than the sequence of current assets; however, Notes Payable customarily precedes Accounts Payable.

A current section of a balance sheet is shown in Exhibit 8–3 to illustrate the presentation of items discussed in this chapter.

Because they are financial rather than operating items, we often separate Interest Expense and Interest Income from operating items in the income statement. They frequently appear under the classification *Other Income and Expense*, as shown in Exhibit 8–4. With this type of presentation, readers can make intercompany comparisons of operating results that are not influenced by financing patterns of the companies involved (such comparisons are explained more fully in Chapter 20).

EXHIBIT 8–3

Huron Company
Partial Balance Sheet
December 31, 19XX

Current Assets		
Cash		$ 2,000
Notes Receivable—Trade	$24,000	
Interest Receivable	300	24,300
Accounts Receivable—Trade	$50,000	
Less: Allowance for Uncollectible Accounts	1,500	48,500
Inventory		75,000
Prepaid Expenses		200
Total Current Assets		$150,000
Current Liabilities		
Notes Payable—Banks	$ 8,000	
Less: Discount on Notes Payable	60	$ 7,940
Notes Payable—Trade	$20,000	
Interest Payable	400	20,400
Accounts Payable—Trade		30,000
Other Accrued Liabilities		11,660
Total Current Liabilities		$ 70,000

EXHIBIT 8–4

Huron Company
Partial Income Statement
For the Year Ended December 31, 19XX

Sales		$200,000
Cost of Goods Sold		140,000
Gross Profit		$ 60,000
Operating Expenses:		
•		•
•		•
•		•
Total Operating Expenses		40,000
Net Operating Income		$ 20,000
Other Income and Expense:		
Interest Income	$1,400	
Interest Expense	800	600
Net Income		$ 20,600

KEY POINTS TO REMEMBER

(1) When a debt is considered uncollectible, the *direct write-off* method of recording credit losses results in a debit to Uncollectible Accounts Expense and a credit to Accounts Receivable.

(2) The *allowance* method of recording credit losses can be summarized as follows:
   (a) To provide for losses, estimate them in advance, and then debit Uncollectible Accounts Expense and credit Allowance for Uncollectible Accounts. The amount of the entry may be either a percentage of the period's credit sales or an amount necessary to bring the allowance account to a desired balance that is based on an analysis of the receivables.
   (b) To write off accounts, debit Allowance for Uncollectible Accounts and credit Accounts Receivable when accounts are considered uncollectible.

(3) Discount is calculated on the maturity value of a note for the period the bank must hold it. Proceeds of a note are obtained by subtracting the discount from the maturity value.

(4) To record the discounting of a customer's note, we debit Cash for the proceeds, and credit Notes Receivable for the face value of the note. If proceeds exceed face value, we credit the difference to Interest Income. If proceeds are less than face value, we debit the difference to Interest Expense. When a firm discounts its *own* note, Notes Payable is credited.

(5) If the maker of a discounted note receivable fails to pay the note at maturity, the bank notifies the endorser of the default and charges the maturity value (plus any protest fee) to the endorser's bank account. The endorser then records the payment as a debit to Accounts Receivable and a credit to Cash.

(6) When a firm discounts its own note, Discount on Notes Payable is debited for the difference between face value and proceeds. This contra liability account is deducted from the related Notes Payable on the balance sheet. As the term of the note expires, adjusting entries reduce the discount by charging Interest Expense.

SELF-TEST QUESTIONS
(Answers are at the end of this chapter.)

1. A firm on the allowance method of recording credit losses wrote off a customer's account of $500. Later, the customer paid the account. The firm reinstated the account by means of a journal entry, then recorded the collection. The result of these procedures
   (a) Increased total assets by $500.
   (b) Decreased total assets by $500.
   (c) Decreased total assets by $1,000.
   (d) Had no effect on total assets.

2. A firm has accounts receivable of $60,000 and a debit balance of $600 in the Allowance for Uncollectible Accounts. Two-thirds of the accounts receivable are current and one-third is past due. The firm estimates that 2% of the current accounts and 5% of the past due accounts will prove to be uncollectible. The adjusting entry to provide for uncollectible accounts expense should be for

(a) $1,800 (c) $1,200
(b) $2,400 (d) $2,800

3. A firm discounted its own $12,000, 90-day note payable at the bank at 10%. The effective interest rate for this transaction is

(a) 10% (c) 9.74%
(b) 8.33% (d) 10.26%

4. A firm held a $9,000, 10%, 120-day note receivable for 20 days, then discounted the note at the bank at 12%. The entry to record the discounting of the note will show

(a) Interest Income of $300 (c) Interest Expense of $10
(b) Interest Income of $10 (d) Interest Expense of $310

5. On December 1, a firm discounted its own $6,000, 120-day note payable at the bank at 12%. The adjusting entry for interest at December 31 will show a

(a) $60 credit to Discount on Notes Payable.
(b) $60 debit to Discount on Notes Payable.
(c) $60 credit to Interest Expense.
(d) $240 debit to Interest Expense.

QUESTIONS

8–1 What events might cause credit balances in customers' accounts and debit balances in creditors' accounts? How are such items classified in the balance sheet?

8–2 A mail-order firm regularly makes a large proportion of its sales on the installment basis, requiring a 20% down payment and monthly payments over a period of six to 24 months, depending on the type of item sold. Where should the installment receivables be classified in the balance sheet of this mail-order firm?

8–3 How do the direct write-off and allowance methods of handling credit losses differ with respect to the timing of expense recognition?

8–4 When a firm provides for credit losses under the allowance method, why is the Allowance for Uncollectible Accounts credited rather than Accounts Receivable?

8–5 Describe the two most commonly used methods of estimating uncollectible accounts expense when the allowance method is employed.

8–6 The Fisher Company estimates its uncollectibles by aging its accounts and applying percentages to various strata of the aged accounts. This year, it calculated a total of $1,900 in possible losses. On December 31, the Accounts Receivable balance is $90,000 and the Allowance for Uncollectible Accounts has a credit balance of $400 before adjustment. Give the adjusting entry to provide for credit losses. Determine the net amount of Accounts Receivable added into current assets.

8–7 In June of last year, Byrd, Inc., sold $975 worth of merchandise to Vale Company. In November of last year, Byrd, Inc., wrote off Vale's account. In March of this year, Vale Company paid the account in full. Give the entries made by Byrd, Inc., for the write-off and the recovery, assuming that Byrd, Inc., uses (a) the direct write-off method, and (b) the allowance method of handling credit losses.

8–8 Lane Company sold a $600 refrigerator to a customer who charged the sale with a VISA bank credit card. Lane Company's bank charges a credit card fee of 4% of sales. What entry should Lane Company make to record the sale?

8–9 Rivers, Inc., received a 60-day, 12% note for $6,000 on March 12 of this year.
(a) What is the maturity date of the note?
(b) What is the maturity value of the note?
(c) Assuming Rivers, Inc., discounted the note at 12% at the bank on March 27, calculate the proceeds of the note.

8–10 On July 18 of this year, Ralph Wells discounted at the bank his own 120-day note for $7,000 at 12%.
(a) What is the maturity date of the note?
(b) What is the maturity value of the note?
(c) What are the proceeds of the note?

8–11 Why is a discounted customer's note a contingent liability of the endorser?

8–12 The maturity value of a $9,000 customer's note discounted by Timm Company is $9,150. The customer dishonored the note, and the bank charged the $9,150 plus a $12 protest fee to Timm's bank account. What entries should Timm make to record this event?

8–13 Gann Company received a 120-day, 12% note for $18,000 on December 1. What adjusting entry is needed to accrue interest on December 31?

8–14 On December 11, Kay Mills discounted her own 90-day note for $15,000 at the bank at 12% and charged the discount to Discount on Notes Payable. What adjusting entry is necessary on December 31?

8–15 James Todd gave a creditor a 60-day, 10% note for $8,400 on December 16. What adjusting entry should Todd make on December 31?

EXERCISES

Credit losses based on sales

8–16 Miles Company uses the allowance method of handling credit losses. It estimates losses at 1% of credit sales, which were $600,000 during the current year. On December 31 of the current year, the Accounts Receivable balance was $120,000, and the Allowance for Uncollectible Accounts had a credit balance of $700 before adjustment.
(a) Give the adjusting entry to record credit losses for the current year.
(b) Show how Accounts Receivable and the Allowance for Uncollectible Accounts would appear in the December 31 balance sheet.

Credit losses based on accounts receivable

8–17 Bartel, Inc., analyzed its Accounts Receivable balances at December 31 and arrived at the aged balances listed below, along with the percentages of each age group that have proven uncollectible in the past.

Age	Loss (%)	Balance
Current	1	$ 80,000
30–60 days past due	2	16,000
61–120 days past due	5	8,000
121 days–six months past due	10	7,000
Over six months past due	25	6,000
		$117,000

The company handles credit losses with the allowance method. The credit balance of the Allowance for Uncollectible Accounts is $600 on December 31 before any adjustments.

(a) Prepare the adjusting entry for estimated credit losses on December 31.
(b) Give the entry to write off Robert Wade's account in April of the following year, $625.

Allowance vs. direct write-off methods

8–18 On March 10 of this year, Baird, Inc., declared a $750 account receivable from Gordon Company uncollectible and wrote off the account. On November 18 of this year, Baird received a $750 payment on the account from Gordon.

(a) Assume Baird uses the allowance method of handling credit losses. Give the entries to record the write-off and the subsequent recovery of Gordon's account.
(b) Assume Baird uses the direct write-off method of handling credit losses. Give the entries to record the write-off and the subsequent recovery of Gordon's account.
(c) Assume the payment from Gordon arrives on February 5 of next year rather than on November 18 of this year. Give the entries to record the write-off and subsequent recovery of Gordon's account under the allowance method.
(d) Assume the payment from Gordon arrives on February 5 of next year rather than on November 18 of this year. Give the entries to record the write-off and subsequent recovery of Gordon's account under the direct write-off method.

Maturity dates of notes

8–19 Determine the maturity date and compute the interest for each of the following notes:

Date of Note	Principal	Interest Rate (%)	Term
(a) July 6	$ 4,800	12	60 days
(b) April 10	9,000	10	90 days
(c) May 15	2,800	15	120 days
(d) June 6	3,600	12	45 days
(e) October 25	16,000	9	75 days

Discounting note receivable

8–20 Record the following transactions on the books of both Bingham Company and Field, Inc.:

Oct. 1 Field, Inc., gave Bingham Company an $18,000, 60-day, 10% note in payment of account.
21 Bingham Company discounted the note at the bank at 12%.
Nov. 30 On the maturity date of the note, Field, Inc., paid the amount due.

Dishonored note

8–21 Suppose that, in Exercise 8–20, Field, Inc., dishonored its note and the bank notified Bingham Company that it had charged the maturity value plus a $10

432

protest fee to Bingham Company's bank account. What entry should Bingham Company make on the maturity date?

← 112

Discounting note payable

8–22 On November 16, Johnson Company discounted its own $5,600, 60-day note at the bank at 12%.

(a) What is the maturity date of the note?
(b) What are the proceeds of the note?
(c) What amount of interest expense should be recorded as an adjustment at December 31?
(d) What will be the balance in the Discount on Notes Payable account at December 31?
(e) What is the effective interest rate on the note?

Adjusting entries for interest

8–23 The following note transactions occurred during the current year for the Marcus Company:

Nov.	25	Marcus received a 120-day, 10% note for $12,000 from Wynn Company.
Dec.	7	Marcus discounted its own 90-day, $8,000 note at the bank at 12%, charging the discount to Discount on Notes Payable.
	23	Marcus gave Arden, Inc., a $4,500, 10%, 60-day note in payment of account.

Give the general journal entries necessary to adjust the interest accounts at December 31.

Computing accrued interest

8–24 Compute the interest accrued on each of the following notes receivable held by Clinton, Inc., on December 31, 19X6:

Maker	Date of Note	Principal	Interest Rate (%)	Term
Donner	11/16/X6	$9,000	12	120 days
Malone	12/10/X6	12,000	10	90 days
Peters	12/19/X6	4,500	14	60 days

PROBLEMS

Allowance vs. direct write-off methods

8–25 Penco, Inc., which has been in business for three years, makes all sales on account and does not offer cash discounts. The firm's credit sales, collections from customers, and write-offs of uncollectible accounts for the three-year period are summarized below:

Year	Sales	Collections	Accounts Written Off
1	$400,000	$380,000	$2,000
2	600,000	590,000	2,400
3	720,000	704,000	3,000

REQUIRED

(a) If Penco, Inc., had used the direct write-off method of recognizing credit losses during the three years, what amount of Accounts Receivable would appear on the firm's balance sheet at the end of the third year? What total amount of uncollectible accounts expense would have appeared on the firm's income statement during the three-year period?
(b) If Penco, Inc., had used an allowance method of recognizing credit losses and had provided for such losses at the rate of $\frac{3}{4}$% of sales, what amounts

of Accounts Receivable and Allowance for Uncollectible Accounts would appear on the firm's balance sheet at the end of the third year? What total amount of uncollectible accounts expense would have appeared on the firm's income statement during the three-year period?

(c) Comment on the use of the $\frac{3}{4}$% rate to provide for losses in part (b).

Entries for credit losses

8–26 At the beginning of the current year, Savage Company had the following accounts on its books:

Accounts Receivable	$86,000	(debit)
Allowance for Uncollectible Accounts	2,200	(credit)

During this year, credit sales were $700,000 and collections on account were $685,000. The following transactions, among others, occurred during the year:

Feb. 17	Wrote off R. Jackson's account, $700.
May 28	Wrote off M. Driscoll's account, $450.
Oct. 13	M. Driscoll, who is in bankruptcy proceedings, paid $250 in final settlement of the account written off on May 28. This amount is not included in the $685,000 collections.
Dec. 15	Wrote off P. Landon's account, $600.
31	In an adjusting entry, recorded the provision for uncollectible accounts at $\frac{1}{2}$% of credit sales for the year.

REQUIRED

(a) Prepare general journal entries to record the credit sales, the collections on account, and the above transactions.

(b) Show how Accounts Receivable and the Allowance for Uncollectible Accounts would appear in the December 31 balance sheet.

Credit losses based on accounts receivable

8–27 At December 31 of the current year, the Jason Company had a balance of $160,000 in its Accounts Receivable account and a credit balance of $1,700 in the Allowance for Uncollectible Accounts. The Accounts Receivable subsidiary ledger consisted of $161,500 in debit balances and $1,500 in credit balances. The company has aged its accounts as follows:

Current	$134,000
0–60 days past due	15,000
61–180 days past due	8,000
Over six months past due	4,500
	$161,500

In the past, the company has experienced losses as follows: 1% of current balances, 5% of balances 0–60 days past due, 15% of balances 61–180 days past due, and 40% of balances over six months past due. The company bases its provision for credit losses on the aging analysis.

REQUIRED

(a) Prepare the adjusting journal entry to record the provision for credit losses for the year.

(b) Show how Accounts Receivable (including the credit balances) and Allowance for Uncollectible Accounts would appear in the December 31 balance sheet.

Discounting notes payable

8–28 Duluth Products, Inc., had the following transactions for 19X1 and 19X2:

19X1

May 18 Discounted its own $15,000, 90-day note at the bank at 12%.
Aug. 16 Paid the bank the amount due from the May 18 loan.
Oct. 2 Discounted its own $9,600, 120-day note at the bank at 14%.
Dec. 31 Made the appropriate adjusting entry for interest expense.

19X2

Jan. 30 Paid the bank the amount due from the October loan.

REQUIRED

(a) Record the above transactions and adjustment in general journal form.
(b) Compute the effective interest rate on the loan of:
 (1) May 18.
 (2) October 2.

Various entries for accounts and notes

8–29 Cody Company had the following transactions during the current year:

Apr. 8 Received a $7,200, 75-day, 10% note from L. Vance in payment of account.
May 24 Wrote off customer J. Bolt's account against the Allowance for Uncollectible Accounts, $575.
June 22 L. Vance paid note in full.
Sept. 10 Gave a $5,600, 90-day, 11% note to H. Carter in payment of account.
18 J. Bolt paid account written off on May 24.
Dec. 4 Discounted its own $18,000, 90-day note at the bank at 12%.
9 Paid principal and interest due on note to H. Carter.
21 Received a $7,500, 60-day, 12% note from L. Trent on account.

REQUIRED

(a) Record the above transactions in general journal form.
(b) Make any necessary adjusting entries for interest at December 31.

Various entries for accounts and notes

8–30 Randall, Inc., began business on January 1 of the current year. Certain transactions for the current year are given below:

May 1 Borrowed $15,000 from the bank on a six-month, 14% note, interest to be paid at maturity.
June 13 Received an $8,000, 60-day, 12% note on account from S. Weldon.
28 Discounted Weldon's note at the bank at 15%.
Aug. 12 S. Weldon paid her note at the bank, with interest.
Sept. 1 Received a $9,000, 120-day, 10% note from F. Lane on account.
Oct. 11 Discounted Lane's note at the bank at 15%.
Nov. 1 Paid May 1 note, with interest.
21 Discounted its own $7,500, 120-day note at the bank at 12%.
Dec. 16 Received an $8,400, 45-day, 12% note from M. Davis on account.
30 The bank notified Randall, Inc., that F. Lane's note was dishonored. Maturity value of the note plus an $8 protest fee was charged against Randall's checking account at the bank.
31 Wrote off Lane's account as uncollectible. Randall, Inc., uses the allowance method of providing for credit losses.
31 Recorded expected credit losses for the year by an adjusting entry. Write-offs of accounts during this first year have created a debit balance in the

Allowance for Uncollectible Accounts of $9,500. Analysis of aged receivables indicates that the desired balance of the allowance account is $7,800.

Dec. 31 Made the appropriate adjusting entries for interest.

REQUIRED

Record the foregoing transactions and adjustments in general journal form.

Adjusting entries for interest

8–31 At December 31, 19X0, Neptune Corporation held one note receivable and had one note payable outstanding. At December 31, 19X1, Neptune again held one note receivable and had outstanding one note payable. The notes are described below.

	Date of Note	Principal	Interest Rate (%)	Term
December 31, 19X0				
Note Receivable	11/25/X0	$8,000	12	120 days
Note Payable	12/16/X0	5,600	15	30 days
December 31, 19X1				
Note Receivable	12/11/X1	$7,200	12	60 days
Note Payable	12/7/X1	9,000	14	150 days

REQUIRED

(a) Assume that the appropriate adjusting entries were made at December 31, 19X0, but that no reversing or adjusting entries were made in 19X1. Give the journal entries to record payment of the notes that were outstanding December 31, 19X0.

(b) Assume that the appropriate adjusting entries were made at December 31, 19X0. However, no reversing or adjusting entries were made in 19X1, and the bookkeeper neglected to consider the related interest receivable and interest payable when the notes were paid in 19X1. Make the necessary adjusting entries for interest at December 31, 19X1.

ALTERNATE PROBLEMS

Entries for credit losses

8–26A At January 1 of the current year, Blockaid, Inc., had the following accounts on its books:

Accounts Receivable	$110,000	(debit)
Allowance for Uncollectible Accounts	3,800	(credit)

During this year, credit sales were $720,000 and collections on account were $708,000. The following transactions, among others, occurred during the year:

Jan. 11 Wrote off D. Morrow's account, $1,400.

Apr. 29 Wrote off G. Burke's account, $950.

Nov. 15 G. Burke paid debt of $950, written off April 29. This amount is not included in the $708,000 collections.

Dec. 5 Wrote off M. Bell's account, $1,800.

31 In an adjusting entry, recorded the provision for uncollectible accounts at 1% of credit sales for the year.

REQUIRED

(a) Prepare general journal entries to record the credit sales, the collections on account, and the above transactions.

(b) Show how Accounts Receivable and the Allowance for Uncollectible Accounts would appear in the December 31 balance sheet.

Credit losses based on accounts receivable

8–27A At December 31 of the current year, the Lancer Company had a balance of $70,000 in its Accounts Receivable account and a credit balance of $900 in the Allowance for Uncollectible Accounts. The Accounts Receivable subsidiary ledger consisted of $72,400 in debit balances and $2,400 in credit balances. The company has aged its accounts as follows:

Current	$60,000
0–60 days past due	5,000
61–180 days past due	3,800
Over six months past due	3,600
	$72,400

In the past, the company has experienced losses as follows: 2% of current balances, 6% of balances 0–60 days past due, 15% of balances 61–180 days past due, and 30% of balances more than six months past due. The company bases its provision for credit losses on the aging analysis.

REQUIRED

(a) Prepare the adjusting journal entry to record the provision for credit losses for the year.

(b) Show how Accounts Receivable (including the credit balances) and Allowance for Uncollectible Accounts would appear in the December 31 balance sheet.

Discounting notes receivable

8–28A The Hobbs Corporation had the following transactions for 19X3 and 19X4:

19X3

Mar.	6	Sold $4,500 worth of merchandise to C. Lester and received a $4,500, 60-day, 10% note.
	26	Discounted C. Lester's note at the bank at 12%.
May	5	Lester paid the bank the amount due on the March 6 note.
Dec.	11	Received an $8,000, 60-day, 9% note from R. Fleming in settlement of an open account.
	31	Made the appropriate adjusting entry for interest income.

19X4

Jan.	1	Reversed the December 31 adjustment for interest income.
Feb.	9	Received payment from R. Fleming on the December 11 note.

REQUIRED

(a) Record the above transactions, adjustment, and reversal in general journal form.

(b) Assume Hobbs Corporation does not make reversing entries. Give the entry to record the receipt of the note payment from R. Fleming on February 9, 19X4.

Various entries for accounts and notes

8–29A The Fairfield Company had the following transactions during the current year:

July	15	Received a $6,400, 90-day, 11% note from D. Quinn in payment of account.
Sept.	5	Wrote off customer J. Olson's account against the Allowance for Uncollectible Accounts, $725.
	9	Gave a $7,600, 90-day, 10% note to P. Austin in payment of account.
Oct.	13	D. Quinn paid note in full.
	21	J. Olson paid account written off on September 5.
Dec.	8	Paid principal and interest due on note to P. Austin.
	13	Discounted its own $5,000, 90-day note at the bank at 10%.
	19	Received a $4,800, 60-day, 10% note from L. Sage on account.

REQUIRED

(a) Record the above transactions in general journal form.

(b) Make any necessary adjusting entries for interest at December 31.

Various entries for accounts and notes

8–30A Holland, Inc., began business on January 1 of the current year. Several transactions for the current year are given below:

Mar.	1	Borrowed $25,000 from the bank on a five-month, 12% note, interest to be paid at maturity.
May	2	Received a $13,500, 60-day, 10% note on account from R. Dunbar.
	22	Discounted Dunbar's note at the bank at 12%.
July	1	R. Dunbar paid his note at the bank, with interest.
	1	Received a $4,500, 120-day, 10% note from Ida Moore on account.
	25	Discounted Moore's note at the bank at 10%.
Aug.	1	Paid March 1 note, with interest.
Oct.	30	The bank notified Holland, Inc., that Ida Moore's note was dishonored. Maturity value of the note plus a $10 protest fee was charged against Holland's checking account at the bank.
Dec.	1	Discounted its own $15,000, 120-day note at bank at 12%.
	9	Wrote off Moore's account as uncollectible. Holland, Inc., uses the allowance method of providing for credit losses.
	11	Received a $7,000, 90-day, 9% note from J. Sterling on account.
	31	Recorded expected credit losses for the year by an adjusting entry. The Allowance for Uncollectible Accounts has a debit balance of $4,800 as a result of write-offs of accounts during this first year. Analysis of aged receivables indicates that the desired balance of the allowance account is $3,750.
	31	Made the appropriate adjusting entries for interest.

REQUIRED

Record the foregoing transactions and adjustments in general journal form.

BUSINESS DECISION PROBLEM

The latest income statement for Rushmore Sales, Inc.—a wholesaler of electronic parts and equipment—is shown below. Company president William Royce has been dissatisfied with the firm's rate of growth for several years. He believes that increasing sales promotion and liberalizing credit policies would raise gross sales substantially.

Specifically, Royce is fairly confident that gross sales would increase by 25% if the firm adopted the following plan:

(1) Increase certain of the firm's trade discounts. This change would reduce the average selling price of merchandise somewhat, but it would increase sales volume.
(2) Extend credit to an additional number of less "select" customers.

Rushmore Sales, Inc.
Income Statement
For the Year Ended December 31, 19XX

Sales	$750,000	
Less: Sales Discounts	10,000	
Net Sales	$740,000	100%
Cost of Goods Sold	444,000	60
Gross Profit on Sales	$296,000	40%
Selling Expenses (excluding Uncollectible Accounts Expense)	$222,000	30%
Uncollectible Accounts Expense	7,400	1
Administrative Expenses	37,000	5
Total Expenses	$266,400	36%
Net Income	$ 29,600	4%

The controller for Rushmore Sales, Inc., makes the following comments after analyzing Royce's proposal for its likely impact on other income statement items:

(1) Gross Profit on Sales—The slight decline in average selling prices of merchandise resulting from an increase in trade discounts will reduce the gross profit rate from 40% to 38%.

(2) Sales Discounts—The firm has been selling to selected retailers on terms of 2/15, n/30, with about two-thirds of total sales subject to the discount. Even with an increased number of customers, two-thirds of total sales will still be subject to the discount.

(3) Selling Expenses—Excluding uncollectible accounts expense, selling expenses will remain at 30% of net sales. Because of the expected 25% increase in sales, selling expenses, including promotion outlays, will rise accordingly.

(4) Uncollectible Accounts Expense—Uncollectible accounts expense has been about 1% of net sales for several years. The proposed liberalization of credit policies will increase this expense to 2% of net sales.

(5) Administrative Expenses—These expenses will remain constant even if gross sales increase.

REQUIRED
Prepare an income statement based on Royce's proposal and the controller's comments. Based on your results, should the firm adopt Royce's proposal?

ANSWERS TO SELF-TEST QUESTIONS

1. (d) 2. (b) 3. (d) 4. (c) 5. (a)

9

Inventories

Chapter Objectives

- **Discuss the basic concepts of accounting for inventories.**
- **Describe the pricing of inventory using the (1) specific identification method, (2) weighted average method, (3) FIFO method, and (4) LIFO method.**
- **Analyze the effects inventory pricing methods have on gross profits, income, matching of costs and revenue, and income taxes.**
- **Apply the lower of cost or market rule to inventory measurements.**
- **Describe the gross profit and retail inventory methods of estimating inventories.**
- **Describe and illustrate the perpetual inventory system.**

Good merchandise finds a ready buyer.

PLAUTUS

Inventories constitute the lifeblood of merchandising and manufacturing firms. For these firms, inventory is a significant asset, and the sale of inventory provides the major source of revenue. This chapter focuses on inventory accounting for merchandisers—firms that buy finished products to sell to their customers. Inventories of manufacturing companies are covered in a later chapter.

We have already introduced the special source documents, business transactions, and accounting techniques related to routine inventory transactions. Now we build on these facts by briefly considering the basic notions of inventories, examining and illustrating the problems of inventory determination, and comparing the consequences for periodic income determination of various inventory pricing methods.

REVIEW OF BASIC CONCEPTS

Before discussing new material, let us review some of the pertinent concepts covered earlier.

Inventory is all merchandise owned by a company and held for resale to customers in the ordinary course of business. Inventories are current assets because they typically will be sold within one year, or during a firm's normal operating cycle if it should be longer than a year. For retailing firms, inventories are often the largest or most valuable current asset.

Inventory costs are all costs necessary to acquire the merchandise and bring it to the site of sale. Inventory costs include the purchase price, plus any transportation or freight in, less purchases returns and allowances and purchases discounts.

The **cost of goods sold** is the net acquisition cost of the goods sold to customers in generating the sales revenue of an operating period. The following is a typical example of the computation of the cost of goods sold:

Beginning Inventory			$10,000
Add: Net Cost of Purchases			
Purchases		$31,000	
Less: Purchases Returns and Allowances	$2,100		
Purchases Discounts	400	2,500	
		$28,500	
Add: Transportation In		500	29,000
Cost of Goods Available for Sale			$39,000
Less: Ending Inventory			9,000
Cost of Goods Sold			$30,000

THE NEED FOR INVENTORIES

Most well-managed merchandisers find it necessary and desirable to maintain large, varied inventories. As a consumer, you have probably experienced a favorable buyer reaction to the availability of a wide assortment of colors, sizes, qualities, and types of the goods for which you shop. The prevailing affluence of our society and the related buyer habits have probably made large, varied inventories an operating necessity for most retail firms.

Other business factors can justify the existence of relatively large inventories. Clearly, a firm can sell more goods in a period than it can purchase or produce only by having beginning inventories. Beginning inventories are particularly important to seasonal industries or markets. Attractive quantity discounts may justify a firm's buying in excess of its current sales requirements and therefore creating additional inventories. Strategic purchases offer still another reason for carrying inventories. Many firms—especially those that sell in seasonal markets—buy in excess of their needs when supply prices are favorable. They store the goods and can then maintain sales during a period of unfavorable supply prices.

Progressive firms take into account customer preferences, competitors' merchandising patterns, and favorable market situations in determining inventory size and balance, but they must also consider the cost of carrying large inventories. Often, savings obtained by purchasing in large quantities or under favorable market conditions may be more than offset by increased carrying costs. Storage and handling costs for large inventories can increase substantially. In addition, the firm may suffer losses from inventory deterioration and obsolescence. Finally, inventories tie up working capital that might be used more profitably elsewhere. These latter factors often cause merchandisers to contract inventory during recessionary periods.

INCOME DETERMINATION AND INVENTORY MEASUREMENT

Proper income determination depends on the appropriate measurement of all assets; higher asset amounts result in higher reported income amounts. Because inventories are often relatively large and their sizes fluctuate, accounting correctly for inventories is important in determining net income properly. Other things being equal, **changing the dollar amount of ending inventory changes net income dollar for dollar** (ignoring any income tax effects), as Exhibit 9–1 illustrates. Note that sales, beginning inventory, and purchases are identical in all four cases. As ending inventory increases by a given amount—$1,000 from A to B, $2,000 from B to D, for example—cost of goods sold decreases and income increases by the same amount.

Accountants must be concerned with the problems of inventory measurement because of its role in the determination of reported income. We consider these problems in the remainder of this chapter.

EXHIBIT 9–1
Relationship of Inventory Measurements to Reported Income

	Amounts (in Thousands of Dollars)			
Assumed Data	**A**	**B**	**C**	**D**
Sales	$25	$25	$25	$25
Beginning inventory	$ 3	$ 3	$ 3	$ 3
Purchases	20	20	20	20
Goods available for sale	$23	$23	$23	$23
Ending inventory	4	5	6	7
Cost of goods sold	$19	$18	$17	$16
Reported income	$ 6	$ 7	$ 8	$ 9

THE EFFECT OF INVENTORY ERRORS

To determine the effect of inventory errors on income determination, we must consider the method for calculating cost of goods sold. We illustrate why in Exhibit 9–2, where we assume that the ending inventory of period 1 was overstated by $1,000.

Because the ending inventory in period 1 is overstated by $1,000, the cost of goods sold is understated by $1,000, and thus reported income is overstated by that amount. Because the ending inventory in period 1 is also the beginning

EXHIBIT 9–2
Effect of Inventory Error on Two Operating Periods

	Amounts (in Thousands of Dollars)							
	Period 1				Period 2			
	Correct		Erroneous		Erroneous		Correct	
Sales		$80		$80		$100		$100
Beginning inventory	$20		$20		$14		$13	
Net cost of purchases	50		50		66		66	
Goods available	$70		$70		$80		$79	
Ending inventory	13		14		10		10	
Cost of goods sold		57		56		70		69
Gross profit		$23		$24		$ 30		$ 31
Overstatement or (understatement) of net income			$1				($1)	

inventory in period 2, the reported income for both periods will be misstated unless the error is corrected. Note, however, that the error in period 2 causes a misstatement of reported income that is equal in amount ($1,000) to the error in period 1 but opposite in direction (an understatement); thus, the errors in the two periods offset each other.

Therefore, uncorrected errors in ending inventories affect income determination for two periods. Overstating or understating ending inventory overstates or understates income, respectively. Regardless of the direction of the error, it will cause an offsetting error of like amount in the second period if it is not corrected.

INVENTORY MEASUREMENT

The dollar amount of an inventory depends on two variables—quantity and price. We usually express inventories as the aggregate dollar value (Quantity × Price) of the goods on hand at a specific time. "Taking" an inventory consists of (1) counting the items involved, (2) pricing each item, and (3) summing the amounts. Exhibit 9–3 illustrates these three steps.

Inventory counts can be extremely complicated and expensive. Even moderate-sized firms may have thousands of items, hundreds of types, sizes, and qualities, purchased at a variety of unit prices, and located in dozens of warehouses, stores, branches, and departments. Proper planning and coordination are imperative if all items are to be counted—only once—and properly priced. Although some firms "close" for inventory-taking, many continue operations during the count and must, of course, know if counted or uncounted merchandise is sold during the inventory period.

Another problem in inventory counts is deciding what goods should be counted. Often the proper inventory is not simply "all merchandise on site." By definition, the inventory should include—and be limited to—goods *owned* by the firm and *available* for resale. Ownership transfers when title to the goods

EXHIBIT 9–3
The Three Steps of Taking an Inventory

(1) PHYSICAL COUNT		(2) PRICING	(3) SUMMATION
Merchandise Item	Unit Count	Unit Price	Extension
A	30	$6	$180
B	40	7	280
C	50	8	400
			$860

passes from the seller to the buyer. Title may pass at any time expressly agreed to by these two parties. In the absence of a specific agreement, title generally passes when the seller completes performance with regard to delivery. Therefore, a firm purchasing merchandise on terms F.O.B. shipping point may acquire title to the goods before it physically receives the goods. Such items (often called *goods in transit*) should be included in the inventory count.

Merchandise whose title has passed to customers does not belong in the inventory count, even if it has not been removed from the store or warehouse. A buyer, for example, may agree to pick up the goods at the seller's place of business. When the seller identifies the goods that fulfill the contract, title transfers to the buyer. These goods should be excluded from the seller's inventory count because they are no longer owned or available for resale. Similarly, goods held for resale on consignment from another firm are not included in the inventory count, because the goods are not owned by the firm holding them.

We see, therefore, that although a firm's ownership of merchandise often is indicated by the physical presence of goods, a firm can also own goods that it has not yet received and not own goods that it still possesses.

INVENTORY PRICING METHODS

In general, inventories are priced at their cost. Inventory pricing is quite simple when acquisition prices remain constant. When prices for like items change during the accounting period, however, it is not always apparent which price should be used to measure the ending inventory. Consequently, when cost prices fluctuate, we must either keep track of all costs for specific goods or make assumptions about which goods have been sold and which goods are on hand. The need for such assumptions has led to the commonly used methods of inventory pricing that we illustrate in this section. We illustrate a rising price pattern, which is the most prevalent in our economy.

Two terms—*goods flow* and *cost flow*—are useful in considering the problems of pricing inventories under fluctuating prices. **Goods flow** describes the actual physical movement of goods in the firm's operations. Goods flow is a result of physical events. **Cost flow** is the real or *assumed* association of unit costs with goods either sold or on hand. The assumed cost flow does not always reflect the actual goods flow. Furthermore, generally accepted accounting principles permit the use of an assumed cost flow that does *not* reflect the real goods flow. There is nothing illicit about this practice; in fact, there are often compelling reasons for adopting it.

We introduce four generally accepted methods of pricing inventories: (1) specific identification; (2) weighted average; (3) first-in, first-out; and (4) last-in, first-out. Again, the four methods illustrated use historical costs. In this section, we concentrate primarily on the computational technique of each method. A comparative evaluation is presented in the following section.

To compare more easily the four inventory methods, we illustrate all four with identical data. In each case, goods available for sale during the period are as follows:

Beginning inventory	60 units @ $10 =	$ 600
Purchases:	100 units @ 11 =	1,100
	100 units @ 13 =	1,300
	40 units @ 15 =	600
Totals	300 units	$3,600

Therefore, in each illustration:

(1) Beginning inventory is priced at $600.

(2) Three purchases are made during the period, as listed above.

(3) Goods available for sale during the period amount to 300 units at a total cost of $3,600.

In each case, 220 units are sold during the period, leaving an ending inventory of 80 units. The four inventory methods differ in the way they assign costs to the units sold and to those remaining in inventory.

By assigning costs we are simply dividing the cost of goods available for sale between cost of goods sold and ending inventory. Therefore, we can compute costs by:

(1) Pricing out *either* the cost of goods sold or the ending inventory.

(2) Subtracting the amount determined in step (1) from the cost of goods available for sale.

(3) Assigning the residual to the element not priced in (1).

It will usually be advantageous to price out the ending inventory (and assign the residual amount to cost of goods sold), because the ending inventory involves fewer units than cost of goods sold. We use this approach in our illustrations.

Specific Identification

The **specific identification** method involves (1) keeping track of the purchase price of each specific unit, (2) knowing which specific units are sold, and (3) pricing the ending inventory at the actual prices of the specific units not sold. Obviously, this approach is not practical for merchandise having large unit volumes and small unit prices. Accounting students may consider specific identification the most "precise" way of evaluating inventory because the actual unit costs are attached to a given inventory. We shall see, however, that there is compelling justification for using other inventory pricing methods.

Assume that the 80 unsold units consist of 20 units from beginning inventory, 10 units from each of the first two purchases, and all 40 of the last units purchased. The costs assigned to the ending inventory and cost of goods sold are

EXHIBIT 9–4
Specific Identification Inventory Pricing

	Goods Available			Ending Inventory		
	Units	Cost	Total	Units	Cost	Total
Beginning inventory	60 @	$10 =	$ 600	20 @	$10 =	$ 200
Purchases:	100 @	11 =	1,100	10 @	11 =	110
	100 @	13 =	1,300	10 @	13 =	130
	40 @	15 =	600	40 @	15 =	600
	300		$3,600	80		$1,040

Cost of goods available for sale	$3,600
Less: Ending inventory	1,040
Cost of goods sold	$2,560

shown in Exhibit 9–4. Note that the full $3,600 cost of the goods available for sale has been assigned as either ending inventory or as cost of goods sold.

Weighted Average

The **weighted average** method spreads the total dollar cost of the goods available for sale equally among all units. In our illustration, this figure is $3,600/300, or $12 per unit. Exhibit 9–5 diagrams the assignment of costs under this method. Note again that the entire cost of goods available for sale has divided between ending inventory and cost of goods sold.

It would be incorrect to use a *simple* average of the prices. The average price paid is ($10 + $11 + $13 + $15)/4 = $12.25; this figure fails to take into account the different numbers of units available at the various prices. The simple average yields the same figure as the weighted average only when the same number of units are purchased at each price.

EXHIBIT 9–5
Weighted Average Inventory Pricing

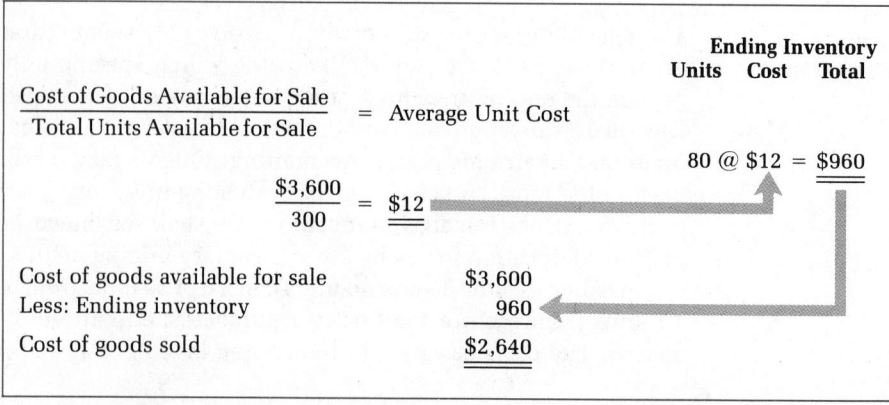

$$\frac{\text{Cost of Goods Available for Sale}}{\text{Total Units Available for Sale}} = \text{Average Unit Cost}$$

$$\frac{\$3,600}{300} = \$12$$

Ending Inventory		
Units	Cost	Total
80 @	$12 =	$960

Cost of goods available for sale	$3,600
Less: Ending inventory	960
Cost of goods sold	$2,640

First-in, First-out (FIFO)

First-in, first-out (FIFO) pricing assumes that the oldest goods on hand (or earliest purchased) are sold first. Thus, ending inventories are always made up of the most recent purchases. Under FIFO, goods in the beginning inventory can also be in the ending inventory only when the number of units sold is less than the number of units in the beginning inventory. A FIFO approach would result in the cost allocations as shown in Exhibit 9–6. This method assumes the first 220 units acquired are sold and the last 80 units purchased are still on hand.

Last-in, First-out (LIFO)

The **last-in, first-out (LIFO)** approach assumes that the most recent purchases are sold first. Thus, unless sales exceed purchases, the beginning inventory remains on hand as part of the ending inventory. Exhibit 9–7 shows how LIFO works. This method assumes the 220 units most recently purchased are sold, and the 80 oldest units available for sale (60 units from the beginning inventory and 20 units from the period's first purchase) remain on hand at the end of the period.

EXHIBIT 9–6
First-in, First-out Inventory Pricing

	Goods Available Units	Cost	Total	Ending Inventory Units	Cost	Total
Beginning inventory	60 @	$10 =	$ 600			
Purchases:	100 @	11 =	1,100			
	100 @	13 =	1,300	40 @	$13 =	$ 520
	40 @	15 =	600	40 @	15 =	600
	300		$3,600	80		$1,120

Cost of goods available for sale	$3,600
Less: Ending inventory	1,120
Cost of goods sold	$2,480

EXHIBIT 9–7
Last-in, First-out Inventory Pricing

	Goods Available Units	Cost	Total	Ending Inventory Units	Cost	Total
Beginning inventory	60 @	$10 =	$ 600	60 @	$10 =	$600
Purchases:	100 @	11 =	1,100	20 @	11 =	220
	100 @	13 =	1,300			
	40 @	15 =	600			
	300		$3,600	80		$820

Cost of goods available for sale	$3,600
Less: Ending inventory	820
Cost of goods sold	$2,780

COMPARATIVE ANALYSIS OF INVENTORY PRICING METHODS

In this section, we consider the effects of and reasons for using the various inventory pricing methods just illustrated.

Variations in Income Patterns

For comparative purposes, let us assume that the 220 units in our illustration were sold for $20 each. Exhibit 9–8 shows the differences among gross profit figures resulting from each of the inventory pricing methods. Remember that these differences in reported gross profit result from assumptions made about cost flows, not from any difference in actual goods flows. Pretax income will also reflect these differences if operating expenses are equal in each case.

Cost Flows

The specific identification method is most appropriate for operations that involve somewhat differentiated products of relatively high unit values. New automobiles and construction equipment are good examples of merchandise that would justify the cost of maintaining the price of each inventory unit and specifically identifying each sale. Specific identification is not feasible when products have low unit values and involve large volumes.

Specific identification offers limited potential for income manipulation. To the degree that like units of inventory are available at various cost figures, we can maximize reported income by "choosing" to sell the unit with the lowest cost. Income could be minimized by choosing to sell the unit with the highest cost.

The weighted average approach to inventory measurement is best suited to operations that store a large volume of undifferentiated goods in common areas.

EXHIBIT 9–8
Differential Gross Margins on Sales
Based on Various Inventory Pricing Methods

	Inventory Pricing Method			
	Sp. Id.	Average	FIFO	LIFO
Sales (220 units @ $20)	$4,400	$4,400	$4,400	$4,400
Beginning inventory	$ 600	$ 600	$ 600	$ 600
Total purchases	3,000	3,000	3,000	3,000
Cost of goods available for sale	$3,600	$3,600	$3,600	$3,600
Less: Ending inventory (See earlier computations)	1,040	960	1,120	820
Cost of goods sold	$2,560	$2,640	$2,480	$2,780
Gross profit on sales	$1,840	$1,760	$1,920	$1,620
Increased gross profit compared with LIFO	$220	$140	$300	

Liquid fuels, grains, and other commodities are good examples. To some degree, the weighted average cost represents all the various costs of accumulating the goods currently on hand. Consequently, weighted average costs typically fall between the extreme cost figures that can result from other methods.

As a matter of good business, most companies—especially those with perishable or style-affected goods—attempt to sell the oldest merchandise first. This is especially true of companies dealing in foods, certain chemicals, or drugs. In these cases, FIFO most nearly matches the cost flow to the probable goods flow.

Finding an example of a business operation in which LIFO represents the natural flow of goods is difficult. Purchases of coal or a similar commodity may all be dumped onto one pile from an overhead trestle, and sales may be taken from the top of the pile by a crane. If beginning inventories have been maintained or increased, we conclude that the firm's original purchases are still in inventory. In this case, LIFO represents the actual goods flow. Although LIFO is not the goods flow for most businesses, an estimated 50% or more of major businesses use LIFO to price some of their inventories. We explore the reasons for this choice later in this chapter.

In summary:

(1) In a physical sense, specific identification best presents actual cost of goods sold.

(2) Weighted average can best be associated with business operations in which like goods are commingled.

(3) FIFO probably represents most accurately the actual goods flow for most firms.

(4) Although LIFO represents the least plausible goods flow for most businesses, many major firms use it.

MATCHING COSTS AND REVENUE Because the use of FIFO and LIFO can result in extreme differences during times of changing prices (see Exhibit 9–8), we examine the effects of these two methods.

Consider the data below, taken from our earlier computations, which show that FIFO matches the older costs against current revenue and LIFO matches the most recent costs against current revenue. Under FIFO, therefore, the ending inventory is measured at relatively recent prices, whereas under LIFO, the ending inventory amount reflects older prices.

	Units	Cost	Total
Beginning inventory	60 @	$10 =	$ 600
Purchases:	100 @	11 =	1,100
	100 @	13 =	1,300
	40 @	15 =	600

FIFO		LIFO	
Cost of goods sold:	$2,480 (oldest 220 units)	Cost of goods sold:	$2,780 (latest 220 units)
Ending inventory:	1,120 (latest 80 units)	Ending inventory:	820 (oldest 80 units)

LIFO DISCLOSURES

The footnotes to financial statements generally contain additional information about the accounting for a company's inventories. In particular, the LIFO method generates a variety of disclosures. A few examples of these disclosures are presented below.

Beginning in the 1970s, a large number of companies have switched to the LIFO method. In 1973, for example, 150 of 600 companies surveyed annually used LIFO to price at least some portion of their inventories. By 1983, 408 of the 600 companies surveyed used LIFO.[1] Companies switch to LIFO primarily to reduce their phantom (inventory) profits during inflation and to generate greater cash flows due to smaller income tax liabilities. The change usually has a significant impact on net income and on the inventory amount in the balance sheet. Here is how Arden Group, Inc., described its 1983 change to LIFO:

> In 1983, the Company adopted the last-in first-out (LIFO) method of determining the cost of its nonperishable grocery merchandise ($26,943,000). Perishable merchandise and all other inventory is valued at the lower of first-in, first-out (FIFO) cost or market. The company believes that the use of the LIFO method for nonperishable grocery merchandise results in a better matching of costs and revenues. At December 31, 1983, inventories valued by the LIFO method would have been $637,445 higher if they had been stated at the lower of FIFO cost or market. The effect on net income and income per share for the fifty-two weeks ended December 31, 1983, was a decrease of approximately $562,000 ($.20 per share).[2]

The early 1980s were characterized by very high interest rates and a recessionary economy. In such an environment, companies typically reduce their inventory levels (that is, units sold exceed units purchased during the year). When companies on the LIFO method reduce their inventory, the process is known as a LIFO liquidation. A LIFO liquidation means that some unusually low costs (costs incurred in prior periods) will be charged to cost of goods sold. LIFO liquidations, then, distort the matching of current costs with current revenue. Because of this distortion, companies generally disclose the impact of LIFO liquidations on income. Inland Steel's 1983 annual report, for example, contains the following disclosure:

> During each of the years 1983 through 1981, various inventory quantities were reduced, resulting in liquidations of LIFO inventory quantities carried at lower costs prevailing in prior years as compared with current year costs. The effect of these liquidations on continuing operations in 1983 was to decrease cost of goods sold by $18.3 million as compared to $12.8 million in 1982 and $7.0 million in 1981.[3]

LIFO inventory amounts are not measured at costs currently being incurred by a company. As a result, companies often disclose the difference between the LIFO inventory amount and a more current inventory measure. Georgia–Pacific Corporation's 1984 annual report states:

> The last-in, first-out (LIFO) method of inventory valuation is utilized for the majority of inventories at manufacturing facilities and the Corporation's manufactured inventories located at its building products distribution centers. The average cost method is used for all other inventories.
>
> If LIFO inventories were valued at the lower of average cost or market, the inventories would have been $134 million and $117 million higher than those reported at December 31, 1984 and 1983, respectively.[4]

The 1983 fiscal year report for R. H. Macy & Co. contains this disclosure:

> The LIFO inventory amount at July 30, 1983, and July 31, 1982, was less than the FIFO amount of such inventory by $65,849,000 and $60,961,000.[5]

[1] American Institute of Certified Public Accountants, *Accounting Trends & Techniques*, twenty-eighth edition (1974) and thirty-eighth edition (1984).
[2] Arden Group, Inc., *Annual Report*, 1983.
[3] Inland Steel Company, *Annual Report*, 1983.
[4] Georgia–Pacific Corporation, *Annual Report*, 1984.
[5] R. H. Macy & Co., Inc., *Annual Report*, July 30, 1983.

Most accountants agree that when prices are rising, FIFO tends to overstate income because older, lower unit costs are included in cost of goods sold and matched against current sales prices. In other words, in our example, some of the units sold are charged to costs of goods sold at unit costs of $10, $11, and $13. If our latest purchases reflect current acquisition prices, the units sold must be replaced by units costing $15 (or more if prices continue to rise). Thus, we can argue that when prices rise, LIFO better matches current costs against current revenue, because the cost of the most recent purchases constitutes cost of goods sold.

However, while LIFO associates the current, most significant, unit prices with cost of goods sold, it consequently prices the ending inventory at the older, less realistic unit prices. Because of this, the LIFO inventory figure on the balance sheet is often meaningless in terms of current prices. As we noted earlier, when inventory quantities are maintained or increased, the LIFO method prevents the older prices from appearing in the cost of goods sold. No doubt, some firms still carry LIFO inventories at unit prices that prevailed more than 25 years ago.

Phantom Profits and Income Tax Advantage

A highly simplified example will illustrate how to reduce the undesirable effects of *phantom profits* that result from the use of FIFO during times of rising prices. The same computations will show a related tax advantage of using LIFO during such periods.

Assume that a firm has an opening inventory of five units costing $500 each. The firm sells the five units for $750 each and replaces its inventory by purchasing five more units costing $650 per unit. All transactions are for cash and, for simplicity, we also assume that operating expenses are zero and the applicable income tax rate is 40%. Exhibit 9–9 shows how FIFO produces a phantom profit that is avoided under LIFO and also shows the tax benefit of LIFO when purchase prices are rising.

Note that under FIFO, $750 of net income is reported, but the amount of cash from sales is only enough to replace the inventory sold and pay the income tax on the $1,250 pretax income. Thus, the net income of $750 is not realized in cash that can be declared as dividends or reinvested in the business; it is considered *phantom profit* (or *inventory profit*). We can easily imagine how the phantom profit element causes problems in the planning of dividend policy and the use of net income as a source of capital investments.

When prices rise, LIFO's tax benefit is obvious. Under LIFO, inventories are measured at older (lower) prices, which causes cost of goods sold to increase and pretax income (and therefore income taxes payable) to decrease. Use of LIFO during times of *falling* prices, however, can have quite the opposite tax consequence.

Disclosure

A firm's financial statements should disclose its inventory pricing methods. This is often done in footnotes to the financial statements or parenthetically within the appropriate section of the statements.

EXHIBIT 9–9
FIFO–LIFO Comparison: Phantom Profit Effect and Tax Benefit

	FIFO		LIFO	
	Income Statement	**Cash In (Out)**	**Income Statement**	**Cash In (Out)**
Sales (5 @ $750)	$3,750	$3,750	$3,750	$3,750
Cost of goods sold:				
Beginning inventory (5 @ $500)	$2,500		$2,500	
Purchases (5 @ $650)	3,250	(3,250)	3,250	(3,250)
Goods available (10 units)	$5,750		$5,750	
Ending inventory:				
5 @ FIFO	3,250			
5 @ LIFO			2,500	
Cost of goods sold	$2,500		$3,250	
Pretax income	$1,250		$ 500	
Income tax at 40%	500	(500)	200	(200)
Net income	$ 750		$ 300	
Net cash proceeds		$ 0		$ 300

DEPARTURES FROM COST

Inventories are generally measured at cost. The measurement may be reduced below cost, however, if there is evidence that the inventory's utility has fallen below cost. Such *inventory write-downs* may occur when (1) merchandise must be sold at reduced prices because it is damaged or otherwise not in normal salable condition, or (2) the cost of replacing items in the ending inventory has declined below their recorded cost.

Net Realizable Value

Damaged, physically deteriorated, or obsolete merchandise should be measured and reported at **net realizable value** when this value is less than cost. Net realizable value is the estimated selling price less the expected cost of disposal. For example, assume that an inventory item cost $300 but can be sold for only $200 because it is damaged. Related selling costs are an estimated $20. We should write down the item to $180 ($200 estimated selling price less $20 estimated disposal cost) and reflect a $120 loss for this period.

Lower of Cost or Market

The **lower of cost or market (LCM) rule** provides for the recognition of a loss when prices decline on new inventory items. Under this rule, the loss is reported in the period when the prices decline, rather than during a subsequent period of sale. *Market* is defined as the current replacement cost of the merchandise. If applicable, the LCM rule simply measures inventory at the lower (replacement) market figure. Consequently, reported income decreases by the amount that the ending inventory has been written down. When the ending inventory becomes part of the cost of goods sold in a future period of lower selling prices, its reduced carrying value helps maintain normal profit margins in the period of sale.

To illustrate, let us assume an inventory item that cost $80 has been selling for $100 during the year, yielding a gross profit of 20% on sales. At year-end, the item's replacement cost has dropped to $60—a 25% decline—and a proportionate reduction in the selling price to $75 is expected. In this case, the inventory would be written down to the $60 replacement cost, reducing the current period's net income by the $20 loss. When the item is sold in a subsequent period for $75, a normal gross profit of 20% on sales will be reported ($75 − $60 = $15 gross profit).

Because of the scale and complexity of modern markets, not all decreases in replacement prices are followed by proportionate reductions in selling prices. In these cases, the application of the LCM rule is modified as follows:

(1) If selling price is not expected to drop, inventory may be carried at cost even though it exceeds replacement cost. Using the above example, if the selling price remains at $100 even though the replacement cost drops to $60, we need not write down the inventory.

(2) If selling price is expected to drop—but less than proportionately to the decline in replacement cost—inventory is written down only to the extent necessary to maintain a normal gross profit in the period of sale. Referring again to the above example, if the selling price drops from $100 to $90 when the replacement cost declines to $60, inventory would be written down to $72. This amount maintains a 20% gross profit when the item is sold ($90 − $72 = $18 gross profit).

We may apply the LCM rule to (1) each inventory item, (2) the totals of major inventory classes or categories, or (3) the total inventory. The following simple illustration shows the application of two of these alternatives and indicates that the inventory amount obtained depends on how the rule is applied.

		Unit Price			**Inventory Amounts**	
Inventory Item	**Quantity**	**Cost**	**Market**	**Cost**	**Market**	**LCM (by Item)**
A	4	$4	$3	$16	$12	$12
B	3	6	7	18	21	18
				$34	$33	$30

If we apply LCM to the total inventory, our result is $33. Applied by item, however, the LCM amount is $30. Although the item by item procedure is used most often, either way is acceptable, but one method should be used consistently. Inventory market values appear in such sources as current price catalogs, purchase contracts with suppliers, and other forms of price quotations.

ESTIMATING INVENTORIES

Several good reasons exist for estimating inventories. When taking physical inventory counts for interim financial statements is impractical, an estimate is sufficient. The adequacy of inventory insurance coverage may be determined on the basis of an inventory estimate. Finally, an estimate may be necessary to determine the loss from merchandise destroyed by fire or other disaster. Therefore, we should examine some methods for estimating inventories.

Gross Profit Method

The **gross profit method** of estimating inventories merely rearranges the cost of goods sold section of the income statement—estimated cost of goods sold is deducted from the cost of goods available for sale to derive the estimated ending inventory. Subtracting an estimated gross profit amount from sales provides the estimated cost of goods sold figure. For the gross profit method to be valid, the gross profit percentage used must be representative of the merchandising activities leading up to the date of the inventory estimate.

Suppose that over the past three years a company's gross profit averaged 30% of net sales. Assume also that the net sales for the current year's first interim period are $80,000; the inventory at the beginning of the period was $20,000; and net cost of purchases for the period are $50,000. Exhibit 9–10 shows how to estimate the ending inventory using the gross profit method.

Retail Method

The **retail method** represents another approach to estimating inventories. It is widely used by retail businesses, such as department stores, that keep periodic inventory records. Such firms typically mark each item of merchandise with the retail price and record purchases at both cost and retail price. A firm can estimate its ending inventory at *retail* price merely by subtracting sales from the retail price of merchandise available for sale. To determine the inventory *cost*, the firm applies a cost-to-retail price percentage, which is the ratio of cost to retail price of merchandise available for sale. In Exhibit 9–11 this ratio is 70%, which yields a cost amount of $21,000 when applied to the $30,000 retail value of the inventory.

EXHIBIT 9–10
Gross Profit Method of Estimating Inventory

Beginning inventory		$20,000
Net cost of purchases		50,000
Cost of goods available for sale		$70,000
Net sales	$80,000	
Estimated gross profit (30%)	24,000	
Estimated cost of goods sold		56,000
Estimated ending inventory		$14,000

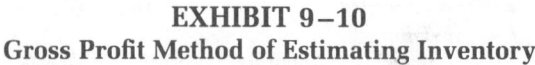

EXHIBIT 9–11
Retail Method of Estimating Inventory

	Cost	Retail Price
Beginning inventory	$14,000	$ 22,000
Net purchases	70,000	98,000
Total merchandise available for sale	$84,000	$120,000
Cost-to-retail percentage: $\frac{\$84,000}{\$120,000} = 70\%$		
Less: Sales during period		90,000
Estimated ending inventory at retail prices		$ 30,000
Applicable cost percentage		× 0.70
Estimated ending inventory at cost		$ 21,000

The cost-to-retail ratio can also be used to compute the cost of a physical inventory taken at retail prices. Thus, the firm saves the considerable effort and expense of determining cost prices for each inventory item. Suppose, for example, that sales clerks count their stock and determine that the ending inventory has an aggregate retail value of $40,000. If the cost-to-retail price ratio is 70%, management could easily obtain the estimated cost of the inventory, $28,000, that is needed to prepare financial statements.

The accuracy of the retail method depends on the assumption that the ending inventory contains the same proportion of goods at the various mark-up percentages as did the original group of merchandise available for sale. To the extent that the mix of mark-up percentages does not remain constant, the accuracy of the estimate is impaired.

PERPETUAL INVENTORY PROCEDURES

Thus far in our discussion, we have assumed that all inventory situations involve a *periodic* system. This system (1) records acquisitions of merchandise as debits to a Purchases account, (2) makes no entry at the time of sale for the cost of goods sold, and (3) only periodically (hence its name) updates the Inventory account when closing entries are made. The periodic system is most suitable for businesses that have many sales transactions of relatively small unit product costs—for example, retail grocery, drug, variety, or department stores.

Other types of business firms, notably those with fewer sales transactions but relatively high unit product costs, may use a **perpetual** inventory system.

Under the perpetual inventory system (also descriptively named), the Inventory account is "perpetually," or continually (as opposed to periodically), maintained. Perpetually updating the Inventory account requires (1) that at the time of purchase, merchandise acquisitions be recorded as debits to the Inventory account and (2) that at the time of sale, the cost of goods sold be determined and recorded by a debit to a Cost of Goods Sold account and a credit to the Inventory account. With a perpetual inventory system, Cost of Goods Sold is an actual account in the general ledger rather than merely a category on the income statement as it is with a periodic inventory system.

Perpetual Inventory Entries

When a firm employs perpetual inventory procedures, the Inventory account shows the amount of inventory on hand at the end of the period—assuming that no theft, spoilage, or error has occurred. However, even if there is little chance for or suspicion of inventory discrepancy, most companies take a physical inventory count at least once a year. At that time, the account is adjusted for any inaccuracies discovered.

The following entries demonstrate the recording procedures followed under the perpetual inventory system, contrasted with the periodic system.

Journal Entries

Periodic Inventory System			Perpetual Inventory System		
(1) Purchased $1,200 worth of merchandise on account, terms 2/10, n/30 (recorded at invoice price).					
Purchases	1,200		Inventory	1,200	
Accounts Payable		1,200	Accounts Payable		1,200
(2) Returned $200 worth of merchandise to vendors.					
Accounts Payable	200		Accounts Payable	200	
Purchases Returns and Allowances		200	Inventory		200
(3) Paid for merchandise (discount taken).					
Accounts Payable	1,000		Accounts Payable	1,000	
Purchases Discounts		20	Inventory		20
Cash		980	Cash		980
(4) Sold goods costing $500 for $800 on account.					
Accounts Receivable	800		Accounts Receivable	800	
Sales		800	Sales		800
			Cost of Goods Sold	500	
			Inventory		500

(5) Counted inventory at end of period, $19,800. The balance in the Inventory account under the periodic system is $25,000 (the beginning inventory). The balance in the Inventory account under the perpetual system is $20,000.

(Closing entries for periodic inventory)					
Income Summary	25,000		Loss on Inventory Shrinkage	200	
Inventory		25,000	Inventory		200
Inventory	19,800				
Income Summary		19,800			

Note that under a perpetual system the Inventory account is increased by purchases and decreased by the cost of goods sold, purchases returns and allowances, and discounts. Therefore, at the end of the period, one entry brings the Inventory account balance into agreement with the amount of the physical inventory. Because we assumed the physical inventory of goods on hand amounted to $19,800, and the Inventory account had a balance of $20,000, we charged the $200 difference to Loss on Inventory Shrinkage and reduced the Inventory account balance to $19,800.

Perpetual Inventory Pricing Methods

When purchase prices for inventory items change during an accounting period, we must select a perpetual inventory pricing method so that the debit to Cost of Goods Sold for each sale may be determined. The same four methods we examined under the periodic inventory system are available—specific identification, average, FIFO, and LIFO. To illustrate these methods on a perpetual basis, we shall use the following data about an inventory item:

		Units	Unit Cost	Total Cost
January 1	Beginning inventory	5	$30.00	$150.00
January 15	Purchase	10	33.00	330.00
September 12	Sale	(9)		
September 29	Purchase	10	36.00	360.00

We must compute the cost of goods sold amount for the nine units sold on September 12.

SPECIFIC IDENTIFICATION When specific identification is used, the actual costs of the specific items sold constitute the cost of goods sold. Assuming two of the nine units sold are from the beginning inventory and the remaining seven units are from the January 15 purchase, the cost of goods sold is $291 [(2 × $30) + (7 × $33)]. Of course, the costs remaining in inventory are the actual costs of the specific items that are unsold. Specific identification gives the same results for both perpetual and periodic systems.

MOVING AVERAGE The average method under a perpetual inventory system is called the **moving average** method. Each time goods are purchased, a new average unit cost is computed for the goods on hand. Cost of goods sold for each sale is computed by multiplying the average unit cost at that time by the number of units sold. On September 12, the average unit cost is $32 ($480 total cost ÷ 15 units available for sale). Therefore, the cost of goods sold is $288 (9 × $32). On September 29, a new average unit cost of $34.50 is computed ($552 total cost ÷ 16 units available for sale).

Because unit average costs are recomputed each time a purchase occurs, the moving average method gives different answers from those obtained by using the weighted average method under a periodic inventory system.

FIRST-IN, FIRST-OUT Under the perpetual FIFO method, each time a sale is made the costs of the oldest goods on hand are charged to cost of goods sold. In our illustration, the FIFO cost of goods sold on September 12 is $282 [(5 × $30) + (4 × $33)]. The FIFO method applied on a perpetual basis results in the same total cost of goods sold amount—and the same ending inventory—as that achieved under the periodic FIFO method.

EXHIBIT 9–12
Perpetual Inventory Record—FIFO Basis

INVENTORY CONTROL

Part No. 1342

Description Fastener cam (3/8") | Maximum 16

Prime Supplier Hill Machinery Company | Reorder Level 6

Location Small Parts Warehouse (Bin 32) | Reorder Quantity 10

Date		Received			Sold			Balance		
		Units	Cost/Unit	Total	Units	Cost/Unit	Total	Units	Cost/Unit	Total
19XX										
Jan.	1	Balance Fwd.						5	$30	$150
	15	10	$33	$330				5	30	
								10	33	480
Sept.	12				5	$30	$150			
					4	33	132	6	33	198
	29	10	36	360				6	33	
								10	36	558

LAST-IN, FIRST-OUT When perpetual LIFO is used, each time a sale is made the costs of the most recent purchases are charged to cost of goods sold. For the September 12 sale, the most recent costs for nine units were incurred on January 15. Thus, cost of goods sold is $297 (9 × $33).

Perpetual LIFO normally gives results different from periodic LIFO for both the total cost of goods sold for a period and the period's ending inventory.

Perpetual Inventory Records

When a perpetual inventory system is used, a detailed perpetual inventory record must be maintained—manually or by computer—for each inventory item. The perpetual inventory records must provide for both the inflow and outflow of merchandise as well as disclose the quantities and prices of items at any time. Although these records are continually maintained, their accuracy should be verified at least once each year by physical counts of merchandise.

Exhibit 9–12 illustrates a perpetual inventory record for an inventory item priced on the FIFO basis. At year-end, the balances on all the perpetual inventory records are added, and their total dollar amount should agree with the amount in the Inventory account, which serves as a control account.

DEMONSTRATION PROBLEM FOR REVIEW

Mackenzie, Inc., began operations on April 1 of the current year. Sales revenue for April totaled $90,000. The company uses the periodic inventory system. Its beginning inventory was $4,000, consisting of 2,000 units at $2 per unit. A summary of April purchases appears below.

April 8	5,000 units	@ $2.50 =	$12,500
19	10,000	@ 3.00 =	30,000
29	6,000	@ 3.50 =	21,000
		Total	$63,500

At the end of April, 7,000 units were on hand.

REQUIRED

(a) How much gross profit on sales would Mackenzie, Inc., report for April under (1) first-in, first-out inventory pricing, and (2) last-in, first-out inventory pricing?

(b) Calculate Mackenzie's gross profit on sales for April under (1) first-in, first-out, and (2) last-in, first-out if the April 29 purchase had been postponed until May.

(c) Calculate Mackenzie's gross profit on sales for April under (1) first-in, first-out, and (2) last-in, first-out if the April 29 purchase had been 9,000 units instead of 6,000 units.

(d) Based on your answers to parts (a), (b), and (c), what can you conclude about the impact of the timing or amount of end-of-period purchases on the gross profit on sales computed under the (1) first-in, first-out, and (2) last-in, first-out methods of inventory pricing?

SOLUTION TO DEMONSTRATION PROBLEM

(a)

		FIFO	LIFO
Sales		$90,000	$90,000
Cost of Goods Sold:			
Beginning Inventory		$ 4,000	$ 4,000
Add: Purchases		63,500	63,500
Cost of Goods Available for Sale		$67,500	$67,500
Less: Ending Inventory			
FIFO: 6,000 × $3.50 =	$21,000		
1,000 × $3.00 =	3,000	24,000	
LIFO: 2,000 × $2.00 =	$ 4,000		
5,000 × $2.50 =	12,500		16,500
Cost of Goods Sold		$43,500	$51,000
Gross Profit on Sales		$46,500	$39,000

(b) If the April 29 purchase of 6,000 units was postponed until May, the April 30 inventory would have been 1,000 units and purchases for April would have totaled $42,500 ($12,500 on April 8 + $30,000 on April 19). The gross profit on sales would then be computed as follows:

	FIFO	LIFO
Sales	$90,000	$90,000
Cost of Goods Sold:		
Beginning Inventory	$ 4,000	$ 4,000
Add: Purchases	42,500	42,500
Cost of Goods Available for Sale	$46,500	$46,500
Less: Ending Inventory		
FIFO: 1,000 × $3.00	3,000	
LIFO: 1,000 × $2.00		2,000
Cost of Goods Sold	$43,500	$44,500
Gross Profit on Sales	$46,500	$45,500

(c) If 9,000 units were purchased on April 29, then the April 30 inventory would have been 10,000 units and purchases for April would have totaled $74,000 ($12,500 on April 8 + $30,000 on April 19 + $31,500 on April 29). The gross profit on sales would then be computed as follows:

			FIFO	LIFO
Sales			$90,000	$90,000
Cost of Goods Sold:				
Beginning Inventory			$ 4,000	$ 4,000
Add: Purchases			74,000	74,000
Cost of Goods Available for Sale			$78,000	$78,000
Less: Ending Inventory				
FIFO:	9,000 × $3.50 =	$31,500		
	1,000 × $3.00 =	3,000	34,500	
LIFO:	2,000 × $2.00 =	$ 4,000		
	5,000 × $2.50 =	12,500		
	3,000 × $3.00 =	9,000		25,500
Cost of Goods Sold			$43,500	$52,500
Gross Profit on Sales			$46,500	$37,500

(d) Gross profit on sales under the FIFO method is the same in all three cases. The gross profit is unaffected by changes in the amount or timing of end-of-period purchases.

Gross profit on sales under the LIFO method is different in each case. Gross profit is affected by changes in the amount or timing of end-of-period purchases, because—under the periodic LIFO method—the costs of the most recently purchased goods are the first costs charged to cost of goods sold.

KEY POINTS TO REMEMBER

(1) Cost of goods sold under a periodic system is calculated as beginning inventory plus net cost of purchases less ending inventory.

(2) Other things being equal, changing the dollar amount of ending inventory changes reported pretax income by a like amount.

(3) Uncorrected ending inventory measurement errors cause the reported income of two periods to be misstated. The errors are equal in amount, opposite in direction, and therefore offsetting.

(4) Taking inventory consists of three stages: (a) counting, (b) pricing, and (c) summation.

(5) An inventory amount under a periodic system can be calculated by using any of the following methods: specific identification; weighted average; first-in, first-out (FIFO); and last-in, first-out (LIFO). Reported income can be influenced by choosing among inventory pricing methods.

(6) When prices are rising, LIFO matches current costs against revenue and results in lower reported income than FIFO does and thus may provide a related tax benefit.

(7) Inventories can be estimated by the gross profit method or the retail method. The gross profit method requires the use of a representative gross profit percentage. An appropriate cost-to-retail price percentage must be computed under the retail method.

(8) A perpetual inventory system (a) does not use a Purchases account, (b) records cost of goods sold at the time of sale, and (c) continually updates the balance in the Inventory account. Pricing methods under a perpetual system are specific identification, moving average, FIFO, and LIFO.

SELF-TEST QUESTIONS
(Answers are at the end of this chapter.)

1. Which inventory pricing method assumes that the goods most recently purchased are sold first?
   (a) FIFO.
   (b) Specific identification.
   (c) Weighted average.
   (d) LIFO.
2. Which inventory pricing method reflects the most recently incurred purchase costs in the ending inventory?
   (a) FIFO.
   (b) LIFO.
   (c) Retail.
   (d) Weighted average.
3. Boyer Company started 19X4 with a $140,000 inventory. Purchases totaled $300,000 during the first three months of 19X4. Sales during the same period were $500,000. Boyer's gross profit averages 45% of sales. Using the gross profit method, Boyer's March 31, 19X4, inventory is estimated at
   (a) $165,000
   (b) $275,000
   (c) $225,000
   (d) $215,000
4. Clipper, Inc., returned $600 of merchandise purchased on account. Under a perpetual inventory system, the account credited in the journal entry to record the return is
   (a) Purchases.
   (b) Purchases Returns and Allowances.
   (c) Inventory.
   (d) Accounts Payable.
5. The average inventory pricing method under a perpetual inventory system is called the
   (a) Weighted average method.
   (b) Moving average method.
   (c) Composite average method.
   (d) Simple average method.

QUESTIONS

9–1 List six factors (or cost categories) typically included in the cost of goods sold computation under a periodic inventory system and indicate whether the amount of each normally increases or decreases the cost of goods sold figure.

9–2 Define *inventory* and identify the costs that should be included as inventory costs.

9–3 Under a periodic inventory system, why is reported income affected dollar-for-dollar (disregarding income taxes) by any change in the dollar amount of ending inventory?

9–4 Welch Company overstated its 19X1 ending inventory by $10,000. Assuming the error was not discovered, what was the effect on income for 19X1? For 19X2?

9–5 For a physical inventory count, explain (a) the three steps involved, (b) why firms maintaining perpetual inventory records still take physical counts, and (c) what merchandise should be included.

9–6 What is meant by *goods flow* and *cost flow?*

9–7 Briefly describe each of the following inventory pricing methods under a periodic inventory system: (a) specific identification; (b) weighted average; (c) first-in, first-out; and (d) last-in, first-out.

9–8 Describe an appropriate operating situation (that is, goods flow corresponds with cost flow) for each of the four approaches to inventory pricing listed in Question 9–7.

9–9 Why do relatively stable purchase prices reduce the significance of the choice of an inventory pricing method?

9–10 Briefly explain the nature of *phantom profits* during periods of rising merchandise purchase prices.

9–11 If prices have been rising, which inventory pricing method—weighted average; first-in, first-out; or last-in, first-out—yields (a) the lowest inventory amount? (b) The lowest net income? (c) The largest inventory amount? (d) The largest net income?

9–12 Even though it does not represent their goods flow, why might firms adopt last-in, first-out inventory pricing during periods when prices are consistently rising?

9–13 Identify two situations in which merchandise may be inventoried at an amount less than cost.

9–14 At year-end, Tony's Appliance Shop has a refrigerator on hand that has been used as a demonstration model. The refrigerator cost $500 and sells for $750 when new. In its present condition, the refrigerator will be sold for $475. Related selling costs are an estimated $15. At what amount should the refrigerator be carried in inventory?

9–15 Discuss the effect on reported income of applying the lower of cost or market rule.

9–16 Under what circumstances might firms estimate the dollar amount of their inventories rather than actually count them?

9–17 Contrast the accounting procedures for periodic and perpetual inventory systems.

9–18 Which inventory pricing methods give the same results (ending inventory and total cost of goods sold) when applied under a perpetual inventory system and a periodic inventory system?

EXERCISES

Periodic and perpetual systems

9–19 Lewis Stores, Inc., uses the periodic inventory system. Its accounting records include the following balances:

Accounts Payable (all for merchandise)	$ 5,100
Delivery Expense (to customers)	3,000
Inventory	13,000
Purchases	66,000
Purchases Discounts	1,200
Purchases Returns and Allowances	1,800
Sales	98,000
Sales Discounts	1,700
Sales Returns and Allowances	2,000
Transportation In	2,700

(a) Assuming that the ending inventory, determined by physical count, is $15,000, compute the cost of goods sold.
(b) How would the above accounts differ if the firm used a perpetual inventory system?

Ending inventory count

9–20 The December 31, 19XX, inventory of Miller Company was $76,000. In arriving at this amount, the following items were considered:

(1) Included in the inventory count were goods on hand costing $5,000 owned by Ward Company but on consignment to Miller Company.
(2) Included in the inventory count were goods in transit at December 31 to Miller Company from Tyler, Inc. These goods, costing $8,000, were shipped F.O.B. destination and arrived on January 3.
(3) Excluded from the inventory count were goods sitting on Miller Company's shipping dock on December 31. These goods, costing $4,000, were sold to Ovett, Inc., on December 31 and were picked up by an Ovett truck on January 2.
(4) Included in the inventory count were goods in transit at December 31 to Miller Company from Adler, Inc. The goods, costing $6,000, were shipped F.O.B. shipping point and arrived on January 2.

Compute the correct December 31, 19XX, inventory amount for Miller Company. Miller has no specific agreement with any party concerning the passage of title to goods bought or sold.

Inventory pricing methods—periodic

9–21 The following information is for the Bock Company for May 19XX. Bock sells just one product.

	Units	Unit Cost
Beginning inventory	40	$ 6
Purchases: May 11	70	8
18	60	10
23	30	11

During May, 150 units were sold, leaving an ending inventory of 50 units. Assume periodic inventory procedures and compute the ending inventory and the cost of goods sold using (a) first-in, first-out; (b) last-in, first-out; and (c) weighted average.

Inventory pricing methods—periodic

9–22 Ortega Company, which uses the periodic inventory system, has the following records for July:

		Units	Unit Cost
Beginning inventory		32	$18
Purchases: July	6	80	17
	15	50	15
	28	28	14

Ending inventory for July was 55 units. Compute the ending inventory and the cost of goods sold using (a) first-in, first-out; (b) weighted average; and (c) last-in, first-out.

Departures from cost

9–23 Determine the proper inventory amount for each of the following items in Delta Company's year-end inventory.

(a) Delta has 500 video games in stock. The games cost $30 each, but their year-end replacement cost is $24. Delta has been selling these games for $60, but competitors are now selling them for $48. Delta plans to drop its price to $48. Delta's normal gross profit rate on video games is 50%.

(b) Delta has 600 rolls of camera film that are past the expiration date marked on each film's box. The films cost $1.50 each and are normally sold for $3.00. New replacement films still cost $1.50. To clear out these old films, Delta will drop their selling price to $1.00. There are no related selling costs.

(c) Delta has 50 binoculars in stock that cost $100 each. They are priced to sell for $200 (for a normal gross profit rate of 50%). At year-end, the replacement cost is $90 each. Delta is the exclusive area retailer for this brand of binoculars. Even though the replacement cost has dropped, Delta believes it will not have to lower the selling price for the binoculars on hand.

Gross profit method

9–24 Over the past several years Allen Company's gross profit has averaged 45% of net sales. During the first six months of the current year, net sales are $600,000 and net cost of purchases totals $320,000. Inventory at the beginning of the period was $58,000. The company prepares quarterly interim financial statements. Use the gross profit method to determine the estimated cost of inventory at the end of the current six-month period.

Retail method

9–25 Dodge Company's April 1 inventory had a cost of $28,000 and a retail value of $46,000. During April, Dodge's net merchandise purchases cost $65,000 and had a net retail value of $104,000. Net sales for April totaled $120,000.

(a) Compute the estimated cost of the April 30 inventory using the retail method.

(b) What key assumptions underlie the validity of this estimate of inventory cost?

Inventory error corrections

9–26 The following information is available for Foley Company during four consecutive operating periods:

	Amounts by Period			
	1	2	3	4
Beginning inventory	$17,000	$22,000	$20,000	$18,000
Net cost of purchases	80,000	52,000	64,000	43,000
Cost of goods available for sale	$97,000	$74,000	$84,000	$61,000
Ending inventory	22,000	20,000	18,000	16,000
Cost of goods sold	$75,000	$54,000	$66,000	$45,000

Assuming that the company made the following errors, compute the revised cost of goods sold figure for each period.

Period	Error in Ending Inventory	
1	Overstated	$4,000
2	Overstated	3,000
3	Understated	2,000

Periodic and perpetual systems

9–27 Present journal entries to record the following transactions if (a) a periodic inventory system is used and (b) a perpetual inventory system is used.

(1) Merchandise is purchased for (and recorded at) $3,400, terms 2/10, n/30.
(2) Goods originally costing $400 (in the preceding transaction) are returned to the seller before payment is made.
(3) The remainder of the purchase in transaction (1) is paid for and the related discount is taken.
(4) Goods costing $1,800 are sold on account for $2,900.
(5) The proper balance in the Inventory account is established at the end of the period. A physical inventory at the end of the period shows goods costing $1,690 on hand. Assume that the beginning balance in this account was $600.

Inventory pricing methods—perpetual

9–28 The following are July inventory data for Merrit Company, which uses perpetual inventory procedures.

July	1	Beginning inventory, 75 units @ $30 per unit.
	10	Purchased 50 units @ $35 per unit.
	15	Sold 90 units.
	26	Purchased 80 units @ $36 per unit.

Compute the cost of goods sold for July 15 using (a) first-in, first-out; (b) last-in, first-out; and (c) moving average.

PROBLEMS

Inventory pricing methods

9–29 Pierce Sales, Inc., had a beginning inventory for May comprising 500 units that had cost $40 per unit. A summary of purchases and sales during May follows:

		Unit Cost	Units Purchased	Units Sold
May	2			300
	6	$43	1,000	
	10			800
	19	45	600	
	23			700
	30	48	300	

REQUIRED

(a) Assuming Pierce uses a periodic inventory system, calculate the amount of ending inventory under each of the following pricing methods: first-in, first-out; last-in, first-out; and weighted average.

(b) Which inventory pricing method would you choose:
(1) to reflect what is probably the physical flow of goods?
(2) to minimize income tax for the period?
(3) To report the largest amount of income for the period?
Justify your answers.

(c) Assuming Pierce uses a perpetual inventory system, calculate cost of goods sold amounts on May 2, May 10, and May 23 under each of the following pricing methods: first-in, first-out; last-in, first-out; and moving average.

Effects of FIFO and LIFO

9–30 Examine the July data below for Lambert, Inc., which prices inventory on the last-in, first-out basis and uses the periodic inventory system.

Beginning inventory: 4,000 units @ $3 each

Purchases		Sales	
July 5	9,000 @ $4	July 8	8,000 @ $ 7
19	20,000 @ 6	21	17,000 @ 9
30	5,000 @ 7	28	6,000 @ 10

REQUIRED

(a) How much gross profit on sales would Lambert, Inc., report for July?
(b) By what amount would Lambert's reported gross profit for July change if the final merchandise purchase had been postponed for several days?
(c) How would Lambert's reported gross profit differ if the final purchase had been for 16,000 units instead of for 5,000 units?
(d) Assuming Lambert used the first-in, first-out method, calculate the answers to parts (a), (b), and (c).

Income effects of inventory pricing methods

9–31 The following is a summary of Kallis Company's inventory amounts at the end of each of its first three years of operations, assuming various inventory pricing procedures.

Year-end	First-in, First-out	Last-in, First-out	Weighted Average
1	$3,900	$3,500	$3,650
2	5,200	4,700	5,000
3	4,600	4,300	4,450

REQUIRED

Answer each of the following questions, providing supporting computations or other reasoning (disregard income tax effects).

(a) For year 1, by how much could reported income change simply by choosing among the three inventory pricing methods?
(b) For year 2, which inventory pricing method would result in the *highest* reported income?
(c) For year 3, which inventory pricing method would result in the *lowest* reported income?
(d) For year 3, by how much and in what direction would reported income differ under first-in, first-out compared with weighted average?
(e) Which inventory pricing method would result in the *highest* reported income for the *three years combined?*

Lower of cost or market rule

9–32 The Grand Company had the following inventory at December 31, 19X7:

	Quantity	Unit Price Cost	Unit Price Market
Fans			
Model X1	300	$14	$16
Model X2	200	20	19
Model X3	400	28	25
Heaters			
Model B7	150	22	21
Model B8	180	30	32
Model B9	60	39	37

REQUIRED

(a) Determine the ending inventory amount by applying the lower of cost or market rule to:
  (1) each item of inventory.
  (2) each major category of inventory.
  (3) the total inventory.

(b) Which of the LCM procedures from part (a) result in the lowest net income for 19X7? Explain.

Retail method

9–33 Sales clerks for Carlene Company, a retail concern, took a year-end physical inventory at retail prices and determined that the total retail value of the ending inventory was $90,000. The following information for the year is available:

	Cost	Selling Price
Beginning inventory	$ 58,900	$ 86,000
Net purchases	224,000	324,000
Sales		312,000

Management estimates its inventory loss from theft and other causes by comparing its physical ending inventory at retail prices with an estimated ending inventory at retail prices (determined by subtracting sales from goods available for sale at selling prices) and reducing this difference to cost by applying the proper cost ratio.

REQUIRED

(a) Compute the estimated cost of the ending inventory using the retail method. This inventory amount will appear in the balance sheet, and the calculation should be based on the physical inventory taken at retail prices.

(b) Compute the estimated inventory loss for the year from theft and other causes.

Comparison of FIFO and LIFO

9–34 Selected operating data follow for Perco, Inc., a franchised distributor of compact disc players:

Beginning inventory	250 units	@ $300 each
Purchases:	500	@ 350
	200	@ 380
Sales	700	@ 500
Operating expenses	$57,500	

Perco uses the periodic inventory system priced at first-in, first-out. Assume all sales, purchases, operating expenses, and taxes are paid in cash and that a 30% income tax rate is applicable.

REQUIRED

(a) What is Perco's net income for the period?

(b) What is the net amount of cash generated by the period's activity?

(c) Why are the amounts in parts (a) and (b) different? How would you explain this to a stockholder who expected a cash dividend equal to one-half of the reported net income?

(d) What would be your answers to parts (a) and (b) if the firm used the last-in, first-out method to price its ending inventory?

(e) Briefly explain the nature of any phantom profit on inventory in part (a). Also, explain the nature of any tax advantage of the last-in, first-out inventory pricing in part (d).

(f) Contrast the inventory carrying values in parts (a) and (d). Which figure is more meaningful? Why?

(g) Contrast the reported income in parts (a) and (d). Which figure is more meaningful? Why?

Gross profit method

9–35 Ryder Company, an automobile parts supplier, was robbed of a portion of its inventory on the night of August 16, 19X4. The company does not keep perpetual inventory records and must, therefore, estimate the theft loss. To aid in this determination, the accounting staff compiles the following information:

Inventory, August 1, 19X4	$290,000
Inventory, August 16, 19X4 (not stolen)	132,000
Purchases, August 1–16, 19X4	84,000
Purchases returns, August 1–16, 19X4	4,000
Sales, August 1–16, 19X4	225,000
Average gross profit margin	42%

REQUIRED

Use the gross profit method to estimate the amount of the inventory theft loss.

Periodic and perpetual systems

9–36 Assume that Lemly Company had a $20,000 ending inventory balance at the close of the last period. The following sales and purchase transactions occurred during the current period:

(1) Purchased merchandise on account, $9,500, terms 1/10, n/30.

(2) Returned part of the above merchandise that had an original gross purchase price of $500.

(3) Paid the balance of the purchase in time to receive the purchases discount.

(4) Sold goods costing $16,000 for $25,000. Cash of $6,500 was received, with the balance due on account.

REQUIRED

(a) Record these transactions assuming that (1) a periodic inventory system is used and (2) a perpetual inventory system is used. Assume also that accounts payable are initially recorded at the full invoice price.

(b) Suppose that a physical inventory at the end of the current period shows inventory costing $12,300 to be on hand. Present the journal entries (if any) required under each inventory system to establish the proper balance in the Inventory account.

(c) Which system would best disclose any possible inventory loss in the income statement? Why?

Inventory pricing methods—perpetual

9–37 Hunt Company uses a perpetual inventory system. Transactions for an inventory item during April were as follows:

April	1	Beginning inventory, 40 units @ $210 per unit.
	9	Purchased 10 units @ $225 per unit.
	14	Sold 30 units @ $400 per unit.
	23	Purchased 20 units @ $227 per unit.
	29	Sold 15 units @ $420 per unit.

REQUIRED

Record the beginning inventory, purchases, cost of goods sold, and the continuous (perpetual) inventory balance for April on an inventory control record like the one illustrated in Exhibit 9–12, page 346. Use the (a) first-in, first-out method; (b) last-in, first-out method; and (c) moving average method.

ALTERNATE PROBLEMS

Inventory pricing methods

9–29A Mellow Sales, Inc., had a beginning inventory for July comprising 1,800 units that had cost $24 per unit. A summary of purchases and sales during July follows:

	Unit Cost	Units Purchased	Units Sold
July 3			1,000
8	$26	1,200	
13			1,500
19	27	700	
23	29	1,300	
28			500

REQUIRED

(a) Assuming Mellow uses a periodic inventory system, calculate the amount of ending inventory under each of the following pricing methods: first-in, first-out; last-in, first-out; and weighted average.

(b) Which inventory pricing method would you choose:
(1) to reflect what is probably the physical flow of goods?
(2) to minimize income tax for the period?
(3) to report the largest amount of income for the period?
Justify your answers.

(c) Assuming Mellow uses a perpetual inventory system, calculate cost of goods sold amounts on July 3, July 13, and July 28 under each of the following pricing methods: first-in, first-out; last-in, first-out; and moving average.

Effects of FIFO and LIFO

9–30A Examine the April data below for Salem, Inc., which prices inventory on the last-in, first-out basis and uses the periodic inventory system.

Beginning inventory: 6,000 units @ $5 each

Purchases		Sales	
Apr. 5	4,000 @ $6	Apr. 8	3,000 @ $ 9
12	10,000 @ 7	16	12,000 @ 10
21	15,000 @ 8	22	13,000 @ 11
30	8,000 @ 9	27	5,000 @ 12

REQUIRED

(a) How much gross profit on sales would Salem, Inc., report for April?

(b) By what amount would Salem's reported gross profit for April change if the final merchandise purchase had been postponed for several days?

(c) How would Salem's reported gross profit differ if the final purchase had been for 20,000 units instead of for 8,000 units?

(d) Assuming Salem used the first-in, first-out method, calculate the answers to parts (a), (b), and (c).

Lower of cost or market rule

9–32A Lopez Company had the following inventory at December 31, 19X4:

	Quantity	Unit Price Cost	Unit Price Market
Desks			
Model 9001	75	$150	$140
Model 9002	40	200	210
Model 9003	30	300	305
Cabinets			
Model 7001	150	50	56
Model 7002	35	80	74
Model 7003	40	100	105

REQUIRED

(a) Determine the ending inventory amount by applying the lower of cost or market rule to:
   (1) each item of inventory.
   (2) each major category of inventory.
   (3) the total inventory.

(b) Which of the LCM procedures from part (a) result in the lowest net income for 19X4? Explain.

Retail method

9–33A Sales clerks for Garver Company, a retail concern, took a year-end physical inventory at retail prices and determined that the total retail value of the ending inventory was $150,000. The following information for the year is available:

	Cost	Selling Price
Beginning inventory	$ 55,000	$ 90,000
Net purchases	534,000	860,000
Sales		790,000

Management estimates its inventory loss from theft and other causes by comparing its physical ending inventory at retail prices with an estimated ending inventory at retail prices (determined by subtracting sales from goods available for sale at selling prices) and reducing this difference to cost by applying the proper cost ratio.

REQUIRED
(a) Compute the estimated cost of the ending inventory using the retail method. This inventory amount will appear in the balance sheet, and the calculation should be based on the physical inventory taken at retail prices.
(b) Compute the estimated inventory loss for the year from theft and other causes.

Periodic and perpetual systems

9–36A Assume that Heritage Appliance Shop had a $7,000 ending inventory balance at the close of the last period. The following sales and purchase transactions occurred during the current period:
(1) Purchased merchandise on account, $6,200, terms 2/10, n/30.
(2) Returned part of the above merchandise that had an original gross purchase price of $700.
(3) Paid the balance of the purchase in time to receive the purchases discount.
(4) Sold goods costing $8,200 for $16,000. Cash of $10,000 was received, with the balance due on account.

REQUIRED
(a) Record these transactions assuming that (1) a periodic inventory system is used and (2) a perpetual inventory system is used. Assume also that accounts payable are initially recorded at the full invoice price.
(b) Suppose that a physical inventory at the end of the current period shows inventory costing $3,900 to be on hand. Present journal entries (if any) required under each inventory system to establish the proper balance in the Inventory account.
(c) Which system would best disclose any possible inventory loss in the income statement? Why?

Inventory pricing methods—perpetual

9–37A Howland Company uses a perpetual inventory system. Transactions for an inventory item during June were as follows:

June	1	Beginning inventory, 50 units @ $83 per unit.
	5	Purchased 10 units @ $95 per unit.
	13	Sold 40 units @ $190 per unit.
	25	Purchased 30 units @ $90 per unit.
	29	Sold 18 units @ $180 per unit.

REQUIRED
Record the beginning inventory, purchases, cost of goods sold, and the continuous (perpetual) inventory balance for June on an inventory control record like the one illustrated in Exhibit 9–12, page 346. Use the (a) first-in, first-out method; (b) last-in, first-out method; and (c) moving average method.

BUSINESS DECISION PROBLEM

Nolan Company's entire inventory and many of its accounting records were destroyed by fire early in the morning of April 1, 19X3. Nolan filed an inventory loss claim of $100,000 with Dependable Insurance Company. As Dependable's representative, you must evaluate the reasonableness of Nolan's claim. You and Nolan's head bookkeeper have gathered the following information from various sources:

(1) The January 1, 19X3, inventory figure of $40,000 was found on a copy of a personal property tax declaration filed with the local municipality.

(2) From a statistical summary filed with a trade association, the sales and cost of goods sold for the preceding three years were as follows:

	19X0	**19X1**	**19X2**
Net Sales	$720,000	$840,000	$940,000
Cost of goods sold	420,800	484,000	545,200

(3) Nolan buys an estimated 70% of its merchandise from three wholesale suppliers. According to these three suppliers, Nolan's purchases for the first three months of 19X3 were as follows:

Supplier	**Purchases**
Jackson Corporation	$35,000
Levin Company	60,000
Pohl, Inc.	45,000

(4) Nolan's sales average 10% cash and the balance on credit. Adding machine tapes totaling the accounts receivable subsidiary ledger were found and showed $30,000 and $39,000, respectively, for December 31, 19X2, and March 31, 19X3. An analysis of bank deposit slips indicates that collections from credit customers deposited in the bank in 19X3 were: $75,000 for January; $100,000 for February; and $68,000 for March.

REQUIRED

Based on the preceding data, use the gross profit method to estimate Nolan Company's ending inventory destroyed by fire. Is Nolan's loss claim reasonable?

ANSWERS TO SELF-TEST QUESTIONS

1. (d) 2. (a) 3. (a) 4. (c) 5. (b)

10

Plant Assets: Measurement and Depreciation

Chapter Objectives

- **Provide the background to understand the various problems related to the measurement of plant assets.**
- **Identify the guidelines relating to the initial measurement of plant assets.**
- **Discuss the nature of the depreciation process.**
- **Illustrate four generally accepted methods of computing periodic depreciation.**
- **Discuss the distinction between revenue and capital expenditures.**

Little of all we value here
Wakes on the morn of its hundredth year.

OLIVER WENDELL HOLMES

In this chapter and Chapter 11, we discuss the accounting problems related to the acquisition, use, and disposal of assets whose benefits to a firm extend over many accounting periods. These long-term assets fall in three major balance sheet categories—**plant assets, natural resources,** and **intangible assets.** Plant assets, or *fixed assets,* refer to a firm's *property, plant,* and *equipment.*

The carrying values of these long-term assets are normally based on historical costs. As with other business assets, the costs related to the use of long-term assets must be properly calculated and matched against the revenue they help generate, so that periodic net income is determined correctly. Each period's expired portion of the asset's cost is called *depreciation, depletion,* or *amortization,* depending on the type of asset involved. All of these terms have the same meaning in accounting, that is, periodic charging to expense.

Exhibit 10–1 gives several specific examples within each asset category. The exhibit also associates the term for the periodic write-off to expense with the proper asset category. Note that site land—that is, a place on which to operate—usually has an indefinite useful life and therefore does not require any periodic write-off to expense.

EXHIBIT 10–1
Classification of Long-term Assets and Related Write-off

Asset Category	Examples	Term for Periodic Write-off to Expense
Plant Assets	Buildings, equipment, tools, furniture, fixtures, and vehicles	Depreciation
	Land for site use	No periodic write-off; considered to have an indefinite life.
Natural Resources	Oil, timber, coal, and other mineral deposits	Depletion
Intangible Assets	Patents, copyrights, leaseholds, franchises, trademarks, and goodwill	Amortization

OVERVIEW OF PLANT ASSET PROBLEMS

We consider the problems associated with plant assets in the order shown in Exhibit 10–2. This exhibit is a graphic presentation of the typical accounting problems created by plant assets in relation to an asset's life cycle.

Measurement problems associated with plant assets include identifying the types and amounts of expenditures that make up the original recorded cost of the particular asset. During the use period of a limited-life asset, it is important to charge the appropriate amounts against yearly revenue to reflect the asset's consumption. This involves estimating the asset's useful life and its probable salvage value at disposal. Also during the use period, expenditures for simple maintenance (expense) must be properly differentiated from expenditures that increase the capacity or extend the life of the asset (added to asset costs). On disposal, the adjusted accounting cost of the asset must be compared with the net proceeds from disposal in order to determine any related gain or loss. We consider this last problem in Chapter 11.

EXHIBIT 10–2
Typical Problems of Plant Asset Accounting

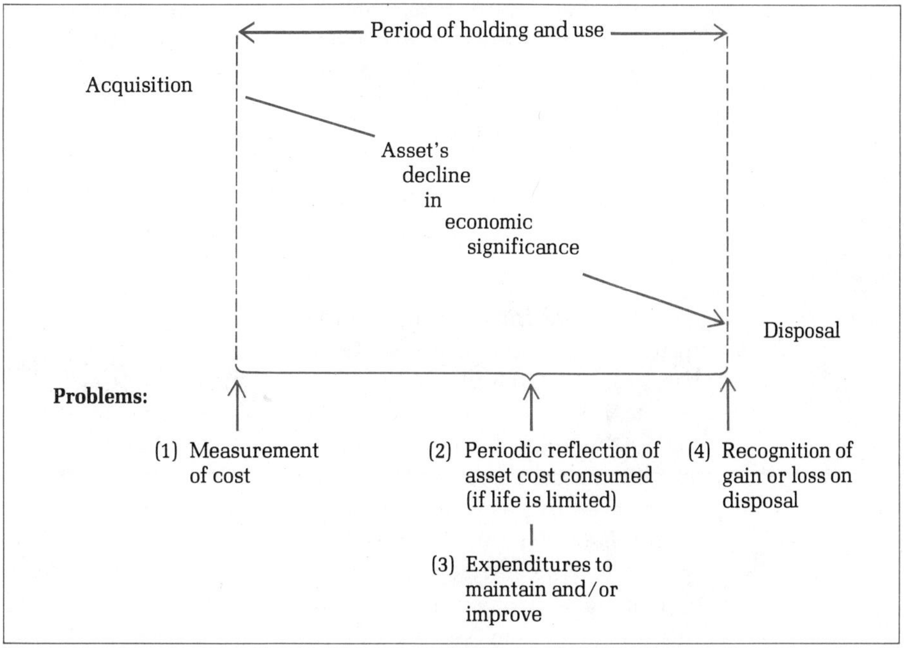

ORIGINAL MEASUREMENT OF PLANT ASSETS

Plant assets are originally recorded at their cost. These measures are also called *historical costs* because they provide the basis for accounting for the assets in subsequent periods. Usually we do not attempt to reflect subsequent changes in market values for plant assets. In general, the initial cost of a plant asset is equal to the cash and/or the cash equivalent of that which is given up in order to acquire the asset *and* to prepare it for use. In other words, initial cost includes the asset's (1) implied cash price and (2) cost of preparation for use.

The expenditures to acquire and prepare the asset for use must be reasonable and necessary to be considered part of the asset's cost. Accountants do not capitalize (charge to an asset account) wasteful or inefficient expenditures. Costs of waste and inefficiency are expensed when incurred. For example, suppose equipment is damaged while it is being installed or a firm's receiving dock is damaged while equipment is being unloaded. Expenditures made to repair these damages are not part of the cost of the equipment; they are instead charged to expense.

Cash and Noncash Purchases

Often an asset's historical cost is simply the amount of cash paid when the asset is acquired and readied for use. Consider, for example, the following expenditures for a certain piece of equipment:

Purchase price factors:		
Gross invoice price	$10,000	
Less: Cash discount (1/10, n/30)	(100)	
Sales tax	500	$10,400
Related expenditures:		
Freight charges	$ 200	
Installation costs	500	
Testing of installed machine	300	1,000
Cost of equipment		$11,400

The total initial equipment cost is $11,400, consisting of a cash purchase price of $10,400 and preparation costs of $1,000. The sales tax is a necessary component of the purchase price and should not be charged to a tax expense account. Similarly, the costs of freight, installation, and testing are expenditures necessary to get the asset in condition and location for use.

If an asset's purchase price is not immediately paid in cash, we determine the cash equivalent purchase price at the acquisition date and record that amount in the asset account. Suppose we purchased the above equipment on a financing plan requiring a $1,500 cash down payment and a non-interest-bearing note for $10,000 due in one year. The implied cash price remains $10,400, even though the financing plan is used. The difference between the $10,400 and the $11,500 total disbursement under the financing plan ($1,500 down payment plus $10,000

UNFIXED ASSETS

Corporations of all types are finding that prosaic assets such as office buildings and empty lots can turn into cash cows. They are syndicating their real estate, borrowing on it and spinning it off into separate companies. They are using real estate for everything from bankrolling corporate overhauls to increasing bank reserves. And some companies are using it to launch or fend off takeover attempts.

The new awareness of the possibilities of real estate has dawned slowly. A 1983 Harvard Business Review study found that at least 25% of the average company's assets were tied up in real estate. American companies held between $700 billion and $1.4 trillion worth of property, including up to 14 billion square feet of office space and 140 million acres of undeveloped land. But, the study said, "Most treat property as an overhead cost like stationery and paper clips."

"The big thing is getting [companies] to think of real estate as they do of cash," says William D. Saunders, the chairman of LaSalle Partners. Adds Carl Kane, a partner of Kenneth Leventhal & Co., an accounting firm: "When you start looking at it, real estate isn't a fixed asset anymore. It's no longer illiquid."

But real estate can hurt unwary companies. For example, they may fall prey to corporate raiders well aware that the book value of real estate may bear little relation to its market value. Land and buildings are recorded on corporate balance sheets at the price originally paid, and the buildings are depreciated every year; so, the book value of real estate is constantly diminishing even though its market value may be increasing substantially.

Take Castle & Cooke, Inc., the San Francisco food company best known for its Dole brand of fruit. The company attracted the attention of three takeover artists, David H. Murdock, Irwin L. Jacobs and Charles Hurwitz, largely because of its 150,000 acres of Hawaiian land. Analysts say the land—much of it ripe for resort or office development—could fetch more than enough to pay off the company's $440 million of debt.

Castle & Cooke ultimately caved in and agreed to a takeover by Mr. Murdock's Flexi-Van Corp. last March. Castle & Cooke's real estate was immediately turned into a weapon to fend off other suitors. As part of the acquisition agreement, the real estate was rolled into a "poison pill." The pill, which gives Flexi-Van an option to buy up to $300 million of Castle & Cooke's best Hawaiian property, would be activated if a group unaffiliated with Flexi-Van begins a tender offer for Castle & Cooke.

Another anti-takeover ploy gaining adherents calls for a company to spin off its real estate into a partnership or real-estate investment trust. REITs are stock companies that invest in real estate and distribute most of their earnings to shareholders.

Raiders often acquire companies through leveraged buyouts, in which they buy a company primarily with debt and then pay off the debt by selling company assets.

International Paper Co. put seven million acres of timberland into a partnership last year, at a time when the company was rumored to be a takeover target. More recently, Crown Zellerbach Corp., another forest-products company, thwarted a hostile bid from Sir James Goldsmith. Crown proposed a restructuring that included spinning off its timber assets into an $800 million liquidating partnership.

A simpler defense is a straight sale of real estate. Carson Pirie Scott & Co., a Chicago retail chain, is another perennially rumored takeover target, largely because of the value of its real estate.

The company, however, is making any takeover attempt difficult. Last year, it sold two resorts that it owned near Chicago, making a $21.4 million profit over book value while keeping control by staying on as manager.

. . . Real estate can work for a company. A popular tactic, particularly among banks, is to sell and lease back office buildings. Last July, Security Pacific Corp. sold its Los Angeles headquarters for $300 million; the tower cost only $110 million to build in 1975. In October, Crocker National Corp., hurt by a portfolio of poor-quality loans, sold its building for $358 million, for an after-tax gain of $185 million.

From Joanne Lipman, "Real Estate Is Turning Into Big Source of Cash For Many Companies," *The Wall Street Journal*, July 1, 1985, p. 1. Reprinted by permission of *The Wall Street Journal*,

payment on note) represents the interest cost of the financing plan. The entry to record the purchase of the asset under the financing plan would be:

Equipment	10,400	
Discount on Notes Payable	1,100	
Cash		1,500
Notes Payable		10,000
To record purchase of equipment.		

Of course, the expenditures for freight, installation, and testing are still debited to the Equipment account when they are incurred.

Capitalization of Interest

Interest cost is part of an asset's initial cost if a period of time is required to get the asset ready for use. For example, the construction of a factory building takes time to complete. Accordingly, an appropriate portion of the actual interest cost incurred during the construction period is added to the factory building's cost. We compute the amount of interest capitalized by multiplying the periodic interest rate times the period's average accumulated construction expenditures.

To illustrate, let us assume Miller Company borrowed $500,000 at 12% to finance the construction of a factory building. Interest of $5,000 is paid monthly. During the first month, construction expenditures total $300,000. The interest cost capitalized this first month is $1,500, computed as follows:

Average accumulated construction expenditures:			
Accumulated construction expenditures, beginning of month	$ -0-		
Accumulated construction expenditures, end of month	300,000		
Average accumulated construction expenditures for the month	$300,000	÷ 2 =	$150,000
Monthly interest rate (1%)			0.01
Interest capitalized for the month			$ 1,500

The entry to record the first month's interest payment is

Factory Building	1,500	
Interest Expense	3,500	
Cash		5,000
To record interest payment, of which $1,500 is capitalized to factory building.		

Interest is capitalized until the factory building is completed. Of course, in subsequent months, the average accumulated construction expenditures increase, so larger amounts of interest cost are capitalized. If the average accumulated construction expenditures exceed $500,000, then additional computations based on the company's other borrowings are needed to determine the interest cost associated with the expenditures over $500,000. These computations are covered in intermediate accounting texts.

Related Expenditures

A purchase of land often raises some interesting questions about related expenditures. Suppose a firm retains a local real estate broker at a fee of $2,000 to locate an appropriate site for its new office building. The property eventually chosen has an old residence on it, which will be razed. The terms of the sale include a payment of $40,000 to the seller, with the buyer paying off an existing mortgage of $10,000 and $300 of accrued interest. In addition, the buyer agrees to pay accrued real estate taxes of $800. Other related expenditures include legal fees of $400 and a title insurance premium of $500. A local salvage company will raze the old residence, level the lot, keep all the materials, and pay the firm $200. If we apply the general plant asset measurement rule, we compute the initial cost of the land as follows:

Payment to the seller	$40,000
Commission for finding property	2,000
Payment of mortgage and interest due at time of sale	10,300
Payment of property taxes owed by seller	800
Legal fees	400
Title insurance premium	500
	$54,000
Less: Net recovery from razing	(200)
Cost of land	$53,800

Again, expenditures for the taxes, insurance, legal fees, and interest should be capitalized as part of the land, because they were necessary for its acquisition and preparation for use. Removing the old residence prepares the land for its intended use. The $200 net recovery from razing, therefore, reduces the land's cost. A net payment to remove the old building would have increased the land's cost.

When a land site is acquired in an undeveloped area, the firm may pay special assessments to the local government for such property improvements as streets, sidewalks, and sewers. These improvements are normally maintained by the local government and, accordingly, are considered relatively permanent improvements by the firm. In these circumstances, the company capitalizes the special assessments as part of the cost of the land.

The firm may make property improvements that have limited lives. Paved parking lots, driveways, private sidewalks, and fences are examples. These expenditures are charged to a separate account, **Land Improvements**, which is depreciated over the estimated lives of the improvements.

Package Purchases

Sometimes several types of assets are purchased concurrently as a package. For example, assume that a company purchased a small freight terminal including land, a building, and some loading equipment for a total price of $190,000. For accounting purposes, the total purchase price should be divided among the three asset forms because (1) they are reported in different accounts, (2) only the building and equipment are subject to depreciation, and (3) the equipment will have an estimated useful life different from that of the building.

The price of package purchases is commonly allocated on the basis of relative market or appraisal values. We assume estimated market values to illustrate this approach.

Asset	Estimated Market Value	Percent of Total	Allocation of Purchase Price	Estimated Useful Life
Land	$ 60,000	30	$ 57,000	Indefinite
Building	120,000	60	114,000	30 years
Equipment	20,000	10	19,000	8 years
Totals	$200,000	100	$190,000	

Actually, the firm may obtain realistic market values from a knowledgeable employee, a professional appraiser, or from assessed values on related property tax bills.

Nonroutine Acquisitions

Not all asset acquisitions involve specific amounts of money. Often nonmonetary assets are traded for other nonmonetary assets, and therefore the implied cash price is not readily apparent. Generally accepted accounting principles normally provide that the transaction price should be the market value of either the asset given up or the asset received, whichever is more objectively determinable. General-purpose property and equipment (standard office or factory equipment) and widely traded securities usually have more objectively determinable market values than do highly specialized buildings or equipment and securities that are new or seldom traded. In the latter instances, the accountant must exercise professional judgment.

An exception to this guideline is the exchange of a nonmonetary productive asset for a similar asset. We consider this exception in Chapter 11 in our discussion of exchanges of similar plant assets.

THE NATURE OF DEPRECIATION

With the exception of site land, the use of plant assets to generate revenue consumes their economic potential. At some point of reduced potential—usually before they are totally worthless—these assets are disposed of and possibly replaced. We can diagram the typical pattern of plant asset utilization (indicated in Exhibit 10–2) as follows:

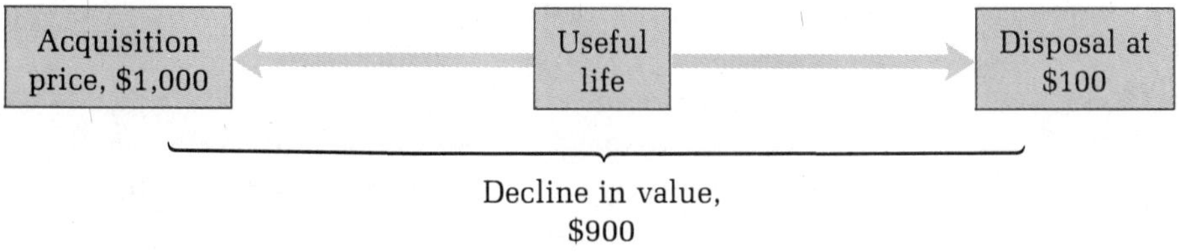

The asset is acquired for $1,000, used for several accounting periods, and then sold for $100. The $900 decline in value is, in every sense of the word, an expense of generating the revenue realized during the periods that the asset was used. Therefore, if the income figure is to be meaningful, $900 of expense must be allocated to these periods and matched against the revenue. Failure to do so would overstate income for these periods.

Note that in this process we estimate an asset's useful life and salvage value as well as properly determine its acquisition cost. **Useful life** is the expected period of economic usefulness to the current entity—the period from date of acquisition to expected date of disposal. **Salvage value** (or residual value) is the expected net recovery (Sales proceeds − Disposal costs) when the asset is sold or removed from service. When the salvage value is insignificant, it may be ignored in the depreciation process.

Allocation versus Valuation

Although the idea is theoretically appealing, accountants do not specifically base depreciation on the changes in market value or on the measured wear of assets—primarily because a reliable, objective, and practical source for such data rarely exists. Rather, depreciation accounting attempts to allocate in a rational and systematic manner the difference between acquisition cost and estimated salvage value over the *estimated* useful life of the asset. Depreciation accounting techniques are convenient expedients for measuring asset expirations and are therefore not precise. Though tentative, depreciation estimates and allocations clearly provide better income determination than would result from completely expensing the asset at either the date of acquisition or the date of disposal.

Several factors are naturally related to the periodic allocation of depreciation. Depreciation can be caused by wear from use, natural deterioration through interaction of the elements, and technical obsolescence. Each factor reduces the value of the asset. To some extent maintenance (lubrication, adjustments, parts replacements, and cleaning) may partially arrest or offset wear and deterioration. Quite logically, then, when useful life and salvage values are estimated, a given level of maintenance is assumed. Therefore, the cost of using plant assets tends to be the sum of periodic maintenance expenditures plus some measure of the depreciation that occurs despite the maintenance performed. Maintenance expense normally increases toward the latter stages of most assets' lives.

How to allocate depreciation expense is just one facet of the overall problem of matching revenue and expenses. The most defensible reason for choosing one allocation pattern over another is that one pattern may better portray the pattern of services received each period from using the asset. It would be only coincidence if the book value of a particular asset were exactly equal to its market value at any time during its useful life. On the other hand, the general pattern of an asset's book value may be closely related to its decline in market value. Indeed, the goal is that at the end of an asset's useful life, its book value and market value (that is, salvage value) should be the same.

COMPUTATIONS OF PERIODIC DEPRECIATION

We now illustrate four widely used methods of computing periodic depreciation. For each illustration, we assume that the asset costs $1,000 and has an estimated useful life of five years. The estimated salvage value at the end of the five-year period is $100. Our computations illustrate different ways to *allocate* the amount depreciated among each of the five accounting periods in the asset's life.

Straight Line

Straight-line depreciation is probably the simplest to compute. An equal amount of depreciation expense is allocated to each full period of the asset's useful life. Using straight-line depreciation,

$$\text{Annual Depreciation} = \frac{\text{Original Cost} - \text{Salvage Value}}{\text{Periods of Useful Life}}$$

which in our example is

$$\frac{\$1{,}000 - \$100}{5 \text{ years}} = \$180/\text{year}$$

The basic entry to record each period's depreciation expense is:

Depreciation Expense	180	
Accumulated Depreciation—Equipment		180
To record depreciation expense for the year.		

Like other expense accounts, Depreciation Expense is deducted from revenue in determining net income and is closed at year-end to the Income Summary account. The offsetting credit is posted to the contra account, Accumulated Depreciation, which is deducted from the related asset account on the balance sheet to compute the asset's book value, or carrying value. In this manner, the original cost of an asset is maintained in the asset account, and the cumulative balance of depreciation taken is carried in the contra account as long as the asset is in service. When an asset is disposed of, the related cost and accumulated depreciation are removed from the accounts.

For our simple illustration, the table below shows account balances and the progression of certain amounts during the asset's five-year life.

Period	Balance of Asset Account	Periodic Depreciation Expense	End-of-Period Balance Accumulated Depreciation Account	Asset's Book Value
1	$1,000	$180	$180	$820
2	1,000	180	360	640
3	1,000	180	540	460
4	1,000	180	720	280
5	1,000	180	900	100
	Total depreciation	$900		

Observe that (1) the asset account always shows the original cost of the asset, (2) each period reflects $180 of depreciation expense, (3) the Accumulated Depreciation account balance is cumulative and shows the portion of the original cost taken as depreciation to date, (4) the asset's book value is the original cost less total accumulated depreciation to date, and (5) the asset's book value at the end of five years equals the estimated salvage value. Thus, the book value decreases to the estimated salvage value as the asset is depreciated during its useful life.

The book value of the asset is shown on the balance sheet by deducting the Accumulated Depreciation account (normally a credit balance) from the asset account (normally a debit balance). At the end of the second year, for example, the asset's balance sheet presentation is as follows:

Equipment (original cost)	$1,000
Less: Accumulated Depreciation	360
Equipment (book value)	$ 640

For periods of less than one year, straight-line depreciation amounts are simply proportions of the annual amount. For example, if the asset had been acquired on April 1, depreciation for the period ended December 31 would be $\frac{9}{12} \times \$180 = \$135$. Assets acquired or disposed of during the first half of any month are usually treated as if the acquisition or disposal occurred on the first of the month. When either event occurs during the last half of any month, we assume it occurred on the first of the following month.

Straight-line allocation is best suited to an asset with a relatively uniform periodic usage and a low obsolescence factor. Examples include pipelines, storage tanks, fencing, and surface paving. These types of assets can provide approximately equal utility during all periods of their useful lives.

Units of Production

The **units-of-production method** allocates depreciation in proportion to the asset's use in operations. First, the depreciation per unit of production is computed by dividing the total expected depreciation (in our example, $900) by the asset's projected units-of-production capacity. Therefore,

$$\text{Depreciation per Unit} = \frac{\text{Original Cost} - \text{Salvage Value}}{\text{Estimated Total Units of Production}}$$

Units-of-production capacity may represent miles driven, tons hauled, or number of cuttings, drillings, or stampings of parts. Assume that our example is a drilling tool that will drill an estimated 45,000 parts during its useful life. The depreciation per unit of production is

$$\frac{\$1{,}000 - \$100}{45{,}000 \text{ parts}} = \$0.02 \text{ per part}$$

To find periodic depreciation expense, we multiply the depreciation per unit of production by the number of units produced during the period. If 8,000 units are produced during the first year, then 8,000 × \$0.02 = \$160 is the year's depreciation expense. If 12,000 parts are drilled the next year, that year's depreciation expense is 12,000 × \$0.02 = \$240.

The units-of-production approach is particularly appropriate when wear is the major cause of depreciation and the amount of use varies from period to period. Of course, if use is uniformly spread over the asset's life, the same allocation of depreciation would result from either the straight-line or units-of-production method. The units-of-production method may necessitate some extra record keeping to express the periodic use in terms of production capacity. However, this data may already be tabulated as part of a periodic production report.

Sum of the Years' Digits

The **sum-of-the-years'-digits (SYD) method** accelerates depreciation expense so that the amounts recognized in the early periods of an asset's useful life are greater than those recognized in the later periods. The SYD is found by estimating an asset's useful life in years, assigning consecutive numbers to each year, and totaling these numbers. For N years,

$$\text{SYD} = 1 + 2 + 3 + \ldots + N$$

In our example, the SYD for a five-year asset life is 1 + 2 + 3 + 4 + 5 = 15.

Determining the SYD factor by simple addition can be somewhat laborious for long-lived assets. For these assets, the formula $N(N + 1)/2$, where N = the number of periods in the asset's useful life, can be applied to derive the SYD. In our example, we have

$$\frac{5(5 + 1)}{2} = \frac{30}{2} = 15$$

The yearly depreciation is then calculated by multiplying the total depreciable amount for the asset's useful life by a fraction whose numerator is the remaining useful life and whose denominator is the SYD. Thus, the formula for yearly depreciation is

$$\text{Annual Depreciation} = (\text{Original Cost} - \text{Salvage Value}) \times \frac{\text{Remaining Useful Life}}{\text{SYD}}$$

The calculations for our example are shown below:

Year of Useful Life	Fraction of Total Depreciation Taken Each Year		Original Cost Less Salvage Value		Annual Depreciation Allocation
1	$\frac{5}{15}$	×	$900	=	$300
2	$\frac{4}{15}$	×	900	=	240
3	$\frac{3}{15}$	×	900	=	180
4	$\frac{2}{15}$	×	900	=	120
5	$\frac{1}{15}$	×	900	=	60
SYD 15					Total $900

When the acquisition of an asset does not coincide with the beginning of the fiscal period, the annual depreciation amounts are allocated proportionately to the appropriate fiscal periods. For example, assume we purchased the asset on April 1. Depreciation for the period ended December 31 would be $\frac{9}{12} \times \$300 = \$225$. For the next fiscal year, a full year's depreciation would be calculated as $(\frac{3}{12} \times \$300) + (\frac{9}{12} \times \$240) = \$255$.

As an accelerated depreciation method, the SYD approach is most appropriate when the asset renders greater utility during its early life and less in its later life. Accelerated depreciation is suitable for assets with either a high technological obsolescence factor in the early life phase or a high maintenance factor in the late life phase.

Double Declining Balance

Another accelerated depreciation method is the **double declining-balance method,** which derives its name from the fact that a *constant percentage* factor of twice the straight-line rate is applied each year to the *declining balance* of the asset's book value.

The *straight-line rate* is simply the number of years in the asset's useful life divided into 100%. In our example, this would be 100%/5 = 20%. Double the straight-line rate is then 40%. In equation form,

$$\text{Double Declining-balance Rate} = \frac{100\%}{\text{Years of Useful Life}} \times 2$$

To determine the annual double declining-balance depreciation expense, we simply *multiply the asset's book value at the beginning of the period by the constant rate (or percentage)*. Remember that an asset's book value at any time is its original cost less its accumulated depreciation to date. The book value of a depreciable asset *declines* as it is depreciated. The important thing to remember is that the percentage depreciation rate remains constant; the book value—to which the percentage is applied—declines. Salvage value is not considered in the calculations, except that depreciation stops when the asset's book value equals its estimated salvage value.

Applying the general rule for double declining-balance depreciation to our example, we obtain the accelerated depreciation pattern shown in the following table (amounts to nearest dollar).

Year of Useful Life	Original Cost	Beginning Accumulated Depreciation	Beginning Book Value		Twice Straight-line Percentage		Amount of Depreciation Expense
1	$1,000	$ 0	$1,000	×	40%	=	$400
2	1,000	400	600	×	40%	=	240
3	1,000	640	360	×	40%	=	144
4	1,000	784	216	×	40%	=	86
5	1,000	870	130				30
			Total depreciation taken				$900

Observe that in the fifth year depreciation expense is only $30, the amount needed to reduce the asset's book value to the estimated salvage value of $100. Assets are not depreciated below their salvage values. If no salvage value has been estimated, the double declining-balance technique automatically provides one. When a fraction (40%, or $\frac{4}{10}$, for example) is applied to an asset's book value, the entire original cost can never be depreciated; some balance, though small, will always remain.

If an asset is purchased during the fiscal period, a pro-rata allocation of the first year's depreciation is necessary. If we acquired our asset on April 1, depreciation for the period ended December 31 would be $\frac{9}{12} \times (40\% \times \$1{,}000) = \$300$. In subsequent periods, the usual procedure is followed; that is, the asset's book value at the beginning of the period is multiplied by the constant rate. The next year, for example, depreciation would be $40\% \times (\$1{,}000 - \$300) = \$280$.

Because double declining-balance depreciation is also an accelerated depreciation method, it is appropriate in the same situations as the SYD method.

REVISION OF DEPRECIATION

We have stressed that depreciation allocations are based on estimates of both useful lives and salvage values. Circumstances change, however, and original estimates may be too high or too low. Once it is determined that original estimates are wrong, the computation of periodic depreciation expense for the asset's remaining useful life must be revised. We revise a depreciation estimate by allocating the revised undepreciated balance of the asset over the revised remaining useful life. To illustrate this revision procedure, we use the data from our previous examples in which an asset costing $1,000 has a five-year life and an estimated salvage value of $100.

If, based on the original estimates, straight-line depreciation of $180 has been recorded for each of the first three years, the accumulated depreciation would be $3 \times \$180 = \$540$. Now suppose that just before recording the fourth year's depreciation, circumstances indicate that the asset's life will be six years instead of five and that its salvage value at the end of the sixth year will be $40. The revised depreciation expense to be taken during the revised remaining useful life is computed as follows:

Original asset cost		$1,000
Depreciation already recorded (3 years @ $180)		540
Book value at start of fourth year		$ 460
Revised salvage value		40
Revised remaining depreciation		$ 420
Revised remaining useful life		3 years
Revised periodic depreciation expense for fourth, fifth, and sixth years	$420/3 =	$140 per year

The revision process does not change depreciation amounts recorded in earlier periods. The earlier computations utilized the best estimates available at the time. A change in an estimate, then, causes depreciation expense to be revised in the year of change and subsequent periods only.

DEPRECIATION FOR TAX PURPOSES

Depreciation expense is deducted by a business on its federal income tax return. The amount on the tax return, however, may differ from the amount reported in the firm's income statement. Indeed, different tax depreciation guidelines apply to property acquired before 1981 than apply to property acquired after 1980.

Property acquired before 1981 is depreciated for income tax purposes over its useful life. Depreciation methods acceptable for tax purposes include straight line, units of production, sum of the years' digits, and double declining balance. The method used on the tax return, however, need not be the same method used in the financial statements. Typically, a firm uses an accelerated depreciation method for tax purposes and the straight-line method in its financial statements. In a sense, accelerated depreciation provides an interest-free loan to the firm because the accelerated methods allow the firm to pay less tax in the early phase of an asset's life and more in the later phase. During the intervening time, the firm can use the amount of funds equal to the postponed income tax payments.

The **Accelerated Cost Recovery System (ACRS)** applies to property acquired after 1980 and eliminates the concept of useful life. Instead, ACRS establishes classes of property with prescribed lives—currently there are eight property classes with prescribed lives ranging from three years to 31.5 years. Most machinery and equipment, for example, is in a five-year class. When acquired, property is placed in the appropriate class (regardless of its useful life) and depreciated over the prescribed period following the method specified for that class. Property in the five-year class, for example, is depreciated using double declining balance (with a switch to straight line when it gives a larger deduction) and 31.5-year property is depreciated using the straight-line method. Designed to encourage capital investment, ACRS generally permits a faster recovery of an asset's cost, and thus larger tax benefits during the asset's early life, than was previously possible.

Change and modification characterize the history of U.S. tax law. Indeed, ACRS has been modified since it was first introduced. Keep in mind, however, that depreciation changes in the tax law do not affect the depreciation methods a firm may use in preparing its financial statements. Tax depreciation guidelines only apply to the preparation of income tax returns.

REVENUE EXPENDITURES

Revenue expenditures are expenditures relating to plant assets that are expensed when incurred. The following list identifies three types of revenue expenditures:

(1) Expenditures for ordinary maintenance and repairs of existing plant assets.

(2) Expenditures to acquire low-cost items that benefit the firm for several periods.

(3) Expenditures considered unnecessary or unreasonable in the circumstances.

Maintenance and Repairs

Some level of maintenance and repairs must be assumed when estimating useful lives and salvage values of property, plant, and equipment. Obviously, a plant asset that is not maintained or repaired has a shorter useful life than a similar asset that is properly maintained. Periodic upkeep—such as lubrication, cleaning, and replacement of minor parts—is necessary to maintain an asset's expected level and length of usefulness. These periodic upkeep costs are charged to expense as they are incurred.

Low-cost Items

Most businesses purchase items that provide years of service at a relatively small cost, such as paperweights, ashtrays, and wastebaskets. Because of the small dollar amounts involved, establishing these items as assets and depreciating them over their expected useful lives really serves no useful purpose. The effect on the financial statements is not significant. Consequently, expensing these expenditures at the time of purchase is more efficient. The accounting for such low-cost items is thus completed in the period they are purchased. This practice of accounting for small dollar transactions in the most expedient fashion is an example of the basic principle of *materiality.* (We discuss materiality in more detail in Chapter 13.)

Unnecessary or Unreasonable Costs

As noted earlier, costs of waste and inefficiency related to the acquisition of plant assets are expensed when incurred. Because an asset's initial cost includes only necessary and reasonable expenditures, any unnecessary or unreasonable outlays are expensed. An accountant may need to exercise considerable judgment, however, in determining whether a particular expenditure is necessary and reasonable. Identical expenditures may be treated differently, depending on the circumstances. For example, assume a company pays an overtime premium to have a piece of equipment delivered on a holiday. If it is essential that the equipment be available for use on the next workday, then the overtime premium should be added to the equipment's cost as a necessary and reasonable expenditure. In contrast, if the equipment could just as well be delivered on the next workday, then the overtime premium is an unnecessary and wasteful expenditure that should be expensed.

CAPITAL EXPENDITURES

Capital expenditures increase the book value of long-term assets. To *capitalize* an amount, then, means to increase an asset's book value by that amount. Typical capital expenditures related to property, plant, and equipment are as follows:

(1) Initial acquisitions and additions.
(2) Betterments.
(3) Extraordinary repairs.

Initial Acquisitions and Additions

Earlier in this chapter, we discussed the guidelines governing the initial measurement of plant assets. Expenditures equal to the asset's implied cash price plus the costs necessary to prepare the asset for use were debited to the asset account. These amounts were capital expenditures.

The same guidelines apply in accounting for additions to existing plant assets. Adding a new wing to a building or expanding the size of an asphalt parking lot are examples of additions. These capital expenditures should also be debited to an asset account. A separate account (and depreciation schedule) should be used for an addition when its estimated useful life differs from the remaining useful life of the existing plant asset.

Betterments

Betterments improve the quality of services rendered by a plant asset but do not necessarily extend its useful life. Examples include adding a power winch to a highway service truck or air conditioning to an automobile. In each instance, the vehicle's services are enhanced, but its useful life is not changed. Expenditures for betterments are debited to the appropriate asset account, and the subsequent periodic depreciation expense is increased to allocate the additional cost over the asset's remaining useful life.

To illustrate, let us assume Tray Service Station purchased a new service truck for $6,500 on January 2, 19X1. Its estimated useful life is six years with a salvage value of $500. Using the straight-line method, $1,000 of depreciation expense is recorded in 19X1 [($6,500 − $500)/6 = $1,000]. On January 2, 19X2, a power winch costing $700 is added to the truck. The truck's useful life does not change, but its estimated salvage value increases to $600. The January 2, 19X2, entry to record the new winch is

Truck	700	
Cash		700
To record cost of power winch added to truck.		

Annual depreciation expense of $1,120 for 19X2–19X6 is computed as follows:

Original truck cost		$6,500
Power winch cost		700
Total cost		$7,200
Depreciation recorded in 19X1		1,000
Book value after 19X2 betterment		$6,200
Revised salvage value		600
Revised remaining depreciation		$5,600
Remaining useful life		5 years
Revised periodic depreciation expense for 19X2–19X6	$5,600/5 =	$1,120 per year

The December 31, 19X2, entry to record depreciation expense is

Depreciation Expense—Truck	1,120	
Accumulated Depreciation—Truck		1,120
To record 19X2 depreciation on truck.		

Betterments may involve replacing a significant asset component with an improved component. Again, the cost of the new asset component should be added to the asset account and depreciated over the asset's remaining useful life. Further, the cost and accumulated depreciation of the replaced asset component should be removed from the accounts. For example, if a building's gas furnace is replaced by a more efficient model, the cost of the new furnace is added to the Building account, and the cost and applicable depreciation on the old furnace are removed from the accounts. The book value of the old asset component may be difficult to determine if it is not accounted for separately, but a reasonable estimate frequently can be made.

Extraordinary Repairs

extend usefull life

Extraordinary repairs are expenditures that extend an asset's expected useful life beyond the original estimate. These capital expenditures are debited to the asset's Accumulated Depreciation account (which increases the asset's book value). We charge Accumulated Depreciation because some of the previous years' depreciation presumably is recovered by the expenditures that extend the asset's useful life. Depreciation entries after an extraordinary repair should lead to the salvage value at the end of the revised (extended) useful life.

For example, assume $12,800 worth of equipment is purchased; it has an estimated useful life of eight years and a salvage value of $800. Annual straight-line depreciation expense is $1,500 [($12,800 − $800)/8]. At the beginning of the seventh year, the equipment is extensively overhauled at a cost of $2,200. The overhaul extends the equipment's useful life an estimated two years beyond the original eight, with no change in the expected salvage value. The entry to record the overhaul is

Accumulated Depreciation—Equipment	2,200	
Cash		2,200
To record cost of equipment overhaul.		

Beginning with the seventh year, annual depreciation expense is $1,300, computed as follows:

Original cost		$12,800
Less: Depreciation for six years	$9,000	
Less: Extraordinary repairs	2,200	6,800
Book value at start of seventh year		$ 6,000
Salvage value		800
Remaining depreciation		$ 5,200
Revised remaining useful life		4 years
Revised periodic depreciation expense for years 7–10	$5,200/4 =	$1,300 per year

The entry to record depreciation expense at the end of the seventh year is

Depreciation Expense—Equipment	1,300	
Accumulated Depreciation—Equipment		1,300
To record depreciation on equipment.		

In practice, the distinctions among additions, betterments, and extraordinary repairs to plant assets often become blurred. Some expenditures, for example, may improve an asset's quality of services *and* extend its useful life. Accountants must use reasonable judgment to identify (and account for) the primary effect of the transaction.

Preparation of accurate financial statements depends on maintaining the proper distinction between capital expenditures and revenue expenditures. A misclassification of expenditures results in incorrect financial statements for several periods. For example, capitalizing a revenue expenditure overstates the current period's income and understates income in subsequent periods as the amount incorrectly capitalized is depreciated. Similarly, if a capital expenditure is immediately expensed, then the current period's income is understated and income is overstated during the subsequent periods when the incorrectly expensed amount should have been depreciated. Exercising care in analyzing expenditures, of course, will minimize these undesirable effects.

KEY POINTS TO REMEMBER

(1) The major types of long-term assets are plant assets, natural resources, and intangible assets.

(2) The cost (less salvage value) of a long-term asset is periodically charged to expense over its useful life as follows:

Plant assets: Depreciation
Natural resources: Depletion
Intangible assets: Amortization

(3) The initial cost of a plant asset is its implied cash price plus the expenditures necessary to prepare it for use.

(4) The most commonly used depreciation methods are straight line, units of production, sum of the years' digits, and double declining balance.

(5) Revisions of depreciation are accomplished by recalculating depreciation charges for current and subsequent periods.

(6) Revenue expenditures, expensed as incurred, include the performance of ordinary repairs and maintenance, the purchase of low-cost items, and the incurrence of unnecessary or unreasonable outlays.

(7) Capital expenditures, which increase a plant asset's book value, include initial acquisitions, additions, betterments, and extraordinary repairs.

SELF-TEST QUESTIONS
(Answers are at the end of this chapter.)

1. The initial cost of a plant asset is equal to the asset's implied cash price and
(a) The interest paid on any debt incurred to finance the asset's purchase.
(b) The market value of any noncash assets given up to acquire the plant asset.
(c) The reasonable and necessary costs incurred to prepare the asset for use.
(d) The asset's estimated salvage value.

2. Which of the following depreciation methods allocates equal amounts of depreciation to each full period of an asset's useful life?
(a) Units of production.
(b) Straight line.
(c) Double declining balance.
(d) Sum of the years' digits.

3. On January 1, 19X1, Rio Company purchased a delivery truck for $10,000. The company estimates the truck will be driven 80,000 miles over its eight-year useful life. The estimated salvage value is $2,000. The truck was driven 12,000 miles in 19X1. Which method results in the largest 19X1 depreciation expense?
(a) Sum of the years' digits.
(b) Units of production.
(c) Straight line.
(d) Double declining balance.

4. Which of the following statements is false?
   (a) A plant asset's useful life is the period from date of acquisition to date of disposal.
   (b) When the estimate of a plant asset's useful life is changed, depreciation amounts recorded in earlier periods are revised to reflect the new useful life.
   (c) Expenditures for extraordinary repairs are debited to an accumulated depreciation account.
   (d) Capitalizing a revenue expenditure in the current period overstates the current period's net income.
5. Which of the following expenditures is expensed when incurred?
   (a) The cost of regular monthly maintenance on a firm's copying machines.
   (b) The cost of a new table and chairs for a firm's conference room.
   (c) Interest paid that relates to the average monthly accumulated construction expenditures on a building under construction.
   (d) The cost of razing an unwanted building on newly-purchased land.

QUESTIONS

10–1 List three major types of long-term assets, present examples of each, and indicate for each type the term that denotes the periodic write-off to expense.

10–2 In what way is land different from other long-term assets?

10–3 Describe the typical sequence of transactions and related problem areas associated with plant assets.

10–4 In general, what amounts constitute the initial cost of plant assets?

10–5 Fyre Company borrowed $2,000,000 to finance the purchase of a new office building, which was ready for immediate use. May Fyre add a portion of the interest cost on the $2,000,000 to the building's cost? Explain.

10–6 Lane Company bought land with a vacant building for $750,000. Lane will use the building in its operations. Must Lane allocate the purchase price between the land and building? Why or why not? Would your answer be different if Lane intends to raze the building and build a new one? Why or why not?

10–7 Explain why the recognition of depreciation expense is necessary to match revenue and expense properly.

10–8 "Depreciation is a process of periodic reductions in a plant asset's book value to correspond with changes in the asset's market value as it ages." Do you agree? Why or why not?

10–9 How is the use of the contra account Accumulated Depreciation justified when recording depreciation?

10–10 How can we justify the use of accelerated depreciation?

10–11 Briefly describe an operational situation that lends itself naturally to each of the following depreciation methods: (a) straight line, (b) units of production, (c) sum of the years' digits, and (d) double declining balance.

10–12 How should we handle a revision of depreciation charges due to a change in an asset's estimated useful life or salvage value? Which periods—past, present, or future—are affected by the revision?

10–13 Explain the benefit of accelerating depreciation for income tax purposes when the total depreciation taken is no more than if straight-line depreciation is used.

10–14 Identify three types of revenue expenditures. What is the proper accounting for revenue expenditures?

10–15 "We cannot properly estimate an asset's useful life without first considering the level of maintenance employed." Do you agree? Why or why not?

10–16 Oreo Company purchased a $20 set of bookends with an estimated useful life of 25 years. How should Oreo account for this expenditure?

10–17 Identify three types of capital expenditures. What is the proper accounting for capital expenditures?

10–18 What is the difference between an ordinary repair and an extraordinary repair? What is the rationale for charging extraordinary repairs to accumulated depreciation?

EXERCISES

Initial cost of plant asset

10–19 The following data relate to a firm's purchase of a machine used in the manufacture of its product:

Invoice price	$25,000
Applicable sales tax	1,470
Purchase discount taken	500
Freight paid	420
Cost of insurance coverage on machine while in transit	100
Installation costs	1,000
Testing and adjusting costs	350
Repair of damages to machine caused by the firm's employees	400

Compute the initial amount at which the machine should be carried in the firm's accounts.

Capitalization of interest

10–20 On April 1, 19X1, Wyoming Company borrowed $800,000 at 15% to finance the construction of a new wing on its headquarters office building. The construction will take several months. Interest of $10,000 is paid monthly. Construction begins April 1, 19X1, and accumulated construction expenditures are $300,000 at April 30, 19X1. Determine how much interest cost should be capitalized for April.

Allocation of package purchase price

10–21 Redding Company purchased a small established plant from one of its suppliers. The $950,000 purchase price included the land, a building, and factory machinery. Redding also paid $2,000 in legal fees to negotiate the purchase of the plant. The property tax bill for the plant showed the following assessed values for the items purchased:

Property	Assessed Value
Land	$144,000
Building	384,000
Machinery	272,000
	$800,000

Using the assessed valuations on the property tax bill as a guide, allocate the total purchase price of the plant to the land, building, and machinery accounts in Redding Company's records.

Depreciation methods

10–22 A delivery truck costing $12,000 is expected to have a 10% salvage value at the end of its useful life of four years or 120,000 miles.

(a) Assume the truck was purchased on January 2, 19X1. Compute the depreciation expense for 19X1 using each of the following depreciation methods: (1) straight line, (2) sum of the years' digits, (3) double declining balance, and (4) units of production (assume the truck was driven 32,000 miles in 19X1).

(b) Assume the truck was purchased on March 1, 19X1. Compute the depreciation expense for 19X2 using each of the following depreciation methods: (1) straight line, (2) sum of the years' digits, (3) double declining balance, and (4) units of production (assume the truck was driven 42,000 miles in 19X2).

Depreciation methods

10–23 A machine costing $48,600 was purchased January 2, 19X2. The machine should be obsolete after three years and, therefore, no longer useful to the company. The estimated salvage value is $1,800. Compute the depreciation expense for each year of the machine's useful life using each of the following depreciation methods: (a) straight line, (b) sum of the years' digits, and (c) double declining balance.

Depreciation methods

10–24 Assume the machine from Exercise 10–23 was purchased May 1, 19X2. Compute each year's depreciation expense for 19X2–19X5 using each of the following depreciation methods: (a) straight line, (b) sum of the years' digits, and (c) double declining balance.

Revision of depreciation

10–25 On January 2, 19X0, Mullis, Inc., purchased new equipment for $42,000. The equipment was expected to have a $3,000 salvage value at the end of its estimated six-year useful life. Straight-line depreciation has been recorded. Before adjusting the accounts for 19X4, Mullis decided that the useful life of the equipment should be extended by two years and the salvage value decreased to $2,000.

(a) Present a general journal entry to record depreciation expense on the equipment for 19X4.

(b) What is the book value of the equipment at the end of 19X4 (that is, after recording the depreciation expense for 19X4)?

Capital expenditure

10–26 On January 3, 19X1, Breen Company purchased a warehouse for $420,000 with an estimated useful life of 25 years and a salvage value of $45,000. Breen uses straight-line depreciation on the warehouse. In early January, 19X8, Breen spent $30,000 for the installation of a fire detection and sprinkler system in the warehouse. The useful life of the warehouse was unchanged, but its estimated salvage value increased to $48,000.

DDB dont consider salvage until the end of the period

(a) Prepare the general journal entry to record the cost of the fire detection and sprinkler system.
(b) Compute the 19X8 depreciation expense on the warehouse.
(c) Prepare the general journal entry to record the warehouse's 19X8 depreciation expense.

Capital expenditure

10–27 At the end of last year, the balance sheet of Citation Company shows a building with a cost of $830,000 and an accumulated depreciation of $296,000. The company uses the straight-line method to depreciate the building. When acquired, the building had an estimated 40-year useful life, and its salvage value was $90,000. Early in January of the current year, Citation made major structural repairs to the building costing $202,000. Although the capacity of the building was unchanged, the improvements will extend the useful life of the building to an estimated 50 years, rather than the original 40 years. The salvage value remains $90,000.
(a) By the end of last year, how many years had the company depreciated the building?
(b) Present the general journal entry to record the cost of the structural repairs.
(c) Present the general journal entry to record the building's depreciation expense for the current year.

Revenue and capital expenditures

10–28 Amato Company built an addition to its chemical plant. Indicate whether each of the following expenditures related to the addition is a revenue expenditure or a capital expenditure.
(a) Amato's initial application for a building permit was denied by the city as not conforming to environmental standards. Amato disagreed with the decision and spent $5,000 in attorney's fees to convince the city to reverse its position and issue the permit.
(b) Due to unanticipated sandy soil conditions, and upon the advice of construction engineers, Amato spent $25,000 to extend the footings for the addition to a greater depth than originally planned.
(c) Amato spent $4,500 to send each of the addition's subcontractors a side of beef as a thank-you gift for completing the project on schedule.
(d) Amato invited the mayor to a ribbon-cutting ceremony to open the plant addition. Amato spent $30 to purchase the ribbon and scissors.

PROBLEMS

Initial cost of plant assets

10–29 The items below represent expenditures (or receipts) related to the construction of a new home office for the Lippert Company.

Cost of land site, which included an old apartment building appraised at $60,000	$ 170,000
Legal fees, including fee for title search	2,100
Payment of apartment building mortgage and related interest due at time of sale	7,500
Payment of delinquent property taxes assumed by the purchaser	2,800
Cost of razing the apartment building	14,000
Proceeds from sale of salvaged materials	(3,200)
Grading and drainage on land site	6,000

Architect's fees on new building	$ 100,000
Proceeds from sale of excess dirt (from basement excavation) to owner of adjoining property (dirt was used to fill in a low area on property)	(800)
Payment to building contractor	2,500,000
Interest cost incurred during construction (based on average accumulated construction expenditures)	200,000
Payment of medical bills of employee accidentally injured while inspecting building construction	600
Special assessment for paving city sidewalks (paid to city)	12,000
Cost of paving driveway and parking lot	16,000
Cost of installing lights in parking lot	7,300
Premium for insurance on building during construction	5,000
Cost of open house party to celebrate opening of new building	4,500

REQUIRED
From the given data, compute the proper balances for the Land, Building, and Land Improvements accounts of the Lippert Company.

Allocation of package purchase price and depreciation methods

10–30 To expand its business, Reed Company paid $580,000 for most of the property, plant, and equipment of a small trucking company that was going out of business. Before agreeing to the price, Reed hired a consultant for $6,000 to appraise the assets. The appraised values were as follows:

Land	$ 90,000
Building	300,000
Trucks	150,000
Equipment	60,000
	$600,000

Reed issued two checks totaling $586,000 to acquire the assets and pay the consultant on July 1, 19X3. Reed depreciated the assets using the straight-line method on the building, the double declining-balance method on the trucks, and the sum-of-the-years'-digits method on the equipment. Estimated useful lives and salvage values were as follows:

	Useful Life	Salvage Value
Building	18 years	$23,000
Trucks	4 years	11,000
Equipment	7 years	5,400

REQUIRED
(a) Compute the amounts allocated to the various types of plant assets acquired on July 1, 19X3.
(b) Prepare the July 1, 19X3, general journal entries to record the purchase of the assets and the payment of the consultant.
(c) Prepare the December 31, 19X3, general journal entries to record 19X3 depreciation expense on the building, trucks, and equipment.

Depreciation methods

10–31 On January 2, Wabash, Inc., purchased a laser cutting machine to be used in the fabrication of a part for one of its key products. The machine cost $64,000, and its estimated useful life was four years or 400,000 cuttings, after which it could be sold for $4,000.

REQUIRED

Compute the depreciation expense for each year of the machine's useful life under each of the following depreciation methods:

(a) Straight line.
(b) Sum of the years' digits.
(c) Double declining balance.
(d) Units of production. (Assume annual production in cuttings of 120,000; 140,000; 80,000; and 60,000.)

Comprehensive problem

10–32 During the first few days of 19X5, the Lewis Company entered into the following transactions:

(1) Purchased a parcel of land with a building on it for $750,000 cash. The building, which will be used in operations, has an estimated useful life of 25 years and a residual value of $20,000. The assessed valuations for property tax purposes show the land at $65,000 and the building at $585,000.
(2) Paid $22,800 for the construction of an asphalt parking lot for customers. The parking lot is expected to last 12 years and have no salvage value.
(3) Paid $5,000 for the construction of a new entrance to the building.
(4) Purchased store equipment, paying the invoice price (including 7% sales tax) of $42,800 in cash. The estimated useful life of the equipment is nine years, and the salvage value is $3,100.
(5) Paid $350 freight on the new store equipment.
(6) Paid $500 to repair damages to floor caused when the store equipment was accidentally dropped as it was moved into place.
(7) Paid $6,000 for four-year insurance policy on building.

REQUIRED

(a) Prepare general journal entries to record the above transactions.
(b) Prepare the December 31, 19X5, general journal entries to record the proper amounts of depreciation expense and insurance expense for the year. Sum-of-the-years'-digits depreciation is used for the equipment, and straight-line depreciation is used for the building and land improvements.

Comprehensive problem

10–33 Tiempo Corporation had the following transactions related to its delivery truck:

19X1

Jan.	5	Purchased for $10,760 cash a new truck with an estimated useful life of four years and a salvage value of $2,000.
Feb.	20	Installed a new set of rear view mirrors at a cost of $45 cash.
June	9	Paid $180 for an engine tune-up, wheel balancing, and a periodic lubrication.
Aug.	2	Paid a $300 repair bill for the uninsured portion of damages to the truck caused by Tiempo's own driver.
Dec.	31	Recorded 19X1 depreciation on the truck.

19X2

May	1	Installed a set of parts bins in the truck at a cost of $720 cash. This expenditure was not expected to increase the salvage value of the truck.
Dec.	31	Recorded 19X2 depreciation on the truck.

19X3

July 1 Paid $1,690 for a major engine overhaul on the truck. The overhaul should extend the useful life of the truck an additional two years (to December 31, 19X5) with a salvage value now estimated at $1,500.

Dec. 31 Recorded 19X3 depreciation on the truck.

Tiempo's depreciation policies include (1) using straight-line depreciation, (2) recording depreciation to the nearest whole month, and (3) expensing all truck expenditures of $50 or less.

REQUIRED

Present general journal entries to record these transactions.

Revision of depreciation and capital expenditure

10–34 Bridge Company uses straight-line depreciation in accounting for its machines. On January 3, 19X1, Bridge purchased a new machine for $50,000 cash. The machine's estimated useful life was 10 years with a $5,000 salvage value. In 19X3, the company decided its original useful life estimate should be reduced by two years. Beginning in 19X3, depreciation was based on an eight-year total useful life, and no change was made in the salvage value estimate. On January 2, 19X4, Bridge added an automatic guide and a safety shield to the machine at a cost of $3,000 cash. These improvements did not change the machine's useful life, but did increase the estimated salvage value to $5,500.

REQUIRED

(a) Prepare general journal entries to record (1) the purchase of the machine, (2) 19X1 depreciation expense, (3) 19X2 depreciation expense, (4) 19X3 depreciation expense, (5) the 19X4 improvements, and (6) 19X4 depreciation expense.

(b) Compute the book value of the machine at the end of 19X4 (that is, after recording the depreciation expense for 19X4).

Plant asset errors and corrections

10–35 During 19X2, Hallon, Inc., analyzed several transactions relating to its plant assets as described below.

Jan. 2 Paid for robotic equipment purchased and installed today. The invoice price was $100,000 and Hallon was entitled to a 2% cash discount. Entry:

Robotic Equipment	100,000	
Purchases Discounts		2,000
Cash		98,000

Feb. 6 Paid $500 for regular, annual maintenance on the firm's word processors. Entry:

Office Equipment	500	
Cash		500

June 7 Paid $3,000 to clear timber and brush from a land site purchased a few days earlier. Hallon will build a new plant on this land site. Entry:

Land Clearing Expense	3,000	
Cash		3,000

Aug. 1 Paid $20 for a wastebasket purchased today. The wastebasket has an estimated useful life of 40 years. Entry:

Office Equipment	20	
Cash		20

Dec. 30 Paid $14,700 interest on $98,000 borrowed on January 2, 19X2, to finance the purchase of the robotic equipment. Entry:

Robotic Equipment	14,700	
Cash		14,700

Dec. 31 Recorded the 19X2 straight-line depreciation on the robotic equipment purchased January 2, 19X2. The equipment has a 10-year useful life and a $6,000 expected salvage value. The Robotic Equipment account balance before depreciation was $114,700. Entry:

Depreciation Expense	10,870	
Robotic Equipment		10,870

REQUIRED
(a) Identify any errors made by Hallon, Inc., in analyzing the above transactions.
(b) Prepare journal entries at December 31, 19X2, to correct each error noted in part (a). The books have not been closed for 19X2.

ALTERNATE PROBLEMS

Initial cost of plant assets

10–29A The items below represent expenditures (or receipts) related to the construction of a new home office for Kyler Investment Company.

Cost of land site, which included an abandoned railroad spur	$ 215,000
Legal fees relating to land purchase	4,000
Title insurance premiums on property	1,200
Cost of removing railroad tracks	6,000
Payment of delinquent property taxes assumed by the purchaser	4,900
Proceeds from sale of timber from walnut trees cut down to prepare site for construction	(10,000)
Proceeds from sale of salvaged railroad track	(2,500)
Grading and drainage on land site	8,000
Cost of basement excavation (contracted separately)	6,500
Architect's fees on new building	90,000
Payment to building contractor—original contract price	1,750,000
Cost of changes during construction to make building more energy efficient	52,000
Interest cost incurred during construction (based on average accumulated construction expenditures)	122,000
Cost of replacing windows broken by vandals	1,500
Cost of paving driveway and parking lot	20,000

Out-of-court settlement for mud slide onto adjacent property	$ 6,000
Special assessment for paving city sidewalks (paid to city)	18,000
Cost of brick and wrought iron fence installed across front of property	7,400

REQUIRED
From the given data, compute the proper balances for the Land, Building, and Land Improvements accounts of Kyler Investment Company.

Allocation of package purchase price and depreciation methods

10–30A In an expansion move, Rotary Company paid $1,315,000 for most of the property, plant, and equipment of a small manufacturing firm that was going out of business. Before agreeing to the price, Rotary hired a consultant for $10,000 to appraise the assets. The appraised values were as follows:

Land	$ 270,000
Building	540,000
Equipment	600,000
Trucks	90,000
	$1,500,000

Rotary issued two checks totaling $1,325,000 to acquire the assets and pay the consultant on April 1, 19X4. Rotary depreciated the assets using the straight-line method on the building, the sum-of-the-years'-digits method on the equipment, and the double declining-balance method on the trucks. Estimated useful lives and salvage values were as follows:

	Useful Life	Salvage Value
Building	15 years	$42,000
Equipment	10 years	35,000
Trucks	5 years	8,000

REQUIRED
(a) Compute the amounts allocated to the various types of plant assets acquired on April 1, 19X4.
(b) Prepare the April 1, 19X4, general journal entries to record the purchase of the assets and the payment of the consultant.
(c) Prepare the December 31, 19X4, general journal entries to record the 19X4 depreciation expense on the building, equipment, and trucks.

Depreciation methods

10–31A On January 2, 19X1, Powell Company purchased an electroplating machine to help manufacture a part for one of its key products. The machine cost $182,250 and was estimated to have a useful life of six years or 600,000 platings, after which it could be sold for $18,450.

REQUIRED
Compute each year's depreciation expense for 19X1–19X6 under each of the following depreciation methods:
(a) Straight line.
(b) Sum of the years' digits.

(c) Double declining balance.
(d) Units of production. (Assume annual production in platings of: 120,000; 150,000; 100,000; 60,000; 90,000; and 80,000.)

Comprehensive problem

10–33A Rapid Delivery Service had the following transactions related to its delivery truck:

19X3

Mar.	1	Purchased for $12,620 cash a new delivery truck with an estimated useful life of five years and a $1,300 salvage value.
	2	Paid $380 for painting the company name and logo on the truck.
Dec.	31	Recorded 19X3 depreciation on the truck.

19X4

July	1	Installed air conditioning in the truck at a cost of $980 cash. Although the truck's estimated useful life was not affected, its estimated salvage value was increased by $100.
Sept.	7	Paid $275 for truck tune-up and safety inspection.
Dec.	31	Recorded 19X4 depreciation on the truck.

19X5

May	2	Paid $1,630 for a major overhaul of the truck. The overhaul should extend the truck's useful life one year (to February 28, 19X9), when the revised salvage value should be $1,600.
Sept.	3	Installed a set of front and rear bumper guards at a cost of $65 cash.
Dec.	31	Recorded 19X5 depreciation on the truck.

19X6

Dec.	31	Recorded 19X6 depreciation on the truck.

Rapid's depreciation policies include (1) using straight-line depreciation, (2) recording depreciation to the nearest whole month, and (3) expensing all truck expenditures of $75 or less.

REQUIRED
Present general journal entries to record these transactions.

Revision of depreciation and capital expenditure

10–34A Cofield Company uses straight-line depreciation in accounting for its machines. On January 2, 19X1, Cofield purchased a new machine for $75,000 cash. The machine's estimated useful life was eight years with a $7,000 salvage value. In 19X6, the company decided its original useful life estimate should be increased by three years. Beginning in 19X6, depreciation was based on an 11-year total useful life, and no change was made in the salvage value estimate. On January 3, 19X7, Cofield added an automatic cut-off switch and a self-sharpening blade mechanism to the machine at a cost of $4,500 cash. These improvements did not change the machine's useful life, but did increase the estimated salvage value to $7,500.

REQUIRED
(a) Prepare general journal entries to record (1) the purchase of the machine, (2) 19X1 depreciation expense, (3) 19X6 depreciation expense, (4) the 19X7 improvements, and (5) 19X7 depreciation expense.
(b) Compute the book value of the machine at the end of 19X7 (that is, after recording the depreciation expense for 19X7).

BUSINESS DECISION PROBLEM

Kent Desyde, president of Desyde, Inc., wants you to resolve his dispute with Mia Findum over the amount of a finder's fee due Findum. Desyde hired Findum to locate a new plant site to expand the business. By agreement, Findum's fee was to be 15% of the "cost of the property (excluding the finder's fee) measured according to generally accepted accounting principles."

Findum located Site 1 and Site 2 for Desyde to consider. Each site had a selling price of $190,000, and the geographic locations of both sites were equally acceptable to Desyde. Desyde employed an engineering firm to conduct the geological tests necessary to determine the relative quality of the two sites for construction. The tests, which cost $7,000 for each site, showed that Site 1 was superior to Site 2.

The owner of Site 1 initially gave Desyde 30 days—a reasonable period—to decide whether or not to buy the property. However, Desyde procrastinated in contracting the geological tests, and the results were not available by the end of the 30-day period. Desyde requested a two-week extension. The Site 1 owner granted Desyde the additional two weeks but charged him $6,000 for the extension (which Desyde paid). Desyde eventually bought Site 1.

Desyde sent Findum a fee of $29,550, which was 15% of a cost computed as follows:

Sales price, Site 1	$190,000
Geological tests, Site 1	7,000
Total	$197,000

Findum believes she is entitled to $31,500, based on a cost computed as follows:

Sales price, Site 1	$190,000
Geological tests, Site 1	7,000
Geological tests, Site 2	7,000
Fee for time extension	6,000
Total	$210,000

REQUIRED

What fee is Findum entitled to under the agreement? Explain.

ANSWERS TO SELF-TEST QUESTIONS

1. (c) 2. (b) 3. (d) 4. (b) 5. (a)

11

Plant Asset Disposals, Natural Resources, and Intangible Assets

Chapter Objectives

- **Explain and illustrate the accounting for disposals of plant assets.**
- **Identify the records used to provide control over plant assets.**
- **Discuss the nature of and the accounting for natural resources.**
- **Discuss the nature of and the accounting for intangible assets.**
- **Identify and distinguish operating leases and capital leases.**

The meek shall inherit the earth,
but *not* its mineral rights.

J. PAUL GETTY

The preceding chapter dealt with the measurement and depreciation of plant assets. In this chapter, we examine the remaining plant asset problem area—accounting for their disposal. We then consider the accounting issues related to the acquisition and use of natural resources and intangible assets. Although plant assets, natural resources, and intangible assets are separate identifiable categories of long-term assets, the basic accounting procedures related to each category are similar.

DISPOSALS OF PLANT ASSETS

A firm may dispose of a plant asset in a variety of ways. The asset may be sold, retired, exchanged for a dissimilar asset, or traded in as partial payment for a new, similar asset. The asset's usefulness to the firm may also be ended by an unfavorable and unanticipated event—the asset may be stolen or destroyed by a natural disaster.

Depreciation must extend through an asset's total useful life to a firm. Therefore, depreciation must be recorded up to the disposal date, regardless of the manner of the asset's disposal. Should the disposal date not coincide with the end of an accounting period, a journal entry must record depreciation for a partial period (the period from the date depreciation was last recorded to the disposal date). We illustrate this partial period depreciation in two of our subsequent examples.

We use the following basic data to illustrate disposals of plant assets:

Equipment's original cost	$1,000
Estimated salvage value after five years	100
Annual straight-line depreciation	180
(Unless stated otherwise, assume that depreciation to the date of sale has been recorded.)	

Sale of Plant Assets

Firms normally sell their plant assets once they are no longer efficient or useful. Generally, the asset still has some book value and some sales value in the used market.

Most sales of plant assets involve the following related factors:

(1) The sale transaction exchanges a used plant asset for cash. Because the plant asset sold is no longer on hand, the journal entry must remove from both the asset and accumulated depreciation accounts all amounts related to that asset. These amounts reflect the asset's book value.

(2) Because plant assets are most often sold for amounts either greater or less than their book values, gains or losses are produced. Sales proceeds in excess of book values create gains from the sales. Book values in excess of sales proceeds cause losses from the sales.

SOLD FOR MORE THAN BOOK VALUE Assume the equipment is sold for $230 midway through its fifth year. Depreciation was last recorded at the end of the fourth year. The related entries are

Depreciation Expense	90	
Accumulated Depreciation		90
To record depreciation expense for six months.		

Cash	230	
Accumulated Depreciation	810	
Equipment		1,000
Gain on Sale of Plant Assets		40
To record sale of equipment for $230.		

Note that recording depreciation to the date of sale adds $90 to the Accumulated Depreciation account, which totals (4 × $180) + $90 = $810. To reflect the sale properly, we must remove this entire amount of accumulated depreciation from the books. The gain is the proceeds of $230 minus the asset's book value of $190.

SOLD FOR LESS THAN BOOK VALUE Assume the equipment is sold for $30 at the end of the fifth year. The correct entry is

Cash	30	
Loss on Sale of Plant Assets	70	
Accumulated Depreciation	900	
Equipment		1,000
To record sale of equipment for $30.		

The loss equals the book value of $100 minus the sales proceeds of $30. The cash receipt is recorded, and balances from both accounts related to the asset—the asset account and its contra account—are removed from the books.

SOLD FOR BOOK VALUE Assume the equipment is sold for $280 at the end of the fourth year. The proper entry is

Cash	280	
Accumulated Depreciation	720	
Equipment		1,000
To record sale of equipment for $280.		

The equipment's book value at the end of the fourth year is $280 ($1,000 cost − $720 accumulated depreciation). The $280 sales proceeds exactly equal the book value; no gain or loss is involved. Of course, we still remove from the accounts the amounts reflecting the book value of the asset sold.

Retirement of Plant Assets

When a plant asset that has no sales value in the used market is retired from productive service, we record a loss equal to the asset's book value. Assume the equipment in our example is scrapped at the end of five years. The entry to record this event is

Loss on Retirement of Plant Assets	100	
Accumulated Depreciation	900	
Equipment		1,000
To record retirement of equipment.		

Ideally, any plant asset that will be scrapped should have a zero salvage value. Then the asset's book value is zero (accumulated depreciation equals the asset's cost) at the end of its estimated useful life. If the asset is retired on that date, no loss is recorded. The asset's cost and accumulated depreciation, of course, must still be removed from the accounts. To illustrate, let us change our example and assume a zero salvage value for the equipment. Over the equipment's five-year life, we record depreciation totaling $1,000 ($200 per year). The following entry records the equipment's retirement at the end of five years:

Accumulated Depreciation	1,000	
Equipment		1,000
To record retirement of equipment.		

Note, however, that the equipment's book value reaches zero only at the end of five years. Should the equipment be retired before that date, a loss equal to the equipment's book value will be recorded.

Exchange of Dissimilar Plant Assets

A plant asset may be exchanged for a different kind of plant asset. The seller of the new asset establishes a trade-in allowance for the used asset with the balance of the selling price due in cash. The trade-in allowance is not related to the used asset's book value. When it is applied against a legitimate cash selling price, the allowance does represent the used asset's fair value. In some exchanges, the suggested selling price may be higher than the asset's cash selling price; therefore the trade-in allowance is inflated and does not indicate the used asset's fair value.

When dissimilar plant assets are exchanged, the cash equivalent (fair) value of what is given up is not always obvious. Therefore, the new asset should be recorded at the fair value of the assets given up or the fair value of the asset received, whichever is more clearly evident. The used asset's book value, of course, is removed from the accounts. We determine any gain or loss on the transaction by comparing the fair value assigned to the new asset with the total of the used asset's book value plus any cash payment. If the new asset's fair value is larger, a gain is recorded. Should the used asset's book value plus cash paid exceed the new asset's fair value, we reflect a loss.

To illustrate, assume our equipment ($1,000 cost and $100 salvage value) is exchanged for an office desk two-thirds of the way through the second year. The desk's cash selling price is $950. The equipment receives an $800 trade-in allowance, so a $150 cash payment is required. Because equipment depreciation was last recorded at the end of the first year, the correct entries are

Depreciation Expense	120	
Accumulated Depreciation		120
To record depreciation expense for eight months.		

Office Furniture	950	
Accumulated Depreciation	300	
Equipment		1,000
Cash		150
Gain on Exchange of Plant Assets		100
To record trade of equipment for office furniture.		

The $100 gain on the transaction is the excess of the desk's fair value ($950) over the equipment's book value ($700) plus cash paid ($150).

Exchange of Similar Plant Assets

When a plant asset is traded in for a similar new asset, the accounting analysis depends upon whether a loss or a gain is implicit in the transaction. A loss will be reflected in the accounting entry, but a gain will not.

LOSS EXCHANGE Assume that the equipment in our illustration is traded in after three years (accumulated depreciation, $540) on similar new equipment that has a $1,400 cash price. A trade-in allowance of $400 is given, so a $1,000 cash payment must be made. There is a loss inherent in this exchange because the new asset's fair value ($1,400) is less than the sum of the used asset's book value plus the cash payment ($460 + $1,000 = $1,460). We analyze this exchange the same way we analyze exchanges of dissimilar plant assets. The new asset is recorded at its fair value, the used asset's book value is removed from the accounts, the cash payment is shown, and the appropriate loss is recorded. The entry to record the exchange would be:

Equipment (new)	1,400	
Loss on Exchange of Plant Assets	60	
Accumulated Depreciation	540	
Equipment (old)		1,000
Cash		1,000
To record trade of equipment.		

GAIN EXCHANGE If in the preceding exchange the company's trade-in allowance was $600 (rather than $400), then an $800 cash payment is required. Now there is a gain inherent in the exchange because the new asset's fair value ($1,400) exceeds the sum of the used asset's book value and the cash payment ($460 + $800 = $1,260).

The Accounting Principles Board, however, concluded that the exchange of similar productive assets is not an event that should result in an immediate gain to the company acquiring the new asset.[1] Instead, the new asset is recorded at an amount equal to the sum of the book value of the asset traded in plus any cash paid. The following entry records the exchange:

Equipment (new)	1,260	
Accumulated Depreciation	540	
Equipment (old)		1,000
Cash		800
To record trade of equipment.		

The new equipment is recorded at $1,260—the sum of the $460 book value of the old equipment and the $800 cash payment. This treatment departs from the general rule that newly acquired assets are recorded at their implied cash cost. The new equipment has a cash price of $1,400, but it is recorded at $1,260. Essentially, its book value has been reduced by the $140 gain that is not recognized in the exchange.

TRADE-IN AND TAX REGULATIONS The Internal Revenue Code specifies that any gains or losses on trade-in transactions involving similar assets are not reported in the year of exchange. The treatment of gains parallels the analysis discussed above. Losses, however, are treated as adjustments of the carrying value of the new asset. The above loss exchange illustration would be recorded as follows under the income tax guidelines:

Equipment (new) ($1,400 + $60 loss)	1,460	
Accumulated Depreciation	540	
Equipment (old)		1,000
Cash		1,000
To record trade of equipment.		

This treatment does not recognize the loss in the year of exchange, but increases the depreciation available in future years. Generally accepted accounting principles require that significant losses on trade-ins be recognized rather than deferred. Some firms, however, follow the income tax method when losses are immaterial to avoid keeping a separate record for income tax purposes.

Destruction or Theft of Plant Assets

A company's plant assets may be destroyed—by fire, flood, earthquake, tornado, or other natural disaster—or they may be stolen. If an uninsured asset is destroyed or stolen, the firm suffers a loss measured by the asset's book value. Assume the equipment in our example is uninsured and after three years is destroyed by fire.

[1] *Opinions of the Accounting Principles Board, No. 29*, "Accounting for Nonmonetary Transactions" (New York: American Institute of Certified Public Accountants, 1973).

Its book value when destroyed is $460 ($1,000 cost − $540 accumulated depreciation). The proper journal entry is

Fire Loss	460	
Accumulated Depreciation	540	
Equipment		1,000
To record equipment fire loss.		

Business firms normally insure their property to eliminate, or reduce, the risk of loss by destruction or theft. When an insured asset is destroyed or stolen, a claim is filed with the insurance company. The maximum amount recoverable from the insurance company is the asset's fair market value. Because the accounting records reflect a plant asset's book value—not its fair market value—the accounting analysis of the asset's theft or destruction may show a gain or loss, even when the asset is insured. The gain or loss is the difference between the insurance settlement and the asset's book value. To illustrate, assume the equipment from the preceding example is insured and has a fair market value of $500 when destroyed by fire. The $500 insurance claim exceeds the equipment's book value, so we reflect a $40 gain from the insurance settlement in the following entry:

Receivable from Insurance Company	500	
Accumulated Depreciation	540	
Equipment		1,000
Gain on Insurance Settlement		40
To record insurance claim on equipment destroyed by fire.		

Cash is debited and Receivable from Insurance Company is credited when the $500 check settling the claim is received from the insurance company.

CONTROL OF PLANT ASSETS

Firms with a large number of plant assets use a system of control accounts and subsidiary ledgers to account for and manage these assets. The general ledger becomes unwieldy if it contains a separate account for each plant asset. Instead, plant assets are divided into functional groups and only the control accounts (asset and accumulated depreciation accounts) for each functional group appear in the general ledger. The plant asset functional groupings will vary somewhat from company to company, but typical control accounts include Land Improvements, Buildings, Furniture and Fixtures, Factory Equipment, and Delivery Equipment.

A subsidiary ledger supports each plant asset control account in the general ledger. The subsidiary ledger contains a detailed record for each specific asset in the control group. The subsidiary ledger may be maintained by a manual or a computerized system. Regardless of the record's form, the following basic data are usually incorporated:

Description
Firm's assigned serial number and accounting classification
Date purchased
Assigned physical location
Insurance coverage
Person accountable
Original cost
Major modifications and repairs
Depreciation method and data
Disposition data (date, price, remarks)

Exhibit 11–1 portrays the relationship between control accounts for a plant asset functional group (Delivery Equipment) and the related subsidiary ledger. Each purchase and sale of delivery equipment is recorded in the control account and on a separate detailed record in the subsidiary ledger. In this illustration, two delivery vans were purchased in 19X1 and they represent the firm's total delivery equipment. Annual depreciation for the individual vans is noted on the subsidiary ledger records and then totaled to get the amount for the general journal entry to record the delivery equipment's annual depreciation. At the end of the accounting period, the control account balances should equal the sum of the balances of the individual assets in the subsidiary ledger (as shown in Exhibit 11–1). The detailed information in the subsidiary ledger is particularly helpful in determining (1) periodic depreciation and (2) a plant asset's book value at time of disposal.

Most firms assign a specific serial number to each plant asset when it is purchased. This is usually done by small decals, stampings, or etchings that are not easily removed or altered. Periodically, the existence and condition of these assets should be verified by a physical count.

NATURAL RESOURCES

Natural resources include such items as timber, petroleum, natural gas, coal, and other mineral deposits mined by the extractive industries. These resources are also known as *wasting assets*. As with plant assets, natural resources are initially accounted for at their cost. When known deposits are purchased, the initial measurement is quite simple. When the natural resource is discovered after extensive exploration, however, determining its initial cost is more difficult. Because not all exploration activities are successful, we must determine which activities were necessary to discover the resource. Expenditures for these activities are capitalized as the cost of the resource, and the remaining amounts are expensed. The cost of developing the site so the natural resource may be extracted is another component of initial cost. Expenditures to remove land overburdens, build access roads, and construct mine entrances illustrate these development costs.

EXHIBIT 11–1
Plant Asset Control Accounts and Subsidiary Ledger

General Ledger Control Accounts

Delivery Equipment **Account No. 164**

Date		Description	Post. Ref.	Debit	Credit	Balance
19X1						
Jan.	1		J1	9,000		9,000
July	1		J8	10,400		19,400

Accumulated Depreciation—Delivery Equipment **Account No. 165**

Date		Description	Post. Ref.	Debit	Credit	Balance
19X1						
Dec.	31		J14		2,640	2,640

Delivery Equipment Subsidiary Ledger

Item Ford Delivery Van, Blue **Account No.** 164
Purchased From Mann Ford, Madison **Serial No.** V280
Person Responsible Store 1 Manager **Insurance** Allgroup, #8750
Service Life 5 years **Location** Store 1
Depreciation: **Salvage Value** $600
Method Straight line **Per Year** $1,680 **Per Mo.** $140

Date	Descrip.	Asset Dr.	Asset Cr.	Asset Balance	Accumulated Depreciation Dr.	Accumulated Depreciation Cr.	Accumulated Depreciation Balance
19X1							
Jan. 1		9,000		9,000			
Dec. 31						1,680	1,680

Item Ford Delivery Van, Tan **Account No.** 164
Purchased From Mann Ford, Madison **Serial No.** V281
Person Responsible Store 2 Manager **Insurance** Allgroup, #8750
Service Life 5 years **Location** Store 2
Depreciation: **Salvage Value** $800
Method Straight line **Per Year** $1,920 **Per Mo.** $160

Date	Descrip.	Asset Dr.	Asset Cr.	Asset Balance	Accumulated Depreciation Dr.	Accumulated Depreciation Cr.	Accumulated Depreciation Balance
19X1							
July 1		10,400		10,400			
Dec. 31						960	960

Depletion

The term **depletion** refers to the allocation of the cost of natural resources to the units extracted from the ground or, in the case of timberland, the board feet of timber cut. Accounting for the depletion of natural resources is comparable to units-of-production depreciation of plant assets. The average depletion cost per unit of natural resource is computed as follows:

$$\text{Depletion per Unit} = \frac{\text{Cost of Natural Resource} - \text{Residual Value}}{\text{Estimated Total Units of Resource}}$$

The unit measure used depends on the natural resource; the unit may be barrels, tons, board feet, cubic feet, or some other unit appropriate for the resource. Once depletion per unit is computed, periodic depletion is determined as follows:

$$\text{Periodic Depletion} = \text{Depletion per Unit} \times \text{Units Extracted in Current Period}$$

For example, assume that a company acquires for $520,000 a parcel of land whose major commercial value is a soft coal mine that contains an estimated 800,000 tons of extractable coal. Development costs of $100,000 are incurred to prepare the site for mining coal. The property's estimated residual value is $20,000. The coal deposit's initial cost is $620,000 ($520,000 acquisition cost + $100,000 development costs). We calculate the depletion per ton of mined coal as follows:

$$\frac{\$620{,}000 - \$20{,}000}{800{,}000 \text{ tons}} = \$0.75 \text{ per ton}$$

If, during the first period, 60,000 tons are extracted, that period's depletion charge would be 60,000 × $0.75 = $45,000. We would make the following entry:

Depletion of Coal Deposit	45,000	
Accumulated Depletion		45,000
To record depletion of coal deposit.		

In the balance sheet, Accumulated Depletion is a contra account deducted from the cost of the natural resource as follows:

Coal Deposit (original cost)	$620,000
Less: Accumulated Depletion	45,000
Coal Deposit (book value)	$575,000

This treatment is similar to handling Accumulated Depreciation accounts.

The disposition of the periodic depletion charge depends on whether the extracted units are sold or on hand at the end of the period. The depletion amount of units sold is deducted in the income statement as part of the cost of the resource sold. Units on hand at year-end, however, constitute inventory items, so their depletion charge appears in the balance sheet as part of the inventory cost. In addition to the depletion charge, the costs of extracting and processing the natural resource are part of the inventory cost.

Assume, for example, that $81,000 of extracting and processing costs are incurred the first period to mine the 60,000 tons of coal. The total cost of the

60,000 mined tons is $126,000 ($45,000 depletion + $81,000 extracting and processing costs); the average cost per ton is $2.10 ($126,000/60,000 tons). If 40,000 tons are sold during the first period, $84,000 (40,000 tons × $2.10 per ton) is expensed in the income statement as the cost of coal sold. The year-end balance sheet will show a mined coal inventory of $42,000 (20,000 tons × $2.10 per ton).

Revision of Depletion

Estimating accurately the recoverable units of a natural resource is difficult. Imagine trying to estimate the barrels of oil or the ounces of silver located underground. After extracting activities begin, better information may result in revisions of such estimates. When an estimate of recoverable units changes, a revised depletion per unit is computed. The revised depletion per unit becomes effective in the period the estimate of recoverable units changes—depletion amounts computed in prior periods are not changed. The revised depletion per unit is computed as follows:

$$\text{Revised Depletion per Unit} = \frac{\text{Book Value of Natural Resource} - \text{Residual Value}}{\text{Revised Estimate of Remaining Units of Resource}}$$

To illustrate, assume that at the beginning of the second year of our coal mining example, the estimated total amount of recoverable coal is changed to 560,000 tons. Because 60,000 tons have already been mined, an estimated 500,000 tons remain underground. The coal deposit's book value at the start of the second year is $575,000 (Cost − Accumulated Depletion). Therefore, the revised depletion per ton is $1.11, determined as follows:

$$\frac{\$575{,}000 - \$20{,}000}{500{,}000 \text{ tons}} = \$1.11 \text{ per ton}$$

Depletion for Tax Purposes

The Internal Revenue Code permits a deduction for the depletion of natural resources sold. The depletion deduction may be based on the resource's cost, using the procedures illustrated. Companies mining certain resources, however, may use **percentage depletion** if it gives a larger deduction. Under percentage depletion, the depletion deduction is a specified percentage of the gross revenue from mining activities, with certain limitations. The depletion percentages range from 5%–22%, depending on the natural resource. Percentage depletion is not limited by the resource's cost and may, over a period of years, result in income tax depletion deductions that exceed total cost. Percentage depletion is a special income tax feature; it is not permitted under generally accepted accounting principles for financial reporting purposes.

On-site Equipment

The extraction of many natural resources requires the construction of *on-site* equipment, such as drilling and pumping devices, crushing equipment, and conveyor systems. Often in remote places, this equipment may be abandoned when the natural resource is exhausted. If the useful life of these assets expires before the resources are exhausted, ordinary depreciation techniques are appropriate. When the reverse is true—natural resources are exhausted, and the asset is abandoned before the end of its physical life—depreciation should be based on the length of the extraction period. Alternatively, we could employ the units-of-production approach based on the estimated total resource to be extracted.

For example, assume coal mining equipment was acquired at a cost of $210,000 in our preceding example. The equipment has an estimated $10,000 salvage value after the coal is mined. If the units-of-production method were used, depreciation per ton for the first year would be

$$\frac{\$210{,}000 - \$10{,}000}{800{,}000 \text{ tons}} = \$0.25 \text{ per ton}$$

The first year's depreciation, when 60,000 tons are mined, is 60,000 × $0.25 = $15,000.

Under the units-of-production method, depreciation per unit must be revised if the estimate of extractable resource units changes. The process is similar to the depletion per unit revision discussed earlier. We compute the revised depreciation per unit by dividing the asset's book value (less any salvage value) by the revised remaining resource units. For example, at the beginning of the second year, the coal mining equipment's book value is $195,000 ($210,000 cost − $15,000 accumulated depreciation). If the coal remaining underground is now estimated at 500,000 tons, then depreciation per ton, beginning in the second year, is $0.37, computed as follows:

$$\frac{\$195{,}000 - \$10{,}000}{500{,}000 \text{ tons}} = \$0.37 \text{ per ton}$$

Supplemental Disclosures

Many companies in the extractive industries—especially oil- and gas-producing companies—are holding for future operations large discovered and proven reserve fields. Most often these reserves are carried at historical cost figures that may represent only a small fraction of their current values. In such cases, the financial statements may contain supplemental disclosures about reserve quantities and other data useful in estimating reserve values.[2]

INTANGIBLE ASSETS

In accounting, intangible assets include certain resources that benefit an enterprise's operations but lack physical substance. Several intangible assets are exclusive rights or privileges obtained from a governmental unit or by legal contract—such as patents, copyrights, franchises, trademarks, and leaseholds. Other intangible assets (1) arise from the creation of a business enterprise—namely, organization costs—or (2) reflect a firm's ability to generate above-normal earnings—that is, goodwill.

[2]Specific disclosure requirements have been established for oil- and gas-producing companies. For details, see *Statement of Financial Accounting Standards No. 69*, "Disclosures about Oil and Gas Producing Activities" (Stamford, CT: Financial Accounting Standards Board, 1982).

The term *intangible asset* is not used with precision in accounting literature. By convention, only certain assets are included in the intangible category. Some resources that lack physical substance—such as prepaid insurance, receivables, and investments—are not classified as intangible assets. Because intangible assets lack physical characteristics, the related accounting procedures may be more subjective and arbitrary than for tangible assets.

Measurement of Intangible Assets

A firm should record intangible assets acquired from outside entities initially at their cost. Similarly, some intangible assets created internally by a firm are measured at their cost. For example, the costs of forming a business are charged to an Organization Costs account, and the costs to secure a trademark—such as attorney's fees, registration fees, and design costs—are charged to a Trademarks account.

Most expenditures related to internally created intangible assets are expensed rather than capitalized. Because these intangibles are not acquired from outside entities, accountants lack an objective measure for the asset account. The accountant responds to uncertainty about an intangible asset's existence, or its proper measure, by expensing the related amounts. This situation is particularly evident in accounting for research and development costs.

RESEARCH AND DEVELOPMENT COSTS American industry annually spends billions of dollars searching for new knowledge and translating this knowledge into new or significantly improved products or processes. These **research and development costs** are important, but usually a significant uncertainty exists about the future benefits of specific research and development efforts. Only a small portion of research and development projects culminate in a new product or process, and then, commercial success is not certain. The market failure rate is high for new products. Uncertain future benefits of research and development costs influenced the Financial Accounting Standards Board's development of the following accounting guideline: *All research and development costs related to a firm's products and its production processes must be expensed when incurred.*[3]

The preceding guideline does not apply to a firm's selling and administrative activities nor to the unique exploration and development efforts of firms in the extractive industries. Also, legal costs of obtaining or defending a patent for a new product or process may be capitalized.

COMPUTER SOFTWARE The widespread use of computers has spawned an entire industry of companies that produce computer software for sale or lease. The industry's unique product and the rapidly changing computer technology caused the Financial Accounting Standards Board to consider specifically how to account for the costs of developing and producing computer software for sale or lease. The Board's conclusions illustrate the application of measurement guidelines relating to research and development costs and intangible assets to a par-

[3]*Statement of Financial Accounting Standards No. 2*, "Accounting for Research and Development Costs" (Stamford, CT: Financial Accounting Standards Board, 1974).

ticular industry. It assigns the various development and production costs to three different categories, as follows:[4]

(1) **Expensed as research and development costs** All costs incurred to establish the software's technological feasibility are expensed as research and development costs. This covers all costs of those activities—such as planning, designing, coding, and testing—necessary to establish that the software can be produced to achieve the design specifications.

(2) **Capitalized as an intangible asset** After technological feasibility has been established, the rest of the costs incurred to produce the product masters are capitalized as computer software production costs, an intangible asset. Product masters are the completed versions of the software, documentation, and training materials which are then copied to produce the items for sale or lease.

(3) **Capitalized as inventory** The costs incurred to duplicate and physically package the computer software, documentation, and training materials are capitalized in the company's inventory account.

Computer software purchased by a company to use in its selling or administrative activities may be capitalized when it clearly benefits future periods. For example, the purchase cost of a computer software package designed to serve a firm's general management information needs should be capitalized if it will be used several years. Similarly, if a firm develops its own software for internal selling or administrative uses, the development costs may be capitalized when the software will be useful for several periods. Many firms, however, follow a policy of expensing immediately all costs of developing software for internal use.

Amortization of Intangibles

The **amortization** of an intangible asset is the periodic write-off to expense of the asset's cost over the term of its expected useful life. Because salvage values are ordinarily not involved, amortization typically entails (1) determining the asset's cost, (2) estimating the period over which it benefits the firm, and (3) allocating the cost in equal amounts to each accounting period involved. The Accounting Principles Board modified this general approach by specifying that the period of amortization for intangibles should not exceed 40 years.[5] As a result, intangibles are treated as if they have a limited life—even though some, such as trademarks, may legally have indefinite lives. Straight-line amortization must be used for intangible assets unless another method is shown to be more appropriate.[6]

[4] *Statement of Financial Accounting Standards No. 86*, "Accounting for the Costs of Computer Software to Be Sold, Leased, or Otherwise Marketed" (Stamford, CT: Financial Accounting Standards Board, 1985).

[5] *Opinions of the Accounting Principles Board, No. 17*, "Accounting for Intangible Assets" (New York: American Institute of Certified Public Accountants, 1970).

[6] Annual amortization of computer software production costs, however, is to be the greater of (1) the straight-line amount or (2) an amount computed using the ratio of the current revenue for the software product to the total current and estimated future revenue for the product.

The amortization entry debits the appropriate amortization expense account. The entry's credit may go to an accumulated amortization account—a contra account to the related intangible asset. In amortizing intangibles, however, frequently the asset account is credited directly; that is, no contra account is used.

Intangible assets originally deemed to have specific useful lives should be reviewed periodically to determine if their value or their economic lives have decreased. If so, an immediate write-off or a plan of periodic amortization at an increased rate is appropriate.

Patents

A **patent** is an exclusive right, granted by the federal government for 17 years, to use a specific process or to make a specific product. Patent laws were originated to encourage inventors by protecting them from imitators who might usurp the invention for commercial gain. Just what a patentable idea is has become quite complex in the modern realm of technical knowledge. Consequently, long periods of patent "searching" and, frequently, successful defense of infringement suits may precede the validation of a patent. Even though patents have a legal life of 17 years, changes in technology or consumer tastes may shorten their economic life. Because of their uncertain value, patents should probably be accounted for conservatively. When patents are purchased some time after having been granted, the buyer enjoys the privilege at most for only the remaining legal life.

To illustrate the accounting for patents, assume that, early in January, a company pays $34,000 legal costs to obtain a patent on a new product. The journal entry is

Patents	34,000	
Cash		34,000
To record legal costs of acquiring patent.		

The company expects the patent to provide benefits for 17 years. If a contra asset account is used, the following entry records the first year's straight-line amortization:

Patent Amortization Expense	2,000	
Accumulated Amortization—Patents		2,000
To record patent amortization.		

The expense would be deducted from revenue, and the Accumulated Amortization—Patents contra account would be deducted from the related asset account on the balance sheet as follows:

Patents (original cost)	$34,000
Less: Accumulated Amortization	2,000
Patents (book value)	$32,000

If the asset account is credited directly (no contra account is used), the amortization entry would be as follows:

Patent Amortization Expense	2,000	
Patents		2,000
To record patent amortization.		

When no contra account is used, the asset account reflects the asset's book value, and the balance sheet presentation would be

Patents (cost less amortization to date)	$32,000

Copyrights

Copyrights protect the owner against the unauthorized reproduction of a specific written work or artwork. A copyright lasts for the life of the author plus 50 years. The purchase price of valuable copyrights can be substantial, and proper measurement and amortization are necessary for valid income determination. But even with the related legal fees, the cost of most copyrights is seldom sufficiently material to present accounting problems.

A copyright's legal life exceeds the 40-year maximum amortization period allowed for intangibles. However, copyright costs are generally amortized over periods much shorter than 40 years. Copyright costs should be amortized over the period that the copyrighted work produces revenue—for a proper matching of revenue and expense—which may be only a few years.

Franchises

Franchises most often involve exclusive rights to operate or sell a specific brand of products in a given geographical area. Franchises may be for definite or indefinite periods. Although many franchises are agreements between two private firms, various governmental units award franchises for public utility operations within their legal jurisdictions. The right to operate a Kentucky Fried Chicken restaurant or to sell Midas Mufflers in a specific area illustrates franchise agreements in the private sector.

Some franchise agreements require a substantial initial payment by the party acquiring the franchise. This amount should be debited to the intangible asset account Franchise and amortized on a straight-line basis over the franchise period or 40 years, whichever is shorter.

Trademarks and Trade Names

Trademarks and **trade names** represent the exclusive and continuing right to use certain terms, names, or symbols, usually to identify a brand or family of products. An original trademark or trade name can be registered with the federal government at nominal cost. A company may spend considerable time and money to determine an appropriate name or symbol for a product. Also, the purchase of well-known, and thus valuable, trademarks or trade names may involve substantial amounts of funds. When the cost of a trademark or trade name is material, the amount is debited to an appropriate intangible asset account—Trademarks, for example—and amortized over the period of expected benefit (not exceeding 40 years).

Organization Costs

Expenditures incurred in launching a business (usually a corporation) are called **organization costs.** These expenditures, which may include attorney's fees, fees

NAME THAT BRAND

These days a good name is hard to find. The R. J. Reynolds Tobacco division of R. J. Reynolds Industries thought the perfect brand name for a new cigarette aimed at fashion-conscious, young women smokers would be Ritz, as in puttin' on the. . . . Not so fast, said the Ritz Hotel in Paris, haunt of several generations of American romantics. The hotel, which, as it happens, markets a brand of cigarettes called Ritz Paris, brought a trademark infringement suit against Reynolds.

Was RJR intentionally infringing the Paris hotel's trademark? That's for the courts to decide; the suit is pending in a New York federal court. But name overlap can happen innocently these days. In the last four years alone more than 150,000 trademarks were registered with the U.S. Patent & Trademark Office. That's double the number of names registered in the preceding four years. It makes picking a name a big problem.

But be of good cheer. Some smart businessmen are willing to relieve you of the problem. For a price. "The days when clients asked their advertising agencies to crank out a few names or held a company contest are over," declaims Frank Delano, chairman of the New York firm of Delano Goldman & Young, Inc. Its business is making up names. "We can clear a name in North America in about four hours and foreign countries in about five days."

What's in a name? Plenty, says Larry Goldman, Delano's partner. Apple Computer's name was a good choice, he explains, because it separated the company from thousands of others using the word computer as part of their trademark. Goldman claims he told Apple that Lisa was a poor name choice for its later product. "Too feminine," says Goldman.

Where do companies get their names? Some let their computers spew out thousands of letter combinations. Other sources include foreign words, trees, flowers, even words that don't mean anything but do imply desirable qualities—such as Ford's Merkur, which sounds, as it is intended to, German and vaguely high tech. The challenge in these cases is to match the name with the image of the product.

For big jobs, like naming cars or motorcycles, Delano Goldman & Young might charge $100,000 or more. A smaller job might cost $20,000. Clearly, the name business is profitable. Delano says that last year his company generated $1.2 million in revenues, with pretax earnings of 22%, and he expects to do $2 million in 1985.

Delano Goldman is not without competition. NameLab, Inc., in San Francisco, works from morphemes—the core semantic unit within a word. For example, "tra" in transport, used by NameLab in the name Softra for a California software distributor. There are approximately 6,200 morphemes in the English language, the root of most of the 150,000-word stock of the language. Ira Bachrach, NameLab's president, says he has programmed each morpheme into his computer through the use of a notational system. The end result: coinages like Compaq (morpheme: pak, meaning a small object).

"Most of the morphemes are Indo-European, the root of most of the major Western languages. By choosing the right morphemes," says Bachrach, "you can create names that have an impact worldwide." One example: Acura, the name of Honda's new luxury car. Bachrach thinks the word conveys precision—as in accurate—which was Honda's intention. Acura also meets the technical demands of a coined word, Bachrach explains. Because it ends with the suffix *a*, it is read as a noun and, therefore, a name. The word also starts and ends with the same letter, making it more memorable, and contains three clearly voiced syllables in only five letters.

Suzanne Leff, vice president of Interbrand, Inc., a New York company in the name business, points to Lozol, a drug for treating high blood pressure, manufactured by USV Laboratories, a unit of Revlon. "The name is a palindrome—it is spelled the same backwards and forwards—which is an advantage because such words tend to have pleasant sounds and are well balanced," says Leff.

Needless to say, the name was created by Leff's company.

From *Forbes*, April 8, 1985, pages 128 and 130. "Name That Brand," by Jeffrey A. Trachtenberg.

paid to the state, and other costs related to preparation for operations, are debited to the intangible asset account Organization Costs. Theoretically, these expenditures benefit the firm throughout its operating life, but all intangibles must be amortized over 40 years or less. Most firms amortize organization costs over a five- to 10-year period. Income tax guidelines reinforce this practice by permitting the amortization of organization costs for tax purposes over a period of at least five years.

Goodwill

Goodwill is the value derived from a firm's ability to earn more than a normal rate of return on its specific, identifiable net assets. The measurement of goodwill is complex, because it can stem from any factor that can make income rates high relative to investment. Examples of such factors include exceptional customer relations, advantageous location, operating efficiency, superior personnel relations, favorable financial sources, and even monopolistic position. Furthermore, goodwill cannot be severed from a firm and sold separately. Because measuring goodwill is difficult, a firm records it in the accounts only when another firm is purchased and the amount paid to acquire it exceeds the recognized value of the identifiable net assets involved. Determining the amount of goodwill often requires complex negotiations, but the agreed-on amount is almost always based on the anticipated above-normal earnings.

Accountants expense immediately all costs associated with the internal development or maintenance of goodwill. This means many firms that have created goodwill through their operations do not reflect it in the accounts because it was not purchased.

To illustrate the concept of goodwill, assume Carley Company is for sale. We know the following information about the company and the industry in which it operates:

Fair market value of Carley Company's identifiable net assets	$2,000,000
Normal rate of return on net assets for industry	× 11%
Normal earnings on $2,000,000 of identifiable net assets	$ 220,000
Average annual earnings for Carley Company (past four years)	286,000
Above-average earnings for Carley Company	$ 66,000

Carley's $66,000 of superior earnings suggests the presence of an asset—not specifically identifiable—that helps generate these excess earnings. That asset is goodwill—a combination of factors unique to Carley Company that generates the above-average rate of return on its identifiable net assets. The price paid for Carley will exceed $2,000,000 because the goodwill is also being purchased.

How much should be paid for goodwill? Although above-average earnings in the past are evidence of goodwill, the purchaser is interested in future earnings performance. Goodwill estimates are subject to uncertainty about how long the superior earnings may be sustained. A purchaser may use several methods to estimate a goodwill amount. We illustrate the following two methods:

(1) Goodwill may be estimated by capitalizing the superior earnings at the normal rate of return. *Capitalizing earnings* here means dividing earnings by the

rate of return; this computation for Carley Company is $66,000/0.11 = $600,000. The $600,000 represents the dollar investment that, at an 11% rate of return, will earn $66,000 each year. However, this approach implies that *every* future year will generate the $66,000 excess earnings—a tenuous assumption in a competitive environment. Sometimes excess earnings are capitalized at an above-normal rate of return in recognition of the greater risk of continued superior earnings. The higher the capitalization rate used, the lower the goodwill estimate.

(2) Goodwill may be estimated as some multiple of the superior earnings. Carley's purchaser, for example, may pay five times the above-average earnings for goodwill, or 5 × $66,000 = $330,000.

Of course, the seller also estimates goodwill in determining an overall value for the firm. When the buyer and seller agree on the firm's total purchase price, we can establish the portion assignable to goodwill. The difference between the total purchase price and the fair value of the specific, identifiable net assets is the goodwill measure. For example, if Carley Company is purchased for $2,400,000, $2,000,000 is assigned to the identifiable net assets and $400,000 is assigned to goodwill.

Shown as an intangible asset in the financial statements, goodwill must be amortized over 40 years or less.

Leases

A firm may rent property for a specified period under a contract called a **lease.** The company acquiring the right to use the property is the **lessee;** the owner of the property is the **lessor.** The rights transferred to the lessee are called a **leasehold.** Examples of leased assets are land, buildings, trucks, factory machinery, office equipment, and automobiles. A lessee's accounting treatment depends on whether a lease is an operating lease or a capital lease.

OPERATING LEASE The typical rental agreement illustrates an **operating lease**—the lessee pays for the use of an asset for a limited period, and the lessor retains the usual risks and rewards of owning the property. The lessee usually charges each lease payment to rent expense. Sometimes leases extending over long periods require advance payments from the lessee. The lessee debits these payments to a **Leasehold** account, then allocates the amount to rent expense over the period covered by the advance payment. For example, assume Graphic Company makes an $18,000 advance payment for the final year's rent on a 10-year lease of office space. The following entry records the advance payment:

Leasehold	18,000	
Cash		18,000
To record advance lease payment.		

The leasehold amount is an intangible asset. In this illustration, the advance payment relates specifically to year 10, so the $18,000 is classified as an intangible asset for nine years. In year 10, the $18,000 is expensed. The following entry recognizes a full year's rent expense at the end of year 10:

Office Rent Expense	18,000	
Leasehold		18,000
To record annual rent expense.		

Expenditures made by a lessee to alter or improve property leased under an operating lease are called **leasehold improvements.** For example, a company may construct a building on leased land or make improvements to a leased building. The improvements or alterations become part of the leased property and revert to the lessor at the end of the lease. Thus, the cost of leasehold improvements should be amortized over the life of the lease or the life of the improvements, whichever is shorter. The classification of leasehold improvements varies—some businesses classify them as intangible assets, whereas others include them in the property, plant, and equipment section of the balance sheet.

To illustrate, assume Graphic Company improves the office space leased for 10 years by adding new interior walls and built-in bookshelves. The improvements were made at the start of the lease, cost $40,000, and have an estimated life of 40 years. Graphic Company records the expenditures for the improvements as follows:

Leasehold Improvements	40,000	
Cash		40,000
To record office improvements.		

Because Graphic Company benefits from these leasehold improvements only for the 10-year lease period, it should amortize the improvements over 10 years. The following entry is made in each of the 10 years (assuming a contra account is not used):

Leasehold Improvements Amortization Expense	4,000	
Leasehold Improvements		4,000
To record amortization of leasehold improvements.		

CAPITAL LEASE A **capital lease** transfers to the lessee substantially all of the benefits and risks related to the ownership of the property. A lease meeting at least one of the following criteria is a capital lease:[7]

(1) The lease transfers ownership of the property to the lessee by the end of the lease term.

(2) The lease contains a bargain purchase option.

(3) The lease term is at least 75% of the estimated economic life of the leased property.

[7] *Statement of Financial Accounting Standards No. 13*, "Accounting for Leases" (Stamford, CT: Financial Accounting Standards Board, 1976).

(4) The present value of the lease payments[8] is at least 90% of the fair value of the leased property.

The economic effect of a capital lease is similar to that of an installment purchase. The lessee accounts for a capital lease by recording the leased property as an asset and establishing a liability for the lease obligation. The present value of the future lease payments determines the dollar amount of the entry. The leased property is then depreciated over the period it benefits the lessee. Part of each lease payment made by the lessee is charged to interest expense and the remainder reduces the lease obligation.

We have identified the basic differences between operating and capital leases. Accounting for capital leases is quite complex. Similar complexities face lessors because they may treat some leases as sales or financing transactions rather than as typical rental agreements. These areas, beyond the scope of this text, are covered in intermediate accounting texts.

BALANCE SHEET PRESENTATION

Plant assets, natural resources, and intangible assets usually are presented in the balance sheet below the sections for current assets and investments. Exhibit 11–2 (page 416) shows how these assets may appear on a balance sheet.

DEMONSTRATION PROBLEM FOR REVIEW

Rochelle Company has an office copier that originally cost $10,250 and that has an $800 expected salvage value at the end of an estimated seven-year useful life. Straight-line depreciation on the machine has been recorded for five years; the last depreciation entry was made at the end of the fifth year. Two months into the sixth year, Rochelle disposes of the copier.

REQUIRED

(a) Prepare the journal entry to record depreciation expense to the date of disposal.

(b) Prepare journal entries to record the machine's disposal in the following unrelated situations:

(1) Sale of the machine for cash at its book value.

(2) Sale of the machine for $3,000 cash.

(3) Sale of the machine for $5,000 cash.

[8]Present values are discussed in Appendix A to Chapter 17.

EXHIBIT 11–2
Balance Sheet Presentation of Plant Assets, Natural Resources, and Intangible Assets (in Thousands of Dollars)

Plant Assets		
Land		$ 800
Buildings	$4,600	
Less: Accumulated Depreciation	1,200	3,400
Fixtures	$ 90	
Less: Accumulated Depreciation	20	70
Equipment	$1,400	
Less: Accumulated Depreciation	300	1,100
Total Plant Assets		$5,370
Natural Resources		
Timberland	$ 500	
Less: Accumulated Depletion	200	$ 300
Coal Deposit	$ 900	
Less: Accumulated Depletion	150	750
Total Natural Resources		$1,050
Intangible Assets (cost less amortization to date)		
Patents		$ 200
Goodwill		500
Organization Costs		100
Total Intangible Assets		$ 800

(4) Exchange of the machine for a new office copier costing $13,000. The trade-in allowance received for the old copier is $4,200. The $8,800 balance is paid in cash. Follow generally accepted accounting principles in recording this transaction.

(5) Destruction of the machine by flood. Unfortunately, Rochelle does not carry flood insurance.

SOLUTION TO DEMONSTRATION PROBLEM

(a)	Depreciation Expense	225	
	Accumulated Depreciation		225
	To record depreciation expense for two months.		

Annual depreciation: $\frac{\$10,250 - \$800}{7} = \$1,350$

Two months' depreciation: $\$1,350 \times \frac{2}{12} = \$225$

(b) (1)	Cash		3,275	
	Accumulated Depreciation		6,975	
	Office Equipment			10,250
	To record sale of machine for book value.			
	Cost	$10,250		
	Accumulated depreciation:			
	5 years × $1,350 = $6,750			
	2 months 225	6,975		
	Book value	$ 3,275		
(2)	Cash		3,000	
	Loss on Sale of Plant Assets		275	
	Accumulated Depreciation		6,975	
	Office Equipment			10,250
	To record sale of machine for $3,000.			
(3)	Cash		5,000	
	Accumulated Depreciation		6,975	
	Office Equipment			10,250
	Gain on Sale of Plant Assets			1,725
	To record sale of machine for $5,000.			
(4)	Office Equipment (new)		12,075	
	Accumulated Depreciation		6,975	
	Office Equipment (old)			10,250
	Cash			8,800
	To record trade of office copiers.			
(5)	Flood Loss		3,275	
	Accumulated Depreciation		6,975	
	Office Equipment			10,250
	To record flood loss to machine.			

KEY POINTS TO REMEMBER

(1) When a firm disposes of a plant asset, depreciation must be recorded on the asset up to the disposal date.

(2) Gains and losses on plant asset dispositions are determined by comparing the assets' book values to their sales proceeds. Gains are not recognized on exchanges of similar productive assets, although losses on such exchanges are recognized.

(3) Depletion is the allocation of a natural resource's cost to the resource units as they are mined, cut, or otherwise extracted from their source.

(4) The units-of-production depreciation method may be appropriate for equipment used exclusively in the mining and extracting of natural resources.

(5) Amortization is the periodic write-off to expense of an intangible asset's cost over the asset's useful life or 40 years, whichever is shorter.

(6) Intangible assets and natural resources are initially measured at their cost.

(7) Research and development costs related to a firm's products and its production processes are expensed as incurred.

(8) Goodwill reflects a firm's ability to generate above-normal earnings. Goodwill may be shown in the accounts only when it has been purchased.

SELF-TEST QUESTIONS
(Answers are at the end of this chapter.)

1. On the first day of the current year, Blakely Company sold equipment for less than its book value. Which of the following is part of the journal entry to record the sale?
(a) A debit to Equipment.
(b) A credit to Accumulated Depreciation.
(c) A credit to Gain on Sale of Plant Assets.
(d) A debit to Loss on Sale of Plant Assets.

2. Wilde Company maintains factory equipment control accounts (asset and accumulated depreciation accounts) in its general ledger, supported by a factory equipment subsidiary ledger. The annual depreciation expense on a particular piece of equipment is determined by reference to the:
(a) Factory equipment asset control account in the general ledger.
(b) Factory equipment accumulated depreciation control account in the general ledger.
(c) Factory equipment subsidiary ledger.
(d) General journal entry recording total factory equipment depreciation expense for the year.

3. Accounting for the periodic depletion of natural resources is similar to which depreciation method?
(a) Straight line.
(b) Units of production.
(c) Sum of the years' digits.
(d) Double declining balance.

4. Certain costs related to a firm's products and its production processes must be expensed when incurred. These costs are:
(a) Research and development costs.
(b) Computer software production costs.
(c) Costs of forming the business (organization costs).
(d) Legal costs to obtain a patent for a new product.

5. The value derived from a firm's ability to earn more than a normal rate of return on its specific, identifiable net assets is called:
(a) A franchise.
(b) Goodwill.
(c) A patent.
(d) Organization costs.

QUESTIONS

11–1 Identify three ways that a firm may dispose of a plant asset.

11–2 What factors determine the gain or loss on the sale of a plant asset?

11–3 Under what condition does a firm show neither a gain nor a loss from (a) the sale of a plant asset and (b) the retirement of a plant asset?

11–4 Talbot Company depreciates a piece of equipment $360 per year on a straight-line basis. After the last depreciation entry on December 31, 19X4, the equipment's book value is $2,300. On July 31, 19X5, the equipment is sold for $2,700 cash. What is the gain (or loss) on the sale of the equipment?

11–5 Blough, Inc., exchanged a used microcomputer with an $800 book value and $500 cash for office furniture having a cash selling price of $1,600. At what amount should Blough record the office furniture? What is the gain (or loss) on the exchange of assets?

11–6 Assume a company exchanged a used microcomputer with an $800 book value and $500 cash for a new microcomputer having a cash selling price of $1,600. At what amount should the company record the new microcomputer? What is the gain (or loss) on the exchange of assets?

11–7 How is the amount of loss determined when an uninsured plant asset is destroyed by flood?

11–8 Cisco Company has a Buildings subsidiary ledger. Identify the general ledger control accounts which are supported by this subsidiary ledger.

11–9 Ziegler, Inc., has a Furniture and Fixtures subsidiary ledger. When Ziegler purchases furniture, should the purchase be reflected in the general ledger? The subsidiary ledger?

11–10 Define *depletion*. The total depletion charge for a period may not all be expensed in the same period. Explain.

11–11 Lyal Company installed a conveyor system that cost $48,000. The system can only be used in the excavation of gravel at a particular site. Lyal expects to excavate gravel at the site for ten years. Over how many years should the conveyor be depreciated if its physical life is estimated at (a) eight years and (b) twelve years?

11–12 Why is computing the depletion of natural resources similar to computing units-of-production depreciation?

11–13 List and briefly explain the nature of six different types of intangible assets.

11–14 How should a firm account for research and development costs related to its products and production processes?

11–15 Which costs of developing and producing computer software for sale or lease are to be capitalized as an intangible asset?

11–16 Urban Company purchased for $6,500 computer software that is designed to process the firm's payroll, bill customers, and process customer payments. The software should be useful without significant modification for five years. What is the proper accounting for the software's cost?

11–17 What is the maximum amortization period for an intangible asset?

11–18 Briefly describe two methods for estimating the goodwill amount for a firm that is generating above-average earnings.

11–19 What is the difference between an operating lease and a capital lease?

EXERCISES

Sale of plant asset

11–20 Becker Company has a machine that originally cost $48,000. Depreciation has been recorded for five years using the straight-line method, with a $3,000 estimated salvage value at the end of an expected nine-year life. After recording depreciation at the end of the fifth year, Becker sells the machine. Prepare the journal entry to record the machine's sale for
(a) $29,000 cash.
(b) $23,000 cash.
(c) $19,000 cash.

Disposal of plant asset

11–21 On January 2, 19X1, Gammon, Inc., purchased a floor maintenance machine costing $3,500. Gammon estimates the machine's useful life at seven years with no salvage value. Straight-line depreciation is recorded each year on December 31. Prepare the journal entry to record the machine's disposal in the following situations:
(a) The machine is scrapped on December 31, 19X7. Assume 19X7 depreciation has been recorded.
(b) The machine is scrapped on June 30, 19X6. Prepare an entry to update depreciation before recording the machine's disposal.
(c) The machine is traded in on a lawn tractor (a dissimilar asset) on December 31, 19X5. The tractor's cash selling price is $2,100. Gammon's trade-in allowance is $1,400, and it pays the remaining $700 in cash. Assume 19X5 depreciation has been recorded.

Disposal of plant asset

11–22 Refer to Exercise 11–21. Assume Gammon, Inc., had estimated a $350 salvage value for the floor maintenance machine, and all other data remain the same. Prepare the journal entry to record the machine's disposal in the three situations described in Exercise 11–21.

Exchange of plant asset

11–23 Holden Company exchanges used equipment costing $50,000 (on which $35,000 of depreciation has accumulated) for similar new equipment. The new equipment's cash price, with no trade-in, is $60,000.
(a) Following generally accepted accounting principles, prepare the journal entry to record Holden's trade-in transaction when
   (1) The equipment's trade-in allowance is $12,000, and the balance is paid in cash.
   (2) The equipment's trade-in allowance is $16,000, and the balance is paid in cash.
(b) Following income tax guidelines, prepare the journal entry to record Holden's trade-in transaction when
   (1) The equipment's trade-in allowance is $12,000, and the balance is paid in cash.
   (2) The equipment's trade-in allowance is $16,000, and the balance is paid in cash.

Exchange of plant asset

11–24 Assume Caldwell Company trades a used machine for a new machine with a cash price of $28,000. The old machine originally cost $22,000 and has $16,000 of accumulated depreciation. The seller allows $7,500 as a trade-in for the old machine; Caldwell pays the balance in cash. Following generally accepted accounting principles, prepare the journal entry to record Caldwell's trade-in transaction assuming

(a) The machines are dissimilar plant assets.
(b) The machines are similar plant assets.

Destruction of plant asset

11–25 A storage building owned by Noble Company was destroyed by flood exactly eight years after its purchase. The building, purchased for $250,000, had an estimated 20-year useful life and a $20,000 salvage value. Depreciation was up to date when the building was destroyed. Prepare the journal entry to record the destruction of the building assuming

(a) The building was not insured.
(b) The building was insured, and Noble expects a $165,000 insurance settlement.
(c) The building was insured, and Noble expects a $150,000 insurance settlement.

Computation of depletion and depreciation

11–26 Cooper Copper Company recently acquired a parcel of land containing an estimated 800,000 tons of commercial grade copper ore. Cooper paid $7,100,000 for the land and acquired extraction equipment at a cost of $920,000. Although the equipment will be worthless when the ore is depleted, Cooper estimates that the land can be sold for $500,000 after the mining operations are completed.

(a) Compute the proper depletion charge for a period during which 90,000 tons of ore are extracted and sold.
(b) Compute the proper depreciation expense on the extraction equipment, using the units-of-production method, for a period during which 90,000 tons of ore are extracted and sold.

Computation and recording of amortization expense

11–27 For each of the following unrelated situations, calculate the annual amortization expense and present a general journal entry to record the expense. Assume contra accounts are not used for accumulated amortization.

(a) A two-year-old patent was purchased for $600,000. The patent will probably be commercially exploitable for another eight years.
(b) Certain sales counter fixtures, costing $78,000, were constructed and permanently installed in a building leased from another firm. The physical life of the counters was an estimated 20 years. When the counters were installed, the operating lease had 12 years to run and contained no provision for the removal of the fixtures.
(c) A trademark is carried at a cost of $92,000, which represents the out-of-court settlement paid to another firm that has agreed to refrain from using or claiming the trademark or one similar to it. The trademark has an indefinite life.
(d) A patent was acquired on a device designed by a production worker. Although the cost of the patent to date consisted of $30,600 in legal fees for handling the patent application, the patent should be commercially valuable during its entire legal life and is currently worth approximately $255,000.
(e) A franchise granting exclusive distribution rights for a new solar water heater within a four-state area for three years was obtained at a cost of

$42,000. Satisfactory sales performance over the three years permits renewal of the franchise for another three years (at an additional cost determined at renewal).

Goodwill estimation

11–28 Green Company, which is for sale, has identifiable net assets with a fair value of $8,000,000 and no recorded goodwill. Green's annual net income in recent years has averaged $920,000 in an industry which considers 10% a normal rate of return on net assets.

(a) Compute Green's above-normal earnings.
(b) Estimate Green's goodwill amount by capitalizing the above-normal earnings at the normal rate of return on net assets.
(c) How much will the goodwill estimate from part (b) change if the excess earnings are capitalized at 15%?

PROBLEMS

Disposals of plant asset

11–29 Bayside Company has a used executive charter plane that originally cost $590,000. Straight-line depreciation on the plane has been recorded for six years, with a $50,000 expected salvage value at the end of its estimated eight-year useful life. The last depreciation entry was made at the end of the sixth year. Eight months into the seventh year, Bayside disposes of the plane.

REQUIRED

Prepare journal entries to record

(a) Depreciation expense to the date of disposal.
(b) Sale of the plane for cash at its book value.
(c) Sale of the plane for $155,000 cash.
(d) Sale of the plane for $132,000 cash.
(e) Exchange of the plane for a new aircraft costing $630,000. The trade-in allowance received is $165,000, and the balance is paid in cash. Follow generally accepted accounting principles in recording this transaction.
(f) Destruction of the plane in a fire. Bayside expects a $125,000 insurance settlement.
(g) Exchange of the plane for a new yacht costing $630,000. The trade-in allowance received is $165,000, and the balance is paid in cash.

Exchange of plant assets

11–30 On July 1, 19X1, Ruhl Construction Company purchased a small bulldozer for $12,400. Ruhl estimates a six-year useful life and a $1,000 salvage value for the bulldozer. On October 1, 19X1, the company purchased a flatbed truck for $10,000. Ruhl estimates the truck's useful life at seven years and its salvage value at $900. Ruhl uses straight-line depreciation for all plant assets and records depreciation on December 31 each year.

On March 31, 19X6, Ruhl traded in the truck for a new truck. The manufacturer's "sticker" price on the new truck was $13,500, but the dealer's cash price was $13,000. After the dealer deducted the allowance for the old truck, Ruhl paid $9,500 cash for the new truck. Ruhl estimates the new truck will last five years and have a $1,000 salvage value.

On June 30, 19X6, Ruhl exchanged the bulldozer for a new bulldozer with a cash price of $15,000. Ruhl's trade-in allowance for the old bulldozer was $4,000, and the company paid $11,000 cash. The new bulldozer's estimated useful life is six years; its estimated salvage value is $1,300.

REQUIRED

Following generally accepted accounting principles, prepare journal entries to record the following events in 19X6:

Mar. 31	Update depreciation on the truck.
31	Exchange of trucks.
June 30	Update depreciation on the bulldozer.
30	Exchange of bulldozers.
Dec. 31	Depreciation for 19X6 on new truck and new bulldozer.

Depletion accounting

11–31 Pitz Gravel, Inc., has just purchased a site containing an estimated 2,500,000 tons of high-grade aggregate rock. Pitz makes the following expenditures before starting production:

Purchase price of property	$1,120,000
Legal fees to acquire title and secure proper zoning for operations	8,000
Removal of overburden and grading for drainage	42,000
Construction of on-site crushing, washing, and loading facilities	315,000

Once the rock deposits are no longer commercially valuable, Pitz estimates the land will sell for $120,000. Certain parts of the on-site crushing, washing, and loading facilities have an estimated salvage value of $15,000 when operations are terminated.

REQUIRED

(a) Compute the total depletion charge for the first year, during which 250,000 tons of rock are extracted from the quarry.

(b) Compute the amount of depreciation on the crushing, washing, and loading facilities during the first year, in which 250,000 tons of rock are extracted. Use the units-of-production depreciation method.

(c) Compute the cost of a 25,000-ton inventory of rock at the end of the first year for which all extraction and processing costs except depletion and depreciation of crushing, washing, and loading facilities average $0.70 per ton.

(d) At the beginning of the second year, Pitz estimates that only 1,500,000 tons of rock remain in the quarry. Compute the revised (1) depletion per ton of rock and (2) depreciation per ton of rock.

Accounting for intangible assets

11–32 Woodstock Company owns several retail outlets. In 19X1, it expands operations and enters into the following transactions:

Jan. 2	Signed an eight-year operating lease for additional retail space for an annual rent of $28,800. Woodstock pays the first and last years' rent in advance on this date. (Hint: Debit the first year's rent to Prepaid Rent.)
3	Paid $10,000 to contractor for installation of new oak floor in leased facility. The oak floor's life is an estimated 50 years with no salvage value.
3	Purchased new cash register for $4,980. The cash register initially will be used in the leased outlet, but may eventually replace a cash register at

another location. The cash register's estimated useful life is 14 years with a $500 salvage value.

REQUIRED
(a) Prepare general journal entries to record these transactions.
(b) Prepare the necessary adjusting entries on December 31, 19X1, for these transactions. Woodstock makes adjusting entries once a year. Woodstock uses straight-line depreciation and amortization but does not use contra accounts when amortizing intangible assets.

Accounting for plant and intangible assets

11–33 Selected 19X6 transactions and events for the Raycon Company are given below:

Jan. 2	Paid $17,000 for a four-year franchise to distribute a product line locally.
Mar. 31	Discovered a computer was stolen from the accountant's office. Raycon carries no theft insurance. The computer cost $9,960 when purchased on January 2, 19X3, and was being depreciated over six years with a $600 salvage value. Straight-line depreciation was last recorded on December 31, 19X5.
Apr. 1	Entered into a nine-year operating lease for additional warehouse space. Paid in advance the final month's rent of $1,500 when the lease was signed.
June 30	Discarded office equipment and realized no salvage value. A $500 salvage value, after a six-year useful life, had been estimated when the equipment was acquired for $5,900 on July 1, 19X0. Straight-line depreciation was last recorded on December 31, 19X5.
Aug. 1	Paid a $2,500 cash bonus to employee for designing and developing a new product.
Sept. 1	Paid a $9,000 legal services fee to obtain a new product patent, which was granted today. Raycon estimates the patent will provide effective protection from competitors for ten years.
Oct. 1	Constructed storage bins at a cost of $7,650 in the warehouse space leased April 1. The physical life of the storage bins is an estimated 15 years. The lease contains no provision for the removal of the bins; the lessor takes control of the bins at the end of the lease.
Nov. 1	Exchanged a used forklift truck for a similar new truck. The used truck cost $6,700 and had accumulated depreciation of $5,600 (through October 31, 19X6). The new truck's cash price was $8,000. Raycon's trade-in allowance was $1,400, and the company paid $6,600 cash. Raycon estimates a ten-year useful life and an $800 salvage value for the new truck.

REQUIRED
(a) Prepare general journal entries to record these transactions.
(b) Prepare the December 31, 19X6, general journal entries to record the proper amounts of depreciation and amortization expense for assets acquired during the year. Raycon uses straight-line depreciation and amortization but does not use contra accounts when amortizing intangible assets.

Preparation of balance sheet

11–34 Kraft Company's December 31, 19X4, post-closing trial balance contains the following normal balances:

Cash	$ 3,000
Accounts Payable	6,000
Stone Quarry	175,000
Building	200,000
Notes Payable (long term)	375,000
T. Kraft, Capital	362,000
Accumulated Depreciation—Equipment	89,000
Leasehold	4,000
Accumulated Depletion—Stone Quarry	40,000
Land	25,000
Accounts Receivable	8,000
Timberland	320,000
Accumulated Depreciation—Building	60,000
Wages Payable	2,000
Patent (net of amortization)	20,000
Accumulated Depletion—Timberland	96,000
Notes Payable (short term)	65,000
Inventory	90,000
Equipment	250,000

REQUIRED
Prepare a December 31, 19X4, classified balance sheet for Kraft Company.

ALTERNATE PROBLEMS

Disposals of plant asset

11–29A Breslin Company has a used delivery truck that originally cost $10,300. Straight-line depreciation on the truck has been recorded for three years, with a $700 expected salvage value at the end of its estimated six-year useful life. The last depreciation entry was made at the end of the third year. Three months into the fourth year, Breslin disposes of the truck.

REQUIRED
Prepare journal entries to record
(a) Depreciation expense to the date of disposal.
(b) Sale of the truck for cash at its book value.
(c) Sale of the truck for $6,000 cash.
(d) Sale of the truck for $4,600 cash.
(e) Exchange of the truck for a new truck costing $14,200. The trade-in allowance received is $4,800, and the balance is paid in cash. Follow generally accepted accounting principles in recording this transaction.
(f) Theft of the truck. Breslin carries no insurance for theft.
(g) Exchange of the truck for golf carts costing $14,200 for the company golf course. The trade-in allowance received is $5,300, and the balance is paid in cash.

Exchange of plant assets

11–30A On April 1, 19X1, Dohm Excavators, Inc., purchased a tractor for $23,600. Dohm estimates a nine-year useful life and a $2,000 salvage value for the tractor. On September 1, 19X1, the company paid $30,000 for a new trenching machine. Dohm estimates the machine's useful life at five years and its salvage value at $1,500. Dohm uses straight-line depreciation for all plant assets and records depreciation on December 31 each year.

On June 30, 19X6, Dohm traded in the tractor for a new tractor with a cash price of $29,000. The dealer allowed a trade-in value of $9,000 for the old tractor, and Dohm paid the remaining $20,000 in cash. Dohm estimates the new tractor will last seven years and have a $1,000 salvage value.

On August 31, 19X6, Dohm exchanged the trenching machine for a new trenching machine with a cash price of $37,000. Dohm's trade-in allowance for the old trenching machine was $2,500, and the company paid $34,500 cash. The new machine's estimated useful life is six years; its estimated salvage value is $2,700.

REQUIRED

Following generally accepted accounting principles, prepare journal entries to record the following events in 19X6:

June 30	Update depreciation on the tractor.
30	Exchange of tractors.
Aug. 31	Update depreciation on the trenching machine.
31	Exchange of trenching machines.
Dec. 31	Depreciation for 19X6 on new tractor and new trenching machine.

Depletion accounting

11–31A Central Mining Company has just purchased a site containing an estimated 1,800,000 tons of coal. Central makes the following expenditures before starting operations:

Cost of land survey	$ 18,000
Purchase price of property	1,375,000
Legal fees to acquire title and secure proper zoning for operations	17,000
Construction of on-site conveyance and loading facilities	420,000

After all the coal has been extracted, Central expects to sell the property for $150,000 and certain parts of the conveyance and loading facilities for $42,000.

REQUIRED

(a) Compute the total depletion charge for the first year, during which 200,000 tons of coal are extracted from the mine.

(b) Compute the amount of depreciation on the conveyance and loading facilities during the first year, in which 200,000 tons of coal are extracted. Use the units-of-production depreciation method.

(c) Compute the cost of a 30,000-ton inventory of coal at the end of the first year for which all extraction and processing costs except depletion and depreciation of conveyance and loading facilities average $2.15 per ton.

(d) At the beginning of the second year, Central estimates that only 1,400,000 tons of coal remain underground. Compute the revised (1) depletion per ton of coal and (2) depreciation per ton of coal.

Accounting for intangible assets

11–33A During the first few days of 19X2, York Company began business and entered into the following transactions:

(1) Paid $8,500 in attorney's fees and other costs related to the organization of the company.
(2) Purchased an existing patent on a product for $75,000. The patent's legal protection and useful life cover 12 more years.
(3) Entered into a six-year operating lease for additional office space. Paid in advance the final month's rent of $1,800 when the lease was signed.
(4) Paid $5,400 to have recessed lighting installed in the leased office space. The lighting is estimated to last 20 years with no salvage value.
(5) Paid $130,000 for a 20-year franchise to distribute a product line in a three-state region.
(6) Spent $10,000 on the initial research for a promising new product to complement the patented product.
(7) Purchased a computer software package to aid the controller's financial planning and budgeting activities. The software cost $5,600, should be useful without significant modification for four years, and has no salvage value.

REQUIRED

(a) Prepare general journal entries to record these transactions.
(b) Prepare the December 31, 19X2, general journal entries to record the proper amounts of amortization expense for the year. Organization costs are amortized over five years. York uses straight-line amortization but does not use contra accounts when amortizing intangible assets.

Preparation of balance sheet

11–34A Menard Company's December 31, 19X5, post-closing trial balance contains the following normal account balances:

Interest Payable	$ 25,000
Accumulated Depreciation—Equipment	80,000
Inventory	125,000
Organization Costs (net of amortization)	20,000
Copper Deposit	750,000
Notes Payable (short term)	100,000
Cash	5,000
Accumulated Depletion—Coal Deposit	150,000
Building	250,000
Accounts Receivable	15,000
Patent (net of amortization)	60,000
Equipment	320,000
C. Menard, Capital	737,000
Accumulated Depreciation—Building	50,000
Accounts Payable	18,000
Accumulated Depletion—Copper Deposit	280,000
Land	195,000
Notes Payable (long term)	900,000
Coal Deposit	600,000

REQUIRED

Prepare a December 31, 19X5, classified balance sheet for Menard Company.

BUSINESS DECISION PROBLEM

Keith Flynn wants to buy Lamb Company from Sara Lamb. His first offer was rejected, and he seeks your advice as he prepares another offer. Your discussions with Flynn and an analysis of related data disclose the following:

(1) Flynn's first offer of $1,200,000 was equal to the fair value of Lamb Company's identifiable net assets. Flynn and Lamb agree this amount represents the fair value of these net assets.
(2) Lamb rejected the first offer because she believes her company has exceptionally good supplier, customer, and employee relationships. These attributes do not appear on the balance sheet, but they are a component of the company's overall value and should be reflected in the purchase price.
(3) Flynn recognizes Lamb Company's favorable relationships. However, he is uncertain how long they will last when Lamb leaves the company after the sale.
(4) Flynn is willing to incorporate a goodwill amount in his offer and accepts a "capitalization of excess earnings" approach to estimating goodwill. In light of his uncertainty about the long-run continuation of superior earnings, however, the capitalization rate must be twice the average rate of return for the industry.
(5) The industry's average rate of return on identifiable net assets is 14%.
(6) Over the past several years, Lamb Company's net income has averaged $280,000.

REQUIRED

Estimate a goodwill amount for Lamb Company, and recommend a purchase price that Keith Flynn should offer Sara Lamb.

ANSWERS TO SELF-TEST QUESTIONS

1. (d) 2. (c) 3. (b) 4. (a) 5. (b)

12

Current Liabilities and Payroll Accounting

Chapter Objectives

- Define and illustrate the most common types of current and contingent liabilities.
- Explain and illustrate the deductions made in computing net pay and the items included in employers' payroll taxes.
- Describe and illustrate the records required in payroll accounting.

Owe money to be paid at Easter, and Lent will seem short.

ITALIAN PROVERB

Liabilities, one of the three elements in the accounting equation, generally represent a firm's obligations to nonowners. Total liabilities are divided into two subcategories—current liabilities and long-term liabilities. In this chapter, we focus on current liabilities, and because several liabilities are associated with a firm's payroll, we will examine payroll accounting procedures and requirements in some depth.

THE NATURE OF LIABILITIES

Liabilities are obligations resulting from past transactions that require the firm to pay money, provide goods, or perform services in the future. The existence of a past transaction is an important element in the definition of liabilities. For example, a purchase commitment is actually an agreement between a buyer and a seller to enter into a *future* transaction. The performance of the seller that will create the obligation on the part of the buyer is, at this point, a future transaction; hence, a purchase commitment is not a liability. Another example is a company's long-term salary contract with an executive. When the agreement is signed, each party is committed to perform in the future—the executive to render services and the company to pay for those services. The company does not record a liability when the contract is signed, because at this point the executive has not yet rendered any services.

Although they involve definite future cash payments, the foregoing examples are not reported as liabilities because they are related to future transactions. However, significant purchase commitments and executive compensation commitments should be disclosed in footnotes to the balance sheet.

In general, items shown as liabilities are often not legally due and payable on the balance sheet date. For example, the routine accrual of wages expense incurred but not paid during the period results in a credit balance account titled Wages Payable. In most cases, accrued wages are not legally due until several days after the balance sheet date. In the case of other accrued expenses—such as property taxes and executive bonuses—payment may not be legally due until months after the balance sheet date. Bonds payable, although shown as liabilities, may not be actually payable for several decades. These items are all reported as liabilities, however, because they are obligations resulting from past transactions that will be settled as the business continues to operate.

The determination of liabilities is basic to accounting properly for a firm's operations. For example, if a liability is omitted, then either an asset or an expense has been omitted also. If expense is involved, then income and owners' equity are misstated as well. Thus, the balance sheet or the income statement, or both, may be affected if liabilities are not reported correctly.

Most liabilities are satisfied by the eventual remittance of cash. Some may require a firm to furnish goods—for instance, a publisher obligated to provide issues of a magazine to customers who have subscribed in advance. Other liabilities may be obligations to provide services, for example, product warranties and maintenance contracts that accompany a new appliance or automobile.

Definition of Current Liabilities

For many years, current liabilities were considered obligations to be paid during the coming year—a simple and useful rule. The rule was subsequently made more flexible and broader in scope. The present version designates current liabilities as all obligations that will require within the coming year or the operating cycle, whichever is longer, (1) the use of existing current assets or (2) the creation of other current liabilities. We contrast the two versions of the rule by noting, for example, that a one-year note payable satisfied by the issuance of another short-term note is a current liability only under the later version of the rule. Also, the newer version has significant effects on firms in industries (for example, distilling and lumber) with operating cycles longer than one year.

Obligations that do not meet these guidelines are long-term liabilities. Two examples are mortgage notes payable and bonds payable, which we examine in Chapter 17.

Measurement of Current Liabilities

Generally speaking, current liabilities should be measured and shown in the balance sheet at the money amount necessary to satisfy the obligation. Of course, when future provision of services or goods is involved, the related dollar amount is only an estimate of the costs. The liability for product warranties, for example, may have to be estimated. Interest included in the face amount of a note payable is subtracted from the face amount when presenting the liability in the balance sheet. For example, if a company discounts its own note at the bank, the Discount on Notes Payable arising from this transaction is a contra account to the Notes Payable account.

EXAMPLES OF CURRENT LIABILITIES

In this section, we review the common types of current liabilities. Although not exhaustive, these concepts should enable you to look deeper into the accounting problems and techniques involved.

Trade Accounts and Notes Payable

In a balance sheet listing of current liabilities, amounts due to short-term creditors on open accounts or notes payable are commonly shown first. Most of the accounting procedures for accounts and notes payable are fairly routine and have been discussed in previous chapters. However, we should carefully account for transactions that occur shortly before and after the end of the accounting period. At the end of the period, recently received inventory items must be reflected as accounts payable, if unpaid, and as purchases of the period. Likewise, items that the company owns and for which a payable has been recorded must be included in inventory whether or not the items have been received. In other words, we need a proper "cut-off" of purchases, payables, and inventory for valid income determination and presentation of financial position.

Dividends Payable

Ordinary dividends are distributions of corporate earnings to stockholders. We discuss many of the accounting problems related to dividends in Chapter 16. Because the corporate board of directors determines the timing and amounts of dividends, they do not accrue as does interest expense. Instead, dividends are shown as liabilities only on formal declaration. Once declared, however, dividends are binding obligations of the corporation. Dividends are current liabilities because they are almost always paid within several weeks of the time they are declared.

Portions of Long-term Debt

The repayment of many long-term obligations is a series of installments over several years. To report liabilities involving installments properly, we should show the principal amount of the installments due within one year (or the operating cycle, if longer) as a current liability.

Sales and Excise Taxes

Many products and services are subject to sales and excise taxes. The laws governing these taxes usually require the retail (or selling) firm to collect the tax at the time of sale and to remit the collections periodically to the appropriate taxing agency. Assume that a particular product selling for $1,000 is subject to a 4% state sales tax and a 10% federal excise tax. Each tax should be figured on the basic sales price only. We record the above sale as follows:

Accounts Receivable (or Cash)	1,140	
Sales		1,000
Sales Tax Payable		40
Excise Tax Payable		100
To record sales and related taxes.		

Recording this transaction as a $1,140 sale is incorrect, because this overstates revenue and may lead to the omission of the liabilities for the taxes collected. The selling firm periodically completes a tax reporting form and remits the period's tax collections with it. The tax liability accounts are then debited and Cash is credited.

As an expedient, some firms record sales at the gross amount, including taxes collected. Then, to convert this type of revenue figure to actual sales, we divide the transaction total of $1,140 by 1.14 to yield $1,000 as the basic sales price and $140 as the total tax.

Estimated or Accrued Liabilities

Estimated or accrued liabilities are often referred to as *accrued expenses*. Generally they are the credits offsetting a series of debits to various expense accounts that are necessary for matching periodic revenue and expenses. Examples are the accrual of incurred (but unpaid) product warranty expense, various taxes, and vacation pay.

PRODUCT WARRANTIES Many firms guarantee their products for a period of time after the sale. Proper matching of revenue and expenses requires that the estimated costs of providing these warranties be recognized as an expense of the period of sale rather than of a later period when the warranty costs may actually be paid.

Let us suppose that a firm sells a product for $300 per unit, which includes a 30-day warranty against defects. Past experience indicates that 3% of the units will prove defective and that the average repair cost is $40 per defective unit. Furthermore, during a particular month, product sales were $240,000, and 13 of the units sold in this month were defective and were repaired during the month. Using this information, we calculate the accrued liability for product warranties at the end of the month as follows:

Number of units sold ($240,000/$300)	800
Rate of defective units	× 0.03
Total units expected to fail	24
Less: Units failed in month of sale	13
Units expected to fail in the remainder of the warranty period	11
Average repair cost per unit	× $ 40
Estimated liability for product warranty provision at end of period	$440

This accrued liability would be recorded at the end of the period of sale as

Product Warranty Expense	440	
Estimated Liability for Product Warranty		440
To record estimated warranty expense.		

When a unit fails in a future period, the repair costs will be recorded by debiting the accrued liability, Estimated Liability for Product Warranty, and crediting Cash, Supplies, and so forth.

PROPERTY TAXES Property taxes are a primary source of revenue for city and county governments. The property taxes paid by business firms are, to some extent, the price for the many governmental services from which the firms benefit. Thus, property taxes are considered an operating expense that applies pro rata to each operating period.

Although procedures vary widely, property taxes are usually assessed annually. A typical sequence involves

(1) Determination of the tax rate by relating the total revenue needed to the total value of property taxed.

(2) Assessment of specific amounts of taxes against specific property parcels—at this time, the taxes are usually liens against the property.

(3) Payment of taxes, usually in one or two installments.

Taxes may be assessed and paid after or before the tax year to which they relate. For example, if property taxes are assessed during the fiscal year to which the taxes relate, firms must accrue an estimated amount of property tax expense (and the related liability) until they know their actual tax liability. To illustrate, let us assume Willetts Company, which ends its accounting year on December 31, is located in a city whose fiscal year runs from July 1 to June 30. City taxes are assessed on October 1 (for the fiscal year started the preceding July 1) and are paid by November 15. Willetts Company estimates in July that its property taxes for the next year will be $18,000. At the end of July, August, and September, the following entry would reflect the estimated monthly property taxes ($18,000/12 = $1,500):

Property Tax Expense	1,500	
Estimated Property Taxes Payable		1,500
To record estimated property tax expense.		

On October 1, Willetts Company receives a $19,008 property tax bill from the city. Willetts' estimate for July–September is too low by $252 ($19,008/12 = $1,584; $1,584 − $1,500 = $84; $84 × 3 months = $252). The $252 difference may be handled as an increase in the property taxes for October. The entry to record the October taxes would then be:

Property Tax Expense ($1,584 + $252)	1,836	
Estimated Property Taxes Payable		1,836
To record estimated property tax expense.		

The Estimated Property Taxes Payable account has a balance of $6,336 after the October entry. The entry on November 15 to record the property tax payment in full is:

Estimated Property Taxes Payable	6,336	
Prepaid Property Taxes	12,672	
Cash		19,008
To record payment of property taxes.		

The balance in the Prepaid Property Taxes account is amortized to Property Tax Expense from November–June—$1,584 each month.

In contrast with the preceding illustration, if property taxes are assessed and paid before the taxing agency's fiscal year begins, the entire tax payment is initially charged to Prepaid Property Taxes. No estimates are necessary; the prepayment is simply amortized over the year to which the taxes apply.

INCOME TAXES The federal government, most states, and some municipalities levy income taxes against corporations, individuals, estates, and trusts. Sole proprietorships and partnerships are not taxable entities—their owners include the businesses' income on their personal tax returns. In the United States, income is generally reported annually on one or more income tax forms, and taxpayers compute (or assess themselves) the amount of tax due. The tax due is determined in accordance with generally accepted accounting principles, modified by the various tax laws, rulings of the taxing agencies, and many applicable court decisions. Because administration of tax laws is quite complex and many honest differences exist in their interpretation, the final tax liability for certain firms may not be settled until several years after a given tax year. Thus, the liability for income taxes is often an estimated obligation for some period of time.

Because corporations are separate taxable entities, they ordinarily incur a legal obligation for income taxes whenever corporate income is earned. Therefore, corporate financial statements are routinely adjusted for income tax liabilities. This adjustment is often recorded as follows:

Income Tax Expense	XXX	
Income Tax Payable		XXX
To record estimated income tax.		

Income Tax Expense may be included among the operating expenses in the income statement. Alternatively, to highlight the impact of income taxes, some companies derive an intermediate figure in the income statement labeled "income before income taxes." All expenses except income taxes are subtracted from revenue to derive this figure. Income taxes are then subtracted last in the income statement. Income taxes are discussed more fully in Chapter 28.

VACATION PAY Most employees enjoy vacation privileges—typically, at least two weeks per year with regular pay. Depending on the particular agreement, an employee may earn some fraction of his or her annual vacation each payroll period. Other contracts may require a full year's employment before any vacation is given. In the latter case, the proportion of employees who earn annual vacations depends on the employee turnover rate.

Generally, an employer accrues vacation benefit expense if the employees' vacation benefits relate to service already rendered and they vest over time, as long as payment is probable and can be estimated.[1] Assume that a firm provides an annual two-week vacation for employees who have worked 50 weeks and that with the employee turnover rate, 80% of the staff will, in fact, receive vacation benefits. These employees earn the two weeks' vacation pay during the 50 weeks worked each year, or at the rate of 4% (2 weeks vacation/50 weeks worked). The proper accrual of vacation benefits expense for a $10,000 payroll would be

$$\$10{,}000 \times 0.04 \times 0.8 = \$320$$

The appropriate journal entry would be

Vacation Benefits Expense	320	
Estimated Liability for Vacation Benefits		320
To record estimated vacation benefits.		

[1] *Statement of Financial Accounting Standards No. 43*, "Accounting for Compensated Absences" (Stamford, CT: Financial Accounting Standards Board, 1980).

When the vacation benefits are paid, the amount would be recorded as follows:

Estimated Liability for Vacation Benefits	XXX	
Cash		XXX
To record payment of vacation benefits.		

This treatment reflects the annual vacation expense in the appropriate periods and recognizes throughout the year the accrued liability for vacation benefits.

CONTINGENT LIABILITIES

A contingent liability is an obligation that *may* develop out of an existing situation. Whether or not the obligation develops depends on the occurrence of a future event.

If the future event will probably occur and the amount of the liability can be reasonably estimated, the liability should be recorded in the accounts.[2] The estimated liability for product warranty discussed earlier in the chapter is an example of this situation. Our analysis assumed that customers were likely to make claims under warranties for goods they had purchased and that a reasonable estimate of the amount of warranty obligation could be made.

When the future event will likely not occur or the amount of the liability cannot be reasonably estimated, contingent liabilities are not recorded in the accounts. They should, when significant, be disclosed in the financial statements either in a parenthetical note in the body of the statements or as a footnote to the balance sheet. Some common examples of contingent liabilities are given below.

Notes receivable discounted As explained in Chapter 8, firms that discount (sell to others) notes receivable with recourse are contingently liable for their payment should the original maker fail to honor the note. We noted that this contingent liability is usually disclosed in a footnote to the balance sheet.

Credit guarantees To accommodate important but less financially secure suppliers or customers, a firm may guarantee the other company's debt by cosigning a note. Until the original debtor satisfies the obligation, the cosigning firm is contingently liable for the debt.

Lawsuits In the course of its operations, a firm may be the defendant in a lawsuit involving potential damage awards. During the time a lawsuit is pending, the firm should disclose in its financial statements the nature of the suit and any potential liability.

Additional income tax assessments Earlier in this chapter, we explained that many aspects of income tax laws and rulings are subject to a significant

[2] *Statement of Financial Accounting Standards No. 5*, "Accounting for Contingencies" (Stamford, CT: Financial Accounting Standards Board, 1975).

degree of interpretation. Consequently, many firms do not know their final income tax liability for a given tax period until the related return has been audited or until the applicable statute of limitations becomes effective. The federal statute of limitations for income taxes is three years. No statute of limitations exists in cases of fraud or failure to file returns. Proposed assessments for additional taxes often are contested in court for extended periods. During this time, the taxpaying firm is contingently liable for the proposed additional tax.

PAYROLL ACCOUNTING

Wages and salaries represent a major element in the cost structure of most businesses. Indeed, the largest single expense incurred by some service businesses may be the compensation paid to employees. As we examine the procedures and requirements associated with accounting for salaries and wages, we see that several different current liabilities are related to a company's payroll expense.

IMPACT OF LEGISLATION ON PAYROLL PROCEDURES

Payroll accounting procedures are influenced significantly by legislation enacted by the federal and state governments. These laws levy taxes based on payroll amounts, establish remittance and reporting requirements for employers, and set up certain minimum standards for wages and hours.

Levy of Taxes

FEDERAL INSURANCE CONTRIBUTIONS ACT In the mid-1930s, the federal government enacted a national Social Security program to provide workers with a continuing source of income during retirement. The program has been expanded several times since then, one example being the 1965 enactment of the Medicare program of hospital and medical insurance for persons 65 years of age and older. Today, in addition to health insurance benefits for eligible people, Social Security provides monthly payments to workers and their dependents when a worker retires, is disabled, or dies.

Monthly benefit payments and hospital insurance protection under Medicare are financed by taxes levied on employees, their employers, and self-employed people. Approximately 9 out of 10 employed persons in the United States currently earn Social Security protection through this process. Medical insurance under Medicare is financed by premiums paid by persons who enroll for this protection and from the general revenue of the federal government. Because we focus on payroll accounting in this chapter, we consider in more detail the financing provided by a tax on employees and their employers.

The Federal Insurance Contributions Act (FICA) establishes the tax levied on *both* employee and employer. A schedule of tax rates and the amount of earnings subject to the tax are amended at intervals. At this writing, the following rate schedule is expected to be used for the next few years:

Calendar Year	FICA Rate
1986–87	7.15%
1988–89	7.51
1990	7.65

The FICA tax applies to wages paid to employees during a calendar year, up to a certain amount per employee. For example, in 1986 the tax is applied to the first $42,000 of an employee's wages. At a 7.15% rate, the maximum tax on any one employee in a year would be 7.15% × $42,000 = $3,003. The amount of earnings subject to the FICA tax is adjusted yearly for changes in the Consumers Price Index. Near the end of each year, the Social Security Administration announces the earnings base for the following year.

The employee's tax is deducted from each paycheck by the employer. The amount of tax levied on the employer and the employee is the same. At a 7.15%

CHALLENGES FOR THE SOCIAL SECURITY SYSTEM

Since its founding over 50 years ago, Social Security has become the most important source of income for most elderly Americans. For example, in 1950, only 20 percent of the people over age 65 received Social Security benefits; today, well over 90 percent do. In 1950, the average monthly benefit, adjusted for inflation, was about $125 in 1980 dollars. In the early 1980s, the average benefit exceeded $300 per month.*

Since its inception, the Social Security system has been financed by payroll taxes, shared equally by employers and employees. The system is essentially a "pay-as-you-go" system, in which the aggregate tax collections from all employers and workers are used to pay benefits as they come due. Thus, Social Security can be viewed as an intergenerational transfer program, since it collects revenues from one generation (that is, workers) and passes them on to another (that is, retirees). At the inception of the program, the payroll tax amounted to 1 percent (2 percent for employer and employee combined) of the first $3,000 of earnings. In 1986, the rate exceeded 7 percent (14 percent combined), and the earnings base was $42,000.

In the past, the system's traditional political and social acceptance has rested on low tax rates and the belief that today's payments would assure tomorrow's benefits. However, in recent years, it has been recognized that the system is in serious financial trouble. Increased benefits, lower birth rates, longer life expectancies, and slower economic growth are some of the important factors that all add up to a vast increase in the number of retired nonworkers being supported by a decreasing proportion of workers. In 1960, for example, there were 20 Social Security beneficiaries for every 100 workers; by 1980, the rate had risen to 31 beneficiaries per 100 contributing workers. According to some estimates, this ratio is expected to rise to a range of 40 to 70 by the middle of the next century.†

The tax increases scheduled for the immediate future will undoubtedly not prove sufficient to

rate, the employer's total tax for a year would equal 0.0715 times the total amount of employees' wages subject to FICA tax during the year. For simplicity in calculations, we use a 7% rate in our illustrations and problems.

FEDERAL UNEMPLOYMENT TAX ACT The Federal Unemployment Tax Act (FUTA) is also part of the federal Social Security program. The states and the national Social Security Administration work together in a joint unemployment insurance program. FUTA raises funds to help finance the administration of the unemployment compensation programs operated by the states. Generally, funds collected under this act are not paid out as unemployment compensation benefits, but are used to pay administrative costs at the federal and state levels. In times of high unemployment, however, the federal government may appropriate funds from its general revenue to provide extended unemployment benefits.

FUTA generates funds by a payroll tax levied only on the employer. At the time of this writing, the rate is 6.2% of the first $7,000 of an employee's wages. However, the employer is entitled to a credit against this tax for unemployment taxes paid to the state. The maximum credit allowed is 5.4% of the first $7,000

---

meet the costs of Social Security as it goes into the next century. Using intermediate estimates, the Social Security Administration has estimated that, under the current structure, combined employer and employee tax rates will need to rise to 16.6 percent of payroll in 2010 and to 25.4 percent in 2030. Certain pessimistic forecasts (based on slower economic growth, lower birth rates, and substantially lower mortality rates) have the combined tax rate going to 21.4 percent, 36.3 percent, and 45.3 percent in 2010, 2030, and 2050, respectively. Even if more modest predictions prevail, there are serious implications for consumer purchasing power and the ability of individuals to save. In addition, higher taxes levied on employers may increase the price of goods and services and have adverse effects on employment and new investment.

Many proposals have been advanced to relieve the impending crises. Some of these, related to the present structure, include postponing eligibility for benefits to an age later than 62 or 65, taxing certain benefits of retirees above stipulated income levels, and curtailing benefit levels. The first two of these proposals are already in the process of implementation. However, many people believe that the structure of the system should be changed. A number of proposals suggest that Social Security should provide only a basic floor of retirement income for virtually all retirees, supplemented by employer pension plans with improved funding and broader coverage, and by personal saving. Many of these proposals call for income tax reform to provide more incentive for savings, such as the incentives in Individual Retirement Plans (IRAs) and Keough plans, which allow the deferral of taxes. There are also proposals to have funding, at least in part, from general tax revenues.

Clearly, Social Security is entering a new era. The combined forces of inflation, slow economic growth, demographic change, and the maturing of the system itself, have brought about the financial crises. The challenge that policy makers face is how to reshape the system so that the costs to the working generation are kept manageable and yet still fulfill the social and economic goal of providing benefits to retirees.[‡]

*Sylvester J. Schieber, *Social Security: Perspectives on Preserving the System* (Washington, D.C.: Employee Benefit Research Institute, 1982), p. xxii.

†Committee of the Committee for Economic Development, *Reforming Retirement Policies* (New York: Committee for Economic Development, 1981), p. 28.

‡Committee of the Committee for Economic Development, p. 29.

of each employee's wages. Often, states set their basic unemployment tax rates at this maximum credit. In these states, the effective FUTA rate on the employer is generally 0.8% (6.2% − 5.4%). In our illustrations and problems, the rates used, unless otherwise stated, are 5.4% for state unemployment tax and 0.8% for the federal unemployment tax.

STATE UNEMPLOYMENT COMPENSATION TAXES Benefit payments to compensate individuals for wages lost during unemployment are handled through unemployment compensation programs administered by each state. Generally, a worker who becomes unemployed through no fault of his or her own, is able to work, and is available for work is eligible for unemployment benefits. The duration and amount of benefits typically depend on the worker's length of employment and average wage during a previous base period.

The funds for unemployment benefits are generated in most states by a payroll tax levied exclusively on *employers*. In a few states, the employee must also contribute. Because of the credit allowed against the FUTA tax, states often establish their unemployment tax rate for new employers at 5.4% of the first $7,000 of wages paid each employee. However, the rate may vary over time according to an employer's experience rating. Employers with records of stable employment may pay less than the basic rate, while employers with irregular employment records may pay more than the basic rate. An employer with a favorable experience rating who pays less than the basic rate is still entitled to the maximum 5.4% credit against the federal unemployment tax.

We should remember that FICA, FUTA, and state unemployment taxes are levied on certain maximum amounts of payroll. Throughout the calendar year, employers must be alert to the fact that a greater amount of each period's wages may no longer be subject to one or more of these taxes. The following schedule indicates the possible divergence between the total payroll for a period and the payroll subject to the FICA and unemployment taxes.

Total payroll	$205,000
Wages subject to FICA tax (In 1986, for example, excludes any wages in excess of $42,000 per employee.)	176,000
Wages subject to FUTA and state unemployment taxes (Excludes any wages in excess of $7,000 per employee.)	59,000

FEDERAL INCOME TAX WITHHOLDING Employers are required to withhold federal income taxes from wages and salaries paid to employees. Current withholding of income taxes facilitates the government's collection of the tax and also eliminates the possible burden on the employee of having to pay a tax on income after the income has been used for other purposes.

The amount of income tax withheld from each employee is based on the amount of the employee's wage or salary, the employee's marital status, and the number of withholding allowances to which the employee is entitled. When first employed, each employee reports his or her marital status, Social Security number, and number of withholding allowances to the employer on an *Employee's*

Withholding Allowance Certificate, also known as *Form W-4*. Employees file new W-4s if withholding allowances or marital status change. Employees are entitled to each of the withholding allowances for which they qualify, including one for the employee, one for his or her spouse, and one for each dependent. Additional allowances may be claimed if the employee is (1) 65 or older, or (2) blind, or if the employee's spouse is (3) 65 or older, or (4) blind. An employee may also claim one or more additional allowances based on expected excessive itemized deductions on his or her annual income tax return.

Employers usually use the government's wage-bracket tables to determine the amount of federal income taxes to withhold from each employee. These tables indicate the amounts to withhold at different wage levels for different numbers of withholding allowances. Exhibit 12–1 illustrates a few lines from a recent wage-bracket table.

Alternatively, employers may use the percentage method, which is especially useful when no wage-bracket tables pertain to the length of the payroll period in question. Both the wage-bracket tables and the percentage method incorporate a graduated system of withholding. That is, the withholding rates increase as the earnings subject to withholding increase.

STATE INCOME TAX WITHHOLDING Most states now have an income tax that is withheld by employers. Payroll procedures for withholding state income taxes are similar to those for withholding federal income taxes.

INCIDENCE OF PAYROLL TAXES Taxes related to payroll amounts may be levied on the employee, the employer, or both. Exhibit 12–2 summarizes the incidence of the various payroll taxes we have just discussed.

EXHIBIT 12–1
Wage-bracket Table

WEEKLY Payroll Period—Employee MARRIED												
And the wages are—		And the number of withholding allowances claimed is—										
At least	But less than	0	1	2	3	4	5	6	7	8	9	10 or more
		The amount of income tax to be withheld shall be—										
$300	$310	$37.10	$33.80	$30.50	$27.30	$24.00	$20.70	$17.50	$14.90	$12.60	$10.30	$ 8.00
310	320	38.80	35.50	32.20	29.00	25.70	22.40	19.20	16.10	13.80	11.50	9.20
320	330	40.50	37.20	33.90	30.70	27.40	24.10	20.90	17.60	15.00	12.70	10.40
330	340	42.20	38.90	35.60	32.40	29.10	25.80	22.60	19.30	16.20	13.90	11.60
340	350	43.90	40.60	37.30	34.10	30.80	27.50	24.30	21.00	17.70	15.10	12.80
350	360	45.60	42.30	39.00	35.80	32.50	29.20	26.00	22.70	19.40	16.30	14.00

EXHIBIT 12–2
Incidence of Taxes Related to Payroll Amounts

Tax	Employer	Employee
Federal Insurance Contributions Act	X	X
Federal Unemployment Tax Act	X	
State Unemployment Compensation Taxes	X	In a few states
Federal Income Tax Withholding		X
State Income Tax Withholding		X

Employee versus Independent Contractor

Salaries and wages paid to employees provide the basis for withholding taxes from employees and levying payroll taxes on the employer. Independent contractors are not subject to withholding and are therefore distinguished from employees. In general, an *employee* performs services subject to the supervision and control of another party known as the employer. The following variables establish the existence of an employer–employee relationship: (1) the employer has the power to discharge the individual worker, (2) the employer sets the work hours for the individual worker, and (3) the employer furnishes a place to work. An *independent contractor,* on the other hand, may also perform services for a business firm, but that firm does not have the legal right to direct and control the methods used by this person. Independent contractors are in business for themselves; examples are certified public accountants, lawyers, and physicians.

Wages are the earnings of employees who are paid on an hourly or piecework basis. A *salary* is the compensation of employees paid on a monthly or annual basis. In practice, however, these terms are used more or less synonymously. Amounts paid to independent contractors are identified as *fees*. For example, the expense account Audit Fees may be charged for the amounts paid to a certified public accountant for audit work and Legal Fees may be charged for payments to a lawyer for legal work.

Remittance and Reporting Requirements

The legislation levying various taxes on payroll amounts also specifies the procedures for remitting these taxes to the government and establishes the reports an employer must file. A sound system of payroll accounting ensures that these payments are made and reports are filed on time.

FICA TAXES AND FEDERAL INCOME TAXES WITHHELD Employer remittance and reporting requirements are the same for both employer's and employees' FICA taxes and federal income taxes withheld, because these taxes are combined for payment and reporting purposes. Generally, remittances are deposited in a Federal Reserve bank or authorized commercial bank. The specific remittance requirements vary depending on the combined dollar amount of the taxes. An employer has three banking days to make a deposit if the unpaid taxes are at least $3,000 by the 3rd, 7th, 11th, 15th, 19th, 22nd, 25th, or last day of the month. At the end of any month, undeposited taxes of $500–$3,000 must be deposited within 15 days. If the undeposited taxes are less than $500 at the end of a calendar quarter, the amount must be deposited within one month (or paid with the employer's quarterly tax return).

Each quarter, employers file an Employer's Quarterly Federal Tax Return, Form 941, with the Internal Revenue Service. On this form, the employer schedules a record of its liability for FICA taxes and withheld income taxes throughout the quarter and reports its deposits of these taxes.

By January 31, an employer must give each employee two copies of *Form W-2, Wage and Tax Statement,* which specifies the employee's total wages paid, the federal income taxes withheld, the wages subject to FICA tax, and the FICA tax withheld for the preceding calendar year. The worker attaches one copy of Form W-2 to his or her federal income tax return. The employer sends a copy of each employee's Form W-2 to the Social Security Administration, which, in turn, provides the Internal Revenue Service with the income tax data that it needs from these forms.

FEDERAL UNEMPLOYMENT INSURANCE TAXES The amount due on federal unemployment insurance taxes must be reviewed quarterly. If undeposited taxes exceed $100 at the end of any of the first three quarters of a year, a deposit must be made in a Federal Reserve bank or authorized commercial bank during the first month after the quarter. If the amount due is $100 or less, no deposit is necessary. By January 31, each employer must file a Form 940, Employer's Annual Federal Unemployment Tax Return, for the preceding year. If the annual tax reported on Form 940, less deposits made, exceeds $100, the entire amount due must be deposited by January 31. If this amount is $100 or less, it may be either deposited or remitted with Form 940.

STATE UNEMPLOYMENT COMPENSATION TAXES The filing and payment requirements for unemployment compensation taxes vary among the states. Often, however, employers must pay the taxes when they file quarterly reports. Some states require payments more frequently, sometimes monthly, if the taxes owed by an employer exceed a preestablished level.

Wages and Hours

FAIR LABOR STANDARDS ACT The Fair Labor Standards Act establishes minimum wage, overtime pay, and equal pay standards for employees covered by the act and sets record-keeping requirements for their employers. The act's coverage has been amended several times since its passage in 1938. Its provisions now extend, with certain exemptions, to employees directly or indirectly engaged in interstate commerce and to domestic service workers. Executive, administrative, and professional employees are exempt from the act's minimum wage and overtime provisions.

At this writing, for example, the minimum wage that an employee must receive in 1986 is $3.35 per hour. Of course, employers and employees may agree to higher wages. Employers often operate under contracts negotiated with their employees' unions that provide more favorable terms to employees than the standards provided by the Fair Labor Standards Act.

A covered employee must be paid an amount equal to at least $1\frac{1}{2}$ times that employee's regular pay rate for every hour beyond 40 that he or she works in a week. The following are some examples of overtime pay computations under this standard; the examples differ by the basic method of compensating the employee.

(1) Jody Green receives \$5.10 per hour as her regular rate of pay. Her overtime rate of pay is \$7.65 (\$5.10 + \$2.55) per hour. This week she worked 44 hours. Her gross earnings this week are \$234.60, computed as (40 hours × \$5.10/hour) + (4 hours × \$7.65/hour).

(2) Jack Tyler is paid on a piece rate basis. His earnings this week, before any overtime compensation, are \$206.40 for 43 hours of work. For overtime pay computations, his regular hourly rate of pay is determined by dividing his weekly earnings on a piece rate basis by the number of hours worked in that week, or \$206.40/43 = \$4.80. For each hour worked over 40 in the week, Tyler is entitled to an overtime premium of \$2.40 ($\frac{1}{2}$ of \$4.80). Therefore, his total earnings this week are \$206.40 + \$7.20 (3 hours × \$2.40) = \$213.60.

The act permits an alternative way to compute overtime for piece rate workers, if agreed upon in advance of the work. This method pays $1\frac{1}{2}$ times the piece rate for each piece produced during overtime hours.

(3) Bill Jantz receives a salary of \$240 for a 40-hour workweek. This week he worked 46 hours. Bill's regular rate of pay is computed at \$6 per hour (\$240/40); his overtime rate of pay is \$6 × $1\frac{1}{2}$, or \$9 per hour. Bill's gross earnings for the current 46-hour week are \$240 + (6 × \$9), or \$294.

Again, we note that employees may negotiate overtime pay rates in excess of the minimum standard illustrated in the preceding discussion. A union contract, for example, may require double the regular pay rate for hours worked on Sundays and holidays.

Under the Fair Labor Standards Act, employers may not discriminate on the basis of sex in the rates paid to men and women employees performing equal work on jobs demanding equal skill, effort, and responsibility and having similar working conditions. The equal pay provisions also provide that employers must eliminate illegal pay differentials by a means other than reducing employee pay rates. The law does permit wage differentials between men and women when due to a job-related factor other than sex, such as a difference based on a bona fide seniority or merit system.

Employers are required under the law to maintain a detailed record of each employee's wage and hours, including the hour and day the employee's workweek begins, the regular hourly rate of pay, the total overtime pay for any week in which more than 40 hours are worked, the deductions from and additions to wages, and the employee's total wages paid each period. The law does not prescribe any particular form for these records. The payroll records maintained in a typical payroll accounting system contain much of this information, which is also needed to comply with other laws and regulations.

OTHER PAYROLL DEDUCTIONS

In addition to FICA taxes, federal income taxes, and perhaps state and local income taxes, other items may be deducted from an employee's gross earnings in arriving at the net *take-home* pay for the period. Each additional deduction must be authorized by the employee; often this is done individually, although in some instances the union contract provides the authorization needed by the employer. Examples of these items are payments for

(1) Union dues.

(2) Premiums on life, accident, hospital, surgical care, or major medical insurance.

(3) Installment loan from employees' credit union.

(4) Advance from employer.

(5) U.S. savings bonds.

(6) Contributions to charitable organizations.

(7) Retirement plan.

NET PAY COMPUTATION FOR INDIVIDUAL EMPLOYEE

To illustrate the computation of an individual employee's net pay for a payroll period, let us assume Donald Bork's regular salary is $320 for a 40-hour workweek. He is married and claims three withholding allowances on Form W-4. He has authorized his employer to deduct $3 per week from his earnings for group hospital insurance and $2 per week as a contribution to the United Way Charity. During the current week, he works 42 hours. Prior to the current week, his gross earnings for the year are $1,328. The applicable FICA tax rate is 7%. The amount paid to Donald Bork is shown in the following summary:

Gross earnings		$344.00
Deductions:		
FICA tax (@ 7%)	$24.08	
Federal income tax withheld	34.10	
Group hospital insurance	3.00	
United Way Charity contribution	2.00	
Total deductions		63.18
Net earnings		$280.82

An explanation of these amounts follows:

(1) Gross earnings—Bork's regular hourly pay rate is $320 ÷ 40 hours, or $8. His overtime pay rate is $1\frac{1}{2} \times \$8$, or $12 per hour. Because Bork worked two hours overtime, his overtime pay is 2 × $12 = $24. His gross pay equals his regular salary plus his overtime pay ($320 + $24 = $344).

(2) FICA tax—Bork's gross earnings to date for the year ($1,672) have not yet exceeded the maximum to which the FICA tax applies. Therefore, the FICA tax on Bork's earnings is 7% × $344 = $24.08.

(3) Federal income tax withheld—We apply the wage-bracket table of Exhibit 12–1 to this illustration. From this table, we see that the income tax withheld from a married employee with three withholding allowances earning wages of at least $340 but less than $350 per week is $34.10.

(4) Group hospital insurance and charitable contribution—Bork has specifically authorized his employer to make these deductions.

PAYROLL RECORDS

The precise nature of an enterprise's payroll records and procedures depends to a great extent on the size of the work force and the degree to which the record keeping is automated. In some form, however, two records are basic to most payroll systems—the payroll register and individual employee earnings records.

The Payroll Register

The **payroll register,** prepared each pay period, lists the company's complete payroll in detail. Each employee's earnings and deductions for the period are contained in the payroll register. Exhibit 12–3 illustrates a typical payroll register for a firm with a small number of employees. The pay period covered by this payroll register is one week.

In Exhibit 12–3, the column immediately after each employee's name shows the total hours worked by that employee during the week. Data on the hours worked are taken from time cards or similar documents maintained for each employee. In this illustration, each employee is paid a regular salary for a 40-hour workweek. The regular salary is shown in the first column of the earnings section of the register. Overtime pay, computed at $1\frac{1}{2}$ times the regular hourly rate (Regular weekly salary ÷ 40), is presented in the next column. The employees' gross earnings appear in the final column in the earnings section.

The 7% FICA tax is deducted from each employee's gross earnings. Because the payroll illustrated is early in the calendar year (the week ended February 4), no employee's earnings have exceeded the maximum amount of wages subject to the FICA tax. As discussed earlier, the federal income tax withheld is based on an employee's earnings, marital status, and number of withholding allowances. In Exhibit 12–3, for example, David Plank's relatively high federal income tax withheld is due to the fact that he is single and claims only one withholding allowance. The deductions for hospital insurance, contributions to charity, and purchases of U.S. savings bonds are specifically authorized by each employee affected by the deductions. The hospital insurance premiums vary with the number of persons covered by the plan.

EXHIBIT 12–3
Payroll Register
For the Week Ended February 4, 19X1

Employee	Total Hours	Earnings			Deductions					Payment		Distribution	
		Regular	Overtime	Gross	FICA Tax	Federal Income Tax	Hospital Insurance	Other (see key)	Total Deductions	Net Earnings	Check No.	Office Salaries	Sales Salaries
Donald Bork	42	320	24	344	24.08	34.10	3.00	(A) 2.00	63.18	280.82	566	344	
Jane Latt	40	210		210	14.70	24.30	2.00	(B) 5.00	46.00	164.00	567		210
Raul Lopez	44	200	30	230	16.10	18.60	3.00		37.70	192.30	568		230
David Plank	40	300		300	21.00	41.90	2.00	(B) 5.00	69.90	230.10	569		300
Myra Smiken	44	280	42	322	22.54	33.90	3.00		59.44	262.56	570		322
Fred Wells	40	180		180	12.60	19.30	2.00	(A) 1.50	35.40	144.60	571	180	
Beth White	40	200		200	14.00	22.40	2.00		38.40	161.60	572	200	
Totals		1,690	96	1,786	125.02	194.50	17.00	13.50	350.02	1,435.98		724	1,062

Key: A—United Way Charity
B—U.S. Savings Bonds

An employee receives an amount equal to gross earnings less total deductions for the pay period. These net earnings are shown in the payment section of the payroll register, along with the number of the check issued by the company in payment of the wages.

In the last two columns of the payroll register, gross earnings are distributed between the office salaries and sales salaries categories. This division permits the total salaries for the period to be recorded in the proper expense accounts.

Recording the Payroll and Related Taxes

For some businesses, the payroll register is a special journal; in these cases the pertinent payroll register information is posted directly to the general ledger. Often, however, the payroll register is the basis for a general journal entry that is then posted to the general ledger. The journal entry to record the weekly payroll shown in Exhibit 12–3 would be

Office Salaries Expense	724.00	
Sales Salaries Expense	1,062.00	
FICA Tax Payable		125.02
Federal Income Tax Withholding Payable		194.50
Hospital Insurance Premiums Payable		17.00
United Way Contributions Payable		3.50
U.S. Savings Bond Deductions Payable		10.00
Payroll Payable		1,435.98
To record payroll for week ended February 4.		

The employer company may, when recording each payroll, also record its payroll tax liabilities. The year-to-date gross earnings for the employees in Exhibit 12–3 have not exceeded the maximum limits for either the FICA or unemployment taxes. The entry to record the employer's taxes for the week's payroll follows:

Payroll Tax Expense	235.75	
FICA Tax Payable (7% × $1,786)		125.02
Federal Unemployment Tax Payable (0.8% × $1,786)		14.29
State Unemployment Tax Payable (5.4% × $1,786)		96.44
To record payroll tax expense for week ended February 4.		

Payment of the Liabilities

The various liabilities established in the entries recording the payroll and the employer's payroll taxes are settled when the employer makes payments to the appropriate parties. The issuance of the employees' payroll checks results in the following entry:

Payroll Payable	1,435.98	
Cash		1,435.98
To pay net payroll for week ended February 4.		

The FICA taxes, federal income taxes withheld, and federal unemployment insurance taxes are remitted to a depository bank in accordance with the remittance requirements discussed earlier. The state unemployment compensation taxes are remitted to the appropriate state agency, according to the state's requirements. The hospital insurance premiums are sent to the company providing the coverage, the United Way contributions are paid to that charitable organization, and the deductions for the purchase of U.S. savings bonds are remitted to the financial institution handling the acquisition of the bonds. If any of these liabilities remain unpaid when financial statements are prepared, they are classified as current liabilities in the balance sheet.

Accrual of Employer Payroll Taxes

Employer payroll taxes are based on employees' salaries and wages. A company that accrues wages and salaries with a year-end adjusting entry should also record the related employer payroll taxes as year-end adjustments. Payroll taxes are properly an expense of the period during which the related salaries and wages were earned, although the employer is *legally* obligated for these taxes in the period the salaries and wages are actually paid. This circumstance, coupled with a possibly immaterial amount of payroll taxes, leads some companies to an alternative procedure: they record the total amount of payroll taxes only in the year the payroll is paid.

Individual Employee Earnings Record

Employers maintain an **individual earnings record** for each employee. This record contains much of the information needed for the employer to comply with the various taxation and reporting requirements established by law. Exhibit 12–4 illustrates Donald Bork's individual earnings record, for the first five weeks of 19X1.

The individual earnings record contains the details on earnings and deductions shown earlier in the payroll register. In addition, the cumulative gross earnings column alerts the employer when an employee's yearly earnings have exceeded the maximum amounts to which the FICA and unemployment taxes apply.

Employers prepare Form W-2—the Wage and Tax Statement sent to every employee each year—from the individual employee earnings records. Although Form W-2 is sent only once and covers an entire year, employers typically provide employees with an earnings statement each pay period, detailing the earnings and deductions for that period. These earnings statements may be a detachable portion of the employee's paycheck or may be enclosed as a separate document with the paycheck.

PAYMENT TO EMPLOYEES

A company with a small number of employees may pay them with checks drawn on the firm's regular bank account. A company with a large number of employees usually establishes a separate bank account to pay the payroll.

EXHIBIT 12–4
Individual Employee Earnings Record

Employee's Name: Donald Bork	Social Security No.: 719-23-4866			Employee No.: 6
Address: 510 Many Lane	Male: X	Single:		Weekly Pay Rate: $320.00
Archer, Florida 32600	Female:	Married: X		Hourly Equivalent: $8.00
Date of Birth: May 6, 1946	Withholding Allowances: 3			
Position: Clerk-Analyst	Date of Employment: June 1, 19X0			
	Date Employment Ended:			

19X1		Earnings			Deductions					Payment		
Period Ended	Total Hours	Regular	Overtime	Gross	FICA Tax	Federal Income Tax	Hospital Insurance	Other: A—United Way B—Savings Bonds	Total Deductions	Net Earnings	Check No.	Cumulative Gross Earnings
Jan. 7	40	320.00		320.00	22.40	30.70	3.00	A2.00	58.10	261.90	412	320.00
Jan. 14	44	320.00	48.00	368.00	25.76	37.50	3.00	A2.00	68.26	299.74	447	688.00
Jan. 21	40	320.00		320.00	22.40	30.70	3.00	A2.00	58.10	261.90	480	1,008.00
Jan. 28	40	320.00		320.00	22.40	30.70	3.00	A2.00	58.10	261.90	525	1,328.00
Feb. 4	42	320.00	24.00	344.00	24.08	34.10	3.00	A2.00	63.18	280.82	566	1,672.00

Payroll Bank Account

A company with a separate payroll bank account draws a check on its regular bank account each pay period in an amount equal to the total net earnings of the employees. This check is deposited in the payroll bank account. Individual payroll checks are then drawn on this account and delivered to the employees. The issuance of the payroll checks reduces to zero the book balance in the payroll bank account.

One advantage of maintaining a separate payroll bank account is that it divides the work between the preparation and issuance of regular company checks and payroll checks. A related advantage is that it simplifies the monthly reconciliation of the regular bank account. The large number of payroll checks, many of which may be outstanding at month-end, are not run through the regular bank account. Of course, the payroll bank account must also be reconciled, but the only reconciling items for this bank account are payroll checks outstanding.

Payment in Cash

Sometimes employees are paid in currency and coin rather than by check. This may happen, for example, if the employees work in a location where it may not be convenient for them to deposit or cash checks. The company prepares and cashes its own checks for the payroll amount. Each employee's pay is delivered to the employee in an envelope. For internal control, and to have evidence of the payment, an employee signs a receipt for the payroll envelope. Often the outside of the envelope contains an itemization of the employee's gross earnings and deductions for the period.

KEY POINTS TO REMEMBER

(1) Liabilities are obligations resulting from past transactions to pay money, provide goods, or perform services in the future.

(2) Current liabilities must be satisfied within the coming year or the operating cycle, whichever is longer. To meet these obligations, a firm must use existing current assets or create other current liabilities.

(3) Failure to accrue liabilities properly will cause a misstatement of financial position and reported income.

(4) A contingent liability is an obligation that depends on the occurrence of a future event. A contingent liability is recorded in the accounts if the future event will probably occur and if the amount of the liability can be reasonably estimated.

(5) Payroll accounting is influenced significantly by several legislative acts. Payroll transactions involve a series of withholdings from the employee's wages and a series of payroll taxes levied against the employer.

(6) A payroll register lists information on the gross earnings and deductions of all employees for each payroll period. Individual employee earnings records contain information on gross earnings and deductions for each employee for all payroll periods during the year.

SELF-TEST QUESTIONS
(Answers are at the end of this chapter.)

1. Which of the following is *not* considered to be a contingent liability?
   (a) Discounted notes receivable.
   (b) Estimated liability for product warranty.
   (c) Credit guarantees.
   (d) Lawsuit.
2. A firm sold merchandise on account for $1,380, which included a 10% excise tax and a 5% sales tax. The entry to record this sale would include
   (a) A debit of $1,200 to Accounts Receivable.
   (b) A debit of $1,587 to Accounts Receivable.
   (c) A credit of $1,200 to Sales.
   (d) A credit of $1,380 to Sales.
3. A firm sells a product for $400 per unit, which includes a 30-day warranty against defects. Experience indicates that 4% of the units will prove defective, requiring an average repair cost of $40 per unit. During the first month of business, product sales were $320,000 and 20 of the units sold were defective and repaired during the month. The accrued liability for product warranties at month-end is
   (a) $800 (b) $480 (c) $1,280 (d) $1,680
4. Which of the following payroll-related taxes does not represent a deduction from the employees' earnings?
   (a) FICA taxes.
   (b) Income taxes.
   (c) Federal unemployment taxes
   (d) All of the above are deductions from employees' earnings.
5. James Sheldon, who is covered by the Fair Labor Standards Act, receives a salary of $360 for a 40-hour workweek. This week he worked 44 hours. Income tax withheld amounts to $47.50. His prior gross earnings for the year were $4,320, and the FICA tax rate is 7%. Sheldon's net pay is
   (a) $337.52 (b) $320.78 (c) $354.26 (d) $341.30

QUESTIONS

12–1 For accounting purposes, how are *liabilities* defined?

12–2 Present a general rule for measuring current liabilities on the balance sheet.

12–3 Define *current liabilities*.

12–4 "Because they are a matter of governmental discretion, property taxes should be recognized as expense in the period in which the assessment becomes a lien against the property involved." Comment on this statement.

12–5 Under what conditions must an employer accrue employees' vacation benefits?

12–6 Define *contingent liabilities*. List three examples of contingent liabilities. When should contingent liabilities be recorded in the accounts?

12–7 On whom is the FICA tax levied? What does the FICA tax finance?

12–8 On whom are the federal and state unemployment insurance taxes levied? What do these taxes finance?

12–9 Why does an employee file a Form W-4, Employee's Withholding Allowance Certificate, with his or her employer?

12–10 What is the difference between an employee and an independent contractor?

12–11 What does Form W-2, Wage and Tax Statement, report? Who receives copies of this form?

12–12 George Walker is employed at $9.50 per hour. Under the Fair Labor Standards Act, how many hours in a week must he work before he is entitled to overtime pay? What is the minimum overtime rate of pay he must receive?

12–13 List at least five examples of deductions from an employee's gross earnings other than FICA taxes and federal income taxes withheld.

12–14 What is a payroll register? How does it differ from an individual employee earnings record?

12–15 If earned but unpaid wages are accrued at year-end, should employer payroll taxes on these wages be accrued at the same time? Explain.

12–16 List two advantages of maintaining a special payroll bank account for the payment of a net payroll.

EXERCISES

Current liabilities in balance sheet

12–17 For each of the following situations, indicate the amount shown as a liability on the balance sheet of Yates, Inc., at December 31, 19X2.

(a) Yates has trade accounts payable of $75,000 for merchandise included in the 19X2 ending inventory.
(b) Yates has agreed to purchase a $24,000 drill press in January 19X3.
(c) During November and December of 19X2, Yates sold products to a firm and guaranteed them against product failure for 90 days. Estimated costs of honoring this provision during 19X3 are $1,200.
(d) On December 15, 19X2, Yates declared a $50,000 cash dividend payable on January 15, 19X3, to stockholders of record on December 31, 19X2.
(e) Yates provides a profit-sharing bonus for its executives equal to 5% of the reported before-tax income for the current year. The estimated income (as defined above) for 19X2 is $360,000.

Excise and sales tax calculations

12–18 Brent Company has just billed a customer for $742.40, an amount that includes a 10% excise tax and a 6% state sales tax.
(a) What amount of revenue is recorded?
(b) Present a general journal entry to record the transaction on the books of Brent Company.

Providing for vacation benefits

12–19 Rider, Inc.'s current vacation policy for its production workers provides four weeks paid vacation at the end of a full year's employment. An analysis of the company's employee turnover rates indicates that approximately 15% of the employees will forfeit their vacation benefits.
(a) Compute the proper provision for estimated vacation benefits for a four-week period in which the total pay earned by the employee group was $264,300.
(b) Present a general journal entry to recognize the above vacation benefits.

Providing for warranty costs

12–20 Universal Company sells an electric timer that carries a 60-day unconditional warranty against product failure. Based on a reliable statistical analysis, Universal knows that between the sale and lapse of the product warranty, 2% of the units sold will require repair at an average cost of $30 per unit. The following data reflect Universal's recent experience.

	October	November	December
Units sold	32,000	28,000	40,000
Known product failures from sales of:			
October	160	320	160
November		80	280
December			180

Calculate and prepare a general journal entry to record properly the estimated liability for product warranties at December 31. Assume that warranty costs of known failures have already been reflected in the records.

Payroll calculations for an employee

12–21 Daniel Lynn is an employee subject to the Fair Labor Standards Act. His regular pay rate is $7.50 per hour, and he is paid overtime at $1\frac{1}{2}$ times his regular pay rate. He worked 44 hours in the current week. His gross earnings prior to the current week are $10,200. He is married and claims four withholding allowances on Form W-4. No deductions other than FICA and federal income taxes are subtracted from his paycheck. Compute the following amounts related to Lynn's current week's wages:
(a) Regular earnings.
(b) Overtime earnings.
(c) FICA taxes (assume 7% rate).
(d) Federal income tax withheld (use wage-bracket table in Exhibit 12–1).
(e) Net earnings.

Recording payroll taxes

12–22 Arrow Company's August payroll register shows total gross earnings of $184,000. Of this amount, $14,000 is not subject to FICA taxes, and $162,000 is above the maximum amount subject to federal and state unemployment taxes. Arrow Company has a favorable employment record, so its state unemployment tax rate is 2%. It is subject to a 7% FICA tax and a 0.8% federal unemployment tax. Prepare the general journal entry to record Arrow Company's payroll tax expense for August.

Payroll calculations for an employee

12–23 Jan Carter is an employee subject to the Fair Labor Standards Act who is paid on a piece rate basis. Her earnings for the current week, before any overtime compensation, are $324 for 45 hours of work. For each hour over 40 worked in a week, she receives an overtime premium of one-half her regular hourly pay rate based on the total hours worked in that week. Her gross earnings prior to the current week were $7,200. She is married and claims one withholding allowance on Form W-4. No deductions other than FICA and federal income taxes are subtracted from her paycheck. Compute the following amounts related to Carter's current week's wages:
(a) Regular hourly pay rate.
(b) Gross earnings.
(c) FICA taxes (assume 7% rate).
(d) Federal income tax withheld (use wage-bracket table in Exhibit 12–1).
(e) Net earnings.

PROBLEMS

Property tax calculations

12–24 Royal Company prepares monthly financial statements and ends its accounting year on December 31. Its headquarters building is located in the city of Wingate. City taxes are assessed on September 1 each year, are paid by October 15, and relate to the city's fiscal year which ends the next June 30 (10 months after assessment). For the city tax year 19X5–19X6, Royal paid $50,000 in property taxes on its headquarters building.

REQUIRED

(a) What amount of property tax expense should be accrued on the financial statements for July 19X6, if property taxes for 19X6–19X7 are an estimated 8% higher than the preceding year?

(b) Assume that the 19X6–19X7 tax bill received on September 1, 19X6, was for $56,400 and that the estimate in part (a) was used through August. What is the proper monthly property tax expense for September 19X6, if the deficiencies in the monthly property tax estimates through August are handled as an increase in the property tax expense for September 19X6?

(c) How does the payment of the tax bill on October 15, 19X6, affect the amount of property tax expense recognized for October?

Recording payroll and payroll taxes

12–25 Torrance Corporation had the following payroll for March 19X1:

Officers' salaries	$24,000
Sales salaries	72,000
Income taxes withheld	21,500
FICA taxes withheld	6,720
Hospital insurance premiums deducted	1,250
United Way contributions deducted	650
Salaries (included above) subject to unemployment taxes	80,000

REQUIRED

Present general journal entries to record:

(a) Accrual of the payroll.

(b) Payment of the net payroll.

(c) Accrual of employer's payroll taxes. (Assume that the FICA tax matches the amount withheld, the federal unemployment tax is 0.8%, and the state unemployment tax is 5.4%.)

(d) Payment of all liabilities related to this payroll. (Assume all are settled at the same time.)

Excise and sales tax calculations

12–26 Ensign Corporation initially records its sales at amounts that include any related excise and sales taxes. During June 19XX, Ensign recorded total sales of $171,200. An analysis of June sales indicated the following:

(1) Three-tenths of sales were subject to both a 10% excise tax and a 5% sales tax.

(2) One-half of sales were subject only to the sales tax.

(3) The balance of sales were for labor charges not subject to either excise or sales tax.

REQUIRED

Calculate the amount of sales revenue for June 19XX, and the related liabilities for excise and sales taxes.

Recording payroll and payroll taxes

12–27 The following data are taken from Rockton Wholesale Company's May 19X5 payroll:

Administrative salaries	$36,000
Sales salaries	54,000
Custodial salaries	8,000
Total payroll	$98,000
Salaries subject to FICA tax	$84,000
Salaries subject to FUTA and state unemployment taxes	12,000
Income taxes withheld from all salaries	21,400

Assume that (1) FICA taxes are 7% each for the employee and the employer and (2) the company is subject to a 2% state unemployment tax (due to a favorable experience rating) and a 0.8% federal unemployment tax on the first $7,000 paid to each employee.

REQUIRED
Record the following in general journal form:
(a) Accrual of the payroll.
(b) Payment of the net payroll.
(c) Accrual of the employer's payroll taxes.
(d) Payment of the above payroll-related liabilities. (Assume all are settled at the same time.)

Preparing payroll register and recording payroll

12–28 The Beaumont Company employs five persons, one of whom receives a $550 salary for a 40-hour week; the other four are paid an hourly rate. All employees receive overtime pay at $1\frac{1}{2}$ times their regular pay rate. Data relating to the payroll for the week ended March 31 are given below:

Employee	Hours Worked	Pay Rate	Gross Earnings to End of Prior Week
Carl Adler	44	$7.00 per hour	$3,920
James Cruz	40	$550 per week	6,600
Amy Moore	46	$8.00 per hour	4,160
Arthur Reed	40	$9.00 per hour	4,680
Mark Wild	40	$6.00 per hour	3,120

Additional Data:
(1) James Cruz's salary is charged to Office Salaries Expense; the gross earnings of the other employees are charged to Sales Salaries Expense.
(2) All salaries and wages are subject to FICA tax; a 7% rate is assumed.
(3) The federal unemployment tax is 0.8%, and the state unemployment tax is 5.4% of the first $7,000 of salaries and wages.
(4) Each employee has a $3.50 per week deduction for group medical insurance.
(5) Assume the federal income tax withheld the last week in March is:

Adler	$33.90
Cruz	67.90
Moore	39.30
Reed	40.70
Wild	20.30

REQUIRED

(a) Prepare the payroll register for the week ended March 31, using the following column headings:

	Earnings			Deductions				
Employee	Regular	Overtime	Gross	FICA Tax	Federal Income Tax	Medical Insurance	Total	Net Earnings

(b) Prepare the general journal entry to record:
   (1) The week's payroll.
   (2) The employer's payroll taxes for the week.
   (3) The payment of the net payroll.

(c) Beaumont Company remits the group medical insurance premiums to the Puritan Insurance Company monthly. Total premiums withheld in March were $72. Prepare the general journal entry to record the monthly remittance of these premiums.

(d) The March 31 balances in the FICA Tax Payable and Federal Income Tax Withholding Payable accounts—after posting the entries from part (b)—are $1,225 and $1,042, respectively. Prepare the general journal entry to record the monthly remittance of these taxes to an authorized commercial bank.

(e) Beaumont Company's total federal unemployment tax for the quarter ended March 31 is $182.20—after posting the entries from part (b). Beaumont Company deposits the taxes quarterly in an authorized commercial bank. Prepare the general journal entry to record this remittance.

(f) The total state unemployment tax for the quarter ended March 31 is $1,228.20—after posting the entries from part (b). Prepare the general journal entry to record the quarterly remittance of this tax.

ALTERNATE PROBLEMS

Property tax calculations

12–24A Rankin Company prepares monthly financial statements and ends its accounting year on December 31. The company owns a factory in the city of Dover, where city taxes are assessed on March 1 each year, are paid by May 1, and relate to the city's fiscal year which ends the next June 30 (four months after assessment). For the city tax year 19X1–19X2, Rankin paid $36,000 in property taxes on its factory.

REQUIRED

(a) What amount of property tax expense should be accrued on the financial statements for July 19X2, if property taxes for 19X2–19X3 are an estimated 10% higher than they were the preceding year?

(b) Assume that the 19X2–19X3 tax bill received on March 1, 19X3, was for $41,400 and that the estimate in part (a) was used through February. What is the proper monthly property tax expense for March 19X3, if the deficiencies in the monthly property tax estimates through February are handled as an increase in the property tax expense for March 19X3?

(c) How does the payment of the tax bill on May 1, 19X3, affect the amount of property tax expense recognized for May?

Recording payroll and payroll taxes

12–25A Waters, Inc., had the following payroll for March 19X8:

Officers' salaries	$28,000
Sales salaries	52,000
Income taxes withheld	18,300
FICA taxes withheld	5.600
Hospital insurance premiums deducted	1,800
Salaries (included above) subject to unemployment taxes	62,000

REQUIRED
Present general journal entries to record:
(a) Accrual of the payroll.
(b) Payment of the net payroll.
(c) Accrual of employer's payroll taxes. (Assume that the FICA tax matches the amount withheld, the federal unemployment tax is 0.8%, and the state unemployment tax is 5.4%.)
(d) Payment of all liabilities related to this payroll. (Assume all are settled at the same time.)

Excise and sales tax calculations

12–26A Harris Corporation initially records its sales at amounts that include any related excise and sales taxes. During May 19XX, Harris recorded total sales of $256,320. An analysis of May sales indicated the following:
(1) Two-tenths of sales were subject to both a 10% excise tax and a 6% sales tax.
(2) Six-tenths of sales were subject only to the sales tax.
(3) The balance of sales were for labor charges not subject to either excise or sales tax.

REQUIRED
Calculate the amount of sales revenue for May 19XX, and the related liabilities for excise and sales taxes.

Recording payroll and payroll taxes

12–27A The following data are taken from Gilbert Plumbing Company's March 19X4 payroll:

Administrative salaries	$21,000
Sales salaries	42,000
Custodial salaries	5,000
Total payroll	$68,000
Salaries subject to FICA tax	$68,000
Salaries subject to FUTA and state unemployment taxes	42,000
Income taxes withheld from all salaries	14,600

Assume that (1) FICA taxes are 7% each for the employee and the employer and (2) the company is subject to a 5.4% state unemployment tax and an 0.8% federal unemployment tax on the first $7,000 paid to each employee.

REQUIRED
Record the following in general journal form:
(a) Accrual of the payroll.

(b) Payment of the net payroll.
(c) Accrual of the employer's payroll taxes.
(d) Payment of the above payroll-related liabilities. (Assume all are settled at the same time.)

Preparing payroll register and recording payroll

12–28A The Dalton Company employs five persons, one of whom receives a $600 salary for a 40-hour week; the other four are paid an hourly rate. All employees receive overtime pay at $1\frac{1}{2}$ times their regular pay rate. Data relating to the payroll for the week ended March 31 are given below:

Employee	Hours Worked	Pay Rate	Gross Earnings to End of Prior Week
Lynn Brown	43	$8.00 per hour	$4,160
David Harding	40	$600 per week	7,200
James Moore	46	$7.20 per hour	3,744
Lyle Sims	42	$7.20 per hour	3,852
Willis Young	40	$9.00 per hour	4,680

Additional Data:
(1) David Harding's salary is charged to Office Salaries Expense; the gross earnings of the other employees are charged to Sales Salaries Expense.
(2) All salaries and wages are subject to FICA tax; a 7% rate is assumed.
(3) The federal unemployment tax is 0.8%, and the state unemployment tax is 5.4% of the first $7,000 of salaries and wages.
(4) Each employee has a $4.00 per week deduction for group medical insurance.
(5) Assume the federal income tax withheld the last week in March is:

Brown	$39.00
Harding	85.20
Moore	35.80
Sims	30.50
Young	44.00

REQUIRED
(a) Prepare the payroll register for the week ended March 31, using the following column headings:

	Earnings			Deductions				
Employee	**Regular**	**Overtime**	**Gross**	**FICA Tax**	**Federal Income Tax**	**Medical Insurance**	**Total**	**Net Earnings**

(b) Prepare the general journal entry to record:
  (1) The week's payroll.
  (2) The employer's payroll taxes for the week.
  (3) The payment of the net payroll.
(c) Dalton Company remits the group medical insurance premiums to the Badger Insurance Company monthly. Total premiums withheld in March were $100. Prepare the general journal entry to record the monthly remittance of these premiums.

(d) The March 31 balances in the FICA Tax Payable and Federal Income Tax Withholding Payable accounts—after posting the entries from part (b)—are $1,187 and $1,166, respectively. Prepare the general journal entry to record the monthly remittance of these taxes to an authorized commercial bank.

(e) Dalton Company's total federal unemployment tax for the quarter ended March 31 is $143.39—after posting the entries from part (b). Prepare the general journal entry to record this remittance.

(f) The total state unemployment tax for the quarter ended March 31 is $967.59—after posting the entries from part (b). Prepare the general journal entry to record the quarterly remittance of this tax.

BUSINESS DECISION PROBLEM

Carley Enterprises manages office buildings in several Midwestern cities. The firm maintains its own janitorial staff for all buildings managed. The firm manages ten buildings in Rock Falls, where it maintains a staff of 40 people, with a total annual payroll of $540,000. All of the staff earn more than $7,000 per year each. Only one employee's salary, a supervisor's, exceeds the maximum amount subject to FICA tax, by the amount of $3,200. The annual nonpayroll costs of the janitorial service are:

Supplies	$42,000
Depreciation on Equipment	24,000
Insurance	18,000
Miscellaneous	4,000
	$88,000

Carley pays a 7% FICA tax on its payroll and is subject to a 5.4% state unemployment tax. Its federal unemployment compensation tax rate is 0.8%. The firm also pays part of the employees' health insurance costs, averaging $56 per employee.

The firm has a high employee turnover rate and has not always kept tenants happy with the janitorial service. President Michael Carley has been approached by Kleenit, Inc., a commercial janitorial service chain, which has submitted a bid of $675,000 annually to provide janitorial service for the ten buildings in Rock Falls. This firm is noted for efficiency and satisfactory service. Carley estimates that hiring an outside firm would save $7,500 annually in bookkeeping costs and costs of contracting with other commercial firms for substitutes for regular help. These costs are not included in the above list of nonpayroll costs.

REQUIRED

Prepare a cost analysis for Carley to help him decide whether to accept the bid of Kleenit, Inc. Assume that unemployment taxes apply to the first $7,000 paid to each employee.

ANSWERS TO SELF-TEST QUESTIONS

1. (b) 2. (c) 3. (b) 4. (c) 5. (a)

13

Accounting Principles and Financial Statement Disclosures

Chapter Objectives

- Provide a framework for understanding the development of generally accepted accounting principles.
- Identify the basic principles underlying accounting theory.
- Discuss the process of revenue recognition and the matching of expenses with revenue.
- Identify and describe the various types of financial statement disclosures.
- Discuss the adjustments used to disclose the impact of inflation on financial statements.

Every why hath a wherefore.

WILLIAM SHAKESPEARE

In Chapter 1, we touched briefly on the role of generally accepted accounting principles as the rules by which financial accounting statements are prepared. The phrase *generally accepted accounting principles* encompasses a wide spectrum of accounting guidelines, ranging from basic concepts and standards to detailed methods and procedures. There are principles covering almost every aspect of financial accounting and reporting. We have already discussed many of the methods and procedures within the domain of generally accepted accounting principles, such as inventory pricing methods and depreciation methods. In this chapter, we focus on the fundamental and pervasive principles of accounting, an understanding of which is indispensable to anyone who uses financial accounting data. We also consider the topic of financial statement disclosures.

HISTORICAL DEVELOPMENT

In contrast to the physical sciences, accounting has no immutable or natural laws, such as the law of gravity. The closest approximation to a law in accounting is probably the use of arithmetic functions and logic. Because no basic natural accounting law exists, accounting principles have developed on the basis of their *usefulness*. Consequently, the growth of accounting is more closely related to experience and practice than to the foundation provided by ultimate law. As such, accounting principles tend to evolve rather than be discovered, to be flexible rather than precise, and to be subject to relative evaluation rather than be ultimate or final.

Conventional accounting comprises a relatively recent body of knowledge. Although the origin of double-entry bookkeeping has been traced back to the fourteenth century, most important accounting developments have occurred in the last century.

The recent rapid development of accounting as an information system is largely explained by the economic history of the last eight to ten decades. This period included (1) the development of giant industrial firms, (2) the existence of large stockholders' groups, (3) the pronounced separation of ownership and management of large corporate firms, (4) the rapid growth of industrial and economic activity, and (5) the expansion of government regulation of industry. These factors helped create the large groups of interested parties who require a constant stream of reliable financial information concerning the economic entities they own, manage, or regulate. This information is meaningful only when prepared according to some agreed-on standards and procedures.

Accounting principles—like common law—originate from problem situations such as changes in the law, tax regulations, new business organizational arrangements, or new financing or ownership techniques. In response to the effect such problems have on financial reports, certain accounting techniques or procedures are tried. Through comparative use and analysis, one or more of these techniques are judged most suitable, obtain substantial authoritative support, and are then considered a generally accepted accounting principle. Organizations such as the Financial Accounting Standards Board (FASB), the American Institute of Certified Public Accountants (AICPA), the Securities and Exchange Commission (SEC), the Internal Revenue Service, and the American Accounting Association—and the literature each publishes—are instrumental in the development of most accounting principles.

The general acceptance of accounting principles is not determined by a formal vote or survey of practicing accountants. An accounting principle must have substantial authoritative support to qualify as generally accepted. References to a particular accounting principle in authoritative accounting literature constitute substantive evidence of its general acceptance.

Pronouncements by the FASB are the most direct evidence of whether or not a specific accounting principle is generally accepted. Organized in 1973, the FASB has issued more than 90 statements dealing with generally accepted accounting principles. Before the creation of the FASB, pronouncements by the AICPA—many of which are still in effect—represented the most authoritative indicators of general acceptance.

During the two decades ending in 1959, the AICPA issued 51 *Accounting Research Bulletins*. These bulletins dealt with a variety of problems and, although they lacked formal legal status, they considerably influenced generally accepted practice. In 1959, the AICPA established the Accounting Principles Board (APB) to issue authoritative *opinions* on problems related to generally accepted accounting principles. Many of the 31 opinions issued during its existence were preceded by considerable research, wide circulation of *exposure drafts*, and partial revisions based on the resulting feedback. These opinions increased in importance in 1964 when the AICPA required that any departure from an opinion be disclosed in a footnote to the financial statements or in the accompanying auditor's report. When the FASB succeeded the APB in 1973, this requirement was extended to cover FASB pronouncements.

CONCEPTUAL FRAMEWORK

The FASB has developed an overall conceptual framework to guide the formulation of specific accounting principles. The conceptual framework is a cohesive set of interrelated objectives and fundamentals for external financial reporting. For business enterprises, the framework consists of (1) financial reporting objectives, (2) qualitative characteristics of accounting information, (3) financial statement elements, and (4) recognition criteria for financial statement items. A recurrent theme throughout the conceptual framework is the importance of providing information that is useful to financial statement readers.

The financial reporting objectives focus primarily on information useful to investors and creditors, who share a common interest in assessing a firm's ability to generate favorable future cash flows. Financial reports should help an investor or creditor predict a firm's future performance or evaluate earlier expectations, or both. Accordingly, financial reports should contain information about a firm's economic resources, obligations, owners' equity, and periodic financial performance.

The conceptual framework also identifies the qualities of accounting information that contribute to decision usefulness. The two primary qualities are **relevance** and **reliability**. Relevant information, of course, contributes to the predictive and evaluative decisions made by investors and creditors. Reliable information contains no bias or material error, and faithfully portrays what it intends to represent.

Financial statement elements are the significant components used to put financial statements together. They include assets, liabilities, owners' equity, investments by owners, distributions to owners, revenue, expenses, gains, losses, and comprehensive income.[1] The conceptual framework identifies and defines these elements, noting that they reflect the economic resources, claims to resources, and events that are relevant to decisions made by investors and creditors.

The recognition criteria specify in broad terms the criteria that must be satisfied before a particular asset, liability, revenue, expense, or the like may be recorded in the accounts. Essentially, the item under consideration must meet the definition of an element and be measurable, and the resultant information about the item should be relevant and reliable.

Various pieces of this conceptual framework were already a part of the accounting discipline before their consideration by the FASB. Integrating the pieces into a cohesive framework is important, however. The FASB's intent is to solve individual accounting issues and formulate specific accounting principles within the context of the conceptual framework. Consequently, accounting principles based on this framework should form a consistent and coherent set of guidelines for financial reporting. The framework was essentially completed in the mid-1980s; it will be several years before its impact may be properly evaluated.

BASIC PRINCIPLES

The accounting principles we consider in this section are among the most important ideas in accounting theory. Though less than exhaustive, the treatment here should provide sufficient background for further accounting studies. The discussion of each principle begins with a brief description.

[1]Comprehensive income includes all changes in owners' equity during a period except investments by or distributions to owners and is a concept not yet achieved in practice. For example, prior period adjustments (discussed in Chapter 16) are not included in the income statement under current accounting principles.

Accounting Entity

Each entity should be accounted for separately.

The most fundamental concept in accounting is the entity. An accounting entity is an economic unit with identifiable boundaries for which accountants accumulate and report financial information. Before accountants can analyze and report activities, they must identify the particular entity (and its boundaries) for which they are accounting. Every financial report specifies the entity in its heading.

Each proprietorship, partnership, and corporation is a separate entity, and separate accounting records should be kept for each unit. In accumulating financial information, we must separate the activities of an accounting entity from the other economic and personal activities of its owners. For example, Matt and Lisa Cook own the Good Cook Inn restaurant as partners. The Good Cook Inn partnership is an accounting entity. Matt Cook is also an attorney whose activities constitute a proprietorship. Therefore, he keeps a set of accounting records for his legal activities separate from Good Cook Inn's records of its business activities. Lisa Cook's activities as a realtor also constitute a proprietorship. She keeps a set of accounting records for her realty activities separate from both the records of Good Cook Inn and of Matt Cook, attorney.

An accounting entity may be a unit other than a proprietorship, partnership, or corporation. Data for two or more corporations may be combined to provide financial reports for a larger economic entity. For example, a parent corporation and its wholly owned subsidiaries (corporations in their own right) may consolidate their individual financial reports into a set of consolidated statements covering the group of corporations. (This process is a topic of Chapter 18.) In contrast, internal reports to corporate management may contain financial data concerning the activities of units as small as a division, a department, a profit center, or a plant. In this type of financial reporting, the entity is the division, the department, the profit center, or the plant.

The entity concept does not negate the legal fact that an all-inclusive legal liability exists in proprietorships and partnerships. In other words, business assets are available to personal creditors, and business creditors may have legal access to both business and personal assets in these noncorporate business organizations.

Accounting Period

Accounting reports relate to specific periods—typically, one year.

The operations of most businesses are virtually continuous except for some changes associated with cyclical time periods, seasons, or dates. Thus, any division of the total life of a business into segments based on annual periods is somewhat artificial. However, the idea of accounting periods is useful. Many taxes are assessed on an annual basis, and comprehensive reports to corporation stockholders are made annually. In addition, many other noneconomic factors tend to consider the year a natural division of time.

For special purposes, accounting reports may cover other periods. For instance, many companies prepare *interim* financial reports for time spans of less than one year, such as quarterly (three months) or even monthly periods.

EXHIBIT 13–1

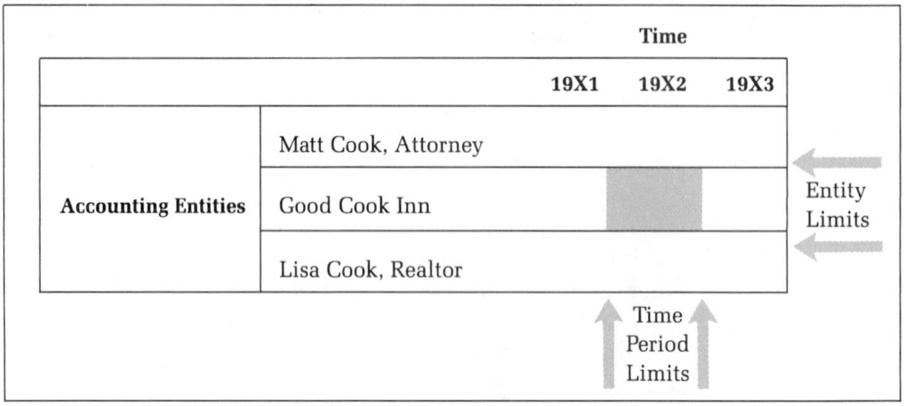

The combined effect of the entity and periodicity concepts is illustrated in Exhibit 13–1, which uses the Good Cook Inn and its two owners as an example. The shaded box isolates Good Cook Inn's activities for 19X2. Proper accounting requires that both the entity and the period be identified in financial reports.

As useful as it is, the idea of artificially "cutting off" the business at the end of a certain period presents many problems. Transactions incurred and consummated entirely within one accounting period present few problems. However, many transactions bridge two or more periods, and their total effect on the entity must often be properly allocated among these periods. Problems of *periodicity* are closely related to the concept of matching revenue and expense, which is developed later in the chapter.

Materiality

Accounting transactions so insignificant that they would not affect the actions of financial statement users are recorded as is most expedient.

Sound accounting procedures require effort and cost money. When the amounts involved are too small to affect the overall picture significantly, the application of theoretically correct accounting procedures is hardly worth its cost. For example, accounting theory asserts that assets acquired and used over several accounting periods should first be recorded as assets, with systematic amounts of depreciation expense recognized in each of the periods in which the assets are used (directly or indirectly) to earn revenue. The principle of *materiality,* however, permits a firm to expense the costs of such items as small tools, pencil sharpeners, and waste paper baskets when acquired because they are "immaterial" in amount. Many firms set dollar limits—such as $25 or $100—below which the costs of all items are expensed.

The concept of materiality is relative—an immaterial amount for General Motors Corporation may be material for smaller companies. Also, the nature of the transaction should be considered. A difference of $1,000 in depreciation expense might be immaterial, but the same discrepancy in cash could be material.

The materiality of an item in a financial statement is usually judged in comparison to a related amount. For example, to determine the effect of the inclusion or omission of an income statement item, we express it as a percentage of net income; a current asset item might be expressed as a percentage of total current assets, and so on. Accounting literature is not precise about what quantitative proportions are deemed material. In specific instances, 5–15% of related amounts have been considered material, but this matter is best subject to judgment. Always remember, however, that although a given series of transactions might *each* be considered immaterial in amount, their aggregate effect could be material in certain circumstances.

Conservatism

Accounting measurements take place in a context of significant uncertainties, and possible errors in measurement of net assets and income should tend toward understatement rather than overstatement.

Accounting determinations are often based on estimates of future events and are therefore subject to a range of optimistic or pessimistic interpretations. In the early 1900s, many abuses were perpetrated on financial statement users who were given overly optimistic measurements of assets and estimates of income. Consequently, the investor was reassured when a company used the "most conservative" accounting procedures. In some instances, banks would write down handsome multistory office buildings, showing them on the balance sheet at a nominal value of $1. The intention was to emphasize the understatement of assets as evidence of conservative accounting and financial strength.

More recently, accountants have recognized that intentional understatement of net assets and income can be as misleading as overly optimistic accounting treatments. For example, stockholders might erroneously decide to sell their stock in a company that grossly understates its income through overly conservative accounting procedures. Also, a conservative treatment in one accounting period may cause the overstatement of reported income for many other periods. For example, the bank that writes its building down to $1 is, in a sense, "overdepreciating" and therefore understating both assets and income for that period. During the building's remaining useful life, the bank's income is overstated because the related building depreciation expense is omitted from the income statements of those periods.

Today, *conservatism* is the accountant's reaction to situations in which significant uncertainties exist about the outcomes of transactions still in progress. In contrast to the intentional understatements of net assets and income, accountants follow conservative accounting procedures when they are unsure of the proper measure to use. For example, if two estimates of future amounts to be received are about equally likely, conservatism requires the less optimistic estimate be used. Thus, possible errors in measuring net assets and income should tend toward understatement rather than overstatement.

Consistency

Unless otherwise disclosed, accounting reports are prepared on a basis consistent with the preceding period.

In many instances, more than one method of applying a generally accepted accounting principle is possible. In other words, two firms that have identical operating situations might each choose a different—but equally acceptable—accounting method and report different amounts for the same types of transactions.

Changes in accounting procedures that lead to different reported values may affect the amount of reported income. Under certain circumstances, a firm could, by design, increase or decrease its reported earnings simply by changing from one generally accepted accounting principle to another that yields different values. This situation justifies the *consistency* principle. Consistency means the same accounting methods are used from one accounting period to the next. Consistency enhances the utility of financial statements when comparative data for a firm are analyzed.

Of course, there are instances when it is appropriate for a firm to change an accounting method. Indeed, progress in improving accounting data almost dictates that some changes will occur. In these cases, financial statement users should know when and to what extent reported earnings result from changes in accounting techniques. In Chapter 16, we discuss how to report the effects of changes in accounting principles.

Objectivity

Whenever possible, accounting entries must be based on objectively determined evidence.

The concept of *objectivity* requires bias-free and verifiable accounting data. Users want accounting data that are not subject to the capricious whim of either management or the accountant who prepares or audits the statements. Consequently, whenever possible, accounting determinations are based on actual invoices, documents, bank statements, and physical counts of items involved.

Not all accounting determinations can be totally objective. Periodic depreciation and estimates of the eventual collectibility of credit sales are examples of relatively subjective factors routinely incorporated into accounting reports. Several accountants required to determine independently the depreciation expense for a given period on an item of special-purpose equipment would probably come up with a range of suggested amounts. We might expect the range to be in some proportion to the degree of subjectivity involved.

Obviously, variations in accounting measurements lead to variations in reported income. Thus, the more subjective accounting records are, the greater variety there may be in reported income. Because highly subjective determinations are not readily verifiable, a user of a subjectively derived accounting report does not know where this particular statement falls in the range of reportable income figures. An even greater disadvantage is that the user has no way of knowing the motives of the individual preparing the statements. Was he or she trying to be "fair" or attempting to minimize or maximize reported income? We have no reliable source of answers to this question. For this reason, accountants—particularly independent auditors—look for objective evidence to support the accounting data in financial reports.

Going Concern **In the absence of evidence to the contrary, a business is assumed to have an indefinite life.**

With few exceptions, business organizations have no anticipated termination date. Most firms operate profitably for indefinite periods and are, in fact, *going concerns*. Firms that do not succeed usually have indications of impending termination for some time before operations actually cease.

The going concern assumption has important implications for accounting procedures. It allows firms to defer costs—such as ending inventories, prepaid expenses and undepreciated asset balances—that will be charged against the revenue of future periods. Furthermore, the going concern concept assumes the use of cost-based accounting measures rather than market-based liquidation values. Firms that expect to continue profitable operations do not ordinarily sell their operating assets; therefore, potential liquidation prices for these assets at the end of an accounting period may not be especially relevant. In this sense, the going concern assumption justifies the use of historical cost as the primary basis for accounting entries.

Measuring Unit **The unit of measure in accounting is the basic unit of money.**

Although other descriptive information is often relevant, money is the common measure for recording accounting transactions. By expressing all assets and equities in terms of money, the accountant creates a common denominator that permits addition and subtraction of all forms of assets and equities and makes possible the preparation of financial statements. Expressing all statement items in money terms also permits the comparison of (1) various elements in the financial statements of a firm, (2) different sets of statements for the same firm, and (3) the statements of two or more firms. This principle also assumes the unit of measure is stable; that is, changes in its general purchasing power are not considered sufficiently important to require adjustments to the basic financial statements.

Historical Cost **Accounting measures are primarily based on historical costs.**

The dollar amounts in account balances represent the accounting measures of the items about which information is collected. Possible sources of these measures are opinions of management, professional appraisals, current market prices, and historical costs. Accountants have experimented with all of these sources at various times, but with few exceptions, they have used historical cost whenever it is available. Most practicing accountants feel that other sources are so subjective that their use should be seriously limited.

We can describe *historical cost* as an item's "historical exchange price." It represents the amount of cash, or its equivalent, paid to acquire an asset or received when a liability is incurred. Most accountants agree that no item has a single ultimate value and that for the millions of exchanges that occur daily, the exchange price probably best indicates the value of an item at the time of the transaction. Usually we do not attempt to reflect subsequent changes in market values for assets and liabilities, so the initial exchange price of an item becomes known as its historical cost.

Historical costs tend to be highly objective because under classical assumptions they are derived in the marketplace by informed, rational, and independent parties. Also, the details of the original transaction can easily be verified by consulting the documents that are customarily executed at the time of exchange (deeds, bills of sale, checks, and mortgages). An overlooked advantage of historical cost measurement is that the data are a natural byproduct of the exchange transaction itself and are therefore available at little additional cost or effort. Relative objectivity may be the primary justification for historical cost-based accounting measures, but their natural availability at negligible cost is also an important factor—especially when the historical cost method is compared with more expensive sources of values such as professional appraisals.

Matching Expenses with Revenue

To the extent feasible, all expenses related to given revenue are matched with and deducted from that revenue for the determination of periodic income.

The income determination process relates, or matches, expenses and revenue in the following ways:

(1) Costs that relate to specific revenue are recognized as expenses whenever the related revenue is recognized. For example, cost of goods sold relates to the specific revenue from the sale of goods. Cost of goods sold is recorded, therefore, in the same accounting period as the sales revenue.

(2) Costs that relate to the revenue of several accounting periods are expensed in a systematic and rational manner throughout these periods. The impact of some assets benefiting several periods cannot be traced to any specific revenue amounts. Instead, the asset's cost is matched with each period's overall revenue through appropriate depreciation and amortization procedures. The depreciation of office equipment illustrates this category of matching.

(3) Costs that relate only to the current period's overall revenue are expensed immediately. Expenditures that benefit only the current accounting period, such as office salaries expense, fit this category.

The proper matching of expenses and revenue is accomplished primarily through the accrual accounting techniques illustrated throughout the text.

Revenue Recognition at Point of Sale

With limited exceptions, revenue is recognized at the point of sale.

At first, this principle may seem obvious. However, modern business operations are often so complicated and so extended that practical questions arise concerning the point at which revenue should be recognized. With the exceptions discussed later in this section, generally accepted accounting principles require the recognition of revenue in the accounting period in which the sale occurs. Moreover, the matching principle (explained above) dictates that we match any related expenses with this revenue in that period. Thus, the combined effect of the two principles requires the recognition of revenue and related expenses in the period of sale.

For services, the sale is deemed to occur when the service is performed. When merchandise is involved, the sale takes place when title to the goods transfers from seller to buyer. In many situations this coincides with the delivery of the merchandise. As a result, accountants usually record revenue when goods are delivered.

To understand the logic of and the exceptions to the principle of recognizing revenue at point of sale, we must consider some underlying factors. Most firms have some sort of cash-to-cash operating cycle, which is diagramed in Exhibit 13–2. In reality, most firms are engaged in many partially overlapping operating cycles represented by the following diagram:

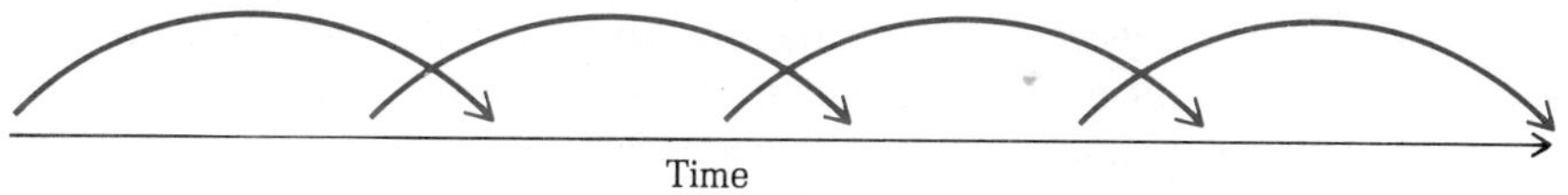

For our purposes, it is sufficient to consider the isolated cycle. In Exhibit 13–2, the firm starts with \$100 cash and then uses the cash to acquire, handle, store, promote, display, and finally sell the inventory. In a cash sale, inventory is immediately converted to \$120 cash. If the sale is made on credit terms, the collection process must be accomplished. The \$20 difference between the cash at the cycle's beginning and at its end, reduced by any applicable noncash expenses, is the income generated by the operating cycle.

EXHIBIT 13–2
Typical Operating Cycle for a Firm

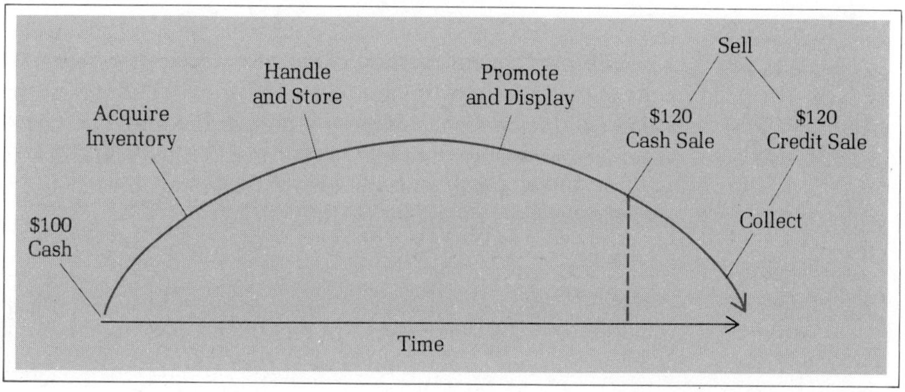

Throughout the cycle, the firm works toward the eventual sale of the goods and collection of the sales price. This cycle is the firm's "earning process" and it should be substantially complete before revenue is recorded. Also, the revenue should be realized before it is recorded in the accounts. Realized means the goods (or services) are exchanged for cash or claims to cash. It is at the point of sale, then, that the two important conditions for revenue recognition are met—at that time the revenue is both (1) **earned** and (2) **realized.**[2]

Other Bases for Revenue Recognition

COLLECTION BASES For selected exceptions, revenue recognition occurs at times other than the point of sale. Methods that delay recognition until cash is collected are **collection basis methods.** These methods usually relate to installment credit sales. A conservative method, known as the **cost recovery method,** considers all cash collections a return of costs until all costs are recovered; the remaining collections are considered gross profit.

A more widely used collection basis method is the **installment method.** The installment method takes its name from the popular sales term for purchases of moderate to large dollar amounts. In effect, the installment method treats each dollar received as part return of cost and part gross profit. The specific proportion of each is determined by the relationship between the cost and the sales price of the merchandise involved. For example, assume that on October 1, 19X7, a refrigerator costing $450 is sold for $600, with installment terms consisting of a 20% down payment and the balance due in 24 equal payments of $20 on the last day of each month. Under the installment basis, because the cost was 75% of the selling price ($450/$600), each dollar collected will be considered 75% return of cost and 25% gross profit. The resulting gross profit during the three years would be recognized as follows:

	19X7		19X8	19X9	
	Down Payment	**Three $20 Payments**	**Twelve $20 Payments**	**Nine $20 Payments**	**Totals**
Total received (100%)	$120	$60	$240	$180	$600
Considered return of cost (75%)	90	45	180	135	450
Considered gross profit (25%)	30	15	60	45	150

The installment method of revenue recognition should be used when firms cannot reasonably estimate the extent of collectibility of the installment receivables. Companies that can reasonably predict and make accruals for future losses should not employ the installment method. Instead, they should recognize revenue at point of sale and match with it an appropriate estimate of uncollectible accounts. With certain limitations, however, these companies may still use the

[2]*Statement of Financial Accounting Concepts No. 5,* "Recognition and Measurement in Financial Statements of Business Enterprises" (Stamford, CT: Financial Accounting Standards Board, 1984).

installment method to recognize some gross profit for income tax purposes (because it may be desirable to delay gross profit recognition for tax purposes).

PERCENTAGE OF COMPLETION Some operations—such as the construction of roads, dams, and large office buildings—take a long time and therefore cover several accounting periods. In such situations, the point-of-sale recognition method (called the completed contract method when referring to long-term contract accounting) does not work very well, because the earnings from several years of construction work may be reported as the income of only the period in which the project was completed and sold. Consequently, another method of revenue recognition, **percentage of completion (POC),** may be used.

The POC method simply allocates the estimated total gross profit on a contract among the several accounting periods involved, in proportion to the estimated percentage of the contract completed each period. To use this method, we must have a reasonably accurate and reliable procedure for estimating periodic progress on the contract. Most often, estimates of the percentage of contract completion are tied to the proportion of total costs incurred.

For example, assume that a dam is to be constructed during a two-year period beginning July 1, 19X1. The contract price is $3 million, and estimated total costs are $2.4 million; thus, estimated gross profit is $600,000. If the total cost incurred in 19X1 is $720,000 (that is, 30% of the estimated total), then $180,000 (or 30% of the estimated total gross profit) is recognized in 19X1. Similarly, if another 50% of the total estimated costs is incurred in 19X2, then 50% of the estimated total gross profit (or $300,000) is recognized in 19X2. Under the POC method, the gross profit is reflected among the three calendar years as follows:

(Dollars in Thousands)

	19X1	**19X2**	**19X3**	**Total**
Cost incurred	$720	$1,200	$480	$2,400
Percent of total costs	30%	50%	20%	100%
Gross profit recognized	$180	$ 300	$120	$ 600

Clearly, in long-term construction, the POC method of revenue recognition more reasonably reflects reported income as an indicator of productive effort than the completed contract basis.

Full Disclosure

All information necessary for the users' understanding of the financial statements must be disclosed.

Accounting's purpose is to provide useful information to various parties interested in a firm's financial performance and position. Often facts or conditions exist that, although not specifically part of the data in the accounts, have considerable influence on the understanding and interpretation of the financial statements. To inform users properly, a firm should disclose this additional information.

In the following section, we expand on this basic principle of full disclosure.

FINANCIAL STATEMENT DISCLOSURES

Disclosures related to financial statements fall into one of three categories: (1) parenthetical disclosures on the face of the financial statements, (2) notes to the financial statements, and (3) supplementary information. Most disclosures amplify or explain information contained in the financial statements. Some disclosures, however, add new kinds of information.

Parenthetical Disclosures

Parenthetical disclosures are placed next to an account title or other descriptive label in the financial statements. Their purpose is to provide succinctly some additional detail about the item. The information disclosed parenthetically could instead be disclosed by a note to the statements. The selection of the particular disclosure technique is at the discretion of individual companies. Because they are presented on the face of the financial statements, parenthetical disclosures probably stand a better chance of being noticed by statement readers than do footnote disclosures.

Several types of parenthetical disclosures follow, illustrated with examples that relate to topics we have discussed in earlier chapters.

(1) A parenthetical disclosure may report contra asset amounts, such as the allowance for uncollectible accounts or accumulated depreciation.

	19X7	**19X6**
Accounts Receivable, less allowances for uncollectible accounts (19X7—$30,000, 19X6—$26,500)	$215,000	$174,000
Plant and Equipment, less accumulated depreciation (19X7—$530,000, 19X6—$450,000)	997,000	892,000

(2) The measurement technique used may be revealed by a parenthetical disclosure.

	19X7	**19X6**
Inventories (at last-in, first-out cost)	$620,000	$710,000
Intangibles (cost less amortization to date)	75,000	80,000

(3) An alternate financial measure for the item reported may be disclosed parenthetically.

	19X7	**19X6**
Short-term Stock Investments, at market (cost, $250,000 at December 31, 19X7, and $600,000 at December 31, 19X6)	$210,000	$525,000
Inventories (at last-in, first-out cost; cost using first-in, first-out would have been: 19X7—$1,200,000, 19X6—$1,000,000)	950,000	800,000

(4) A parenthetical disclosure may report an amount that is not otherwise separately reported, such as the amount of interest capitalized during the year.

	19X7	**19X6**
Interest Expense (net of capitalized amounts of $29,000 and $11,000, respectively)	$187,000	$162,000

(5) Accounts which have been combined and reported as a single figure in the financial statements may be broken down in a parenthetical disclosure.

	19X7	**19X6**
Cash and Cash Equivalents (including short-term investments of $300,000 and $270,000 at December 31, 19X7 and 19X6, respectively)	$540,000	$420,000

Notes to Financial Statements

Although much information is gathered, summarized, and reported in financial statements, the statements alone are limited in their ability to convey a complete picture of a firm's financial status. Notes are added to financial statements to help fill in the gaps. In fact, accountants have given so much attention to financial statement notes in recent years that today it is not unusual for the notes to take up more space than the statements themselves. Notes may cover a wide variety of topics. Typically, they will deal with significant accounting policies, explanations of complex or special transactions, details of reported amounts, commitments, contingencies, segments, quarterly data, and subsequent events.

SIGNIFICANT ACCOUNTING POLICIES Accounting principles contain several instances where alternative procedures are acceptable. For example, there are several acceptable depreciation and inventory pricing methods, revenue on long-term construction contracts may be recognized using either the percentage-of-completion or completed contract method, and revenue from some installment sales may be recognized using collection basis methods. The particular procedures selected obviously affect the financial data presented. Further, unique or complex events may require innovative applications of accounting principles. Knowledge of a firm's specific accounting principles and methods of applying these principles helps users understand the financial statements. Accordingly, these principles and methods are disclosed in a **summary of significant accounting policies.** The summary is either the initial note to the financial statements or immediately precedes the notes. The number of policies listed, of course, will vary from firm to firm, but the policies relating to inventory pricing methods, depreciation methods, and consolidation practices (discussed in Chapter 18) are invariably included.

EXPLANATIONS OF COMPLEX OR SPECIAL TRANSACTIONS The complexity of certain transactions means that not all important aspects are likely to be reflected in the accounts. Financial statement notes, therefore, report the additional relevant details about such transactions. Typical examples include notes discussing financial aspects of pension plans, profit sharing plans, acquisitions of other companies, borrowing agreements, stock option and other incentive plans, and income taxes.

Transactions with related parties are special transactions requiring disclosure in the financial statement notes.[3] Related party transactions include transactions between a firm and its (1) principal owners, (2) members of management, (3) subsidiaries, or (4) affiliates. The transactions may be sales or purchases of property, leases, borrowings or lendings, and the like. These transactions are not arm's length transactions; that is, they are not between independent parties each acting in their own best interests (as is true in most transactions). Because of the relationships between the parties, one party may exert significant influence over the other party and the results may differ from what would occur in an arm's length transaction (for example, the interest rate for funds borrowed may be below the current market rate). A user trying to compare a firm's financial data with that of prior periods or other similar companies will find related party information useful. It may help identify and explain differences in the data.

DETAILS OF REPORTED AMOUNTS Financial statements often summarize several groups of accounts into a single dollar amount. For example, a balance sheet may show as one asset an amount labeled "property, plant, and equipment" or it may list "long-term debt" as a single amount among the liabilities. These aggregated amounts may be sufficient for some financial statement users, but others want more detail about these items. Notes will report this detail, presenting schedules that list the types and amounts of property, plant, and equipment and long-term debt. Other items that may be summarized in the financial statements and detailed in the notes include inventories, other current assets, notes payable, accrued liabilities, owners' equity, and income tax expense.

COMMITMENTS A firm may have contractual arrangements existing at a balance sheet date where both parties to the contract still have acts to perform. If performance under these **commitments** will have a significant financial impact on the firm, the existence and nature of the commitments should be disclosed in the financial statement notes. Examples of commitments reported in footnotes are commitments under operating leases, contracts to purchase materials or equipment, contracts to construct facilities, salary commitments to executives, commitments to retire or redeem stock, and commitments to deliver goods.

CONTINGENCIES We discussed contingent liabilities in Chapter 12. As noted there, if the future event that would turn a contingency into an obligation is not likely to occur, or if the liability amount cannot be reasonably estimated, the contingency is disclosed parenthetically or in a note to the financial statements. Typical contingencies disclosed in notes are lawsuits, possible income tax assessments, credit guarantees, and discounted notes receivable.

[3] *Statement of Financial Accounting Standards No.* 57, "Related Party Disclosures" (Stamford, CT: Financial Accounting Standards Board, 1982).

SEGMENTS Many firms diversify their activities and operate in several different industries. The firms' financial statements combine information from all operations into aggregate amounts. This complicates the users' ability to analyze the statements because the interpretation of financial data is influenced by the industry in which a firm operates. Different industries face different types of risk and have different rates of profitability. In making investment and lending decisions, users evaluate risk and required rates of return. Having financial data available by industry segments is helpful to such evaluations.

The FASB recognizes the usefulness of industry data to investors and lenders. Public companies with significant operations in more than one industry must report certain information by industry segments. Typically, these disclosures are in the financial statement notes. The major disclosures by industry segment are revenue, operating profit or loss, and identifiable assets (the assets used by the segment).

Other types of segment data may also be disclosed. Obviously, operations in different parts of the world are subject to different risks and opportunities for growth. Thus, public firms with significant operations in foreign countries must report selected financial data by foreign geographic area. The data disclosed are revenue, operating profit or loss (or other profitability measure), and identifiable assets. Also, if a firm has export sales or sales to a single customer that are 10% or more of total revenue, the amount of such sales must be separately disclosed.

QUARTERLY DATA Interim financial reports cover periods shorter than one year. Companies that issue interim reports to investors and others generally do so quarterly. These reports provide users with timely information on a firm's progress and are most useful in predicting what the annual financial results will be. The SEC requires certain companies to disclose selected quarterly financial data in their annual reports to stockholders. Included among the notes, the data reported for each quarter include sales, gross profit, net income, and earnings per share. Quarterly data permit users to analyze such things as the seasonal nature of operations, the impact of diversification on quarterly activity, and whether the firm's activities lead or lag general economic trends.

SUBSEQUENT EVENTS If a company issues a large amount of securities or suffers a casualty loss after the balance sheet date, this information should be reported in a note to the readers, even though the situation arose subsequent to the balance sheet date. Firms are responsible for disclosing any significant events that occur between the balance sheet date and the date the financial statements are issued. This guideline recognizes that it takes several weeks for financial statements to be prepared and audited before they are issued. Events occurring during this period that may have a material effect on the firm's operations are certainly of interest to readers and should be disclosed. Other examples of subsequent events requiring disclosure are sales of assets, significant changes in long-term debt, and acquisitions of other companies.

Supplementary Information

Supplementing the financial statements are several additional disclosures—management's financial discussion and analysis of the statements, selected financial data covering a five-to-ten year period, and information on the impact of inflation. These disclosures are either required of certain companies by the SEC or recommended (but not required) by the FASB.

MANAGEMENT'S DISCUSSION AND ANALYSIS Management may increase the usefulness of financial statements by sharing some of their knowledge about the company's financial condition and operations. This is the purpose of the disclosure devoted to management's discussion and analysis. In this supplement to the financial statements, management identifies and comments on events and trends influencing the firm's liquidity, operating results, and financial resources. Management's closeness to the company not only gives them insights unavailable to outsiders, but also may introduce certain biases into the analysis. Nonetheless, management's comments, interpretations, and explanations should contribute to a better understanding of the financial statements.

COMPARATIVE SELECTED FINANCIAL DATA The analysis of financial performance is enhanced if a firm's financial data for several years are available. By analyzing trends over time, the analyst learns much more about a company than is possible from only a single year's data. Year-to-year changes may give clues as to future growth or may highlight areas for concern. Corporate annual reports to stockholders present complete financial statements in comparative form, showing the current year and one or two preceding years. Beyond this, however, the financial statements are supplemented by a summary of selected key financial statistics for a five- or ten-year period. The financial data presented in this historical summary usually include sales, net income, dividends, earnings per share, working capital, and total assets.

INFLATION ACCOUNTING Inflation has an impact on virtually every aspect of economic affairs, including investment decisions, pricing policies, marketing strategies, and salary and wage negotiations. Persons making economic decisions utilize financial data prepared by accountants. Conventional financial statements, however, contain no explicit adjustments for the impact of inflation on the financial data. In response to this, the FASB encourages companies to disclose supplementary information about the effects of changing prices on the firm's financial data.[4]

The supplementary data combine two types of adjustments for changing prices. One, **constant dollar accounting,** adjusts financial data for changes in the general purchasing power of the dollar. The other, **current cost accounting,** reflects the impact of specific price changes on a firm by incorporating current value measurements into the data. We now examine the nature of these adjustments.

[4]For several years the Financial Accounting Standards Board required large, publicly-held companies to disclose this supplementary information. After reviewing the experiences of financial statement users and preparers with such data, the FASB made these disclosures optional in 1987.

Constant dollar accounting The general purchasing power of the dollar is a measure of its ability to buy goods and services. **Price-level changes** are changes in the prevailing exchange ratio between money and goods or services. Whenever a rise in the general level of prices for goods and services occurs, the general purchasing power of the dollar declines; this is **inflation.** In contrast, **deflation** is an increase in the dollar's general purchasing power as the general level of prices declines. Our discussion is in the context of inflation, the prevailing price-level movement of the last several decades.

Price indexes measure price-level changes. A **price index** represents a series of measurements, stated as percentages, indicating the relationship between (a) the weighted average price of a sample of goods and services at various points in time and (b) the weighted average price of a similar sample of goods and services at a common, or base, date.

For example, assume we wish to construct a price index for a single commodity that was priced at $1.60 in December 19X2, $2 in December 19X3, and $2.50 in December 19X4. If we select December 19X3 as our base date, our price index expresses the price of this commodity in December of 19X2, 19X3, and 19X4 as a percentage of its price in December 19X3. The 19X2 price is

21-DIGIT INFLATION

During the period 1979–1981, the United States' annual rate of inflation was in the 10–13% range. This double-digit inflation rate was considered high for the United States, but it was modest in comparison with the inflation rates in several other countries. Some countries, such as Argentina, Brazil, and Israel, had inflation rates exceeding 100% during this period. By 1984, though, Bolivia's annual inflation rate dwarfed these other rates—it was 2,000% and climbing. Bolivia has probably experienced the most out-of-control inflation within the past decade. Yet even its rate pales before the all-time record, noted in the following excerpt.

> No, the famous hyper-inflation of the German mark in 1923 is not the world's record. That distinction is held by Hungary, whose inflation in 1946 was a *thousand* times worse. In 1939, just before World War II, one American dollar bought 3.38 Hungarian pengös. In July 1946, the same dollar was worth 500,000,000,000,000,000,000 (500 million trillion) pengös. Never before—or since—has so much been worth so little.
>
> After the war, rural Hungarians quickly abandoned money in favor of primitive barter, but people in Budapest had to cope with the monetary system. Wages were raised daily, but prices rose by the hour. Shoppers carried their money in large bags, as high-speed presses raced to turn out currency notes in ever larger denominations. Savings evaporated and the moneyed classes were wiped out. The $100,000 worth of pengös one had banked in 1939 weren't worth the trouble it took to withdraw them in 1946. Not when a haircut cost 800 trillion pengös in Budapest, and the average annual income there would buy only $50 worth of merchandise on the black market—the only place where consumer goods could be purchased.*

*From "21-Digit Inflation," Irving Wallace, David Wallechinsky, and Amy Wallace, in "Significa," *Parade* Magazine, October 18, 1981, page 20.

80% ($1.60/$2) of the 19X3 price, and the 19X4 price is 125% ($2.50/$2) of the 19X3 price. The percentage relationship on the base date is, of course, always 100%. The price index for each date is as follows (the percent sign is understood and usually not shown with index numbers):

December 19X2	80
December 19X3	100
December 19X4	125

Prominent examples of price indexes are the Consumer Price Index for All Urban Consumers and the Gross National Product Implicit Price Deflator. The FASB recommends the use of the Consumer Price Index for any general purchasing power adjustments. The monthly calculation of the Consumer Price Index is one advantage it has over the GNP Implicit Price Deflator, which is calculated quarterly.

With index numbers, amounts stated in terms of dollars of general purchasing power at a particular time may be restated in terms of dollars of different purchasing power at another time. We simply multiply the amount to be restated by the following **conversion factor:**

$$\frac{\text{Index You Are Converting TO}}{\text{Index You Are Converting FROM}}$$

For example, suppose we acquired a parcel of land for $5,000 in December 19X3, when the general price index was 100. Suppose also that the general price indexes for various times were as follows:

December 19X2	80
December 19X3	100
December 19X4	125
Average for 19X4	110

We restate the cost of the land in terms of the December 19X4 dollar by multiplying the $5,000 by the conversion factor 125/100 (December 19X4 index/December 19X3 index). The resulting measure is $6,250, the cost of the land stated in dollars of December 19X4 general purchasing power. The cost of the land in terms of the 19X4 average dollar is $5,000 × 110/100 = $5,500. The amounts $5,000, $6,250, and $5,500 each represent the cost of the land, but the cost is expressed in a different unit of measure in each case.

Current market values may also be expressed in different units of general purchasing power. Assume at December 31, 19X4, the current market value of the land is $7,500. This amount exceeds the land's historical cost adjusted for changes in the dollar's general purchasing power to December 31, 19X4 ($6,250), indicating the specific price of this land has increased more than prices in general. The land's current market value is a financial measure taken at December 31, 19X4, so it is stated in terms of the dollar's general purchasing power at that date (price index of 125). As with any dollar amount, we may restate this measure to other units of general purchasing power by using the proper conversion factor. For example, the land's December 31, 19X4, current market value restated to the 19X4 average purchasing power of the dollar is $7,500 × 110/125 = $6,600.

Generally accepted accounting principles use the dollar as a measuring unit and assume it is stable (that is, that no significant general price-level changes occur); therefore, all dollars are considered economically equal. Obviously, some single-year levels of inflation have strained the stable dollar assumption, and certainly, some multiyear periods have invalidated it. A benefit of adjusting for changes in the general purchasing power of the dollar is that better comparisons of financial data through time are achieved.

To illustrate, assume that the average price-level indexes and Company A's sales revenue for 19X2–19X4 are as shown:

	Average Price-level Index	Unadjusted Sales
19X2	75	$1,500,000
19X3	88	1,650,000
19X4	110	1,900,000

Events that occur fairly evenly throughout the year, such as sales, are assumed to be initially stated in dollars of the average purchasing power for the year. The 19X2 unadjusted sales, then, are stated in dollars of 19X2 average purchasing power; 19X3 sales are measured in dollars of 19X3 average purchasing power; and 19X4 sales are stated in dollars of 19X4 average purchasing power.

The unadjusted sales figures indicate a healthy increase in sales. However, if we convert the dollars stated in the average price-level for 19X2, 19X3, and 19X4 to a common unit of general purchasing power—a dollar with the 19X4 average purchasing power—we discover the following sales levels:

	Average Price-level Index	Unadjusted Sales	Conversion Factor	Restated Sales
19X2	75	$1,500,000	110/75	$2,200,000
19X3	88	1,650,000	110/88	2,062,500
19X4	110	1,900,000	110/110	1,900,000

Adjusting the data to a common dollar indicates a decrease in sales activity rather than an increase. During periods of significant inflation, other comparative data, such as net income and earnings per share, may be similarly affected. Putting comparative data in the same unit of general purchasing power, then, may help users to better analyze and interpret the data.

A new item computed from constant dollar adjustments is the **purchasing power gain or loss on net monetary items.** This gain or loss is among the recommended FASB disclosures. Net monetary items are monetary assets less monetary liabilities. Monetary assets include cash and other assets—such as receivables—that represent the right to receive a fixed number of dollars in the future, regardless of price-level changes. Monetary liabilities are obligations to disburse a fixed number of dollars in the future, regardless of price-level changes. Most liabilities are monetary. By their nature, monetary items in a balance sheet are stated in dollars of current purchasing power at the balance sheet date.

Holding monetary items during a period of rising prices creates purchasing power gains and losses on these items. For example, suppose you hold $1,000 cash during a period when the general price level increases from 100 to 125. Obviously, at the end of the period, your $1,000 will buy fewer goods and services than it would at the beginning of the period. This decrease in your ability to buy goods and services as a result of inflation is a *purchasing power loss on cash*. The amount of the loss, stated in end-of-year general purchasing power, is $250, calcuated by multiplying the percentage increase in prices, 25%, by the $1,000 cash you held.

Assume you also had a note payable of $800 outstanding during the time the general price index increased from 100 to 125. As a result of inflation, you owe dollars whose general purchasing power at the end of the period is less than it was at the beginning of the period. The decrease in the general purchasing power of the dollars with which you will settle the liability represents a *purchasing power gain on the note payable*. The amount of the gain, stated in end-of-year general purchasing power, is $200 (25% × $800).

Combining the $250 purchasing power loss on cash and the $200 purchasing power gain on the note payable gives a $50 purchasing power loss on *net* monetary items, stated in year-end general purchasing power. Purchasing power gains and losses have no counterpart in conventional financial statements. They are computed only by making constant dollar adjustments. The net purchasing power gain or loss is one indicator of how well management handled monetary items during a period of inflation or deflation and may, therefore, be useful to financial statement readers.

Current cost accounting Current cost accounting is a system for incorporating current values into the financial data. The current cost of an asset is the estimated cost to acquire a similar asset at current prices. Under a system of current cost accounting, net income is determined by subtracting from revenue the current cost of assets used in the earning process. Assets at year-end are measured at their current cost. Changes in the current cost of an asset are reflected in the period in which the change in value occurs.

A simple example illustrates the basic concepts of current cost accounting. Assume Densmore, Inc., started business on January 1, 19X4, with the following assets:

Cash	$10,000
Inventory (7,500 units @ $10)	75,000
Land	15,000

During 19X4, Densmore, Inc., sold 5,000 inventory units at $16 each and incurred cash operating expenses of $18,000. Densmore's 19X4 historical cost income statement follows:

Historical Cost		
Sales	$80,000	(5,000 units @ $16)
Cost of Goods Sold	$50,000	(5,000 units @ $10)
Operating Expenses	18,000	
Total Expenses	$68,000	
Net Income	$12,000	

Now assume that before any inventory was sold in 19X4, its current cost increased to $11 per unit and remained there until year-end. Densmore's 19X4 income statement using current cost procedures follows:

Current Cost		
Sales	$80,000	
Cost of Goods Sold	$55,000	(5,000 units @ $11)
Operating Expenses	18,000	
Total Expenses	$73,000	
Net Income	$ 7,000	

The $7,000 current cost net income shows earnings after first providing for the replacement of assets used in operations. Expenses are measured at their current costs when incurred. Current cost net income, therefore, indicates the profitability of operations at the company's current level of operating costs. It also represents the maximum dividend the company could pay and still maintain its present level of operations.

Changes in the specific prices of assets held during the year are identified using current cost procedures. To continue our Densmore, Inc., illustration, assume the replacement cost of land increased to $19,000 by year-end. Current cost procedures will show a 19X4 increase of $11,500 in the current cost of inventory and land held during the year, computed as follows:

Inventory: Increase from $10 to $11 on 7,500 units	$ 7,500
Land: Increase from $15,000 to $19,000	4,000
Increase in current cost during 19X4	$11,500

Note the current cost increase includes $5,000 that relates to the inventory units sold during 19X4. The increase in their replacement cost occurred before they were sold so the increase does belong as part of the value change that occurred while Densmore held the assets.

One issue in current cost accounting is whether the changes in the current costs of assets held should be included as part of net income or handled separately. The FASB disclosures contain the latter treatment—the current cost increase or decrease in inventory and plant assets is disclosed as an amount separate from net income.

FASB disclosures The supplementary disclosures recommended by the FASB are the result of several years of experimentation with, and evaluation of, various constant dollar and current cost disclosures. Most of the present disclosures are current cost amounts stated in a constant unit of general purchasing power. It is hoped that this combination encompasses the best aspects of both constant dollar and current cost accounting. Constant dollar adjustments stabilize the purchasing power of the unit of measure and reveal the purchasing power gain or loss on net monetary items, while current cost calculations show the impact of specific price changes during the period. Complete procedures for combining current cost and constant dollar accounting, however, are beyond the scope of this textbook.

The FASB disclosures consist of a five-year summary of selected data as well as a few current year disclosures. All financial data in the five-year summary are in the same unit of general purchasing power (usually the average purchasing power of the dollar for the current year). The five-year summary reports:

(1) Net sales and other operating revenue.

(2) Net income[5] computed using current cost accounting.

(3) Purchasing power gain or loss on net monetary items.

(4) Increase or decrease in the current cost of inventory and property, plant, and equipment.

(5) Year-end net assets on a current cost basis.

(6) Foreign currency translation adjustment on a current cost basis, if applicable.[6]

(7) Income per share on a current cost basis.

(8) Cash dividends declared per common share.

(9) Year-end market price per common share.

(10) The Consumer Price Index for each year.

The current year disclosures include (1) net income computed using current cost accounting, showing certain components not presented in the five-year summary, (2) the purchasing power gain or loss on net monetary items, (3) the increase (or decrease) in the current cost of inventory and property, plant, and equipment, both before and after eliminating the effects of inflation, and (4) the current cost of inventory and property, plant, and equipment at the end of the current year.

Concluding Remarks

The preceding catalogue of parenthetical disclosures, notes, and supplementary information demonstrates the breadth and detail of data that accompanies a set of financial statements. Not all firms classify every disclosure the same way. For example, the inflation accounting disclosure may be among the notes rather than

[5]If a company reports extraordinary items or discontinued operations, then income from continuing operations rather than net income is reported on a current cost basis. We discuss extraordinary items, discontinued operations, and income from continuing operations in Chapter 16.
[6]Foreign currency translation adjustments are discussed in Appendix C.

after the notes, and quarterly data may be after the notes rather than among the notes. The important thing, of course, is to disclose the information. Examples of many of the disclosures we have discussed may be found in the financial report of the Whirlpool Corporation, shown on pages 1110–1123.

To some, the vast and increasing array of financial statement disclosures threatens to turn a wealth of information into an information "overload." Whether there is too much information, of course, depends on the needs and financial sophistication of users. Nonetheless, it is obvious that much may be learned by reading these disclosures.

KEY POINTS TO REMEMBER

(1) Each of the following is an important basic accounting principle:

accounting entity	going concern
accounting period	measuring unit
materiality	historical cost
conservatism	matching expenses with revenue
consistency	point-of-sale revenue recognition
objectivity	full disclosure

(2) The installment method of revenue recognition treats each dollar received as part return of cost and part gross profit.

(3) The percentage-of-completion method recognizes gross profit in proportion to the amount of the total contract completed in each period.

(4) Financial statement disclosures provide additional information about financial performance and position and appear as parenthetical disclosures, notes, or supplementary information.

(5) Inflation accounting disclosures combine constant dollar adjustments and current cost adjustments.

(6) Constant dollar adjustments restate financial data to dollars of the same general purchasing power.

(7) Current cost adjustments reflect operating expenses at their current costs and measure assets at current costs.

SELF-TEST QUESTIONS
(Answers are at the end of this chapter.)

1. Which of the following is not included in the overall conceptual framework for business enterprises?
(a) Financial reporting objectives.
(b) Financial statement elements.
(c) Inflation accounting disclosures.
(d) Qualitative characteristics of accounting information.

2. Plant assets are depreciated over their useful lives. Which basic principle of accounting does this procedure reflect?
(a) Historical cost.
(b) Matching expenses with revenue.
(c) Consistency.
(d) Objectivity.

3. On August 1, 19X5, Perry Company sold a computer costing $3,500 for $5,000. The customer paid 25% down with the balance due in 30 equal monthly payments of $125 starting September 1, 19X5. Using the installment method, how much gross profit is recognized in 19X5?
(a) $525 (b) $1,500 (c) $150 (d) $1,225

4. During 19X5, Switzer Company made interest-free loans totaling $2,500,000 to certain of its officers. The money is used to finance construction of a special facility which will then be leased to Switzer. Switzer discloses this situation in a note to its 19X5 financial statements. This note is an example of a
(a) Contingency disclosure.
(b) Significant accounting policy disclosure.
(c) Related party disclosure.
(d) Subsequent event disclosure.

5. Assume constant dollar adjustments are made. Which of the following items will generate a purchasing power loss if held by a company during an inflationary period?
(a) Accounts payable.
(b) Land.
(c) Wages payable.
(d) Accounts receivable.

QUESTIONS

13–1 How would you determine whether a particular accounting procedure is a generally accepted accounting principle?

13–2 Discuss the origin of accounting principles.

13–3 Why has the FASB developed a conceptual framework?

13–4 Identify two primary qualities of accounting information that contribute to decision usefulness.

13–5 In one sentence, describe each of the following accounting principles:

accounting entity	going concern
accounting period	measuring unit
materiality	historical cost
conservatism	matching expenses with revenue
consistency	point-of-sale revenue recognition
objectivity	full disclosure

13–6 Why is the accounting entity the most fundamental accounting concept?

13–7 Why do accounting principles emphasize historical cost as a basis for measuring assets?

13–8 How do accountants justify using the point of sale for revenue recognition?

13–9 Explain the procedures and justification for using the following methods of revenue recognition: (a) the installment method and (b) the percentage-of-completion method.

13–10 Identify the three categories of financial statement disclosures.

13–11 Emery Air Freight Corporation provides overnight air courier and cargo transportation services. Where in Emery's financial report should you look to determine how they account for aircraft maintenance and repair costs?

13–12 The Times Mirror Company operates principally in six industries: newspaper publishing, newsprint and forest products, book publishing, information services, broadcast television, and cable television. What financial information about these industry activities should be available in the Times Mirror financial report? Where and why is this information disclosed?

13–13 Identify and briefly explain two types of adjustments to financial data to reflect the impact of changing prices.

13–14 Explain how price-level indexes can be used to convert the dollars of one year to those of another year.

13–15 Define *inflation*. What difficulty does inflation cause for financial accounting?

13–16 Define *monetary assets* and *monetary liabilities*. Give examples of each.

13–17 What is a purchasing power loss on net monetary items?

13–18 How is net income computed in a current cost accounting system?

13–19 What disclosures about the current cost of assets are recommended by the FASB?

EXERCISES

Basic principles

13–20 Indicate the basic principle or principles of accounting that underlie each of the following independent situations:

(a) Dr. Fowler is a practicing pediatrician. Over the years, she has accumulated a personal investment portfolio of securities, virtually all of which have been purchased from her earnings as a pediatrician. The investment portfolio is not reflected in the accounting records of her medical practice.

(b) A company purchases a desk tape dispenser for use by the office secretary. The tape dispenser cost $12 and has an estimated useful life of 20 years. The purchase is debited to the Office Supplies Expense account.

(c) A company sells a product that has a two-year warranty covering parts and labor. In the same period that sales are recorded, an estimate of future warranty costs is debited to the Product Warranty Expense account.

(d) A company pays $72,000 for a patent that has an estimated useful life of 12 years and no salvage value. The amount, debited to the Patent account, is amortized over a 12-year period.

(e) A company purchased a parcel of land several years ago for $35,000. The land's estimated current market value is $50,000. The Land account balance is not increased, but remains at $35,000.

(f) A company has a calendar-year accounting period. On January 8, 19X2, a tornado destroyed its largest warehouse, causing a $600,000 loss. This information is reported in a footnote to the 19X1 financial statements.

Revenue recognition

13–21 For each of the following independent situations, determine how much revenue should be reported in the current period and how much should be deferred to a future period. If either the installment method or percentage-of-completion method applies, determine the appropriate gross profit amounts rather than revenue amounts.

(a) Purchased merchandise for $25,000 that will be sold early in the next period for $38,000.
(b) Took a special order for merchandise that is both acquired and delivered to the customer during the next period. The merchandise costs $5,400 and sells for $8,000.
(c) Began work on a long-term construction contract with a price of $900,000. Expected costs total $640,000, of which $96,000 were incurred this period.
(d) Sold undeveloped real estate lots for $80,000 on installment terms. Of the $80,000, 25% was collected during this period. No reasonable estimate of the collectibility of the remaining balances is possible. The cost of the property sold is $48,000.
(e) Accomplished approximately 65% of the work on an order of machinery that will be completed during the first month of the next period and sold for $74,000. Total estimated cost for the machinery when completed is $56,000.

Revenue recognition

13–22 On October 1, 19X2, Hampton Appliance Company sold a combination refrigerator–freezer for $900 on terms of 20% down on the purchase date, and 24 equal monthly payments beginning November 1, 19X2. The appliance cost $540. Compute the amount of gross profit shown in each calendar year involved using the following revenue recognition methods:

(a) The cost recovery method.
(b) The installment method.
(c) The point-of-sale method.

Financial statement notes

13–23 Notes to financial statements present information on significant accounting policies, complex or special transactions, details of reported amounts, commitments, contingencies, segments, quarterly data, and subsequent events. Indicate which type of note disclosure is illustrated by each of the following notes.

(a) The company has an option to purchase eight British Aerospace Jetstream 31 aircraft for an aggregate purchase price of $21,200,000. A refundable $25,000 deposit for all eight aircraft was made in April of the current year. Tentative delivery dates are between the second and fourth quarter of next year.
(b) The company has deferred certain costs related to major accounting and information systems enhancements which are anticipated to benefit future years. Upon completion, the related cost is amortized over a period not exceeding five years.
(c) The company has guaranteed loans and leases of independent distributors approximating $26.8 million as of December 31 of the current year.
(d) Sales to an airline company accounted for approximately 43% of the company's net sales in the current year.
(e) An officer of the company is also a director of a major raw material supplier of the company. The amount of raw material purchases from this supplier approximated $365,000 in the current year.

Constant dollar accounting

13–24 In 19X1, the Piper Company purchased a parcel of land for $40,000 when the general price-level index was 120. By the end of 19X5, the land's current market value was $72,000. General price-level indexes for 19X2–19X5 follow:

December 19X2	132
December 19X3	150
December 19X4	156
December 19X5	180
Average for 19X5	171

(a) Restate the land's cost in terms of the dollar's general purchasing power at (1) December 19X2, (2) December 19X3, (3) December 19X4, (4) December 19X5, and (5) for the year 19X5 (average for 19X5).

(b) Restate the land's December 19X5 market value in terms of the dollar's average purchasing power for 19X5.

Constant dollar accounting

13–25 Moon Corporation has reported sales revenue for the past three years as follows:

19X5	$3,100,000
19X6	4,000,000
19X7	4,900,000

The average general price-level indexes for these three years are as follows: 19X5, 120; 19X6, 150; and 19X7, 180. The price-level index at the end of 19X7 is 198. Prepare a schedule of sales revenue for 19X5–19X7 stated in the general purchasing power of the dollar (a) at the end of 19X7, and (b) for the year 19X7 (average for 19X7).

Purchasing power gain or loss on monetary items

13–26 Listed below are the year-end monetary assets and liabilities of March Company and the general price-level index on the date each account balance was established.

	Balance	Price-level Index
Cash	$40,000	256
Accounts Receivable	70,000	250
Notes Receivable	21,000	300
Accounts Payable	12,300	246
Notes payable	15,000	240

The year-end price index is 320. Assume the balance of each monetary item has not changed since it was established.

(a) Compute the purchasing power gain or loss on each monetary item, stated in terms of the year-end purchasing power of the dollar.

(b) What is the purchasing power gain or loss on net monetary items?

Current cost accounting

13–27 On January 2, 19X5, Cheny Company started business and bought 6,000 inventory items at $60 each. On January 3, the unit purchase price increased to $64 and remained there until year-end. During 19X5, Cheny sold 3,400 of these items (and made no more purchases). If Cheny followed current cost accounting procedures, what would be the amount of (a) the 19X5 cost of goods sold expense, and (b) the increase in the current cost of inventory during 19X5?

PROBLEMS

Basic principles

13–28 The following are certain unrelated accounting situations and the accounting treatment, in general journal form, that has been followed in each firm's records.

(1) Toonin Company mounts a $250,000, year-long advertising campaign on a new national cable television network. The television network required full payment in December at the beginning of the campaign. Accounting treatment is

Advertising Expense	250,000	
Cash		250,000

(2) Because of a local bankruptcy, machinery worth $90,000 was acquired at a "bargain" purchase price of $76,000. Accounting treatment is

Machinery	76,000	
Cash		76,000

(3) Curt Jewell, a consultant operating a sole proprietorship, withdrew $8,000 from the business and purchased securities as a gift to his wife. Accounting treatment is

Investments	8,000	
Cash		8,000

(4) The Steady State Bank, by action of the board of directors, wrote down the book value of its home office building to a nominal amount of $100. The objective was to bolster its customers' confidence in the bank's financial strength by obviously understating bank assets. Accounting treatment is

Retained Earnings	1,199,900	
Buildings		1,199,900

(5) Hayward, Inc., ends its fiscal year on June 30. Financial statements for the year just ended are prepared on July 10. During the July 4 holiday weekend, a fire destroyed most of the inventories of the company. Because the company may have violated local fire regulations, the loss may not be covered by insurance. This possible loss is reflected in the financial statements for the year just ended. Accounting treatment is

Fire Loss	227,000	
Merchandise Inventory		227,000

(6) Blier Company received a firm offer of $65,000 for a parcel of land it owns which cost $49,000 two years ago. The offer was refused, but the indicated gain was recorded in the accounts. Accounting treatment is

Land	16,000	
Income from Increase in Value of Land		16,000

(7) Because of an increase in the general level of prices, Darrow, Inc., determined that the recorded depreciation expense of its store building was understated by approximately $5,500. The company reflects this in its accounts. Accounting treatment is

Depreciation Expense	5,500	
Accumulated Depreciation		5,500

REQUIRED

(a) In each of the given situations, indicate which generally accepted accounting principles apply and whether they have been used appropriately.

(b) If you decide the accounting treatment is not generally accepted, discuss the effect of the departure on the balance sheet and the income statement.

Accrual versus cash basis accounting

13–29 The following events relate to the sale of a machine by Grogan Equipment Company in April 19X1:

March — Grogan received a sales order accompanied by a $1,000 deposit from the customer, as is usual when special devices are custom ordered for the machine. The machine was acquired on account from a local supplier for $5,900. Purchase terms required net cash payment in May.

April — The machine was modified at an additional cash cost of $700 to Grogan. The machine was sold for a total price of $9,200 (including the deposit) on terms that required the customer to pay an additional $5,000 at the time of sale and the balance before the end of May.

May — Grogan paid its supplier for the machine. The customer made the final payment on the machine.

REQUIRED

(a) Calculate the amount of gross profit (or loss) that would be reported each month if a cash basis accounting treatment (cash receipts less cash disbursements) were used.

(b) Prepare journal entries to reflect properly the accrual accounting treatment of these transactions. (*Hint:* For the first March transaction, credit the liability account Customer Deposit.) What is each month's reported gross profit? Assume a perpetual inventory method.

(c) Comment briefly on the usefulness of each method in parts (a) and (b) to a manager concerned with evaluating the effect of these transactions on the firm's operations.

Installment method

13–30 On December 1, 19X7, Excalibur Company initiated a policy of permitting customers to buy goods on an installment basis. Sales of $240,000 were made during December on an installment basis. Terms were 30% down on the date of purchase, and 20 equal monthly payments beginning January 2, 19X8. The cost of goods sold on the installment basis was $132,000. Excalibur Company elects the installment method to report the gross profit from these sales on its income tax return. On its books, the company recognizes the revenue and related cost of goods sold when the sale is made.

REQUIRED

(a) Comment on why Excalibur Company would elect the installment method to report the gross profit on its income tax return.

(b) Assuming all installment payments are collected as scheduled, how much gross profit from these December installment sales will Excalibur Company report on its income tax return for (1) 19X7, (2) 19X8, and (3) 19X9?

(c) Assuming all installment payments are collected as scheduled, how much gross profit from these December installment sales will Excalibur Company report on its books for (1) 19X7, (2) 19X8, and (3) 19X9?

Percentage of completion accounting

13–31 On December 1, 19X1, Comstar, Inc., signed a contract to build a communications satellite. Completion and sale of the satellite were scheduled for November 19X3. The total contract price for the satellite was $35,000,000, and total estimated cost was $28,000,000. The contract specified the following cash payments by the buyer:

$6,500,000 on signing the contract;
$15,000,000 when the satellite is considered one-half completed;
$10,000,000 when the satellite is completed; and
$3,500,000 90 days after completion.

The degree of completion is considered equal to the proportion of estimated total cost incurred by the builder. Comstar accounts for operations on a calendar-year basis. Costs for the satellite were incurred and paid as follows:

December 19X1	$ 4,200,000
19X2	16,800,000
19X3	7,000,000

The satellite was finished and the sale was consummated November 8, 19X3.

REQUIRED

(a) Calculate the gross profit (or loss) that would be reported each year if a cash basis of accounting (cash receipts less cash disbursements) were used.
(b) Calculate the gross profit that would be reported each year on an accrual basis of accounting using (1) the completed contract (point-of-sale) method of revenue recognition; and (2) the percentage-of-completion method of revenue recognition.
(c) Comment on the relative usefulness of these approaches to periodic income determination.

Financial statement notes — quarterly data

13–32 Selected 19X7 quarterly data are presented below for Company A and Company B. One of these companies manufactures and sells greeting cards while the other company manufactures and sells office furniture. Both companies are on a calendar year basis.

	First Quarter	Second Quarter	Third Quarter	Fourth Quarter	Year
		(Amounts in thousands)			
Company A					
Net sales	$95,500	$92,000	$100,000	$109,500	$397,000
Gross profit	28,400	25,700	29,000	31,300	114,400
Net income	4,400	3,100	4,300	5,000	16,800
Company B					
Net sales	40,200	42,000	89,500	128,300	300,000
Gross profit	23,500	25,000	46,000	63,200	157,700
Net income	3,200	2,200	10,300	12,700	28,400

REQUIRED

(a) Compute the percent of annual net sales generated each quarter by Company A. Round to the nearest percent.

(b) Compute the percent of annual net sales generated each quarter by Company B. Round to the nearest percent.

(c) Which company has the most seasonal business? Briefly explain.

(d) Which company is in the greeting card business? The office furniture business? Briefly explain.

(e) Which company's interim quarterly data is probably most useful for predicting annual results? Briefly explain.

Constant dollar accounting

13–33 Appearing below are the 19X2 year-end asset accounts of Gentry Company under historical cost accounting and the general price-level index that reflects the purchasing power of the dollar used to measure each asset.

	Balance	Price-level Index
Cash	$ 60,000	150
Notes Receivable	80,000	150
Supplies on Hand	20,000	125
Building (net of accumulated depreciation)	600,000	60
Equipment (net of accumulated depreciation)	240,000	80
Total Assets	$1,000,000	

The average general price-level index for 19X2 is 135, while the year-end index is 150.

REQUIRED

(a) Restate each asset balance to a constant unit of general purchasing power—the 19X2 year-end purchasing power of the dollar—and compute the total assets.

(b) Restate each asset balance to a constant unit of general purchasing power—the 19X2 average purchasing power of the dollar—and compute the total assets.

(c) Prepare a schedule showing the percent of total assets each asset represents using (1) historical cost measures, (2) constant dollar (end-of-year dollar) measures, and (3) constant dollar (average-for-the-year dollar) measures. Round answers to the nearest percent.

(d) Based on your answers to (c), does changing the unit of measure from one constant dollar to another constant dollar alter the relationships among assets?

Current cost accounting

13–34 Schorr Corporation began operations on January 2, 19X2, with the following assets:

Cash	$ 50,000
Inventory (10,000 units @ $17)	170,000
Land	100,000

During 19X2, Schorr sold 4,000 inventory units at $32 each and incurred cash operating expenses of $31,000. Schorr's historical cost income statement for 19X2 was as follows:

Sales		$128,000
Cost of Goods Sold	$68,000	
Operating Expenses	31,000	
Total Expenses		99,000
Net Income		$ 29,000

Schorr did not purchase any inventory units after January 2, 19X2. Before any inventory was sold, its current cost increased to $20 per unit and remained there until year-end. The current cost of the land at December 31, 19X2, was $115,000.

REQUIRED

(a) Prepare a schedule showing Schorr's 19X2 net income using current cost accounting procedures.
(b) Prepare a schedule showing the year-end current cost of inventory and land, and a schedule showing the year-end historical cost of inventory and land.
(c) Prepare a schedule showing the increase in the current cost of inventory and land that occurred during 19X2.
(d) How much of the increase computed in (c) relates to inventory units sold during 19X2 and how much relates to assets on hand at year-end?

ALTERNATE PROBLEMS

Basic principles

13–28A The following are several unrelated accounting practices:

(1) A recession has caused slow business and low profits for Bacon Company. Consequently, the firm takes no depreciation on its plant assets this year.
(2) Kyle Mann, a consultant operating a sole proprietorship, used his business car for a personal, month-long vacation. A full year's depreciation on the car is charged to the firm's depreciation expense account.
(3) Knott Company purchased a new $18 snow shovel that is expected to last six years. The shovel is used to clear the firm's front steps during the winter months. The shovel's cost is debited to the Snow Shovel asset account and will be depreciated over six years.
(4) Borg Corporation has been named as the defendant in a $20,000,000 pollution lawsuit. Because the lawsuit will take several years to resolve and the outcome is uncertain, Borg's management decides not to mention the lawsuit in the current year financial statements.
(5) Snow Corporation's portfolio of short-term stock investments has an aggregate market value below cost. Management believes that stock prices will rise soon and, therefore, does not write down the portfolio at year-end to its lower market value amount.
(6) The management of Dryer Corporation prefers the financial results using constant dollar adjustments and issues financial statements in constant dollars (rather than the conventional statements) to stockholders.

REQUIRED

(a) For each of the given practices, indicate which generally accepted accounting principles apply and whether they have been used appropriately.

(b) For each inappropriate accounting practice, indicate the proper accounting procedure.

Installment method

13–30A Allen Company makes all sales on an installment basis. Selected financial data for its first three years of operations are shown below.

	19X1	19X2	19X3
Sales	$300,000	$500,000	$600,000
Cost of Goods Sold	180,000	275,000	300,000
Gross Profit	$120,000	$225,000	$300,000
Cash collections from 19X1 sales	$135,000	$150,000	$ 15,000
Cash collections from 19X2 sales		240,000	200,000
Cash collections from 19X3 sales			312,000

Allen Company elects the installment method to report the gross profit from its installment sales on its income tax return. On its books, the company recognizes the revenue and related cost of goods sold when the sale is made.

REQUIRED

(a) What is the gross profit percentage on sales for 19X1, 19X2, and 19X3?

(b) How much gross profit will Allen report on its income tax returns in 19X1, 19X2, and 19X3?

(c) For the three year period 19X1–19X3, how much less gross profit will Allen have reported on its income tax returns compared with the gross profit recorded on its books?

Percentage of completion accounting

13–31A On November 1, 19X2, Atlantic, Inc., signed a contract to build a large seagoing oil tanker. Completion and sale of the ship were scheduled for October 19X4. The total contract price for the ship was $20,000,000 and the total estimated cost was $15,000,000. The contract specified the following cash payments by the buyer:

$1,000,000 on signing the contract;
$10,000,000 when the ship is considered one-half completed;
$7,000,000 when the ship is completed;
$2,000,000 90 days after completion.

The degree of completion is considered equal to the proportion of estimated total cost incurred by the builder. Atlantic accounts for operations on a calendar-year basis. Costs for the ship were incurred and paid as follows:

November and December, 19X2	$1,800,000
19X3	7,950,000
19X4	5,250,000

The ship was finished and the sale was consummated October 20, 19X4.

REQUIRED

(a) Calculate the gross profit (or loss) that would be reported each year if a cash basis of accounting (cash receipts less cash disbursements) were used.

(b) Calculate the gross profit that would be reported each year on an accrual basis of accounting using (1) the completed contract (point-of-sale) method of revenue recognition; and (2) the percentage-of-completion method of revenue recognition.

(c) Comment on the relative usefulness of these approaches to periodic income determination.

Constant dollar accounting

13–33A Appearing below are Webster Company's sales for three years under historical cost accounting and the average general price-level index for each year.

	Sales	Average price-level index
19X6	$5,400,000	120
19X7	6,750,000	144
19X8	9,450,000	160

The 19X8 year-end general price-level index is 180.

REQUIRED

(a) Restate each year's sales amount to a constant unit of general purchasing power—the 19X8 year-end purchasing power of the dollar.

(b) Restate each year's sales amount to a constant unit of general purchasing power—the 19X8 average purchasing power of the dollar.

(c) Prepare a schedule showing the percent of sales increase from 19X6 to 19X7, and from 19X7 to 19X8 using (1) historical cost measures, (2) constant dollar (end-of-year dollar) measures, and (3) constant dollar (average-for-the-year dollar) measures. Round to the nearest percent.

(d) Based on your answers to (c), does changing the unit of measure from one constant dollar to another constant dollar change the year-to-year relationships between sales amounts?

Current cost accounting

13–34A Anchor Corporation began operations on January 2, 19X5, with the following assets:

Cash	$ 30,000
Inventory (6,000 units @ $20)	120,000
Land	80,000

During 19X5, Anchor sold 4,400 inventory units at $30 each and incurred cash operating expenses of $12,000. Anchor's historical cost income statement for 19X5 was as follows:

Sales		$132,000
Cost of Goods Sold	$88,000	
Operating Expenses	12,000	
Total Expenses		100,000
Net Income		$ 32,000

Before any inventory was sold, its current cost increased to $22 per unit. After the last sale in 19X5, Anchor's supplier announced a year-end price increase to $23 per unit. The current cost of the land at December 31, 19X5, was $88,000.

REQUIRED

(a) Prepare a schedule showing Anchor's 19X5 net income using current cost accounting procedures.
(b) Prepare a schedule showing the year-end current cost of inventory and land, and a schedule showing the year-end historical cost of inventory and land.
(c) Prepare a schedule showing the increase in the current cost of inventory and land that occurred during 19X5.
(d) How much of the increase computed in (c) relates to inventory units sold during 19X5 and how much relates to assets on hand at year-end?

BUSINESS DECISION PROBLEM

Copter, Inc., started operations on January 1, 19X1. Its primary assets are two helicopters, which are used in the following ways:

(1) For carrying passengers between a major air terminal and a downtown heliport. As a new business promotion, the company sold 600 booklets of one-way tickets. Each booklet contained ten tickets and was priced at $200. During 19X1, purchasers of the booklets used 3,200 tickets.
(2) For passenger charter flights. A local corporation charters a helicopter to transport executives to and from an island conference facility. A deposit of 25% of the charter fee is required when a charter flight is booked. On December 31, 19X1, the company had deposits of $4,000 for scheduled charter flights. The company received a total of $28,000 for charter flights flown during 19X1.
(3) For construction material and equipment transportation. Building contractors rent a helicopter for $140 per hour for moving material and equipment to and from construction sites. Contractors used the helicopters a total of 150 hours during 19X1. Of this total, 30 hours occurred in December, for which the company has not yet received payment.
(4) For "Save A Life" efforts during holidays. The state rents a helicopter for $90 per hour on holiday weekends to carry a medical team to accident locations. The state used the helicopters a total of 300 hours in 19X1. The company has not yet collected for 48 hours of use in December.

Copter's bookkeeper has prepared the following schedule of revenue for 19X1:

One-way ticket booklets (600 @ $200)	$120,000
Charter flights made	28,000
Deposits on charter flights scheduled	4,000
Contractors (120 hours @ $140)	16,800
"Save A Life" program (252 hours @ $90)	22,680
Total Revenue	$191,480

The president of Copter, Inc., has asked you to evaluate whether the bookkeeper has correctly determined the 19X1 revenue in accordance with generally accepted accounting principles.

REQUIRED

Has the bookkeeper correctly determined the 19X1 revenue? If not, prepare a revised 19X1 revenue schedule. Give reasons for any changes you make from the bookkeeper's schedule.

ANSWERS TO SELF-TEST QUESTIONS

1. (c) 2. (b) 3. (a) 4. (c) 5. (d)

COMPREHENSIVE PROBLEM—PART 2

This comprehensive problem utilizes the financial statement disclosure data of four actual companies. In each case, we give a brief profile of the company and selected disclosure data from a recent annual report to stockholders, followed by questions relating to certain accounting principles and practices discussed thus far in the text.

(I) NATURE'S SUNSHINE PRODUCTS, INC.

PROFILE

Nature's Sunshine Products, Inc., manufactures a variety of nutritional and personal care products, including encapsulated herbs, vitamins, food supplements, grooming aids, cosmetics, a water purifier, and a weight loss program. These products are sold directly to consumers by means of an independent sales force situated throughout the United States, Canada, Australia, and New Zealand. At the end of 1984, total assets were $11.9 million and sales revenue exceeded $33 million for 1984.

DISCLOSURE DATA (from note on Significant Accounting Policies in 1984 annual report)

Revenue Recognition

The Company generally receives its product sales price in cash accompanying orders from independent sales force members. A volume incentive payment related to product orders is made in the month following the sale. Sales and related volume incentives are generally recorded when the merchandise is shipped. Cash received for unshipped merchandise is recorded as a liability.

Selling Expenses

Independent sales force members may earn Company-paid attendance at conventions by achieving the required levels of product purchases within the qualification period. The paid attendance costs and expenses are accrued over the qualification period as they are earned.

REQUIRED

(a) Why doesn't Nature's Sunshine Products, Inc., record revenue when it receives the sales orders and cash from its sales force members? Why does it wait until the merchandise is shipped?

(b) The volume incentives are part of the firm's direct sales marketing program and represent compensation paid to independent sales force members for reaching certain levels of sales performance and organizational development. In 1984, volume incentives amounted to $16,317,488 (49.1% of sales). What accounting principle underlies the firm's procedure of recording volume incentives as an expense when merchandise is shipped?

(c) The firm's December 31, 1984, balance sheet shows Accrued Volume Incentives of $1,201,837 as a current liability. Why is this item classified as a current liability?

(d) What accounting principle underlies the firm's procedure of accruing Company-paid convention attendance costs and expenses over the qualification period rather than expensing these amounts when they are paid at the time of the convention?

(II) FRIGITRONICS, INC.

PROFILE

Frigitronics, Inc., manufactures and sells intraocular lenses, contact lenses, auxiliary ophthalmic products, and surgical, testing, and diagnostic instruments. The firm also sells prescription eye wear through about 350 company-owned locations (Benson Optical), making it the third largest chain of retail eye wear stores in the country. Total revenue for the year ended May 31, 1985, was $129 million and assets exceeded $71 million at May 31, 1985.

DISCLOSURE DATA (from notes to financial statements in 1985 annual report)

Patent Litigation

On July 3, 1985, the U.S. District Court for the District of Delaware affirmed a jury verdict in favor of Schering Corporation in its suit against Precision–Cosmet Co., Inc., a wholly-owned subsidiary, for patent infringement. In accordance with Financial Accounting Standards Board Statement No. 5, the Company has made a provision for its estimated potential liability plus the Company's own costs associated with this action. On July 26, 1985, the Company reached a tentative agreement for settlement and believes the provision will be adequate to cover all costs. The agreement is expected to be finalized in several weeks.

Contingent Liabilities

At May 31, 1985, one of the subsidiaries was contingently liable for approximately $5,543,000 of notes issued by customers in payment for equipment and discounted with recourse at banks. These notes are collateralized by security interests in the equipment.

REQUIRED

(a) Frigitronics' 1985 fiscal year ends on May 31. The jury verdict against the firm in the patent litigation was not affirmed until July 1985. Yet the company has made an entry as of May 31, 1985, regarding its contingent liability in this lawsuit. Why?

(b) The contingent liability recorded for the patent litigation was $5,000,000. Prepare the journal entry to record this liability. Should this liability be classified as a current or a long-term liability? Why?

(c) By May 31, 1985, Frigitronics has not made an entry regarding its contingent liability on customers' discounted notes. Why?

(III) HOUSE OF FABRICS, INC.

PROFILE

House of Fabrics, Inc., is the largest home sewing/craft retailer in the United States, with 760 stores located in 47 states, selling medium-priced fabrics, crafts, and sewing machines. Assets at January 31, 1985, were $126 million, and sales for the year ended on that date were $278 million.

DISCLOSURE DATA (from note on Significant Accounting Policies in 1985 annual report)

Lease Commitments

Total rental expense for the years ended January 31, 1985, 1984, and 1983, were $22,998,000, $19,391,000, and $15,914,000, respectively. . . . Maximum future rentals under operating leases in effect at January 31, 1985, are as follows:

1986	$17,963,000	1990	$11,302,000
1987	16,703,000	1991–1995	33,201,000
1988	15,139,000	1996–2000	2,416,000
1989	13,238,000		

REQUIRED

(a) Would you expect a long-term liability for lease commitments to appear on the firm's January 31, 1985, balance sheet, relating to the rentals shown on the foregoing schedule? Why or why not?

(b) The firm shows $22.6 million for leasehold improvements on its January 31, 1985, balance sheet. Generally, how should this asset be amortized? What is the longest period over which any of the leasehold improvements now on the balance should be amortized?

(IV) SHELBY WILLIAMS INDUSTRIES, INC.

PROFILE

Shelby Williams Industries, Inc., designs, manufactures, and distributes chairs and other related seating products for the hotel and food service industries, for the executive and general office, and for institutional markets. Customers include, among others, Holiday Inns, Inc., Wendy's International, Hyatt, Hilton, Marriott, Sheraton, and Howard Johnson Hotels, and many widely known chain restaurants. In 1984, total assets were $52.5 million and net sales were $100.7 million.

DISCLOSURE DATA (from the seven-year sales summary in the 1984 annual report)

	1984	**1983**	**1982**	**1981**	**1980**	**1979**	**1978**
Sales (in $000s)	$100,676	$81,767	$71,016	$63,448	$56,544	$50,130	$43,693

REQUIRED

(a) Calculate, as a percentage of 1978 sales, the sales of each year for the period 1979–1984. (Example: for 1979, the percentage is calculated as $50,130/$43,693 = 114.7%.)

(b) Restate the sales figures for each year of the period in terms of 1984 purchasing power, using the following average consumers price index for the period:

	1984	1983	1982	1981	1980	1979	1978
Consumers Price Index, 1967 = 100	311.1	298.4	289.1	272.4	246.8	217.4	195.4

(Example: for 1978, restated sales are \$43,693 × 311.1/195.4 = \$69,564.)

(c) Recalculate, as a percentage of 1978 restated sales, the restated sales of each year for the period 1979–1984. Compare these percentages with those calculated in (a) and comment on the differences.

Part Three

Partnership and Corporation Accounting

14

Partnership Accounting

Chapter Objectives

- Describe the partnership form of organization and the formation of a partnership.
- Illustrate various methods for the division of profits and losses.
- Describe the methods for admitting a new partner.
- Describe the alternatives when a partner retires.
- Explain how partnerships are liquidated.

We are the two halves of a pair of scissors, when apart, Perksniff, but together we are something.

CHARLES DICKENS

The essence of the partnership form of business organization is captured by the proverb, "Two heads are better than one." A **partnership** is a voluntary association of two or more persons for the purpose of conducting a business for profit. The Uniform Partnership Act governs the formation and operation of partnerships in many states. A partnership is easily formed—the parties need only agree to the partnership. The ease of formation makes the partnership an attractive form of organization for a business that requires more capital than a single proprietor can provide or for persons who want to combine specialized talents. Professional people, such as physicians, attorneys, and public accountants, as well as many small business concerns, often operate as partnerships.

Partnership agreements may be oral, but sound business practice demands a written agreement to avoid misunderstandings. A written partnership agreement constitutes the **articles of co-partnership.** The articles of co-partnership should detail the important provisions of the partnership arrangement, including the name and location of the partnership, the nature and duration of the business, the duties of partners, the capital contribution of each partner, the procedure for sharing profits and losses, permitted withdrawals of assets, the manner of keeping the books, the procedure for withdrawals of partners, and the procedure for dissolving the business.

CHARACTERISTICS OF A PARTNERSHIP

Although a partnership is an accounting entity, it is not a legal entity separate from its owners. Several characteristics—in addition to ease of formation—relate to this aspect of partnerships.

Mutual Agency

Mutual agency means that every partner is an agent for the firm, with the authority to bind the partnership to contracts. This authority applies to all acts typical of a partner engaging in the usual activities of the firm. Although the partners may limit the authority of one or more partners to act on customary matters, a partner acting in contravention of a restriction may still contractually bind the partnership if the other party to the contract is unaware of the limitation. The partnership would not be bound, however, if the other party knew of the restriction.

MAKING A PARTNERSHIP WORK

The "together we are something" epigraph at the opening of this chapter describes a happy, successful business partnership. For many partnerships, however, an ancient Arab adage might apply: "A pot belonging to partners is neither hot nor cold." A recent study of 170 small businesses started by partners seems to support this adage: more than two-thirds broke up, usually because a partner's interests changed or there were personal conflicts among the partners. Less than a third were truly successful.

In his article "Making a Partnership Work,"* David H. Bennet, a founding partner in Dynamic Systems, Inc. (an engineering and management consulting firm), identifies what he believes to be the "most critical factor" in the success or failure of a partnership, as explained by a banker friend: "A partnership is very much like a marriage," his friend told him. "As you work with each other, you will get to know each other's strengths, limitations, idiosyncrasies, goals, values, skills and behavior patterns. How well these human characteristics complement or conflict with one another and how much they help or harm a young company are the often-hidden forces that heavily influence long-term success." Based on his own company's experience, Bennet has discovered that a successful partnership is the result of careful partnership selection and cooperation.

Partners should be chosen "with the long-term health of the company in mind," not just according to a specific need for funds, marketing contacts, or other requirements. The values of all the participants should be considered. As Bennet explains, "the level of acceptable risk varies widely among individuals; yet, when company decisions are made, all parties are subjected to the same degree of risk and reward. If one individual is looking for minimum risk and is willing to accept a minimum return, while another partner desires a fast, hefty return on investment and is willing to take high risks to get it, the partners are headed for conflict."

Though values should be similar, partners' abilities and strengths should complement, not duplicate, each other's. For example, when one individual is particularly strong in financial management and another has a natural instinct for human relations, "it is obvious which responsibilities each should have in the organization—and where each should yield to another's strengths."

Effective communication among partners is also essential to a firm's success. All partners must convey a unified corporate image, both to their employees and to the community. Partners should be open and straight-forward about their own long- and short-term goals and about how their own fundamental values affect their views of the world, decision-making processes, and opportunities. They should establish, in advance, the ground rules for operation—what the firm's philosophy should be, how decisions are to be made, what the equity will be, and who will run the firm. Discussions by the partners of Bennet's firm indicated that they wanted a firm that would be known for absolute integrity, competence, and fast response. Their decisions are made by a majority vote; evenly split decisions count as a negative vote. They decided on equal shares of the partnership because they "wanted to create an environment in which if one person was successful, everybody would be successful, and if anyone had problems, everybody would suffer."

Bennet believes that partners' spouses should also be kept informed of the operations and the status of the business. Oftentimes partners' personal assets are at risk, so the spouse must also live with the consequences of a firm's decisions. It is only fair that spouses know the risks and are aware of what the firm is doing. Bennet has found that the spouses should share the same aspirations as those of the partners to avoid potential conflicts as the company grows. Above all, when disagreement occurs, Bennet believes that everyone should focus on the good of the firm—as he states it, "antagonizing or running down another individual . . . hurts the organization. And hurting the organization hurts every partner."

*"Making a Partnership Work," *Nation's Business*, May, 1984, pp. 66–67.

Unlimited Liability

Each partner in a **general partnership** is individually liable for the firm's obligations regardless of the amount of personal investment. Thus, creditors of a general partnership unable to pay its debts may obtain payment from the personal assets of individual partners. In addition to at least one general partner, a **limited partnership** has one or more limited partners. The liability of a limited partner is restricted to his or her capital investment. A limited partner who becomes active in the control of the firm, however, assumes the status—and unlimited liability—of a general partner, as provided in the Uniform Limited Partnership Act.

Limited Life

Because a partnership is a voluntary association of persons, many events may cause its dissolution. These events include the expiration of the agreed-on partnership term; the accomplishment of the business objective; the admission of a new partner; the withdrawal, death, or bankruptcy of an existing partner; and the issuance of a court decree because of a partner's incapacity or misconduct. Even though a change in membership dissolves a partnership, business continuity is often unaffected. A new partnership continues the operations of the former partnership without interruption.

Co-ownership of Property

Assets contributed by partners become partnership property jointly owned by all partners. Individual partners no longer separately own the specific resources invested in the firm. Unless an agreement to the contrary exists, each partner has an equal right to the firm's property for partnership purposes.

Nontaxable Entity

Although a partnership must file an information return for federal income tax purposes, the organization itself is not a taxable entity. The information return shows the distributive shares of the partnership's net income that the partners include on their individual tax returns. The individual members must pay income taxes on their respective shares of partnership earnings whether or not these amounts have been withdrawn from the firm.

ADVANTAGES AND DISADVANTAGES OF A PARTNERSHIP

In contrast with a corporation, a partnership is easier and less expensive to organize and is subject to less government regulation and fewer reporting requirements. Certain corporate actions require the approval of stockholders or directors; partners have fewer constraints on their actions. Businesses of modest size or of planned short duration may find these features advantageous. The same may be true for new businesses hesitant to incur the cost of incorporation until their ventures prove successful.

Disadvantages of the partnership form of organization are mutual agency, unlimited liability, and limited life. The first two in particular underscore the importance of selecting partners with great care and are no doubt partially responsible for the rule that no person may be admitted to a partnership without the consent of all existing partners. A corporation, which offers limited liability to investors, is better able than a partnership to raise large amounts of capital.

The impact of taxes varies from one circumstance to the next. A partnership is a nontaxable entity; a corporation is a taxable entity. Partners' earnings are taxable whether distributed or not; corporate income is taxable a second time, but only when distributed as dividends. The tax rate on individuals in high tax brackets exceeds the corporate tax rate. To determine the most advantageous form of organization for tax purposes requires careful analysis of existing tax laws and the tax status of the persons going into business.

CAPITAL, DRAWING, AND LOAN ACCOUNTS

Accounting for partnerships is similar in most respects to accounting for sole proprietorships. Each partner has a capital account and a drawing account that serve the same functions as the related accounts for a sole proprietor. A partner's capital account is credited for his or her investments, and each individual drawing account is debited to reflect assets withdrawn from the partnership. At the end of each accounting period, the balances in the drawing accounts are closed to the related capital accounts.

Occasionally a partner may advance amounts to the partnership beyond the intended permanent investment. These advances should be credited to the partner's loan account and classified among the liabilities, separate from liabilities to outsiders. By the same token, if a partner withdraws money with the intention of repaying, the debit should go to the partner's advance (or loan receivable) account and be classified separately among the partnership's receivables.

The formation of partnerships, the division of profits and losses, the admission and retirement of partners, and the liquidation of partnerships represent areas of particular interest in accounting for these entities. We focus on these issues in the remainder of the chapter.

FORMATION OF A PARTNERSHIP

A partnership's books are opened with an entry reflecting the net contribution of each partner to the firm. Asset accounts are debited for assets invested in the partnership, liability accounts are credited for any liabilities assumed by the partnership, and a separate capital account is credited for the amount of each partner's net investment (Assets − Liabilities).

Assume that Earl Ames, a sole proprietor, and John Baker form a partnership. Ames invests $8,000 cash, office equipment with a current fair value of $25,000, and office supplies worth $2,000. The partnership agrees to assume the $5,000 balance on a note issued by Ames when he acquired the equipment. Baker invests

$10,000 cash. The following opening entries on the books of the partnership record the investments of Ames and Baker:

Cash	8,000	
Office Equipment	25,000	
Office Supplies on Hand	2,000	
Notes Payable		5,000
E. Ames, Capital		30,000
To record Ames' investment in the partnership of Ames and Baker.		

Cash	10,000	
J. Baker, Capital		10,000
To record Baker's investment in the partnership of Ames and Baker.		

Assets invested in the partnership should be recorded at their current fair values. These assets (less any liabilities assumed by the partnership) determine the opening capital balances for each partner. If the assets are not recorded initially at their fair values, inequities develop among the partners in terms of their respective capital balances.

For example, assume the office equipment invested by Ames was recorded incorrectly at $22,000 (its book value from his proprietorship records). If the partnership immediately sold the equipment for its current fair value of $25,000, the resulting $3,000 gain, on closing, would increase the capital balances of both Ames and Baker. This is not equitable. The $3,000 "gain" was not added to the asset by the operations of the partnership. Baker should not be credited with any part of this amount. A similar inequity develops if the equipment is used in operations rather than sold. Owing to a lower total depreciation over the life of the equipment, income would be $3,000 greater over the same period. To avoid such inequities, the partnership records the office equipment initially at $25,000. The values assigned to assets invested in a partnership are important and should be agreeable to all partners.

DIVISION OF PARTNERSHIP PROFITS AND LOSSES

In the absence of a profit and loss sharing agreement, partnership profits and losses are divided equally. Partners who do not wish to share profits equally must specify, preferably in a formal written agreement, the manner in which profit and loss distributions are made. Such arrangements may specify a fixed ratio (such as $\frac{2}{3}$ to $\frac{1}{3}$, 60% to 40%, or 5:3) or a sharing formula of some kind based on the relative financial participation of the partners, the services performed by the partners, or both. Any arrangement can be made, and losses may be shared differently from profits. If an agreement specifies the manner of sharing profits but is silent on the sharing of losses, losses will be divided in the same fashion as profits. In the following sections, we discuss several common arrangements.

Capital Ratios

When the services performed or skills provided by the various partners are considered equal, profits and lòsses may be divided according to the partners' relative investments in the firm. Assume that the Ames and Baker partnership had a profit of $18,000 for the year and that the partners' capital balances before any profit distribution at year-end were as follows:

E. Ames, Capital			J. Baker, Capital		
	19XX			19XX	
	Jan. 1	30,000		Jan. 1	10,000
				July 1	10,000

The $18,000 profit might be divided according to the beginning capital investment ratio or the average capital investment ratio for the year.

BEGINNING CAPITAL RATIO At the beginning of the year, the total capital investment in the firm was $40,000—$30,000 for Ames and $10,000 for Baker. If they shared according to the ratio of beginning capital balances, the profit distribution would be 3 to 1, or $13,500 for Ames and $4,500 for Baker, computed as follows:

	Beginning Capital	Percent of Total	Division of Profit
Ames	$30,000	75	$13,500
Baker	10,000	25	4,500
	$40,000	100	$18,000

The following entry would be made to distribute the balance in the Income Summary account:

Income Summary	18,000	
E. Ames, Capital		13,500
J. Baker, Capital		4,500
To close the Income Summary account.		

AVERAGE CAPITAL RATIO Because partners' investments may change during the year, the partners may decide that using *average* capital balances rather than beginning capital balances provides a more equitable division of profits. Under this scheme, investment balances are *weighted* by multiplying the amount of the investment by the portion of the year that these funds were invested. Because Baker invested an additional $10,000 on July 1, his average capital would be based on a $10,000 investment for the first six months and a $20,000 investment for the last six months. The computation might be as follows:

		Dollars × Months			Average Investment
Ames					
$30,000 × 12 months		$360,000	÷ 12	=	$30,000
Baker					
$10,000 × 6 months	$ 60,000				
$20,000 × 6 months	120,000	180,000	÷ 12	=	15,000
		$540,000			$45,000

Profit Distribution

Ames: $\frac{\$30,000}{\$45,000} \times \$18,000 = \$12,000$

Baker: $\frac{\$15,000}{\$45,000} \times \$18,000 = 6,000$

$\$18,000$

The entry to close the Income Summary account would credit E. Ames, Capital with $12,000 and J. Baker, Capital with $6,000.

Salary and Interest Allowances

A sharing agreement may provide for variations in the personal services contributed by partners and in their relative investments. **Salary allowances** provide for differences in personal services; **allowances for interest** on capital balances provide for differences in the financial participation of partners.

The terms *salary allowances* and *allowances for interest* describe only the process of dividing net income among partners. These terms should not be confused with any salary expense and interest expense appearing in the firm's records or with any cash withdrawals the partners make. For example, the partnership agreement may provide that partners may make withdrawals equal to their salary allowances. These withdrawals would be debited to each partner's drawing account, which is eventually closed to his or her capital account. The cash withdrawals in no way affect the division of net income among partners—the division of net income is governed by the sharing agreement.

SALARY ALLOWANCE Suppose Ames and Baker render different degrees of personal services and therefore specify a salary allowance in their sharing agreement—$6,000 for Ames and $4,000 for Baker. The remainder of net income is divided equally. The division of the $18,000 net income is as follows:

	Ames	Baker	Total
Earnings to be divided			$18,000
Salary allowances:			
Ames	$ 6,000		
Baker		$4,000	10,000
Remainder			$ 8,000
Remainder ($8,000) divided equally	4,000	4,000	
Partners' shares	$10,000	$8,000	

The $18,000 balance in the Income Summary account would be closed by crediting E. Ames, Capital for $10,000 and J. Baker, Capital for $8,000.

SALARY AND INTEREST ALLOWANCES Next, assume that Ames and Baker wish to acknowledge the differences in their financial involvement as well as in their personal services. They have the following sharing agreement: salaries of $6,000 to Ames and $4,000 to Baker; 8% interest on *average* capital balances; and the remainder divided equally. We computed average investments for Ames and Baker earlier at $30,000 and $15,000, respectively. The $18,000 net income would therefore be divided as follows:

	Ames	Baker	Total
Earnings to be divided			$18,000
Salary allowances:			
Ames	$ 6,000		
Baker		$4,000	10,000
			$ 8,000
Allowance for interest on average capital:			
Ames ($30,000 × 0.08)	2,400		
Baker ($15,000 × 0.08)		1,200	3,600
Remainder			$ 4,400
Remainder ($4,400) divided equally	2,200	2,200	
Partners' shares	$10,600	$7,400	

The entry closing the $18,000 net income in the Income Summary account would credit E. Ames, Capital for $10,600 and J. Baker, Capital for $7,400.

If Ames and Baker had withdrawn cash equal to their salary allowances, their drawing accounts at the end of the year would contain debit balances of $6,000 and $4,000, respectively. The entry to close the drawing accounts would be

E. Ames, Capital	6,000	
J. Baker, Capital	4,000	
E. Ames, Drawing		6,000
J. Baker, Drawing		4,000
To close the partners' drawing accounts.		

ALLOWANCES EXCEED EARNINGS Unless a special provision is included in the sharing agreement, the same allocation procedures apply in the event of a loss or of earnings insufficient to cover allowances for salary and interest. For example, assume that net income for the year was only $8,000. After salary and interest allowances are allocated, a *sharing agreement loss* of $5,600 would be divided equally between the partners to fulfill their agreement. The computations are shown below:

	Ames	Baker	Total
Earnings to be divided			$ 8,000
Salary allowances	$6,000	$4,000	
Interest allowances	2,400	1,200	
Total salary and interest	$8,400	$5,200	13,600
Remainder (sharing agreement loss)			($ 5,600)
Remainder divided equally	(2,800)	(2,800)	
Partners' shares	$5,600	$2,400	

The entry closing the $8,000 net income in the Income Summary account would credit E. Ames, Capital with $5,600 and J. Baker, Capital with $2,400.

PARTNERSHIP FINANCIAL STATEMENTS

A few unique features of partnership financial statements arise because a partnership consists of co-owners. The partnership income statement may show, at the bottom, how the net income is divided among the partners. A capital account for each partner appears in the owners' equity section of the balance sheet. The statement of partners' (or owners') capital portrays the changes in the capital balances of each partner, as shown in Exhibit 14–1.

EXHIBIT 14–1

Ames and Baker
Statement of Partners' Capital
For the Year Ended December 31, 19XX

	Ames	Baker	Total
Capital Balances, January 1, 19XX	$30,000	$10,000	$40,000
Add: Additional Contributions		10,000	10,000
Net Income for 19XX	10,600	7,400	18,000
Totals	$40,600	$27,400	$68,000
Less: Withdrawals	6,000	4,000	10,000
Capital Balances, December 31, 19XX	$34,600	$23,400	$58,000

ADMISSION OF A PARTNER

New partners may be admitted to a partnership either by purchasing an interest from current members or by investing in the firm. When a person buys an interest from one or more of the current partners, the assets of the firm are not affected. Payment is made personally to the member or members from whom the interest is obtained, resulting in merely a transfer among capital accounts. When an investment is made in the firm, however, total assets increase by the amount contributed.

Economic circumstances usually dictate a new partner's mode of entry. A firm with sufficient capital may seek the skills and services of a particular new partner. Or, current partners may wish to liquidate part of their interests and scale down their individual investments. In these situations, the firm may sell an interest in the current partnership. On the other hand, if additional capital is needed, adding a partner who will contribute assets may be a proper solution.

For the benefit of the existing partners, the net assets of the current partnership should reflect their current fair values when a new partner is admitted. This may require a revaluation of certain assets. The resultant gain or loss would be apportioned to the current partners in their profit and loss sharing ratio. If the net assets do not reflect their fair values, the new partner may share in gains and losses that developed before admission to the firm. In the following examples of new partner admissions, we assume that the recorded book values of the current partnership's assets do not require restatement.

Purchase of an Interest

Suppose that Ames and Baker have capital balances of $30,000 and $10,000, respectively, and that Ames sells one-half of his interest to Susan Carter. For Carter to become a partner, both Ames and Baker must consent to the sale. The entry to record Carter's admission would be

E. Ames, Capital	15,000	
S. Carter, Capital		15,000
To record admission of Carter.		

The actual cash amount paid to Ames is entirely a personal matter between the two persons and is not relevant in recording Carter's admission. Whether an interest is purchased from one partner or several, a transfer of capital is made only for the amounts of the interests purchased without regard to the payment made. Suppose that Carter purchased a one-fourth interest in the firm by obtaining one-fourth of each partner's current share. One-fourth interest would amount to $10,000 (one-fourth of $40,000 present capital). The entry for Carter's admission would be

E. Ames, Capital	7,500	
J. Baker, Capital	2,500	
S. Carter, Capital		10,000
To record admission of Carter.		

Admission by Investment

Clearly, if an incoming partner contributes assets to the firm, total capital increases. If the current partners' capital balances are realistically stated, the new partner simply contributes assets equal to the desired proportionate interest in the total capital of the new firm. In our example, present capital is $40,000—$30,000 for Ames and $10,000 for Baker. Carter wants to contribute enough cash to obtain one-third interest in the new firm. The current partners' capital of $40,000 represents two-thirds of the new firm's capital; therefore, Carter should contribute $20,000. The entry for admission would be

Cash	20,000	
S. Carter, Capital		20,000
To record admission of Carter.		

BONUS TO CURRENT PARTNERS If a partnership interest is especially attractive because of a superior earnings record or the promise of exceptional future earnings, the current partners may require the new partner to pay an additional amount as a "bonus" for admission. Suppose that Ames and Baker required a $35,000 payment for a one-third interest in the new firm. The total capital of the new firm would then be $75,000, of which a one-third interest would be $25,000, as follows:

E. Ames, Capital	$30,000
J. Baker, Capital	10,000
Present Capital	$40,000
Contribution of Carter	35,000
Capital of New Firm	$75,000
One-third Interest	$25,000

The $10,000 difference between Carter's payment of $35,000 and her interest of $25,000 is a bonus to the former partners, to be divided according to their profit and loss sharing ratio. If the agreement provides for equal sharing, the entry to admit Carter is

Cash	35,000	
E. Ames, Capital		5,000
J. Baker, Capital		5,000
S. Carter, Capital		25,000
To record admission of Carter.		

BONUS TO NEW PARTNER A firm eager to add a partner who has ready cash or unique skills, management potential, or other desirable characteristics may award the new partner a larger interest than would be warranted by his or her contribution. Because the capital of the new partner will be greater than his or her asset contribution, the current partners must make up the difference (bonus to new partner) by reducing their capital balances. Assume that Carter receives a one-third interest by contributing only $14,000 to the new firm. The capital of the new firm increases to $54,000 ($40,000 + $14,000), of which a one-third interest is $18,000, as shown below:

E. Ames, Capital	$30,000
J. Baker, Capital	10,000
Present Capital	$40,000
Contribution of Carter	14,000
Capital of New Firm	$54,000
One-third Interest	$18,000

The $4,000 difference between Carter's $14,000 contribution and her $18,000 interest is a bonus to Carter. Ames and Baker reduce their capital balances accordingly, with amounts based on the profit and loss sharing ratio. With equal sharing, the entry to admit Carter as a partner in the firm is

Cash	14,000	
E. Ames, Capital	2,000	
J. Baker, Capital	2,000	
S. Carter, Capital		18,000
To record admission of Carter.		

RETIREMENT OF A PARTNER

A retiring partner may (1) sell his or her interest to an outsider, (2) sell that interest to one or more of the remaining partners, or (3) receive payment for the interest from partnership funds.

Sale of Partnership Interest

INTEREST SOLD TO NEW PARTNER The procedure for recording the sale of a retiring partner's interest to an outsider is similar to that illustrated earlier for the purchase of an interest. Suppose that retiring partner Baker, with the firm's approval, sells his $10,000 interest to Stan Dodge. Regardless of the personally determined amount of Dodge's actual payment to Baker, the entry to record Dodge's admission and Baker's departure is

J. Baker, Capital	10,000	
S. Dodge, Capital		10,000
To record Dodge's purchase of Baker's interest.		

INTEREST SOLD TO REMAINING PARTNERS This transaction is a personal one between Baker and his partners. If Baker sells his interest to remaining partners Ames and Carter, Baker's interest is merely transferred to their capital accounts, regardless of the actual amount of the payments. If Baker sells equal portions of his interest to the remaining partners, the entry is

J. Baker, Capital	10,000	
E. Ames, Capital		5,000
S. Carter, Capital		5,000
To record sale of Baker's interest to Ames and Carter.		

Payment from Partnership Funds

SETTLEMENT EXCEEDS CAPITAL BALANCE A partner's retirement may be an occasion for reviewing partners' capital balances. Because of such factors as appreciation of assets or an exceptional partnership performance record, the capital balances may not provide a realistic basis for determining the value of partnership interests. In such situations, the partners may recognize any amount by which the current fair value of the retiring partner's partnership interest exceeds his or her capital balance by paying a bonus to the retiring partner.

If the retiring partner receives funds from the partnership for his or her interest, any difference between the amount of this interest and the sum paid affects the capital balances of the remaining partners. For example, assume that the capital balances of Ames, Baker, and Carter are $35,000, $15,000, and $25,000, respectively, when Baker retires and that the firm pays $20,000 for Baker's interest. Baker's $5,000 bonus is divided by the other partners according to their profit and loss sharing ratio (assumed here to be equal). The entry would be:

E. Ames, Capital	2,500	
S. Carter, Capital	2,500	
J. Baker, Capital	15,000	
Cash		20,000
To record Baker's withdrawal from the partnership.		

When the fair value of a retiring partner's interest exceeds his or her related capital balance, the remaining partners might revalue total partnership assets proportionately upward, distribute the increase to all partners in their profit and loss sharing ratio, and then pay the retiring partner an amount equal to his or her new capital balance. Such an approach, however, obviously departs from the principle of historical cost. Although the increased value of the partnership interest is properly considered in settling with the retiring partner, revaluing total partnership assets above their historical cost is not acceptable.

CAPITAL BALANCE EXCEEDS SETTLEMENT In certain circumstances, a retiring partner may accept a settlement less than his or her capital balance. Examples include a history of poor partnership earnings or recognition of operating disadvantages resulting from the partner's retirement. In such cases, the excess of the retiring partner's capital balance over the settlement constitutes a bonus to the remaining partners. Assume that Baker, who has a capital balance of $15,000, accepts $11,000 rather than $20,000 for his interest. The $4,000 bonus is allocated to the remaining partners in their profit and loss sharing ratio (assumed here to be equal). The entry to record this bonus is

J. Baker, Capital	15,000	
E. Ames, Capital		2,000
S. Carter, Capital		2,000
Cash		11,000
To record Baker's withdrawal from the partnership.		

LIQUIDATION OF A PARTNERSHIP

The situations that arise during partnership liquidations can be quite complex. Because liquidations are treated comprehensively in advanced accounting texts, we shall provide only a basic approach to them here. When a business partnership is discontinued, the assets are sold, liabilities are paid, and the remaining cash is distributed to the partners. The conversion of the partnership assets into cash (by selling the assets) is called **realization**. Essentially, gains and losses realized in selling assets are carried to the partners' capital accounts (in the established profit and loss sharing ratio), and each partner eventually receives the balance remaining in his or her capital account.

Let us suppose that Ames, Baker, and Carter share profits and losses in the ratio of 40%, 40%, and 20%, respectively, and that before liquidation the partnership's balance sheet can be summarized as follows (assume that for the final operating period, the partnership books have been adjusted and closed and the profit or loss allocated to each partner):

Cash	$ 15,000	Liabilities	$ 40,000
Other Assets (net)	100,000	E. Ames, Capital	35,000
		J. Baker, Capital	15,000
		S. Carter, Capital	25,000
	$115,000		$115,000

Capital Balances Exceed Losses

If the noncash assets in the balance sheet in our example are sold for $80,000, the firm sustains a $20,000 loss. Because the partners share the loss, their capital balances are ultimately reduced by the following amounts: Ames, $8,000; Baker, $8,000; and Carter, $4,000. The appropriate entries might be as follows:

Cash	80,000	
Loss on Realization of Assets	20,000	
Other Assets (net)		100,000
To record loss on sale of other assets.		

E. Ames, Capital	8,000	
J. Baker, Capital	8,000	
S. Carter, Capital	4,000	
Loss on Realization of Assets		20,000
To distribute loss on sale of other assets.		

After these entries have been recorded, the firm's balance sheet accounts would be as follows:

Cash	$95,000	Liabilities	$40,000
		E. Ames, Capital	27,000
		J. Baker, Capital	7,000
		S. Carter, Capital	21,000
	$95,000		$95,000

Finally, the entries to pay the liabilities and distribute the remaining cash to the partners would be:

Liabilities	40,000	
Cash		40,000
To record payment of liabilities.		
E. Ames, Capital	27,000	
J. Baker, Capital	7,000	
S. Carter, Capital	21,000	
Cash		55,000
To record cash distribution to partners.		

Observe that *only gains* and *losses* on liquidation are shared in the profit and loss sharing ratio—not the residual cash. Remaining funds are distributed to partners *in the amounts of their capital balances* after all gains and losses have been shared.

Losses Exceed Partner's Capital

When liquidation losses occur, a partner's share of losses may exceed his or her capital balance. That partner will be expected to contribute cash to the partnership to offset the capital account debit balance. For example, suppose that in our illustration the $100,000 of other assets are sold for only $60,000. The resulting $40,000 loss on realization of assets is recorded and then distributed in the 40%:40%:20% sharing ratio, reducing partners' capital accounts as follows: Ames, $16,000; Baker, $16,000; and Carter, $8,000. Entries to record and distribute the loss and to pay the liabilities are

Cash	60,000	
Loss on Realization of Assets	40,000	
Other Assets (net)		100,000
To record loss on sale of other assets.		
E. Ames, Capital	16,000	
J. Baker, Capital	16,000	
S. Carter, Capital	8,000	
Loss on Realization of Assets		40,000
To distribute loss on sale of other assets.		

Liabilities	40,000	
Cash		40,000
To record payment of liabilities.		

After recording and distributing the loss on the sale of other assets and payment of the liabilities, the following account balances remain:

Cash	$35,000	E. Ames, Capital	$19,000
		J. Baker, Capital (debit)	(1,000)
		S. Carter, Capital	17,000
	$35,000		$35,000

Note that Baker's $16,000 share of the loss on realization of the other assets absorbs his $15,000 capital balance and leaves a $1,000 capital deficit (debit balance) in his capital account.

If Baker pays the firm $1,000 to make up his deficit, the resulting $36,000 cash balance is the amount distributed to Ames ($19,000) and Carter ($17,000). If Baker cannot make the contribution, the $1,000 is treated as a loss distributed to Ames and Carter in their profit and loss sharing ratio. Because the ratio of their respective shares is 40:20, Ames sustains 40/60, or two-thirds, of the $1,000 loss and Carter, 20/60, or one-third. The entry to redistribute Baker's debit balance would be

E. Ames, Capital	667	
S. Carter, Capital	333	
J. Baker, Capital		1,000
To record distribution of Baker's capital deficit to Ames and Carter.		

The $35,000 cash is then paid to Ames and Carter in the amounts of their final capital balances.

E. Ames, Capital	18,333	
S. Carter, Capital	16,667	
Cash		35,000
To record cash distribution to partners.		

Sometimes a partner with a capital account deficit may be uncertain about making up the deficit. At the same time, the other partners may want to distribute whatever cash is available after creditors have been paid. In our illustration, if Ames and Carter had doubts about receiving $1,000 from Baker, cash might be distributed as shown in the last entry—$18,333 to Ames and $16,667 to Carter. This would leave sufficient amounts in their capital accounts—$667 for Ames and $333 for Carter—to absorb a $1,000 loss in the sharing ratio if Baker defaults on payment. If he does contribute the amount needed, the other partners will be paid the balances of their capital accounts.

Statement of Partnership Liquidation

Liquidation of a partnership can continue over an extended period. To provide interested parties with a comprehensive report of the initial assets and liabilities, the sale of noncash assets, the payment of liabilities, and the final distribution of cash to the partners, the partnership may prepare a statement of partnership liquidation. Using data from our illustration, Exhibit 14–2 presents a statement of liquidation for the Ames, Baker, and Carter partnership. We assume that noncash assets are sold for $60,000 and that Baker does not cover his $1,000 capital deficit.

Observe the following about the statement of partnership liquidation:

(1) The statement is dated to reflect the period during which the liquidation took place.

(2) The initial numbers on the statement reflect the partnership balance sheet at the beginning of the liquidation (see page 519 in our illustration).

EXHIBIT 14–2

Ames, Baker, and Carter (Partnership)
Statement of Partnership Liquidation
From January 1 to March 31, 19XX

	Cash	Noncash Assets	Liabilities	E. Ames, Capital (40%)	J. Baker, Capital (40%)	S. Carter, Capital (20%)	Realization Gain (Loss)
Beginning Balances	$15,000	$100,000	$40,000	$35,000	$15,000	$25,000	
Sale of Noncash Assets	60,000	(100,000)					($40,000)
	$75,000	$ –0–	$40,000	$35,000	$15,000	$25,000	($40,000)
Allocation of Loss to Partners				(16,000)	(16,000)	(8,000)	40,000
	$75,000		$40,000	$19,000	$ (1,000)	$17,000	$ –0–
Payment of Liabilities	(40,000)		(40,000)				
	$35,000		$ –0–	$19,000	$ (1,000)	$17,000	
Allocation of Baker's Capital Deficit				(667)	1,000	(333)	
	$35,000			$18,333	$ –0–	$16,667	
Final Distribution of Cash	(35,000)			(18,333)		(16,667)	
	$ –0–			$ –0–		$ –0–	

(3) Each line that reflects a step in the liquidation (sale of noncash assets, allocation of loss, payment of liabilities, allocation of partner's capital deficit, and final cash distribution) matches related journal entries in the illustration (see pages 520–21).

(4) The statement shows how each step affects the liquidation and is therefore an excellent vehicle for analysis.

DEMONSTRATION PROBLEM FOR REVIEW

J. Porter and M. Kantor have been partners for several years, operating Fast Moves, a moving business. The business has had its ups and downs, but overall has been quite successful. In recognition of Porter's administrative responsibilities, the profit and loss sharing agreement allows him a salary of $5,000, with the remainder shared equally.

On January 1, 19X1, Porter and Kantor had capital balances of $14,000 and $9,000, respectively. During 19X1, Porter withdrew $4,000 cash from the partnership, and 19X1 net income was $11,000. On December 31, 19X1, the partnership had the following assets and liabilities: Cash, $4,000; Other Assets, $29,000; and Accounts Payable, $3,000.

Porter and Kantor liquidate the partnership on January 1, 19X2. On that date, other assets are sold for $35,000, creditors are paid, and the partners receive the remaining cash.

REQUIRED

(a) Prepare a schedule showing how the $11,000 net income for 19X1 should be divided between Porter and Kantor.

(b) Prepare a statement of partners' capital for 19X1.

(c) Prepare a balance sheet at December 31, 19X1.

(d) Give the January 1, 19X2, journal entries to record the sale of other assets and recognition of any related gain or loss, the distribution of any gain or loss to partners' capital accounts, the payment of liabilities, and the distribution of cash to the partners.

SOLUTION TO DEMONSTRATION PROBLEM

(a)

	Porter	Kantor	Total
Earnings to be divided			$11,000
Salary allowance	$5,000		5,000
Remainder			$ 6,000
Remainder divided equally	3,000	$3,000	
Partners' shares	$8,000	$3,000	

(b)

Fast Moves
Statement of Partners' Capital
For the Year 19X1

	Porter	Kantor	Total
Capital Balances, January 1, 19X1	$14,000	$ 9,000	$23,000
Add: Net Income for 19X1	8,000	3,000	11,000
Totals	$22,000	$12,000	$34,000
Less: Withdrawals	4,000		4,000
Capital Balances, December 31, 19X1	$18,000	$12,000	$30,000

(c)

Fast Moves
Balance Sheet
December 31, 19X1

Assets		Liabilities		
Cash	$ 4,000	Accounts Payable		$ 3,000
Other Assets	29,000			
		Owners' Equity		
		J. Porter, Capital	$18,000	
		M. Kantor, Capital	12,000	30,000
Total Assets	$33,000	Total Liabilities and Owners' Equity		$33,000

(d)

19X2			
Jan. 1	Cash	35,000	
	Other Assets		29,000
	Gain on Realization of Assets		6,000
	To record sale of other assets.		
Jan. 1	Gain on Realization of Assets	6,000	
	J. Porter, Capital		3,000
	M. Kantor, Capital		3,000
	To distribute gain on sale of other assets.		
Jan. 1	Accounts Payable	3,000	
	Cash		3,000
	To record payment of liabilities.		
Jan. 1	J. Porter, Capital	21,000	
	M. Kantor, Capital	15,000	
	Cash		36,000
	To record cash distribution to partners.		

KEY POINTS TO REMEMBER

(1) A partnership is a voluntary association of persons who agree to become joint owners of a business. Each general partner is an agent for the partnership, has unlimited liability for partnership obligations, and co-owns firm property with all partners. A partnership is a nontaxable entity and may be dissolved by any membership change or by court decree.

(2) Partnership assets should be recorded initially at their current fair values, which precludes future inequities in partners' capital balances resulting from the use of these assets.

(3) Partnership profits and losses are divided among partners according to their sharing agreement. If no sharing agreement exists, profits and losses are divided equally.

(4) New partners may be admitted to a partnership either by purchasing an interest or by investing assets. Because the purchase of an interest is a personal transaction between the incoming partner and one or more current partners, the firm's assets do not change. Admission of a partner through an investment increases the assets of the partnership.

(5) A retiring partner may sell his or her interest to an outsider, to one or more of the remaining partners, or receive payment for the interest from partnership funds.

(6) The liquidation of a partnership involves conversion of assets to cash, recognition and distribution of any related gain or loss, payment of creditors, and distribution of any remaining cash to partners. The final distribution of cash to partners is based on their capital balances.

SELF-TEST QUESTIONS
(Answers are at the end of this chapter.)

1. Partners A and B have beginning investments of $40,000 and $60,000, respectively. Profit and loss sharing is as follows: interest at 20% on beginning capital balances, salaries to A and B of $10,000 and $5,000, respectively, and the remainder shared in the ratio 2:3. How much of $30,000 net income would be distributed to A?

   (a) $18,000 (b) $16,000 (c) $15,500 (d) $14,000

2. Partners Hill and Dale have capital balances of $50,000 and $30,000, respectively, and share profits and losses equally. Brown purchases one-half of Hill's interest for $28,000. The entry for Brown's admission is:

(a) Hill, Capital	28,000	
Brown, Capital		28,000
(b) Cash	28,000	
Brown, Capital		28,000

(c) Hill, Capital	25,000	
Brown, Capital		25,000
(d) Hill, Capital	26,500	
Dale, Capital	1,500	
Brown, Capital		28,000

3. Byrd and Carr have capital balances of $80,000 and $70,000, respectively, and share profits and losses equally. Drumm invests an amount to give him exactly a one-third interest in the firm. No bonuses are to be awarded to any partners.
   (a) Drumm should invest $75,000 and be credited with $75,000.
   (b) Drumm should invest $50,000 and be credited with $50,000.
   (c) Drumm should invest $50,000 and be credited with $75,000.
   (d) Drumm should invest $75,000 and be credited with $50,000.

4. Partners Doyle, Farr, and Gibbs have capital balances of $50,000, $60,000, and $70,000, respectively, and share profits and losses in the ratio 3:2:1. Doyle retires and is paid $56,000 with partnership funds. The entry to record Doyle's retirement will include a
   (a) Debit to Doyle, Capital for $56,000.
   (b) Debit to Farr, Capital for $3,000.
   (c) Credit to Farr, Capital for $4,000.
   (d) Debit to Gibbs, Capital for $2,000.

5. Partners Hughes, Judd, and King share profits and losses in the ratio 3:5:2. Just before liquidation, the partnership has the following balance sheet:

Cash	$ 20,000	Hughes, Capital	$ 60,000
Other Assets	140,000	Judd, Capital	20,000
		King, Capital	80,000
	$160,000		$160,000

   Other Assets are sold for $80,000. Assuming that none of the partners can make up any resulting capital deficit, the final cash distribution to partner King is
   (a) $68,000 (b) $64,000 (c) $20,000 (d) $72,000

QUESTIONS

14–1 What is meant by *mutual agency*? By *unlimited liability*?

14–2 A corporation is said to have continuity of existence, whereas a partnership is characterized by a limited life. Name several events that may cause the dissolution of a partnership.

14–3 Lange understands that a partnership is a nontaxable entity and believes that if she does not withdraw any assets from the firm this year, she will not have any taxable income from her partnership activities. Is Lange correct? Why or why not?

14–4 Hughes invests in his partnership a machine that originally cost him $16,000. At the time of the investment, his personal records carry it at a book value of

$7,000. Its current market value is $10,000. At what amount should the partnership record the machine? Why?

14–5 What factors should persons going into partnership consider in deciding how to share profits and losses?

14–6 If a partnership agreement is silent on the sharing of profits and losses, how will they be divided? What if the agreement indicates the method of sharing profits, but states nothing about the sharing of losses?

14–7 What are salary allowances? What is the difference between a salary allowance and a salary expense?

14–8 In what ways do the financial statements of a partnership differ from those of a sole proprietorship? What is the purpose of a statement of partners' capital?

14–9 Distinguish between the admission of a partner by the purchase of an interest and by investment in the firm.

14–10 What circumstances might cause (a) current partners to receive a bonus when admitting a new partner and (b) an incoming partner to receive a bonus?

14–11 Reed and Dunn, who share profits and losses equally, admit Allen as a new partner. Allen contributes $60,000 for a one-fourth interest in the new firm. The entry to admit Allen shows a $10,000 bonus each to Reed and Dunn. What is the apparent total capital of the new partnership?

14–12 When a partner retires, are the assets and capital of the partnership reduced? Explain.

14–13 When a partnership liquidates, how do accountants handle the gains and losses realized in selling the assets?

14–14 In a partnership liquidation, the residual cash is distributed to partners in the amounts of their capital balances just prior to the distribution. Why is this the proper distribution procedure?

14–15 Assume that during liquidation a debit balance arises in a partner's capital account and the partner is unable to contribute any more assets to the partnership. How does the partnership dispose of the debit balance in the capital account?

14–16 How is a statement of partnership liquidation dated and what accounting information does this statement contain?

EXERCISES

Partnership formation

14–17 Burns and Eaton form a partnership on May 1. Burns contributes $60,000 cash and Eaton contributes the following items from a separate business:

Marketable securities—cost of $10,000; current fair value of $12,000
Equipment—cost of $40,000; accumulated depreciation of $15,000; current fair value of $35,000
Land—cost of $35,000; current fair value of $47,000
Note payable (secured by equipment)—$14,000 assumed by partnership

Give the opening general journal entries of the partnership to record the investments of Burns and Eaton.

Profit and loss sharing

14–18 Walker and Lowe are partners whose profit and loss sharing agreement gives salary allowances of $14,000 to Walker and $6,000 to Lowe, with the remainder divided equally.

(a) Net income for the year is $40,000. Give the general journal entry to distribute the income to Walker and Lowe.

(b) Assume a $10,000 net loss for the year. Give the general journal entry to distribute the loss to Walker and Lowe.

Statement of partners' capital

14–19 Use the following data to prepare a 19XX statement of partners' capital for Reese and Wade, who share profits and losses in the ratio of 60% to Reese and 40% to Wade.

Reese, Capital, January 1, 19XX	$80,000
Wade, Capital, January 1, 19XX	40,000
Reese, Drawing	25,000
Wade, Drawing	15,000
Additional investments by Reese	10,000
Net income for 19XX	30,000

Admission of a partner

14–20 Bond and Ellis are partners with capital balances of $80,000 and $60,000, respectively. They share profits and losses in the ratio of 75% to Bond and 25% to Ellis. Wood receives a one-fourth interest in the firm by investing $60,000 cash on May 4.

(a) Give the general journal entry to record Wood's admission assuming a bonus is allowed Bond and Ellis.

(b) Briefly explain circumstances that might cause existing partners to receive a bonus when admitting a new partner.

Retirement of a partner

14–21 Burr, Lins, and Niven are partners sharing profits and losses in the ratio 5:3:2, respectively. Their capital balances are Burr, $65,000; Lins, $40,000; and Niven, $50,000. Burr retires from the firm on June 30 and is paid $70,000 from partnership funds.

(a) Give the general journal entry to record Burr's retirement, assuming that Lins and Niven absorb the bonus paid Burr.

(b) Briefly explain circumstances that might cause a retiring partner to receive a bonus.

Partnership liquidation

14–22 In the liquidation of the ABC Partnership, noncash assets were sold for $25,000 and the related gain or loss on realization resulted in debits to the capital accounts of partners A, B, and C for $6,000, $4,500, and $4,500, respectively.

(a) Were the noncash assets sold at a gain or a loss? How do you know? How much was the gain or the loss?

(b) What is the partners' apparent profit and loss sharing ratio?

(c) What was the apparent book value of the noncash assets sold?

Partnership liquidation

14–23 Just before liquidation, the balance sheet of Ward and Sills, who share profits and losses equally, appeared as follows:

Cash	$26,000	Liabilities	$10,000
Other Assets	44,000	Ward, Capital	40,000
		Sills, Capital	20,000
	$70,000		$70,000

(a) If other assets are sold for $40,000, what amounts will Ward and Sills receive as the final cash distribution?

(b) If other assets are sold for $50,000, what amounts will Ward and Sills receive as the final cash distribution?

(c) If Ward receives $28,000 and Sills receives $8,000 as the final (and only) cash distribution, what amount was received from the sale of the other assets?

Partnership liquidation

14–24 Doan, Gage, Hill, and Larson are liquidating their partnership. All assets have been converted to cash, and all liabilities have been paid. At this point, the capital accounts show the following: Doan, $8,000 credit balance; Gage, $7,000 credit balance; Hill, $6,000 debit balance; and Larson, $9,000 credit balance. Profits and losses are shared equally.

(a) How much cash is available to distribute to partners?

(b) If there is doubt concerning Hill's ability to make up the $6,000 deficit, how should the available cash be distributed?

Partnership liquidation

14–25 The following is a summary of a statement of partnership liquidation. Each numbered line represents some aspect of the liquidation. Amounts in parentheses represent decreases or losses. Briefly describe what each numbered line represents, indicating the apparent partners' sharing ratio when appropriate.

	Cash	Noncash Assets	Liabilities	A, Capital	B, Capital	Gain or Loss on Realization
(1)	$20,000	$60,000	$24,000	$40,000	$16,000	
(2)	50,000	($60,000)				($10,000)
(3)	(24,000)		($24,000)			
(4)				(6,000)	(4,000)	$10,000
(5)	($46,000)			($34,000)	($12,000)	

PROBLEMS

Profit and loss sharing

14–26 Martin and Johnson form a partnership and invest $50,000 and $30,000, respectively. During its first year, the partnership earned a $16,000 net income.

REQUIRED

(a) Give the entry to close the Income Summary account and distribute the $16,000 net income under each of the following independent assumptions:

(1) The partnership agreement is silent on the sharing of profits and losses.

(2) Profits and losses are shared in the ratio of beginning capital investments.

(3) Profits and losses are shared by allowing 10% interest on beginning capital investments, with the remainder divided equally.

(b) Assume the partnership had a $24,000 loss in its first year. Give the entry to close the Income Summary account and distribute the $24,000 loss under each of the foregoing assumptions.

Profit and loss sharing

14–27 The capital accounts and the Income Summary account of the Read, Kell, and Turner partnership appear below. None of the partners withdrew capital during the year.

Read, Capital

	19XX	
	Jan. 1	12,000
	July 1	16,000

Kell, Capital

	19XX	
	Jan. 1	16,000
	Oct. 1	16,000

Turner, Capital

	19XX	
	Jan. 1	40,000

Income Summary

	19XX	
	Dec. 31	30,000

REQUIRED

(a) Give the entry to distribute the $30,000 net income if Read, Kell, and Turner share profits and losses:
   (1) Equally.
   (2) In the ratio 5:3:2, respectively.
   (3) In the ratio of *average* capital balances for the year.
   (4) Under an agreement allowing $16,000 salary to Turner, 10% interest on *beginning* investments, with the remainder shared equally.

(b) Assume that net income was $14,400 rather than $30,000. Give the entry to distribute the $14,400 earnings if the agreement allows $16,000 salary to Turner, 10% interest on beginning investments, with the remainder shared equally.

Admission of a partner

14–28 Barton and Kelly are partners with capital balances of $40,000 and $14,000, respectively. Profits and losses are shared equally.

REQUIRED

Give the entries to record the admission of a new partner, Dorn, under each of the following separate circumstances:

(a) Dorn purchases one-half of Kelly's interest, paying Kelly $10,000 personally.
(b) Dorn invests sufficient funds to receive exactly a one-fourth interest in the new partnership. (No bonuses are recorded.)
(c) Dorn invests $16,000 for a one-fifth interest, with any bonus distributed to the capital accounts of Barton and Kelly.
(d) Dorn invests $14,000 for a one-fourth interest, with any bonus credited to Dorn's capital account.
(e) In parts (c) and (d) above, what do the terms of admission imply regarding the relative negotiating positions of the new partner and the old partners?

Retirement of a partner

14–29 Gibbs, Lane, and Perry are partners with capital balances of $80,000, $45,000, and $60,000, respectively. Profits and losses are shared equally. Perry retires from the firm.

REQUIRED

Record the entries for Perry's retirement in each of the following separate circumstances:

(a) Perry's interest is sold to Markham, a new partner, for $65,000.
(b) One-half of Perry's interest is sold to each of the remaining partners for $36,000 apiece.

(c) Perry receives $64,000 of partnership funds for his interest. The remaining partners absorb the bonus paid Perry.
(d) The partners agree that Perry's abrupt retirement presents operating disadvantages and therefore Perry should receive only $54,000 for his interest. Payment is from partnership funds, with any bonuses going to Gibbs and Lane.

Sharing of loss, admission and withdrawal of partners

14–30 Bell and Harms formed a partnership on January 1, 19X1, with capital investments of $32,000 and $54,000, respectively. The profit and loss sharing agreement allowed Bell a salary of $16,000, with the remainder divided equally. During the year, Harms made withdrawals of $9,000; no other investments or withdrawals were made in 19X1. The partnership incurred a net loss of $20,000 in 19X1.

On January 1, 19X2, Field was admitted to the partnership. Field purchased one-third of Harms' interest, paying $10,000 directly to Harms. Bell, Harms, and Field agreed to share profits and losses in the ratio 3:5:2, respectively. No provision was made for salaries. The partnership earned a net income of $30,000 in 19X2.

On January 1, 19X3, Harms withdrew from the partnership. Harms received $35,000 of partnership funds for her interest. Bell and Field absorbed the bonus paid Harms.

REQUIRED
(a) Give the December 31, 19X1, entry to close the Income Summary account and distribute the $20,000 loss for 19X1.
(b) Compute the capital balances of Bell and Harms at December 31, 19X1.
(c) Give the entry to record the admission of Field on January 1, 19X2.
(d) Give the December 31, 19X2, entry to close the Income Summary account and distribute the $30,000 income for 19X2.
(e) Compute the December 31, 19X2, capital balances of Bell, Harms, and Field.
(f) Give the January 1, 19X3, entry to record Harms' withdrawal.

Statement of partners' capital

14–31 Lewis and Gray formed a partnership in 19X1, agreeing to share profits and losses equally. On December 31, 19X1, their capital balances were Lewis, $60,000; Gray, $36,000.

On January 1, 19X2, White was admitted to a one-fourth interest in the firm by investing $48,000 cash. White's admission was recorded by according bonuses to Lewis and Gray. The profit and loss sharing agreement of the new partnership allowed salaries of $12,000 to Lewis and $16,000 to White, with the remainder divided in the ratio 3:3:2 among Lewis, Gray, and White, respectively.

Net income for 19X2 was $76,000. Lewis and White withdrew cash during the year equal to their salary allowances. Immediately after the net income had been closed to the partners' capital accounts, White retired from the firm. White received $68,000 of partnership funds for his interest, and the remaining partners absorbed the bonus paid White.

REQUIRED
Prepare a statement of partners' capital for 19X2.

Partnership liquidation

14–32 Ray, Mack, and Clark are partners who share profits and losses in the ratio of 5:3:2, respectively. Just before the partnership's liquidation, its balance sheet accounts appear as follows:

Cash	$ 30,000	Accounts Payable	$ 40,000
Other Assets	160,000	Ray, Capital	30,000
		Mack, Capital	80,000
		Clark, Capital	40,000
	$190,000		$190,000

REQUIRED

(a) Assuming that other assets are sold for $140,000, give the entries to record the sale of the other assets and distribute the related loss, pay liabilities, and distribute the remaining cash to the partners.

(b) Assuming that other assets are sold for $80,000, give the entries to record the sale of the other assets and distribute the related loss, pay liabilities, apportion any partner's deficit among the other partners (assuming any such deficit is not made up by the partner involved), and distribute the remaining cash to the appropriate partners.

(c) Assuming that liquidation procedures occurred between January 1 and February 15, 19X4, prepare a statement of partnership liquidation using the data in part (b).

Sharing of loss and partnership liquidation

14–33 Allen, Burt, Curtis, and Dawes are partners who share profits and losses in the ratio of 4:3:2:1, respectively. Their partnership agreement provides for annual interest at 20% on partners' beginning capital balances and annual salaries of $10,000 and $4,000 to Allen and Burt, respectively.

Due to a history of modest earnings, they liquidate their partnership at December 31, 19X4. Just prior to completing the closing of the partnership books for 19X4, the trial balance is summarized as follows:

Cash	$ 62,000	Liabilities	$ 50,000
Noncash Assets (net)	85,000	Allen, Capital	30,000
Allen, Drawings	10,000	Burt, Capital	60,000
Curtis, Drawings	3,000	Curtis, Capital	20,000
Income Summary	20,000	Dawes, Capital	20,000
	$180,000		$180,000

REQUIRED

(a) Assuming that none of the partners made any capital contributions during the year, prepare journal entries to complete the closing of the books at December 31, 19X4.

(b) Starting with the partnership post-closing trial balance at December 31, 19X4, prepare a statement of partnership liquidation assuming that
   (1) Noncash assets were sold for $40,000 cash.
   (2) All liabilities were paid in cash.
   (3) Any partner experiencing a capital deficit would be unable to make up the deficit to the partnership.
   (4) The final distribution of cash to partners was made on February 20, 19X5.

ALTERNATE PROBLEMS

Profit and loss sharing

14–26A Holt and Wilson form a partnership and invest $80,000 and $40,000, respectively. During its first year, the partnership earned an $18,000 net income.

REQUIRED

(a) Give the entry to close the Income Summary account and distribute the $18,000 net income under each of the following independent assumptions:
  (1) The partnership agreement is silent on the sharing of profits and losses.
  (2) Profits and losses are shared in the ratio of beginning capital investments.
  (3) Profits and losses are shared by allowing 10% interest on beginning capital investments with the remainder divided equally.

(b) Assume the partnership had a $9,000 loss in its first year. Give the entry to close the Income Summary account and distribute the $9,000 loss under each of the foregoing assumptions.

Profit and loss sharing

14–27A The capital accounts and the Income Summary account of the Brady, Flood, and Gann partnership appear below. None of the partners withdrew capital during the year.

Brady, Capital

	19XX	
	Jan. 1	30,000
	July 1	20,000

Flood, Capital

	19XX	
	Jan. 1	20,000
	Oct. 1	60,000

Gann, Capital

	19XX	
	Jan. 1	50,000

Income Summary

	19XX	
	Dec. 31	48,000

REQUIRED

(a) Give the entry to distribute the $48,000 net income if Brady, Flood, and Gann share profits and losses:
  (1) Equally.
  (2) In the ratio 3:2:1, respectively.
  (3) In the ratio of *average* capital balances for the year.
  (4) Under an agreement allowing $26,000 salary to Brady, 10% interest on *beginning* investments, with the remainder shared equally.

(b) Assume that net income was $33,000 rather than $48,000. Give the entry to distribute the $33,000 earnings if the agreement allows $26,000 salary to Brady, 10% interest on beginning investments, with the remainder shared equally.

Admission of a partner

14–28A Casey and Dobson are partners with capital balances of $54,000 and $30,000, respectively. Profits and losses are shared equally.

REQUIRED

Give the entries to record the admission of a new partner, Gordon, under each of the following separate circumstances:

(a) Gordon purchases one-half of Dobson's interest, paying Dobson $24,000 personally.

(b) Gordon invests sufficient funds to receive exactly a one-fourth interest in the new partnership. (No bonuses are recorded.)
(c) Gordon invests $31,000 for a one-fifth interest, with any bonus distributed to the capital accounts of Casey and Dobson.
(d) Gordon invests $24,000 for a one-fourth interest, with any bonus credited to Gordon's capital account.
(e) In parts (c) and (d) above, what do the terms of admission imply regarding the relative negotiating positions of the new partner and the old partners?

Retirement of a partner

14–29A Archer, Kyle, and Nunn are partners with capital balances of $80,000, $60,000, and $60,000, respectively. Profits and losses are shared equally. Nunn retires from the firm.

REQUIRED
Record the entries for Nunn's retirement in each of the following separate circumstances:
(a) Nunn's interest is sold to Green, a new partner, for $65,000.
(b) One-half of Nunn's interest is sold to each of the remaining partners for $32,000 apiece.
(c) Nunn receives $72,000 of partnership funds for his interest. The remaining partners absorb the bonus paid to Nunn.
(d) The partners agree that Nunn's abrupt retirement presents operating disadvantages and therefore Nunn should receive only $52,000 for his interest. Payment is from partnership funds, with any bonuses going to Archer and Kyle.

Partnership liquidation

14–32A Barr, Steele, and Timm are partners who share profits and losses in the ratio of 5:3:2, respectively. Just before the partnership's liquidation, its balance sheet appears as follows:

Cash	$18,000	Accounts Payable	$16,000
Other Assets (net)	78,000	Barr, Capital	15,000
		Steele, Capital	25,000
		Timm, Capital	40,000
	$96,000		$96,000

REQUIRED
(a) Assuming that other assets are sold for $58,000, give the entries to record the sale of the other assets and distribute the related loss, pay liabilities, and distribute the remaining cash to the partners.
(b) Assuming that other assets are sold for $43,000, give the entries to record the sale of the other assets and distribute the related loss, pay liabilities, apportion any partner's deficit among the other partners (assuming any such deficit is not made up by the partner involved), and distribute the remaining cash to the appropriate partners.
(c) Assuming that liquidation procedures occurred between January 1 and February 8, 19X5, prepare a statement of partnership liquidation using the data in part (b).

Sharing of loss and partnership liquidation

14–33A Cole, Hanley, Upton, and Wild are partners who share profits and losses in the ratio of 5:3:1:1, respectively. Their partnership agreement provides for annual interest at 20% on partners' beginning capital balances and annual salaries of $10,000 and $20,000 to Cole and Hanley, respectively.

Due to a history of modest earnings, they liquidate their partnership on December 31, 19X5. Just prior to completing the closing of the partnership books for 19X5, the trial balance is summarized as follows:

Cash	$ 54,000	Liabilities	$ 34,000
Noncash Assets (net)	160,000	Cole, Capital	50,000
Cole, Drawings	20,000	Hanley, Capital	40,000
Hanley, Drawings	30,000	Upton, Capital	100,000
Income Summary	20,000	Wild, Capital	60,000
	$284,000		$284,000

REQUIRED

(a) Assuming that none of the partners made any capital contributions during the year, prepare journal entries to complete the closing of the books at December 31, 19X5.

(b) Starting with the partnership post-closing trial balance at December 31, 19X5, prepare a statement of partnership liquidation assuming the following:
   (1) Noncash assets were sold for $120,000 cash.
   (2) All liabilities were paid in cash.
   (3) Any partner experiencing a capital deficit would be unable to make up the deficit to the partnership.
   (4) The final distribution of cash to partners was made on January 31, 19X6.

BUSINESS DECISION PROBLEM

Braden and Coyle were in business for several years, sharing profits and losses equally. Because of Coyle's poor health, they liquidate the partnership. Braden managed the liquidation because Coyle was in the hospital. Just before liquidation, the partnership balance sheet contained the following information:

Cash	$ 50,000	Liabilities	$ 30,000
Other Assets	150,000	Braden, Capital	70,000
		Coyle, Capital	100,000
	$200,000		$200,000

Braden (1) sold the other assets at the best prices obtainable, (2) paid off all the creditors, and (3) divided the remaining cash between Coyle and himself equally, according to their profit and loss sharing ratio.

Coyle received a note from Braden that read "Good news—sold other assets for $180,000. Have $100,000 check waiting for you. Get well soon." Because he will not be released from the hospital for several days, Coyle asks you to review Braden's liquidation and cash distribution procedures.

REQUIRED

Do you approve of Braden's liquidation and cash distribution procedures? Explain. If you believe Braden erred, what amount of final cash settlement should Coyle receive?

ANSWERS TO SELF-TEST QUESTIONS

1. (b) 2. (c) 3. (a) 4. (d) 5. (b)

15

Corporations: Organization and Capital Stock

Chapter Objectives

- Define and discuss the corporate form of organization.
- Identify and discuss the types of stock and their basic rights.
- Explain the difference between par and no-par value stock.
- Describe the accounting for issuances of stock for cash, by subscription, and for noncash assets.
- Explain the accounting for reacquired and reissued shares of stock.
- Define and discuss the terms book value, market value, and liquidation value per share of stock.

The genius of the industrial system lies in its organized use of capital and technology.

JOHN KENNETH GALBRAITH

"It was once said that the sun never set on the British Empire. Today the sun does set on the British Empire, but not on the scores of corporate empires. . . ."[1] Without a doubt, the modern corporation dominates the national and international economic landscape. In the United States, corporations generate well over three-fourths of the combined business receipts of corporations, partnerships, and proprietorships, even though fewer than one of every five businesses is organized as a corporation. The corporate form of organization is used for a variety of business efforts—from the large, multinational corporation with more than a million owners operating in countries all over the world to the small, family-owned business in a single community.

In this and the next three chapters, we consider various aspects of accounting for the corporation. In this chapter, we emphasize the organization of the corporation and the accounting procedures for its capital stock transactions.

NATURE AND FORMATION OF A CORPORATION

A corporation is a legal entity—an artificial legal "person"—created on the approval of the appropriate governmental authority. The right to conduct business as a corporation is a privilege granted by the state in which the corporation is formed. All states have laws specifying the requirements for creating a corporation. In some instances—such as the formation of a national bank—the federal government must approve the creation of a corporation.

To form a corporation, the incorporators (often at least three are required) must apply for a charter. The incorporators prepare and file the **articles of incorporation**, which delineate the basic structure of the corporation, including the purposes for which it is formed, the amount of capital stock to be authorized, and the number of shares into which the stock is to be divided. If the incorporators meet the requirements of the law, the government issues a charter or certificate of incorporation. After the charter has been granted, the incorporators (or, in some states, the subscribers to the corporation's capital stock) hold an organization meeting to elect the first board of directors and adopt the corporation's bylaws.

Because assets are essential to corporate operations, the corporation issues **certificates of capital stock** to obtain the necessary funds. As owners of the

[1] Lester R. Brown, "How Big Are the Multinationals?" *The Saturday Evening Post*, March 1974.

corporation, **stockholders,** or **shareholders,** are entitled to a voice in the control and management of the company. Stockholders with voting stock may vote at the annual meeting and participate in the election of the board of directors. The board of directors is responsible for the overall management of the corporation. Normally, the board selects such corporate officers as a president, one or more vice-presidents, a controller, a treasurer, and a secretary. The officers implement the policies of the board of directors and actively manage the day-to-day affairs of the corporation.

Creating a corporation is more costly than organizing a proprietorship or partnership. The expenditures incurred to organize a corporation are charged to Organization Costs, an intangible asset account. These costs include attorney's fees, fees paid to the state, and costs of promoting the enterprise. As we discussed in Chapter 11, organization costs typically are amortized over a period of five to ten years.

CHARACTERISTICS OF CORPORATIONS

Separate Legal Entity

A business with a corporate charter is empowered to conduct business affairs apart from its owners. The corporation, as a legal entity, may acquire assets, incur debt, enter into contracts, sue, and be sued—all in its own name. The owners, or stockholders, of the corporation receive stock certificates as evidence of their ownership interests; the stockholders, however, are separate and distinct from the corporation. This characteristic contrasts with proprietorships and partnerships, which are accounting entities but not legal entities apart from their owners. Owners of proprietorships and partnerships can be held responsible separately and collectively for unsatisfied obligations of the business.

Limited Liability

The liability of shareholders with respect to company affairs is usually limited to their investment in the corporation. Because of this limited liability, state laws restrict distributions to shareholders. Most of these laws have fairly elaborate provisions that define the various forms of owners' equity and describe distribution conditions. To protect creditors, the state controls the distribution of contributed capital. Distributions of retained earnings (undistributed profits) are not legal unless the board of directors formally declares a dividend. Because of the legal delineation of owner capital available for distribution, corporations must maintain careful distinctions in the accounts to identify the different elements of stockholders' equity.

Transferability of Ownership

Shares in a corporation may be routinely transferred without affecting the company's operations. The corporation merely notes such transfers of ownership in the stockholder records (ledger). Although a corporation must have stockholder records to notify shareholders of meetings and to pay dividends, the price at which shares transfer between owners is not recognized in the corporation's accounts.

Continuity of Existence

Because routine transfers of ownership do not affect a corporation's affairs, the corporation is said to have continuity of existence. In this respect, a corporation is completely different from a partnership. In a partnership, any change in ownership technically results in discontinuance of the old partnership and formation of a new one. (Many large professional service partnerships, however, follow procedures that provide for continuity with changes in ownership.)

In a partnership, the individual partners' capital accounts indicate their relative interests in the business. The stockholders' equity section of a corporate balance sheet does not present individual stockholder accounts. A shareholder, however, can easily compute his or her interest in the corporation by calculating the proportion of the total shares outstanding that his or her shares represent. For example, if only one class of stock is outstanding and it totals 1,000 shares, an individual owning 200 shares has a 20% interest in the corporation's total stockholders' equity, which includes all contributed capital and retained earnings. The dollar amount of this interest, however, is a book amount, rarely coinciding with the market value. A stockholder who liquidates his or her investment would sell it at a price negotiated with a buyer or, if the stock is traded on a stock exchange, at the exchange's quoted market price.

Capital-raising Capability

The limited liability of stockholders and the ease with which shares of stock may be transferred from one investor to another are attractive features to potential stockholders. These characteristics enhance the ability of the corporation to raise large amounts of capital by issuing shares of stock. Because both large and small investors may acquire ownership interests in a corporation, a wide spectrum of potential investors exists. Corporations with thousands of stockholders are not uncommon. The ability to accumulate and use tremendous amounts of capital makes the corporation the dominant form of business organization in the U.S. economy.

Taxation

As legal entities, corporations are subject to federal income taxes on their earnings, whether distributed or not. In addition, shareholders must pay income taxes on earnings received as dividends. In many small corporations in which the shareholders themselves manage the business affairs, large salaries may reduce earnings to a point where the double taxation feature is not onerous. However, the firm may have to justify the reasonableness of such salaries to the Internal Revenue Service. Under certain circumstances, a corporation with 35 or fewer shareholders may elect partnership treatment for tax purposes. Although partnerships must submit "information" tax returns, an income tax is not imposed on their earnings. Instead, the partners report their respective shares of partnership earnings on their individual income tax returns.

Usually, corporations are subject to state income taxes in the states in which they are incorporated or are doing business. They may also be subject to real estate, personal property, and franchise taxes.

Regulation and Supervision

Corporations are subject to greater degrees of regulation and supervision than are proprietorships and partnerships. Each state has the right to regulate the corporations it charters. State laws limit the powers a corporation may exercise, identify reports that must be filed, and define the rights and liabilities of stockholders. If stock is issued to the public, the corporation must comply with the laws governing the sale of corporate securities. Furthermore, corporations whose stock is listed and traded on organized security exchanges—such as the New York Stock Exchange—are subject to the various reporting and disclosure requirements of these exchanges.

OWNERS' EQUITY AND ORGANIZATIONAL FORMS

Differences arise between accounting for the owners' equity of a corporation and for that of a sole proprietorship or partnership. In a sole proprietorship, only a single owner's capital account is needed to reflect increases from capital contributions and net earnings as well as decreases from withdrawals and net losses. In practice, as explained in Chapter 2, many sole proprietors keep a separate drawing account to record withdrawals of cash and other business assets. This separate record is kept only for convenience, however; no subdivision of the owner's capital account is required either by law or by accounting principles.

A similar situation exists in most partnerships, which customarily maintain capital and drawing accounts for each partner. A partnership is simply an association of two or more persons who agree to become joint owners of a business. Because more than one individual is involved in the business, a written agreement should govern the financial participation and business responsibilities of the partners. However, no legal or accounting requirement demands that a distinction be maintained between contributed capital and undistributed earnings.

A corporation, on the other hand, is subject to certain legal restrictions imposed by the government approving its creation. These restrictions focus on the distinction between contributed capital and retained earnings and make accounting for the owners' equity somewhat more complex for corporations than for other types of business organizations. Note that much of the accounting for corporate owners' equity is actually a polyglot of legal prescription and accounting convention. The detailed reporting of stockholders' equity transactions, however, provides analytical information that is often useful and, in many instances, required by law.

TYPES OF STOCK

The amounts and kinds of stock that a corporation may issue are enumerated in the company's charter. Providing for several classes of stock permits the company to raise capital from different types of investors. The charter also specifies the corporation's **authorized stock**—the maximum number of shares of each class of stock that may be issued. A corporation that wishes to issue more shares than its authorized number must first amend its charter. Shares that have been sold and issued to stockholders constitute the **issued stock** of the corporation. Some of this stock may be repurchased by the corporation. Shares actually held by stockholders are called **outstanding stock,** whereas those reacquired by the corporation are **treasury stock.** We discuss treasury stock later in the chapter.

Common Stock

When only one class of stock is issued, it is called **common stock.** Common shareholders compose the basic ownership class. They have rights to vote, to share in earnings, to participate in additional issues of stock, and—in the case of liquidation—to share in assets after prior claims on the corporation have been settled. We now consider each of these rights.

As the owners of a corporation, the common shareholders elect the board of directors and vote on other matters requiring the approval of owners. Common shareholders are entitled to one vote for each share of stock they own. Owners who do not attend the annual stockholders' meetings may vote by proxy (this may be the case for most stockholders in large corporations).

A common stockholder has the right to a proportionate share of the corporation's earnings that are distributed as dividends. All earnings belong to the corporation, however, until the board of directors formally declares a dividend.

Each shareholder of a corporation has a **preemptive right** to maintain his or her proportionate interest in the corporation. If the company issues additional shares of stock, current owners of that type of stock receive the first opportunity to acquire, on a pro-rata basis, the new shares. In certain situations, management may request shareholders to waive their preemptive rights. For example, the corporation may wish to issue additional stock to acquire another company. Further, stockholders of firms incorporated in some states do not receive preemptive rights.

A liquidating corporation converts its assets to a form suitable for distribution, usually cash, which it then distributes to parties having claims on the corporate assets. Any assets remaining after all claims have been satisfied belong to the residual ownership interest in the corporation—the common stockholders. These owners are entitled to the final distribution of the balance of the assets.

A company may occasionally use **classified** common stock; that is, it may issue more than one class of common stock. Two classes of common stock issued are identified as Class A and Class B. The two classes usually differ in either their respective dividend rights or their respective voting powers. Usually, classified common stock is issued when the organizers of the corporation wish to acquire funds from the public while retaining voting control. To illustrate, let us assume 10,000 shares of Class A stock are issued to the public at $40 per share, while 20,000 shares of Class B stock are issued to the organizers at $5 per share. If each shareholder receives one vote per share of stock, the Class B stockholders have twice as many votes as the Class A stockholders. Yet the total investment of Class B stockholders is significantly less than that of the Class A stockholders. To offset the difference in the voting power per dollar of investment, the Class A stockholders may have better dividend rights, such as being entitled to dividends in early years, while the Class B stockholders may not receive dividends until a certain level of earning power is reached.

Preferred Stock

Preferred stock is a class of stock with various characteristics that distinguish it from common stock. Preferred stock has one or more preferences over common stock, usually with reference to (1) dividends and (2) assets when the corporation liquidates. To determine the features of a particular issue, we must examine the stock contract. The majority of preferred issues, however, have certain typical features, which we discuss below.

DIVIDEND PREFERENCE When the board of directors declares a distribution of earnings, preferred stockholders are entitled to a certain annual amount of dividends before common stockholders receive any distribution. The amount is usually specified in the preferred stock contract as a percentage of the face value (called par value) of the stock or in dollars per share if the stock does not have a par value. (Par value and no-par value stock are discussed later in this chapter.) Thus, if the preferred stock has a $100 par value and a 6% dividend rate, the preferred shareholders receive $6 per share in dividends. However, the amount is owed to the stockholders only if declared.

Preferred dividends are usually **cumulative**—that is, regular dividends to preferred stockholders omitted in past years must be paid in addition to the current year's dividend before any distribution is made to common shareholders. For example, a dividend may not be declared in an unprofitable year. If the $6 preferred stock dividend mentioned above is one year in arrears and a dividend is declared in the current year, preferred shareholders would receive $12 per share before common shareholders received anything. If a preferred stock is noncumulative, omitted dividends do not carry forward. Because investors normally consider the noncumulative feature unattractive, noncumulative preferred stock is rarely issued.

Dividends in arrears (that is, omitted in past years) on cumulative preferred stock are not an accounting liability and do not appear in the liability section of the balance sheet. They do not become an obligation of the corporation until the board of directors formally declares such dividends. Any arrearages are typically disclosed to investors in a footnote to the balance sheet.

Ordinarily, preferred stockholders receive a fixed amount and do not participate further in distributions made by the corporation. In rare circumstances, however, the stock contract may make the preferred a **participating** stock. To illustrate the participating feature, let us assume that a company had outstanding 1,000 shares of $100 par value, 6% *fully participating* cumulative preferred stock and 2,000 shares of $100 par value common stock. Assume also that the company declared total dividends of $27,000 and that no preferred dividends were in arrears. The distribution would be made as follows:

	Preferred	Common	Total
Outstanding stock (total par value)	$100,000	$200,000	$300,000
Preferred dividends in arrears	$-0-		$-0-
Regular dividend (6%) and matching rate to common (6%)	6,000	$12,000	18,000
Remainder of $9,000 ($27,000 − $18,000) divided to give each class the same rate: $9,000/$300,000 = 3%	3,000	6,000	9,000
Total distribution	$9,000	$18,000	$27,000
Rate of distribution (based on total par value)	9%	9%	

Note that, after the preferred stock is accorded its regular 6% dividend, a like rate of 6% ($12,000) is allocated to the common stock. The remaining $9,000 is then apportioned so both classes of stock receive the same *rate* of distribution. This rate is determined by dividing the remainder to be distributed by the total par value of both classes of stock ($300,000). It is important to note that the preferred stock does not participate until the common stock is accorded an amount corresponding to the regular preferred dividend rate.

Preferred stock may also be *partially* participating. For example, suppose that the preferred shares participate to 8%. They would then be entitled only to an additional 2% over their regular 6% dividend, and any remaining amount would be accorded to the common shares.

Any arrearage on cumulative preferred stock must first be awarded to the preferred shareholders. Therefore, had there been one year's arrearage on the fully participating stock in the foregoing example, $12,000 ($6,000 dividends in arrears and $6,000 current dividends) would have been allocated to the preferred stock and then the normal 6%, or $12,000, to the common stock. Of the remaining $3,000, $1,000 would be assigned to the preferred stock and $2,000 to the common stock.

Of course, if either the common stock or the preferred stock is no-par value stock, preferred stock participation is determined on some basis other than total par values. For example, the participation may be achieved by allocating dividends of equal dollar amounts per share to each class of stock.

ASSET DISTRIBUTION PREFERENCE Preferred stockholders normally have a preference over common stockholders as to the receipt of assets when a corporation liquidates. As the corporation goes out of business, the claims of creditors are settled first. Then preferred stockholders have the right to receive assets equal to the par value of their stock or a larger stated liquidation value per share before any assets are distributed to common stockholders. The preferred stockholders' preference to assets in liquidation also includes any dividends in arrears.

OTHER FEATURES Although preferred shareholders do not ordinarily have the right to vote in the election of directors, this right can be accorded by contract. Some state laws require that all stock issued by a corporation be given voting rights. Sometimes, a preferred stock contract confers full or partial voting rights under certain conditions—for example, when dividends have not been paid for a specified period.

Preferred stock contracts may contain features that cause the stock to resemble the common stock equity at one end of a spectrum or a debt obligation at the other end. The stock may, for example, be **convertible** into common stock at some specified rate. With this feature, the market price of the preferred often moves with that of the common. When the price of the common stock rises, the value of the conversion feature is enhanced. Preferred stock may also be convertible into long-term debt securities (bonds).

Preferred stock may be **callable**, which means the corporation can redeem the stock after a length of time and at a price specified in the contract. The call feature makes the stock similar to a bond, which frequently is callable or has a limited life. Most preferred stocks are callable, with the call or redemption price set slightly above the original issuance price.

To be successful in selling its preferred stock, a corporation often must cater to current market vogues. Features are added or omitted, depending on market conditions and the desires of the investor group the corporation wishes to attract. Management must balance market requirements with its own goals. Sometimes management must compromise and issue securities that it hopes to change over time, perhaps through conversion or refinancing, to arrive at the desired financial plan.

Preferred stocks appeal to investors who want a steady rate of return that is normally somewhat higher than that on bonds. These investors often feel that preferred stock entails less risk than common stock, although the common will pay off more if the company does well.

From both the legal and the accounting standpoint, all types of preferred stock, whatever their features, are part of stockholders' equity. Dividends are distributions of earnings and, unlike interest on bonds, are not shown as expenses on the income statement. Also, because of the legal classification of preferred stock as stockholders' equity, the company cannot deduct dividends as expenses for income tax purposes, whereas interest on debt can be deducted as an expense.

PAR AND NO-PAR VALUE STOCK

The corporate charter may specify a face value, or **par value**, for each share of stock of any class. Although this face value may relate to the initial price of the stock, it is often arbitrary and has no connotation of value once operations begin. Par value may have legal implications, however, because it invariably is used to determine the *legal capital* of the business. State laws normally define this term and restrict the distribution of legal capital. For this reason, accountants carefully segregate and record the par value amount of stock transactions in an appropriate capital stock account.

Because investors may confuse par value with realistic values, many states have permitted **no-par** stock since the early 1900s. Most states, however, permit a company's directors to set a **stated value** on the shares (some states insist on this). Again, this figure is arbitrary, but in contrast to par value, the stated value is not printed on the stock certificates. For accounting purposes, stated value amounts are treated in a fashion similar to par value amounts.

A **premium** is the amount in excess of par value received when a corporation issues stock. The excess of par value over the amount received may be called **discount.** In some states, persons purchasing stock for less than par value may have a liability for the discount should creditor claims remain unsatisfied after the company's liquidation. Stocks are rarely sold at a discount—in certain states this practice is even forbidden. When no-par stock with a stated value is sold, the price received invariably exceeds the stated value. In accounting, the difference is called *excess of amount paid in over stated value;* the terms *premium* and *discount* are not used with no-par stock.

To record differences between amounts received for shares and par value, the accountant uses appropriately descriptive accounts. When an amount greater than par value is received, we may use the account Paid-in Capital in Excess of Par Value, or simply Premium on Stock. The account Excess of Par Value over Amount Paid In or simply Discount on Stock, can be used when a discount is involved. For no-par stock with a stated value, accounts have titles such as Paid-in Capital in Excess of Stated Value.

To illustrate how the stockholders' equity accounts present the amounts paid in for stock, let us assume that in its first year of operations, a corporation had the following transactions:

(1) Sold 1,000 shares of $100 par value, 9% preferred stock at $107 per share.

(2) Sold 1,000 shares of $100 par value, 6% preferred stock at $98 per share.

(3) Sold 5,000 shares of no-par common stock at $30 per share. Stated value is $20 per share.

(4) The company earned $50,000 during the year. After paying dividends of $9,000 on the 9% preferred stock, $6,000 on the 6% preferred stock, and $10,000 to the common shareholders, the company had $25,000 in retained earnings.

The stockholders' equity section of the company's December 31 balance sheet appears in Exhibit 15–1.

EXHIBIT 15–1
Stockholders' Equity

Paid-in Capital:		
9% Preferred Stock, $100 Par Value, 1,000 shares authorized, issued, and outstanding	$100,000	
Paid-in Capital in Excess of Par Value	7,000	$107,000
6% Preferred Stock, $100 Par Value, 1,000 shares authorized, issued, and outstanding	$100,000	
Excess of Par Value over Amount Paid In	(2,000)	98,000
No-par Common Stock, Stated Value $20, 10,000 shares authorized; 5,000 shares issued and outstanding	$100,000	
Paid-in Capital in Excess of Stated Value	50,000	150,000
Total Paid-in Capital		$355,000
Retained Earnings		25,000
Total Stockholders' Equity		$380,000

In the illustration, we assume that all authorized amounts of both classes of preferred stock and half of the 10,000 shares of common stock authorized have been issued. Note that both the premium on the 9% preferred stock and the excess received over stated value of the no-par common stock are added to the par and stated values, respectively. On the other hand, the $2,000 discount on the 6% preferred stock is deducted from par value to show the amount received for this class. All the accounts in the illustration have credit balances in the general ledger, except Excess of Par Value over Amount Paid In on the 6% preferred stock, which has a $2,000 debit balance.

Corporate owners' equity accounts are presented in a variety of ways in published reports. One popular format groups the par and stated values of the three classes of stock together under the heading Capital Stock—a total of $300,000 in our example. The remainder of the paid-in capital items are placed under a heading such as Paid-in Capital. In our example, the paid-in amounts in excess of par and stated values less the excess of par value over amount received on the 6% preferred stock total $55,000. This type of presentation is not as clear as Exhibit 15–1, because the capital stock of a firm is really part of total paid-in capital.

STOCK ISSUANCES FOR CASH

In issuing its stock, a corporation may use the services of an investment banker, a specialist in marketing securities to investors. The investment banker may *underwrite* a stock issue—that is, the banker buys the stock from the corporation and resells it to investors. The corporation does not risk being unable to sell its stock. The underwriter bears this risk in return for the profits generated by selling the stock to investors at a price higher than that paid the corporation. An investment banker who is unwilling to underwrite a stock issue may handle it on a *best efforts* basis. In this case, the investment banker agrees to sell as many shares as possible at a set price, but the corporation bears the risk of unsold stock.

The stock issues in Exhibit 15–1, which were all for cash, would have been entered in the corporation's books by the following entries:

(1) Sale of 1,000 shares of $100 par value, 9% preferred stock at $107 per share.

Cash	107,000	
9% Preferred Stock		100,000
Paid-in Capital in Excess of Par Value		7,000

(2) Sale of 1,000 shares of $100 par value, 6% preferred stock at $98 per share.

Cash	98,000	
Excess of Par Value over Amount Paid In	2,000	
6% Preferred Stock		100,000

(3) Sale of 5,000 shares of no-par common stock, stated value $20, at $30 per share.

Cash	150,000	
Common Stock		100,000
Paid-in Capital in Excess of Stated Value		50,000

The appropriate capital stock account is always credited with the par value of shares, or if the stock is no-par, with its stated value, if any. Cash received is debited, and any difference is placed in an appropriately named account. The $7,000 premium on the 9% preferred stock may be credited to an account called Premium on Preferred Stock. Similarly, the $2,000 discount on the 6% preferred stock may be debited to an account called Discount on Preferred Stock. The account titles we have used in the illustration, however, are most common.

When no-par stock has a stated value, as in entry (3), the stated value of the total shares issued is credited to the proper capital stock account and any additional amount received is credited to an account called Paid-in Capital in Excess of Stated Value. This amount, though treated similarly to a stock premium, should not be regarded as a premium—the stated value is arbitrarily set by the board of directors. If no stated value for no-par stock exists, the entire proceeds should be credited to the appropriate capital stock account. In entry (3), if the common stock had no stated value, the entire $150,000 amount would have been credited to the Common Stock account.

STOCK SUBSCRIPTIONS

Sometimes a corporation sells stock directly to investors rather than through an investment banker. The corporation may obtain signatures of prospective purchasers on *subscription contracts* prior to issuing shares. Frequently, such contracts provide for installment payments. When subscriptions are obtained, the corporation debits a receivable account, Stock Subscriptions Receivable. Instead of crediting the regular Common Stock account, the firm credits a temporary paid-in capital account called Common Stock Subscribed. The use of a temporary account signifies that the shares have not yet been paid for or issued. Until the shares are paid for, the account is shown separately in the stockholders' equity section of the balance sheet. Stock Subscriptions Receivable appears with the current assets. After all payments have been received and the stock is issued, the corporation debits the temporary account, Common Stock Subscribed, and credits the regular account, Common Stock.

To illustrate the journal entries for stock subscription transactions, let us assume that 500 shares of $100 par value stock were sold on subscription for $120 a share, paid in installments of $40 and $80. The entries would be:

To record receipt of subscriptions

Stock Subscriptions Receivable—Common	60,000	
Common Stock Subscribed		50,000
Paid-in Capital in Excess of Par Value		10,000
Received subscriptions for 500 shares at $120 per share.		

To record collection of first installment

Cash	20,000	
Stock Subscriptions Receivable—Common		20,000
Collected first installment of $40 per share.		

To record collection of final installment and issuance of shares

Cash	40,000	
Stock Subscriptions Receivable—Common		40,000
Collected final installment of $80 per share.		
Common Stock Subscribed	50,000	
Common Stock		50,000
To record issuance of 500 shares.		

STOCK ISSUANCES FOR ASSETS OTHER THAN CASH

When stock is issued for property other than cash or for services, the accountant must carefully determine the amount recorded. We should not assume that the par or stated value of the shares issued automatically sets a value for the property or services received. In the early years of U.S. corporations, such an assumption frequently resulted in the recording and reporting of excessive asset valuations.

Property or services acquired should be recorded at their current fair value or at the fair value of the stock issued, whichever is more clearly determinable. If the stock is actively traded on a securities exchange, the market price of the stock issued may indicate an appropriate value. For example, if the current market price is $140 per share and 500 shares are issued for a parcel of land, this land may be valued, in the absence of other price indicators, at $70,000. An effort should be made, however, to determine a fair value for the property. Certainly, all aspects of the transaction should be carefully scrutinized to ascertain that the number of shares issued was objectively determined. Obviously, if no market value for the stock is available, we would seek an independently determined value for the property or services received.

Let us suppose the stock issued for the land is $100 par value common stock and its market value is the best indicator of the property's fair value. The entry to record the transaction would be

Land	70,000	
Common Stock		50,000
Paid-in Capital in Excess of Par Value		20,000
To record issuance of 500 shares of common stock for land valued at $70,000.		

TREASURY STOCK

When a corporation reacquires its own outstanding shares for a purpose other than retiring them, the reacquired shares are called *treasury stock*. Treasury stock may be purchased for a variety of reasons, which include reissuing them to officers and employees in profit-sharing schemes or stock-option plans. Whatever the purpose, the corporation is reducing owner capital for a period of time. Consequently, treasury stock is not regarded as an asset. The shares do not carry voting privileges or preemptive rights, are not paid dividends, and do not receive assets on the corporation's liquidation.

Because treasury stock is stock that has been issued before, it differs in one significant way from unissued stock. If the treasury stock was fully paid for when first issued (that is, it was initially issued for an amount equal to or more than its par value), then it may be reissued at less than par value without any discount liability attaching to it. As we mentioned earlier, some states may attach a liability to shares initially issued at a discount, whereas other states do not even permit such issuances.

Accountants commonly record treasury stock at cost, debiting a Treasury Stock account. The aggregate cost is deducted from total stockholders' equity in the balance sheet. Suppose a corporation had outstanding 2,000 shares of $100 par value common stock and then repurchased 100 shares at $120 per share. The entry for the repurchase would be

Treasury Stock	12,000	
Cash		12,000
To record purchase of 100 shares of treasury stock at $120 per share.		

The corporation may accept any price for the reissue of treasury stock. Treasury stock transactions are not part of a firm's normal operating activities, and any additional capital obtained from reissuing such shares at more than cost is not regarded as earnings and is not added to retained earnings. The corporation should regard any additional amounts paid by subsequent purchasers as paid-in

GREENMAIL AND TREASURY STOCK ACCOUNTING

During the early 1980s, the word "greenmail" entered the lexicon of business terminology. Greenmail is a corporate takeover ploy in which an investor purchases stock in a corporation and then sells it back to the company at a premium price.

The greenmail procedure begins when an investor identifies a target company—a company the investor believes is undervalued (that is, a company whose underlying net assets are worth more than the price of its stock). The investor buys a substantial number of shares in the company and then announces to the corporate management that an effort will be made to take control of the company. The investor will have lined up sizeable financial resources to wage the threatened takeover bid. Viewing the proposed takeover bid as a hostile maneuver, the corporate management takes action to resist it. One action is to buy the stock from the investor at a price well above its current market price, thus netting the investor a tidy profit. Indeed, the investor may even have encouraged this particular management action. The premium paid to make the investor "be quiet and go away" is viewed by some as a form of corporate financial blackmail (although not illegal); hence the name "greenmail."

Other stockholders of the target company may believe it is unfair and a waste of assets to pay a premium price to a greenmailer—a price the long-term stockholder cannot currently obtain. In response, corporate management typically notes the stock is currently undervalued in the market and the shares eventually will be worth more and that almost any action that will retain the company's independence is in the best long-run interest of the stockholders.*

Saul Steinberg and Carl Icahn are examples of individuals who executed sizeable greenmail maneuvers. Saul Steinberg led a group of investors in a 1984 greenmailing of Walt Disney Productions. To buy off the investors, Walt Disney Productions paid $325 million—$12 per share above the market price.† Carl Icahn led greenmail procedures against such companies as Hammermill Paper Company and Saxon Industries. Saxon's management bought out Icahn's 767,700 shares at $10.50 a share, a 60% premium over the market price at that time.‡

Making greenmail payments to repurchase outstanding shares does affect the accounting for treasury stock. The Financial Accounting Standards Board decided that purchasing treasury stock at a price well above its current market price is evidence the price includes payment for something in addition to the stock reacquired.§ Having the selling shareholder agree to abandon certain acquisition plans or to agree not to purchase additional shares for a stated time period are examples. Only the fair value of the shares reacquired should be accounted for as their cost and debited to the Treasury Stock account. The excess amount paid to elicit certain actions from the selling stockholder must be charged to the current period as an expense.

Greenmailing is a controversial and, to many, an unpopular procedure. Amendments to corporate charters or even governmental legislation may be enacted to discourage greenmailing. A corporate charter could be amended, for example, to provide that—unless approved by a majority vote of the disinterested stockholders—the corporation could not purchase any shares for more than their market price from a stockholder holding a sizeable number (5% or more) of the outstanding shares.‖

Regardless of greenmailing's future, it has already impacted a number of corporations as well as the guidelines for treasury stock accounting.

*John Perham, "Should Companies Pay Takeover Ransom?," *Dun's Review*, May 1981, p. 104.
†Anne B. Fisher, "Oops! My Company Is on the Block," *Fortune*, July 23, 1984, p. 17.
‡"Saxon: A Paper Profit?," *Forbes*, October 12, 1981, p. 244.
§*FASB Technical Bulletin No. 85–6*, "Accounting for a Purchase of Treasury Shares at a Price Significantly in Excess of the Current Market Price of the Shares and the Income Statement Classification of Costs Incurred in Defending against a Takeover Attempt," December 31, 1985, p. 2.
‖Martin A. Siegel, "How to Foil Greenmail," *Fortune*, January 21, 1985, p. 158.

capital. Therefore, increases in capital from the reissue of purchased treasury shares are credited to a paid-in capital account such as Paid-in Capital from Treasury Stock. Decreases on reissue of treasury stock at less than cost offset previously recorded paid-in capital from treasury stock transactions or, if that is not possible, retained earnings.

Let us assume that 50 shares of the treasury stock reacquired are resold by the corporation at $130 per share. The entry to record the reissue would be

Cash	6,500	
Treasury Stock		6,000
Paid-in Capital from Treasury Stock		500
To record sale of 50 shares of treasury stock at $130 per share.		

Observe that Treasury Stock is credited at the cost price of $120 per share, a basis consistent with the original debit to the account. The excess over cost is credited to Paid-in Capital from Treasury Stock. If a balance sheet is prepared after this transaction, the stockholders' equity section would appear as shown below (assuming retained earnings of $40,000):

Stockholders' Equity

Paid-in Capital:	
Common Stock, $100 Par Value, authorized and issued 2,000 shares; 50 shares in treasury, 1,950 shares outstanding	$200,000
Paid-in Capital from Treasury Stock	500
Retained Earnings	40,000
	$240,500
Less: Treasury Stock (50 shares) at Cost	6,000
Total Stockholders' Equity	$234,500

Note that the $200,000 par value of all *issued* stock is shown, although 50 shares are no longer outstanding. The total cost of the 50 shares, however, is later deducted from total stockholders' equity.

In the above owners' equity situation, the corporation apparently has $40,000 retained earnings unfettered by any legal restrictions; the entire amount might be distributed as dividends if the corporation's cash position permits. In some states, however, the corporation must restrict (reduce) the retained earnings available for declaration of dividends by the cost of any treasury stock held. Then, in our illustration, only $34,000 in retained earnings would be available for dividends, and the reason would be disclosed in the stockholders' equity section. Methods of disclosing retained earnings restrictions are discussed in Chapter 16. The statutory restriction exists because a corporation that reduces its paid-in capital by repurchasing shares must protect creditors by "buffering" the reduced capital with its retained earnings in an amount equal to resources expended.

DONATED CAPITAL

Occasionally, a corporation may acquire treasury stock by a shareholder's donating shares to the corporation. Perhaps the donor received the shares in exchange for a patent on a product and now wishes the corporation to raise additional capital to promote and market the product. As noted, because treasury shares represent stock that has been issued once, they can be reissued at any price. Thus, the corporation may find it easier to market these shares than to sell unissued shares, especially if investors have shown little interest in the venture and the unissued shares could be sold only at a discount.

The reacquisition of treasury shares by donation, whatever the reason, is usually not recorded—except for a memorandum entry—at the time of reacquisition. When such shares are subsequently sold, the amount received is credited to Donated Capital, a form of paid-in capital. To illustrate, suppose a stockholder donates 100 shares of common stock to a corporation, which then resells the shares at $125 per share. The entries for these transactions would be

To record receipt of donated treasury shares

(Memorandum) Received 100 shares of donated common stock.

To record sale of donated treasury shares

Cash	12,500	
Donated Capital		12,500
To record sale of 100 donated shares at $125 per share.		

The Donated Capital account may also be credited for the fair market value of any property donated to the corporation, assuming that a value can be determined objectively. For example, communities wanting to attract industry have donated land sites to corporations. If fair values can be established by appraisal or by study of prices for similar local property, the amount may be recorded. In any event, amounts acquired through donation should never be credited to Retained Earnings, because this account is used solely for accumulating earnings from operations.

Assume that a city donates a plant site to a corporation. An independent appraiser values the land at $26,000, which is accepted by the board of directors as an appropriate valuation. The entry to record the donation would be

Land	26,000	
Donated Capital		26,000
To record receipt of donated land valued at $26,000.		

REDEMPTION OF PREFERRED STOCK

Corporations often retain the right to call or redeem their outstanding preferred stock by paying the preferred stockholders the par value of the stock plus a premium. For example, assume that a company has issued 1,000 shares of $100 par value preferred stock at $105 per share. After such issue, the stockholders' equity would include the following accounts:

Preferred Stock, $100 Par Value, 1,000 shares issued and outstanding	100,000
Paid-in Capital in Excess of Par Value	5,000

Suppose that 500 shares are then redeemed at $102 per share. When the redemption is recorded, the amounts in the above accounts related to the 500 redeemed shares must be eliminated. In other words, half of the preferred stock ($50,000) and half of the original premium ($2,500) must be removed from the accounts. Because the shares were redeemed for $3 less per share than the issue price, the $1,500 difference is recognized as paid-in capital from the stock redemption. The entry to record the redemption is as follows:

Preferred Stock	50,000	
Paid-in Capital in Excess of Par Value	2,500	
Cash		51,000
Paid-in Capital from Stock Redemption		1,500
To record redemption of 500 shares of preferred stock at $102 per share.		

When preferred stock is redeemed at a price higher than the issue price, the excess is debited to Retained Earnings, inasmuch as it represents a distribution of earnings to stockholders. If the redemption price in the above situation had been $106 per share, the appropriate entry would have been

Preferred Stock	50,000	
Paid-in Capital in Excess of Par Value	2,500	
Retained Earnings	500	
Cash		53,000
To record redemption of 500 shares of preferred stock at $106 per share.		

BOOK VALUE PER SHARE

Book value per share is often calculated for a class of stock, particularly common stock. **Book value per share,** which is the dollar amount of net assets represented by one share of stock, is computed by dividing the amount of stockholders' equity associated with a class of stock by the number of outstanding shares in that class. The computation uses stockholders' equity, because a corporation's net assets (Assets − Liabilities) equals its stockholders' equity. The measure is based on amounts recorded in the books and presented in the balance sheet—hence, the term *book* value per share.

For example, assume the following stockholders' equity section of a balance sheet:

Stockholders' Equity

Paid-in Capital:	
Common Stock, $50 Par Value, 5,000 shares authorized, issued, and outstanding	$250,000
Paid-in Capital in Excess of Par Value	100,000
Retained Earnings	80,000
Total Stockholders' Equity	$430,000

Because this corporation has only one class of stock, the book value per share is the total stockholders' equity divided by the shares outstanding, that is, $430,000/5,000 = $86. Note that the divisor is shares outstanding; it does not include shares of unissued common stock or treasury stock.

To compute book values per share when more than one class of stock is outstanding, we must determine the portion of stockholders' equity attributable to each class of stock. Preferred stocks are assigned the amounts their owners would receive if the corporation liquidated—that is, the liquidation preference of preferred stock plus any dividend arrearages on cumulative stock. The common shares receive the remainder of the stockholders' equity. For example, assume the following stockholders' equity section:

Stockholders' Equity

Paid-in Capital:	
9% Preferred Stock, $100 Par Value, 1,000 shares authorized, issued, and outstanding	$100,000
Paid-in Capital in Excess of Par Value—Preferred Stock	5,000
No-par Common Stock, Stated Value $40, 3,000 shares authorized, issued, and outstanding	120,000
Paid-in Capital in Excess of Stated Value—Common Stock	6,000
Retained Earnings	73,000
Total Stockholders' Equity	$304,000

If the stated liquidation preference is $103 per share for the preferred stock (with no dividends in arrears), then the book value per share for the preferred stock is also $103. The computation for the common stock follows:

Total Stockholders' Equity	$304,000
Less: Equity Applicable to Preferred Stock	103,000
Equity Allocated to Common Stock	$201,000
Shares of Common Stock Outstanding	3,000
Book Value per Share of Common Stock ($201,000/3,000)	$67

The book value per share of common stock may be used in many ways. Management may include the book value per share—and any changes in it for the year—in the annual report to stockholders. Two corporations negotiating a merger through an exchange of stock may find their respective book values per share to be one of several factors influencing the final exchange ratio. Or an individual may acquire an option to buy stock in the future, with the purchase price related to the future book value of the stock.

MARKET VALUE AND LIQUIDATION VALUE

The book value of common stock is different from its market value and its liquidation value. The **market value per share** is the current price at which the stock may be bought or sold. This price reflects such things as the earnings potential of the company, dividends, book values, capital structure, and general economic conditions. Because book value is only one of several variables influencing market price (and usually not the most significant one at that), market values and book values rarely coincide.

The **liquidation value per share** of common stock is the amount that would be received if the corporation liquidated. The amounts recorded in the books do not portray liquidation proceeds, so no correlation exists between liquidation values and book values of common stocks. Liquidation values may not be easy to determine, but corporate managements must be alert to the relationship between the market value and the approximate liquidation value of their common stock. A corporation whose liquidation value exceeds its market value may be the object of a "raid." A raider acquires control of a corporation (by buying stock at market values) and then liquidates the business (at liquidation values), keeping the difference as a gain.

KEY POINTS TO REMEMBER

(1) A corporation is a separate legal entity chartered by the state in which it is formed or, in some cases, by the federal government.

(2) The liability of corporate shareholders is usually limited to their ownership investment, whereas claims against partners and sole proprietors may extend to their personal resources.

(3) Unlike proprietorships and partnerships, corporations must report paid-in equity capital separately from the accumulated balance of retained earnings. Distributions to shareholders are limited by the amount of retained earnings and other capital as specified by state law.

(4) Common stock represents a corporation's basic ownership class of stock. Preferred stocks may differ from common stock in any of several characteristics. Typically, preferred stocks have some type of dividend preference and a prior claim to assets in liquidation.

(5) In financial statements, the par values or stated values of different forms of stock (preferred, common) are shown separately, along with any excess or deficiency received for the shares. These differences are called premium and discount, respectively, for par value stock. For no-par stock with a stated value, an appropriate title (for example, paid-in capital in excess of stated value) describes the difference.

(6) Treasury stock represents repurchased shares of the firm's own stock. It is commonly recorded at cost and deducted from total stockholders' equity in the balance sheet.

(7) Donated capital results from gifts to the corporation which, if feasible, should be recorded at fair market value.

(8) The book value per share of common stock indicates the net assets, based on recorded amounts, associated with a share of common stock. Common stock book values are different from market values or liquidation values.

SELF-TEST QUESTIONS
(Answers are at the end of this chapter.)

1. The liability of stockholders for corporation actions is usually
   (a) Unlimited.
   (b) Limited to the par or stated value of the stock they hold.
   (c) Limited to the amount of their investment in the corporation.
   (d) Limited to the amount of the corporation's retained earnings.
2. Which type of stock may have dividends in arrears?
   (a) Cumulative preferred stock.
   (b) Common stock.
   (c) Noncumulative preferred stock.
   (d) Treasury stock.
3. Wyler Company issues 20,000 shares of $10 par value common stock in exchange for a building with a current fair value of $1,000,000. In recording this transaction, what amount should be credited to Paid-in Capital in Excess of Par Value?
   (a) $1,000,000
   (b) $200,000
   (c) $800,000
   (d) $980,000
4. Which of the following accounts has a normal debit balance?
   (a) Common Stock Subscribed.
   (b) Paid-in Capital from Stock Redemption.
   (c) Donated Capital.
   (d) Treasury Stock.

5. Caffey Corporation has a total stockholders' equity of $1,860,000. Caffey has 20,000 shares of $25 par value, 6% preferred stock issued and outstanding, and 60,000 shares of $10 par value common stock issued and outstanding. The preferred stock has a liquidation preference of $27 per share and no dividends in arrears. What is the book value per share of common stock?
   (a) $31.00
   (b) $22.00
   (c) $22.67
   (d) $10.00

QUESTIONS

15–1 Explain the meaning of each of the following terms and, when appropriate, how they interrelate: corporation, articles of incorporation, corporate charter, board of directors, corporate officers, and organization costs.

15–2 What is meant by the limited liability of a shareholder? Does this characteristic enhance or reduce a corporation's ability to raise capital?

15–3 Contrast the federal income taxation of corporations with that of sole proprietorships and partnerships. Which of the three types of organizations must file a federal income tax return?

15–4 What is the preemptive right of a shareholder?

15–5 What are the basic differences between preferred stock and common stock? What are the typical features of preferred stock?

15–6 What features make preferred stock similar to debt? Similar to common stock?

15–7 What is meant by dividend arrearage on preferred stock? If dividends are three years in arrears on $250,000 of 8% preferred stock and dividends are declared this year, what amount of total dividends must preferred shareholders receive before any distributions can be made to common shareholders?

15–8 What is fully participating preferred stock? Partially participating preferred stock?

15–9 Distinguish between authorized stock and issued stock. Why might the number of shares issued be greater than the number of shares outstanding?

15–10 Distinguish between premium and discount on stock. Where do such amounts appear in the balance sheet?

15–11 What is no-par stock? How is the stated value, if any, of no-par stock determined?

15–12 A company acquired machines with a fair market value of $85,000 in exchange for 1,200 shares of $50 par value common stock. How should this transaction be recorded in the accounts?

15–13 Define *treasury stock*. Why might a corporation acquire treasury stock? How is treasury stock shown in the balance sheet?

15–14 If a corporation purchases 400 shares of its own common stock at $25 per share and resells it at $30 per share, where would the $2,000 increase in capital appear in the financial statements? Why is no gain reported?

15–15 A corporation has total stockholders' equity of $221,400 and one class of $40 par value common stock. The company has issued 6,000 shares and currently holds 600 shares as treasury stock. What is the book value per share?

15–16 A corporation has total stockholders' equity of $3,600,000 and one class of $20 par value common stock. The corporation has 100,000 shares authorized; 90,000 shares issued; 80,000 shares outstanding; and 10,000 shares as treasury stock. What is the book value per share?

15–17 Define and contrast the terms book value, market value, and liquidation value per share of common stock.

EXERCISES

Stock issuances for cash

15–18 On June 1, Locke, Inc., issued 3,000 shares of $30 par value preferred stock at $47 per share and 8,000 shares of no-par common stock at $25 per share. The common stock had no stated value. All issuances were for cash.
(a) Give the general journal entries to record the issuances.
(b) Give the entry for the issuance of the common stock, assuming it had a stated value of $20 per share.
(c) Give the entry for the issuance of the common stock, assuming it had a par value of $15 per share.

Stock subscriptions

15–19 On May 1, the Vidot Company received subscriptions for 4,000 shares of $10 par value common stock at $35 per share, paid as follows: 50% with subscription, 30% on June 15, and 20% on July 1. All payments were received on schedule, and the shares were issued on July 1. Give the general journal entries made on May 1, June 15, and July 1.

Noncash stock issuances

15–20 Haven Corporation was organized in 19X4. The company's charter authorizes 100,000 shares of $20 par value common stock. The attorney who helped organize the corporation billed Haven $4,500 for services rendered. On August 1, 19X4, the attorney accepted 150 shares of Haven common stock in settlement of the bill. On October 15, 19X4, Haven issued 1,200 common shares to acquire a vacant land site appraised at $39,000. Give the general journal entries to record the stock issuances on August 1 and October 15.

Dividend distribution

15–21 The Unger Company has outstanding 6,000 shares of $50 par value, 7% cumulative preferred stock and 25,000 shares of $10 par value common stock. The company declared cash dividends amounting to $110,000.
(a) If no arrearage on the preferred stock exists, how much in total dividends, and in dividends per share, is paid to each class of stock?
(b) If one year's dividend arrearage on the preferred stock exists, how much in total dividends, and in dividends per share, is paid to each class of stock?
(c) Assume that no arrearage on the preferred stock exists but that the stock is fully participating. How much in total dividends, and in dividends per share, is paid to each class of stock?

Treasury stock

15–22 Sunray Corporation issued 12,000 shares of $20 par value common stock at $26 per share and 5,000 shares of $60 par value, 8% preferred stock at $65 per share. The company then repurchased 2,000 shares of common stock at $29 per share.

(a) Give the general journal entries to record the stock issuances and the repurchase of the common shares.

(b) Assume that Sunray resold 1,400 shares of the treasury stock at $32 per share. Give the general journal entry to record the resale of this treasury stock.

(c) Assume that Sunray resold the remaining 600 shares of treasury stock at $27 per share. Give the general journal entry to record the resale of this treasury stock.

Stock issuance and treasury stock

15–23 Mauer, Inc., recorded certain capital stock transactions shown in the following respective journal entries: (1) issuance of common stock for $35 cash per share; (2) subsequent repurchase of some shares at $39 per share; and (3) reissuance of some of the reacquired shares.

(1) Cash	595,000	
Common Stock		510,000
Paid-in Capital in Excess of Par Value		85,000
(2) Treasury Stock	97,500	
Cash		97,500
(3) Cash	63,000	
Treasury Stock		58,500
Paid-in Capital from Treasury Stock		4,500

(a) How many shares were originally issued?

(b) What was the par value of the shares issued?

(c) How many shares of treasury stock were reacquired?

(d) How many shares of treasury stock were reissued?

(e) At what price per share was the treasury stock reissued?

Donated capital

15–24 Yeager Company has 8,000 shares of $5 par value common stock outstanding. Prepare the general journal entries (if required) to record the following transactions:

Aug.	12	The community in which Yeager Company is building a new plant donated the land site to the company. The appraised value of the land is $60,000.
Oct.	7	Shareholders donated 400 shares to the corporation.
	22	The company sold the donated shares for $24 cash per share.

Preferred stock redemption

15–25 Paar Corporation has 10,000 shares outstanding of 6%, $75 par value preferred stock that were originally issued at par. The company redeemed all of the stock at $78 per share.

(a) Prepare the journal entry to record the redemption of the stock.

(b) Assume that the original issue price was $83 per share; prepare the journal entry to record the redemption.

Book value per share

15–26 The stockholders' equity section of the Griffin Company appears as follows:

Paid-in Capital:		
8% Cumulative Preferred Stock, $50 Par Value, 6,000 shares authorized, issued, and outstanding	$300,000	
Paid-in Capital in Excess of Par Value—Preferred Stock	66,000	$366,000
No-par Common Stock, $15 Stated Value, 25,000 shares authorized, issued, and outstanding	$375,000	
Paid-in Capital in Excess of Stated Value—Common Stock	100,000	475,000
Paid-in Capital from Treasury Stock		19,000
Total Paid-in Capital		$860,000
Retained Earnings		130,000
Total Stockholders' Equity		$990,000

The preferred stock has a liquidation preference of $52 per share, and no dividends are in arrears. Compute the book value per share of the common stock.

PROBLEMS

Stockholders' equity—transactions and balance sheet presentation

15–27 The Halley Corporation was organized on April 1 of the current year with an authorization of 10,000 shares of 7%, $60 par value preferred stock and 100,000 shares of $20 par value common stock. During April, the following transactions affecting stockholders' equity occurred:

Apr.	1	Issued 6,000 shares of preferred stock for $81 cash per share and 40,000 shares of common stock at $28 cash per share.
	3	Issued 500 shares of common stock to attorneys and promoters in exchange for their services in organizing the corporation. The services were valued at $14,000.
	8	Issued 750 shares of preferred stock in exchange for equipment with a fair market value of $61,500.
	17	Received land valued at $90,000 as a donation from the city to attract Halley to its present location. The land will allow Halley to have adequate parking for its operations.
	20	Issued 4,000 shares of common stock for cash at $29 per share.
	30	Closed the $30,000 net income for April from the Income Summary account to Retained Earnings.

REQUIRED

(a) Prepare general journal entries to record the foregoing transactions.

(b) Prepare the stockholders' equity section of the balance sheet at April 30.

Dividend distribution

15–28 The Piper Corporation has outstanding 20,000 shares of $100 par value, 8%, cumulative preferred stock and 80,000 shares of $15 par value common stock. The company has declared cash dividends of $448,000.

REQUIRED

(a) Calculate the total dividends and the dividends per share paid to each class of stock. There are no dividend arrearages.
(b) Assuming that one year's dividend arrearage exists on the preferred stock, calculate the total dividends and the dividends per share paid to each class of stock.
(c) Assuming that the 8% preferred stock is participating only to 10% (and no dividend arrearages exist), calculate the total dividends and the dividends per share paid to each class of stock.
(d) Assuming that the 8% preferred stock is fully participating (and no dividend arrearages exist), calculate the total dividends and the dividends per share paid to each class of stock.

Stockholders' equity—transactions, balance sheet presentation, and book value per share

15–29 The stockholders' equity of the Street Corporation at January 1 of the current year appears below:

6% Preferred Stock, $25 Par Value, 10,000 shares authorized; 5,200 shares issued and outstanding	$130,000
Paid-in Capital in Excess of Par Value—Preferred Stock	78,000
Common Stock, $10 Par Value, 200,000 shares authorized; 60,000 shares issued and outstanding	600,000
Retained Earnings	325,000

During the current year, the following transactions occurred:

Jan.	10	Issued 11,000 shares of common stock for $13 cash per share.
	23	Repurchased 6,000 shares of common stock for the treasury at $14 per share.
Mar.	2	Shareholders donated 2,600 shares of common stock to the corporation.
	14	Sold one-half of the treasury shares acquired January 23 for $17 per share.
	14	Sold the donated shares at $17 per share.
July	15	Issued 1,200 shares of preferred stock to acquire special equipment with a fair market value of $54,000.
Sept.	15	Received subscriptions to 10,000 shares of common stock at $21 per share. One-third of the subscription price was received in cash.
Nov.	15	Received the balance due on the September 15 stock subscriptions in cash, and issued the stock certificates.
Dec.	31	Closed the net income of $95,800 from the Income Summary account to Retained Earnings.

REQUIRED

(a) Set up T accounts for the stockholders' equity accounts at the beginning of the year, and enter January 1 balances.
(b) Prepare general journal entries to record the foregoing transactions, and post to T accounts (set up any additional T accounts needed). Determine the ending balances for the stockholders' equity accounts.
(c) Prepare the December 31 stockholders' equity section of the balance sheet.
(d) Assume the preferred stock has a liquidation preference of $27 per share. No dividends are in arrears. Compute the book value per share of common stock at December 31.

Stockholders' equity—information and entries from comparative data

15–30 Comparative stockholders' equity sections from two successive years' balance sheets of Ripley, Inc., are as follows:

	Dec. 31, 19X2	Dec. 31, 19X1
Paid-in Capital:		
8% Preferred Stock, $50 Par Value, authorized 9,000 shares; issued and outstanding, 19X1: 9,000 shares; 19X2: 6,500 shares	$ 325,000	$ 450,000
Paid-in Capital in Excess of Par Value—Preferred Stock	143,000	198,000
Common Stock, No-par Value, $10 Stated Value, authorized 50,000 shares; outstanding, 19X1: 25,000 shares; 19X2: 38,000 shares	380,000	300,000
Paid-in Capital in Excess of Stated Value—Common Stock	259,000	195,000
Paid-in Capital from Stock Redemption—Preferred	20,000	
Paid-in Capital from Treasury Stock	10,000	
Donated Capital	60,000	
Retained Earnings	286,000	204,000
		$1,347,000
Less: Treasury Stock (5,000 shares common) at Cost		85,000
Total Stockholders' Equity	$1,483,000	$1,262,000

No dividends were declared or paid during 19X2. The company received a donated parcel of land from the city in 19X2.

REQUIRED

(a) What was the redemption price in 19X2 per share of preferred stock?

(b) For what price per share was the treasury stock sold in 19X2?

(c) Prepare the general journal entries for the transactions affecting stockholders' equity that evidently occurred during 19X2.

Book value per share

15–31 Handel Corporation has the following stockholders' equity section in its balance sheet:

Paid-in Capital:		
6% Preferred Stock, $100 Par Value, 5,000 shares authorized, issued, and outstanding	$ 500,000	
Paid-in Capital in Excess of Par Value—Preferred Stock	30,000	
Common Stock, $30 Par Value, 50,000 shares authorized; 40,000 shares issued and outstanding	1,200,000	
Paid-in Capital in Excess of Par Value—Common Stock	80,000	
Paid-in Capital from Treasury Stock	14,000	$1,824,000
Retained Earnings		280,000
Total Stockholders' Equity		$2,104,000

REQUIRED

For each of the following independent cases, compute the book value per share for the preferred stock and the common stock.

(a) The preferred stock is noncumulative, nonparticipating, and has a liquidation preference of $104 per share.

(b) The preferred stock is cumulative, nonparticipating, and has a liquidation preference per share equal to par value plus dividends in arrears. No dividends are in arrears.

(c) The preferred stock is cumulative, nonparticipating, and has a liquidation preference of $102 per share plus dividends in arrears. Dividends are three years in arrears.

Stockholders' equity—transactions and balance sheet presentation

15–32 The stockholders' equity section of Dresden Corporation's balance sheet at January 1 of the current year is shown below:

7% Preferred Stock, $40 Par Value, 20,000 shares authorized; 7,000 shares issued and outstanding	$ 280,000
Paid-in Capital in Excess of Par Value—Preferred Stock	14,000
Common Stock, $5 Par Value, 100,000 shares authorized; 60,000 shares issued and outstanding	300,000
Paid-in Capital in Excess of Par Value—Common Stock	420,000
Retained Earnings	315,000
Total Stockholders' Equity	$1,329,000

The following transactions, among others, occurred during the year:

Jan.	12	Redeemed all the preferred stock at $43 per share (and retired the shares).
	20	Received subscriptions for the sale of 16,000 shares of common stock at $14 per share. Received one-half of the subscription price in cash.
Feb.	9	Received the remainder of payment for the shares subscribed on January 20 in cash, and issued the stock certificates.
Apr.	14	Received a plant site valued at $110,000 as a gift from the city.
June	1	Acquired equipment with a fair market value of $45,000 in exchange for 3,000 shares of common stock.
Sept.	1	Reacquired 2,000 shares of common stock for cash at $17 per share.
Oct.	12	Resold 200 treasury shares at $19 per share.
Nov.	30	Received subscriptions for the sale of 6,000 shares of common stock at $18 per share. Received one-third of the subscription price in cash.
Dec.	28	Resold 1,000 of the remaining treasury shares at $16 per share.
	31	Closed the Income Summary account, with net earnings of $75,000, to Retained Earnings.

REQUIRED

(a) Set up T accounts for the stockholders' equity accounts at the beginning of the year and enter January 1 balances.

(b) Prepare general journal entries for the given transactions, and post them to the T accounts (set up any additional T accounts needed). Determine the ending balances for the stockholders' equity accounts.

(c) Prepare the stockholders' equity section of the balance sheet at December 31 of the current year.

Stockholder's equity—transaction descriptions from account data

15–33 The T accounts below contain keyed entries representing seven transactions involving the stockholders' equity of Lawson, Inc.

Cash

(1)	29,600	(4)	3,000
(2)	40,000	(7)	2,610
(6)	2,160		

Land

(3)	60,000		
(5)	25,000		

Preferred Stock, $25 Par

(7)	2,250	(1)	20,000

Paid-in Capital in Excess of Par Value—Preferred Stock

(7)	1,080	(1)	9,600

Common Stock, $10 Par

		(2)	40,000
		(3)	50,000

Paid-in Capital in Excess of Par Value—Common Stock

		(3)	10,000

Treasury Stock

(4) (200 shares of common)	3,000	(6)	1,800

Paid-in Capital from Treasury Stock

		(6)	360

Donated Capital

		(5)	25,000

Paid-in Capital from Stock Redemption

		(7)	720

REQUIRED

Using this information, give detailed descriptions, including number of shares and price per share when applicable, for each of the seven transactions.

ALTERNATE PROBLEMS

Stockholders' equity—transactions and balance sheet presentation

15–27A The Selmon Corporation was organized on July 1 of the current year with an authorization of 15,000 shares of $4 no-par value preferred stock ($4 is the annual dividend) and 50,000 shares of $25 par value common stock. During July, the following transactions affecting stockholders' equity occurred:

July 1 Issued 4,000 shares of preferred stock for $55 cash per share and 18,000 shares of common stock at $30 cash per share.

5 The local municipality donated a vacant building to the corporation as an inducement to operate the business in the community. The fair market value of the building was $400,000.

July 12 Issued 2,500 shares of common stock in exchange for equipment with a fair market value of $80,000.
15 Issued 1,000 shares of preferred stock for cash at $53 per share.
23 Received subscriptions for 7,000 shares of common stock at $33 per share. A 25% cash down payment accompanied the subscriptions. The balance of the subscription price is due on August 31.
31 Closed the $41,000 net income for July from the Income Summary account to Retained Earnings.

REQUIRED
(a) Prepare general journal entries to record the foregoing transactions.
(b) Prepare the stockholders' equity section of the balance sheet at July 31.

Dividend distribution

15–28A Colter Corporation has outstanding 6,000 shares of $50 par value, 9%, cumulative preferred stock and 45,000 shares of $20 par value common stock. The company has declared cash dividends of $180,000.

REQUIRED
(a) Calculate the total dividends and the dividends per share paid to each class of stock. There are no dividend arrearages.
(b) Assuming that two years' dividend arrearages exist on the preferred stock, calculate the total dividends and the dividends per share paid to each class of stock.
(c) Assuming that the 9% preferred stock is participating only to 12% (and no dividend arrearages exist), calculate the total dividends and the dividends per share paid to each class of stock.
(d) Assuming that the 9% preferred stock is fully participating (and no dividend arrearages exist), calculate the total dividends and the dividends per share paid to each class of stock.

Stockholders' equity—transactions, balance sheet presentation, and book value per share

15–29A The stockholders' equity of the Marino Corporation at January 1 of the current year appears below:

Common Stock, $30 Par Value, 60,000 shares authorized; 30,000 shares issued and outstanding	$900,000
Paid-in Capital in Excess of Par Value—Common Stock	105,000
Retained Earnings	476,000

During the current year, the following transactions occurred:

Jan. 5 Issued 8,000 shares of common stock for $35 cash per share.
18 Repurchased 2,500 shares of common stock for the treasury at $34 per share.
Mar. 10 Shareholders donated 1,000 shares to the corporation.
12 Sold one-half of the treasury shares acquired January 18 for $36 per share.

Mar 12	Sold the donated shares at $36 per share.
July 17	Sold 625 shares of the remaining treasury stock for $32 per share.
Sept. 20	Received subscriptions to 5,000 shares of common stock at $37 per share. Received one-fourth of the subscription price in cash.
Nov. 25	Received the balance due on the September 20 stock subscription in cash, and issued the stock certificates.
Dec. 31	Closed the net income of $72,000 from the Income Summary account to Retained Earnings.

REQUIRED

(a) Set up T accounts for the stockholders' equity accounts at the beginning of the year, and enter January 1 balances.

(b) Prepare general journal entries to record the foregoing transactions, and post to T accounts (set up any additional T accounts needed). Determine the ending balances for the stockholders' equity accounts.

(c) Prepare the December 31 stockholders' equity section of the balance sheet.

(d) Compute the book value per share of common stock at December 31.

Book value per share

15–31A Daniels, Inc., has the following stockholders' equity section in its balance sheet:

Paid-in Capital:		
7% Preferred Stock, $75 Par Value, 8,000 shares authorized, issued, and outstanding	$600,000	
Paid-in Capital in Excess of Par Value—Preferred Stock	28,000	
Common Stock, $15 Par Value, 80,000 shares authorized; 50,000 shares issued and outstanding	750,000	
Paid-in Capital in Excess of Par Value—Common Stock	80,000	
Donated Capital	32,000	$1,490,000
Retained Earnings		220,000
Total Stockholders' Equity		$1,710,000

REQUIRED

For each of the following independent cases, compute the book value per share for the preferred stock and the common stock.

(a) The preferred stock is noncumulative, nonparticipating, and has a liquidation preference of $77 per share.

(b) The preferred stock is cumulative, nonparticipating, and has a liquidation preference per share equal to par value plus dividends in arrears. No dividends are in arrears.

(c) The preferred stock is cumulative, nonparticipating, and has a liquidation preference of $78 per share plus dividends in arrears. Dividends are two years in arrears.

Stockholders' equity—transactions and balance sheet presentation

15–32A The following is the stockholders' equity section of Skyking Corporation's balance sheet at January 1 of the current year:

8% Preferred Stock, $50 Par Value, 5,000 shares authorized; 3,000 shares issued and outstanding	$ 150,000
Paid-in Capital in Excess of Par Value—Preferred Stock	30,000
Common Stock, $10 Par Value, 100,000 shares authorized; 60,000 shares issued and outstanding	600,000
Paid-in Capital in Excess of Par Value—Common Stock	240,000
Retained Earnings	310,000
Total Stockholders' Equity	$1,330,000

The following transactions, among others, occurred during the year:

Jan.	12	Issued 1,000 shares of preferred stock for $65 cash per share.
	20	Received subscriptions for the sale of 5,000 shares of common stock at $17 per share. Received one-half of the subscription price in cash.
Feb.	9	Received the remainder of payment for the shares subscribed on January 20 in cash, and issued the stock certificates.
Apr.	14	Received a vacant school building valued at $475,000 as a gift from the city. The company plans to remodel the building for additional office space.
May	18	Redeemed all the preferred stock at $55 per share (and retired the shares).
June	1	Acquired equipment with a fair market value of $80,000 in exchange for 4,000 shares of common stock.
Sept.	1	Reacquired 3,000 shares of common stock for cash at $22 per share.
Oct.	12	Resold 1,100 treasury shares at $23 per share.
Nov.	30	Received subscriptions for the sale of 8,000 shares of common stock at $22 per share. Received one-fifth of the subscription price in cash.
Dec.	28	Resold 900 of the remaining treasury shares at $20 per share.
	31	Closed the Income Summary account, with net earnings of $65,000, to Retained Earnings.

REQUIRED

(a) Set up T accounts for the stockholders' equity accounts at the beginning of the year and enter January 1 balances.

(b) Prepare general journal entries for the given transactions, and post them to the T accounts (set up any additional T accounts needed). Determine the ending balances for the stockholders' equity accounts.

(c) Prepare the stockholders' equity section of the balance sheet at December 31 of the current year.

BUSINESS DECISION PROBLEM

William Renk has operated Renk's Variety very successfully as a sole proprietorship. He feels that the continued growth and success of his business depends on increasing its scale of operations, which requires additional working capital. He also wishes to relocate his store from its rented quarters to a new retail shopping area. After exploring several opportunities that would result in large personal debts, Renk incorporates his business, taking in as stockholders Dr. Davis, who invests cash, and Ms. Stein, a real estate developer who owns land and a suitable vacant building in the desired shopping area.

As an initial step, Renk and his attorney secure a corporate charter for Varieties, Inc., authorizing it to issue 25,000 shares of $20 par value common stock. On June 1 of the current year, the date of incorporation, the post-closing trial balance of Renk's Variety is as follows:

	Debit	Credit
Cash	$ 4,500	
Accounts Receivable	9,600	
Allowance for Uncollectible Accounts		$ 200
Merchandise Inventory	120,000	
Store Equipment	54,000	
Accumulated Depreciation—Store Equipment		25,000
Accounts Payable		10,800
Note Payable (due two years hence)		30,000
W. Renk, Capital		122,100
	$188,100	$188,100

Other details of the agreement follow:

(1) After a detailed review of the accounts of Renk's Variety, the new stockholders agree that:
   (a) The allowance for uncollectible accounts should increase by $300.
   (b) Because of damaged and shopworn goods, the merchandise inventory should be written down by $10,000.
   (c) The store equipment will be recorded in the corporate accounts at its fair market value of $35,000 with no accumulated depreciation.
   (d) The new corporation assumes at face value the recorded liabilities of the proprietorship.

(2) Renk has agreed to accept shares in the new corporation at par value in exchange for his adjusted equity in the assets of the proprietorship. He will purchase for cash at par value any additional shares necessary to bring his total holdings to the next even 100 shares.

(3) The total value of Stein's building and land is agreed to be $120,000, of which $20,000 is associated with the land. Stein has agreed to accept stock at $25 per share for her land and building.

(4) In an effort to stimulate local business, the Business Development Commission of the local city government has deeded to the corporation, for a token fee of $500, a small strip of land that will provide better delivery access to the rear of Stein's building. The fair value of the parcel is $5,000.

(5) Davis has agreed to purchase for cash 2,200 shares at $25 per share. He will subscribe to an additional 500 shares at $28 per share, paying 20% of the issue price on subscription and the balance in two equal installments, 90 and 180 days later.

(6) Legal and accounting costs of $6,000 associated with acquiring the corporate charter and issuing the stock are paid from corporate funds. (Treat these as the asset, Organization Costs.)

REQUIRED

(a) As Renk's accountant, you must prepare a balance sheet for the new corporation reflecting the shares issued, the stock subscription received, the parcel of land received from the city, and payment of legal and accounting costs. (*Hint:* You may wish to prepare a worksheet with the following headings:

	Renk's Variety Trial Balance		Adjustments and Organizational Transactions		Varieties, Inc. Trial Balance	
Accounts	**Dr.**	**Cr.**	**Dr.**	**Cr.**	**Dr.**	**Cr.**

Properly combining and extending the amounts in the first two pairs of columns provide amounts for the trial balance of Varieties, Inc. When recording the Renk's Variety trial balance, leave extra lines for the several transactions that will affect the Cash and W. Renk, Capital accounts. Also, leave extra lines when entering the Common Stock and Paid-in Capital in Excess of Par Value accounts on the worksheet. For purposes of review, you may wish to key your adjustments and transactions to the letters and numbers used in the problem data.)

(b) In contrast to what they contributed to the corporation, what specifically do Renk and Stein "own" after the incorporation?

(c) From Renk's viewpoint, what are the advantages and disadvantages of incorporating the variety store?

ANSWERS TO SELF-TEST QUESTIONS

1. (c) 2. (a) 3. (c) 4. (d) 5. (b)

16

Corporations: Earnings Disclosure, Dividends, and Retained Earnings

Chapter Objectives

- **Identify the income statement sections used to report certain types of transactions.**
- **Discuss the nature of and accounting for prior period adjustments and changes in accounting estimates.**
- **Discuss and illustrate the computation and disclosure of earnings per share data.**
- **Identify and distinguish between cash dividends and stock dividends.**
- **Define stock splits and distinguish them from stock dividends.**
- **Discuss the process of appropriating retained earnings.**

All things have their place, knew we how to place them.

GEORGE HERBERT

Profits play a significant role in the organization and functioning of economic activity in the United States. A corporation's profitability is vitally important both to its owners and to potential investors. For this reason, earnings data are usually considered the most important financial information presented by corporate entities. Earnings data encompass not only the net income or loss for the period, but also any prior period adjustments and earnings per share amounts.

As explained earlier, the balance of the Retained Earnings account represents the stockholders' equity arising from the corporation's retention of assets generated from profit-directed activities. At the end of an accounting period, the Retained Earnings account is credited with the corporation's net income (when the Income Summary account is closed to it) or debited with a net loss. A debit balance in the Retained Earnings account resulting from accumulated losses is called a **deficit.** In certain instances, Retained Earnings is charged or credited directly to correct errors made in past periods; these items do not appear in the income statement.

The board of directors may decide, based on the income performance of the corporation, to distribute assets to stockholders, in which case they declare a *dividend*. The board of directors may also decide to retain some of the assets resulting from profitable operations for an identifiable purpose, such as expansion of operations or as a buffer for possible losses. They may then appropriate or restrict a portion of retained earnings.

Because of the importance of income data, accountants have developed several guidelines for their disclosure. In this chapter, we discuss the procedures for reporting earnings data and accounting for dividends and appropriations of retained earnings.

INCOME STATEMENT SECTIONS

Accountants believe that the usefulness of the income statement is enhanced if certain types of transactions and events are reported in separate sections. For this reason, information about extraordinary items, discontinued operations, and effects of changes in accounting principles are disclosed separately in an income statement. Segregating these categories of information from the results of ordinary, continuing operations should make it easier for financial statement users to estimate the future earnings performance of the company.

The creation of several sections in the income statement, however, complicates the reporting of income tax expense. Items affecting the overall amount of income tax expense may appear in more than one section. If this is the case, accountants allocate the income tax expense among those sections of the statement in which the items affecting the tax expense appear.

We now examine these areas in more detail.

EXTRAORDINARY ITEMS

Extraordinary items are transactions and events that are *unusual in nature* and *occur infrequently.*[1] An item that is unusual in nature is highly abnormal and significantly different from the firm's ordinary and typical activities. To determine a firm's ordinary and typical activities, we must consider such things as the type of operations, lines of business, operating policies, and the environment in which the firm operates. The operating environment includes the characteristics of the industry, the geographic location of the firm's facilities, and the type of government regulations imposed. A transaction or event is considered to occur infrequently if the firm does not expect it to recur in the foreseeable future.

The two criteria—unusual nature and infrequent occurrence—considerably restrict the events and transactions that qualify as extraordinary items. For example, suppose a tobacco grower suffers crop loss from a flood, which normally happens every few years in this area. The history of floods creates a reasonable expectation that another flood will occur in the foreseeable future. The loss, therefore, does not meet the criteria for an extraordinary item. Now consider a different tobacco grower who suffers flood damage to his crop for the first time from a broken dam. The dam is repaired and is not expected to fail in the foreseeable future. The flood loss in this circumstance is an extraordinary item.

Other events that may generate extraordinary losses are earthquakes, expropriation of property, and prohibitions under newly enacted laws (such as a government ban on a product currently marketed). An extraordinary gain may result from a nonrecurring sale of an asset never used in operations. Assume a manufacturing company acquired land several years ago for future use but then changed its plans and held the land for appreciation. If this is the only land the company owns and it will not speculate in land in the foreseeable future, any gain from the sale of the land is considered extraordinary.

One exception to the criteria defining extraordinary items relates to gains and losses incurred when a company extinguishes its own debt. These gains and

[1]*Opinions of the Accounting Principles Board, No. 30,* "Reporting the Results of Operations—Reporting the Effects of Disposal of a Segment of a Business, and Extraordinary, Unusual and Infrequently Occurring Events and Transactions" (New York: American Institute of Certified Public Accountants, 1973).

EXHIBIT 16–1

Pacific Corporation
Income Statement
For the Year Ended December 31, 19XX

Sales		$700,000
Cost of Goods Sold		360,000
Gross Profit on Sales		$340,000
Less: Selling Expenses	$90,000	
Administrative Expenses	80,000	
Loss from Plant Strike	45,000	215,000
Income before Taxes and Extraordinary Item		$125,000
Less: Income Taxes		50,000
Income before Extraordinary Item		$ 75,000
Extraordinary Item:		
Gain from Sale of Z Company Stock	$80,000	
Less: Income Taxes	22,400	57,600
Net Income		$132,600

losses are aggregated and, if material, classified as extraordinary items.[2] An example of a debt extinguishment loss is presented in Chapter 17.

Exhibit 16–1 is an income statement for a corporation with an extraordinary item. During 19XX, the Pacific Corporation, a manufacturing concern, sold a block of common stock of Z Company, a publicly traded company, at a gain of $80,000. The shares of stock were the only security investment the company had ever owned, and it does not plan to acquire other stocks in the foreseeable future. For Pacific Corporation, this gain is unusual, infrequent, and properly considered an extraordinary item. The gain, taxed at 28%, is reported net of $22,400 income taxes, as shown in Exhibit 16–1.

UNUSUAL OR NONRECURRING ITEMS

Events and transactions that are unusual or nonrecurring, but not both, are not extraordinary items. *Accounting Principles Board Opinion No. 30* notes several examples of gains and losses that are not extraordinary either because they are typical or because they may recur as a result of continuing business activities. Examples of such items are gains and losses from (a) the write-down or write-off

[2]Unless the gains or losses result from extinguishments of debt made to satisfy sinking-fund requirements that must be met within one year. See *Statement of Financial Accounting Standards No. 64*, "Extinguishments of Debt Made to Satisfy Sinking-fund Requirements" (Stamford, CT: Financial Accounting Standards Board, 1982).

of receivables, inventories, and intangible assets; (b) the exchange or translation of foreign currencies; (c) the sale or abandonment of property, plant, or equipment used in the business; (d) the effects of a strike; and (e) the adjustments of long-term contract accruals. An unusual or infrequently occurring item of a material amount should be reported as a separate component of income before extraordinary items.

Assume that during 19XX the Pacific Corporation incurred a $45,000 loss because of a labor strike at one of its plants. The strike was not part of the company's ordinary activities, but Pacific Corporation has a history of labor difficulties. Therefore, even though the strike loss was unusual, it was not infrequent because it will likely happen again in the foreseeable future. Because it did not qualify as an extraordinary item, the before-tax amount of the strike loss was reported as a separate item among the ordinary expenses, as shown in Exhibit 16–1.

TAX ALLOCATION WITHIN A PERIOD

Note that the extraordinary gain in Exhibit 16–1 is shown net of applicable income taxes. Pacific Corporation's total income tax expense of $72,400 has been allocated to two parts of the income statement: $50,000 deducted in deriving income before extraordinary items, and $22,400 deducted in the extraordinary items section. This process, known as **tax allocation within a period**, reports the tax effect of an extraordinary item in the same section of the income statement as the item itself. By the same token, the income taxes deducted in the income before extraordinary items section relate only to the revenue and expenses disclosed in that section. Thus, tax allocation within a period portrays normal relationships within the income statement between income taxes and the items affecting their calculation.

A tax reduction due to an extraordinary loss would be deducted from the loss in the extraordinary items section. Suppose that instead of the $80,000 gain, Pacific Corporation incurred an extraordinary flood loss of $30,000, which reduced income subject to a 40% tax rate. The lower portion of the company's income statement, after tax allocation, would appear as follows:

Income before Taxes and Extraordinary Item		$125,000
Less: Income Taxes		50,000
Income before Extraordinary Item		$ 75,000
Extraordinary Item:		
Flood Loss	$30,000	
Less: Tax Reduction from Flood Loss	12,000	18,000
Net Income		$ 57,000

An alternative way of reporting the tax effects of extraordinary items is to disclose them parenthetically. Using this procedure, the extraordinary gain would be shown as

Gain from Sale of Z Company Stock (net of $22,400 of income taxes)	$57,600

The extraordinary loss would be reported as follows:

Flood Loss (net of $12,000 reduction of income taxes)	$18,000

DISCONTINUED OPERATIONS

When a company sells, abandons, or otherwise disposes of a segment of its operations, a **discontinued operations** section of the income statement reports information about the discontinued segment. The discontinued operations section presents two categories of information:

(1) The income or loss from the segment's operations for the portion of the year before its discontinuance.

(2) The gain or loss from the disposal of the segment.

The section is placed after information about ordinary, continuing operations and before any extraordinary items.

A **segment** of a business is a unit—such as a department or a division—whose activities constitute a separate major line of business or serve a particular class of customer. The assets and operating results of the segment must be clearly distinguishable from the rest of the company. For example, a furniture manufacturing division of a diversified manufacturing company is a segment of the business.

To illustrate the reporting of discontinued operations, we assume that on July 1 of the current year, Atlantic Corporation sold its Division Y. From January 1 through June 30, Division Y had operated at a loss, net of taxes, of $15,000 ($25,000 operating loss less a $10,000 reduction in income taxes caused by the operating loss). The loss, net of taxes, from the sale of the division was $42,000 ($70,000 loss on the sale less a $28,000 reduction in income taxes caused by the loss). Exhibit 16–2 illustrates the income statement for Atlantic Corporation, including the information about Division Y in the discontinued operations section. Note that when there is a discontinued operations section, the difference between the ordinary revenue and expenses is labeled "income from continuing operations."

CHANGES IN ACCOUNTING PRINCIPLES

Occasionally a company may change an accounting principle, that is, switch from one generally accepted principle to another. Examples include a change in inventory pricing method—such as from FIFO to weighted average—or a change in

EXHIBIT 16–2

Atlantic Corporation
Income Statement
For the Year Ended December 31, 19XX

Sales		$1,900,000
Expenses:		
Cost of Goods Sold	$1,100,000	
Selling Expenses	200,000	
Administrative Expenses	180,000	
Interest Expense	20,000	
Income Tax Expense	160,000	
Total Expenses		1,660,000
Income from Continuing Operations		$ 240,000
Discontinued Operations:		
Loss from Operations of Discontinued Division Y (net of $10,000 reduction of income taxes)	$ 15,000	
Loss on Disposal of Division Y (net of $28,000 reduction of income taxes)	42,000	57,000
Income before Extraordinary Item and Cumulative Effect of a Change in Accounting Principle		$ 183,000
Extraordinary Item:		
Earthquake Loss (net of $16,000 reduction of income taxes)		(24,000)
Cumulative Effect on Prior Years of Changing to a Different Depreciation Method (net of $8,000 income taxes)		12,000
Net Income		$ 171,000

depreciation method—such as from double declining balance to straight line. Because the comparability of financial data through time is enhanced by the consistent use of accounting principles, a company should change principles only when it can demonstrate that the new principle is preferable.

Almost all changes in accounting principles introduce a new item into the income statement—the **cumulative effect of a change in principle.** This item represents the total difference in the cumulative income for all prior years had the new principle been used in those years. It is equal to the difference between (a) the retained earnings at the beginning of the year and (b) the retained earnings amount at the beginning of the year had the new principle been used in all years in which the previous principle was followed for the items in question. The cumulative effect is disclosed between the extraordinary items section and the net income figure.

To illustrate the reporting of the cumulative effect of a change in principle, we assume the Atlantic Corporation in Exhibit 16–2 changed its method of depreciating plant equipment in 19XX, switching from an accelerated method to the straight-line method. Cumulative income before income taxes for years prior to 19XX would have been $20,000 greater if the straight-line method had been used to depreciate the plant equipment in those years. If we assume an income tax rate of 40%, the $12,000 after-tax amount of the effect of the change in principle would be reported on Atlantic Corporation's income statement as shown in Exhibit 16–2.

In addition to reporting the cumulative effect, the company should, in a note to the financial statements, justify the change and disclose the effect of the change on the current year's income exclusive of the cumulative adjustment. The effect of the change on earnings per share should also be reported.

Annual financial reports often include financial statements for prior periods for comparative purposes. These prior period statements are not revised to reflect the new principle adopted this period. For each period reported, however, the income before extraordinary items, net income, and the related earnings per share amounts are recomputed as if the new principle had been in effect in that period. Each period's income statement will disclose these recomputed amounts.

The above disclosure requirements accommodate two conflicting positions on the appropriate method of disclosing a change in accounting principle. One position stresses the possible dilution of public confidence in financial statements if previously reported statements are revised to reflect a new principle—hence, the inclusion of a cumulative effect on prior years' income in the current year's income statement with no revision of prior period statements. The other position emphasizes the importance of consistency in the use of accounting principles for comparative analysis of data—hence, the disclosure of selected, significant pieces of information, recomputed using the new principle, for all periods presented in the financial statements.

SINGLE-STEP AND MULTIPLE-STEP INCOME STATEMENTS

Exhibit 16–2 (page 577) illustrates a **single-step** income statement, in which the ordinary, continuing income of the business is derived in one step—by subtracting total expenses from total revenue. In Exhibit 16–2, all the expenses, totaling $1,660,000, are combined and then subtracted from the total revenue of $1,900,000. The single-step statement is a popular reporting format.

Exhibit 16–1 (page 574) is an example of a **multiple-step** income statement, in which one or more intermediate amounts are derived before the ordinary, continuing income is reported. In Exhibit 16–1, "gross profit on sales" and "income before taxes and extraordinary item" are intermediate amounts presented before the "income before extraordinary item" figure. Both the multiple-step and the single-step formats are acceptable procedures.

PRIOR PERIOD ADJUSTMENTS

Essentially, **prior period adjustments** correct errors made in financial statements of prior periods.[3] Errors may result from mathematical mistakes, oversights, incorrect applications of accounting principles, or improper analyses of existing facts when the financial statements are prepared.

Prior period adjustments are not included in the current year's income statement. Instead, corrections of material errors of past periods are charged or credited directly to Retained Earnings and are reported as adjustments to the beginning balance of Retained Earnings in the current year's retained earnings statement. For example, in 19X2, a company discovered that several mathematical errors caused its December 31, 19X1, inventory to be understated by $30,000, a material amount. Assuming an applicable income tax rate of 30%, the company reports the $21,000 prior period adjustment on the retained earnings statement. A partial statement showing this disclosure follows (beginning balance assumed):

Retained Earnings Balance, January 1, 19X2	$43,000
Add: Correction of Prior Period Inventory Error (net of $9,000 income taxes)	21,000
Retained Earnings Adjusted Balance, January 1, 19X2	$64,000

Exhibit 16–4 (page 591) contains this prior period adjustment.

Of course, a current period error does not require a prior period adjustment. The correction of current period errors was discussed in Chapter 3. As noted there, a journal entry posted to the wrong account is most easily corrected by making a new journal entry that transfers the amount to the proper account. An error that involves the right accounts but the wrong amounts may be corrected by drawing a line through the wrong amounts, entering the correct amounts above, and initialing the correction. Because the errors and corrections occur in the same period, the financial statements reflect the correct data.

CHANGES IN ACCOUNTING ESTIMATES

Estimates play an integral part in accounting. In preparing periodic financial statements, we estimate the effects of transactions continuing in the future. For example, we must estimate uncollectible accounts, useful lives of plant and intangible assets, salvage values of plant assets, and product warranty costs. As a normal consequence of such estimates, new information, changed conditions, or more experience may require the revision of previous estimates.

[3] *Statement of Financial Accounting Standards No. 16*, "Prior Period Adjustments" (Stamford, CT: Financial Accounting Standards Board, 1977).

The effect of a change in an estimate should be reflected in the income statements of current and future periods to the extent appropriate in each case. The effect may not be treated as a prior period adjustment and bypass the income statement.

The total impact of some changes in estimates is included in the current year's income statement. A revision of an estimated liability recorded in prior periods is one example. Assume that unanticipated cost increases have caused a company to underestimate its liability for product warranty carried into the current year by $900. The estimated liability is revised as follows:

Product Warranty Expense	900	
Estimated Liability for Product Warranty		900
To record estimated warranty expense.		

An estimate revision may affect both the period of change and future periods. If so, the effect of the revision should be accounted for over the current and future periods. The revision of depreciation discussed on page 376 illustrates this type of change.

The Accounting Principles Board concluded in its *Opinion No. 20*, "Accounting Changes," that the restatement of amounts reported in prior period financial statements is an inappropriate way to account for changes in estimates. Presumably, the previous estimates were the best possible, given the information then available. Thus, amounts reported for those periods should not be changed.

SUMMARY OF REPORTING FORMAT

Reporting the income of a corporation with the variety of items discussed in this chapter can be complex. Exhibit 16–3 summarizes these items and indicates their placement on the income or retained earnings statement, the order in which they are normally reported, and whether each is reported before or net of its income tax effect. Each of these items on the financial statements is keyed with the number of its related explanation.

Note that all items except prior period adjustments are reported on the income statement. Changes in accounting estimates and unusual or nonrecurring items are reported without any related income tax amounts because they are included in the computation of income from continuing operations. Income tax expense in this section relates to all preceding items of revenue and expense. All items below income from continuing operations are reported at amounts net of their income tax effects. The income statement in Exhibit 16–3 is a single-step income statement. Income from continuing operations is computed in one step, subtracting total expenses from sales. Of course, a single-step statement may include sections other than income from continuing operations.

EXHIBIT 16–3
Summary of Reporting Format

EXPLANATIONS

1 Changes in Accounting Estimates
Before-tax amounts are reported as part of related ordinary expenses.

2 Unusual or Nonrecurring Items
Before-tax amounts are separate items listed among the ordinary expenses.

3 Income Tax Expense
The initial allocation of income taxes applies to the net of all preceding revenue and expense items. All items appearing below income from continuing operations are reported net of income taxes.

4 Discontinued Operations
Involves reporting separately for the discontinued segment:
(a) Gain or loss from operations net of income taxes.
(b) Gain or loss on disposal net of income taxes.

5 Extraordinary Items
Reported net of income taxes.

6 Cumulative Effect of Change in Accounting Principle
Reported net of income taxes as the last item before net income on the income statement.

7 Prior Period Adjustments
Reported net of income taxes as a separate item leading to an adjusted beginning balance of retained earnings.

ABC Corporation
Income Statement
For the Year Ended December 31, 19XX

Sales		$XXX
Expenses:		
1 Ordinary Expenses (including effects of changes in accounting estimates)	$XX	
2 Unusual or Nonrecurring Items	XX	
3 Income Tax Expense	XX	
Total Expenses		XXX
Income from Continuing Operations		$XXX
4 Discontinued Operations:		
Gain or Loss from Operations (net of income taxes)	$XX	
Gain or Loss on Disposal (net of income taxes)	XX	XX
Income before Extraordinary Items and Cumulative Effect of a Change in Accounting Principle		$XXX
5 Extraordinary Items (net of income taxes)		XX
6 Cumulative Effect on Prior Years of Change in Accounting Principle (net of income taxes)		XX
Net Income		$XXX

ABC Corporation
Retained Earnings Statement
For the Year Ended December 31, 19XX

Balance, January 1, 19XX	$XXX
7 Add (Less): Prior Period Adjustments (net of income taxes)	XX
Adjusted Balance, January 1, 19XX	$XXX
Add (Less): Net Income (Loss)	XXX
	$XXX
Less: Dividends Declared	XX
Balance, December 31, 19XX	$XXX

EARNINGS PER SHARE

A financial statistic of great interest to corporation shareholders and potential investors is the earnings per share of common stock. Consequently, earnings per share data are widely disseminated, reaching interested persons through such channels as annual stockholder reports, financial newspapers, and financial statistical services. Because this financial information is so important, accounting guidelines require the disclosure of earnings per share data on the income statement.[4]

In determining the presentation of earnings per share data, accountants distinguish between corporations with simple capital structures and those with complex capital structures. A **simple capital structure** contains no securities that, if exercised or converted, reduce (dilute) earnings per share of common stock. Convertible debt, convertible preferred stock, stock options, and stock warrants are examples of potentially dilutive securities, because if they are exercised or converted, the number of outstanding shares of common stock increases. A **complex capital structure** contains one or more potentially dilutive securities. Corporations with simple capital structures make a single presentation of earnings per share, while corporations with complex capital structures make a dual presentation.

Simple Capital Structure

Corporations with simple capital structures calculate earnings per share by dividing net income by a weighted average of the shares of common stock outstanding during the year. If preferred stock also is outstanding, its dividend requirements are first subtracted from net income to derive earnings available to common stockholders.

Suppose that the Owens Corporation has a net income of $39,000 for 19XX. On January 1, 19XX, 10,000 shares of common stock were outstanding. An additional 6,000 shares were issued on July 1. The company has no preferred stock. The weighted average of the shares of common stock outstanding during the year is computed as follows:

Shares		Months Outstanding		Share Months
10,000	×	6	=	60,000
16,000	×	6	=	96,000
		12		156,000

$$\text{Weighted Average of Common Shares Outstanding} = \frac{156{,}000}{12} = 13{,}000$$

$$\text{Earnings per Share} = \frac{\text{Net Income}}{\text{Weighted Average of Common Shares Outstanding}}$$

$$= \frac{\$39{,}000}{13{,}000} = \$3.00$$

[4] *Opinions of the Accounting Principles Board, No. 15,* "Earnings Per Share" (New York: American Institute of Certified Public Accountants, 1969).

Complex Capital Structure

The dual presentation for corporations with complex capital structures consists of primary earnings per share and fully diluted earnings per share data. The computation of **primary earnings per share** considers the common stock outstanding during the year plus any potentially dilutive securities that are equivalent to common stock. (Accounting guidelines contain criteria for determining when a potentially dilutive security is a common stock equivalent.) The calculation of **fully diluted earnings per share** is based on the *assumption* that all dilutive securities are converted into common stock. The difference between the two per-share amounts shows the maximum possible dilution in earnings per share from any outstanding dilutive securities that are not common stock equivalents.

To illustrate the computation of primary and fully diluted earnings per share, let us suppose the Bodeen Company had a net income of $90,000 for the current year. All year the company had 40,000 shares of common stock and 5,000 shares of convertible preferred stock outstanding. The annual dividend on the convertible preferred stock is 80 cents per share, and each share is convertible into one share of common stock. The convertible preferred stock is a potentially dilutive security; we assume it is not a common stock equivalent.

Primary Earnings per Share

Net Income	$90,000
Less: Preferred Stock Dividend Requirement (5,000 shares × $0.80)	4,000
Earnings Available to Common Stockholders	$86,000
Weighted Average of Common Shares Outstanding	40,000

$$\text{Primary Earnings per Share} = \frac{\$86{,}000}{40{,}000} = \$2.15$$

Fully Diluted Earnings per Share*

Net Income (under the assumption of preferred stock conversion, there is no deduction for a preferred stock dividend requirement)	$90,000
Weighted Average of Common Shares Outstanding (40,000 shares of common stock + 5,000 shares from assumed conversion of preferred stock)	45,000

$$\text{Fully Diluted Earnings per Share} = \frac{\$90{,}000}{45{,}000} = \$2.00$$

*Assumes all preferred stock was converted into common stock at the beginning of the year.

Additional per-Share Disclosures

The form in which earnings per share data are disclosed should correspond with the income statement contents. Thus, if a firm reports extraordinary gains or losses, an earnings per share amount should be disclosed for income before extraordinary items as well as for net income. Companies may also disclose the per-share effect of each extraordinary item. Similar disclosures should be made if the income statement contains an adjustment for the cumulative effect of a change in accounting principle. The following hypothetical data from a comparative income statement for a company with 10,000 outstanding shares of common stock illustrate the proper disclosure:

	19X2	19X1
Income before Extraordinary Items	$50,000	$60,000
Extraordinary Gain (net of tax)	18,000	
Net Income	$68,000	$60,000
Earnings per Share of Common Stock:		
Income before Extraordinary Items	$5.00	$6.00
Extraordinary Gain (net of tax)	1.80	
Net Income	$6.80	$6.00

This form of disclosure precludes drawing misleading inferences from comparative earnings per share data. Note that although the earnings per share for net income increase from 19X1 to 19X2, the data for 19X2 are influenced by an extraordinary (and therefore unusual and nonrecurring) gain. A per-share comparison of income before extraordinary items shows a decrease from 19X1 to 19X2.

The variety of potentially dilutive securities and of events that affect outstanding common stock can make the computations of earnings per share quite complex. The analysis required for such computations is covered in advanced courses.

DIVIDENDS

A corporation can distribute dividends to shareholders only after its board of directors has formally declared a distribution. Dividends are usually paid in cash but may also be property or additional shares of stock in the firm. Legally, declared dividends are an obligation of the firm, and an entry to record the dividends payable is made on the **declaration date.** Cash and property dividends payable are carried as liabilities, and stock dividends to be distributed are shown in the stockholders' equity section of the balance sheet. At the declaration, a **record date** and **payment date** are established. For example, on April 25 (declaration date), the board of directors might declare a dividend payable June 1 (payment date) to those who own stock on May 15 (record date). Stockholders owning stock on the record date receive the dividend even if they dispose of their shares before the payment date. Therefore, shares sold between the record date and payment date are sold **ex-dividend** (without right to the dividend).

Most dividend declarations reduce the balance of Retained Earnings; under certain conditions, however, state laws may permit distributions from paid-in capital. Shareholders should be informed of the source of such dividends, because, in a sense, they are a return of capital rather than a distribution of earnings.

Cash Dividends The majority of dividends distributed by corporations are paid in cash. Although companies may pay such dividends annually, many large firms pay quarterly dividends. Some companies occasionally pay an extra dividend at year-end. Usually this is done when the company wishes to increase the total annual distri-

DIVIDEND REINVESTMENT PLANS

As a means of attracting capital and promoting goodwill among shareholders, dividend reinvestment plans (DRPs) were devised. Originally begun in 1969 by Allegheny Power Company, these plans became increasingly popular during the 1970s. There are currently over 1,000 companies offering DRPs, and about 200 of them use the plan to issue new common stock.

The DRPs allow participants to automatically reinvest any cash dividends in common shares of the company. The shareholder notifies the company of a willingness to participate in the plan, and then instead of reciving cash dividends, the shareholder receives an equivalent value of stock. This provides a simple, convenient, systematic method for the investor to increase equity investment in the company. Because the expenses for the new issue plans are absorbed by the company, the new issue DRPs are also an inexpensive method of investment.

Many companies have added other features to their plans. Some issue shares of stock through DRPs at a discount from the market price (typically 5%). In addition, many plans permit the investor to contribute limited amounts of additional cash to the plan, ranging from $1,000 to $25,000 per quarter.

This investment method has had special appeal to the small shareholder. Surveys conducted by several companies have indicated that over 75% of the participants in DRPs hold fewer than 200 shares of the company's stock.

The benefits of DRPs to the individual shareholder are numerous. They allow the shareholder to decide whether to be paid dividends in the form of cash or stock. By selecting the stock alternative, the shareholder has access to a simple, systematic investment vehicle which provides the advantages of dollar cost averaging of the investments as well as the benefits of compounding. The plans also allow the investor to invest small amounts without incurring transaction costs.

From the national economic standpoint, DRPs are also beneficial. By providing an economical means of obtaining new equity capital, the plans assist in raising needed capital to improve productivity and to revitalize industry. They also encourage small investors to participate in the equity market. This provides needed stability to the markets.

DRPs also have important advantages for the issuing companies. The relatively low issuance costs of the DRP stock make the plans an inexpensive means of raising common equity capital.

Because the plans provide a relatively stable, assured, and continuous flow of new equity capital, companies are able to reduce the number and size of public equity offerings and the associated downward pressure on the market price. The market has demonstrated an ability to accept a small steady stream of new common stock without a significant impact on the market price, while an equivalent number of new shares issued at one time in a public offering could result in a significant decrease in the stock price.

By strengthening the equity base of companies, DRPs provide a means of improving their competitive capabilities. The benefits of an improved capital base have been noted by several credit rating agencies, including Moody's and Duff and Phelps, who have stated that the use of DRPs could lead to improved credit ratings for firms.

From Brent Wilson, "Reinvesting Dividends: A Way To Revitalize Your Company," *Financial Executive*, December 1982, pages 42–43.

bution without departing from a standard quarterly amount that was established by custom or announced in advance.

In declaring cash dividends, a company must have both an appropriate amount of retained earnings and the necessary amount of cash. Uninformed investors often believe that a large Retained Earnings balance automatically permits generous dividend distributions. A company, however, may successfully accumulate earnings and at the same time not be sufficiently liquid to pay large dividends. Many companies, especially new firms in the so-called growth industries, use retained earnings for expansion and pay out only a small portion, or perhaps none, of their earnings.

Cash dividends are based on the number of shares of stock outstanding. When a company's directors declare a cash dividend, an entry is made debiting Retained Earnings and crediting Dividends Payable, a current liability account. Assume, for example, that a company has outstanding 1,000 shares of $100 par value, 6% preferred stock and 3,000 shares of $50 par value common stock. If the company declares the regular $6 dividend on the preferred stock and a $4 dividend on the common stock, the dividend payment totals $18,000. The following entry is made at the declaration date:

Retained Earnings	18,000	
Dividends Payable—Preferred Stock		6,000
Dividends Payable—Common Stock		12,000
To record declaration of $6 dividend on preferred stock and $4 dividend on common stock.		

Unpaid cash dividends are carried as a current liability on the balance sheet. On the payment date, the following entry is made:

Dividends Payable—Preferred Stock	6,000	
Dividends Payable—Common Stock	12,000	
Cash		18,000
To record payment of dividends on preferred and common stocks.		

Some companies, especially those paying quarterly dividends, debit an account called Dividends on the declaration date. Dividends is a contra account to Retained Earnings until it is closed by a debit to Retained Earnings at year-end.

Stock Dividends

Companies frequently distribute shares of their own stock as dividends to shareholders in lieu of, or in addition to, cash dividends. A company may issue **stock dividends** when it does not wish to deplete its working capital by paying a cash dividend. Distribution of a stock dividend may also signify management's desire to "plough back" earnings into the company. The distribution transfers a portion of retained earnings to the paid-in capital accounts. The so-called permanent capital is thereby increased although no new assets are acquired. Young and growing companies often issue stock dividends, inasmuch as earnings are needed to acquire new facilities and to expand. The use of stock dividends is by no means confined to such companies, however.

Although stock dividends may take a number of forms, usually common shares are distributed to common shareholders. We limit our discussion to this type of distribution.

For small stock dividends—additional shares issued are fewer than 20–25% of the number previously outstanding—an amount equal to the market value of the shares issued is transferred from Retained Earnings to Paid-in Capital. In some respects, the issuance of new shares in the form of a dividend can be viewed as a transaction that avoids the test of the marketplace. If the shareholders receive cash and immediately purchase additional shares of the firm's stock, the purchases are made at market value. Thus, the number of shares issued in exchange for a given amount of retained earnings should be related to the market value of the shares.

To illustrate the entries reflecting a declaration of a stock dividend, we assume that the stockholders' equity of a company is as follows before declaration of a 10% stock dividend:

Common Stock, $50 Par Value, 2,000 shares issued and outstanding	$100,000
Paid-in Capital in Excess of Par Value	5,000
Retained Earnings	80,000
Total Stockholders' Equity	$185,000

With 2,000 shares outstanding, declaration of a 10% stock dividend requires the issuance of an additional 200 shares. Let us assume that the market price per share is $70. The amount transferred from Retained Earnings is $14,000, of which $10,000 (par value of the shares) is credited to the Stock Dividend to Be Issued account. The premium of $20 per share, or $4,000, is credited to Paid-in Capital in Excess of Par Value.

Retained Earnings	14,000	
Stock Dividend to Be Issued		10,000
Paid-in Capital in Excess of Par Value		4,000
To record declaration of 10% stock dividend on common shares.		

When the stock is distributed, the following entry is made:

Stock Dividend to Be Issued	10,000	
Common Stock		10,000
To record issuance of stock dividend on common shares.		

After the stock dividend is distributed, the stockholders' equity appears as follows:

Common Stock, $50 Par Value, 2,200 shares issued and outstanding	$110,000
Paid-in Capital in Excess of Par Value	9,000
Retained Earnings	66,000
Total Stockholders' Equity	$185,000

If a balance sheet is prepared between the declaration date and distribution date of a stock dividend, the Stock Dividend to Be Issued account is shown as a separate item added to the Common Stock account.

The relative position of a common shareholder is not altered by the receipt of a common stock dividend. If a 10% stock dividend is distributed, all shareholders increase their proportionate holdings by 10%, while the total stock outstanding is increased in the same proportion. No income is realized by the shareholders. If the stock dividend distributed is not large in relation to the outstanding shares, little or no change may occur in the market value of the stock. If the market value does not decrease and the company continues the same cash dividends per share, shareholders have benefited by the distribution.

When the number of shares issued as a stock dividend is large enough to reduce materially the per-share market value, the shareholders may not perceive the same benefits as they do for small stock dividends. The transaction is analogous to a stock split, whereby a company increases the number of outstanding shares and proportionately reduces the par or stated value of its stock. For this reason, the accounting analysis is different for large stock dividends (in excess of 20–25%). The amount transferred from Retained Earnings to Paid-in Capital is the minimum required by law (that is, the legal capital). Usually this amount is the par or stated value of the stock.

STOCK SPLITS

Occasionally, a corporation reduces the par or stated value of its common stock and issues additional shares to its stockholders. This type of transaction, called a **stock split**, does not change the balances of the stockholders' equity accounts—only a memorandum entry is made in the records to show the altered par or stated value of the stock. For example, if a company that has 1,000 shares outstanding of $100 par value common stock announced a 2 for 1 stock split, it would simply reduce the par value of its stock to $50 per share. After the stock split, each shareholder would have twice the number of shares held before the split.

Note the difference between accounting for a stock split, which requires a memorandum entry, and accounting for a large stock dividend, which requires a transfer equal to the legal capital from Retained Earnings to Paid-in Capital. A stock split reduces the par or stated value of the stock and therefore does not change the total par or stated value of shares outstanding. In a stock dividend, no change occurs in the par or stated value per share, so an entry must reflect the increased legal capital associated with the additional shares issued.

The major reason for a stock split is to reduce the market price of the stock. Some companies like their stock to sell within a certain price range. They may feel that higher prices narrow the breadth of their market, because investors often prefer to buy 100-share lots (purchases of fewer shares are odd-lot purchases and may be subject to higher brokers' fees), and obviously, many small investors cannot purchase high-priced stocks in 100-share lots.

When shares are selling below the desired price, a *reverse split* can be accomplished by increasing the par value of the shares and reducing the number outstanding. Such transactions are encountered less frequently than stock splits.

APPROPRIATIONS OF RETAINED EARNINGS

Portions of the Retained Earnings balance are often restricted so that these amounts cannot be paid out as dividends. The amounts so segregated are called **retained earnings appropriations**, or *retained earnings reserves*.

In some instances, appropriations of retained earnings may be entirely *voluntary*—the board of directors may restrict dividends to use corporate funds for a specific internal purpose. For example, the company may want to enlarge its plant or establish a buffer against possible adversity. By appropriating retained earnings, the directors inform the shareholders of the need to restrict dividend payments.

Other types of retained earnings appropriations may be *statutory* or *contractual*. In Chapter 15, we mentioned a statutory appropriation in connection with treasury stock purchases—some states require that retained earnings be restricted in an amount equal to the cost of treasury stock purchased by the corporation. A contractual restriction may result from agreements made when a company issues long-term debt. The debt agreement may limit the amount of dividends the company may pay until the debt is settled. Such an agreement helps protect the availability of the company's working capital for debt payment purposes.

Retained earnings may be appropriated by making an entry in the company's records. For example, if the board of directors appropriates $60,000 for plant expansion, the following entry is made:

Retained Earnings	60,000	
Retained Earnings Appropriated for Plant Expansion		60,000
To record retained earnings appropriation for plant expansion.		

The appropriated amount is presented in the balance sheet as follows:

Retained Earnings	
Appropriated for Plant Expansion	$ 60,000
Unappropriated	90,000
Total Retained Earnings	$150,000

Note that this company has total retained earnings of $150,000, of which only $90,000 is available for the declaration of dividends.

Certain points should be emphasized regarding the appropriation of retained earnings. First, segregating retained earnings for a particular objective only restricts dividend amounts. The procedure does not ensure that funds will be available for the avowed objective, because a company may have a large Retained Earnings balance without having an ample amount of liquid assets. When a company appropriates earnings for plant expansion, for example, management may also *fund* the appropriation. This is accomplished by setting aside funds, as they become available, in a special asset account to permit eventual *spending* for plant expansion.

Second, expenditures are never charged against retained earnings appropriations. When the purpose is accomplished or the event transpires for which the appropriation was made, the restricted amount is returned, intact, to unappropriated retained earnings. For example, suppose that the company in our preceding illustration implemented its expansion plans, spending $55,000 for new facilities. After recording the purchase by debiting plant assets and crediting Cash for the amount spent, the company reverses the entry made to appropriate retained earnings:

Retained Earnings Appropriated for Plant Expansion	60,000	
Retained Earnings		60,000
To return appropriation to Retained Earnings.		

As an alternative to segregating retained earnings formally, a note to the balance sheet may inform shareholders of restrictions on retained earnings. The following note from an annual report of Georgia–Pacific Corporation illustrates this type of disclosure:

> Certain loan agreements place a limitation on cash dividends that can be paid. The amount of retained earnings available for cash dividends under the most restrictive covenants of the loan agreements is approximately $365 million. In addition, certain agreements require the corporation to maintain a minimum of $250 million of consolidated working capital and impose certain limitations on additional borrowings.

RETAINED EARNINGS STATEMENT

A **retained earnings statement** is an analysis of the Retained Earnings accounts (both appropriated and unappropriated) for the accounting period and is usually presented with the other corporate financial statements. The form of the statement is not standardized, and sometimes it is combined with the income statement. An example of a retained earnings statement is shown in Exhibit 16–4.

DEMONSTRATION PROBLEM FOR REVIEW

Information related to the income and retained earnings of Alpha, Inc., for 19X1 is listed below. For simplicity, amounts are limited to three digits. Using these data, prepare a single-step income statement and a retained earnings statement for Alpha, Inc., for 19X1. Assume that all changes in income are subject to a 30% income tax rate. Use the format in Exhibit 16–3 and disregard earnings per share disclosures.

EXHIBIT 16–4

Holmes Corporation
Retained Earnings Statement
For the Year Ended December 31, 19X2

Appropriated			
Appropriated for Plant Expansion:			
Balance, January 1, 19X2		$40,000	
Appropriated in 19X2		10,000	$ 50,000
Unappropriated			
Balance, January 1, 19X2		$43,000	
Add: Correction of Prior Period Inventory Error (net of $9,000 income taxes)		21,000	
Adjusted Balance, January 1, 19X2		$64,000	
Add: Net Income		35,000	
		$99,000	
Less: Dividends Declared	$15,000		
Appropriation for Plant Expansion (see above)	10,000	25,000	74,000
Total Retained Earnings, December 31, 19X2			$124,000

Additional uncollectible accounts expense due to revised estimate of percentage of anticipated uncollectible accounts (considered a selling expense)	$ 20	Increase in prior years' reported income before income taxes due to change in depreciation method	$ 20
Cost of goods sold	420	Loss from labor strike (considered unusual but recurring)	40
Dividends declared	70	Loss from operations of discontinued Beta Division	50
Overstatement of 19X0 ending inventory (caused by error)	10	Other operating expenses	230
Gain on condemnation of property (considered unusual and infrequent)	40	Retained earnings balance at end of 19X0	454
Gain on disposal of discontinued Beta Division	80	Sales	980
		Selling and administrative expenses (before revised estimate of uncollectible accounts)	170

SOLUTION TO DEMONSTRATION PROBLEM (Selected computations appear as notes to the financial statements.)

Alpha, Inc.
Income Statement
For the Year Ended December 31, 19X1

Sales		$980
Expenses:		
Cost of Goods Sold	$420	
Other Operating Expenses	230	
Selling and Administrative Expenses (Note A)	190	
Loss from Labor Strike	40	
Income Tax Expense (Note B)	30	
Total Expenses		910
Income from Continuing Operations		$ 70
Discontinued Operations:		
Loss from Operations of Discontinued Beta Division (net of $15 reduction of income taxes) (Note C)	($ 35)	
Gain on Disposal of Discontinued Beta Division (net of $24 income taxes) (Note D)	56	21
Income before Extraordinary Item and Cumulative Effect of a Change in Accounting Principle		$ 91
Extraordinary Item:		
Gain on Condemnation of Property (net of $12 income taxes) (Note E)		28
Cumulative Effect on Prior Years of Changing to a Different Depreciation Method (net of $6 income taxes) (Note F)		14
Net Income		$133

Alpha, Inc.
Retained Earnings Statement
For the Year Ended December 31, 19X1

Balance, January 1, 19X1	$454
Less: Correction of Prior Period Inventory Error (net of $3 reduction of income taxes) (Note G)	7
Adjusted Balance, January 1, 19X1	$447
Add: Net Income	133
	$580
Less: Dividends Declared	70
Balance, December 31, 19X1	$510

Notes to financial statements:

(A) $170 + $20 = $190
(B) 30% [$980 − ($420 + $230 + $190 + $40)] = $30
(C) $50 − [0.3 ($50)] = $35
(D) $80 − [0.3 ($80)] = $56
(E) $40 − [0.3 ($40)] = $28
(F) $20 − [0.3 ($20)] = $14
(G) $10 − [0.3 ($10)] = $7

KEY POINTS TO REMEMBER

(1) Special sections of the income statement are used to report
  (a) Gains and losses from discontinued operations.
  (b) Extraordinary items, that is, items that are both unusual and unlikely to recur.
  (c) The cumulative effects of most changes in accounting principles.

(2) Tax allocation within a period improves the reporting of income taxes by disclosing both the tax effect and the items causing that effect in the same location in financial statements.

(3) Corrections of material errors made in previous periods are charged or credited directly to Retained Earnings.

(4) The effects of changes in accounting estimates are spread over the appropriate current and future periods.

(5) Corporations with complex capital structures present data on both primary earnings per share and fully diluted earnings per share. A single presentation of earnings per share is appropriate for a corporation with a simple capital structure.

(6) Some of the major transactions related to retained earnings are
  (a) Cash dividends, which reduce retained earnings and are a current liability when declared.

(b) Stock dividends, which represent a transfer of retained earnings to the appropriate stock and paid-in capital accounts at the market value of the shares for small stock dividends and at the legal minimum for large stock dividends.
(c) Appropriations, which are segregations of retained earnings. The appropriated amount reduces the retained earnings available for dividends.

(7) Stock splits change the par or stated value of stock and affect the number of shares outstanding. Only a memorandum notation records stock splits.

SELF-TEST QUESTIONS
(Answers are at the end of this chapter.)

1. Assume an income statement contains each of the four sections listed below. Which will be the last section in the income statement?
(a) Extraordinary item.
(b) Cumulative effect of a change in accounting principle.
(c) Income from continuing operations.
(d) Discontinued operations.

2. Which of the following items will appear in either a single-step or a multiple-step income statement for a merchandising firm?
(a) Appropriation of retained earnings.
(b) Gross profit on sales.
(c) Income before extraordinary item.
(d) Prior period adjustment.

3. Which of the following events decreases a corporation's stockholders' equity?
(a) A 3 for 1 stock split.
(b) A declaration of a 6% stock dividend.
(c) A $100,000 retained earnings appropriation.
(d) A declaration of a $1.00 cash dividend per share of preferred stock.

4. In 19X3, Corliss, Inc., discovered an arithmetic error had been made in 19X2, causing 19X2's depreciation expense to be overstated. Corliss corrected the error in 19X3 with a journal entry that included a credit to Retained Earnings. This situation illustrates a:
(a) Prior period adjustment.
(b) Change in an accounting estimate.
(c) Change in an accounting principle.
(d) Restriction on retained earnings.

5. A corporation will make a dual presentation of earnings per share (primary and fully diluted earnings per share) when it
(a) Has two classes of stock outstanding (preferred and common stock).
(b) Uses a multiple-step income statement format.
(c) Has a capital structure that contains at least one potentially dilutive security (a complex capital structure).
(d) Has restrictions on the amount of earnings that may be paid out as dividends.

QUESTIONS

16–1 Define *extraordinary items*. How are extraordinary items shown in the income statement?

16–2 A manufacturing plant of the Barnet Corporation was destroyed by an earthquake, which is rare in the region where the plant was located. Where should this loss be classified in the income statement?

16–3 A Florida citrus grower incurs substantial frost damage to crops. Frost damage typically is experienced every few years. How should the loss on the crops be shown in the income statement?

16–4 What is meant by *tax allocation within a period?* What is the purpose of this type of tax allocation?

16–5 Define a business *segment*. Why are gains and losses from a discontinued segment reported in a separate section of the income statement?

16–6 This year, the Warren Company switched from the FIFO method of inventory pricing to the weighted average method. Cumulative income before income taxes for previous years would have been $60,000 lower if the weighted average method had been used.

(a) Assuming a 35% income tax rate, how should the effect of this inventory pricing change be shown in the income statement?

(b) If a comparative income statement is presented in the annual report, should Warren revise last year's income statement using the weighted average method?

16–7 What is the difference between a single-step income statement and a multiple-step income statement?

16–8 Which one of the following amounts would appear only in a multiple-step income statement?

Income from Continuing Operations
Income before Extraordinary Item
Gross Profit on Sales
Net Income

16–9 The Musket Company discovered this year that a significant portion of its inventory was overlooked during its inventory count at the end of last year. How should the correction of this error be disclosed in the financial statements?

16–10 Distinguish between an error and a change in an estimate. How is reporting corrections of errors different from reporting changes in accounting estimates?

16–11 Distinguish between corporations with simple capital structures and those with complex capital structures. What does the type of capital structure imply regarding the presentation of earnings per share data?

16–12 In 19XX, Haynen Company earned a net income of $127,500. The company, which has a simple capital structure, started the year with 15,000 shares of common stock outstanding and issued an additional 6,000 shares on September 1. What is Haynen Company's 19XX earnings per share?

16–13 What assumption underlies the computation of fully diluted earnings per share? What does the difference between the amounts of primary earnings per share and fully diluted earnings per share reveal?

16–14 What is a stock dividend? How does a common stock dividend paid to common shareholders affect their respective ownership interests?

16–15 Distinguish between a stock dividend and a stock split by indicating (a) the effect of each on shareholders' individual interests, (b) the possible effect of each on the market price of stock, and (c) the entries necessary to record these events in the accounting records.

16–16 What is an *appropriation* of retained earnings? Why and by whom are such appropriations made?

16–17 Where do the following accounts (and their balances) appear in the balance sheet?
(a) Dividends Payable—Common Stock
(b) Stock Dividend to Be Issued
(c) Retained Earnings Appropriated for Contingencies

EXERCISES

Income statement sections

16–18 During the current year, Reed Corporation incurred an extraordinary tornado loss of $150,000 and sold a segment of its business at a gain of $200,000. Until it was sold, the segment had a current period operating loss of $90,000. Also, the company discovered that an error caused last year's ending inventory to be understated by $20,000 (a material amount). The company had $600,000 income from continuing operations for the current year. Prepare the lower part of the income statement, beginning with the $600,000 income from continuing operations. Follow tax allocation procedures, assuming all changes in income are subject to a 40% income tax rate. Disregard earnings per share disclosures.

Accounting changes and prior period adjustment

16–19 For each of the following current year events for Doring, Inc., (1) identify the type of accounting change or other category of event involved; (2) indicate where each would be reported on the current year's income or retained earnings statement; and (3) illustrate how each would be disclosed including the relevant dollar amounts. Assume all changes in income are subject to a 30% income tax rate.

(a) The company changed from the sum-of-the-years'-digits to the straight-line method of depreciating its equipment. Cumulative income before income taxes for prior years would have been $60,000 higher under the straight-line method.

(b) The company discovered that, because of a new employee's oversight, depreciation of $25,000 on an addition to the plant had been omitted last year. The amount is material.

(c) A patent acquired at a cost of $54,000 six years ago (including the current year) has been amortized under the straight-line method using an estimated useful life of 15 years. In reviewing accounts for the year-end adjustments, the company revised its estimate of the total useful life to 11 years.

Earnings per share

16–20 The Ewing Corporation began the year with a simple capital structure consisting of 34,000 shares of common stock outstanding. On April 1, 10,000 additional shares were issued, and another 6,000 shares were issued on August 1. The company had a net income for the year of $209,000.

(a) Compute the earnings per share of common stock.

(b) Assume that the company also had 11,000 shares of 6%, $40 par value cumulative preferred stock outstanding throughout the year. Compute the earnings per share of common stock.

Earnings per share

16–21 During 19X3, the Daly Corporation had 25,000 shares of $10 par value common stock and 5,000 shares of 7%, $20 par value convertible preferred stock outstanding. The preferred stock is not a common stock equivalent. Each share of preferred stock may be converted into two shares of common stock. Daly Corporation's 19X3 net income was $77,000.

(a) Compute the primary earnings per share for 19X3.
(b) Compute the fully diluted earnings per share of 19X3.

Earnings per share

16–22 Wilson, Inc., discloses earnings per share amounts for extraordinary items. Use the following summarized income data for the current year to prepare earnings per share disclosures for the company, assuming that a 40% income tax rate is applicable and that 15,000 shares of common stock were outstanding during the year.

Sales	$860,000
Total operating expenses (excluding income taxes)	640,000
Extraordinary flood loss	50,000

Cash and stock dividends; stock split

16–23 Bowser Corporation has 8,000 shares of $30 par value common stock outstanding and retained earnings of $315,000. The company declares a cash dividend of $2.50 per share and a 4% stock dividend. The market price of the stock at the declaration date is $35 per share.

(a) Give the general journal entries for (1) the declaration of dividends and (2) the payment (or issuance) of the dividends.
(b) Assume that the company declares a 50% stock dividend rather than a 4% stock dividend. Give the general journal entries for (1) the declaration of the stock dividend and (2) the issuance of the stock dividend.
(c) Assume that the company splits its stock 1.5 shares for 1 share and reduces the par value from $30 to $20 per share rather than declaring a 50% stock dividend. How does the accounting for the stock split differ from the accounting for the 50% stock dividend?

Retained earnings appropriation

16–24 In both 19X3 and 19X4, the Kerr Construction Company appropriated $60,000 of retained earnings for a future truck crane acquisition. In 19X5, the company acquired the truck crane for $115,000 cash. Prepare general journal entries to record the appropriations of retained earnings in 19X3 and 19X4, the purchase of the truck crane in 19X5, and the disposition of the balance in the appropriated retained earnings account after the purchase.

Stockholders' equity section

16–25 Use the following data to prepare the stockholders' equity section of Faber Corporation's balance sheet.

Unappropriated Retained Earnings	$263,000
Paid-in Capital in Excess of Par Value—Common Stock	75,000
Paid-in Capital in Excess of Par Value—Preferred Stock	30,000
Retained Earnings Appropriated—Treasury Stock Purchases	21,000
7% Preferred Stock, $40 Par Value, 6,000 shares outstanding	240,000
Common Stock, $20 Par Value, 30,000 shares issued	600,000
Treasury Stock (Common), 500 shares (at cost)	21,000
Retained Earnings Appropriated—Plant Expansion	210,000

Retained earnings statement

16–26 Use the following data to prepare a retained earnings statement for the Beach Corporation for 19X2. Assume a 30% tax rate.

Total retained earnings originally reported at December 31, 19X1, of which $100,000 is appropriated for future plant expansion	$325,000
Cash dividends declared in 19X2	50,000
Net income reported for 19X2	150,000
Additional appropriation of retained earnings in 19X2 for future plant expansion	25,000
Understatement of 19X1 ending inventory discovered late in 19X2 (caused by arithmetic errors)	10,000

PROBLEMS

Income statement sections and format

16–27 The following information from Willow Company's 19X1 operations is available:

Administrative expenses	$ 82,000
Cost of goods sold	630,000
Sales	975,000
Flood loss (considered unusual and infrequent)	25,000
Selling expenses	124,000
Interest expense	9,000
Loss from operations of discontinued segment	60,000
Gain on disposal of discontinued segment	40,000
Income taxes:	
Amount applicable to ordinary operations	39,000
Reduction applicable to flood loss	7,500
Reduction applicable to loss from operations of discontinued segment	18,000
Amount applicable to gain on disposal of discontinued segment	12,000

REQUIRED
(a) Prepare a multiple-step income statement for the Willow Company for 19X1.
(b) Prepare a single-step income statement for the Willow Company for 19X1.

Earnings per share

16–28 The Tanner Corporation began 19XX with 26,000 shares of common stock and 2,000 shares of convertible preferred stock outstanding. On March 1 an additional 2,000 shares of common stock were issued. On August 1, another 6,000 shares of common stock were issued. On November 1, 1,000 shares of common stock were reacquired for the treasury. The preferred stock has a $1.50 per-share dividend rate, and each share may be converted into one share of common. The preferred stock is not a common stock equivalent. Tanner Corporation's 19XX net income is $120,000.

REQUIRED
(a) Compute primary earnings per share for 19XX.
(b) Compute fully diluted earnings per share for 19XX.
(c) If the preferred stock were not convertible, Tanner Corporation would have a simple capital structure. What would be its earnings per share for 19XX?

Earnings per share and multiple-step income statement

16–29 Roseland Corporation discloses earnings per share amounts for extraordinary items. The following summarized data relate to the company's 19X3 operations:

Sales	$635,000
Cost of goods sold	350,000
Selling expenses	50,000
Administrative expenses	77,000
Loss from earthquake damages (considered unusual and infrequent)	48,000
Loss on sale of equipment	8,000

Shares of common stock:	
Outstanding at January 1, 19X3	12,000 shares
Additional issued at May 1, 19X3	4,000 shares
Additional issued at November 1, 19X3	2,000 shares

REQUIRED
Prepare a multiple-step income statement for Roseland Corporation for 19X3. Assume a 30% income tax rate. Include earnings per share disclosures for 19X3 at the bottom of the income statement.

Income statement and dividend relationships

16–30 Graff Company presented the following earnings per share data:

Earnings per Share of Common Stock:	
Income before Extraordinary Item	$5.02
Extraordinary Gain (net of tax)	.48
Net Income	$5.50

The company, which has a simple capital structure, began the year with 33,000 shares of $10 par value common stock and 10,000 shares of 6%, $25 par value preferred stock outstanding. On October 1, an additional 12,000 shares of common stock were issued. Cash dividends were distributed to both preferred and common stockholders.

REQUIRED
(a) What is the annual preferred stock dividend requirement?
(b) What was the net income for the current year for Graff Company?
(c) What was the amount of the extraordinary gain, net of the tax effect? What was the amount of the gain before the tax effect, assuming a 40% tax rate on the gain?
(d) If the tax rate on ordinary income is 40%, what amount of income tax expense was reported in the income before extraordinary item section of the income statement?

Retained earnings—transactions and statement

16–31 The stockholders' equity of the Hernandez Corporation at January 1, 19X2, appears below:

Common Stock, $20 Par Value, 50,000 shares authorized; 30,000 shares issued and outstanding	$600,000
Paid-in Capital in Excess of Par Value—Common Stock	195,000
Unappropriated Retained Earnings	292,000

During 19X2, the following transactions occurred:

June 7	The board of directors appropriated $80,000 of retained earnings for future land acquisition.
Dec. 10	Declared a cash dividend of $1.60 per share and a 5% stock dividend. Market value of the common stock was $28 per share.
31	Closed the net income of $146,000 from the Income Summary account to Retained Earnings.

REQUIRED

(a) Prepare general journal entries to record the foregoing transactions.
(b) Prepare a retained earnings statement for 19X2.
(c) The cash dividend was paid and the stock dividend was issued on January 17, 19X3. Make the necessary journal entries.
(d) The board of directors dropped its plan to acquire land in the future and on January 25, 19X3, eliminated the appropriation for future land acquisition. Make the necessary journal entry.

Retained earnings—transactions and statement

16–32 The stockholders' equity of the Redwing Corporation at January 1, 19X4, follows.

5% Preferred Stock, $40 Par Value, 10,000 shares authorized; 6,000 shares issued and outstanding	$ 240,000
Common Stock, $15 Par Value, 80,000 shares authorized; 45,000 shares issued and outstanding	675,000
Paid-in Capital in Excess of Par Value—Common Stock	180,000
Retained Earnings Appropriated for Plant Expansion	225,000
Unappropriated Retained Earnings	320,000
Total Stockholders' Equity	$1,640,000

The following transactions, among others, occurred during 19X4:

Feb. 10	Discovered the bookkeeper overlooked a 19X3 adjusting entry for $5,000 of goodwill amortization. Goodwill amortization is not deductible for tax purposes, so this error has no income tax effect. Redwing Corporation does not use a contra account when recording goodwill amortization.
June 18	Declared a 6% stock dividend on all outstanding shares of common stock. The market value of the stock was $21 per share.
July 1	Issued the stock dividend declared on June 18.
Sept. 8	The board of directors appropriated an additional $75,000 of retained earnings for plant expansion.
Dec. 20	Declared the annual cash dividend on the preferred stock and a cash dividend of $1.70 per share of common stock, payable on January 20 to stockholders of record on December 28.

Dec. 31 Closed the Income Summary account, with net earnings of $218,000, to Retained Earnings.

REQUIRED
(a) Prepare general journal entries to record the foregoing transactions.
(b) Prepare a retained earnings statement for 19X4.

Stockholders' equity—transactions and financial statement presentations

16–33 The stockholders' equity of the Hoppe Corporation at January 1, 19X2, is shown below:

8% Preferred Stock, $60 Par Value, 8,000 shares authorized; 7,000 shares issued and outstanding	$ 420,000
Paid-in Capital in Excess of Par Value—Preferred Stock	56,000
Common Stock, $40 Par Value, 40,000 shares authorized; 22,000 shares issued and outstanding	880,000
Paid-in Capital in Excess of Par Value—Common Stock	110,000
Unappropriated Retained Earnings	412,000
Total Stockholders' Equity	$1,878,000

The following transactions, among others, occurred during 19X2:

Jan. 15 Hoppe Corporation carries life insurance on its key officers (with the corporation as beneficiary), and in 19X1 it paid insurance premiums of $3,000 covering 19X1 and 19X2. Today the company discovered that the full $3,000 had been charged to Insurance Expense in 19X1. These premiums are not deductible for tax purposes, so this error has no tax effect.

May 1 Announced a 2 for 1 stock split, reducing the par value of the common stock to $20 per share. The authorization was increased to 80,000 shares.

Sept. 1 Reacquired 4,000 shares of common stock for cash at $23 per share.

2 Appropriated an amount of retained earnings equal to the cost of the treasury shares acquired September 1.

Dec. 5 Declared a 5% stock dividend on all outstanding shares of common stock. The market value of the stock was $25 per share.

15 Issued the stock dividend declared on December 5.

16 Declared the annual cash dividend on the preferred stock and a cash dividend of $1.30 per common share, payable on January 10 to stockholders of record on December 30.

31 Recorded the annual patent amortization expense. In reviewing the accounts for year-end adjustments, management revised the estimated total useful life of the patent from 17 years to 11 years. The patent cost $71,400 when acquired at the beginning of last year. The company uses the straight-line method for amortization and does not use a contra account.

31 Closed the Income Summary account, with net earnings of $195,000, to Retained Earnings.

REQUIRED
(a) Prepare general journal entries to record the foregoing transactions.
(b) Prepare a retained earnings statement for 19X2.
(c) Prepare the stockholders' equity section of the balance sheet at December 31, 19X2.

ALTERNATE PROBLEMS

Single-step income statement and retained earnings statement

16–27A The information listed below is related to Coleman Corporation's 19X3 income and retained earnings.

Administrative expenses	$ 38,000
Appropriation of retained earnings in 19X3 for plant expansion	100,000
Cash dividends declared	80,000
Cost of goods sold	461,000
Understatement of 19X2 depreciation expense (caused by an error)	15,000
Increase in prior years' income before income taxes due to change in inventory pricing method (from weighted average to FIFO)	45,000
Loss from uninsured portion of brushfire damages (considered unusual but recurring)	12,000
Loss from expropriation of property by foreign government (considered unusual and infrequent)	85,000
Retained earnings appropriated for plant expansion (balance at December 31, 19X2)	300,000
Unappropriated retained earnings (balance at December 31, 19X2)	530,000
Sales	894,000
Selling expenses	73,000
Income taxes:	
Amount applicable to ordinary operations	124,000
Reduction applicable to loss from expropriation of property	34,000
Amount applicable to increase in prior years' income before income taxes due to change in inventory pricing method	18,000
Reduction applicable to 19X2 depreciation expense error	6,000

REQUIRED

(a) Prepare a single-step income statement for the Coleman Corporation for 19X3.

(b) Prepare a retained earnings statement for the Coleman Corporation for 19X3.

Earnings per share

16–28A The Shoreline Corporation began the year 19XX with 10,000 shares of common stock and 3,000 shares of convertible preferred stock outstanding. On May 1, an additional 8,000 shares of common stock were issued. On July 1, 2,000 shares of common stock were reacquired for the treasury. On September 1, the 2,000 treasury shares of common stock were reissued. The preferred stock has a $2 per-share dividend rate, and each share may be converted into two shares of common. The preferred stock is not a common stock equivalent. Shoreline Corporation's 19XX net income is $84,000.

REQUIRED

(a) Compute primary earnings per share for 19XX.

(b) Compute fully diluted earnings per share for 19XX.

(c) If the preferred stock were not convertible, Shoreline Corporation would have a simple capital structure. What would be its earnings per share for 19XX?

Earnings per share and multiple-step income statement

16–29A Kasten Corporation discloses earnings per share amounts for extraordinary items. The following summarized data are related to the company's 19X2 operations:

Sales	$1,460,000
Cost of goods sold	800,000
Selling expenses	145,000
Administrative expenses	90,000
Gain from expropriation of property by foreign government (considered unusual and infrequent)	100,000
Loss from plant strike	50,000
Shares of common stock:	
Outstanding at January 1, 19X2	50,000 shares
Additional issued at April 1, 19X2	10,000 shares
Additional issued at August 1, 19X2	6,000 shares

REQUIRED

Prepare a multiple-step income statement for Kasten Corporation for 19X2. Assume a 40% income tax rate. Include earnings per share disclosures for 19X2 at the bottom of the income statement.

Retained earnings—transactions and statement

16–31A The stockholders' equity of the Adler Corporation at January 1, 19X8, appears below:

Common Stock, $10 Par Value, 60,000 shares authorized; 40,000 shares issued and outstanding	$400,000
Paid-in Capital in Excess of Par Value—Common Stock	180,000
Unappropriated Retained Earnings	235,000

During 19X8, the following transactions occurred:

May 12	Fearing a strike early next year, the board of directors appropriated $50,000 of retained earnings for contingencies.
Dec. 5	Declared a cash dividend of 75 cents per share and a 7% stock dividend. Market value of the common stock was $19 per share on this date.
31	Closed the net income of $125,000 from the Income Summary account to Retained Earnings.

REQUIRED

(a) Prepare general journal entries to record the foregoing transactions.
(b) Prepare a retained earnings statement for 19X8.
(c) The cash dividend was paid and the stock dividend was issued on January 20 of the following year. Make the necessary journal entries.
(d) The expected employee strike did not materialize, and the board of directors on January 22 eliminated the appropriation for contingencies. Make the necessary journal entry.

Retained earnings—transactions and statement

16–32A The stockholders' equity of the Waverly Corporation at January 1, 19X5, appears below:

6% Preferred Stock, $50 Par Value, 8,000 shares authorized; 5,000 shares issued and outstanding	$ 250,000
Common Stock, $30 Par Value, 40,000 shares authorized; 15,000 shares issued and outstanding	450,000
Paid-in Capital in Excess of Par Value—Common Stock	135,000
Retained Earnings Appropriated for Future Litigation	90,000
Unappropriated Retained Earnings	410,000
Total Stockholders' Equity	$1,335,000

The following transactions, among others, occurred during 19X5:

Jan. 22	Discovered the bookkeeper made an arithmetic error in 19X4 causing a $12,000 overstatement of goodwill amortization for that year. Goodwill amortization is not deductible for tax purposes, so this error has no income tax effect. Waverly Corporation does not use a contra account when recording goodwill amortization.
Aug. 10	Declared an 8% stock dividend on all outstanding shares of common stock. The market value of the stock was $40 per share.
26	The board of directors appropriated an additional $30,000 of retained earnings for possible future litigation.
Sept. 5	Issued the stock dividend declared on August 10.
Dec. 5	Declared the annual cash dividend on the preferred stock and a cash dividend of $2.10 per share of common stock, payable on January 25 to stockholders of record on December 27.
30	Appropriated $75,000 of retained earnings for general contingencies.
31	Closed the Income Summary account, with net earnings of $163,000, to Retained Earnings.

REQUIRED

(a) Prepare general journal entries to record the foregoing transactions.
(b) Prepare a retained earnings statement for 19X5.

Stockholders' equity—transactions and financial statement presentations

16–33A The stockholders' equity of the Prairie Corporation at January 1, 19X4, is shown below:

5% Preferred Stock, $100 Par Value, 8,000 shares authorized; 2,000 shares issued and outstanding	$ 200,000
Paid-in Capital in Excess of Par Value—Preferred Stock	40,000
Common Stock, $60 Par Value, 30,000 shares authorized; 20,000 shares issued and outstanding	1,200,000
Paid-in Capital in Excess of Par Value—Common Stock	74,000
Unappropriated Retained Earnings	521,000
Total Stockholders' Equity	$2,035,000

The following transactions, among others, occurred during 19X4:

Feb. 12 Prairie Corporation carries life insurance on its key officers (with the corporation as beneficiary), and in 19X3 it paid insurance premiums of $7,800 covering the three-year period 19X3–19X5. Today the company discovered that none of the $7,800 had been charged to Insurance Expense in 19X3 (it all remained in Prepaid Insurance). These premiums are not deductible for tax purposes, so this error has no tax effect.

Apr. 1 Announced a 3 for 1 stock split, reducing the par value of the common stock to $20 per share. The authorization was increased to 90,000 shares.

Aug. 11 Reacquired 6,000 shares of common stock for cash at $25 per share.

12 Appropriated an amount of retained earnings equal to the cost of the treasury shares acquired August 11.

Dec. 7 Declared a 3% stock dividend on all outstanding shares of common stock. The market value of the stock was $30 per share.

17 Issued the stock dividend declared on December 7.

20 Declared the annual cash dividend on the preferred stock and a cash dividend of $1.50 per common share, payable on January 15 to stockholders of record on December 31.

31 Recorded the annual patent amortization expense. In reviewing the accounts for year-end adjustments, management revised the estimated total useful life of the patent from 9 years to 14 years. The patent cost $58,500 when acquired at the beginning of last year. The company uses the straight-line method for amortization and does not use a contra account.

31 Closed the Income Summary account, with net earnings of $236,000, to Retained Earnings.

REQUIRED

(a) Prepare general journal entries to record the foregoing transactions.
(b) Prepare a retained earnings statement for 19X4.
(c) Prepare the stockholders' equity section of the balance sheet at December 31, 19X4.

BUSINESS DECISION PROBLEM

The stockholders' equity section of Golden Corporation's comparative balance sheet at the end of 19X7 and 19X8—part of the financial data just reviewed at a stockholders' meeting—is presented below:

	December 31, 19X8	**December 31, 19X7**
Common Stock, $10 Par Value, 500,000 shares authorized; issued at December 31, 19X8, 290,000 shares; 19X7, 250,000 shares	$2,900,000	$2,500,000
Paid-in Capital in Excess of Par Value	1,820,000	1,500,000
Retained Earnings:		
Appropriated for Plant Expansion	900,000	750,000
Unappropriated	1,166,000	1,805,000
Total Stockholders' Equity	$6,786,000	$6,555,000

The following items were also disclosed at the stockholders' meeting: net income for 19X8 was $666,000; a 16% stock dividend was issued December 14, 19X8; when the stock dividend was declared, the market value was $18 per share; the market value per share at December 31, 19X8, was $16; management plans to borrow $200,000 to help finance a new plant addition, which is expected to cost a total of $1,000,000; and the customary $1.74 per-share cash dividend had been revised to $1.50 when declared and issued the last week of December, 19X8.

As part of their stockholders' goodwill program, during the stockholders' meeting management asked stockholders to write any questions they might have concerning the firm's operations or finances. As assistant controller, you are given the stockholders' questions.

REQUIRED

Prepare brief but reasonably complete answers to the following questions:

(a) What did Golden do with the cash proceeds from the stock dividend issued in December?
(b) What was my book value per share at the end of 19X7 and 19X8?
(c) I owned 5,000 shares of Golden in 19X7 and have not sold any shares. How much more or less of the corporation do I own at December 31, 19X8, and what happened to the market value of my interest in the company?
(d) I heard someone say that stock dividends don't give me anything I didn't already have. Why did you issue one? Are you trying to fool us?
(e) Instead of a stock dividend, why didn't you declare a cash dividend and let us buy the new shares that were issued?
(f) Why are you cutting back on the dividends I receive?
(g) If you have $900,000 put aside for the new plant addition, which will cost $1,000,000, why are you borrowing $200,000 instead of just the $100,000 needed?

ANSWERS TO SELF-TEST QUESTIONS

1. (b) 2. (c) 3. (d) 4. (a) 5. (c)

17

Long-term Liabilities and Bond Investments

Chapter Objectives

- Describe mortgages and various kinds of bonds.
- Discuss the relationship of bond prices to interest rates, and illustrate accounting for bond issuance, interest, and amortization.
- Illustrate the classification of bonds payable, premium, and discount on the balance sheet.
- Illustrate the retirement of bonds and the use of sinking funds.
- Describe and illustrate accounting for long-term bond investments.
- Describe the basic ideas of pension accounting.
- Describe and illustrate interperiod tax allocation.
- Provide a review of a corporation balance sheet.

**Don't put your trust in money,
put your money in trust.**

OLIVER WENDELL HOLMES

Some of the most frequently encountered or significant long-term liabilities of business firms are mortgage notes payable, bonds payable, employee pension liability, deferred income taxes payable, and capital lease liabilities. We discuss the accounting treatment of the first four of these long-term liabilities in this chapter; accounting for capital leases, a direct method of financing plant and equipment, was discussed in Chapter 11. Because accounting for long-term bond investments is similar to that for bonds payable, this chapter also includes a discussion of such investments.

MORTGAGE NOTES AND BONDS PAYABLE

At various times in the course of business operations, particularly during phases of expansion, firms must secure additional long-term funds. Often they choose long-term borrowing, rather than issue additional capital stock, to avoid diluting the ownership interests or because the borrowed funds may have a lower net cost to current stockholders.[1] The interest cost of long-term debt has identifiable limits; that is, creditors do not receive an increased return on investment if profits grow. Furthermore, the borrowing firm may deduct interest payments on debt for tax purposes, but it may not deduct dividend distributions to owners.

Not all aspects of long-term debt are necessarily desirable for the borrowing company. In contrast with dividends on common stock, interest on debt represents a fixed periodic expenditure that the firm is contractually obligated to make. Fixed interest charges can be a financial burden when operations do not develop as favorably as expected. Because long-term debt normally has a definite maturity date, the firm must also provide for repayment of the obligation. Finally, a long-term borrowing agreement may restrict the company's financial policies while the debt is outstanding.

Mortgage Notes Payable

A firm may borrow long-term funds by issuing a **mortgage note,** which is actually two related agreements. The note is an agreement to repay the principal and to pay specified interest amounts on certain dates; the mortgage is a legal agreement pledging certain property of the borrower as security for repayment of the note.

[1]The concept of investment leverage is explained in Chapter 20.

Usually, a mortgage note is used when all the funds are borrowed from one lender. Sometimes a firm finds it more strategic or even necessary to borrow large amounts of funds from several lenders. In these latter cases, issuing bonds is more practical.

Bonds Payable

Bonds are, in essence, notes payable. Their special characteristics are dictated by the specific objectives of a given borrowing situation. Because a complete discussion of the wide variety of bonds is beyond the scope of this text, only the more significant characteristics of bonds are described below.

Bonds are used most often when a borrower receives funds from a large number of lenders contributing various amounts. Consequently, bonds are usually drawn up to be negotiable. Because many parties are involved, the borrower should select a **trustee**—often a large bank—to represent the group of bondholders. As a third party to the transaction, the trustee may take security title to any pledged property and is likely to initiate any action necessitated by failure to meet the terms of the bond agreement.

If the borrower fails to meet the provisions of the bond agreement, the bondholders, represented by the trustee, may institute a variety of actions. Examples of less significant actions are enforcing agreements restricting dividend payments, prescribing minimum cash balances or financial operating ratios, placing restrictions on additional financing, and electing new members to the board of directors. The ultimate action, of course, is to bring foreclosure proceedings. The trustee may also maintain a record of current bond owners and may act as disbursing agent for the interest and principal payments.

CHARACTERISTICS OF BONDS Bond agreements may be formulated to capitalize on certain lending situations, appeal to special investor groups, or provide special repayment patterns. We now list some common bond characteristics.

Secured bonds pledge some specific property as security for meeting the terms of the bond agreement. The specific title of the bonds may indicate the type of property pledged—for example, real estate mortgage bonds (land and/or buildings), chattel mortgage bonds (machinery or equipment), and collateral trust bonds (negotiable securities). If property is subject to two or more mortgages, the relative priority of each mortgage is denoted by its identification as a "first," "second," or even "third" mortgage.

Bonds that have no specific property pledged as security for their repayment are **debenture bonds.** Holders of such bonds rely on the borrower's general credit reputation. Because the lender's risk is usually greater than with secured bonds, the sale of unsecured bonds may require offering a higher interest rate.

The maturity dates of **serial bonds** are staggered over a series of years. For example, a serial bond issue of $15 million may provide for $1 million of the bonds to mature each year for 15 years. An advantage of serial bonds is that lenders can choose bonds with maturity dates that correspond with their desired length of investment.

The issuing corporation (or its trustee) maintains a record of the owners of **registered bonds.** At appropriate times, interest payments are mailed to the registered owners. Interest on **coupon bonds** is paid in a different manner. A coupon for interest payable to the bearer is attached to the bond for each interest period. Whenever interest is due, the bondholder detaches a coupon and deposits it with his or her bank for collection.

Callable bonds allow the borrower to *call in* (retire) the bonds and pay them off after a stated date. Usually, an extra amount or premium must be paid to the holders of the called bonds. Callable bonds offer borrowers an additional flexibility that may be significant if funds become available at interest rates substantially lower than those being paid on the bonds. To some degree, borrowers can in effect "call" any of their bonds by buying them in the open market.

Convertible bonds grant the holder the right to convert them to capital stock at some specific exchange ratio. This provision gives an investor the security of a creditor during a certain stage of a firm's life, with the option of becoming a stockholder if the firm becomes sufficiently profitable.

BOND PRICES Most bonds are sold in units of $1,000 face (maturity) value, and the market price is expressed as a percentage of face value. For example, a $1,000 face value bond quoted at 98 sells for $980, and a bond quoted at 103 sells for $1,030. Generally, bond prices fluctuate in response to changes in market interest rates, which are determined by government monetary policies (managing the demand and supply of money) and economic expectations. Obviously, they are also affected by the outlook for the issuing firm. Market prices are quoted in the financial news at the nearest $\frac{1}{8}$% of the true market price.

RECORDING BOND ISSUES Firms often authorize more bonds than they actually anticipate issuing at one time. Authorization of bonds usually includes (1) formal action by the board of directors, (2) application to and approval of some government agency, (3) retention of a trustee, and (4) all the attendant negotiations and legalities. For secured bonds, the total value of the bonds authorized is typically some fraction of the value of the property pledged. The difference between the dollar amount of the bonds issued and the value of the pledged property represents a margin of safety to bondholders.

Because individual bond issues may have widely varying characteristics, separate accounts with reasonably descriptive titles should be used for each bond issue. When the bonds are authorized, an account is opened in the general ledger, and a memorandum entry may be made in the account stating the total amount of bonds authorized.

The *face value* of a bond is the amount of principal to be repaid at the maturity date. Interest on bonds is usually paid semiannually, with the payments six months apart (such as January 1 and July 1). The annual rate of interest—also called the *coupon* or *nominal* rate of interest—payable on a bond is stated in the bond agreement. The amount of interest paid semiannually on such bonds is the face value multiplied by one-half the nominal rate of interest. If financial statements are prepared between interest payment dates, the periodic interest expense and the related liability for interest payable are accrued to the date of the statements.

To provide a simple illustration, we use informal account titles and an unrealistically short bond life. Assume that on January 1, Reid, Inc., issues at face value ten \$10,000, 10% bonds that mature in four years with interest paid on June 30 and December 31. The following entry records the bond issue:

Jan. 1	Cash	100,000	
	Bonds Payable		100,000
	To record issuance of bonds.		

Interest of \$5,000 (\$100,000 $\times$ 0.10 $\times$ $\frac{6}{12}$) will be paid on each of the eight payment dates (four years, semiannual payments). For example, the entry on June 30, the first interest payment date, is

June 30	Bond Interest Expense	5,000	
	Cash		5,000
	To record payment of semiannual interest on bonds payable.		

When the bonds mature, Reid, Inc., records their retirement in the following manner:

(final year)			
Dec. 31	Bonds Payable	100,000	
	Cash		100,000
	To record retirement of bonds.		

BOND PRICES AND INTEREST RATES In our illustration, we assume that the Reid, Inc., bonds are issued at par or face value. Often, the issue price differs from the face value because the market rate of interest for the bonds differs from the **nominal** or **contract** rate on the bond certificate. The nominal rate dictates the amount of interest paid each period, whereas the **market** rate—sometimes called the **effective** rate—is the rate of return investors expect on their investment. Market rates of interest fluctuate constantly.

When the market rate of interest on the bonds exceeds the nominal rate, investors expect the bonds to sell at a *discount* (Face Value − Price). When the market rate falls below the nominal rate, investors expect to pay a *premium* (Price − Face Value).

Since bonds are usually printed and sold at different times, the two interest rates often differ. Also, a firm may desire a nominal rate expressed in even percents or in easily recognized fractions of a percent (that is, 10% or $9\frac{1}{2}$%), whereas the market rate for a particular bond issue may be expressed in a more complex fraction or decimal amount.

Bonds issued at a discount If the nominal rate of interest on the bonds issued is less than the current market rate of interest for the type and quality of the bonds, they can be sold only at a price less than their face value. In such cases, investors "discount" the bonds to earn the amount of interest reflected in the current money market. For example, assume that Reid, Inc.'s \$100,000 issue of 10%, four-year bonds are sold on January 1 at 98—98% of their face value—

because the applicable market rate exceeds the 10% nominal rate. The following entry records the issue of these bonds:

Jan. 1	Cash	98,000	
	Bond Discount	2,000	
	Bonds Payable		100,000
	To record issuance of bonds at 98.		

The $2,000 discount is not an immediate loss or expense to Reid, Inc. Rather, it represents an adjustment of interest expense over the life of the bonds. We illustrate this by comparing the funds Reid, Inc., receives with the funds it must pay to the bondholders. Regardless of their selling price, the bonds are an agreement to pay $140,000 to the bondholders ($100,000 principal plus eight semiannual interest payments of $5,000 each).

Total funds paid to bondholders	$140,000
Total funds received from bond sale	98,000
Difference equals total interest paid	$ 42,000
Average expense per year ($42,000/4)	$ 10,500

Although Reid, Inc., makes only two $5,000 interest payments—a total of $10,000—each year, its full annual interest expense on the bonds exceeds that amount. To reflect the larger periodic interest expense, the bond discount is *amortized*. Amortization of bond discount means that periodically an amount is transferred from bond discount to interest expense.

Basically, there are two methods of amortization—the straight-line method and the effective interest method. Under the *straight-line method*, equal amounts are transferred from bond discount to interest expense for equal periods of time. For Reid, Inc., this amount is $250 every six months ($2,000 total bond discount ÷ 8 semiannual interest periods). Some companies may amortize the discount annually rather than semiannually; the annual amortization for Reid, Inc., is $500. The more complex *effective interest method* reflects a constant rate of interest over the life of the bonds. The effective interest method is discussed later in this chapter.

Assuming the straight-line method of amortization, the journal entries each year to record interest expense for Reid, Inc., are as follows. (We assume that the bond sale is already recorded as illustrated above and that the bonds were issued on the day they are dated.)

June 30	Bond Interest Expense	5,000	
	Cash		5,000
	To record first semiannual interest payment.		
30	Bond Interest Expense	250	
	Bond Discount		250
	To record semiannual amortization of bond discount.		

Dec. 31	Bond Interest Expense	5,000	
	Cash		5,000
	To record second semiannual interest payment.		
31	Bond Interest Expense	250	
	Bond Discount		250
	To record semiannual amortization of bond discount.		

These entries result in four debits to the Bond Interest Expense account each year, a total of $10,500 annual interest expense. Amortizing the bond discount over the four-year life of the bonds at $250 every six months leaves a zero balance in the Bond Discount account at the maturity date of the bonds. The retirement of the bonds is then recorded by debiting Bonds Payable and crediting Cash for $100,000, the amount of their face value.

Bonds issued at a premium If the market rate of interest had been below the 10% offered by Reid, Inc.'s bonds, investors would have been willing to pay a premium for them. Like a bond discount, a bond premium is considered an adjustment of interest expense over the life of the bonds. We just saw that bond discount increases interest expense; now we see that bond premium reduces interest expense. The following entries illustrate the sale of Reid, Inc., bonds at 104 (104% of face value), the payments of interest, the amortization of bond premium, and the retirement of the bonds at maturity:

Jan. 1	Cash	104,000	
	Bonds Payable		100,000
	Bond Premium		4,000
	To record sale of bonds at a premium.		
June 30	Bond Interest Expense	5,000	
	Cash		5,000
	To record first semiannual interest payment.		
	Bond Premium	500	
	Bond Interest Expense		500
	To record semiannual amortization of bond premium.		
Dec. 31	Bond Interest Expense	5,000	
	Cash		5,000
	To record second semiannual interest payment.		
31	Bond Premium	500	
	Bond Interest Expense		500
	To record semiannual amortization of bond premium.		

(final year)			
Dec. 31	Bonds Payable	100,000	
	Cash		100,000
	To retire bonds at maturity.		

The eight semiannual $500 debit entries to the Bond Premium account leave it with a zero balance when the bonds mature. We can verify the $9,000 total annual interest expense reflected by the above entries as follows:

Total funds paid to bondholders	$140,000
Total funds received from bondholders	104,000
Difference equals total interest paid	$ 36,000
Average interest expense per year ($36,000/4)	$ 9,000

The related interest expense account would have a balance of $9,000, shown in the following T account:

Bond Interest Expense

First semiannual interest payment	5,000	First semiannual amortization of bond premium	500
Second semiannual interest payment	5,000	Second semiannual amortization of bond premium	500

Year-end or interim adjustments When a periodic interest payment date does not correspond with year-end, adjustment of the general ledger accounts should include an entry reflecting the amount of interest expense incurred but not paid and an entry reflecting a pro-rata amortization of bond discount or bond premium for the portion of the year involved. Similar adjustments are appropriate when interim financial statements are prepared and the interim date does not correspond with an interest payment date.

Assume the bonds issued by Reid, Inc., at 98 were issued on April 1 and had interest payment dates on April 1 and October 1. At December 31 of each year, the following entries would be made:

Dec. 31	Bond Interest Expense	2,500	
	Bond Interest Payable		2,500
	To accrue interest expense for three months ($\$100,000 \times 0.10 \times \frac{3}{12}$).		
31	Bond Interest Expense	125	
	Bond Discount		125
	To amortize bond discount for three months ($500 annual amortization/4).		

If the bonds were issued at a premium rather than at a discount, an entry would amortize the bond premium for three months. The Bond Interest Payable account is classified as a current liability in the balance sheet.

Issuance between interest dates Not all bonds are sold on the exact day on which their interest begins to accumulate (the date on the bond certificates). For example, issuance may be delayed in anticipation of a more favorable bond market. Investors who buy bonds after the interest begins to accrue are expected to "buy" the accrued interest. Such bonds are said to be sold at some price "plus accrued interest." To illustrate, let us assume that Reid, Inc., sold its $100,000, 10%, four-year bonds at 104 on April 1 instead of on January 1, the date on the bond certificates. The entry would be

Apr. 1	Cash	106,500	
	Bonds Payable		100,000
	Bond Premium		4,000
	Bond Interest Payable		2,500
	To record bond issuance at 104 plus three months' accrued interest.		

The interest accrued on the bonds on April 1 is $2,500 ($100,000 × 0.10 × $\frac{3}{12}$). On the first interest payment date, June 30, Reid, Inc., would make the following entry:

June 30	Bond Interest Payable	2,500	
	Bond Interest Expense	2,500	
	Cash		5,000
	To record payment of semiannual interest on bonds payable.		

This entry records interest expense of $2,500, the appropriate amount for the three months the bonds have been outstanding. The other $2,500 represents the return of the accrued interest collected from the bond purchasers on April 1.

In this situation, the $4,000 bond premium would be amortized over the period the bonds are outstanding, or 45 months. Therefore, on June 30, the amount of the premium to be amortized is $266.67 [($4,000/45) × 3 months, rounded]. The entry would be

June 30	Bond Premium	266.67	
	Bond Interest Expense		266.67
	To amortize bond premium for three months [($4,000/45) × 3].		

Thus, the bond interest expense for the three months ended June 30 consists of the $2,500 net interest paid, less the $266.67 amortization of premium, or $2,233.33.

A similar treatment would be used if the bonds had been sold at a discount. In other words, the amortization period for premium or discount extends from the date of sale to the maturity date of the bonds.

BONDS PAYABLE ON THE BALANCE SHEET In this section, we use the data relating to Reid, Inc., bonds with interest payment dates of June 30 and December 31 and straight-line amortization. Exhibit 17–1 shows that regardless of whether bond premium or bond discount is involved, the book value of bonds progresses toward and equals their face value at the time of maturity.

Assume that Reid, Inc., issued bonds on January 1, 19X1, corresponding to each of the examples above. At the end of the second year, the firm's trial balance would include the following accounts:

	Debit	Credit
Bond Discount, Second Mortgage Series	$1,000	
Bonds Payable, 10%, 19X4, First Mortgage Series		$100,000
Bonds Payable, 10%, 19X4, Second Mortgage Series		100,000
Bond Premium, First Mortgage Series		2,000

The Bond Premium and Bond Discount accounts are classified properly as an addition to and as a deduction from, respectively, the face value of the bonds in the balance sheet, as follows:

Long-term Liabilities:		
Bonds Payable, 10%, 19X4, First Mortgage Series	$100,000	
Add: Unamortized Premium	2,000	$102,000
Bonds Payable, 10%, 19X4, Second Mortgage Series	$100,000	
Less: Unamortized Discount	1,000	99,000

EXHIBIT 17–1
Amortization Schedule

	Reid, Inc., Bonds Sold at 104 (Premium) (Straight-line Amortization)			Reid, Inc., Bonds Sold at 98 (Discount) (Straight-line Amortization)		
	Balances			Balances		
At Year-end	Bonds Payable (Credit)	Bond Premium (Credit)	Book Value	Bonds Payable (Credit)	Bond Discount (Debit)	Book Value
At issue	$100,000	$4,000	$104,000	$100,000	$2,000	$ 98,000
19X1	100,000	3,000	103,000	100,000	1,500	98,500
19X2	100,000	2,000	102,000	100,000	1,000	99,000
19X3	100,000	1,000	101,000	100,000	500	99,500
19X4	100,000	0	100,000	100,000	0	100,000

Bonds payable maturing within the next year should be classified as a current liability. An exception to this guideline arises when a bond sinking fund, a noncurrent asset, is used to retire the bonds. In that case, because a current asset is not utilized to retire the bonds, the bonds payable may be classified as long-term liabilities.

EFFECTIVE INTEREST METHOD OF AMORTIZATION Many business firms use the straight-line method of amortizing bond discount and premium because of its simplicity. This method recognizes equal amounts of interest expense each year. However, because the **book value (carrying value)** of the bonds changes each year (see Exhibit 17–1), the interest, expressed as a percentage of the book value, changes over the life of the bonds. Theoretically, this percentage should be constant; otherwise, the firm's borrowing rate appears to change each year. The **effective interest method** of amortization corrects this deficiency. With this method, a constant percentage of the book value of the bonds is recognized as interest expense each year, resulting in unequal recorded amounts of interest expense. In *APB Opinion No. 21*, the Accounting Principles Board recommends the use of the effective interest method whenever the two methods yield materially different results.

To obtain a period's interest expense under the effective interest method, we multiply the bonds' book value at the beginning of each period by the effective interest rate. The difference between this amount and the amount of interest paid (Nominal Interest Rate × Face Value of Bonds) is the amount of discount or premium amortized. When using the effective interest method of amortization, accountants often prepare an amortization schedule similar to Exhibit 17–2, explained in the following example.

Bonds issued at a discount Assume that, on April 1, 19X1, a firm issues four-year bonds of $100,000 face value with an 8% annual interest rate and interest dates of April 1 and October 1. The selling price is $93,552, which provides an effective interest rate of 10%.[2] Exhibit 17–2 gives an amortization schedule for the life of the bonds, with amounts rounded to the nearest dollar.

The schedule shows six-month interest periods; therefore, the interest rates shown in columns (A) and (B) are one-half the annual rates. Column (A) lists the constant amounts of interest paid each six months, that is, the nominal interest rate times face value (4% × $100,000). The amounts in column (B) are obtained by multiplying the book value at the beginning of each period [column (E)] by the 5% effective interest rate. For example, the $4,678 interest expense for the first period is 5% of $93,552; for the second period, it is 5% of $94,230, or $4,712, and so on. Note that the amount changes each period. For discounted bonds, the amount increases each period because the book value increases over the life of the bonds until it reaches face value at the maturity date. The amount of discount amortization for each period, given in column (C), is the difference between the

[2] See Appendix A for a discussion of effective interest rates and the determination of issue prices.

EXHIBIT 17–2
Bonds Sold at a Discount: Periodic Interest Expense, Amortization, and Book Value of Bonds

Year	Interest Period	(A) Interest Paid (4% of face value)	(B) Interest Expense (5% of bond book value)	(C) Periodic Amortization (B − A)	(D) Balance of Unamortized Discount (D − C)	(E) Book Value of Bonds, End of Period ($100,000 − D)
(at issue)					$6,448	$ 93,552
1	1	$4,000	$4,678	$678	5,770	94,230
	2	4,000	4,712	712	5,058	94,942
2	3	4,000	4,747	747	4,311	95,689
	4	4,000	4,784	784	3,527	96,473
3	5	4,000	4,824	824	2,703	97,297
	6	4,000	4,865	865	1,838	98,162
4	7	4,000	4,908	908	930	99,070
	8	4,000	4,930*	930	0	100,000

*Adjusted for cumulative rounding error of $24.

corresponding amounts in columns (A) and (B). Column (D) lists the amount of unamortized discount at the end of each period.

The amounts recorded for the issuance of the bonds and each interest payment can be read directly from the amortization schedule. The following entry records the issuance:

Apr. 1	Cash	93,552	
	Bond Discount	6,448	
	Bonds Payable		100,000
	To record issuance of bonds.		

The following entry records interest expense and discount amortization on October 1, 19X1:

Oct. 1	Bond Interest Expense	4,678	
	Bond Discount		678
	Cash		4,000
	To record semiannual interest expense and discount amortization.		

Bonds issued at a premium Suppose that the bonds in our illustration carried an 8% nominal interest rate but that the effective interest rate was 6%. These bonds would be issued at $106,980 (for computations, see Appendix A). The amortization schedule for the bond issue is given in Exhibit 17–3. The nominal interest rate of 4% in column (A) and the effective interest rate of 3% in

EXHIBIT 17–3
Bonds Sold at a Premium: Periodic Interest Expense, Amortization, and Book Value of Bonds

Year	Interest Period	(A) Interest Paid (4% of face value)	(B) Interest Expense (3% of bond book value)	(C) Periodic Amorti- zation (A − B)	(D) Balance of Unamor- tized Premium (D − C)	(E) Book Value of Bonds, End of Period ($100,000 + D)
(at issue)					$6,980	$106,980
1	1	$4,000	$3,209	$791	6,189	106,189
	2	4,000	3,186	814	5,375	105,375
2	3	4,000	3,161	839	4,536	104,536
	4	4,000	3,136	864	3,672	103,672
3	5	4,000	3,110	890	2,782	102,782
	6	4,000	3,083	917	1,865	101,865
4	7	4,000	3,056	944	921	100,921
	8	4,000	3,079*	921	0	100,000

*Adjusted for cumulative rounding error of $51.

column (B) are one-half the annual rates for the bonds, because the calculations are for six-month periods. The issuance of the bonds is recorded as follows:

Apr. 1	Cash	106,980	
	Bonds Payable		100,000
	Bond Premium		6,980
	To record issuance of bonds.		

The entry to record interest expense and premium amortization on October 1, 19X1, is

Oct. 1	Bond Interest Expense	3,209	
	Bond Premium	791	
	Cash		4,000
	To record semiannual interest expense and premium amortization.		

Year-end adjusting entries We record interest and premium amortization for the bonds in our example on April 1 and October 1. Therefore, at December 31, three months' interest should be accrued.

The amounts recorded can be computed from those shown for the second interest period in the amortization schedule in Exhibit 17–3. One-half of the amount in column (A) [($4,000/2) = $2,000] is the interest payable. Similarly, [($3,186/2) = $1,593] is the interest expense, and [($814/2) = $407] is the premium amortization. The year-end adjusting entry is

Dec. 31	Bond Interest Expense	1,593	
	Bond Premium	407	
	Bond Interest Payable		2,000
	To accrue interest for three months and amortize one-half of the premium for the interest period.		

Retirement of Bonds before Maturity

Bonds are usually retired at their maturity dates with an entry debiting Bonds Payable and crediting Cash for the amount of the face value of the bonds. However, bonds may be retired before maturity—for example, to take advantage of more attractive financing terms.

In accounting for the retirement of bonds before maturity, the following factors should be considered:

(1) Amortization of any related premium or discount as of the retirement date.

(2) Removal of both the bond liability account and any related Bond Premium or Bond Discount accounts.

(3) Recognition of any gain or loss on the retirement of the bonds.

For this example, assume that the Reid, Inc., bonds issued at 104 were called for retirement at 105 plus accrued interest on April 1 of their fourth and final year. Exhibit 17–1 shows that the related account balances at the end of their third year are

Bonds Payable	$100,000
Bond Premium	1,000

If interest is paid semiannually on June 30 and December 31, and financial statements are prepared annually, no premium amortization entry has been made since the end of the third year. Thus, the following entries properly reflect the retirement of the bonds on April 1:

Apr. 1	Bond Premium	250	
	Bond Interest Expense		250
	To amortize bond premium for three months ($1000/4).		
1	Bonds Payable	100,000	
	Bond Premium	750	
	Bond Interest Expense	2,500	
	Loss on Bond Retirement	4,250	
	Cash		107,500
	To retire bonds at 105 plus interest and record the loss on retirement.		

The loss on retirement is the difference between the retirement amount ($105,000) and the book value of the bonds at retirement ($100,750). The amount of interest paid at retirement ($2,500) does not affect the gain or loss on retirement. The gain or loss, if material, should be classified as an extraordinary item on the income statement.

Conversion of Bonds

Few convertible bonds are redeemed for cash, since at some point, these bonds are usually converted into common stock. Because, as noted earlier, the conversion feature is attractive to potential investors, a company may issue convertible bonds at a lower interest rate than it would pay without the conversion feature.

A company may also issue convertible bonds to reduce the dilutive effect that a common stock issue would have on earnings per share. This occurs because the conversion price is higher than the current market price of the stock when the convertible bonds are issued. For example, suppose a company that needs $100,000 of funds could issue additional common stock at $20 per share. The company needs to issue 5,000 shares to obtain $100,000. Alternatively, the firm may issue $100,000 of convertible bonds and establish a conversion price of $25 per share. When the bonds are converted into stock (and the company expects this to happen), the number of common shares issued will be 4,000 ($100,000/$25). The fewer number of common shares associated with the convertible bonds produces higher earnings per share than if common stock had been issued initially.

Convertible bonds include a call feature. When the market value of the stock to be received on conversion is significantly higher than the call price on the bond, a company may force conversion by calling in the bonds. Of course, one of the risks of issuing convertible bonds is that the market price of the stock may not increase in the future. Bondholders may then decide it is not to their advantage to convert the bonds, and the company cannot force conversion by exercising the call feature.

The entry to record a bond conversion transfers the book value of the bonds to the common stock accounts. For example, assume that the Reid, Inc., bonds issued at 98 were convertible into 2,000 shares of $40 par value common stock. All the bonds were converted into stock on January 1 of the third year. Exhibit 17–1 shows that the book value of the bonds at the end of the second year is $99,000. The following entry records the conversion:

Jan. 1	Bonds Payable	100,000	
	Bond Discount		1,000
	Common Stock		80,000
	Paid-in Capital in Excess of Par Value		19,000
	To record conversion of bonds into 2,000 shares of $40 par value common stock.		

BOND SINKING FUNDS

As additional security to bondholders, some bond agreements require the borrower to make periodic cash deposits to a **bond sinking fund**, which is used to retire the bonds. The fund is often controlled by a trustee—usually a bank or a trust company. The trustee invests the cash deposited periodically in the sinking fund in income-producing securities. The objective is to accumulate investments and investment income sufficient to retire the bonds at their maturity.

We now illustrate typical transactions for a simple bond sinking fund managed by a trustee. Assume that Reid, Inc., establishes such a fund to retire its $100,000 bond issue, which matures in four years. Reid, Inc., makes equal annual deposits to the sinking fund at the end of each of the four years.

PERIODIC DEPOSIT OF CASH TO THE FUND The amount of the equal periodic contributions is determined by compound interest tables and assumes an average annual rate of net investment income. If the trustee estimates that the sinking-fund securities will earn 8% annually, Reid, Inc.'s annual cash payment to the trustee should be $22,192. Earning 8% annually, the fund will grow to $100,000 after four years, as follows:

Year	Annual Cash Deposit	8% Annual Interest	Fund Balance at Year-end
1	$22,192	—	$ 22,192
2	22,192	$1,775	46,159
3	22,192	3,693	72,044
4	22,192	5,764	100,000

The entry to record the annual cash deposit is

Bond Sinking Fund	22,192	
Cash		22,192

INCOME REPORTED ON SINKING-FUND SECURITIES Reid, Inc., records on its books the trustee's periodic reports on the earnings of the sinking-fund securities. For example, if the fund earned $1,775 during the second year, Reid, Inc., makes the following journal entry:

Bond Sinking Fund	1,775	
Bond Sinking-fund Income		1,775

RETIREMENT OF BONDS Usually, the trustee sells the sinking-fund securities and pays the bondholders with the proceeds. Reid, Inc., then records the retirement of the bonds as follows:

Bonds Payable	100,000	
Bond Sinking Fund		100,000

Any deficit in the sinking fund needed to retire the bonds requires an additional cash payment from Reid, Inc. Any surplus is transferred to the Cash account in closing out the sinking fund.

The Bond Sinking Fund is classified in the balance sheet as an investment. Bond Sinking-fund Income is reported under Other Income and Expenses in the income statement.

LONG-TERM BOND INVESTMENTS

Corporate bonds may be acquired by a variety of investors, including individuals, partnerships, corporations, mutual funds, pension funds, foundations, and trusts. Our discussion focuses on bond investments by corporations.

Bonds may be purchased when they are originally issued or at some time thereafter from an investor. Bond investments are recorded by the purchaser at cost plus any brokerage commission. Because bonds acquired as a long-term investment may be held for extended periods, the related premium or discount is usually amortized to interest income. The straight-line method of amortization is commonly used; however, as we mentioned earlier, the effective interest method should be used when the two methods yield materially different results. In our example, we use the straight-line method.

Assume that a firm purchases ten National Telephone $10,000, 8% bonds at 98 on a semiannual interest date (January 1) ten years prior to maturity. Brokerage commission is $200. Because the bonds will have a maturity value of $100,000 in ten years, the bond discount is $1,800, which is amortized (using the straight-line method) at a rate of $90 at the end of each of the 20 remaining semiannual interest periods ($1,800/20 = $90). The following entry records the purchase:

Jan. 1	National Telephone Bonds	98,200	
	Cash		98,200
	To record purchase of ten bonds at 98 on interest date plus commission of $200.		

Note that although the bond discount is amortized, no Bond Discount account is established. The investment is initially recorded at cost, and the discount amortization entry is made directly to the asset account. For example, on the next interest date, the following entries record the receipt of interest and amortization of discount:

July 1	Cash	4,000	
	Bond Interest Income		4,000
	To record receipt of semiannual interest on National Telephone bonds.		
1	National Telephone Bonds	90	
	Bond Interest Income		90
	To record semiannual amortization of discount on National Telephone bonds.		

As in the case of Bonds Payable on the books of borrowers, the carrying value of the bonds increases until they reach their maturity value on their maturity date.

When the purchase price of a bond exceeds its maturity value, the bond is still recorded at cost and the related premium amortization entry is a debit to Bond Interest Income and a credit to the Investment account. Thus, the carrying value of bonds acquired at a premium progresses downward toward maturity value. Also, the net amount of interest income reported is less (by the amount of premium amortized) than the cash received as interest income each period.

Bonds may be sold before they reach maturity. Assume that on January 1, five years after they were purchased, the National Telephone bonds were sold at $99\frac{1}{2}$ less a $150 commission. Discount amortization over the ten semiannual interest periods during which the bonds were held would have raised their carrying value to $99,100 [$98,200 + (10 × $90) = $99,100]. Again, we figure the accounting gain by comparing the book value of the asset to the net proceeds from the sale. The sale is recorded as follows:

Jan. 1	Cash	99,350	
	National Telephone Bonds		99,100
	Gain on Sale of Investments		250
	To record sale of bond investment at $99\frac{1}{2}$ less a commission of $150.		

PENSION PLANS

Many companies have established plans to pay benefits to their employees after they retire. The cost of these **pension plans** may be paid entirely by the employer. Sometimes, the employees pay part of the cost through deductions from their salaries and wages. The employer and employee contributions are usually paid into a pension fund which is managed by another company. Retirement benefits are paid from the assets in the pension fund.

The employer's pension plan cost must be expensed during the years the employees work for the company. For some plans, this accounting analysis is fairly simple; for other plans, it is not. In a *defined contribution* plan, for example, the employer's responsibility is to contribute a certain defined amount to the pension fund each year (a percentage of employee salaries, perhaps). The assets available in the pension fund, then, determine the size of the retirement benefits. The employer's pension accounting analysis is straightforward—when the required contribution is made, Pension Expense is debited and Cash is credited.

The analysis becomes more complex in *defined benefit* plans. These plans specify the retirement benefits to be received in the future; typically, the retirement benefits are a function of the number of years an employee works for the company and the salary or wage level at or near retirement. One complexity under such plans is the determination of the periodic pension expense and contribution amounts. These amunts are influenced by such factors as employee turnover, employee life expectancies, future salary and wage levels, and pension fund investment performance. Actuaries are utilized to make the required pension estimates.

When a defined benefit plan is first adopted, the company usually gives employees credit for their years of employment prior to the plan's adoption. The cost of providing the retirement benefits earned by this earlier service is called **prior service cost.** Prior service cost may be quite sizeable and the company may take many years to fund it. A similar situation may develop when a company amends a plan to increase benefit levels. Another complexity in a defined benefit plan, then, is that the accumulated pension retirement benefits may exceed the assets in the pension fund. In such cases, the FASB requires companies to record a liability equal to the excess amount.[3] This liability may run into the millions or hundreds of millions of dollars for some companies.

DEFERRED INCOME TAXES

Business firms often adopt income tax methods of determining taxable net income that differ from the methods of determining accounting net income. Almost invariably, the firms adopt tax accounting methods that defer tax payments; ordinarily, these methods defer revenue recognition or accelerate expense recognition for tax purposes. Accounting for such timing differences of revenue or expense recognition often results in *deferred tax credits*, which are classified as long-term liabilities.

Timing Differences

When **timing differences** exist, the revenue and expense items that affect pretax accounting income in one period enter into the calculation of taxable income in a different period. Eventually, however, the total amount of revenue or expense reported in both sets of records over a period of time will be the same. Timing differences arise because tax laws either (1) require recognition of certain revenue and expense items in different periods than do generally accepted accounting principles or (2) permit the use of a different method of accounting for revenue or expenses on the tax return than is used in determining pretax accounting income. In the latter case, businesses normally select a tax accounting method that minimizes their current tax liability.

A typical example of a timing difference concerns depreciation methods. A company may use an accelerated depreciation method in the tax return and straight-line depreciation in arriving at accounting income. As another example, a firm may recognize losses from uncollectible accounts using the allowance method in determining accounting income but use the direct write-off method to reflect credit losses for tax purposes.

Whenever timing differences cause pretax accounting income to differ from taxable income, the income tax expense included in the income statement should be based on the revenue and expense amounts reported in the income statement (that is, the tax expense should be based on the pretax accounting income). To do otherwise presents distorted information in the income statement.

[3] *Statement of Financial Accounting Standards No. 87*, "Employers' Accounting for Pensions" (Stamford, CT: Financial Accounting Standards Board, 1985). This requirement is quite controversial; companies have until 1989 to implement it.

The process of apportioning income tax expense to the income statement over the periods affected by timing differences is known as **interperiod income tax allocation.** To illustrate this process and the distortions that result if it is not employed, assume the following data: On January 1, 19X1, the Cascade Company paid $36,000 for a plant asset with a useful life of four years and no expected salvage value. Cascade Company uses straight-line depreciation on its books, deducting $9,000 depreciation expense annually for four years. For tax purposes,

---

ROLLOVER

The liability side of Anheuser-Busch's 1980 balance sheet shows "deferred income taxes, $267.7 million." That's no small sum—equal to 19% of total liabilities and 26% of stockholders' equity. Anheuser is not an isolated case. But are deferred taxes really a *liability*?

That's a question many accountants are asking themselves these days. Says Harvey D. Moskowitz, national director of accounting and auditing for Seidman & Seidman, "The deferred taxes on the balance sheet bear no relationship to what is actually going to be owed. So the current method of income tax accounting makes it impossible for the investor to evaluate a company's liquidity, solvency, or cash flow."

Here's the explanation for this curious state of affairs: Anheuser-Busch had pretax income of $271.5 million, so, using standard corporate tax rates (less credits), it owed $99.7 million to Uncle Sam. That's what it set aside as "provision for income taxes" on its income statement. But it's not what the company actually paid. Like most businesses Anheuser keeps two sets of books, one for tax purposes, one for stock owners. It uses accelerated depreciation for taxes but straight line for reporting to investors. It expenses interest for tax purposes but often capitalizes it on the books. So, out-of-pocket, it really had to pay only $31.9 million in taxes in 1980—the line marked "current" on the income statement. The other $67.8 million, called "deferred," represents cash that's squirreled away in liabilities on the balance sheet, under the assumption that the company will pay those taxes *eventually*—when accelerated depreciation runs out, for example.

That assumption is probably wrong, though. As long as the company keeps growing—in real terms or because of inflation—it will keep adding new assets and new interest costs to replace the ones that are running out. That means those deferred taxes, instead of getting paid, will simply roll over. And over and over and over. It could almost make you dizzy.

Dennis Beresford, national head of accounting standards for Ernst & Whinney, recently took a look at the 1980 annuals of the 250 largest industrial companies in America. He found 26 that had deferred taxes in excess of 20% of stockholders' equity, with the average for those companies being 27%. That's up sharply from 1971, when the same group of companies' deferred taxes were only 10% of equity. Clearly, these folks aren't just staying even in the rollover game—they're getting ahead of themselves. It's like the Sorcerer's Apprentice sequence in Disney's *Fantasia*, where the enchanted broomsticks dump ten buckets of water on the cellar floor for every one bucket Mickey Mouse manages to bail out. Only in this case it's cash.

In a sense then, both profits and net worth are seriously understated. "Many of these large companies say this is unrealistic reporting," says Beresford. "'We'll never pay those amounts,' they say, 'so why do we have to set them up as liabilities? They should really be considered part of our income and stockholders' equity.'"

From *Forbes*, January 18, 1982, page 75, "Rollover," by Jane Carmichael.

Authors' note: The Financial Accounting Standards Board is reviewing the guidelines for accounting for income taxes. Although some changes may result, the basic process of interperiod income tax allocation will most likely be retained.

the accelerated cost recovery system (ACRS) over a three-year period is used, resulting in depreciation charges of $12,000, $16,000, and $8,000 for 19X1–19X3, respectively. This represents Cascade Company's only timing difference between information collected in the accounts and the tax return. For simplicity, we assume that the firm generates $90,000 of income before depreciation and taxes and that its income tax rate is 35%.

Cascade Company's taxable income and income tax payable to the Internal Revenue Service for 19X1–19X4 are as follows:

	19X1	19X2	19X3	19X4
Income before depreciation and taxes	$90,000	$90,000	$90,000	$90,000
Depreciation (ACRS)	12,000	16,000	8,000	—
Taxable income	$78,000	$74,000	$82,000	$90,000
Income tax liability (35% of taxable income)	$27,300	$25,900	$28,700	$31,500

The pretax accounting income for each of the four years differs from the taxable income because of the timing difference in recognizing depreciation expense.

	19X1	19X2	19X3	19X4
Income before depreciation and taxes	$90,000	$90,000	$90,000	$90,000
Depreciation (straight line)	9,000	9,000	9,000	9,000
Pretax accounting income	$81,000	$81,000	$81,000	$81,000

The reporting of taxes in the income statement without income tax allocation (that is, income tax expense equals the actual tax liability for the year) is shown in part A of the following schedule. Part B shows how income tax allocation affects income tax expense and net income.

	19X1	19X2	19X3	19X4
A. Without Income Tax Allocation				
Pretax Accounting Income	$81,000	$81,000	$81,000	$81,000
Income Tax Expense	27,300	25,900	28,700	31,500
Net Income	$53,700	$55,100	$52,300	$49,500
B. With Income Tax Allocation				
Pretax Accounting Income	$81,000	$81,000	$81,000	$81,000
Income Tax Expense	28,350	28,350	28,350	28,350
Net Income	$52,650	$52,650	$52,650	$52,650

Accountants consider the presentation in A distorted because the relationship between pretax accounting income and income tax expense is not normal (in this example, 35%). Based on the amounts reported in the four years, the percentage relationship is 33.7%, 32%, 35.4%, and 38.9%, respectively. A related distortion occurs in the net income figure. In this illustration, pretax accounting income fluctuates throughout the four-year period even though pretax accounting income is constant during that period. The reason, of course, is the timing difference, with income tax expense in part A based on taxable income, not on pretax accounting income.

In part B, income tax expense is allocated to each year according to the pretax accounting income. This income tax allocation procedure produces a normal annual relationship between pretax accounting income and income tax expense. Also, net income moves in harmony with pretax accounting income (in this example, they both remain constant from one year to the next).

Deferred Tax Accounts

Under income tax allocation, the annual charge to Income Tax Expense does not equal the income tax liability for the period. **Deferred tax** accounts are needed to balance the analysis. The journal entries recording income tax expense for Cascade Company for 19X1–19X4 illustrate this point.

19X1	Income Tax Expense	28,350	
	Income Tax Payable		27,300
	Deferred Tax Credits		1,050
	To record 19X1 income tax.		
19X2	Income Tax Expense	28,350	
	Income Tax Payable		25,900
	Deferred Tax Credits		2,450
	To record 19X2 income tax.		
19X3	Income Tax Expense	28,350	
	Deferred Tax Credits	350	
	Income Tax Payable		28,700
	To record 19X3 income tax.		
19X4	Income Tax Expense	28,350	
	Deferred Tax Credits	3,150	
	Income Tax Payable		31,500
	To record 19X4 income tax.		

The balance in the Deferred Tax Credits account represents the tax effect of timing differences. For example, the $1,050 balance at the end of 19X1 equals the tax rate, 35%, times the timing difference in 19X1 of $3,000. The balance in the account is deferred for allocation to income tax expense (as a reduction of the expense) in the future. Once the timing differences have completely worked themselves out, the Deferred Tax Credits account has a zero balance. This occurs at the end of 19X4 for the Cascade Company, as shown in the following T account:

Deferred Tax Credits

19X3	350	19X1	1,050
19X4	3,150	19X2	2,450

The balance in the Deferred Tax Credits account should be classified in the balance sheet as a liability. The amounts disclosed are frequently quite large; deferred tax credits reported by major corporations often run into millions of dollars. Because firms continually engage in transactions causing timing differences, large deferred tax liabilities persist over time.

Some timing differences will first cause pretax accounting income to be less than taxable income. Initially, then, the income tax payable exceeds the charge to income tax expense, and a Deferred Tax Charges account is debited to balance the analysis. This account balance reflects the amount of tax payments allocated to income tax expense (as an increase in the expense) in the future. As with the Deferred Tax Credits account, the Deferred Tax Charges account has a zero balance after the timing differences have completely worked themselves out. Deferred tax charges should be classified in the balance sheet as an asset.

CORPORATION BALANCE SHEET

Exhibit 17–4 is a comprehensive illustration of a corporation's balance sheet that contains many of the items discussed in this chapter and in Chapters 15 and 16.

KEY POINTS TO REMEMBER

(1) To sell bonds payable is to borrow money for which interest expense is incurred.

(2) The amount of bond discount or premium (a) is determined by the difference between the nominal interest rate on the bonds and the applicable market rate of interest, and (b) should be considered a long-term adjustment of interest expense.

(3) Bonds payable should be presented in the balance sheet at their face value plus any related premium or less any related discount.

(4) Premium or discount on bonds payable is usually amortized to interest expense over the life of the bonds using the straight-line method of amortization. However, the effective interest method should be used when the two methods yield materially different results.

(5) When convertible bonds are converted, the book value of the bonds is transferred to the common stock accounts.

(6) Investments in bonds are recorded at cost plus any brokerage fee, and related interest income is accrued. Bond premium and discount are normally amortized on long-term investments.

(7) Pension plans generally are of two kinds: defined contribution plans and defined benefit plans. Often, under defined benefit plans, accumulated retirement benefits, including prior service costs, may exceed pension fund assets, resulting in a liability for the excess.

EXHIBIT 17–4

Superior Corporation
Balance Sheet
December 31, 19XX

ASSETS

Current Assets				
Cash			$ 20,000	
Short-term Investments (at lower of cost or market)			10,000	
Accounts Receivable		$65,000		
Less: Allowance for Uncollectible Accounts		5,000	60,000	
Inventories (at lower of cost or market)			120,000	
Prepaid Expenses			10,000	
Total Current Assets				$220,000
Investments				
Sinking Fund for Bond Retirement			$ 20,400	
Long-term Bond Investments			29,600	
Total Investments				50,000
Plant Assets	**Cost**	**Accumulated Depreciation**	**Book Value**	
Machinery and Equipment	$170,000	$30,000	$140,000	
Buildings	100,000	20,000	80,000	
Land	30,000	—	30,000	
Total Plant Assets				250,000
Intangible Assets (cost less amortization to date)				
Goodwill			$ 28,000	
Patents			12,000	
Total Intangible Assets				40,000
Total Assets				$560,000

(8) When timing differences exist in recognizing revenue and expense items per books and per tax return, income tax expense per books should be based on the firm's pretax accounting income. This procedure often results in the appearance of deferred tax credits, which are classified as a liability.

SELF-TEST QUESTIONS
(Answers are at the end of this chapter.)

1. On May 1 of the current year, a firm issued $400,000, 12-year, 12% bonds payable at $96\frac{1}{2}$ plus accrued interest. The bonds are dated January 1 of the current year, and interest is payable on January 1 and July 1 of each year. The amount the firm receives on May 1 is
(a) $370,000 (b) $402,000 (c) $430,000 (d) $398,000

EXHIBIT 17–4 (continued)

Superior Corporation
Balance Sheet
December 31, 19XX (continued)

LIABILITIES		
Current Liabilities		
Accounts Payable	$ 45,000	
Income Tax Payable	18,000	
Dividends Payable	15,000	
Accrued Payables	2,000	
Total Current Liabilities		$ 80,000
Long-term Liabilities		
First Mortgage, 9% Bonds Payable (due 1990)	$100,000	
Premium on First Mortgage Bonds	6,000	
	$106,000	
Deferred Income Tax Credits	30,000	
Total Long-term Liabilities		136,000
Total Liabilities		$216,000
STOCKHOLDERS' EQUITY		
Paid-in Capital		
Common Stock, $100 Par Value, authorized and issued 2,000 shares; 50 shares in treasury	$200,000	
Paid-in Capital in Excess of Par Value	20,000	
Total Paid-in Capital		$220,000
Retained Earnings		
Appropriated for Plant Expansion	$ 44,000	
Appropriated for Treasury Stock	6,000	
Unappropriated	80,000	
Total Retained Earnings		130,000
		$350,000
Less: Treasury Stock (50 shares) at Cost		6,000
Total Stockholders' Equity		$344,000
Total Liabilities and Stockholders' Equity		$560,000

2. The amount of discount on the bonds in Question (1) to be amortized (straight-line) on July 1 of the current year is
(a) $200 (b) $195.44 (c) $600 (d) $583.33

3. A firm issued $500,000, ten-year, 12% bonds payable on January 1 of the current year for $562,360, yielding an effective rate of 10%. Interest is payable on January 1 and July 1 each year. The firm records amortization on each

interest date. Bond interest expense for the first six months of this year, using effective interest amortization, is

(a) $30,000 (b) $33,741.60 (c) $28,118 (d) $26,882

4. A firm purchased $20,000, ten-year, 9% bonds as an investment at 96 on January 1, 19X1, ten years before maturity. The firm records interest and amortization on interest dates. On January 1, three years from the purchase date, the firm sold the bonds at 98. The gain or loss to be recorded on the date of sale is

(a) $160 loss (b) $160 gain (c) $240 loss (d) $240 gain

5. A firm that employs interperiod tax allocation deducted a $10,000 expense on its tax return in 19X1, but reported it in its income statement in 19X2. The firm's pretax accounting income was $100,000 in 19X1 and $90,000 in 19X2 (after deducting the $10,000 item). The income tax rate is 40%. At the end of 19X1, the Deferred Tax Credits account has a balance of

(a) $6,000 credit (b) $10,000 debit (c) $4,000 debit (d) $4,000 credit

QUESTIONS

17–1 Define the following terms:

(a) mortgage notes
(b) bonds payable
(c) trustee
(d) secured bonds
(e) serial bonds
(f) callable bonds
(g) convertible bonds
(h) face value
(i) nominal interest rate
(j) bond discount
(k) bond premium
(l) amortization of bond premium or discount

17–2 Explain how issuing bonds at a premium or discount "adjusts the nominal rate to the applicable market rate of interest."

17–3 A $1,000,000 issue of ten-year, 10% bonds was sold at 97 plus accrued interest three months after the bonds were dated. What net amount of cash is received?

17–4 Regardless of whether premium or discount is involved, what generalization can be made about the change in the book value of bonds payable during the period in which they are outstanding?

17–5 How should premium and discount on bonds payable be presented in the balance sheet?

17–6 On April 30, 19X5, eight months before maturity, the Bolton Company retired $50,000 of 12% bonds payable at 101 plus accrued interest. The book value of the bonds on April 30 was $47,500. Bond interest was last paid on December 31, 19X4. What is the gain or loss on the retirement of the bonds?

17–7 Give reasons why a convertible bond may be attractive to both an investor and the issuing company. Why do corporations typically include a call feature in a convertible bond?

17–8 What is the purpose of a bond sinking fund? Where is the bond sinking fund classified in the balance sheet?

17–9 Under what conditions should the effective interest method be used to amortize discount or premium on bonds payable and on long-term bond investments?

17–10 If the effective interest amortization method is used for bonds payable, how does the periodic interest expense change over the life of the bonds when they are issued (a) at a discount and (b) at a premium?

17–11 The Lowell Company invested in bonds at a premium on a long-term basis. Should the bond premium be amortized? Where should the bond investment be classified in the balance sheet?

17–12 In employee pension plans, what does the term "prior service cost" mean?

17–13 What accounting analysis is required when the accumulated retirement benefits under a firm's pension plan exceed the assets in the pension fund?

17–14 What are timing differences between pretax accounting income and taxable income? Give an example of a timing difference.

17–15 What is meant by *interperiod tax allocation?* Why do accountants employ interperiod tax allocation?

17–16 What does the balance in the Deferred Tax Credits account reflect? Where should the account be classified in the financial statements?

17–17 How does interperiod tax allocation differ from tax allocation within a period (discussed in Chapter 16)?

EXERCISES

Bonds payable entries; conversion

17–18 On January 1, the Leeds Company issued $100,000 of ten-year, 10% convertible bonds at 102. Interest is payable semiannually on June 30 and December 31. Each $1,000 bond may be converted into 20 shares of $50 par value common stock. Present journal entries to reflect (a) the issuance of the bonds, (b) the payment of interest for the first six months, (c) the premium amortization for the first six months (straight-line), and (d) the conversion of $50,000 face amount of bonds into stock exactly five years after the issuance of the bonds.

Bonds payable entries; retirement

17–19 The Wade Company issued $600,000 of ten-year, 9% bonds at 98. The bonds were issued on March 1, 19X1, with interest payable semiannually on March 1 and September 1. Present journal entries to reflect (a) the issuance of the bonds, (b) the payment of interest for the first six months, (c) the discount amortization for the first six months (straight-line), and (d) the retirement of the bonds at 101 plus accrued interest on June 1, 19X5.

Bonds payable on balance sheet

17–20 The adjusted trial balance for the Barton Corporation at the end of the current year contains the following accounts:

Bond Interest Payable	$ 71,000
9% Bonds Payable	800,000
10% Bonds Payable	500,000
Discount on 9% Bonds Payable	4,000
Premium on 10% Bonds Payable	3,000
Sinking Fund for Bond Retirement	120,000
Long-term Bond Investment	80,200

Prepare the long-term liabilities section of the balance sheet. Indicate the proper balance sheet classification for accounts listed above that do not belong in the long-term liabilities section.

Effective interest amortization

17–21 Parker, Inc., issued $800,000 of ten-year, 8% bonds payable on January 1, 19X1. The bonds were sold for $700,384, yielding an effective interest rate of 10%. Semiannual interest is payable on January 1 and July 1, and the effective interest method is used to amortize the discount.

(a) Prepare an amortization schedule showing the necessary information for the first two interest periods. Round amounts to the nearest dollar.

(b) Give the entries to record interest expense and discount amortization on July 1 and December 31.

Effective interest amortization

17–22 Refer to Exhibit 17–3 on page 621 of this chapter. The $100,000, 8% bonds in the example were issued on April 1, 19X1, and sold at a premium. Interest payment dates were April 1 and October 1. Give the adjusting entry to record interest expense and premium amortization on December 31, 19X2.

Bond investment entries

17–23 As a long-term investment, six ten-year, $1,000, 10% bonds were purchased at 104 on the first day of their first semiannual interest period. Present journal entries to record (a) their purchase for cash, (b) the receipt of the first two semiannual interest payments, (c) the semiannual amortizations of bond premium for the first year (straight-line), and (d) the sale of the bonds at 102 two years after they were purchased.

Bond investment entries

17–24 Assume that the bonds in Exercise 17–23 were purchased at 97 on the first day of their first semiannual interest period. Present journal entries to record (a) their purchase for cash, (b) the receipt of the first two semiannual interest payments, (c) the semiannual amortizations of bond discount for the first year (straight-line), and (d) the sale of the bonds at 98 two years after they were purchased.

Income tax allocation

17–25 The bottom portion of Porter, Inc., income statements for 19X1 and 19X2 is as follows:

	19X2	19X1
Income before Income Taxes	$70,000	$50,000
Income Tax Expense	24,000	24,000
Net Income	$46,000	$26,000

In 19X1, Porter, Inc., received an advance payment of $10,000, which was subject to income tax in 19X1, but not reported in accounting income until 19X2. The income tax rate is 40%. Porter did not employ interperiod income tax allocation.

(a) Identify the distortions in Porter's income statements that arise from the failure to use interperiod income tax allocation.

(b) Redo the bottom portion of Porter's income statements, using interperiod income tax allocation.

PROBLEMS

Bonds payable entries

17–26 On January 1, 19X4, Winslow, Inc., sold at 97 a $600,000 issue of 9% bonds that mature in ten years. Bond interest is payable on June 30 and December 31. Winslow's accounting year ends on December 31. The firm uses the straight-line method of amortization.

REQUIRED

(a) Show all entries pertaining to the bonds for 19X4.

(b) Present the entries necessary to record properly the retirement of one-half the bonds at 99 plus accrued interest on March 1, 19X7.

Bonds payable entries

17–27 Page, Inc., which closes its books on December 31, is authorized to issue $900,000 of 10%, 12-year bonds dated April 1, 19X1, with interest payments on October 1 and April 1.

REQUIRED

Present general journal entries to record the following events, assuming the bonds were (a) sold at 96 on April 1, 19X1; and (b) sold at $103\frac{1}{2}$ plus accrued interest on August 1, 19X1.

(1) The bond issue.

(2) Payment of the first semiannual period's interest and amortization on that date of any related bond premium or discount (straight-line).

(3) Accrual of bond interest expense and any related bond premium or discount amortization at December 31, 19X1.

(4) Retirement of $300,000 of the bonds at 101 on April 1, 19X7.

Effective interest amortization

17–28 On January 1, 19X5, Webster, Inc., issued $750,000 face value, 10%, ten-year bonds for $664,125, yielding an effective interest rate of 12%. Semiannual interest is payable on January 1 and July 1 each year. The firm uses the effective interest method to amortize the discount.

REQUIRED

(a) Prepare an amortization schedule showing the necessary information for the first two interest periods. Round amounts to the nearest dollar.

(b) Prepare the journal entry for the bond issuance on January 1, 19X5.

(c) Prepare the entry to record bond interest expense and discount amortization at July 1, 19X5.

(d) Prepare the adjusting entry to record interest expense and discount amortization at December 31, 19X5, the close of the firm's accounting year.

Effective interest amortization

17–29 On April 1, 19X5, Craig, Inc., issued $1,000,000 face value 10%, ten-year bonds for $1,135,500, yielding an effective interest rate of 8%. Semiannual interest is payable on April 1 and October 1 each year. The firm uses the effective interest method to amortize the premium.

REQUIRED

(a) Prepare an amortization schedule showing the necessary information for the first two interest periods. Round amounts to the nearest dollar.

(b) Prepare the journal entry for the bond issuance on April 1, 19X5.

(c) Prepare the entry to record bond interest expense and premium amortization at October 1, 19X5.

(d) Prepare the adjusting entry to record interest expense and premium amortization at December 31, 19X5, the close of the firm's accounting year.

Sinking-fund entries

17–30 Gilman, Inc., issued $150,000 of bonds and is required by its bond agreement to maintain a bond sinking fund managed by a trustee. The following transactions relate to the fund at various times in its life.

(1) Gilman remits a periodic cash deposit of $8,250 to the fund.

(2) The trustee reports sinking fund earnings of $1,855 during the period.

(3) The trustee reports the sale of sinking-fund securities and the retirement of the $150,000 of outstanding bonds. Just before this report, the Bond

Sinking Fund account for Gilman, Inc., showed a balance of $150,000. The trustee also reports the sale of the securities generated an unexpected gain of $2,750, and a check for this amount accompanies the trustee's report (credit to Bond Sinking-fund Income).

REQUIRED
Present general journal entries for these sinking-fund transactions.

Bonds payable and bond investment entries

17–31 The following are selected transactions of the Reese Corporation for 19X1 and 19X2. The company closes its books on December 31.

19X1

Jan. 1 Issued $400,000 of 9%, ten-year convertible bonds at 97. Interest is payable on January 1 and July 1. The holder of each $1,000 bond may convert it into 18 shares of $50 par value Reese Corporation common stock.

July 1 Paid semiannual interest and recorded semiannual discount amortization (straight-line) on convertible bonds.

1 Purchased, as a long-term investment, forty $1,000, 12% Bell Company bonds at 103. The bonds pay interest on July 1 and January 1 and mature in ten years.

Dec. 31 Recorded accrued interest payable and semiannual discount amortization on convertible bonds and accrued interest receivable and semiannual premium amortization on Bell Company bonds. (Reese Corporation does not use reversing entries.) Straight-line amortization is used both for bonds payable and bond investments.

19X2

Jan. 1 Paid semiannual interest on convertible bonds and received semiannual interest on Bell Company bonds.

2 Converted $40,000 of convertible bonds to common stock.

May 1 Sold one-half the Bell Company bonds at 102 plus accrued interest.

REQUIRED
Record these transactions in general journal form.

Bond investment entries

17–32 The following transactions relate to certain bonds acquired by Allen Corporation as a long-term investment.

19X2

Mar. 1 Purchased $600,000 face value of Clinton, Inc., 20-year, 10% bonds dated January 1, 19X2, directly from the issuing company for $609,520 plus accrued interest. Interest is paid January 1 and July 1.

July 1 Received semiannual interest on Clinton, Inc., bonds and amortized the related bond premium. The straight-line method of amortization is used.

Dec. 31 Accrued interest receivable on Clinton, Inc., bonds and amortized the related bond premium. (Allen Corporation does not use reversing entries.)

19X4

Jan. 2 Received semiannual interest on Clinton, Inc., bonds

May 1 Sold the Clinton, Inc., bonds at 101 plus accrued interest. A selling commission of $700 was deducted from the proceeds. Amortized bond premium to date of sale.

REQUIRED
Record these transactions in general journal form.

Income tax allocation

17–33 On January 1, 19X1, Valley Company entered a three-year construction contract that had an estimated gross profit of $150,000. The firm uses the percentage of completion method of recognizing gross profit on its books and reports construction contract income during 19X1–19X3 of $30,000, $75,000, and $45,000, respectively. A different procedure is used for income tax purposes and the firm reports construction contract income on the tax return during 19X1–19X3 of $12,000, $30,000, and $108,000, respectively. This is the only difference between pretax accounting income and taxable income. The firm had income before construction contract income and taxes of $120,000, $180,000, and $160,000, respectively, for 19X1, 19X2, and 19X3. The applicable tax rate is 35%.

REQUIRED

(a) Prepare a schedule deriving taxable income and income tax liability for 19X1–19X3.

(b) Prepare a schedule deriving pretax accounting income for 19X1–19X3.

(c) Prepare journal entries to record (1) income taxes for 19X1–19X3, using interperiod income tax allocation, and (2) the payment of taxes. Assume that Valley Company pays its tax liability in full in the year following its recognition in the accounts.

ALTERNATE PROBLEMS

Bonds payable entries

17–26A On January 1, 19X6, Dixon, Inc., sold at 103 a $400,000 issue of 10% bonds that mature in 20 years. Bond interest is payable on June 30 and December 31. Dixon's accounting year ends on December 31. The firm uses the straight-line method of amortization.

REQUIRED

(a) Show all entries pertaining to the bonds for 19X6.

(b) Present the entries necessary to record properly the retirement of one-half of the bonds at 101 plus accrued interest on April 1, 19X9.

Bonds payable entries

17–27A Orion, Inc., which closes its books on December 31, is authorized to issue $800,000 of 9%, 20-year bonds dated March 1, 1987, with interest payments on March 1 and September 1.

REQUIRED

Present general journal entries to record the following events, assuming the bonds were (a) sold for $776,000 on March 1, 1987; and (b) sold for $816,520 plus accrued interest on July 1, 1987.

(1) The bond issue.

(2) Payment of the first semiannual period's interest and amortization on that date of any related bond premium or discount (straight-line).

(3) Accrual of bond interest expense and any related bond premium or discount amortization at December 31, 1987 (compute to the nearest dollar).

(4) Retirement of $200,000 of the bonds at 101 on March 1, 1997.

Effective interest amortization

17–28A On April 1, 19X6, Nolan, Inc., issued $300,000 face value, 9%, ten-year bonds for $281,337, yielding an effective interest rate of 10%. Semiannual interest is payable on April 1 and October 1 each year. The firm uses the effective interest method to amortize the discount.

REQUIRED

(a) Prepare an amortization schedule showing the necessary information for the first two interest periods. Round amounts to the nearest dollar.

(b) Prepare the journal entry for the bond issuance on April 1, 19X6.
(c) Prepare the entry to record bond interest expense and discount amortization at October 1, 19X6.
(d) Prepare the adjusting entry to record interest expense and discount amortization at December 31, 19X6, the close of the firm's accounting year.

Effective interest amortization

17–29A Complete the requirements of Problem 17–28A assuming that the bonds were issued for $320,265, yielding an effective interest rate of 8%. The firm uses the effective interest method to amortize the premium.

Bonds payable and bond investment entries

17–31A The following are selected transactions of the Pacific Corporation for 19X7 and 19X8. The company closes its books on December 31.

19X7

Jan. 1 Issued $500,000 of 10%, 20-year bonds payable at 102. Interest is payable on January 1 and July 1.
June 30 Purchased, as a long-term investment, fifty $1,000, 9% Knox Company bonds at 96. The bonds pay interest on June 30 and December 31 and mature in ten years.
July 1 Paid semiannual interest and recorded semiannual discount amortization (straight-line) on bonds payable.
Dec. 31 Received semiannual interest on Knox Company bonds.
31 Recorded accrued interest payable and semiannual premium amortization on bonds payable and discount amortization on Knox Company bonds. (Pacific Corporation does not use reversing entries.) Straight-line amortization is used both for bonds payable and bond investments.

19X8

Jan. 1 Paid semiannual interest on bonds payable.
2 Retired $100,000 of bonds payable at 101.
Apr. 1 Sold Knox Company bonds at 99 plus accrued interest.

REQUIRED
Record these transactions in general journal form.

Bond investment entries

17–32A The following transactions relate to certain bonds acquired by Walker Corporation as a long-term investment.

19X4

Feb. 1 Purchased $2,000,000 face value of Holt, Inc., 20-year, 9% bonds dated January 1, 19X4, directly from the issuing company for $1,971,320 plus accrued interest. Interest is paid January 1 and July 1.
July 1 Received semiannual interest on Holt, Inc., bonds and amortized the related bond discount. The straight-line method of amortization is used.
Dec. 31 Accrued interest receivable on Holt, Inc., bonds and amortized the related bond discount. (Walker Corporation does not use reversing entries.)

19X6

Jan. 2 Received semiannual interest on Holt, Inc., bonds.
May 1 Sold the Holt, Inc., bonds at 99 plus accrued interest. A selling commission of $1,200 was deducted from the proceeds. Amortized bond discount to date of sale.

REQUIRED
Record these transactions in general journal form.

Income tax allocation

17–33A In 19X1, Hickory Company made an expenditure of $30,000, which was deductible for income taxes in 19X1 but was reported in the firm's income statement as an expense in 19X2. The firm's pretax accounting income was $90,000 in 19X1 and $85,000 in 19X2 (after the $30,000 expense item). The applicable income tax rate is 40%.

REQUIRED

(a) Prepare a schedule deriving taxable income and income tax liability for 19X1 and 19X2.

(b) Prepare a schedule deriving income tax expense for 19X1 and 19X2.

(c) Prepare journal entries to record (1) income taxes for 19X1 and 19X2, using interperiod income tax allocation, and (2) the payment of taxes. Assume that Hickory Company pays its tax liability in full in the year following its recognition in the accounts.

BUSINESS DECISION PROBLEM

On January 1, 19X1, Jim Cooper, president of Cooper Appliance Service, Inc., tells you that the firm plans to expand its business. The expansion involves the acquisition of special tools costing $225,000. The tools have an estimated useful life of five years and no salvage value. Cooper has furnished you with the following projection of income before depreciation and taxes for the next five years:

19X1	$200,000
19X2	220,000
19X3	250,000
19X4	280,000
19X5	300,000

Cooper is concerned about the income tax and accounting implications of the expansion. You indicate that the special tools will be depreciated on the books over five years using the straight-line method. For tax purposes, however, the special tools will be depreciated over three years as follows:

19X1	$ 75,000
19X2	100,000
19X3	50,000

This is the firm's only timing difference and you explain how the firm would employ interperiod income tax allocation.

REQUIRED

Answer Cooper's questions, shown below, based on the given data. Assume an income tax rate of 35%.

(a) What will the income tax liability be for each of the five years?

(b) What amount of income tax expense will appear on the firm's income statements for each of the five years?

(c) What will the accounting net income be for each of the five years?

(d) What balance for Deferred Tax Credits will appear in the balance sheet for each of the five years, and how will this amount be classified?

(e) What is the purpose of interperiod income tax allocation?

ANSWERS TO SELF-TEST QUESTIONS

1. (b) 2. (a) 3. (c) 4. (b) 5. (d)

APPENDIX A

PRESENT VALUES AND EFFECTIVE INTEREST AMORTIZATION

In this appendix, we explain the concept of present value and the techniques of bond valuation to expand on the subject of effective interest amortization, which was introduced in Chapter 17.

PRESENT VALUES

Concept of Present Value

Would you rather receive a dollar now or a dollar one year from now? Most persons would answer, "a dollar now." Intuition tells us that a dollar received now is more valuable than the same amount received sometime in the future. Sound reasons exist for choosing the earlier dollar, the most obvious of which concerns risk. Because the future is always uncertain, some event may prevent us from receiving the dollar at the later date. To avoid this risk, we choose the earlier date.

A second reason for choosing the earlier date is that the dollar received now could be invested; one year from now, we could have not only the dollar, but also the interest income for the period. Using these risk and interest factors, we can generalize that (1) the right to receive an amount of money now—its *present value*—is normally worth more than the right to receive the same amount later—its future value; (2) the longer we must wait to receive an amount, the less attractive the receipt is; and (3) the difference between the present value of an amount and its future value is a function of interest (Principal × Interest Rate × Time). The more risk associated with any situation, the higher the appropriate interest rate.

We support these generalizations with an illustration. What amount could we accept now that would be as valuable as receiving $100 one year from now if the appropriate interest rate is 10%? We recognize intuitively that with a 10% interest rate, we should accept less than $100, or approximately $91. We base this estimate on the realization that the $100 received in the future must equal the present value (100%) plus 10% interest on the present value. Thus, in our example, the $100 future receipt must be 1.10 times the present value. Dividing ($100/1.10), we obtain a present value of $90.90. In other words, under the given conditions we would do as well to accept \$90.90 now as to wait one year and receive \$100. To confirm the equality of a \$90.90 receipt now to a \$100 receipt one year later, we calculate the future value of \$90.90 at 10% for one year as follows:

$$\$90.90 \times 1.10 \times 1 \text{ year} = \$100 \text{ (rounded)}$$

Thus, we compute the present value of a future receipt by discounting (deducting an interest factor) the future receipt back to the present at an appropriate interest rate. We present this schematically below:

Present value, \$90.90 ← Discounted for one year at 10% ← Future value, \$100

If either the time period or the interest rate were increased, the resulting present value would decrease. If more than one time period is involved, compound interest computations are appropriate.

Use of Present Value Tables

Because present value tables, such as Table I on page 1073, are widely available, we need not present here the various formulas for interest computations. Table I can be used to compute the present value amounts in the illustrations and problem materials that follow. Simply stated, present value tables provide a multiplier for many combinations of time periods and interest rates, that when applied to the dollar amount of a future receipt determines its present value.

Present value tables are used as follows. First, determine the number of interest compounding periods involved (three years compounded annually is three periods, three years compounded semiannually is six periods, three years compounded quarterly is 12 periods, and so on). The extreme left-hand column indicates the number of periods covered in the table.

Next, determine the interest rate per compounding period. Note that interest rates are usually quoted on a *per year* basis. Therefore, only in the case of annual compoundings is the quoted interest rate the interest rate per compounding period. In other cases, the rate per compounding period is the annual rate divided by the number of compounding periods in a year. For example, an interest rate of 10% per year would be 10% for one compounding period if compounded annually, 5% for two compounding periods if compounded semiannually, and $2\frac{1}{2}$% for four compounding periods if compounded quarterly.

Locate the factor that is to the right of the appropriate number of compounding periods and beneath the appropriate interest rate per compounding period. Multiply this factor by the number of dollars involved.

Note the logical progressions among multipliers in Table I. All values are less than 1.0 because the present value is always smaller than the \$1 future amount if the interest rate is greater than zero. Also, as the interest rate increases (moving from left to right in the table) or the number of periods increases (moving from top to bottom), the multipliers become smaller.

EXAMPLE 1 Compute the present value of \$100 one year hence, at 10% interest compounded annually.

Number of periods (one year, annually) = 1
Rate per period (10%/1) = 10%
Multiplier = 0.909
Present value = $100.00 × 0.909 = $90.90
(Note that this agrees with our earlier illustration.)

EXAMPLE 2 Compute the present value of $116.99 two years hence, at 8% compounded semiannually.

Number of periods (two years, semiannually) = 4
Rate per period (8%/2) = 4%
Multiplier = 0.855
Present value = $116.99 × 0.855 = $100 (rounded)

Annuity Form of Cash Flows

Using present value tables like Table I, we can compute the present value of any single future receipt or series of future receipts. One frequent pattern of cash receipts, however, is subject to a more convenient treatment. This pattern, known as the **annuity form**, can be described as *equal amounts equally spaced over a period.*

For example, $100 is to be received at the end of each of the next three years as an annuity. As shown below, the present value of this annuity can be computed from Table I by computing the present value of each of the three individual receipts and summing them (assuming 5% annual interest).

Future Receipts (annuity) Yr. 1	Yr. 2	Yr.3		PV Multiplier (Table I)		Present Value
$100			×	0.952	=	$ 95.20
	$100		×	0.907	=	90.70
		$100	×	0.864	=	$ 86.40
				Total present value		$272.30

Table II (page 1074) provides a single multiplier for computing the present value of a series of future cash receipts in the annuity form. Referring to Table II in the "3 periods" row and the 5% column, we see that the multiplier is 2.723. When applied to the $100 annuity amount, the multiplier gives a present value of $272.30. Of course, the same present value is derived from the several multipliers of Table I. For annuities of 5,10, or 20 years, the computations avoided by using annuity tables are considerable.

Bond Valuations

In Chapter 17, we explained that (1) the essence of a bond investment is lending money; (2) the amount received by the lender consists of a series (usually semiannual) of interest income amounts and a single lump-sum repayment of the bond principal; and (3) bonds are sold at premiums or discounts to adjust their effective interest rates to the prevailing market rate when they are issued.

Because of the role of interest in bond investments, the selling price (or valuation) of a bond that is necessary to yield a specific rate can be determined as follows:

EXHIBIT A–1
Valuation of a Bond Issue Using Present Value Tables

Future Cash Receipts	Multiplier (Table I)	Multiplier (Table II)	Present Values
Principal repayment, $100,000 (a single amount received eight semiannual periods hence)	0.731		$ 73,100
Interest receipts, $4,000 at end of each of eight semiannual interest periods		6.733	26,900 (rounded)
Total present value (or issue price) of bond			$100,000

(1) Use Table I to compute the present value of the future principal repayment at the desired (or effective) rate of interest.

(2) Use Table II to compute the present value of the future series of interest receipts at the desired (or effective) rate of interest.

(3) Add the present values obtained in (1) and (2).

We illustrate in Exhibit A–1 the valuation of a $100,000 issue of 8%, four-year bonds paying interest semiannually and sold on the date of issue to yield 8%.

We use the 4% column in both tables because the interest rate is 8% compounded semiannually (8%/2 = 4% per compounding period), and we use the eight periods hence line because there are eight semiannual periods in four years. The multiplier from Table I is applied to the $100,000 because the principal repayment is a single sum. Because the eight semiannual interest receipts are in the annuity form, we use the multiplier from Table II to compute their present value. Note that the computation in Exhibit A–1 confirms the observation that the price of 8% bonds sold to yield 8% should be face (or par) value.

EFFECTIVE INTEREST AMORTIZATION

Most bonds sell at more or less than their face value, and therefore accounting for them involves amortizing bond premium or bond discount. For the remainder of this illustration, we show (1) how the $100,000, 8% bond issue used earlier would be valued if it were sold to yield either 6% or 10% compounded semiannually, and (2) how the bond discount and premium amounts would be determined under the effective interest method of amortization.

We calculate the amount of discount and premium in our illustration as follows:

	Bonds Sold at Discount (to yield 10%)		Bonds Sold at Premium (to yield 6%)	
Future Cash Receipts	**Present Value Multiplier**	**Present Value**	**Present Value Multiplier**	**Present Value**
Principal receipt of $100,000 (eight semiannual periods hence, factors from Table I)	0.677	$67,700	0.789	$ 78,900
Interest receipts of $4,000 each (a series of eight in annuity form, factors from Table II)	6.463	25,852	7.020	28,080
Selling price of bond issues		$93,552		$106,980
Amount of bond discount or premium		$ 6,448		$ 6,980

According to these results, an investor wishing to earn 10%, compounded semiannually, must discount the bonds by $6,448 (that is, pay only $93,552 for them). An investor paying as much as a $6,980 premium for the bonds would still earn 6%, compounded semiannually, on the investment.

As we explained in Chapter 17, the book value of bonds consists of their face value plus any unamortized premium or less any unamortized discount. Thus, at issuance, the book value of the bonds is equal to their selling price. To calculate the periodic amount of amortization using the effective interest method:

(1) Determine the period's interest expense by multiplying the bonds' book value at the beginning of the period involved by the desired (or effective) interest rate.

(2) Determine the period's amortization by comparing the period's interest expense [step (1) above] to the amount of interest actually paid. If the interest expense is greater than the amount of interest paid, the difference is discount amortization; if the expense is less than the interest paid, the difference is premium amortization.

Face value of bonds	$100,000
Less: Discount	6,448
Book value of bonds at beginning of period	$ 93,552
Multiply by the interest rate per interest period (10%/2 = 5%)	× 0.05
Interest expense for first period (rounded)	$ 4,678
Actual interest paid ($100,000 × 0.08 × $\frac{6}{12}$)	4,000
First period's discount amortization	$ 678

Exhibits A–2 and A–3 summarize the calculations, related account balances, and the general progressions involved in the other periods of our illustration. These amortization schedules also appear in Chapter 17 and are explained there. We repeat them here for your convenience.

The effective interest method of amortization is often justified as being more precise than the straight-line method. This contention probably rests on the fact that, by incorporating a changing amount of total interest expense, the effective interest method results in a uniform interest rate throughout the life of the bonds. Obviously, this increased precision is offset by the added complexity and the fact that the difference between the two methods is often considered immaterial.

EXHIBIT A–2
Bonds Sold at a Discount: Periodic Interest Expense, Amortization, and Book Value of Bonds

Year	Interest Period	(A) Interest Paid (4% of face value)	(B) Interest Expense (5% of bond book value)	(C) Periodic Amortization (B − A)	(D) Balance of Unamortized Discount (D − C)	(E) Book Value of Bonds, End of Period ($100,000 − D)
(at issue)					$6,448	$ 93,552
1	1	$4,000	$4,678	$678	5,770	94,230
	2	4,000	4,712	712	5,058	94,942
2	3	4,000	4,747	747	4,311	95,689
	4	4,000	4,784	784	3,527	96,473
3	5	4,000	4,824	824	2,703	97,297
	6	4,000	4,865	865	1,838	98,162
4	7	4,000	4,908	908	930	99,070
	8	4,000	4,930*	930	0	100,000

*Adjusted for cumulative rounding error of $24.

EXHIBIT A–3
Bonds Sold at a Premium: Periodic Interest Expense, Amortization, and Book Value of Bonds

Year	Interest Period	(A) Interest Paid (4% of face value)	(B) Interest Expense (3% of bond book value)	(C) Periodic Amortization (A − B)	(D) Balance of Unamortized Discount (D − C)	(E) Book Value of Bonds, End of Period ($100,000 + D)
(at issue)					$6,980	$106,980
1	1	$4,000	$3,209	$791	6,189	106,189
	2	4,000	3,186	814	5,375	105,375
2	3	4,000	3,161	839	4,536	104,536
	4	4,000	3,136	864	3,672	103,672
3	5	4,000	3,110	890	2,782	102,782
	6	4,000	3,083	917	1,865	101,865
4	7	4,000	3,056	944	921	100,921
	8	4,000	3,079*	921	0	100,000

*Adjusted for cumulative rounding error of $51.

PROBLEMS

Note: Use Tables I and II (pages 1073 and 1074, respectively) to solve the following problems.

Computing various present values

A–1 Compute the present value of each of the following:

(a) $60,000 ten years hence if the annual interest rate is:
   (1) 8% compounded annually.
   (2) 8% compounded semiannually.
   (3) 8% compounded quarterly.

(b) $600 received at the end of each year for the next eight years if money is worth 12% per year compounded annually.

(c) $200 received at the end of each six months for the next nine years if the interest rate is 10% per year compounded semiannually.

(d) $500,000 inheritance ten years hence if money is worth 10% per year compounded annually.

(e) $500 received each half-year for the next ten years plus a single sum of $25,000 at the end of ten years if the interest rate is 8% per year compounded semiannually.

Computing present value of annuity

A–2 Using Table II, calculate the present value of a five-year, $5,000 annuity if the interest rate is 10% per year compounded annually. Verify your answer by using Table I. Briefly explain how these tables are related.

Determining bond purchase price

A–3 You have an opportunity to purchase a bond issued by a local hospital. The bond has a face value of $20,000, will pay 10% interest per year in semiannual payments, and will mature in five years. How much should you pay for the bond if you want to earn 12% interest per year compounded semiannually on your investment?

Determining bond selling price

A–4 Sharpe, Inc., plans to issue $500,000 of 10% bonds that will pay interest semiannually and mature in five years. Assume that the effective interest rate is 12% per year compounded semiannually.

(a) Compute the selling price of the bonds.

(b) Construct a table similar to Exhibit A–2 for the first two years of the bonds' life. Round amounts to the nearest dollar.

Determining bond selling price

A–5 Complete the requirements of Problem A–4 assuming the effective interest rate is 8% per year compounded semiannually. For requirement (b), construct a table similar to Exhibit A–3.

Comparing straight-line and effective interest amortization

A–6 A $400,000, ten-year, 10% bond issue (with interest paid semiannually) is sold when the effective interest rate is 12% per year compounded semiannually.

(a) Compute the selling price of the bonds.

(b) Prepare a schedule similar to Exhibit A–2 for the first five years of the bonds' life. Round amounts to the nearest dollar.

(c) For the first five years, compute the amount of bond premium or discount amortized each year (1) under the straight-line method and (2) under the effective interest method.

(d) Compare the differences in reported income *each year* under the two methods in part (c). Do you consider these differences material? Why?

(e) What arguments might we advance for (or against) each of the approaches to bond premium and discount amortization in part (c)?

18

Long-term Stock Investments and Consolidated Financial Statements

Chapter Objectives

- **Describe the various kinds of long-term stock investments and the accounting for them.**
- **Define parent–subsidiary relationships and illustrate how their balance sheet data are consolidated.**
- **Discuss the treatment of acquisitions when cost exceeds the book value acquired in a subsidiary.**
- **Explain and illustrate the consolidation of parent and subsidiary income statements.**
- **Provide an overview of accounting for acquisitions under the "pooling of interests" method.**

'Tis sweet to know that stocks will stand
When we with daisies lie,
That commerce will continue,
and trades as briskly fly.

EMILY DICKINSON

In previous chapters, we have discussed the nature and accounting treatment of short-term investments and long-term bond investments. Now we examine the nature and accounting treatment of long-term stock investments.

Firms purchase the shares of other companies on a long-term basis for a variety of reasons. Sometimes modest investments are made simply because the shares promise a good yield or an increase in value over time. Sizeable long-term stock investments—particularly controlling interests in other firms—are more often made for such economic reasons as growth, product diversification, market penetration, assurance of raw material supplies, and tax savings. Most business combinations today are achieved by stock acquisitions. Practically all of the corporations listed on the organized stock exchanges own all or a majority of the voting stock of other companies. Accounting for such business combinations is treated later in this chapter.

TYPES OF OWNERSHIP INTEREST

Although all long-term investments in stock are first entered in the accounts at cost, the subsequent accounting procedures differ according to the circumstances. Basically, the accounting treatment employed depends on whether the ownership interest acquired is a controlling interest—that is, an interest that permits the investor company to exercise significant influence over the company whose stock is held—or an interest that is neither controlling nor influential.

Noncontrolling and Noninfluential Interest

Long-term investments of less than 20% of a corporation's voting stock are considered small enough to preclude the investor company from significantly influencing the policies of the company whose stock is acquired. Such investments are initially recorded at cost, and, depending on company policy, cash dividends are recorded as income either when declared or received. These procedures are known as the **cost method** of accounting for investments. On the balance sheet, however, these investments are carried at the lower of cost or market value of the portfolio, determined at the balance sheet date. Thus, like temporary stock investments, their carrying value may increase or decrease from period to period (but never above cost). Unlike temporary stock investments, however, any unrealized losses or recoveries of unrealized losses are not shown in the income statement; instead, the net unrealized loss on the portfolio of long-term stock investments is reported separately as a contra stockholders' equity account in the balance sheet.

The journal entries for noncontrolling and noninfluential investments are similar to those for temporary stock investments, shown in Chapter 7. For convenience, we review certain typical entries here.

Suppose 100 shares of Hytex, Inc., common stock are acquired on October 1 at a cost of $6,600, including commissions and taxes. The investment is recorded as follows:

Oct. 1	Investment in Hytex Stock	6,600	
	Cash		6,600
	To record purchase of 100 shares of common stock for $6,600.		

DIVIDENDS As in the case of temporary investments, cash dividends received are credited to a Dividend Income account, whereas a memorandum entry records any stock dividends received, since they do not constitute income. The entry for the stock dividend reveals the new average cost of the stock held. Assume that on December 10, Hytex, Inc., paid a cash dividend of $2 per share and a stock dividend of 10%. The following entries record the cash and stock dividends:

Dec. 10	Cash	200	
	Dividend Income		200
	To record receipt of $200 dividend on Hytex, Inc., stock.		

(Memorandum) Received ten shares of Hytex, Inc., common stock as stock dividend. Average cost per share of 110 shares held is now $60 ($6,600/110).

LOWER OF COST OR MARKET FOR PORTFOLIO All of a company's noncontrolling and noninfluential investments in long-term stocks constitute a portfolio. At the end of the accounting period, they are reported on the balance sheet at the lower of the aggregate cost or market value of the portfolio. Should the aggregate market value drop below total cost, an unrealized loss is recorded and a contra asset account (to offset long-term stock investments) is credited. To illustrate, assume a company has the following portfolio of long-term stock investments at the end of its first year of operations:

Stock	Cost	Market Value
Hytex, Inc., Common	$ 6,600	$ 4,800
Intersouth, Inc., Common	20,000	21,500
Wade Corporation Common	15,400	12,000
Total	$42,000	$38,300

Because the total market value ($38,300) is less than total cost ($42,000), the company makes the following journal entry:

Dec. 31	Unrealized Loss on Long-term Investments	3,700	
	Allowance to Reduce Long-term Investments to Market		3,700
	To record unrealized losses on portfolio of long-term stock investments.		

The unrealized loss on long-term investments is considered temporary and is therefore reported separately as a contra stockholders' equity account in the balance sheet (thereby reducing total stockholders' equity). On the balance sheet, the Allowance to Reduce Long-term Investments to Market account balance is deducted from the cost of long-term investments or the investment is shown in the following condensed form:

Long-term Stock Investments, at market (cost $42,000)	$38,300

If the portfolio's market value exceeds its total cost, the investments are reported at cost and no allowance is created.

SALE OF LONG-TERM INVESTMENTS When a long-term stock investment is sold, a gain or loss is recorded equal to the difference between the sale proceeds and the stock's original cost (or the original cost adjusted for the effect of a stock dividend). For example, if all 110 shares of Hytex, Inc., stock discussed above were sold on March 1 of the next year for $4,800, the following entry would be made:

Mar. 1	Cash	4,800	
	Loss on Sale of Investments	1,800	
	Investment in Hytex Stock		6,600
	To record sale of stock for $4,800.		

RECOVERY OF UNREALIZED LOSS The difference between the total cost and market value of a stock portfolio will likely change from one year-end to the next because of changes in market values or in the portfolio's composition. Thus, the contra asset account increases or decreases each year-end to reflect the net unrealized portfolio loss at that time. If the net unrealized loss at year-end is smaller than it was the year before, the adjusting entry records a recovery of an unrealized loss. Assume the company whose investments we have been analyzing has the following portfolio of long-term stock investments at the end of its second year of operations:

Stock	Cost	Market Value
Intersouth, Inc., Common	$20,000	$22,100
Wade Corporation Common	15,400	12,800
Total	$35,400	$34,900

The net unrealized loss is now $500 ($35,400 − $34,900); at the end of the preceding year, it had been $3,700. The following entry would adjust the allowance account:

Dec. 31	Allowance to Reduce Long-term Investments to Market	3,200	
	Unrealized Loss on Long-term Investments		3,200
	To record decrease in net unrealized loss on long-term stock investments.		

On the year-end balance sheet, the contra amount to stockholders' equity is only $500, and the long-term investments would be shown at market value ($35,400 cost − $500 allowance).

Influential but Noncontrolling Interest

A corporation that owns 20% or more of another corporation's voting stock may exert a significant influence on the operating or financial decisions of that company. However, if 50% or less of the total voting stock is owned, the investment will not usually represent a controlling interest. Investments in the 20–50% ownership range may therefore be considered influential but noncontrolling interests. The **equity method** of accounting is appropriate for investments in this category.

Under the equity method, the investor company records as income or loss each period its proportionate share of the income or loss reported for that period by the company whose stock is held. For example, if Warner Company owns 30% of Rose Corporation's voting stock and Rose Corporation reports earnings of $20,000 for the current year, Warner Company makes the following entry:

Investment in Rose Corporation Stock	6,000	
Income from Investment in Rose Corporation		6,000
To record as income 30% of Rose Corporation's current year earnings of $20,000.		

As this entry shows, when the investor company records its share of the other corporation's income, the investment amount also increases. When cash dividends are received, however, the investor company reports no income. The receipt of a dividend is treated as a reduction of the investment balance. To illustrate, assume Rose Corporation declared and paid a $7,000 dividend for the current year. Warner Company's entry on receipt of its share of the dividend is

Cash	2,100	
Investment in Rose Corporation Stock		2,100
To record receipt of $2,100 dividend from Rose Corporation.		

Controlling Interest

A company holding more than 50% of another corporation's stock owns a controlling interest. In some cases—such as by agreement with other stockholders—control may exist with a lesser percentage of stock ownership. The financial data of controlled corporations are usually consolidated (combined) with the data of the investor company in **consolidated financial statements**. Either the cost or equity method may be used for investments in these controlled corporations; in either case, the application of consolidation procedures yields the same result. The equity method should be used for controlling-interest investments in corporations whose data is not consolidated.

PARENT–SUBSIDIARY RELATIONSHIP

A corporation that controls the policies and operations of other corporations through ownership of their stock commonly presents financial statements of the combined group in published reports. Such consolidated statements portray the financial position and operating results of affiliated companies as a single economic unit. The company holding all or a majority of the stock of the others is the **parent company**, and the wholly owned or majority-held companies are **subsidiaries**. It is important to observe that the individual companies of a group are *legal entities*, each with separate financial statements. When the financial data of these legal entities are combined, the resulting statements portray the group as an *economic entity*, as shown in Exhibit 18–1.

Consolidated financial statements present both the total resources controlled by a parent company and the aggregate results of the group's operations that are difficult to perceive when viewing only the separate reports of the individual companies. Consolidated statements are particularly valuable to the managers and stockholders of the parent company. In addition, creditors, government agencies, and the general public are informed of the magnitude and scope of an economic enterprise through consolidated statements.

Most companies prepare consolidated statements when they hold more than 50% of the subsidiary's stock. With this kind of control, the parent can usually direct the policies and activities of the subsidiary. On the other hand, the accounts of some wholly or majority owned subsidiaries may be excluded from consoli-

EXHIBIT 18–1

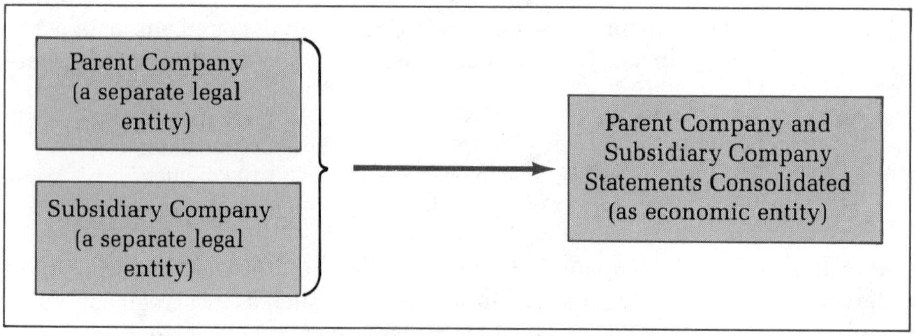

dated statements. For example, subsidiaries engaged in activities completely unrelated to those of the parent and other affiliates are normally excluded from consolidated statements. Sears, Roebuck and Company does not include its insurance firm, Allstate, in its consolidated statements, because the economic operations of an insurance company (and its accounts) are not compatible with the merchandising and manufacturing activities of the companies in Sears' consolidated statements. For similar reasons, Ford, General Motors, and FMC Corporation exclude the accounts of their wholly owned finance and insurance companies when they prepare consolidated financial statements.

Sometimes wholly or majority owned subsidiaries are located in foreign countries that restrict the parent's control of assets and operations; when the restrictions are severe, the subsidiaries' accounts may be excluded from the consolidated statements.

Whenever a subsidiary firm's accounts are not included in the consolidated statements, the parent company's investment is shown in the consolidated balance sheet as Investment in Unconsolidated Subsidiary.[1] As we mentioned earlier, the investment is accounted for under the equity method.

ACQUISITION OF SUBSIDIARIES

A corporation may obtain a subsidiary either by establishing a new firm and holding more than 50% of its voting stock or by acquiring more than 50% of the voting stock of an existing firm. Both methods have been extensively used. When an existing firm is acquired, however, the method of acquisition may play an important role in the manner of accounting for the subsidiary.

One common method of acquiring an existing firm is to give up cash, other assets, notes, or debt securities. Generally, this is a *purchase* of a subsidiary, and the **purchase method** of reporting is used in consolidated financial statements. We discuss this method of acquisition first. Another method, called *pooling of interests*, involves exchanging stock of the acquiring company for substantially all of the shares of another firm. We discuss the **pooling method** of accounting and reporting later in the chapter.

WHOLLY OWNED SUBSIDIARIES—CONSOLIDATION AT ACQUISITION DATE

Creating a Subsidiary Company

Let us assume that, on January 1, 19XX, P Company established a new, wholly owned subsidiary, S Company, to market P Company's products. P Company acquired all of S Company's common stock for $100,000 cash. To record this

[1] Often firms report condensed financial statements of unconsolidated subsidiaries in footnotes to the consolidated balance sheet.

EXHIBIT 18–2

Before Creating S Company		After Creating S Company			
P Company Balance Sheet January 1, 19XX		**P Company Balance Sheet January 1, 19XX**		**S Company Balance Sheet January 1, 19XX**	
Cash and Other Assets	$750,000	Cash and Other Assets	$650,000	Cash	$100,000
		Investment in S Company	100,000		
	$750,000		$750,000		$100,000
Liabilities	$200,000	Liabilities	$200,000	Liabilities	$ —
Common Stock	400,000	Common Stock	400,000	Common Stock	100,000
Retained Earnings	150,000	Retained Earnings	150,000	Retained Earnings	—
	$750,000		$750,000		$100,000

Reciprocal Items

transaction, P Company debits Investment in S Company and credits Cash for $100,000. In its records, S Company debits Cash and credits Common Stock for $100,000. Condensed balance sheets before and after the creation of the subsidiary are given in Exhibit 18–2.

Notice that the only change in P Company's balance sheet is a shift of $100,000 from Cash and Other Assets to Investment in S Company. The latter represents the 100% ownership of S Company common stock, giving P Company control over the resources of S Company ($100,000 cash). Thus, the $100,000 Investment in S Company on P Company's balance sheet and the $100,000 stockholders' equity (Common Stock) on the subsidiary's balance sheet are reciprocal items. If we combine (consolidate) the accounts on the balance sheets of the two companies at January 1, the reciprocal items must be eliminated. Otherwise, assets and stockholders' equity would be "double-counted." The eliminating entry made in a consolidated worksheet debits Common Stock (S Company) for $100,000 and credits Investment in S Company for $100,000. Exhibit 18–3 is the worksheet showing how the balance sheets are consolidated. Note that after eliminating the reciprocal elements, the consolidated balance sheet (the right-hand column in Exhibit 18–3) is identical with that of P Company before the creation of the subsidiary. This is logical because P Company commands no more resources than it did formerly. Also, observe that the stockholders' equity on the consolidated balance sheet is the parent company's—that is, *outside* shareholders. *The intercompany equity existing on the balance sheets is always eliminated.*

Acquisition of an Existing Firm

The general concept of consolidating affiliated companies is always the same, whether a subsidiary is created or an existing firm is acquired. Intercompany items—such as intercompany stockholders' equity—are eliminated so that the

EXHIBIT 18–3

P and S Companies
Consolidated Balance Sheet Worksheet
January 1, 19XX

			Eliminations		Consolidated
	P Company	**S Company**	**Debit**	**Credit**	**Balance Sheet**
Cash and Other Assets	650,000	100,000			750,000
Investment in S Company	100,000	—		100,000	—
	750,000	100,000			750,000
Liabilities	200,000	—			200,000
Common Stock					
P Company	400,000				400,000
S Company		100,000	100,000		—
Retained Earnings					
P Company	150,000				150,000
	750,000	100,000	100,000	100,000	750,000

consolidated statements show only the interests of outsiders. (Later we dicuss the elimination of other intercompany items.)

Suppose that P Company, instead of creating a new firm, purchased 100% of the common stock of an existing firm, Z Company, for $100,000. In this case, we assume that Z Company *already has* $100,000 in Cash and Other Assets and no liabilities. The only difference from our previous example is that Z Company's $100,000 of stockholders' equity is composed of $80,000 of Common Stock and $20,000 of Retained Earnings.

The entry on P Company's books to record the acquisition debits Investment in Z Company for $100,000 and credits Cash for $100,000. Z Company makes no entry because payment is made directly to current shareholders of Z Company. Therefore, the balance sheets of the two companies *immediately after the acquisition* are as shown in Exhibit 18–4.

The only significant difference between the balance sheets in Exhibit 18–4 and the balance sheets after acquisition in Exhibit 18–2 is that the stockholders' equity of Z Company consists of $80,000 Common Stock and $20,000 Retained Earnings rather than $100,000 Common Stock. In this case, the reciprocal items are the $100,000 Investment in Z Company on P Company's balance sheet and the Common Stock and Retained Earnings ($80,000 + $20,000) on Z Company's balance sheet. To avoid double-counting assets and stockholders' equity, we must eliminate these items when consolidating the accounts of the two firms. The worksheet entry debits Common Stock (Z Company) for $80,000, debits Retained Earnings (Z Company) for $20,000, and credits Investment in Z Company for $100,000. The worksheet to prepare the consolidated balance sheet is shown in Exhibit 18–5.

EXHIBIT 18–4

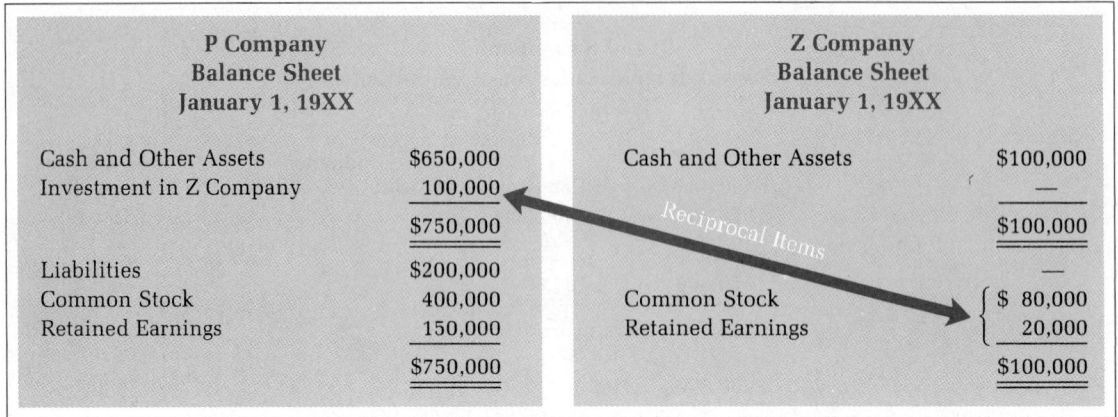

P Company
Balance Sheet
January 1, 19XX

Cash and Other Assets	$650,000
Investment in Z Company	100,000
	$750,000
Liabilities	$200,000
Common Stock	400,000
Retained Earnings	150,000
	$750,000

Z Company
Balance Sheet
January 1, 19XX

Cash and Other Assets	$100,000
	—
	$100,000
	—
Common Stock	$ 80,000
Retained Earnings	20,000
	$100,000

Reciprocal Items

EXHIBIT 18–5

P and Z Companies
Consolidated Balance Sheet Worksheet
January 1, 19XX

	P Company	Z Company	Eliminations Debit	Eliminations Credit	Consolidated Balance Sheet
Cash and Other Assets	650,000	100,000			750,000
Investment in Z Company	100,000	—		100,000	—
	750,000	100,000			750,000
Liabilities	200,000	—			200,000
Common Stock					
P Company	400,000				400,000
Z Company		80,000	80,000		—
Retained Earnings					
P Company	150,000				150,000
Z Company		20,000	20,000		—
	750,000	100,000	100,000	100,000	750,000

WHOLLY OWNED SUBSIDIARIES—CONSOLIDATION AFTER ACQUISITION DATE

In accounting periods following a parent–subsidiary affiliation, the parent company may account for its investment in the subsidiary by either the cost or the equity method. In all of our examples and problems, we use the equity method, because it is easier to understand.[2] Recall that under this method, the parent periodically reflects on its own records its share (100% in our example) of the subsidiary's earnings by debiting the Investment in Subsidiary account and crediting Income from Investment in Subsidiary. The latter item eventually increases the parent company's retained earnings. (If the subsidiary has a loss, the entry would be a debit to Loss from Investment in Subsidiary and a credit to Investment in Subsidiary, the debit eventually reducing the parent's retained earnings.) Whenever the subsidiary pays dividends, the parent company debits Cash and credits the Investment in Subsidiary account for the amount received.

To illustrate, let us return to the example (Exhibit 18–2) in which P Company created a subsidiary by purchasing 100% of S Company's stock for $100,000 cash. We assume that during the year following acquisition, P Company earned $40,000 *before* adding its earnings from S Company and paid no dividends. We also assume that S Company earned $20,000, paying $10,000 in dividends.

To record its share of S Company's earnings and to record the dividends received, P Company makes the following entries *in its own records:*

Investment in S Company	20,000	
Income from Investment in S Company (Retained Earnings)		20,000
To record 100% of S Company's earnings for the current year.		
Cash	10,000	
Investment in S Company		10,000
To record dividends received from S Company.		

The balance sheets of P Company and S Company at December 31, 19XX, are given in Exhibit 18–6.

[2] As we mentioned earlier in this chapter, both methods yield the same results when appropriate procedures are used. Consolidation procedures for both methods are taught in advanced accounting courses.

EXHIBIT 18–6

P Company
Balance Sheet
December 31, 19XX

Cash and Other Assets	$700,000
Investment in S Company	110,000
	$810,000
Liabilities	$200,000
Common Stock	400,000
Retained Earnings	210,000
	$810,000

S Company
Balance Sheet
December 31, 19XX

Cash and Other Assets	$115,000
	—
	$115,000
Liabilities	$ 5,000
Common Stock	100,000
Retained Earnings	10,000
	$115,000

Let us review the changes that have occurred in these two balance sheets since the date of acquisition. P Company's Cash and Other Assets has increased $50,000. This increase consists of P Company's own net income of $40,000 plus $10,000 in dividends received from S Company. (For simplicity, we assume that all of P Company's net income increases Cash and Other Assets, with liabilities remaining unchanged.) The Investment in S Company has increased $10,000 ($20,000 S Company earnings less $10,000 dividends received). P Company's Retained Earnings has increased $60,000 ($40,000 of its own net income plus $20,000 S Company net income).

For S Company, Cash and Other Assets has increased $15,000, along with a $5,000 increase in liabilities. Thus, net assets have increased $10,000. The corresponding $10,000 increase in Retained Earnings resulted from $20,000 net income less $10,000 dividends declared and paid. Exhibit 18–7 shows a worksheet to prepare a consolidated balance sheet at December 31, 19XX.

Whenever consolidated statements are prepared after the acquisition date, the worksheet entries eliminate the intercompany equity existing *at the date of the consolidated statements.* P Company's 100% interest in S Company includes all of the subsidiary's common stock and retained earnings. Therefore, the eliminating entry on the worksheet debits Common Stock (S Company) for $100,000, debits Retained Earnings (S Company) for $10,000, and credits Investment in S Company for $110,000.

A formal consolidated balance sheet is given in Exhibit 18–8. Note that the Cash and Other Assets of both firms have been combined, as well as the liabilities.

EXHIBIT 18–7

P and S Companies
Consolidated Balance Sheet Worksheet
December 31, 19XX

	P Company	S Company	Eliminations Debit	Eliminations Credit	Consolidated Balance Sheet
Cash and Other Assets	700,000	115,000			815,000
Investment in S Company	110,000	—		110,000	—
	810,000	115,000			815,000
Liabilities	200,000	5,000			205,000
Common Stock					
P Company	400,000				400,000
S Company		100,000	100,000		—
Retained Earnings					
P Company	210,000				210,000
S Company		10,000	10,000		—
	810,000	115,000	110,000	110,000	815,000

EXHIBIT 18–8

P and S Companies
Consolidated Balance Sheet
December 31, 19XX

Cash and Other Assets	$815,000	Liabilities	$205,000
		Common Stock	400,000
		Retained Earnings	210,000
	$815,000		$815,000

The intercompany equity—100% of S Company stockholders' equity—has been eliminated; therefore, the stockholders' equity is that of the parent company.

MAJORITY-HELD SUBSIDIARIES—CONSOLIDATION AT ACQUISITION DATE

When a firm owns more than a 50% but less than a 100% interest in another firm, the parent company's interest is a **majority interest.** The interest of the other (outside) stockholders of the subsidiary company is called the **minority interest.** In preparing a consolidated balance sheet for a parent company and a majority-held subsidiary, the assets and liabilities of the affiliated companies are combined in the usual way to show their total resources and liabilities. The parent company's equity in the subsidiary at the date of the consolidated statements is eliminated as before, but in this case, the equity represents less than 100% of the subsidiary's common stock and retained earnings. The amount of the subsidiary's common stock and retained earnings not eliminated, which represents the minority interest in the subsidiary, will appear on the consolidated balance sheet.

For example, assume that P Company purchased 80% of Q Company's voting stock on January 1, 19XX, for $160,000. After the acquisition, the separate balance sheets of the two firms appeared as shown in Exhibit 18–9.

Note that Q Company's stockholders' equity is $200,000 ($150,000 Common Stock and $50,000 Retained Earnings). The equity acquired by P Company is therefore $160,000 (80% of $200,000), which is the amount P Company paid for its interest. This intercompany equity at the date of the consolidated statements is eliminated. The remaining 20% minority interest, however, must be shown in the consolidated balance sheet. In other words, the minority, or outside, shareholders have a $40,000 interest in the stockholders' equity of Q Company (20% of $200,000). The worksheet entry to eliminate the intercompany equity and to reflect the minority interest debits Common Stock (Q Company) for $150,000, debits Retained Earnings (Q Company) for $50,000, credits Investment in Q Com-

EXHIBIT 18–9

P and Q Companies
Balance Sheets
January 1, 19XX

	P Company	Q Company
Cash and Other Assets	$590,000	$220,000
Investment in Q Company	160,000	—
	$750,000	$220,000
Liabilities	$200,000	$ 20,000
Common Stock	400,000	150,000
Retained Earnings	150,000	50,000
	$750,000	$220,000

pany for $160,000, and credits Minority Interest for $40,000. The worksheet to prepare the consolidated balance sheet is given in Exhibit 18–10.

A formal consolidated balance sheet for the two companies, prepared from the right-hand column of the worksheet, is given in Exhibit 18–11. Note that the total consolidated stockholders' equity of $590,000 consists of the parent com-

EXHIBIT 18–10

P and Q Companies
Consolidated Balance Sheet Worksheet
January 1, 19XX

	P Company	Q Company	Eliminations Debit	Eliminations Credit	Consolidated Balance Sheet
Cash and Other Assets	590,000	220,000			810,000
Investment in Q Company	160,000	—		160,000	—
	750,000	220,000			810,000
Liabilities	200,000	20,000			220,000
Minority Interest				40,000	40,000
Common Stock					
P Company	400,000				400,000
Q Company		150,000	150,000		—
Retained Earnings					
P Company	150,000				150,000
Q Company		50,000	50,000		—
	750,000	220,000	200,000	200,000	810,000

EXHIBIT 18–11

P and Q Companies
Consolidated Balance Sheet
January 1, 19XX

Cash and Other Assets	$810,000	Liabilities		$220,000
		Stockholders' Equity:		
		Minority Interest	$ 40,000	
		Common Stock	400,000	
		Retained Earnings	150,000	590,000
	$810,000			$810,000

pany's common stock and retained earnings (totaling $550,000) and the $40,000 minority interest. Thus, the interests of outside shareholders (the parent firm's shareholders and the subsidiary's minority shareholders) are portrayed in the consolidated balance sheet. Sometimes, in formal consolidated balance sheets, the minority interest amount is shown between the liabilities and the stockholders' equity. Most financial analysts, however, consider the minority interest part of stockholders' equity, and it is probably a better practice to classify it with the stockholders' equity.

MAJORITY-HELD SUBSIDIARIES—CONSOLIDATION AFTER ACQUISITION DATE

Assume that the separate balance sheets of P Company and Q Company (of our previous example) one year after the acquisition date are as shown in the first two columns of Exhibit 18–12. During the year following acquisition, Q Company earned $25,000 net income and paid $5,000 in dividends. Therefore, its Retained Earnings increased by $20,000, to $70,000. Since P Company would reflect 80% of the increase in its Investment in Q Company under the equity method, the balance of this account at year-end would be $176,000 ($160,000 + $16,000). As shown in Exhibit 18–12, this amount would be eliminated in preparing a consolidated balance sheet. Likewise, the Common Stock and Retained Earnings of Q Company would be eliminated, and 20% of the $220,000 total stockholders' equity of Q Company would be established as minority interest, $44,000. Note that the $4,000 increase in this amount consists of 20% of the increase in Q Company's retained earnings since acquisition. The formal consolidated balance sheet taken from the last column of the worksheet is shown in Exhibit 18–13.

EXHIBIT 18–12

P and Q Companies
Consolidated Balance Sheet Worksheet
December 31, 19XX

	P Company	Q Company	Eliminations Debit	Eliminations Credit	Consolidated Balance Sheet
Cash and Other Assets	624,000	250,000			874,000
Investment in Q Company	176,000	—		176,000	—
	800,000	250,000			874,000
Liabilities	210,000	30,000			240,000
Minority Interest				44,000	44,000
Common Stock					
P Company	400,000				400,000
Q Company		150,000	150,000		—
Retained Earnings					
P Company	190,000				190,000
Q Company		70,000	70,000		—
	800,000	250,000	220,000	220,000	874,000

EXHIBIT 18–13

P and Q Companies
Consolidated Balance Sheet
December 31, 19XX

Cash and Other Assets	$874,000	Liabilities		$240,000
		Stockholders' Equity:		
		Minority Interest	$ 44,000	
		Common Stock	400,000	
		Retained Earnings	190,000	634,000
	$874,000			$874,000

DIFFERENCES BETWEEN ACQUISITION COST AND BOOK VALUE

So far in our examples, we have assumed that the amount paid by the parent company to acquire a particular interest in a subsidiary exactly equals the book value of the interest acquired. In the real world this rarely happens. In fact, the parent firm almost always pays more for its interest than the book values shown on the subsidiary's balance sheet. This occurs for one of two reasons, or a combination of them. First, the recorded values of the subsidiary's assets are often understated in terms of current fair market values, a common situation given the impact of inflation. Second, the parent firm may be willing to pay an additional amount for an unrecorded asset of the subsidiary—goodwill—if the subsidiary's

GHOSTS OF ACQUISITIONS PAST

Nobody ever denied that takeovers like U.S. Steel's merger with Marathon Oil or Occidental Petroleum's gobbling up of Cities Service are expensive. But a recent Supreme Court opinion could make some of these giant acquisitions far pricier than stockholders or corporate officers ever expected. The decision sides squarely with the IRS on the tax benefit rule—an issue that has divided appellate courts for years and could cost several corporations millions in additional taxes.

When one company purchases another company using cash or notes instead of swapping stock, for example, it usually writes up the value of its new property's assets and then starts to expense them again. After all, the acquiring company pays a premium because it sees more value in its acquisition target than the balance sheet reveals. The bottom line: one asset, two tax savings.

Sadly, however, those days may soon be over. The IRS has been trying to stop this so-called double dipping for years, and the Supreme Court has just lent authority to the service's argument. "We could look at any transaction and apply the tax benefit rule to it," says one high-ranking IRS source who requested anonymity. "I can't give you a number because I have no statistics, but it will affect everyone that has stepped up the value of the assets they bought." Since company books are open to the IRS for three years and often longer, even old transactions will be subject to scrutiny.

"There have been almost no major acquisitions for cash or notes in the last several years in which the companies don't have some exposure to the IRS," says Robert Willens, Peat Marwick Mitchell's widely respected tax partner. "If a corporate taxpayer took an aggressive position—and there is no doubt that many did—they don't have any argument to make anymore. The IRS rule applies."

Particularly vulnerable are companies that paid a premium for intangible assets such as patents or acquired large quantities of short-lived assets such as tools and supplies. These are items that often have little value on an acquired company's books, though they often contribute a great deal to the worth of an acquisition. "If an acquiring company put a value on a patent, the government may now say, 'Well, you will have to pay taxes on the R&D expense that went into that patent,'" explains Richard Berkowitz, a tax partner in Arthur Andersen's mergers and acquisitions group.

Take a look a the potential impact on a company like Warner-Lambert, which bought IMED, a designer of electronic medical instruments, for $468 million last August. IMED had expensed over $4 million in research and development costs during 1982 alone. If Warner elected to write up the value of assets associated with IMED's research, it could suddenly wind up owing the IRS taxes on at least that amount.

Naturally, much of the potential liability here still depends on how aggressively the IRS takes advantage of its newfound clout. But companies that have rejoiced over winning nasty takeover battles in the last several years have good reason to worry. Their success may become a lot more expensive. And for companies interested in takeovers of the future, acquisition costs have just gone up.

From Forbes, May 23, 1983, page 122, "Ghosts of Acquisitions Past," by Ellyn Spragins.

EXHIBIT 18–14

P Company
Balance Sheet
January 1, 19XX

Cash and Other Assets	$XXX,XXX
Investment in Y Company	125,000
	$XXX,XXX
Liabilities	$XXX,XXX
Common Stock	XXX,XXX
Retained Earnings	XXX,XXX
	$XXX,XXX

Y Company
Balance Sheet
January 1, 19XX

Current Assets	$ 40,000
Plant and Equipment	60,000
	$100,000
Liabilities	$ —
Common Stock	80,000
Retained Earnings	20,000
	$100,000

earning power or its potential earning power is higher than normal for similar firms.

Suppose that P Company acquires a 100% interest in Y Company's voting stock for $125,000 when Y Company has the balance sheet depicted in Exhibit 18–14. Obviously, P Company is paying $125,000 for a 100% interest in a firm with a net book value of $100,000. Negotiations for the purchase, however, reveal that Y Company's plant and equipment are undervalued by $15,000 and that its potential for future superior earnings is valued at an additional $10,000.

In preparing a consolidated balance sheet, we make a worksheet entry that eliminates the intercompany equity and reflects the additional asset values established by the acquisition. The entry includes the following debits: Common Stock (Y Company), $80,000; Retained Earnings (Y Company), $20,000; Plant and Equipment, $15,000; and Goodwill from Consolidation, $10,000. A credit of $125,000 would be made to Investment in Y Company. Thus, the intercompany equity in the recorded book values of the subsidiary is eliminated, and an additional amount of assets, $25,000, is reflected in the consolidated balance sheet. The goodwill from consolidation[3] appears as an intangible asset on the consolidated balance sheet. In the consolidated statements of subsequent years, the amount paid in excess of the equity acquired in the subsidiary is amortized over the life of the assets to which the amount has been assigned. In the case of goodwill, the period cannot exceed 40 years.

We rarely encounter a situation in which the parent company pays less than the equity acquired for a particular interest in a subsidiary company. If this situation occurs, an analogous treatment is used to prepare a consolidated balance sheet. If the difference is attributed to an overvaluation of subsidiary assets, the eliminating entry on the worksheet credits such assets. On the other hand, if the

[3] Often this is called Excess of Cost over Book Value of Investment in Subsidiary. Many accountants and financial analysts, however, prefer to call it Goodwill from Consolidation.

difference is attributed to the subsidiary's poor earnings record, an account called Excess of Book Value of Investment in Subsidiary over Cost of Equity Acquired is credited. In a consolidated balance sheet, such an amount is probably best subtracted from total consolidated assets.

CONSOLIDATED INCOME STATEMENT

So far we have dealt only with consolidated balance sheets. Now we look at the problem of consolidating the income statements of affiliated firms. If we wish to show the scope of operations of affiliated companies as an entity, combining the revenue, cost of goods sold, and expenses of the several companies is logical. In preparing a consolidated income statement, however, we should present only the results of transactions with firms and individuals *outside* the entity. Any intercompany transactions—such as intercompany sales and purchases—should be eliminated. Likewise, revenue and expense amounts representing services rendered by one firm to an affiliated firm should be eliminated. Otherwise, the consolidated income statement would distort the extent of the group's operations.

For example, if a single company has two divisions—one manufacturing products and another marketing them—transfers of products from the manufacturing division to the marketing division are not regarded as sales transactions. Only sales by the marketing division are reflected in the firm's income statement. The same situation exists when two separate firms make up one consolidated entity.

To illustrate the procedures for preparing a consolidated income statement, we use Exhibit 18–15, the separate income statements of P Company and its 75%-held subsidiary, S Company. For simplicity, we assume that P Company has not yet reflected its 75% share of S Company's net income in its own income statement.[4]

We have indicated in the income statements that $30,000 of S Company's sales were to P Company. Assume that P Company, in turn, sold all of this merchandise to outsiders. In preparing a consolidated income statement, we must eliminate $30,000 from the sales reported by S Company and from the purchases (in cost of goods sold) reported by P Company. The worksheet to prepare a consolidated income statement for the two firms is given in Exhibit 18–16.

In Exhibit 18–16, the $30,000 in S Company's sales and the reciprocal amount in P Company's cost of goods sold have been eliminated so that only sales to outsiders are reflected in the consolidated income statement. Notice that this elimination does not affect consolidated net income, because the same amount is excluded from both sales and cost of goods sold. It does, however, avoid distorting the sales volume and costs of the group. Of the $60,000 aggregate net income of the two firms, the $5,000 minority interest (25% of S Company's net

[4]If P Company had already included its share of S Company's earnings in its own income statement, this amount would have to be eliminated to avoid double-counting when the revenue and expenses of the two firms are consolidated.

EXHIBIT 18–15

P Company
Income Statement
For the Year Ended December 31, 19XX

Sales	$500,000
Cost of Goods Sold (including $30,000 of purchases from S Company)	300,000
Gross Profit	$200,000
Operating Expenses (including income taxes)	160,000
Net Income	$ 40,000

S Company
Income Statement
For the Year Ended December 31, 19XX

Sales (including $30,000 sold to P Company)	$200,000
Cost of Goods Sold	140,000
Gross Profit	$ 60,000
Operating Expenses (including income taxes)	40,000
Net Income	$ 20,000

EXHIBIT 18–16

P and S Companies
Consolidated Income Statement Worksheet
For the Year Ended December 31, 19XX

	P Company	S Company	Eliminations Debit	Eliminations Credit	Consolidated Income Statement
Sales	500,000	200,000	30,000		670,000
Cost of Goods Sold	300,000	140,000		30,000	410,000
Gross Profit	200,000	60,000			260,000
Expenses (including income taxes)	160,000	40,000			200,000
Net Income	40,000	20,000			60,000
Minority Interest in Net Income of S Company (25% of $20,000)					(5,000)
Consolidated Net Income					55,000

income) is deducted, so the consolidated net income of the affiliated firms is $55,000. Thus, the $55,000 consolidated net income consists of $40,000 (the parent's net income from its own operations) plus $15,000 (the parent's 75% interest in the $20,000 subsidiary net income). The consolidated net income statement, shown in Exhibit 18–17, is prepared directly from the last column of the worksheet.

EXHIBIT 18–17

P and S Companies
Consolidated Income Statement
For the Year Ended December 31, 19XX

Sales	$670,000
Cost of Goods Sold	410,000
Gross Profit	$260,000
Expenses (including income taxes)	200,000
Net Income before Minority Interest	$ 60,000
Less: Minority Interest in Net Income of S Company	5,000
Consolidated Net Income	$ 55,000

CONSOLIDATED RETAINED EARNINGS STATEMENT

Preparation of a consolidated retained earnings statement for affiliated firms is a relatively simple task, and worksheets are rarely required. Using our previous example, assume that the January 1, 19XX, balance of consolidated retained earnings for P and S companies amounted to $260,000 and that P Company declared cash dividends of $25,000 during 19XX. The 19XX consolidated retained earnings statement for the two companies is given in Exhibit 18–18.

Observe that the consolidated retained earnings balance is increased by consolidated net income, which consisted of P Company's earnings plus its 75% share of S Company's earnings ($40,000 + $15,000 = $55,000). P Company enters the $15,000 income from S Company on its books by increasing the Investment

EXHIBIT 18–18

P and S Companies
Consolidated Retained Earnings Statement
For the Year Ended December 31, 19XX

Consolidated Retained Earnings, January 1	$260,000
Add: Consolidated Net Income for the Year	55,000
	$315,000
Less: Dividends Declared (by P Company)	25,000
Consolidated Retained Earnings, December 31	$290,000

in S Company account. Only dividends declared by the parent company appear in the consolidated retained earnings statement. We pointed out earlier that dividends received by the parent company from the subsidiary are credited to the Investment in Subsidiary account. Dividends paid by the subsidiary to the minority shareholders reduce the minority interest in the consolidated balance sheet.

OTHER INTERCOMPANY ACCOUNTS

Because affiliated companies often engage in a variety of intercompany transactions, treating the resulting amounts in consolidated statements can be fairly complex. For example, transactions may include intercompany loans, intercompany bond and preferred stockholdings, or plant and equipment transfers. Because this chapter is only an introduction to consolidated statements, we discuss here only some of the most commonly encountered relationships—intercompany receivables and payables and intercompany profit in assets.

Intercompany Receivables and Payables

In our example of the preparation of a consolidated income statement (Exhibit 18–16), S Company, a 75%-held subsidiary, sold merchandise to P Company for $30,000 during the year. Suppose that at year-end, P Company still owed $15,000 to S Company for some of the merchandise. P Company therefore had an account payable to S Company for $15,000 in its balance sheet at year-end, and S Company showed a receivable from P Company for the same amount. The consolidated balance sheet should show receivables and payables only with *outsiders;* otherwise both total receivables and payables of the consolidated entity are overstated. Therefore, the reciprocal receivable and payable of $15,000 must be eliminated in preparing the consolidated balance sheet, as shown in the following partial worksheet:

			Eliminations		Consolidated
	P Company	S Company	Debit	Credit	Balance Sheet
Assets					
Accounts Receivable	80,000	60,000		15,000	125,000
⋮					
Liabilities					
Accounts Payable	45,000	40,000	15,000		70,000
⋮					

Unrealized Intercompany Profit in Assets

In the above example, when S Company sold P Company $30,000 worth of merchandise, we assumed that P Company in turn sold all of it to outside parties. As far as the entity is concerned, a profit was *realized* on *all* of the merchandise.

If the merchandise had cost S Company $22,000, and P Company eventually sold all of it to outsiders for $36,000, the entity would have made a profit of $14,000 on the merchandise. Remember that the only elimination necessary to avoid double-counting was excluding $30,000 from S Company sales and $30,000 from P Company's cost of goods sold.

Suppose, however, that P Company still had $10,000 worth of the merchandise in its inventory at year-end. Also assume that S Company's cost for the remaining $10,000 worth of merchandise had been $8,000. In this situation, the $2,000 of S Company profit residing in P Company's inventory is *unrealized* from the standpoint of the entity. In a consolidated balance sheet, the $2,000 is eliminated from P Company's inventory amount and from S Company's retained earnings. This elimination is made in addition to the $30,000 elimination from S Company's sales and P Company's cost of goods sold.

In addition to merchandise, a firm may sell an affiliate such assets as securities, plant, and equipment. Following our general rule, any intercompany profit residing in the assets of the entity must be eliminated in preparing consolidated financial statements; only profits earned in dealing with outsiders can be reflected in consolidated net income and in consolidated retained earnings statements.

The technical procedures for handling these detailed adjustments in preparing consolidated financial statements are somewhat complex; they are explored in detail in advanced accounting courses.

CONSOLIDATED STATEMENTS—POOLING METHOD

In all of the foregoing examples, we assumed that an acquiring company *purchased* a controlling interest in the shares of another firm by issuing cash, other assets, or debt. Thus, a purchase and sale transaction occurred, and we used the *purchase method* to prepare consolidated statements.

On the other hand, if the acquiring company obtains substantially all (90% or more) of a subsidiary company's shares by *issuing its own shares* (and by meeting certain other criteria[5]), a **pooling of interests** has occurred. In a pooling of interests, stockholders of the subsidiary company become stockholders of the parent company. Basically, two sets of interests "unite" rather than have a purchase and sale transaction take place.

If a combination is a pooling of interests, the parent's investment and the consolidated financial statements are prepared according to the pooling method of accounting. In a consolidated balance sheet prepared under the pooling method, the *book values* of the affiliated companies are combined. Of course, the market

[5]The criteria for determining whether a pooling has occurred are set forth in *Opinions of the Accounting Principles Board, No. 16*, "Business Combinations" (New York: American Institute of Certified Public Accountants, 1970), page 297.

values of each firm's stock play an important part in determining the number of shares exchanged for the subsidiary's shares. However, once the negotiations are completed, the market values of the shares play no role in recording the parent's investment or in preparing consolidated financial statements.

Because the consolidated statements reflect the book values of the subsidiary's assets, we do not revalue these assets, nor does any goodwill (excess of cost over equity acquired) emerge from the consolidation. However, under the purchase method, the subsidiary's assets are revalued (almost invariably upward during periods of rising prices), and goodwill often appears in the consolidated balance sheet. Also, the increase in tangible assets and any goodwill are amortized over future periods. Consequently, future yearly consolidated earnings are less under the purchase method than under the pooling method.

Another facet of the pooling method is that the subsidiary's and the parent's net incomes for the entire period of the acquisition year can be combined regardless of the date of acquisition. For example, suppose a parent company earned $500,000 net income in the year that it used the pooling method to acquire a 100% interest in a subsidiary that earned $400,000. The acquisition occurred October 1, and the subsidiary's earnings for the last quarter were $100,000. The pooling method combines the subsidiary's entire $400,000 with the parent's earnings, for a total consolidated net income of $900,000. With the purchase method, only the last quarter's earnings of the subsidiary ($100,000) are combined with the parent's $500,000 earnings, for a net income of $600,000.

We summarize the pooling method as follows:

(1) With the pooling method, total consolidated assets do not increase, because book values of each firm are combined. With the purchase method, asset revaluation and goodwill (excess of cost over equity acquired) often increase total consolidated assets.

(2) Without amortization of revaluation increases or goodwill, the pooling method results in higher future earnings than the purchase method.

(3) When pooling is used, parent company and subsidiary earnings for the entire year are combined in the year of acquisition. With the purchase method, only the subsidiary's earnings after the acquisition date are included with parent company earnings.

Combination by pooling was widely used in the 1960s, because this method enabled companies to show an immediate (often synthetic) improvement in their earnings records *purely as a result of the combination* rather than through improved operations. Combining firms were allowed wide latitude in their methods of recording and consolidation, regardless of the nature of the exchange, with the result that the pooling method was selected for most combinations. In 1970, however, the Accounting Principles Board issued *Opinion No. 16*, "Business Combinations," which curtailed certain abuses by specifying more restrictive criteria that combining firms must meet to use the pooling method of accounting.

USEFULNESS OF CONSOLIDATED STATEMENTS

Consolidated statements present an integrated report of an economic unit comprising a number of business enterprises related through stock ownership. In fact, no other way can depict, fairly concisely, the extent of resources and scope of operations of many companies subject to common control.

The statements do have certain limitations, however. The status or performance of weak constituents in a group can be "masked" through consolidation with successful units. Rates of return, ratios, and trend percentages calculated from consolidated statements may sometimes prove deceptive because they are really composite calculations. Shareholders and creditors of controlled companies who are interested in their legal rights and prerogatives should examine the separate financial statements of the relevant constituent companies.

In recent years, supplemental disclosures have improved the quality of consolidated statements, particularly those of *conglomerates*—entities with diversified lines of business. Both the Financial Accounting Standards Board and the Securities and Exchange Commission have stipulated that certain firms disclose information regarding revenue, income from operations, and identifiable assets for various business segments.

DEMONSTRATION PROBLEM FOR REVIEW

On January 1, 19XX, the Montana Company purchased 75% of the common stock of the Utah Company for $180,000. On that date, the stockholders' equity of Utah Company consisted of $200,000 of common stock and $40,000 in retained earnings. Separate balance sheets of the two firms at December 31, 19XX, follow.

Montana and Utah Companies
Balance Sheets
December 31, 19XX

Assets	**Montana**	**Utah**
Investment in Utah	$195,000	—
Other Assets	305,000	$300,000
	$500,000	$300,000
Liabilities and Stockholders' Equity		
Liabilities	$100,000	$ 40,000
Common Stock	300,000	200,000
Retained Earnings	100,000	60,000
	$500,000	$300,000

Neither firm declared or paid dividends during the year. At year-end, Utah Company owed $7,000 to Montana Company on a loan made during the year.

REQUIRED
Prepare a consolidated balance sheet worksheet at December 31, 19XX.

SOLUTION TO DEMONSTRATION PROBLEM

Montana and Utah Companies
Consolidated Balance Sheet Worksheet
December 31, 19XX

	Montana	Utah	Eliminations Debit		Eliminations Credit		Consolidated Balance Sheet
Investment in Utah	195,000	—			(1)	195,000	—
Other Assets	305,000	300,000			(2)	7,000	598,000
	500,000	300,000					598,000
Liabilities	100,000	40,000	(2)	7,000			133,000
Minority Interest					(1)	65,000	65,000
Common Stock							
Montana Company	300,000						300,000
Utah Company		200,000	(1)	200,000			—
Retained Earnings							
Montana Company	100,000						100,000
Utah Company		60,000	(1)	60,000			—
	500,000	300,000		267,000		267,000	598,000

Utah Company had earnings of $20,000 during the year, because its retained earnings increased from $40,000 to $60,000 and no dividends were declared. At December 31, Montana Company's $195,000 investment consisted of the $180,000 originally paid plus $15,000—its 75% share of Utah Company's earnings. At December 31, the minority interest is $65,000—25% of the total stockholders' equity of Utah Company (25% of $260,000).

KEY POINTS TO REMEMBER

(1) Long-term stock investments are of three types:
  (a) Noncontrolling and noninfluential interest, that is, amounting to less than 20% of the investee's voting stock. Such investments are recorded at cost, and the portfolio is valued at the lower of total cost or market at each year-end. Unrealized losses are shown contra to stockholders' equity.
  (b) Influential but noncontrolling interest, that is, amounting to 20–50% of the investee's voting stock. Such investments are recorded at cost, then adjusted periodically according to the equity method. The firm's share of the investee's earnings is added to and dividends are deducted from the investment's carrying value.
  (c) Controlling interest, that is, amounting to over 50% of the investee's voting stock. The investment may be carried on either the cost or equity basis;

the application of consolidation procedures results in the same consolidated statements under either method.

(2) When a firm acquires another company's stock by exchanging cash, assets, notes, or debt securities, the acquisition is a purchase. If less than 90% of another firm's stock is acquired, the acquisition is a purchase, regardless of the media of exchange. However, if the acquiring firm obtains 90% or more of the other firm's shares by issuing its own shares, the transaction is usually regarded as a pooling of interests.

(3) In a purchase combination, the acquiring company initially records its investment at cost. Any amount in excess of the book value of the acquired firm's net assets is allocated among specific assets when possible. Any unallocated amount is goodwill, which must be amortized over a period of years.

(4) In a pooling combination, the parent firm records its investment in accordance with the book value of the acquired firm's net assets. Cost (as measured by the market value of shares exchanged) is ignored. The acquired firm's retained earnings at acquisition date are added to those of the acquiring company. Earnings of both companies for the period when the acquisition occurred are likewise combined.

(5) A parent company that carries its investment in a subsidiary under the equity method—as illustrated in this chapter—uses the following accounting procedures:
   (a) The parent periodically debits Investment in Subsidiary and credits Income from Subsidiary for its share of subsidiary earnings. Dividends received from the subsidiary are debited to Cash and credited to Investment in Subsidiary.
   (b) The parent eliminates its equity in the subsidiary existing when the consolidated balance sheet is prepared.

SELF-TEST QUESTIONS
(Answers are at the end of this chapter.)

1. A firm purchased noncontrolling and noninfluential long-term investments that cost $65,000. At the close of the year, the portfolio had a market value of $60,000. The entry to adjust the carrying value of the investments at the end of the year includes a
   (a) Credit of $5,000 to Unrealized Loss on Long-term Investments.
   (b) Debit of $5,000 to Long-term Stock Investments.
   (c) Credit of $5,000 to Allowance to Reduce Long-term Investments to Market.
   (d) Debit of $60,000 to Long-term Stock Investments.
2. Artway Company purchased 30% of the voting stock of the Barton Company for $60,000 on January 1 of the current year. During the year, Barton Company earned $50,000 net income and paid $15,000 in dividends. At the end of the year, Artway Company's account, Investment in Barton Company, should have a balance of
   (a) $110,000 (b) $70,500 (c) $95,000 (d) $60,000

3. X Company purchased an 80% interest in Y Company for $225,000 at the beginning of the current year. At that time, X Company had $500,000 common stock and $150,000 retained earnings, and Y Company had $200,000 common stock and $60,000 retained earnings. On the consolidated balance sheet prepared at the time of the acquisition, consolidated retained earnings should be
(a) $150,000 (b) $210,000 (c) $198,000 (d) $48,000

4. Suppose that Y Company, in Question 3 above, earned $40,000 net income and paid $10,000 dividends during the year following acquisition. The minority interest to be shown on a consolidated balance sheet prepared at the end of the year should be
(a) $232,000 (b) $60,000 (c) $18,000 (d) $58,000

5. Brown Company, which owns 70% of Greene Company's voting stock, sold merchandise during the year to Greene Company for $60,000. The merchandise had cost Brown Company $40,000. Greene Company sold all of the merchandise to outsiders during the year. The eliminating entry to prepare a consolidated income statement for the year should reduce the sales amount and the cost of goods sold amount by
(a) $60,000 (b) $40,000 (c) $20,000 (d) $28,000

QUESTIONS

18–1 What is a noncontrolling and noninfluential long-term stock investment?

18–2 How are noncontrolling and noninfluential long-term stock investments reported in the balance sheet? Where are unrealized losses on the portfolio of such investments reported?

18–3 Describe the accounting procedures used when a stock investment represents from 20–50% of the voting stock.

18–4 Describe the accounting procedures used when a stock investment represents over 50% of the voting stock.

18–5 What is the purpose of consolidated financial statements?

18–6 In a recent annual report, FMC Corporation's consolidated financial statements showed an amount under Investments that included a 100% interest in FMC Finance Corporation and a 50% interest in Ketchikan Pulp Corporation and its subsidiaries. The latter investment represents a 50–50 joint venture with Louisiana–Pacific Corporation. Explain why the accounts of these firms are not consolidated with the accounts of FMC and its other subsidiaries. On what accounting basis are the investments in these unconsolidated subsidiaries carried?

18–7 What is the difference between a *purchase* acquisition and a *pooling of interests*?

18–8 P Company purchases all of the common stock of S Company for $500,000 when S Company has $400,000 of common stock and $100,000 of retained earnings. If a consolidated balance sheet is prepared immediately after the acquisition, what amounts are eliminated in preparing it?

18–9 Suppose, in Question 18–8, that P Company acquires only 75% of S Company's common stock by paying $375,000. If a consolidated balance sheet is prepared immediately after the acquisition, what amounts are eliminated in preparing this statement? What amount of minority interest appears in the consolidated balance sheet?

18–10 Explain the entries made in a parent company's records under the equity method of accounting to (a) reflect its share of the subsidiary's net income for the period and (b) record the receipt of dividends from the subsidiary.

18–11 On January 1 of the current year, P Company purchased 80% of the common stock of S Company for $600,000. During the year, S Company had $80,000 of net income and paid $30,000 in cash dividends. At year-end, what amount appears in P Company's balance sheet as Investment in S Company under the equity method?

18–12 Howell Company purchased an interest in Ward Company for $265,000 when Ward Company had $200,000 of common stock and $50,000 of retained earnings.

(a) If Howell Company had acquired a 100% interest in Ward Company, what amount of Goodwill from Consolidation would appear on the consolidated balance sheet? (Assume that Ward's assets are fairly valued.)

(b) If Howell had acquired only a 90% interest in Ward Company, what amount of Goodwill from Consolidation would appear?

18–13 Benson Company purchased a 75% interest in Gates Company on January 1 of the current year. Benson Company had $250,000 net income for the current year before reflecting its share of Gates Company's net income. If Gates Company had net income of $80,000 for the year, what is the consolidated net income for the year?

18–14 Regent Company, which owns 80% of Hayes Company, sold merchandise during the year to Hayes Company for $80,000. The merchandise cost Regent Company $60,000. If Hayes Company in turn sold all of the merchandise to outsiders for $100,000, what eliminating entry related to these transactions does Regent make in preparing a consolidated income statement for the year?

18–15 Suppose, in Question 18–14, that Hayes Company still owed Regent Company $35,000 for the merchandise acquired during the year. What eliminating entry is made for this item in preparing a consolidated balance sheet at year-end?

18–16 P Company acquired 100% of S Company on September 1 of the current year. Explain why the consolidated earnings of the two firms for the current year might be greater if the transaction is treated as a pooling of interests rather than as a purchase.

18–17 What are the inherent limitations of consolidated financial statements?

EXERCISES

Entries for a noncontrolling and noninfluential investment

18–18 As a long-term investment, 2,000 shares of Spencer Company common stock were acquired on March 10, 19X1, at a total cost of $82,600. The investment represented 15% of the company's voting stock. On December 28, 19X1, Spencer Company declared a cash dividend of $1.50 per share, which was received on January 15, 19X2. Dividend income is recorded when received. Present the necessary journal entries to reflect (a) the purchase of the stock and (b) the receipt of the cash dividend.

Entries for an influential but noncontrolling investment

18–19 Assume the 2,000 shares purchased in Exercise 18–18 represent 25% of Spencer Company's voting stock. Spencer Company's 19X1 net income was $60,000. Using the equity method, present the journal entries to reflect (a) the purchase of the stock, (b) the proportionate share of Spencer Company's 19X1 net income (dated December 31, 19X1), and (c) the receipt of the cash dividend.

Calculating unrealized loss in investment portfolio

18–20 During its first year of operations, a firm purchased the following noncontrolling and noninfluential long-term investments:

1,000 shares of A Company stock at $50 per share
2,000 shares of B Company stock at $60 per share

At year-end, the market value of the A Company stock was $44 per share, and the market value of the B Company stock was $61 per share. What was the unrealized loss at year-end, and where does it appear in the firm's financial statements?

Eliminating entry and stockholders' equity in consolidation

18–21 On January 1 of the current year, Gates Company purchased all of the common shares of Jordan Company for $240,000 cash. On this date, the stockholders' equity of Gates Company consisted of $400,000 in common stock and $80,000 in retained earnings. Jordan Company had $200,000 in common stock and $40,000 in retained earnings.

(a) Give the worksheet eliminating entry to prepare a consolidated balance sheet on the acquisition date.
(b) What amount of total stockholders' equity appears on the consolidated balance sheet?

Stockholders' equity in consolidated balance sheet

18–22 Nolan Company purchased 75% of the common stock of Root Company for $180,000 in cash and notes when the stockholders' equity of Root Company consisted of $200,000 in common stock and $40,000 in retained earnings. On the acquisition date, the stockholders' equity of Nolan Company consisted of $700,000 in common stock and $150,000 in retained earnings. Present the stockholders' equity section in the consolidated balance sheet prepared on the acquisition date.

Eliminating entry including asset revaluation and goodwill

18–23 On January 1 of the current year, Wynn Company purchased all of the common shares of Oakwell Company for $525,000 cash and notes. Balance sheets of the two firms immediately after the acquisition were as follows:

	Wynn	**Oakwell**
Current Assets	$1,200,000	$120,000
Investment in Oakwell Company	525,000	—
Plant and Equipment	2,275,000	380,000
	$4,000,000	$500,000
Liabilities	$ 600,000	$ 20,000
Common Stock	3,000,000	400,000
Retained Earnings	400,000	80,000
	$4,000,000	$500,000

During the negotiations for the purchase, Oakwell's plant and equipment were appraised at $400,000. Furthermore, Wynn concluded that an additional $25,000 demanded by Oakwell's shareholders was warranted because Oakwell's earning power was somewhat better than the industry average. Give the worksheet eliminating entry to prepare a consolidated balance sheet on the acquisition date.

Determining investment balance using the equity method

18–24 Tinker Company purchased a 70% interest in Star Company for $480,000 cash on January 1 of the current year. During the year, Star Company earned $30,000 net income and declared and paid half its earnings in dividends. Tinker Company carries its investment in Star Company on the equity method. What is the carrying value of Tinker Company's Investment in Star Company account at year-end?

Eliminating entry for intercompany sales

18–25 Prairie Company has an 80% interest in Meadow Company. During the current year, Meadow Company sold merchandise costing $45,000 to the Prairie Company for $60,000. Assuming Prairie Company sold all of the merchandise to outsiders, what worksheet eliminating entry should be made in preparing a consolidated income statement for the period?

Calculating amounts on consolidated statements

18–26 On January 1, 19XX, Beacon Company purchased for $240,000 cash a 90% stock interest in Clayton, Inc., which then had common stock of $200,000 and retained earnings of $50,000. On December 31, 19XX, after Beacon had taken up its share of Clayton's earnings, the balance sheets of the two companies were as follows:

	Beacon	**Clayton, Inc.**
Investment in Clayton, Inc., (at equity)	$267,000	—
Other Assets	283,000	$320,000
	$550,000	$320,000
Liabilities	$ 50,000	$ 40,000
Common Stock	400,000	200,000
Retained Earnings	100,000	80,000
	$550,000	$320,000

Clayton, Inc., did not declare or pay dividends during the year.

(a) What was the net income of Clayton, Inc., for the year?

(b) The consolidated balance sheet prepared December 31, 19XX, would show
  (1) What amount of common stock?
  (2) What amount of retained earnings?
  (3) What amount of minority interest?

(c) Assuming that Clayton, Inc., assets are properly stated, what amount of goodwill from consolidation is reported?

PROBLEMS

Entries for noninfluential and noncontrolling investments

18–27 The following selected transactions and information are for the Monterey Corporation for 19X1 and 19X2.

19X1

July 1 Purchased, as a long-term investment, 1,000 shares of Wheeler, Inc., common stock at a total cost of $54,600. This interest is noninfluential and noncontrolling.

Oct. 1 Purchased, as a long-term investment, 2,000 shares of Langdon, Inc., common stock at a total cost of $74,200, and 2,000 shares of Gammon, Inc., common stock at a total cost of $60,000. Both investments are noninfluential and noncontrolling interests.

Nov. 9 Received a cash dividend of 60 cents per share on the Langdon, Inc., stock.

Dec. 31 The Wheeler, Inc., shares have a market value of $52 per share; the Langdon, Inc., shares have a market value of $33 per share; and the Gammon, Inc., shares have a market value of $31 per share. (An entry should be made to adjust the carrying value of the portfolio to the lower of cost or market.)

19X2

Feb. 1 Sold the Langdon, Inc., stock for $34 per share less a $60 commission fee.

Dec. 31 The market value of the long-term stock investment portfolio is as follows: Wheeler, Inc., $53 per share; Gammon, Inc., $29 per share. (An entry should be made to adjust the carrying value of the investments and the unrealized loss account.)

REQUIRED

Give the journal entries to record these transactions and adjustments.

Contrasting entries for influential and noninfluential investments

18–28 On January 2, 19X1, Lancer Corporation purchased, as a long-term investment, 6,000 shares of Rider Company common stock for $28 per share, including commissions and taxes. On December 31, 19X1, Rider Company announced a net income of $48,000 for the year and a dividend of $1.50 per share, payable January 20, 19X2, to stockholders of record on January 10, 19X2. Lancer Corporation received its dividend on January 23, 19X2.

REQUIRED

(a) Assume the stock acquired by Lancer Corporation represents 15% of Rider Company's voting stock. Prepare all journal entries appropriate for this investment, beginning with the purchase on January 2, 19X1, and ending with the receipt of the dividend on January 23, 19X2. (Lancer Corporation recognizes dividend income when received.)

(b) Assume the stock acquired by Lancer Corporation represents 25% of Rider Company's voting stock. Prepare all journal entries appropriate for this investment, beginning with the purchase on January 2, 19X1, and ending with the receipt of the dividend on January 23, 19X2.

Determining eliminations and consolidated data on date of acquisition (wholly owned subsidiary)

18–29 Allied Company purchased all of Post Company's common stock for cash on January 1, 19XX, after which the separate balance sheets of the two corporations appeared as follows:

Allied and Post Companies
Balance Sheets
January 1, 19XX

	Allied	Post
Investment in Post Company	$ 520,000	—
Other Assets	1,480,000	$600,000
	$2,000,000	$600,000
Liabilities	$ 700,000	$140,000
Common Stock	1,000,000	400,000
Retained Earnings	300,000	60,000
	$2,000,000	$600,000

During the negotiations for the purchase, Allied Company determined that the appraised value of Post Company's Other Assets amounted to $640,000.

REQUIRED

(a) Give the worksheet entry to eliminate the intercompany equity and to reflect the appraised value of Post Company's assets.
(b) What amount of total assets should appear on a January 1 consolidated balance sheet?
(c) What amount of total stockholders' equity should appear on a January 1 consolidated balance sheet?

Determining intercompany data one year after acquisition (wholly owned subsidiary)

18–30 On January 1, 19XX, Spokane Company purchased all of the common stock of Portland Company for $220,000 cash. The stockholders' equity of Portland consisted of $200,000 in common stock and $20,000 in retained earnings. On December 31, 19XX, the separate balance sheets of the two firms were as follows:

Spokane and Portland Companies
Balance Sheets
December 31, 19XX

	Spokane	Portland
Cash	$ 45,000	$ 40,000
Accounts Receivable	85,000	50,000
Investment in Portland Company (at equity)	240,000	—
Other Assets	330,000	210,000
	$700,000	$300,000
Accounts Payable	$ 80,000	$ 60,000
Common Stock	500,000	200,000
Retained Earnings	120,000	40,000
	$700,000	$300,000

During the year, Portland Company had net income of $30,000. At December 31, Portland owed Spokane $15,000 on account for merchandise.

REQUIRED

(a) What amount of dividends did Portland Company declare and pay during the year?

(b) Give Spokane Company's journal entries that affect the Investment in Portland Company account.

(c) What amount of total assets would appear in a December 31, 19XX, consolidated balance sheet?

Preparing consolidated balance sheet worksheet on acquisition date

18–31 On January 1, 19XX, Kingston Company purchased 75% of the common stock of Dixon Company for $520,000 cash, after which the separate balance sheets of the two firms were as follows:

Kingston and Dixon Companies
Balance Sheets
January 1, 19XX

	Kingston	**Dixon**
Investment in Dixon Company	$ 520,000	—
Other Assets	980,000	$700,000
	$1,500,000	$700,000
Liabilities	$ 300,000	$ 60,000
Common Stock	1,000,000	500,000
Retained Earnings	200,000	140,000
	$1,500,000	$700,000

REQUIRED

Prepare a consolidated balance sheet worksheet at January 1, 19XX. Assume that any amount paid by Kingston Company in excess of the equity acquired in Dixon Company's net assets is attributable to goodwill.

Preparing consolidated income statement worksheet

18–32 Signet Company owns 70% of the common stock of Lake Company. The income statements of the two companies for the current year are shown below. In its income statement, Signet Company has not recorded its share of Lake Company's net income.

Signet and Lake Companies
Income Statements
For the Current Year

	Signet	**Lake**
Sales	$480,000	$260,000
Cost of Goods Sold	340,000	180,000
Gross Profit	$140,000	$ 80,000
Expenses (including income taxes)	84,000	46,000
Net Income	$ 56,000	$ 34,000

During the year, Signet Company sold Lake Company merchandise for $50,000, which had cost Signet $35,000. Lake Company sold all of this merchandise to outsiders.

REQUIRED
Prepare a consolidated income statement worksheet for the current year.

Analyzing data from statements consolidated a year after acquisition

18–33 On January 1, 19XX, Astro Company acquired an interest in Cyprus Company for $240,000, consisting of $100,000 cash and $140,000 in notes payable. The following information is available about the two companies at December 31, 19XX:

	Astro	Cyprus	Consolidated
Assets			
Cash	$ 50,000	$ 30,000	$ 80,000
Accounts Receivable	60,000	50,000	100,000
Inventory	120,000	70,000	190,000
Investment in Cyprus (at equity)	270,000	—	
Other Assets	300,000	200,000	500,000
Excess of Cost over Equity Acquired in Cyprus			20,000
Total Assets	$800,000	$350,000	$890,000
Liabilities and Stockholders' Equity			
Accounts Payable	$ 80,000	$ 60,000	$130,000
Notes Payable	150,000	40,000	190,000
Common Stock	450,000	200,000	450,000
Retained Earnings	120,000	50,000	120,000
Total Liabilities and Stockholders' Equity	$800,000	$350,000	$890,000

REQUIRED
(a) Is the acquisition of Cyprus Company by Astro Company a purchase or a pooling of interests? Explain.
(b) What ownership percentage of Cyprus Company did Astro Company acquire?
(c) What were Cyprus Company's 19XX earnings? Cyprus declared and paid no dividends in 19XX.
(d) How much of Cyprus Company's retained earnings is included in the consolidated retained earnings?
(e) What were the amounts of intercompany receivables and payables at December 31?

Parent's entries for acquisition, income, and dividends of majority-held subsidiary

18–34 On January 1, 19XX, Windsor Company purchased 80% of the common shares of Blair Company for $620,000 cash. At that time, the stockholders' equity of Blair Company consisted of $600,000 of common stock and $100,000 of retained earnings. At December 31, 19XX, the separate balance sheets of the two firms were as follows:

Windsor and Blair Companies
Balance Sheets
December 31, 19XX

	Windsor	Blair
Investment in Blair (at equity)	$ 660,000	—
Other Assets	1,340,000	$900,000
	$2,000,000	$900,000
Liabilities	$ 750,000	$150,000
Common Stock	1,000,000	600,000
Retained Earnings	250,000	150,000
	$2,000,000	$900,000

REQUIRED

(a) Give Windsor Company's general journal entry to record the purchase of Blair Company's shares on January 1, 19XX.

(b) Blair Company's 19XX net income was $90,000. Blair declared and paid $40,000 in dividends near the end of 19XX.

(1) Give Windsor Company's general journal entry to record its share of Blair's net income for the year.

(2) Give Windsor Company's general journal entry to record the receipt of dividends from Blair Company.

(c) Prepare a consolidated balance sheet for the two firms at December 31, 19XX. Assume that two-thirds of any amount paid by Windsor Company in excess of the equity acquired in Blair's net assets at January 1 is goodwill. The remaining one-third represents an appraisal increase of Blair's Other Assets. At December 31, Blair Company owed $75,000 to Windsor Company for a loan made during the year.

ALTERNATE PROBLEMS

Entries for noninfluential and noncontrolling investments

18–27A The following selected transactions and information are for the Atwood Corporation for 19X1 and 19X2.

19X1

Aug. 1 Purchased, as a long-term investment, 1,500 shares of Hunt, Inc., common stock at a total cost of $79,500. This interest is noninfluential and noncontrolling.

Nov. 3 Purchased, as a long-term investment, 3,000 shares of Sydney, Inc., common stock at a total cost of $171,000, and 1,000 shares of Cooper, Inc., common stock at a total cost of $32,000. Both investments are noninfluential and noncontrolling interests.

21 Received a cash dividend of $2 per share on the Sydney, Inc., stock.

Dec. 31 The Hunt, Inc., shares have a market value of $49 per share; the Sydney, Inc., shares have a market value of $50 per share; and the Cooper, Inc., shares have a market value of $33 per share. (An entry should be made to adjust the carrying value of the portfolio to the lower of cost or market.)

19X2

Jan. 15 Sold the Sydney, Inc., stock for $54 per share less a $150 commission fee.

Dec. 31 The market value of the long-term investment portfolio is as follows: Hunt, Inc., $51 per share; Cooper, Inc., $30 per share. (An entry should be made to adjust the carrying value of the investments and the unrealized loss account.)

REQUIRED

Give the journal entries to record these transactions and adjustments.

Contrasting entries for influential and noninfluential investments

18–28A On January 2, 19X1, Curtis, Inc., purchased, as a long-term investment, 20,000 shares of Yuma, Inc., common stock for $36 per share, including commissions and taxes. On December 31, 19X1, Yuma, Inc., announced a net income of $160,000 for the year and a dividend of 80 cents per share, payable January 15, 19X2, to stockholders of record on January 5, 19X2. Curtis, Inc., received its dividend on January 18, 19X2.

REQUIRED

(a) Assume the stock acquired by Curtis, Inc., represents 16% of Yuma, Inc.'s voting stock. Prepare all journal entries appropriate for this investment, beginning with the purchase on January 2, 19X1, and ending with the receipt of the dividend on January 18, 19X2. (Curtis, Inc., recognizes dividend income when received.)

(b) Assume the stock acquired by Curtis, Inc., represents 30% of Yuma, Inc.'s voting stock. Prepare all journal entries appropriate for this investment, beginning with the purchase on January 2, 19X1, and ending with the receipt of the dividend on January 18, 19X2.

Determining eliminations and consolidated data on date of acquisition (majority-held subsidiary)

18–29A Eagle Company purchased 70% of Mann Company's voting stock on January 1, 19XX, after which the separate balance sheets of the two companies appeared as follows:

Eagle and Mann Companies
Balance Sheets
January 1, 19XX

	Eagle	Mann
Investment in Mann Company	$ 445,000	—
Other Assets	955,000	$650,000
	$1,400,000	$650,000
Liabilities	$ 250,000	$ 50,000
Common Stock	800,000	450,000
Retained Earnings	350,000	150,000
	$1,400,000	$650,000

In purchasing Mann Company's shares, Eagle Company attributed the excess of the amount paid over the equity acquired in Mann entirely to that company's superior earning potential.

REQUIRED

(a) Give the worksheet entry to eliminate the intercompany equity and to reflect the goodwill.
(b) What amount of total assets should appear on a January 1 consolidated balance sheet?
(c) What amount of total stockholders' equity should appear on a January 1 consolidated balance sheet?

Determining intercompany data one year after acquisition (wholly owned subsidiary)

18–30A On January 1, 19XX, Oxford Company purchased all of the common stock of Harris Company for $370,000 cash. The stockholders' equity of Harris Company consisted of $300,000 of common stock and $50,000 of retained earnings. On December 31, 19XX, the separate balance sheets of the two firms were as follows:

Oxford and Harris Companies
Balance Sheets
December 31, 19XX

	Oxford	**Harris**
Cash	$ 60,000	$ 70,000
Accounts Receivable	110,000	160,000
Investment in Harris Company (at equity)	410,000	—
Other Assets	380,000	290,000
	$960,000	$520,000
Accounts Payable	$120,000	$130,000
Common Stock	700,000	300,000
Retained Earnings	140,000	90,000
	$960,000	$520,000

During the year, Harris Company had net income of $60,000. At December 31, Harris owed Oxford $15,000 on account for merchandise.

REQUIRED

(a) What amount of dividends did Harris Company declare and pay during the year?
(b) Give Oxford Company's journal entries that affect the Investment in Harris Company account.
(c) What amount of total assets would appear in a December 31, 19XX consolidated balance sheet?

Preparing consolidated balance sheet worksheet one year after acquisition

18–31A On January 1, 19XX, Vista, Inc. purchased 75% of the voting stock of Dakota, Inc., for $335,000. At that date, Dakota had $300,000 in common stock outstanding and $100,000 in retained earnings. On December 31, 19XX, the separate balance sheets of the two companies were as follows:

Vista, Inc., and Dakota, Inc.
Balance Sheets
December 31, 19XX

	Vista	Dakota
Investment in Dakota, Inc. (at equity)	$ 357,500	—
Other Assets	842,500	$520,000
	$1,200,000	$520,000
Liabilities	$ 160,000	$ 90,000
Common Stock	800,000	300,000
Retained Earnings	240,000	130,000
	$1,200,000	$520,000

During the year, Dakota, Inc., paid $20,000 in dividends.

REQUIRED

Prepare a consolidated balance sheet worksheet at December 31, 19XX. Assume that any amount paid by Vista in excess of the equity acquired in Dakota is attributable to goodwill.

Preparing consolidated income statement worksheet

18–32A Topaz Company purchased a 60% interest in Grant Company on January 1, 19XX. The income statements for the two companies for 19XX are given below. Topaz Company has not yet recorded its share of Grant Company's net income.

Topaz and Grant Companies
Income Statements
For the Year Ended December 31, 19XX

	Topaz	Grant
Sales	$840,000	$450,000
Cost of Goods Sold	580,000	310,000
Gross Profit	$260,000	$140,000
Operating Expenses (including taxes)	185,000	108,000
Net Income	$ 75,000	$ 32,000

Grant Company did not pay any dividends in 19XX. During the year, Topaz sold merchandise costing $64,000 to Grant for $85,000, all of which Grant sold to outsiders.

REQUIRED

Prepare a consolidated income statement worksheet for 19XX.

BUSINESS DECISION PROBLEM

Kleenaire, Inc., manufactures furnaces, filter systems, and air conditioning equipment. It has a 75% interest in Chinook Company, which manufactures humidifiers. It also has a 100% interest in Kleenaire Finance Company, created by the parent company to finance sales of its products to consumers. The parent company's only other investment is a 10% interest in the common stock of Scott, Inc., which manufactures controls for both Kleenaire, Inc., and Chinook Company. A condensed consolidated balance sheet for the entity for the current year is given below:

Kleenaire, Inc., and Subsidiaries
Consolidated Balance Sheet
December 31, 19XX

Assets		
Current Assets		$24,300,000
Investment in Stock of Kleenaire Finance Company (100%) at Underlying Equity		15,500,000
Investment in Stock of Scott, Inc. (10%) at Cost		2,700,000
Other Assets		47,900,000
Excess of Cost over Equity Acquired in Net Assets of Chinook Company		1,600,000
Total Assets		$92,000,000
Liabilities and Stockholders' Equity		
Current Liabilities		$10,500,000
Long-term Liabilities		14,000,000
Stockholders' Equity:		
Minority Interest	$ 3,600,000	
Common Stock	50,000,000	
Retained Earnings	13,900,000	67,500,000
Total Liabilities and Stockholders' Equity		$92,000,000

This balance sheet, along with other financial statements, was furnished to shareholders before their annual meeting, and all shareholders were invited to submit questions to be answered at the meeting. As chief financial officer of Kleenaire, Inc., you have been appointed to respond to the questions at the meeting.

REQUIRED

Answer the following stockholder questions:

(a) What is meant by *consolidated financial statements?*
(b) Why are investments in Scott, Inc., and Kleenaire Finance Company shown on the balance sheet, while the investment in Chinook Company is omitted?
(c) What is meant by the carrying value at *underlying equity* for the investment in Kleenaire Finance Company?
(d) Why is the investment in Scott, Inc., shown at cost, while the investment in Kleenaire Finance Company is shown at underlying equity?
(e) Explain the meaning of the asset Excess of Cost over Equity Acquired in Net Assets of Chinook Company.
(f) What is meant by *minority interest* and to what company is this account related?

ANSWERS TO SELF-TEST QUESTIONS

1. (c) 2. (b) 3. (a) 4. (d) 5. (a)

COMPREHENSIVE PROBLEM—PART 3

This comprehensive problem utilizes the financial statement disclosure data of three actual companies. In each case, we give a brief profile of the company and selected disclosure data from a recent annual report to stockholders, followed by questions relating to certain accounting principles and practices discussed thus far in the text.

(I) COLLINS FOODS INTERNATIONAL, INC.

PROFILE

Collins Foods International, Inc., is one of the largest franchisees of Kentucky Fried Chicken Corporation, the majority stockholder of Sizzler Restaurants International, Inc., and owner of Collins Foodservice, a wholesale distribution business. At April 30, 1985, total assets amounted to $264.5 million and total sales for the year then ended were $589.8 million. The firm has been publicly held since 1968 and its common stock is currently traded on the New York Stock Exchange and the Pacific Stock Exchange.

DISCLOSURE DATA (from Notes to Consolidated Financial Statements)

Stock Splits

On November 16, 1984, the Company effected a three-for-two stock split. All data regarding common shares, common equivalents, options, warrants, and per share amounts have been restated to reflect the effects of the split.

REQUIRED

(a) There are two ways a corporation may increase its outstanding common stock by 50%: (1) implement a formal three-for-two stock split or (2) declare and distribute a 50% stock dividend. What is the difference in the accounting analysis for a formal three-for-two stock split compared with the analysis for a 50% stock dividend?

(b) Collins' analysis of its stockholders' equity accounts for the year ended April 30, 1985, shows that the three-for-two stock split was recorded by debiting Retained Earnings and crediting Common Stock for $438,000. Was Collins' three-for-two stock split a formal stock split or was it a 50% stock dividend? Briefly explain.

DISCLOSURE DATA (from Notes to Consolidated Financial Statements)

Principles of Consolidation

The consolidated financial statements include the accounts of Collins Foods International, Inc., and all domestic and foreign subsidiaries (the "Company"). The Company's investment in unconsolidated joint ventures are accounted for by the equity method (see below). Minority interest in the net income of Sizzler Restaurants International, Inc., is shown in the consolidated statements of income under the caption "Minority Interest." All significant intercompany accounts and transactions have been eliminated in consolidation.

Minority Interest

Sizzler Restaurants International, Inc. ("Sizzler"), a public company, is a 70 percent owned subsidiary of the Company.

Investments in Unconsolidated Joint Ventures

The Company's investments in unconsolidated joint ventures, which are accounted for under the equity method, consist primarily of interest in four oil and gas ventures. They include a 99 percent working interest in Devon–Collins, Ltd., a limited partnership between the Company and Devon Energy Corp., a 22 percent interest in a joint venture with Nance Petroleum Corporation and a 50 percent interest in a joint venture with Whitmar Exploration Company.

REQUIRED

(c) Why is the 99 percent interest in Devon–Collins, Ltd., accounted for by the equity method and not consolidated with the Collins' financial statements, while Sizzler Restaurants International, Inc., a 70 percent owned company, is consolidated?

(d) In the firm's consolidated income statement for the year ended April 30, 1985, the minority interest in the net income of Sizzler Restaurants International, Inc., was shown at $3,002,000. What was the net income of this subsidiary for the year ended April 30, 1985?

(e) In the firm's consolidated balance sheet at April 30, 1985, the minority interest in Sizzler Restaurants International, Inc., was shown at $17,831,000. What was the total common shareholders' equity of Sizzler at April 30, 1985?

(II) ZAYRE CORP.

PROFILE

Zayre Corp. is a leading operator of self-service discount department stores and off-price specialty shops located primarily in the eastern half of the United States. Its three major divisions are Zayre Stores (290 general merchandise discount department stores), T.J. Maxx (156 apparel "supermarts" marketing off-price, brand-name family apparel), and Hit or Miss (401 shops selling off-price apparel for women). At January 26, 1985, total assets exceeded $1.1 billion and sales for the year ended January 26, 1985, exceeded $3.1 billion.

DISCLOSURE DATA (from consolidated financial statements)

Analysis of Retained Earnings (amounts in thousands)

Balance, January 28, 1984	$230,433
Net income	80,316
Cash dividends on common stock	(7,729)
10% common stock dividend	(59,360)
Balance, January 26, 1985	$243,660

REQUIRED

(a) Zayre's common stock is $1 par value stock. On January 24, 1984, the company had 17,953,297 common shares outstanding. Prepare journal entries to reflect (1) Zayre's declaration of a 10% common stock dividend during the year ended January 26, 1985, and (2) the distribution of the stock dividend to shareholders (round entries to the nearest dollar).

(b) In addition to the 10% common stock dividend, other events increased outstanding common stock by another 31,354 shares during the year ended January 26, 1985. What is the per share amount of the cash dividend declared and paid by Zayre for the year ended January 26, 1985?

(III) LA-Z-BOY CHAIR COMPANY

PROFILE
La-Z-Boy Chair Company is a manufacturer of residential upholstered furniture and office furniture. La-Z-Boy is a widely recognized name in reclining and motion furniture. La-Z-Boy products are manufactured in eight United States plants and one Canadian plant. Total assets at April 27, 1985, exceeded $193 million and sales for the year then ended were over $282 million.
DISCLOSURE DATA (from consolidated balance sheets and income statements)

Balance Sheet	**April 27, 1985**	**April 28, 1984**
Shareholders' Equity		
Common Shares, $1.00 par value, authorized—20,000,000 in 1985 and 1984; issued—4,660,185	$ 4,660,185	$ 4,660,185
Capital in excess of par value	5,514,340	5,540,441
Retained earnings	122,335,619	106,843,050
Currency translation adjustments	(654,512)	(271,286)
	$131,855,632	$116,772,390
Less: Treasury shares, at cost (91,510 in 1985 and 14,355 in 1984)	2,361,265	153,973
Total shareholders' equity	$129,494,367	$116,618,417

Income Statement Year Ended	*April 27, 1985*	*April 28, 1984*
Net income for the year	$21,358,949	$23,285,286
Weighted average number of shares outstanding	4,574,424	4,639,884
Net income per share	$4.67	$5.02

REQUIRED
La-Z-Boy had no change in its common shares issued from the end of fiscal 1984 to the end of fiscal 1985. Why is the weighted average number of shares outstanding less for fiscal 1985 than it is for fiscal 1984?

APPENDIX B

ACCOUNTING FOR BRANCHES

Many business firms expand by opening new outlets, or **branches**, at different locations. The development of suburban shopping centers has provided the impetus for branch marketing of goods and services by many firms, especially retail stores, banks, and savings and loan companies. Both wholesale and retail merchandising companies have expanded their marketing territories through widespread branch operations.

Typically, the various branches offer the same goods or services and follow fairly standardized operations. A manager appointed for each branch normally is responsible for that outlet's profitability. From a managerial viewpoint, each branch is an accounting entity, even though branches are usually segments of a single legal entity—a corporation, partnership, or sole proprietorship. The principal outlet, from which the firm's activities are normally directed, is often referred to as the **home office.**

Generally, merchandising policies, advertising, and promotion are directed or heavily influenced by the home office. Although branches may be given some latitude in acquiring merchandise, often the major portion of goods is purchased centrally.

The accounting system for branch operations should furnish management with complete and timely information to measure branch profitability. The size and complexity of branch operations, geographic location, and degree of autonomy, among other things, may influence the type of accounting system adopted. Most systems, however, are variations of two basic schemes—centralized accounting by the home office and decentralized accounting by the branch.

CENTRALIZED BRANCH RECORDS

Under a **centralized** accounting system, the home office maintains most of the records needed to account for branch operations. Thus, separate asset, liability, revenue, and expense records for each branch are maintained at the home office. Typically, cash is transferred to the branch to establish a working fund for small disbursements. This fund is ordinarily kept on an imprest basis (like a petty cash fund) and replenished regularly by the home office on the basis of expense vouchers or summaries submitted by the branch. A branch that collects any amounts in its operations must often deposit such amounts in a home office bank account and transmit deposit slips and lists of the remittances to the home office for recording. The branch also transmits other documents such as copies of sales invoices and credit memos to the home office for recording. The data needed to record branch transactions may be transmitted by a telecommunication or similar device, with the documents forwarded periodically. In some cases, the documents may be filed at the branch, with periodic audits by either home office auditors or independent accountants.

DECENTRALIZED BRANCH RECORDS

Under a **decentralized** accounting system, each branch ordinarily maintains a comprehensive set of accounting records for its operations and forwards periodic financial statements to the home office. Normally, the forms of the records and statements are standardized for all branches, so that they may be conveniently analyzed by the home office and integrated into the financial reports of the whole organization. Emphasis is often placed on the operating, or income statement, accounts. Also, the branch may keep accounts for current assets—such as cash, accounts receivable, and inventory—but the home office may retain the accounts for equipment, fixtures, and accumulated depreciation.

In place of owners' equity accounts, the branch has an account called **Home Office,** which represents amounts of advances or assets received from the home office plus accumulated branch earnings not transferred to the home office. A reciprocal account called **Branch Office** is maintained in the ledger of the home office. When both accounts are posted and up to date, the dollar balances should be identical.

From the branch's viewpoint, the Home Office account may be regarded as either a capital account or a liability. Likewise, the Branch Office balance on the books of the home office may be viewed either as an investment or as a receivable. The classification of these accounts is not especially important; the branch is only an accounting segment, and when its accounts are combined with those of the home office, the balances of these two accounts offset each other and do not appear in the combined financial statements.

ILLUSTRATION OF DECENTRALIZED ACCOUNTING

Assume that on May 1 of the current year the Foto-Art Company, retailer of photographic equipment, opened its Western Branch in another city, leasing the store facilities and fixtures. The home office transferred $20,000 cash and $40,000 in merchandise to the branch to begin operations. The following entries record the transfer establishing the branch:

Home Office Records			Western Branch Records		
Western Branch	60,000		Cash	20,000	
Cash		20,000	Shipments from Home Office	40,000	
Shipments to Western Branch		40,000	Home Office		60,000

This entry established the investment in the branch (or receivable from the branch) for the amount of cash and merchandise advanced to the new outlet. The $60,000 amount shown in Western Branch's reciprocal account equals the amount of capital received from the home office.

Generally, merchandise shipped from the home office to the branch should be differentiated from branch acquisitions purchased from outsiders. Therefore, a Shipments to Branch account is credited on the home office records, and a Shipments from Home Office account is debited on the branch records whenever the home office transfers merchandise to the branch. On the home office records, the Shipments to Branch account can be considered a contra account to the Purchases account. On the branch records, the Shipments from Home Office debit balance can be considered a purchases amount. When the branch closes its books, it closes the Shipments from Home Office account to the Income Summary account. Likewise, the home office closes the Shipments to Branch balance to its own Income Summary account.

The following transactions, including the asset transfer establishing the branch, are shown in summary form:

Summary of May Transactions	Home Office Records			Western Branch Records		
(1) Home office opened Western Branch, transferring $20,000 cash and $40,000 merchandise.	Western Branch	60,000		Cash	20,000	
	Cash		20,000	Shipments from Home Office	40,000	
	Shipments to Western Branch		40,000	Home Office		60,000
(2) Purchased $15,000 merchandise from outsiders.				Purchases	15,000	
				Accounts Payable		15,000
(3) Sold merchandise on account for $30,000				Accounts Receivable	30,000	
				Sales		30,000
(4) Incurred $5,000 selling expenses and $3,000 general expenses; of the total, $2,000 was on account.				Selling Expenses	5,000	
				General Expenses	3,000	
				Cash		6,000
				Accounts Payable		2,000
(5) Collected $24,000 on account from customers.				Cash	24,000	
				Accounts Receivable		24,000

EXHIBIT B–1

Foto-Art Company
Western Branch
Trial Balance
May 31, 19XX

	Debit	Credit
Cash	$16,000	
Accounts Receivable	6,000	
Home Office		$51,000
Accounts Payable		5,000
Sales		30,000
Purchases	15,000	
Shipments from Home Office	40,000	
Selling Expenses	5,000	
General Expenses	4,000	
	$86,000	$86,000

(6) Paid $12,000 to creditors on account.				Accounts Payable	12,000	
				Cash		12,000
(7) Sent $10,000 cash to home office.	Cash	10,000		Home Office	10,000	
	Western Branch		10,000	Cash		10,000
(8) Attributed $1,000 home office general expenses to Western Branch.	Western Branch	1,000		General Expenses	1,000	
	General Expenses		1,000	Home Office		1,000

After the foregoing entries have been posted to Western Branch's ledger, the trial balance for the branch would appear as shown in Exhibit B–1.

Western Branch next records any necessary end-of-period adjustments in the usual fashion. For the sake of simplicity, we assume that none are needed.

BRANCH FINANCIAL STATEMENTS

After the branch has recorded any necessary adjusting entries, financial statements can be prepared. Exhibits B–2 and B–3 show the May income statement and the May 31 balance sheet for Western Branch. Note in the balance sheet that the net income for the period is added to the balance of the Home Office account. Actually, the branch's net income would be closed to the Home Office account at the end of the accounting period, as shown later in the closing entries.

EXHIBIT B–2

Foto-Art Company
Western Branch
Income Statement
For the Month of May, 19XX

Sales		$30,000
Cost of Goods Sold:		
Beginning Inventory	—	
Purchases	$15,000	
Shipment from Home Office	40,000	
Goods Available for Sale	$55,000	
Less: Ending Inventory	37,000	
Cost of Goods Sold		18,000
Gross Profit on Sales		$12,000
Operating Expenses:		
Selling Expenses	$ 5,000	
General Expenses	4,000	
Total Operating Expenses		9,000
Net Income		$ 3,000

EXHIBIT B–3

Foto-Art Company
Western Branch
Balance Sheet
May 31, 19XX

Assets		Liabilities and Home Office Equity		
Cash	$16,000	Accounts Payable		$ 5,000
Accounts Receivable	6,000	Home Office	$51,000	
Inventory	37,000	Net Income	3,000	54,000
	$59,000			$59,000

COMBINED FINANCIAL STATEMENTS

At the end of the accounting period, the various branches submit their financial statements (or alternatively, adjusted trial balances) to the home office, which combines the data into a single set of statements for the whole enterprise. The worksheets in Exhibit B–4 provide a convenient vehicle for compiling and inte-

EXHIBIT B–4

Foto-Art Company
Home Office and Western Branch
Income Statement Worksheet
For the Month of May, 19XX

	Home Office	Western Branch	Eliminations	Combined Income Statement
Sales	$65,000	$30,000		$95,000
Cost of Goods Sold:				
Inventory, May 1	$38,000	—		$ 38,000
Purchases	70,000	$15,000		85,000
Shipments to Branch	(40,000)		$40,000	
Shipments from Home Office		40,000	(40,000)	
Goods Available for Sale	$68,000	$55,000		$123,000
Less: Inventory, May 31	28,000	37,000		65,000
Cost of Goods Sold	$40,000	$18,000		$ 58,000
Gross Profit on Sales	$25,000	$12,000		$ 37,000
Operating Expenses:				
Selling Expenses	$9,000	$5,000		$14,000
General Expenses	7,000	4,000		11,000
Total Operating Expenses	$16,000	$ 9,000		$ 25,000
Net Income	$ 9,000	$ 3,000		$ 12,000

Foto-Art Company
Home Office and Western Branch
Balance Sheet Worksheet
May 31, 19XX

	Home Office	Western Branch	Eliminations	Combined Balance Sheet
Assets				
Cash	$ 20,000	$16,000		$ 36,000
Accounts Receivable	36,000	6,000		42,000
Inventory	28,000	37,000		65,000
Western Branch	54,000		($54,000)	
Plant Assets, Net of Accumulated Depreciation	80,000			80,000
Total Assets	$218,000	$59,000	($54,000)	$223,000
Liabilities and Stockholders' Equity				
Accounts Payable	$ 18,000	$ 5,000		$ 23,000
Accrued Liabilities	2,000			2,000
Home Office		54,000	($54,000)	
Common Stock	150,000			150,000
Retained Earnings	48,000			48,000
Total Liabilities and Stockholders' Equity	$218,000	$59,000	($54,000)	$223,000

grating the data for the company. In the illustration, the data for home office operations are assumed. Note that the reciprocal amounts of $40,000 representing shipments from the home office to the branch are eliminated and the accounts do not appear in the combined income statement. Likewise, the home office and branch office accounts, with $54,000 balances, are eliminated when the combined balance sheet is prepared.

CLOSING ENTRIES

After financial statements are prepared, the following closing entries are recorded by the branch:

May 31	Income Summary	64,000	
	Purchases		15,000
	Shipments from Home Office		40,000
	Selling Expenses		5,000
	General Expenses		4,000
	To close income statement accounts with debit balances.		
31	Inventory	37,000	
	Sales	30,000	
	Income Summary		67,000
	To record the ending inventory and to close income statement account with credit balance.		
31	Income Summary	3,000	
	Home Office		3,000
	To close the Income Summary account to the Home Office account.		

On May 31, the home office reflects the branch net income by making a corollary entry to the last entry shown above:

May 31	Western Branch	3,000	
	Net Income—Western Branch		3,000
	To reflect net income of Western Branch.		

In closing its records, the home office closes the Net Income—Western Branch account to its Income Summary account.

PROBLEMS

Entries to Home Office account by branch

B–1 Midtown Branch had a beginning balance of $28,000 in its Home Office account. During the current month, Midtown received $40,000 in merchandise shipments from the home office. At month-end, the branch's share of home office general expenses was $3,800. After closing its records, Midtown Branch determined its net income as $21,500. The branch then sent $15,000 cash to the home office.

REQUIRED

(a) Give the branch's journal entry made on receiving the $40,000 in merchandise from the home office.

(b) What amount would be in the Home Office account after all entries were posted for the current month?

Entries on branch and home office records

B–2 Bradley Branch of Harding Tax Service, which has decentralized accounting records, opened on July 1 of the current year and had the following July transactions:

July	1	The home office transferred $9,000 cash and $20,000 in equipment to the branch.
	15	The branch collected $8,000 service fees.
	20	The branch paid $5,200 in operating expenses.
	30	The home office allocated $2,200 of home office general expenses to the branch. (Debit Operating Expenses for branch.)
	31	The branch collected $6,500 service fees and sent $8,000 cash to the home office.
	31	The branch recorded depreciation on equipment, $100. (Debit Operating Expenses.)
	31	The branch made the appropriate entries to close the books at the end of July. The branch has one revenue account (Fee Revenue) and one expense account (Operating Expenses).
	31	The branch reported its net income of $7,000 to the home office.

REQUIRED

Journalize the foregoing entries on the branch books and on the home office books.

Entries on branch and home office records

B–3 Forbes, Inc., which operates a large music store in Chicago, arranged in May of the current year to open a branch in Rockford. Record keeping for the branch is decentralized. A summary of the branch's transactions for May is given below:

May	1	The Chicago store transferred $50,000 cash and $75,000 in mechandise to the Rockford branch.
	3	Purchased $36,000 in merchandise on account from various dealers.
	10	Paid $15,000 on accounts payable.
	15	Sales to date: cash, $11,000; on account $14,000.
	18	Collected $7,200 on account from customers.
	20	Selling expenses for the branch were $8,000 and general expenses were $4,500; of the total, $1,500 was on account and the remainder paid in cash.

May 25 Sent $15,000 cash to the Chicago store.
30 Sales during the last half of the month: cash, $12,000; on account, $16,000.

REQUIRED
(a) Journalize the May transactions on the books of the Rockford branch.
(b) Make the necessary closing entries on the Rockford branch records, assuming that the May 31 inventory is $81,000.
(c) Journalize the May transactions requiring entries on the books of the Chicago home office, including the entry to record the branch's net income.
(d) State the May 31 Home Office account balance in the Rockford branch's ledger.

Reconciling Branch account with Home Office account

B–4 The reciprocal accounts of the home office and branch operations of Ryan Specialty Stores as they appear near the end of the accounting year are shown below.

Branch Account (Home Office Records)

Date		Description	Debit	Credit	Balance
Nov.	30	Balance			52,600
Dec.	5	Merchandise shipped	14,600		67,200
	28	Equipment sent	1,500		68,700

Home Office (Branch Records)

Date		Description	Debit	Credit	Balance
Nov.	30	Balance			52,600
Dec.	5	Merchandise received		16,400	69,000
	31	Net income		8,600	77,600
	31	Cash remitted	7,000		69,600

REQUIRED
(a) Review these accounts in terms of any needed updating and the appropriateness of their ending balances. If you discover any apparent bookkeeping errors, assume that the home office records are correct. Prepare any needed adjusting journal entries.
(b) Prepare a brief analysis leading to what you consider to be the correct year-end balances for these accounts.
(c) What eliminating entry would be appropriate on a worksheet used to prepare combined balance sheets for the home office and the branch?

Entries on branch and home office records

B–5 Ross, Inc., operates a store selling men's shoes, hosiery, and other men's furnishings in Houston. The firm opened a branch in Austin on June 1 of the current year. A summary of the branch's June transactions follows:

June 1 Received $40,000 cash and $80,000 merchandise from the home office in Houston.

June 12 Purchased $28,000 merchandise on account from various dealers.
15 Sales to date: cash, $16,000; on account, $19,000.
19 Collected $8,600 on account from customers.
21 Paid $15,000 on accounts payable.
25 Selling expenses for the branch were $14,500 and general expenses were $3,800; of the total, $6,500 was on account and the remainder paid in cash.
26 The home office informed the Austin branch that $2,200 home office general expense was allocated to the branch.
30 Sales during the last half of the month: cash: $18,000; on account, $11,000.

REQUIRED

(a) Journalize the June transactions on the Austin branch's books.
(b) Make the necessary closing entries on the Austin branch's records, assuming that the June 30 inventory is $72,000.
(c) Journalize the June transactions requiring entries on the home office's books, including the entry to record the branch's net income.
(d) Prepare an analysis of the June 30 balance in the Home Office account in the Austin branch's ledger.

APPENDIX C

INTERNATIONAL ACCOUNTING

WORLD TRADE AND MULTINATIONAL CORPORATIONS

The market today for consumer and capital goods is truly a world market. An individual in the United States, for example, may drink Brazilian coffee, jog in West German running shoes, drive a Japanese automobile, snack on a Swiss chocolate bar, and enjoy English records played on a stereo system with Danish components.

United States export and import levels indicate the extensive involvement of U.S. firms in international trade. Annual merchandise exports and imports each amount to several hundred billions of dollars. In 1984, the combined exports of the nation's 50 largest industrial exporters topped $64 billion. Indeed, the four largest industrial exporters—General Motors, Ford Motor, General Electric, and Boeing—had combined exports exceeding $20 billion.[1]

As world trade has grown, so have the number and size of multinational corporations. A **multinational corporation** conducts operations in more than one country by locating branches, divisions, or subsidiaries outside its home country. Exxon Corporation, for example, has divisions and affiliated companies operating in the United States and over 80 other countries. Exhibit C–1 lists the ten largest U.S. multinational corporations in 1984.

[1]"The 50 Leading Exporters," *Fortune*, August 5, 1985, p. 60–1.

EXHIBIT C–1
Ten Largest U.S. Multinationals in 1984

Rank	Company	Foreign Revenue (millions)	Foreign Assets (millions)
1	Exxon	$63,042	$27,198
2	Mobil	31,900	17,249
3	Texaco	23,729	11,372
4	Chevron	20,964	13,757
5	IBM	18,536	15,464
6	Phibro-Salomon	17,300	5,300
7	Ford Motor	15,578	13,022
8	General Motors	14,534	11,065
9	EI du Pont de Nemours	11,429	6,984
10	Citicorp	10,200	76,642

Source: *Forbes*, July 29, 1985.

The existence of world markets and U.S. multinational corporations impacts on accounting because currencies other than the U.S. dollar are involved in accounting transactions. Financial data stated in a foreign currency must be converted to U.S. dollars. We explain two basic conversion situations in this appendix: (1) the translation of foreign currency transactions, and (2) the conversion of foreign currency financial statements. Before examining these situations, however, we consider foreign currency exchange rates.

FOREIGN CURRENCY EXCHANGE RATES

Exchange rates are used to convert one currency into a different currency. An **exchange rate** states the price, in terms of one currency, at which one unit of another currency may be bought or sold. Because our focus is on accounting in U.S. dollars, we express foreign currency exchange rates in terms of the U.S. dollar.

Exhibit C–2 presents exchange rates for several foreign currencies. The exhibit shows, for example, that one Canadian dollar converts to $0.7194; that is, it takes $0.7194 to purchase one Canadian dollar. Similarly, one British pound converts to $1.529, or it takes $1.529 to purchase one British pound. Currencies are bought and sold like other goods. Thus, a currency's price (its exchange rate) is determined by the supply and demand for that currency. Exchange rates change frequently so the rates in Exhibit C–2 (which are for a particular date) are illustrative only. Current exchange rates, no doubt, are different.

EXHIBIT C–2
Exchange Rates with the U.S Dollar

Country	Currency Unit	Price of One Unit in U.S. Dollars
Brazil	Cruzado	$0.07241
Canada	Dollar	0.7194
Denmark	Krone	0.1217
France	Franc	0.1416
Great Britain	Pound	1.5290
Italy	Lira	0.0006566
Japan	Yen	0.005708
Netherlands	Guilder	0.3986
Switzerland	Franc	0.5420
West Germany	Deutsche Mark	0.4509

Source: *Wall Street Journal*, April 18, 1986.

TRANSLATION OF FOREIGN CURRENCY TRANSACTIONS

Transactions a U.S. business may have with a foreign entity include the purchase or sale of goods and the borrowing or lending of funds. A transaction is a **foreign currency transaction** if it is *denominated* in a foreign currency; that is, if its terms are fixed in the amount of foreign currency to be paid or received. A steel purchase from a Japanese firm requiring payment of a fixed number of yen is a foreign currency transaction. Similarly, an export sale to an English enterprise that requires settlement in a fixed number of British pounds is a foreign currency transaction.

Accounting at Transaction Date

A U.S. firm keeps its financial records in U.S. dollars. All foreign currency transactions, therefore, must be translated into U.S. dollars so they may be properly recorded. When journalized, each transaction component is translated into U.S. dollars using the exchange rate at the transaction date.

To illustrate, assume a U.S. firm purchases merchandise on account from a Canadian firm on June 1, 19X1. The cost is 10,000 Canadian dollars (C$). Payment is due in 30 days. The exchange rate for Canadian dollars on June 1 is $0.80. Using the June 1 exchange rate, the U.S. firm translates the C$10,000 to $8,000 (C$10,000 × $0.80) and makes the following entry:

June 1	Purchases	8,000	
	Accounts Payable		8,000
	To record purchase of merchandise on account (C$10,000 × $0.80 = $8,000).		

Accounting at Settlement Date

Exchange rates may change before the settlement date for a foreign currency payable or receivable. Should this occur, a **foreign exchange gain or loss** is recorded at the settlement date. The foreign exchange gain or loss measures the change in the U.S. dollar equivalent required to settle the transaction. Foreign exchange gains and losses are reported in the income statement. A company experiencing both foreign exchange gains and foreign exchange losses during the same period may combine them and report a net foreign exchange gain or loss in its income statement.

We continue our previous example. Assume on July 1, the U.S company settles its account payable with the Canadian firm. The exchange rate on July 1 is $0.78. On July 1, it costs the U.S. firm $7,800 to purchase the 10,000 Canadian dollars needed to settle the account. The exchange rate decline creates a $200 foreign exchange gain ($8,000 − $7,800) for the U.S. firm. The July 1 settlement is recorded as follows:

July 1	Accounts Payable	8,000	
	Cash		7,800
	Foreign Exchange Gain		200
	To record payment of account payable (C$10,000 × $0.78 = $7,800) and foreign exchange gain.		

Unsettled Foreign Currency Transactions

Foreign currency receivables and payables that are not settled at a balance sheet date are adjusted to reflect the exchange rate at that date. Such adjustments place foreign exchange gains and losses in the period when exchange rates change. Any foreign exchange gain or loss at the settlement date, then, relates only to exchange rate changes since the latest balance sheet date.

To illustrate, assume on December 15, 19X1, our U.S. firm purchases more merchandise on 30-day account from the Canadian firm. The merchandise costs 15,000 Canadian dollars. The U.S. firm's accounting period ends on December 31, 19X1. The account payable is settled on January 14, 19X2. Exchange rates for the Canadian dollar are:

December 15	$0.77
December 31	0.79
January 14	0.76

The U.S. firm accounts for this foreign currency transaction as follows:

Dec. 15	Purchases	11,550	
	Accounts Payable		11,550
	To record purchase of merchandise on account (C$15,000 × $0.77 = $11,550).		

Dec. 31	Foreign Exchange Loss	300	
	Accounts Payable		300
	To adjust accounts payable to current exchange rate (C$15,000 × $0.79 = $11,850; $11,850 − $11,550 = $300) and record foreign exchange loss.		
Jan. 14	Accounts Payable	11,850	
	Cash		11,400
	Foreign Exchange Gain		450
	To record payment of account payable (C$15,000 × $0.76 = $11,400) and foreign exchange gain.		

On December 31, 19X1, a $300 foreign exchange loss is recorded to reflect the impact of the strengthening of the Canadian dollar between December 15 and December 31. Because the account payable is not settled on this date, the loss is unrealized. It is included, however, in the 19X1 income statement. The account payable is settled on January 14, 19X2. The Canadian dollar has weakened since December 31, 19X1, so a $450 foreign exchange gain is recorded and included in the 19X2 income statement.

Transactions Denominated in U.S. Currency

A U.S. firm's transactions with foreign entities that are denominated in U.S. dollars are *not* foreign currency transactions. No translation is required (the transaction is initially stated in U.S. dollars) and no foreign exchange gains or losses develop. For example, assume a U.S. firm sells merchandise to a Swiss firm on account. The sales price is $6,000 U.S. dollars, due in 30 days. Because the transaction is denominated in U.S. dollars, the U.S. firm accounts for the transaction no differently than if the customer was in the United States. The Swiss firm, in contrast, must translate its foreign currency transaction into Swiss francs and faces gains and losses from exchange rate changes.

CONVERSION OF FOREIGN CURRENCY FINANCIAL STATEMENTS

U.S. multinational corporations frequently use foreign subsidiary companies to conduct their foreign activities. If the foreign subsidiary is more than 50% owned, its financial statements are usually consolidated with the U.S. parent's statements. Of course, when the subsidiary's accounting records are kept in the foreign currency, its financial statements must be converted to U.S. dollars before consolidation can occur.

There are two different procedures that may be used to convert foreign financial statements to U.S. dollars:

(1) Translation procedures.

(2) Remeasurement procedures.

The **functional currency** of a foreign subsidiary determines which of these two procedures is used. As defined by the Financial Accounting Standards Board:

> An entity's functional currency is the currency of the primary economic environment in which the entity operates; normally, that is the currency of the environment in which an entity primarily generates and expends cash.[2]

Depending on the circumstances, the functional currency may be either the foreign currency or the U.S. dollar. For example, a West German subsidiary manufactures and sells its own products. Its expenses as well as cash generated by its operations are primarily in deutsche marks and have little impact on its parent's cash flows. This subsidiary's operations are well integrated with the West German economy. Thus, its functional currency is the foreign currency (deutsche mark). In contrast, consider a West German subsidiary that is a sales outlet for its U.S. parent's goods. The subsidiary takes orders, bills and collects the invoice price, warehouses the goods to facilitate delivery, and remits its net cash flows primarily to the parent. This subsidiary is essentially an agent for the parent company. Its functional currency would be the U.S. dollar.

The functional currency is also the U.S. dollar for foreign subsidiaries that operate in highly inflationary economies (economies whose cumulative inflation over a three-year period is approximately 100 percent or more). The U.S. dollar is deemed the functional currency because it is the more stable currency; the foreign currency is too unstable. Argentina and Israel are recent examples of countries whose three-year cumulative inflation exceeds 100 percent.

Once the functional currency is determined, the specific conversion procedures are selected as follows:

(1) Foreign currency is functional currency—use translation procedures.

(2) U.S. dollar is functional currency—use remeasurement procedures.

To illustrate these two procedures for converting foreign financial statements to U.S. dollars, we assume Wyso Company was organized in West Germany on January 1, 19X1, as a wholly-owned subsidiary of Minor Corporation, a U.S. company. Wyso's opening balance sheet, in West German deutsche marks (DM), consisted of the following assets and stockholders' equity:

Assets		**Stockholders' Equity**	
Cash	DM 40,000	Common Stock	DM800,000
Inventory	160,000		
Plant Assets	600,000		
Total	DM800,000		

Wyso's 19X1 income statement and December 31, 19X1, balance sheet, in deutsche marks, follow.

[2]*Statement of Financial Accounting Standards No. 52*, "Foreign Currency Translation" (Stamford, CT: Financial Accounting Standards Board, 1981), p. 3.

Wyso Company
Income Statement
For the Year Ended December 31, 19X1

Sales		DM750,000
Cost of Goods Sold	DM500,000	
Depreciation Expense	30,000	
Other Expenses	70,000	
Total Expenses		600,000
Net Income		DM150,000

Wyso Company
Balance Sheet
December 31, 19X1

Assets		**Liabilities**		
Cash	DM 60,000	Accounts Payable		DM 30,000
Accounts Receivable (net)	140,000	**Stockholders' Equity**		
Inventory	210,000	Common Stock	DM800,000	
Plant Assets (net)	570,000	Retained Earnings	150,000	950,000
Total Assets	DM980,000	Total Liabilities and Stockholders' Equity		DM980,000

Exchange rates for the deutsche mark are:

January 1, 19X1	$0.48
Average for 19X1	0.44
December 31, 19X1	0.40

Translation Procedures

Assume Wyso Company's operations are fully integrated with West Germany's economy. Thus, its functional currency is the deutsche mark and translation procedures are used. **Translation procedures** convert foreign financial statements to U.S. dollars as follows:

(1) All asset and liability accounts are converted using the exchange rate at the balance sheet date (current rate).

(2) Capital stock accounts are converted using the exchange rate on the date the stock was issued (historical rate).

(3) All revenue and expense accounts are converted using the exchange rate at the date these items were recognized. If revenue and expenses are generated in a relatively uniform pattern during the year, an average exchange rate for the year may be used (average rate).

The purpose of these translation procedures is to retain, in the converted data, the financial results and relationships among assets and liabilities that were created by the subsidiary's operation in its foreign environment.

Exhibit C–3 shows these translation procedures applied to Wyso Company's financial statements. Note the $70,000 **translation adjustment** in the exhibit, shown as a reduction of stockholders' equity in U.S. dollars. Translation procedures create a translation adjustment. The translation adjustment balances the balance sheet and arises because the same exchange rate is not used to convert all accounts. The $70,000 may be calculated as:

Common stock × (historical rate − current rate)	
DM800,000 × ($0.48 − $0.40) =	$64,000
Net income × (average rate − current rate)	
DM150,000 × ($0.44 − $0.40) =	6,000
Translation adjustment	$70,000

The translation adjustment is reported as a separate component of stockholders' equity. Depending on the direction of exchange rate changes, it may reduce stockholders' equity (as in our illustration) or increase stockholders' equity.

EXHIBIT C–3
Translation of Wyso Company Financial Statements
December 31, 19X1
Deutsche Mark = Functional Currency

	Deutsche Marks	Exchange Rate	U.S. Dollars
Balance Sheet			
Cash	DM 60,000	$0.40	$ 24,000
Accounts Receivable (net)	140,000	0.40	56,000
Inventory	210,000	0.40	84,000
Plant Assets (net)	570,000	0.40	228,000
Total	DM980,000		$392,000
Accounts Payable	DM 30,000	0.40	$ 12,000
Common Stock	800,000	0.48	384,000
Retained Earnings	150,000	See Net Income	66,000
Translation Ajustment			(70,000)
Total	DM980,000		$392,000
Income Statement			
Sales	DM750,000	$0.44	$330,000
Cost of Goods Sold	DM500,000	0.44	$220,000
Depreciation Expense	30,000	0.44	13,200
Other Expenses	70,000	0.44	30,800
Total Expenses	DM600,000		$264,000
Net Income	DM150,000		$ 66,000

Remeasurement Procedures

Now assume Wyso Company's operations are essentially a direct extension of Minor Corporation's (the parent) activities. In this circumstance, Wyso's functional currency is the U.S. dollar and remeasurement procedures are used. **Remeasurement procedures** convert foreign financial statements to U.S. dollars as follows:

(1) Monetary asset and liability accounts (basically all cash, receivables, and payables) are converted using the exchange rate at the balance sheet date (current rate).

(2) All other balance sheet accounts are converted using the exchange rate in effect when the item was initially recorded on the books (historical rate).

(3) Revenue and expense accounts are converted using the exchange rate related to the transaction. Generally, the average exchange rate for the period is used. However, expenses that relate to assets converted at historical rates are converted at the appropriate historical rate. Depreciation expense and cost of goods sold are in this latter category.

The objective of these remeasurement procedures is to produce the same U.S. dollar financial statements as if the foriegn entity's accounting records had been initially maintained in the U.S. dollar.

Exhibit C–4 shows these remeasurement procedures applied to Wyso Company's financial statements. Schedule A in the exhibit details the remeasurement of cost of goods sold, which requires converting the beginning inventory, purchases, and ending inventory at historical exchange rates. The average rate for the year ($0.44) applies to the purchases of DM550,000 while a rate of $0.42 applies to the ending inventory (the average exchange rate during the latter part of the year when the ending inventory was acquired). Also, note the $8,400 foreign exchange loss among the income statement expenses in U.S. dollars.[3] Remeasurement procedures produce foreign exchange gains or losses—the effects on assets and liabilities of exchange rate changes. These foreign exchange gains and losses are included in net income.

Generally Accepted Accounting Principles

At present, there are no international accounting principles that are broadly accepted and enforced. Accounting principles vary among countries because legal, economic, and regulatory systems differ, as well as social values and traditions. Foreign company financial statements, therefore, may vary in some respects from U.S. generally accepted accounting principles. If they do, the statements must be changed to conform to U.S. generally accepted accounting principles before the conversion to U.S. dollars may occur.

[3]The $8,400 foreign exchange loss in our illustration is the amount needed to obtain a $36,800 net income. When transferred to retained earnings, the $36,800 balances the balance sheet.

EXHIBIT C–4
Remeasurement of Wyso Company Financial Statements
December 31, 19X1
U.S. Dollar = Functional Currency

	Deutsche Marks	Exchange Rate	U.S. Dollars
Balance Sheet			
Cash	DM 60,000	$0.40	$ 24,000
Accounts Receivable (net)	140,000	0.40	56,000
Inventory	210,000	0.42	88,200
Plant Assets (net)	570,000	0.48	273,600
Total	DM980,000		$441,800
Accounts Payable	DM 30,000	0.40	$ 12,000
Common Stock	800,000	0.48	384,000
Retained Earnings	150,000	Set Net Income	45,800
Total	DM980,000		$441,800
Income Statement			
Sales	DM750,000	0.44	$330,000
Cost of Goods Sold	DM500,000	See Schedule A	$230,600
Depreciation Expense	30,000	0.48	14,400
Other Expenses	70,000	0.44	30,800
Foreign Exchange Loss			8,400
Total Expenses	DM600,000		$284,200
Net Income	DM150,000		$ 45,800
Schedule A			
Inventory (beginning)	DM160,000	0.48	$ 76,800
Purchases	550,000	0.44	242,000
	DM710,000		$318,800
Inventory (ending)	210,000	0.42	88,200
Cost of Goods Sold	DM500,000		$230,600

PROBLEMS

Translation of foreign currency transactions

C–1 On June 18, 19X3, Drexel, Inc., a U.S. company, purchased merchandise on account from Seine Company, a French firm. The merchandise cost was 85,000 French francs. Drexel paid the amount due (in francs) on July 10, 19X3. Drexel's fiscal year ends on June 30. Exchange rates for the French franc were:

June 18, 19X3	$0.16
June 30, 19X3	0.14
July 10, 19X3	0.13

REQUIRED
(a) Prepare the journal entries to account for the Seine Company transaction on Drexel's records for June 18, 19X3, June 30, 19X3, and July 10, 19X3.
(b) Assume Drexel's accounting year ends December 31 rather than June 30. Prepare the necessary journal entries on Drexel's records in 19X3 to account for the foreign currency transaction with Seine Company.
(c) Assume Drexel's accounting year ends June 30 and the exchange rates for the French franc were:

June 18, 19X3	$0.12
June 30, 19X3	0.15
July 10, 19X3	0.13

Prepare the journal entries to account for the Seine Company transaction on Drexel's records for June 18, 19X3, June 30, 19X3, and July 10, 19X3.

Translation of foreign currency transactions

C–2 On December 20, 19X5, Baylite, Inc., a U.S. firm, sold merchandise on account to Santama Company, a Japanese company. The sales price was 6,000,000 yen. Baylite received the amount due (in yen) on January 18, 19X6. Baylite ends its accounting year on December 31. Exchange rates for the Japanese yen were:

December 20, 19X5	$0.0047
December 31, 19X5	0.0054
January 18, 19X6	0.0057

REQUIRED
(a) Prepare the journal entries to account for the Santama Company transaction on Baylite's records for December 20, 19X5, December 31, 19X5, and January 18, 19X6.
(b) Assume Baylite's accounting year ends October 31 rather than December 31. Prepare the necessary journal entries on Baylite's records in 19X5 and 19X6 to account for the foreign currency transaction with Santama Company.
(c) Assume Baylite's accounting year ends December 31 and the exchange rates for the Japanese yen were:

December 20, 19X5	$0.0058
December 31, 19X5	0.0053
January 18, 19X6	0.0049

Prepare the journal entries to account for the Santama Company transaction on Baylite's records for December 20, 19X5, December 31, 19X5, and January 18, 19X6.

Translation of foreign currency transactions

C–3 Listed below are selected 19X1 transactions and adjustments of Macklin, Inc., a U.S. company.

Oct. 7 Purchased merchandise on account from Lafarge Company, a French firm. The merchandise cost 70,000 French francs and payment is due within 30 days. The exchange rate today for the French franc is $0.14.

19 Sold merchandise for 19,000 deutsche marks on account to Saarberg

Company, a West German firm. Payment is due within 30 days. The exchange rate today for the deutsche mark is $0.49.

Nov. 5 Paid French francs to settle the account payable with Lafarge Company (see October 7 transaction). The exchange rate today for the French franc is $0.15.

16 Received full payment on account, in deutsche marks, from Saarberg Company (see October 19 transaction). The exchange rate today for the deutsche mark is $0.46.

Dec. 8 Sold merchandise for 200,000 cruzados on account to Bimento Company, a Brazilian firm. Payment is due within 30 days. The exchange rate today for the Brazilian cruzado is $0.07445.

10 Purchased merchandise on account from Palace Company, an English firm. The merchandise cost 14,000 British pounds and payment is due within 30 days. The exchange rate today for the British pound is $1.5425.

31 Adjusted the account receivables with Bimento Company (see December 8 transaction) and the account payable with Palace Company (see December 10 transaction) to reflect current exchange rates. The exchange rate today is $0.07675 for the Brazilian cruzado and $1.5285 for the British pound.

REQUIRED

Prepare journal entries to record the above transactions and adjustments of Macklin, Inc.

Conversion of foreign currency financial statements—translation procedures

C–4 Danthur Company was organized in Switzerland on January 1, 19X1, as a wholly-owned subsidiary of Hailand, Inc., a U.S. company. Danthur's opening balance sheet, in Swiss francs (SF), consisted of the following assets and stockholders' equity:

Assets		**Stockholders' Equity**	
Cash	SF 15,000	Common Stock	SF650,000
Inventory	135,000		
Plant Assets	500,000		
Total	SF650,000		

Danthur's 19X1 income statement and December 31, 19X1, balance sheet, in Swiss francs, follow.

Danthur Company
Income Statement
For the Year Ended December 31, 19X1

Sales		SF800,000
Cost of Goods Sold	SF450,000	
Depreciation Expense	40,000	
Other Expenses	60,000	
Total Expenses		550,000
Net Income		SF250,000

Danthur Company
Balance Sheet
December 31, 19X1

Assets		**Liabilities**		
Cash	SF 85,000	Accounts Payable		SF 30,000
Accounts Receivable (net)	125,000	**Stockholders' Equity**		
Inventory	260,000	Common Stock	SF650,000	
Plant Assets (net)	460,000	Retained Earnings	250,000	900,000
Total Assets	SF930,000	Total Liabilities and Stockholders' Equity		SF930,000

Exchange rates for the Swiss franc are:

January 1, 19X1	$0.53
Average for 19X1	0.48
December 31, 19X1	0.45

REQUIRED
Assume the functional currency for Danthur Company is the Swiss franc. Use translation procedures to convert Danthur's 19X1 income statement and December 31, 19X1, balance sheet to U.S. dollars. Follow the format of Exhibit C–3.

Conversion of foreign currency financial statements—remeasurement procedures

C–5 Refer to the data given for the Danthur Company in Problem C–4. In addition, the historical exchange rate applicable to the ending inventory is $0.46 and the historical exchange rate applicable to the 19X1 purchases of SF575,000 is $0.48.

REQUIRED
Assume the functional currency for Danthur Company is the U.S. dollar. Use remeasurement procedures to convert Danthur's 19X1 income statement and December 31, 19X1, balance sheet to U.S. dollars. There is a 19X1 foreign exchange loss of $6,150 from the remeasurement procedures. Follow the format of Exhibit C–4.

Part Four

Analysis of Cash Flows and of Financial Statements

19

Statement of Cash Flows

Chapter Objectives

- **Provide a basis for understanding a statement of cash flows.**
- **Discuss and illustrate the direct method of determining cash flow from operations.**
- **Discuss and illustrate the indirect method of determining cash flow from operations.**
- **Illustrate a worksheet approach to preparing a statement of cash flows using the direct method.**
- **Illustrate a worksheet approach to preparing a statement of cash flows using the indirect method.**
- **Discuss the disclosure of significant noncash investing and financing activities.**

Happiness is . . . Positive Cash Flow.

FREDERICK R. ADLER

The **statement of cash flows** is a basic financial statement that summarizes information about the flow of cash into and out of a company. The statement of cash flows complements the balance sheet and the income statement. The balance sheet reports the company's financial position at a point in time (the end of each period) while the statement of cash flows explains the change in one component of financial position—cash—from one balance sheet date to the next. The income statement reveals the results of the company's operating activities for the period, and these operating activities are a major contributor to the change in cash reported in the statement of cash flows.

The statement of cash flows replaces the statement of changes in financial position.[1] The statement of changes in financial position was a required financial statement for over 15 years and presented information on a firm's sources and uses of funds. When preparing the statement of changes in financial position, firms had the option of defining funds as either working capital (current assets less current liabilities) or cash. Initially, most companies prepared the statement with a focus on working capital. Dissatisfaction with this format by various users caused many firms to switch to a cash format. By the mid-1980s, a majority of firms were utilizing the cash format. When prepared in a cash format, the statement of changes in financial position bore many similarities to the statement of cash flows discussed in this chapter. Replacing the statement of changes in financial position with the statement of cash flows, in essence, completed the transition from a working capital to a cash focus.

CASH AND CASH EQUIVALENTS

Even though it is titled a statement of cash flows, the statement actually encompasses a somewhat broader concept than just cash. More precisely, the statement is to explain the change in a firm's cash and cash equivalents. Cash equivalents are the short-term, highly liquid investments that firms acquire with cash in

[1]On July 31, 1986, the Financial Accounting Standards Board proposed the statement of cash flows replace the statement of changes in financial position beginning July 1, 1987. This chapter's content is based on the FASB's proposal.

excess of their immediate needs. Examples of cash equivalents are Treasury bills, commerical paper, and money market funds. When preparing the statement of cash flows, the cash and cash equivalents are added together and treated as a single sum.

Cash equivalents are covered by the statement of cash flows because the purchase and sale of such investments are considered to be part of a firm's overall management of cash rather than a source or use of cash. Similarly, as statement users evaluate and project cash flows, it may matter very little to them whether the cash is on hand, deposited in a bank account, or invested in cash equivalents.

When discussing the statement of cash flows, accountants generally use the word "cash" rather than the term "cash and cash equivalents." We shall follow the same practice in this chapter.

CLASSIFICATIONS IN STATEMENT OF CASH FLOWS

A statement of cash flows classifies cash receipts and payments into three major categories: operating activities, investing activities, and financing activities. Grouping cash flows into these categories identifies the effects on cash of each of the major activities of a firm.

Operating Activities

A company's income statement reflects the transactions and events that constitute its operating activities. Generally, the cash effects of these transactions and events are what determine the net cash flow from operating activities (also referred to as "cash flow from operations").

The primary operating cash inflows are cash receipts from customers, either as a result of sales made or services rendered. Other operating sources of cash include cash received as dividends and interest. Typical operating cash outflows include cash payments for merchandise purchased, cash payments to employees, cash payments to outside suppliers for various services and supplies, and cash payments for taxes.

Investing Activities

A firm's transactions involving (1) the acquisition and disposal of plant assets and intangible assets, (2) the purchase and sale of stocks, bonds, and other securities (that are not cash equivalents), and (3) the lending and subsequent collection of money constitute the basic components of its investing activities. The related cash receipts and payments appear in the investing activities section of the statement of cash flows. Cash inflows would come from such events as cash sales of plant assets and intangible assets, cash sales of investments in stocks and bonds, and loan repayments from borrowers. Cash payments to purchase plant assets and intangible assets, cash payments to purchase stocks and bonds, and cash loaned to borrowers would comprise the typical cash outflows related to investing activities.

Financing Activities

A firm engages in financing activities when it obtains resources from owners, returns resources to owners, borrows resources from creditors, and repays amounts borrowed. Cash flows related to these events are reported in the financing activities section of the statement of cash flows. Cash transactions involving owners include cash received from issuing preferred stock and common stock, cash paid to reacquire treasury stock, and cash paid as dividends. Cash transactions with creditors include cash received by issuing bonds, mortgage notes, and other notes, and cash paid to settle these debts. Observe that paying cash to settle such obligations as accounts payable, wages payable, and income tax payable are operating activities, not financing activities.

The classification of cash flows into three categories of activities helps financial statement users interpret cash flow data. To illustrate, assume companies D, E, and F are similar companies operating in the same industry. Each company showed a $100,000 cash increase during the current year. Their current-year statements of cash flows are summarized below.

	D	E	F
Net Cash Flow from Operating Activities	$100,000	$ -0-	$ -0-
Cash Flows from Investing Activities:			
Sale of Plant Assets	-0-	100,000	-0-
Cash Flows from Financing Activities:			
Issuance of Notes Payable	-0-	-0-	100,000
Net Increase in Cash	$100,000	$100,000	$100,000

Although each company's cash increase was the same, the source of the increase varied by company. This variation affects the analysis of the cash flow data, particularly for potential short-term creditors who must evaluate the likelihood of obtaining repayment in the future for any funds loaned to the company. Based only on this cash flow data, a potential creditor would feel more comfortable lending money to D than to either E or F. D's cash increase came from its operating activities while both E and F could only break even on their cash flows from operations. E's cash increase came from the sale of plant assets, and this is not a source that is likely to recur regularly. F's cash increase came entirely from borrowed funds. F faces additional cash burdens in the future when the interest and principal payments on the note payable become due.

USEFULNESS OF STATEMENT OF CASH FLOWS

The conceptual framework developed by the Financial Accounting Standards Board includes a statement of cash flows as a necessary component in a full set of financial statements.[2] The FASB believes one objective of financial reporting

[2] *Statement of Financial Accounting Concepts No. 5*, "Recognition and Measurement in Financial Statements of Business Enterprises" (Stamford, CT: Financial Accounting Standards Board, 1984), p. 6.

is to help external users assess the amount, timing, and uncertainty of future cash flows to the enterprise.[3] These assessments will help users evaluate their own prospective cash receipts from their investments in, or loans to, the firm. Although statements of cash flows report past cash flows, these statements should be useful for assessing the future cash flows noted by the FASB.

A statement of cash flows shows the periodic cash effects of a firm's operating, investing, and financing activities. Distinguishing among these different categories of cash flows helps users compare, evaluate, and predict cash flows. With cash flow information, creditors and investors are better able to assess a firm's ability to settle its liabilities and pay its dividends. A firm's need for outside financing may also be better evaluated. Over time, the statement of cash flows permits users to observe and analyze management's investing and financing policies.

A statement of cash flows also provides information useful in evaluating a firm's *financial flexibility*. Financial flexibility is a firm's ability to generate sufficient amounts of cash to respond to unanticipated needs and opportunities. Information about past cash flows, particularly cash flows from operations, helps in assessing financial flexibility. An evaluation of a firm's ability to survive an unexpected drop in demand, for example, may include a review of its past cash flows from operations. The larger these cash flows, the greater will be the firm's ability to withstand adverse changes in economic conditions. Other financial statements, particularly the balance sheet and its notes, also contain information useful for judging financial flexibility.

Some investors and creditors find the statement of cash flows useful in evaluating the "quality" of a firm's income. As we know, determining income under accrual accounting procedures requires many accruals, deferrals, allocations, and valuations. These adjustment and measurement procedures introduce more subjectivity into income determination than some financial statement users prefer. These users will relate a more objective performance measure—cash flow from operations—to net income. To these users, the higher this ratio is, the higher is the quality of the income.

Compared with its predecessor statement (the statement of changes in financial position), one advantage of a statement of cash flows is that it does focus on cash. Frequently, companies prepared the statement of changes in financial position to explain changes in working capital rather than cash. There can be significant differences between working capital flows and cash flows. Working capital may increase, but this does not necessarily mean that the company is financially healthy. During an economic recession, for example, growth in accounts receivable and inventory may cause a working capital increase even though cash decreases. If the focus is on working capital flows, the overall growth in working

[3] *Statement of Financial Accounting Concepts No. 1*, "Objectives of Financial Reporting by Business Enterprises" (Stamford, CT: Financial Accounting Standards Board, 1978), p. 18. The FASB also believes information should be reported about earnings. It notes that earnings measured by accrual accounting are a better indicator of periodic financial performance than information about current cash receipts and payments.

capital may mask the fact that the company faces financial problems (uncollectible receivables and excessive inventory). The statement of cash flows helps users avoid this possible misinterpretation of data.

CASH FLOWS VERSUS WORKING CAPITAL FLOWS

You can trace the history of the cash versus working capital controversy back to 1975. The problem is perspective. Busy accountants are aware of the many incidents that created support for a cash-based funds statement; they just have not had the time to put the whole picture together.

The W. T. Grant controversy

It took a major business failure to trigger serious interest in the cash-based funds statement. The 1975 W. T. Grant bankruptcy shocked investors everywhere. "With all the facts and figures churned out by Grant," declared one bitter shareholder, "where was the truth? Why couldn't we see this coming?" Analysts point an accusing finger at the working-capital-based funds statement.

W. T. Grant's operations were users, not providers, of cash from 1966–1975. In the decade preceding the bankruptcy, cash provided by operations was in the black for only two years. Until collapse was imminent, however, Grant's working capital from operations remained positive and fairly stable. Grant's funds statement hid a major liquidity problem.

W. T. Grant finally choked to death on its own inventory. Its failure served notice that there is an important difference between cash flows and working capital flows.

The General Electric experience

The W. T. Grant bankruptcy took most investors by surprise. Back in 1975, earnings per share was king; cash management was an unheard of art.

General Electric woke up to the importance of cash-flow information earlier than many other corporations did. In 1976, GE launched a massive campaign to force operating managers to pay closer attention to cash flow. The results were startling: At the beginning of the program, declining liquidity threatened GE's triple A bond rating; by the end of the program, the company had freed up over $1 billion in excess cash.

The financial analysts

General Electric showed business executives that cash-flow information offers a significant financial opportunity. When it became clear that companies that manage cash flow outperform those that do not, the financial analysts soon jumped on the bandwagon. As one analyst put it, "If cash-flow information makes good financial sense, it probably makes good financial reporting sense." The analysts embraced cash-flow analysis with a missionary zeal, and results were a rude surprise to a lot of business people.

Companies with good earnings records discovered their performance didn't measure up using the cash-flow yardstick. "Cannibalizing its capital structure to keep stock prices up," reads one report. "Neglecting plant and equipment and paying dividends with money that's not there," huffs another. "A perfect formula for earnings success if you don't mind rusting plants, inferior R&D and yesterday's technology," preaches a third.

Financial analysts found a powerful tool in cash-flow analysis. Although earnings information might tell them how much money a company was making, only cash-flow information could say whether that money was real.

From Richard S. Clark, "Statement of Changes: In Need of a Change?" *CA Magazine*, February 1983, pages 26–30. Excerpted, with permission, from *CA Magazine*, February 1983, published by the Canadian Institute of Chartered Accountants, Toronto, Canada.

CASH FLOW FROM OPERATIONS

In Chapter 1 we defined a cash basis system of accounting. Such a system records revenue when cash is received and expenses when cash is disbursed. This system is particularly relevant when we focus on a firm's cash flow from operations. Essentially, a firm's net cash flow operating activities is equal to its income computed on a cash basis.

Of course, most business firms compute income using accrual accounting, not cash basis accounting. To calculate cash flow from operations, then, it is often necessary to convert amounts computed using accrual accounting to the corresponding cash basis amounts. To better understand the process of converting from accrual measures to cash amounts, let us consider the following financial data for Bennett Company:

Balance Sheet at December 31, 19X1

Cash	$ 10,000	Accounts Payable	$ 19,000
Accounts Receivable	34,000	Wages Payable	4,000
Inventory	60,000	Income Tax Payable	1,000
Prepaid Insurance	4,000	Common Stock	180,000
Plant Assets	200,000	Retained Earnings	64,000
Accumulated Depreciation	(40,000)	Total Liabilities	
Total Assets	$268,000	and Stockholders' Equity	$268,000

Transactions During 19X2

(1) Made sales on account of $250,000.

(2) Collected accounts receivable of $245,000.

(3) Purchased merchandise on account of $134,000.

(4) Determined cost of goods sold was $140,000.

(5) Paid accounts payable (for merchandise purchased) of $143,000.

(6) Paid wages to employees of $52,500.

(7) Accrued wages expense (and wages payable) of $1,500 at December 31, 19X2.

(8) Paid insurance premium of $18,000 to extend coverage for three years.

(9) Allocated $5,000 of prepaid insurance to insurance expense.

(10) Paid income taxes to government of $11,500 (paid final portion of 19X1 taxes and initial installments of 19X2 taxes).

(11) Recorded 19X2's total income tax expense (and income tax payable) of $13,000.

As a result of these transactions, Bennett's 19X2 income statement and December 31, 19X2 balance sheet appear as shown in Exhibit 19–1 (the 19X1 year-end balance sheet is also included for comparative purposes).

EXHIBIT 19–1

Bennett Company
Balance Sheets

Assets	Dec. 31, 19X2	Dec. 31, 19X1	Liabilities and Stockholders' Equity	Dec. 31, 19X2	Dec. 31, 19X1
Cash	$ 30,000	$ 10,000	Accounts Payable	$ 10,000	$ 19,000
Accounts Receivable	39,000	34,000	Wages Payable	1,500	4,000
Inventory	54,000	60,000	Income Tax Payable	2,500	1,000
Prepaid Insurance	17,000	4,000	Common Stock	180,000	180,000
Plant Assets	200,000	200,000	Retained Earnings	96,000	64,000
Accumulated Depreciation	(50,000)	(40,000)			
Total Assets	$290,000	$268,000	Total Liabilities and Stockholders' Equity	$290,000	$268,000

Bennett Company
Income Statement
For the Year Ended December 31, 19X2

Sales		$250,000
Cost of Goods Sold		140,000
Gross Profit		$110,000
Wages Expense	$50,000	
Insurance Expense	5,000	
Depreciation Expense	10,000	
Income Tax Expense	13,000	
Total Expenses		78,000
Net Income		$32,000

Direct Method

First, we will determine and present Bennett's 19X2 cash flow from operations using the **direct method.** The direct method shows the major categories of operating cash receipts and payments and is, in essence, a cash basis income statement. Using the direct method, we may determine the cash amounts for the various categories either by (1) reviewing and classifying the firm's cash transactions or (2) converting the firm's accrual basis revenues and expenses to corresponding cash amounts.

REVIEW AND CLASSIFY CASH TRANSACTIONS A review of Bennett's 19X2 transactions shows that transactions 2, 5, 6, 8, and 10 reflect the cash receipts and disbursements from its operating activities. The direct method presents the cash flow from operations by reporting these cash receipts and payments as follows:

Cash Received from Customers		$245,000
Cash Disbursed for Operating Activities:		
Cash Paid for Merchandise Purchased	$143,000	
Cash Paid to Employees	52,500	
Cash Paid for Insurance	18,000	
Cash Paid for Taxes	11,500	225,000
Net Cash Flow from Operating Activities		$ 20,000

CONVERT REVENUES AND EXPENSES Alternatively, Bennett's major categories of cash receipts and payments may be determined by starting with its accrual basis revenue and expense amounts and converting them to the corresponding cash amounts. We will now explain and illustrate these conversion procedures.

Convert sales to cash received from customers During 19X2, accounts receivable increased $5,000. This increase means that during 19X2 cash collections on account (which decrease accounts receivable) were less than credit sales (which increase accounts receivable). We compute cash received from customers, then, as follows:

Sales	$250,000
+ Beginning Accounts Receivable	34,000
− Ending Accounts Receivable	(39,000)
= Cash Received from Customers	$245,000

Convert cost of goods sold to cash paid for merchandise purchased The conversion of cost of goods sold to cash paid for merchandise purchased is a two-step process. First, cost of goods sold is adjusted for the change in inventory to determine the amount of purchases during the year. Then, the purchases amount is adjusted for the change in accounts payable to derive the cash paid for merchandise purchased.

Inventory decreased from $60,000 to $54,000 during 19X2. This $6,000 decrease indicates that the cost of goods sold exceeded the cost of goods purchased during the year. The year's purchases amount is computed as:

Cost of Goods Sold	$140,000
+ Ending Inventory	54,000
− Beginning Inventory	(60,000)
= Purchases	$134,000

During 19X2, accounts payable decreased $9,000. This decrease reflects the fact that cash payments for merchandise purchased on account (which decrease accounts payable) exceeded purchases on account (which increase accounts payable). The cash paid for merchandise purchased, therefore, is computed as:

Purchases	$134,000
+ Beginning Accounts Payable	19,000
− Ending Accounts Payable	(10,000)
= Cash Paid for Merchandise Purchased	$143,000

Convert wages expense to cash paid to employees Wages payable decreased from $4,000 at December 31, 19X1 to $1,500 at December 31, 19X2. This $2,500 decrease means that cash paid to employees as wages in 19X2 (which includes $4,000 charged to expense in 19X1) exceeds 19X2's wages expense (which includes $1,500 accrued but not paid at year-end). This change in wages payable is used to convert wages expense to cash paid to employees, as follows:

Wages Expense	$50,000
+ Beginning Wages Payable	4,000
− Ending Wages Payable	(1,500)
= Cash Paid to Employees	$52,500

Convert insurance expense to cash paid for insurance Prepaid insurance increased $13,000 during 19X2. The $13,000 increase reflects the excess of cash paid for insurance during 19X2 (which increases prepaid insurance) over the year's insurance expense (which decreases prepaid insurance). Starting with insurance expense, then, the cash paid for insurance is computed as:

Insurance Expense	$ 5,000
+ Ending Prepaid Insurance	17,000
− Beginning Prepaid Insurance	(4,000)
= Cash Paid for Insurance	$18,000

Convert income tax expense to cash paid for taxes The increase in income tax payable from $1,000 at December 31, 19X1 to $2,500 at December 31, 19X2 means that 19X2's income tax expense (which increases income tax payable) was $1,500 larger than 19X2's tax payments (which decrease income tax payable). If we start with income tax expense, then we calculate cash paid for taxes in the following manner:

Income Tax Expense	$13,000
+ Beginning Income Tax Payable	1,000
− Ending Income Tax Payable	(2,500)
= Cash Paid for Taxes	$11,500

Eliminate Depreciation Expense Depreciation expense is a noncash expense. Because it does not represent a cash payment, depreciation expense is completely

EXHIBIT 19–2

Accrual Basis →			Cash Basis
Sales	+ Beginning – Ending Acc. Receivable	=	Receipts
Cost of Goods Sold	+ Ending – Beginning Inventory + Beginning – Ending Accounts Payable	=	Payments for Goods
Operating Expenses and Income Taxes (except depreciation and similar write-offs)	+ Ending – Beginning Prepaid Expenses + Beginning – Ending Accrued Liab.	=	Payments for Expense
Depreciation (and similar write-offs)	Eliminated	=	0

eliminated as we convert accrual expense amounts to the corresponding amounts of cash payments. If Bennett Company had any amortization expense, it also would be eliminated for the same reason. The amortization of an intangible asset is entirely a noncash expense.

We have now applied the proper adjustments to convert each accrual basis revenue and expense amount to the corresponding cash amount. Note that the computed cash receipts and cash payments are exactly the same amounts as identified in transactions 2, 5, 6, 8, and 10 for Bennett Company. Exhibit 19–2 summarizes the procedures for converting individual revenues and expenses from an accrual to a cash basis.

Indirect Method

A second method of determining and presenting cash flow from operations is the **indirect** (or **reconciliation**) **method.** The indirect method begins with the accrual basis net income and applies a series of adjustments to convert the income to a cash basis. In contrast to the direct method, the indirect method does not show categories of cash receipts and payments.

The adjustments to accrual basis net income consist of the adjustments we just reviewed in converting individual revenue and expense amounts to a cash basis. However, the adjustments are applied to net income rather than to the individual revenues and expenses. Also, to be more efficient, just the changes in the balance sheet accounts are used rather than using both the beginning and ending account balances.

Under the indirect method, then, noncash expenses such as depreciation and amortization are added to net income to eliminate the effect they had on net income. Changes during the year in accounts receivable, inventory, prepaid expenses, accounts payable, and accrued liabilities (such as wages payable and income tax payable) are either added to or subtracted from net income, depending on which account we are analyzing and whether the change was an increase or a decrease. The following schedule summarizes the treatment of these account changes.

	Change in Account: Adjustment of Accrual Basis Net Income to Convert to Cash Flow from Operations	
Account	**Add**	**Deduct**
Accounts Receivable	Decrease	Increase
Inventory	Decrease	Increase
Prepaid Expenses	Decrease	Increase
Accounts Payable	Increase	Decrease
Accrued Liabilities	Increase	Decrease

For example, we add a decrease in accounts receivable during the period to accrual net income to convert to a cash basis figure. We deduct an increase in accounts receivable from accrual net income. The remainder of the schedule is interpreted in a similar fashion.

In summary, then, the procedures used in the indirect method to convert an accrual basis net income amount to a cash flow from operations figure are as follows:

Accrual Basis Net Income
+ Depreciation and Similar Write-offs
+ or − Changes in Accounts Receivable, Inventory, Prepaid Expenses, Accounts Payable, and Accrued Liabilities
= Net Cash Flow from Operating Activities

Applying these procedures to the data in our illustration, we present Bennett Company's cash flow operations under the indirect method as follows:

Net Income	$32,000
Add (Deduct) Items to Convert Net Income to Cash Basis:	
Depreciation	10,000
Accounts Receivable Increase	(5,000)
Inventory Decrease	6,000
Prepaid Insurance Increase	(13,000)
Accounts Payable Decrease	(9,000)
Wages Payable Decrease	(2,500)
Income Tax Payable Increase	1,500
Net Cash Flow from Operating Activities	$20,000

If there is a net loss for the period, the indirect method begins with the net loss. It is possible, of course, for the net amount of add-backs to exceed the loss so that there is a positive cash flow from operating activities even when there is an accrual basis net loss.

EXHIBIT 19–3

Bennett Company
19X2 Cash Flow from Operations

Direct Method		
Cash Received from Customers		$245,000
Cash Disbursed for Operating Activities:		
Cash Paid for Merchandise Purchased	$143,000	
Cash Paid to Employees	52,500	
Cash Paid for Insurance	18,000	
Cash Paid for Taxes	11,500	225,000
Net Cash Flow from Operating Activities		$ 20,000

Indirect Method	
Net Income	$32,000
Add (Deduct) Items to Convert Net Income to Cash Basis:	
Depreciation	10,000
Accounts Receivable Increase	(5,000)
Inventory Decrease	6,000
Prepaid Insurance Increase	(13,000)
Accounts Payable Decrease	(9,000)
Wages Payable Decrease	(2,500)
Income Tax Payable Increase	1,500
Net Cash Flow from Operating Activities	$20,000

Comparison of Methods

Exhibit 19–3 presents Bennett Company's cash flow from operations under both the direct method and the indirect method. Although both methods show the same final cash flow from operations, the financial presentation deriving the final amount is quite different. The direct method shows the specific sources and uses of cash from operations. The indirect method shows the adjustments to convert net income to a cash basis amount.

Both the direct and indirect methods have strengths and weaknesses. One advantage of the direct method is its understandability for financial statement users. A presentation of cash flow from operations as the difference between operating cash receipts and cash payments is a simple and easily understood presentation. In contrast, the rationale for the additions to and deductions from net income under the indirect method may not be clear to the users of cash flow data.

Because it begins with net income, an advantage of the indirect method is that it provides a direct linkage with the income statement. The direct method does not provide any income statement linkage—no cash flow component under the direct method necessarily agrees with any amount in the income statement. All other things being equal, accountants prefer to have their various financial statements articulate, or tie together, as much as possible.

The method most useful for predicting future cash flows from operations probably varies among users. Some users may wish to estimate future cash flows from operations by predicting both operating cash inflows and outflows, in which case the cash sources and uses reported under the direct method is helpful. Other users may estimate future cash flows from operations by first estimating future net income and then converting that estimate to a cash flow by allowing for expected differences between net income and cash flow. Because the indirect method highlights the differences between income and cash flow, the historical information provided may help these users in estimating future differences.

The indirect method eliminates the need for any special treatment of uncollectible accounts expense, while the direct method requires that it be specifically considered. Although this expense is a noncash expense, it is *not* eliminated in the process of converting accrual measures to cash amounts. When uncollectible accounts expense is recorded, it also reduces accounts receivable (net of the allowance for uncollectible accounts). This reduction in accounts receivable, however, is not caused by the collection of cash. Because we use the change in accounts receivable under the direct method when converting from sales to cash received from customers, we must adjust for the effect of uncollectible accounts expense. We do so by deducting uncollectible accounts expense in the computation. If there is uncollectible accounts expense, then, cash received from customers is computed as:

Sales
+ Beginning Accounts Receivable (net)
− Ending Accounts Receivable (net)
− Uncollectible Accounts Expense
= Cash Received from Customers

Under the indirect method, we do not compute cash received from customers, but only the final net cash flow from operations. Uncollectible accounts expense has already been deducted in arriving at net income, the starting point for the indirect method. The indirect method, then, does not require any special consideration of uncollectible accounts expense.

Some companies believe the direct method may require more preparation costs than the indirect method. Because their accounting records are kept on the accrual basis, these companies do not routinely collect the information on cash receipts and payments required by the direct method. Indeed, analyzing and classifying a year's cash receipts and disbursements may be costly. However, if operating cash flows are determined by converting accrual revenues and expenses to cash amounts, there should not be significant differences in preparation costs between the two methods. This is particularly so if revenues and expenses are combined into just a few categories of operating cash flows.

In the remainder of this chapter, we use three categories of operating cash outflows under the direct method—cash paid to suppliers, cash paid to employees, and cash paid for taxes. We will determine operating cash flows by converting accrual revenues and expenses to cash amounts. Cash paid to suppliers includes not only cash paid for merchandise purchased, but also payments for other services and supplies acquired from outsiders. Accordingly, we will combine cost of goods sold with most operating expenses (excluding uncollectible accounts expense, wages expense, and income tax expense) as the starting point for computing cash paid to suppliers.

PREPARATION OF STATEMENT OF CASH FLOWS

The preparation of a statement of cash flows involves three steps:

(1) Compute the net increase or decrease in cash during the year.

(2) Prepare a worksheet to identify the cash flows for the year.

(3) Prepare the statement of cash flows using information from the worksheet.

To demonstrate these three steps, we use the financial data of XYZ Company. Exhibit 19–4 shows comparative balance sheets for 19X2 and 19X3, and Exhibit 19–5 presents the income statement for 19X3. Assume that during 19X3 the following transactions took place, in addition to routine transactions:

(1) Sold plant assets having a book value of $4,000 ($7,000 cost - $3,000 accumulated depreciation) for $4,000 cash.

(2) Purchased new plant assets for $8,000 cash.

(3) Issued additional common stock at par value for $10,000 cash.

(4) Declared and paid cash dividends of $3,000.

We will illustrate the three steps to construct a statement of cash flows under both the direct and indirect methods.

EXHIBIT 19–4

XYZ Company
Balance Sheets

Assets	**Dec. 31, 19X3**	**Dec. 31, 19X2**
Cash	$ 23,000	$ 16,000
Accounts Receivable	18,000	10,000
Inventory	34,000	30,000
Plant Assets	56,000	55,000
Accumulated Depreciation	(12,000)	(10,000)
Total Assets	$119,000	$101,000
Liabilities and Stockholders' Equity		
Accounts Payable	$ 20,700	$ 18,200
Wages Payable	800	300
Income Tax Payable	500	1,500
Common Stock	60,000	50,000
Retained Earnings	37,000	31,000
Total Liabilities and Stockholders' Equity	$119,000	$101,000

EXHIBIT 19–5

XYZ Company
Income Statement
For the Year Ended December 31, 19X3

Sales		$59,000
Cost of Goods Sold		30,000
Gross Profit		$29,000
Wages Expense	$10,000	
Depreciation Expense	5,000	
Other Operating Expenses	3,000	
Income Tax Expense	2,000	20,000
Net Income		$ 9,000

Direct Method

STEP 1 Determine the net increase or decrease in cash during the year by comparing the cash balances on the comparative balance sheets. XYZ Company's cash increased $7,000 (from $16,000 to $23,000) during 19X3.

STEP 2 Prepare a worksheet to analyze the changes in the noncash accounts and identify, by type of activity, the sources and uses of cash for the period. Our general approach in determining the sources and uses of cash is to review all balance sheet accounts (except Cash) to identify the events affecting cash flows. Exhibit 19–6 shows the worksheet for XYZ Company under the direct method.

Heading and form The worksheet heading includes the name of the company, an identification of the statement the worksheet deals with, and the period covered by the analysis.

The worksheet form illustrated in Exhibit 19–6 has a description column and four money columns. Each of the two headings Changes in Noncash Accounts and Analyzing Entries has a debit and credit column.

Changes in noncash accounts The content of the worksheet focuses on the company's noncash accounts.

(1) First, a list of all noncash accounts is entered in the description column. The debit or credit change in each account balance for the period is entered in the appropriate column under the Changes in Noncash Accounts heading. Accounts Receivable, for example, increased from $10,000 at December 31, 19X2, to $18,000 at December 31, 19X3; the $8,000 increase is entered in the debit column. Inventory and Plant Assets also increased during 19X3 and their increases are handled the same way as the Accounts Receivable increase. During 19X3, Accummulated Depreciation increased from $10,000 to $12,000; the $2,000 increase is entered in the credit column. The 19X3 increases in

EXHIBIT 19–6

XYZ Company
Worksheet for Statement of Cash Flows (Direct Method)
For the Year Ended December 31, 19X3

Description	Changes in Noncash Accounts		Analyzing Entries	
	Debit	Credit	Debit	Credit
Accounts Receivable	8,000		(2) 8,000	
Inventory	4,000		(3) 4,000	
Plant Assets	1,000		(9) 8,000	(8) 7,000
Accumulated Depreciation		2,000	(8) 3,000	(5) 5,000
Accounts Payable		2,500		(4) 2,500
Wages Payable		500		(6) 500
Income Tax Payable	1,000		(7) 1,000	
Common Stock		10,000		(10) 10,000
Retained Earnings		6,000	(11) 3,000	(1) 9,000
	14,000	21,000		
Increase in Cash	7,000			
	21,000	21,000		
Cash Flows from Operating Activities				
Cash Received from Customers			(1) 59,000	
Less: Accounts Receivable Increase				(2) 8,000
Cash Paid to Suppliers				(1) 38,000
Add: Inventory Increase				(3) 4,000
Less: Accounts Payable Increase			(4) 2,500	
Less: Depreciation			(5) 5,000	
Cash Paid to Employees				(1) 10,000
Less: Wages Payable Increase			(6) 500	
Cash Paid for Taxes				(1) 2,000
Add: Income Tax Payable Decrease				(7) 1,000
Cash Flows from Investing Activities				
Sale of Plant Assets			(8) 4,000	
Purchase of Plant Assets				(9) 8,000
Cash Flows from Financing Activities				
Issuance of Common Stock			(10) 10,000	
Payment of Dividends				(11) 3,000
			108,000	108,000

Accounts Payable, Wages Payable, Common Stock, and Retained Earnings are also entered in the credit column. The decrease in Income Tax Payable is entered in the debit column.

(2) After entering the changes for all noncash accounts, the two columns are totaled. The difference between the column totals equals the cash change calculated in step 1. The cash change is entered on the worksheet—an increase in the debit column, a decrease in the credit column—and the two columns are totaled and double ruled to show their equality. Exhibit 19—6 shows the $7,000 cash increase for XYZ Company in the debit column.

(3) At this point, the phrase "cash flows from operating activities" is written in the description column. Beneath this heading, enter labels for the following categories of operating cash flows (and allow two or three lines of space for each category): "cash received from customers," "cash paid to suppliers," "cash paid to employees," and "cash paid for taxes." Next, the phrase "cash flows from investing activities" is written in the description column. Several lines are skipped and the phrase "cash flows from financing activities" is entered in the column. The worksheet is now ready for the analyzing entries.

Analyzing entries Analyzing entries explain the changes that occurred in the noncash accounts during the period. If the change affected cash flows, we enter the appropriate amount on the worksheet in the proper cash flow category. When all changes in noncash accounts have been explained, our analysis is complete.

Essentially, the analysis consists of two sets of analyzing entries. The initial set determines the various operating cash flows. The first analyzing entry shows the effect net income had on retained earnings and places the income statement data on the worksheet. Revenue and expense amounts are the starting points for computing operating cash receipts and payments. The first analyzing entry sets up these starting points as follows:

Sales (net of any uncollectible accounts expense) is the starting point for computing cash received from customers and is debited to that worksheet category.

Cost of goods sold plus all operating expenses other than uncollectible accounts expense, wages expense, and income tax expense is the starting point for computing cash paid to suppliers and is credited to that worksheet category.

Wages expense is the starting point for computing cash paid to employees and is credited to that worksheet category.

Income tax expense is the starting point for computing cash paid for taxes and is credited to that worksheet category.

To complete the entry, net income is credited to retained earnings. Note that all income statement accounts are included in the first analyzing entry. This is true even though some expenses, such as depreciation and amortization, will subsequently be eliminated.

After the first analyzing entry is recorded, we then prepare analyzing entries to reflect the adjustments needed to convert accrual basis revenues and expenses to cash amounts. As discussed earlier, changes in accounts receivable, inventory, prepaid expenses, accounts payable, and accrued liabilities affect these conversions. Changes in these accounts are added to the "starting points" if the change means the cash flow exceeds the accrual amount. The changes are deducted from the "starting points" if the change means the cash flow is smaller than the accrual amount. The initial set of analyzing entries also eliminates any depreciation or amortization expense from the "starting points." We do this by debiting cash paid to suppliers and crediting the appropriate balance sheet account.

The second set of analyzing entries explains the changes in the noncash accounts that were not analyzed in determining the operating cash flows. This set of entries derives any cash flows from investing or financing activities. We review each noncash account whose change during the period has not been fully explained by the first set of analyzing entries and reconstruct the entries, in summary form, to explain these changes. Any effects of these transactions on cash are entered in the worksheet's lower portion as either a cash inflow or a cash outflow. Cash inflows are entered as debits and cash outflows are entered as credits. Of course, not every analyzing entry has to affect cash. Issuing stock to acquire land, for example, does not affect cash. It requires an analyzing entry, though, because it causes a change in the noncash accounts and we must explain all changes completely. (We discuss noncash events in more detail later.)

We now explain the analyzing entries in Exhibit 19–6. Entries (1)–(7) derive the operating cash flows, and entries (8)–(11) explain the remaining changes in the noncash accounts.

(1) Entry (1) establishes the starting points for computing operating cash flows. The entry debits cash received from customers for $59,000 (the Sales amount), credits cash paid to suppliers for $38,000 (the sum of Cost of Goods Sold, Depreciation Expense, and Other Operating Expenses), credits cash paid to employees for $10,000 (the Wages Expense amount), credits cash paid for taxes for $2,000 (the Income Tax Expense amount), and credits Retained Earnings for the $9,000 net income.

(2) An $8,000 increase in accounts receivable during 19X3 means that cash collected from customers was less than sales revenue. Entry (2) reflects this effect by debiting Accounts Receivable and crediting cash received from customers for $8,000.

(3) An inventory increase is added when converting cost of goods sold to a related cash payment amount. To reflect this effect, entry (3) debits Inventory and credits cash paid to suppliers for the $4,000 19X3 inventory increase.

(4) A 19X3 increase in accounts payable means that cash payments for goods and services during 19X3 were less than the related expense amounts. This adjustment is handled in entry (4) which debits cash paid to suppliers and credits Accounts Payable for the $2,500 increase.

(5) Entry (5) eliminates depreciation expense by debiting cash paid to suppliers and crediting Accumulated Depreciation for $5,000.

(6) Entry (6) debits cash paid to employees and credits Wages Payable for the $500 increase in wages payable. This increase indicates that cash payments to employees during 19X3 were less than wages expense.

(7) Income tax payable decreased $1,000 during 19X3, indicating that income taxes paid exceeded income tax expense. Entry (7) records this effect by debiting Income Tax Payable and crediting cash paid for taxes for $1,000.

(8) The sale of plant assets was an investing activity that increased cash by $4,000, decreased Accumulated Depreciation by $3,000, and decreased Plant Assets by $7,000, as shown in entry (8).

(9) The purchase of plant assets was an investing activity that used $8,000 cash. Entry (9) portrays this cash outflow and the corresponding increase in Plant Assets.

(10) The issuance of common stock was a financing event that caused a $10,000 cash inflow. Entry (10) debits this event to cash flows from financing activities and credits Common Stock for $10,000.

(11) The dividend of $3,000 declared and paid in 19X3 was a financing event that reduced cash. Entry (11) reconstructs the entry for the dividend payment, debiting Retained Earnings and crediting the cash outflow to cash flows from financing activities.

For each noncash account, the debit or credit balance of the analyzing entries now equals the change shown in the first two columns. Our analysis is complete, and we total and double rule the last two columns to complete the worksheet. The analyzing entries help us compile information for a statement of cash flows; they are not recorded in the accounts.

STEP 3 Prepare the statement of cash flows from the information in the worksheet. The worksheet already classifies cash flows in the proper categories for the statement of cash flows. The sum of the cash flows from the operating, investing, and financing sections of the statement will equal the change in cash calculated in step 1. The statement of cash flows for the XYZ Company, using the direct method, is shown in Exhibit 19–7.

Cash inflows and outflows from similar areas of investing and financing activities are reported separately (rather than reporting only the net difference). For example, in Exhibit 19–7, proceeds from the sale of plant assets are reported separately from outlays made to acquire plant assets. Similarly, funds borrowed would be reported separately from debt repayments, and proceeds from issuing stock would be reported separately from outlays to acquire treasury stock.

Indirect Method

The procedures to prepare a statement of cash flows using the indirect method are quite similar to the procedures under the direct method. The differences, of course, relate to determining and reporting the cash flow from operations. We will review the steps for the indirect method, with emphasis on the differences from the direct method.

STEP 1 Determine the net increase or decrease in cash during the year. This step is the same as under the direct method. XYZ Company's cash balance increased $7,000 during 19X3.

EXHIBIT 19–7
Statement of Cash Flows
Direct Method

XYZ Company Statement of Cash Flows For the Year Ended December 31, 19X3		
Cash Flows from Operating Activities		
Cash Received from Customers		$51,000
Cash Disbursed for Operating Activities:		
Cash Paid to Suppliers	$34,500	
Cash Paid to Employees	9,500	
Cash Paid for Taxes	3,000	47,000
Net Cash Flow from Operating Activities		$ 4,000
Cash Flows from Investing Activities		
Sale of Plant Assets	$ 4,000	
Purchase of Plant Assets	(8,000)	
Net Cash Used by Investing Activities		(4,000)
Cash Flows from Financing Activities		
Issuance of Common Stock	$10,000	
Payment of Dividends	(3,000)	
Net Cash Provided by Financing Activities		7,000
Net Increase in Cash		$ 7,000

STEP 2 Prepare a worksheet to identify the cash flows for the year. The basic worksheet approach under the indirect method is the same as the direct method. The changes in the noncash balance sheet accounts are analyzed to identify, by area of activity, the cash inflows and outflows. The worksheet heading, description column, and money columns are identical to the format under the direct method. Exhibit 19–8 shows the worksheet for XYZ Company using the indirect method.

Changes in noncash accounts As under the direct method, we begin the worksheet by listing all noncash accounts and their account balance changes in the proper columns. We total the two columns showing these changes in the noncash accounts and then enter the change in cash as a balancing amount.

At this point we enter the labels for the cash flow categories in the description column. Under the indirect method, only one label relating to operating cash flows is entered—"net cash flow from operating activities." Several lines are skipped to allow for the determination of cash flow from operations. The remaining two labels entered in the description column are the same as for the direct method—"cash flows from investing activities" and "cash flows from financing activities."

EXHIBIT 19–8

XYZ Company
Worksheet for Statement of Cash Flows (Indirect Method)
For the Year Ended December 31, 19X3

	Changes in Noncash Accounts		Analyzing Entries	
Description	**Debit**	**Credit**	**Debit**	**Credit**
Accounts Receivable	8,000		(3) 8,000	
Inventory	4,000		(4) 4,000	
Plant Assets	1,000		(9) 8,000	(8) 7,000
Accumulated Depreciation		2,000	(8) 3,000	(2) 5,000
Accounts Payable		2,500		(5) 2,500
Wages Payable		500		(6) 500
Income Tax Payable	1,000		(7) 1,000	
Common Stock		10,000		(10) 10,000
Retained Earnings		6,000	(11) 3,000	(1) 9,000
	14,000	21,000		
Increase in Cash	7,000			
	21,000	21,000		
Net Cash Flow from Operating Activities				
Net Income			(1) 9,000	
Add: Depreciation			(2) 5,000	
Less: Accounts Receivable Increase				(3) 8,000
Less: Inventory Increase				(4) 4,000
Add: Accounts Payable Increase			(5) 2,500	
Add: Wages Payable Increase			(6) 500	
Less: Income Tax Payable Decrease				(7) 1,000
Cash Flows from Investing Activities				
Sale of Plant Assets			(8) 4,000	
Purchase of Plant Assets				(9) 8,000
Cash Flows from Financing Activities				
Issuance of Common Stock			(10) 10,000	
Payment of Dividends				(11) 3,000
			58,000	58,000

Analyzing entries The analyzing entries have the same purpose as under the direct method. Again, the analysis consists of two sets of analyzing entries. The initial set determines cash flow from operations using the indirect method. The first analyzing entry establishes the starting point for computing cash flow from operations—accrual basis net income. On the worksheet, the net income is debited to net cash flow from operating activities and credited to retained earnings. We then reflect, as analyzing entries, the adjustments needed to convert the net income from an accrual to a cash basis. As previously discussed, these adjustments involve depreciation and amortization expense, and changes in accounts receivable, inventory, prepaid expenses, accounts payable, and accrued liabilities. Adjustments which are added to net income are debited to net cash flow from operating activities and adjustments which are deducted are credited to net cash flow from operating activities. For example, the entry analyzing depreciation expense debits net cash flow from operating activities and credits accummulated depreciation. Or, if accounts receivable increased during the period, our analyzing entry would debit accounts receivable and credit net cash flow from operating activities.

The second set of analyzing entries explain the remaining changes in the noncash accounts and identify the investing and financing cash flows. The entries in this set are constructed exactly the same way as under the direct method.

Analyzing entries (1)–(7) in Exhibit 19–8 are explained below. These entries derive the cash flow from operations. Entries (8)–(11) are identical to those under the direct method (in Exhibit 19–6) and are not explained again here.

(1) Entry (1) debits the $9,000 accrual basis net income to net cash flow from operating activities and credits Retained Earnings.

(2) Entry (2) adds depreciation expense to the accrual basis net income as part of the conversion to a cash basis net income. The entry debits net cash flow from operating activities and credits Accumulated Depreciation.

(3) Accounts receivable increases are deducted when converting an accrual basis net income to a cash basis amount. Entry (3) debits Accounts Receivable and credits net cash flow from operating activities for this $8,000 adjustment.

(4) Inventory increases are also deducted in converting from an accrual basis to a cash basis net income. Entry (4) debits Inventory and credits net cash flow from operating activities for the $4,000 inventory increase.

(5) Entry (5) adds the increase in accounts payable to the accrual basis net income as another part of the conversion to a cash basis amount. The entry debits net cash flow from operating activities and credits Accounts Payable for $2,500.

(6) Increases in accrued liabilities are added to accrual basis net income in the process of converting to a cash basis amount. Entry (6) adds the $500 increase in wages payable by debiting net cash flow from operating activities and crediting Wages Payable for $500.

(7) Entry (7) deducts the decrease in income tax payable from the accrual basis net income to complete the conversion to a cash basis amount. The entry debits Income Tax Payable and credits net cash flow from operating activities for $1,000.

STEP 3 Prepare the statement of cash flows using the information in the worksheet. Again, the worksheet has compiled the cash flows in the proper categories for the statement of cash flows. Exhibit 19–9 shows the statement of cash flows,

EXHIBIT 19–9
Statement of Cash Flows
Indirect Method

XYZ Company Statement of Cash Flows For the Year Ended December 31, 19X3		
Net Cash Flow from Operating Activities		
Net Income	$ 9,000	
Add (Deduct) Items to Convert Net Income to Cash Basis:		
Depreciation	5,000	
Accounts Receivable Increase	(8,000)	
Inventory Increase	(4,000)	
Accounts Payable Increase	2,500	
Wages Payable Increase	500	
Income Tax Payable Decrease	(1,000)	
Net Cash Flow from Operating Activities		$4,000
Cash Flows from Investing Activities		
Sale of Plant Assets	$ 4,000	
Purchase of Plant Assets	(8,000)	
Net Cash Used by Investing Activities		(4,000)
Cash Flows from Financing Activities		
Issuance of Common Stock	$10,000	
Payment of Dividends	3,000	
Net Cash Provided by Financing Activities		7,000
Net Increase in Cash		$7,000

using the indirect method, for XYZ Company. The only difference from the statement of cash flows prepared under the direct method is in the presentation of the net cash flow from operating activities.

NONCASH INVESTING AND FINANCING ACTIVITIES

A secondary objective of the statement of cash flows is to present information about a firm's investing and financing activities. Of course, many of these activities affect cash and are therefore already included in the investing and financing sections of the statement of cash flows. Some significant investing and financing events, however, do not affect current cash flows. Examples of such events are the issuance of stocks or bonds in exchange for plant assets or intangible assets and the conversion of long-term debt into common stock. Information about these events must be reported in the statement of cash flows.

Noncash investing and financing transactions generally do impact on future cash flows. Issuing bonds payable to acquire equipment, for example, requires future cash payments for interest and principal on the bonds. On the other hand, converting bonds payable into common stock eliminates future cash payments related to the bonds. Knowledge of these types of events, therefore, should be helpful to users of cash flow data who wish to assess a firm's future cash flows.

The need to report noncash investing and financing activities causes no change in the worksheet used to compile information for the statement of cash flows. As analyzing entries are prepared, note must be made of any significant noncash investing or financing transactions (referencing these events with a special mark on the worksheet, perhaps). Information on these events will then be placed in the statement of cash flows when the statement is prepared.

There are two ways data on noncash investing and financing transactions may be disclosed. They may be reported in a supplementary schedule to the statement of cash flows or they may be integrated into the investing and financing sections of the statement itself. If integrated into the body of the statement, however, there must be a clear distinction made between the events affecting current cash flows and the noncash events. We illustrate both disclosure procedures in the comprehensive illustration that follows.

COMPREHENSIVE ILLUSTRATION

We now present a comprehensive exercise to introduce additional events that impact on the statement of cash flows and to review the procedures for preparing the statement. The illustration covers both the direct and indirect methods.

The comparative balance sheets and income statement for the Superior Corporation are presented in Exhibits 19–10 and 19–11, respectively. During 19X2, the following transactions occurred, in addition to routine transactions:

(1) Sold a parcel of land, which originally cost $10,000, for $35,000 cash.

(2) Purchased equipment for $32,000 cash.

(3) Acquired custom-built equipment worth $30,000 by issuing 300 shares of common stock.

(4) Paid cash to retire bonds payable of $20,000 at par value.

(5) Issued 100 shares of common stock at par value for cash.

Under both the direct and indirect methods, we first determine the change in cash experienced by Superior Corporation during 19X2. The comparative balance sheets in Exhibit 19–10 show cash increased $12,000 during 19X2. We must explain this cash increase in the statement of cash flows.

EXHIBIT 19–10

Superior Corporation
Balance Sheets

	Dec. 31, 19X2	Dec. 31, 19X1	Increase (Decrease)
ASSETS			
Current Assets			
Cash	$ 25,000	$ 13,000	$12,000
Accounts Receivable (net)	55,000	60,000	(5,000)
Inventory	94,000	80,000	14,000
Prepaid Expenses	13,000	10,000	3,000
Total Current Assets	$187,000	$163,000	$24,000
Plant Assets			
Plant	$235,000	$183,000	$52,000
Accumulated Depreciation	(47,000)	(34,000)	13,000
Total Plant Assets	$188,000	$149,000	$39,000
Total Assets	$375,000	$312,000	$63,000
LIABILITIES AND STOCKHOLDERS' EQUITY			
Current Liabilities			
Accounts Payable	$ 30,000	$ 40,000	($10,000)
Wages Payable	2,000	4,000	(2,000)
Income Tax Payable	2,000	1,000	1,000
Total Current Liabilities	$ 34,000	$ 45,000	($11,000)
Long-term Debt			
Bonds Payable	$ 50,000	$ 70,000	($20,000)
Stockholders' Equity			
Common Stock ($100 par value)	$175,000	$135,000	$40,000
Retained Earnings	116,000	62,000	54,000
Total Stockholders' Equity	$291,000	$197,000	$94,000
Total Liabilities and Stockholders' Equity	$375,000	$312,000	$63,000

Direct Method

Next, we prepare a worksheet for the statement of cash flows. Exhibit 19–12 shows the worksheet for Superior Corporation using the direct method. The analyzing entries are explained below. Entries (1)–(8) derive cash flow from operations and entries (9)–(13) explain the remaining changes in the noncash accounts.

(1) The first analyzing entry places the accrual basis income statement data on the worksheet. Superior's income statement reflects a $25,000 gain from the sale of land. The sale of land is an investing activity. Any gain (or loss) from

EXHIBIT 19–11

Superior Corporation
Income Statement
For the Year Ended December 31, 19X2

Sales		$360,000
Cost of Goods Sold		240,000
Gross Profit		$120,000
Wages Expense	$45,000	
Depreciation Expense	13,000	
Other Operating Expenses	21,000	
Gain on Sale of Land	(25,000)	
Income Tax Expense	12,000	66,000
Net Income		$ 54,000

investing activities should not affect cash flows from operating activities, so the $25,000 gain is debited as a separate item to the cash flows from investing activities section (a loss on the sale of plant assets would be credited to cash flows from investing activities). A later analyzing entry [entry (9)] will eliminate the gain completely because we are interested in the cash inflow from the sale, not the gain.

The complete first entry debits cash received from customers, $360,000 (the Sales amount); debits Gain on Sale of Land (within cash flows from investing activities), $25,000; credits cash paid to suppliers, $274,000 (the sum of Cost of Goods Sold, Depreciation Expense, and Other Operating Expenses); credits cash paid to employees, $45,000 (the Wages Expense amount); credits cash paid for taxes, $12,000 (the Income Tax Expense amount); and credits Retained Earnings for the $54,000 net income.

(2) Entry (2) adds the $5,000 decrease in accounts receivable to the $360,000 sales amount to convert it from an accrual to a cash amount. The entry debits cash received from customers and credits Accounts Receivable for $5,000.

(3), (4), (5), and **(6)** Entries (3)–(6) reflect the adjustments to convert cash paid to suppliers from its accrual basis starting point to a cash amount. Entries (3) and (4) add the $14,000 inventory increase and the $3,000 prepaid expenses increase to the starting point. The entries debit the respective asset accounts and credit cash paid to suppliers. Entry (5) adds the $10,000 decrease in accounts payable by debiting Accounts Payable and crediting cash paid to suppliers. Depreciation expense is eliminated in entry (6); the entry debits cash paid to suppliers and credits Accummulated Depreciation for $13,000.

(7) Entry (7) adds the $2,000 decrease in Wages Payable to the $45,000 wages expense to convert it from an accrual to a cash amount. The entry debits Wages Payable and credits cash paid to employees for $2,000.

(8) Entry (8) deducts the $1,000 increase in Income Tax Payable from income

EXHIBIT 19–12

Superior Corporation
Worksheet for Statement of Cash Flows (Direct Method)
For the Year Ended December 31, 19X2

Description	Changes in Noncash Accounts		Analyzing Entries	
	Debit	Credit	Debit	Credit
Accounts Receivable (net)		5,000		(2) 5,000
Inventory	14,000		(3) 14,000	
Prepaid Expenses	3,000		(4) 3,000	
Plant Assets	52,000		(10) 32,000	(9) 10,000
			(11)* 30,000	
Accumulated Depreciation		13,000		(6) 13,000
Accounts Payable	10,000		(5) 10,000	
Wages Payable	2,000		(7) 2,000	
Income Tax Payable		1,000		(8) 1,000
Bonds Payable	20,000		(12) 20,000	
Common Stock		40,000		(11)* 30,000
				(13) 10,000
Retained Earnings		54,000		(1) 54,000
	101,000	113,000		
Increase in Cash	12,000			
	113,000	113,000		
Cash Flows from Operating Activities				
Cash Received from Customers			(1) 360,000	
Add: Accounts Receivable Decrease			(2) 5,000	
Cash Paid to Suppliers				(1) 274,000
Add: Inventory Increase				(3) 14,000
Add: Prepaid Expenses Increase				(4) 3,000
Add: Accounts Payable Decrease				(5) 10,000
Less: Depreciation			(6) 13,000	
Cash Paid to Employees				(1) 45,000
Add: Wages Payable Decrease				(7) 2,000
Cash Paid for Taxes				(1) 12,000
Less: Income Tax Payable Increase			(8) 1,000	
Cash Flows from Investing Activities				
Gain on Sale of Land			(1) 25,000	(9) 25,000
Sale of Land			(9) 35,000	
Purchase of Equipment				(10) 32,000
Cash Flows from Financing Activities				
Retirement of Bonds Payable				(12) 20,000
Issuance of Common Stock			(13) 10,000	
			560,000	560,000

tax expense to convert it from an accrual to a cash amount. The entry debits cash paid for taxes and credits Income Tax Payable for $1,000.

(9) Entry (9) reconstructs the entry for the sale of land. The transaction generated a cash inflow of $35,000 which is debited to cash flows from investing activities, the $10,000 land cost is credited to Plant Assets, and the $25,000 gain is credited to Gain on Sale of Land in the cash flows from investing activities section. The $25,000 credit thus eliminates the gain from the worksheet [it was debited in entry (1)]. We eliminate the gain because, in a statement of cash flows, we must report the cash inflows from sales and not the gains or losses from sales.

(10) Cash of $32,000 was used to purchase equipment. Entry (10) reflects this investment event with a debit to Plant Assets and a credit to cash flows from investing activities for $32,000.

(11) Entry (11) reconstructs the entry for the acquisition of equipment in exchange for common stock. The entry debits Plant Assets and Credits Common Stock for $30,000. This event is a significant noncash investing and financing transaction that must be disclosed in the statement of cash flows. We highlight the analyzing entry with an asterisk (*) to identify it as an event requiring special disclosure treatment.

(12) The retirement of bonds payable utilized $20,000 of cash. Entry (12) shows this financing transaction by debiting Bonds Payable for $20,000 and crediting $20,000 to cash flows from financing activities for the retirement of bonds.

(13) Entry (13) reconstructs the entry for the issuance of common stock for cash. This financing event increased cash $10,000. The entry debits cash flows from financing activities and credits Common Stock for $10,000.

Once the worksheet is completed, we prepare the statement of cash flows for Superior Corporation, under the direct method, shown in Exhibit 19–13. One disclosure treatment for noncash investing and financing transactions is to report them in a supplementary schedule to the statement of cash flows. This disclosure treatment is used in Exhibit 19–13.

Indirect Method

Exhibit 19–14 presents Superior Corporation's worksheet for a statement of cash flows using the indirect method. Analyzing entries (1)–(9) are explained below. Entries (1)–(9) determine the net cash flow from Superior's operating activities [entry (3) also reflects the cash inflow from the sale of land]. Entries (10)–(13) are exactly the same entries as entries (10)–(13) under the direct method illustrated in Exhibit 19–12. Refer to our previous discussion for an explanation of these four entries.

(1) Entry (1) debits the $54,000 accrual basis net income to net cash flow from operating activities and credits Retained Earnings.

(2) Entry (2) eliminates depreciation expense from net income by debiting net cash flow from operating activities and crediting Accumulated Depreciation.

(3) Entry (3) reconstructs the entry for the sale of land. The sale created a $25,000 gain which is included in the $54,000 net income. The gain must be eliminated from net income because it does not reflect the cash flow from the

EXHIBIT 19–13
Statement of Cash Flows—Direct Method with Noncash Investing and Financing Activities in a Supplementary Schedule

Superior Corporation
Statement of Cash Flows
For the Year Ended December 31, 19X2

Cash Flows from Operating Activities		
Cash Received from Customers		$365,000
Cash Disbursed for Operating Activities:		
Cash Paid to Suppliers	$288,000	
Cash Paid to Employees	47,000	
Cash Paid for Taxes	11,000	346,000
Net Cash Flow from Operating Activities		$ 19,000
Cash Flows from Investing Activities		
Sale of Land	$ 35,000	
Purchase of Equipment	(32,000)	
Net Cash Provided by Investing Activities		3,000
Cash Flows from Financing Activities		
Issuance of Common Stock	$ 10,000	
Retirement of Bonds Payable	(20,000)	
Net Cash Used by Financing Activities		(10,000)
Net Increase in Cash		$ 12,000
Schedule of Noncash Investing and Financing Activities:		
Issuance of Common Stock to Acquire Equipment		$ 30,000

sale nor does it relate to an operating activity. The analyzing entry credits the gain to net cash flow from operating activities; this credit eliminates the gain from net income.

The complete analyzing entry debits cash flows from investing activities for the $35,000 cash inflow from the sale of land, credits Plant Assets for the $10,000 cost of the land sold, and credits net cash flow from operating activities for the $25,000 gain.

(4), (5), (6), (7), (8), and (9) Entries (4)–(9) reflect the impact of changes in various current asset and current liability accounts on the conversion of accrual basis net income to a cash amount. Entry (4) adds the decrease in accounts receivable to net income with a debit to net cash flow from operating activities and a credit to Accounts Receivable for $5,000. Entries (5) and (6) subtract the increases in inventory ($14,000) and prepaid expenses ($3,000) from net income by debit-

EXHIBIT 19–14

Superior Corporation
Worksheet for Statement of Cash Flows (Indirect Method)
For the Year Ended December 31, 19X2

	Changes in Noncash Accounts		Analyzing Entries	
Description	**Debit**	**Credit**	**Debit**	**Credit**
Accounts Receivable (net)		5,000		(4) 5,000
Inventory	14,000		(5) 14,000	
Prepaid Expenses	3,000		(6) 3,000	
Plant Assets	52,000		(10) 32,000	(3) 10,000
			(11)* 30,000	
Accumulated Depreciation		13,000		(2) 13,000
Accounts Payable	10,000		(7) 10,000	
Wages Payable	2,000		(8) 2,000	
Income Tax Payable		1,000		(9) 1,000
Bonds Payable	20,000		(12) 20,000	
Common Stock		40,000		(11)* 30,000
				(13) 10,000
Retained Earnings		54,000		(1) 54,000
	101,000	113,000		
Increase in Cash	12,000			
	113,000	113,000		
Net Cash Flow from Operating Activities				
Net Income			(1) 54,000	
Add: Depreciation			(2) 13,000	
Less: Gain on Sale of Land				(3) 25,000
Add: Accounts Receivable Decrease			(4) 5,000	
Less: Inventory Increase				(5) 14,000
Less: Prepaid Expenses Increase				(6) 3,000
Less: Accounts Payable Decrease				(7) 10,000
Less: Wages Payable Decrease				(8) 2,000
Add: Income Tax Payable Increase			(9) 1,000	
Cash Flows from Investing Activities				
Sale of Land			(3) 35,000	
Purchase of Equipment				(10) 32,000
Cash Flows from Financing Activities				
Retirement of Bonds Payable				(12) 20,000
Issuance of Common Stock			(13) 10,000	
			229,000	229,000

ing the respective current asset accounts and crediting net cash flow from operating activities. Entries (7) and (8) subtract the decreases in accounts payable ($10,000) and wages payable ($2,000) from net income; the entries debit the respective current liability accounts and credit net cash flow from operating activities. Entry (9) adds the $1,000 increase in income tax payable to net income by debiting net cash flow from operating activities and crediting Income Tax Payable for $1,000.

Superior Corporation's statement of cash flows in Exhibit 19–15 uses the indirect method and is prepared from the worksheet shown in Exhibit 19–14.

EXHIBIT 19–15
Statement of Cash Flows—Indirect Method with Noncash Investing and Financing Activities Integrated into the Statement

Superior Corporation
Statement of Cash Flows
For the Year Ended December 31, 19X2

Net Cash Flow from Operating Activities			
Net Income		$54,000	
Add (Deduct) Items to Convert Net Income to Cash Basis:			
Depreciation		13,000	
Gain on Sale of Land		(25,000)	
Accounts Receivable Decrease		5,000	
Inventory Increase		(14,000)	
Prepaid Expenses Increase		(3,000)	
Accounts Payable Decrease		(10,000)	
Wages Payable Decrease		(2,000)	
Income Tax Payable Increase		1,000	
Net Cash Flow from Operating Activities			$19,000
Cash Flows from Investing Activities			
Sale of Land		$35,000	
Acquisition of Equipment	$62,000		
Less: Equipment Acquired by Issuing Common Stock	30,000		
Cash Outflow for Equipment		(32,000)	
Net Cash Provided by Investing Activities			3,000
Cash Flows from Financing Activities			
Issuance of Common Stock	$40,000		
Less: Common Stock Issued to Acquire Equipment	30,000		
Cash Proceeds from Issuance of Common Stock		$10,000	
Retirement of Bonds Payable		(20,000)	
Net Cash Used by Financing Activities			(10,000)
Net Increase in Cash			$12,000

This statement of cash flows integrates the noncash investing and financing transaction into the body of the statement. The noncash event is both an investing transaction (acquisition of equipment) and a financing transaction (issuance of common stock) so it appears in each of these sections in the statement of cash flows. The presentation must clearly identify the noncash events while also preserving the statement's focus on cash flows. We accomplish this by first combining together similar cash and noncash events (the acquisition of equipment is one type of event and the issuance of common stock is another type of event) and then removing the noncash aspects of the transactions. Superior Corporation acquired equipment totaling $62,000 and issued common stock amounting to $40,000. These amounts are shown in the statement of cash flows and then the noncash amounts are removed ($30,000 in both instances). The remainders represent the cash flows associated with these events.

KEY POINTS TO REMEMBER

(1) The statement of cash flows explains the net increase or decrease in cash during the period.

(2) The statement of cash flows separates cash flows into operating, investing, and financing categories.

(3) Cash flows from operations may be presented using the direct method or the indirect method. The direct method shows the major categories of cash receipts and payments. The indirect method reconciles net income to the cash flow from operations amount.

(4) A worksheet may aid in the preparation of a statement of cash flows. The worksheet contains entries analyzing the changes in all noncash balance sheet accounts and identifies the transactions affecting cash flows.

(5) Significant noncash investing and financing transactions must be reported in the statement of cash flows. They may be disclosed in a supplementary schedule or be integrated into the body of the statement.

SELF-TEST QUESTIONS
(Answers are at the end of this chapter.)

1. Which of the following is not disclosed in a statement of cash flows?
   (a) The amount of cash on hand at year-end.
   (b) Cash outflows from investing activities during the period.
   (c) Cash inflows from financing activities during the period.
   (d) Cash provided by operations during the period.
2. A worksheet for a statement of cash flows analyzes the changes in
   (a) Each of the firm's bank accounts.
   (b) All of the firm's noncash accounts.

(c) The firm's working capital accounts only.
(d) The firm's noncurrent accounts only.

3. Tyler Company has an accrual basis net income of $39,000 and the following related items:

Depreciation expense	$ 7,000
Accounts receivable decrease	2,000
Inventory increase	10,000
Accounts payable increase	4,000

Using the indirect method, what is Tyler's cash flow from operations?
(a) $42,000 (b) $46,000 (c) $44,000 (d) $34,000

4. Which of the following events will appear in the cash flows from financing activities section of the statement of cash flows?
(a) Cash purchase of equipment.
(b) Cash purchase of bonds issued by another company.
(c) Cash received as repayment for funds loaned.
(d) Cash purchase of treasury stock.

5. Which of the following cash flows does not appear in a statement of cash flows prepared using the indirect method?
(a) Net cash flow from operating activities.
(b) Cash received from customers.
(c) Cash inflow from sale of equipment.
(d) Cash outflow from dividend payment.

QUESTIONS

19–1 Define *cash equivalents.* Give three examples of cash equivalents.

19–2 Why are cash equivalents included with cash in a statement of cash flows?

19–3 Why is a statement of cash flows a useful financial statement?

19–4 Identify the three major types of activities classified on a statement of cash flows and give an example of a cash inflow and a cash outflow in each classification.

19–5 What limitation of the prodecessor statement of changes in financial position (focusing on working capital changes) is overcome by a statement of cash flows?

19–6 Distinguish between the direct method and the indirect (reconciliation) method of presenting net cash flow from operating activities.

19–7 What are the two methods of determining cash flows from operating activities using the direct method? Generally, which of these methods is simplest to use?

19–8 A firm is converting its accrual basis revenues and expenses to corresponding cash amounts using the direct method. Sales on the income statement are $220,000. Beginning and ending accounts receivable on the balance sheet are $28,000 and $32,000, respectively. What is the amount of cash received from customers?

19–9 The firm in Question 8 is converting the $130,000 cost of goods sold on its income statement to cash paid for merchandise purchased. Beginning and ending inventories are $40,000 and $50,000, respectively, and beginning and ending accounts payable (for merchandise purchased) are $21,000 and $18,000, respectively. What is the amount of cash paid for merchandise purchased?

19–10 The firm in Question 8 is converting the $60,000 wages expense on its income statement to cash paid to employees. If beginning and ending wages payable are $2,500 and $1,300, respectively, what is the amount of cash paid to employees?

19–11 Star Company sold for $32,000 cash long-term investments originally costing $14,000. The company recorded a gain on the sale of $18,000. Describe how this event is handled in a statement of cash flows using (a) the direct method, and (b) the indirect method.

19–12 In determining net cash flow from operating activities using the indirect method, why must we add depreciation back to net income? Give an example of another item that is added back to net income under the indirect method.

19–13 Explain how uncollectible accounts expense is handled under the direct method of reporting net cash flow from operating activities.

19–14 Foster Company sold equipment for $1,500 cash that had cost $12,000 and had $9,600 of accumulated depreciation. Describe how this event is handled in a statement of cash flows using (a) the direct method, and (b) the indirect method.

19–15 Identify in which of the three activity categories of a statement of cash flows each of the following items would appear, and indicate for each item whether it represents a cash inflow or a cash outflow:
(a) Cash purchase of equipment
(b) Collections on loans
(c) Cash dividends paid
(d) Cash dividends received
(e) Cash proceeds from issuing stock
(f) Cash receipts from customers

19–16 A firm uses the indirect method of presenting net cash flow from operating activities. Calculate this net cash flow using the following information:

Net income	$15,000
Accounts receivable decrease	3,000
Inventory increase	4,000
Accounts payable decrease	2,500
Wages payable increase	1,200
Depreciation expense	7,000

19–17 What is the purpose of the analyzing entries on a worksheet for a statement of cash flows?

19–18 If a business had a net loss for the year, under what circumstances would the statement of cash flows show a positive net cash flow from operating activities?

19–19 Kyle Company acquired a $900,000 building by issuing $900,000 worth of bonds payable. Describe two ways this transaction may be reported in a statement of cash flows.

19–20 Why are significant noncash investing and financing transactions included in a statement of cash flows?

EXERCISES

Operating cash flows

19–21 Victory Company's current year income statement contains the following data:

Sales	$760,000
Cost of Goods Sold	500,000
Gross Profit	$260,000

Victory's comparative balance sheets show the following data (accounts payable relate to merchandise purchases):

	End of Year	Beginning of Year
Accounts Receivable (net)	$ 43,000	$52,000
Inventory	110,000	94,000
Prepaid Expenses	7,000	9,000
Accounts Payable	31,000	36,000

(a) Compute Victory's current year cash received from customers and cash paid for merchandise purchased.

(b) Assume Victory's income statement shows uncollectible accounts expense of $4,000. Compute the current year cash received from customers.

Cash flow from operations

19–22 The Lucky Company, a sole proprietorship which owns no plant assets, had the following income statement for the current year:

Sales		$440,000
Cost of Goods Sold		300,000
Gross Profit		$140,000
Operating Expenses:		
Wages Expense	$60,000	
Rent Expense	24,000	
Insurance Expense	12,000	96,000
Net Income		$ 44,000

Additional information about the company follows:

	End of Year	Beginning of Year
Accounts Receivable	$48,000	$42,000
Inventory	60,000	76,000
Prepaid Insurance	6,000	4,000
Accounts Payable	28,000	16,000
Wages Payable	5,000	8,000

Use the preceding information to calculate the net cash flow from operating activities using the direct method.

Cash flow from operations

19–23 Refer to the information in Exercise 19–22. Calculate the net cash flow from operating activities using the indirect method.

Cash flow from operations

19–24 The following information was obtained from the Forrest Company's comparative balance sheets.

	Dec. 31, 19X1	Dec. 31, 19X0
Cash	$ 15,000	$19,000
Accounts Receivable	35,000	22,000
Inventory	51,000	36,000
Prepaid Rent	2,000	3,000
Plant Assets	106,000	86,000
Accumulated Depreciation	(23,000)	(16,000)
Accounts Payable	25,000	20,000
Income Tax Payable	1,000	4,000
Common Stock	95,000	85,000
Retained Earnings	65,000	41,000

Assume Forrest Company's 19X1 income statement showed depreciation expense of $7,000 and a net income of $30,000. Calculate the net cash flow operating activities using the indirect method.

Classification of cash flows

19–25 Refer to the information in Exercise 19–24. During 19X1 Forrest Company purchased plant assets for cash and issued common stock for cash. The firm also declared and paid cash dividends in 19X1. What items and amounts will appear in the (a) Cash Flows from Investing Activities and the (b) Cash Flows from Financing Activities sections of a 19X1 statement of cash flows?

Classification of cash flows

19–26 For each of the items below, indicate in which of the three categories [Cash Flows from Operating Activities (Direct Method), Cash Flows from Investing Activities, and Cash Flows from Financing Activities] the item should appear, and whether it is an inflow or an outflow of cash.

(a) Cash receipts from customers
(b) Sale of long-term investments for cash
(c) Acquisition of plant assets for cash
(d) Payment of taxes
(e) Bonds issued for cash
(f) Dividends paid
(g) Dividends received
(h) Cash loaned to borrowers
(i) Preferred stock issued for cash

Cash flow from operations

19–27 Rocket Company had a $10,000 net loss from operations for 19X2. Depreciation expense for 19X2 was $6,500 and a 19X2 dividend of $4,000 was declared and paid. Balances of the current asset and current liability accounts at the beginning and end of 19X2 are as follows:

	End	Beginning
Cash	$ 3,000	$ 9,000
Accounts Receivable	12,000	17,000
Inventory	40,000	39,000
Prepaid Expenses	1,500	3,500
Accounts Payable	8,500	6,000
Accrued Liabilities	1,000	4,000

Did Rocket Company's 19X2 operations provide or use cash? Use the indirect method to determine your answer.

Cash flow from operations

19–28 The following information is taken from the financial statements of Packer Corporation:

From the 19X5 income statement:

Net income	$106,000
Depreciation Expense	12,000
Goodwill Amortization Expense	4,000
Loss on Sale of Long-term Investments	1,000

From the 19X4 and 19X5 year-end balance sheets:

	Dec. 31, 19X5	Dec. 31, 19X4
Accounts Receivable	$31,000	$34,000
Inventory	98,000	92,000
Accounts payable	19,000	26,000
Accrued Liabilities	20,000	14,000

Calculate the 19X5 net cash flow from operating activities using the indirect method.

PROBLEMS

Statement of cash flows—direct method

19–29 Madden Company's 19X1 income statement and comparative balance sheets at December 31 of 19X1 and 19X0 are shown below.

Madden Company
Income Statement
For the Year Ended December 31, 19X1

Sales		$280,000
Cost of Goods Sold		180,000
Gross Profit		$100,000
Wages Expense	$41,000	
Depreciation Expense	9,000	
Other Operating Expenses	16,000	
Income Tax Expense	5,000	71,000
Net Income		$ 29,000

Madden Company
Balance Sheets

Assets	Dec. 31, 19X1	Dec. 31, 19X0
Cash	$ 9,000	$ 7,000
Accounts Receivable (net)	18,000	15,000
Inventory	39,000	28,000
Prepaid Expenses	2,000	4,000
Plant Assets	100,000	75,000
Accumulated Depreciation	(30,000)	(21,000)
Total Assets	$138,000	$108,000

Liabilities and Stockholders' Equity		
Accounts Payable	$ 4,600	$ 9,000
Wages Payable	2,400	1,700
Income Tax Payable	1,000	1,300
Bonds Payable	20,000	—
Common Stock	60,000	60,000
Retained Earnings	50,000	36,000
Total Liabilities and Stockholders' Equity	$138,000	$108,000

Cash dividends of $15,000 were declared and paid during 19X1. Plant assets were purchased for cash, and later in the year, bonds payable were issued for cash.

REQUIRED

(a) Prepare a worksheet for a 19X1 statement of cash flows using the direct method.

(b) Prepare a 19X1 statement of cash flows using the direct method.

Statement of cash flows—direct method

19–30 Novak Company's income statement for the current year and comparative balance sheet at December 31 of this year and last year are presented below.

Novak Company
Income Statement
For the Current Year

Sales		$385,000
Cost of Goods Sold		227,000
Gross Profit		$158,000
Uncollectible Accounts Expense	$ 1,000	
Wages Expense	58,000	
Depreciation Expense	24,000	
Goodwill Amortization Expense	4,000	
Other Operating Expenses	19,000	
Income Tax Expense	10,000	116,000
Net Income		$ 42,000

Novak Company
Balance Sheets

	Dec. 31, This Year	**Dec. 31, Last Year**
Assets		
Cash	$ 19,000	$ 13,000
Accounts Receivable (net)	40,000	38,000
Inventory	84,000	91,000
Prepaid Expenses	5,000	4,000
Plant Assets	255,000	220,000
Accumulated Depreciation	(70,000)	(60,000)
Goodwill (net)	32,000	36,000
Total Assets	$365,000	$342,000

Liabilities and Stockholders' Equity		
Accounts Payable	$ 30,000	$ 24,000
Wages Payable	5,000	6,000
Income Tax Payable	2,000	4,000
Bonds Payable	75,000	100,000
Common Stock	140,000	120,000
Retained Earnings	113,000	88,000
Total Liabilities and Stockholders' Equity	$365,000	$342,000

During the year, the company sold for $6,000 old equipment that had cost $20,000 and had $14,000 accumulated depreciation. New equipment was purchased for cash. A portion of the bonds matured this year and were retired for cash. A $17,000 cash dividend was declared and paid this year. All stock issuances were for cash.

REQUIRED
(a) Prepare a worksheet for a statement of cash flows for this year using the direct method.
(b) Prepare a statement of cash flows for this year using the direct method.

Statement of cash flows—direct method

19–31 The Burton Company's comparative balance sheets at December 31 of this year and last year and its income statement for the current year are shown below.

Burton Company
Balance Sheets

	Dec, 31, This Year	Dec. 31, Last Year
Assets		
Cash	$ 21,000	$ 26,000
Accounts Receivable (net)	48,000	39,000
Inventory	99,000	87,000
Prepaid Expenses	13,000	10,000
Long-term Investments	10,000	28,000
Land	120,000	70,000
Buildings	360,000	260,000
Accumulated Depreciation—Buildings	(78,000)	(55,000)
Equipment	183,000	215,000
Accumulated Depreciation—Equipment	(45,000)	(46,000)
Patents (net)	30,000	15,000
Total Assets	$761,000	$649,000
Liabilities and Stockholders' Equity		
Accounts Payable	$ 42,000	$ 26,000
Wages Payable	7,000	5,500
Income Tax Payable	5,000	8,500
Bonds Payable	250,000	225,000
Preferred Stock ($100 par value)	120,000	100,000
Common Stock ($50 par value)	210,000	190,000
Paid-in Capital in Excess of Par Value—Common	12,000	8,000
Retained Earnings	115,000	86,000
Total Liabilities and Stockholders' Equity	$761,000	$649,000

Burton Company
Income Statement
For the Current Year

Sales		$850,000
Cost of Goods Sold		578,000
Gross Profit		$272,000
Wages Expense	$85,000	
Depreciation Expense	43,000	
Patent Amortization Expense	5,000	
Other Operating Expenses	41,000	
Loss on Sale of Equipment	4,000	
Gain on Sale of Investments	(8,000)	
Income Tax Expense	27,000	197,000
Net Income		$ 75,000

During the year, the following transactions occurred:
(1) Purchased land for $50,000 cash.
(2) Sold long-term investments, costing $18,000, for $26,000 cash.
(3) Capitalized an expenditure of $100,000 made to improve the building.
(4) Sold equipment for $7,000 cash that originally cost $32,000 and had $21,000 accumulated depreciation.
(5) Issued $25,000 of bonds payable at face value.
(6) Acquired a patent with a fair value of $20,000 by issuing 200 share of preferred stock at par value.
(7) Declared and paid a $46,000 cash dividend.
(8) Issued 400 shares of common stock for cash at $60 per share.
(9) Recorded depreciation of $23,000 on buildings and $20,000 on equipment.

REQUIRED
(a) Prepare a worksheet for a statement of cash flows for this year using the direct method.
(b) Prepare a statement of cash flows for this year using the direct method. Place noncash investing and financing events in a supplementary schedule.

Statement of cash flows—direct method

19–32 Polk Company's 19X1 income statement and comparative balance sheets at December 31 of 19X1 and 19X0 are shown below.

Polk Company
Income Statement
For the Year Ended December 31, 19X1

Sales		$160,000
Cost of Goods Sold		100,000
Gross Profit		$ 60,000
Wages Expense	$29,000	
Depreciation Expense	8,000	
Other Operating Expenses	34,000	
Gain on Sale of Land	(4,000)	67,000
Net Loss		$ 7,000

Polk Company
Balance Sheets

	Dec. 31, 19X1	Dec. 31, 19X0
Assets		
Cash	$ 7,000	$ 15,000
Accounts Receivable (net)	16,000	12,000
Inventory	34,000	28,000
Prepaid Expenses	2,000	4,000
Plant Assets	102,000	65,000
Accumulated Depreciation	(28,000)	(20,000)
Total Assets	$133,000	$104,000
Liabilities and Stockholders' Equity		
Accounts Payable	$ 10,000	$ 13,000
Wages Payable	1,000	2,000
Bonds Payable	45,000	—
Common Stock	60,000	60,000
Retained Earnings	22,000	29,000
Treasury Stock	(5,000)	—
Total Liabilities and Stockholders' Equity	$133,000	$104,000

During 19X1, Polk sold land for $15,000 that had originally cost $11,000. Polk also purchased equipment for cash, reacquired treasury stock for cash, and issued bonds payable for cash.

REQUIRED
(a) Prepare a worksheet for a 19X1 statement of cash flows using the direct method.
(b) Prepare a 19X1 statement of cash flows using the direct method.

Statement of cash flows—indirect method

19–33 Refer to the data given for the Madden Company in Problem 19–29.

REQUIRED
(a) Prepare a worksheet for a 19X1 statement of cash flows using the indirect method.
(b) Prepare a 19X1 statement of cash flows using the indirect method.

Statement of cash flows—indirect method

19–34 Refer to the data given for the Novak Company in Problem 19–30

REQUIRED
(a) Prepare a worksheet for a statement of cash flows for this year using the indirect method.
(b) Prepare a statement of cash flows for this year using the indirect method.

Statement of cash flows—indirect method

19–35 Refer to the data given for the Burton Company in Problem 19–31.

REQUIRED
(a) Prepare a worksheet for a statement of cash flows for this year using the indirect method.
(b) Prepare a statement of cash flows for this year using the indirect method. Place noncash investing and financing events in a supplementary schedule.

Statement of cash flows—indirect method

19–36 Refer to the data given for the Polk Company in Problem 19–32.

REQUIRED

(a) Prepare a worksheet for a 19X1 statement of cash flows using the indirect method.

(b) Prepare a 19X1 statement of cash flows using the indirect method.

ALTERNATE PROBLEMS

Statement of cash flows—direct method

19–29A Terry Company's 19X1 income statement and comparative balance sheets at December 31 of 19X1 and 19X0 are shown below.

Terry Company
Income Statement
For the Year Ended December 31, 19X1

Sales		$390,000
Cost of Goods Sold		235,000
Gross Profit		$155,000
Wages Expense	$63,000	
Depreciation Expense	14,000	
Other Operating Expenses	26,000	
Income Tax Expense	17,000	120,000
Net Income		$ 35,000

Terry Company
Balance Sheets

Assets	**Dec. 31, 19X1**	**Dec. 31, 19X0**
Cash	$ 16,000	$ 30,000
Accounts Receivable (net)	28,000	35,000
Inventory	110,000	84,000
Prepaid Expenses	12,000	8,000
Plant Assets	178,000	130,000
Accumulated Depreciation	(76,000)	(62,000)
Total Assets	$268,000	$225,000
Liabilities and Stockholders' Equity		
Accounts Payable	$ 27,000	$ 14,000
Wages Payable	6,000	2,500
Income Tax Payable	3,000	4,500
Common Stock	135,000	125,000
Retained Earnings	97,000	79,000
Total Liabilities and Stockholders' Equity	$268,000	$225,000

Cash dividends of $17,000 were declared and paid during 19X1. Plant assets were purchased for cash, and later in the year, additional common stock was issued for cash.

REQUIRED
(a) Prepare a worksheet for a 19X1 statement of cash flows using the direct method.
(b) Prepare a 19X1 statement of cash flows using the direct method.

Statement of cash flows—direct method

19–30A Sagan Company's income statement for the current year and comparative balance sheets at December 31 of this year and last year are presented below.

Sagan Company
Income Statement
For the Current Year

Sales		$445,000
Cost of Goods Sold		240,000
Gross Profit		$205,000
Uncollectible Accounts Expense	$ 2,000	
Wages Expense	74,000	
Depreciation Expense	26,000	
Other Operating Expenses	35,000	
Gain on Sale of Equipment	(6,000)	
Income Tax Expense	20,000	151,000
Net Income		$ 54,000

Sagan Company
Balance Sheets

Assets	Dec. 31, This Year	Dec. 31, Last Year
Cash	$ 12,000	$ 15,000
Accounts Receivable (net)	37,000	21,000
Inventory	109,000	86,000
Prepaid Expenses	8,000	9,000
Plant Assets	430,000	362,000
Accumulated Depreciation	(84,000)	(72,000)
Total Assets	$512,000	$421,000
Liabilities and Stockholders' Equity		
Accounts Payable	$ 40,000	$ 34,500
Wages Payable	7,000	4,000
Income Tax Payable	4,000	1,500
Bonds Payable	150,000	100,000
Common Stock	205,000	205,000
Retained Earnings	120,000	76,000
Treasury Stock	(14,000)	—
Total Liabilities and Stockholders' Equity	$512,000	$421,000

During the year, Sagan Company sold equipment for $11,000 cash that had cost $19,000 and had $14,000 accumulated depreciation. New equipment was purchased for cash. Additional bonds payable were issued for cash. Cash dividends of $10,000 were declared and paid this year. At the end of this year, shares of treasury stock were purchased for cash.

REQUIRED
(a) Prepare a worksheet for a statement of cash flows for this year using the direct method.
(b) Prepare a statement of cash flows for this year using the direct method.

Statement of cash flows—direct method

19–32A Comparative balance sheets and an income statement for Corona Company are shown below.

Corona Company
Balance Sheets

Assets	**Dec. 31, 19X2**	**Dec. 31, 19X1**
Cash	$ 20,000	$ 9,000
Accounts Receivable (net)	30,000	19,000
Inventory	40,000	32,000
Land	30,000	30,000
Building	153,000	130,000
Accumulated Depreciation—Building	(31,000)	(25,000)
Equipment	70,000	50,000
Accumulated Depreciation—Equipment	(19,000)	(15,000)
Patents (net)	22,000	12,000
Total Assets	$315,000	$242,000
Liabilities and Stockholders' Equity		
Accounts Payable	$ 19,800	$ 12,400
Wages Payable	4,200	5,800
Income Tax Payable	1,000	1,800
Bonds Payable	45,000	—
Common Stock ($25 par value)	212,000	200,000
Retained Earnings	33,000	22,000
Total Liabilities and Stockholders' Equity	$315,000	$242,000

Corona Company
Income Statement
For the Year Ended December 31, 19X2

Sales		$300,000
Cost of Goods Sold		200,000
Gross Profit		$100,000
Wages Expense	$49,000	
Depreciation Expense	10,000	
Patent Amortization Expense	2,000	
Other Operating Expenses	19,000	
Income Tax Expense	4,000	84,000
Net Income		$ 16,000

During 19X2, $5,000 of cash dividends were declared and paid. A patent valued at $12,000 was obtained in exchange for 480 shares of common stock.

Bonds payable were sold for cash. Most of the bond proceeds were used to pay for structural improvements to the building and new equipment.

REQUIRED
(a) Prepare a worksheet for a 19X2 statement of cash flows using the direct method.
(b) Prepare a 19X2 statement of cash flows using the direct method. Place noncash investing and financing events in a supplementary schedule.

Statement of cash flows—indirect method

19–33A Refer to the data given for the Terry Company in Problem 19–29A.

REQUIRED
(a) Prepare a worksheet for a 19X1 statement of cash flows using the indirect method.
(b) Prepare a 19X1 statement of cash flows using the indirect method.

Statement of cash flows—indirect method

19–34A Refer to the data given for the Sagan Company in Problem 19–30A.

REQUIRED
(a) Prepare a worksheet for a statement of cash flows for this year using the indirect method.
(b) Prepare a statement of cash flows for this year using the indirect method.

Statement of cash flows—indirect method

19–36A Refer to the data given for the Corona Company in Problem 19–32A.

REQUIRED
(a) Prepare a worksheet for a 19X2 statement of cash flows using the indirect method.
(b) Prepare a 19X2 statement of cash flows using the indirect method. Place noncash investing and financing events in a supplementary schedule.

BUSINESS DECISION PROBLEM

Recently hired as assistant controller for Shure, Inc., you are sitting next to the controller as he responds to questions at the annual stockholders' meeting. The firm's financial statements contain a statement of cash flows prepared using the indirect method. A stockholder raises her hand.

Stockholder: "I notice depreciation expense is shown as an addition in the calculation of the net cash flow from operating activities."

Controller: "That's correct."

Stockholder: "What depreciation method do you use?"

Controller: "We use the straight-line method for all plant assets."

Stockholder: "Well, why don't you switch to an accelerated depreciation method, such as double declining balance, increase the annual depreciation amount, and thus increase the net cash flow from operating activities?"

The controller pauses, turns to you, and replies: "My assistant will answer your question."

REQUIRED
Prepare an answer to the stockholder's question.

ANSWERS TO SELF-TEST QUESTIONS

1. (a) 2. (b) 3. (a) 4. (d) 5. (b)

20

Analysis and Interpretation of Financial Statements

Chapter Objectives

- **Describe and illustrate horizontal analysis of financial statements.**
- **Describe and illustrate vertical analysis of financial statements.**
- **Explain measures for evaluating operating performance.**
- **Discuss the use of earnings per share, price–earnings ratios, and dividend yields in evaluating a firm.**
- **Define and illustrate "trading on the equity."**
- **Explain measures for evaluating financial strength.**
- **Discuss the limitations of financial analysis.**

Look ere you leap, see ere you go,
It may be for thy profit so.

THOMAS TUSSER

Many individuals and groups are interested in the data appearing in a firm's financial statements, including managers, owners, prospective investors, creditors, labor unions, governmental agencies, and the public. These parties are usually interested in the profitability and financial strength of the firm in question, although such factors as size, growth, and the firm's efforts to meet its social responsibilities may also be of interest. Managers, owners, and prospective investors may ask the following questions: How do profits compare with those of previous years? How do profits compare with those of other firms in the industry? Creditors may ask: Will our debt be repaid on time? Will the interest payments be met? Unions may ask: How can we show that the firm can support a particular wage increase? Regulatory agencies may ask: What rate of return should the firm be permitted? Is the firm enjoying windfall profits? These kinds of questions can be answered by interpreting the data in financial reports.

Various techniques are used to analyze and interpret financial statement data. In the following pages, we concentrate on some widely used methods of evaluation. In many cases, management may profitably use these techniques to plan and control its own operations, but in this discussion our viewpoint is primarily that of an outsider.

SOURCES OF INFORMATION

Except for closely held companies, business firms publish financial statements at least annually, and most large companies also issue them quarterly. Normally, annual statements are attested to by certified public accountants, and the careful analyst reads the accountants' opinion to determine the reliability of the given data. Companies listed on stock exchanges submit annual statements to the Securities and Exchange Commission. These statements, which are available to any interested parties, are generally more useful than annual reports because they furnish a greater amount of detail. Even more detail can be found in prospectuses submitted to the SEC by certain companies issuing large amounts of new securities.

For data not provided by the financial statements, a trained analyst has a number of sources: personal interviews with company management, contacts with research organizations, trade association data, and subscriptions to financial services that periodically publish analytical data for many firms. The analyst also can obtain useful information from financial newspapers—such as *The Wall Street Journal* and *Barron's*—and from magazines devoted to financial and economic reporting—such as *Business Week* and *Forbes*. Data on industry norms, average ratios, and other relationships are available from such agencies as Dun & Bradstreet and Robert Morris and Associates. The analyst may want to compare the performance of a particular firm with that of the industry. Both Dun & Bradstreet and Robert Morris and Associates compile industry statistics for a variety of manufacturers, wholesalers, and retailers. In addition, the Dun & Bradstreet statistics report not only median performance, but the performance of firms in the upper and the lower quartiles of the industry. Robert Morris and Associates reports statistics by size of organization.

ANALYTICAL TECHNIQUES

Absolute dollar amounts of profits, sales, assets, and other key data are not meaningful when studied individually. For example, knowing that a company's annual earnings are $1 million is of little value unless these earnings can be related to other data. A $1 million profit might represent excellent performance for a company with less than $10 million in invested capital. On the other hand, such earnings would be meager for a firm that has several hundred million dollars in invested capital. Thus, the most significant information derived in analysis concerns the relationships between two or more variables, such as earnings to assets, earnings to sales, and earnings to stockholders' investment. To describe these relationships clearly and to make comparisons easy, the analyst states these relationships in terms of ratios and percentages.

For example, we might express the relationship of $15,000 in earnings to $150,000 in sales as a 10% ($15,000/$150,000) rate of earnings on sales. To describe the relationship between sales of $150,000 and inventory of $20,000, we might use a ratio or a percentage; ($150,000/$20,000) may be expressed as 7.5, 7.5:1, or 750%.

Often, changes in selected items compared in successive financial statements are expressed as percentages. For example, if a firm's earnings increased from $40,000 last year to $48,000 this year, the $8,000 increase related to the base year is expressed as a 20% increase ($8,000/$40,000). To express a dollar increase or decrease as a percentage, however, the analyst must make the base year amount a positive figure. If, for example, a firm had a net loss of $4,000 in one year and earnings of $20,000 in the next, the $24,000 increase cannot be expressed as a percentage. Similarly, if a firm showed no marketable securities in last year's balance sheet but showed $15,000 of such securities in this year's statement, the $15,000 increase cannot be expressed as a percentage.

When evaluating a firm's financial statements for two or more years, analysts often use **horizontal analysis.** This type of analysis is useful in detecting improvement or deterioration in a firm's performance and in spotting trends. The term **vertical analysis** describes the study of a single year's financial statements.

Horizontal Analysis

COMPARATIVE FINANCIAL STATEMENTS The form of horizontal analysis encountered most often is **comparative financial statements** for two or more years, showing dollar and percentage changes for important items and classification totals. Dollar increases and decreases are divided by the earliest year's data

EXHIBIT 20–1

Alliance Company
Comparative Balance Sheets
(Thousands of Dollars)

	Dec. 31, 19X5	Dec. 31, 19X4	Increase (Decrease)	Percent Change
Assets				
Current Assets:				
Cash	$ 5,500	$ 4,200	$ 1,300	31.0
Marketable Securities	1,500	2,400	(900)	(37.5)
Accounts Receivable (less allowance for uncollectible accounts of $2,400 in 19X5 and $2,000 in 19X4)	61,600	52,000	9,600	18.5
Inventory [lower of cost (first-in, first-out) or market]	76,000	63,000	13,000	20.6
Prepaid Expenses	900	600	300	50.0
Total Current Assets	$145,500	$122,200	$23,300	19.1
Long-term Assets:				
Property, Plant, and Equipment (net of accumulated depreciation)	$ 45,000	$ 40,000	$ 5,000	12.5
Investments	1,800	1,600	200	12.5
Total Long-term Assets	$ 46,800	$ 41,600	$ 5,200	12.5
Total Assets	$192,300	$163,800	$28,500	17.4
Liabilities and Stockholders' Equity				
Liabilities				
Current Liabilities:				
Notes Payable	$ 5,700	$ 3,000	$ 2,700	90.0
Accounts Payable	22,000	24,100	(2,100)	(8.7)
Accrued Liabilities	30,000	27,300	2,700	9.9
Total Current Liabilities	$ 57,700	$ 54,400	$ 3,300	6.1
Long-term Liabilities:				
12% Debenture Bonds Payable	$ 25,000	$ 20,000	$ 5,000	25.0
Total Liabilities	$ 82,700	$ 74,400	$ 8,300	11.2
Stockholders' Equity				
10% Preferred Stock, $100 Par Value	$ 8,000	$ 8,000	$ —	—
Common Stock, $5 Par Value	20,000	14,000	6,000	42.9
Paid-in Capital in Excess of Par Value	7,500	5,500	2,000	36.4
Retained Earnings	74,100	61,900	12,200	19.7
Total Stockholders' Equity	$109,600	$ 89,400	$20,200	22.6
Total Liabilities and Stockholders' Equity	$192,300	$163,800	$28,500	17.4

to obtain percentage changes. The 19X4 and 19X5 financial statements of Alliance Company, an electronic components and accessories manufacturer, are shown in Exhibits 20–1, 20–2, and 20–3. We use the data in these statements throughout this chapter to illustrate various analytical techniques.

When examining financial statements, the analyst focuses immediate attention on significant items only. Large percentage changes frequently occur in items whose dollar amounts may not be significant compared with other items on the statements. For example, although a large percentage change in Alliance Company's balance sheet occurred in Prepaid Expenses, the analyst would scarcely notice this item in an initial examination of changes. Instead, attention would be directed first to changes in totals—current assets, long-term assets, total assets, current liabilities, and so on. Next, changes in significant individual items, such as receivables and inventory, would be examined. These changes may be related to certain changes in income statement items to determine whether they are favorable.

For example, Alliance Company's total assets increased 17.4% (Exhibit 20–1), and sales increased 29.7% (Exhibit 20–2). A fairly large percentage increase in sales was supported by a much smaller rate of increase in assets. Furthermore, the 20.6% increase in inventory was also considerably less than the increase in

EXHIBIT 20–2

Alliance Company
Comparative Income Statements
(Thousands of Dollars)

	Year Ended Dec. 31, 19X5	Year Ended Dec. 31, 19X4	Increase (Decrease)	Percent Change
Net Sales	$415,000	$320,000	$95,000	29.7
Cost of Goods Sold	290,000	230,000	60,000	26.1
Gross Profit	$125,000	$ 90,000	$35,000	38.9
Operating Expenses:				
Selling Expenses	$ 39,500	$ 27,300	$12,200	44.7
Administrative Expenses	49,640	32,600	17,040	52.3
Total Operating Expenses	$ 89,140	$ 59,900	$29,240	48.8
Operating Income	$ 35,860	$ 30,100	$ 5,760	19.1
Interest Expense	3,000	2,400	600	25.0
Income before Income Taxes	$ 32,860	$ 27,700	$ 5,160	18.6
Income Tax Expense	14,100	12,300	1,800	14.6
Net Income	$ 18,760	$ 15,400	$ 3,360	21.8
Earnings per Share	$5.28	$5.21		
Dividends per Share	1.44	0.81		

EXHIBIT 20–3

Alliance Company
Comparative Retained Earnings Statements
(Thousands of Dollars)

	Year Ended Dec. 31, 19X5	Year Ended Dec. 31, 19X4	Increase (Decrease)	Percent Change
Retained Earnings, Jan. 1	$61,900	$49,580	$12,320	24.8
Net Income	18,760	15,400	3,360	21.8
Total	$80,660	$64,980	$15,680	24.1
Dividends:				
On Preferred Stock	$ 800	$ 800	$ —	—
On Common Stock	5,760	2,280	3,480	152.6
Total	$ 6,560	$ 3,080	$ 3,480	113.0
Retained Earnings, Dec. 31	$74,100	$61,900	$12,200	19.7

sales. These results reflect quite favorably on the firm's performance. In addition, the 29.7% increase in sales was accompanied by an increase in accounts receivable of only 18.5%; on the surface, the company's sales growth was not associated with a relaxation in credit policy.

We see on the income statement that the 38.9% gross profit increase outstripped the rate of increase in sales, indicating a higher mark-up rate in the latest year. Net income, however, increased only 21.8%; therefore, expenses must have grown disproportionately. Indeed, selling and administrative expenses increased 44.7% and 52.3%, respectively.

From this limited analysis of comparative financial statements, an analyst would conclude that operating performance for the latest year appeared favorable. Further analysis using some of the techniques described later in the chapter, however, might cause the analyst to modify that opinion. The foregoing analysis has revealed one reservation—operating expenses, particularly administrative expenses, have increased at a fairly high rate. Many selling expenses—such as sales salaries, commissions, and advertising—should rise somewhat proportionately with sales, but administrative expenses should not. An investigation of the reasons for the large increase in the latter expense might be indicated.

TREND ANALYSIS To observe percentage changes over time in selected data, analysts compute **trend percentages.** Most companies provide summaries of data for the past five or ten years in their annual reports. With such information, the analyst may examine changes over a period longer than two years. For example, suppose you were interested in sales and earnings trends for Alliance Company for the past five years. The dollar data, taken from the company's published annual report in the fifth year (19X5) of the period, are shown below:

Alliance Company
Annual Performance (Millions of Dollars)

	Year 1	Year 2	Year 3	Year 4	Year 5
Sales	$202.0	$215.0	$243.0	$320.0	$415.0
Net Earnings	10.9	11.7	13.5	15.4	18.8

By inspecting the above data, we perceive a fairly healthy growth pattern for this company, but we can determine the pattern of change from year to year more precisely by calculating trend percentages. To do this, we select a base year and then divide the data for each of the other years by the base year data. The resultant figures are actually indexes of the changes occurring throughout the period. If we choose year 1 as the base year, all data for years 2 through 5 will be related to year 1, which is represented as 100%.

To create the following table, we divided each year's sales—from year 2 through year 5—by $202, the year 1 sales in millions of dollars. Similarly, the net earnings for years 2 through 5 were divided by $10.9, the year 1 net earnings in millions of dollars.

Annual Performance (Percentage of Base Year)

	Year 1	Year 2	Year 3	Year 4	Year 5
Sales	100	106	120	158	205
Net Earnings	100	107	124	141	172

The trend percentages reveal that the growth in earnings outstripped the growth in sales for years 2 and 3, then fell below the sales growth in the last two years. We saw in our analysis of comparative statements that a disproportionate increase in operating expenses emerged in 19X5 (year 5). We might therefore analyze the 19X4 data to determine if net income was affected for the same reason or if the reduced growth was caused by other factors.

We must exercise care in interpreting trend percentages. Remember that all index percentages are related to the *base year.* Therefore, the change between the year 2 sales index (106%) and the year 3 sales index (120%) represents a 14% increase in terms of *base year* dollars. To express the increase as a percentage of year 2 dollars, we divide the 14% increase by the 106% year 2 sales index, to obtain an increase of 13%. We must also carefully select a representative base year. For example, consider the following sales and earnings data during the identical period for a competing company (which we call Century Company):

Century Company
Annual Performance

	Year 1	Year 2	Year 3	Year 4	Year 5
Sales (millions of dollars)	$192.3	$204.4	$225.0	$299.0	$414.6
(Percentage of base year)	100	106	117	155	216
Net Earnings (millions of dollars)	$ 1.9	$ 3.0	$ 4.0	$ 6.5	$ 10.0
(Percentage of base year)	100	158	210	342	526

Note that Century Company's sales growth pattern is similar to Alliance Company's. When judged from trend percentages, however, the net earnings growth is over three times that of Alliance Company. Using an unrepresentative base year for Century Company—when earnings were depressed—makes the earnings trend misleading. In year 1, Century Company earned less than 1% of sales ($1.9/$192.3). But in the later years of the period, a more normal relationship between earnings and sales prevailed, and earnings were roughly 2 to $2\frac{1}{2}$% of sales. The earnings/sales relationship for Alliance Company was relatively normal in year 1.

Other data that the analyst may relate to sales and earnings over a period of years include total assets, plant investment, and expenditures for research and development.

EFFECT OF INFLATION As we saw in Chapter 13, financial information reported on a historical cost basis during a period of inflation may not portray economic reality. Comparisons made for a firm over time and with other firms may be deceptive. In the foregoing analysis, for example, sales and net earnings growth for Alliance Company would be considerably less if the data were adjusted for the effects of inflation. Many other relationships would likewise be distorted unless adjusted for inflation. Relationships between income statement items—such as sales—and balance sheet items may be distorted because the sales figure is expressed in current-year dollars, and inventories (especially LIFO inventories) and plant and equipment include dollar amounts of earlier price levels.

The financial analyst should therefore attempt to determine the effect of inflation on the data being examined. Certain inflation-adjusted operating data will be available for some companies because the FASB encourages its disclosure in supplementary form (see Chapter 13). When analyzing the financial reports of firms not making these disclosures, the analyst must make the necessary inquiries and estimates of the effects of inflation on the data.

Vertical Analysis

The relative importance of various items in financial statements can be highlighted by showing them as percentages of a key figure or total. Calculation of such percentages is particularly useful in presenting income statement data. For example, each item on the income statement may be shown as a percentage of the sales figure, as illustrated in Exhibit 20–4 for Alliance Company's 19X5 income statement.

COMMON-SIZE STATEMENTS **Common-size** financial statements contain the percentages of a key figure alone, without the corresponding dollar figures. Common-size income statements for Alliance Company are compared with Century Company's in Exhibit 20–5.

We see from Exhibit 20–5 that Century Company has a smaller gross profit margin percentage than does Alliance Company. The disparity might be due either to lower sales prices or to higher production costs for Century Company. Selling and administrative expenses as a percentage of sales are fairly comparable, except that, combined, they are a higher percentage of the sales dollar for Alliance Com-

EXHIBIT 20–4

Alliance Company
Income Statement
For the Year Ended December 31, 19X5
(Thousands of Dollars)

Net Sales	$415,000	100.0%
Cost of Goods Sold	290,000	69.9
Gross Profit	$125,000	30.1%
Operating Expenses:		
Selling Expenses	$ 39,500	9.5%
Administrative Expenses	49,640	12.0
Total Operating Expenses	$ 89,140	21.5%
Operating Income	$ 35,860	8.6%
Interest Expense	3,000	0.7
Income before Income Taxes	$ 32,860	7.9%
Income Tax Expense	14,100	3.4
Net Income	$ 18,760	4.5%

EXHIBIT 20–5

Alliance and Century Companies
Common-size Income Statements
(Percentage of Net Sales)

	Alliance Company		Century Company	
	Year Ended Dec. 31, 19X5	Year Ended Dec. 31, 19X4	Year Ended Dec. 31, 19X5	Year Ended Dec. 31, 19X4
Net Sales	100.0%	100.0%	100.0%	100.0%
Cost of Goods Sold	69.9	71.9	73.8	74.9
Gross Profit	30.1%	28.1%	26.2%	25.1%
Operating Expenses:				
Selling Expenses	9.5%	8.5%	8.6%	8.2%
Administrative Expenses	12.0	10.2	12.3	11.4
Total Operating Expenses	21.5%	18.7%	20.9%	19.6%
Operating Income	8.6%	9.4%	5.3%	5.5%
Interest Expense	0.7	0.8	1.0	0.8
Income before Income Taxes	7.9%	8.6%	4.3%	4.7%
Income Tax Expense	3.4	3.8	2.1	2.3
Net Income	4.5%	4.8%	2.2%	2.4%

pany than for Century Company in 19X5. The interest expense as a percentage of sales in 19X5 is somewhat higher for Century Company than for Alliance Company. If we consider Century Company's low rate of net income to net sales (2.2% in 19X5), the interest percentage is significant. Yet Alliance Company's higher rate of return on sales (about double that of Century Company) is due mainly to its better gross profit margin.

We may also employ common-size percentages to analyze balance sheet data, although less successfully than with income statement data. For example, if for a period of several years we state current assets and long-term assets as a percentage of total assets, we can determine whether a company is becoming more or less liquid. By determining each current asset's percentage of total current assets, we may observe any changes in these ingredients of working capital.

The best use of common-size statements with balance sheet data is probably with the sources of capital (equities). The proportions of the total capital supplied by short-term creditors, long-term creditors, preferred stockholders, and common stockholders of Alliance Company are shown below for 19X5:

	Amount (Millions of Dollars)	Common-size Percentage
Current debt	$ 57.7	30
Long-term debt	25.0	13
Preferred stock equity	8.0	4
Common stock equity	101.6	53
	$192.3	100

These percentages reveal that 53% of Alliance Company's capital is supplied by the common shareholders and 47% by preferred stockholders and creditors. We shall discover shortly that such percentages are useful in appraising the financial structure of a firm.

ANALYSIS OF OPERATING PERFORMANCE

In evaluating the operating performance of a firm, the analyst invariably uses **rate of return** analysis. This analysis, which deals with the firm's profitability, relates either the operating income or the net income to some base, such as average total assets, average stockholders' equity, or the year's sales. The resultant percentage can be compared with similar rates for the firm in past years or to other firms. The most important relationships are

(1) Return on assets.

(2) Return on common stockholders' equity.

(3) Return on sales.

Return on Assets

The rate of return on the total assets available to a firm is probably one of the most useful measures of the firm's profitability and efficiency. It is calculated by dividing the year's operating income (income before deducting interest expense and income tax expense) by the average total assets employed during the year.

$$\text{Rate of Return on Assets} = \frac{\text{Operating Income}}{\text{Average Total Assets}}$$

Because the return for a year is earned on assets employed throughout the year and assets may vary during that time, we compute the return on the *average* amount of assets. We obtain the approximate average by summing the beginning and ending asset totals and dividing by two.

If the percentage is a true index of productivity and accomplishment, it should not be influenced by the manner in which the company is financed. Therefore, we use income before interest charges as a measure of the dollar return in the numerator. As a result, we may compare the return for a company having a relatively high proportion of debt with that of a company using mostly owners' equity to finance its assets.

For example, assume that Company X and Company Y each have $500,000 in average total assets and that each has income of $70,000 before interest expense and taxes. Suppose that Company X has no interest-bearing debt but Company Y has $200,000 of 10% bonds payable outstanding. The bottom portions of the income statements of these two companies (rearranged to highlight the effect of interest and taxes) are shown in Exhibit 20–6 (for simplicity, we assume a 40% effective income tax rate).

Company X and Company Y earn the same percentage return—14%—on their assets ($70,000 income before interest and taxes divided by $500,000 average total assets). Company Y, however, is financed partially by bonds. Thus, its interest expense of $20,000 less a 40% tax benefit of $8,000 makes its final net income $12,000 less than that of Company X. This difference is due solely to the manner in which the two companies are financed and is unrelated to their *operational accomplishment*. For this reason, the return on assets is normally measured before interest and income taxes. We demonstrate later that judicious use of debt in financing may benefit the owners of a business.

EXHIBIT 20–6

Partial Income Statements

	Company X	**Company Y**
Operating Income (before interest expense and income tax expense)	$70,000	$70,000
Interest Expense (10% of $200,000)	—	20,000
	$70,000	$50,000
Income Tax Expense (40%)	28,000	20,000
Net Income	$42,000	$30,000

The return on assets, sometimes called the **productivity ratio,** is useful for comparing similar companies operating in the same industry. It also aids management in gauging the effectiveness of its asset utilization. When we consider this ratio along with such relationships as return on stockholders' equity and return on sales (explained below), we gain much insight about a firm's operating performance.

Alliance Company's return on assets for 19X5 and 19X4 is calculated below:

		19X5	19X4
Operating Income		$ 35,860	$ 30,100
Total Assets:			
Beginning of Year	(a)	$163,800	$142,500
End of Year	(b)	192,300	163,800
Average [(a + b)/2]		178,050	153,150
Rate of Return on Average Assets		20.1%	19.7%

Return on Common Stockholders' Equity

The rate of return to common shareholders is calculated using net income less preferred stock dividend requirements. This ratio measures the ultimate profitability of the investment to the common stockholders. Although the ratio can be figured before taxes, it is commonly done after taxes as follows:

$$\text{Rate of Return on Common Stockholders' Equity} = \frac{\text{Net Income} - \text{Preferred Dividend Requirements}}{\text{Average Common Stockholders' Equity}}$$

The return is earned on the stockholders' equity invested *throughout* the year. Because this amount varies during the year, we commonly approximate the average investment by summing the beginning and ending balances and dividing by two.

The rate of return for Alliance Company in 19X5 and 19X4 is calculated below:

		19X5	19X4
Net Income		$ 18,760	$15,400
Less: Preferred Dividend Requirements (10% of $8,000)		800	800
Common Stock Earnings		$ 17,960	$14,600
Common Stockholders' Equity:			
Beginning of Year	(a)	$ 81,400	$63,500
End of Year	(b)	101,600	81,400
Average [(a + b)/2]		91,500	72,450
Rate of Return on Common Stockholders' Equity		19.6%	20.2%

Return on Sales

Another important measure of operating performance is the rate of return on the net sales of a firm. The most commonly used version of this ratio is **net income to net sales.** When common-size percentages, or component percentages, are available with the income statement, return on sales equals the net income percentage, calculated as follows:

$$\text{Rate of Return on Sales} = \frac{\text{Net Income}}{\text{Net Sales}}$$

The calculations for Alliance Company are given below:

	19X5	19X4
Net Income	$ 18,760	$ 15,400
Net Sales	415,000	320,000
Rate of Return on Sales	4.5%	4.8%

Net income to net sales percentages are performance indexes used solely when studying similar companies in the same industry or when comparing different periods for the same company. The rate of return on sales varies widely from industry to industry. Some industries are characterized by low profit margins and high turnover of principal assets. (The ratio of net sales to average total assets is called *asset turnover.*) For example, meat processing companies and supermarkets seldom have a net income to net sales ratio exceeding 2%. They have huge sales volumes, however, and turn over their assets (especially inventory) many times. In contrast, a company manufacturing and selling fine grand pianos might have an extremely high net income to net sales ratio. Because production capabilities of making pianos are inherently limited, turnover of assets is low. As a general rule, firms that deal in slow-moving products involving fairly long production periods require higher profit margins for a respectable rate of return on assets and on the owners' investments.

USING THE NET INCOME FIGURE

When analyzing the operating performance of a company, intelligent analysts make their own evaluations of a firm's reported net income. Because they are interested in the prospects for future income, they analyze carefully the factors influencing the net income figure. If possible, they wish to determine which segments of the business contribute the most to net income and what the future prospects are for these segments. In this respect, the analysts' inquiries frequently lead to information sources other than the financial statements. However, an analyst can usually determine from the statements themselves (1) how representative the net income figure is and (2) whether it was determined by conservative accounting principles.

The analyst scrutinizes a firm's income statement to determine whether its net income is representative of its earning capability. Often, any unusual and/or nonrecurring items included in the determination of net income are eliminated for analytical purposes. Such items as gains and losses on sales of plant assets or securities, casualty losses, and the like, are either omitted or apportioned to a number of years' income calculations.

The analyst also examines such factors as inventory pricing techniques and depreciation methods (and rates) to determine their effect on net income. Company policies for investment tax credits (whether included in income immediately or deferred to future periods) and for recording fringe benefit costs (such as pension costs) must also be reviewed. The analyst wants to know whether the company's net income falls in the low (conservative) or high side of the spectrum of possible amounts. Once this is determined, the analyst may develop a more informed evaluation of a company's operating performance, stock values, growth potential, and so on.

Earnings per Share

Because stock market prices are quoted on a per-share basis, it is useful to calculate a firm's earnings on the same basis. *Earnings per share* for common stock are usually prominent in reports because both analysts and investors consider the relationship of prices and earnings to be quite important. An independent public accountant computing earnings per share for reporting purposes should follow procedures described in Accounting Principles Board *Opinion No. 15*, "Earnings Per Share," published by the AICPA. We discussed these procedures in Chapter 16.

Analysts may use the earnings-per-share figures that are available in annual reports—if they find such computations meaningful—or they may compute their own figures. We compute earnings per share by dividing common stock earnings (net income less any preferred dividend requirements) by the average number of shares outstanding during the year, as follows:[1]

$$\text{Earnings per Share} = \frac{\text{Net Income} - \text{Preferred Dividend Requirements}}{\text{Average Number of Common Shares Outstanding}}$$

The following calculations are made for Alliance Company:

		19X5	19X4
Net Income		$18,760	$15,400
Less: Preferred Dividend Requirements (10% of $8,000)		800	800
Common Stock Earnings		$17,960	$14,600
Common Shares Outstanding:			
Beginning of Year	(a)	2,800	2,800
End of Year	(b)	4,000	2,800
Average [(a + b)/2]		3,400	2,800
Earnings per Share		$5.28	$5.21

Alliance Company's earnings per share increased only slightly in 19X5 because a large number of additional shares were issued during the year.

[1] Analysts usually use the number of shares outstanding at year-end in this calculation. However, the average number of shares outstanding during the year is a more meaningful figure. The AICPA's Accounting Principles Board suggests the use of a weighted average that takes into account the periods during which various amounts of stock were outstanding.

Price–Earnings Ratio

The **price–earnings ratio** is the result of dividing the market price of a share of stock by the earnings per share. For many analysts and investors, this ratio is an important tool in assessing stock values. For example, after evaluating the strong and weak points of several companies in an industry, the analyst may compare price–earnings ratios to determine the "best buy."

When determing the price–earnings ratio, we customarily use the latest market price and the common stock earnings for the last four quarters of a company's operations. In our calculation for Alliance Company, we use 19X5 common stock earnings and the market price at year-end, \$37.50.

$$\text{Price–Earnings Ratio} = \frac{\text{Market Price per Common Share}}{\text{Common Stock Earnings per Share}} = \frac{\$37.50}{\$5.28} = 7.1$$

In other words, the market price of a share of Alliance Company common stock was approximately seven times the amount that share earned for the year. By itself, this multiplier is not particularly meaningful, although price–earnings ratios well below 10 often indicate a depressed market price. A prospective investor might compare this ratio with that of Century Company or with the average for the (electronic accessories) industry. Coupled with a fair evaluation of the strengths and weaknesses of several investment prospects and some knowledge of the industry itself, the price–earnings ratio might indicate whether the stock is overvalued in the market or an attractive investment.

Yield and Dividend Payout

Investors' expectations vary a great deal with personal economic circumstances and with the overall economic outlook. Some investors are more interested in price appreciation of a stock investment than in present income in the form of dividends. When shares are disposed of in the future, only part of the gains may be taxed under the capital gains provision of the income tax laws, whereas dividends are almost fully taxable. Other investors are more concerned with dividends than with price appreciation. Such investors desire a high **yield**—or dividend rate of return—on their investments. Yield is normally calculated by dividing the current annual dividends per share by the current price of the stock. For Alliance Company, we use the 19X5 dividends and the year-end price per share to calculate yield, as follows:

$$\text{Dividend Yield} = \frac{\text{Common Dividends per Share}}{\text{Market Price per Share}} = \frac{\$1.44}{\$37.50} = 3.8\%$$

Investors who emphasize the yield on their investments may also be interested in a firm's **dividend payout ratio,** which is the percentage of the common stock earnings paid out in dividends. The payout ratio indicates whether a firm has a conservative or a liberal dividend policy and may also indicate whether the firm is conserving funds for internal financing of growth. For Alliance Company, we calculate the payout ratio for 19X5 as follows:

$$\text{Dividend Payout Ratio} = \frac{\text{Common Dividends per Share}}{\text{Common Stock Earnings per Share}} = \frac{\$1.44}{\$5.28} = 27.3\%$$

Both the yield and the dividend payout ratio for the common shares of Alliance Company were relatively low in 19X5. The firm has embarked on an expansion program and is conserving funds to finance acquisitions internally.

Low payout ratios can have a depressing effect on the market price of a stock, and reducing the payout ratio may have a dramatic effect on the stock price. For example, General Motors once reduced its payout ratio by cutting its year-end dividend, and within two weeks the common stock price skidded down 10%.

Payout ratios for typical, seasoned industrial corporations vary between 40% and 60%. Many corporations, however, need funds for internal financing of growth and pay out little or nothing in dividends. At the other extreme, some companies—principally utility companies—may pay out as much as 80% or 90% of their earnings. Utilities have less need of retaining funds for growth because the bulk of their financing is through long-term debt. They are said to "trade on the equity" to a large extent. We discuss this idea in greater detail in the next section.

TRADING ON THE EQUITY

The expression **trading on the equity** designates the use of borrowed funds, particularly long-term debt, in the capital structure of a firm. Trading *profitably* on the equity means that the borrowed funds generate a higher rate of return than the interest rate paid for the use of the funds. The excess, of course, accrues to the benefit of the common shareholders because it magnifies, or increases, their earnings. To illustrate, let us return to the example in Exhibit 20–6, in which both companies X and Y have assets of $500,000. Company X has its entire capital in common stockholders' equity, while Company Y has $200,000 in 10% bonds payable and $300,000 in common stockholders' equity. Both firms have $70,000 operating income (income before interest and taxes). For clarity, we repeat the net income calculation below, together with percentages earned on assets and on stockholders' equity.

	Company X	Company Y
Operating income	$70,000	$70,000
Interest expense (10% of $200,000)	—	20,000
	$70,000	$50,000
Income tax expense (40%)	28,000	20,000
Net income	$42,000	$30,000
Return on assets:		
For both companies: $70,000/$500,000 =	14%	14%
Return on stockholders' equity:		
For Company X: $42,000/$500,000 =	8.4%	
For Company Y: $30,000/$300,000 =		10%

Note that Company Y achieved a higher return on its stockholders' investment than did Company X. We account for this additional 1.6% on stockholders' equity as follows:

14% earned on $200,000 borrowed	$28,000
10% interest paid for use of funds	20,000
Trading on equity gain before income tax	$ 8,000
Less: 40% income tax	3,200
Trading on equity gain after taxes	$ 4,800
$4,800 gain ÷ $300,000 stockholders' equity =	1.6%

Because Company Y earned 14% on its assets (including the $200,000 borrowed) and paid only 10% on the money borrowed, it had an $8,000 gain before income taxes. After deducting 40% for taxes, the gain was $4,800. The after tax gain of $4,800 is a 1.6% return on the stockholders' equity of $300,000. Magnifying gains for the shareholders in this manner is sometimes referred to as the use of **leverage.**

Leverage in the capital structure must be used judiciously because some risk is involved. Leverage can also magnify losses. Suppose that operating income had been only $30,000, representing a 6% return on the assets of $500,000. The after tax return for Company Y would be only $6,000 [$30,000 − ($20,000 interest + $4,000 taxes)]. The return on stockholders' equity would then be only 2% ($6,000/$300,000) compared with a return of 3.6% for Company X ($30,000 − $12,000 taxes = $18,000; $18,000/$500,000 = 3.6%).

In general, companies with stable earnings can afford more debt in their capital structure than those with fluctuating earnings. Because of their stable earnings, utility companies may have as much as 70% of their financial structure in debt, whereas most industrial companies rarely have more than 50% debt financing.

ANALYSIS OF FINANCIAL STRENGTH

Because the ultimate source of any company's financial strength is its earning power, our discussion has stressed the operating performance and earning power of the business firm. However, certain other relationships in the financial statements give the analyst insight into the financial strength of a company. The first of these relationships concerns the company's financial structure and its fixed charges. The second relates to the company's working capital position.

Equity Ratio

To determine the manner in which a company is financed, we calculate the **equity ratio,** which is the common stockholders' equity divided by the company's total assets.

$$\text{Equity Ratio} = \frac{\text{Common Stockholders' Equity}}{\text{Total Assets}}$$

We commonly use year-end balances for the elements in this ratio rather than averages because we are interested in the capital structure at a particular point in time. The calculations for Alliance Company are as follows:

	19X5	19X4
Common Stockholders' Equity	$101,600	$ 81,400
Total Assets	$192,300	$163,800
Equity Ratio	53.0%	49.7%

The equity ratio is readily available in common-size percentages calculated from the balance sheet (see page 770). At the close of 19X5, 53% of Alliance Company's capital was provided by common shareholders and 47% by debtors and preferred shareholders. Because the analyst's concern is whether the company may be trading on the equity too heavily, the equity ratio indicates the extent of the firm's borrowing in relation to its assets.

When we analyze a firm's leverage, we may question the treatment of any preferred stock outstanding. Remember that the dividends on ordinary preferred stock are not a fixed charge, such as bond interest, but a contingent charge—contingent on a declaration by the firm's board of directors. Despite this fact, most analysts treat regular preferred stock as debt when examining a company's long-term position. They evidently feel that preferred dividends should be treated as a fixed charge, because ordinarily such dividends must be paid before distributions are made to common shareholders. Usually, preferred stock is included with stockholders' equity *for analytical purposes* only when the preferred stock is convertible into common and is likely to be converted in the near future.

Although no explicit rules of thumb or standards exist for equity ratios, the analyst may have a general idea of what a company's financial structure should be. An equity ratio that falls outside the analyst's subjective range of percentages will be investigated further.

Bond Interest Coverage

To evaluate further the size of a company's debt, an analyst may observe the relationship of interest charges to earnings. For example, an extremely low equity ratio for a company may indicate heavy borrowing. However, if its earnings are sufficient, even in poor years, to meet the interest charges on the debt several times over, the analyst may regard the situation quite favorably.

Analysts, particularly long-term creditors, almost always calculate the **bond interest coverage**, sometimes called **times interest earned.** This ratio is determined by dividing the operating income (income before bond interest and income taxes) by the annual bond interest:

$$\text{Bond Interest Coverage} = \frac{\text{Operating Income}}{\text{Annual Bond Interest}}$$

The computations for Alliance Company are as follows:

	19X5	19X4
Operating Income	$35,860	$30,100
Annual Bond Interest (12% of Bonds Payable)	$ 3,000	$ 2,400
Times Interest Earned	12.0	12.5

In other words, Alliance Company's income available to meet interest charges each year was approximately 12 times the amount of its interest expense. Obviously, Alliance Company has an exceptionally good margin of safety. Generally speaking, a company that earns its interest several times before taxes in its poor years is regarded as a satisfactory risk by long-term creditors.

Preferred Dividend Coverage

Quite naturally, preferred stockholders would like some assurance that dividends will continue to be paid. They may therefore wish to calculate their **dividend coverage.** To compute the number of times preferred dividends are earned, we divide operating income (income before interest and income taxes) by the sum of the annual bond interest and preferred dividend requirements, as follows:

$$\text{Preferred Dividend Coverage} = \frac{\text{Operating Income}}{\text{Annual Bond Interest} + \text{Preferred Dividend Requirements}}$$

The following calculations for Alliance Company show ample protection for the preferred dividends:

	19X5	19X4
Operating Income	$35,860	$30,100
Annual Bond Interest	$ 3,000	$ 2,400
Preferred Dividend Requirements	800	800
	$ 3,800	$ 3,200
Times Preferred Dividends Earned	9.4	9.4

The preferred dividend requirement is combined with the bond interest in the calculations because bond interest is a prior charge against earnings—that is, it must be paid before any preferred dividends are distributed.[2] An inexperienced analyst may calculate the preferred dividend coverage by dividing net income after income taxes by the dividend requirement. If we did this for Alliance Company in 19X5, the result would be a coverage of 23.5 times ($18,760/$800). This result is obviously absurd, since the bond interest coverage is only 12 times. Inasmuch as bond interest is a prior charge, the protection for dividends on a junior security such as preferred stock cannot be better than the protection for the bond interest.

Analysis of Working Capital Position

A firm's working capital is the difference between its current assets and current liabilities. Adequate working capital enables a firm to meet its current obligations on time and take advantage of available discounts. Shortages of working capital can sometimes force a company into disadvantageous borrowing at inopportune times and unfavorable interest rates and can also affect its ability to pay interest and dividends. Many long-term debt contracts contain provisions that require the borrowing firm to maintain an adequate working capital position.

[2]Because bond interest is tax deductible and preferred dividends are not, some analysts place the dividends on the same basis as the interest by dividing them by (1 − tax rate). With a 40% tax rate, the dividends would be $1,333. We have ignored this technicality in our discussion.

Analysis of a firm's working capital, or current position, involves looking at the firm's current assets and current liabilities and relating various elements to other accounts, such as sales and cost of goods sold. In the remainder of this chapter we examine the current position of Alliance Company, whose working capital in 19X5 (in thousands of dollars) was $87,800 ($145,500 current assets − $57,700 current liabilities).

The adequacy of a firm's working capital is indicated in its relation to sales and in the ratio between current assets and current debt. Compare the following sets of 19X5 data for Alliance Company and Century Company:

	(Thousands of Dollars) Alliance	Century
Current Assets	$145,500	$139,549
Current Liabilities	57,700	90,136
Working Capital	$ 87,800	$ 49,413
Sales	$415,000	$414,644

In this example, the ratio of sales to working capital (called **working capital turnover**) is 4.7 for Alliance ($415,000/$87,800) and 8.4 for Century ($414,644/$49,413). We might wonder about this disparity. How much working capital should support a given amount of sales? We can determine which of the two companies has a better defensive position by calculating the current ratio.

CURRENT RATIO The current ratio is simply the current assets divided by the current liabilities.

$$\text{Current Ratio} = \frac{\text{Current Assets}}{\text{Current Liabilities}}$$

This ratio is a measure of a firm's ability to meet its current obligations on time and to have funds readily available for current operations. The calculations below show that Alliance Company improved its position in 19X5 and has a current ratio of 252%.

	19X5	19X4
Current Assets	$145,500	$122,200
Current Liabilities	$ 57,700	$ 54,400
Current Ratio	2.52	2.25

This represents a better current position than that of Century Company, which had a ratio of only 155% ($139,549/$90,136). Century Company's working capital may be too small to support its volume of sales.

For many years, some short-term creditors have relied on a rule of thumb that the current ratio for industrial companies should exceed 200%. This arbitrary guideline probably developed from the premise that, because inventories frequently amount to as much as one-half of current assets, the remaining, more liquid current assets should at least equal the current debt. The rule is not completely reliable, since many companies have operated successfully with lower current ratios. Nonetheless, the 200% can be used as a general guide. When a company's current ratio is low, the analyst should attempt to determine if the situation is temporary and if the company has access to a line of credit so that refinancing can be accomplished easily in the event of difficulty.

QUICK RATIO Sometimes analysts calculate the ratio between the liquid, or *quick*, current assets and the current liabilities. **Quick current assets** are cash, marketable securities, and receivables. The main item omitted is the inventory. Prepaid items are also omitted, but they are usually not material in amount. The quick ratio may give a better picture than the current ratio of a company's ability to meet current debts and to take advantage of discounts offered by creditors. The quick ratio and the current ratio together indicate the influence of the inventory figure in the company's working capital position. For example, a company might have an acceptable current ratio, but if its quick ratio falls much below 100%, the analyst might be uneasy about the size of the inventory and analyze the inventory position more carefully. Again, the 100% rule of thumb for the quick ratio is an arbitrary standard used only to alert the analyst to the need for further scrutiny.

We calculate the quick ratio for Alliance Company as follows:

$$\text{Quick Ratio} = \frac{\text{Cash + Marketable Securities + Receivables}}{\text{Current Liabilities}}$$

	19X5	**19X4**
Cash, Marketable Securities, and Receivables	$68,600	$58,600
Current Liabilities	$57,700	$54,400
Quick Ratio	1.19	1.08

INVENTORY TURNOVER An analyst concerned about a company's inventory position may compute the company's average **inventory turnover.** This figure indicates whether the inventory amount is disproportionate to the amount of sales. Excessive inventories not only tie up company funds and increase storage costs but may also lead to subsequent losses if the goods become outdated or unsaleable. The computation always involves dividing some measure of sales volume by a measure of the typical inventory level. Most accountants use cost of goods sold as a measure of sales volume and the average inventory for the year as a measure of the typical inventory level, as follows:

$$\text{Inventory Turnover} = \frac{\text{Cost of Goods Sold}}{\text{Average Inventory}}$$

Using this measure for Alliance Company gives the following results:

		19X5	19X4
Cost of Goods Sold		$290,000	$230,000
Beginning Inventory	(a)	$ 63,000	$ 48,000
Ending Inventory	(b)	76,000	63,000
Average Inventory [(a + b)/2]		69,500	55,500
Inventory Turnover		4.17	4.14

We use cost of goods sold in the calculation because the inventory measure in the denominator is a *cost* figure; we should therefore use a cost figure in the

GOOD-LOOKING BALANCE SHEETS CAN BE ASSETS FOR COMPANIES

Lenders judge businesses by their financial statements. So common sense dictates that they look as good as possible. Year-end is "the one time of the year they take a picture of your company," says Steven N. Delit, of the New York CPA firm of Delit Friedman & Co., "and you want it to look its best."

There are a number of perfectly legitimate things a business can do to put the best face on its balance sheet. Some can be done near the end of the year, but it is better to operate a company with financial results in mind all the time.

Business owners need "an element of perspicacity" about producing a good balance sheet each year, says James McNeil Stancil, a professor of finance at the University of Southern California. As an example, he cites a company that borrows regularly against its receivables from a finance company, as many companies do.

The business normally takes cash it collects on its receivables and promptly pays off the finance company. One day its bank balance is impressive, the next it is anemic. If it has a skimpy bank balance the last day of the year, Mr. Stancil says, its balance sheet will look bad. It wouldn't matter that the company "has $5 million of assets," he says. "Someone will look at the cash account and say, 'My God! You are broke!'"

That can be avoided by having the finance company agree to slower repayment for a week or more near year-end, so the business can accumulate cash for its balance sheet.

Ratio analysis is a common way lenders analyze balance sheets. Most familiar is the current ratio, computed by dividing current assets—cash, accounts receivable, inventory—by current liabilities, or debt due within a year.

A company can strengthen this ratio by paying off current debt. If a business has, say, $40,000 cash (its only current asset) and $20,000 of current liabilities, its current ratio is 2:1. If $10,000 of the cash is used to reduce debt, however, the ratio improves significantly to 3:1.

A financial statement can be enhanced by borrowing long term to pay-off short-term debt. "If you can get debt out of short term into long term, it cleans up the balance sheet," says Edward H. Pendergast, chairman of Kennedy & Lehan CPAs Inc., North Quincy, Mass. But this isn't mere window dressing, he says. "The company is much stronger because it is more liquid. Current demands on the business have been reduced considerably."

numerator. However, many credit agencies and analysts commonly use the sales amount instead of cost of goods sold to calculate inventory turnover. Calculated in this manner, Alliance Company's turnover is 5.97 times in 19X5. Analysts who compare a firm's inventory turnover with industry averages computed in this manner should use the sales figure in the calculations.

Usually, the average inventory is obtained by adding the year's beginning and ending inventories and dividing by two. Since inventories taken at the beginning and end of the year are likely to be lower than the typical inventory, an unrealistically high turnover ratio may result. We should use a 12-month average if monthly inventory figures are available. Furthermore, we should be careful in calculating inventory turnover ratios for companies that use last-in, first-out

---

Bankers look carefully at the equity a small business has in relationship to debt. "There's nothing like equity," says the executive vice president of a $7 billion bank. "It's your cushion in the event something comes up that could damage the company." In the past, nothing less than a one-to-one debt-equity ratio would satisfy most banks. Nowadays, debt one and a half times greater than equity is usually acceptable. And some banks won't balk if it exceeds this, says David F. Nasman, president of Bellingham National Bank, Tacoma, Wash.

High debt-equity ratios could be acceptable, Mr. Nasman says, for a young company "that is strong and operating and growing well." But, he says, a bank would view with alarm "a company in business for 25 years whose debt-equity ratio starts to slide." The difference, he says, is that the young profitable company probably can "increase its equity along the way."

Profits left in the business become retained earnings and increase equity. However, small-business owners usually try to minimize profits for income tax purposes, and often do this by paying themselves year-end bonuses. One way to satisfy tax considerations and bolster the financial statement is for the owner to take the bonus, providing the company a tax deduction, and then loan the money back to the company.

"If you indicate that the company doesn't have to pay the owner back for a year," says Herbert C. Speiser, a partner at Touche Ross & Co., CPAs, "a banker will consider it equity."

Such a solution isn't always possible, however. "Sometimes tax planning goes against the financial statement, says Irwin Math, a partner in the CPA firm of Laventhol & Horwath. "Sometimes I tell a client to pay taxes and strengthen your statement." In some small companies this means valuing year-end inventory as high as possible to maximize profits, and thus incur higher taxes.

Manufacturers should try to reduce raw materials inventory by turning it into finished goods, Mr. Math says. Large year-end raw-materials inventory suggests "you have a problem of not being able to sell your product," he says. A bulge in finished-goods inventory looks better because "finished goods are what you can convert to cash quickly."

However, when the business is having a terrible year, says John J. O'Leary, partner in the accounting firm of Alexander Grant & Co., "you can't pull a rabbit out of the hat in the last quarter." Don't wait for year-end to tell the bank the business is in trouble, he says. "It rubs bankers the wrong way."

Henry R. Pearson, a Dallas CPA, says he doesn't window dress statements for clients. "We dress down; we are very conservative." The way to impress lenders is to repay them on time, he says. "If you're not paying your debts," he says, "no matter what you say to your banker he isn't going to be happy."

Sanford L. Jacobs, "Good-Looking Balance Sheets Can Be Assets for Companies." *Wall Street Journal*, September 23, 1985, p. 31. Reprinted by permission of *Wall Street Journal*,

inventory measurement methods. In calculating inventory turnover, company management may restate the inventories at current prices using price indexes or other available data. Outside analysts may not be able to make such adjustments and may have to make some subjective allowance for overstatement of turnover.

A low inventory turnover can, of course, result from an overextended inventory position or from inadequate sales volume. For this reason, appraisal of inventory turnover should be accompanied by scrutiny of the quick ratio and analysis of trends in both inventory and sales. Inventory turnover figures vary considerably from industry to industry, and analysts frequently compare a firm's experience with industry averages.

AVERAGE COLLECTION PERIOD We can measure the average quality of a firm's trade receivables by calculating the **average collection period.** This calculation, sometimes called **day's sales outstanding,** is made as follows:

$$\text{Average Collection Period} = \frac{\text{Trade Accounts Receivable}}{\text{Year's Sales}} \times 365$$

Note that this equation results from first calculating the average day's sales (Sales/365) and then dividing this figure into the accounts receivable balance to determine how many average days' sales are uncollected. In the computation, the numerator should be the year-end receivables before deducting the allowance for uncollectible accounts, and only credit sales should be in the denominator. In the following calculations, we assume that all of Alliance Company's sales were credit sales.

	19X5	19X4
Year-end Receivables (before allowance for uncollectible accounts)	(a) $ 64,000	$ 54,000
Net Credit Sales	(b) 415,000	320,000
Average Collection Period [(a/b) × 365]	56 days	62 days

Analysts calculate the average collection period to discover whether the accounts receivable are slow or overdue. A rough rule of thumb sometimes used by credit agencies is that the average collection period should not exceed $1\frac{1}{3}$ times the net credit period. For example, the average collection period of a firm selling on 30-day net terms should probably not exceed 40 days.

LIMITATIONS OF FINANCIAL ANALYSIS

The ratios, percentages, and other relationships we have described in this chapter are merely the result of analytical techniques. They may only isolate areas requiring further investigation. Moreover, we must interpret them with due consideration to general economic conditions, conditions of the industry in which the companies operate, and the positions of individual companies within the industry.

We should also be aware of the inherent limitations of financial statement data. Problems of comparability are frequently encountered. Companies otherwise similar may employ different accounting methods, which can cause problems in comparing certain key relationships. For instance, inventory turnover is different for a company using LIFO than for one using FIFO inventory costing. Inflation may distort certain computations, especially those resulting from horizontal analysis. For example, trend percentages calculated from unadjusted data may be deceptive. Sometimes, gains over time in sales, earnings, and other key figures disappear when the underlying data are adjusted for changes in price levels.

We must be careful even when comparing companies in a particular industry. Such factors as size, diversity of product, and mode of operations can make the firms completely dissimilar. Some firms, particularly conglomerates, are difficult to classify by industry. If segment information—particularly product-line data—is available, the analyst may compare the statistics for several industries. Often, trade associations like the American Meat Institute prepare industry statistics that are stratified by size of firm or type of product, making analysis easier.

KEY POINTS TO REMEMBER

The important ratios covered in this chapter are summarized below:

Analysis of Operating Performance

$$\text{Rate of Return on Assets} = \frac{\text{Operating Income}}{\text{Average Total Assets}}$$

$$\text{Rate of Return on Common Stockholders' Equity} = \frac{\text{Net Income} - \text{Preferred Dividend Requirements}}{\text{Average Common Stockholders' Equity}}$$

$$\text{Rate of Return on Sales} = \frac{\text{Net Income}}{\text{Net Sales}}$$

$$\text{Price–Earnings Ratio} = \frac{\text{Market Price per Common Share}}{\text{Common Stock Earnings per Share}}$$

$$\text{Dividend Yield} = \frac{\text{Common Dividends per Share}}{\text{Market Price per Share}}$$

$$\text{Dividend Payout Ratio} = \frac{\text{Common Dividends per Share}}{\text{Common Stock Earnings per Share}}$$

Analysis of Financial Strength

$$\text{Equity Ratio} = \frac{\text{Common Stockholders' Equity}}{\text{Total Assets}}$$

$$\text{Bond Interest Coverage} = \frac{\text{Operating Income}}{\text{Annual Bond Interest}}$$

$$\text{Preferred Dividend Coverage} = \frac{\text{Operating Income}}{\text{Annual Bond Interest} + \text{Preferred Dividend Requirements}}$$

$$\text{Current Ratio} = \frac{\text{Current Assets}}{\text{Current Liabilities}}$$

$$\text{Quick Ratio} = \frac{\text{Cash} + \text{Marketable Securities} + \text{Receivables}}{\text{Current Liabilities}}$$

$$\text{Inventory Turnover} = \frac{\text{Cost of Goods Sold}}{\text{Average Inventory}}$$

$$\text{Average Collection Period} = \frac{\text{Trade Accounts Receivable}}{\text{Year's Sales}} \times 365$$

SELF-TEST QUESTIONS
(Answers are at the end of this chapter.)

All of the self-test questions are based on the following data:

Thermo Company
Balance Sheet
December 31, 19XX

Cash	$ 40,000	Current Liabilities	$ 80,000
Accounts Receivable (net of $2,000 Allowance for Uncollectible Accounts	80,000	10% Bonds Payable	120,000
Inventory	130,000	Common Stock	200,000
Plant and Equipment	250,000	Retained Earnings	100,000
	$500,000		$500,000

Net sales for the year were $800,000, gross profit was $320,000, and net income was $36,000. The income tax rate was 40%. A year ago inventory was $110,000, and common stockholders' equity was $260,000.

1. The current ratio of Thermo Company at 12/31, calculated from the above data, was 3.125, and the working capital was $170,000. If the firm paid $20,000 of its current liabilities, immediately after this transaction,
   (a) Both the current ratio and the working capital would decrease.
   (b) Both the current ratio and the working capital would increase.
   (c) The current ratio would increase, but the working capital would remain the same.
   (d) The current ratio would increase, but the working capital would decrease.
2. The firm's inventory turnover for the year is
   (a) 6.67 times (b) 4 times (c) 6 times (d) 3.69 times

3. The firm's return on common stockholders' equity was
   (a) 25.71% (b) 12.86% (c) 17.14% (d) 21.43%
4. The firm's average collection period for receivables was
   (a) 36.5 days (b) 37.41 days (c) 35.59 days (d) 18.25 days
5. The firm's bond interest coverage for the year was
   (a) 4 times (b) 3 times (c) 5 times (d) 6 times

QUESTIONS

20–1 What are trend percentages, and how are they calculated? What pitfalls must an analyst avoid when preparing trend percentages?

20–2 Distinguish between horizontal analysis and vertical analysis of financial statements.

20–3 The following data are taken from the income statements of the Lindsay Company. Using year 1 as the base year, calculate trend percentages.

	Year 1	Year 2	Year 3	Year 4
Sales	$500,000	$570,000	$610,000	$640,000
Earnings	20,000	23,200	24,000	30,200

20–4 During the past year, Sawyer Company had net income of $2 million, and Maxwell Company had net income of $5 million. Both companies manufacture electrical components for the building trade. What additional information would you need to compare the profitability of the two companies? Discuss your answer.

20–5 Under what circumstances can return on sales be used to appraise the profitability of a company? Can this ratio be used to compare the profitability of companies from different industries? Explain.

20–6 Why do we calculate the rate of return on assets? Give reasons why the income measure used in this calculation is not reduced for interest or income taxes.

20–7 What does the rate of return on common stockholders' equity measure? Why are interest expense and income taxes deducted from the income measure in this ratio?

20–8 What are common-size percentages, and how are they used?

20–9 Datron, Inc., earned $6.50 per share of common stock in the current year and paid dividends of $3.50 per share. The most recent market price of the common stock is $55.25 per share. Calculate (a) the price–earnings ratio, (b) the dividend yield, and (c) the dividend payout ratio.

20–10 Explain, by giving an example, what is meant by *trading on the equity.*

20–11 Why is it dangerous for a company with unstable earnings to trade heavily on the equity?

20–12 Discuss the significance of the equity ratio, and explain how it is computed.

20–13 Why do we determine bond interest coverage, and how is it calculated?

20–14 List three important ratios for evaluating the current position of a firm, and state how they are used.

20–15 What is meant by the *yield* on a common stock investment? Give an example of a computation of yield.

20–16 Utility companies have a high "payout" ratio compared with industrial companies. What is meant by a *payout ratio*? Why would utility companies continue high payout ratios?

EXERCISES

In the following exercises, inventory turnover is calculated using cost of goods sold in the numerator.

Comparative and common-size statements

20–17 Consider the following income statement data from the Jensen Company for this year and last year:

	This Year	Last Year
Sales	$840,000	$720,000
Cost of Goods Sold	520,800	432,000
Selling Expenses	168,000	151,200
General Expenses	84,000	86,400
Income Tax Expense	12,600	10,080

(a) Prepare a comparative income statement, showing increases and decreases in dollars and in percentages.
(b) Prepare common-size income statements for each year.
(c) Comment briefly on the changes between the two years.

Current ratio and working capital

20–18 Royal Company has a current ratio of 220% (2.2 to 1) on December 31 of the current year. On that date its current assets are as follows:

Cash		$ 45,000
Accounts Receivable	$80,000	
Less: Allowance for Uncollectible Accounts	5,000	75,000
Merchandise Inventory		150,000
Prepaid Expenses		5,000
		$275,000

(a) What is the firm's working capital on December 31?
(b) What is the quick ratio on December 31?
(c) If the company pays a current note payable of $10,000 immediately after December 31, how does the transaction affect the current ratio? Working capital?

Collection of receivables and inventory turnover

20–19 Royal Company, whose current assets are shown in Exercise 20–18, had net sales of $650,000 during the current year. The beginning inventory for the year was $125,000. Cost of goods sold for the year amounted to $425,000.
(a) What was the average collection period for receivables?
(b) What was the average inventory turnover for the year?

Current ratio and working capital

20–20 The following data are taken from a recent annual report of Dow Jones & Company, Inc., publishers of *The Wall Street Journal* and *Barron's*. Calculate the working capital and the current ratio.

Current Assets	$213,894,000
Current Liabilities:	
Notes Payable	$ 30,694,000
Accounts Payable and Accrued Liabilities	57,252,000
Profit Sharing and Retirement Contributions Payable	14,511,000
Income Taxes Payable	17,454,000
Unexpired Subscriptions	111,571,000
Total Current Liabilities	$231,482,000

Does any of this data suggest a modification of the normal way in which the working capital and the current ratio are calculated?

Earnings and dividend ratios

20–21 The Lund Corporation pays a quarterly dividend of $3.75 per share of common stock. Its earnings after taxes during the past four quarters of operation were $2,150,000. The company has 100,000 shares of $100 par value common stock and 30,000 shares of $50 par value, 10% preferred stock outstanding. The current market price of the common shares is $172.
(a) Calculate the earnings per share for the common stock.
(b) Calculate the price–earnings ratio for the common stock.
(c) What is the current dividend yield on the common stock?

Long-term debt vs. stock financing

20–22 The Weston Company has total assets of $1,500,000 and earns an average of $150,000 before income taxes. Currently, the company has no long-term debt outstanding. The company needs an additional $500,000 in funds on which it plans to earn 16% before income taxes. It can borrow the money at 10% or issue additional common stock. The effective tax rate is 40%. The company has 15,000 shares of common stock outstanding. Calculate the earnings per share expected (a) if the additional funds are borrowed and (b) if an additional 5,000 shares are sold.

Various ratios

20–23 The following information is available for the Anchor Company:

	Dec. 31, This Year	**Dec. 31, Last Year**
Total Assets	$4,000,000	$3,200,000
Current Liabilities	$ 800,000	$ 500,000
12% Bonds Payable	900,000	900,000
Common Stock ($100 Par Value)	1,800,000	1,500,000
Retained Earnings	500,000	300,000
	$4,000,000	$3,200,000

For this year, net sales amounted to $6,144,000, and net income was $307,200. The income tax rate was 40%. Calculate the following for this year:
(a) Return on assets.
(b) Return on common stockholders' equity.
(c) Return on sales.
(d) Bond interest coverage.
(e) Equity ratio.

PROBLEMS

Note: Unless otherwise indicated, inventory turnover is calculated using cost of goods sold in the numerator in the following problems.

Trend percentages

20–24 Net sales, net income, and total asset figures for Rainbow Paint, Inc., for five consecutive years are given below:

	Annual Amounts (Thousands of Dollars)				
	Year 1	**Year 2**	**Year 3**	**Year 4**	**Year 5**
Net Sales	$52,800	$57,300	$64,200	$69,500	$76,800
Net Income	2,430	2,590	3,020	3,350	3,830
Total Assets	32,500	34,200	37,800	40,600	42,400

REQUIRED

(a) Calculate trend percentages, using year 1 as the base year.

(b) Calculate the return on sales for each year. (Rates above 3% are considered good for paint and varnish companies; rates above 4.8% are considered *very* good.)

(c) Comment on the results of your analysis.

Changes in various ratios

20–25 Selected information follows for the Nu-Tech Company, taken from the current year's and last year's financial statements:

	This Year	**Last Year**
Net Sales	$840,000	$600,000
Cost of Goods Sold	580,000	450,000
Bond Interest Expense	18,000	18,000
Income Tax Expense	18,000	14,000
Net Income (after income taxes)	45,000	36,000
Accounts Receivable, December 31 (before allowance for uncollectible accounts)	136,000	90,000
Inventory, December 31	220,000	170,000
Common Stockholders' Equity	370,000	350,000
Total Assets	650,000	540,000

REQUIRED

(a) Calculate the following ratios and relationships for this year. Last year's results are given for comparative purposes.

	Last Year
(1) Return on assets.	13.2%
(2) Return on sales.	6.0%
(3) Return on common stockholders' equity.	10.3%
(4) Average collection period.	55 days
(5) Inventory turnover.	2.7 times
(6) Bond interest coverage.	3.8 times

(b) Comment on the changes between the two years.

Ratios from comparative and common-size data

20–26 Consider the following financial statements for the Sigma Company for the past two years.

During the year just ended, management obtained additional bond financing to enlarge its production facilities. The company faced higher production costs during the year for such things as fuel, materials, and freight. Because of temporary government price controls, a planned price increase on products was delayed several months.

As a holder of both common and preferred stock, you analyze the financial statements for the past two years.

Sigma Company
Balance Sheets
(Thousands of Dollars)

	Dec. 31, This Year	Dec. 31, Last Year
Assets:		
Cash	$ 12,000	$ 10,000
Accounts Receivable (net of allowance for uncollectible accounts)	35,000	32,000
Inventory	75,000	70,000
Prepaid Expenses	10,000	8,000
Plant and Other Assets (net)	288,000	240,000
	$420,000	$360,000
Liabilities and Stockholders' Equity:		
Current Liabilities	$ 50,000	$ 53,000
12% Bonds Payable	150,000	100,000
9% Preferred Stock, $50 Par Value	50,000	50,000
Common Stock, $10 Par Value	125,000	125,000
Retained Earnings	45,000	32,000
	$420,000	$360,000

Sigma Company
Income Statements
(Thousands of Dollars)

	This Year	Last Year
Sales	$560,000	$480,000
Cost of Goods Sold	375,200	307,200
Gross Profit	$184,800	$172,800
Operating Expenses	120,400	108,000
Operating Income	$ 64,400	$ 64,800
Bond Interest Expense	18,000	12,000
Income before Income Taxes	$ 46,400	$ 52,800
Income Tax Expense	18,400	21,000
Net Income	$ 28,000	$ 31,800

REQUIRED

(a) Calculate the following for each year: current ratio, quick ratio, inventory turnover (inventory was $66 million two years ago), equity ratio, times interest earned, preferred dividend coverage, return on assets (total assets were $340 million two years ago), and return on common stockholders' equity (common stock equity was $140 million two years ago).

(b) Calculate common-size percentages for each year's income statement.

(c) Calculate the apparent amount of common dividends per share paid during the year just ended. (Use number of shares at year-end.)

(d) Comment on the results of your analysis.

Ratios compared with industry averages

20–27 Because you own both preferred and common stock of the Ridgeway Corporation, a manufacturer of motor vehicle parts and accessories, you are analyzing the firm's performance for the most recent year. The following data are taken from the firm's last annual report.

	Dec. 31, This Year	Dec. 31, Last Year
Total Assets	$7,200,000	$6,400,000
Current Liabilities	$ 900,000	$ 700,000
12% Bonds Payable	1,800,000	1,800,000
10% Preferred Stock, $100 Par Value	900,000	900,000
Common Stock, $50 Par Value	3,000,000	2,500,000
Retained Earnings	600,000	500,000
Total Liabilities and Stockholders' Equity	$7,200,000	$6,400,000

For this year, net sales amount to $14,500,000, and net income is $774,000. The income tax rate is 40%.

REQUIRED

(a) Calculate the following for this year:
   (1) Return on sales.
   (2) Return on assets.
   (3) Return on common stockholders' equity.
   (4) Equity ratio.
   (5) Bond interest coverage.
   (6) Preferred dividend coverage.

(b) Trade association statistics and information provided by credit agencies reveal the following data on industry norms:

	Median	Upper Quartile
Return on sales	4.57%	6.09%
Return on assets	16.2	21.3
Return on stockholders' equity	12.5	19.4
Equity ratio	52.0	61.0

Compare Ridgeway Corporation's performance with industry performance.

Constructing statements from ratio data

20–28 The following are the 19X8 financial statements for Celtic Company, with almost all dollar amounts missing.

Celtic Company
Balance Sheet
December 31, 19X8

Cash	$?	Current Liabilities	$?
Accounts Receivable (net of allowance for uncollectible accounts)	?	10% Bonds Payable	?
Inventory	?	Common Stock	?
Equipment (net)	?	Retained Earnings	300,000
Total Assets	$1,500,000	Total Liabilities and Stockholders' Equity	$1,500,000

Celtic Company
Income Statement
For the Year Ended December 31, 19X8

Net Sales	$?
Cost of Goods Sold	?
Gross Profit	?
Operating Expenses	?
Operating Income	?
Bond Interest Expense	?
Income before Income Taxes	?
Income Tax Expense (40%)	?
Net Income	$150,000

The following information is available about Celtic Company's 19X8 financial statements:

(1) Quick ratio, 1.6:1.
(2) Inventory turnover (inventory at January 1, 19X8 was $400,000), 3.5 times.
(3) Return on sales, 6%.
(4) Average collection period, 17.52 days. Allowance balance is $10,000.
(5) Gross profit rate, 30%.
(6) Return on assets (total assets at January 1, 19X8 were $1,300,000), 20%.
(7) Equity ratio, 70%.
(8) The interest expense relates to the bonds payable that were outstanding all year.

REQUIRED
Compute the missing amounts, and complete the financial statements of Celtic Company. *Hint:* Complete the income statement first.

Ratios compared with industry averages

20–29 Westport Plastics, Inc., manufactures various plastic and synthetic products. Financial statement data for the firm are as follows:

	(Thousands of Dollars)
This Year:	
Net Sales	$750,000
Net Income (after income taxes)	39,000
Dividends	18,000
Interest Expense	7,500
Income Tax Expense	24,000

Westport Plastics, Inc.
Balance Sheets
(Thousands of Dollars)

Assets	**Dec. 31, This Year**	**Dec. 31, Last Year**
Cash	$ 10,800	$ 9,000
Accounts Receivable (net of allowance for uncollectible accounts of $5,400 last year and $4,800 this year)	84,200	84,600
Inventory	195,000	164,400
Total Current Assets	$290,000	$258,000
Plant Assets (net)	152,000	96,600
Other Assets	8,000	5,400
Total Assets	$450,000	$360,000
Liabilities and Stockholders' Equity		
Notes Payable—Banks	$ 15,000	$ 12,000
Accounts Payable	58,500	43,500
Income Tax Payable	8,100	9,000
Accrued Liabilities	29,400	25,500
Total Current Liabilities	$111,000	$ 90,000
Long-term Debt	75,000	75,000
Total Liabilities	$186,000	$165,000
Common Stock, $100 Par Value	$180,000	$132,000
Retained Earnings	84,000	63,000
Total Stockholders' Equity	$264,000	$195,000
Total Liabilities and Stockholders' Equity	$450,000	$360,000

REQUIRED

(a) Using the given data, calculate items (1) through (8) for this year. Compare the performance of Westport Plastics, Inc., with industry averages (given below), and comment on its operations.

	Median Ratios for Manufacturers of Plastic and Synthetic Products
(1) Current ratio.	3.42
(2) Quick ratio.	1.30
(3) Average collection period.	51 days
(4) Net sales to ending inventory.	5.3 times

(5) Equity ratio.	52.6%
(6) Return on assets.	19.1%
(7) Return on stockholders' equity.	11.8%
(8) Return on sales.	3.4%

(b) Calculate the dividends paid per share of common stock. (Use average number of shares outstanding during the year.) What was the payout ratio?

(c) If the most recent price per share of common stock is $177.50, what is the price–earnings ratio? The dividend yield?

ALTERNATE PROBLEMS

Note: Unless otherwise indicated, inventory turnover is calculated using cost of goods sold in the numerator in the following problems.

Trend percentages **20–24A** Net sales, net income, and total asset figures for Culhane Meat Processing, Inc. for five consecutive years are given below:

	Annual Amounts (Thousands of Dollars)				
	Year 1	**Year 2**	**Year 3**	**Year 4**	**Year 5**
Net Sales	$412,000	$420,000	$448,000	$470,000	$560,000
Net Income	6,400	9,200	11,700	9,800	12,500
Total Assets	112,000	120,000	130,000	134,000	145,000

REQUIRED

(a) Calculate trend percentages, using year 1 as the base year.

(b) Calculate the return on sales for each year. (Rates above 1% are considered good for meat processing companies; rates above 1.5% are considered very good.)

(c) Comment on the results of your analysis.

Various ratios **20–25A** Selected information follows for the Diamond Company, taken from the current year's and last year's financial statements:

	This Year	**Last Year**
Net Sales	$540,000	$475,000
Cost of Goods Sold	324,000	310,000
Bond Interest Expense	13,000	9,000
Income Tax Expense	6,100	4,800
Net Income (after income taxes)	24,000	19,200
Accounts Receivable, December 31 (before allowance for uncollectible accounts)	75,000	60,500
Inventory, December 31	64,000	52,000
Common Stockholders' Equity	160,000	152,000
Total Assets	270,000	260,000

REQUIRED

Calculate the following for this year:

(a) Return on assets.

(b) Return on sales.

(c) Return on common stockholders' equity.
(d) Average collection period.
(e) Inventory turnover.
(f) Bond interest coverage.

Ratios from comparative and common-size data

20–26A Consider the following financial statements for the Syncro Company for the past two years.

During the year just ended, management obtained additional bond financing to enlarge its production facilities. The plant addition would produce a new high-margin product, which is supposed to improve the average rates of gross profit and return on sales.

As a holder of both common and preferred stock, you analyze the financial statements for the past two years.

Syncro Company
Balance Sheets
(Thousands of Dollars)

	Dec. 31, This Year	Dec. 31, Last Year
Assets:		
Cash	$ 24,000	$ 36,000
Accounts Receivable (net of allowance for uncollectible accounts)	36,000	40,000
Inventory	115,000	75,000
Prepaid Expenses	2,500	4,000
Plant and Other Assets (net)	497,500	445,000
	$675,000	$600,000
Liabilities and Stockholders' Equity:		
Current Liabilities	$ 92,000	$ 70,000
10% Bonds Payable	200,000	170,000
9% Preferred Stock, $50 Par Value	50,000	50,000
Common Stock, $10 Par Value	250,000	250,000
Retained Earnings	83,000	60,000
	$675,000	$600,000

Syncro Company
Income Statements
(Thousands of Dollars)

	This Year	Last Year
Sales	$936,000	$780,000
Cost of Goods Sold	599,040	522,600
Gross Profit	$336,960	$257,400
Operating Expenses	238,660	191,800
Operating Income	$ 98,300	$ 65,600
Bond Interest Expense	20,000	17,000
Income before Income Taxes	$ 78,300	$ 48,600
Income Tax Expense	31,300	17,600
Net Income	$ 47,000	$ 31,000

REQUIRED

(a) Calculate the following for each year: current ratio, quick ratio, inventory turnover (inventory was $69 million two years ago), equity ratio, times interest earned, preferred dividend coverage, return on assets (total assets were $580 million two years ago), and return on common stockholders' equity (common stock equity was $290 million two years ago).

(b) Calculate common-size percentages for each year's income statement.

(c) Calculate the apparent amount of common dividends per share paid during the year just ended.

(d) Comment on the results of your analysis.

Constructing statements from ratio data

20–28A The following are the 19X8 financial statements for Daniels Company, with almost all dollar amounts missing:

Daniels Company
Balance Sheet
December 31, 19X8

Cash	$?	Current Liabilities	$?
Accounts Receivable (net of allowance for uncollectible accounts)	?	8% Bonds Payable	?
Inventory	?	Common Stock	?
Equipment (net)	?	Retained Earnings	280,000
Total Assets	$1,800,000	Total Liabilities and Stockholders' Equity	$1,800,000

Daniels Company
Income Statement
For the Year Ended December 31, 19X8

Net Sales	$?
Cost of Goods Sold	?
Gross Profit	?
Operating Expenses	?
Operating Income	?
Bond Interest Expense	?
Income before Income Taxes	?
Income Tax Expense (40%)	?
Net Income	$180,000

The following information is available about Daniels Company's 19X8 financial statements:

(1) Quick ratio, 1.5:1.

(2) Inventory turnover (inventory at January 1, 19X8 was $410,000), 6 times.

(3) Return on sales, 5%.

(4) Average collection period, 51.71 days. Allowance balance is $10,000. (Round Accounts Receivable balance to nearest $1,000.)

(5) Gross profit rate, 30%.
(6) Return on assets (total assets at January 1, 19X8 were $1,400,000), 20%.
(7) Equity ratio, 60%.
(8) The interest expense relates to the bonds payable that were outstanding all year.

REQUIRED
Compute the missing amounts, and complete the financial statements of Daniels Company. *Hint:* Complete the income statement first.

BUSINESS DECISION PROBLEM

Crescent Lighting, Inc., which manufactures electric lighting and wiring equipment, has been in business five years. The company has had modest profits and has experienced few operating difficulties until this year, when president James Thorpe discusses his company's working capital problems with you, a loan officer at Midtown Bank. Thorpe explains that expanding his firm has created difficulties in meeting obligations when they come due and in taking advantage of cash discounts offered by manufacturers for timely payment. He would like to borrow $50,000 from Midtown Bank. At your request, Thorpe submits the following financial data for the past two years:

	This Year	Last Year
Net Sales	$1,200,000	$1,000,000
Net Income (after income taxes)	37,000	35,000
Dividends	20,000	15,000
Interest Expense	21,000	18,000
Income Tax Expense	9,000	8,000
Total Assets Two Years Ago		540,000
Total Stockholders' Equity Two Years Ago		270,000

Crescent Lighting, Inc.
Balance Sheets

Assets	Dec. 31, This Year	Dec. 31, Last Year
Cash	$ 45,000	$ 35,000
Accounts Receivable (net of allowance for uncollectible accounts of $6,000 last year and $8,000 this year)	180,000	135,000
Inventory	340,000	260,000
Prepaid Expenses	15,000	10,000
Total Current Assets	$580,000	$440,000
Plant Assets (net)	300,000	260,000
Total Assets	$880,000	$700,000

Liabilities and Stockholders' Equity

Notes Payable—Banks	$ 40,000	$ 25,000
Accounts Payable	235,000	140,000
Income Tax Payable	3,000	2,000
Accrued Liabilities	42,000	35,000
Total Current Liabilities	$320,000	$202,000
10% Mortgage Payable	180,000	160,000
Total Liabilities	$500,000	$362,000
Common Stock	$325,000	$300,000
Retained Earnings	55,000	38,000
Total Stockholders' Equity	$380,000	$338,000
Total Liabilities and Stockholders' Equity	$880,000	$700,000

You calculate the following items for both years from the given data and compare them with the typical ratios for electric lighting and wiring equipment manufacturers provided by a commercial credit firm:

	Typical Ratios for Electric Lighting and Wiring Equipment Manufacturers
(a) Current ratio.	2.66
(b) Quick ratio.	1.3
(c) Average collection period.	46 days
(d) Net sales to ending inventory.	4.8 times
(e) Equity ratio.	49%
(f) Return on assets.	13.1%
(g) Return on stockholders' equity.	11.9%
(h) Return on sales.	4.08%

REQUIRED
Based on your analysis, decide whether and under what circumstances you would grant Thorpe's request for a loan. Explain the reasons for your decision.

ANSWERS TO SELF-TEST QUESTIONS

1. (c) 2. (b) 3. (b) 4. (b) 5. (d)

COMPREHENSIVE PROBLEM—PART 4

This comprehensive problem utilizes the financial statement disclosure data of two actual companies. In each case, we give a brief profile of the company and selected disclosure data from a recent annual report to stockholders, followed by questions relating to certain accounting principles and practices discussed thus far in the text.

(I) CHESEBROUGH–POND'S, INC.

PROFILE

Chesebrough–Pond's, Inc., is a diversified worldwide manufacturer and marketer of branded consumer products and hospital products. Its popular brand names include

Prince tennis products, Prince Matchabelli fragrances, Ragú spaghetti sauces, Vaseline petroleum jelly, Bass footwear, and Pond's creams. At December 31, 1985, total assets were over $3 billion and sales for the year then ended were approximately $2.7 billion.

DISCLOSURE DATA (from 1984 and 1983 annual reports to stockholders)

Selected financial data (all amounts in thousands except dividends per share)

	1984	1983	1982	1981
For the Year				
Net sales	$1,857,330	$1,685,417	$1,623,190	
Cost of products sold	935,098	806,980	779,475	
Income from operations	227,834	231,321	223,581	
Net income	119,529	127,828	125,265	
At Year-end				
Current assets	1,006,445	850,611	727,470	
Quick current assets	465,620	423,530	350,278	
Inventories	502,894	396,515	354,847	$ 361,527
Total assets	1,447,310	1,171,910	1,043,420	1,067,973
Current liabilities	506,927	340,288	226,215	
Common stockholders' equity	625,617	649,945	625,082	565,436
Common Stock Data				
Weighted average shares outstanding	35,132	35,768	35,196	
Dividends per share	$1.92	$1.84	$1.72	

REQUIRED

(a) Compute the following ratios for Chesebrough–Pond's, Inc., for 1984, 1983, and 1982:
1. Rate of return on assets
2. Rate of return on common stockholders' equity (there is no outstanding preferred stock)
3. Rate of return on sales
4. Equity ratio
5. Current ratio
6. Quick ratio
7. Inventory turnover
8. Earnings per share
9. Dividend payout ratio

(b) Based on the ratios computed above, comment on Chesebrough's financial performance and strength during the 1982–1984 period.

(II) LOCTITE CORPORATION

PROFILE

Loctite Corporation is a worldwide producer and marketer of high-performance adhesives, sealants, coatings, and other specialty chemicals. The product line includes thread locking sealants, structural adhesives, instant adhesives, gasketing compounds, rust treatments, sealants for electronic components, and automobile body repair components. Total assets exceeded $219 million at June 30, 1985, and sales for the year then ended exceeded $231 million.

DISCLOSURE DATA (from consolidated Statement of Changes in Financial Position for the year ended June 30, 1985)

Loctite's presentation of cash provided by operations is as follows (amounts in thousands):

Net earnings	$20,443
Add (deduct) items not affecting cash in the period:	
Depreciation and amortization	6,369
Deferred income taxes	(425)
Other	(130)
Change in:	
Trade and other receivables	6,926
Inventory	2,661
Other current assets	(465)
Accounts payable and accrued expenses	(4,700)
Taxes payable	555
Cash provided by operations	$31,234

REQUIRED

Loctite's fiscal 1985 income tax expense was $11,042,000. How much cash did Loctite disburse for taxes in fiscal 1985?

Part Five

Accounting in Manufacturing Companies

21

Accounting for Manufacturing Operations

Chapter Objectives

- **Identify the key differences between a merchandising firm and a manufacturing firm.**
- **Explain the unique aspects of manufacturing accounting.**
- **Introduce the special accounts used in manufacturing accounting and present the formats of manufacturing financial statements.**
- **Describe the costing of manufacturing inventories.**
- **Outline end-of-period accounting procedures for a manufacturing firm.**

Man is made to create,
from the poet to the potter.

BENJAMIN DISRAELI

So far, our discussion of accounting systems and procedures has related mainly to merchandising firms and service firms. Another important segment of industry comprises manufacturing firms.

Although the accounting principles and techniques described earlier apply to manufacturing firms, accounting for manufacturing operations is usually more complex because more activities are involved in producing a product than in simply purchasing a product, as in a merchandising firm. Because specific purchase prices are known, the cost of goods purchased for resale is relatively easy to determine. In manufacturing operations, however, the costs of all inputs must be accumulated and allocated to calculate the cost of the units produced. In addition, manufacturers must account for the buying, selling, and administrative activities that are common to other types of firms.

Manufacturing operations vary widely in complexity. In this chapter, a general accounting system is adapted to a relatively simple manufacturing operation using the periodic inventory method. No specific product costing system is involved. The two primary cost accounting systems—*job order costing* and *process costing*—are considered in Chapters 22 and 23.

KEY CONCEPTS IN MANUFACTURING ACCOUNTING

Cost of Goods Manufactured

The primary difference between merchandising and manufacturing firms is that merchandising firms *buy* finished products to sell whereas manufacturers *make* the products they sell. This difference is apparent in the following comparative illustration of cost of goods sold for each:

Merchandising Firm		Manufacturing Firm	
Beginning Merchandise Inventory	$ 80	Beginning Finished Goods Inventory	$ 80
Add: Net Cost of Merchandise Purchases	620	Add: Cost of Goods Manufactured	620
Cost of Goods Available for Sale	$700	Cost of Goods Available for Sale	$700
Less: Ending Merchandise Inventory	100	Less: Ending Finished Goods Inventory	100
Cost of Goods Sold	$600	Cost of Goods Sold	$600

Note on the manufacturing firm's statement that cost of goods manufactured corresponds to net cost of merchandise purchases on the merchandising firm's statement. In both cases, these amounts represent costs of finished goods ready for sale.

Product and Period Costs

Product costs are all costs necessary to bring a manufactured product to completion. Thus, all the costs of factory materials and labor, as well as such other factory costs as utilities, depreciation, insurance, and repairs, are incorporated into the total cost of the products manufactured.

When accounting for service and merchandising organizations, we immediately expense such items as wages, salaries, depreciation, and utilities. In man-

THE U.S. ECONOMIC BASE: AGRICULTURE→ MANUFACTURING→?

A basic variable in a country's welfare is the industry that dominates production of its gross national product. Initially for the United States, this industry was agriculture. For the past several decades, however, manufacturing has dominated U.S. production, and less than 5% of the labor force are now employed in agriculture.

Today, observers theorize that the U.S. economy is rapidly shifting from its manufacturing base as more and more products are manufactured in foreign countries. Automobiles, textiles, high-quality optics, and even the basic commodity of steel represent product lines manufactured abroad. Although its causes are complex, the shift to foreign manufacturers is primarily explained by a pursuit of low labor rates. Many so-called developing countries have large labor forces readily available at wage rates a fraction of the U.S. minimum wage. Ironically, companies losing manufacturing jobs in the United States may be considered victims of the relatively high U.S. living standard.

Personal services was first identified as the industry base that would replace manufacturing. This theory was primarily supported by recognizing that a number of manufacturing jobs have disappeared and that the new jobs are in the personal services area—such as fast-food clerks, banking clerks, personal health and beauty care clerks, and government clerks. However, well-documented theses now argue that the new U.S. economic base will be information, not personal services. In other words, the United States will increasingly create and distribute technological information rather than manufactured products. Critical events underlying this theme are the rampant technological developments in telecommunications, space satellites, and computers and the lead the United States enjoys in these phenomena.* Probably the most widely read proponent of the technology thesis is John Naisbitt, who, in his bestseller *Megatrends*, listed the shift from an industrial society to an information society as the first of his 10 "megashifts" that are transforming our lives.†

Implications stemming from such basic economic changes are difficult to state. Certainly, the quality and emphases of public education must be reexamined. In their career choices, students should consider the possibility of significantly altered opportunities in manufacturing-based companies. Accountants, for example, play a primary role in the decisions of manufacturing operations, but as information technologists, they are assured a vital place in the new information society.

*For a fascinating review of these events, see Daniel Bell, *The Winding Passage* (Cambridge, MA: ABT Books, 1980), especially Chapter 2, titled "Teletext and Technology: New Networks of Knowledge and Information in Postindustrial Society," pages 34–65.

†John Naisbitt, *Megatrends: Ten New Directions Transforming Our Lives* (New York: Warner Books, Inc., 1980).

ufacturing accounting, however, all such costs for the factory are product costs and, thus, are initially taken into inventory. They will be expensed (as cost of goods sold) in the period in which the related products are sold to customers.

Period costs are charged to expense in the period incurred. The benefits associated with such costs are considered to expire in that period rather than relate to whatever product may have been produced in that period. Traditionally, selling expenses and nonfactory administrative expenses are considered period costs. Some functions in a manufacturing firm—such as a personnel department and a company security department—may benefit both factory and nonfactory activities. The costs of such functions are partly product cost and partly period cost.

Based on the above concepts, income statements for manufacturing firms have the following form:

Sales		$900
Cost of Goods Sold (product costs of units sold)		600
Gross Profit on Sales		$300
Operating Expenses (period costs):		
Selling Expenses	$160	
Nonfactory Administrative Expenses	80	240
Net Income		$ 60

Multiple Inventory Accounts

At any point in time, manufacturing operations typically have units of products at various stages of completion. Consequently, three inventory accounts are usually maintained:

(1) The Materials Inventory account reflects factory materials that have been acquired but not yet placed into production. (Even though these items may be finished products for the supplying firm, they are raw materials for the using firm.) Materials are carried at their net delivered cost.

(2) The Work in Process Inventory account reflects all factory costs associated with units of product started but not completed on the date the firm's financial statements are prepared.

(3) The Finished Goods Inventory account reflects all factory costs associated with the units of product completed but not yet sold.

All three inventory accounts represent current assets.

Manufacturing Cost Categories

Factory costs are usually accounted for in the following three categories:

(1) **Direct material** includes all of the important materials or component parts that physically comprise the product. Examples are sheets of steel, electric motors, and microprocessors. Incidental material items—such as glue and fasteners—are considered indirect materials and are included in factory overhead. Supply items—such as cleaning supplies and lubricants—are considered factory supplies and are included in factory overhead.

(2) **Direct labor** includes the salary and wage costs of factory employees who work directly on the product. Machine operators, assemblers, and painters are examples of such workers. The salary and wage costs of factory employees who work indirectly on the product—such as supervisors, inspectors, material handlers, and maintenance workers—are considered indirect labor costs and are included in factory overhead.

(3) **Factory overhead**, sometimes called manufacturing overhead or factory burden, includes all other manufacturing costs not included in direct material or direct labor. Examples of items included in factory overhead are indirect material, factory supplies used, indirect labor, factory payroll taxes and fringe benefits, factory utilities (natural gas and electricity), factory building and equipment costs (insurance, property taxes, repairs and maintenance, and depreciation), and other factory costs.

Factory overhead specifically excludes selling expenses and nonfactory administrative expenses since these are not incurred in the manufacturing process.

Exhibit 21–1 illustrates the relationship of the multiple inventory accounts, the manufacturing cost categories, the manufacturing process, and the selling process. Materials are purchased and placed in the Materials Inventory. Direct material, direct labor, and factory overhead are combined to create products. Completed products are stored until they are sold to customers.

EXHIBIT 21–1
Relationship of Multiple Inventory Accounts, Manufacturing Cost Categories, Manufacturing Process, and Selling Process

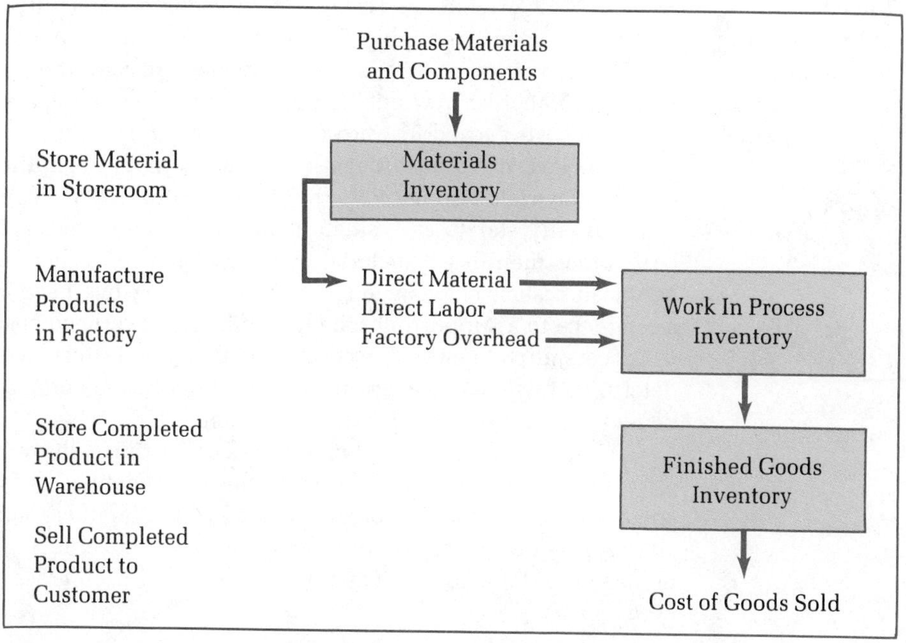

FINANCIAL STATEMENT FEATURES UNIQUE TO MANUFACTURING ACCOUNTING

Financial statement features unique to manufacturing accounting are concentrated in the cost of goods manufactured statement and the income statement.

Calculating Cost of Goods Manufactured

Cost of goods manufactured is the cost of goods whose manufacture is completed during the accounting period. Cost of goods manufactured is calculated as follows:

Beginning Work in Process Inventory		$ 30,000
Add: Direct Material Used	$190,000	
Direct Labor	240,000	
Factory Overhead	180,000	610,000
Cost of Work in Process During the Period		$640,000
Less: Ending Work in Process Inventory		20,000
Cost of Goods Manufactured		$620,000

The $620,000 cost of goods manufactured represents this period's total manufacturing cost ($610,000) adjusted for the change in work in process inventories. In other words, the cost of goods manufactured during this period is the cost of partially completed products carried forward from last period ($30,000) plus the total manufacturing cost this period ($610,000) less the cost of partially completed products this period ($20,000) that are carried forward and completed in the next period. Remember that ending inventories of one period become the beginning inventories of the subsequent period.

Illustrations of Financial Statements

Exhibit 21–2 presents a formal cost of goods manufactured statement and an income statement for a typical manufacturing firm. All amounts are assumed.

The cost of goods manufactured statement presents the several cost categories in the general order in which they are incurred. In a sense, the first costs incurred are those costs carried forward from the preceding period as beginning work in process. Next, direct material used is determined (Beginning Inventory + Net Cost of Materials Purchased − Ending Inventory). The cost of direct labor follows, usually shown as a single figure. Factory overhead—a list of all factory costs other than direct material and direct labor—is then added. If the list of overhead costs is extensive, only the total factory overhead may be shown with a reference to a supporting schedule of factory overhead costs. Beginning work in process, direct material used, direct labor, and factory overhead are added to determine total cost of work in process. Finally, the ending work in process is deducted to derive cost of goods manufactured.

On the income statement of a manufacturing firm, the cost of goods sold and gross profit are determined in much the same manner as for a merchandising concern—except that cost of goods manufactured, rather than merchandise purchases, is added to the beginning finished goods inventory. Selling expense and nonfactory administrative expense are deducted from gross profit to determine net income.

EXHIBIT 21–2

A Manufacturing Company
Cost of Goods Manufactured Statement
For the Year Ended December 31, 19XX

Beginning Work in Process Inventory		$ 30,000
Direct Material Used:		
Beginning Materials Inventory	$ 50,000	
Net Cost of Materials Purchased	250,000	
Cost of Materials Available	$300,000	
Less: Ending Materials Inventory	110,000	
Direct Material		190,000
Direct Labor		240,000
Factory Overhead:		
Depreciation	$ 25,000	
Utilities	34,000	
Insurance	15,000	
Property Taxes	28,000	
Indirect Labor	39,000	
Factory Supplies Used	21,000	
Other Factory Overhead	18,000	
Total Factory Overhead		180,000
Total Cost of Work in Process During 19XX		$640,000
Less: Ending Work in Process Inventory		20,000
Cost of Goods Manufactured		$620,000

A Manufacturing Company
Income Statement
For the Year Ended December 31, 19XX

Net Sales		$900,000
Cost of Goods Sold:		
Beginning Finished Goods Inventory	$ 80,000	
Cost of Goods Manufactured	620,000	
Cost of Goods Available for Sale	$700,000	
Less: Ending Finished Goods Inventory	100,000	
Cost of Goods Sold		600,000
Gross Profit on Sales		$300,000
Operating Expenses:		
Selling Expenses	$160,000	
Administrative Expenses	80,000	240,000
Net Income		$ 60,000
Earnings per Share of Capital Stock		$3

SPECIAL ACCOUNTS FOR MANUFACTURING

Many accounts appearing in a manufacturing firm's ledger—such as Cash, Accounts Receivable, and Sales—are similar to those of service and merchandising firms. The unique aspects of manufacturing, however, have led to the use of several special accounts, particularly Materials Inventory, Materials Purchases, Materials Returns and Allowances, Work in Process Inventory, Finished Goods Inventory, and Manufacturing Summary accounts.

Accounts Related to Materials

When the periodic inventory method is used, accounting for the acquisition and use of materials is similar to the accounting for merchandise purchases by a retailer. The manufacturer uses separate accounts to record purchases of materials (Material Purchases), related returns and adjustments (Material Returns and Allowances), and costs of transporting material purchases to the factory (Transportation In). At the end of the accounting period, the balances of these accounts are used to calculate the net cost of materials purchased and are closed to the Manufacturing Summary account.

Entries in the Materials Inventory account are made only when the end-of-period physical inventory count is taken. During the period, the transfer of material into production is not recorded. Determining the ending materials inventory involves counting all units on hand, identifying an appropriate cost price per unit (perhaps from a recent purchase invoice or supply catalog), multiplying quantity by price, and combining all items for a total inventory figure.

Work in Process Inventory Account

The Work in Process Inventory account reflects the costs of products that have been begun but are not completed at the end of the accounting period. All or part of direct material may have been added, but portions of direct labor and factory overhead have not. In a general accounting system using periodic inventory procedures, the amount of work in process is estimated at the end of the period, usually by a production supervisor or someone familiar with the manufacturing process. An illustrative calculation of estimated work in process inventory using assumed amounts appears below:

	Estimated Cost per Finished Unit of Product	Average Proportion Applied	
Direct Material:			
Material A (wood)	$2	100%	$ 2
Material B (paint)	4	25	1
Direct Labor	8	50	4
Factory Overhead	6	50	3
			$ 10
Number of Units in Ending Work in Process			× 2,000
Estimated Cost of Ending Work in Process			$20,000

Estimating the ending work in process inventory typically involves (1) estimating the amount of each manufacturing cost element associated with a finished unit of product, (2) multiplying each cost by an appropriate estimate of the average proportion applied, (3) summing the estimated costs for the various factors, and (4) multiplying by the number of units in the ending inventory. This new work in process figure is the recorded amount of work in process for the end of the current period. Both the beginning and ending balances of work in process are used to calculate the cost of goods manufactured for the period.

Finished Goods Inventory

The balance in the Finished Goods Inventory account represents the cost of finished products awaiting sale to customers. In a periodic inventory system, the ending finished goods inventory is determined by (1) estimating the average cost per finished unit of product for each manufacturing cost element, (2) making a physical count of the unsold finished units of product on hand, (3) multiplying the units by the estimated total cost per unit, and (4) aggregating the total finished goods inventory cost. An illustrative calculation of finished goods inventory costing using assumed amounts follows:

Product	Direct Material A	Direct Material B	Direct Labor	Factory Overhead	Total Unit Cost	Units on Hand	Total Cost of Inventory
101	$3	$0	$ 4	$3	$10	2,500	$ 25,000
102	4	2	8	6	20	3,000	60,000
103	3	1	12	9	25	600	15,000
Totals						6,100	$100,000

Notice that different amounts of each manufacturing cost may be applied to various products. Entries to the Finished Goods Inventory account occur only at the end of the accounting period when a new balance is determined. Both the beginning and ending balances of Finished Goods Inventory are involved in computing the cost of goods sold for the period.

Determining both work in process and finished goods inventories requires a knowledge of product design specifications and cost data relating to various production inputs. The cost of direct material and direct labor is reasonably estimated as some normal or average quantity of materials or direct labor multiplied by some normal or average cost or rate for each factor. Factory overhead, however, can only be related *indirectly* to units of product. The appropriate amounts per unit of product for such costs as factory supervision, depreciation, utilities, and property taxes are not readily apparent. Most firms therefore assume that the amount of factory overhead assigned to products is in proportion to some other known and important production variable such as direct labor hours or direct labor costs. A *factory overhead rate* is determined by dividing the total overhead cost by the total of the base used to assign overhead. For example, the cost of goods manufactured statement in Exhibit 21–2 shows total direct labor costs of $240,000 and total factory overhead of $180,000. Thus, this firm might compute its factory overhead rate as:

$$\text{Factory Overhead Rate} = \frac{\text{Total Factory Overhead}}{\text{Total Direct Labor Costs}} = \frac{\$180{,}000}{\$240{,}000} = 75\% \text{ of Direct Labor Costs}$$

Using this factory overhead rate, an ending work in process inventory that involved \$5,000 of direct labor would be assigned \$3,750 (0.75 × \$5,000) of factory overhead.

Manufacturing Summary Account

Manufacturing firms use both a Manufacturing Summary account and an Income Summary account. As its name implies, the Manufacturing Summary account summarizes the total manufacturing costs for the period and determines the cost of goods manufactured. As is true for the Income Summary account, entries are made only during the closing procedures, after which the account itself is closed. Stated simply, the balance of the Manufacturing Summary account equals the cost of goods manufactured for the period when (1) all accounts for factory costs are closed to the Manufacturing Summary account, and (2) the Materials Inventory and Work in Process Inventory accounts are closed to the Manufacturing Summary account (beginning balances debited and ending balances credited). The Manufacturing Summary and Income Summary accounts are illustrated in Exhibit 21–3 in T-account form, using the data from Exhibit 21–2.

The balance of the Manufacturing Summary account comprises a series of entries reflecting (1) debits for the manufacturing costs carried forward to this period as beginning materials and work in process inventories, and the other manufacturing costs incurred during this period—such as materials purchases, transportation in, direct labor, and factory overhead—and (2) credits representing the ending materials and work in process inventories. In effect, we deduct these latter amounts because they are carried forward as costs of the subsequent manufacturing period. Had materials returns and allowances been involved in this illustration, the debit for purchases would have included the gross amount of purchases, and an additional credit would appear in the Manufacturing Summary account for materials returns and allowances. In turn, the Manufacturing Summary account is closed to Income Summary, therefore becoming an important factor in determining the period's net income.

Notice that the finished goods inventory is not part of the cost of goods manufactured. Rather, the beginning and ending finished goods inventory amounts are closed to and appear, respectively, as a debit and a credit in the Income Summary account. This procedure combines the cost of goods manufactured, the beginning finished goods inventory, and the ending finished goods inventory, so that the cost of goods sold can be determined.

END-OF-PERIOD PROCEDURES FOR A MANUFACTURING FIRM

Most end-of-period procedures for manufacturing firms are similar to those presented for other types of firms in Chapters 4 and 5. In the remainder of this chapter, we present a comprehensive illustration of these procedures for a man-

EXHIBIT 21–3

Manufacturing Summary

19XX			19XX		
Dec. 31	Work in Process Inventory (Beginning)	30,000	Dec. 31	Work in Process Inventory (Ending)	20,000
31	Materials Inventory (Beginning)	50,000	31	Materials Inventory (Ending)	110,000
31	Materials Purchases	250,000	31	(To close to Income Summary)	620,000
31	Direct Labor	240,000			
31	Factory Overhead (total)	180,000			
		750,000			750,000

Income Summary

19XX			19XX		
Dec. 31	Finished Goods Inventory (Beginning)	80,000	Dec. 31	Sales	900,000
31	Cost of Goods Manufactured	620,000	31	Finished Goods Inventory (Ending)	100,000
31	Selling Expenses (total)	160,000			
31	Nonfactory Administrative Expenses (total)	80,000			
31	(To close to Retained Earnings)	60,000			
		1,000,000			1,000,000

ufacturing firm, including preparation and use of the worksheet to adjust the general ledger accounts, preparation of financial statements from worksheet data, and procedures for closing the temporary accounts at year-end. The illustration highlights the unique aspects of manufacturing accounting.

Worksheet for a Manufacturing Firm

Remember from Chapter 4 that a worksheet facilitates adjusting the general ledger accounts and preparing financial statements because

(1) It places in one location the debit and credit balances of all general ledger accounts.

(2) It makes apparent the effects of any adjustment.

(3) It groups all adjusted account balances involved in preparing each financial statement.

Worksheets for manufacturing firms differ from those presented in Chapters 4 and 5. An additional set of columns is provided for the accounts contained in the cost of goods manufactured statement, and three, rather than one, inventory accounts are involved. Also, note that the adjusted trial balance columns have been omitted. Instead, the adjusted amounts are computed and placed directly in the proper financial statement column. This more efficient procedure is considered appropriate at this stage of your study. The following basic aspects of the worksheet are similar for all firms:

(1) The unadjusted trial balance is transcribed from the general ledger to the first set of money columns.
(2) Appropriate adjustments are formulated in the second set of money columns.
(3) Unadjusted account balances and any related adjustments are combined to derive adjusted balances for all accounts, which are then extended to the appropriate set of columns representing the cost of goods manufactured, the income statement, and the balance sheet. Special procedures are used to extend the beginning inventory balances and to record the ending inventory balances.
(4) Each set of statement columns is balanced in turn, to check the arithmetical accuracy of the worksheet.

Exhibit 21–4 (pages 818–19) presents the worksheet for Lollar Manufacturing, Inc., for an accounting year ended December 31, 19XX. Remember that in preparing monthly or quarterly financial statements, worksheet adjustments are not recorded and posted to the general ledger. When annual statements are prepared, however, both adjusting and closing entries are recorded in the general journal and posted to the general ledger.

Adjusting entry data for our year-end illustration are as follows:

(1) Unexpired insurance on factory machinery, $1,000.
(2) Unpaid wages and salaries at year-end (by category): direct labor, $4,000; indirect labor, $3,000; office salaries, $1,000; and sales salaries, $2,000.
(3) Depreciation on factory machinery, $6,000.
(4) Accrued interest payable at year-end, $1,000.
(5) Uncollectible accounts expense is an estimated 2% of sales.
(6) Factory supplies on hand, $4,000.
(7) Office supplies on hand, $2,000.
(8) Estimated income taxes, $17,000.

Because these adjustments are routine and parallel those of other firms, related journal entries with explanations are not presented here. Related amounts in the adjustments columns of the worksheet in Exhibit 21–4 are keyed to the parenthetical numbers of each data item.

MANUFACTURING INVENTORIES IN THE WORKSHEET Worksheet procedures for manufacturing inventories under the periodic method parallel those illustrated in Chapter 5 for merchandising companies. Recall that inventory amounts in a manufacturing firm's trial balance are debits representing the *beginning* balances for each inventory. Also, only materials and work in process inventories are involved in determining cost of goods manufactured. Finished goods inventories are involved in determining cost of goods sold (in the income statement).

The worksheet inventory procedures result in (1) beginning inventory balances being added to—and ending inventory balances being deducted from—other related net debit amounts for determining cost of goods manufactured and cost of goods sold, and (2) the ending balances of all three inventories being reflected as assets on the balance sheet. These procedures are as follows:

(1) Extend the beginning balances of materials and work in process inventories as debits in the cost of goods manufactured columns.

(2) Extend the beginning finished goods inventory as a debit in the income statement columns.

(3) At the bottom of the worksheet, record all three inventory account titles and record the ending balances of materials and work in process inventories as credits in the cost of goods manufactured columns, and the ending balance of finished goods inventory as a credit in the income statement columns.

(4) On the same respective lines used in step (3), record the ending balance of each inventory account as a debit in the balance sheet columns.

We represent these procedures schematically in the chart below [the parenthetical (+) and (−) signs indicate the respective effects on cost of goods manufactured, cost of goods sold, and total assets on the balance sheet].

	Cost of Goods Manufactured		**Income Statement**		**Balance Sheet**	
	Debit	**Credit**	**Debit**	**Credit**	**Debit**	**Credit**
Extension of Beginning Balances:						
Materials inventory	(+)					
Work in process inventory	(+)					
Finished goods inventory			(+)			
Recording Ending Balances at Bottom of Worksheet:						
Materials inventory		(−)			(+)	
Work in process inventory		(−)			(+)	
Finished goods inventory				(−)	(+)	

Review of Exhibit 21–4 shows the effects of these procedures in the worksheet illustrated there.

EXHIBIT 21–4

Lollar Manufacturing, Inc.
Manufacturing Worksheet
For the Year Ended December 31, 19XX

Description	Trial Balance		Adjustments		Cost of Goods Manufactured		Income Statement		Balance Sheet	
	Debit	Credit	Debit	Credit	Debit	Credit	Debit	Credit	Debit	Credit
Cash	13,000								13,000	
Accounts Receivable	45,000								45,000	
Allowance for Uncollectible Accounts		1,000		(5) 9,000						10,000
Materials Inventory	10,000				10,000					
Work in Process Inventory	6,000				6,000					
Finished Goods Inventory	20,000						20,000			
Factory Supplies on Hand	17,000			(6) 13,000					4,000	
Office Supplies on Hand	5,000			(7) 3,000					2,000	
Prepaid Insurance	4,000			(1) 3,000					1,000	
Factory Machinery	90,000								90,000	
Accumulated Depreciation—Factory Machinery		20,000		(3) 6,000						26,000
Accounts Payable		7,000								7,000
Long-term Notes Payable—10%		40,000								40,000
Common Stock—$10 Par Value		50,000								50,000
Retained Earnings		20,000								20,000
Dividends	4,000								4,000	
Sales		450,000						450,000		
Materials Purchases	114,000				114,000					
Transportation In	2,000				2,000					
Direct Labor	77,000		(2) 4,000		81,000					
Indirect Labor	43,000		(2) 3,000		46,000					

Factory Utilities	20,000				20,000					
Factory Repairs	10,000				10,000					
Factory Rent	40,000				40,000					
Administrative Rent Expense	7,000						7,000			
Sales Rent Expense	23,000						23,000			
Office Salaries Expense	12,000		(2) 1,000				13,000			
Sales Salaries Expense	16,000		(2) 2,000				18,000			
Advertising Expense	7,000						7,000			
Interest Expense	3,000		(4) 1,000				4,000			
	588,000	588,000								
Factory Insurance			(1) 3,000		3,000					
Wages Payable				(2) 10,000						10,000
Factory Depreciation—Machinery			(3) 6,000		6,000					
Interest Payable				(4) 1,000						1,000
Uncollectible Accounts Expense			(5) 9,000				9,000			
Factory Supplies Expense			(6) 13,000		13,000					
Office Supplies Expense			(7) 3,000				3,000			
Income Tax Expense			(8) 17,000				17,000			
Income Tax Payable				(8) 17,000						17,000
Ending Inventories: Materials						18,000			18,000	
Work in Process						8,000			8,000	
Finished Goods								26,000	26,000	
			62,000	62,000	351,000	26,000				
Cost of Goods Manufactured						325,000	325,000			
					351,000	351,000	446,000	476,000	211,000	181,000
Net Income							30,000			30,000
							476,000	476,000	211,000	211,000

TOTALING AND BALANCING THE WORKSHEET After all other relevant amounts are extended, the cost of goods manufactured columns are added; the amount needed to balance them (a credit of $325,000) is the cost of goods manufactured figure for this period. The $325,000 credit needed to balance the cost of goods manufactured columns is then extended as a debit to the income statement columns. The $30,000 debit needed to balance these columns represents net income for the period. The $30,000 is then extended as a credit to balance the balance sheet columns. When operating losses occur, the *credit* needed to balance the income statement columns is extended as a debit to balance the balance sheet columns. This completes the worksheet.

Preparation of Financial Statements

Properly completed, the worksheet contains all the data necessary to prepare the cost of goods manufactured statement, the income statement, the retained earnings statement, and the balance sheet. Exhibit 21–5 presents those statements for

EXHIBIT 21–5
Financial Statements of Lollar Manufacturing, Inc.

Lollar Manufacturing, Inc.
Cost of Goods Manufactured Statement
For the Year Ended December 31, 19XX

Beginning Work in Process Inventory		$ 6,000
Direct Material Used:		
Beginning Materials Inventory	$ 10,000	
Materials Purchases	114,000	
Transportation In	2,000	
Cost of Materials Available	$126,000	
Less: Ending Materials Inventory	18,000	
Direct Material		108,000
Direct Labor		81,000
Factory Overhead:		
Indirect Labor	$ 46,000	
Factory Utilities	20,000	
Factory Repairs	10,000	
Factory Rent	40,000	
Factory Supplies Used	13,000	
Factory Insurance	3,000	
Factory Depreciation—Machinery	6,000	
Total Factory Overhead		138,000
Total Cost of Work in Process During 19XX		$333,000
Less: Ending Work in Process Inventory		8,000
Cost of Goods Manufactured		$325,000

Lollar Manufacturing, Inc., prepared from the data on the worksheet in Exhibit 21–4. Observe that the key income statement figures—cost of goods manufactured and net income—agree with the amounts that balance the related worksheet columns.

Closing Entries Recall that closing procedures occur only at the end of the operating year. The worksheet provides all the data necessary to prepare closing entries for manufacturing cost accounts and expense accounts and to record inventory changes at

EXHIBIT 21–5 (continued)
Financial Statements of Lollar Manufacturing, Inc.

Lollar Manufacturing, Inc.
Income Statement
For the Year Ended December 31, 19XX

Net Sales			$450,000
Cost of Goods Sold:			
Beginning Finished Goods Inventory		$ 20,000	
Cost of Goods Manufactured		325,000	
Cost of Goods Available for Sale		$345,000	
Less: Ending Finished Goods Inventory		26,000	
Cost of Goods Sold			319,000
Gross Profit on Sales			$131,000
Operating Expenses:			
Selling Expenses:			
Sales Rent Expense	$23,000		
Sales Salaries Expense	18,000		
Advertising Expense	7,000		
Total Selling Expenses		$ 48,000	
Administrative Expenses:			
Administrative Rent Expense	$ 7,000		
Office Salaries Expense	13,000		
Uncollectible Accounts Expense	9,000		
Office Supplies Expense	3,000		
Total Administrative Expenses		32,000	
Total Operating Expenses			80,000
Income from Operations			$ 51,000
Less: Interest Expense			4,000
Income before Income Taxes			$ 47,000
Less: Income Tax Expense			17,000
Net Income			$ 30,000
Earnings per Share of Capital Stock			$6

EXHIBIT 21–5 (continued)
Financial Statements of Lollar Manufacturing, Inc.

Lollar Manufacturing, Inc.
Balance Sheet
December 31, 19XX

ASSETS		
Current Assets		
Cash		$ 13,000
Accounts Receivable	$45,000	
Less: Allowance for Uncollectible Accounts	10,000	35,000
Inventories:		
Materials	$18,000	
Work in Process	8,000	
Finished Goods	26,000	52,000
Prepaid Expenses:		
Factory Supplies on Hand	$ 4,000	
Office Supplies on Hand	2,000	
Prepaid Insurance	1,000	7,000
Total Current Assets		$107,000
Plant Assets		
Machinery and Equipment	$90,000	
Less: Accumulated Depreciation	26,000	64,000
Total Assets		$171,000
LIABILITIES AND STOCKHOLDERS' EQUITY		
Current Liabilities		
Accounts Payable		$ 7,000
Wages Payable		10,000
Interest Payable		1,000
Income Tax Payable		17,000
Total Current Liabilities		$ 35,000
Long-term Notes Payable (10%, due 5 years hence)		40,000
Total Liabilities		$ 75,000
Stockholders' Equity		
Common Stock, $10 Par Value, 5,000 Shares Authorized and Issued	$50,000	
Retained Earnings	46,000	96,000
Total Liabilities and Stockholders' Equity		$171,000

EXHIBIT 21–5 (continued)
Financial Statements of Lollar Manufacturing, Inc.

Lollar Manufacturing, Inc.
Retained Earnings Statement
For the Year Ended December 31, 19XX

Retained Earnings, January 1	$20,000
Add: Net Income for 19XX	30,000
	$50,000
Less: Dividends Declared	4,000
Retained Earnings, December 31	$46,000

year-end. Using compound journal entries when appropriate, we use the following closing procedures:

(1) Close the beginning Materials and Work in Process inventory accounts and all manufacturing cost accounts with *debit* balances and debit the total to the Manufacturing Summary account.

(2) Record (as debits) the ending materials and work in process inventories, close any manufacturing cost accounts with *credit* balances, and credit the total to the Manufacturing Summary account. (The balance of the Manufacturing Summary account should now equal the total cost of goods manufactured.)

(3) Close the beginning Finished Goods Inventory account, the Manufacturing Summary account, and all other income statement accounts with *debit* balances, and debit the total to the Income Summary account.

(4) Record (as a debit) the ending Finished Goods Inventory account, close any income statement account with a *credit* balance, and credit the total to the Income Summary account. (The balance of the Income Summary account should now equal net income.)

(5) Close the Income Summary account to Retained Earnings.

(6) Close the Dividends account to Retained Earnings.

The closing entries for Lollar Manufacturing, Inc., follow (entries are parenthetically numbered to indicate the related closing step involved):

(1)	Manufacturing Summary	351,000	
	Materials Inventory (beginning)		10,000
	Work in Process Inventory (beginning)		6,000
	Materials Purchases		114,000
	Transportation In		2,000
	Direct Labor		81,000
	Indirect Labor		46,000

	Factory Utilities		20,000
	Factory Repairs		10,000
	Factory Rent		40,000
	Factory Supplies Used		13,000
	Factory Insurance		3,000
	Factory Depreciation—Machinery		6,000
	To close beginning Materials and Work in Process accounts and manufacturing cost accounts having debit balances to the Manufacturing Summary account.		
(2)	Materials Inventory (ending)	18,000	
	Work in Process Inventory (ending)	8,000	
	Manufacturing Summary		26,000
	To record the ending materials and work in process inventories.		
(3)	Income Summary	446,000	
	Finished Goods Inventory (beginning)		20,000
	Administrative Rent Expense		7,000
	Sales Rent Expense		23,000
	Office Salaries Expense		13,000
	Office Supplies Expense		3,000
	Sales Salaries Expense		18,000
	Advertising Expense		7,000
	Interest Expense		4,000
	Uncollectible Accounts Expense		9,000
	Income Tax Expense		17,000
	Manufacturing Summary		325,000
	To close the beginning finished goods inventory, all expense accounts, and the Manufacturing Summary account to the Income Summary account.		
(4)	Finished Goods Inventory (ending)	26,000	
	Sales	450,000	
	Income Summary		476,000
	To record the ending finished goods inventory and close Sales to the Income Summary account.		
(5)	Income Summary	30,000	
	Retained Earnings		30,000
	To close the Income Summary account to Retained Earnings.		

(6)	Retained Earnings	4,000	
	Dividends		4,000
	To close the Dividends account to Retained Earnings.		

After the closing entries are recorded and posted, the general ledger reflects only the balances of those assets, liabilities, and stockholders' equity accounts that are carried forward as beginning balances for the next year.

In manufacturing accounting, a general accounting system using the periodic inventory method may be satisfactory for small, stable, single-product firms. The limitations of this approach are critical, however, in more complex, multiproduct manufacturing operations. When periodic inventory procedures are used, the amounts of materials used and cost of goods sold are merely residual figures that offer little opportunity for management control. Also, periodic inventory procedures permit accurate income determination only at the end of the period, when ending inventories are taken. However, management may need reliable current product cost data on a day-to-day basis. Because multiple products may involve widely varying types and amounts of materials, different production techniques, and a variety of production routines in a series of departments, product cost accounting requires a more sophisticated approach. Therefore, cost accounting systems using perpetual inventories have been developed. Cost accounting systems are discussed in Chapters 22 and 23.

KEY POINTS TO REMEMBER

(1) Product costs comprise all costs necessary to bring the manufactured product to completion.

(2) Manufacturers have three inventory accounts—Materials, Work in Process, and Finished Goods.

(3) Manufacturing costs are accounted for in three categories: (1) direct material, (2) direct labor, and (3) factory overhead, which includes all manufacturing costs other than direct material and direct labor.

(4) In manufacturing accounting, all product costs—direct material, direct labor, and factory overhead—are capitalized; that is, they become the cost of goods manufactured.

(5) Cost of goods manufactured equals the total of all manufacturing costs incurred adjusted for the change in work in process inventory.

(6) Cost of goods sold equals cost of goods manufactured adjusted for the change in finished goods inventory.

(7) Neither cost of goods manufactured nor cost of goods sold includes selling expenses or nonfactory administrative expenses.

(8) Worksheets for manufacturing firms have an additional set of columns for cost of goods manufactured.

(9) Closing procedures for manufacturers incorporate a Manufacturing Summary

account to which beginning Materials and Work in Process Inventory account balances and all accounts related to the cost of goods manufactured are closed. Ending Materials and Work in Process Inventory account balances are recorded as credits in the Manufacturing Summary account and as debits in the related balance sheet asset accounts. Beginning finished goods inventory, the Manufacturing Summary account, and all income statement accounts are closed to the Income Summary account. Ending finished goods inventory is recorded as a credit in the Income Summary account and as a debit in the related balance sheet asset account.

SELF-TEST QUESTIONS
(Answers are at the end of this chapter.)

1. Which of the following is not an element of factory overhead?
   (a) Factory office salaries.
   (b) Plant manager's salary.
   (c) Product inspector's salary.
   (d) President's salary.
2. Which of the following is never an element of product cost?
   (a) Insurance.
   (b) Advertising.
   (c) Utilities.
   (d) Supplies.
3. Which of the following is extended to the Income Statement columns on a manufacturing worksheet?
   (a) Beginning materials inventory.
   (b) Beginning work in process inventory.
   (c) Beginning finished goods inventory.
   (d) Dividends.
4. Which of the following would typically not be a factor in determining an overhead rate?
   (a) Pounds of material.
   (b) Direct labor hours.
   (c) Total overhead costs.
   (d) Direct labor cost.
5. Under the periodic inventory method, entries are made in the materials inventory:
   (a) When materials are purchased.
   (b) When materials are used.
   (c) At the end of the accounting period.
   (d) All of the above.

QUESTIONS

21–1 In what two important ways is accounting for a manufacturing firm more complex than accounting for a merchandising firm?

21–2 How are product costs accounted for differently from period costs? Give examples of each.

21–3 What is the basic format for the income statement of a manufacturing firm?

21–4 Name the three inventory accounts maintained by manufacturing firms and briefly describe the nature of each.

21–5 Name and briefly describe the three major categories used to account for manufacturing costs.

21–6 List six examples of factory overhead costs.

21–7 In what way is the total manufacturing cost during the year different from cost of goods manufactured?

21–8 If cost of work in process during the year is $400,000 and ending work in process inventory is $30,000, what is the amount of cost of goods manufactured?

21–9 If beginning and ending finished goods inventories are $60,000 and $80,000, respectively, and the cost of goods sold is $380,000, what is the cost of goods manufactured?

21–10 Identify and briefly describe the normal balances and typical entries in the four accounts usually maintained for the purchase and use of materials.

21–11 What information is necessary to estimate the ending work in process inventory? The ending finished goods inventory?

21–12 Briefly describe the nature and timing of the entries expected in the Manufacturing Summary account.

21–13 Briefly outline a typical worksheet format for a manufacturing company. What four steps are followed to prepare such a worksheet?

21–14 "Preparation of a worksheet does not specifically affect the general ledger." Do you agree or disagree with this statement? Why?

21–15 Briefly explain the year-end closing procedures for a manufacturing firm.

21–16 In what important way is the assignment of factory overhead to the work in process and finished goods inventories different from the assignment of direct material and direct labor costs? Briefly explain the approach that is widely used to assign factory overhead.

EXERCISES

Cost of goods manufactured statement

21–17 The following account balances are available from the Lawrence Manufacturing Company ledger:

	Beginning of Year	End of Year
Materials Inventory	$40,000	$ 30,000
Work in Process Inventory	50,000	70,000
Finished Goods Inventory	60,000	55,000
Direct Labor		140,000
Materials Purchases		90,000
Indirect Labor		45,000
Depreciation—Factory		15,000
Factory Supplies Used		8,000
Repairs and Maintenance—Factory		11,000
Selling Expenses (total)		32,000
Nonfactory Administrative Expenses (total)		29,000

Prepare a cost of goods manufactured statement for the current year.

Income statement

21–18 Lawrence Manufacturing Company (see Exercise 21–17) sold 15,000 units of product for $26 each during the current year. At year-end, 5,000 shares of capital stock are outstanding. Prepare an income statement for the year.

Cost of goods sold

21–19 For each of the following unrelated columns of data, compute the cost of goods manufactured and the cost of goods sold:

	A	B	C
Selling Expenses	$ 240	$ 396	$ 288
Factory Insurance	120	96	168
Nonfactory Administrative Expenses	108	192	132
Ending Finished Goods Inventory	540	1,200	1,560
Factory Taxes	156	120	108
Materials Inventory (beginning)	240	384	144
Direct Labor	1,200	960	2,520
Factory Maintenance	96	144	228
Materials Purchased	540	780	600
Beginning Finished Goods Inventory	360	1,440	1,320
Increase (Decrease) in Work in Process	120	0	(324)
Factory Utilities	108	360	864
Depreciation—Factory	240	1,080	720
Indirect Labor	372	252	1,320
Factory Supplies Used	156	204	456
Materials Inventory (ending)	204	300	108

Factory overhead rate and assigning overhead

21–20 During the current year, Johnson Factories, Inc., recorded the following costs and expenses:

Direct Material	$ 50,000
Direct Labor	110,000
Factory Supplies Used	30,000
Indirect Labor	40,000
Sales Commissions	15,000
Factory Supervision	20,000
Nonfactory Administrative Expenses	18,000
Other Factory Overhead	9,000

Assume that Johnson assigns factory overhead on the basis of direct labor costs.

(a) Compute the factory overhead rate.

(b) Indicate the total cost of the ending work in process inventory that has been assigned $5,000 of direct material cost and $11,000 of direct labor cost.

Estimated cost of inventories

21–21 Marshall Manufacturing Company's accounting department has estimated that each completed unit of its product involves an average of 3 pounds of direct material costing $3 per pound and 5 hours of direct labor costing $9 per hour. Factory overhead is assigned on the basis of total direct labor cost incurred, which for the current year are $98,000 and $140,000, respectively.

(a) Determine the proper cost of an ending finished goods inventory that comprises 4,000 units.

(b) Determine the proper cost of an ending work in process inventory that involves 800 units, to which all direct material has been added but for which only 60% of the direct labor has been assigned.

Assigning overhead and estimated cost of inventories

21–22 The only product of Statz Manufacturers, Inc., is produced in a continuous process. At the end of the current year, the ending inventories of work in process and finished goods were as follows:

	Estimated Amounts Assigned per Unit		
	Direct Material	Direct Labor	Total Units
Work in Process	$7	$ 8	4,000
Finished Goods	9	15	6,000

Assuming that factory overhead is assigned at the rate of 80% of direct labor cost, compute the cost of the ending work in process and finished goods inventories.

Recording changes in inventory and closing entries

21–23 Using the following summarized data, prepare the compound journal entries (similar to those illustrated in the chapter) to record the changes in inventories and to close the manufacturing accounts at year-end to Manufacturing Summary and, in turn, to close Manufacturing Summary to Income Summary.

	Beginning of Year	End of Year
Materials Inventory	$ 11,000	$12,000
Work in Process Inventory	6,000	9,000
Materials Purchases	80,000	
Direct Labor	100,000	
Factory Overhead (total)	75,000	
Selling Expenses (total)	15,000	
Nonfactory Administrative Expenses (total)	35,000	

Cost of goods manufactured statement

21–24 The following cost of goods manufactured columns are from a Taylor Manufacturing, Inc., worksheet at the end of the current year. Simple, summarized data are used.

	Cost of Goods Manufactured	
	Debit	Credit
Materials Inventory (beginning)	9	
Work in Process Inventory (beginning)	12	
Materials Purchases	89	
Direct Labor	63	
Transportation In—Purchases	14	
Indirect Labor	35	
Factory Supervision	21	
Factory Utilities	13	
Factory Supplies Used	8	
Depreciation—Equipment	16	
Depreciation—Factory Building	20	
Other Factory Overhead	26	
Ending Inventories:		
Materials Inventory		10
Work in Process Inventory		7
	326	17
Cost of Goods Manufactured		309
	326	326

Using these data, prepare a cost of goods manufactured statement for the current year.

PROBLEMS

Cost of goods manufactured and income statement

21–25 Selected account balances from the completed year-end worksheet of the Butler Manufacturing Company appear below:

Nonfactory Administrative Salaries	$23,000	Work in Process, Jan. 1	$ 5,000
Advertising and Promotion Expense	14,000	Finished Goods, Jan. 1	21,000
Depreciation—Machinery	9,000	Materials, Dec. 31	6,000
Nonfactory Administrative Depreciation—Equipment	7,000	Work in Process, Dec. 31	12,000
Depreciation—Sales Fixtures	6,000	Finished Goods, Dec. 31	17,000
Direct Labor	70,000	Maintenance—Machinery	5,000
Factory Rent	6,000	Nonfactory Administrative Rent	12,000
Factory Supervision	10,000	Other Factory Overhead	11,000
Factory Supplies Used	8,000	Other Selling Expenses	9,000
Indirect Labor	7,000	Materials Purchases	31,000
Inventories:		Sales	280,000
Materials, Jan. 1	4,000	Sales Salaries Expense	25,000
		Transportation In	3,000

REQUIRED

Using the above data, prepare a cost of goods manufactured statement and an income statement for the current year (disregard income tax and earnings per share considerations).

Cost of goods manufactured

21–26 The following journal entries recorded the changes in inventories and closed the manufacturing accounts of Weber Factory, Inc., at year-end:

Manufacturing Summary	563,000	
Materials Inventory (beginning)		20,000
Work in Process Inventory (beginning)		12,000
Direct Labor		150,000
Indirect Labor		75,000
Transportation In		8,000
Depreciation—Factory		26,000
Depreciation—Equipment		21,000
Factory Repairs and Maintenance		16,000
Factory Supplies Used		9,000
Other Factory Overhead		32,000
Materials Purchases		194,000
To close the beginning materials and work in process inventories and the manufacturing cost accounts having debit balances to the Manufacturing Summary account.		

Materials Inventory (ending)	27,000	
Work in Process Inventory (ending)	14,000	
Manufacturing Summary		41,000
To record the ending materials and work in process inventories.		

REQUIRED
Using the above information, prepare a cost of goods manufactured statement for the current year.

Cost of goods manufactured and sold

21–27 The data below relate to three independent production periods of Allied Manufacturing Company. Missing data are indicated by question marks.

	A	B	C
Materials:			
Beginning Inventory	$ 26	$ 82	$ 55
Purchases	?	350	250
Ending Inventory	37	50	?
Direct Material	165	?	220
Direct Labor	290	480	400
Factory Overhead:			
Factory Supplies Used	48	?	60
Indirect Labor	80	75	175
Other	?	100	170
Total Factory Overhead	260	240	?
Work in Process Inventories:			
Beginning	?	45	130
Ending	35	?	50
Finished Goods Inventories:			
Beginning	?	200	40
Ending	165	60	165
Cost of Goods Manufactured	740	?	?
Cost of Goods Sold	720	1,000	?

REQUIRED
Using the above data, calculate the cost of goods manufactured and cost of goods sold. (You should list in order the items appearing on the cost of goods manufactured statement and the cost of goods sold computation, fill in the known data, and calculate the missing amounts.)

Cost per unit and inventory costing

21–28 The following data relate to estimating the ending work in process and finished goods inventories of the Carter Manufacturing Company:

		Estimated Cost of Completed Unit of Product	Estimated Proportions Assigned to Work in Process
Direct Material:	A	3 lb @ $8/lb	100%
	B	5 lb @ $6/lb	60%
Direct Labor:	Cutting	1 hr @ $12/hr	70%
	Assembly	2 hr @ $8/hr	40%

For the manufacturing period, total direct labor was $300,000, and total factory overhead was $240,000. Factory overhead is assigned to products on the basis of direct labor cost.

REQUIRED
Using the above data, calculate the cost of (a) an ending finished goods inventory of 800 units and (b) an ending work in process inventory of 600 units.

Statements and closing entries

21–29 The following balances appear in the cost of goods manufactured and the income statement columns of a December 31 worksheet for the current year's operations of the Franklin Corporation.

	Cost of Goods Manufactured		Income Statement	
	Debit	Credit	Debit	Credit
Materials Inventory (beginning)	20,000			
Work in Process Inventory (beginning)	12,000			
Finished Goods Inventory (beginning)			30,000	
Sales				330,000
Materials Purchases	80,000			
Transportation In	3,200			
Direct Labor	95,000			
Indirect Labor	24,000			
Utilities	1,500			
Repairs and Maintenance	2,500			
Depreciation—Machinery	2,700			
Insurance	3,100			
Property Taxes	3,300			
Selling Expenses			36,000	
Administrative Expenses			28,000	
Income Tax Expense			7,500	
Ending Inventories:				
Materials Inventory		15,000		
Work in Process Inventory		14,000		
Finished Goods Inventory				23,000
	247,300	29,000		
Cost of Goods Manufactured		218,300	218,300	
	247,300	247,300	319,800	353,000
Net Income			33,200	
			353,000	353,000

REQUIRED

(a) Prepare a cost of goods manufactured statement and an income statement for the Franklin Corporation. Assume that 4,000 shares of capital stock are outstanding at year-end.

(b) Prepare general journal entries to reflect the changes in inventories and to close the manufacturing accounts, the Manufacturing Summary account, the revenue and expense accounts, and the Income Summary account.

Cost of goods manufactured and income statement

21–30 Two inventors, organized as Modern, Inc., consult you regarding a planned new product. They have estimates of the costs of materials, labor, overhead, and other expenses involved but need to know how much to charge for each unit to earn a pretax profit in the first year equal to 10% of their estimated total long-term investment of $300,000.

Their plans indicate that each unit of the new product requires:

Direct Material
3 lb of a material costing $4/lb

Direct Labor
2 hr of a metal former's time at $10/hr
0.5 hr of an assembler's time at $8/hr

Major items of production overhead would be annual rent of $46,000 on a factory building and $26,000 on machinery. Other production overhead is an estimated 50% of total direct labor costs. Selling expenses are an estimated 30% of total sales revenue while nonfactory administrative expenses are 20% of total sales.

The consensus at Modern is that during the first year 10,000 units of product should be produced for selling and another 2,000 units for the next year's beginning inventory. Also, an extra 3,000 pounds of materials will be purchased as beginning inventory for the next year. Because of the nature of the manufacturing process, all units started must be completed, so work in process inventories are negligible.

REQUIRED

(a) Incorporate the above data into a projected cost of goods manufactured statement and compute the unit production cost.

(b) Prepare a projected income statement that would provide the target amount of profit.

(c) What unit sales price should the company charge for the new product?

Worksheet and financial statements

21–31 The trial balance for the Greene Manufacturing Corporation at the end of the current year follows:

	Debit	Credit
Cash	$ 10,000	
Accounts Receivable	62,000	
Allowance for Uncollectible Accounts		$ 1,400
Materials Inventory, January 1	41,000	
Work in Process Inventory, January 1	18,000	
Finished Goods Inventory, January 1	23,000	
Land	35,000	
Factory Buildings	200,000	
Accumulated Depreciation—Factory Buildings		46,000
Factory Machinery	175,000	
Accumulated Depreciation—Factory Machinery		17,000
Accounts Payable		36,000
Long-term Notes Payable—8%		56,000
Common Stock, $200 Par Value (all outstanding)		280,000
Retained Earnings		57,000
Sales		420,000
Materials Purchases	95,000	
Direct Labor	126,000	
Indirect Labor	31,000	
Factory Utilities	4,900	
Repairs and Maintenance	4,000	
Factory Property Taxes	4,500	
Selling Expenses	48,000	
Nonfactory Administrative Expenses	36,000	
	$913,400	$913,400

The following information is available for adjusting and closing the accounts:

(1) December 31 inventories are: materials, $34,000; work in process, $20,000; and finished goods, $16,000.

(2) Accrued wages and salaries at December 31 are: direct labor, $2,100; indirect labor, $700; and sales salaries, $2,800.

(3) Annual amounts of depreciation are: factory buildings, $11,000; factory machinery, $7,000.

(4) Accrued utilities payable at December 31, $500.

(5) Uncollectible accounts expense, $\frac{1}{2}$% of sales. (Debit this expense to Selling Expenses.)

(6) Assume an income tax rate of 30%.

REQUIRED

(a) Prepare a manufacturing worksheet for the year.

(b) Prepare a cost of goods manufactured statement and an income statement.

(c) Prepare a balance sheet.

(d) Prepare closing entries similar to those illustrated in this chapter.

Worksheet, financial statements, and closing entries

21–32 The trial balance of the Diamond Company at December 31 of the current year is given below, together with the worksheet adjustments.

	Trial Balance		Adjustments	
	Debit	**Credit**	**Debit**	**Credit**
Cash	14,000			
Materials Inventory, Jan. 1	18,000			
Work in Process Inventory, Jan. 1	13,900			
Finished Goods Inventory, Jan. 1	21,000			
Prepaid Insurance	1,400			(1) 700
Factory Machinery	120,000			
Accumulated Depreciation—Factory Machinery		25,000		(2) 8,500
Unamortized Cost of Patents	20,400			(3) 1,600
Accounts Payable		30,600		
Common Stock, $100 Par Value		85,000		
Retained Earnings		22,900		
Dividends	10,200			
Sales		310,000		
Materials Purchases	71,400			
Direct Labor	88,400		(4) 2,000	
Indirect Labor	30,000		(4) 500	
Factory Utilities	4,100			
Repairs and Maintenance—Factory	2,200			
Factory Buildings Rent	9,000			
Sales Salaries Expense	26,000			
Advertising Expense	6,800			
Nonfactory Administrative Expenses	16,700			
	473,500	473,500		
Insurance—Factory			(1) 700	
Depreciation—Factory Machinery			(2) 8,500	
Amortization of Patents			(3) 1,600	
Wages Payable				(4) 2,500
Income Tax Expense			(5) 10,000	
Income Tax Payable				(5) 10,000
			23,300	23,300

Additional information:

(1) December 31 inventories are: materials, $26,000; work in process, $15,000; and finished goods, $21,000.

(2) Patent amortization applies to factory operations.

REQUIRED
(a) Complete the manufacturing worksheet.
(b) Prepare a cost of goods manufactured statement and an income statement.
(c) Prepare closing entries similar to those illustrated in this chapter.

ALTERNATE PROBLEMS

Cost of goods manufactured and income statement

21–25A Selected account balances from the completed year-end worksheet of the Barnes Manufacturing Company appear below in alphabetical order:

Administrative Salaries*	$30,000	Work in Process, Jan. 1	$ 11,000
Advertising and Promotion		Finished Goods, Jan. 1	41,000
Expense	31,500	Materials, Dec. 31	24,000
Depreciation—Machinery	19,500	Work in Process, Dec. 31	18,000
Depreciation—Office Equipment*	15,000	Finished Goods, Dec. 31	22,000
Depreciation—Sales Fixtures	9,000	Maintenance—Machinery	12,000
Direct Labor	134,000	Materials Purchases	87,000
Factory Rent	23,000	Nonfactory Area Rent*	19,000
Factory Supervision	13,000	Other Factory Overhead	9,500
Factory Supplies Used	6,000	Other Selling Expenses	10,000
Indirect Labor	16,000	Sales	450,000
Inventories:		Sales Salaries Expense	24,000
Materials, Jan. 1	9,000	Transportation In	4,000

*These amounts relate to nonfactory administration.

REQUIRED
Using the above data, prepare a cost of goods manufactured statement and an income statement for the current year (disregard income tax and earnings per share considerations).

Cost per unit and inventory costing

21–28A The following data relate to estimating the ending work in process and finished goods inventories of the Conway Manufacturing Company:

	Estimated Cost of Completed Unit of Product	Estimated Proportions Assigned to Work in Process
Direct Material:		
A	3 lb @ $3/lb	100%
B	4 lb @ $5/lb	70%
Direct Labor:		
Cutting	3 hr @ $8/hr	60%
Assembly	2 hr @ $6/hr	25%

For the manufacturing period, total direct labor was $400,000 and total factory overhead was $500,000. Factory overhead is assigned to products on the basis of direct labor cost.

REQUIRED
Using the above data, calculate the cost of (a) an ending finished goods inventory of 1,000 units and (b) an ending work in process inventory of 800 units.

Statements and journal entries

21–29A The following balances appear in the cost of goods manufactured and the income statement columns of a December 31 worksheet for the current year's operations of the Fulton Corporation.

	Cost of Goods Manufactured Debit	Cost of Goods Manufactured Credit	Income Statement Debit	Income Statement Credit
Materials Inventory (beginning)	23,000			
Work in Process Inventory (beginning)	16,000			
Finished Goods Inventory (beginning)			62,000	
Sales				840,000
Materials Purchases	242,000			
Transportation In	17,000			
Direct Labor	150,000			
Indirect Labor	66,000			
Factory Utilities	9,000			
Factory Repairs and Maintenance	11,000			
Depreciation—Machinery	5,000			
Factory Insurance	3,000			
Factory Property Taxes	7,000			
Selling Expenses			53,000	
Administrative Expenses			37,000	
Income Tax Expense			64,000	
Ending Inventories:				
Materials Inventory		32,000		
Work in Process Inventory		12,000		
Finished Goods Inventory				36,000
	549,000	44,000		
Cost of Goods Manufactured		505,000	505,000	
	549,000	549,000	721,000	876,000
Net Income			155,000	
			876,000	876,000

REQUIRED

(a) Prepare a cost of goods manufactured statement and an income statement for the Fulton Corporation. Assume that 10,000 shares of capital stock are outstanding at year-end.

(b) Prepare general journal entries to reflect the changes in inventories and to close the manufacturing accounts, the Manufacturing Summary account, the revenue and expense accounts, and the Income Summary account.

Cost of goods manufactured and income statement

21–30A You are consulted by Mutual, Inc., a group of investors planning a new product. They have estimates of the costs of materials, labor, overhead, and other expenses involved but need to know how much to charge for each unit of the new product to earn a pretax profit in the first year equal to 10% of their estimated investment of $200,000.

Their plans indicate that each unit of the new product requires:

Direct Material

3 lb of a material costing $5/lb

Direct Labor
3 hr of a die cutter's time at $8/hr
2 hr of an assembler's time at $7/hr

Major items of production overhead would be annual rent of $58,000 on the factory building and $25,000 on machinery. Other production overhead is an estimated 80% of total direct labor costs. Selling expenses are an estimated 20% of total sales revenue while nonfactory administrative expenses are 10% of total sales.

The consensus at Mutual is that during the first year 4,000 units of product should be produced for selling and another 1,000 units for the next year's beginning inventory. Also, an extra 6,000 pounds of materials will be purchased as beginning inventory for the next year. Because of the nature of the manufacturing process, all units started must be completed, so work in process inventories are negligible.

REQUIRED

(a) Incorporate the above data into a projected cost of goods manufactured statement and compute the unit production cost.
(b) Prepare a projected income statement that would provide the target amount of profit.
(c) Rounded to the nearest dollar, what unit sales price should the company charge for the new product?

Worksheet and financial statements

21–31A The trial balance for the Gordon Boatbuilders Corporation at the end of the current year follows:

	Debit	Credit
Cash	$ 20,000	
Accounts Receivable	75,600	
Allowance for Uncollectible Accounts		$ 3,600
Materials Inventory, January 1	32,000	
Work in Process Inventory, January 1	16,000	
Finished Goods Inventory, January 1	40,000	
Land	52,000	
Factory Buildings	275,000	
Accumulated Depreciation—Factory Buildings		74,000
Factory Machinery	370,000	
Accumulated Depreciation—Factory Machinery		54,000
Accounts Payable		58,000
Long-term Notes Payable—9%		108,000
Common Stock, $50 Par Value (all outstanding)		180,000
Retained Earnings		255,000
Sales		738,000
Materials Purchases	208,000	
Direct Labor	148,000	
Indirect Labor	55,000	
Factory Utilities	15,000	
Repairs and Maintenance	9,000	
Property Taxes	12,000	
Selling Expenses	86,000	
Nonfactory Administrative Expenses	57,000	
	$1,470,600	$1,470,600

The following information is available for adjusting and closing the accounts:

(1) December 31 inventories are: materials, $25,000; work in process, $22,000; and finished goods, $27,000.

(2) Accrued wages and salaries at December 31 are: direct labor, $3,000; indirect labor, $500; and sales salaries, $1,800.

(3) Annual amounts of depreciation are: factory buildings, $16,000; factory machinery, $13,000.

(4) Accrued utilities payable at December 31, $900.

(5) Uncollectible accounts expense, 1% of sales. (Debit this expense to Selling Expenses.)

(6) Assume an income tax rate of 40%.

REQUIRED

(a) Prepare a manufacturing worksheet for the year.

(b) Prepare a cost of goods manufactured statement and an income statement.

(c) Prepare a balance sheet.

(d) Prepare closing entries similar to those illustrated in this chapter.

Worksheet and financial statements

21–32A The trial balance of the Danton Company at December 31 of the current year is given below, together with the worksheet adjustments.

	Trial Balance		Adjustments	
	Debit	Credit	Debit	Credit
Cash	17,000			
Materials Inventory, Jan. 1	34,000			
Work in Process Inventory, Jan. 1	25,000			
Finished Goods Inventory, Jan. 1	42,000			
Prepaid Insurance	5,000			(1) 2,500
Factory Machinery	285,000			
Accumulated Depreciation—Factory Machinery		24,000		(2) 11,200
Unamortized Cost of Patents	49,000			(3) 3,000
Accounts Payable		67,000		
Common Stock, $200 Par Value		112,000		
Retained Earnings		94,000		
Dividends	16,000			
Sales		950,000		
Materials Purchases	252,000			
Direct Labor	238,000		(4) 7,000	
Indirect Labor	90,000		(4) 3,000	
Factory Utilities	13,000			
Repairs and Maintenance—Factory	6,000			

Factory Buildings Rent	15,000			
Sales Salaries Expense	67,000			
Advertising Expense	31,000			
Nonfactory Administrative Expenses	62,000			
	1,247,000	1,247,000		
Insurance—Factory			(1) 2,500	
Depreciation—Machinery			(2) 11,200	
Amortization of Patents			(3) 3,000	
Wages Payable				(4) 10,000
Income Tax Expense			(5) 53,000	
Income Tax Payable				(5) 53,000
			79,700	79,700

Additional information:

(1) December 31 inventories are: materials, $39,000; work in process, $17,000; and finished goods, $33,000.

(2) Patent amortization applies to factory operations.

REQUIRED

(a) Complete the manufacturing worksheet.

(b) Prepare a cost of goods manufactured statement and an income statement.

(c) Prepare closing entries similar to those illustrated in this chapter.

BUSINESS DECISION PROBLEM

Raymond Kane, an engineer, needs some accounting advice. In their spare time during the past year, Kane and his college-aged son, Greg, have manufactured a small weed-trimming sickle in a rented building near their home. Greg, who has had one accounting course in college, keeps the books.

Kane is pleased about the results of their first year's operations. He asks you to look over the following income report prepared by Greg before they leave on a well-deserved vacation to the Bahamas, after which they plan to expand their business significantly.

Sales (18,500 units at $24 each)		$444,000
Costs of producing 20,000 units:		
Materials:		
Precast blades at $4 each	$ 84,000	
Preturned handles at $3 each	66,000	
Labor costs of hired assemblers	33,600	
Labor costs of hired painters	42,000	
Rent on building	20,000	
Rent on machinery	8,000	
Utilities for production	10,000	
Other production costs	11,000	
Advertising expense	36,400	
Sales commissions	50,000	
Delivery of products to customers	13,000	
Total costs	$374,000	
Less: Ending inventory of 1,500 units at average production costs of $18.70 (or $374,000/20,000 units)	28,050	
Cost of sales		345,950
Net Income		$ 98,050

After you examine the income report, Kane responds to your questions and assures you that (1) no theft or spoilage of materials has occurred, (2) no partially completed units are involved, and (3) he and his son have averaged about 30 hours each per week in the business, and (4) he is in approximately the 40% income tax bracket (before considering the sickle venture).

REQUIRED

(a) Identify any apparent discrepancy in the income report in the cost of materials used.

(b) Recalculate the cost of goods manufactured, the average cost per unit produced, and the net income for the year, including a provision for estimated income taxes on the earnings.

(c) What factors should Kane consider regarding the profitability of his venture before deciding to expand it significantly?

ANSWERS TO SELF-TEST QUESTIONS

1. (d) 2. (b) 3. (c) 4. (a) 5. (c)

22

Cost Accounting Systems: Job Order Costing

Chapter Objectives

- **Discuss the limitations of cost determinations.**
- **Provide a framework for understanding cost accounting systems.**
- **Present the conceptual framework of job order costing systems.**
- **Outline the entries necessary in a job order costing system.**

So soon as we begin to count the cost, the cost begins.

HENRY DAVID THOREAU

In Chapter 21, we introduced the concepts of multiple manufacturing inventories, cost of goods manufactured, and financial statements for a manufacturing concern. Our approach presented a general accounting system for a simple manufacturing operation using periodic inventory procedures. The limitations of that system justify the development of specialized cost accounting systems and the use of perpetual inventories to provide cost data which are more meaningful for managerial decision making. In this and the following chapter, we introduce important aspects of cost accounting and illustrate two important types of cost accounting systems for manufacturing firms.

LIMITATIONS OF COST DETERMINATIONS

There are inherent limitations in most cost determinations. Misconceptions prevail that accounting cost figures are exact and that a precise cost can be assigned to any asset, product, or unit of activity. Although an exhaustive consideration of these issues is beyond the scope of this chapter, a review of several examples should provide a realistic perspective.

We determine cost basically by accumulating the total costs incurred in doing something and then allocating these costs among the various units of accomplishment. Any unit of activity, service rendered, or product manufactured may be involved. Accounting procedures for both the accumulation and the allocation of costs may necessarily involve somewhat arbitrary choices. Often no single cost measurement or allocation scheme is demonstrably better than any other. Therefore, the accountant must choose from among a group of equally defensible approaches to cost measurement and allocation. Following are several examples, the first two of which were mentioned in previous chapters.

Assumed cost flows The purchase prices of materials often vary throughout the year. Assigning costs to cost of goods sold and ending inventories may involve arbitrarily assuming a cost flow such as FIFO, LIFO, or some form of average cost.

Depreciation estimates The service potential of plant assets is utilized over many operating periods. No method can determine the precise amount of the asset's cost to be allocated to a given period. Instead, periodic depreciation expense is based on estimates of useful life and salvage value as well as on an often arbitrary choice among several depreciation methods.

Allocated joint costs Joint costs are common to two or more products or manufacturing processes. Costs of materials, supervisors' salaries, and service department costs are often joint costs. In a lumbering mill operation, for example, no single precise method can allocate the cost of a whole log to the several wood products that result—prime clear boards used for furniture, rough construction-grade boards, the bark sold as mulching to landscapers, and the sawdust used for paper. Joint product costs are often allocated arbitrarily on the basis of the relative sales value, weights, or volumes of each joint product. In Chapter 23, we illustrate accepted allocation techniques for joint products and service departments.

Realistically then, *the* cost of something is actually determined by our choices from among a series of perhaps equally valid assumptions.

Another aspect of the limitations of cost determination is that the concept of cost varies and different versions may be useful for different purposes. Ordinarily, cost systems provide *full average cost*, or the total of all costs divided by all output. For example, if costs of $100,000 are incurred in producing 80,000 units of product, the average unit cost is $1.25 ($100,000/80,000). Suppose that in evaluating the opportunity to accept an additional overseas order for 10,000 units, production engineers advise that producing the additional 10,000 units would raise total costs to $108,000. In its decision to accept or reject the offer, management could consider the new average unit cost of $1.20 ($108,000/90,000 units) or the incremental unit cost of 80 cents (the $8,000 increase in cost divided by the 10,000 unit increase in production). Neither of these costs is wrong, nor the other right. Rather, depending on certain management decision situations, either one may be defended as more appropriate. This and other instances of management's use of "different cost for different purposes" are illustrated in subsequent chapters.

It is important to realize that, as necessary and useful as cost data are, they are complex and have inherent limitations. Users of cost data must be aware of the specific assumptions made, the costing procedures used, and the proper application of the variations of cost data.

THE NATURE AND ADVANTAGES OF COST ACCOUNTING SYSTEMS

Any orderly method of developing cost information constitutes cost accounting. Typically, some amount of cost is accumulated and related to some unit of activity or accomplishment. Examples include accumulating the costs of cutting or forming materials, assembling parts, and the painting and finishing that might result in a completed unit of product such as a lawnmower, a computer, or a custom-designed executive jet aircraft. Although a cost system could be maintained independently of a firm's formal accounting records, most comprehensive cost systems are integrated into the formal accounting system.

Cost accounting systems are usually illustrated in the context of a manufacturing situation involving unit product costs. Remember, however, that reliable cost-per-unit-of-accomplishment data are vital to decision makers in all economic endeavors. For example, a municipality may need to know the cost per ton of snow removal; a hospital, the cost per patient of providing various surgical or diagnostic services; and an insurance company, the cost of providing various combinations of homeowner protection to specific groups of policyholders. Many of the costing concepts and techniques used in manufacturing costing systems also apply to nonmanufacturing situations.

Use of Perpetual Inventories

The inherent weaknesses of using periodic inventory procedures for manufacturing operations were discussed in Chapter 21. Cost of materials used and cost of goods sold tend to be residual (or *plug*) figures when periodic inventory procedures are used. Also, relatively current cost data are available only at end-of-period intervals, and many significant departmental cost details are not readily apparent.

Cost accounting systems usually incorporate perpetual inventory procedures. That is, additions to and deductions from all inventory accounts—materials, work in process, and finished goods—are recorded as they occur. The more current cost information and greater cost controls justify the additional bookkeeping costs of perpetually maintaining the inventory accounts.

Perpetual inventory records are customarily verified by physical inventory counts at least once a year. Necessary adjustments for errors and unrecorded inventory shrinkages can then be made. The flow of product costs—direct material, direct labor, and factory overhead—through the various perpetual inventory accounts of a cost accounting system should be apparent in both the simple and more comprehensive illustrations appearing in this chapter.

Timely Product Costing

A cost accounting system must provide for the timely determination of product costs. Product costs are needed to arrive at inventory amounts for work in process and for finished goods; these amounts are required in the preparation of financial statements. Obviously, to determine income properly, we must have some method of identifying costs with the products sold and the products that remain on hand in a finished or unfinished state.

Management uses engineering studies and cost analyses to establish cost standards and budgets. Only by knowing product costs can management compare actual costs with standards and budgets and take necessary remedial action.

Management also needs product cost data to establish price lists and to submit bids on special orders for its products. Although many factors, including marketing and legal constraints, affect pricing decisions, unit product costs are often an important determinant. Furthermore, once prices are established, knowledge of costs enables management to determine profit margins and to direct its efforts intelligently to the promotion of its more profitable items.

To identify costs with a product or a group of products, a manufacturer must trace factory costs—direct material, direct labor, and factory overhead—to lots or batches of product. Tracing material and labor costs to products is fairly routine.

To account for the material used, a firm may keep track of the costs of material requisitioned for production. Labor costs can similarly be accounted for by timekeeping methods or by identifying the product with the payroll costs of personnel in those operations or departments that produce the product. A firm cannot directly determine the amount of factory overhead that should be identified with different products or groups of products. Consequently, a firm typically assigns overhead costs throughout the production period by using a predetermined overhead rate.

Use of Predetermined Overhead Rates

Many of the concepts and procedures underlying the use of **predetermined overhead rates** are extensive and complex. In this chapter, we present only a basic treatment, sufficient to convey a general understanding of the use of these rates in product costing.

Before the beginning of an accounting period, management normally prepares budgets. Sales forecasts are translated into production budgets, which in turn permit estimates of plant utilization in terms of a common measure of activity. This common measure is normally direct labor hours, direct labor costs, or machine hours. Using historical data and projected activity levels, management can estimate the total factory overhead cost to be incurred. The overhead rate is computed by dividing the estimated total factory overhead by the selected measure of activity. Calculations of predetermined overhead rates are usually based on year-long production periods.

Assume that the number of direct labor hours used is the most appropriate measure of activity for applying overhead in a given situation. If the estimated number of direct labor hours is 100,000 and the estimated total factory overhead is $150,000, the overhead rate may be calculated

$$\text{Overhead Rate} = \frac{\text{Estimated Factory Overhead for the Year}}{\text{Estimated Direct Labor Hours for the Year}}$$

$$= \frac{\$150{,}000}{100{,}000 \text{ hours}}$$

$$= \$1.50/\text{direct labor hour}$$

If, during the accounting period, a particular product requires 50 direct labor hours of production time, $75 of overhead (50 × $1.50) is charged to this product.

Before selecting the basis for applying overhead to products, a firm should carefully analyze the relationship between overhead incurred and various alternative measures of activity. The most common bases are direct labor hours or direct labor costs. In situations with a high degree of equipment use relative to manual labor, however, machine-hours may be a more appropriate base.

Using a predetermined overhead rate, management can estimate the overhead costs of any job at any stage of production, computing "costs to date" both for control purposes and for inventory costing. This method also eliminates wide fluctuations in unit costs that might result if actual recorded overhead costs were assigned to products during short interim periods when production departed markedly from average levels.

For example, assume that normal production is 100,000 direct labor hours per year and that production fluctuates seasonally throughout the year. Suppose also that a large share of actual factory overhead cost is spread fairly evenly over the year. (Such costs as depreciation, maintenance, utilities, and supervisory costs remain fairly constant from month to month.) Exhibit 22–1 illustrates the possible differences between assigned overhead costs based on actual monthly overhead rates and those based on an annual overhead rate. The estimated annual rate in this example is $1.50 per direct labor hour ($150,000/100,000 direct labor hours). The actual monthly rates vary from $3.10 in February to $1.10 in July, with only the months of April, September, and October even approaching the annual average of $1.50 per direct labor hour. Using actual monthly rates and assuming that a particular unit of product requires three direct labor hours, a unit produced in July when production activity was highest would be assigned overhead costs of $3.30 (3 × $1.10). In contrast, a unit produced in February when production activity was lowest would be assigned overhead costs of $9.30 (3 × $3.10). The $6 difference is hardly defensible, especially when the two units of product may be virtually indistinguishable physically. Clearly, basing product costs on allocations of actual monthly overhead amounts is unrealistic. The use of a predetermined overhead rate employing a yearly average produces more meaningful unit cost figures.

EXHIBIT 22–1
Comparison of Actual Monthly and Estimated Annual Overhead Rates

	Factory Overhead Costs Incurred Each Month*	Direct Labor Hours Worked Each Month	Actual Monthly Overhead Rates	Estimated Annual Overhead Rate
January	$ 9,900	4,000	$2.48	$1.50
February	9,300	3,000	3.10	1.50
March	10,500	5,000	2.10	1.50
April	12,300	8,000	1.54	1.50
May	14,100	11,000	1.28	1.50
June	14,700	12,000	1.23	1.50
July	16,500	15,000	1.10	1.50
August	15,300	13,000	1.18	1.50
September	13,500	10,000	1.35	1.50
October	12,300	8,000	1.54	1.50
November	11,100	6,000	1.85	1.50
December	10,500	5,000	2.10	1.50
Annual Amounts	$150,000	100,000		

*Assumed to be $7,500 each month plus 60 cents per direct labor hour.

Flow of Product Costs

The simple illustration on the next few pages introduces the basic ideas of cost accounting systems. The final part of this chapter presents a more detailed example for assigning costs to manufactured products. The simple illustration below identifies a first phase of accumulating product costs and a second phase of tracing these costs as they sequentially become (1) work in process, during manufacturing operations; (2) finished goods, when completed; and (3) costs of goods sold, when sold. Remember in this illustration that all product costs are capitalized (treated as assets).

ACCUMULATING PRODUCT COSTS The basic relationships in this illustration underlie all cost accounting systems, although the account titles used vary in practice. For simplicity in presenting these basic concepts, we assume no beginning inventory. Each entry is explained and its effect keyed to related accounts shown here in T-account form.

(1) Recording Acquisition of Materials and Supplies

Materials Inventory	1,000	
Accounts Payable		1,000

Materials Inventory	
(1) 1,000	

Accounts Payable	
	(1) 1,000

The perpetual inventory procedures for purchasing merchandise explained in Chapter 9 are used to derive this entry.

(2) Recording Factory Payroll

Factory Payroll	600	
Factory Payroll Payable		600

Factory Payroll	
(2) 600	

Factory Payroll Payable	
	(2) 600

Here, the total factory payroll includes both direct and indirect labor. Later, these two items will be handled separately. Data for this entry would come from a detailed analysis of factory payroll records.

(3) Recording Other Factory Costs as Overhead

Factory Overhead	1,000	
Accumulated Depreciation		400
Utilities Payable		300
Prepaid Insurance		200
Property Tax Payable		100

Factory Overhead	
(3) 1,000	

Accumulated Depreciation	
	(3) 400

Utilities Payable	
	(3) 300

Prepaid Insurance	
	(3) 200

Property Tax Payable	
	(3) 100

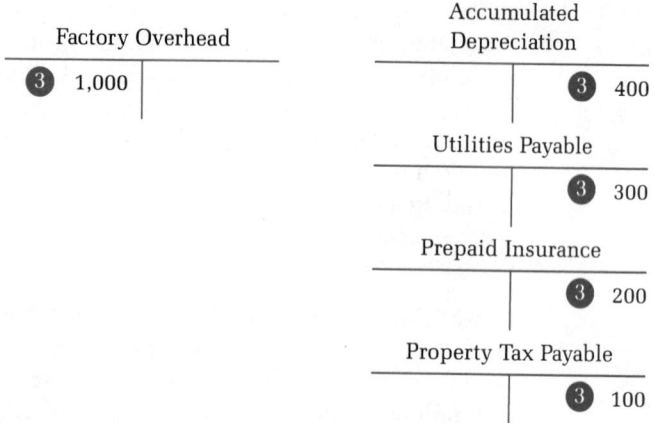

Realistically, factory overhead includes many more items than are shown here. We chose these particular items to illustrate depreciation, accruals, and the write-off of prepaid items.

At this point, all product costs have been accumulated into debit balances in the Materials Inventory, Factory Payroll, and Factory Overhead accounts. We now trace these costs through to Cost of Goods Sold.

TRACING PRODUCT COSTS In this phase of our illustration, we show how the product costs accumulated earlier are transferred sequentially through the Work in Process Inventory and Finished Goods Inventory accounts to the Cost of Goods Sold account. Descriptions, journal entries, and explanations for each step are keyed to the cost flow diagram in Exhibit 22–2. As you read the material, trace each entry in the cost flow diagram.

(4) Recording Requisitions of Direct Material and Factory Supplies

Work in Process Inventory	600	
Factory Overhead	200	
Materials Inventory		800

This entry reflects the requisition of all materials and supplies used in production by the various parties. Direct material is charged directly to the Work in Process Inventory account. Costs of factory supplies (or indirect materials) are part of factory overhead. We assume here (as is often the case in practice) that the Materials Inventory account is the control account for both direct material and factory supplies.

(5) Recording Distribution of Factory Payroll

Work in Process Inventory	500	
Factory Overhead	100	
Factory Payroll		600

EXHIBIT 22–2
Tracing Product Costs Through a Cost Accounting System

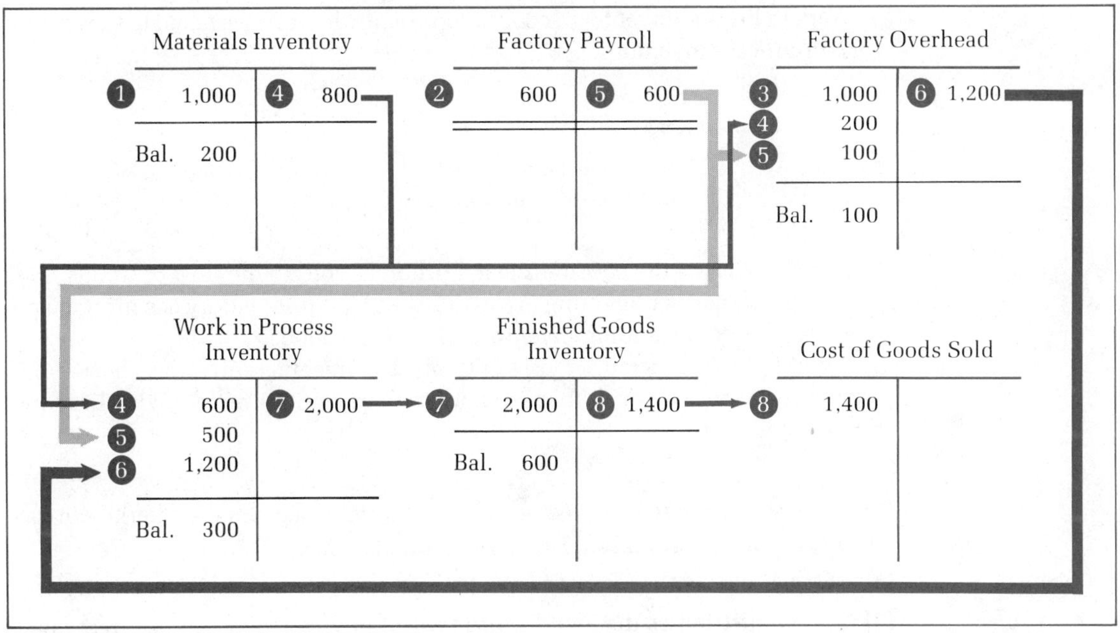

Work in Process Inventory is debited for $500 of direct labor, and Factory Overhead is debited for $100 of indirect labor. Observe that the total factory payroll is distributed, leaving a zero balance in the Factory Payroll account. The division of total factory payroll into direct and indirect labor is based on a detailed analysis of each employee's job description, wage rates, and hours worked.

6 Recording Application of Factory Overhead

Work in Process Inventory	1,200	
Factory Overhead		1,200

This entry adds the third and final category of factory costs to work in process. Note that the amount of this entry is not equal to the $1,300 of actual factory overhead incurred to date. As explained earlier, most firms do *not* apply the actual amount of overhead incurred each period to the goods manufactured during that period. Instead, they apply a predetermined overhead rate that reflects estimates of total annual production volume and total annual overhead costs.

7 Recording Completed Production

Finished Goods Inventory	2,000	
Work in Process Inventory		2,000

This entry assigns costs to completed production and transfers those costs from Work in Process Inventory to Finished Goods Inventory. As explained later, the amount of this entry is derived from production records, the details of which vary with the firm's particular product costing system. The balance remaining in the Work in Process Inventory account represents the costs assigned to the ending work-in-process inventory.

8 Recording Cost of Goods Sold

Cost of Goods Sold	1,400	
Finished Goods Inventory		1,400

This entry transfers the cost of finished products sold to the Cost of Goods Sold account. The balance remaining in the Finished Goods Inventory account reflects costs assigned to the ending inventory of finished goods.

Exhibit 22–2 diagrams the results of the foregoing entries as the various product costs move through the manufacturing accounts. The following list summarizes these entries:

(1) Entries 1–3 accumulate factory costs into three accounts—Materials Inventory, Factory Payroll, and Factory Overhead.

(2) Entry 4 reflects the requisition of both direct material and factory supplies.

(3) Entry 5 distributes the total factory payroll to direct labor and indirect labor. At this point, debits in the Factory Overhead account reflect the actual factory overhead incurred.

(4) Entry 6 applies an amount of factory overhead based on a predetermined overhead rate. The $100 balance in the Factory Overhead account represents an amount of actual overhead incurred but not yet applied to work in process, the nature and disposition of which are explained later in the chapter. After entry 6, the Work in Process Inventory account has been charged for all three categories of product costs—direct material, direct labor, and applied factory overhead.

(5) Entry 7 transfers to Finished Goods Inventory the costs assigned to completed production. The $300 balance in the Work in Process Inventory account is the cost assigned to the goods that are only partially completed at this point.

(6) Entry 8 transfers to Cost of Goods Sold the costs of the finished goods sold. The balance in the Finished Goods Inventory account represents the cost assigned to the goods that are finished but not yet sold.

So far, we have presented the important aspects of cost accounting systems including the use of perpetual inventory procedures, the provision of timely product costs, the use of predetermined overhead rates, and an illustration of the flow of product costs through a cost accounting system. We now turn to an illustration of the widely used *job order* cost accounting system.

JOB ORDER COSTING SYSTEMS

The two basic types of cost accounting systems are job order cost accounting and process cost accounting. **Job order cost accounting** (sometimes called **specific order** costing) is appropriate when production is characterized by a series of different products or jobs undertaken either to fill specific orders from customers or to produce a general stock of products from which future orders are filled. This type of costing is widely used in construction, printing, and machine shop operations. Often the products or batches of products vary in their material components and manner of production. In contrast, **process cost accounting** lends itself most readily to the production of a large volume of products manufactured in a "continuous flow" operation, such as distillation of fuels or manufacture of paint, chemicals, wire, and similar items. Essentially the same ingredients and operations are involved during each period of manufacture.

Either system primarily allocates manufacturing costs to products to determine unit costs. In a job order system, costs are identified with specific jobs to determine the cost of products manufactured. In a process system, costs are identified with production processes and averaged over the products made during the period. This chapter describes a job order costing system; the basic concepts of process costing are presented in Chapter 23.

Exhibits 22–3 through 22–7 show some of the important accounting forms used in job order costing as they might appear during use. In a job order costing system, each of the three inventory accounts—Materials Inventory, Work in Process Inventory, and Finished Goods Inventory—has a subsidiary ledger in which unit costs are accounted for. **Materials ledger cards** (Exhibit 22–3) for each type of material or factory supply used make up the subsidiary record for the Materials Inventory account; the cards show quantities received, issued, and on hand, unit costs, and total amounts. **Materials requisition forms** (Exhibit 22–4) contain the initial recording of issuances of direct material for various jobs or of factory supplies for general factory use. **Time tickets** (Exhibit 22–5) initially record the amount of time spent and the individual employee labor cost incurred for each individual job or as a part of factory overhead.

Job cost sheets (Exhibit 22–6) are the subsidiary records for the Work in Process Inventory account. For each job in process, the sheets indicate the costs of direct material, direct labor, and applied overhead identified with the job. When a job is completed, the total cost is divided by the number of units in the lot to obtain a unit cost. Also at this time, the job's cost sheet is removed from the Work in Process ledger and an entry is made in the **finished goods ledger** (Exhibit 22–7), which is the subsidiary record for Finished Goods Inventory. The cards in this last ledger identify the stock number and name of the product and show quantities, unit costs, and total costs of the various lots of product awaiting sale.

We now turn to the comprehensive illustration of job order costing, which shows how to use these forms. In this illustration, we make the following three assumptions:

(1) Condor Company uses materials A and B to produce products Y and Z.

(2) The company also uses material C, which is classified as factory supplies because it is employed in all parts of the factory and is not incorporated directly into products Y and Z.

(3) Condor uses a predetermined overhead rate based on direct labor hours to assign factory overhead to products.

EXHIBIT 22–3
Materials Ledger Card

Materials Ledger Card

Stock No. 32
Description 1/8″ Steel Wire
Supplier Steel Supply Corp.
Reorder Quantity 4,000 ft.
Minimum Quantity 1,000 ft.

	Received				Issued				Balance		
Date	Rec'g. Report No.	Units	Price	Total Price	Mat'l. Req'n. No.	Units	Price	Total Price	Units	Price	Total Price
19XX											
8/1	320	4,000	0.20	800.00					4,000	0.20	800.00
8/5					567	700	0.20	140.00	3,300	0.20	660.00
8/9	332	4,000	0.21	840.00					{3,300	0.20	660.00}
									{4,000	0.21	840.00}

EXHIBIT 22–4
Materials Requisition Form

Materials Requisition

Date 8/5/XX Job. No. 372 Requisition No. 567

Item	Quantity Authorized	Quantity Issued	Unit Price	Amount
Stock No. 32 (1/8″ wire)	700 ft.	700 ft.	0.20	$140
Total				$140

Authorized by: J.E.K. Issued by: J.A.P. Received by: F.W.E.

EXHIBIT 22–5
Time Ticket

Time Ticket

Employee Name James L. Kitt — Employee No. 42

Skill Specification Wire Former — Payroll Period Ending 8/16/XX

Time Started	Time Stopped	Total Time	Hourly Labor Rate	Department	Job No.	Total Cost
8:00	12:00	4.0	$8.00	B	372	$32.00
1:00	2:00	1.0	8.00	B	372	8.00
Totals		5.0				$40.00

Approved by C.L.T.

EXHIBIT 22–6
Job Cost Sheet

Job Cost Sheet

Customer Ace Fabricators, Inc. — Job No. 372

Product Bracket-H3 — Date Promised 9/1/XX

Quantity 200 — Dates: Started 8/1/XX Completed 8/20/XX

Direct Material		Direct Labor			Cost Summary	
Mat'l. Req'n. No.	Amount	Payroll Summary Dated	Dept.	Amount		
567	140.00	8/2	A	70.00	Direct Material	700.00
573	180.00	8/9	A	240.00	Direct Labor	600.00
591	200.00	8/16	B	190.00	Factory Overhead (applied at):	
603	180.00	8/23	B	100.00	150% of direct labor cost	900.00
					Total Cost	2,200.00
Totals	700.00			600.00	Units Finished 200 — Unit Cost	11.00

EXHIBIT 22–7
Finished Goods Ledger Card

Finished Goods Ledger Card

Stock No. H3

Item Bracket-H3 Minimum Quantity 50

Manufactured			Sales			Balance			
Job No.	Quantity	Total Cost	Invoice No.	Quantity	Total Cost	Date	Quantity	Unit Cost	Total Cost
372	200	2,200.00				8/20	200	11.00	2,200.00
			123	100	1,100.00	8/25	100	11.00	1,100.00

Accounting for Materials

A materials clerk records the amounts of materials received in the materials ledger as additions to the balances on the appropriate ledger cards. At the end of the accounting period, the total purchases for the period are posted from the invoice register to the Materials Inventory account. The amount added to this account equals the sum of the amounts added to the materials ledger cards during the period.

When direct material (A and B, in this case) is requisitioned for specific orders or jobs, the materials clerk records the reductions on the appropriate materials ledger cards. Cost clerks then enter these amounts in the materials section of the job cost sheets for the specific jobs in which the material is used. Amounts on requisitions representing factory supplies (material C) are handled by the materials clerk in the same fashion as amounts for direct material. The amounts, however, are charged to the Factory Overhead account, because they cannot be identified feasibly with particular jobs.

For example, assume the following:

(1) The Condor Company purchased $2,500 of material A, $1,500 of material B, and $500 of material C during its first month of operations. (Total: $4,500.)

(2) $1,700 of materials were requisitioned: $1,000 of material A for job 1; $500 of material B for job 2; and $200 of material C for general factory use.

The effect of these transactions is shown in Exhibit 22–8. Notice that in each subsidiary ledger, *matching* postings (debits for debits and credits for credits) totaling each entry are made to the related general ledger control account.

Accounting for Labor

To identify labor costs with specific jobs, firms use time tickets to accumulate the hours spent on various jobs by each employee. Hourly wage rates can then be used to compute the labor costs for the various jobs. Periodically, these records

EXHIBIT 22–8
Entries for Purchase and Requisition of Materials and Factory Supplies

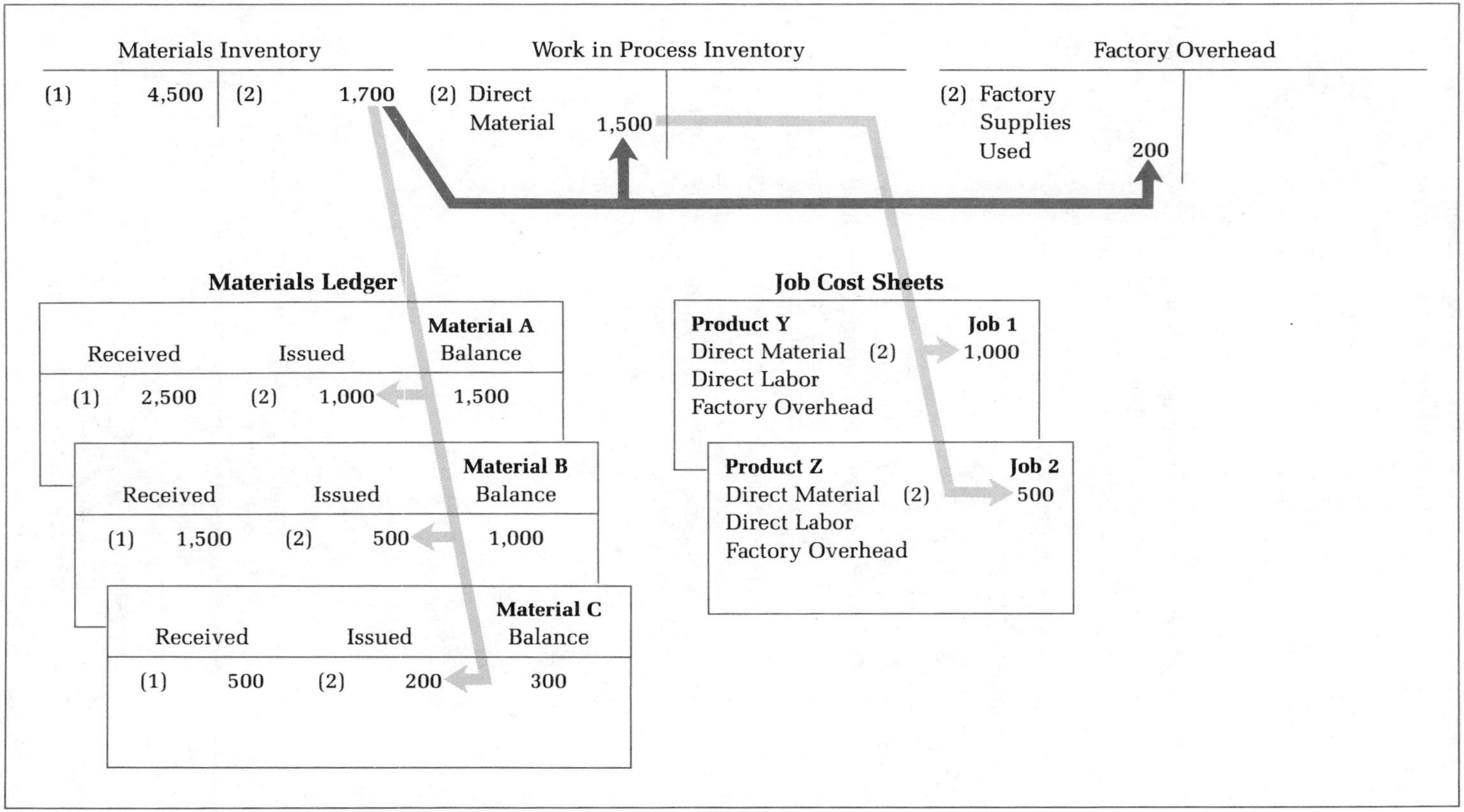

are sorted and the direct labor amounts posted to the job cost sheets. To continue our example, we assume the following:

(3) Total direct labor hours used and charges incurred during the period ($2,400):
Job 1—200 hours, $1,600 total direct labor
Job 2—100 hours, $800 total direct labor

(4) Indirect labor payroll for the period, $1,000.

The effect of these transactions is shown in Exhibit 22–9, where we use the Work in Process Inventory account, its subsidiary ledger (the job cost sheets), the Factory Overhead account, and the Factory Payroll account. We do not show the Factory Payroll account debit entry that would be part of the entry to record accrual of the factory payroll liability.

Accounting for Overhead

Exhibits 22–8 and 22–9 demonstrate how factory supplies used and indirect labor costs for the period are introduced into the accounts. In our example, the cost of the factory supplies amounted to $200 and the indirect labor costs were $1,000. Other overhead costs are charged to the Factory Overhead account as incurred or through adjusting entries at the end of the accounting period. For instance, assume that in addition to the factory supplies used and indirect labor costs, the following overhead costs were incurred during the period: utilities, $50; repairs, $60; depreciation, $180; and insurance, $40. The general journal entry to record these items is given below:

(5)	Factory Overhead—Utilities	50	
	Factory Overhead—Repairs	60	
	Factory Overhead—Depreciation	180	
	Factory Overhead—Insurance	40	
	Cash (or Accounts Payable)		110
	Accumulated Depreciation		180
	Prepaid Insurance		40

The debits in entry (5) are shown as they would appear in the Factory Overhead account (see Exhibit 22–10). The accounts credited in the entry—Cash, Accumulated Depreciation, and Prepaid Insurance—are omitted from the exhibit.

As explained earlier, actual overhead is not identified directly with specific jobs. Instead, through the use of a predetermined overhead rate, the Work in Process Inventory account is charged with overhead applied. We assume that the Condor Company charges overhead to jobs on the basis of direct labor hours. Its forecasting and budgeting process has determined an overhead rate of $5 per direct labor hour. Because job 1 accumulated 200 hours, Condor applies $1,000 of overhead cost to this job, while job 2, requiring 100 hours, receives $500 of

EXHIBIT 22–9
Entries for Assignment of Factory Payroll

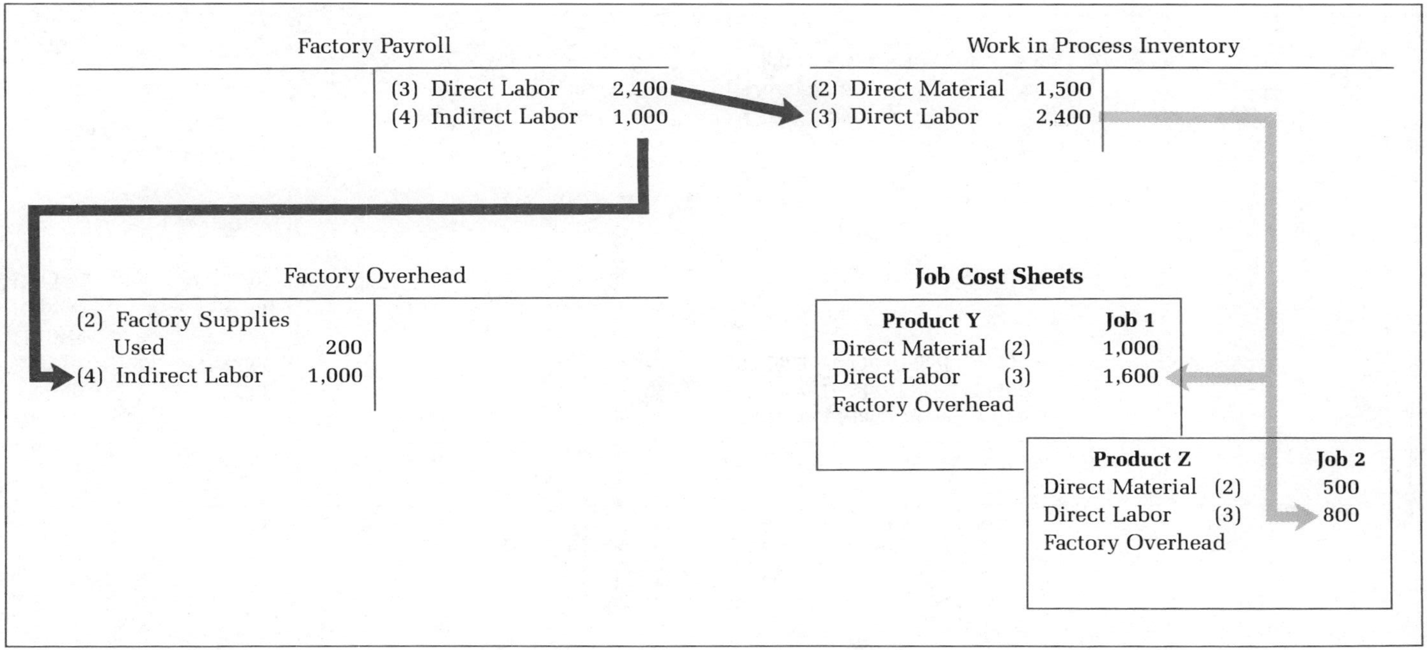

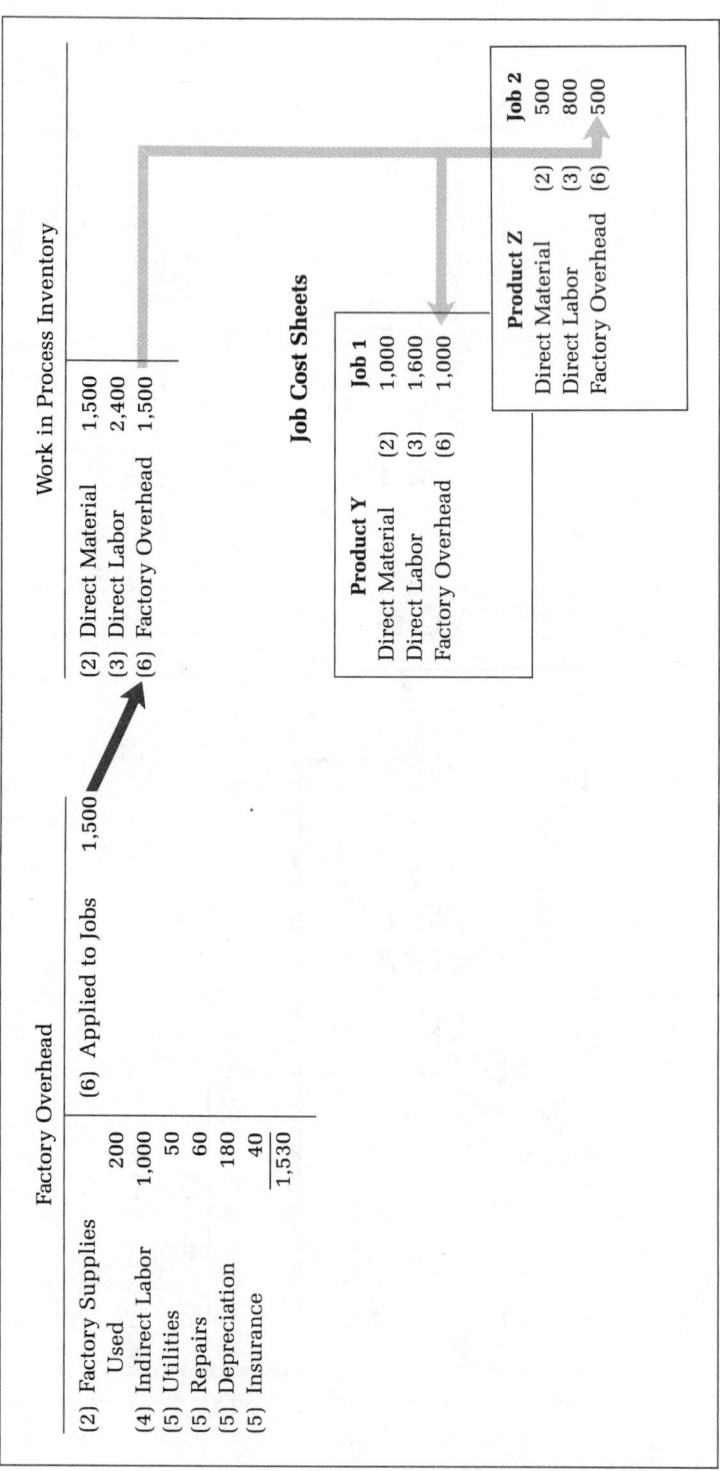

EXHIBIT 22–10
Entries for Assignment of Factory Overhead

Factory Overhead

Debit		Credit	
(2) Factory Supplies Used	200	(6) Applied to Jobs	1,500
(4) Indirect Labor	1,000		
(5) Utilities	50		
(5) Repairs	60		
(5) Depreciation	180		
(5) Insurance	40		
	1,530		

Work in Process Inventory

Debit		Credit
(2) Direct Material	1,500	
(3) Direct Labor	2,400	
(6) Factory Overhead	1,500	

Job Cost Sheets

Product Y		Job 1
Direct Material	(2)	1,000
Direct Labor	(3)	1,600
Factory Overhead	(6)	1,000

Product Z		Job 2
Direct Material	(2)	500
Direct Labor	(3)	800
Factory Overhead	(6)	500

overhead cost. The general journal entry to charge work in process inventory with applied overhead would be

(6)	Work in Process Inventory	1,500	
	Factory Overhead		1,500
	(Job 1, $1,000; job 2, $500)		

Exhibit 22–10 shows how the accounts reflect overhead items.

After overhead cost has been entered on the job cost sheets, all elements of cost to date—direct material, direct labor, and factory overhead—can be totaled. This sum represents the cost of the job from its inception to its present stage of production. In our example, we see that $3,600 ($1,000 + $1,600 + $1,000) has been accumulated on job 1 by the end of the accounting period. Frequently, management compares the calculated cost for a job not yet completed with the costs of similar jobs in the past. Knowing such costs, management may take any necessary steps to control costs. In addition, accumulating cost by jobs permits an evaluation of the work in process inventory.

Note that the amount of overhead applied to jobs during the period is $30 less than the actual overhead incurred ($1,530). In fact, it would be unusual in any month for the amount applied to equal the actual overhead cost. There are several reasons for this. First, estimates of the total annual overhead cost and the activity in labor hours were used to calculate the overhead rate. Second, production activity normally fluctuates from month to month. Third, the actual pattern of incurring overhead cost may also vary from month to month. Therefore, we can expect either debit or credit balances monthly in the Factory Overhead account. A debit balance in the account is called **underapplied** (or **underabsorbed**) overhead. A credit balance would be **overapplied** (or **overabsorbed**) overhead. On interim financial statements, the Factory Overhead account balance can be shown on the balance sheet as a deferred debit or a deferred credit. An existing balance at year-end is usually closed to the Cost of Goods Sold account. For example, if the Factory Overhead had a $30 debit balance at year-end, the following entry might be made:

Cost of Goods Sold	30	
Factory Overhead		30
To close the Factory Overhead account.		

Accounting for Finished Goods

When job orders are completed, the unit cost of items is obtained by dividing the total accumulated cost by the number of units produced. The job cost sheets can then be removed from the work in process subsidiary ledger and filed in the completed jobs file. At the same time, entries are made in the finished goods subsidiary ledger, showing quantities, unit cost, and total cost of the items entered. At the end of the period, a journal entry credits Work in Process Inventory and debits Finished Goods Inventory for the total cost of the jobs completed during the period. When units of product are sold, the cost of those units is removed from the finished goods ledger cards; at the end of the accounting period, an entry made in the general ledger credits Finished Goods Inventory and debits Cost of Goods Sold.

To illustrate the entries made in accounting for finished goods, assume that job 1, costing $3,600, was completed during the current period, resulting in 1,000 units of product Y, and that 400 units of product Y were sold for $6 each. Job 2 was still in process at the end of the period. The following entries record the transfer of the units of product Y to finished goods and reflect the sale of 400 units:

JOB ORDER COSTING IN SERVICE INDUSTRIES

Many firms in service industries use variations of job order costing systems for accumulating costs and developing billings to customers. Manufacturing firms typically accumulate costs by job or product while service firms accumulate costs by client (accounting and law firms), by patient (hospitals and clinics), or by project (engineering and architectural firms).

For example, hospitals use patient accounting systems to accumulate the costs of all services provided to each patient during a stay in the hospital and to develop the amounts to be billed to the patient or the patient's health insurance company for each service. A typical hospital bill includes a variety of items.

EXAMPLE HOSPITAL

September 30, 19XX

John R. Thatcher
1620 Adams Street
Lansing, Minnesota 98203

INVOICE for hospital stay:
9/10/XX through 9/14/XX

X-rays	$ 36
Room supplies	42
Surgeon's fee	875
Private duty nurse	440
Room charge	1,250
TOTAL	$2,643

Each of the items in this bill can be related to the job costing framework. X-rays were taken by a separate group of radiologists that billed the hospital $36 for the x-rays. They were billed to the patient at the same amount. The room supplies were taken from the hospital's material inventory. They had an original cost of $30 but were billed to the patient at $42, incorporating a $12 gross profit. X-rays and room supplies represent material charges.

Two types of labor charges are included in the bill—the surgeon's fee and the private duty nurse charge. The $875 surgeon's fee was based on 2.5 hours of surgery at $350 per hour, a direct parallel to factory direct labor. The private duty nurse charge represents four shifts of eight hours. The nurses are paid $85 per shift while each shift is billed to the patient at $110, incorporating a total gross profit of $100.

Many other costs cannot be directly identified with each patient in an efficient manner. These overhead-type cost items (such as staff interns, general nursing care, food service, building depreciation, and utilities) are allocated to individual patients using a daily room charge. This charge is primarily a predetermined overhead rate, but also incorporates a gross profit. The bill for Mr. Thatcher includes five days of room charge at $250 per day which consists of $1,050 of allocated cost and $200 of gross profit.

The patient accounting system accumulates these charges in an account the equivalent of work in process, with subsidiary records by patient. When the billing is prepared for a patient, the billed amount is removed from the work in process account and placed in an account which is the equivalent of cost of goods sold. There is no equivalent of finished goods inventory.*

*For further discussion of cost accounting in hospitals, see James D. Suver and Bruce R. Neumann, *Management Accounting for Healthcare Organizations*, Revised Edition (Chicago: Pluribus Press, Inc., and Oakbrook, Illinois: Healthcare Financial Management Association, 1985).

(7)	Finished Goods Inventory	3,600	
	Work in Process Inventory		3,600
	Job 1 completed, producing 1,000 units of product Y at $3.60 per unit.		
(8)	Cost of Goods Sold	1,440	
	Finished Goods Inventory		1,440
	Cost of 400 units of product Y at $3.60 each.		
(9)	Accounts Receivable	2,400	
	Sales		2,400
	Sold 400 units of product Y at $6 per unit.		

After transactions (7)–(9) are entered, the relevant accounts and subsidiary records would appear as shown in Exhibit 22–11. Note three points: an obvious

EXHIBIT 22–11
Entries for Completion and Sale of Product

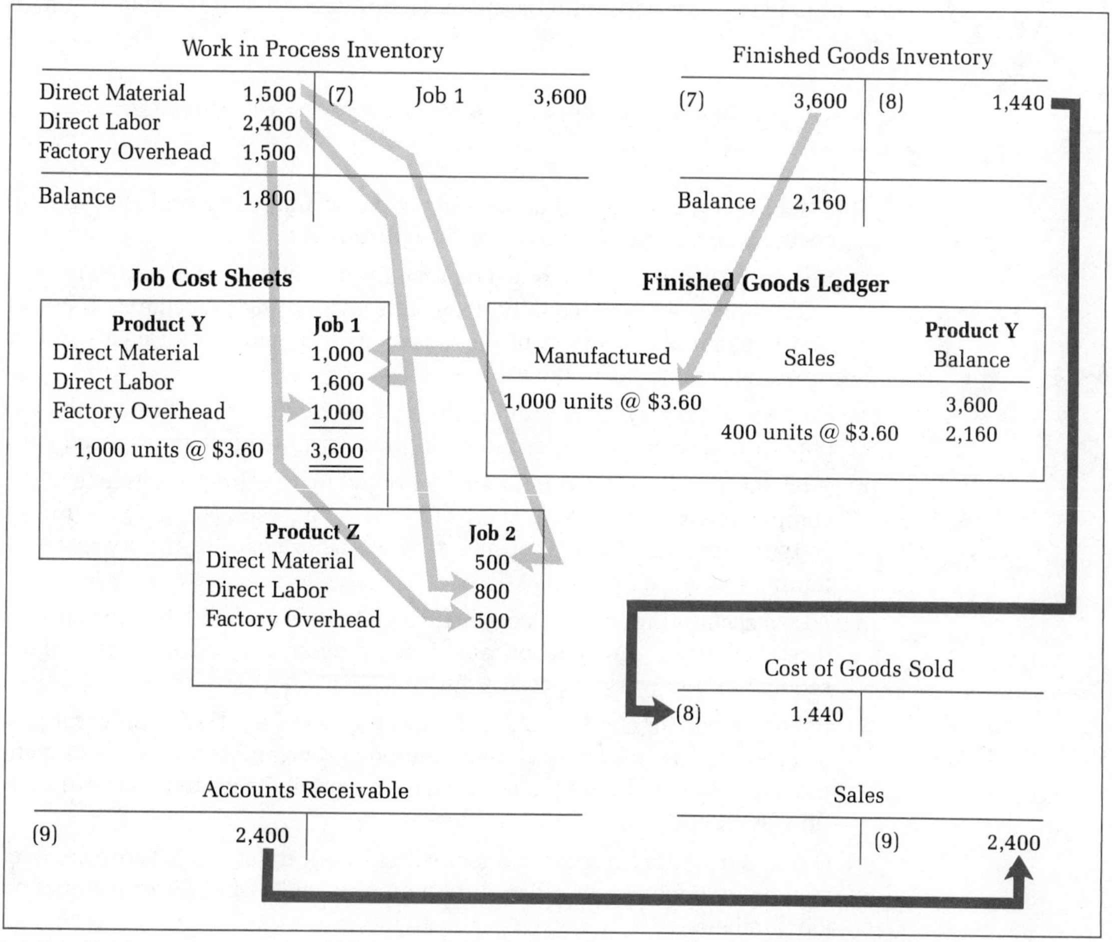

parallel exists between the physical flow of goods and the related accounting entries; the various subsidiary ledgers contain a detailed analysis of the aggregate balances in their related general ledger control accounts; and the sale of finished goods involves entries at both the selling price and the related cost amount.

COST ACCOUNTING SYSTEMS AND FINANCIAL STATEMENTS

When perpetual inventory procedures are used in cost accounting systems, the ending balances of all three inventory accounts reflect the period's routine transactions that increase and decrease inventories. These ending balances are adjusted only if a discrepancy appears in year-end physical inventory counts. Note also that the cost of goods sold figure has been accumulated throughout the year in a general ledger account and can be placed directly on the income statement. Detailed information is available in the related accounts for preparing analyses of cost of goods manufactured and cost of goods sold. The format of financial statements for firms using cost accounting systems is similar to that illustrated in Chapter 21.

KEY POINTS TO REMEMBER

(1) The basic concept of cost accounting is the accumulation and allocation of cost to some unit of activity or accomplishment.

(2) Virtually all cost data are based on assumptions about—and relatively arbitrary choices among—equally defensible accounting procedures. Users of cost data should be aware of the variations inherent in cost data and any resulting limitations to the data used.

(3) Cost accounting systems provide timely unit product costs through the use of perpetual inventory procedures and predetermined factory overhead rates.

(4) Predetermined overhead rates are computed by dividing an estimate of the coming year's total factory overhead cost by an estimate of some unit of activity (such as direct labor hours, direct labor costs, or factory machine hours).

(5) A cost accounting system is basically a method of accumulating the costs of direct material, direct labor, and factory overhead and allocating them sequentially to work in process, finished goods, and cost of goods sold.

(6) Job order costing lends itself to the production of a series of different jobs or products that may vary in their component materials and mode of manufacture. Process costing is most useful for products made in a continuous flow operation.

(7) Detailed inventory records and requisitions must differentiate between direct material and factory supplies and accumulate the cost of direct material by job number.

(8) Detailed payroll records and time tickets must differentiate among direct labor, indirect labor, and nonfactory labor costs and accumulate direct labor costs by job number.

(9) When all related postings are complete, the materials ledger cards, job cost sheets, and finished goods ledger should present a detailed analysis of the balances in the Materials Inventory, Work in Process Inventory, and Finished Goods Inventory accounts, respectively.

(10) Under- or overapplied overhead, which is expected at the end of interim accounting periods, is shown as deferred debits or credits on interim balance sheets. The balance at the end of the year is closed to Cost of Goods Sold.

SELF-TEST QUESTIONS
(Answers are at the end of this chapter.)

1. Which of the following statements is true about perpetual inventories?
(a) Cost of materials used and cost of goods sold tend to be residual (or plug) figures.
(b) Relatively current cost data are available only at end-of-period intervals.
(c) Additions to and deductions from inventory accounts are recorded as they occur.
(d) Physical inventory counts are not needed.

2. Predetermined overhead rates should be:
(a) Greater than actual overhead rates.
(b) Less than actual overhead rates.
(c) Based on monthly budgets.
(d) Based on annual budgets.

3. Which account is debited to record the issuance of material to production for incorporation into the product?
(a) Direct material.
(b) Materials inventory.
(c) Work in process inventory.
(d) Factory supplies.

4. Which of the following is usually not found on a Job Cost Sheet?
(a) Factory overhead applied.
(b) Finished units currently on hand.
(c) Direct material.
(d) Unit cost.

5. When should the balance of the Factory Overhead account be zero?
(a) At the end of each month.
(b) Only after year-end closing.
(c) Never.
(d) Each time a job is completed.

QUESTIONS

22–1 What are the two primary objectives of cost accounting systems?

22–2 What are the limitations of most cost determinations?

22–3 In a manufacturing operation, what important advantages do perpetual inventory procedures have over periodic inventory procedures?

22–4 Identify several important uses of unit product costs. Why might management need unit product costs before the operating year-end?

22–5 What is a predetermined factory overhead rate, and how, in general, is it determined?

22–6 Briefly justify the use of an annual predetermined factory overhead rate as opposed to actual monthly factory overhead.

22–7 A manufacturing company employs an overhead rate of 140% of direct labor cost. The job 301 cost sheet shows that $4,000 in direct material has been used and that $10,000 in direct labor has been incurred. If 1,000 units of product have been produced on job 301, what is the unit cost of the product?

22–8 Briefly explain the sequential flow of product costs through a cost accounting system.

22–9 For what types of manufacturing activities are job order costing systems most appropriate? For what types are process costing systems most appropriate?

22–10 What type of records would be used or maintained for the following manufacturing activities?
(a) Determining the amount of a specific material on hand.
(b) Issuing direct material for production.
(c) Assigning the direct labor costs for a particular worker.
(d) Accumulating the cost of a particular product or batch of products.
(e) Determining the amounts and cost of completed products on hand.

22–11 Explain the general format and give examples of the data that would appear on (a) a materials ledger card, (b) a job cost sheet, and (c) a finished goods ledger card.

22–12 Briefly explain (a) the concept of a control account and a subsidiary ledger, (b) the three inventory accounts in a manufacturing cost system that are often control accounts, (c) the name of the subsidiary ledger record for each account in part (b), and (d) how to determine that a control account and subsidiary ledger agree.

22–13 Why can we say that the sale of a manufactured product is recorded at two different amounts?

22–14 The Dalton Company records both actual overhead and applied overhead in a single Factory Overhead account. On January 31, the account has a credit balance. Has overhead been underapplied or overapplied during January? What is the significance of this balance, and how should it be treated in the January financial statements?

22–15 Outline the disposition of an amount of underapplied overhead, assuming it exists either at the end of an interim accounting period or at year-end.

22–16 Johnson Manufacturing Company applies factory overhead at the rate of 150% of direct labor cost. During the current period, Johnson incurred $80,000 of direct labor costs and $116,000 of factory overhead costs. What is the amount of over- or underapplied factory overhead?

EXERCISES

Calculate and use overhead rate

22–17 Selected data for the Fabrication Department of Madison Manufacturing, Inc., are presented below:

Estimated factory overhead cost for the year	$172,800
Estimated direct labor cost for the year (@ $9/hr)	144,000
Actual factory overhead cost for January	13,000
Actual direct labor cost for January (1,200 hours)	11,000

Assuming that direct labor cost is the basis for applying factory overhead:
(a) Calculate the predetermined overhead rate.
(b) Present a journal entry that applies factory overhead for January.
(c) By what amount is factory overhead over- or underapplied in January?
(d) How would the amount in part (c) be reflected in January's financial statements?

Calculate and use overhead rate

22–18 Using the data in Exercise 22–17, but assuming that the basis for applying factory overhead is direct labor *hours*, complete requirements (a) through (d).

Calculate and use overhead rate

22–19 During the coming accounting year, Morton, Inc., anticipates the following costs, expenses, and operating data:

Direct Material (18,000 lb)	$36,000
Direct Labor (@ $10/hr)	60,000
Factory Supplies Used	5,000
Indirect Labor	8,000
Sales Commissions	16,000
Factory Administration	6,000
Nonfactory Administrative Expenses	9,000
Other Factory Overhead*	23,000

*Provides for operating 35,000 machine hours.

(a) Calculate the predetermined overhead rate for the coming year for each of the following application bases: (1) direct labor hours, (2) direct labor costs, and (3) machine hours.
(b) For each case in part (a), determine the proper application of factory overhead to job No. 63, to which 8 direct labor hours, $70 of direct labor cost, and 50 machine hours have been charged.

Applied vs. actual overhead

22–20 Adams Manufacturing Corporation applies factory overhead on the basis of 80% of direct labor cost. An analysis of the related accounts and job cost sheets indicates that during the year total factory overhead incurred was $132,000 and that at year-end Work in Process Inventory, Finished Goods Inventory, and Cost of Goods Sold included $9,000, $36,000, and $108,000, respectively, of direct labor charges incurred during the current year.
(a) Determine the amount of over- or underapplied overhead at year-end.
(b) Prepare a journal entry to close the Factory Overhead account at year-end.

Flow of product costs through accounts

22–21 Assuming a routine manufacturing activity, present journal entries (account titles only) for each of the following transactions:
(a) Purchased direct material on account.
(b) Recorded factory payroll earned but not paid.

(c) Requisitioned both material and factory supplies.
(d) Assigned direct and indirect factory payroll costs.
(e) Recorded factory depreciation, property tax expense, and insurance expense.
(f) Applied factory overhead to production.
(g) Completed monthly production.
(h) Sold finished goods.

Flow of product costs through accounts

22–22 The following is a cost flow diagram similar to Exhibit 22–2 in which all or part of typical manufacturing transactions (or account entries) are indicated by parenthetical letters on the debit or credit side of each account.

Materials Inventory	
(a)	(c)

Factory Payroll	
(b)	(d)

Factory Overhead	
(c)	(f)
(d)	
(e)	

Work in Process Inventory	
(c)	(g)
(d)	
(f)	

Finished Goods Inventory	
(g)	(h)

Cost of Goods Sold	
(h)	

For each parenthetical letter, present a general journal entry indicating the apparent transaction or procedure that has occurred (disregard amounts).

Job cost records

22–23 For each of the manufacturing transactions or activities indicated by the parenthetical letters in the cost flow diagram in Exercise 22–22, briefly identify the detailed forms, records, or documents (if any) that would probably underlie each journal entry.

Perpetual inventories

22–24 The following summary data are from the job cost sheets of the Thompson Company:

Job No.	Dates: Started	Finished	Shipped	Total Costs Assigned at April 30	Total Production Costs Added in May
1	4/10	4/20	5/9	$5,400	
2	4/18	4/30	5/20	4,000	
3	4/24	5/10	5/25	2,000	$4,300
4	4/28	5/20	6/3	2,700	3,400
5	5/15	6/10	6/20		1,800
6	5/22	6/18	6/28		3,000

Using the above data, compute (a) the finished goods inventory at May 1 and May 31, (b) the work in process inventory at May 1 and May 31, and (c) the cost of goods sold for May.

Finished goods and cost of goods sold

22–25 Before the completed production for June is recorded, the Work in Process Inventory account for the Grand Company appears as follows:

Work in Process Inventory

Balance, June 1	6,000		
Direct Material	18,000		
Direct Labor	15,000		
Factory Overhead	11,000		

Assume that completed production for June includes jobs 107, 108, and 109 with total costs of $10,000, $20,000, and $12,000, respectively.

(a) Determine the cost of unfinished jobs at June 30 and prepare a journal entry recording completed production.

(b) Using general journal entries, record the sale of job 107 for $16,000 on account.

Job cost sheet

22–26 A manufacturing company has the following account in its cost records:

Work in Process Inventory

Direct Material	42,000	To Finished Goods	82,000
Direct Labor	28,000		
Factory Overhead	21,000		

The company applies overhead to production at a predetermined rate based on direct labor costs. Assume that the company uses a job order costing system and that job 110, the only job in process at the end of the period, has been charged with direct material of $2,000. Complete the following cost sheet for job 110.

Cost Sheet—Job 110 (in process)

Direct Material	______
Direct Labor	______
Factory Overhead	______
Total Cost	______

PROBLEMS

Note: In all problems, assume perpetual inventory procedures, a single Factory Overhead account, first-in, first-out costing of inventories, and that the Materials Inventory account is the control account for both direct material and factory supplies.

Determine and use overhead rate

22–27 Verona Manufacturing, Inc., expects the following costs and expenses during the coming year:

Direct Material	$ 30,000
Direct Labor (@ $7/hr)	105,000

Sales Commissions	$ 23,000
Factory Supervision	15,000
Indirect Labor	28,000
Factory Depreciation	20,000
Factory Taxes	5,000
Factory Insurance	4,000
Factory Supplies Used	8,000
Factory Utilities	10,000

REQUIRED

(a) Compute a predetermined factory overhead rate applied on the basis of direct labor hours.

(b) Present a general journal entry to apply factory overhead during an interim period when 1,200 direct labor hours were worked.

(c) What amount of overhead would be assigned to job 466, to which $56 in direct labor had been charged?

Determine and use overhead rate

22–28 The following selected ledger accounts of the Princeton Company are for February (the second month of its accounting year):

Materials Inventory

Feb. 1 Bal.	20,000	February Credits	75,000
February Debits	68,000		

Factory Overhead

February Debits	91,000	Feb. 1 Bal.	7,000
		February Credits	80,000

Work in Process Inventory

Feb. 1 Bal.	14,000	February Credits	230,000
February Debits:			
Direct Material	61,000		
Direct Labor	100,000		
Factory Overhead	80,000		

Factory Payroll Payable

February Debits	129,000	Feb. 1 Bal.	30,000
		February Credits	117,000

Finished Goods Inventory

Feb. 1 Bal.	51,000	February Credits	255,000
February Debits	230,000		

REQUIRED
(a) Determine the amount of factory supplies requisitioned for production during February.
(b) How much indirect labor cost was apparently incurred during February?
(c) Calculate the factory overhead based on direct labor cost.
(d) Was factory overhead for February under- or overapplied, and by what amount?
(e) Was factory overhead for the first two months of the year under- or overapplied, and by what amount?
(f) What is the cost of production completed in February?
(g) What is the cost of goods sold in February?

Job cost journal entries

22–29 Ralston Manufacturing had the following inventories at the end of its last fiscal year:

Materials Inventory	$22,000
Work in Process Inventory	9,000
Finished Goods Inventory	17,000

During the first month of the current year, the following transactions occurred:
(1) Purchased materials on account, $40,000.
(2) Incurred factory payroll, $79,000.
(3) Requisitioned direct material of $37,000 and factory supplies of $15,000.
(4) Assigned total factory payroll, of which $13,000 was considered indirect labor.
(5) Incurred other factory overhead, $25,000. (Credit Accounts Payable.)
(6) Applied factory overhead on the basis of 70% of direct labor costs.
(7) Determined completed production, $123,000.
(8) Determined cost of goods sold, $105,000.

REQUIRED
(a) Prepare general journal entries to record these transactions.
(b) If the above transactions covered a full year's operations, present a journal entry to dispose of the overhead account balance.

Job cost journal entries and T accounts

22–30 At the beginning of the current year, the Elgin Company estimated that it would incur $76,800 of factory overhead cost during the year, using 12,000 direct labor hours to produce the desired volume of goods. On January 1 of the current year, beginning balances of Materials Inventory, Work in Process Inventory, and Finished Goods Inventory were $14,000, $–0–, and $22,000, respectively.

REQUIRED
Prepare general journal entries to record the following transactions for the current year:
(a) Purchased materials on account, $20,000.
(b) Of the total dollar value of materials used, $16,000 represented direct material and $6,000 were factory supplies used.
(c) Determined total factory labor, $88,000 (11,000 hours at $8/hr).
(d) Of the factory labor, 80% was direct and 20% indirect.
(e) Applied factory overhead based on direct labor hours to work in process.
(f) Determined actual factory overhead other than those items already recorded, $28,000. (Credit Accounts Payable.)

(g) Ending inventories of work in process and finished goods were $16,000 and $30,000, respectively. (Make separate entries.)
(h) Closed the balance in Factory Overhead to Cost of Goods Sold.

Job cost journal entries and T accounts

22–31 Following are certain operating data for Mayer Manufacturing Company during its first month of the current year's operations.

	Materials Inventory	Work in Process Inventory	Finished Goods Inventory
Beginning Inventory	$21,000	$ 9,000	$84,000
Ending Inventory	12,000	15,000	18,000

Total sales were $660,000, on which the company earned a 40% gross profit. Mayer uses a predetermined factory overhead rate of 110% of direct labor costs. Factory overhead applied was $132,000. Exclusive of factory supplies used, total factory overhead incurred was $90,000; it was overapplied by $9,000.

REQUIRED
Compute the following items. (Set up the T accounts involved in the manufacturing cost flows as shown in Exhibit 22–2, fill in the known amounts, and then use the normal relationships among the various accounts to compute the unknown amounts.)
(a) Cost of goods sold.
(b) Cost of goods manufactured.
(c) Direct labor incurred.
(d) Direct material used.
(e) Factory supplies used.
(f) Total materials purchased.

Determine overhead rate and analyze accounts

22–32 The following summary of job cost sheets relates to the production of Jonathon Manufacturing, Inc., during the first month of the current operating year. Jonathon uses the same overhead rate for all jobs.

Job No.	Direct Material	Direct Labor	Factory Overhead
109	$ 760	$ 580	$ 464
110	1,080	720	576
111	2,160	2,520	2,016
112	1,800	1,440	1,152
113	1,120	940	752

Job 109 was in process at the end of the preceding year, when it had incurred direct labor charges of $350 and total charges of $1,170. Job 113 is the current month's ending work in process.

REQUIRED
(a) What is the apparent factory overhead rate?
(b) Determine the total direct material requisitioned in the current month.
(c) What is the total direct labor incurred in the current month?
(d) If factory overhead is underapplied by $500 at the end of the current month, what is the total factory overhead incurred during the month?
(e) If finished goods inventory decreased during the month by $1,300, what is the cost of goods sold for the month?

Job cost journal entries and T accounts

22–33 Summarized data for the first month's operations of Sterling Welding Foundry are presented below. A job order costing system is used.

(1) Materials purchased on account, $24,000.
(2) Amounts of materials requisitioned and foundry labor used:

Job No.	Materials	Foundry Labor
1	$1,800	$1,100
2	2,900	2,100
3	1,300	1,000
4	5,000	1,800
5	1,900	1,200
6	600	500
Foundry supplies used	2,600	
Indirect labor		1,400

(3) Foundry overhead is applied at the rate of 200% of direct labor costs.
(4) Miscellaneous foundry overhead incurred:

Prepaid foundry insurance written off	$ 600
Property taxes on foundry building accrued	1,000
Foundry utilities payable accrued	2,200
Depreciation on foundry equipment	3,100
Other costs incurred on account	4,300

(5) Ending work in process consisted of jobs 4 and 6.
(6) Jobs 1 and 3 and one-half of job 2 were sold on account for $8,400, $7,200, and $6,000, respectively.

REQUIRED

(a) Open general ledger T accounts for Materials Inventory, Foundry Payroll, Foundry Overhead, Work in Process Inventory, Finished Goods Inventory, and Cost of Goods Sold. Also set up subsidiary T accounts as job cost sheets for each job.
(b) Prepare general journal entries to record the summarized transactions for the month, and post appropriate entries to any accounts listed in part (a). Key each entry to the related parenthetical number in the problem data.
(c) Determine the balances of any accounts necessary and prepare schedules of jobs in ending work in process and jobs in ending finished goods to confirm that they agree with the related control accounts.

Complex job cost journal entries and analysis

22–34 During June, its first month of operations, Bradley Manufacturing Company completed the transactions listed below. Bradley uses a simple job order costing system. Materials requisitions and the factory payroll summary are analyzed on the fifteenth and the last day of each month, and charges for direct material and direct labor are entered directly on specific job cost sheets. Factory overhead at the rate of 140% of direct labor costs is recorded on individual job cost sheets when a job is completed and at month-end for any job then in process. At month-end, entries to the general ledger accounts summarize materials requisitions, distribution of factory payroll costs, and the application of factory overhead for the month. All other entries to general ledger accounts are made as they occur.

(1) Purchased materials on account, $81,000.
(2) Paid miscellaneous factory overhead costs, $20,200.
(3) Paid the semimonthly factory payroll, $61,800.
(4) An analysis of materials requisitions and the factory payroll summary for June 1–15 indicates the following cost distribution:

Job No.	Materials	Factory Labor
1	$13,500	$23,000
2	6,500	10,000
3	2,700	6,700
Factory supplies used	4,800	
Indirect labor		22,100
	$27,500	$61,800

(5) Jobs 1 and 2 were completed on June 15 and transferred to Finished Goods Inventory on the next day. (Enter the appropriate factory overhead amounts on the job cost sheets, mark them completed, and make a general journal entry transferring the appropriate amount of cost to the Finished Goods Inventory account.)
(6) Paid miscellaneous factory overhead costs, $14,600.
(7) Sold job 1 on account, $116,000 (recognized its cost of sales in the general journal).
(8) Paid the semimonthly factory payroll, $59,000.
(9) An analysis of materials requisitions and factory payroll summary for June 16–30 indicates the following cost distribution:

Job No.	Materials	Factory Labor
3	$14,300	$10,500
4	11,300	20,200
5	4,900	8,100
6	1,900	2,700
Factory supplies used	4,300	
Indirect labor		18,400
	$36,700	$59,900

(10) Jobs 3 and 4 were completed on June 30 and transferred to Finished Goods Inventory on the same day. [See instruction (5).]
(11) Sold job 3 on account, $97,200 (recognized its cost of sales in the general journal).
(12) Recorded the following additional factory overhead:

Depreciation on factory building	$16,200
Depreciation on factory equipment	9,500
Expiration of factory insurance	2,700
Accrual of factory taxes payable	4,300
	$32,700

(13) Recorded monthly general journal entry for the costs of all materials used.
(14) Recorded monthly general journal entry for the distribution of factory payroll costs.
(15) Recorded factory overhead on the job cost sheets for jobs in ending work in process and in the general journal for all factory overhead applied during the month.

REQUIRED
(a) Set up the following general ledger T accounts: Materials Inventory, Factory Payroll Summary, Factory Overhead, Work in Process Inventory, Finished Goods Inventory, Cost of Goods Sold, and Sales.
(b) Set up subsidiary ledger T accounts for each of jobs 1–6 as job cost sheets.
(c) Noting the accounting procedures described in the first paragraph of the problem, do the following:
  (1) Record general journal entries for all transactions. Note that general journal entries are *not* required in transactions (4) and (9). Post only those portions of these entries affecting the general ledger accounts set up in part (a).
  (2) Enter the applicable amounts directly on the appropriate job cost sheets for transactions (4), (5), (9), (10), and (15). Note parenthetically the nature of each amount entered.
(d) Present a brief analysis showing that the general ledger accounts for Work in Process Inventory and for Finished Goods Inventory agree with the related job cost sheets.
(e) Explain in one sentence each what the balance of each general ledger account established in part (a) represents.

ALTERNATE PROBLEMS

Determine and use overhead rate

22–27A Eastside Manufacturing, Inc., expects the following costs and expenses during the coming year:

Direct Material	$ 39,000
Direct Labor (@ $6/hr)	144,000
Sales Commissions	23,000
Factory Supervision	38,000
Indirect Labor	72,000
Factory Depreciation	31,000
Factory Taxes	9,000
Factory Insurance	7,000
Factory Supplies Used	22,000
Factory Utilities	13,000

REQUIRED
(a) Compute a predetermined factory overhead rate applied on the basis of direct labor hours.
(b) Present a general journal entry to apply factory overhead during an interim period when 2,000 direct labor hours were worked.

(c) What amount of overhead would be assigned to job 325, to which $90 in direct labor had been charged?

Job cost journal entries

22–29A Cutler Manufacturing had the following inventories at the end of its last fiscal year:

Materials Inventory	$13,000
Work in Process Inventory	11,000
Finished Goods Inventory	20,000

During the first month of the current year, the following transactions occurred:
(1) Purchased materials on account, $44,000.
(2) Incurred factory payroll, $70,000.
(3) Requisitioned total materials of $40,000, of which $7,000 was considered factory supplies.
(4) Assigned total factory payroll, of which $10,000 was considered indirect labor.
(5) Incurred other factory overhead, $26,000. (Credit Accounts Payable.)
(6) Applied factory overhead on the basis of 80% of direct labor costs.
(7) Determined ending work in process, $20,000.
(8) Determined ending finished goods, $35,000.

REQUIRED
(a) Prepare general journal entries to record these transactions.
(b) If the above transactions covered a full year's operations, present a journal entry to dispose of the overhead account balance.

Job cost journal entries and T accounts

22–30A At the beginning of the current year, the Davis Company estimated that it would incur $51,000 of factory overhead cost during the year, using 17,000 direct labor hours to produce the desired volume of goods. On January 1 of the current year, beginning balances of Materials Inventory, Work in Process Inventory, and Finished Goods Inventory were $16,000, $–0–, and $29,000, respectively.

REQUIRED
Prepare general journal entries to record the following transactions for the current year:
(a) Purchased materials on account, $41,000.
(b) Of the total dollar value of materials used, $34,000 represented direct material and $8,000 were factory supplies used.
(c) Determined total factory labor, $126,000 (18,000 hours @ $7/hr).
(d) Of the factory labor, 75% was direct and 25% indirect.
(e) Applied factory overhead based on direct labor hours to work in process.
(f) Determined actual factory overhead other than those items already recorded, $9,400. (Credit Accounts Payable.)
(g) Ending inventories of work in process and finished goods were $19,000 and $39,000, respectively. (Make separate entries.)
(h) Closed the balance in Factory Overhead to Cost of Goods Sold.

Determine overhead rate and analyze accounts

22–32A The following summary of job cost sheets relates to the production of Harrison Manufacturing, Inc., during the first month of the current operating year. Harrison uses the same overhead rate for all jobs.

Job No.	Direct Material	Direct Labor	Factory Overhead
109	$1,000	$1,200	$ 840
110	1,800	900	630
111	4,500	3,800	2,660
112	3,000	2,300	1,610
113	1,300	1,100	770

Job 109 was in process at the end of the preceding year, when it had incurred direct labor charges of $350 and total charges of $1,120. Job 113 is the current month's ending work in process.

REQUIRED

(a) What is the apparent factory overhead rate?
(b) Determine the total direct material requisitioned in the current month.
(c) What is the total direct labor incurred in the current month?
(d) If factory overhead is overapplied by $1,000 at the end of the current month, what is the total factory overhead incurred during the month?
(e) If finished goods inventory increased during the month by $1,500, what is the cost of goods sold for the month?

Job cost journal entries and T accounts

22–33A Summarized data for the first month's operations of Northbrook Foundry are presented below. A job order costing system is used.

(1) Materials purchased on account, $42,000.
(2) Amounts of materials requisitioned and foundry labor used:

Job No.	Materials	Foundry Labor
1	$2,200	$1,700
2	2,500	2,900
3	1,800	4,300
4	6,600	5,900
5	3,100	3,400
6	1,800	900
Foundry supplies used	5,400	
Indirect labor		8,000

(3) Foundry overhead is applied at the rate of 150% of direct labor costs.
(4) Miscellaneous foundry overhead incurred:

Prepaid foundry insurance written off	$ 900
Property taxes on foundry building accrued	1,800
Foundry utilities payable accrued	2,100
Depreciation on foundry equipment	4,000
Other costs incurred on account	7,000

(5) Ending work in process consisted of jobs 4 and 6.
(6) Jobs 1 and 3 and one-half of job 2 were sold on account for $12,000, $15,000, and $9,000, respectively.

REQUIRED
(a) Open general ledger T accounts for Materials Inventory, Foundry Payroll, Foundry Overhead, Work in Process Inventory, Finished Goods Inventory, and Cost of Goods Sold. Also set up subsidiary T accounts as job cost sheets for each job.
(b) Prepare general journal entries to record the summarized transactions for the month, and post appropriate entries to any accounts listed in part (a). Key each entry to the related parenthetical letter in the problem data.
(c) Determine the balances of any accounts necessary and prepare schedules of jobs in ending work in process and jobs in ending finished goods to confirm that they agree with the related control accounts.

BUSINESS DECISION PROBLEM

Columbia Manufacturing Company plans to make and sell a newly designed fuel director valve for use in small aircraft manufactured by other companies. If made with traditional materials, the valve would require the following materials and labor:

Materials	
A	5 lb @ $5 each
B	6 lb @ $7 each
C	4 lb @ $13 each
Labor	
Casting	3 hr @ $5/hr
Finishing	3 hr @ $6/hr
Assembling	2 hr @ $7/hr

Overhead costs in these departments should be $12 per direct labor hour.

Management may also use a new synthetic material, D, perfected in space technology. Making the body of the valve out of material D would alter the cost and manufacturing procedures as follows: Eight pounds of D, costing $11 per pound, would replace both materials A and B. Casting and finishing labor time would be reduced by 50%. However, each valve would require four hours of machining labor costing $10 per hour and performed on a highly specialized, partially automated machine. Factory overhead in the machining department is applied at the rate of $8 per machine hour.

Columbia's marketing department advises management that the valve made of traditional materials would sell for 150% of the company's cost and that aircraft manufacturers would pay 170% of the company's cost for the valve made of the new lightweight material D.

REQUIRED
Present an analysis showing the gross profit per unit for each manufacturing alternative. Based on this analysis, recommend whether or not the new material should be used.

ANSWERS TO SELF-TEST QUESTIONS

1. (c) 2. (d) 3. (c) 4. (b) 5. (b)

23

Cost Accounting Systems: Process Costing

Chapter Objectives

- Describe the basic concepts of a process costing system.
- Present techniques and procedures for unit cost determination under process costing.
- Illustrate cost flows through a process costing system.
- Analyze the costs transferred between or among departments using a production cost report.
- Describe the procedures for cost allocation for service departments.
- Identify joint product costs and by-product costs and describe techniques to account for them.

For which of you, desiring to build a tower, does not first sit down and count the cost . . . ?

LUKE 14:28

The early sections of this chapter explain and illustrate the concepts and procedures typical of a process costing system that involves more than one processing department. The concluding sections of the chapter deal with accounting for the costs of service departments, joint products, and byproducts.

In Chapter 22, we explained that a process costing system is appropriate in accounting for costs in the production of a large volume of relatively homogeneous products manufactured in a "continuous flow" operation. Producers of fuel, chemicals, cement, paint, and similar goods find this system useful.

In job order costing, cost must be identified with the specific job or order being produced before unit costs can be determined. In contrast, costs in a process system are identified with a **cost center**, or production department, *during a period of time*—usually a month. Monthly product costs are accumulated in separate Work in Process accounts for each processing or production department. At month-end, costs are summarized for each cost center in a separate **production cost report.** This report provides the unit cost information that can be used to determine costs of goods transferred from process to process and finally into the finished goods inventory.

A job order system has one Work in Process account supported by a number of job order cost sheets, while a process system has several Work in Process accounts, each supported by a monthly production cost report (one for each department).

Exhibit 23–1 illustrates process cost flows for a liquid product, the production of which involves only two successive processes—department A and department B. To simplify the illustration, we assume no incomplete production in process at the beginning or end of the period. We also assume that materials inventory and finished goods inventory were zero at the beginning of the period.

It is important to note the following about Exhibit 23–1:

(1) Materials purchased, factory payroll accrued, and factory overhead incurred are initially recorded in the Materials Inventory account, Factory Payroll account, and Factory Overhead account, respectively—the same as for job order costing. These amounts are indicated by XX in the accounts.

(2) Material requisitioned as direct material is charged to the work in process accounts of the departments to which the material was issued [see (a) and (e)]; factory payroll is distributed as direct labor [see (b) and (f)]; and factory overhead is allocated to the work in process accounts of the departments benefited [see (c) and (g)].

EXHIBIT 23–1
Illustration of Cost Flows in a Simplified Process Costing System

Materials Inventory

XX	(a)	1,400
	(e)	1,600

Factory Payroll

XX	(b)	2,000
	(f)	1,700

Factory Overhead

XX	(c)	800
	(g)	1,800

Work in Process Department A

(a)	1,400	(d)	4,200
(b)	2,000		
(c)	800		
	4,200		4,200

Work in Process Department B

(d)	4,200	(h)	9,300
(e)	1,600		
(f)	1,700		
(g)	1,800		
	9,300		9,300

Finished Goods Inventory

(h)	9,300	(i)	9,100

Cost of Goods Sold

(i)	9,100	

(3) Goods completed in department A are transferred to department B for further processing; goods completed in department B are transferred to the warehouse as product ready for sale; goods are shipped to customers when they are sold.

(4) Similarly, the product cost of goods completed in department A are transferred from the department A work in process account to the department B work in process account [see (d)]; the product cost of goods completed in department B are transferred from the department B work in process account to the finished goods inventory account [see (h)]; and the product cost of goods sold is transferred from the finished goods inventory account to the cost of goods sold account [see (i)].

DETERMINING UNIT COSTS

To trace the cost of products transferred from one processing department to another and then into finished goods, we must calculate unit costs. If unit costs are calculated on a monthly basis, a firm can compare its current costs with those of prior periods and determine when cost control measures are needed.

Unit cost determination is basically an averaging process. Exhibit 23–1 shows that during January of the current year, Department A incurred $1,400 of direct material cost, $2,000 of direct labor cost, and $800 of overhead cost in processing 800 gallons of product. The unit cost for each gallon would be

$$\frac{\text{Total Costs for January}}{\text{Total Work Accomplished}} = \frac{\$4{,}200}{800 \text{ gallons}} = \$5.25 \text{ per gallon}$$

Equivalent Units

In the above computation, we assumed that the 800 gallons were begun and completed during the month. Suppose, however, that unfinished units were in process in department A at the beginning and end of the period. Assume that, of the 800 gallons handled during January, 200 were 20% complete at the end of December and 100 were 40% complete at the end of January. Clearly, determining the January unit cost by treating all 800 gallons as if they had been started and finished in January is incorrect. Instead, we should convert the processing done on 800 gallons into a smaller number of **equivalent units** of completed product. The 100 gallons 40% completed during the period are equivalent to 40 gallons begun and completed; 200 gallons 80% completed are equivalent to 160 gallons begun and completed. In our example, we would calculate the equivalent units of work in department A for January as follows:

	Total Units Involved (gallons)		Proportion Completed This Month		Equivalent Units
Beginning inventory	200	×	80%	=	160
Begun and finished in January	500	×	100%	=	500
Ending inventory	100	×	40%	=	40
	800				700

If we assume that materials, labor, and overhead are added gradually throughout processing, the correct unit cost for department A for January would be

$$\frac{\text{Total Costs for January}}{\text{Equivalent Units Processed}} = \frac{\$4{,}200}{700 \text{ gallons}} = \$6 \text{ per gallon}$$

In process cost systems, unit cost calculations may be complicated by the fact that materials are added at a different rate or at a different time than are labor and overhead, which are grouped together and called *conversion costs*. For example, materials may be added at the beginning of the process, while conversion costs are added evenly throughout the process. In this case, the number of equivalent units used to calculate the unit cost of materials is different from the number of equivalent units used to compute the unit cost of conversion.

Exhibit 23–2 graphically presents the revised computation of equivalent units when all materials are added initially and conversion costs are incurred evenly throughout the process. Because all materials for beginning work in process were added during the previous period (when these units were started), this batch has no equivalent units for materials in this period. However, any unit of product begun this period has all materials added this period, so the 500 units begun and completed and the 100 units only begun (ending work in process) are assigned full equivalent units for materials. For conversion costs, (1) the 200 units in

EXHIBIT 23–2
Graphic Illustration of Equivalent Units in Department A: Material Added Initially; Conversion Incurred Evenly Throughout Period

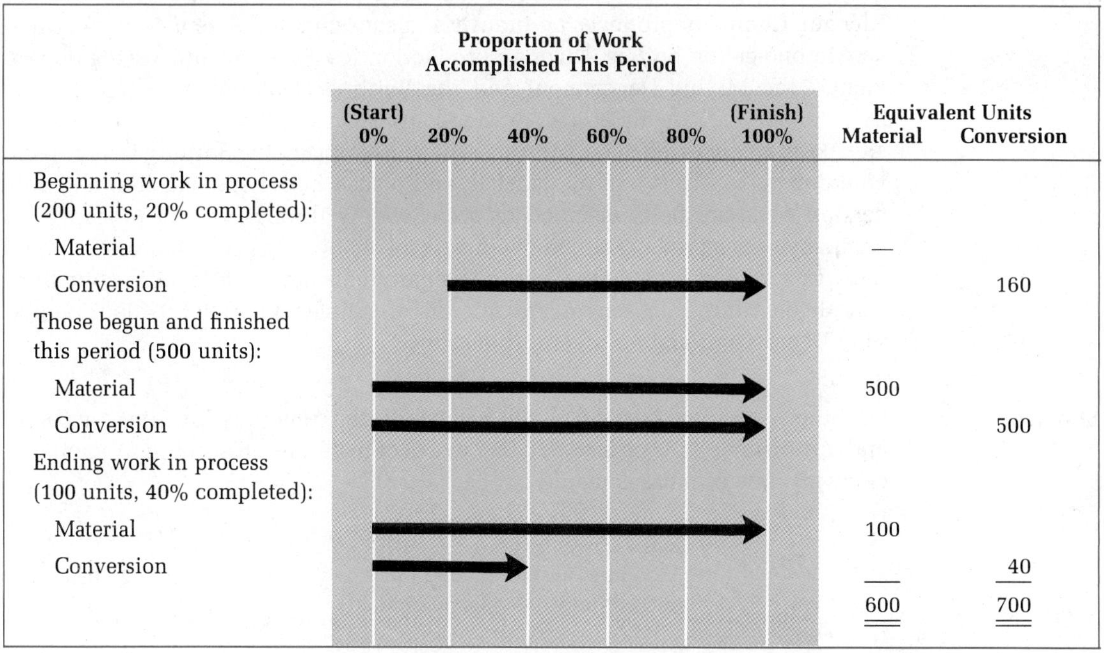

beginning work in process represent only 160 (80% × 200) equivalent units because only the final 80% of processing occurred this period; (2) each of the 500 units of product begun and completed this period equals one equivalent unit because all conversion was accomplished this period; and (3) the 100 units in ending work in process equal only 40 (40% × 100) equivalent units because only 40% of their processing was accomplished this period. Under these assumptions, the number of equivalent units completed for the period is not the same for materials as for conversion costs. Consequently, the computation of cost per equivalent unit requires separate calculations for the two cost components, which are then totaled. In our illustration, these are:

$$\frac{\text{Material Cost}}{\text{Equivalent Units}} = \frac{\$1{,}400}{600} = \$2.333 \text{ for material}$$

$$\frac{\text{Conversion Costs}}{\text{Equivalent Units}} = \frac{\$2{,}000 + \$800}{700} = \$4.000 \text{ for conversion}$$

Total cost for a unit processed this period $6.333

Note again that equivalent unit costs are average costs for a specific period and are derived by dividing the total costs for the period by the related amount of work accomplished during that period.

COST FLOWS ILLUSTRATED

For an example of the operation of a process costing system, assume that the Kleenup Company produces an industrial cleanser called Kleeno, which it markets in one-gallon bottles. Kleeno's production involves two processing departments—the Mixing Department and the Bottling Department. In the Mixing Department, various materials are added at the start of the process, and conversion costs are incurred evenly throughout processing. In the Bottling Department, where the cleanser is bottled, labeled, and placed in cartons, material and conversion costs are both assumed to occur evenly throughout the process. The company uses a predetermined overhead rate of 50% of direct labor costs in both departments. On June 1, the Mixing Department had 6,000 gallons, one-third complete with respect to conversion costs; this inventory cost $8,400. The Bottling Department had no inventory on June 1.

Material

On June 1, the firm had a $15,000 balance in the Materials Inventory account, and during June it purchased $20,000 worth of materials on account. A summary entry for June purchases would be:

Materials Inventory	20,000	
Accounts Payable		20,000
To record June materials purchased.		

The direct material requisitioned during June for each processing department and the supplies for general factory use are shown in the following summary entry:

Work in Process—Mixing Department	26,000	
Work in Process—Bottling Department	2,100	
Factory Overhead	3,000	
Materials Inventory		31,100
To record materials and supplies used in June.		

Labor

During June, the company accrued $43,400 of factory payroll. A summary entry to record this payroll would be:

Factory Payroll	43,400	
Wages Payable, etc.		43,400
To record the factory payroll for June.		

The factory payroll for June indicated that direct labor costs were $28,000 in the Mixing Department, and $8,400 in the Bottling Department. Indirect labor costs of supervisors amounted to $7,000. The following summary entry distributes these costs:

Work in Process—Mixing Department	28,000	
Work in Process—Bottling Department	8,400	
Factory Overhead	7,000	
Factory Payroll		43,400
To distribute June payroll.		

Factory Overhead

So far, we have charged $3,000 of factory supplies and $7,000 of indirect labor to the Factory Overhead account. Assume that other overhead costs (maintenance, utilities, depreciation, and so on) total $8,300. In recording these amounts, we credit various accounts such as Accumulated Depreciation, Accounts Payable, and Prepaid Expenses. For simplicity, we credit Other Accounts in the following summary entry:

Factory Overhead	8,300	
Other Accounts		8,300
To record various factory expenses.		

The Kleenup Company allocates factory overhead to each department at a rate of 50% of direct labor costs. (As explained in Chapter 22, a firm determines this rate at the beginning of the year by estimating factory overhead and direct labor costs.) The following entry charges the Mixing and Bottling Departments with factory overhead:

Work in Process—Mixing Department (50% of $28,000)	14,000	
Work in Process—Bottling Department (50% of $8,400)	4,200	
Factory Overhead		18,200
To charge overhead to processing departments.		

Actual costs charged to the Factory Overhead account total $18,300, but the foregoing entry allocates only $18,200 to the processing departments, resulting in $100 of underapplied overhead. Recall that accumulated amounts of under- or overapplied overhead can be carried as deferred balance sheet charges or credits until year-end and then closed to Cost of Goods Sold.

As a result of the journal entries recorded during the month, the two Work in Process accounts contain the following balances as of the end of the month:

	Mixing Department	Bottling Department
Beginning Balance	$ 8,400	$ –0–
Direct Material	26,000	2,100
Direct Labor	28,000	8,400
Factory Overhead	14,000	4,200
	$76,400	$14,700

At the end of the month, additional journal entries are needed to reflect the goods transferred from mixing to bottling, from bottling to finished goods, and from finished goods to cost of goods sold.

COST OF GOODS TRANSFERRED OUT AND INVENTORIES

We have explained how material and conversion costs are charged to Work in Process accounts for each processing department during the month. At the end of each month, we must calculate the cost of goods transferred out and the cost of goods remaining uncompleted for each department. Calculations can be performed on either the first-in first-out (FIFO) accounting method or the weighted average accounting method. We illustrate the FIFO accounting method in this chapter.

Exhibit 23–3 shows the June production report for the two processing departments. Note the following key observations regarding the production report:

(1) All unit figures are in whole gallons rather than in equivalent units.

(2) In the Mixing Department, the beginning work in process (6,000) plus units started (26,000) constitute the total number of units to be accounted for (32,000). The 32,000 units are accounted for as units transferred out (24,000) plus units in ending work in process (8,000) of the Mixing Department.

(3) For the Bottling Department, the beginning work in process (0) plus units transferred in from the Mixing Department (24,000) constitute the total number of units to be accounted for (24,000). The 24,000 units are accounted for as units transferred out to finished goods (20,000) plus units in ending work in process (4,000) of the Bottling Department.

EXHIBIT 23–3

Kleenup Company
Production Report (gallons)
For the Month of June, 19XX

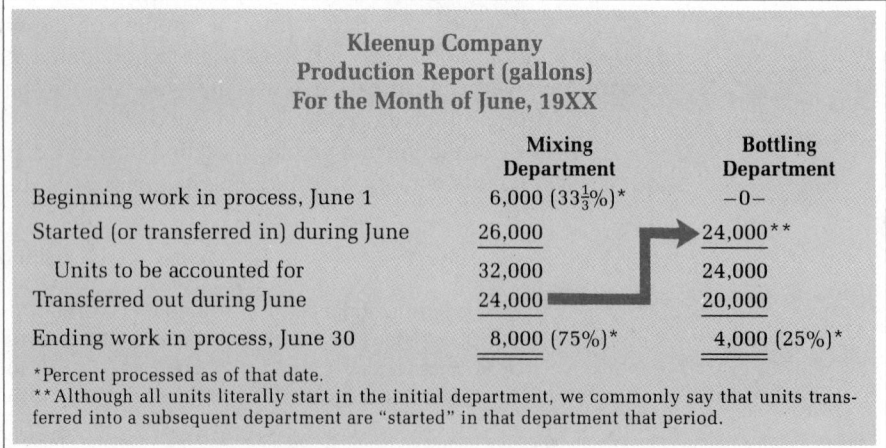

	Mixing Department	Bottling Department
Beginning work in process, June 1	6,000 ($33\frac{1}{3}$%)*	–0–
Started (or transferred in) during June	26,000	24,000**
Units to be accounted for	32,000	24,000
Transferred out during June	24,000	20,000
Ending work in process, June 30	8,000 (75%)*	4,000 (25%)*

*Percent processed as of that date.
**Although all units literally start in the initial department, we commonly say that units transferred into a subsequent department are "started" in that department that period.

(4) Units started minus units in ending work in process inventory constitute the units started *and* completed in that period.

(5) The number of units transferred out of the Mixing Department (24,000) is equal to the number of units transferred into the Bottling Department (24,000).

We now examine how costs are allocated to the various units, beginning with the Mixing Department.

Mixing Department

Remember that in the Mixing Department, materials are added at the start of the mixing process, but conversion costs are incurred evenly throughout the process. Therefore, we must calculate equivalent units and cost per equivalent unit separately for material and conversion costs. Exhibit 23–4 presents these calculations in a cost per equivalent unit report.

In allocating costs to various units of product, three batches of Kleeno are considered: (1) units completed from the June 1 inventory, (2) units begun and completed in June, and (3) units begun but not completed in June. The compo-

EXHIBIT 23–4

Kleenup Company
Mixing Department
Cost per Equivalent Unit Report
For the Month of June, 19XX

			Equivalent Units	
	Total Units Involved	Conversion Completed This Month	Materials (added initially)	Conversion (added throughout)
Transferred Out:				
Beginning inventory	6,000	$66\frac{2}{3}$%	–0–	4,000
Started and completed	18,000	100%	18,000	18,000
Total transferred out	24,000			
Ending Inventory:	8,000	75%	8,000	6,000
Units acounted for	32,000			
Total equivalent units			26,000	28,000
Current Costs:				
Materials			$26,000	
Conversion:				
Direct labor				$28,000
Factory overhead				14,000
				$42,000
Current Cost per Equivalent Unit			$1.00	$1.50

sition of costs for the three batches of product handled by the Mixing Department is explained below and in the production cost report shown in Exhibit 23–5:

(1) **Beginning inventory** The 6,000 gallons in the beginning inventory had all the material and one-third of the required conversion work added in May, for an $8,400 total cost in that month. The remaining two-thirds of the conversion work was completed in June. We multiply the conversion cost of a full unit ($1.50) by the equivalent units (4,000 gallons) to obtain the $6,000 cost to complete this batch. Thus, this batch cost $14,400.

(2) **Started and completed in June** During June, all required material and conversion work were applied to the 18,000 gallons started and completed. The material added this month at $1.00 per gallon and the conversion work completed at $1.50 per unit are applied to each of the 18,000 units, resulting in a cost of $45,000. The total cost of the 24,000 gallons in the two batches

EXHIBIT 23–5

Kleenup Company
Mixing Department
Production Cost Report
For the Month of June, 19XX

	Total Cost	Unit Cost
Costs to Be Accounted for:		
Beginning work in process	$ 8,400	
Direct material	26,000	
Direct labor	28,000	
Factory overhead	14,000	
Costs to be accounted for	$76,400	
Transferred Out:		
Beginning work in process:		
Prior month cost	$ 8,400	
Material	–0–	
Conversion (4,000 × $1.50)	6,000	
Started and completed:		
Material (18,000 × $1.00)	18,000	
Conversion (18,000 × $1.50)	27,000	
Transferred out (24,000 units)	$59,400	$2.475
Ending Work in Process:		
Material (8,000 × $1.00)	$ 8,000	
Conversion (6,000 × $1.50)	9,000	
Ending work in process	$17,000	
Total Costs Accounted For	$76,400	

transferred to the Bottling Department amounts to $59,400, and the average cost of the two batches is $2.475 per gallon ($59,400/24,000).

(3) **Ending inventory** The 8,000 units begun but not completed in June contain all required material but only three-fourths of the needed conversion work. Therefore, we multiply the per-unit material cost of $1.00 by 8,000 gallons to obtain the $8,000 material cost. We then multiply the $1.50 conversion cost by the equivalent units of conversion work performed ($8{,}000 \times \frac{3}{4} = 6{,}000$) to obtain the $9,000 conversion cost.

Notice that the production cost report fully accounts for both the 32,000 units of product involved and the total costs of $76,400 charged to the Mixing Department for June.

The following entry transfers the cost of the work completed in the Mixing Department during June to the Bottling Department:

Work in Process—Bottling Department	59,400	
Work in Process—Mixing Department		59,400
To transfer cost of completed work from Mixing to Bottling		

The Work in Process account for the Mixing Department would now appear as follows:

Work in Process—Mixing Department

June 1 (beginning balance)	8,400	Transferred to Bottling Department	59,400
Direct Material	26,000		
Direct Labor	28,000		
Factory Overhead	14,000		
June 30 (ending balance)	17,000		

Note that all costs charged to this account have been accounted for as either transferred out or as ending inventory.

Bottling Department

Because this department had no beginning inventory, the units handled during June consisted only of the 24,000 gallons received from the Mixing Department. These units cost $2.475 per gallon, for a total cost of $59,400. We assume that the costs of the added direct material, direct labor, and factory overhead are incurred evenly throughout the bottling process. We must convert the work performed into equivalent units and obtain costs per equivalent unit. These computations are shown in the cost per equivalent unit report in Exhibit 23–6.

The production cost report in Exhibit 23–7 (page 891) shows the cost allocation for the Bottling Department. Note that the total cost of the 20,000 gallons transferred to finished goods is $63,500 and the related unit cost is $3.175 per gallon ($63,500/20,000). Also note that the 4,000 units of ending work in process contain a full unit of the Mixing Department's cost ($2.475 per gallon), even

EXHIBIT 23–6

Kleenup Company
Bottling Department
Cost per Equivalent Unit Report
For the Month of June, 19XX

	Total Units Involved	Conversion Completed This Month	Equivalent Units: Materials (added throughout)	Equivalent Units: Conversion (added throughout)
Transferred Out:				
Beginning inventory	–0–		–0–	–0–
Started and completed	20,000	100%	20,000	20,000
Total transferred out	20,000			
Ending Inventory:	4,000	25%	1,000	1,000
Units accounted for	24,000			
Total equivalent units			21,000	21,000
Current Costs:				
Materials			$2,100	
Conversion:				
Direct labor				$ 8,400
Factory overhead				4,200
				$12,600
Current Cost per Equivalent Unit			$0.10	$0.60

though they are only one-fourth complete in the Bottling Department. Therefore, the Mixing Department unit cost of $2.475 is multiplied by 4,000 gallons to obtain the $9,900 total cost from that department.

The cost allocations in the production cost report are reflected in the journal entry transferring the cost of completed units ($63,500) to Finished Goods Inventory and as the ending balance of Work in Process—Bottling Department ($10,600).

The following entry transfers the cost of completed work in the Bottling Department during June:

Finished Goods Inventory	63,500	
Work in Process—Bottling Department		63,500
To transfer cost of completed work from the Bottling Department to Finished Goods Inventory.		

The Work in Process account for the Bottling Department would now appear as follows:

EXHIBIT 23–7

Kleenup Company
Bottling Department
Production Cost Report
For the Month of June, 19XX

	Total Cost	Unit Cost
Costs to Be Accounted for:		
Beginning work in process	$ –0–	
Transferred from Mixing Department	59,400	
Direct material	2,100	
Direct labor	8,400	
Factory overhead	4,200	
Costs to be accounted for	$74,100	
Transferred Out:		
Beginning work in process	$ –0–	
Started and completed:		
Mixing Department costs (20,000 × $2.475)	49,500	
Material (20,000 × $0.10)	2,000	
Conversion (20,000 × $0.60)	12,000	
Transferred out (20,000 units)	$63,500	$3.175
Ending Work in Process:		
Mixing Department costs (4,000 × $2.475)	$ 9,900	
Material (1,000 × $0.10)	100	
Conversion (1,000 × $0.60)	600	
Ending work in process	$10,600	
Total Costs Accounted For	$74,100	

Work in Process—Bottling Department

June 1 (beginning balance)	–0–	Transferred to Finished Goods	63,500
Transferred in from Mixing Department	59,400		
Direct Material	2,100		
Direct Labor	8,400		
Factory Overhead	4,200		
June 30 (ending balance)	10,600		

Again, note that all costs accumulated to this point have been accounted for.

Finished Goods and Cost of Goods Sold

In the cost flows for a process costing system, the journal entries to record sales are similar to those made in a job order system. We assume that during June the Kleenup Company sold goods costing $45,000 for $60,000. In summary form, the following entries reflect the sales:

Accounts Receivable	60,000	
Sales		60,000
To record June sales.		
Cost of Goods Sold	45,000	
Finished Goods Inventory		45,000
To record cost of goods sold in June.		

FLEXIBLE MANUFACTURING SYSTEMS

The clean, brightly colored building contains rows of large, complex machining centers, each serviced by a series of robot arms and remotely guided conveyor belts and carts. Through closed-circuit television, a supervisor monitors perhaps 10 or 12 machining centers that turn out high-quality, precision-machined metal parts. During the day, a skeleton crew of supervisors and maintenance personnel work with the machines; the machines work virtually alone during the night. Such is the scenario in modern automated factories utilizing "flexible manufacturing systems" (FMS). Some of these factories exist in the United States, but most can be found in Japan.

FMS is the latest stage in the evolution of automated machines that began about 30 years ago when a machine's operation was guided through relatively crude digital-based taped instructions. Intervening years have seen first computer-aided design and then computer-aided manufacturing. A major advantage of FMS is the capacity to be quickly and easily reprogrammed to produce different products. Hence, relatively small batches of many different products may now be manufactured. Because fixed manufacturing systems require extensive down-time and expense to retool and realign for changes in products, only large batches of identical products are feasible. In contrast, FMS can be applied to a wide array of products and production volumes.

As expected, FMS installations are comparatively costly. However, the relative productivity of FMS easily passes cost effectiveness criteria. In some cases, the FMS approach requires only 10% of the labor and production time and perhaps only one-fourth the number of machines required by traditional manufacturing procedures. Potential profits to be generated by FMS are just as spectacular.

FMS installations are more widely used for machining than for assembling processes. Apparently, all but the more routine assembly of a small number of components are still best done by human hands. As technology improves, the capacity of FMS to handle complex assembly processes will improve.

Development of FMS rests heavily on computer technology, other microcircuitry technology, the availability of highly skilled labor, and sufficient capital to fund purchase and installation. Companies—and nations—dominating the FMS phenomenon will certainly be tough competitors. Most people living today will probably have their standards of living affected by the technological revolution known as FMS.*

*For further discussion of flexible manufacturing systems, see Gene Bylinsky, "The Race to the Automated Factory," *Fortune*, February 21, 1983, pages 52–64, and Lynn Adkins, "FMS Creates a Sci-Fi Factory," *Dun's Business Month*, March 1985, pages 65 & 67.

An Overview of Process Costing

As you review the Kleenup Company example, note these basic patterns and relationships in process costing:

(1) Product costs are accumulated in three pools: direct material, direct labor, and factory overhead; the latter two are grouped together and called conversion costs.

(2) Physical units to be accounted for include any beginning work in process and any units started (or transferred in). Physical units are accounted for by transferring them out or retaining them as ending work in process.

(3) All cost factors, including any beginning inventory costs, are combined as work in process and must be accounted for.

(4) Through equivalent unit computations, the production accomplished in a period is measured in whole units and divided into the related total cost amounts to determine the period's equivalent unit cost.

(5) In addition to any beginning inventory costs, equivalent unit costs for the current period are assigned to units transferred out and ending work in process, the total of which should equal the cost to be accounted for in (3).

ACCOUNTING FOR SERVICE DEPARTMENTS

Most factories are so large and so complex that a high degree of organizational specialization naturally exists in their operations. Production usually involves a series of specialized departments, such as cutting, preshaping, grinding, subassembly, final assembly, painting, and packaging. In addition to these production departments, a typical factory also has highly specialized *service* departments, which may engage in purchasing, materials handling, personnel, warehousing, inspection, maintenance, and even factory cafeterias. Whereas production departments work directly on products, service departments provide production departments with support services that contribute indirectly to the completion of products.

Service Departments as Cost Centers

Service departments are often viewed by management as cost centers. As such, the costs of each service department are accumulated so management can identify the total cost of such services as repairs and building maintenance. Also, unit costs for each service—such as maintenance cost per square foot of floor space—can be derived for comparison with other operating periods and/or other sources of the service such as outside contractors. A well-designed accounting system accounts for service departments as cost centers.

Service Department Costs as Product Costs

Although service departments do not perform actual work on specific products, they do provide essential services to the production departments. Thus, service department costs are appropriately considered among the related production department's costs and are included in final product costs. This section explains how service costs are accumulated and assigned to individual products.

By their nature, service departments do not use direct material or direct labor. Their costs are part of factory overhead. However, these departments do not work directly on a product, so overhead rates, in the strict sense, are not computed for them. Instead, service department costs are usually allocated to various production departments according to the approximate benefits received by each production department. In other words, service department costs become part of product costs by being allocated among several production departments, using the most appropriate allocation base for each, and becoming part of each production department's overhead to be applied to work in process.

The T-account diagram (with typical titles and amounts) in Exhibit 23–8 illustrates how service department costs: (1) are accumulated on a cost center basis, (2) are allocated to one or more production departments, and (3) become part of the product costs when factory overhead is applied to work in process for each production department. To simplify this illustration, we assume these amounts result in no over- or underapplied overhead.

Note that $4,000 is accumulated as the total cost for the Maintenance Department, then $1,000 and $3,000 are allocated to the Mixing and Bottling Departments, respectively. The allocated service department costs are in turn included in the totals of $18,000 and $12,000 of overhead costs applied from the respective production departments. Similar observations can be made for the Utilities Department.

Method of Cost Allocation

Costs are allocated among various departments on a base that reflects the proportion of the service or activity that benefits each department. Some examples of allocated costs and their possible allocation bases are listed below:

Service Cost	Possible Allocation Base
Personnel salaries	Number of employees in each department
Building depreciation	Square feet of floor space used
Utilities	Machine hours used
Building maintenance	Square feet of floor space used
Machine maintenance	Machine hours used
Heat and light	Cubic feet of building space used

Of course, the concern for cost control may justify the use of elaborate devices and schemes to measure service benefits. Some examples are departmental electric meters, vouchers or tickets reflecting actual hours of services requested and used, and elaborate weighting techniques in which requests for rush or peak hour services are assigned higher costs than requests honored at the convenience of the service department.

To allocate a particular cost, we simply divide the total cost among a series of departments in proportion to departmental shares of the appropriate base activity. For example, suppose that $8,000 of personnel department cost is allocated between a mixing department with 15 employees and a bottling department with 25 employees. The number of production employees is the allocation base. The two distinct steps involved and illustrative calculations follow:

EXHIBIT 23–8
Allocation of Service Department Costs to Production Departments' Overhead Accounts

Maintenance Department (a service department)

(Various costs either identifiable with or allocated to this service department)	4,000	Allocated to:	
		Mixing	1,000
		Bottling	3,000
	4,000		4,000

Utilities Department (a service department)

(Various costs either identifiable with or allocated to this service department)	6,000	Allocated to:	
		Mixing	4,000
		Bottling	2,000
	6,000		6,000

Factory Overhead—Mixing Department

(Various overhead costs either identifiable with or allocated to this production department)	13,000	Applied to Work in Process	18,000
Allocations from:			
Maintenance Department	1,000		
Utilities Department	4,000		
	18,000		18,000

Factory Overhead—Bottling Department

(Various overhead costs either identifiable with or allocated to this production department)	7,000	Applied to Work in Process	12,000
Allocations from:			
Maintenance Department	3,000		
Utilities Department	2,000		
	12,000		12,000

Work in Process—Mixing Department

Direct Material	XX	
Direct Labor	XX	
Factory Overhead	18,000	

Work in Process—Bottling Department

Direct Material	XX	
Direct Labor	XX	
Factory Overhead	12,000	

(1)

$$\frac{\text{Total Cost to Be Allocated}}{\text{Total Allocation Base}} = \text{Allocation Rate}$$

$$\frac{\$8{,}000}{40 \text{ employees}} = \$200 \text{ per employee}$$

(2) $$\frac{\text{Allocation}}{\text{Rate}} \times \frac{\text{Amount of Allocation Base}}{\text{Related to Department}} = \frac{\text{Specific Amount}}{\text{Allocated}}$$

$$\$200 \times 15 \text{ employees} = \$3{,}000 \text{ (for mixing)}$$

$$\$200 \times 25 \text{ employees} = \$5{,}000 \text{ (for bottling)}$$

As a final step, we should check allocations and verify that the sum of allocated amounts equals the total amount allocated.

Exhibit 23–9 illustrates a worksheet often used to accumulate and allocate factory overhead in a multidepartment factory operation that includes service departments. Note the following:

(1) Three categories of costs are involved:
   (a) Those directly identifiable with departments.
   (b) Those requiring allocations to production and service departments.
   (c) Service department costs allocated to production departments.

(2) A total overhead amount is first accumulated for each service department and each production department.

(3) After service department costs are allocated, the total overhead is assigned to the production departments only.

(4) The final amounts assigned to each production department are used to calculate departmental overhead rates. (See the footnotes to Exhibit 23–9).

The amounts, proportions, and variety of costs shown in Exhibit 23–9 have been chosen for simplicity of presentation to stress the basic concepts.

Obviously, we might ask why service department costs are not allocated to other service departments. More sophisticated allocation techniques may involve allocations of some service department costs to other service departments and even mutual assignment of all of one or more service departments' costs to all other service departments. In many instances, these refinements do not result in materially different allocations; such detailed discussions are beyond our present objectives.

JOINT PRODUCTS

Often, the processing of direct material results in two or more products of significant commercial value. Such products derived from a common input are **joint products**, and the related cost of the direct material is a **joint product cost.** An obvious example of a direct material whose processing results in joint products is crude oil, from which a variety of fuels, solvents, lubricants, and residual petrochemical pitches are derived. Cattle, from which the meat packer obtains many cuts and grades of meat, hides, and other products, are another example.

EXHIBIT 23–9

Overhead Distribution Worksheet
For the Year Ended December 31, 19XX

		Service Departments		Production Departments		
	Totals	**Building Maintenance**	**Machine Repairs**	**Mixing**	**Bottling**	**Allocation Base**
Directly Identifiable with Departments						
Indirect labor	85,000	8,000	20,000	38,500	18,500	Factory payroll analysis
Factory supplies used	24,000	3,000	2,000	9,000	10,000	Requisition forms
Allocated to Production and Service Departments						
Building depreciation	6,000	600	1,200	3,000	1,200	Square feet of floor space
Personal property taxes	4,000	400	800	1,500	1,300	Assessed value of equipment used
Total Cost to Be Allocated	119,000	12,000	24,000	52,000	31,000	
Allocation of Service Departments						
Building maintenance (assumed as $\frac{2}{3}$ for mixing and $\frac{1}{3}$ for bottling)		(12,000)		8,000	4,000	Square feet of factory area used
		–0–				
Machinery repairs (assumed as $\frac{1}{6}$ for mixing and $\frac{5}{6}$ for bottling)			(24,000)	4,000	20,000	Machine hours
Totals	119,000		–0–	64,000*	55,000**	

*Assuming a factory overhead allocation base of 20,000 machine hours, the overhead rate for the Mixing Department is $3.20 per machine hour ($64,000/20,000 machine hours).

**Assuming a factory overhead allocation base of $110,000 direct labor, the overhead rate for the Bottling Department is 50 cents per direct labor dollar ($55,000/$110,000 direct labor).

It is impossible to allocate a joint product cost among joint products in such a way that management can decide whether to continue production or what price to charge for a joint product. To decide to produce one joint product is to decide to produce all related joint products, even if some are discarded. Therefore, to make informed decisions about joint products, management must compare the total revenue generated by all joint products with their total production costs.

The primary reason for allocating a joint product cost among two or more products is to price the ending inventories of joint products when determining periodic income. The most popular method of allocating joint product costs for inventory pricing purposes is the **relative sales value** method. Like the cost allocations explained earlier, this approach uses arithmetic proportions. The total joint product cost is allocated to the several joint products in the proportions of their individual sales values to the total sales value of all joint products at the split-off point—that is, where physical separation takes place. For example, assume that 50,000 55-gallon barrels of crude oil costing $1,200,000 are processed into 800,000 gallons of fuel selling for 75 cents per gallon; 400,000 gallons of lubricants selling for $2 per gallon; and 1,000,000 gallons of petrochemical residues selling for 20 cents per gallon. The following calculations illustrate the joint product cost allocation using the relative sales value approach:

Joint Products	Quantity Produced (gallons)		Unit Sales Value		Product Sales Value	Proportion of Total Sales Value
Fuel	800,000	×	$0.75	=	$ 600,000	6/16
Lubricants	400,000	×	2.00	=	800,000	8/16
Residues	1,000,000	×	0.20	=	200,000	2/16
Total sales value					$1,600,000	16/16

Allocations of joint product costs would be undertaken as follows:

	Proportion of Materials Cost	Allocated Cost		Quantity Produced		Cost per Unit
Fuel	6/16 × $1,200,000	$ 450,000	÷	800,000	=	$0.5625 per gallon
Lubricants	8/16 × $1,200,000	600,000	÷	400,000	=	$1.50 per gallon
Residues	2/16 × $1,200,000	150,000	÷	1,000,000	=	$0.15 per gallon
		$1,200,000				

Note that the relative sales value approach results in assigned unit costs that are the same percentage of the selling price for each product. In our illustration, the cost per unit equals 75% of the sales value per unit.

BYPRODUCTS

Byproducts have relatively little sales value compared with the other products derived from a particular process. Byproducts are considered incidental to the manufacture of the more important products. For example, the sawdust and shavings generated in a lumber planing mill or in a furniture factory's cutting department are byproducts.

We may account for byproducts by assigning them a cost equal to their sales value less any disposal costs. This net amount is charged to an inventory account for the byproduct and credited to the work in process account that was charged with the original materials. For example, consider a furniture factory in which walnut boards are processed through a cutting and shaping department. In processing $40,000 worth of lumber, 800 bushels of sawdust and shavings are generated, which, after treatment costing $80, can be sold for $1 per bushel. The following accounts illustrate the amounts and entries involved:

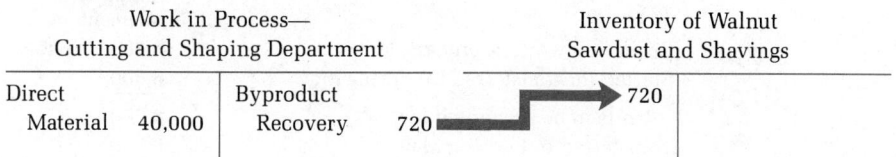

Work in Process— Cutting and Shaping Department			
Direct Material	40,000	Byproduct Recovery	720 →

Inventory of Walnut Sawdust and Shavings	
→ 720	

This procedure reduces the costs of the main products by the net amount recovered from byproducts.

DEMONSTRATION PROBLEM FOR REVIEW

Luster, Inc., produces a liquid furniture polish in two sequential processes organized as the Mixing Department and the Bottling Department. Direct material is added initially in the Mixing Department; all other costs in both departments are incurred evenly throughout the processes. The following are cost data for May:

	Mixing Department	**Bottling Department**
Beginning work in process inventory	$ 588	$ –0–
May's operating costs:		
Direct material	2,400	650
Direct labor	3,500	2,600
Factory overhead	1,400	1,950
	$7,888	$5,200

Beginning work in process consisted of 800 gallons, 50% processed; 8,000 gallons were started in the Mixing Department. Ending work-in-process inventories were 2,000 gallons, 30% processed, in the Mixing Department and 400 gallons, 25% processed, in the Bottling Department.

REQUIRED

(a) Prepare a Production Report for May for both departments.

(b) For each department: (1) prepare a Cost per Equivalent Unit Report for May, (2) prepare a Production Cost Report for May, and (3) prepare journal entries to record the transfer of completed units.

SOLUTION TO DEMONSTRATION PROBLEM

(a)

Luster, Inc.
Production Report (gallons)
For the Month of May, 19XX

	Mixing Department		Bottling Department	
Beginning work in process, May 1	800	(50%)	–0–	
Started (or transferred in) during May	8,000		6,800	
Units to be accounted for	8,800		6,800	
Transferred out during May	6,800		6,400	
Ending work in process, May 31	2,000	(30%)	400	(25%)

(b) (1) (Mixing Department)

Luster, Inc.
Mixing Department
Cost per Equivalent Unit Report
For the Month of May, 19XX

			Equivalent Units	
	Total Units Involved	Conversion Completed This Month	Materials (added initially)	Conversion (added throughout)
Transferred Out:				
Beginning inventory	800	50%	–0–	400
Started and completed	6,000	100%	6,000	6,000
Total transferred out	6,800			
Ending Inventory:	2,000	30%	2,000	600
Units accounted for	8,800			
Total equivalent units			8,000	7,000
Current Costs:				
Materials			$2,400	
Conversion:				
Direct labor				$3,500
Factory overhead				1,400
				$4,900
Current Cost per Equivalent Unit			$0.30	$0.70

(2) (Mixing Department)

Luster, Inc.
Mixing Department
Production Cost Report
For the Month of May, 19XX

	Total Cost	Unit Cost
Costs to Be Accounted for:		
Beginning work in process	$ 588	
Direct material	2,400	
Direct labor	3,500	
Factory overhead	1,400	
Costs to be accounted for	$7,888	
Transferred Out:		
Beginning work in process:		
Prior month cost	$ 588	
Material	–0–	
Conversion (400 × $0.70)	280	
Started and completed:		
Material (6,000 × $0.30)	1,800	
Conversion (6,000 × $0.70)	4,200	
Transferred out (6,800 units)	$6,868	$1.01
Ending Work in Process:		
Material (2,000 × $0.30)	$ 600	
Conversion (600 × $0.70)	420	
Ending work in process	$1,020	
Total Costs Accounted For	$7,888	

(3) (Mixing Department)

Work in Process—Bottling Department	6,868	
Work in Process—Mixing Department		6,868
To record completion of 6,800 units at a cost of $1.01 per unit and their transfer to the Bottling Department.		

(b) (1) (Bottling Department)

Luster, Inc.
Bottling Department
Cost per Equivalent Unit Report
For the Month of May, 19XX

	Total Units Involved	Conversion Completed This Month	Equivalent Units: Materials (added throughout)	Equivalent Units: Conversion (added throughout)
Transferred Out:				
Beginning inventory	–0–		–0–	–0–
Started and completed	6,400	100%	6,400	6,400
Total transferred out	6,400			
Ending Inventory	400	25%	100	100
Units accounted for	6,800			
Total equivalent units			6,500	6,500
Current Costs:				
Materials			$ 650	
Conversion:				
Direct labor				$2,600
Factory overhead				1,950
				$4,550
Current Cost per Equivalent Unit			$0.10	$0.70

(2) (Bottling Department)

Luster, Inc.
Bottling Department
Production Cost Report
For the Month of May, 19XX

	Total Cost	Unit Cost
Costs to Be Accounted for:		
Beginning work in process	$ –0–	
Transferred from Mixing Department	6,868	
Direct material	650	
Direct labor	2,600	
Factory overhead	1,950	
Costs to be accounted for	$12,068	

Transferred Out:		
Beginning work in process	$ –0–	
Started and completed:		
Mixing Department costs (6,400 × $1.01)	6,464	
Material (6,400 × $0.10)	640	
Conversion (6,400 × $0.70)	4,480	
Transferred out (6,400 units)	$11,584	$1.81
Ending Work in Process:		
Mixing Department costs (400 × $1.01)	$ 404	
Material (100 × $0.10)	10	
Conversion (100 × $0.70)	70	
Ending work in process	$ 484	
Total Costs Accounted For	$12,068	

(3) (Bottling Department)

Finished Goods Inventory	11,584	
Work in Process—Bottling Department		11,584
To record completion of 6,400 units at a cost of $1.81 per unit and their transfer to Finished Goods Inventory.		

KEY POINTS TO REMEMBER

(1) Process cost accounting averages the total process costs for a period over the related amount of production accomplished during that period.

(2) When ending work-in-process inventory exists, the measurement of work accomplished in a period requires that partially completed units be converted to equivalent units.

(3) When materials are added and conversion is accomplished at different rates (or unevenly), equivalent units must be computed separately for each cost factor.

(4) The manufacturing cost flows and related journal entries are similar for process and job order costing systems.

(5) The total of all costs in beginning inventories and all costs charged to work in process must be accounted for as cost of ending work in process plus cost of goods transferred out.

(6) In assigning manufacturing costs, we consider three batches of products: units transferred out from beginning work-in-process inventories, units both begun and completed this period, and units remaining in ending work-in-process inventories.

(7) The total cost accounted for in a department includes any cost associated with units transferred in from another department.

(8) Service department costs are overhead costs that are allocated to production departments and eventually assigned to products as part of the production departments' overhead.

(9) Joint products are products of significant value originating from a common direct material or process. Joint product costs are allocated among joint products primarily for inventory costing purposes.

(10) Byproducts have relatively insignificant sales values and are assigned costs equal to their net recoverable value, which is removed from the related Work in Process account and charged to an appropriate inventory account.

SELF-TEST QUESTIONS
(Answers are at the end of this chapter.)

1. Which of the following costs will not be part of product cost when using a process costing system?
   (a) Prior department cost.
   (b) Conversion cost.
   (c) Subsequent department cost.
   (d) Material cost.

2. For which of the following account titles will there be multiple accounts in the general ledger when using process costing?
   (a) Finished Goods.
   (b) Work in Process.
   (c) Materials.
   (d) Factory Payroll.

3. Which of the following will be excluded from the calculation of equivalent units when FIFO is used?
   (a) Prior department units transferred in.
   (b) Ending inventory units.
   (c) Beginning inventory units.
   (d) Units sold.

4. Which of the following is not one of the categories of cost involved in the allocation of service department costs?
   (a) Service department costs allocated to production departments.
   (b) Costs directly identifiable with departments.
   (c) Costs requiring allocation to departments.
   (d) Selling department costs.

5. What basis should be used to allocate joint product costs to the individual products?
   (a) Quantity sold × unit sales price.
   (b) Quantity produced × unit sales price.
   (c) Quantity sold × unit cost.
   (d) Quantity produced × unit cost.

QUESTIONS

23–1 What are the important differences between job order and process costing systems? Give two examples of industries that might use each system.

23–2 How are all manufacturing costs for a series of processing departments accumulated as finished goods inventory?

23–3 Why do unit cost computations in a manufacturing process require equivalent unit computations?

23–4 Why do we say that process cost accounting is basically an averaging computation?

23–5 What is meant by the term *equivalent unit?*

23–6 Why must we sometimes compute equivalent units separately for materials and for conversion costs?

23–7 Describe the three batches of products that are typically involved in a period's production under the FIFO accounting method. In what special situation are there only two batches?

23–8 What is meant by the expression that in each department's Work in Process account all charges must be accounted for, either as being transferred out or as ending work in process inventory?

23–9 Contrast service departments with production departments. Give three examples of service departments.

23–10 Why might service departments be treated as cost centers?

23–11 Explain what each of the following statements means:
(a) Service departments do not work directly on products.
(b) Service department costs are factory overhead costs.
(c) Overhead rates are not used for service departments.
(d) In spite of part (c), service department costs become part of product costs.

23–12 How do we choose a base for allocating a cost to several departments?

23–13 How is an allocation rate calculated? How is the specific amount allocated to a department calculated?

23–14 Briefly describe the general format, data, and calculations that would appear on an overhead distribution worksheet for a company with a number of production and service departments.

23–15 Define *joint product,* and give two examples of industries that have joint products because of the nature of the materials used.

23–16 If allocated joint product costs are irrelevant for management decisions, how do we justify allocating joint costs among joint products?

23–17 Define *byproduct,* and briefly describe an accepted procedure in accounting for them.

EXERCISES

Product report and equivalent units

23–18 James Corporation makes a powdered rug shampoo concentrate in two sequential departments, Compounding and Drying. Materials are added initially in the Compounding Department. All other costs are added evenly throughout each process. In the Compounding Department, beginning work in process was 5,000 pounds (70% processed), 34,000 pounds were started in process, 31,000 pounds transferred out, and ending work in process was 60% processed. In the Drying Department, there was no beginning work in process, 27,000 pounds were transferred out, and the ending work in process was 40% processed. Prepare a production report for the current month, and calculate the relevant amounts of equivalent units for each department.

Cost flows through journal entries

23–19 The Mixing Department performs the last of a series of processes in which a fluid chemical is emulsified. Records indicate that the Mixing Department has been charged with $87,000 of transfer-in costs from the Compounding Department and $30,000 of direct labor costs. The factory overhead rate is 150% of direct labor costs. Beginning work in process was $20,000, and ending work in process totaled $14,000. One-half of this period's completed product is sold on account at a price equal to 160% of its cost. Prepare journal entries to record: (1) various costs charged to the Mixing Department this period, (2) transfer of this period's completed product, and (3) sale of one-half of this period's production.

Equivalent units calculations

23–20 The following are selected operating data for the Blending Department for April. Tinting and packaging operations are carried out subsequently in other departments.

Beginning inventory	10,000 units, 60% complete
Units both begun and completed	39,000 units
Ending inventory	12,000 units, 30% complete

Calculate the equivalent units accomplished, assuming that:
(a) all materials are added and conversion accomplished evenly throughout the process;
(b) all materials are added initially and conversion costs are incurred evenly throughout.

Equivalent units and product cost assignment

23–21 In its first month's operation, Department No. 1 incurred charges for direct material (6,000 units) of $108,000, direct labor of $35,000, and factory overhead of $17,800. At month-end, 4,400 units had been completed and transferred out; those remaining were completed with respect to materials but only 25% complete with respect to conversion. Assuming materials are added initially and conversion occurs evenly, compute:
(a) The equivalent units for materials and conversion.
(b) The cost per equivalent unit for materials and conversion.
(c) The total cost assigned to the units transferred out.
(d) The total cost assigned to the ending inventory. Prove that your solutions to parts (c) and (d) account for the total cost involved.

Equivalent units and costs analyses

23–22 Following is the Work in Process account (and certain annotations) for the first of four departments in which Maryland Company makes its only product.

Work in Process—Department 1

Beginning Balance (1,200 units, 70% complete)	18,400	Transferred to Department 2:	
Direct Material (9,600 units)	52,800	Beginning Inventory (1,200 units)	______ (a)
Direct Labor	60,000	Current Period's Production (7,200 units)	______ (b)
Factory Overhead	21,600		
Ending Balance [(c) ______ units, 25% complete]	(d) ______		

Assuming that materials are added initially and conversion costs are incurred evenly throughout, compute the amounts necessary to fill in the four blanks.

Equivalent units and product cost assignment

23–23 Following are the June charges (and certain annotations) appearing in the Work in Process account for the Glendale Company's final processing department:

Beginning inventory (700 units, 40% complete)	$ 5,460
Transferred in from preceding department (5,000 units)	25,000
Direct labor	22,000
Factory overhead applied	14,050

Assuming that conversion costs are incurred evenly throughout and that ending work in process totals 900 units, 70% complete, compute the unit costs for:

(a) Goods transferred out from June's beginning inventory.
(b) Goods transferred out from current production.
(c) Ending work-in-process inventory.

Service department cost allocation

23–24 Presented below are certain operating data for the four departments of Castle Manufacturing Company.

	Departments			
	Service		Production	
	1	2	1	2
Total overhead costs either identifiable with or allocated to each department	$30,000	$48,000	$53,000	$72,000
Square feet of factory floor space			30,000	60,000
Number of factory workers			20	60
Planned direct labor hours for the year			25,000	32,000

Allocate to the two production departments the costs of Service Departments 1 and 2 using factory floor space and number of workers, respectively, as bases. What is the apparent overhead rate for each production department if planned direct labor hours is the overhead application base?

Joint product cost allocation

23–25 Woodfield, Inc., produces joint products A, B, and C from a common material, a batch of which costs $900,000. At the point at which each product is separated, the following quantities and unit sales prices are available.

Product	Quantity (pounds)	Selling Price/Pound
A	72,000	$ 5.00
B	60,000	12.00
C	240,000	0.50

Using the relative sales value approach, calculate the amount of joint product cost assigned to a pound of each product.

PROBLEMS

Note: The firms in all of the following problems use the first-in, first-out method (as illustrated in the chapter) to compute equivalent units and cost inventories.

Calculate units started and equivalent units

23–26 Oakbrook Corporation manufactures quality placemats in three consecutive processing departments: Cutting, Printing, and Packaging. The following information is taken from July's unit product reports:

	Units in Beginning Inventory	Percent Complete	Units Started in July	Units in Ending Inventory	Percent Complete
Cutting Department	9,000	70	52,000	14,000	40
Printing Department	12,000	40	?	17,000	60
Packaging Department	8,000	30	?	10,000	50

Materials are added at the start of the process in the Cutting Department and evenly throughout processing in the Packaging Department. No materials are used in the Printing Department. Conversion costs are incurred evenly in all processing departments.

REQUIRED

(a) Calculate the number of units started or transferred in during July in the Printing and Packaging Departments.

(b) Calculate the equivalent units relating to materials and conversion costs in each department.

Calculate equivalent units and costs; journal entries

23–27 Carson, Inc., produces a film developer in two sequential processes designated Phase I and Phase II. Carson shut down during June, when all employees took their annual vacations. Production began on July 1. The following operating data apply to July:

	Phase I	Phase II
Units started in process	188,000	
Units transferred in from Phase I		156,000
Units in ending work in process (on the average, 40% processed)	32,000	39,000
Costs charged to departments:		
Direct material	$337,600	$198,900
Direct labor	82,580	112,820
Factory overhead	52,460	119,230

Assume all manufacturing costs are incurred evenly throughout each process and that 80% of July's production was sold on account at a price equal to 150% of its cost.

REQUIRED
(a) Briefly explain the July 31 status of the units started in process during July.
(b) For each department, prepare a cost per equivalent unit report for July.
(c) Prepare journal entries to record the completion and transfer of products from each department and the sale of 80% of July's production.

Calculate units, costs, and transferred costs

23–28 Speer Manufacturing, Inc., operates a plant that produces its own regionally marketed Speer Steak Sauce. The sauce is produced in two processes, blending and bottling. In the Blending Department, all materials are added at the start of the process, and labor and overhead are incurred evenly throughout the process. The Work in Process—Blending Department account for January follows:

Work in Process—Blending Department

January 1 Inventory (4,800 gallons, 60% processed)	26,000	Transferred to Bottling Department (34,000 gallons)	______
January charges:			
Direct Material (32,000 gallons)	96,000		
Direct Labor	44,680		
Factory Overhead	29,750		
January 31 Inventory (______ gallons, 70% processed)	______		

REQUIRED
Calculate the following amounts for the Blending Department:
(a) Number of units in the January 31 inventory.
(b) Equivalent units for materials cost and conversion cost.
(c) January cost per equivalent unit for conversion.
(d) Cost of the units transferred to the Bottling Department.
(e) Cost of the incomplete units in the January 31 inventory.

Calculate units, costs, and transferred costs

23–29 The Galena Company processes a food seasoning powder through a Compounding Department and a Packaging Department. In the Packaging Department, costs of direct material, direct labor, and factory overhead are incurred evenly throughout the process. Costs in the Packaging Department for August were:

Inventory, August 1 (6,000 units, 50% complete)	$ 18,500
Transferred in from Compounding Department (29,000 units)	72,500
Direct material	9,485
Direct labor	35,595
Factory overhead	17,250
	$153,330

At August 31, 7,000 units were in process, 30% completed.

REQUIRED

Calculate the following for the Packaging Department:

(a) Equivalent units during August.

(b) Costs per equivalent unit.

(c) Total cost of units transferred to Finished Goods Inventory.

(d) Inventory cost at August 31.

Journal entries with supporting calculations

23–30 Batavia Laboratories, Inc., produces one of its products in two successive departments. All materials are added at the beginning of the process in Department 1; no materials are used in Department 2. Conversion costs are incurred evenly in both departments. January 1 inventories are as follows:

Materials Inventory	$20,000
Work in Process—Department 1 (2,000 units, 35% complete)	10,760
Work in Process—Department 2	–0–
Finished Goods Inventory (2,000 units @ $13.60)	27,200

During January, the following transactions occurred:

(1) Purchased materials on account, $40,000.

(2) Placed 20,000 units of materials at $2.20 per unit into process in Department 1.

(3) Distributed total payroll costs—$100,800 of direct labor to Department 1, $43,200 of direct labor to Department 2, and $32,000 of indirect labor to Factory Overhead.

(4) Incurred other actual factory overhead costs, $30,000. (Credit Other Accounts.)

(5) Applied overhead to the two processing departments—$50,400 to Department 1 and $25,200 to Department 2.

(6) Transferred 19,000 completed units from Department 1 to Department 2. The 3,000 units remaining in Department 1 were 20% completed with respect to conversion costs.

(7) Transferred 15,000 completed units from Department 2 to Finished Goods Inventory. The 4,000 units remaining in Department 2 were 75% completed with respect to conversion costs.

(8) Sold 6,000 units on account at $18 per unit. The company uses FIFO inventory costing.

REQUIRED
(a) Record the January transactions in general journal form.
(b) State the balances remaining in Materials Inventory, in each Work in Process account, and in Finished Goods Inventory.

Production cost report

23–31 Dayton Manufacturing Corporation produces a cosmetic product in three consecutive processes. The costs of Department 2 for May were as follows:

Cost from Department 1		$496,800
Costs added in Department 2:		
Direct material	$56,700	
Direct labor	81,000	
Factory overhead	32,400	170,100

Department 2 had no May 1 inventory, but it handled the following units during May:

Units transferred in from Department 1	34,500
Units transferred to Department 3	27,000
Units in process, May 31	7,500

Of the units in process on May 31, one-half were 80% complete and one-half 40% complete. Both materials and conversion costs occur evenly throughout the process in Department 2.

REQUIRED
Prepare the production cost report for Department 2 for May.

Overhead distribution worksheet

23–32 The following are selected operating data for the production and service departments of Richmond Company for the current operating period.

	Departments			
	Service		Production	
	1	2	1	2
Overhead costs (identified by department)				
Factory supplies used	$32,000	$53,600	$169,600	$344,000
Indirect labor	$64,800	$96,000	$216,000	$960,000
Square feet of building floor space used	4,800	7,200	12,000	24,000
Assessed value of equipment used	$14,000	$42,000	$ 84,000	$140,000
Cubic yards of factory space used			88,000	132,000
Machine hours			51,200	204,800
Direct labor			$125,000	$250,000

Building depreciation of $128,000 is allocated on the basis of square feet of floor space. Personal property taxes of $48,000 are allocated on the basis of assessed values of equipment used. Costs for Service Departments 1 and 2 are allocated to production departments on the basis of cubic yards of factory space and machine hours, respectively.

REQUIRED

(a) Prepare an overhead distribution worksheet similar to Exhibit 23–9.

(b) Compute the factory overhead rates for Production Departments 1 and 2 using machine hours and direct labor costs, respectively, for allocation bases.

Allocating joint product costs

23–33 The Paxton Company produces joint products A and B and byproduct B-1 from a common material and manufacturing process involving sequential processing departments for blending and distilling. After distilling, the three products are separable and considered finished goods.

Because of the nature of the operation, no beginning or ending work in process inventories exist. For the current period, charges to Work in Process—Distilling Department were

Transferred in from Blending Department	$ 87,400
Direct labor	22,400
Factory overhead	35,400
	$145,200

REQUIRED

Assume that the following quantities and sales prices are available when the products are separable:

Product	Quantity (pounds)	Unit Price
A	4,000	$ 7.00
B	6,000	12.00
B-1	1,000	2.00*

*Special freight charges of $400 are incurred in selling product B-1 for this price.

(a) Allocate the joint product costs to each joint product on the basis of relative sales value.

(b) Prepare journal entries to record the current period's product completion in and transfer from the Distilling Department to Finished Goods Inventory.

ALTERNATE PROBLEMS

Calculate equivalent units and costs; journal entries

23–27A Chandler, Inc., produces a shoe polish in two sequential processes designated Phase I and Phase II. Chandler shut down during August, when all employees took their annual vacations. Production began again on September 1. The following operating data apply to September:

	Phase I	Phase II
Units started in process	61,000	
Units transferred in from Phase I		54,000
Units in ending work in process (on the average, 30% processed)	7,000	14,000
Costs charged to departments:		
Direct material	$ 42,075	$ 77,350
Direct labor	118,520	131,480
Factory overhead	63,805	56,370

Assume all manufacturing costs are incurred evenly throughout each process and that three-fourths of September production was sold on account at a price equal to 140% of its cost.

REQUIRED

(a) Briefly explain the September 30 status of the units started in process during September.
(b) For each department, prepare a cost per equivalent unit report for September.
(c) Prepare journal entries to record the completion and transfer of products from each department and the sale of three-fourths of September's production.

Calculate units, costs, and transferred costs

23–28A Shaw Manufacturing, Inc., operates a plant that produces its own regionally marketed Shaw Salad Dressing. The dressing is produced in two processes, blending and bottling. In the Blending Department, all materials are added at the start of the process, and labor and overhead are incurred evenly throughout the process. The Work in Process—Blending Department account for January follows:

Work in Process—Blending Department

January 1 Inventory (3,000 gallons, 75% complete)	32,700	Transferred to Bottling Department (40,500 gallons)	______
January charges:			
Direct material (45,000 gallons)	369,000		
Direct labor	117,240		
Factory overhead	75,135		
January 31 Inventory (______ gallons, 60% complete)	______		

REQUIRED

Calculate the following amounts for the Blending Department:

(a) Number of units in the January 31 inventory.
(b) Equivalent units for materials cost and conversion cost.
(c) January cost per equivalent unit for conversion.
(d) Cost of the units transferred to the Bottling Department.
(e) Cost of the incomplete units in the January 31 inventory.

Calculate units, costs, and transferred costs

23–29A The Golden Company processes a scouring powder through a Compounding Department and a Packaging Department. In the Packaging Department, costs of direct material, direct labor, and factory overhead are incurred evenly throughout the process. Costs charged to the Packaging Department in October were:

Inventory, October 1 (10,000 units, 25% complete)	$ 20,250
Transferred in from Compounding Department (95,000 units)	161,500
Direct material	66,500
Direct labor	35,000
Factory overhead	22,000
	$305,250

At October 31, 15,000 units were in process, 50% completed.

REQUIRED
Calculate the following for the Packaging Department:
(a) Equivalent units during October.
(b) Costs per equivalent unit.
(c) Total cost of units transferred to Finished Goods Inventory.
(d) Inventory cost at October 31.

Journal entries with supporting calculations

23–30A Bingham Laboratories, Inc., produces one of its products in two successive departments. All materials are added at the beginning of the process in Department 1; no materials are used in Department 2. Conversion costs are incurred evenly in both departments. August 1 inventories are as follows:

Materials Inventory	$10,000
Work in Process—Department 1 (6,000 units, 25% complete)	12,250
Work in Process—Department 2	–0–
Finished Goods Inventory (4,000 units @ $6.60)	26,400

During August, the following transactions occurred:
(1) Purchased materials on account, $34,000.
(2) Placed 16,000 units of materials at $2.50 per unit into process in Department 1.
(3) Distributed total payroll costs—$56,550 of direct labor to Department 1, $29,920 of direct labor to Department 2, and $13,400 of indirect labor to Factory Overhead.
(4) Incurred other actual factory overhead costs, $19,400. (Credit Other Accounts.)
(5) Applied overhead to the two processing departments: Department 1, $11,700, Department 2, $7,480.
(6) Transferred 20,000 completed units from Department 1 to Department 2. The 2,000 units remaining in Department 1 were 50% completed with respect to conversion costs.
(7) Transferred 15,000 completed units from Department 2 to Finished Goods Inventory. The 5,000 units remaining in Department 2 were 40% completed with respect to conversion costs.
(8) Sold 9,000 units on account at $14 per unit. The company uses FIFO inventory costing.

REQUIRED
(a) Record the August transactions in general journal form.
(b) State the balances remaining in Materials Inventory, in each Work in Process account, and in Finished Goods Inventory.

Production cost report

23–31A Delta Manufacturing Corporation produces a dandruff shampoo in three consecutive processes. The costs of Department 2 for June were as follows:

Cost from Department 1		$43,200
Costs added in Department 2:		
Direct material	$15,000	
Direct labor	38,400	
Factory overhead	11,100	64,500

Department 2 had no June 1 inventory, but it handled the following units during June:

Units transferred in from Department 1	18,000
Units transferred to Department 3	12,000
Units in process, June 30	6,000

Of the units in process on June 30, one-half were 75% complete and one-half were 25% complete. Both materials and conversion costs occur evenly throughout the process in Department 2.

REQUIRED
Prepare the production cost report for Department 2 for June.

BUSINESS DECISION PROBLEM

Tracy Corporation makes a new high-tech adhesive in a single process that blends and bottles the product, which currently sells for $16 per gallon. Market demand for the product seems good, but management is not satisfied with the product's seemingly low profit margin and has sought your advice.

Because of its concern, management has allocated a $45,000 fund for a program of product promotion or cost reduction, or both. Members of the firm's controller's office and marketing staff have identified the following three possible plans:

(1) Plan A—Devote all funds to product promotion, which allows all costs and the sales volume to remain the same, but permits a $2 per gallon sales price increase.

(2) Plan B—Spend $30,000 on product promotion and $15,000 on cost reduction techniques, which maintains sales volume, permits a price increase of $1 per gallon, and reduces direct labor costs by 20% per gallon.

(3) Plan C—Devote all funds to cost reduction efforts. Sales volume and price do not change. For each gallon produced, however, direct material cost decreases 5%, direct labor cost decreases 30%, and factory overhead decreases 15%.

The controller's office also provides you with the following operating data for a typical period (all materials are added initially; conversion costs occur evenly throughout the process):

Beginning work in process (4,500 gallons, 60% processed)	$ 50,400
Units started in process (33,000 gallons)	
Ending work in process (7,500 gallons, 60% processed)	
Costs charged to the department:	
Direct material	214,500
Direct labor	174,264
Factory overhead	86,496
	$525,660

Using the data from this representative production period, analyze the apparent relative benefits derived from each plan and make a recommendation supported by relevant calculations. Assume sales will equal units completed.

ANSWERS TO SELF-TEST QUESTIONS

1. (c) 2. (b) 3. (d) 4. (d) 5. (b)

COMPREHENSIVE PROBLEM—PART 5

The managerial accounting system used by a firm of certified public accountants (CPAs) incorporates many of the aspects of job order costing used by manufacturing firms.

(A) Each client is accounted for as a separate job.

(B) The individual client accounts collectively represent the detailed subsidiary ledger for the work in process inventory.

(C) A variation of normal product costing is typically used to accumulate product cost (plus gross profit) by client.

- **(1)** Items such as postage, photocopies, and travel expense are charged to client accounts as direct material.
- **(2)** The time spent by the professional accountants and the clerical staff working on clients' projects is charged to client accounts as direct labor. Direct labor is the first component of the predetermined billing rates.
- **(3)** Other expenses such as rent, utilities, management, training, and depreciation are charged to client accounts as overhead. Overhead is the second component of the predetermined billing rates.
- **(4)** Gross profit is also charged to client accounts. Gross profit is the third component of the predetermined billing rates.

The managerial accounting system for a CPA firm is often known as the Client Accounting System, which consists of two major subsystems—Client Work In Process and Client Accounts Receivable.

JONES & STRATFORD, CPAs The basic input record for Client Work In Process is the Employee Timesheet. Two employees of Jones and Stratford, CPAs, have completed their time sheets for March 20, 19XX, as follows:

Employee name: Mary J. Albertson — **Employee number:** 109

Billable Time				Nonbillable Time		
Date	**Client**	**Description**	**Hours**	**Date**	**Description**	**Hours**
3–20	Clark	Meeting with Banker	1.5	3–20	Training	2.0
3–20	Jensen	Tax return	3.0			
3–20	Martin	Projection	2.0			

Employee name: Jonathon Frank **Employee number:** 216

Billable Time				Nonbillable Time		
Date	**Client**	**Description**	**Hours**	**Date**	**Description**	**Hours**
3–20	Jensen	Tax return	1.0	3–20	Meeting	2.5
3–20	Martin	Tax return	4.0			
3–20	Martin	Meeting to explain taxes	1.5			

One of these forms is completed by each professional accountant and clerical employee of the CPA firm. The left side of the form accumulates time that will be billable to clients (direct labor) while the right side of the form accumulates the time that will not be billable to clients (overhead).

Billable time is posted to Client Work In Process using the time recorded on the Employee Timesheets and the predetermined billing rates for the appropriate employees. The amount posted represents direct labor, overhead, and gross profit.

REQUIRED

(a) Calculate the billing rates for Mary and Jonathon, using the formula that billing rate equals 2.5 times rate of pay. Mary is paid $12 per hour while Jonathon is paid $16 per hour.

(b) Post the time for clients Clark, Jensen, and Martin in the Client Work In Process subsidiary ledger accounts, which have the following column headings—Date, Employee Number, Hours, Billable Amount, Amount Billed, and Balance to be Billed.

(c) Post the expenses specifically incurred for the clients in the Client Work In Process subsidiary ledger accounts, using March 31 as the date and employee number 900 to identify the item as an expense. The expenses are: Clark = $28, Jensen = $100, and Martin = $45.

MONTHLY BILLING At the end of each month, the management of the CPA firm will typically review the Balance to Be Billed for each client and determine whether to bill the client and how much to bill. The amount billed is posted in the Amount Billed column and deducted from the Balance to Be Billed column of the Client Work In Process subsidiary ledger accounts. The amount is also set up in the Client Accounts Receivable subsidiary ledger accounts.

(d) Post the March 31 amount billed in the Client Work In Process subsidiary ledger accounts, assuming that Clark and Martin were billed for their entire balances while the billing for Jensen was deferred until the next month.

(e) Prepare general journal entries to reflect the transactions described in (b), (c), and (d) above and payment in full by Clark on April 10, 19XX. Assume Jones & Stratford uses accrual accounting and has general ledger control accounts for Client Work In Process and Client Accounts Receivable.

The balance of the general ledger control account for Client Work In Process will equal the sum of the individual Client Work In Process account balances, while the balance of the general ledger control account for Client Accounts Receivable will equal the sum of the individual Client Accounts Receivable account balances. There is no account equivalent to finished goods.

Many managerial reports can be prepared from the Work In Process and Accounts Receivable files, including (1) aging of accounts receivable, (2) aging of balance to be billed, (3) percent of total time that is billable with detail by employee, and (4) time spent on each client during the year with detail by employee. The Client Accounting System not only keeps track of amounts billable to and collectible from each client but also provides the management of the CPA firm with valuable information about the firm's practice.

Part Six

Planning, Control, and Decision Making

24

Cost–Volume–Profit Relationships

Chapter Objectives

- Develop an understanding of how specific types of costs change in response to volume changes.
- Define the concept of relevant range.
- Outline the approach to developing cost formulas.
- Present a discussion of and formulas for calculating the break-even point.
- Define contribution margin and contribution margin ratio.
- Discuss approaches to planning net income using cost–volume–profit analyses.

We lose money on every sale—but make it up on volume.

ANONYMOUS

Management must study a number of factors when planning the future course for an organization. One of the most important factors is the relationship of sales (revenue), costs (expenses), and profit (net income). Cost–volume–profit analysis is used to study this relationship.

Cost–volume–profit analysis is appropriately used by for-profit organizations as well as not-for-profit organizations. The latter type of organization uses the analysis with a target profit of zero. All of the relationships studied in the analysis are equally valid for both types of organizations.

COST BEHAVIOR ANALYSIS

Each specific cost incurred by an organization may be affected differently by changes in the volume of business activity. Some costs will increase proportionately as volume increases, some costs will change disproportionately, and some costs will remain the same. Other factors besides volume can also cause changes in specific costs—an increase in the assessment rate, for example, can increase property tax expense, while a decrease in electricity rates can decrease utility expense. These types of changes, however, are not typically caused by fluctuation in volume of business activity.

The Activity Base

For meaningful managerial analysis, costs must be related to some measure of volume of business activity. In a manufacturing operation, such measures include units of product, direct labor hours, machine hours, and percent of capacity. The cost analyst must consider the use of the analysis when selecting the most relevant and useful activity base to which costs can be related. For example, if management uses the analysis for control purposes and for establishing reponsibility for costs, the analyst selects measures that are meaningful to those responsible for incurring costs. We may use several bases, depending on the objectives of the analysis.

Cost–Volume Graphs

One of the most useful analytic tools for relating cost changes to volume changes is the cost–volume graph. Exhibits 24–1 and 24–2 are examples of cost–volume graphs. In these two exhibits, costs (in thousands of dollars) are measured on the vertical axis, and business volume (in thousands of units) is measured on the horizontal axis. Point A in Exhibit 24–1 shows that at a volume level of 30,000

EXHIBIT 24–1
Graphic Presentation of Cost–Volume Relationships

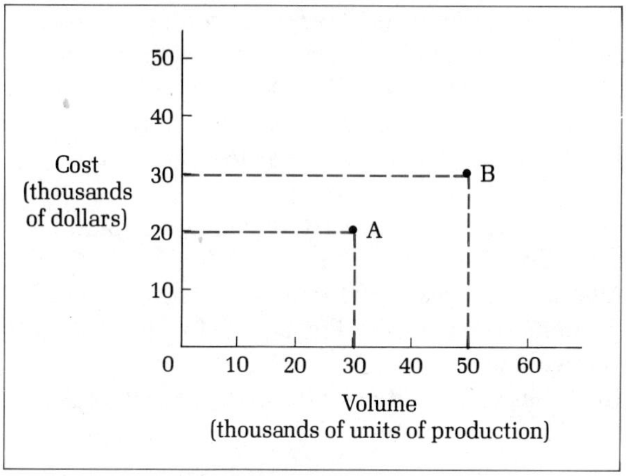

EXHIBIT 24–2
Estimation of Cost–Volume Relationships from Known Data

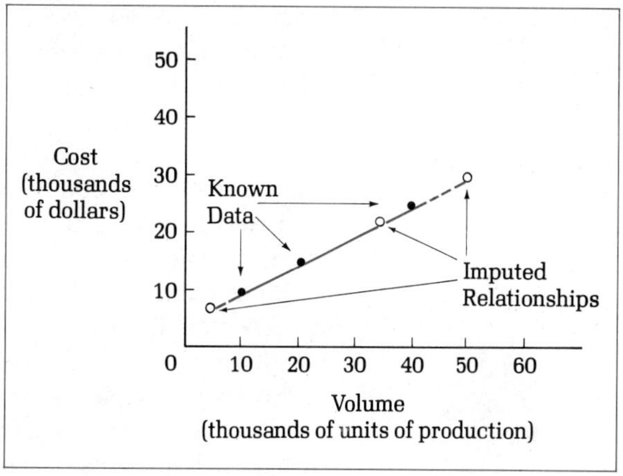

units the associated cost is $20,000. Similarly, point B in Exhibit 24–1 represents a cost of $30,000 for a volume level of 50,000 units.

Cost–volume graphs are particularly valuable when available cost–volume data are plotted on the same graph and other cost–volume relationships are estimated by fitting a line to the known points. In Exhibit 24–2, for example, we use three known data points (a greater number of known data points should be used to develop a reliable graph). The known data points, represented by solid points, are:

Volume (units)	Cost (dollars)
10,000	10,000
20,000	15,000
40,000	25,000

By connecting the known data points with a straight line, we may impute the costs associated with other levels of volume. For example, the open points indicate that for volumes of 5,000, 35,000, and 50,000 units, the related costs would be $7,500, $22,500, and $30,000, respectively. Some important limitations to the validity of this type of imputed cost–volume relationship are discussed later in the chapter.

Classifications of Cost Behavior Patterns

For purposes of analyzing their behavior patterns, costs are usually classified as *variable, fixed,* or *semivariable.* However, the classification of costs into these distinct groups is seldom a simple matter.

Despite the difficulties of classification, the study of approximate cost behavior patterns can aid in planning and analyzing operations. Let us examine the ways in which cost–volume graphs vary among the three cost classifications.

Variable costs change proportionately with changes in the volume of activity. Direct material cost and direct labor cost, for example, are variable costs.

Exhibit 24–3 is a typical variable cost graph. As illustrated here, a purely variable cost pattern always passes through the origin, because zero cost is associated with zero volume. Also, because variable costs respond in direct proportion to changes in volume, a variable cost line always slopes upward to the right. The steepness of the slope depends on the amount of cost associated with each unit of volume; the greater the unit cost the steeper the slope. In Exhibit 24–3, volume is measured in direct labor hours, and the total variable dollar cost is twice as great at 40,000 hours as at 20,000 hours, as expected.

Fixed costs do not change when the volume of activity changes. Examples are depreciation on buildings and property taxes.

Since fixed costs do not respond to changes in volume, they are represented by horizontal lines on a cost–volume graph. In Exhibit 24–4, fixed costs are $80,000 regardless of the volume level considered.

Semivariable costs—sometimes called *mixed costs*—can be described analytically as having both fixed and variable components. A semivariable cost changes linearly with changes in activity, but is some positive amount at zero activity, as shown in Exhibit 24–5. Changes in total semivariable costs are therefore not proportional to changes in operating volume.

As an example of a semivariable cost, consider a firm's utility expense. Even if the firm shuts down production for one period, it must pay a minimum amount for utilities. When production resumes, the costs of heat, light, and power increase as production increases.

For purposes of cost analysis, a semivariable cost is divided into its fixed and variable components. We accomplish this by any one of several approaches that vary in their degree of sophistication. One simple method entails plotting on a graph the amount of cost experienced at several levels of volume. If cost

EXHIBIT 24–3
Variable Cost Pattern

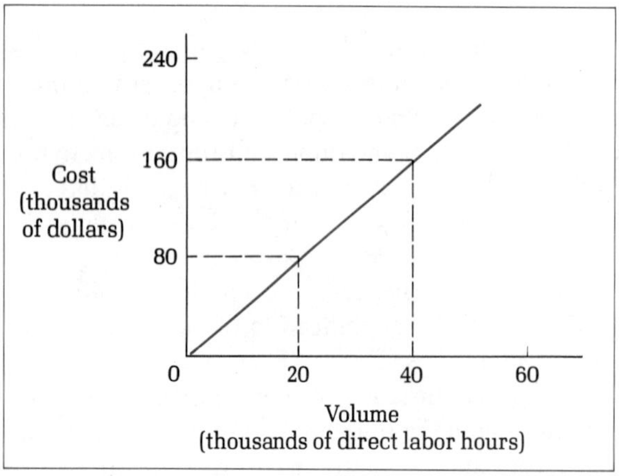

EXHIBIT 24–4
Fixed Cost Pattern

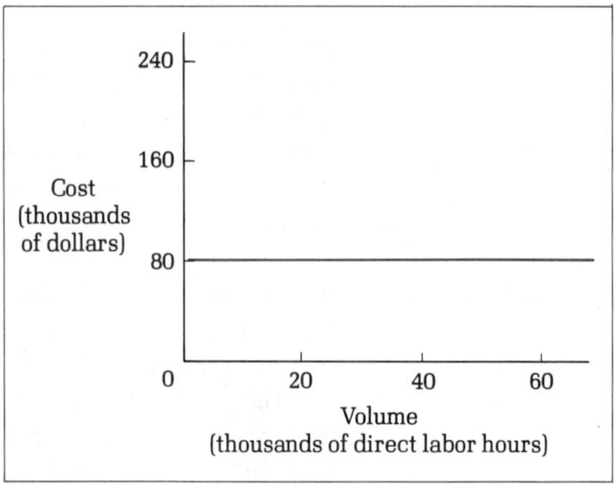

EXHIBIT 24–5
Semivariable Cost Pattern

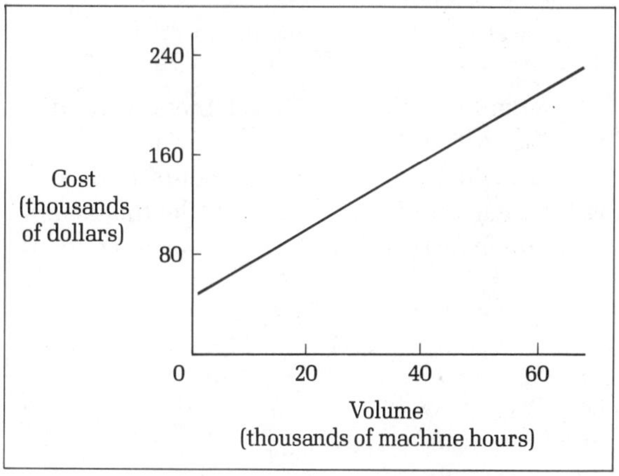

EXHIBIT 24–6
Analysis of Semivariable Cost

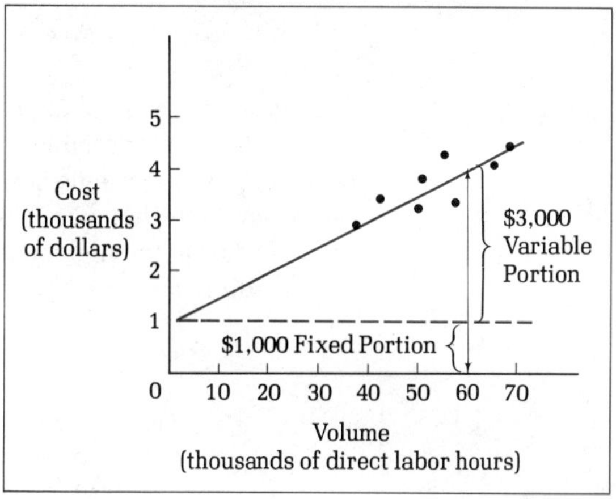

behavior in actual situations were perfectly correlated, the observations (points) would form a straight line. More realistically, however, we expect only a discernible pattern as shown in Exhibit 24–6.

The line in Exhibit 24–6 has been subjectively determined to approximate the pattern of data points. Extending this line to the vertical axis indicates a $1,000 fixed portion. We subtract this $1,000 fixed cost from the total $4,000 cost at 60,000 direct labor hours to find a total variable portion of $3,000. Therefore, the rate of variation is $3,000/60,000, or 5 cents, per direct labor hour. Hence, we could describe this semivariable cost as $1,000 plus 5 cents per direct labor hour.

We can obtain a better approximation by fitting the line to the cost observation pattern (data points) by the method of least squares. That technique, which is beyond the scope of this text, is illustrated in most introductory statistics texts.

High–Low Method

When too few cost observations are available to plot a graph, or when the analyst wishes to avoid fitting lines to data, the **high–low** method is sometimes used to approximate the position and slope of the cost line. This relatively simple method compares costs at the highest and lowest levels of activity for which representative cost data are available. The variable cost per activity unit (here, per direct labor hour) is determined by dividing the difference in costs at these two levels by the difference in activity. The fixed element of cost is then isolated by multiplying the variable cost per unit by either the top or bottom level of activity and then subtracting the resulting product from the total cost at the selected activity level.

For example, assume that the lowest and highest levels of activity are 40,000 and 60,000 direct labor hours, respectively, and that total costs for these two levels are shown below:

	Level of Activity	Total Cost
High	60,000 direct labor hours	$4,200
Low	40,000 direct labor hours	3,000
Difference	20,000 (increase)	$1,200 (increase)

Because an increase of 20,000 direct labor hours causes a $1,200 increase in total cost (and only the variable portion of the cost could increase), the variable portion of the total semivariable cost must be $1,200/20,000 direct labor hours, or 6 cents per direct labor hour. Subtracting the total variable portion from the total semivariable cost at the high and low activity levels gives us the fixed portion of total cost as follows:

	Volume Levels	
	Low	High
Total semivariable cost	$3,000	$4,200
Less variable portions:		
$0.06 × 40,000 direct labor hours	2,400	
$0.06 × 60,000 direct labor hours		3,600
Fixed portion of total cost	$ 600	$ 600

The high–low analysis tells us that any volume level has $600 of fixed cost plus a variable portion of 6 cents per direct labor hour, which can be formulated as

$$\text{Total Cost} = \$600 + (\$0.06 \times \text{Direct Labor Hours})$$

In other words, we can now easily compute the total cost for varying levels of direct labor hours. Obviously, if either the high or low value used in this method is not representative of the actual cost behavior, the resulting cost formula is inexact.

Relevant Range

The foregoing illustrations of cost behavior are oversimplified because they portray linear cost behavior over the entire range of possible activity. Actually, plotting costs against volume may not always produce a single straight line. For example, certain costs may increase abruptly at intervals in a "step" pattern; others may exhibit a curvilinear pattern when plotted over a wide range of activity. Examples of these cost patterns are shown graphically in Exhibit 24–7.

Clearly, an assumption of linear costs over the entire scale on either axis in these two cases causes some degree of error. The significance of this error is often minimized by the fact that many of the firm's decisions involve relatively small changes in volume around some relevant range of activity. The actual cost pattern at extremely low- or high- volume levels is not relevant to the firm's decisions. The cost pattern need only be reasonably linear within the relevant range of activity.

Total Versus Per-unit Costs

The cost–volume relationships for fixed cost, variable cost, and semivariable cost typically remain the same for only one range of activity and for only one time period (frequently one year). Fixed, variable, and semivariable costs are assumed to react only to changes in volume within the relevant range during the given

EXHIBIT 24–7
Illustrations of Relevant Ranges

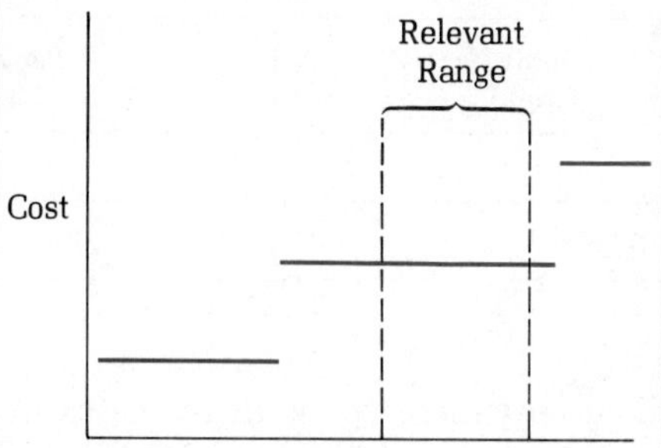

Step Cost

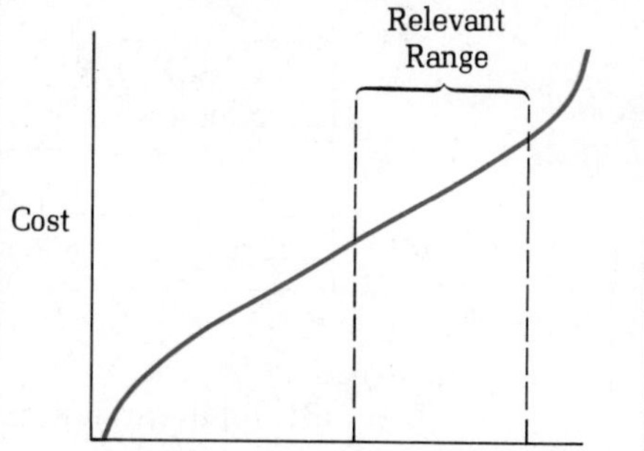

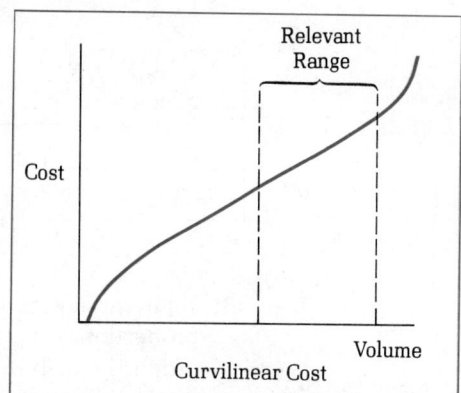

Curvilinear Cost

time period. The cost relationships, however, may change when moving to a different range of activity or a different time period. For example, a higher level of activity (above the current relevant range) could require a higher level of supervisory personnel, which would result in a higher level of fixed salary expense. Similarly, next year could have a higher fixed property tax expense due to a higher property tax assessment rate.

It is important for many forms of managerial analysis to fully understand the behavior patterns of total fixed and variable costs and per-unit fixed and variable costs. Exhibit 24–8 presents an example of total and per-unit cost behavior for a relevant range of 200 to 1,000 units.

An analysis of Exhibit 24–8 reveals that:

(1) Total variable cost increases proportionately with increases in volume, while per-unit variable cost remains constant.

(2) Total fixed cost remains constant with increases in volume, while per-unit fixed cost decreases proportionately.

EXHIBIT 24–8
Analysis of Total and Per-unit Costs

Activity Volume	Variable Cost ($1.00 per unit)		Fixed Cost ($600 per month)		Total Cost ($600 + $1.00 per unit)	
Units	**Total**	**Per-unit**	**Total**	**Per-unit**	**Total**	**Per-unit**
200	$ 200	$1.00	$600	$3.00	$ 800	$4.00
600	600	1.00	600	1.00	1,200	2.00
1,000	$1,000	1.00	600	0.60	1,600	1.60

EXHIBIT 24–9
Patterns of Total and Per-unit Costs as Volume Increases

Cost Category	Total Costs	Per-unit Costs
Variable	Increase proportionately	Remain constant
Fixed	Remain constant	Decrease proportionately

(3) Total variable plus fixed cost increases with increases in volume (but not proportionately), while per-unit variable plus fixed cost decreases (but not proportionately).

These patterns hold true for all feasible relevant ranges and are summarized in Exhibit 24–9.

Total fixed costs and per-unit variable costs are *stable* cost expressions, because they remain constant as volume is changed. Per-unit fixed costs and total variable costs are *unstable* cost expressions because they are valid at only one volume level. In the following section, we show how the stable forms of cost expressions—*total* fixed cost and *per-unit* variable cost—are incorporated in a general formula for total cost that is valid over a wide range of operating volumes.

Planning Total Costs

Budgeting for a business firm, which is treated in detail in Chapter 26, is usually a financial plan that reflects anticipated or planned amounts of such items as revenue, costs, cash balances, and net income. Underlying most aspects of budgeting is some assumed volume of activity or sales, as well as an analysis of the total cost incurred for that level of operation.

As stated previously, all costs are variable, semivariable, or fixed. For most cost analyses, semivariable costs are separated into their two components, fixed and variable, with the variable component added to the variable costs and the fixed component added to the fixed costs. The following formula and example use this approach.

For an example, we assume that total fixed cost is \$10,000, semivariable cost has a fixed portion of \$5,000 and a variable portion of \$2 per unit, and that variable costs are \$4 per unit. The formulation for planning or budgeting a total cost, using the stable forms of cost expression, is:

$$\text{Total Cost} = \text{Total Fixed Cost} + \left(\begin{array}{c}\text{Variable}\\ \text{Cost}\\ \text{per Unit}\end{array} \times \text{Volume}\right)$$

In our example:

$$\text{Total cost} = \$15{,}000 + (\$6 \times \text{Volume})$$

Therefore, at zero volume, total cost is $15,000, or the total of all fixed costs. At 5,000 units of volume, total cost is $45,000, or [$15,000 + ($6 × 5,000)]. At 10,000 units of volume, total cost is $75,000, or [$15,000 + ($6 × 10,000)]. Notice that when volume doubles from 5,000 to 10,000 units, total cost responds, but less than proportionately.

By using this formula, a firm can forecast costs at different levels of activity. In Exhibit 24–10, each type of cost behavior pattern is considered in the formula. The dollar amounts have been chosen for ease of manipulation, and the 10,000-unit activity level is incorporated for illustrative purposes.

We see from Exhibit 24–10 that by combining the various cost factors into the aggregate formula, we determine expected costs not only at the 10,000-unit level but also at other levels simply by inserting the appropriate volume figure in the final formula. For example, total planned cost at 8,000 units is [$15,000 + ($6 × 8,000) = $63,000]; at 12,000 units, it is [$15,000 + ($6 × 12,000) = $87,000].

A word of caution is appropriate here. Because the cost formula relies so heavily on cost analysis, all the limitations of the latter (assumed linearity, relevant ranges, and so on) apply. Also, we repeat, analyzing many costs into fixed and variable components is often quite complex and inexact. All these limitations to some degree affect the potential contribution of managerial accounting. In many cases, the analytical approach presented here is the best available.

EXHIBIT 24–10
Cost Factors in a Formula for Total Cost at 10,000 Units of Volume

Type of Cost	Total Cost	=	Total Fixed Cost	+	(Variable Cost per Unit	×	Volume)
Direct Material (variable)	$20,000	=			($2.00	×	10,000 units)
Direct Labor (variable)	25,000	=			(2.50	×	10,000 units)
Factory Overhead:							
Factory Supplies (variable)	10,000	=			(1.00	×	10,000 units)
Property Taxes (fixed)	4,000	=	$ 4,000				
Maintenance (semivariable)	7,000	=	5,000	+	(0.20	×	10,000 units)
Selling and Administrative Expense (semivariable)	9,000	=	6,000	+	(0.30	×	10,000 units)
Total Cost	$75,000	=	$15,000	+	($6.00	×	10,000 units)
Aggregate Formula:	Total Cost	=	$15,000	+	($6.00	×	10,000 units)

COST–VOLUME–PROFIT ANALYSIS

For purposes of illustration, we use the following data for Johnson Company throughout the next several sections.

Johnson Company
Condensed Income Statement

Sales (10,000 units @ $20)		$200,000
Costs:		
Variable Cost (10,000 units @ $12)	$120,000	
Total Fixed Cost	60,000	
Total Cost		180,000
Net Income		$ 20,000

This information assumes that any semivariable costs have been divided into their fixed and variable components and combined with the fixed and variable cost elements. We now examine some of the uses of this information.

Break-even Analysis

Management frequently wants to know the level of revenue or number of units of sales at which there is no net income or loss. The level at which total revenue equals total cost is the **break-even point.** Typically it is expressed in dollars or in units of sales. Let us calculate Johnson Company's break-even point, using the above condensed income statement data.

THE BREAK-EVEN CHART For the break-even chart we use the same basic graph employed earlier to explain and portray cost behavior patterns. In Exhibit 24–11 the vertical axis measures both total revenue and total cost. As before, volume is measured along the horizontal axis. For the Johnson Company, the activity base is units of product. Total revenue and total cost are measured in thousands of dollars along the vertical axis.

With zero revenue for zero sales, the graph of total revenue always passes through the origin, which is one point on the line. In general, then, we draw the total revenue line by connecting the origin with any other point that represents total revenue for some volume amount. For Johnson Company, total revenue for 10,000 units is $200,000—point A in Exhibit 24–11. To construct the total revenue line, we simply draw a straight line from the origin to point A and extend it beyond point A.

We now construct the total cost line in the same manner. With fixed costs of $60,000, the total cost line must intersect the vertical axis at $60,000. For Johnson Company, we are given total cost of $180,000 for 10,000 units. From this we can plot point B and draw the total cost line for Johnson Company as shown in Exhibit 24–11.

Extending the dashed lines as indicated from the point of intersection of the two graphed lines to the two axes, we find Johnson Company's break-even point

EXHIBIT 24–11
Break-even Chart

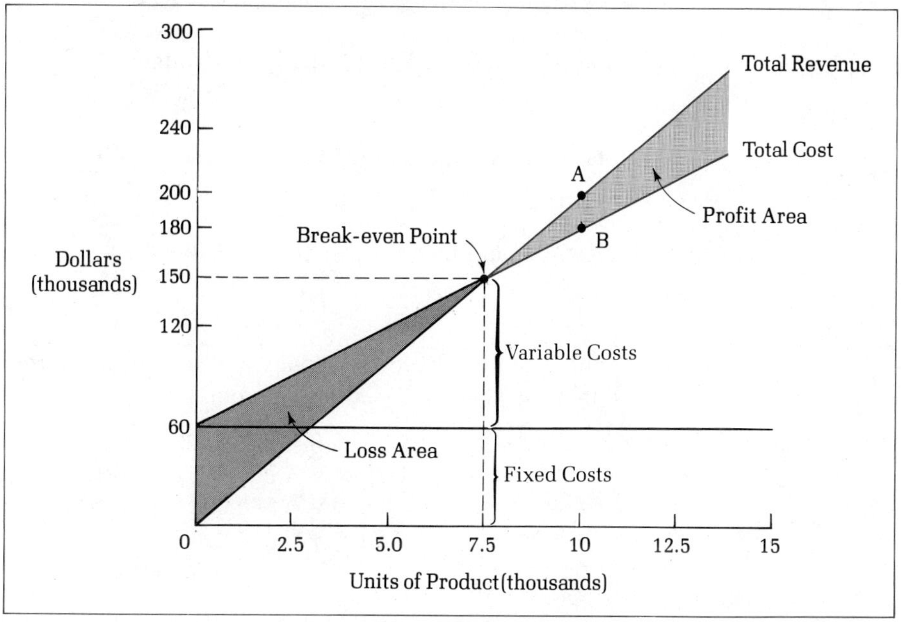

(where total revenue equals total cost) to be 7,500 units of production, or $150,000 of total sales revenue. Note that all points lying below the break-even point indicate a loss, and points above the break-even level represent profit. The profit and loss areas are shaded on our graph. The amount of profit or loss at any volume level is determined by measuring the vertical distance between the total cost and total revenue lines. Clearly, a profit is indicated when the total revenue line is above the total cost line, and a loss is indicated when the reverse is true.

ASSUMPTIONS IN BREAK-EVEN ANALYSIS In our construction of a break-even chart, we assumed linear relationships over a wide range of activity. This approach implies that:

(1) Total fixed cost and variable cost per unit are constant over the entire range of analysis.
(2) Selling price per unit remains the same regardless of the volume of sales.
(3) When more than one product is involved and sales volume varies, each product's percent of total sales (sales mix) does not change.

Even though these assumptions limit the usefulness of break-even analysis somewhat, it is still a convenient method of measuring the effect of changes in sales, costs, volumes, and profits.

BREAK-EVEN FORMULAS We will use the following basic formulas throughout our discussion of break-even analysis to reflect the basic relationship that the break-even point is that point where total revenue equals total cost:

(1) Sales = Unit Sales Price × Units of Volume

$$S = USP \times V$$

(2) Total Variable Cost = Unit Variable Cost × Units of Volume

$$VC = UVC \times V$$

(3) Sales = Total Fixed Cost + Total Variable Cost

$$S = FC + VC$$

Using the data for Johnson Company and the formulas from above, we can calculate Johnson Company's break-even point:

$$\begin{aligned} S &= FC + VC \\ USP \times V &= FC + (UVC \times V) \\ \$20 \times V &= \$60{,}000 + (\$12 \times V) \\ \$8 \times V &= \$60{,}000 \\ V &= 7{,}500 \text{ units} \end{aligned}$$

$$7{,}500 \text{ units} \times \$20 = \$150{,}000$$

These answers, 7,500 units and $150,000, agree with the graphic solutions, which they should.

CONTRIBUTION MARGIN Since variable costs change proportionately with changes in revenue, each time additional revenue is generated, additional variable cost is also generated. The difference between the revenue generated and the variable cost generated is called **contribution margin.** The formula for calculating contribution margin is:

(4) Contribution Margin = Sales − Variable Cost

$$CM = S - VC$$

The formula for calculating unit contribution margin (contribution margin per unit) is similar:

(5) Unit Contribution Margin = Unit Sales Price − Unit Variable Cost

$$UCM = USP - UVC$$

Using the data for Johnson Company, we can calculate unit contribution margin:

$$\begin{aligned} UCM &= USP - UVC \\ UCM &= \$20 - \$12 = \$8 \end{aligned}$$

CONTRIBUTION MARGIN RATIO A related concept that is used in break-even analysis is **contribution margin ratio,** which is the ratio of contribution margin to sales. The formula to calculate contribution margin ratio can use either total amounts or per-unit amounts:

$$\textbf{(6)}\ \text{Contribution Margin Ratio} = \frac{\text{Contribution Margin}}{\text{Sales}}$$

$$\text{CMR} = \text{CM/S}$$

or

$$\textbf{(7)}\ \text{Contribution Margin Ratio} = \frac{\text{Unit Contribution Margin}}{\text{Unit Sales Price}}$$

$$\text{CMR} = \text{UCM/USP}$$

Using the data for Johnson Company:

$$\text{CMR} = \text{UCM/USP}$$
$$\text{CMR} = \$8/\$20 = 0.4$$

ALTERNATE BREAK-EVEN FORMULAS There are two alternate break-even formulas which can be used to calculate the break-even point either in units or in dollars:

$$\textbf{(8)}\ \begin{matrix}\text{Break-even Volume}\\ \text{(in units)}\end{matrix} = \frac{\text{Total Fixed Costs}}{\text{Unit Contribution Margin}}$$

$$\text{BEV} = \text{FC/UCM}$$

$$\textbf{(9)}\ \begin{matrix}\text{Break-even Sales}\\ \text{(in dollars)}\end{matrix} = \frac{\text{Total Fixed Costs}}{\text{Contribution Margin Ratio}}$$

$$\text{BES} = \text{FC/CMR}$$

Using the data for Johnson Company, we can calculate the break-even point using both formulas:

Using formula (8):

$$\text{BEV} = \text{FC/UCM}$$
$$\text{BEV} = \$60{,}000/\$8 = 7{,}500 \text{ units}$$

Using formula (9):

$$\text{BES} = \text{FC/CMR}$$
$$\text{BES} = \$60{,}000/0.4 = \$150{,}000$$

The results of either formula can be translated to the results of the other formula as follows:

$$7{,}500 \text{ units} \times \$20 \text{ per unit} = \$150{,}000$$
$$\$150{,}000/\$20 \text{ per unit} = 7{,}500 \text{ units}$$

The results of any of the break-even formulas can be verified by placing the results in income statement format and determining that net income does equal zero.

Planning Net Income

Business firms use a more generalized form of break-even analysis when they are analyzing cost–volume–profit relationships. Rather than make the calculations for break-even, they use formulas which include a desired profit. These formulas are similar to the break-even formulas:

(10) Desired Sales = Fixed Cost + Variable Cost + Desired Net Income Before Income Tax

$$S = FC + VC + NIBT$$

(11) $\text{Desired Volume} = \dfrac{\text{Fixed Cost + Desired Net Income Before Income Tax}}{\text{Unit Contribution Margin}}$

$$V = \frac{FC + NIBT}{UCM}$$

(12) $\text{Desired Sales} = \dfrac{\text{Fixed Cost + Desired Net Income Before Income Tax}}{\text{Contribution Margin Ratio}}$

$$S = \frac{FC + NIBT}{CMR}$$

Assume that Johnson Company wants to attain a Net Income Before Taxes of $24,000. Using the formulas above, we make the following calculations:

Using formula (10):

$$\begin{aligned} S &= FC + VC + NIBT \\ S &= \$60{,}000 + VC + \$24{,}000 \\ \$20 \times V &= \$60{,}000 + (\$12 \times V) + \$24{,}000 \\ \$8 \times V &= \$84{,}000 \\ V &= 10{,}500 \text{ units} \end{aligned}$$

Using formula (11):

$$V = \frac{FC + NIBT}{UCM}$$

$$V = \frac{\$60{,}000 + \$24{,}000}{\$8}$$

$$V = 10{,}500 \text{ units}$$

Using formula (12):

$$V = \frac{FC + NIBT}{CMR}$$

$$V = \frac{\$60{,}000 + \$24{,}000}{0.4}$$

$$V = \$210{,}000$$

Again, the results can be translated using the unit sales price:

$$10{,}500 \text{ units} \times \$20 \text{ per unit} = \$210{,}000$$
$$\$210{,}000/\$20 \text{ per unit} = 10{,}500 \text{ units}$$

Effect of Income Taxes

A company's management might want to develop plans using Net Income (after tax) rather than Net Income Before Tax. In this case, Net Income must be converted to Net Income Before Tax so the formulas can be used:

(13) $$\text{Net Income Before Tax} = \frac{\text{Net Income}}{1 - \text{Tax Rate}}$$

Assume that Johnson Company's management wants to attain a Net Income of $16,800 when the income tax rate is 30%. Net Income Before Tax can be calculated as follows:

$$\text{Net Income Before Tax} = \frac{\$16{,}800}{1 - 0.3} = \frac{\$16{,}800}{0.7} = \$24{,}000$$

A brief income statement verifies the calculations made in the preceding sections:

Sales (10,500 units × $20)		$210,000
Variable Cost (10,500 units × $12)	$126,000	
Fixed Cost	60,000	
		186,000
Net Income Before Tax		$ 24,000
Income Tax ($24,000 × 0.30)		7,200
Net Income		$ 16,800

Margin of Safety

Margin of safety is the amount by which the actual sales level of a company exceeds the break-even sales level. If sales decrease by more than the margin of safety, then the company will incur an operating loss. The formula for calculating margin of safety is:

(14) Margin of Safety = Actual Sales − Break-even Sales

Using Cost–Volume–Profit Relationships

Cost–volume–profit relationships can be used in a number of ways during planning and budgeting sessions to test possible courses of action. The following three independent situations reveal ways that Johnson Company might use cost–volume–profit relationships.

SITUATION 1 Assume that Johnson Company is considering reducing the price per unit from \$20 to \$18. How would this change impact the break-even point in units?

Using formula 8:

$$\begin{aligned} BEV &= FC/UCM \\ BEV &= \$60{,}000/(\$18 - \$12) \\ BEV &= 10{,}000 \text{ units} \end{aligned}$$

The \$2 price decrease would cause the break-even point to increase from 7,500 units (see page 933) to 10,000 units.

SITUATION 2 Assume that Johnson Company is considering an advertising campaign which would increase fixed costs by \$10,000 and allow a price increase from \$20 to \$22 per unit. How would this change impact the break-even point in units?

Using formula 8:

$$\begin{aligned} BEV &= FC/UCM \\ BEV &= \$70{,}000/(\$22 - \$12) \\ BEV &= 7{,}000 \text{ units} \end{aligned}$$

The \$10,000 advertising campaign and the related \$2 price increase would cause the break-even point to decrease from 7,500 units to 7,000 units.

SITUATION 3 Assume that Johnson Company is considering installing robots to replace some of the direct labor plant workers. This change would decrease unit variable cost from \$12 to \$9 and would increase fixed costs from \$60,000 to \$83,000. Unit sales price would remain at \$20. If the company wants to achieve a net income of \$42,000 and if the income tax rate is 30%, what would the impact be on desired sales volume of installing robots?

Using formula 11:

$$V = (FC + NIBT)/UCM$$

Without robots:

$$\text{Desired Volume} = \frac{\$60{,}000 + \dfrac{\$42{,}000}{1 - 0.3}}{\$20 - \$12} = 15{,}000 \text{ units}$$

With robots:

$$\text{Desired Volume} = \frac{\$83{,}000 + \dfrac{\$42{,}000}{1 - 0.3}}{\$20 - \$9} = 13{,}000 \text{ units}$$

The installation of robots would decrease the desired volume from 15,000 units to 13,000 units. As a result, Johnson Company would be able to sell 2,000 fewer units at the same price and still attain the same desired net income.

Break-even Analysis and Multiple Products

As indicated earlier, we must assume in break-even analysis that only one product is involved or that the product mix (the ratio of units of each product sold to the total units sold) is constant. Break-even sales can be computed for a sales mix of two or more products by calculating the weighted average unit contribution margin.

Assume that a company sells products A and B, has a product sales mix of 75% A and 25% B, and has fixed costs of $88,000. Also assume that the following

COST–VOLUME–PROFIT ANALYSIS FOR RESTAURANTS

Most retailing industries have developed relationships between product cost and retail price that need to be maintained in order to be profitable. Each segment of each industry has its own ideal relationship. For example, a men's clothing store would typically have a lower ratio of retail price to product cost than a retail furrier, while a down-hill ski shop would typically have a higher ratio than a department store.

Many restaurants strive to have the price of their meals set at 2.5 times the cost of the food used in the meal. Portion control is a key element in applying this ratio. For each food item or ingredient to be included in one portion or meal, a standard quantity (weight or volume) is established. This standard recipe can be used to determine the food cost of a meal. For example, 8 ounces of ingredient A costing 35 cents per ounce plus 2 ounces of ingredient B costing 25 cents per ounce would yield a food cost of $3.30 per portion and a target price of $8.25.

Retail establishments also have variable staffing levels. The number of employees on duty will vary, depending on the time of day. For example, a restaurant might have 2 cooks and 5 waiters working from 11:00 am to 2:00 pm, 1 cook and 2 waiters working from 2:00 pm to 5:00 pm, and 2 cooks and 5 waiters working from 5:00 pm to 9:00 pm. The number and type of employees to have on duty has to be predetermined. Therefore, the cost of these employees is fixed. They are typically paid the same amount regardless of how many meals are served.

These concepts have to be incorporated into cost–volume–profit analysis for a restaurant If a restaurant serves only three types of meals with per meal food costs of $4.00, $3.60, and $2.80, then the related prices should be $10.00, $9.00, and $7.00 if the 2.5 ratio is used. If 20% of the meals sold were sold for $10.00, 50% were sold for $9.00, and 30% were sold for $7.00, then the average revenue per meal sold would be $8.60 and the average food cost would be $3.44:

$10.00 × 0.20 =	$2.00	$4.00 × 0.20 =	$0.80
$ 9.00 × 0.50 =	4.50	$3.60 × 0.50 =	$1.80
$ 7.00 × 0.30 =	2.10	$2.80 × 0.30 =	$0.84
	$8.60		$3.44

The weighted average unit contribution margin, therefore, is $8.60 − $3.44 = $5.16.

If the total fixed costs, including personnel, are $60,000 for a typical 30-day month when the restaurant is open every day for the scheduled hours, the break-even volume would be calculated as follows:

$$\frac{\$60,000}{\$5.16} = 11,627.9 \text{ or } 11,628 \text{ meals per month}$$

relationships between selling price and variable cost exist:

	A	B
Unit selling price	$14.00	$7.00
Unit variable cost	8.00	3.00
Unit contribution margin	$ 6.00	$4.00

The weighted average unit contribution margin can be calculated as follows:

Product A: $6.00 × 0.75	=	$4.50
Product B: $4.00 × 0.25	=	1.00
Weighted Average UCM		$5.50

The break-even volume can then be calculated:

$$\text{Break-even Volume} = \frac{\text{Fixed Cost}}{\text{Weighted Average Unit Contribution Margin}}$$

$$= \frac{\$88{,}000}{\$5.50} = 16{,}000 \text{ units}$$

The 16,000 units are comprised of units of A and units of B. The exact mix and related contribution margin are calculated as follows:

Product	Product Mix	Volume Sold	Unit Contribution Margin	Total Contribution Margin
A	.75	12,000	$6.00	$72,000
B	.25	4,000	4.00	16,000
Total		16,000		$88,000

These concepts could be applied to any product mix or number of products.

A Perspective on Cost Analysis

Managing costs is a prevailing concern of management. The concepts introduced in this chapter underlie most efforts to analyze and project cost in a variety of decision situations. In practice, because projections of future costs are subject to many complicating factors, for most companies they are *estimates* of *probable* costs rather than precise determinations. Properly used—with full recognition of their limitations—cost behavior analyses can be highly useful to management.

KEY POINTS TO REMEMBER

(1) Behavior of total cost in response to volume changes are divided into three basic categories within a relevant range:

(a) Variable, which responds proportionately, with zero cost at zero volume.

(b) Fixed, which is constant.

(c) Semivariable, which responds, but less than proportionately, owing to a fixed component.

(2) Total cost for most firms is best represented by the semivariable cost pattern.

(3) Semivariable costs may be divided into fixed and variable subelements using graphic plottings, the high–low method, or statistical methods.

(4) We can often assume linearity of cost because it is approximately true within the range of volume relevant to the analysis.

(5) Per-unit costs behave as follows when volume is increased:
(a) Variable costs remain constant.
(b) Fixed costs decrease proportionately.

(6) A general formula for planning total cost is:

Total Cost = Total Fixed Cost + (Variable Cost per Unit × Volume)

(7) The break-even point (Revenue = Costs) can be derived by graph, formula, or contribution margin analysis.

(8) Contribution Margin = Revenue − Variable Costs.

(9) Break-even and contribution margin formulas can be restated to provide estimates of target sales for planning net income.

(10) Break-even computations involving multiple products incorporate the concept of a weighted average unit contribution margin.

SELF-TEST QUESTIONS
(Answers are at the end of this chapter.)

1. When moving from the low end of a relevant range to the high end, straight line depreciation expense per unit:
(a) Increases.
(b) Decreases.
(c) Remains the same.
(d) Changes unpredictably.

2. In a typical cost formula:
(a) Fixed costs are per unit and variable costs are per unit.
(b) Fixed costs are per unit and variable costs are in total.
(c) Fixed costs are in total and variable costs are in total.
(d) Fixed costs are in total and variable costs are per unit.

3. At the break-even point:
(a) Contribution margin = fixed costs.
(b) Variable costs = fixed costs.
(c) Sales = contribution margin.
(d) Contribution margin = 0.
(e) Gross profit = contribution margin.

4. Contribution margin ratio is:
(a) Unit sales price/unit contribution margin.
(b) 1/margin of safety.

(c) Total contribution margin/sales.
(d) Variable cost/fixed cost.

5. Net income before tax is:
(a) Net income/1 − tax rate.
(b) Tax rate/net income.
(c) Net income + contribution margin.
(d) Net income/tax rate.

QUESTIONS

24–1 Define the terms *cost behavior* and *relevant range*.

24–2 Identify some common activity bases in terms of which the volume of a manufacturing operation might be stated. What general criterion might be used in choosing a base?

24–3 Name, define, and plot on a graph the three most widely recognized cost behavior patterns. Plot activity horizontally and cost vertically.

24–4 Explain (a) how a semivariable cost can be considered "partly fixed and partly variable," and (b) why a firm's total cost is best represented by the semivariable cost pattern.

24–5 Briefly describe two techniques for dividing a semivariable cost into its fixed and variable subelements.

24–6 "Actual costs often behave in a nonlinear fashion. Therefore, assumptions of linearity invalidate most cost behavior analyses." Do you agree or disagree with this statement? Briefly defend your position.

24–7 Describe how fixed and variable costs per-unit respond to volume increases.

24–8 Present a formula for planning total costs, and explain how semivariable costs are incorporated into the formula.

24–9 Define and briefly explain three approaches to break-even analysis.

24–10 The Tasty Donut Shop has fixed costs per month of $1,200, and variable costs are 60% of sales. What amount of monthly sales allows the shop to break even?

24–11 The Swift Car Wash has fixed costs per month of $2,800, and variable costs are 30% of sales. The average amount collected per car serviced during the past year has been $5. How many cars must be serviced per month to break even?

24–12 You have graphed the cost–volume–profit relationships for a company on a break-even chart, after being informed of certain assumptions. Explain how the lines on the chart would change (a) if fixed costs increased over the entire range of activity, (b) if selling price per unit decreased, and (c) if variable costs per unit increased.

24–13 Define *contribution margin*. Is it best expressed as a total amount or as a per-unit amount? In what way is the term descriptive of the concept?

24–14 Explain the approach to break-even analysis that is used for a mix of two or more products.

24–15 Explain how break-even formulas can provide income-planning analyses.

24–16 In planning net income, how can net income be incorporated into the planning formula?

EXERCISES

Cost–volume graph

24–17 Set up a cost–volume graph similar to those presented in the chapter with proportional sales from 0–24,000 (in 4,000-unit increments) for cost and volume. Plot each of the following groups of cost data using different marks for each group. After completing the graph, indicate the type of cost behavior exhibited by each group.

Volume (applicable to each group)	Group A Costs	Group B Costs	Group C Costs
2,000	$ 6,600	$ 2,400	$8,000
6,000	9,800	7,200	8,000
10,000	13,000	12,000	8,000
20,000	21,000	24,000	8,000

High–low method

24–18 Apply the high–low method of cost analysis to the three cost data groups in Exercise 24–17. What cost behavior patterns are apparent? Express each as a cost formula.

High–low method

24–19 The highest and lowest levels of activity for the Princeton Company were 60,000 direct labor hours and 36,000 direct labor hours, respectively. If maintenance costs were $180,000 at the 60,000-hour level and $120,000 at the 36,000-hour level, what cost might we expect at an operating level of 40,000 direct labor hours?

High–low method

24–20 During the past year, Sunset, Inc., operated within the relevant range of its fixed costs. Monthly production volume during the year ranged from 40,000 to 60,000 units of product and corresponding average manufacturing costs ranged from $2.20 to $2.40 per unit. Determine the total cost behavior pattern experienced by Sunset, Inc.

High–low method

24–21 The following selected data relate to the major cost categories experienced by Newton Company at varying levels of operating volumes. Assuming that all operating volumes are within the relevant range, calculate the appropriate costs in each column where blanks appear:

	Total Cost (at 3,000 units)	Total Cost (at 4,000 units)	Variable Cost per Unit	Fixed Cost	Total Cost (at 5,000) units)
Direct labor (variable)	$6,000	$8,000	______	______	______
Factory supervision (semivariable)	5,000	6,500	______	______	______
Factory depreciation (fixed)	3,000	3,000	______	______	______

Cost formula

24–22 The Baseline Company has analyzed its overhead costs and derived a general formula for their behavior: $25,000 + $6 per direct labor hour employed. The company expects to utilize 50,000 direct labor hours during the next accounting period. What overhead rate per direct labor hour should be applied to jobs worked during the period?

Cost formula

24–23 The following amounts of various cost categories are experienced by Larson Factories in producing and selling its only product:

Direct material	$4 per unit of product
Direct labor	$8 per direct labor hour*
Factory overhead	$10,000 + $6 per direct labor hour
Selling expenses	$13,000 + $2 per unit of product
Administrative expenses	$7,000 + $0.30 per unit of product

*Each unit of product requires one-half direct labor hour.

Combine the various cost factors into a general total cost formula for Larson Factories, and determine the total cost for producing and selling 12,000 units.

Break-even chart

24–24 Set up a break-even chart similar to Exhibit 24–11 with proportional scales from 0–$72,000 (in $6,000 increments) on the vertical axis and from 0–12,000 units of production (in 2,000-unit increments) on the horizontal axis. Prepare a break-even chart for Marten Company, assuming total fixed costs of $18,000 and unit selling price and unit variable cost for the company's one product of $6 and $4, respectively.

Break-even calculations

24–25 Compute the break-even point in units of production for each of the following independent situations. Confirm each answer using contribution margin ratio analysis.

	Unit Selling Price	Unit Variable Cost	Total Fixed Cost
(a)	$10	$7	$30,000
(b)	12	9	48,000
(c)	5	3	18,000

Net income planning

24–26 In each of the three situations presented in Exercise 24–25, what unit sales volume is necessary to earn the following related amounts of net income before income taxes? (a) $6,000; (b) $9,000; and (c) equal to 20% of sales revenue.

Cost–volume–profit analysis

24–27 The Alpha Company sells a single product for $18 per unit. Variable costs are $11 per unit and fixed costs are $49,000 at an operating level of 10,000 units.

(a) What is the Alpha Company's break-even point in units?
(b) How many units must be sold to earn $35,000 before income taxes?
(c) How many units must be sold to earn $36,750 after income taxes, assuming a 30% tax rate?

Multiple product break-even

24–28 Douglas Company has $96,600 total fixed costs and sells products A and B with a product mix of 40% A and 60% B. Selling prices and variable costs for A and B result in contribution margins per unit of $7 and $3, respectively. Compute the break-even point.

Net income planning

24–29 Jackson Corporation earned a net income of $300,000 last year. Fixed costs were $900,000. The selling price per unit of its product was $160, of which $40 was a contribution to fixed cost and net income. The income tax rate was 40%.

(a) How many units of product were sold last year?

(b) What was the break-even point in units last year?

(c) The company wishes to increase its net income by 20% this year. If selling prices and the income tax rate remain unchanged, how many units must be sold?

Cost patterns

24–30 The graphs below represent approximations of cost behavior patterns. The horizontal axis of each graph represents units of production while the vertical axis represents total dollars of cost.

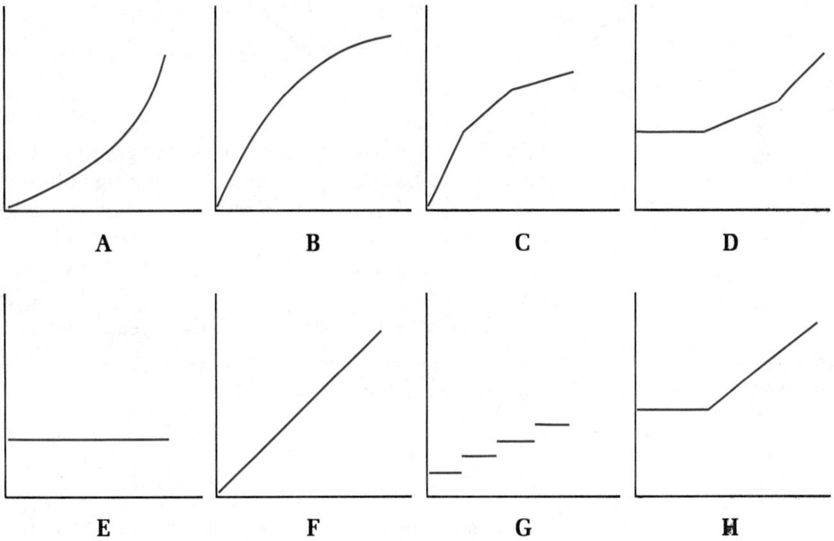

Select the graph that best matches each of the situations described below. Each graph may be selected more than once.

(a) Straight-line depreciation of a factory building.

(b) Utility bill for electricity which includes a fixed charge per month plus a constant usage rate per hour for hours in excess of 100.

(c) Cost of microcomputers incorporated into a product.

(d) Labor cost of machine operators who become more productive as they gain experience.

(e) Water bill which includes a flat fee for the first 50,000 gallons used plus an increasing usage charge for each additional 10,000 gallons used.

(f) Cost of factory supplies, where increasing quantities bring cost discounts as each price break level is attained.

(g) Salaries of quality inspectors, where one additional inspector is hired for each 20,000 units produced.

(h) Cost of an advertising campaign.

PROBLEMS

Cost patterns

24–31 The following graph depicts cost–volume relations for the Anchor Company:

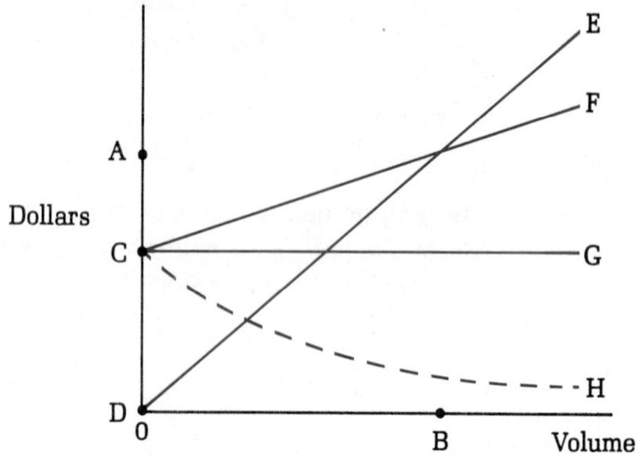

REQUIRED
Choose a labeled point or line on the graph that *best* represents the behavior of each of the following items as operating volume is increased. Answers may be the same for more than one item. Answer each item independently.

(a) Total sales revenue
(b) Total cost for the firm
(c) Variable cost per unit
(d) Total variable cost
(e) Total fixed cost
(f) Fixed cost per unit
(g) Total semivariable cost
(h) Break-even point

Net income planning

24–32 Selected operating data for Redwood Company in four independent situations are shown below:

	A	B	C	D
Sales	$192,000	$____	$____	$160,000
Variable expense	$____	$48,000	$____	$____
Fixed expense	$____	$24,000	$28,800	$ 83,200
Net income (loss)	$ 16,000	$16,000	$19,200	($ 19,200)
Units sold	20,000	____		
Unit contribution margin	$3.20	$4.00		
Contribution margin ratio			0.40	____

REQUIRED
Fill in the blanks for each independent situation. Show your calculations.

Graphing semivariable cost

24–33 During a recent six-month period, Shaw Corporation has the following monthly volume of production and total monthly maintenance expense:

	Units Produced	Maintenance Expense
Mar.	21,000	$ 70,400
Apr.	15,000	56,000
May	30,000	92,000
June	27,500	86,000
July	35,000	104,000
Aug.	25,000	80,000

REQUIRED

Assume all volumes are in the relevant range.

(a) Explain why the data indicate that the maintenance expense is neither a fixed nor a variable expense.

(b) Construct a graph similar to Exhibit 24–6 and plot the above cost observations.

(c) Fit a line (by sight) to the cost observation dots, and estimate the cost formula.

(d) Confirm your answer in part (c) with high–low analysis.

Cost formulas

24–34 Turner Manufacturing produces a single product requiring the following direct material and direct labor:

Description	Cost per Unit of Input	Required Amount per Unit of Product
Material A	$ 8/lb	10 oz
Material B	5/lb	8 oz
Material C	20/gal	0.3 gal
Cutting labor	9/hr	30 min
Shaping labor	11/hr	15 min
Finishing labor	12/hr	45 min

Factory overhead consists of factory supplies, 60 cents per unit of product; indirect labor, $1,000 per month plus 70 cents per unit of product; factory maintenance, $14,000 per year plus 55 cents per unit of product; factory depreciation, $15,000 per year; and annual factory property taxes, $8,000. Selling and administrative expenses include the salaries of a sales manager, $30,000 per year; an office manager, $18,000 per year; and two salespersons, each of whom is paid a base salary of $11,000 per year and a commission of $3 per unit sold. Advertising and promotion of the product are done through a year-round media package program costing $1,000 per week.

REQUIRED

(a) Analyze all cost and expense factors to determine a general formula (based on units of production) for total cost.

(b) Assuming a relevant range of 10,000 to 20,000 units, what is the estimated unit cost for producing and selling 10,000 units? 20,000 units? Explain the variation in unit cost at the two levels of production.

(c) If 15,000 units are produced and sold in a year, what selling price results in a net income before taxes of $60,000?

High–low and cost formula

24–35 The Northern Company has accumulated the following total factory overhead costs for two levels of activity (within the relevant range):

	Low	High
Activity (direct labor hours)	80,000	120,000
Total factory overhead	$201,000	$255,000

The total overhead costs include variable, fixed, and semivariable (mixed) costs. At 120,000 direct labor hours, the total cost breakdown is as follows:

Variable costs	$90,000
Fixed costs	75,000
Semivariable costs	90,000

REQUIRED

(a) Using the high–low method of cost analysis, determine the variable portion of the semivariable costs per direct labor hour. Determine the total fixed cost component of the semivariable cost.

(b) What should the total planned overhead cost be at 100,000 direct labor hours?

Cost formula

24–36 The following total cost data are for Lancaster Manufacturing Company, which has a normal capacity per period of 25,000 units of product that sell for $20 each. For the foreseeable future, sales volume should continue at normal capacity of production.

Direct material	$118,000
Direct labor	80,000
Variable overhead	37,000
Fixed overhead (Note 1)	65,000
Selling expense (Note 2)	40,000
Administrative expense (fixed)	26,000
	$366,000

(1) Beyond normal capacity, fixed overhead costs increase $4,000 for each 1,000 units *or fraction thereof* until a maximum capacity of 30,000 units is reached.

(2) Selling expenses are a 5% sales commission plus shipping costs of 60 cents per unit.

REQUIRED

(a) Using the information available, prepare a formula to estimate Lancaster's total costs at various production volumes up to normal capacity.

(b) Prove your answer in part (a) against the above total cost figure at 25,000 units.

(c) Calculate the planned total cost at 20,000 units, and explain why total cost did not decrease in proportion to the reduced volume.

(d) If Lancaster were operating at normal capacity and accepted an order for 500 more units, what would it have to charge for the order to make a $6 profit per unit on the new sale?

Net income planning

24–37 Delwood Corporation sells a single product for $60 per unit, of which $24 is contribution margin. Total fixed costs are $72,000 and net income before tax is $28,800.

REQUIRED

Determine the following (show key computations):

(a) The present sales volume in dollars.

(b) The break-even point in units.

(c) The sales volume necessary to attain a net income before tax of $52,800.

(d) The sales volume necessary to attain a net income before tax equal to 20% of sales revenue.

(e) The sales volume necessary to attain a net income of $54,000 if the tax rate is 40%.

Break-even and net income planning

24–38 The controller of the Concord Company is preparing data for a conference concerning certain *independent* aspects of its operations.

REQUIRED

Prepare answers to the following questions for the controller:

(a) Total fixed costs are $600,000 and a unit of product is sold for $5 in excess of its unit variable cost. What is break-even unit sales volume?

(b) The company will sell 60,000 units of product—each having a unit variable cost of $10—at a price that will enable the product to absorb $270,000 of fixed costs. What minimum unit sales price must be charged to break even?

(c) Net income before taxes of $120,000 is desired after covering $600,000 of fixed costs. What minimum contribution margin ratio must be maintained if total sales revenue is to be $1,800,000?

(d) Net income before taxes is 10% of sales revenue, the contribution margin ratio is 30%, and the break-even dollar sales volume is $300,000. What is the amount of total revenue?

(e) Total fixed costs are $480,000, variable cost per unit is $10, and unit sales price is $30. What dollar sales volume will generate a net income of $36,000 when the income tax rate is 40%?

Break-even and net income planning

24–39 Hubbard Company has recently leased facilities for the manufacture of a new product. Based on studies made by its accounting personnel, the following data are available:

Estimated annual sales: 40,000 units

Estimated Costs	Amount	Unit Cost
Direct material	$290,000	$ 7.25
Direct labor	230,000	5.75
Factory overhead	160,000	4.00
Administrative expenses	78,000	1.95
	$758,000	$18.95

Selling expenses are expected to be 10% of sales, and the selling price is $30 per unit. Ignore income taxes in this problem.

REQUIRED

(a) Compute a break-even point in dollars and in units. Assume that factory overhead and administrative expenses are fixed but that other costs are variable.

(b) What would net income before tax be if 30,000 units were sold?

(c) How many units must be sold to make a profit of 10% of sales?

Break-even and net income planning

24–40 Baxter Company manufactures and sells the three products below:

	Economy	Standard	Deluxe
Unit sales	10,000	6,000	4,000
Unit sales price	$20	$32	$48
Unit variable cost	$12	$20	$28

REQUIRED
Assume that total fixed costs are $174,000. Ignore income taxes in this problem.
(a) Compute the net income based on the sales volumes shown above.
(b) Compute the break-even point in total dollars of revenue and in specific unit sales volume for each product.
(c) Prove your break-even calculations by computing the total contribution margin related to your answer in part (b).

ALTERNATE PROBLEMS

Net income planning

24–32A Selected operating data for Rockville Company in four independent situations are shown below:

	A	B	C	D
Sales	$320,000	$_____	$_____	$280,000
Variable expense	$_____	$48,000	$_____	_____
Fixed expense	$_____	$56,000	$120,000	$120,000
Net income (loss)	$ 40,000	$16,000	$ 48,000	($ 8,000)
Units sold	7,000	_____		
Unit contribution margin	$20.00	$9.00		
Contribution margin ratio			0.70	_____

REQUIRED
Fill in the blanks for each independent situation. Show your calculations.

Graphing semivariable cost

24–33A During the past operating year, Scott Corporation had the following monthly volume of production and total monthly maintenance expense:

	Units Produced	Maintenance Expense		Units Produced	Maintenance Expense
Jan.	120,000	$11,200	July	124,000	$11,400
Feb.	144,000	12,700	Aug.	154,000	13,300
Mar.	156,000	13,400	Sept.	128,000	11,700
Apr.	130,000	11,600	Oct.	160,000	13,600
May	140,000	12,500	Nov.	152,000	13,200
June	150,000	13,200	Dec.	156,000	13,400

REQUIRED
Assume all volumes are in the relevant range.
(a) Explain why the data indicate that the maintenance expense is neither a fixed nor a variable expense.
(b) Construct a graph similar to Exhibit 24–6 and plot the above cost observations.
(c) Fit a line (by sight) to the cost observation dots, and estimate the cost formula.
(d) Confirm your answer in part (c) with high–low analysis.

Cost formulas

24–34A Thomas Manufacturing produces a single product requiring the following direct material and direct labor:

Description	Cost per Unit of Input	Required Amount per Unit of Product
Material A	$ 9/lb	24 oz
Material B	6/lb	12 oz
Material C	12/gal	0.5 gal
Cutting labor	10/hr	45 min
Shaping labor	12/hr	15 min
Finishing labor	11/hr	30 min

Factory overhead consists of factory supplies, 80 cents per unit of product; indirect labor, $10,000 per year plus $1.20 per unit of product; factory maintenance, $1,000 per month plus 60 cents per unit of product; factory depreciation, $22,000 per year; and annual factory property taxes, $20,000. Selling and administrative expenses include the salaries of a sales manager, $30,000 per year, an office manager, $18,000 per year, and two salespersons, each of whom is paid a base salary of $12,000 per year and a commission of $4 per unit sold. Advertising and promotion of the product are done through a year-round media package program costing $600 per week.

REQUIRED

(a) Analyze all cost and expense factors to determine a general formula (based on units of production) for total cost.
(b) Assuming a relevant range of 20,000 to 40,000 units, which is the estimated unit cost for producing and selling 20,000 units? 40,000 units? Explain the variation in unit cost at the two levels of production.
(c) If 35,000 units are produced and sold in a year, what selling price results in a net income before taxes of $56,800?

High–low and cost formula

24–35A The Nichols Company has accumulated the following total factory overhead costs for two levels of activity (within the relevant range):

	Low	High
Activity (direct labor hours)	30,000	50,000
Total factory overhead	$130,000	$176,000

The total overhead costs include variable, fixed, and semivariable (mixed) costs. At 50,000 direct labor hours, the total cost breakdown is as follows:

Variable costs	$100,000
Fixed costs	40,000
Semivariable costs	36,000

REQUIRED

(a) Using the high–low method of cost analysis, determine the variable portion of the semivariable costs per direct labor hour. Determine the total fixed cost component of the semivariable cost.
(b) What should the total planned overhead cost be at 40,000 direct labor hours?

Net income planning

24–37A Dakota Corporation sells a single product for $70 per unit, of which $40 is contribution margin. Total fixed costs are $80,000 and net income before tax is $20,000.

REQUIRED

Determine the following (show key computations):

(a) The present sales volume in dollars.

(b) The break-even point in units.

(c) The sales volume necessary to attain a net income before tax of $30,000.

(d) The sales volume necessary to attain a net income before tax equal to 20% of sales revenue.

(e) The sales volume necessary to attain a net income of $36,000 if the tax rate is 40%.

Break-even and net income planning

24–38A The controller of the Clearwater Company is preparing data for a conference concerning certain *independent* aspects of its operations.

REQUIRED

Prepare answers to the following questions for the controller:

(a) Total fixed costs are $240,000, and a unit of product is sold for $5.00 in excess of its unit variable cost. What is break-even unit sales volume?

(b) The company will sell 20,000 units of product—each having a unit variable cost of $7—at a price that will enable the product to absorb $90,000 of fixed costs. What minimum unit sales price must be charged to break even?

(c) Net income before taxes of $55,000 is desired after covering $190,000 of fixed costs. What minimum contribution margin ratio must be maintained if total sales revenue is to be $700,000?

(d) Net income before taxes is 20% of sales revenue, the contribution margin ratio is 60%, and the break-even dollar sales volume is $80,000. What is the amount of total revenue?

(e) Total fixed costs are $245,000, variable cost per unit is $27, and unit sales price is $42. What dollar sales volume will generate a net income of $42,000 when the income tax rate is 40%?

Break-even and net income planning

24–40A Bayview Company manufactures and sells the three products below:

	Race	Shaft	Bearing
Unit sales	20,000	30,000	50,000
Unit sales price	$14	$30	$6
Unit variable cost	$ 8	$18	$4

REQUIRED

Assume that total fixed costs are $156,600. Ignore income taxes in this problem.

(a) Compute the net income based on the sales volumes shown above.

(b) Compute the break-even point in total dollars of revenue and in specific unit sales volume for each product.

(c) Prove your break-even calculations by computing the total contribution margin related to your answer in part (b).

BUSINESS DECISION PROBLEM

The following total cost data are for Janesville Manufacturing Company, which has a normal capacity per period of 10,000 units of product that sell for $18 each. For the foreseeable future, regular sales volume should continue at normal capacity of production.

Direct material	$ 43,000
Direct labor	28,000
Variable overhead	14,000
Fixed overhead (Note 1)	22,000
Selling expense (Note 2)	18,000
Administrative expense (fixed)	5,000
	$130,000

(1) Beyond normal capacity, fixed overhead costs increase $1,000 for each 500 units *or fraction thereof* until a maximum capacity of 16,000 units is reached.
(2) Selling expenses are a 10% sales commission plus shipping costs of 30 cents per unit. Janesville pays only one-half of the regular sales commission rate on any sale of 500 or more units.

Janesville's sales manager has received a special order for 1,200 units from a large discount chain at a special price of $16 each, F.O.B. factory. The controller's office has furnished the following additional cost data related to the special order:
(1) Changes in the product's construction will reduce direct material $1.80 per unit.
(2) Special processing will add 25% to the per-unit direct labor costs.
(3) Variable overhead will continue at the same proportion of direct labor costs.
(4) Other costs should not be affected.

REQUIRED
(a) Present an analysis supporting a decision to accept or reject the special order. Assume Janesville's regular sales are not affected by this special order.
(b) What is the lowest unit sales price Janesville could receive and still make a before-tax profit of $1,000 on the special order?

ANSWERS TO SELF-TEST QUESTIONS

1. (b) 2. (d) 3. (a) 4. (c) 5. (a)

25

Special Analyses for Management

Chapter Objectives

- **Describe management's use of accounting information in the decision-making process.**
- **Present an overview of reporting of operations for segments of a business.**
- **Outline the procedures for reporting revenue and expenses by department and allocating indirect expenses.**
- **Introduce the concept of multiple-level performance reporting.**
- **Describe the use of differential analysis.**
- **Provide illustrations of the use of differential analysis in decision-making.**
- **Discuss the differences between variable costing and absorption costing.**

The traditional measurement is not the right measurement; if it were, there would be no need for decisions.

PETER DRUCKER

A well-developed accounting system is a continuing source of operational information for management. The quality of information available to management will influence the success of the operating decisions based on that information. In this chapter, we consider the management decision-making process and some cost concepts that are used in managerial analyses.

MANAGEMENT AND THE DECISION-MAKING PROCESS

There are many definitions of *management*. In the broad sense, anyone who directs the activities of others is a manager. For a typical manufacturing firm, this includes shop supervisors, department heads, plant supervisors, division managers, and the company president. A large, complex firm has many management levels.

As depicted in Exhibit 25–1, top management is responsible for establishing long-range goals and policies, including major financial arrangements, expansion into foreign markets, and mergers with other firms. Middle-level management may deal with the strategies and tactics related to the automation of a department, the establishment of new product lines, and the direction of the merchandising plan. Such matters as daily production quotas, compliance with planned costs, and other detailed operating concerns are the responsibility of lower-level management. To varying degrees, therefore, all levels of management are involved in decision making.

Decision making requires that a choice be made among alternatives. Probably the finest analogy of the business decision process is the play of a well-organized football team. Virtually all the elements of decision making are present in football—the awareness of the objectives and goals that lead to winning; the balancing of such short-run goals as first downs with the long-run goals of winning games and conference championships; the presence of organization, strategy, and tactics in a "hostile" environment where inaction and poor performance result in losses; the development of plays with the hope of achieving particular results; the moment of commitment in the huddle, immediately followed by the period of execution; and finally, the informal evaluation of performance on the field followed by a formal evaluation when game films are analyzed.

EXHIBIT 25–1
Management Responsibilities

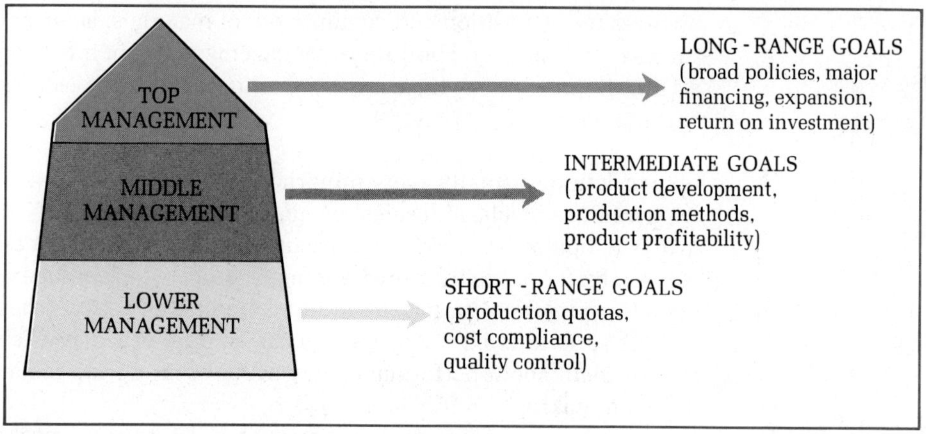

Phases of Decision Making

Decision making may be divided roughly into a planning phase, an execution phase, and an evaluation phase incorporating some form of remedial feedback. The following diagram illustrates the sequential nature of the elements of most decision processes:

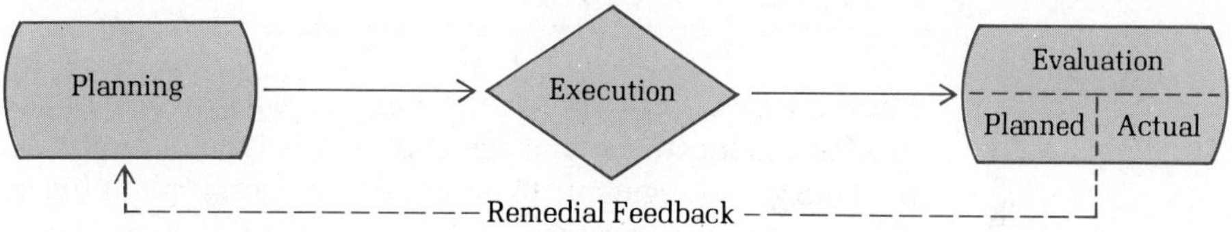

The **planning phase** begins with *goal identification,* the specification of objectives to be sought or accomplished. One of the most common business goals is the long-run optimization of net income. Other goals include target growth rates in sales revenue or total assets and target shares in various markets. Still other goals—such as leadership in product research, innovation, and quality—are difficult to measure. Probably the most widely recognized goal is a specified return on assets.

The next steps in planning are identifying feasible alternative courses of action for achieving desired goals and estimating their qualitative and quantitative effects on the specified goals. All planning involves the future. As a result, data related to the alternative courses of action must be estimated and projected in an environment of uncertainty.

The **execution phase** begins with the actual moment of decision—management's commitment to a specific plan of action. Because of the complexity of modern industry, some elaborate plans may need lead times of several years. Poor planning, or the absence of planning, may lead to operating crises that carry significant penalties for the firm in terms of extra costs, lost opportunities, and—in extreme cases—bankruptcy.

Once a decision has been made, the plan is implemented, which usually involves the acquisition and commitment of materials, labor, and long-lived assets such as machinery and buildings. Management is kept informed through periodic accounting reports on the acquisition and use of these facilities during the execution phase.

In the **evaluation phase**, steps are taken to *control* the outcome of a specific plan of action. Virtually every important aspect of business—costs, product quality, inventory levels, and sales revenue—must be reasonably well controlled if a firm is to operate successfully. Measuring performance is an essential element of control. Performance measurement must compare current operations with desired operations to allow management to take remedial action when significant unfavorable variations exist. Accounting data and reports play a key role in informing management about performance in various areas during the evaluation phase of decision making.

Decision processes do not, however, fall into three neatly divided phases. Changes in competition, technology, and customer demand must be considered. Furthermore, most management teams are engaged in all three decision-making phases at any given time. They may be planning decisions in one area, executing them in a second, and evaluating them in a third.

BUSINESS SEGMENTS

Many business entities are very complex, with diverse divisions and departments in multiple locations. Management of this type of entity finds it useful to divide the entity into segments to enhance managerial planning and control. Segments usually are based on organizational units (divisions or departments) or areas of economic activity (geographic regions or product lines). Many large companies have found that segmentation by organizational unit is the approach which proves most useful. It is important that the managerial accounting systems and procedures which develop information for planning and control decisions be structured to reflect the segmentation.

In Chapter 13 we discussed certain segment disclosures that public companies must include in financial reports to stockholders and other outside parties. Now we focus on the internal reporting of segment data, including departmental operations.

INTERNAL REPORTING OF SEGMENT OPERATIONS

Internal reporting of segment operations deals primarily with the measurement of operating performance. As a result, segmented reports usually take the format of an income statement or a portion of an income statement. These statements may provide information to answer the following types of questions:

(1) What amount is each segment contributing to sales and operating income of the entity as a whole?

(2) How do revenues and expenses for each segment compare to planned or budgeted amounts?

(3) What is the rate of profitability of each segment? Should any segment be expanded, reduced, or eliminated?

(4) Which areas need corrective action and what should be done?

(5) Where should promotional effort be directed?

Segments such as divisions or departments are usually classified as cost centers or profit centers. The manager of a *cost center* is responsible only for the costs and expenses of that segment of the business. There is no responsibility for revenue generation. An example of a cost center would be the machining department of a manufacturer of consumer products. The output of this department is only a part or an intermediate product which is not sold to consumers outside the company. As a result, no revenue is generated directly by this department.

The manager of a *profit center* is responsible for revenue generation as well as for cost and expense control. An example of a profit center would be a division which completely produces a product and sells it to consumers outside the company.

Managerial reports which measure the operating performance of a business entity and its segments reflect whether the segments are profit centers or cost centers. Revenue, expenses, and profitability are reported for segments which are profit centers, while only expenses are reported for cost centers. The examples in this chapter are profit centers.

One of the concepts which is typically built into segment reporting is the classification of costs or expenses as controllable or noncontrollable. Segment managers (profit center or cost center) should be held responsible only for costs and expenses which are controllable. Frequently, costs are considered controllable at one level of management but not at other levels. For example, the vice president of marketing may be responsible for decisions related to advertising. Even though the cost of advertising is incurred at the division level, the manager of the division should not be held responsible for that expense if a higher-level manager makes all the decisions relative to that cost or expense.

DEPARTMENTAL OPERATIONS

Departmentalization is a common and logical type of segmentation for many firms. In manufacturing and merchandising firms, departments are generally classified by product sold. The very term "department store" signifies a type of merchandising by product. Food stores are also commonly departmentalized by products such as meat, produce, groceries, delicatessen, and so forth. Sometimes departments are also classified by type of customer. For example, firms selling such products as floor coverings, lighting fixtures, and heating and air conditioning units may separate commercial sales operations from residential sales operations.

The methods of accounting and reporting for departmental operating activity depend on the performance measures used and the degree of analysis desired by management. Some firms may desire only to identify gross profit by department. In others, management may wish to determine a net income figure for each department. Still others may adopt an intermediate performance measure, such as gross profit less only those expenses directly incurred by the department.

Departmental Gross Profit

The main reason for analyzing gross profit by department is that it permits management to review pricing policies and supplier costs. Comparisons can be made among departments to determine areas with high gross profit margins and in which areas major promotional efforts should be made. Comparisons can also be made with gross profit margins achieved in other periods, or with average percentage statistics for other firms selling the same lines. (These statistics may be obtained from trade association publications and credit agencies.) Often, very low gross profit margins signal a need to investigate purchasing policies or to revise prices.

To obtain gross profit figures by department, a firm will customarily keep separate departmental accounts for sales, purchases, inventory, discounts, returns, and allowances related to sales and purchases transactions. Transportation costs on purchases must also be segregated. Because firms frequently receive incoming shipments for a number of departments, it is often easier to analyze freight costs by department at the end of the accounting period than by individual freight bills being received and recorded throughout the accounting period.

Exhibit 25–2 is a departmental income statement for Decorator Lighting Company, which accumulates gross profit data by department. This firm, segmented into two departments—residential and commercial—sells lighting fixtures in a large retail outlet for retail residential customers and for individual builders who purchase fixtures for single-home construction. In addition, the company sells in a market that supplies lighting fixtures for large-scale contractors engaged in the construction of office buildings, motels, and other commercial installations.

Departmental Net Income

Ordinarily, it is not difficult to maintain an accounting system in which departmental reporting is carried only to the point of measuring gross profit. A firm that desires a more refined measure of operating performance, however, is faced with the problem of assigning operating expenses to the departments. If a measure of departmental net income is desired, it is necessary to trace *all* expenses to departments.

Some expenses may be readily identified with the operation of particular departments, while others cannot be. To identify expenses with departments, it is helpful to classify them into the following two general categories:

Direct expenses: Those operating expenses traceable to and incurred for the benefit of a single department and thus ordinarily controllable by the department.

EXHIBIT 25–2

Decorator Lighting Company
Departmental Income Statement
For the Year Ended December 31, 19XX

	Residential Dept.	Commercial Dept.	Total
Sales	$330,000	$220,000	$550,000
Less: Sales Returns and Allowances	(4,000)	(5,500)	(9,500)
Sales Discounts	(6,000)	(4,500)	(10,500)
Net Sales	$320,000	$210,000	$530,000
Cost of Goods Sold:			
Inventory, Jan. 1	$ 88,000	$ 42,000	$130,000
Purchases	194,000	144,000	338,000
Less: Purchases Returns	(4,500)	(2,000)	(6,500)
Purchases Discounts	(3,500)	(3,000)	(6,500)
Transportation In	6,000	4,000	10,000
Cost of Goods Available for Sale	$280,000	$185,000	$465,000
Less: Inventory, Dec. 31	72,000	38,000	110,000
Cost of Goods Sold	$208,000	$147,000	$355,000
Gross Profit on Sales	$112,000	$ 63,000	$175,000
Operating Expenses:			
Selling Expenses			$ 70,000
Administrative Expenses			60,000
Total Operating Expenses			$130,000
Income before Tax			$ 45,000
Income Tax Expense			15,100
Net Income			$ 29,900

Indirect expenses: Those operating expenses incurred for the benefit of many departments and thus neither traceable to nor controllable by a specific department.

For example, payroll expense related to personnel who work exclusively in one department is a *direct expense* of that department. Payroll expense related to administrative personnel whose work benefits all departments is an *indirect expense* of the operating departments. A firm usually has many indirect expenses, incurred for the benefit of more than one department. Some examples are heat, light, maintenance, depreciation, and other occupancy expenses, office salaries, executive salaries, and a variety of other administrative expenses. These expenses must be fairly apportioned to the operating departments if the measure of departmental net income is to be meaningful. Because it is difficult and cumbersome to attempt any apportionment of indirect expenses at the time they are incurred, they are usually analyzed and allocated to departments at the end of the accounting period.

Assume that the $130,000 operating expenses for Decorator Lighting Company in Exhibit 25–2 consisted of the following:

Sales Salaries Expense	$ 45,000
Advertising Expense	15,000
Delivery Expense	10,000
Insurance Expense (on merchandise)	6,000
Occupancy Expense	16,000
Uncollectible Accounts Expense	3,000
Office Salaries Expense	20,000
Other Administrative Expense	15,000
	$130,000

In preparing a departmental income statement, Decorator Lighting might analyze and allocate these expenses and the income tax expense of $15,100 as follows:

Sales Salaries Expense. The sales force for the residential department is separate from that of the commercial department. Therefore, the sales salaries for each department can be directly determined from payroll records, which show $25,000 for the residential department and $20,000 for the commercial department.

Advertising Expense. Of the company's $15,000 advertising expense, $7,000 was spent on newspaper and television advertising of residential lighting products, $3,000 on producing illustrated brochures with price lists for commercial customers, and $5,000 on general newspaper advertising directed at both markets. The latter amount was allocated on the basis of relative sales. ($330,000/$550,000 = 60% residential; $220,000/$550,000 = 40% commercial.)

	Residential	Commercial	Total
Direct Advertising	$ 7,000	$3,000	$10,000
Indirect Advertising	3,000	2,000	5,000
	$10,000	$5,000	$15,000

Delivery Expense. Products are delivered to all commercial customers via Ace Trucking Service at a cost of $2,000. All residential deliveries are made with the company's own truck or via United Delivery Service and total $8,000. Thus, departmental delivery costs can be determined directly.

Insurance Expense *(on merchandise)*. The cost of insurance is based on the average inventories of the two departments:

Residential ($88,000 + $72,000)/2 =	$ 80,000	80/120 × $6,000 =	$4,000
Commercial ($42,000 + $38,000)/2 =	$ 40,000	40/120 × $6,000 =	2,000
	$120,000		$6,000

Occupancy Expense. Rent, maintenance, and utility expenses are included in this item, which is allocated on the basis of square feet of floor space used by each department. Of the total floor space, $\frac{5}{8}$ is occupied by the residential department and $\frac{3}{8}$ by the commercial department. Of the $16,000 total cost, $10,000 is apportioned to the residential department and $6,000 to the commercial department.

Uncollectible Accounts Expense. The firm maintains a separate customers' ledger for each department and detemines its expense from uncollectible accounts by aging the accounts. Estimated uncollectible accounts totaled $1,600 for residential customers and $1,400 for commercial customers.

Office Salaries and Other Administrative Expense. Often, salaries of office personnel and other administrative expenses are allocated to departments on the basis of the relative sales of each department, since a good share of this cost is related to billings, collections, and customer inquiries. The alternative is to attempt an analysis of time spent by office employees on the affairs of each department and to estimate administrative supplies used, correspondence, and other office expenses by department. Such analysis is liable to be costly and time-consuming, and it may not provide much additional accuracy. Decorator Lighting uses relative sales as a basis, apportioning 60% of the expenses to the residential department and 40% to the commercial department:

	Residential 60%	Commercial 40%	Total
Office Salaries Expense	$12,000	$ 8,000	$20,000
Other Administrative Expense	9,000	6,000	15,000
	$21,000	$14,000	$35,000

Income Tax Expense. Because Decorator Lighting Company is a corporation, it must pay federal income taxes at the appropriate rates on various portions of its taxable income. Here we assume that the total tax on $45,000 income is $15,100. The only realistic way to apportion the tax expense is on the basis of income before taxes. These amounts must be calculated by department (see Exhibit 25–3) before income tax expense can be allocated to the departments. Thus, $32,400/$45,000 × $15,100 = $10,872 tax expense for the residential department, and $12,600/$45,000 × $15,100 = $4,228 tax expense for the commercial department. Some accountants believe that, because departments are not taxable entities, allocation of tax expense among them does not result in meaningful performance measures; they would extend the departmental figures only to income before taxes.

A summary of the operating expenses and income tax expense, giving the direct expenses and allocated indirect expenses of each department, follows.

	Residential Dept.			Commercial Dept.		
	Direct	Indirect	Total	Direct	Indirect	Total
Sales Salaries Expense	$25,000		$25,000	$20,000		$20,000
Advertising Expense	7,000	$ 3,000	10,000	3,000	$ 2,000	5,000
Delivery Expense	8,000		8,000	2,000		2,000
Insurance Expense (on merchandise)	4,000		4,000	2,000		2,000
Occupancy Expense		10,000	10,000		6,000	6,000
Uncollectible Accounts Expense	1,600		1,600	1,400		1,400
Office Salaries Expense		12,000	12,000		8,000	8,000
Other Administrative Expense		9,000	9,000		6,000	6,000
	$45,600	$34,000	$79,600	$28,400	$22,000	$50,400
Income Tax Expense		$10,872			$ 4,228	

This departmental expense distribution was used to prepare the income statement for Decorator Lighting Company shown in Exhibit 25–3, which extends the departmental operating results through net income.

EXHIBIT 25–3

Decorator Lighting Company
Departmental Income Statement
For the Year Ended December 31, 19XX

	Residential Dept.	Commercial Dept	Total
Net Sales	$320,000	$210,000	$530,000
Cost of Goods Sold	208,000	147,000	355,000
Gross Profit on Sales	$112,000	$ 63,000	$175,000
Operating Expenses:			
Sales Salaries Expense	$ 25,000	$ 20,000	$ 45,000
Advertising Expense	10,000	5,000	15,000
Delivery Expense	8,000	2,000	10,000
Insurance Expense (on merchandise)	4,000	2,000	6,000
Occupancy Expense	10,000	6,000	16,000
Uncollectible Accounts Expense	1,600	1,400	3,000
Office Salaries Expense	12,000	8,000	20,000
Other Administrative Expense	9,000	6,000	15,000
Total Operating Expenses	$ 79,600	$ 50,400	$130,000
Income before Tax	$ 32,400	$ 12,600	$ 45,000
Income Tax Expense	10,872	4,228	15,100
Net Income	$ 21,528	$ 8,372	$ 29,900

Departmental Contribution to Indirect Expenses

Operating statements that extend departmental results to net income measures are often criticized on the grounds that the indirect or common expenses are not controllable at the departmental level and therefore should not be assigned to departments when measuring performance. A further criticism is that the bases for assignment of indirect expenses are frequently arbitrary.

Some accountants favor an intermediate type of performance measure as a means of appraising departmental operating results. The **departmental contribution to indirect expenses** is obtained by deducting the direct departmental expenses from departmental gross profit. The resulting amount is a measure of the department's contribution to the firm's pool of common or indirect expenses incurred for the benefit of all operating units. Using this measure eliminates the need for allocating the indirect expenses. Athough this approach emphasizes

MEASUREMENT AND CONTROL OF DIVISIONAL PERFORMANCE

To measure divisional performance by means of a profit figure arrived at after deducting items which are neither controllable at divisional level nor directly related to divisional activity is to use a measure which is arbitrary to the extent that the allocations are arbitrary. It is not independent of conditions outside the division, and may lead divisions into courses of action detrimental to the company. It could, moreover, mislead head office executives into thinking that a division was making a loss or a very small profit, and that therefore it should be liquidated. This could happen even though the facts were that, while the division was failing to make an adequate contribution to the head office expenses and profit, it was making *some* contribution, sufficient perhaps to keep it operating in the hope of eventual recovery.

Most company executives are aware of these arguments against expense allocations but are not always convinced by them. The counterargument most commonly used is that divisions must be made aware that there are nondivisional costs to be covered out of their earnings before the company as a whole can show a profit. Unless this awareness is sharpened by showing the central expense allocations on the divisional profit statements each month, the division may, in pricing policies and other marketing decisions, plan to contribute less than its due share of the company's net income. Moreover, it is argued, if the division were an independent company it would have a top administration of its own.

These counterarguments are not convincing. It is true that some methods of overhead allocation (e.g., allocations based on divisional sales) create possibilities for a division to diminish its contribution to the company's over-all profitability while increasing its own apparent net profit. But such aberrations result simply from the fact of allocation itself. Apart from such allocation practices, *so long as corporate (i.e., nondivisional) expenses are independent of divisional activity,* whatever policies maximize divisional net profits will also maximize divisional contributions to corporate profits before the allocation of corporate expenses. In the general case, in other words, corporate net profits will not suffer if corporate fixed expenses are left unallocated.

SOURCE: David Solomons, *Divisional Performance: Measurement and Control*, Financial Executives Research Foundation, Inc., New York, 1965. Reprinted by permission.

EXHIBIT 25–4

Decorator Lighting Company
Departmental Income Statement
Showing Contributions to Indirect Expenses
For the Year Ended December 31, 19XX

	Residential Dept.	Commercial Dept.	Total
Net Sales	$320,000	$210,000	$530,000
Cost of Goods Sold	208,000	147,000	355,000
Gross Profit on Sales	$112,000	$ 63,000	$175,000
Direct Operating Expenses:			
Sales Salaries Expense	$ 25,000	$ 20,000	$ 45,000
Advertising Expense	7,000	3,000	10,000
Delivery Expense	8,000	2,000	10,000
Insurance Expense (on merchandise)	4,000	2,000	6,000
Uncollectible Accounts Expense	1,600	1,400	3,000
Total Direct Expenses	$ 45,600	$ 28,400	$ 74,000
Contribution to Indirect Expenses	$ 66,400	$ 34,600	$101,000
Indirect Operating Expenses:			
Advertising Expense			$ 5,000
Occupancy Expense			16,000
Office Salaries Expense			20,000
Other Administrative Expense			15,000
Total Indirect Expenses			$ 56,000
Income before Tax			$ 45,000
Income Tax Expense			15,100
Net Income			$ 29,900

direct expenses, it should not be assumed that all aspects of direct expenses are controllable at the departmental level. Higher management may direct that a certain amount of expense be incurred by a department. The expense is properly described as direct and no allocation is required, but to say it is fully controllable at the departmental level would be incorrect. A departmental operating statement showing departmental contributions appears in Exhibit 25–4.

PERFORMANCE REPORTING

Performance reports are usually constructed periodically for each profit center and cost center. They contain different levels of detail for different levels of management. In general, top managers need highly summarized information while lower-level managers need specialized reports with greater detail.

EXHIBIT 25–5

Performance Report—Supervisor of Drilling Department
For the Month of August, 19XX

	Budgeted Cost	Actual Cost	Over (Under)
Direct Material	$16,000	$15,800	$(200)
Direct Labor	18,000	16,700	(1,300)
Factory Overhead:			
(listed in detail)	6,200	6,500	300
	$40,200	$39,000	$(1,200)

Performance Report—Manager of Machining Operations
For the Month of August, 19XX

	Budgeted Cost	Actual Cost	Over (Under)
Lathe Department	$ 56,200	$ 51,000	$(5,200)
Drilling Department	40,200	39,000	(1,200)
Finishing Department	25,900	30,000	4,100
	$122,300	$120,000	$(2,300)

Performance Report—Vice-president of Production
For the Month of August, 19XX

	Budgeted Cost	Actual Cost	Over (Under)
Administration	$ 14,700	$ 19,100	$ 4,400
Machining Operations	122,300	120,000	(2,300)
Fabricating Operations	118,600	122,300	3,700
Assembly Operations	118,400	118,600	200
	$374,000	$380,000	$ 6,000

Exhibit 25–5 presents three performance reports for three successively higher levels of management. The arrows show how the totals from the lower-level reports flow to the higher-level reports. While not all performance reports have the exact format of Exhibit 25–5, most will include a comparison of budgeted performance to actual performance.

DIFFERENTIAL ANALYSIS

Differential analysis is based on the widely accepted decision rule that *only the aspects of a choice that differ among alternatives are relevant to a decision*. For example, when you are deciding which theater to attend, the admission price is irrelevant if both theaters charge the same price. However, if the taxi fare is $4 to one and $3 to the other, then the $1 differential cost is relevant to the choice. The decision process is simplified by concentrating only on the factors that are different.

Suppose a firm may use certain facilities to produce and sell either product A or product B. The decision is to be in favor of the product promising the most net income based on the following estimated operating data:

	Alternatives	
	Product A	**Product B**
Units that can be produced and sold	12,000	18,000
Unit selling price	$8	$6
Manufacturing costs:		
Variable (per unit)	$3	$2
Fixed (total)	$32,000	$32,000
Selling and administrative expenses:		
Variable (per unit)	$1	$1
Fixed (total)	$6,000	$6,000

We may compare the alternatives by preparing comparative income statements which would appear as follows:

	Alternatives		
	Product A	**Product B**	**Difference**
Revenue			
(12,000 units @ $8)	$96,000		
(18,000 units @ $6)		$108,000	$12,000
Cost of goods sold (manufacturing costs):			
Variable (12,000 @ $3 per unit)	$36,000		
(18,000 @ $2 per unit)		$ 36,000	$ –0–
Fixed (total)	32,000	32,000	–0–
Selling and administrative expenses:			
Variable (@ $1 per unit)	12,000	18,000	6,000
Fixed (total)	6,000	6,000	–0–
Total expenses	$86,000	$ 92,000	$ 6,000
Net income	$10,000	$ 16,000	$ 6,000

This analysis shows a $6,000 increase in net income associated with alternative B as a result of a $12,000 increase in total revenue that is partially offset by a $6,000 increase in variable selling and administrative expenses.

Differential analysis of the same situation is illustrated below, where consideration is limited to the revenue and expense factors that differ if product B is produced rather than product A.

Differential revenue:	
Revenue foregone on first 12,000 units, ($8 − $6) × 12,000	($24,000)
Additional revenue from increased sales volume, $6 × 6,000 units	36,000
Net additional revenue	$12,000
Differential costs:	
Increase in variable selling and administrative expenses, 6,000 units at $1	6,000
Net differential income in favor of product B	$6,000

Clearly, the differential approach shows the same net advantage for alternative B as the income statements, but does so more concisely. For this reason, management often uses differential analysis in decision making.

ILLUSTRATIONS OF DIFFERENTIAL ANALYSIS

The Special Order

Business firms occasionally receive special orders from purchasers who wish a price concession. The prospective purchaser may suggest a price or ask for a bid. Sometimes the buyer may request that the firm produce a special version of a product to be identified with the buyer's private brand. As long as no overriding qualitative considerations exist, management should evaluate such propositions fully and be receptive to their profit potential.

Assume that Company A makes a nationally advertised automobile accessory, which it sells to distributors for $16. A discount firm has proposed that the company supply 2,000 units of the accessory for $14 per unit. The accessory would carry the brand name of the discount firm. If Company A were to accept the order, a special machine attachment would be needed to differentiate the product and imprint the private brand. This attachment, which costs $1,500, would be discarded after the order was processed. Also assume that Company A has unused production capacity, and thus anticipates no change in fixed capacity costs. The following unit cost data are available for the regular production of the item:

Direct material	$ 5
Direct labor	4
Variable factory overhead	2
Fixed factory overhead (allocated)	3
Total cost per unit	$14

At first glance, the proposal seems unprofitable because the unit cost figure shown here is $14, the same as the buyer's offered price, and an additional cost of $1,500 must be incurred to process the order. However, the fixed overhead of $3 included in the $14 total unit cost is not relevant to the decision and should not be considered, because Company A's total fixed costs will be incurred whether the special order is accepted or not. The following differential cost and revenue analysis reveals that the special order should be accepted:

Increase in revenue (2,000 units × $14)			$28,000
Increase in costs:			
Direct material	$ 5 per unit		
Direct labor	4 per unit		
Variable factory overhead	2 per unit		
	$11 × 2,000 units	$22,000	
Cost of special attachment		1,500	
Total differential cost			23,500
Net advantage in accepting special order			$ 4,500

The differential costs of accepting the order consist of the variable production costs and the additional cost of the attachment needed to differentiate the product. Actually, with any price higher than $11.75 ($23,500 total differential costs ÷ 2,000 units), the company would earn a profit on the order.

Note that excess production capacity is significant to the special order decision. Without sufficient excess capacity, the additional production would probably cause additional amounts of fixed costs to be incurred. Also observe that although the $1,500 special attachment in this example is a fixed cost, it is relevant to this decision.

Specific qualitative factors that should be considered here include ascertaining (1) that the special price does not constitute unfair price discrimination prohibited under the Robinson–Patman Act, (2) that regular sales at regular prices are not unfavorably affected by the sales of the discount store, and (3) that the long-run price structure for the product is not adversely affected by the special order. Significant concern in any of these areas might be a basis for rejecting the special order despite the potential $4,500 profit.

Make or Buy?

Many manufacturing situations require the assembly of large numbers of specially designed components and subassemblies. Usually, the manufacturer must choose between making these components and subassemblies or buying them from outside suppliers. In each situation, management should evaluate the relative costs of the two choices. Because making a component uses some portion of the firm's manufacturing capacity, we assume that no more attractive use of that capacity is available.

To illustrate the make-or-buy decision, we assume that a company has made 10,000 units of a necessary component at the following costs:

Direct material	$10,000
Direct labor	12,000
Variable factory overhead	4,000
Fixed factory overhead	24,000
Total costs	$50,000
Cost per unit ($50,000/10,000)	$5

Investigations by the purchasing department indicate that a comparable component can be purchased in sufficient quantities at a unit price of $4.50, an indicated savings of 50 cents per unit. At first glance, the opportunity to purchase seems most attractive. The analysis of differential costs, however, shows quite the contrary.

A review of operations indicates that by purchasing the component, the firm reduces fixed overhead associated with producing the component to $8,000. A differential analysis follows:

	Make Part	Buy Part	Increase (Decrease) in Cost if Part Is Bought
Cost of 10,000 units:			
Direct material	$10,000		($10,000)
Direct labor	12,000		(12,000)
Variable factory overhead	4,000		(4,000)
Fixed factory overhead	24,000	$ 8,000	(16,000)
Purchase price of components		45,000	45,000
	$50,000	$53,000	$ 3,000

The following approach to this analysis confirms the more comprehensive one above.

Cost to purchase component (10,000 × $4.50)		$45,000
Less costs avoided by purchasing:		
Direct material	$10,000	
Direct labor	12,000	
Variable factory overhead	4,000	
Fixed factory overhead	16,000	42,000
Increase in acquisition cost by purchasing		$ 3,000

These analyses assume that the manufacturing capacity released by the decision to purchase would not be used. However, should an opportunity arise to use this capacity to generate more than $3,000 of contribution margin, then the opportunity to purchase the components would be attractive.

Dropping Unprofitable Segments

Assume that the condensed income statement in Exhibit 25–6 reflects last year's operations of Martin Company. It might seem that the firm's total income could be raised to $125,000 by discontinuing Department C and avoiding that segment's $25,000 operating loss. The following differential analysis, however, indicates that the firm's overall income would decrease, rather than increase, by discontinuing Department C:

Decrease in revenue		$300,000
Decrease in costs and expenses:		
Variable cost of goods sold	$175,000	
Variable operating expenses	70,000	245,000
Decrease in total contribution margin (and net income) from discontinuing Department C		$ 55,000

EXHIBIT 25–6

Martin Company
Condensed Income Statement
For the Year Ended June 30, 19XX
(Thousands of Dollars)

	Total	A	B	C
Sales	$1,400	$700	$400	$300
Variable Costs:				
Manufacturing	$ 600	$300	$125	$175
Operating	130	40	20	70
Total Variable Costs	$ 730	$340	$145	$245
Contribution Margin	$ 670	$360	$255	$ 55
Fixed Costs:				
Manufacturing	$ 400	$200	$150	$ 50
Operating	170	80	60	30
Total Fixed Costs	$ 570	$280	$210	$ 80
Net Income	$ 100	$ 80	$ 45	$ (25)

Even though Department C reports a $25,000 annual loss, it does generate a contribution margin of $55,000 toward the absorption of fixed costs and expenses. Consequently, discontinuing Department C would not increase the firm's income by $25,000 but would decrease it by $55,000. The $80,000 difference ($25,000 + $55,000) represents fixed costs that have been allocated to Department C, which presumably the company would not avoid.

Management must often consider other factors in decisions of this type. Among these are (1) the potential termination of employees and subsequent effects on employee morale and (2) the possible effects on patronage (for example, customers of Departments A and B may go to other firms for all their purchases if Department C's products are no longer available from the same source).

Sell or Process Further?

Firms sometimes face the decision of either selling products at one point in the production sequence or processing them further and selling them at a higher price. Examples are finished versus unfinished furniture, regular versus high-test gasoline, and unassembled kits versus assembled units of product. These process-further decision situations present another opportunity to apply differential analysis.

Assume that Company B makes and sells 50,000 unfinished telephone stands with the following operating figures per unit:

Current sales price		$12.00
Costs:		
Direct material	$4.00	
Direct labor	2.00	
Variable factory overhead	1.50	
Fixed factory overhead*	1.00	8.50
Gross margin per unit		$ 3.50

*Applied at 50% of direct labor costs (total fixed factory overhead is $60,000).

The company now has excess productive capacity, which should remain available in the foreseeable future. Consequently, management believes that part of this excess capacity could be used to paint and decorate the telephone stands and sell them at $15 per unit in the finished furniture market. A study carried out by the company's production department indicates that the additional processing will add $1.30 to the direct material cost and 80 cents to the direct labor cost of each unit and that variable overhead will continue to be incurred at 75% of direct labor cost.

The following differential analysis supports the proposal to process further:

		Per Unit	Totals for 50,000 Units
Differential revenue ($15 − $12)		$3.00	$150,000
Differential costs:			
Direct material	$1.30		$ 65,000
Direct labor	0.80		40,000
Variable factory overhead	0.60		30,000
Fixed factory overhead	0		0
Total differential costs		2.70	$135,000
Excess of differential revenue over differential costs		$0.30	$ 15,000

Both the per-unit and total differential analyses indicate the advantage of processing further.

Product Emphasis

Because most firms produce several products, management must continually examine operating data and decide which combination of products offers the greatest total long-run profit potential. The decisions related to product emphasis are seldom as simple as determining the most profitable product and confining production to that one product. Typically, management faces such operational constraints as limited demand for the most profitable products, the competitive necessity of offering a line of products with a variety of qualities and capacities, and, in seeking better utilization of existing capacity, the need to produce other, less profitable products.

In product emphasis analysis, an important and widely accepted generalization is that *the firm optimizes its income when it maximizes the contribution margin earned per unit of constraining resource.* The concept of constraining resource stems from the realization that as a firm increases its volume, some resource is eventually exhausted and thus constrains, or limits, the continued expansion of the firm. Which resources are constraining depends on the firm, the operating conditions, and even the products under consideration. Typical examples are key materials, labor skills, machine capacities, and factory floor space or storage space. Simply stated, management has optimized the firm's product mix when it maximizes the contribution margin earned on each unit of the particular resource that limits increased production.

To illustrate product emphasis decisions, assume that Beta Company produces products X, Y, and Z, and that factory machine capacity is its constraining resource. Beta Company operates at 90% capacity, and management wants to devote the unused capacity to one of the products. The following data represent Beta Company's current operations:

	Products		
	X	Y	Z
Per-unit data:			
Sales price	$20	$22	$6
Variable costs	8	16	2
Contribution margin	$12	$ 6	$4
Fixed costs*	6	2	1
Net income	$ 6	$ 4	$3

*Allocated on basis of machine hours at $1 per hour.

Intuition suggests that the extra capacity should be devoted either to product Y, which has the highest sales price, or to product X, which has the highest per-unit contribution margin and net income. However, an analysis of the *contribution margin of each product per unit of constraining factor* reveals that product Z should receive the added capacity.

Note that fixed costs are allocated among products on the basis of machine hours—the constraining resource in our example. Furthermore, the unit allocations of fixed costs, above, indicate that product X requires three times as many machine hours as product Y and six times as many as product Z. The contribution per unit of machine capacity for each product follows:

	Products		
	X	Y	Z
Contribution margin per unit	$12	$6	$4
Divided by units of machine capacity required	6	2	1
Contribution margin per unit of machine capacity (the constraining resource)	$ 2	$3	$4

Use of the remaining capacity generates a greater contribution margin if devoted to product Z. As this simple example illustrates, in deciding product emphasis, management should use contribution margin per unit of constraining resource, rather than the relative sales prices, unit contribution margins, or even unit profit of various products.

VARIABLE COSTING

In Chapter 21, we defined product costs as all factory costs—direct material, direct labor, and factory overhead. These costs were capitalized as inventory during the production period and recognized as expense (cost of goods sold) only when the related merchandise was sold. This method of attaching all factory costs to the product is known as **absorption costing.**

In contrast, some firms use **variable costing** to determine the cost of their manufactured products.[1] Under variable costing, only variable manufacturing costs are capitalized as inventory. Any fixed manufacturing costs are expensed in the period incurred. Exhibit 25–7 contrasts the two approaches to costing. The only difference between absorption and variable costing is that fixed factory overhead is capitalized under absorption costing and expensed under variable costing.

In general, variable costing (carrying only variable costs in the inventory accounts) is considered a departure from financial accounting standards. These standards require that published financial reports attested to by CPAs be prepared on an absorption costing basis. In these reports, all factory costs should be attributed to products and inventories of work in process and finished goods should contain their allocable shares of factory costs, both fixed and variable. Likewise, the Internal Revenue Service has generally insisted on the use of absorption costing in determining net income for tax purposes.

[1] Variable costing is also referred to as *direct costing*. The latter is a misnomer, however, because *variable* costs—not *direct* costs—are capitalized under *direct* costing. This distinction is readily apparent in Exhibit 25–7.

EXHIBIT 25–7
Comparison of Absorption and Variable Costing

Typical Manufacturing Cost (or Expense)	Typical Behavior Pattern	Absorption Costing Product Cost	Absorption Costing Period Cost	Variable Costing Product Cost	Variable Costing Period Cost
Direct Costs:					
Direct Material	Variable	X		X	
Direct Labor	Variable	X		X	
Indirect Costs:					
Variable Factory Overhead	Variable	X		X	
Fixed Factory Overhead	Fixed	X			X
Other Expenses:					
Selling	Semivariable		X		X
Nonfactory Administrative	Semivariable		X		X

Although variable costing should not be used to prepare financial statements for external use, management may use variable costing statements for analytical purposes. A principal benefit is that variable costing usually causes net income figures to move in the same direction as sales. With absorption costing, net income may increase in periods when production volume outstrips sales and decrease when the company outsells production and thus reduces inventory levels.

In Exhibit 25–8, a comparison of partial income statements for the Elway Company for four periods, using both absorption costing and variable costing, demonstrates the effects just discussed. For this simple illustration, we assume that a single item is sold for $5 per unit, that variable product costs are $1 per

EXHIBIT 25–8

The Elway Company
Partial Income Statements

ABSORPTION COSTING

	Period 1		Period 2		Period 3		Period 4	
Sales (100 units @ $5)		$500		$500		$500		$500
Cost of Goods Sold:								
Beginning Inventory	$ 0		$ 0		$150		$ 0	
Cost of Goods Manufactured	400		450		350		400	
	$400		$450		$500		$400	
Ending Inventory	0		150		0		0	
Cost of Goods Sold		400		300		500		400
Gross Profit		$100		$200		$ 0		$100

VARIABLE COSTING

	Period 1		Period 2		Period 3		Period 4	
Sales (100 units @ $5)		$500		$500		$500		$500
Cost of Goods Sold:								
Beginning Inventory	$ 0		$ 0		$ 50		$ 0	
Variable Cost of Goods Manufactured	100		150		50		100	
	$100		$150		$100		$100	
Ending Inventory	0		50		0		0	
Variable Cost of Goods Sold		100		100		100		100
		$400		$400		$400		$400
Fixed Product Costs		300		300		300		300
Gross Profit		$100		$100		$100		$100

unit, and that fixed product costs are $300 per period. The following sales and production figures, in units, are given for the four periods:

	Period 1	Period 2	Period 3	Period 4	Total
Sales (in units)	100	100	100	100	400
Production (in units)	100	150	50	100	400

The Elway Company normally produces and sells 100 units per period. Note, however, that in period 2 the company produced an additional 50 units for inventory that are sold in period 3 together with the 50 units produced in period 3.

In the absorption costing statement shown in the top half of Exhibit 25–8, the cost of goods manufactured includes fixed product costs of $300 per period and variable product costs of $1 per unit produced. The $150 inventory shown at the end of period 2 consists of $50 variable costs (50 units × $1) and $100 fixed costs. (Because one-third of the units produced remain in inventory, one-third of the $300 fixed costs is assigned to the inventory.)

In the variable costing statement shown in the lower half of Exhibit 25–8, the cost of goods manufactured includes only variable product costs at $1 per unit produced. Likewise, the inventory at the end of period 2 consists only of $1 variable product cost times the 50 units in the inventory.

A total of $400 gross profit is reported for the four periods under both methods. However, the variable costing method shows the same gross profit figures each period, which are correlated with the constant sales volume over the four periods. On the other hand, under the absorption costing method, gross profit moves up and down with production. The reason, of course, is that the fixed costs are added to the inventory when production outstrips sales and released when the company sells its entire inventory.

To highlight the effect of variable costing on inventories and income in the foregoing illustration, we considered only manufacturing costs. When detailed income statements are prepared under the variable costing method, fixed and variable costs of all types—including selling and administrative expenses—must be properly segregated. An example of a detailed income statement prepared in accordance with the variable costing concept is shown in Exhibit 25–9.

The term **manufacturing margin,** which appears in Exhibit 25–9, sometimes describes the difference between revenue and variable cost of goods sold. Then contribution margin is obtained by deducting variable selling and administrative expenses from the manufacturing margin. Finally, all types of fixed costs and expenses—manufacturing, selling, and administrative—are deducted to arrive at net income.

The following advantages and disadvantages of using variable costing originate in the fact that under variable costing no fixed overhead costs are assigned to inventory carrying values.

Advantages of Variable Costing

(1) Management may be more aware of cost behavior in the firm's operations and may be likely to use this information in short-term decision situations in which contribution margin analysis is most appropriate.

EXHIBIT 25–9

Cawley Company
Variable Costing Income Statement
For the Year Ended December 31, 19XX

Sales (20,000 units @ $5)		$100,000
Variable Cost of Goods Sold:		
Beginning Inventory (12,000 units @ $3)	$36,000	
Cost of Goods Manufactured (18,000 units @ $3)	54,000	
Goods Available for Sale	$90,000	
Ending Inventory (10,000 units @ $3)	30,000	60,000
Manufacturing Margin		$ 40,000
Variable Selling and Administrative Expenses:		
Variable Selling Expense	$ 8,000	
Variable Administrative Expense	4,000	12,000
Contribution Margin		$ 28,000
Fixed Costs and Expenses:		
Fixed Manufacturing Cost	$12,000	
Fixed Selling Expense	5,000	
Fixed Administrative Expense	3,000	20,000
Net Income		$ 8,000

(2) Reported net income tends to follow sales volume. (This may not be true under absorption costing.)

(3) Cost–volume–profit relationships are more easily discerned from variable costing income statements than from conventional absorption costing statements.

Disadvantages of Variable Costing

(1) Accounting measures derived under variable costing are not in accord with generally accepted accounting principles, nor are they acceptable for reporting purposes under the Internal Revenue Code.

(2) Inventories (and therefore working capital and owners' equity) tend to be understated.

(3) Carrying inventories at only their variable costs may lead to long-run pricing decisions that provide for recovery of variable cost only rather than total cost, and thus does not produce net income in the long run.

KEY POINTS TO REMEMBER

(1) Decision making, which is essentially choosing among alternatives, usually comprises three phases: planning, execution, and evaluation.

(2) Business segments may consist of organizational units (departments or divisions) or areas of economic activity (product lines or markets). Accounting and reporting by segment are indispensable to management and are becoming more important to investors, creditors, and other outsiders.

(3) A segment may be (a) a profit center (generating both revenue and expenses), where the manager is responsible for the profitability of the segment, or (b) a cost center, where the manager is responsible for expenses only.

(4) Expenses incurred by, or for the benefit of, a segment are often called direct expenses; expenses incurred for more than one segment are called indirect expenses. The latter expenses are often allocated to segments on some appropriate basis.

(5) Reporting for departments of a firm is typically extended to one of three operating measures: gross profit, contribution to indirect expenses, or net income. When a net income measure is used, both direct and allocated indirect expenses are deducted from gross profit. When a contribution approach is used, only direct expenses are deducted from departmental gross profit.

(6) Differential analysis is the study of those amounts that are expected to differ among alternatives.

(7) In a decision situation, differential analysis is favorable whenever revenue increases more than costs increase or decreases less than costs decrease.

(8) Differential analysis may be applied in the following decision situations:

(a) Whether to accept orders at special prices.
(b) Whether to make or buy needed components.
(c) Whether to drop unprofitable segments.
(d) Whether to sell or process further.
(e) Which products to emphasize.

(9) Variable costing differs from absorption costing in that it does not assign fixed factory overhead as a product cost, but expenses it in the period incurred.

SELF-TEST QUESTIONS
(Answers are at the end of this chapter.)

1. The manager of which of the following segments of a business is responsible for revenue generation as well as for cost and expense control?
(a) Cost center.
(b) Accounting Department.
(c) Profit center.
(d) Assembly line.

2. Which of the following is not considered in determining contribution to indirect expenses?
   (a) Income taxes.
   (b) Cost of goods sold.
   (c) Direct expenses.
   (d) Net sales.
3. In performance reporting, where budgeted cost is compared to actual cost, which performance report must be prepared first?
   (a) Division, consisting of five departments.
   (b) Region, consisting of three divisions.
   (c) Department, consisting of four cost centers.
   (d) Company, consisting of two regions.
4. When using differential analysis to analyze two alternatives to the current operation, what factors should not be considered?
   (a) Direct material costs which are different.
   (b) Direct labor costs that exist only for one alternative.
   (c) Overhead costs that are the same for both alternatives.
   (d) Sales commissions which apply to only one alternative.
5. In determining inventory costs, which of the following cost elements is included when using absorption costing but excluded when using variable costing?
   (a) Selling costs.
   (b) Direct labor cost.
   (c) Administrative costs.
   (d) Fixed overhead.

QUESTIONS

25–1 Give examples of segments for business firms segmented by (a) organizational unit and (b) economic activity.

25–2 Identify three phases of decision making and briefly discuss the role of each phase in the decision process.

25–3 Distinguish between a *profit center* and a *cost center*.

25–4 Distinguish between *direct expenses* and *indirect expenses*. Which are more likely to be controllable at the department level?

25–5 When a firm wishes to measure gross profit by department, what basic modifications are needed in the chart of accounts?

25–6 Suggest an allocation basis for each of the following common expenses of a departmentalized firm that uses a net income measure to determine the profitability of departments:
(a) Janitorial expense.
(b) Firm manager's salary.
(c) Utilities (heat, light, and air conditioning).
(d) Sales salaries.
(e) Uncollectible accounts.
(f) Property taxes.

25–7 What is meant by departmental contribution to indirect expenses? What advantages does this measure have over net income in measuring departmental performance?

25–8 "The higher the management level receiving reports, the more detailed the reports should be." Comment.

25–9 Although separate phases of decision making are identifiable, management is usually involved in all phases at the same time. Explain.

25–10 List several common aspects of decision making that are often not subject to quantification.

25–11 Explain what is meant by the term *differential analysis.*

25–12 Explain how differential analysis can be applied to the following types of decisions:
(a) Accepting special orders.
(b) Making or buying product components.
(c) Dropping unprofitable segments of the firm.
(d) Selling or processing further.
(e) Product emphasis.

25–13 Department H of a discount store shows a contribution to indirect expenses of $13,000 and a net loss of $8,000 (before taxes). The firm believes that discontinuance of Department H will not affect sales, gross profit, or direct expenses of other departments. If total indirect expenses remain unchanged, what effect will discontinuance of Department H have on the income before taxes of the firm?

25–14 Department X of a firm has a gross profit of $80,000, representing 40% of net departmental sales. Direct departmental expenses are $60,000. Management believes that an increase of $7,000 in advertising, coupled with a 5% average increase in sales prices, will permit the physical volume of products sold to remain the same next period but will improve the department's contribution to indirect expenses. If management's expectations are correct, what will be the effect on this contribution?

25–15 Department Y of a firm has a gross profit of $60,000, representing 40% of net departmental sales. Management believes that an increase of $15,000 in advertising will increase volume of product sold by 20%. Other direct departmental expenses are $40,000. What effect will this decision have on Department Y's contribution to indirect expenses?

25–16 Operating at 80% capacity, Kapp Company produces and sells 16,000 units of its only product for $24. Per-unit costs are direct material, $5; direct labor, $7; variable factory overhead, $3; and fixed factory overhead, $3. A special order is received for 1,000 units. Based on this information, what price should Kapp charge to make a $2,000 gross profit on the special order?

25–17 Larson Company produces unassembled picture frames at the following average per-unit costs: direct material, $X; direct labor, $Y; and factory overhead, $Z. The company can assemble the frames at a unit cost of 90 cents and raise the selling price from $5.50 to $6.95. What is the apparent advantage or disadvantage of assembling the frames?

25–18 Explain the concept of *constraining resource,* and present a general rule for optimizing product mixes.

25–19 "In differential analysis, we can generally count on variable cost being relevant and fixed cost being irrelevant." Comment.

25–20 If both approaches to a decision lead to the same conclusion, why might differential analysis be considered superior to a comprehensive analysis that reflects all revenue and costs?

25–21 What is variable costing? List its advantages and disadvantages.

25–22 What generalizations can be made about the difference in income reported under variable and absorption costing?

EXERCISES

Allocating indirect expenses

25–23 Selected data for the Harris Company, which operates three departments, are given below.

	Dept. A	Dept. B	Dept. C
Inventory	$ 20,000	$ 72,000	$28,000
Equipment (average cost)	180,000	108,000	72,000
Payroll	270,000	240,000	90,000
Square feet of floor space	18,000	9,000	3,000

During the year, the company's indirect expenses included the following:

Depreciation on equipment	20,000
Real estate taxes	15,000
Personal property taxes (on inventory and equipment)	9,600
Personnel department expenses	15,000

Using the most causally related bases, prepare a schedule allocating the indirect expenses to the three departments.

Dropping unprofitable department

25–24 The Arnold Corporation has four departments, all of which appear to be profitable except Department 4. Operating data for the current year are as follows:

	Total	Depts. 1-3	Dept. 4
Sales	$820,000	$700,000	$120,000
Cost of Goods Sold	538,000	448,000	90,000
Gross Profit	$282,000	$252,000	$ 30,000
Direct Expenses	$128,000	$108,000	$ 20,000
Indirect Expenses	110,000	97,000	13,000
Total Expenses	$238,000	$205,000	$ 33,000
Net Income (Loss)	$ 44,000	$ 47,000	($ 3,000)

(a) Calculate the gross profit percentage for Departments 1-3 combined and for Department 4.

(b) Assuming that the operating data for next year will be the same as for the current year, what effect would elimination of Department 4 have on total firm net income? (Ignore the effect of income taxes.)

Analyzing operational changes

25–25 Operating results for Department B of the Gillette Company during the current year are as follows:

Sales	$180,000
Cost of Goods Sold	126,000
Gross Profit on Sales	$ 54,000
Direct Expenses	40,000
Indirect Expenses	22,000
Total Expenses	$ 62,000
Net Loss	($ 8,000)

If Department B could maintain the same physical volume of product sold, while raising selling prices an average of 15% and making an additional advertising expenditure of $15,000, what would be the effect on the department's net income or net loss? (Ignore income taxes in your calculations.)

Analyzing operational changes

25–26 Suppose that Department B in Exercise 25–25 could increase physical volume of product sold by 10% if it spent an additional $6,000 on advertising while leaving selling prices unchanged. What effect would this have on the department's net income or net loss? (Ignore income taxes in your calculations.)

Differential analysis

25–27 In each of four independent cases, the amount of differential revenue or differential cost is as follows (parentheses indicate decreases):

	(1)	(2)	(3)	(4)
Increases (decreases) in:				
Revenue	$18,000	$–0–	?	?
Costs	?	?	($12,000)	$–0–

For each case, determine the missing amount that would be necessary for the net differential amount to be:
(a) $10,000 favorable.
(b) $6,000 unfavorable.

Indicate whether your answers reflect increases or decreases.

Special order

25–28 The Anderson Company sells a single product for $18 per unit. At an operating level of 8,000 units, variable costs are $8 per unit and fixed costs $4 per unit.

The Anderson Company has been offered a price of $9 per unit on a special order of 2,000 units by Larson Discount Stores, which would use its own brand name on the item. If Anderson Company accepts the order, material cost will be $1 less per unit than for regular production. However, special stamping equipment costing $3,000 would be needed to process the order; it would then be discarded.

Assuming that volume remains within the relevant range, prepare an analysis of differential revenue and costs to determine whether Anderson Company should accept the special order.

Special order

25–29 Clancy Company regularly sells its only product for $60 per unit and has a 25% profit on each sale. The company has accepted a special order for a number of units, the production of which would absorb part of its unused

capacity. The special order sales price is 50% of the normal price, but the profit margin is only 20% of the regular dollar profit. What, apparently, is
(a) Clancy's profit per unit on the special order?
(b) Clancy's total variable cost per unit?
(c) Clancy's average fixed cost per unit on regular sales?

Make or buy

25–30 Superior Company incurs a total cost of $90,000 in producing 10,000 units of a component needed in the assembly of its major product. The component can be purchased from an outside supplier for $8 per unit. A related cost study indicates that the total cost of the component includes fixed costs equal to 50% of the variable costs involved.
(a) Should Superior buy the component if it cannot otherwise use the released capacity? Present your answer in the form of differential analysis.
(b) What would be your answer to part (a) if the released capacity could be used in a project that would generate $25,000 of contribution margin?

Sell or process further

25–31 Jacobs Manufacturing Company makes a partially completed assembly unit that it sells for $30 per unit. Normally, 42,000 units are sold each year. Variable unit cost data on the assembly are as follows:

Direct material	$10
Direct labor	8
Variable factory overhead	4

The company is now using only 70% of its normal capacity; it could fully use its normal capacity by processing the assembly further and selling it for $37 per unit. If the company does this, material and labor costs will each increase by $2 per unit and variable overhead will go up by $1 per unit. Fixed costs will increase from the current level of $160,000 to $195,000.

Prepare an analysis showing whether Jacobs should process the assemblies further.

Product emphasis

25–32 The following analysis of selected data is for each of the two products Blaine Corporation produces.

	Product A	Product B
Per-unit Data at 10,000 Units		
Sales price	$22	$15
Production costs:		
Variable	8	6
Fixed	5	2
Selling and administrative expenses:		
Variable	4	1
Fixed	3	3

In Blaine's operation, machine capacity is the company's constraining resource. Each unit of A requires 2.5 hours of machine time while each unit of B requires 1 hour of machine time. Assuming that all production can be sold at a normal price, prepare an analysis showing which of the two products should be produced with any unused productive capacity that Blaine might have.

Variable and absorption costing

25–33 Taylor Company sells its product for \$25 per unit. Variable manufacturing costs per unit are \$10, and fixed manufacturing costs per unit at the normal operating level of 12,000 units are \$5. Variable selling expenses are \$4 per unit sold. Fixed administrative expenses total \$26,000. Taylor Company had no beginning inventory in 19X1. During 19X1, the company produced 12,000 units and sold 9,000. Would net income for Taylor Company in 19X1 be higher if calculated using variable costing or using absorption costing? Indicate reported income using each method.

Variable and absorption costing

25–34 During its first year, Randolph, Inc., showed a \$7 per unit profit under absorption costing but would have reported a total profit \$5,600 less under variable costing. If production exceeded sales by 700 units and an average contribution margin of 60% was maintained, what is the apparent
(a) Fixed cost per unit?
(b) Variable cost per unit?
(c) Sales price per unit?
(d) Unit sales volume if total profit under absorption costing was \$49,000?

PROBLEMS

Departmental income statement

25–35 Thomas, Inc., retails floor coverings through two departments, Carpeting and Hard Covering (tile and linoleum). Operating information for the current year appears below.

	Carpeting Dept.	Hard Covering Dept.
Inventory, January 1	\$ 27,000	\$ 11,000
Inventory, December 31	23,000	13,000
Net Sales	350,000	220,000
Purchases	215,000	165,000
Purchases Returns	10,000	3,000
Purchases Discounts	7,000	1,000
Transportation In	8,000	6,000
Direct Departmental Expenses	50,000	25,000

Indirect operating expenses of the firm were \$50,000.

REQUIRED
(a) Prepare a departmental income statement showing departmental contribution to indirect expenses and net income of the firm. Assume an overall effective income tax rate of 30%.
(b) Calculate the gross profit percentage for each department.
(c) If the indirect expenses were allocated 70% to the Carpeting Department and 30% to the Hard Covering Department, what would the net income be for each department?

Allocate indirect expenses

25–36 The following information was obtained from the ledger of Sumner Candies, Inc., at the end of the current year:

Sumner Candies, Inc.
Trial Balance
December 31, 19XX

	Debit	Credit
Cash	$ 14,000	
Accounts Receivable (net)	52,000	
Inventory, December 31	60,000	
Equipment and Fixtures (net)	180,000	
Accounts Payable		$ 36,000
Common Stock		150,000
Retained Earnings		60,000
Sales—Department X		280,000
Sales—Department Y		120,000
Cost of Goods Sold—Department X	140,000	
Cost of Goods Sold—Department Y	72,000	
Sales Salaries Expense	64,000	
Advertising Expense	14,000	
Insurance Expense	8,000	
Uncollectible Accounts Expense	3,000	
Occupancy Expense	12,000	
Office and Other Administrative Expense	27,000	
	$646,000	$646,000

The firm analyzes its operating expenses at the end of each period in order to prepare an income statement that will exhibit net income by department. From payroll records, advertising copy, and other records, the following tabulation was obtained:

	Direct Expense		Indirect	Allocation Basis for
	Dept. X	Dept. Y	Expense	Indirect Expense
Sales Salaries Expense	$49,000	$15,000		
Advertising Expense	6,000	2,000	$ 6,000	Relative sales
Insurance Expense	5,000	3,000		
Uncollectible Accounts Expense	2,000	1,000		
Occupancy Expense			12,000	Floor space
Office and Other Administrative Expense	4,000	3,000	20,000	6 to 4 ratio (X to Y)

Department X occupies 10,000 square feet of floor space and Department Y, 5,000 square feet. Indirect expenses should be allocated to departments as indicated above.

REQUIRED

Prepare a departmental income statement showing net income by department, assuming an overall income tax rate of 35%.

Analyze operational changes

25–37 Manchester's is a retail store with eight departments including a garden department, which has been operating at a loss. The following condensed income statement gives the latest year's operating results:

	Garden Department	All Other Departments
Sales	$224,000	$1,600,000
Cost of Goods Sold	134,400	1,040,000
Gross Profit	$ 89,600	$ 560,000
Direct Expenses	$ 72,000	$ 182,000
Indirect Expenses	32,000	208,000
Total Expenses	$104,000	$ 390,000
Net Income (Loss)	($ 14,400)	$ 170,000

REQUIRED

(a) Calculate the gross profit percentage for the garden department and for the other departments as a group.

(b) Suppose that if the garden department were discontinued, the space occupied could be rented to an outside firm for $12,000 per year, and the indirect expenses of the firm would be reduced by $3,000. What effect would this action have on the firm's net income? (Ignore income taxes in your calculations.)

(c) It is estimated that if an additional $4,000 were spent on advertising, prices in the garden center could be raised an average of 5% without a change in physical volume of products sold. What effect would this have on operating results of the garden department? (Again, ignore income taxes in your calculations.)

Departmental contribution to indirect expenses

25–38 Certain operating information is shown below for the Carbondale Department Store:

	Dept. A	Dept. B	All Other Departments
Sales	$200,000	$300,000	$700,000
Direct Expenses	35,000	55,000	200,000
Indirect Expenses	30,000	40,000	100,000
Gross Profit Percentage	30%	40%	50%

The managers are disappointed with the operating results of Department A. They do not believe that competition will permit raising prices; however, they believe that spending $7,000 more for promoting this department's products will increase the physical volume of products sold by 20%.

An alternative is to discontinue Department A and use the space to expand Department B. It is believed that Department B's physical volume of products sold can thus be increased 37.5%. Special sales personnel are needed, however, and Department B's direct expenses would increase by $30,000. Neither alternative would appreciably affect the total indirect departmental expense.

REQUIRED

(a) Calculate the contribution now being made to indirect expenses by Department A, by Department B, and by the combination of other departments.

(b) Which of the two alternatives should management choose: increase promotional outlays for Department A, or discontinue Department A and expand Department B? Support your answer with calculations.

Special order

25–39 Total cost data follow for Liberty Manufacturing Company, which has a normal capacity per period of 8,000 units of product that sell for $20 each. For the foreseeable future, sales volume should continue to equal normal capacity.

Direct material	$33,600
Direct labor	20,800
Variable factory overhead	15,600
Fixed factory overhead (Note 1)	12,800
Selling expense (Note 2)	11,200
Administrative expense (fixed)	5,000
	$99,000

(1) Beyond normal capacity, fixed overhead costs increase $600 for each 500 units *or fraction thereof* until a maximum capacity of 10,000 units is reached.
(2) Selling expenses consist of a 6% sales commission and shipping costs of 25 cents per unit. Liberty pays only three-fourths of the regular sales commission rate on sales totaling 501 to 1,000 units and only two-thirds the regular commission on sales totaling 1,000 units or more.

Liberty's sales manager has received a special order for 1,200 units from a large discount chain at a price of $12 each, F.O.B. factory. The controller's office has furnished the following additional cost data related to the special order:

(1) Changes in the product's design will reduce direct material costs 50 cents per unit.
(2) Special processing will add 20% to the per-unit direct labor costs.
(3) Variable overhead will continue at the same proportion of direct labor costs.
(4) Other costs should not be affected.

REQUIRED
(a) Present an analysis supporting a decision to accept or reject the special order. (Round computations to nearest cent.)
(b) What is the lowest price Liberty could receive and still make a $1,200 profit before income taxes on the special order?
(c) What general qualitative factors should Liberty consider?

Make or buy

25–40 Gardner Corporation currently makes the nylon convertible top for its main product, a fiberglass boat designed especially for water skiing. The costs of producing the 1,500 tops needed each year are:

Nylon fabric	$67,500
Aluminum tubing	24,000
Frame fittings	6,000
Direct labor	40,500
Variable factory overhead	7,500
Fixed factory overhead	38,000

Dupre Company, a specialty fabricator of synthetic materials, can make the needed tops of comparable quality for $100 each, F.O.B. shipping point. Gardner would furnish its own trademark insignia at a unit cost of $4. Transportation in would be $7 per unit, paid by Gardner Corporation.

Gardner's chief accountant has prepared a cost analysis, which shows that only 20% of fixed overhead could be avoided if the tops are purchased. The tops have been made in a remote section of Gardner's factory building, using equipment for which no alternate use is apparent in the foreseeable future.

REQUIRED

(a) Prepare a differential analysis showing whether or not you would recommend that the convertible tops be purchased from Dupre Company.

(b) Assuming that the production capacity released by purchasing the tops could be devoted to a subcontracting job for another company that netted a contribution margin of $10,400, what maximum purchase price could Gardner Corporation pay for the tops?

(c) Identify two important qualitative factors that Gardner Corporation should consider in deciding whether to purchase the needed tops.

Dropping unprofitable division

25–41 Based on the following analysis of last year's operations of Mendota, Inc., a financial vice-president of the company believes that the firm's total net income could be increased by $30,000 if the Soft Goods Division were discontinued. (Amounts are given in thousands of dollars.)

	Totals	All Other Divisions	Soft Goods Division
Sales	$2,800	$2,000	$800
Cost of Goods Sold:			
Variable	(970)	(650)	(320)
Fixed	(530)	(350)	(180)
Gross Profit	$1,300	$1,000	$300
Operating Expenses:			
Variable	(750)	(500)	(250)
Fixed	(400)	(300)	(100)
Net Income (Loss)	$ 150	$ 200	($ 50)

REQUIRED

Provide answers for each of the following independent situations:

(a) Assuming that fixed costs and expenses would not be affected by discontinuing the Soft Goods Division, prepare an analysis showing why you agree or disagree with the vice-president.

(b) Assume that discontinuance of the Soft Goods Division will enable the company to avoid 20% of the fixed portion of cost of goods sold and 25% of the fixed operating expenses allocated to the Soft Goods Division. Calculate the resulting effect on net income.

(c) Assume that in addition to the cost avoidance in part (b), the production capacity released by discontinuance of the Soft Goods Division can be used to produce 6,000 units of a new product that would have a variable cost per unit of $9 and would require additional fixed costs totaling $17,000.

At what unit price must the new product be sold if the company is to increase its total net income by $30,000?

Product emphasis

25–42 Western Corporation manufactures both a deluxe and a standard model of a household food blender. Because of limited demand, for several years production has been at 80% of estimated capacity, which is thought to be limited by the number of machine hours available. At current operation levels, a profit analysis for each product line shows the following:

	Per-unit Data			
		Deluxe		**Standard**
Sales price		$216		$84
Production costs:				
Direct material	$89		$12	
Direct labor	36		23	
Variable factory overhead	15		11	
Fixed factory overhead*	25	$165	10	$56
Variable operating expenses		18		10
Fixed operating expenses		8		5
Total costs		$191		$71
Operating income		$ 25		$13

*Assigned on the basis of machine hours at normal capacity.

Management wants to utilize the company's current excess capacity by increasing production.

REQUIRED
(a) What general decision guideline applies in this situation?
(b) Assuming that sufficient units of either product can be sold at current prices to use existing capacity fully and that fixed costs will not be affected, prepare an analysis showing which product line should be emphasized if net income for the firm is the decision basis.

Variable and absorption costing

25–43 Lakeland Corporation makes a product with total unit manufacturing costs of $9, of which $6 is variable. No units were on hand at the beginning of 19X0. During 19X0 and 19X1, the only product manufactured was sold for $14 per unit, and the cost structure did not change. The company uses the first-in, first-out inventory method and has the following production and sales for 19X0 and 19X1:

	Units Manufactured	**Units Sold**
19X0	120,000	90,000
19X1	120,000	130,000

REQUIRED
(a) Prepare gross profit computations for 19X0 and 19X1 using absorption costing.
(b) Prepare gross profit computations for 19X0 and 19X1 using variable costing.
(c) Explain how your answers illustrate the related generalizations presented in the chapter regarding the differences between gross profit under absorption and variable costing.

Variable and absorption costing

25–44 Summarized data for the first year's operations of Austin Manufacturing, Inc., are as follows:

Sales (75,000 units)	$3,000,000
Production costs (80,000 units):	
Direct material	880,000
Direct labor	720,000
Factory overhead:	
Variable	544,000
Fixed	320,000
Operating expenses:	
Variable	168,000
Fixed	240,000

REQUIRED

(a) Prepare an income statement based on full absorption costing.
(b) Prepare an income statement based on variable costing.
(c) Assume you must decide quickly whether to accept a special one-time order for 1,000 units for $29 per unit. Which income statement presents the most relevant data? Determine the apparent profit or loss on the special order based solely on this data.
(d) If the ending inventory is destroyed by fire, which costing approach would you use as a basis for filing an insurance claim for the fire loss? Why?

ALTERNATE PROBLEMS

Departmental income statement

25–35A Thornton, Inc., a retail store, has two departments, Appliances and Furniture. Operating information for the current year appears below.

	Appliance Dept.	Furniture Dept.
Inventory, January 1	$ 120,000	$ 90,000
Inventory, December 31	75,600	48,000
Net Sales	1,120,000	760,000
Purchases	640,000	480,000
Purchases Discounts	8,000	6,000
Transportation In	18,000	16,000
Direct Departmental Expenses	199,600	82,000

Indirect operating expenses of the firm were $180,000.

REQUIRED

(a) Prepare a departmental income statement showing departmental contribution to indirect expenses and net income of the firm. Assume an overall effective income tax rate of 40%.
(b) Calculate the gross profit percentage for each department.
(c) If the indirect expenses were allocated 60% to the Appliance Department and 40% to the Furniture Department, what would the net income be for each department?

Allocate indirect expenses

25–36A The following information was obtained from the ledger of Stillwell, Inc., at the end of the current year:

Stillwell, Inc.
Trial Balance
December 31, 19XX

	Debit	Credit
Cash	$ 18,000	
Accounts Receivable (net)	70,000	
Inventory, December 31	45,000	
Equipment and Fixtures (net)	97,000	
Accounts Payable		$ 34,000
Common Stock		120,000
Retained Earnings		30,000
Sales—Department A		360,000
Sales—Department B		140,000
Cost of Goods Sold—Department A	216,000	
Cost of Goods Sold—Department B	70,000	
Sales Salaries Expense	74,000	
Advertising Expense	31,000	
Insurance Expense (on merchandise)	10,000	
Uncollectible Accounts Expense	3,000	
Occupancy Expense	16,000	
Office and Other Administrative Expense	34,000	
	$684,000	$684,000

Analysis of operating expenses at the end of each period enables the firm to prepare a departmental income statement. Analysis of payroll records, advertising copy, and other documents permitted the preparation of the following tabulation:

	Direct Expense		Indirect	Allocation Basis for Indirect
	Dept. A	Dept. B	Expense	Expenses
Sales Salaries Expense	$48,000	$20,000	$ 6,000	Equally
Advertising Expense	15,000	6,000	10,000	Relative sales
Insurance Expense	8,000	2,000		
Occupancy Expense			16,000	Floor space
Uncollectible Accounts Expense	2,000	1,000		
Office and Other Administrative Expense	17,000	9,000	8,000	3 to 1 ratio (A to B)

Department A occupies 5,000 square feet of floor space, while Department B has 3,000 square feet. Indirect expenses should be allocated to departments as indicated above.

REQUIRED

Prepare a departmental income statement showing net income by department. Assume an overall effective income tax rate of 30%.

Analyze operational changes

25–37A The management of Milton's Department Store is concerned about the operation of its sporting goods department, which has not been very successful. The following condensed income statement gives the latest year's results:

	Sporting Goods Department	All Other Departments
Sales	$400,000	$2,000,000
Cost of Goods Sold	300,000	1,300,000
Gross Profit	$100,000	$ 700,000
Direct Expenses	$ 55,000	$ 280,000
Indirect Expenses	38,000	200,000
Total Expenses	$ 93,000	$ 480,000
Net Income	$ 7,000	$ 220,000

REQUIRED

(a) Calculate the gross profit percentage for the Sporting Goods department and for the other departments as a group.

(b) It is estimated that if an additional $10,000 were spent on promotion of sporting goods, average prices can be raised 5% without affecting physical volume of goods sold. What effect would this have on the operating results of the Sporting Goods department? (Ignore the effect of income taxes.)

(c) Alternatively, it is estimated that physical volume of goods sold could be increased 6% if an additional $7,000 were spent on promotion of sporting goods and prices were not increased. Assuming that operating expenses remain the same, what effect would this have on the operating results of the Sporting Goods department? (Ignore the effect of income taxes.)

Special order

25–39A Total cost data follows for Lincoln Manufacturing Company, which has a normal capacity per period of 20,000 units of product that sell for $54 each. For the foreseeable future, regular sales volume should continue to equal normal capacity.

Direct material	$270,000
Direct labor	216,000
Variable factory overhead	129,600
Fixed factory overhead (Note 1)	118,800
Selling expense (Note 2)	128,000
Administrative expense (fixed)	50,000
	$912,400

(1) Beyond normal capacity, fixed overhead costs increase $4,500 for each 1,000 units *or fraction thereof* until a maximum capacity of 24,000 units is reached.

(2) Selling expenses consist of a 10% sales commission and shipping costs of $1 per unit. Lincoln pays only one-half of the regular sales commission rate on any sale amounting to $3,000 or more.

Lincoln's sales manager has received a special order for 2,500 units from a large discount chain at a price of $43 each, F.O.B. factory. The controller's office has furnished the following additional cost data related to the special order:

(1) Changes in the product's design will reduce direct material $4 per unit.
(2) Special processing will add 10% to the per-unit direct labor costs.
(3) Variable overhead will continue at the same proportion of direct labor costs.
(4) Other costs should not be affected.

REQUIRED
(a) Present an analysis supporting a decision to accept or reject the special order.
(b) What is the lowest price Lincoln could receive and still make a profit of $5,000 before income taxes on the special order?
(c) What general qualitative factors should Lincoln consider?

Make or buy

25–40A Glendale Corporation currently makes the nylon mooring cover for its main product, a fiberglass boat designed for tournament bass fishing. The costs of producing the 2,000 covers needed each year are:

Nylon fabric	$80,000
Wood battens	16,000
Brass fittings	8,000
Direct labor	32,000
Variable factory overhead	24,000
Fixed factory overhead	40,000

Calvin Company, a specialty fabricator of synthetic materials, can make the needed covers of comparable quality for $80 each, F.O.B. shipping point. Glendale would furnish its own trademark insignia at a unit cost of $5. Transportation in would be $4 per unit, paid by Glendale Corporation.

Glendale's chief accountant has prepared a cost analysis, which shows that only 30% of fixed overhead could be avoided if the covers are purchased. The covers have been made in a remote section of Glendale's factory building, using equipment for which no alternate use is apparent in the foreseeable future.

REQUIRED
(a) Prepare a differential analysis showing whether or not you would recommend that the mooring covers be purchased from Calvin Company.
(b) Assuming that the production capacity released by purchasing the covers could be devoted to a subcontracting job for another company that netted a contribution margin of $16,000, what maximum purchase price could Glendale pay for the covers?
(c) Identify two important qualitative factors that Glendale Corporation should consider in deciding whether to purchase the needed covers.

Dropping unprofitable division

25–41A Based on the following analysis of last year's operations of Monona, Inc., a financial vice-president of the company believes that the firm's total net income could be increased by $40,000 if the Soft Goods Division were discontinued. (Amounts are given in thousands of dollars.)

	Totals	All Other Divisions	Soft Goods Division
Sales	$4,700	$3,600	$1,100
Cost of Goods Sold:			
Variable	(1,900)	(1,400)	(500)
Fixed	(1,200)	(1,000)	(200)
Gross Profit	$1,600	$1,200	$ 400
Operating Expenses:			
Variable	(840)	(500)	(340)
Fixed	(400)	(300)	(100)
Net Income (Loss)	$ 360	$ 400	($ 40)

REQUIRED
Provide answers for each of the following independent situations:

(a) Assuming that fixed costs and expenses would not be affected by discontinuing the Soft Goods Division, prepare an analysis showing why you agree or disagree with the vice-president.

(b) Assume that discontinuance of the Soft Goods Division will enable the company to avoid 30% of the fixed portion of cost of goods sold and 40% of the fixed operating expenses allocated to the Soft Goods Division. Calculate the resulting effect on net income.

(c) Assume that in addition to the cost avoidance in part (b), the production capacity released by discontinuance of the Soft Goods Division can be used to produce 6,000 units of a new product that would have a variable cost per unit of $15 and require additional fixed costs totaling $17,000. At what unit price must the new product be sold if the company is to increase its total net income by $45,000?

Product emphasis

25–42A Wolff Corporation manufactures both automatic and manual residential water softeners. Because of limited demand, for several years production has been at 90% of estimated capacity, which is thought to be limited by the number of machine hours available. At current operation levels, a profit analysis for each product line shows the following:

	Per-unit Data			
	Automatic		Manual	
Sales price		$500		$260
Production costs:				
Direct material	$ 90		$50	
Direct labor	80		40	
Variable factory overhead	40		20	
Fixed factory overhead*	90	$300	45	$155
Variable operating expenses		50		10
Fixed operating expenses		90		60
Total costs		$440		$225
Operating income		$ 60		$ 35

*Assigned on the basis of machine hours at normal capacity.

Management wants to utilize the company's current excess capacity by increasing production.

REQUIRED

(a) What general decision guideline applies in this situation?

(b) Assuming that sufficient units of either product can be sold at current prices to use existing capacity fully and that fixed costs will not be affected, prepare an analysis showing which product line should be emphasized if net income for the firm is the decision basis.

Variable and absorption costing

25–43A Landover Corporation makes a product with total unit manufacturing costs of \$16, of which \$9 is variable. No units were on hand at the beginning of 19X0. During 19X0 and 19X1, the only product manufactured was sold for \$24 per unit, and the cost structure did not change. The company uses the first-in, first-out inventory method and has the following production and sales for 19X0 and 19X1:

	Units Manufactured	**Units Sold**
19X0	100,000	70,000
19X1	100,000	120,000

REQUIRED

(a) Prepare gross profit computations for 19X0 and 19X1 using absorption costing.

(b) Prepare gross profit computations for 19X0 and 19X1 using variable costing.

(c) Explain how your answers illustrate the related generalizations presented in the chapter regarding the differences between gross profit under absorption and variable costing.

BUSINESS DECISION PROBLEM

Champion Corporation manufactures both an automatic and a manual household dehumidifier. Because of limited demand, for several years production has been at 80% of estimated capacity, which is thought to be limited by the number of machine hours available. At current operation levels, a profit analysis for each product line shows the following:

	Per-unit Data			
	Automatic		**Manual**	
Sales price		\$360		\$130
Production costs:				
Direct material	\$72		\$19	
Direct labor	43		22	
Variable factory overhead	65		14	
Fixed factory overhead*	40	\$220	16	\$ 71
Variable operating expenses		50		18
Fixed operating expenses		30		13
Total costs		\$300		\$102
Operating income		\$ 60		\$ 28

*Assigned on the basis of machine hours at normal capacity.

Management wants to utilize the company's current excess capacity by increasing production.

REQUIRED

Present answers for the following questions in each independent situation:

(a) Assume that sufficient units of either product can be sold at current prices to utilize existing capacity fully and that fixed costs will not be affected.
   (1) To which product should the excess capacity be devoted if the decision basis is maximization of sales revenue?
   (2) What would be your answer to part (1) if the decision were based on contribution margin per unit of product?
   (3) Prepare an analysis showing which product line should be emphasized if the firm's net income is the decision basis.
   (4) What general decision guideline applies in this situation?

(b) Suppose the excess capacity represents 10,000 machine hours, which can be used to make 4,000 automatic units or 10,000 manual units or any proportionate combination. The only market available for these extra units is a foreign market in which the sales prices must be reduced by 20% and in which no more than 6,000 units of either model can be sold. All costs will remain the same except that the selling commission of 10% (included in variable operating expenses) will be avoided. Prepare an analysis showing which product should be emphasized and the effect on the firm's net income.

(c) Assume that the excess capacity can be used as indicated in part (b), and that the firm's market research department believes that the production available from using the excess capacity exclusively on either model can be sold in the domestic market at regular prices if a promotion campaign costing $200,000 is undertaken for the automatic model or $230,000 for the manual model. Prepare an analysis indicating for which product the campaign should be undertaken.

ANSWERS TO SELF-TEST QUESTIONS

1. (c) 2. (a) 3. (c) 4. (c) 5. (d)

26

Budgeting and Standard Costs

Chapter Objectives

- Describe the budgeting process in a business entity.
- Provide an illustration of the development of a business budget.
- Develop an understanding of the use of standard rates for material, labor, and overhead.
- Outline the calculation of cost variances from the standards.
- Describe and illustrate the use of standard costs in financial statements.

Fortune is the arbiter of half our actions, but she still leaves the control of the other half to us.

MACHIAVELLI

Management has a basic responsibility to plan, control, measure performance, and make decisions. In order to carry out this responsibility, management must plan revenues and expenses, compare actual results to planned results, evaluate differences between actual and planned results, and make decisions and take corrective action based on the evaluations. Budgeting and standard costs are two concepts which facilitate this process.

BUDGETING

A budget is a formal, written, financial plan which presents management's planned actions and the projected financial effects of these plans. Budgeting incorporates many of the accounting concepts discussed in previous chapters. The budget usually presents the financial plan in financial statement format, including income statement, balance sheet, and statement of changes in financial position.

All types of entities can derive benefits from the budgeting process—manufacturing firms, retail businesses, governmental agencies, private clubs, sole proprietorships, churches, trade associations. The format of the budget document will differ among the different types of entities, but the basic concepts of budgeting will be the same.

ADVANTAGES OF BUDGETING

A Plan for Accomplishing Objectives

The annual planning process forces management to step back from the daily problems of the entity and methodically examine the entity as a whole and the direction in which it is moving. Management must carefully consider anticipated market demand and recent trends, changes in productive capacity, availability of new technologies, anticipated actions of competitors, performance of outside suppliers, and many other factors. Long-term goals should be reevaluated, and all short-term goals should be reviewed during the planning process.

The budget should then be developed in concert with the goals and objectives that management wants the entity to achieve. The budgeting process will therefore project some of the current operations as they exist and plan to make changes in others.

Control of Operations

The budget provides the planned basis to which actual results can be compared to test whether remedial action is necessary. Reasonably frequent comparison of budgeted and actual operating data is a sound operating procedure. This provides a natural base for the application of management by exception principles.

A Basis of Performance Measurement

A firm is successful because its key personnel do their jobs efficiently, reliably, and with general adherence to plans. For all major aspects of a firm's operation, a well-developed budget includes criteria for a high level of performance. Therefore, *properly used,* a budget can be a significant motivational force because managers at various levels know that their actual performance is evaluated by comparison with a desired level of performance.

BUDGET PREPARATION

Even though specific budgeting procedures vary widely among firms, all business enterprises engaged in comprehensive budgeting must consider certain elements of budget preparation—the budget committee, the budget period, and the master budget.

The Budget Committee

A budget committee generally consists of representatives from all major areas of a firm—such as sales, production, and finance—and is frequently headed by the firm's controller. The committee must coordinate preparation of the budget, initiate budget procedures, collect and integrate data from various organizational units, supervise the review and modification of original estimates, and direct the implementation of the budget. All departments should participate in formulating the budget, so it will be accepted as a reasonable standard of performance. In the absence of such participation, the budget may be viewed as an unreasonable goal imposed by outsiders who do not fully understand the department's operations.

The Budget Period

The period covered by a budget varies according to the nature of the specific activity involved. Cash budgets may cover a week or a month, production budgets a month or a calendar quarter, general operating budgets a calendar quarter or year, and budgets for acquisition of plant assets several years. In **continuous budgeting,** an interesting extension of period-by-period budgeting, the coming year is dealt with in terms of quarterly periods. At any given time, the firm has four sequential quarterly budgets, and it adds a new quarterly budget as each quarter expires. With this system, regardless of the time of the year, the current budget always covers the current calendar quarter plus the next three quarters. Continuous budgeting can also be carried out in monthly periods.

The Master Budget

The **master budget** is a comprehensive document that integrates all the detailed budgets for the firm's various activities. The master budget contains the data necessary to formulate projected financial statements for the budget period.

The details of a master budget vary according to whether the firm's operations are manufacturing, merchandising, or service oriented. In this chapter, we illustrate budgeting for a small manufacturing operation, Baker Corporation. The following key components constitute Baker Corporation's master budget:

Sales budget Production budget Direct material budget Direct labor budget Factory overhead budget Operating expense budget	Provide a basis for projected income statement
Capital expenditures budget Cash budget	Provide a basis for projected balance sheet

ZERO-BASE BUDGETING

Traditional budgeting procedures often start with the preceding year's budget or the preceding year's actual expenditures. In many instances, the budgeting process simply results in last year's figures plus a percentage. Although some adjustments may be made, too often this approach automatically justifies the amounts budgeted or expended last year and limits thorough analysis and justification procedures to the "new money," or the incremental portion of the total budget. The obvious defect in this approach is that portions of last year's expenditures may not deserve continued justification. The firm may want to take funds from existing operations and devote them to more attractive new operations.

Zero-base budgeting (ZBB) avoids the problem in traditional budgeting described above. In general, ZBB requires each of the firm's budgetary units to justify *all* of its expenditures as if the unit's operations were just starting. Hence, the label *zero-base* budgeting.

ZBB may take different forms, but the prevailing procedure is the following:*

(1) The firm is divided into *decision units* (cost or service centers), to which budget decisions naturally relate.
(2) Decision units request funds by preparing *decision packages*, which set forth a statement of goals, a program for achieving them, benefits expected, related alternatives, consequences of not being funded, and required expenditures. Decision packages are often grouped as they relate to continuing a minimum level of operations, increasing the level of continuing operations, and initiating new operations.
(3) Various levels of management participtate in combining and ranking all departments' decision packages.
(4) Decision packages ranked higher than management's cutoff point constitute the plans for the firm's master budget.

A major drawback to ZBB is that it is time consuming—and thus costly—for all departments to justify in detail each year all aspects of their operations. Consequently, some firms use traditional budgeting procedures and have what is termed a *zero-based review* of departments every two or three years. ZBB is much more useful in budgeting for support functions—such as research and development or the utility department—than it is for budgeting direct material and labor.

*For a comprehensive treatment of the subject, see P.A. Pyhrr, *Zero-Base Budgeting* (New York: John Wiley & Sons, Inc., 1975).

The major sequential steps in preparing the master budget are as follows (assuming the prior development of long-run goals and plans):

(1) Prepare sales forecast.
(2) Determine production volume.
(3) Estimate manufacturing costs and operating expenses.
(4) Determine cash flows and other financial effects.
(5) Formulate projected financial statements.

Estimating sales volume is usually the initial step in constructing a master budget. Once sales are forecast, production volume can be set to reflect desired changes, if any, in finished goods inventories. When production volume is known, reliable estimates can be made for direct material, direct labor, factory overhead, and operating expenses. With estimates of these costs and expenses, cash flows and the related effects on other accounts can be projected. Then, with proper consideration for capital expenditures and related financing, projected financial statements can be prepared. Aspects of the detailed budgets may indicate unacceptable situations such as excessive costs, exceeded capacities, or cash shortages for which revisions must be made. Of course, early identification of potential operating problems is a key advantage of budgeting.

ILLUSTRATIONS OF BUDGETS

The following illustrations outline the development of a relatively simple master budget for Baker Corporation. Budgeted financial statements are not illustrated because they would be virtually identical with the financial statements studied earlier throughout the text.

Sales Budget

The sales budget is prepared first. Anticipated unit sales volume is based on a sales forecast that reflects prior periods' sales, expected general economic conditions, related market research, and specific industry trends. This forecast must be prepared very carefully. Overestimating sales volume can lead to large unwanted inventories, which in turn result in extra storage costs and possibly sales price reductions when liquidating the excess inventory. Underestimating sales can lead to loss of sales revenue and customer ill-will stemming from unfilled orders.

The estimated unit sales volume of each product is multiplied by planned unit sales prices to estimate sales revenue. An example of a sales budget is presented in Exhibit 26–1.

Units of Production Budget

The production budget reflects the quantity of each product to be produced during the budget period. Scheduled production should specifically provide for anticipated sales and desired ending inventories and, of course, consider the beginning inventories of each product. Assume Baker Corporation wants to increase its

EXHIBIT 26–1

Baker Corporation
Sales Budget
For the Quarter Ended June 30, 19XX

	Estimated Unit Sales Volume	Planned Unit Sales Price	Budgeted Total Sales
Product A: East Area	40,000	$10	$ 400,000
West Area	28,000	10	280,000
Total product A	68,000		$ 680,000
Product B: East Area	20,000	$13	$ 260,000
West Area	11,000	13	143,000
Total product B	31,000		$ 403,000
Total sales revenue			$1,083,000

inventory of product A by 20% and decrease its inventory of product B by 20%. Baker's production budget appears in Exhibit 26–2. Note that the desired change in inventory of each product is accomplished by scheduling the appropriate production volumes.

Materials Budget

The quantities of materials to be purchased to meet scheduled production and desired ending inventory requirements are presented in the materials budget. Any beginning materials inventory must be considered in estimating purchases for the budget period. The quantities to be acquired are multiplied by the anticipated unit cost prices to calculate the total dollar amounts of materials purchases. In the materials budget illustrated in Exhibit 26–3, we assume that Baker Corporation uses only two direct materials, X and Y, in producing products A and B.

Direct Labor Budget

The direct labor budget presents the number of direct labor hours necessary for the production volume planned for the budget period. These hours are multiplied by the applicable hourly labor rates to determine the total dollar amounts of direct labor costs to be budgeted. In the direct labor budget for Baker Corporation (Exhibit 26–4, page 1004), we have assumed that both products A and B require manufacturing work in the Machining and Finishing departments, as follows:

	Machining Department	Finishing Department
Product A	0.5 hours	0.3 hours
Product B	1.0 hours	0.4 hours

EXHIBIT 26–2

Baker Corporation
Units of Production Budget
For the Quarter Ended June 30, 19XX

	Units of Finished Product A	Units of Finished Product B
Estimated units to be sold	68,000	31,000
Desired ending inventories	12,000	4,000
Amounts to be available	80,000	35,000
Less: Beginning inventories	10,000	5,000
Total production to be scheduled	70,000	30,000

EXHIBIT 26–3

Baker Corporation
Materials Budget
For the Quarter Ended June 30, 19XX

	X	Y
Direct material required:		
Product A: 70,000 × 2.0	140,000	
70,000 × 0.5		35,000
Product B: 30,000 × 2.0	60,000	
30,000 × 2.0		60,000
Desired ending materials inventory	40,000	15,000
Total units to be available	240,000	110,000
Less: Beginning materials inventory	40,000	30,000
Total units to be purchased	200,000	80,000
Unit purchase prices	× $0.60	× $0.80
Total materials purchases	$120,000	$64,000

Factory Overhead Budget

Recall from earlier chapters that factory overhead comprises all factory costs that are not direct material or direct labor. Examples of factory overhead are factory supplies, indirect labor and factory supervisory salaries, utilities, depreciation, maintenance, taxes, and insurance. Because of the variety of cost factors, factory overhead includes both variable and fixed cost elements.

The factory overhead budget should be determined by using a flexible budget approach. A flexible factory overhead budget for the Machining Department of

EXHIBIT 26–4

Baker Corporation
Direct Labor Budget
For the Quarter Ended June 30, 19XX

	Machining Department	Finishing Department
Direct labor hours required for production:		
Product A: (70,000 units × 0.5 hours)	35,000	
(70,000 units × 0.3 hours)		21,000
Product B: (30,000 units × 1.0 hours)	30,000	
(30,000 units × 0.4 hours)		12,000
Total direct labor hours	65,000	33,000
Hourly rate for direct labor	× $7.00	× $8.00
Total direct labor costs	$455,000	$264,000

Baker Corporation is shown in Exhibit 26–5. Note that the budget separates variable and fixed overhead cost elements and presents budgeted factory overhead costs for three different volumes of direct labor hours. A flexible budget may take the columnar form shown in Exhibit 26–5, or it may be stated as a cost formula. For the Machining Department of Baker Corporation for the quarter ended June 30, the overhead formula for the planned operating volume of 65,000 direct labor hours would be:

$$\text{Total Factory Overhead} = \text{Total Fixed Overhead} + \left(\text{Variable Overhead per direct labor hour} \times \text{Production Volume}\right)$$

$$\$169{,}000 = \$104{,}000 + \left(\$1 \times \text{65,000 direct labor hours}\right)$$

Notice that the formula agrees with the related column for 65,000 hours in Exhibit 26–5.

A flexible factory overhead budget should be prepared for each production department. The master budget amount is calculated using the related production volume. In our example, the production volume selected is derived from the direct labor budget (65,000 direct labor hours for the Machining Department), as shown in Exhibit 26–4.

Operating Expense Budget

Operating expenses, composed of selling and general administrative expenses, are often budgeted using the flexible budget approach just illustrated for factory overhead. However, certain variable selling and administrative expenses, such as sales commissions, may vary with *sales volume* rather than with production

EXHIBIT 26–5

Baker Corporation
Machining Department
Factory Overhead Budget
For the Quarter Ended June 30, 19XX

	Variable Cost per Direct Labor Hour	Overhead Costs at 60,000 Direct Labor Hours	Overhead Costs at 65,000 Direct Labor Hours	Overhead Costs at 70,000 Direct Labor Hours
Variable costs:				
Factory supplies	$0.30	$ 18,000	$ 19,500	$ 21,000
Indirect labor	0.40	24,000	26,000	28,000
Utilities	0.20	12,000	13,000	14,000
Maintenance	0.10	6,000	6,500	7,000
Total variable overhead	$1.00	$ 60,000	$ 65,000	$ 70,000
Fixed costs:				
Supervisory salaries		$ 30,000	$ 30,000	$ 30,000
Depreciation on equipment		15,000	15,000	15,000
Utilities		20,000	20,000	20,000
Maintenance		12,000	12,000	12,000
Property taxes and insurance		27,000	27,000	27,000
Total fixed overhead		$104,000	$104,000	$104,000
Total factory overhead		$164,000	$169,000	$174,000

volume. As with factory overhead, for purposes of departmental cost control and performance measurement, various supplemental schedules would be prepared to relate specific portions of total selling and administrative expenses to specific departments or cost centers.

Budgeted Income Statement

With the information available from the budgets discussed above, a budgeted income statement can be prepared. Other income or expense and estimated income taxes would also be incorporated. The budgeted income statement may be supported by a schedule or statement of cost of goods sold.

Capital Expenditures Budget

Expenditures for plant and equipment are among a firm's most important transactions. Chapter 27 considers some approaches to choosing among capital outlay proposals. Because of the large dollar amounts involved and the relatively long lives of capital assets, such expenditures should be well planned. Even companies that are not growing must eventually replace their equipment. For expanding companies—especially those subject to high technological obsolescence—the budgeting of capital expenditures can be most challenging.

EXHIBIT 26–6

Baker Corporation
Capital Expenditures Budget
For the Year Ended December 31, 19XX

	Calendar Quarters Ending			
	March 31	**June 30**	**September 30**	**December 31**
Machinery	$7,000	$10,000		$40,000
Delivery equipment		8,000	$ 8,000	
Conveyor system			40,000	6,000
Computer		32,000		
Totals	$7,000	$50,000	$48,000	$46,000

In its simplest form, a capital expenditures budget is a list of types of equipment and the amounts budgeted for their acquisition in each of a series of future operating periods, as illustrated in Exhibit 26–6. Capital outlay decisions may significantly affect aspects of other budgets, such as production capacities in production budgets, depreciation expense in factory overhead and operating expense budgets, and related cash expenditures in the cash budget. For example, the $50,000 to be spent in the quarter ended June 30 appears as an April cash disbursement in Baker Corporation's cash budget shown in Exhibit 26–7.

Cash Budget

The cash budget portrays the projected flows of cash during the budget period. Cash receipts are shown in terms of their sources and cash disbursements in terms of their uses. The difference between these two flows determines the net periodic change in cash balances.

Because of the characteristic time lags between many routine transactions and their related effects on cash, proper cash budgeting often requires the analysis of certain data contained in other budgets to determine their impact on cash flows. Sales precede collections from customers, purchases precede payments on account, depreciation usually does not represent current cash outlays, and, of course, several types of prepayments may call for cash outlays before the related expenses are recognized in the accounts. Generally, the shorter the budget period, the more significant may be the differences between cash flows and related aspects of the firm's operations.

For an example of one important aspect of cash budgeting, assume that Baker Corporation has analyzed the collection of its total credit sales in any month as follows:

(1) In the month of sale, 30% is collected and receives a 2% cash discount. (The cash received is thus 30% of the credit sales × 0.98.)

(2) In the month following sale, 50% is collected and no discounts are involved.

EXHIBIT 26–7

Baker Corporation
Cash Budget
For the Quarter Ended June 30, 19XX

	April	May	June
Cash receipts:			
Cash sales	$ 18,000	$ 15,000	$ 17,500
Collections from customers	341,780	350,000	358,000
Sale of investments	8,000	—	—
Short-term borrowing	40,000	—	—
Other sources	3,220	6,000	6,500
Total cash receipts	$411,000	$371,000	$382,000
Cash disbursements:			
Manufacturing costs	$280,000	$290,000	$285,000
Operating expenses	60,000	61,000	58,000
Capital expenditures	50,000	—	—
Income taxes	—	—	30,000
Cash Dividends	15,000	—	—
Other disbursements	4,000	9,000	19,000
Total cash disbursements	$409,000	$360,000	$392,000
Net cash provided (applied)	$ 2,000	$ 11,000	($ 10,000)
Beginning cash balance	20,000	22,000	33,000
Ending cash balance	$ 22,000	$ 33,000	$ 23,000

(3) In the second month following sale, 18% is collected. The remaining 2% of accounts are written off as uncollectible.

Assuming estimated credit sales of $350,000 in February, $340,000 in March, and $370,000 in April, Baker Corporation's cash receipts from credit customers for April could be budgeted in the following manner:

		Collections Received During		
	Monthly Credit Sales	**February**	**March**	**April**
February:	$350,000 × (30% × 0.98)	$102,900		
	350,000 × 50%		$175,000	
	350,000 × 18%			$ 63,000
March:	$340,000 × (30% × 0.98)		99,960	
	340,000 × 50%			170,000
April:	$370,000 × (30% × 0.98)			108,780
				$341,780

Baker Corporation's cash budget for the quarter ended June 30, 19XX (Exhibit 26–7), reflects some of the more common examples of cash receipts and disbursements. Note how virtually every other element of the master budget has affected the cash budget.

Budgeted Balance Sheet The budgeted balance sheet presents anticipated balances for the various balance sheet items at the end of the budget period. Assuming all other budgeting procedures have been properly coordinated, the budgeted balance sheet is extremely useful in reviewing the firm's projected financial position. Management can then identify potential financial problems—for example, by assessing the adequacy of the projected current ratio and equity ratio—and can revise plans or take other necessary corrective actions.

STANDARD COSTS

Cost accounting systems generally become more useful to management when they include budgeted amounts to serve as points of comparison with actual results. As previously discussed, budgeted amounts are determined through a complicated process which considers historical amounts, future estimates, and normative values determined in engineering studies. Budgeted amounts can be established as standard costs, which can be used for a number of purposes.

DETERMINATION OF STANDARD COSTS

Standard costs represent the costs that should be incurred during the next year. Standard costs are typically established for reasonably attainable levels of efficiency rather than for theoretically perfect or ideal levels of efficiency. They should serve as a target, and thus be a motivating force as a standard of performance.

Standard costs are usually established at the beginning of the year, during the budgeting process. Standards should be updated during the year only if there are significant changes in vendor costs, production technology, or product design. One of the important uses of standard costs is to compare actual costs to the standard costs to determine variances. These variances will be meaningful only if the standards used represent the reasonably attainable level of efficiency that was planned during the budgeting process.

Ordinarily, a manufacturing firm establishes standard cost specifications for each of its products. Each standard cost consists of a standard direct material cost, a standard direct labor cost, and a standard overhead cost.

Direct Material Standards The standard cost of direct material used to make a finished unit is the product of two factors—**standard usage** and **standard price.** Usually, to determine standard quantities of the material used to make a unit of product, production personnel must determine the needed quality, production runs, normal spoilage, and other factors. Standard prices are often calculated by purchasing department and accounting personnel after specifications, price quotations from suppliers, possible discounts, and related factors have been considered.

To begin our illustration, assume that the Gregg Manufacturing Company makes only one simple product, A, which requires one type of material, M. If the standard usage is two pounds of M to make one unit of A, and the standard price of M is $1 per pound, the standard materials cost for a unit of product A is $2:

$$\text{Standard Usage} \times \text{Standard Price} = \text{Standard Cost per Unit}$$

$$\begin{pmatrix}\text{2 pounds of material M} \\ \text{per unit of product A}\end{pmatrix} \times \begin{pmatrix}\text{\$1 per pound} \\ \text{of material M}\end{pmatrix} = \begin{matrix}\text{\$2 per unit} \\ \text{of product A}\end{matrix}$$

Direct Labor Standards

The standard cost of direct labor used to make a finished unit is also the product of two factors—**standard time** and **standard rate.** Using time-and-motion studies or other analyses, job analysts and other production personnel set the standard time allotted to each labor operation. Union representatives may influence the time standards, since standard rates are usually set by contracts negotiated between management and labor unions. If, for Gregg Manufacturing Company, the standard direct labor time to make a unit of product A was set at one hour and the standard labor rate was $8 per hour, the standard cost for direct labor would be $8 per unit of product A:

$$\text{Standard Time} \times \text{Standard Rate} = \text{Standard Cost per Unit}$$

$$\begin{pmatrix}\text{1 hour of direct labor} \\ \text{per unit of product A}\end{pmatrix} \times \begin{pmatrix}\text{\$8 per direct} \\ \text{labor hour}\end{pmatrix} = \begin{matrix}\text{\$8 per unit} \\ \text{of product A}\end{matrix}$$

Factory Overhead Standards

Typically, formula flexible budgeting is used to estimate the amount of factory overhead costs at the anticipated level of production that the firm considers its normal capacity. For example, the formula flexible budget for Gregg Manufacturing Company would be:

$$\begin{matrix}\text{Total} \\ \text{Factory} \\ \text{Overhead}\end{matrix} = \begin{pmatrix}\text{Total} \\ \text{Fixed} \\ \text{Overhead}\end{pmatrix} + \begin{pmatrix}\begin{matrix}\text{Variable} \\ \text{Overhead} \\ \text{per direct} \\ \text{labor hour}\end{matrix} \times \begin{matrix}\text{Production} \\ \text{volume in} \\ \text{direct labor} \\ \text{hours}\end{matrix}\end{pmatrix}$$

$$\$40{,}000 = (\$30{,}000) + (\$1 \times 10{,}000)$$

A columnar flexible budget for Gregg Manufacturing Company appears in Exhibit 26–8. The budget indicates that overhead is applied on the basis of direct labor hours and that normal capacity is 10,000 standard direct labor hours per month. The standard amounts of overhead at various levels of operation are shown.

Note that overhead is separated into variable and fixed cost elements, that variable overhead increases proportionately with production levels, and that fixed overhead does not respond to changes in production levels. At Gregg Manufacturing Company's normal capacity of 10,000 standard direct labor hours, the

EXHIBIT 26–8

Gregg Manufacturing Company
Flexible Overhead Cost Budget
For the Month of June, 19XX

	Production Levels			
Percent of Normal Capacity	80%	90%	100%	110%
Standard Direct Labor Hours	8,000	9,000	10,000	11,000
Budget Factory Overhead:				
Variable costs:				
Factory supplies used	$ 800	$ 900	$ 1,000	$ 1,100
Indirect labor	1,600	1,800	2,000	2,200
Power	2,400	2,700	3,000	3,300
Other	3,200	3,600	4,000	4,400
Total variable overhead	$ 8,000	$ 9,000	$10,000	$11,000
Fixed costs:				
Supervisory salaries	$12,000	$12,000	$12,000	$12,000
Depreciation	8,000	8,000	8,000	8,000
Other	10,000	10,000	10,000	10,000
Total fixed overhead	$30,000	$30,000	$30,000	$30,000
Total Budgeted Factory Overhead	$38,000	$39,000	$40,000	$41,000

budget indicates a standard variable overhead rate of $1 per direct labor hour ($10,000/10,000 direct labor hours) and a standard fixed overhead rate of $3 per direct labor hour ($30,000/10,000 direct labor hours).

Total Standard Costs

Most firms prepare a summary of the standard costs (direct material, direct labor, and factory overhead) for each product. Based on the preceding concepts, Gregg Manufacturing Company's standard cost summary for product A would appear as in Exhibit 26–9. Thus, under normal conditions and operating at normal

EXHIBIT 26–9

Gregg Manufacturing Company
Standard Cost Summary—Product A

Direct Material (2 lb @ $1/lb)		$ 2
Direct Labor (1 hr @ $8/hr)		8
Factory Overhead (applied on basis of direct labor hours):		
Variable (1 hr @ rate of $1/direct labor hour)	$1	
Fixed (1 hr @ rate of $3/direct labor hour)	3	4
Total standard cost per unit of product A		$14

capacity, product A should be produced for a total cost of $14 per unit. We use these standard costs in our illustration of cost variance determination.

Cost Variances

Even in well-managed companies with carefully established and currently maintained cost standards, actual costs often differ from standard costs. The differences should be analyzed for indications of their cause so that appropriate action may be taken.

Suppose that, during June, Gregg Manufacturing Company produced 9,800 units of product A, for which it incurred the following actual costs (assume no work in process inventories):

Direct Material (20,600 lb @ $1.05/lb)		$ 21,630
Direct Labor (9,700 hr @ $8.10/hr)		78,570
Factory Overhead:		
Variable	$ 8,700	
Fixed	30,000	38,700
Total actual production costs incurred in June		$138,900

In Exhibit 26–10 the actual costs are compared with standard costs for 9,800 units of product, and the differences, or variances, for each cost category are calculated. The standard costs (from our standard cost summary for product A) are multiplied by the actual quantity of 9,800 units produced in June. Note that both favorable and unfavorable variances exist and that the overall net variance of $1,700 is unfavorable. To initiate remedial action, management must analyze the variance for each manufacturing cost element to determine the underlying causal factors related to prices paid, quantities used, and productive capacity utilized. The following paragraphs present these analyses and the related general journal entries (in summary form) for recording variances.

EXHIBIT 26–10
Comparison of Actual and Standard Costs of Product A
For the Month of June, 19XX

	Actual Costs (9,800 units)	Standard Costs (9,800 units)	Variances Favorable	Variances Unfavorable
Direct Material	$ 21,630	$ 19,600		$2,030
Direct Labor	78,570	78,400		170
Factory Overhead:				
Variable	8,700	9,800	$1,100	
Fixed	30,000	29,400		600
	$138,900	$137,200	$1,100	$2,800
Net total variance (unfavorable)			$1,700	

Material Variances

Variances for direct material stem primarily from paying more or less than the standard price and from using more or less than the standard quantity. Gregg Manufacturing Company's material variances for June are computed below.

The material price variance for Gregg would be:

$$\text{Material Price Variance} = \left(\text{Actual Price} - \text{Standard Price}\right) \times \text{Actual Quantity}$$

$$= (\$1.05 - \$1.00) \times 20{,}600 = \$1{,}030 \text{ Unfavorable}$$

The material price variance is unfavorable since actual price is greater than standard price. If actual price had been less than standard price, then the material price variance would have been favorable.

The material quantity variance for Gregg would be:

$$\text{Material Quantity Variance} = \left(\text{Actual Quantity} - \text{Standard Quantity}\right) \times \text{Standard Price}$$

$$= (20{,}600 - 19{,}600) \times \$1.00 = \$1{,}000 \text{ Unfavorable}$$

The standard quantity is the quantity that should have been used to produce 9,800 units (9,800 units × 2 pounds per unit = 19,600 pounds). The material quantity variance is unfavorable since actual quantity is greater than standard quantity. If actual quantity had been less than standard quantity, then material quantity variance would have been favorable.

The total material variance would be:

Material Price Variance	$1,030 Unfavorable
Material Quantity Variance	1,000 Unfavorable
Total Material Variance	$2,030 Unfavorable

Notice that the total material variance agrees with the amount in Exhibit 26–10.

The unfavorable price variance may have been caused by increases in supplier prices, improper purchasing, or other factors. The unfavorable quantity variance may have been caused by inefficient workers, poor-quality material, or other factors.

The general journal entry to record material costs and variances is:

Work in Process (standard price and quantity)	19,600	
Material Price Variance	1,030	
Material Quantity Variance	1,000	
Materials Inventory (actual price and quantity)		21,600

Note that the journal entry debits Work in Process for standard costs, records the two unfavorable variances as debits (analogous to losses or expenses), and records the actual costs of material requisitioned during June.[1]

[1]In our illustration, we recognize and record the material price variance when the materials start into production. Some firms recognize and record the price variance when materials purchases are recorded.

Labor Variances

Variances for direct labor result from paying more or less than the standard wage rates for direct labor and from using more or less than the standard amount of direct labor hours. Gregg Manufacturing Company's direct labor variances are computed and recorded as shown below. Note that the basic calculations are the same as for material, but the term *rate* is used instead of *price* and the term *efficiency* instead of *quantity.*

$$\text{Labor Rate Variance} = \left(\text{Actual Rate} - \text{Standard Rate}\right) \times \text{Actual Hours}$$

$$= (\$8.10 - \$8.00) \times 9{,}700 = \$970 \text{ Unfavorable}$$

$$\text{Labor Efficiency Variance} = \left(\text{Actual Hours} - \text{Standard Hours}\right) \times \text{Standard Rate}$$

$$= (9{,}700 - 9{,}800) \times \$8.00 = 800 \text{ Favorable}$$

Labor Rate Variance	$970 Unfavorable
Labor Efficiency Variance	800 Favorable
Total Labor Variance	$170 Unfavorable

Notice that the total labor variance also agrees with the amount in Exhibit 26–10.

The favorable labor efficiency variance might be credited to the production supervisor, who presumably oversees the production teams. The unfavorable labor rate variance could have resulted from assigning more highly paid employees than specified, paying overtime, or paying increased labor rates because of recently negotiated wage contracts.

The following journal entry records these costs and variances:

Work in Process (standard rate and hours)	78,400	
Labor Rate Variance	970	
Labor Efficiency Variance		800
Factory Payroll Payable (actual rates and hours)		78,570
To record direct labor costs and related cost variances.		

The journal entry shown charges Work in Process with standard direct labor costs, records the unfavorable labor rate variance as a debit and the favorable labor efficiency variance as a credit (analogous to a gain), and records the liability for direct labor at the amount owed, which is determined by actual hours worked and actual rates paid.

Overhead Variances

Variances for overhead are often identified with two major sources. Incurring more or less total overhead cost than the amount budgeted for the production level achieved results in a *controllable* variance. Operating at a production level above or below the normal capacity results in a *volume* variance.[2] The total

[2] Appendix D to this chapter presents an alternate three-variance analysis for factory overhead that isolates variances for spending, efficiency, and volume.

overhead variance is the sum of these two variances or the difference between total actual overhead costs incurred and the total overhead applied at standard rates to the actual units produced. Gregg Manufacturing Company's total factory overhead variance for June is:

Total overhead applied at standard rates (9,800 direct labor hours × $4 per direct labor hour)	$39,200	
Actual overhead ($8,700 variable + $30,000 fixed)	38,700	
Total overhead variance	$ 500	Favorable

Because the actual overhead cost incurred is less than the standard overhead amount, the $500 difference is a favorable variance. Computation of the overhead variances follows:

Overhead Controllable Variance		
Budgeted overhead for actual production level attained [$30,000 fixed + (9,800 × $1 variable)]	$39,800	
Actual overhead	38,700	
Overhead Controllable variance		$1,100 Favorable
Overhead Volume Variance		
Normal capacity in direct labor hours	10,000	
Standard direct labor hours for actual production level attained (9,800 units × 1 hour)	9,800	
Production capacity not used (hours)	200	
Standard fixed overhead rate per hour	× $3	
Overhead Volume variance		600 Unfavorable
Total Overhead Variance		$ 500 Favorable

The following journal entry records these costs and variances:

Work in Process (at standard overhead rates)	39,200	
Overhead Volume Variance	600	
Overhead Controllable Variance		1,100
Factory Overhead (actual overhead costs)		38,700
To record standard factory overhead and related variances.		

OVERHEAD CONTROLLABLE VARIANCE The $1,100 favorable overhead controllable variance measures how well the actual factory overhead costs have been kept within the budget limits. Overhead controllable variances typically originate with variable overhead costs. A small portion of Gregg's favorable controllable variance—$100—resulted from the 9,800 units being produced in only 9,700 hours. This "savings" of 100 hours multiplied by the $1 per direct labor hour variable overhead rate is the overhead cost avoided by producing 9,800 units of product in 100 hours less than the overhead budget allows. The remaining $1,000 of favorable controllable variance results from spending less than the budget allows for various overhead items. Gregg's overhead budget indicates that total overhead for June should be $39,700 ($30,000 fixed overhead + $1 variable overhead for each of the 9,700 direct labor hours actually worked). Because actual overhead incurred was only $38,700, the $1,000 difference represents a savings of overhead costs. A detailed analysis of actual and budgeted overhead costs would indicate to what extent each overhead cost (such as factory supplies and indirect labor) contributed to the favorable variance. Department supervisors are usually responsible for controllable overhead variances.

OVERHEAD VOLUME VARIANCE The overhead volume variance reflects the costs associated with using factory facilities at more or less than normal capacity. Volume variances are the differences between normal capacity and the standard hours allowed for actual units produced times the standard fixed overhead rate. Because Gregg's capacity was 10,000 standard direct labor hours and only 9,800 hours were allowed for June's production of 9,800 units of product, 200 hours of capacity were not utilized.[3] Each of these hours has an implied cost equal to the fixed overhead rate of $3 per direct labor hour, resulting in a total unfavorable overhead volume variance of $600 ($3 × 200). When utilization exceeds normal capacity, the favorable overhead volume variance represents the amount of fixed overhead "saved" by employing the factory facilities beyond normal capacity.

Note that variable overhead costs play no role in volume variances. Because variable overhead costs respond to the level of production, failure to produce means that related variable costs are not incurred and therefore cannot contribute to volume variances. In contrast, fixed overhead does not respond (within the relevant range) to changes in production levels. Failure to produce does not avoid any portion of fixed overhead. Nor does producing beyond normal capacity increase fixed overhead (within the relevant range). Therefore, only fixed factory overhead can cause volume variances.

STANDARD COSTS IN FINANCIAL STATEMENTS

When the standard costs and related variances for direct material, direct labor, and factory overhead are recorded as previously illustrated, the Work in Process account is debited for each in amounts representing standard quantities and standard prices. All variances—favorable or unfavorable—are carried in separate

[3] Although in our example only 9,700 hours were worked, 100 of these hours were avoided by better-than-standard production efficiency (the favorable overhead controllable variance). The other 200 hours, therefore, represent an appropriate measure of plant underutilization.

accounts with appropriate titles. Gregg Manufacturing Company records completed production for June in the following entry:

Finished Goods Inventory (at standard cost)	137,200	
Work in Process (at standard cost)		137,200
To record completion of June's production of 9,800 units at a standard unit cost of $14. ($19,600 material, $78,400 labor, and $39,200 overhead)		

As each month's production is sold, the related amounts of standard costs are transferred from Finished Goods Inventory to Cost of Goods Sold.

Standard costs and related variances are usually reported only in financial reports intended for management's use. The following partial income statement illustrates how variances often appear on interim financial statements for internal use (amounts are assumed).

Gregg Manufacturing Company
Partial Income Statement
For the Month Ended June 30, 19XX

Sales	$166,000
Cost of Goods Sold at Standard Cost	126,000
Gross Profit at Standard Cost	$ 40,000
Less: Net Unfavorable Cost Variance	1,700
Gross Profit	$ 38,300

The total net variance could be broken down into subvariances or possibly detailed in a schedule of variances accompanying the financial statements.

At year-end, firms commonly close the variance accounts by transferring their balances to Cost of Goods Sold. In effect, this transfer converts the Cost of Goods Sold account from standard costs to actual costs. If large variances exist at year-end and there is evidence that the standards may not apply, a firm may be justified in allocating all or part of the variances to Work in Process, Finished Goods Inventory, and Cost of Goods Sold.

DEMONSTRATION PROBLEM FOR REVIEW

The following standard per unit cost data and total actual cost data for Porter Manufacturing Corporation relate to producing 2,800 units of Porter's only product.

	Standard Unit Costs	Total Actual Costs	
Direct material (3 lb @ $2/lb)	$ 6	(8,500 lb @ $1.80/lb)	$15,300
Direct labor (0.5 hr @ $8/hr)	4	(1,500 hr @ $8.10/hr)	12,150
Factory overhead*			
Variable (0.5 hr @ $4/hr)	2		6,000
Fixed (0.5 hr @ $6/hr)	3		9,500
Total	$15		$42,950

*Normal capacity is considered 1,500 direct labor hours.

REQUIRED

(a) Calculate all variances for material, labor, and overhead.

(b) Prove that the difference between total actual and total standard costs equals the total of all variances.

(c) Assume that Porter's standard unit costs will continue to be valid; that Porter will sell 2,500 units next period; that beginning materials and finished goods inventories are 1,200 units and 800 units, respectively; and that Porter wants to increase both inventories 25%. Calculate for the next period (1) the units of finished goods to be produced, (2) the units of material to be purchased, and (3) the budgeted direct labor cost for the period.

SOLUTION TO DEMONSTRATION PROBLEM

(a)

$$\text{Material Price Variance} = \left(\text{Actual Price} - \text{Standard Price}\right) \times \text{Actual Quantity}$$

$$= (\$1.80 - \$2.00) \times 8{,}500 = \qquad \$1{,}700 \text{ Favorable}$$

$$\text{Material Quantity Variance} = \left(\text{Actual Quantity} - \text{Standard Quantity}\right) \times \text{Standard Price}$$

$$= (8{,}500 - 8{,}400^{*}) \times \$2.00 = \qquad 200 \text{ Unfavorable}$$

$$\text{Labor Rate Variance} = \left(\text{Actual Rate} - \text{Standard Rate}\right) \times \text{Actual Hours}$$

$$= (\$8.10 - \$8.00) \times 1{,}500 = \qquad 150 \text{ Unfavorable}$$

$$\text{Labor Efficiency Variance} = \left(\text{Actual Hours} - \text{Standard Hours}\right) \times \text{Standard Rate}$$

$$= (1{,}500 - 1{,}400^{\dagger}) \times \$8.00 = \qquad 800 \text{ Unfavorable}$$

Overhead Controllable Variance:

Actual overhead ($6,000 + $9,500)	$15,500	
Budgeted overhead for actual production level attained [$9,000‡ fixed + (2,800 × $2 variable)]	14,600	
		900 Unfavorable

Overhead Volume Variance:		
Normal capacity in direct labor hours	1,500	
Standard direct labor hours for actual production level attained	1,400†	
Production capacity not used (hours)	100	
Standard fixed overhead rate per direct labor hour	× $6	
		600 Unfavorable
Total variance		$950 Unfavorable

(b)

Total actual costs	$42,950	
Total standard costs (2,800 units × $15)	42,000	
Total variance	$ 950	Unfavorable

(c) (1) Finished goods production:

Units to be sold	2,500
Planned ending inventory (800 × 1.25)	1,000
	3,500
Less beginning inventory	800
Units to be produced	2,700

(2) Material purchases:

Production requirements (2,700 × 3)	8,100
Planned ending inventory (1,200 × 1.25)	1,500
	9,600
Less beginning inventory	1,200
Units to be purchased	8,400

(3) Units to be produced (see part 1 above)	2,700
Labor requirements per unit of product	× 0.5
Labor hours required	1,350
Labor rate	× $8
Budgeted labor costs	$10,800

*2,800 units produced × 3 lb/unit = 8,400 lb
†2,800 units produced × 0.5 hr/unit = 1,400 hr
‡1,500 direct labor hours at normal capacity × $6 fixed overhead rate = $9,000 (fixed overhead rate was calculated at normal capacity level)

KEY POINTS TO REMEMBER

(1) A comprehensive budget provides management with a plan for accomplishing objectives and a basis for controlling operations and measuring performance.

(2) You should know the basic format for and the key data appearing in each of the following budgets:

(a) Sales
(b) Units of production
(c) Materials
(d) Direct labor
(e) Operating expense
(f) Factory overhead
(g) Capital expenditures
(h) Cash

(3) Flexible budgeting allows management to budget amounts that can be appropriately compared with costs incurred at actual operating volumes.

(4) The total net variance for each manufacturing cost element—material, labor, and overhead—is the difference between total actual costs and total standard costs.

(5) You should be able to compute the amount of each of the following variances, label it as favorable or unfavorable, explain its basic implications, and indicate the managerial position typically held responsible:
(a) Material price
(b) Material quantity
(c) Labor rate
(d) Labor efficiency
(e) Overhead controllable
(f) Overhead volume

(6) When standard costs are incorporated into the general ledger, work in process and finished goods inventories are carried at standard costs, with unfavorable variances recorded as debits and favorable variances recorded as credits in appropriately titled accounts.

SELF-TEST QUESTIONS
(Answers are at the end of this chapter.)

1. Which of the following budgets should be prepared before the others?
(a) Overhead.
(b) Materials.
(c) Units of production.
(d) Direct labor.

2. In what terms are standard overhead rates usually stated?
(a) Per dollar.
(b) Per direct labor hour.
(c) Per unit of product.
(d) Per month.

3. The formula [(Actual Price − Standard Price) × Actual Quantity] can be used to calculate which cost variance?
(a) Overhead controllable.
(b) Labor efficiency.
(c) Overhead volume.
(d) Material price.

4. Which variance considers production capacity not used?
(a) Overhead volume.
(b) Labor efficiency.
(c) Overhead controllable.
(d) Material quantity.

5. The gross profit on the interim income statement of a firm using standard costs in work in process includes:
(a) Sales and cost of goods sold at standard.
(b) Sales less cost of goods sold at standard plus net unfavorable variances.
(c) Sales less cost of goods sold at standard less net unfavorable variances.

QUESTIONS

26–1 What is the difference between budgets and standard costs?

26–2 List and briefly explain three advantages of budgeting.

26–3 What is meant by *continuous budgeting?*

26–4 Define *master budget.*

26–5 List, in the order of preparation, the various budgets that might constitute a master budget for a small manufacturing company.

26–6 Why do most firms prepare the sales budget first?

26–7 Beginning finished goods inventory is 8,000 units, anticipated sales volume is 50,000 units, and the desired ending finished goods inventory is 14,000 units. What number of units should be produced?

26–8 Three pounds of material X (costing $4 per pound) and 5 pounds of material Y (costing $2 per pound) are required to make one unit of product Z. If management plans to increase the inventory of material X by 500 pounds and reduce the inventory of material Y by 800 pounds during a period when 3,000 units of product Z are to be produced, what are the budgeted purchases costs of material X and material Y?

26–9 What is the total cost formula used in flexible budgeting?

26–10 Why is a capital expenditures budget an important budget?

26–11 When should standard costs be established and how often should such standards be changed?

26–12 "Standard costs can be set too high or too low for motivational purposes." Comment.

26–13 Norton Company used 4,200 pounds of direct material costing $3.90 per pound for a batch of products that should have taken 4,000 pounds costing $4 per pound. What are the material variances?

26–14 Name and briefly describe two variances included in the total overhead variance.

26–15 How do we justify analyzing the total variance related to material?

26–16 "Total actual cost exactly equals total standard cost, so everything must be okay." Comment.

26–17 Actual overhead is $41,000, budgeted overhead for the production level attained is $39,700, the standard fixed factory overhead rate is $6 per direct labor hour, and actual production is 150 standard direct labor hours beyond normal capacity. What are the overhead variances?

26–18 Who in the firm might be responsible for each of the following variances?
(a) Material price and quantity variances.
(b) Labor rate and efficiency variances.
(c) Overhead controllable and volume variances.

26–19 Briefly explain how standard cost variances are reported on financial statements.

EXERCISES

Budgeting inventories

26–20 For each independent situation below, determine the amounts indicated by the question marks.

Number of Units	A	B	C	D
Beginning inventory	8,000	?	6,000	?
Produced	14,000	26,000	?	57,000
Available	?	?	24,000	89,000
Sold	17,000	27,000	?	?
Ending inventory	?	12,000	7,000	15,000

Budget preparation

26–21 Apache Company is preparing its comprehensive budget for July. Use the given estimates to determine the amounts required in each part below. (Estimates may be related to more than one part.)

(a) What should total sales revenue be if territories A and B are estimating sales of 6,000 and 10,000 units, respectively, and the unit selling price is $32?

(b) If the beginning finished goods inventory is an estimated 1,600 units and the desired ending inventory is 4,000 units, how many units should be produced?

(c) What dollar amount of material should be purchased at $4 per pound if each unit of product requires 3 pounds and beginning and ending material inventories should be 5,000 and 2,200 pounds, respectively?

(d) How much direct labor cost should be incurred if each unit produced requires 1.5 hours at an hourly rate of $9?

(e) How much factory overhead should be incurred if fixed factory overhead is $30,000 and variable factory overhead is $1.50 per direct labor hour?

(f) How much operating expense should be incurred if fixed and variable operating expenses are $28,000 and 70 cents per unit sold, respectively?

Budget preparation

26–22 The Walden Company is preparing its comprehensive budget for May. Use the estimates provided to determine the amounts required in each part below. (Estimates may be related to more than one part.)

(a) What should total sales revenue be if territories A and B are estimating sales of 5,000 and 10,000 units, respectively, and the unit selling price is $36?

(b) If the beginning finished goods inventory is an estimated 1,000 units and the desired ending inventory is 3,000 units, how many units should be produced?

(c) What dollar amount of material should be purchased at $2 per pound if each unit of product requires 2.5 pounds and beginning and ending material inventories should be 4,000 and 2,000 pounds, respectively?

(d) How much direct labor cost should be incurred if each unit produced requires 2 hours at an hourly rate of $7?

(e) How much factory overhead should be incurred if fixed factory overhead is $15,000 and variable factory overhead is 80 cents per direct labor hour?

(f) How much operating expense should be incurred if fixed and variable operating expenses are $12,000 and $1.20 per unit sold, respectively?

Using flexible budgets

26–23 The following summary data are from a performance report for the Simmons Company for June, during which 9,600 units were produced. The budget reflects the company's normal capacity of 10,000 units.

		Budget (10,000 units)	Actual Costs (9,600 units)	Variances over (under) Budget
Direct material		$ 35,000	$ 34,200	($800)
Direct labor		70,000	69,300	(700)
Factory overhead:	variable	24,000	24,600	600
	fixed	18,000	18,100	100
Total		$147,000	$146,200	($800)

(a) What is the general implication of the performance report? Why might Simmons question the significance of the report?

(b) Revise the performance report using flexible budgeting, and comment on the general implication of the revised report.

Budgeting cash collections

26–24 Allied Company, which sells on terms 2/10, n/30, has had gross credit sales for May and June of $40,000 and $60,000, respectively. Analysis of Allied's operations indicates that the pattern of customers' payments on account is as follows (percentages are of total monthly credit sales):

	Receiving Discount	Beyond Discount Period	Totals
In month of sale	50%	20%	70%
In month following sale	15%	10%	25%
Uncollectible accounts, returns, and allowances			5%
			100%

Determine the estimated cash collected on customers' accounts in June.

Budgeting cash flow

26–25 The following various elements relate to Vilas, Inc.'s cash budget for April of the current year. For each item, determine the amount of cash that Vilas should receive or pay in April.

(a) At $20 each, unit sales are 5,000 and 6,000 for March and April, respectively. Total sales are typically 40% for cash and 60% on credit. One-third of credit sales are collected in the month of sale, with the balance collected in the following month. Uncollectible accounts are negligible.

(b) Merchandise purchases were $36,000 and $64,000 for March and April, respectively. Typically, 20% of total purchases are paid for in the month of purchase and a 5% cash discount is received. The balance of purchases are paid for (without discount) in the following month.

(c) Fixed operating expenses, which total $9,000 per month, are paid in the month incurred. Variable operating expenses amount to 20% of total monthly sales revenue, one-half of which is paid in the month incurred, with the balance paid in the following month.

(d) Fixed selling expenses, which total $3,500 per month, are paid in the month incurred. Variable selling expenses, which are 5% of total sales revenue, are paid in the month following their incurrence.

(e) A plant asset originally costing $7,000, on which $5,000 depreciation has been taken, is sold for cash at a loss of $300.

Material and labor variances

26–26 The following actual and standard cost data for direct material and direct labor relate to the production of 2,000 units of a product:

	Actual Costs	Standard Costs
Direct material	3,900 pounds @ $6.30	4,000 pounds @ $6
Direct labor	6,200 hours @ $7.40	6,000 hours @ $7.60

Determine the following variances:

(a) Material price.
(b) Material quantity.
(c) Labor rate.
(d) Labor efficiency.

Overhead variances

26–27 Boston Company considers 6,000 direct labor hours or 3,000 units of product its normal monthly capacity. Its standard variable and fixed factory overhead rates are $4 and $8, respectively, for each direct labor hour. During the current month, $72,000 of factory overhead was incurred in working 5,600 direct labor hours to produce 2,800 units of product. Determine the following overhead variances, and indicate whether each is favorable or unfavorable:

(a) Controllable.
(b) Volume.

Material, labor, and overhead variances

26–28 The following summarized manufacturing data relate to Mead Corporation's May operations, during which 2,000 finished units of product were produced (normal monthly capacity is 1,100 direct labor hours):

	Standard Unit Costs	Total Actual Costs
Direct material:		
Standard (2 lb @ $3/lb)	$ 6	
Actual (4,200 lb @ $3.40/lb)		$14,280
Direct labor:		
Standard (0.5 hr @ $8/hr)	4	
Actual (950 hr @ $7.80/hr)		7,410
Factory overhead:		
Standard		
Variable: ($2/hr)(0.5 hrs/unit)	1	
Fixed: ($4/hr)(0.5 hrs/unit)	2	
Actual		6,300
Total	$13	$27,990

Determine the material price and quantity variances, the labor rate and efficiency variances, and the overhead controllable and volume variances, indicating whether each is favorable or unfavorable.

Working with variances

26–29 From the following data, determine the total actual costs incurred for direct material, for direct labor, and for factory overhead.

	Standard Costs	Variances over (under) Standard
Direct material	$35,000	
Price variance		$1,500
Quantity variance		(300)
Direct labor	27,000	
Rate variance		700
Efficiency variance		900
Factory overhead	68,000	
Controllable variance		(1,300)
Volume variance		(800)

Standard costs in financial statements

26–30 For producing and selling 3,500 units of its only product for the month ended April 30, 19XX, Denton Company's records reflect the following selected data:

	Standard Unit Costs	Actual Unit Costs
Direct material	$ 6.00	$6.40
Direct labor	10.00	9.70
Factory overhead	7.00	7.30

Assuming that the product sells for $30 per unit and that Denton Company uses standard costs in its general ledger accounts, prepare a partial summary income statement (through gross profit) including total net variances.

PROBLEMS

Budgeting cash

26–31 Darwin, Inc., sells on terms of 5% discount for "cash and carry" or 2/10, n/30 and estimates its total gross sales for the second calendar quarter of next year as follows: April, $100,000; May, $80,000; and June, $120,000. An analysis of operations indicates the following customer collection patterns:

	Portions of Total Sales
In month of sale:	
Cash at time of sale	25%
On account, during discount period	15%
On account, after discount period	10%
In month following sale:	
On account, during discount period	20%
On account, after discount period	10%
In second month following sale:	
On account, after discount period	15%
Average portion uncollectible	5%
	100%

REQUIRED
Prepare an estimate of the cash to be collected from customers during June.

Monthly cash budget

26–32 During the first calendar quarter of 19X1, Providence Corporation is planning to manufacture a new product and introduce it in two regions. Market research indicates that sales will be 6,000 units in the urban region at a unit price of $30 and 5,000 units in the rural region at $27 each. Since the sales manager expects the product to catch on, he has asked for production sufficient to generate a 4,000-unit ending inventory. The production manager has furnished the following estimates related to manufacturing costs and operating expenses.

	Variable (per unit)	Fixed (total)
Manufacturing Costs:		
Direct material:		
A (4 lb @ $1.75/lb)	$7.00	—
B (2 lb @ $2.50/lb)	5.00	—
Direct labor (one-half hour per unit)	4.00	—
Factory overhead:		
Depreciation	—	$ 4,500
Factory supplies	0.45	3,000
Supervisory salaries	—	16,000
Other	0.50	11,500
Operating Expenses:		
Selling:		
Advertising	—	4,000
Sales salaries and commissions*	1.00	5,000
Other*	0.60	1,000
Administrative:		
Office salaries	—	1,500
Supplies	0.10	400
Other	0.05	1,200

*Varies per unit sold, not per unit produced.

REQUIRED

(a) Assuming that the desired ending inventories of materials A and B are 4,000 and 6,000 pounds, respectively, and that work-in-process inventories are immaterial, prepare budgets for the calendar quarter in which the new product will be introduced for each of the following operating factors:
(1) Total sales revenue.
(2) Production (in units).
(3) Material purchases cost.
(4) Direct labor costs.
(5) Factory overhead costs.
(6) Operating expenses.

(b) Using data generated in part (a), prepare a projected income statement for the calendar quarter. Assume an overall effective income tax rate of 30%.

Monthly cash budget

26–33 Kemper, Inc., is a wholesaler for its only product, a deluxe wireless electric drill, which sells for $48 each and costs Kemper $30 each. On December 1, 19X1, Kemper's management requested a cash budget for December, and the following selected account balances at November 30 were gathered by the accounting department.

Cash	$ 75,000
Marketable Securities (at cost)	120,000
Accounts Receivable (all trade)	912,000
Inventories (15,000 units)	450,000
Operating Expenses Payable	78,000
Accounts Payable (all merchandise)	324,000
Note Payable	135,000

Actual sales for October and November were 20,000 and 30,000 units, respectively. Projected unit sales for December and January are 50,000 and 40,000, respectively. Experience indicates that 50% of sales should be collected in the month of sale, 30% in the month following sale, and the balance in the second month following sale. Uncollectibles, returns, and allowances are negligible.

Planned purchases should provide ending inventories equal to 30% of next month's unit sales volume; approximately 70% are paid for in the month of purchase and the balance in the following month.

Monthly operating expenses are budgeted at $4.50 per unit sold plus a fixed amount of $105,000 including depreciation of $45,000. Except for depreciation, 60% of operating expenses are paid in the month incurred and the balance in the following month.

Special anticipated year-end transactions include the following:

(1) Declaration of a $15,000 cash dividend to be paid two weeks after the December 20 date of record.

(2) Sale of one-half of the marketable securities held on November 30; a gain of $12,000 is anticipated.

(3) Payment of $33,000 monthly installment (includes interest) on the note payable.

(4) Trade-in of an old computer originally costing $450,000 and now having accumulated depreciation of $360,000 at a gain of $105,000 on a new computer costing $900,000. Sufficient cash will be paid at the time of trade-in so that only 50% of the total price will have to be financed.

(5) Kemper's treasurer has a policy of maintaining a minimum month-end cash balance of $75,000 but wants to raise this to $150,000 at December 31. He has a standing arrangement with the bank to borrow any amount up to a limit of $300,000.

REQUIRED

Prepare a cash budget for Kemper, Inc., for December 19X1. Begin your solution by scheduling collections from customers, payments on account for merchandise, and payments for operating expenses. Pattern your solution after Exhibit 26–7.

Flexible budget application

26–34 The Polishing Department of the Madison Manufacturing Company operated during April 19X1 with the following factory overhead cost budget based on 5,000 hours of monthly productive capacity:

Madison Manufacturing Company
Polishing Department
Overhead Budget
For the Month of April, 19X1

Variable costs:		
Factory supplies	$25,000	
Indirect labor	38,000	
Utilities (Usage charge)	17,000	
Patent royalties on secret process	74,000	
Total variable overhead		$154,000
Fixed costs:		
Supervisory salaries	$40,000	
Depreciation on factory equipment	36,000	
Factory taxes	12,000	
Factory insurance	8,000	
Utilities (Base charge)	20,000	
Total fixed overhead		116,000
Total factory overhead		$270,000

The Polishing Department was operated for 4,600 hours during April and incurred the following factory overhead costs:

Factory supplies	$ 24,380
Indirect labor	34,040
Utilities (usage factor)	20,700
Utilities (base factor)	24,000
Patent royalties	70,104
Supervisory salaries	42,000
Depreciation on factory equipment	36,000
Factory taxes	14,000
Factory insurance	8,000
Total factory overhead incurred	$273,224

REQUIRED

Using a flexible budgeting approach, prepare a report for the Polishing Department for April 19X1 comparing actual overhead costs with budgeted overhead costs for 4,600 hours. Separate overhead costs into variable and fixed components and show the amounts of any variances between actual and budgeted amounts. Label the report a cost performance report.

Calculate variances

26–35 The following summary data relate to the operations of Taylor Company for April, during which 9,000 finished units were produced:

	Standard Unit Costs	Actual Total Costs
Direct material:		
Standard (4 lb @ $1.50/lb)	$ 6	
Actual (38,000 lb @ $1.40/lb)		$ 53,200
Direct labor:		
Standard (2 hr @ $7/hr)	14	
Actual (18,500 hr @ $7.20/hr)		133,200
Factory overhead:		
Standard (Variable costs of $1.50 per direct labor hour and $40,000 fixed costs for normal monthly capacity of 20,000 direct labor hours)	7	
Actual		68,000
Total	$27	$254,400

REQUIRED
Determine the following variances and indicate whether each is 2610favorable or unfavorable:
(a) Material price variance and quantity variance.
(b) Labor rate variance and efficiency variance.
(c) Overhead controllable variance and volume variance.

Variances, entries, and income statement

26–36 A summary of Randall Company's manufacturing variance report for May follows.

	Total Standard Costs (9,200 units)	Total Actual Costs (9,200 units)	Variances
Direct material	$ 36,800	$ 40,180	$3,380 Unfavorable
Direct labor	138,000	137,740	260 Favorable
Factory overhead:			
Variable	16,560	16,400	160 Favorable
Fixed	6,900	7,500	600 Unfavorable
	$198,260	$201,820	$3,560 Unfavorable

Standard material cost per unit of product is 0.5 pounds at $8 each, and standard direct labor cost is 1.5 hours at $10 per hour. The total actual material cost represents 4,900 pounds purchased at $8.20 per pound; total actual labor cost represents 14,200 hours at $9.70 per hour. Standard variable and fixed overhead rates are $1.20 and 50 cents, respectively, per direct labor hour (based on a normal capacity of 15,000 direct labor hours or 10,000 units of product).

REQUIRED
(a) Calculate variances for material price and quantity, labor rate and efficiency, and overhead controllable and volume.
(b) Prepare compound general journal entries to record standard costs, actual costs, and related variances for material, labor, and overhead.
(c) Prepare journal entries to record the transfer of all completed units to Finished Goods Inventory and the subsequent sale of 8,400 units on account at $38 each (assume no beginning finished goods inventory).

(d) Prepare a partial income statement (through gross profit on sales), showing gross profit based on standard costs, the incorporation of variances, and gross profit based on actual costs.

Variances and journal entries

26–37 Chadwick Company manufactures a single product and uses a standard costing system. The nature of its product dictates that material is used as purchased and no ending work-in-process inventories occur. Per-unit standard product costs are: material, $3 (4 pounds); labor, $4 (one-half hour); variable overhead, $3 (based on direct labor hours); and fixed overhead, $5 (based on a normal monthly capacity of 9,000 direct labor hours).

Chadwick accounts for work in process and finished goods inventories and cost of goods sold at standard cost and records each variance in a separate account. The following data relate to May, when 17,700 finished units were produced.

REQUIRED

(a) Assuming that 67,000 pounds of material purchased on account at 80 cents per pound were used in May's production, present a compound journal entry to record actual costs, standard costs, and any material variances.

(b) Assuming that 8,900 direct labor hours were worked at an average hourly rate of $7.70, present a compound journal entry to record actual costs, standard costs, and any labor variances.

(c) Assuming that total overhead incurred was $146,000, present a compound journal entry to record actual and standard overhead costs and any overhead variances.

(d) Set up T accounts for Work in Process, Finished Goods Inventory, and Cost of Goods Sold, and enter the amounts for parts (a), (b), and (c). Assume that no beginning inventories exist, that all production was completed, and that all but 500 units produced were sold. Prepare and post journal entries to (1) record production completed and (2) record costs of goods sold at standard costs.

Variances and total costs

26–38 Seneca Company has established the following standard cost summary for a unit of its only product:

Direct material (2.5 lb @ $4/lb)	$10.00
Direct labor (0.8 hr @ $10/hr)	8.00
Factory overhead (applied on basis of direct labor hours):	
Variable (0.8 hours @ rate of $9 per direct labor hour)	7.20
Fixed (0.8 hours @ rate of $12 per direct labor hour)	9.60
Total	$34.80

Normal monthly capacity is 10,000 units of product. In July, Seneca produced 10,400 units of product, incurring the following actual costs:

Direct material (25,800 pounds)	$107,070
Direct labor (8,400 hours)	82,320
Factory overhead	175,760
Total	$365,150

REQUIRED
(a) Determine both manufacturing cost variances associated with (1) direct material, (2) direct labor, and (3) overhead. Indicate whether each is favorable or unfavorable.
(b) Prove that the sum of each set of variances explains the differences between the related amounts of total standard costs and total actual costs.
(c) Prove that the sum of all six variances equals the difference between the total actual costs and the total standard costs.

ALTERNATE PROBLEMS

Monthly cash budget

26–32A During the first calendar quarter of 19X1, Prospect Corporation is planning to manufacture a new product and introduce it in two regions. Market research indicates that sales will be 8,000 units in the urban region at a unit price of $38 and 6,000 units in the rural region at $32 each. Since the sales manager expects the product to catch on, he has asked for production sufficient to generate a 4,000-unit ending inventory. The production manager has furnished the following estimates related to manufacturing costs and operating expenses.

	Variable (per unit)	**Fixed (total)**
Manufacturing Costs:		
Direct material:		
A (2 lb @ $1.50/lb)	$ 3.00	—
B (5 lb @ $0.80/lb)	4.00	—
Direct labor (two hours per unit)	14.00	—
Factory overhead:		
Depreciation	—	$13,000
Factory supplies	0.30	2,000
Supervisory salaries	—	9,000
Other	0.50	2,700
Operating Expenses:		
Selling:		
Advertising	—	5,000
Sales salaries and commissions*	1.00	8,000
Other*	0.40	2,000
Administrative:		
Office salaries	—	3,000
Supplies	0.10	1,000
Other	0.20	1,500

*Varies per unit sold, not per unit produced.

REQUIRED
(a) Assuming that the desired ending inventories of materials A and B are 4,000 and 20,000 pounds, respectively, and that work-in-process inventories are immaterial, prepare budgets for the calendar quarter in which

the new product will be introduced for each of the following operating factors:

(1) Total sales revenue.
(2) Production (in units).
(3) Material purchases cost.
(4) Direct labor costs.
(5) Factory overhead costs.
(6) Operating expenses.

(b) Using data generated in part (a), prepare a projected income statement for the calendar quarter. Assume an overall effective income tax rate of 40%.

Monthly cash budget

26–33A Kirkland, Inc., is a wholesaler for its only product, a deluxe wireless rechargeable electric shaver, which sells for $44 each and costs Kirkland $28 each. On June 1, 19X1, Kirkland's management requested a cash budget for June, and the following selected account balances at May 31 were gathered by the accounting department:

Cash	$ 28,000
Marketable Securities (at cost)	100,000
Accounts Receivable (all trade)	1,364,000
Inventories (12,000 units)	336,000
Operating Expenses Payable	123,000
Accounts Payable (all merchandise)	526,400
Note Payable	360,000

Actual sales for April and May were 30,000 and 50,000 units, respectively. Projected unit sales for June and July are 40,000 and 20,000, respectively. Experience indicates that 50% of sales should be collected in the month of sale, 30% in the month following sale, and the balance in the second month following sale. Uncollectibles, returns, and allowances are negligible.

Planned purchases should provide ending inventories equal to 30% of next month's sales volume; approximately 60% are paid for in the month of purchase and the balance in the following month.

Monthly operating expenses are budgeted at $6 per unit sold plus a fixed amount of $180,000 including depreciation of $70,000. Except for depreciation, 70% of operating expenses are paid in the month incurred and the balance in the following month.

Special anticipated June transactions include:

(1) Declaration of a $30,000 cash dividend to be paid two weeks after the June 20 date of record.
(2) Sale of all but $20,000 of the marketable securities held on May 31; a gain of $12,000 is anticipated.
(3) Payment of $120,000 installment (includes interest) on the note payable.
(4) Trade-in of an old company plane originally costing $180,000 and now having accumulated depreciation of $120,000 at a gain of $100,000 on a new plane costing $1,200,000. Sufficient cash will be paid at the time of trade-in so that only 50% of the total purchase price will have to be financed.
(5) Kirkland's treasurer has a policy of maintaining a minimum month-end cash balance of $20,000 and has a standing arrangement with the bank to borrow any amount up to a limit of $200,000.

REQUIRED
Prepare a cash budget for Kirkland, Inc., for June 19X1. Begin your solution by scheduling collections from customers, payments on account for merchandise, and payments for operating expenses. Pattern your solution after Exhibit 26–7.

Calculate variances

26–35A The following summary data relate to the operations of Talbot Company for April, during which 4,500 finished units were produced:

	Standard Unit Costs	Total Actual Costs
Direct Material:		
Standard (0.6 lb @ $5/lb)	$ 3	
Actual (3,000 lb @ $5.25/lb)		$ 15,750
Direct labor:		
Standard (0.8 hr @ $7.50/hr)	6	
Actual (3,800 hr @ $7.30/hr)		27,740
Factory overhead:		
Standard (Variable costs of $5 per direct labor hour and $60,000 fixed costs for normal monthly capacity of 4,000 direct labor hours)	16	
Actual		79,600
Total	$25	$123,090

REQUIRED
Determine the following variances and indicate whether each is favorable or unfavorable:
(a) Material price variance and quantity variance.
(b) Labor rate variance and efficiency variance.
(c) Overhead controllable variance and volume variance.

Variances, entries, and income statement

26–36A A summary of Roberts Company's manufacturing variance report for June follows.

	Total Standard Costs (7,600 units)	Total Actual Costs (7,600 units)	Variances
Direct material	$ 36,480	$ 35,650	$ 830 Favorable
Direct labor	51,300	54,900	3,600 Unfavorable
Factory overhead:			
Variable	22,800	22,000	800 Favorable
Fixed	68,400	72,000	3,600 Unfavorable
	$178,980	$184,550	$5,570 Unfavorable

Standard material cost per unit of product is 4 pounds at $1.20 each and standard direct labor cost is 0.75 hours at $9.00 per hour. Total actual material cost represents 31,000 pounds purchased at $1.15 per pound; total actual labor cost represents 6,000 hours at $9.15 per hour. Variable and fixed factory overhead rates are $4 and $12, respectively, per direct labor hour (based on a normal capacity of 6,000 direct labor hours or 8,000 units of product).

REQUIRED

(a) Calculate variances for material price and quantity, labor rate and efficiency, and overhead controllable and volume.
(b) Prepare compound general journal entries to record standard costs, actual costs, and related variances for material, labor, and overhead.
(c) Prepare journal entries to record the transfer of all competed units to Finished Goods Inventory and the subsequent sale of 6,400 units on account at $35 each (assume no beginning finished goods inventory).
(d) Prepare a partial income statement (through gross profit on sales) showing gross profit based on standard costs, the incorporation of variances, and gross profit based on actual costs.

Variances and journal entries

26–37A Clayton Company manufactures a single product and uses a standard costing system. The nature of its product dictates that material is used as purchased and no ending work-in-process inventories occur. Per-unit standard product costs are: material, $2 (one-half pound); labor, $9 (1.5 hours); variable overhead, $3 (based on direct labor hours); and fixed overhead, $12 (based on a normal monthly capacity of 12,000 direct labor hours or 8,000 units of product).

Clayton Company accounts for work in process and finished goods inventories and cost of goods sold at standard cost and records each variance in a separate account. The following data relate to June, when 7,800 finished units were produced.

REQUIRED

(a) Assuming that 4,200 pounds of material purchased on account at $3.70 per pound were used in June's production, present a compound journal entry to record actual costs, standard costs, and any material variances.
(b) Assuming that 12,000 direct labor hours were worked at an average hourly rate of $6.30, present a compound journal entry to record actual costs, standard costs, and any labor variances.
(c) Assuming that total overhead incurred was $122,000, present a compound journal entry to record actual and standard overhead costs and any overhead variances.
(d) Set up T accounts for Work in Process, Finished Goods Inventory, and Cost of Goods Sold, and enter the amounts for parts (a), (b), and (c). Assume that no beginning inventories exist, that all production was completed, and that all but 900 units were sold. Prepare and post journal entries to (1) record production completed and (2) record cost of goods sold at standard costs.

BUSINESS DECISION PROBLEM

Westfield Corporation has just hired Bill Swanson as its new controller. Although Bill has had little formal accounting training, he professes to be highly experienced, having learned accounting "the hard way" in the field. At the end of his first month's work, Bill prepared the following cost variance report:

Westfield Corporation
Cost Variance Analysis
For the Month of June, 19XX

	Total Actual Costs	Total Budgeted Costs	Variances	
Direct material	$107,568	$118,800	$11,232	Favorable
Direct labor	119,340	132,000	12,660	Favorable
Factory overhead	241,500	264,000	22,500	Favorable
	$468,408	$514,800	$46,392	Favorable

In his presentation at Westfield's month-end management meeting, Bill indicated that things were going "fantastically." "The figures indicate," he said, "that the firm is beating its budget in all cost categories." Bill's good news made everyone at the meeting happy and furthered his acceptance as a member of the management team.

After the management meeting, Susan Jones, Westfield's general manager, asked you as an independent consultant to review Bill's report. Susan's concern stemmed from the fact that Westfield has never operated as favorably as Bill's report seems to imply, and Susan cannot explain the apparent significant improvement.

While reviewing Bill's report, you are provided the following cost and operating data for June: Westfield has a monthly normal capacity of 11,000 direct labor hours or 8,800 units of product. Standard costs per unit for its only product are: direct material, 3 pounds at $4.50 each; direct labor, 1.25 hours at $12 each; and variable and fixed overhead rates per direct labor hour of $6 and $18, respectively. During June, Westfield produced 8,000 units of product using 24,900 pounds of material costing $4.32 each, 10,200 direct labor hours at an average rate of $11.70 each, and incurred $241,500 of total factory overhead costs.

After reviewing Westfield's June cost data, you tell Bill that his cost report contains a classic budgeting error, and you explain how he can remedy it. In response to your suggestion, Bill revises his report as follows:

	Total Actual Costs	Total Budgeted Costs	Variances	
Direct material	$107,568	$108,000	$ 432	Favorable
Direct labor	119,340	120,000	660	Favorable
Factory overhead	241,500	240,000	1,500	Unfavorable
	$468,408	$468,000	$ 408	Unfavorable

Bill's revised report is accompanied by remarks expressing regret at the oversight in the original report, but reassuring management that in view of the small variances in the revised report, the company has met its budget in all cost categories and has no basis for concern.

REQUIRED

In your role as consultant:

(a) Verify that Bill's actual cost figures are correct.

(b) Explain how the proportions of Bill's original variances question the validity of the budgeted cost figures.

(c) Identify and explain the classic budgeting error that Bill apparently incorporated into his original cost report.
(d) Verify the apparent correctness of Bill's revised budget figures.
(e) Explain why Bill's revised figures could be considered deficient, even though substantially correct.
(f) Further analyze Bill's revised variances, isolating underlying potential causal factors. How do your analyses indicate bases for concern to management? Briefly suggest initial areas of inquiry that management might take regarding any apparent problem area.

ANSWERS TO SELF-TEST QUESTIONS

1. (c) 2. (b) 3. (d) 4. (a) 5. (c)

APPENDIX D

THREE-VARIANCE ANALYSIS FOR FACTORY OVERHEAD

Chapter 26 illustrates the analysis of total overhead variance into an overhead controllable variance and an overhead volume variance. A refinement to this approach involves dividing the total overhead variance into the following three variances: (1) a *spending* variance, (2) an *efficiency* variance, and (3) a *volume* variance. Because volume variances are the same under either approach, the only difference is the further division of the controllable variance into a spending variance and an efficiency variance. Of course, the total overhead variance is the same, regardless of the number of variances determined. For convenience, the overhead data for Gregg Manufacturing Company from Exhibit 26–10 are repeated here.

	Standard Costs (9,800 units)	**Actual Costs (9,800 units)**	**Variances**
Factory Overhead:			
Variable	$ 9,800	$ 8,700	$1,100 Favorable
Fixed	29,400	30,000	600 Unfavorable
Total	$39,200	$38,700	$ 500 Favorable

At its normal capacity of 10,000 direct labor hours, Gregg's standard overhead rates per direct labor hour are $1 variable and $3 fixed, and 9,700 direct labor hours are used to produce 9,800 units of product.

The three overhead variances for Gregg Manufacturing Company for June are calculated as follows:

Overhead Spending Variance		
Budgeted overhead for the actual hours worked [$30,000 fixed + (9,700 × $1 variable)]	$39,700	
Actual overhead	38,700	
Overhead spending variance		$1,000 Favorable

Overhead Efficiency Variance		
Budgeted overhead for actual production attained [$30,000 fixed + (9,800 units × 1 hour × $1 variable)]	$39,800	
Budgeted overhead for actual hours worked [$30,000 fixed + (9,700 hours × $1 variable)]	39,700	
Overhead efficiency variance		100 Favorable
Overhead Volume Variance		
Normal capacity in direct labor hours	10,000	
Standard direct labor hours for actual production attained (9,800 units × 1 hour)	9,800	
Production capacity not used (hours)	200	
Fixed overhead rate per hour	× $3	
Overhead volume variance		600 Unfavorable
Total Overhead Variance		$ 500 Favorable

The following journal entry records these costs and variances:

Work in Process (at standard rates)	39,200	
Overhead Volume Variance	600	
Overhead Efficiency Variance		100
Overhead Spending Variance		1,000
Factory Overhead (actual overhead costs)		38,700
To record standard factory overhead and related variances.		

OVERHEAD SPENDING VARIANCE

The overhead spending variance reflects how much more (unfavorable) or less (favorable) was spent on factory overhead than the budget allowed for the actual hours worked. Gregg's overhead budget indicated that overhead costs should be $30,000 plus $1 for each hour actually worked. Therefore, the budget allowed a total of $39,700 for the 9,700 direct labor hours worked in June. Because total actual overhead incurred was only $38,700, the $1,000 difference is a favorable overhead spending variance; thus, the company has avoided $1,000 of planned overhead costs.

A review of detailed spending records would show how the $1,000 savings were accumulated from savings in the many types of costs making up overhead—such as factory supplies, indirect labor, factory utilities, and factory repairs. Although exceptions exist, control of spending for overhead is usually the responsibility of production department supervisors. As a general rule, the variable portions of overhead costs account for most of the spending variance. Fixed costs, however, can also vary from the budgeted amount because of price changes occurring after the budget has been prepared and put into use. For example, supervisors' salaries are normally classified as fixed costs; if they increase after the budget has been prepared, actual fixed costs will vary from those budgeted.

OVERHEAD EFFICIENCY VARIANCE

The overhead efficiency variance shows how much overhead cost was either added or saved by operating above or below the standard level of labor efficiency. In June, Gregg's employees worked 9,700 direct labor hours but produced 9,800 units of product, for which the overhead standards would have allowed 9,800 hours. We can say that June's operations have resulted in a savings of 100 direct labor hours, each of which avoided the standard variable overhead rate of $1, giving us a total favorable efficiency variance of $100. Note that fixed overhead does not enter into the efficiency variance; no part of a fixed cost is avoided by operating fewer hours nor is any extra amount of fixed overhead incurred (within the relevant range) by operating more than the normal number of hours for a given amount of production. In other words, a difference in direct labor hours affects only the total variable overhead; fixed overhead remains constant, at least within the relevant range. Since it is so closely tied to the efficiency of production, the overhead efficiency variance is usually the responsibility of the production supervisor.

OVERHEAD VOLUME VARIANCE

The computation and analyses for overhead volume variances are the same for either the two- or the three-variance approach to overhead variances; therefore, the analyses are not repeated here.

The journal entry for overhead costs charges Work in Process with the standard overhead for the actual production attained, records each of the three variances in an appropriately titled variance account, and credits Factory Overhead for the actual overhead costs incurred.

Determining three variances for overhead is often justified because of the clear separation of the controllable variance into a spending element and an efficiency element. This distinction is even more significant when we realize that a controllable variance might approach zero simply because an unfavorable spending variance is virtually offset by a favorable efficiency variance (or vice versa). This potential for offsetting favorable and unfavorable cost elements could "hide" important operating data from management.

PROBLEMS

Three overhead variances

D–1 Using the following data for Harper Corporation, calculate overhead spending, efficiency, and volume variances for each independent situation:

	A	B	C
Total actual overhead	$66,000	$59,000	$134,000
Normal capacity (in direct labor hours)	5,000	8,000	20,000
Standard overhead rates:			
Variable (per direct labor hour)	$3.00	$2.50	$4.00
Fixed (per direct labor hour)	$10.00	$5.00	$2.50
Actual direct labor hours worked	4,800	8,400	19,800
Standard direct labor hours allowed for actual production	4,600	7,700	20,100

Three overhead variances

D–2 Dane Company uses a standard cost system, has a monthly normal production capacity of 10,000 direct labor hours or 5,000 units of product, and has standard variable and fixed overhead rates per direct labor hour of $6 and $10, respectively. During July, Dane incurred $156,600 of total overhead, working 9,700 direct labor hours to produce 4,700 units of product.

REQUIRED

(a) Compute overhead variances for spending, efficiency, and volume.

(b) Briefly explain the meaning of each variance in terms of operating and budgeting variables.

Three overhead variances

D–3 Using the data in Problem 26–35, compute overhead variances for spending, efficiency, and volume.

Three overhead variances

D–4 Using the data in Problem 26–36, compute overhead variances for spending, efficiency, and volume.

Three overhead variances

D–5 Using the data in Problem 26–35A, compute overhead variances for spending, efficiency, and volume.

Three overhead variances

D–6 Using the data in Problem 26–36A, compute overhead variances for spending, efficiency, and volume.

Two and three overhead variances

D–7 Randolph, Inc., uses a standard cost system, has a monthly normal production capacity of 5,000 direct labor hours or 10,000 units of product, and has standard variable and fixed overhead rates per direct labor hour of $4 and $5, respectively. During May, Randolph incurred $45,400 of total overhead costs, working 4,900 direct labor hours to produce 10,200 units of product.

REQUIRED

(a) Compute an overhead controllable variance and an overhead volume variance. Briefly describe the operating implications of the variances.

(b) Compute overhead variances for spending, efficiency, and volume. Briefly describe the operating implications of the variances.

(c) In what significant way does this situation justify a three-variance analysis of overhead?

27

Capital Budgeting

Chapter Objectives

- **Provide a basis for understanding the elements of capital budgeting.**
- **Discuss required rates of return and the time value of money.**
- **Illustrate the use of present value tables.**
- **Discuss and illustrate the determination of after-tax cash flows.**
- **Describe the net present value method of capital expenditure analysis.**
- **Describe the cash payback and average rate of return methods of capital expenditure analysis.**

Prediction is very difficult, especially about the future.

NIELS BOHR

Using accounting data in planning long-term investments in plant assets is known as **capital budgeting.** The term reflects the fact that for most firms the total costs of all attractive investment opportunities exceed the available investment capital. Thus, management must ration, or budget, investment capital among competing investment proposals. In deciding which new long-term assets to acquire, management must seek investments that promise to optimize return on the funds employed.

Capital budgeting is most valuable for organizations in which managers are responsible for the long-run profitability of their area of concern and are therefore encouraged to develop new products and more efficient production processes. Firms often make their most capable employees responsible for capital budgeting decisions, because such decisions determine how large sums of money are invested and commit the firm for extended future periods. Furthermore, investment decision errors are often difficult and costly to remedy or abandon.

Managers as well as accountants should be familiar with the special analytical techniques that evaluate the relative attractiveness of alternative uses of available capital. In this chapter, we first discuss the nature and procedures of capital budgeting, how required investment earning rates are determined, the time value of money, and the effect of income taxes on capital expenditure decisions. We conclude by illustrating three approaches to capital expenditure analysis—the *net present value method, payback analysis,* and the *average rate of return.*

ELEMENTS OF CAPITAL BUDGETING

Many firms have a capital budgeting calendar calling for consideration of capital expenditure proposals at regular intervals—for example, every six months or a year. Proposals are usually examined with respect to (1) compliance with capital budget policies and procedures; (2) aspects of operational urgency, such as the need to replace critical equipment; (3) established criteria for minimum return on capital investments; and (4) consistency with the firm's operating policies and long-run goals. Proposals for relatively small cash outlays may require the approval of low-level management only, whereas comprehensive proposals are subject to approval at high management levels, perhaps including the board of directors. These comprehensive proposals and the decisions based on them profoundly affect a firm's long-run success.

Once approved, capital expenditures should be monitored to ensure that amounts and purposes are consistent with the original proposal. At appropriate intervals, the actual rates of return earned on important expenditures should be compared with projected rates. These periodic reviews encourage those responsible to formulate thorough and realistic proposals, and often provide an incentive for improving overall capital budgeting procedures.

CAPITAL EXPENDITURE ANALYSIS

The scope of capital expenditures varies widely, ranging from the routine replacement of production equipment to the construction of entire factory complexes. Whatever their size, most capital expenditure projects have the following three recognizable stages:

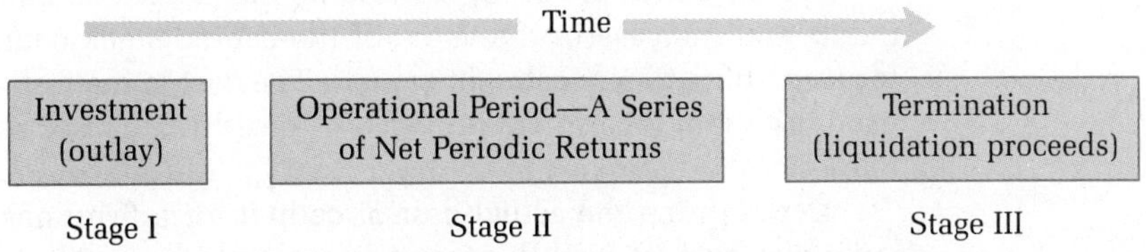

Investment (stage I) consists of the net cash outlay for a project or an asset. Net periodic returns during the life of the project (stage II) may result from either an excess of periodic revenue over related expenses or a periodic saving in some expense. Finally, because most efficient firms replace capital equipment before it becomes worthless, the termination of a project (stage III) often results in some amount of liquidation proceeds.

The attractiveness of a particular investment is determined in large part by the quantitative relationship between the investment in stage I and the receipts expected in stages II and III. This relationship is usually expressed as a ratio known as the *rate of return:*

$$\text{Rate of Return} = \frac{\text{Returns}}{\text{Investment}}$$

All other things being equal, the greater the expected rate of return, the more attractive the investment opportunity. Proposed investments can be ranked according to their expected rates of return, and capital outlays can be allocated among the most attractive investments. In its simplest terms, capital expenditure analysis consists of judging the attractiveness of income-producing or cost-saving opportunities in relation to required investments. The results of this analysis are among the most important input data in capital budgeting decisions.

Three questions of considerable concern in capital budgeting are:

(1) How do we determine an acceptable rate of return for a given project?
(2) How can we meaningfully compare investments made now with returns to be received in the future?
(3) In what terms should investments and returns be measured?

These challenging problems are considered in the following sections of this chapter.

REQUIRED RATES OF RETURN

In determining an acceptable rate of return for a given project, we must consider not only the required capital outlay, but also the costs associated with the acquisition of that capital. The parties providing the funds expect to be reasonably compensated for their use. When the money is borrowed (usually through a bond issue), the interest paid by the firm is obviously a cost of using the funds. When stockholder funds are used, we assume that some combination of dividend payments and increase in the value of the capital stock compensates stockholders for furnishing the investment capital. The cost to the firm of acquiring the funds used in capital investment projects—typically expressed as an annual percentage rate—is called the **cost of capital.**

Determining the actual cost of capital for a firm may require complex calculations, and even well-informed authorities in finance disagree about certain aspects of these calculations. Many firms use an approach that distinguishes among the various sources of financing.

A firm may acquire capital by issuing preferred or common stock, using retained earnings, borrowing, or some combination of these. Consequently, the overall cost of capital for a given project may reflect the cost rates of the several sources of funds in proportion to the amounts obtained from each source. This situation has led to the concept of the **weighted average cost of capital,** illustrated as follows.

Assume that a particular company had acquired capital through all four sources, in the proportions indicated below and with the cost of capital rates as shown.

Source of Capital	Percentage of Total	×	Cost of Capital Rate	=	Weighted Average Cost of Capital Component
Debt	40%		8%		3.2%
Preferred stock	10		9		0.9
Common stock	20		12		2.4
Retained earnings	30		12		3.6
	Weighted average cost of capital				10.1%

Multiplying the percentage of each capital source by its cost of capital rate provides weighted cost factors whose sum is the weighted average cost of capital. This percentage (in this case, 10.1%) can then be used to compare the attractiveness of proposed investments.

Logically, for a capital investment to be considered favorably by a firm, its expected rate of return must be *at least as great* as the cost of capital. Therefore, *the cost of capital represents a minimum required rate of return*. In other words, a firm whose cost of capital is 10% will ordinarily want to invest only in an asset or project whose expected rate of return is greater than 10%. An investment whose return is less than the cost of capital would be economically detrimental, although firms sometimes disregard their cost of capital if qualitative considerations override the quantitative aspects of the decision. Qualitative considerations might include the desire to achieve certain environmental goals, the desire to maintain research leadership in the field, and the need to maintain full employment of the work force during a business slowdown.

Some firms only consider investments whose rates of return are at least a certain number of percentage points higher than the cost of capital. This **buffer margin** acts as a safety factor, because proposals, which rely heavily on estimates of costs and future returns, may involve what will prove to be an erroneous estimated rate of return. Of course, even proposals whose expected rate of return is higher than the **cutoff** or **hurdle rate** (Cost of Capital + Buffer Margin) may be rejected if other investment opportunities offer still higher returns.

THE TIME VALUE OF MONEY

We have seen that in determining the desirability of a proposed capital investment, management compares the amount of investment required at the beginning of a project with its expected returns—typically a series of returns extending several years into the future. This comparison, which is so important in capital outlay decisions, cannot be made properly using the absolute amounts of the future returns because *money has a time value*. As discussed in Appendix A to Chapter 17, the time value of money means that the right to receive an amount of money today is worth more than the right to receive the same amount at some future date, because a current receipt can be invested to earn interest over the intervening period. Thus, if 10% annual interest can be obtained on investments, $100 received today is equal in value to $110 received one year from now. Today's $100 has a **future value** of $110 one year from now; conversely, the **present value**[1] of a $110 receipt expected one year from today is $100.

Obviously, the difference between present and future values is a function of interest rates and time periods. The greater the interest rate or time period involved,

[1]Students not familiar with present values may wish to review the present value discussion in Appendix A.

the greater the amount by which a future value is reduced, or *discounted*, in deriving its present value. For example, Exhibit 27–1 shows just how significant the time value of money can be at various interest rates and time periods. As the table indicates, $100 five years from now has a present value of $78, $62, or $40

KNOWN CUTOFF RATES: YES OR NO?

At least once a year, the senior executives and directors of many corporations address the problem of establishing a capital spending budget and selecting the projects that will be undertaken during the following year. The usual practice is for proposals to be submitted up through the organization; top management selects the most promising proposals, and the directors approve the selection. Some projects are selected for economic reasons; other selections are largely based on nonfinancial considerations such as environmental compliance.

Regardless of the common threads of this process, considerable controversy surrounds the appropriate methodology to be applied to the selection. One of the focal points of this controversy is the determination of capital spending hurdle rates: Should they even be used, and if so, how should they be calculated?

A survey of 136 companies by The Conference Board showed that 62 companies (46%) do not specify minimum cutoff rates for their capital investments. These proportions correspond with my own experience. Many companies do not establish capital spending hurdle rates for three reasons:

(1) Management wishes to reserve the prerogative of determining which proposals should be accepted and which should be turned down or referred. They do not wish to discourage the submission of any capital proposals. However, all proposals should be ranked in the order of their desirability.

(2) It is difficult to determine what "cutoff" or "hurdle rate" should apply, as risks, capital costs, and strategic considerations vary among projects. Moreover, some projects should be considered on a noneconomic basis.

(3) If a hurdle rate is made known to operating management, the figures used in proposals may be "massaged" to pass this rate rather than present the project on an objective basis.

There is merit to the point of view of not using hurdle rates. Good proposals should indeed not be discouraged, particularly those that cannot be supported on a strictly financial basis. It *is* difficult to determine the cost of capital and the impact of risks. Simplistic, arbitrary rates are not a solution either, and operating management *will* tend to play games with capital proposals if hurdle rates are known.

However, not establishing cutoff rates imposes some important disadvantages. Operating managers are not informed about the basic economics of the business. The absence of information encourages the submission of proposals that do not support these economics. It is akin to asking managers to prepare budgets without budget guidelines or objectives, or marketing managers to set selling prices without cost information. Each individual is left to his own devices without any common focus or sense of direction. Unofficial yardsticks as to "what will fly" often emerge from this vacuum. Such yardsticks are communicated through the grapevine and are as apt to provide misinformation as they are to constructively assist with the capital spending proposal and selection process.

From Allen H. Seed, III, "Structuring Capital Spending Hurdle Rates," *Financial Executive*, February 1982, pages 20–21. Reprinted by permission of Financial Executives Institute.

EXHIBIT 27–1
Present Value of $100 Discounted for Years and Interest Rates Shown (rounded to nearest dollar)

Years Discounted	Interest Rates 5%	10%	20%
1	$95	$91	$83
2	91	83	69
3	86	75	58
4	82	68	48
5	78	62	40
10	61	39	16
20	38	15	3
30	23	6	—
40	14	2	—
50	9	1	—

if the applicable interest rates are 5%, 10%, and 20%, respectively. Note also that the greater the time period or the interest rate, the greater the difference between the future value of $100 and its current value. Comparing a current investment with its future returns without discounting the returns to their present value would substantially overstate the economic significance of the returns. Obviously, then, we must recognize the time value of money in capital budgeting procedures.

We should also recognize that techniques for discounting future cash flows to their present values apply to both cash receipts and cash outlays. In other words, the current value of the *right to receive*—or the current value of the *obligation to pay*—a sum in the future is its present value computed at an appropriate interest rate. Of course, we maximize our economic position by arranging to receive amounts as early as possible and postponing amounts to be paid as long as possible. The intrinsic role of these generalizations is apparent in the capital budgeting illustrations later in the chapter.

USING PRESENT VALUE TABLES

Widely available present value tables simplify our work considerably in computing present values. Tables I and II on pages 1073 and 1074 give the present values of $1 for a number of rates and time periods. The amounts in these tables are called **present value factors,** or **discount factors,** because we convert any given cash flow to its present value by multiplying the amount of the cash flow by the appropiate factor.

EXHIBIT 27–2
Present Value of $1 Received in the Future (Excerpted from Table I)

Periods Hence	Rate per Compounding Period						
	2%	3%	4%	5%	6%	8%	10%
1	0.980	0.971	0.962	0.952	0.943	0.926	0.909
2	0.961	0.943	0.925	0.907	0.890	0.857	0.826
3	0.942	0.915	0.889	0.864	0.840	0.794	0.751
4	0.924	0.888	0.855	0.823	0.792	0.735	0.683
5	0.906	0.863	0.822	0.784	0.747	0.681	0.621
10	0.821	0.744	0.676	0.614	0.558	0.463	0.386
20	0.673	0.554	0.456	0.377	0.312	0.215	0.149
30	0.552	0.412	0.308	0.231	0.174	0.099	0.057

Single Sum Flows

Table I gives present value factors for amounts received in a single sum at the end of a specified number of periods. We use Table I to determine the present value of sporadic cash flows—when the returns expected on an investment, or the expenditures it requires, are unequal amounts or are expected at irregular intervals during or at the end of the life of the investment. An excerpt from Table I is presented in Exhibit 27–2.

To illustrate the use of Table I, we assume that an investment project promises a return of $2,000 at the end of two years and another $1,000 at the end of five years. The desired rate of return is 10%. The factor in the 10% column of the table for two periods from now is 0.826; the factor for five periods from now is 0.621. The total present value of the combined flows is $2,273, calculated as follows:

Future Receipts		PV Factor		Present Value
2 years from now	$2,000 ×	0.826	=	$1,652
5 years from now	1,000 ×	0.621	=	621
				$2,273

Annuity Flows

We can compute the present value of a single cash flow sum—or any combinations of single sums—using Table I. Cash flows that are the same each period over two or more periods are an annuity, and using an annuity table is more convenient. Generally, annuity tables are cumulative versions of single sum tables. Table II, for example, is an annuity table based on present value factors from Table I. Exhibit 27–3 is excerpted from Table II.

To illustrate, we assume a project has expected cash inflows of $1,000 at the end of each of the next three periods, and 8% is the appropriate interest rate.

EXHIBIT 27–3
Present Value of $1 Annuity Received at the End of Each Period (Excerpted from Table II)

Periods Hence	Rate per Compounding Period 2%	3%	4%	5%	6%	8%	10%
1	0.980	0.971	0.962	0.952	0.943	0.926	0.909
2	1.942	1.914	1.886	1.859	1.833	1.783	1.736
3	2.884	2.829	2.775	2.723	2.673	2.577	2.487
4	3.808	3.717	3.630	3.546	3.465	3.312	3.170
5	4.714	4.580	4.452	4.330	4.212	3.993	3.791
10	8.983	8.530	8.111	7.722	7.360	6.710	6.145
20	16.351	14.878	13.590	12.462	11.470	9.818	8.514
30	22.397	19.600	17.292	15.373	13.765	11.258	9.427

Using Table I, we compute the total present value as the sum of three individual amounts, as shown below:

Periods Hence	Cash Inflows		PV Factor (Table I @ 8%)		Present Value
1	$1,000	×	0.926	=	$ 926
2	1,000	×	0.857	=	857
3	1,000	×	0.794	=	794
					$2,577

Alternatively, using Table II, we need only multiply the periodic cash flow by a single present value factor for three periods at 8%.

Periods Hence (in annuity)	Periodic Cash Inflow		PV Factor (Table II @ 8%)		Present Value
3	$1,000	×	2.577	=	$2,577

Note that the present value factor for Table II is applied to the periodic cash flow of $1,000, not to the $3,000 total amount of cash flows in the annuity.

The advantage of Table II is that a single present value factor is provided for two or more equal amounts occurring evenly throughout a series of periods. When analyzing investments involving extended series of equal cash flows, the savings in computational effort can be significant.

Tables I and II both assume that all cash flows occur at the end of the periods shown. This assumption is somewhat simplistic, because cash receipts or cost savings from most industrial investments occur in a steady stream throughout the operating period. Nevertheless, businesses use such tables principally because of their availability and ease of use. Obviously, these tables understate present values of flows that are gradual throughout the period, because the present values of cash flows early in the period are greater than similar inflows or outlays at the end of the period. The difference in the factors, however, is normally not material.

MEASUREMENT OF INVESTMENTS AND RETURNS

When present value analysis is used to make investment decisions, investments and returns must be stated in the form of *cash* flows. Present value determinations are basically interest calculations, and therefore, only money amounts—cash flows—are properly used in interest calculations. Furthermore, only the **incremental cash flows** that will occur if the project is accepted should be considered in the analysis.

Typically, financial data available in the accounts are not stated in terms of cash flows because accrual basis accounting is used. Amounts compiled on the accrual basis must be restated to the appropriate cash flows for capital budgeting purposes.[2] For example, apportioning the cost of an asset over its life through depreciation accounting is an important feature of accrual accounting. When present value analysis is used, the cost of an asset is treated as a cash outlay when the asset is paid for. In measuring future returns related to the asset, depreciation expense is irrelevant because it does not represent a cash outlay. However, depreciation provisions affect cash flows indirectly by reducing cash outlays for income tax payments.

Likewise, earnings from projects should reflect the cash inflows rather than the revenue amounts computed using accrual accounting. The timing of the cash collections is important, too, because the essence of present value analysis is that cash received can be reinvested.

If specific accruals or deferrals are not material in amount, or if their amounts at the beginning and end of the period are roughly the same, they are often ignored in restating accrual basis amounts to cash flows. Ignoring the impact of accruals and deferrals in these instances will not adversely affect the capital budgeting analysis.

After-tax Cash Flows

Both federal and state income taxes are important to investment decisions; for many large companies, the combined federal and state income tax rate may approach 40%. Generally, income taxes reduce the economic significance of taxable receipts and deductible outlays. For example, assuming a 40% tax rate, a $40,000 before-tax gain would increase taxable income by $40,000 and income taxes by $16,000 (40% × $40,000), resulting in a $24,000 after-tax gain. A $15,000 before-tax expense would reduce taxable income by $15,000 and income taxes by $6,000

[2]Exhibit 19–1 in Chapter 19 (page 722) illustrates the process of converting accrual basis amounts to cash flows.

(40% of $15,000), resulting in a $9,000 after-tax expense. Because income tax rates can be substantial, management has a continuing responsibility to minimize the firm's income tax. After-tax cash flows are more relevant than before-tax cash flows because they represent the amounts available to retire debt, finance expansions, or pay dividends. For these reasons, investment decision analyses must be formulated in terms of after-tax cash flows.

Illustration of After-tax Cash Flows

Thinking in terms of after-tax cash flows represents a significant departure from the accrual-based accounting for revenue and expenses that dominates much of our earlier study of accounting. Exhibit 27–4 builds on the traditional income statement to illustrate (1) the conversion of net income to after-tax cash flows, (2) the confirmation of that amount as actual cash flows, and (3) the determination of the individual after-tax cash flow effects of receiving revenue, incurring cash expenses, and recording depreciation. An understanding of Exhibit 27–4 provides a basis for studying the comprehensive illustration of capital budgeting later in the chapter.

The area in Exhibit 27–4 set off in color is the traditional income statement, showing that revenue minus operating expenses and income taxes results in a net income of $18,000. For simplicity, we assume revenue and cash expenses involve no significant accruals and that depreciation is the same on both the books and the tax return. Ordinarily, net income does not represent after-tax cash flows because depreciation expense—a noncash expense—is deducted to derive net income. As indicated in column A of Exhibit 27–4, to convert the $18,000 net income to after-tax cash flows, we must add back the depreciation of $10,000,

EXHIBIT 27–4
Illustration of Determining After-tax Cash Flows

		(A) Traditional Income Statement	(B) Income Statement Cash Inflows (Outflows)	(C) Individual After-tax Cash Inflow (Outflow) Effects
Cash revenue (Sales)		$100,000	$100,000	$60,000
Cash operaing expenses	$60,000		(60,000)	(36,000)
Depreciation expense	10,000			4,000
Total operating expenses		70,000		
Pretax income		$ 30,000		
Income tax expense at 40%		12,000	(12,000)	
Net income		$ 18,000		
Add back depreciation		10,000		
After-tax cash flows		$ 28,000	$ 28,000	$28,000

resulting in $28,000 of after-tax cash flows.[3] Present value computations are properly applied to this amount.

Column B of Exhibit 27–4 confirms the $28,000 amount of after-tax cash flows determined in column A. This is accomplished by simply listing the amounts in column A that constitute cash inflows (revenue of $100,000) and cash outflows (cash expenses of $60,000 and income tax payments of $12,000). Depreciation is excluded because it does not represent a cash payment.

Column C in Exhibit 27–4 illustrates the determination of the individual amounts of after-tax cash flows for each item on the income statement. We use this approach in the comprehensive illustration of capital budgeting appearing later in the chapter. Amounts in column C are determined as follows (again, a 40% income tax rate is assumed):

Receipt of $100,000 cash revenue Receipt of $100,000 cash revenue would, by itself, increase taxable income by $100,000, adding $40,000 ($100,000 × 40%) to income taxes. The $60,000 after-tax cash inflow is the difference between the $100,000 cash revenue received and the related $40,000 increase in income taxes (a cash outflow).

Payment of $60,000 in cash operating expenses Payment of $60,000 in cash operating expenses represents a deductible cash outflow that reduces taxable income by $60,000 and thus reduces income taxes by $24,000 ($60,000 × 40%). The $36,000 net cash outflow is the difference between the $60,000 actually paid out for expenses and the $24,000 of income tax payments avoided by virtue of their tax deductibility.

Notice that *avoiding a cash outflow* has the same effect on net cash flows as a cash inflow. In other words, total net cash inflows can be increased by adding to cash inflows or by avoiding cash outflows.

Recording $10,000 of depreciation expense Although depreciation expense is tax deductible, no related cash expenditure occurs during the period. The $10,000 deduction reduces taxable income $10,000 and income taxes $4,000 ($10,000 × 40%). Because the depreciation deduction results in avoidance of an outflow, its after-tax cash flow effect is that of a cash inflow. Depreciation expense and similar noncash expense deductions are often referred to as *tax shields* because they shield an equal amount of income from whatever income tax rate is applicable.

The depreciation amount that provides a tax shield is the depreciation deduction on the tax return. Tax depreciation deductions are governed by tax regulations and not by generally accepted accounting principles. Often the periodic tax depreciation will differ from depreciation expense on the income statement (in Exhibit 27–4 we assume the amounts are equal). When identifying the depreciation tax shield in capital budgeting analysis, then, it is important to use the depreciation amount on the tax return.

[3] If present, other amounts of noncash expenses—such as amortization of intangible assets and discount on bonds payable—are also added back.

Combining the after-tax cash flow effect of each individual amount in column C again confirms that net cash inflows total $28,000. It is helpful to realize that the after-tax cash flow effect of cash receipts and cash expenses is derived by multiplying the before-tax amounts by (1 − the tax rate). In contrast, the after-tax cash flow effect of depreciation deductions is derived by multiplying the before-tax amounts by the tax rate. In our example

Cash revenue $100,000 × (1 − 0.4)	=	$60,000
Cash expenses $60,000 × (1 − 0.4)	=	(36,000)
Depreciation expense $10,000 × 0.4	=	4,000
Net cash flows		$28,000

SUMMARY OF CONCERNS UNDERLYING CAPITAL BUDGETING

(1) The typical investment pattern involves a present investment of funds resulting in anticipated returns, often extending years into the future.

(2) The basic question in capital budgeting is whether present investments are justified by related future returns.

(3) Because money has a time value, returns that occur in the future must be discounted to their present values for a proper comparison with present investments.

(4) To use discounting (interest) calculations properly, we must state amounts in capital budgeting analyses in terms of cash flows.

(5) Because income tax rates are substantial, capital budgeting analyses should be formulated in terms of after-tax cash flows.

In this chapter, we have presented a number of important aspects of capital budgeting as background for the review of several approaches to capital expenditure analysis. These background materials have focused on the analytical concept known as *net present value*. Accountants generally concede that the net present value approach is conceptually and analytically superior to the other two approaches that we illustrate—*cash payback* and *average rate of return*.

NET PRESENT VALUE ANALYSIS

The basic considerations of **net present value** analysis are shown schematically in Exhibit 27–5. Referring to the items in the diagram, we can explain the steps in the net present value approach as follows:

(1) Determine in terms of incremental after-tax cash flows the amount of the investment outlay required.

EXHIBIT 27–5
Schematic Diagram of Net Present Value Analysis

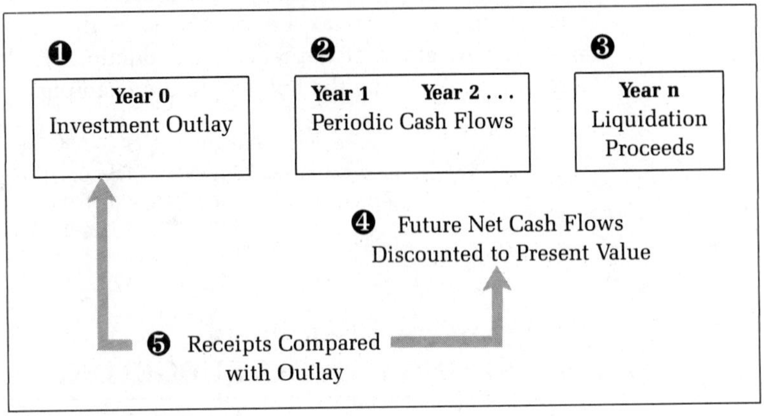

(2) Estimate in terms of incremental after-tax cash flows the amounts and timing of future operating receipts or cost savings.

(3) Estimate any incremental after-tax liquidation proceeds to be received on termination of the project.

(4) Discount all future cash flows to their present value at an appropriate interest rate, usually the minimum desired rate of return on capital.

(5) Subtract the investment outlay from the total present value of future cash flows to determine *net* present value. If net present value is zero or positive (returns equal or exceed investment), then the project's rate of return equals or exceeds the minimum desired rate and should be accepted. Negative net present values indicate that the project's return is less than desired and the project should be rejected.

To illustrate net present value analysis, assume that, with a minimum desired return of 10%, management is considering the purchase of a $12,000 machine that will save $5,000 annually in cash operating expenses; have a useful life of three years; be depreciated over three years on the tax return—$3,000 in year 1, $4,600 in year 2, and $4,400 in year 3; and be sold for $2,000 at the end of the third year. Also, assume that all income and gains are taxed at 40%.

Exhibit 27–6 presents a net present value analysis of the machine as an investment project. Note how the format follows the schematic analysis presented in Exhibit 27–5: future returns are stated in terms of after-tax cash flows; then, from Tables I and II, the present values of future cash flows are determined and compared with the investment. The computations shown in Exhibit 27–6 are explained below.

Annual cash expense savings Cash savings or expense reductions have the same effects as cash revenue, income, or gains. Of course, they also have the same

EXHIBIT 27–6
Illustration of Net Present Value Analysis—After-tax Cash Flows (rounded to nearest dollar)

Analysis of After-tax Cash Flows		Present Value Factors at 10% (Table I or II)	Total Present Value	Projected After-tax Cash Flows Year 0	Year 1	Year 2	Year 3
Annual Cash Expense Savings:							
Annual cash expense saving	$5,000						
Less income tax @ 40%	2,000						
After-tax expense savings	$3,000	(II) 2.487	$ 7,461		$3,000	$3,000	$3,000
Tax Savings from Depreciation Tax Shield:							
Year 1: $3,000 × 40% =	$1,200	(I) 0.909	1,091		1,200		
Year 2: $4,600 × 40% =	$1,840	(I) 0.826	1,520			1,840	
Year 3: $4,400 × 40% =	$1,760	(I) 0.751	1,322				1,760
Liquidation Proceeds:							
Sales price of machine	$2,000						
Tax book value (original cost of $12,000 less accumulated depreciation of $12,000)	-0-						
Gain on sale	$2,000						
Income tax on gain @ 40%	800						
After-tax proceeds of sale	$1,200	(I) 0.751	901				1,200
Total present value of future cash flows			$12,295				
Investment required in machine			(12,000)	($12,000)*			
Net positive present value			$ 295				

*Outflow.

consequence of increasing income taxes. In our example, saving $5,000 in cash expenses each year raises taxable income by $5,000, which leads to a $2,000 ($5,000 × 40%) increase in taxes. Thus, the annual after-tax cash flow is $3,000—the $5,000 savings less the $2,000 tax increase. The $3,000 saved each year for three years can be treated as an annuity. Its present value factor of 2.487 is taken from Table II on the line for three periods and the column for 10% (the minimum return desired). The analysis shows that, with desired return at 10% and income taxes at 40%, saving $5,000 annually for the next three years has a present value of $7,461.

Annual depreciation tax shield The depreciation deduction on the tax return shields an equal amount of income from taxes. The avoided taxes are equal to the depreciation deduction multiplied by the applicable tax rate. In our illustration, the annual tax savings from the depreciation tax shield are as follows:

Year	Depreciation		Tax Rate		Tax Savings
1	$3,000	×	40%	=	$1,200
2	4,600	×	40%	=	1,840
3	4,400	×	40%	=	1,760

The tax savings represent tax payments that are avoided. In analyzing cash flows, tax savings are treated as having an effect similar to that of cash inflows. Present value factors from Table I are used to determine that the present values of these tax savings are $1,091, $1,520, and $1,322, respectively, for each of the three years.

Liquidation proceeds The amount realized when an asset is liquidated contributes to the relative attractiveness of an investment in capital equipment. Liquidation proceeds on long-lived assets are sometimes disregarded because their occurrence is so far in the future that the amounts are difficult to predict, and their present values tend to be small. When useful lives are short, however, liquidation proceeds may be a deciding factor in the analysis. In our illustration, the machine costing $12,000 is sold after three years for $2,000. For tax purposes, salvage value may be ignored in computing depreciation, so the machine is fully depreciated over the three years to a zero book value. The machine's sale for $2,000, then, creates a $2,000 gain on the tax return ($2,000 sales price − $0 book value). The $2,000 gain increases income taxes by $800, which is deducted from the sales price of $2,000 to produce a net after-tax cash flow of $1,200. Because the $1,200 is a single sum received at the end of year 3, its present value of $901 is derived by multiplying the $1,200 by the 0.751 factor from Table I (three periods hence at 10%).

If an asset is sold before the end of its tax depreciation period, a loss may be generated for tax purposes. The loss operates as a tax shield because it shields an equal amount of income from taxes. To illustrate the calculation of cash flows related to a loss sale, assume that the machine was sold after two years for $3,200. The total after-tax cash flow is computed as follows:

Tax book value of machine ($12,000 original cost − $7,600 accumulated depreciation)	$4,400
Less sales price of machine	3,200
Loss on sale	$1,200
Income tax rate	0.40
Income tax savings from loss	$ 480
Plus sales price of machine	3,200
Total after-tax cash flow from sale	$3,680

Required investment Proper consideration of the required investment involves neither an income tax nor a present value calculation. The $12,000 investment itself is not tax deductible; the related depreciation deductions are tax deductible, and are, of course, incorporated into our analysis. Since the investment expenditure is immediate, no discounting for present value is required. Thus, $12,000 represents the after-tax present value of the required investment outflow.

Decision rule With its savings of cash expense, tax savings from the depreciation tax shield, and liquidation proceeds, the $12,000 investment results in future cash flows with a total present value of $12,295 and therefore a net present value of $295. This return on the capital invested, adjusted for the time value of money, exceeds the 10% return rate sought, and the investment is acceptable.

Another interpretation of our anaylsis is that as much as $12,295 could be paid for the machine and still retain the desired 10% rate of return. Paying more than $12,295 for the machine results in a return of less than 10%.

Excess Present Value Index

Alternative capital expenditure proposals may be compared in terms of their **excess present value index,** defined as

$$\text{Excess Present Value Index} = \frac{\text{Total Present Value of Future Cash Flows}}{\text{Initial Investment}}$$

For the investment presented in Exhibit 27–6, the excess present value index would be

$$\frac{\$12{,}295}{\$12{,}000} = 1.025$$

The higher the ratio of return on investment, the more attractive the proposal. Although the excess present value index may be a convenient measure for ranking various proposals, it does not reflect the amount of the investment. Two proposals, requiring initial cash investments of $5,000 and $5,000,000, respectively, could have identical excess present value indexes but could hardly be considered equal investment opportunities.

CASH PAYBACK ANALYSIS

Cash payback analysis is a form of capital expenditure analysis that is considered less sophisticated than net present value analysis. The **cash payback period** is *the time in years that it takes net future after-tax cash inflows to equal the original investment.*

Assume that a firm is considering purchasing either machine A or machine B, for which the following data are given:

Machine	Investment Required	Estimated Annual Net After-tax Cash Inflows	Useful Life
A	$10,000	$2,500	8 years
B	15,000	5,000	3 years

Cash payback is computed as

$$\frac{\text{Original Investment}}{\text{Annual Net Cash Inflows}} = \text{Cash Payback in Years}$$

Thus, for the two machines, we obtain

$$\text{(A)}\quad \frac{\$10{,}000}{\$2{,}500} = \text{4-year cash payback}$$

$$\text{(B)}\quad \frac{\$15{,}000}{\$5{,}000} = \text{3-year cash payback}$$

This analysis shows that machine A will pay back its required investment in four years, and machine B will take only three years. Because the decision rule in cash payback analysis states that *the shorter the payback period the better*, machine B would be considered the better investment.

Concern for the payback of investments is quite natural because the shorter a project's payback period, the more quickly the funds invested in that project are recovered and available for other investments. In high-risk investments, the payback period indicates how soon a firm is "bailed out" of an investment should it prove unattractive.

A primary limitation to cash payback analysis is that the *relative profitability of various investments is not specifically considered*. Note, for example, that in the foregoing illustration, machine B has the better (shorter) cash payback period. However, its useful life, which is ignored in cash payback analysis, indicates that machine B will stop generating cash inflows just when payback is completed. Consequently, there will be no opportunity to generate profit. In contrast, although machine A has the longer payback period, it will generate future cash inflows for four years beyond its payback and therefore promises to be profitable.

Regardless of its failure to consider profitability, cash payback analysis is widely used in industry, probably because of its relative simplicity. It can be useful in conjunction with other analyses or as a preliminary screening device for investment projects under consideration.

AVERAGE RATE OF RETURN

Another approach to capital outlay analysis, **average rate of return** relies heavily on accounting determinations of net income. This measure is calculated as

$$\text{Average Rate of Return} = \frac{\text{Average Annual Net Income from Investment}}{\text{Average Investment}}$$

Note that here the focus is not on after-tax cash flows but on traditional accounting net income (with depreciation deducted).

Assume machine C requires an initial investment of $48,000; provides $12,000 annual cash inflows from operations; and has a useful life of 12 years. Assuming no salvage value, annual straight-line depreciation on machine C would be ($48,000/12), or $4,000. With an income tax rate of 40%, the average annual net income from the investment would be $4,800, computed as follows:

Cash inflow from operations	$12,000
Depreciation expense	4,000
Pretax income from investment	$ 8,000
Income tax expense	3,200
Net income from investment	$ 4,800

We may calculate average investment simply by adding the beginning and ending investments and dividing by 2. The ending investment is the expected salvage value. In our illustration, machine C has no salvage value, so the ending investment is zero. Average investment is therefore ($48,000 + $0)/2 = $24,000.

The average rate of return on machine C is

$$\frac{\$4,800}{\$24,000} = 20\%$$

The decision rule for average rate of return analyses states that *the higher the return, the more attractive the investment.*

As an approach to capital expenditure analysis, the average rate of return is often defended as being most easily understood by management personnel who are accustomed to thinking in accounting terms and concepts. It has two major limitations, however. First, the calculations rely heavily on accounting computations of net income and depreciation, and are thus subject to arbitrary choices, such as the selection of a depreciation method. Second, average rate of return calculations do not consider the time value of money. Future cash flows are treated the same as current cash flows. Our discussion of net present value analysis amply illustrates the often substantial differences between future values and related current values discounted by even moderate interest rates.

As an example of how deceptive the average annual income figures used in average rate of return computations can be, consider three investment proposals that each require a $40,000 initial investment and promise the annual cash inflows shown in Exhibit 27–7. Note that cash flows are concentrated in year 1 in proposal A, are uniform in proposal B, and are concentrated in year 5 in proposal C. Because average rate of return calculations fail to consider the timing of cash flows from operations, these three proposals would have identical 10% average rates of return and therefore would be considered equally attractive. Such an implication is hardly defensible in view of the substantial differences in the relative net present values of the operating cash flows. In our illustration, the difference between the present values of A and C is $12,960, an amount equal to 41% of C's present value.

EXHIBIT 27–7
Present Value Comparison of Equal Annual Average Incomes

		Proposals	
	A	B	C
Annual net cash inflows			
Year 1	$46,000	$10,000	$ 1,000
2	1,000	10,000	1,000
3	1,000	10,000	1,000
4	1,000	10,000	1,000
5	1,000	10,000	46,000
Aggregate net cash inflows	$50,000	$50,000	$50,000
Average annual net cash inflows	$10,000	$10,000	$10,000
Less depreciation ($40,000/5)	8,000	8,000	8,000
Average annual net income	$ 2,000	$ 2,000	$ 2,000
Average rate of return on investment			
$2,000/($40,000/2)	10%	10%	10%
Present value of net cash inflows at 10%:			
(A) One year hence, $45,000 × 0.909	$40,905		
5-year annuity of $1,000 × 3.791	3,791		
	$44,696		
(B) 5-year annuity of $10,000 × 3.791		$37,910	
(C) 5-year annuity of $1,000 × 3.791			$ 3,791
5 years hence, $45,000 × 0.621			27,945
			$31,736

CAPITAL BUDGETING—A PERSPECTIVE

Because it incorporates aspects of such fields as economics, finance, business management, and accounting, the subject of capital budgeting is too complex to treat comprehensively in an introductory accounting book. In this chapter, we have simply provided some insight into problem-solving techniques in capital budgeting by stating decision rules in their simplest form, showing the relevance of present value concepts and after-tax cash flows, and creating an awareness of the potentials and limitations of several widely used approaches to capital expenditure analysis. The illustrations have highlighted key relationships. The rudiments presented here should serve as a basis for further study and an understanding of related subject areas.

KEY POINTS TO REMEMBER

(1) Capital budgeting is the planning of long-lived asset investments; capital expenditure analysis basically examines how well prospective future returns justify related present investments.

(2) Cost of capital is a measure of the firm's cost for investment capital; it usually represents the minimum acceptable return for investment opportunities.

(3) The time value of money concept recognizes that the farther into the future cash flows occur, the less current economic worth they have. Present value tables enable us to convert future cash flows conveniently to their present values at appropriate interest rates.

(4) After-tax cash flows probably represent the most relevant measure of the prospective returns of proposed investments.

(5) We convert cash flows from revenue and expenses into after-tax amounts by multiplying them by the factor $(1 - r)$, where r is the income tax rate. We convert depreciation deductions into their after-tax cash flow effect by multiplying the deduction by the applicable income tax rate.

(6) Net present value analysis compares the present value of net future cash flow returns with the investment. Projects having zero or positive net present values are acceptable.

(7) Cash payback analysis measures the time in years necessary for the net future after-tax cash flows to equal the original investment. In this type of analysis, the shorter the payback period, the more attractive the investment.

(8) Average rate of return analysis compares the annual average net income with the average investment. The higher this ratio, the more attractive the investment.

(9) Cash payback analysis fails to consider the relative profitability of alternative projects. Average rate of return analysis fails to consider the time value of money.

SELF-TEST QUESTIONS
(Answers are at the end of this chapter.)

1. The cost to a firm of acquiring the funds for capital investment projects is known as the
   (a) Payback period.
   (b) Rate of return.
   (c) Cost of capital.
   (d) Time value of money.

2. All other things remaining the same, when the interest rate used to discount future values increases, the present value amount will
   (a) Decrease.
   (b) Increase in proportion to the interest rate increase.
   (c) Remain the same.
   (d) Increase but not in proportion to the interest rate increase.

3. Although depreciation is a noncash expense, it does have an indirect effect on cash flows because it shelters an equal amount of income from income taxes. This feature is known as a
   (a) Buffer margin.
   (b) Cash payback.
   (c) Depreciation flow.
   (d) Tax shield.
4. Whistler Company is considering four investment proposals, each requiring the same amount of initial cash investment. The excess present value index for each proposal is listed below. Using the index as a selection criterion, identify the index of the most attractive proposal.
   (a) 90 (b) 100 (c) 110 (d) 115
5. The primary limitation of the cash payback method is that it
   (a) Uses before-tax cash flows.
   (b) Identifies the length of time it will take to recover the investment outlay in cash.
   (c) Ignores the profitability of one investment project as compared to another.
   (d) Involves a more sophisticated analysis than the net present value method.

QUESTIONS

27–1 What is capital budgeting?

27–2 List three reasons why capital budgeting decisions are often important.

27–3 What are the three stages typical of most investments in plant and equipment?

27–4 Briefly describe the concept of *weighted average cost of capital.*

27–5 In what sense does the cost of capital limit a firm's investment considerations?

27–6 Briefly describe the concept of the *time value of money.*

27–7 In which interest rate columns and periods hence lines in a table showing the present values of $1 received in the future would you expect the smallest factors? Why?

27–8 In which interest rate columns and periods hence lines in a table showing the present values of a $1 annuity would you expect the largest factors? Why?

27–9 What is the relationship between a table showing the present values of $1 and a table showing the present values of a $1 annuity, when both tables use the same interest rates and time periods?

27–10 Explain how to convert before-tax cash operating expenses and depreciation deductions into after-tax amounts.

27–11 What is meant by the term "depreciation tax shield"?

27–12 What amounts are compared in net present value analysis? State the related decision rule.

27–13 What is an excess present value index?

27–14 Define *cash payback*, state the related decision rule, and specify an important limitation of this analysis.

27–15 Define *average rate of return*, state the related decision rule, and specify an important limitation of this analysis.

27–16 You have the right to receive $25,000 at the end of each of the next three years, and money is worth 8%. Using Table II, compute the present value involved. Illustrate how Table I can be used to confirm your answer.

27–17 A company plans to accumulate 70% of its needed investment capital by issuing bonds having a capital cost percentage of 12%; the balance will be raised by issuing stock having a capital cost percentage of 15%. What would be the weighted average cost of capital for the total amount of capital?

27–18 A rich uncle allows you to stipulate which of two ways you receive your inheritance: (a) $825,000 one year after his death or (b) $300,000 on his death and $180,000 each year at the end of the first, second, and third years following his death. If money is worth 10%, what is the relative advantage of the more attractive alternative?

27–19 You can settle a debt with either a single payment now of $50,000 or with payments of $14,000 at the end of each of the next five years. If money is worth 12%, what is the relative advantage of the most attractive alternative? If money is worth 15%, would your answer change? Why?

EXERCISES

Present value computations

27–20 (a) Assuming money is worth 12%, compute the present value of:

(1) $4,500 received 15 years from today.
(2) The right to inherit $2,500,000 fifty years from now.
(3) The right to receive $900 at the end of each of the next six years.
(4) The obligation to pay $500 at the end of each of the next 12 years.
(5) The right to receive $6,000 at the end of the seventh, eighth, ninth, and tenth years from today.

(b) Confirm your answer to part (a)(5) by using Table II and subtracting the present value of a six-year annuity from a ten-year annuity (isolating the four relevant years).

Weighted average cost of capital

27–21 Hyson, Inc., plans to finance its expansion by raising the needed investment capital from the following sources in the indicated proportions and respective capital cost rates:

Source	Proportion	Capital Cost Rate
Bonds	40%	14%
Preferred stock	10	10
Common stock	20	9
Retained earnings	30	8
	100%	

Calculate the weighted average cost of capital.

After-tax cash flows

27–22 For each of the following independent situations, compute the net income and convert it to an after-tax cash flow amount that could be properly incorporated into net present value analyses. Depreciation is the same on both the books and the tax return.

	A	B	C
Cash revenue received	$90,000	$280,000	$130,000
Cash operating expenses paid	60,000	200,000	110,000
Depreciation expense	15,000	30,000	10,000
Income tax rate	30%	40%	20%

After-tax cash flows

27–23 Using the data in Exercise 27–22, (a) calculate—as shown in column C of Exhibit 27–4—the individual after-tax cash flow effect of each relevant item in each independent situation, and (b) confirm that the sum of the individual after-tax cash flows in each situation equals the net income converted to after-tax cash flows.

Net present value analysis

27–24 Loring Company must evaluate two capital expenditure proposals. Loring's cutoff rate is 20%. Data for the two proposals follow.

	Proposal X	Proposal Y
Required investment	$51,000	$51,000
Annual cash inflows	12,000	
Cash inflows at the end of years 3, 6, 9, and 12		36,000
Life of project	12 years	12 years

Using net present value analysis, which proposal is the more attractive? If Loring has sufficient funds available, should both proposals be accepted?

Cash payback

27–25 Refer to the date in Exercise 27–24. What is the cash payback period for proposal X? for proposal Y?

Average rate of return

27–26 Bach Company is considering the purchase of equipment for $60,000. The equipment will expand the company's production and increase revenue by $20,000 per year. Annual cash operating expenses will increase by $8,000. The equipment's useful life is ten years with no salvage value. Bach uses straight-line depreciation. The income tax rate is 35%. What is the average rate of return on the investment?

Depreciation tax shields

27–27 Kettle Company has purchased equipment for $100,000. After it is fully depreciated, the equipment has no salvage value. Kettle may select either of the following depreciation schedules for tax purposes:

Year	Option 1 Depreciation	Option 2 Depreciation
1	$15,000	$10,000
2	22,000	20,000
3	21,000	20,000
4	21,000	20,000
5	21,000	20,000
6	0	10,000

Assuming a 40% tax rate and a 10% desired annual return, compute the total present value of the tax savings provided by these alternative depreciation tax shields. Which depreciation schedule would be the most attractive to Kettle?

PROBLEMS

After-tax cash flows and present value factors

27–28 Below is a list of various capital expenditure proposals that the capital budgeting team of Dynamic, Inc., has incorporated into its net present value analyses during the past year. Unless otherwise noted, the items listed are unrelated to each other. All situations assume a 40% income tax rate and a 12% minimum desired rate of return.

(1) Pretax savings of $3,000 in cash expenses will occur in each of the next three years.
(2) A machine is purchased now for $25,000.
(3) A truck costing $16,000 will be depreciated $4,000, $6,100, and $5,900, respectively, on the tax return over its three-year life.
(4) Machinery costing $200,000 will be depreciated over five years on the tax return in the following amounts: $30,000; $44,000; $42,000; $42,000; and $42,000.
(5) Pretax savings of $3,500 in cash expenses will occur in the third, fourth, and fifth years from now.
(6) Pretax savings of $4,000 in cash expenses will occur in the first, third, and fifth years from now.
(7) The truck described in (3) will be sold after three years for $2,500 cash.
(8) The machinery described in (4) will be sold after four years for $35,000 cash.

REQUIRED
Set up an answer form with the four column headings as shown below. Answer each investment aspect separately. Prepare your calculations on a separate paper and key them to each item. The answer to investment aspect (1) is presented as an example.

Investment Aspect	(A) After-tax Cash Flow Effect(s) (Outflows)	(B) Year(s) of Cash Flow	(C) Applicable Present Value Multiple
(1)	$1,800	1, 2, 3	(II) 2.402

Calculations:

(1)	Pretax cash savings	$3,000
	Less income tax at 40%	1,200
	After-tax cash inflow	$1,800

(a) Calculate and record in column A the related after-tax cash flow effect(s). Place parentheses around outflows.
(b) Indicate in column B the timing of each cash flow shown in column A. Use 0 to indicate immediately and 1, 2, 3, 4, and so on for each year involved.
(c) When relevant, record in column C the present value multiple from Table I or II that you would apply to the cash flow amount shown in column A.

Net present value analysis

27–29 The Skokie Company is considering a contract to provide warranty services for a chain of stores. The contract covers five years. To provide the required services, Skokie would have to purchase additional equipment for $39,000. Skokie estimates the contract will provide annual net cash inflows (before taxes) of $15,400. For tax purposes, the equipment will be depreciated as follows:

Year 1	$5,800
Year 2	8,600
Year 3	8,200
Year 4	8,200
Year 5	8,200

Although salvage value is ignored in the tax depreciation calculations, Skokie estimates the equipment will be sold for $4,500 after five years.

REQUIRED
Assuming a 35% income tax rate and a 15% cutoff rate, compute the net present value of this contract proposal. Using net present value analysis, should Skokie accept the contract? (Round amounts to the nearest dollar.)

Cash payback, average rate of return, and net present value methods

27–30 At a cash cost of $45,000, Bixby Corporation can acquire a machine that will save $16,000 in annual cash operating expenses. No salvage value is expected at the end of its five-year useful life. Assume the machine will be depreciated over five years on a straight-line basis on both the books and the tax return. The income tax rate is 35% and Bixby has a 12% cutoff rate when using a net present value analysis.

REQUIRED
(a) What are the annual after-tax cash savings in operating expenses?
(b) What are the annual tax savings from the depreciation tax shield?
(c) Compute the cash payback period.
(d) Compute the average rate of return.
(e) Compute the net present value and indicate whether it is positive or negative. (Round amounts to the nearest dollar.)
(f) Compute the excess present value index.

Excess present value index and average rate of return

27–31 Catlett Company is evaluating five different capital expenditure proposals. The company's cutoff rate for net present value analyses is 12%. A 10% salvage value is expected from each of the investments. Information on the five proposals is as follows:

Proposal	Required Investment	Present Value at 12% of After-tax Cash Flows	Average Annual Net Income from Investment
A	$90,000	$101,700	$12,600
B	70,000	77,004	10,150
C	50,000	57,554	9,000
D	38,000	40,680	4,920
E	64,000	71,928	8,500

REQUIRED
(a) Compute the excess present value index for the five proposals.
(b) Compute the average rate of return for the five proposals.
(c) Assume Catlett will commit no more than $150,000 to new capital expen-

diture proposals. Using the excess present value index, which proposals would be accepted? Using the average rate of return, which proposals would be accepted?

Cash payback, average rate of return, and net present value methods

27–32 Dannon Amusement Park is considering the construction of a new facility to house a curved, multi-story movie screen. The facility will cost $300,000 and be useful for ten years, with no salvage value. The facility will be depreciated on a straight-line basis over ten years on both the books and the tax return. The following annual results are expected if the facility is constructed:

Increase in annual revenue		$145,000
Increase in expenses:		
Cash operating expenses	$35,000	
Depreciation	30,000	65,000
Pretax income		$ 80,000
Income tax expense (35%)		28,000
Net income		$ 52,000

Dannon uses a 20% cutoff rate when analyzing capital expenditure proposals using net present value.

REQUIRED

(a) What are the annual net cash flows (net inflows) from this project?
(b) Compute the cash payback period.
(c) Compute the average rate of return.
(d) Compute the net present value and indicate whether it is positive or negative.

Net present value analysis

27–33 You have an opportunity to invest in a concession at a world exposition. To exploit the building and exhibits more fully, the venture is expected to cover a five-year period consisting of a preliminary year, the two years of formal exposition, and a two-year period of reduced operation as a regional exposition.

The terms of the concession agreement specify that:

(1) At inception, a $50,000 deposit is paid to Global Expo, Inc., the promoting organization. This amount is returned in full at the end of the five years if the operator maintains the concession in order and keeps it open during scheduled hours. The deposit is not tax deductible, nor is its return subject to income taxes.
(2) The operator must install certain fixtures that will cost $120,000. The fixtures become the property of Global Expo, Inc., at the end of the five years.

After careful investigation and consultation with local experts, you conclude that the following schedule reflects the estimated pretax income of the concession (amounts in thousands of dollars):

	Year 1	Year 2	Year 3	Year 4	Year 5
Sales (all cash)	$100	$285	$325	$200	$165
Operating expenses:					
Cash	$ 62	$158	$175	$ 95	$ 80
Depreciation	18	27	25	25	25
Total expenses	$ 80	$185	$200	$120	$105
Pretax income	$ 20	$100	$125	$ 80	$ 60

REQUIRED

Assuming an income tax rate of 35% and a desired annual return of 12%, what is the net present value of this investment opportunity? What is the maximum amount that could be invested and still earn a 12% annual return? (Round amounts to nearest dollar.)

Weighted average cost of capital and net present value analysis

27–34 Abernathy Company is considering a proposal to acquire new equipment for its research and development division. The equipment will cost $88,000 and be useful for three years. Abernathy expects annual savings in cash operating expenses (before taxes) of $40,000. For tax purposes, the annual depreciation deduction will be $22,000, $33,400, and $32,600, respectively, for the three years. The salvage value is expected to be $5,000. The income tax rate is 40%.

Abernathy establishes a cutoff rate for a net present value analysis at the company's weighted average cost of capital plus one percentage point. Abernathy's capital is provided in the following proportions: debt, 40%; common stock, 50%; and retained earnings, 10%. The cost rates for these capital sources are: debt, 10.5%; common stock, 11%; and retained earnings, 13%.

REQUIRED

(a) Compute Abernathy's (1) weighted average cost of capital, and (2) cutoff rate.

(b) Using Abernathy's cutoff rate, compute the net present value of this capital expenditure proposal. Under net present value analysis, should Abernathy accept the proposal? (Round amounts to the nearest dollar.)

ALTERNATE PROBLEMS

After-tax cash flows and present value factors

27–28A Below is a list of aspects of various capital expenditure proposals that the capital budgeting team of Power Systems, Inc., has incorporated into its net present value analyses during the past year. Unless otherwise noted, the items listed are unrelated to each other. All situations assume a 25% income tax rate and a 20% minimum desired rate of return.

(1) Pretax savings of $5,000 in cash expenses will occur in each of the next three years.

(2) A machine is purchased now for $67,000.

(3) Research and development equipment costing $150,000 will be depreciated $37,500, $57,000, and $55,500, respectively, on the tax return over its three-year life.

(4) A patent purchased for $480,000 will be amortized on a straight-line basis over 16 years on the tax return. No salvage value is expected.

(5) Pretax savings of $8,000 in cash expenses will occur in the fourth, fifth, and sixth years from now.

(6) Pretax savings of $6,000 in cash expenses will occur in the first, fourth, and seventh years from now.

(7) The equipment described in (3) will be sold after three years for $20,000 cash.

(8) A truck with a tax book value of $5,200 after two years will be sold at that time for $3,800.

REQUIRED

Set up an answer form with the four column headings as shown below. Answer each investment aspect separately. Prepare your calculations on a separate paper and key them to each item. The answer to investment aspect (1) is presented as an example.

Investment Aspect	(A) After-tax Cash Flow Effect(s) (Outflows)	(B) Year(s) of Cash Flow	(C) Applicable Present Value Multiple
(1)	$3,750	1, 2, 3	(II) 2.106

Calculations:

(1)	Pretax cash savings	$5,000
	Less income tax at 25%	1,250
	After-tax cash inflow	$3,750

(a) Calculate and record in column A the related after-tax cash flow effect(s). Place parentheses around outflows.
(b) Indicate in column B the timing of each cash flow shown in column A. Use 0 to indicate immediately and 1, 2, 3, 4, and so on for each year involved.
(c) When relevant, record in column C the present value multiple from Table I or II that you would apply to the cash flow amount shown in column A.

Cash payback, average rate of return, and net present value methods

27–30A At a cash cost of $110,000, Deare, Inc., can acquire equipment that will save $34,000 in annual cash operating expenses. No salvage value is expected at the end of its five-year useful life. Assume the machine will be depreciated over five years on a straight-line basis on both the books and the tax return. The income tax rate is 30% and Deare has a 10% cutoff rate when using a net present value analysis.

REQUIRED

(a) What are the annual after-tax cash savings in operating expenses?
(b) What are the annual tax savings from the depreciation tax shield?
(c) Compute the cash payback period.
(d) Compute the average rate of return.
(e) Compute the net present value and indicate whether it is positive or negative. (Round amounts to the nearest dollar.)
(f) Compute the excess present value index.

Excess present value index and average rate of return

27–31A Blazer Corporation is evaluating five different capital expenditure proposals. The company's cutoff rate for net present value analyses is 15%. A 15% salvagc value is expected from each of the investments. Information on the five proposals is as follows:

Proposal	Required Investment	Net Present Value	Average Annual Net Income from Investment
A	$20,000	$3,388	$ 3,300
B	32,000	2,245	9,600
C	45,000	4,584	6,800
D	80,000	5,323	12,700
E	28,000	7,133	5,580

REQUIRED
(a) Compute the excess present value index for the five proposals.
(b) Compute the average rate of return for the five proposals.
(c) Assume Blazer will commit no more than $60,000 to new capital expenditure proposals. Using the excess present value index, which proposals would be accepted? Using the average rate of return, which proposals would be accepted?

Cash payback, average rate of return, and net present value methods

27–32A Freitag Company is considering whether to enter into a franchise agreement which would give the company exclusive distribution rights in a three-state region to a quality line of leisure spas. The franchise agreement will extend eight years and cost $200,000. There is no salvage value. The franchise cost will be amortized on a straight-line basis over eight years on both the books and the tax return. The following annual results are expected if the franchise is acquired:

Increase in annual revenue		$75,000
Increases in expenses:		
Cash operating expenses	$29,000	
Amortization	25,000	54,000
Pretax income		$21,000
Income tax expense (30%)		6,300
Net income		$14,700

Freitag uses a 12% cutoff rate when analyzing capital expenditure proposals using net present value.

REQUIRED
(a) What are the annual net cash flows (net inflows) from this proposal?
(b) Compute the cash payback period.
(c) Compute the average rate of return.
(d) Compute the net present value and indicate whether it is positive or negative. (Round amounts to the nearest dollar.)

Weighted average cost of capital and net present value analysis

27–34A Ripley Company is considering a proposal to purchase robotic equipment at a cost of $281,000. The equipment will be useful for five years and has an expected $40,000 salvage value. Ripley expects annual savings in cash operating expenses (before taxes) of $95,000. For tax purposes, the annual depreciation deduction will be as follows:

Year 1	$42,000
Year 2	62,000
Year 3	59,000
Year 4	59,000
Year 5	59,000

The income tax rate is 35%.

Ripley establishes a cutoff rate for a net present value analysis at the company's weighted average cost of capital plus two percentage points. Ripley's capital is provided in the following proportions: debt, 45%; common stock, 30%; and retained earnings, 25%. The cost rates for these capital sources are: debt, 12%; common stock, 14%; and retained earnings, 13.6%.

REQUIRED

(a) Compute Ripley's (1) weighted average cost of capital, and (2) cutoff rate.

(b) Using Ripley's cutoff rate, compute the net present value of this capital expenditure proposal. Under net present value analysis, should Ripley accept the proposal? (Round amounts to the nearest dollar.)

BUSINESS DECISION PROBLEM

Cabot Corporation recently identified an investment opportunity involving the purchase of a patent which will permit the company to modify its line of video cassette recorders. The patent's purchase price is $250,000 and the legal protection it provides will last for five more years. There is no salvage value. However, after preparing the capital expenditure analysis below, Cabot's treasurer has recommended to Cabot's capital budgeting committee that the investment be rejected. Glenn Mason, chairperson of the capital budgeting committee, finds it difficult to accept the treasurer's analysis because he "feels intuitively" that the investment is attractive. For this reason, he has retained you to review the treasurer's analysis and recommendation. You are provided with the following data and summary of the treasurer's analysis:

(1) Required investment: $250,000 cash for the patent to be amortized on a straight-line basis, five-year useful life, with a zero salvage value.

(2) Projected cash revenue and operating expenses:

Year	Cash Revenue	Cash Expenses
1	$270,000	$ 95,000
2	250,000	70,000
3	140,000	55,000
4	90,000	27,000
5	80,000	18,000
	$830,000	$265,000

(3) Source of capital: Cabot plans to raise 30% of the needed capital by issuing bonds, 40% by issuing stock, and the balance from retained earnings. For these sources, the capital cost rates are 8%, 10%, and 12%, respectively. Cabot has a policy of seeking a return equal to the weighted average cost of capital plus two percentage points as a "buffer margin" for the uncertainties involved.

(4) Income taxes: Cabot assumes an overall income tax rate of 30%.

(5) Treasurer's analysis:

Average cost of capital (8% + 10% + 12%) ÷ 3 = 10%

Total cash revenue		$830,000
Total cash expenses	$265,000	
Total amortization	250,000	
Total operating expenses		515,000
Projected net income over five years		$315,000
Average annual income ($315,000 ÷ 5)		$ 63,000
Present value factor of five-year annuity at 10%		× 3.791
Present value of future returns		$238,833
Required investment		250,000
Negative net present value		$ 11,167

Recommendation: Reject investment because of insufficient net present value.

REQUIRED

(a) Review the treasurer's analysis, identifying any questionable aspects and briefly commenting on the apparent effect of each such item on the treasurer's analysis.

(b) Prepare your own analysis of the investment, including a calculation of the proper cost of capital and cutoff rates, a net present value analysis of the project, and a brief recommendation to Mason regarding the investment.

(c) Because of his concern for the uncertainties of the video cassette recorder business, Mason also has asked you to provide analyses supporting whether or not your recommendation would change:

(1) If estimates of projected cash revenue were reduced by 10%.

(2) If the "buffer margin" were increased from 2% to 5%.

ANSWERS TO SELF-TEST QUESTIONS

1. (c) 2. (a) 3. (d) 4. (d) 5. (c)

APPENDIX E

PRESENT VALUE TABLES

TABLE I
Present Value of $1
Received in the Future

Periods Hence	Rate per Compounding Period 2%	3%	4%	5%	6%	8%	10%	12%	15%	20%
1	0.980	0.971	0.962	0.952	0.943	0.926	0.909	0.893	0.870	0.833
2	0.961	0.943	0.925	0.907	0.890	0.857	0.826	0.797	0.756	0.694
3	0.942	0.915	0.889	0.864	0.840	0.794	0.751	0.712	0.658	0.579
4	0.924	0.889	0.855	0.823	0.792	0.735	0.683	0.636	0.572	0.482
5	0.906	0.863	0.822	0.784	0.747	0.681	0.621	0.567	0.497	0.402
6	0.888	0.838	0.790	0.746	0.705	0.630	0.564	0.507	0.432	0.335
7	0.871	0.813	0.760	0.711	0.665	0.583	0.513	0.452	0.376	0.279
8	0.854	0.789	0.731	0.677	0.627	0.540	0.467	0.404	0.327	0.233
9	0.837	0.766	0.703	0.645	0.592	0.500	0.424	0.361	0.284	0.194
10	0.821	0.744	0.676	0.614	0.558	0.463	0.386	0.322	0.247	0.162
11	0.804	0.722	0.650	0.585	0.527	0.429	0.350	0.287	0.215	0.135
12	0.789	0.701	0.625	0.557	0.497	0.397	0.319	0.257	0.187	0.112
13	0.773	0.681	0.601	0.530	0.469	0.368	0.290	0.229	0.163	0.093
14	0.758	0.661	0.577	0.505	0.442	0.340	0.263	0.205	0.141	0.078
15	0.743	0.642	0.555	0.481	0.417	0.315	0.239	0.183	0.123	0.065
16	0.728	0.623	0.534	0.458	0.394	0.292	0.218	0.163	0.107	0.054
17	0.714	0.605	0.513	0.436	0.371	0.270	0.198	0.146	0.093	0.045
18	0.700	0.587	0.494	0.416	0.350	0.250	0.180	0.130	0.081	0.038
19	0.686	0.570	0.475	0.396	0.331	0.232	0.164	0.116	0.070	0.031
20	0.673	0.554	0.456	0.377	0.312	0.215	0.149	0.104	0.061	0.026
30	0.552	0.412	0.308	0.231	0.174	0.099	0.057	0.033	0.015	0.004
40	0.453	0.307	0.208	0.142	0.097	0.046	0.022	0.011	0.004	0.001
50	0.372	0.228	0.141	0.087	0.054	0.021	0.009	0.003	0.001	—

TABLE II
Present Value of $1 Annuity Received at End of Each Period

Periods Hence	Rate per Compounding Period 2%	3%	4%	5%	6%	8%	10%	12%	15%	20%
1	0.980	0.971	0.962	0.952	0.943	0.926	0.909	0.893	0.870	0.833
2	1.942	1.914	1.886	1.859	1.833	1.783	1.736	1.690	1.626	1.528
3	2.884	2.829	2.775	2.723	2.673	2.577	2.487	2.402	2.283	2.106
4	3.808	3.717	3.630	3.546	3.465	3.312	3.170	3.037	2.855	2.589
5	4.714	4.580	4.452	4.330	4.212	3.993	3.791	3.605	3.352	2.991
6	5.601	5.417	5.242	5.076	4.917	4.623	4.355	4.111	3.784	3.326
7	6.472	6.230	6.002	5.786	5.582	5.206	4.868	4.564	4.160	3.605
8	7.326	7.020	6.733	6.463	6.210	5.747	5.335	4.968	4.487	3.837
9	8.162	7.786	7.435	7.108	6.802	6.247	5.760	5.328	4.772	4.031
10	8.983	8.530	8.111	7.722	7.360	6.710	6.145	5.650	5.019	4.192
11	9.787	9.253	8.761	8.306	7.887	7.139	6.495	5.988	5.234	4.327
12	10.575	9.954	9.385	8.863	8.384	7.536	6.814	6.194	5.421	4.439
13	11.348	10.635	9.986	9.394	8.853	7.904	7.103	6.424	5.583	4.533
14	12.106	11.296	10.563	9.899	9.295	8.244	7.367	6.628	5.724	4.611
15	12.849	11.938	11.118	10.380	9.712	8.560	7.606	6.811	5.847	4.675
16	13.578	12.561	11.652	10.838	10.106	8.851	7.824	6.974	5.954	4.730
17	14.292	13.166	12.166	11.274	10.477	9.122	8.022	7.120	6.047	4.775
18	14.992	13.754	12.659	11.690	10.828	9.372	8.201	7.250	6.128	4.812
19	15.679	14.324	13.134	12.085	11.158	9.604	8.365	7.366	6.198	4.844
20	16.351	14.878	13.590	12.462	11.470	9.818	8.514	7.469	6.259	4.870
30	22.397	19.600	17.292	15.373	13.765	11.258	9.427	8.055	6.566	4.979
40	27.356	23.115	19.793	17.159	15.046	11.925	9.779	8.244	6.642	4.997
50	31.424	25.730	21.482	18.256	15.762	12.234	9.915	8.304	6.661	4.999

28

Income Taxes and Their Effect on Business Decisions

Chapter Objectives

- **Provide an understanding of the purpose and coverage of the tax law.**
- **Describe the format for determining tax liability for individuals.**
- **Discuss the nature and treatment of capital gains and losses.**
- **Illustrate a complete individual tax computation.**
- **Describe and illustrate basic elements of corporate taxation.**
- **Discuss tax avoidance and related business decisions.**

Don't tax you, don't tax me,
tax the fellow behind the tree.

SENATOR RUSSELL LONG

Except for a brief period during Civil War, the United States had no federal income tax until 1913, when its constitutionality was confirmed by ratification of the Sixteenth Amendment. The numerous revenue acts passed since 1913 were first codified in 1939 and then recodified as the Internal Revenue Code of 1954. With the passage of the Tax Reform Act of 1986, another codification has resulted in the Internal Revenue Code of 1986. The federal income tax system is administered by the Internal Revenue Service, an agency of the Treasury department. Regulations interpreting the code are published from time to time by the IRS, but the ultimate interpretative authority lies with the federal court system, which adjudicates controversies between the IRS and taxpayers.

Of the many revenue acts passed in recent years, some of the most sweeping changes in the incidence of taxation on individuals and corporations were made in the Tax Reform Act of 1986. Some of the major purposes of this act were to shift more of the total tax burden to corporations, to exempt low-income taxpayers from income taxes, to simplify somewhat the computations of tax liability for individuals, to reduce the effectiveness of certain tax avoidance schemes (such as tax shelters), and, in general, to produce a more equitable incidence of taxation. As far as possible, we have incorporated the changes made by the 1986 Tax Reform Act in this chapter. Recognize, however, that the tax laws will continue to change in the future, as a result of changes in the political and philosophical views of Congress and the Executive Branch.

The 1986 Tax Reform Act dictates certain transitional changes for the year 1987 and more enduring changes for the year 1988 and beyond. For simplicity, in our illustrations, questions, exercises, and problems, we will use the provisions pertaining to the 1988 taxable year.

Because of the complexity of tax laws, many of the nation's taxpayers have turned to accountants, attorneys, and others for assistance in preparing their tax returns. These professional consultants may also help to arrange business and personal affairs to minimize tax liability. Few business decisions are made without first considering which possible alternatives judged consistent with the business objective have the most desirable tax effect. Indeed, when large amounts of money are involved, this factor is so important that many accountants and attorneys confine their practices to such special areas as estate planning, pension plans, wage and stock option plans, and reorganizations and mergers. Whether they call on professionals for assistance or not, taxpayers generally benefit from a basic understanding of the tax system structure and the options it provides.

PURPOSES OF THE TAX LAW

The primary purpose of the federal income tax laws is raising revenue to pay for the operations of the government. In addition to the primary revenue-producing purpose, many amendments to the Internal Revenue Code have been enacted for other purposes. Federal taxation has changed since 1913 in both purpose and magnitude. The income tax system has become an instrument of the government for economic and social policy.

Through its taxing powers, the government can attempt to distribute income more equitably, stimulate economic growth, combat inflation and unemployment, and finance projects it considers socially desirable. In addition, a number of changes in the tax laws are the result of political influences on Congress, which formulates tax laws. Thus multidimensional influences have contributed to the complexity of rapidly changing income tax laws. Because of these factors, the business manager must be keenly aware of the changing effect of income taxes on the business decision process.

CLASSIFICATION OF TAXPAYERS

The main entities that are recognized for purposes of federal income taxation are individuals, partnerships, corporations, and estates or trusts. Here we cover individuals, partnerships, and corporations, leaving estates and trusts to an advanced course.

Although they are business entities, sole proprietorships and partnerships are not taxable entities. The owners of such firms must include their shares of business income along with income from other sources in their respective individual tax returns. The allocable shares of their business income are taxed directly to them whether or not they have withdrawn such amounts. In conjunction with this requirement, each partnership must file an **information return** showing the results of the firm's operations and the respective shares of net income accorded to each partner.

As taxable entities, corporations are taxed directly on their earnings. Shareholders receiving distributions of earnings must include these amounts as dividend income on their individual returns. Although this practice has led to the allegation that corporate earnings are subject to "double taxation," it is generally conceded that the bulk of corporate taxes are passed on to the consumer in the long run.

Under Subchapter S of the Internal Revenue Code, certain corporations generally are not taxed but pass income and losses through to their owners like partnerships. Firms meeting the Subchapter S criteria are referred to as **S corporations.**

Because of the many technical differences in the tax computations for individuals and corporations, we consider them separately. Thus, we first discuss the

TAXATION OF INDIVIDUALS

Generally, individuals who are citizens of the United States are taxed on all income from whatever source, unless it is specifically excluded by law. Thus, the gross income reported in an individual's tax return consists of total income and gains *less exclusions.* Various deductions and exemptions are permitted to convert gross income to taxable income. Deductions and exemptions must be enumerated in the individual's return (Form 1040) or in supporting schedules.

Although the manner in which this information is detailed in the return varies, a basic, logical format guides the computation of taxable income and the related tax liability. This format, illustrated in Exhibit 28–1, describes the classifications used in the tax laws and is a useful frame of reference in compiling the information needed to prepare an individual's tax return.

THOSE TAXING DAYS OF FORM 1040's INFANCY

If you're about to go crazy doing your federal income tax, just be thankful you weren't around in 1914. That was the first year that Americans had to fill out a Form 1040 after the income tax, or 16th Amendment to the Constitution, was ratified in February 1913. Everything was in a mess.

For one thing, Congress didn't pass the implementing legislation until Oct. 3, 1913, which meant that the handful of officials and clerks authorized by the act had too much to do in too short a time. No tax forms were available until Jan. 8, even though the deadline for submission was March 1. Individuals who planned to be out of the country for the first three months of the year were in a pickle. In fact, a couple of taxpayers simply filled in a sample form printed in their daily newspaper and mailed it before they left. The Internal Revenue people said that was legal, although not preferable. The situation was even worse for Americans living abroad. In Paris, for example, there was almost a storming of consular offices by Americans in search of forms.

The biggest problem was that the Internal Revenue regulations didn't answer all the questions that taxpayers had. "Is the allowance once made a son by his father exempt," wrote one man to his hometown newspaper, "assuming that the father has already paid a tax on this allowance as part of his income?" "Should presents of money," he went on, "such as Christmas or birthday presents, be included in a statement of income, and, if so, can exemption be claimed on such amounts? . . ." One of the most confusing provisions of Form 1040 was the exemption allowed husband and wife filing a joint return: some taxpayers interpreted the authorizing language to permit a $4,000 exemption for both; others saw it as $7,000 for both; and still others were certain that it meant $3,000 to each.

Hardly a day went by that the Treasury Department did not issue a clarifying interpretation. Yes, indeed, women were required to pay taxes even though they didn't have the vote; by all means, returns could be submitted in person until 6 p.m. Saturday, Feb. 28, but mail returns would be timely if received by Tuesday, March 3. As for married couples who were temporarily separated, the married exemption could be claimed provided their separation "was not due to family differences." When the Manhattan Internal Revenue office was

Gross Income

As mentioned above, gross income is income from all sources, less allowable exclusions. Some of the most common types of gross income are wages, salaries, bonuses, fees, tips, interest, dividends, profits or shares of profits from businesses, pensions, annuities, rents, royalties, prizes, and taxable gains on sale of property or securities. The list also includes income from gambling and even illegal income, such as from theft or embezzlement. (Racketeers and other criminals have often been more easily apprehended through income tax investigations than through regular criminal investigations.)

Special rules and procedures apply to certain of these sources of gross income in determining the portion to be included. For example, gains from sale or exchange of capital assets are accorded special treatment. Because of the importance of this subject, we treat it separately later in this chapter.

---

besieged by taxpayers in mid-January over a rumor to the effect that certain exemptions and deductions would be lost if they weren't immediately claimed, its ruling did little to allay anxieties. By Feb. 21, the government threw up its hands, saying that no more clarifying statements would be issued before March 1.

Although only a tiny fraction of the population made enough money to pay the first federal tax, it was still bedlam as the deadline approached—so much so that Col. William H. Osborn, commissioner of Internal Revenue, extended the deadline to Monday, March 2, with local offices on that day staying open until midnight. Of course, his decision may well have been motivated by the fact that his boss, President Wilson, would not be ready to submit the three-page 1040 until that date.

Expectedly, there were numerous errors in the returns. But the Internal Revenue was scarcely precise about the extent of the problem: the range of errors, it announced, was from 30% to 80%. The most common problem involved the tax period covered by the return (March to December 1913), which meant that only five-sixths of income and deductions were to be reported.

A few months later at the National Tax Conference in Denver, experts raked the government's noble experiment with income taxes over the coals. Prof. Charles J. Bullock of Harvard said the tax law was patently discriminatory. "We now have a law," he argued, "that largely exempts holders of corporation securities from the ordinary tax and substantially exempts agricultural industry, while it taxes incomes derived from unincorporated manufacturing or commercial enterprise, and those received in the form of salaries and professional earnings." What was even worse, according to Bullock, were the excessive rates of taxation, rising to 6% on incomes of more than $500,000. "Now the limit of safety, for income taxes," said Bullock, "is probably 10%; and it certainly does not exceed 12. . . ."

A. C. Rearick of New York blamed the confusion of the first year on the taxing verbiage of the congressional act. "To begin with," he said, "the language in which the Act is couched is involved and its rhetoric bewildering. It contains sentences hundreds of words in length, in which clauses are added to clauses and provisos heaped upon provisos." To be sure, Rearick had a better idea. It was called "Simplification of the Federal Income Tax."

Thomas V. DiBacco, "Those Taxing Days of Form 1040's Infancy," *The Wall Street Journal*, March 28, 1985. Reprinted by permission of *The Wall Street Journal*,

EXHIBIT 28–1
Format for Determining Tax Liability of Individuals

Steps		**Explanation**
Determine:	Total Income	All income from whatever source
Less:	Exclusions	Items of income excluded by law (page 1080)
Equals:	Gross Income	Income subject to tax (before deductions and exemptions)
Less:	Deductions from Gross Income	Business-related expenses, losses, and specific deductions from gross income (page 1081)
Equals:	Adjusted Gross Income	Base for computation of limitations on some personal (itemized) deductions
Less:	Itemized Deductions or Standard Deduction	Itemized deductions permitted by law or standard deduction stipulated by law in lieu of itemized deductions (page 1082)
	Personal Exemptions	An amount stipulated by law for taxpayer, spouse, and each dependent. The amount depends on filing status, and it is phased out at certain income levels in 1988 (page 1084)
Equals:	Taxable Income	Amount used to compute the tax from the appropriate tax rate schedule.
Results in:	Income Tax	Taxable income multiplied by appropriate tax rate
Less:	Tax Credits	Specified credits against the tax (page 1088)
Equals:	Tax Liability	Amount of tax owed by the taxpayer

Gross Income

As shown in Exhibit 28–1, **gross income** is income from all sources, less allowable exclusions. Some of the most common types of income are wages, salaries, unemployment compensation (received after December 31, 1986), bonuses, fees, tips, interest, dividends, profits or shares of profits from business, pensions, annuities, rents, royalties, prizes, taxable gains on sales of property or securities, fellowships, and scholarships. The list also includes income from gambling, and even illegal income. (Racketeers and other criminals have often been more easily apprehended through income tax investigations than through regular criminal investigations.) Special rules and procedures apply to certain of these sources of gross income in determining the portion to be included.

Exclusions from Gross Income

Some items excluded by law from gross income include interest on certain state and municipal bonds; Social Security receipts;[1] gifts, bequests, and inheritances; worker's compensation for sickness or injury; certain disability benefits; life

[1]However, taxpayers with "modified" adjusted gross income in excess of certain specified base amounts may have as much as 50% of their Social Security benefits included in taxable income.

insurance proceeds received at the death of the insured; and the portion of scholarships or fellowships for degree candidates that is spent for tuition and course-required materials. (Amounts for room, board, or incidental expenses are not excludable.) The exclusions also exempt amounts of pensions and annuities that are returns of capital invested in them.

Deductions from Gross Income

Individual taxpayers are generally permitted two types of deductions—deductions from gross income to arrive at *adjusted gross income* and deductions from adjusted gross income. The first type is widely characterized as most business expenses and expenses incurred in the production of rents and royalties, whereas the second is generally described as allowable personal deductions.

The calculation of **adjusted gross income** is important in the taxation of individuals because it may affect the amount of certain personal deductions. Generally, we determine adjusted gross income to provide a more equitable base for certain other calculations than that provided by a gross income measure. Thus, a person who generates a large amount of gross income by incurring large amounts of business expenses or other related costs of producing such income is provided a base for determining personal deductions that is fairly comparable to the income of a wage earner or salaried taxpayer who does not have such business expenses.

Deductions permitted the individual taxpayer in arriving at adjusted gross income are as follows (remember these are subject to change):

(1) *Trade and business deductions*—Ordinary and necessary expenses attributable to a trade or business carried on by the taxpayer may be deducted, provided such activity does not consist of performance of services by an employee. (However, if an employee has reimbursed expenses in gross income, they can be deducted.) Only 80% of business meals and entertainment (100% of banquet expense) may be included with trade and business deductions, and certain kinds of entertainment expenses are not deductible.

(2) *Losses from sales or exchanges of property*—Losses from the sale or exchange of business or investment property are deductible in arriving at adjusted gross income. However, losses on the sale or exchange of "personal-use" property are not deductible.

(3) *Net operating loss deduction*—Generally, a business's operating loss in a particular year, which is of no tax benefit for that year, may be carried back to the three preceding years and forward to the next 15 years to reduce the tax liability for those years. After certain adjustments, the loss is carried back to the earliest preceding year first, then successively to each succeeding period, if unused. A taxpayer may forego the carryback and only carry the loss forward 15 years. The Tax Reform Act of 1986 imposed a number of technical limitations on certain carryovers; the act should be read to determine if any of these limitations apply.

(4) *Other deductions*—Certain other deductions, relating to rents, royalties, pensions, profit sharing, bond purchase plans of self-employed individuals, and individual retirement accounts (IRAs) are allowed. Prior to the Tax Reform

Act of 1986, the law allowed an individual to contribute up to $2,000 of compensation to an IRA, plus $250 if there was a nonworking spouse, and deduct the amount contributed. The 1986 Act continues to allow individuals not covered by employer-sponsored qualified pension plans to fully deduct IRA contributions. However, the deduction for IRA contributions is now either limited or completely denied to individuals covered by employer plans. For these individuals, the maximum deduction is phased out between $40,000 and $50,000 of adjusted gross income, if married, and between $25,000 and $35,000, if single.

Itemized Deductions and Standard Deduction

An individual taxpayer may deduct from adjusted gross income certain itemized personal and other expenses specified by the tax law, or may, in lieu of itemizing expenses, take advantage of a **standard deduction.** The amounts of the standard deduction for 1987 and 1988 are given below for single taxpayers and married taxpayers filing jointly.

	1987	**1988**
Single taxpayer	$2,540	$3,000
Married taxpayers filing jointly	3,760	5,000

Beginning in 1987 the above amounts are increased for married individuals if they are elderly or blind by $600 for each condition; for single taxpayers the corresponding amount is $750. In 1989 the standard deduction will be indexed to reflect changes in price levels.

Personal expenses that may be itemized and deducted from adjusted gross income are classified as follows:

(1) *Medical expenses*—With certain limitations, a taxpayer may deduct his or her medical and dental expenses, and those for dependents, not compensated for by insurance or otherwise. Beginning in 1987, the total medical and dental expenses are deductible to the extent that they exceed 7.5% of adjusted gross income. Prescription drugs and insulin are the only drugs which are considered medical expenses.

For example, a taxpayer with an adjusted gross income of $30,000 has the following medical expenses: health insurance premiums, $900; prescription drugs, $620; and other medical expenses not compensated for by insurance, $1,400. The deduction is calculated as follows:

Insurance premiums	$ 900
Prescription drugs	620
Other medical expenses	1,400
	$2,920
Less 7.5% of $30,000 adjusted gross income	2,250
Medical deduction	$ 670

(2) *Taxes*—State and local income taxes, real estate taxes, and personal property taxes are deductible. State and local sales taxes, which were deductible through 1986, are no longer deductible. Federal taxes do not qualify as itemized deductions, nor do flat fees paid for most types of licenses (auto, driver's, pet, and so on). Variable auto license fees required by some states may be deductible. State and local gasoline taxes are not deductible.

(3) *Interest*—Interest on indebtedness incurred to purchase a principal or second home is deductible. However, with certain exceptions, mortgage interest is not deductible on the excess of loans over the purchase price plus improvement costs. The 1986 Tax Reform Act phases out, over five years, the deduction for consumer interest, such as amounts paid for credit card balances and automobile installment loans. The amount of consumer interest to be disallowed is as follows: 1987—35%; 1988—60%; 1989—80%; 1990—90%; and 1991 and later years—100%. Interest on a federal tax deficiency is considered consumer interest.

(4) *Charitable contributions*—The amount of gifts made to religious, scientific, educational, and other charitable organizations officially recognized by the Internal Revenue Service can be deducted but may not exceed 50% of adjusted gross income. Certain other limitations may also apply, as with noncash contributions and gifts to foundations. Gifts to individuals or labor unions and donations to organizations whose major activity is to influence legislation are not deductible. Prior to January 1, 1987, taxpayers not itemizing personal deductions were permitted to deduct charitable contributions, subject to certain limitations. This deduction for non-itemizers has been eliminated.

(5) *Casualty Losses*—To the extent that they exceed $100 for each casualty loss plus 10% of adjusted gross income, certain casualty and theft losses are deductible unless compensated by insurance. Casualty losses must be sudden and unexpected: losses from fire, accident, windstorm, and so forth qualify as deductions. Certain "gradual" losses (such as termite damage and Dutch elm disease) usually do not qualify.

(6) *Miscellaneous deductions*—For the taxable years beginning January 1, 1987, certain itemized miscellaneous deductions are allowed to the extent that they aggregate more than two percent of the taxpayer's adjusted gross income. There are a number of expenses, however, to which the two percent floor does not apply. (For example, gambling losses can still be deducted to the extent of gambling winnings, which must be included in gross income. Also, employee moving expenses are not subject to the two percent floor.) Some of the more common miscellaneous deductions are:

Unreimbursed employee business expenses
Professional dues
Subscriptions to professional publications
Union dues
Cost of job-related work clothing, tools, and safety equipment
Safe-deposit box rental (to store securities)
Fees paid for income tax assistance
Employment agency fees
Certain educational expenses related to present position, incurred to improve or maintain skills, or to meet employer's requirements
Gambling losses (but only to the extent of gains, which are includible in gross income). Not subject to the two percent floor.
Employee moving expenses. Not subject to the two percent floor.

Personal Exemptions

In arriving at taxable income, the individual taxpayer may deduct an amount of each **personal exemption** he or she may legally claim. Married taxpayers filing jointly are allowed an exemption for each spouse and one for each dependent. Through 1986 additional exemptions were granted taxpayers who are 65 or over or blind, but these were repealed by the Tax Reform Act of 1986. Instead, as mentioned earlier, these individuals receive an additional standard deduction amount.

To qualify for a dependency exemption, a person must (1) be closely related to the taxpayer or live in the taxpayer's household for the entire year as a member of the family; (2) have received more than one-half of his or her support from the taxpayer; (3) if married, not be filing a joint return with a spouse; (4) have, with certain exceptions, income less than the exemption amount; and (5) be a U.S. citizen or a resident of the U.S., Canada, or Mexico.

The personal exemption amounts for 1987, 1988, and 1989 are $1,900, $1,950, and $2,000, respectively. In 1990 the amount will be indexed for changes in price levels.

Starting in 1988, the personal exemption is phased out for high income taxpayers (that is, for joint returns beginning at $149,250 of taxable income, and for single taxpayer returns at $89,560). As we explain later in the chapter, first the benefit of the low tax rate in the tax schedules is phased out for high income taxpayers, then the personal exemptions are phased out. For example, the 1988 tax rate schedule for joint returns is: 15% on taxable income up to $29,750, and 28% on taxable income over $29,750. The benefit of having the first $29,750 of taxable income taxed at 15% is phased out starting at $71,900 taxable income and is completely phased out at $149,250. Once taxable income goes beyond $149,250, the personal exemptions are phased out. Increased tax for the phase out is 5% of the *lesser* of (1) the taxable income in excess of the 15% phase out maximum or (2) the phase out *per* exemption times the number of exemptions.

For 1988, the phase out *per* exemption is completed at $10,920:

One exemption:	$1,950 × 28% = $ 546	tax saved per exemption
	$ 546 ÷ 5% = $10,920	amount of taxable income

For 1989, the phase out *per* exemption is completed at $11,200:

One exemption:	$2,000 × 28% = $ 560	tax saved per exemption
	$ 560 ÷ 5% = $11,200	amount of taxable income

Example: Assume that a married couple with four exemptions and taxable income of $170,000 files a joint tax return in 1988. The income tax is determined as follows if the couple itemizes deductions:

Taxable income	$170,000
The full 28% rate applies because the 15% rate is fully phased out	× 28%
	$ 47,600

Phase Out of Personal Exemptions:

Taxable income		$170,000		
Start of exemption phase out		149,250		
		$20,750 :		
			: Smaller	
Phase out amount,			: ×	
per exemption	$10,920		: 5% =	1,038
	× 4	43,680 :		
Federal Income Tax Liability				$ 48,638

CAPITAL GAINS AND LOSSES

Capital gains and losses are those gains and losses that result from the sale or exchange of capital assets. Although they are sometimes difficult to define, capital assets generally include any of the taxpayer's business and investment property except receivables, inventories, real and depreciable business property, certain governmental obligations, and rights to literary and other artistic works. Under certain conditions, however, business real estate and depreciable assets may be treated as capital assets when gains from sales of such assets exceed losses.

Classification by Holding Period

Gains or losses on capital assets sold or exchanged are classified as long term if the assets have been held longer than one year (six months for assets acquired after June 22, 1984, and before January 1, 1988). If the assets have been held for one year or less (six months for assets acquired after June 22, 1984, and before January 1, 1988), disposition results in short-term gains or losses. This basic classification has been retained by the Tax Reform Act of 1986. However, the Act has, at least for the near future, made the holding period irrelevant in the treatment of capital gains and losses for taxpayers.

Net Gains

Through December 31, 1986, 40% of net capital gain was included in adjusted gross income. Thus, with individual tax rates at a 50% maximum, such net capital gain was taxed at a maximum of 20%. In calculating the net capital gain, a taxpayer would take the following steps: (1) offset long-term gains and losses to obtain *net* long-term gain or loss; (2) offset short-term gains and losses to obtain *net* short-term gain or loss; and (3) determine the excess of net long-term gain over net short-term loss. This excess is termed net capital gain.

The Tax Reform Act of 1986 repealed the 60% deduction for years after December 31, 1986 and provided that net capital gains would be taxed at regular rates (but with a maximum rate of 28%) starting in 1987. Thus, both net long-term gains and net short-term gains are treated in the same fashion.

Net Losses

If the net amount from capital transactions is a loss, individuals and other noncorporate taxpayers may offset the loss against ordinary income up to $3,000 in any year. The amount of the losses that are not offset may be carried forward indefinitely to offset capital gains or $3,000 ordinary income in any year.

DETERMINING INDIVIDUAL TAX LIABILITY

Tax Tables and Rate Schedules

Applying the appropriate tax rate to taxable income results in the tax liability, unless there are tax credits, discussed later in this chapter. Individual taxpayers who do not itemize their personal deductions use simplified **tax tables** for various levels of taxable income and the number of claimed exemptions. If deductions are itemized, or if either the taxable income or number of exemptions claimed exceeds those shown in the tables, the taxpayer then uses **tax schedules.** Schedules are provided by the IRS for (1) single taxpayers, (2) married taxpayers filing a joint return (and surviving spouses), (3) married taxpayers filing separately, and (4) unmarried taxpayers who qualify as heads of households. Exhibit 28–2 illustrates the first two of these schedules for 1988, and also gives the 1987 transitional tax rates for single taxpayers and married taxpayers filing jointly (and surviving spouses). All of the illustrations, questions, exercises, and problems in this chapter, however, will utilize the 1988 tax rate schedules.

Head of Household

Unmarried taxpayers who qualify as **heads of households** determine their tax liability from tables or schedules (not shown) which generally determine a tax liability falling between that of single taxpayers and married taxpayers filing jointly. Generally, the qualification can be met by unmarried taxpayers who pay more than one-half the cost of maintaining a home in which a parent resides, if the parent qualifies as a dependent. A taxpayer who pays more than one-half of the cost of maintaining his or her own home where a dependent relative or where unmarried children, adopted stepchildren, or grandchildren reside may also qualify as a head of household.

As indicated in Exhibit 28–2, certain taxpayers with relatively high levels of taxable income gradually lose the benefit of the 15% tax rate for 1988 and subsequent taxable years. This benefit is gradually phased out at certain income levels. As shown, this phase out starts at taxable income of $43,150 for single taxpayers and at $71,900 taxable income for married taxpayers filing jointly. The following example shows how this phase out occurs.

Example: Assume that a single individual in 1988 has one exemption and that taxable income was $55,000. The income tax on this return is determined as follows:

Taxable income	$55,000
Top of 15% bracket	17,850
Taxable income for second bracket	$37,150
Second tax bracket rate	× 28%
Tax on taxable income, second bracket	$10,402

EXHIBIT 28–2
1988 Tax Rate Schedules and 1987 Transitional Rates

1988 Tax Rate Schedules

Single Individuals

If Taxable Income Is Over	But Not Over	Tax Is Amount +	% of	Excess Over
$ 0	$17,850	$ 0	15	$ 0
17,850	—	2,678	28	17,850

The five percent phase out of the benefit of the 15% rate begins at taxable income of $43,150 and is fully phased out at taxable income of $89,560

Married Individuals Filing Joint Returns and Surviving Spouses

If Taxable Income Is Over	But Not Over	Tax Is Amount +	% of	Excess Over
$ 0	$29,750	$ 0	15	$ 0
29,750	—	4,463	28	29,750

The five percent phase out of the benefit of the 15% rate begins at taxable income of $71,900 and is fully phased out at taxable income of $149,250

1987 Transitional Tax Rates

Single Individuals

If Taxable Income Is Over	But Not Over	Tax Is Amount +	% of	Excess Over
$ 0	$ 1,800	$ 0	11	$ 0
1,800	16,800	198	15	1,800
16,800	27,000	2,448	28	16,800
27,000	56,000	5,304	35	27,000
56,000	—	15,454	38.5	56,000

Married Individuals Filing Joint Returns and Surviving Spouses

If Taxable Income Is Over	But Not Over	Tax Is Amount +	% of	Excess Over
$ 0	$ 3,000	$ 0	11	$ 0
3,000	28,000	330	15	3,000
28,000	45,000	4,080	28	28,000
45,000	90,000	8,840	35	45,000
90,000	—	24,590	38.5	90,000

Tax on first $17,850 of taxable income before phase out of 15% rate				
$17,850 × 15% =				2,678
Total				$13,080
Phaseout of 15% rate				
Taxable income		$55,000		
Start of phase out		43,150		
		$11,850	: Smaller	
			: ×	593
End of phase out	$89,560		: 5%	
Start of phase out	43,150	46,410	:	
Federal Income Tax Liability				$13,673

It is probable that the Internal Revenue Service will make available tables or other special forms so that the foregoing calculations may not be necessary.

CREDITS AGAINST THE TAX

Once the income tax has been calculated, certain credits specified in the tax law may reduce the amount owed. Two of the most important of these credits for individual taxpayers are the earned income credit and the dependent care credit.

EARNED INCOME CREDIT The earned income credit provides tax relief to low-income working individuals with children. Beginning in 1987 the credit is 14% of the first $5,714 of earned income permitting a maximum credit of $800. However, this amount is gradually phased out at income levels between $9,000 and $17,000. The maximum amount of income against which the credit applies ($5,714) and the beginning phase out level ($9,000) will be indexed for inflation.

DEPENDENT CARE CREDIT A tax credit is available for taxpayers who maintain a household and incur expenses in caring for a dependent child under 15 years or an incapacitated dependent or spouse, if the expenses incurred permitted the taxpayer to be gainfully employed. The amount of the credit is 20% of the employment-related expenses up to a maximum of $2,400 for one qualifying individual and $4,000 for two or more qualifying individuals.

Two prominent credits that were repealed by the Tax Reform Act of 1986 are the investment tax credit and the political contributions credit. The investment credit was a credit against the tax liability for investments in qualified business property—a stipulated percent of the cost of property meeting certain requirements and used in a trade or business. This credit was repealed, effective for property placed in service after December 31, 1985. The political contributions credit, which permitted a taxpayer to apply 50% of political contributions as a credit against the tax up to a maximum of $50 ($100 in a joint return) was repealed for periods after December 31, 1986.

WITHHOLDING AND ESTIMATED TAX

Ordinarily, tax returns must be filed within $3\frac{1}{2}$ months of the close of the individual's taxable year. Because most taxpayers are on a calendar year basis, they must file their returns by April 15 following the end of the taxable year. During the taxable year, employers of wage earners and salaried employees have withheld tax payments based on the employees' estimated earnings and the number of withholding allowances claimed. Taxpayers who have income not subject to withholding (beyond a certain amount) must estimate income for the current year and file a Declaration of Estimated Tax. The estimated tax, less the amounts expected to be withheld, is paid in four installments. Therefore, when the tax return is filed, the amounts paid through the withholding or declaration process are credits that offset the total tax liability.

INDIVIDUAL TAX COMPUTATION

We present two examples of the common elements of individual tax computations in Exhibits 28–3 and 28–4. Exhibit 28–3 shows the relevant tax data for the joint return of Brian and Mary Fleming, and Exhibit 28–4 shows data for the single taxpayer return of James Malone. Although some of this information would be shown in separate schedules that reveal more detail, we have condensed the data into single schedules to conserve space. Both returns are for the 1988 calendar year.

Brian and Mary Fleming have one child who qualifies as a dependency exemption. Brian operates a tax service and has paid $600 estimated tax quarterly. Mary works part-time as a nurse and has tax withheld from her salary. During the year, Brian sold at a $1,200 gain securities purchased two years ago. The couple has been contributing $4,000 each year to an Individual Retirement Account (IRA). Neither Brian nor Mary are covered by an employer-sponsored retirement plan. The Fleming family's medical expenses were not significant during the year. Notice that the Flemings can deduct their $4,000 contribution to an Individual Retirement Account because they are not covered by an employer retirement plan and they fall below the income levels at which these contributions are not deductible. Brian and Mary are each allowed a $2,000 deductible contribution because both are working. Also notice that their miscellaneous deductions are slightly higher than 2% of adjusted gross income, so that they can deduct a small amount of this expense, and that some of their consumer interest (40%) is deductible.

James Malone, whose 1988 federal income tax data are given in Exhibit 28–4, is single and is covered by an employer-sponsored retirement program. Malone contributed $2,000 to an Individual Retirement Account as he has done for several years. This amount is not deductible in calculating adjusted gross income (both because he is in a retirement program and because of his income level). However, the interest on his IRA is deferred for tax purposes and is not included in adjusted gross income. Malone was transferred by his employer in 1988 and

EXHIBIT 28–3
Brian and Mary Fleming's
1988 Joint Federal Income Tax Return Information

Net income from Fleming Tax Service:			
Fees collected		$48,000	
Ordinary and necessary expenses		18,000	$30,000
Salary (Mary's)			5,600
Interest on savings accounts (excluding IRA interest)			1,400
Dividend income			650
Net capital gain on sale of securities			1,200
Contribution to Individual Retirement Account			(4,000)
Adjusted Gross Income			$34,850
Deductions from adjusted gross income:			
Taxes:			
Property tax on home	$2,200		
State income tax	1,530	$3,730	
Interest on home mortgage		1,620	
Interest on installment and credit card purchases	$ 250		
Less 60% not deductible	150	100	
Charitable contributions		950	
Professional dues, nurse's uniforms, and other miscellaneous deductions	$ 775		
Less 2% of $34,850 adjusted gross income not deductible	697	78	
Total itemized deductions			6,478
			$28,372
Less exemptions 3 × $1,950			5,850
Taxable income			$22,522
Tax: 15% of $22,522 (rounded)			$ 3,378
Less prepayments:			
Tax withheld from salary		$ 680	
Estimated taxes paid quarterly		2,400	
Total tax withheld or prepaid			3,080
Balance of tax due with return			$ 298

had unreimbursed moving expenses of $650 which are fully deductible as miscellaneous expenses. Malone's other miscellaneous expenses are not deductible because they fall below 2% of adjusted gross income. Notice that, because of the level of his taxable income, Malone had phased out part of the tax benefit of the 15% tax bracket. During the year Malone paid estimated tax of $1,300 each quarter (total, $5,200) and had $7,100 withheld from his salary.

EXHIBIT 28–4
James Malone's
1988 Federal Income Tax Return Information

Salary				$56,480
Interest (excluding interest on Individual Retirement Account)				2,410
Dividends				2,190
Net capital gain on sale of securities				1,600
Adjusted Gross Income				$62,680
Deductions from adjusted gross income:				
Taxes:				
Property taxes on home and vacation home		$ 2,250		
State income tax		3,070	$ 5,320	
Interest:				
On home mortgage		$ 2,560		
On vacation home mortgage		200	2,760	
Charitable contributions			1,550	
Miscellaneous expenses:				
Employee moving expense		$ 650		
Other (Safe deposit box rental, dues, subscriptions, etc.)	$ 960			
Less 2% of adjusted gross income	1,254	0	650	
Total itemized deductions				10,280
				$52,400
Less one exemption ($1,950)				1,950
Taxable income				$50,450
Tax:				
Taxable income			$50,450	
Top of 15% bracket			17,850	
Taxable income above first bracket			$32,600	
Second bracket rate			× 28%	
Tax on second bracket income			$ 9,128	
Tax on first $17,850 (× 15%)			2,678	
Total			$11,806	
Phase out of 15% rate:				
Taxable income		$50,450		
Start of phase out		43,150		
		$ 7,300		
End of phase out	$89,560			
Start of phase out	43,150	$46,410		
5% of the smaller amount ($7,300)			365	
Tax liability				$12,171
Less prepayments:				
Tax withheld from salary			$ 7,100	
Estimated taxes paid quarterly			5,200	12,300
Overpayment of tax				$ 129

PARTNERSHIPS

Partnerships are not recognized as separate taxable entities for income tax purposes. Although partnerships are separate business and legal entities, they are treated as conduits for tax purposes, as are S corporations. That is, the ordinary income of the partnership is allocated on a pro-rata basis to the partners, who report this amount on their individual income tax returns (or corporate return, if the partner is a corporation). Items of income other than ordinary income, as well as any deductions that are subject to limitations or special treatment on an individual tax return, are stated separately and flow through to the partners based on their pro-rata shares.

Since each partner must pay the tax on his or her pro-rata share of income, the partners must include the partnership items in adjusted gross income. The partnership pays no federal income tax, but must file an annual information return reflecting the partnership's ordinary income and each partner's individual items. In addition, each partner must include any prospective partnership income in his or her estimate of total personal taxes and pay the related tax quarterly.

TAXATION OF CORPORATIONS

The corporation is a taxable entity, separate from its shareholders, and must file an annual tax return whether or not it owes any tax. Certain corporations—such as banks, insurance companies, and cooperatives—are subject to special tax provisions. Tax regulations even for corporations that are not specially treated can be quite complex. Our discussion is limited to a few of the major distinguishing features of corporate taxation.

Corporate Tax Rates

The following schedule gives the rates applied to the taxable income of corporations through June 30, 1987:

If Taxable Income Is Over	But Not Over	Amount Plus	Tax Is % of	Excess Over
$ 0	$ 25,000	$ 0	15	$ 0
25,000	50,000	3,750	18	25,000
50,000	75,000	8,250	30	50,000
75,000	100,000	15,750	40	75,000
100,000	—	25,750	46	100,000

An additional 5 percent tax is imposed on corporate taxable income in excess of $1,000,000, to a maximum additional tax of $20,250. This provision eliminates the benefits of the graduated rate structure for corporations with taxable income between $1,000,000 and $1,405,000.

The Tax Reform Act of 1986 established the following three-tier tax rate structure, effective July 1, 1987:

If Taxable Income Is Over	But Not Over	Amount Plus	Tax Is % of	Excess Over
$ 0	$50,000	$ 0	15	$ 0
50,000	75,000	7,500	25	50,000
75,000	—	13,750	34	75,000

Corporations with taxable income in excess of $100,000 will pay an additional tax equal to the lesser of (a) 5 percent of the excess over $100,000 or (b) $11,750. This surtax eliminates the benefits of the graduated rates on the first $75,000 of taxable income for corporations with taxable income between $100,000 and $335,000. Corporations with taxable income in excess of $335,000 will thus pay tax at a flat 34% rate. Taxpayers with years that include July 1, 1987, will be subject to blended rates. In our illustrations, exercises, and problems, we will use the new rate schedule and assume taxable years after July 1, 1987.

Corporate taxpayers must pay estimated taxes in quarterly installments, similar to certain individuals. Their final returns, however, are due within $2\frac{1}{2}$ months of the close of their calendar or fiscal years.

Corporate Tax Base

The tax base for corporations is taxable income, that is (Gross Income − All Allowable Deductions). There is no *adjusted gross income* for corporations. Corporation deductions can be classified as ordinary or special. Ordinary deductions are the usual expenses (with certain exceptions) of doing business and producing revenue. The most prominent special deduction is a credit for 80% of dividends received from other domestic corporations (100% if such other corporations are affiliates).

The deduction for dividends received is intended to reduce the effect of "triple" taxation. Without this deduction, the distributing corporation, the receiving corporation, and individual shareholders of the receiving corporation (if they subsequently received the dividends) would all pay tax on the earnings.

The net operating loss deduction, which also applies to sole proprietorships, offsets business losses of a particular year against the income of other years in calculating the ultimate tax liability for those years. Briefly, an operating loss in a particular year can offset the income of three preceding years, beginning with the earliest. Unused losses can be carried forward successively to the next 15 years and used to compute taxable income. The corporation may forego the carryback and only carry the loss forward 15 years. The Tax Reform Act of 1986, through some complex rules, curtails the use of certain net operating loss carryovers when there is a substantial change in stock ownership of a loss corporation or failure to meet certain continuity of business enterprise tests. These rules are designed to forestall profitable firms from acquiring a loss corporation solely to offset their own taxable income with the loss corporation's loss carryover.

Prior to the Tax Reform Act of 1986, net capital gains of corporations were subject to a maximum alternative tax rate of 28%. This rate was utilized when the tax using that rate was lower than the corporation's regular tax. The new law raises the maximum rate to 34%, effective January 1, 1987, subject to certain transitional rules.

The excess of a corporation's capital losses over capital gains is not offset against ordinary income. It is carried back three years and forward five years and offset against capital gains in those years in the manner just described for a net operating loss.

Charitable contributions of corporations are limited to 10% of taxable income, computed before considering the contributions and the special deduction for dividends received. Any contribution in excess of the limitation can be carried forward five years.

Corporate Tax Illustration

The effect of the foregoing items on the corporate tax computation is illustrated in Exhibit 28–5. In this example, we use the following data from the firm's income statement for the year ended December 31, 1988:

Gross profit on sales	$500,000
Dividends from unaffiliated domestic corporations	40,000
Gain on sale of capital asset	10,000
	$550,000
Business expenses, including charitable contributions of $20,000	380,000
Reported income before taxes	$170,000

EXHIBIT 28–5
Corporate Tax Computation
For Calendar Year 1988

Gross profit		$500,000
Dividends from domestic corporations (unaffiliated)		40,000
Gain on sale of capital asset	$10,000	
Less: Net capital loss carryforward	3,000	7,000
		$547,000
Less: Business expenses, less charitable contributions of $20,000		360,000
		$187,000
Charitable contributions, limited to 10% of $187,000		18,700
		$168,300
Dividends received deduction, 80% of $40,000		32,000
Taxable income		$136,300
Tax:		
Regular tax $13,750 + 34% ($136,300 − $75,000)		$ 34,592
Surtax 5% of ($136,300 − $100,000)		1,815
Total tax liability		$ 36,407

The firm also had an unused net capital loss carryforward of $3,000 from preceding years.

BASIS OF DETERMINING TAXABLE INCOME

Many taxpayers' taxable income is determined on a **cash basis.** Taxable earnings from various sources are includible in gross income when received, and deductions are recognized when the allowable related expenditures are paid. Cash basis taxation has wide appeal because it is fairly simple and requires perhaps the least amount of record keeping.

Even a cash basis taxpayer should be aware of certain exceptions provided by the law. Although certain income may not be directly paid to the taxpayer, the law may consider the income a *constructive receipt* if the taxpayer effectively controls it. Thus, interest on savings accounts credited to the taxpayer constitutes taxable income whether or not it is withdrawn. Likewise, any checks received that represent taxable income are taxable whether or not they are cashed before the taxable year-end.

Generally, payments made during the taxable year are deductible in determining the year's taxable income if they meet the criteria for deductions. However, expenditures representing prepayments for a period must usually be allocated to the periods involved. For example, the cost of plant assets must be allocated to the periods of use through depreciation accounting. Likewise, prepayments of insurance, rent, and similar items must be allocated to the years involved rather than deducted totally in the year of payment. Under certain circumstances, real estate taxes paid a year in advance may be deducted; also, in certain cases, prepaid interest has been allowed as a deduction when the prepayment period was not extremely long.

Cash basis taxpayers, particularly those in certain types of service business, sometimes can arrange their pattern of billings and disbursements near year-end to minimize tax liability. For example, an expected tax rate reduction for next year would suggest that billings should be delayed to postpone revenue recognition, but that expenditures qualifying as deductions should be made this year.

For the most part, **accrual basis** accounting must be used by trading or manufacturing firms, because inventories are a factor in determining their income. Revenue must be recognized when sales are made, and inventories must be considered in determining the cost of goods sold.[2] Although some prepayments and accruals may be ignored, the method followed must be consistent and provide a reasonable income determination. Thus, the taxable income of an accrual basis taxpayer will likely not be substantially affected by altering the pattern of receipts or expenditures.

[2] The Tax Reform Act of 1986 imposed an exception to the accrual method of providing for uncollectible accounts expense. Accrual taxpayers, except for certain financial institutions, must now use the direct write-off method, and take into income the existing balance of the allowance for uncollectible accounts over a four-year period.

TAX AVOIDANCE AND BUSINESS DECISIONS

Taxpayers who deliberately misstate their taxable income, whether by omitting income or claiming fraudulently contrived deductions, are practicing **tax evasion.** This, of course, is illegal, and the penalties for such a practice can be severe. However, taxpayers are perfectly within their rights to practice **tax avoidance**—arranging their business affairs to minimize their tax liability. The effectiveness of some methods of tax avoidance, particularly certain tax shelters and deferred methods of income recognition, have been seriously curtailed by the Tax Reform Act of 1986. However, there are still some areas of taxation that permit an informed taxpayer to minimize taxes.

Timing of Transactions

In some instances, taxpayers can minimize taxes by timing certain transactions in a particular way. For example, timing is important when a taxpayer's principal residence is sold at a gain. Under a long-standing Internal Revenue Code provision, the gain is not taxable if an amount at least as great as the selling price[3] is invested in a new residence during the period beginning 24 months before the sale and ending 24 months after the sale. The basis of the new residence is reduced by the gain not recognized; thus, the tax is deferred. Another Code provision, however, grants a once-in-a-lifetime exclusion of $125,000[4] of gain on the sale of a residence for a taxpayer who is at least 55 years old and has used the property as his or her principal residence for three of the five preceding years. Because this exclusion can be used only once in a taxpayer's life, he or she must decide when to use it. If a taxpayer sells a residence at a gain of less than $125,000, he or she must speculate on the possibility of a larger gain being realized on a future residence.

For many years, some taxpayers were able to defer taxes by selling property on the installment plan (reporting income for tax purposes as cash is received in installments, rather than when the sale is made). Although the 1986 Tax Reform Act disallowed the benefits of the installment method for many installment transactions, there are exceptions for real property used in a trade or business or held for rental, where the selling price is less than $150,000, and for casual sales of personal property. Also, in some cases the installment method may be beneficial where the portion of installment sales disallowed is low (the amount disallowed is based on the ratio of outstanding debt to the basis of the assets).

Earlier we mentioned the possibility that cash basic taxpayers may affect their pattern of receipts and expenditures. For example, some taxpayers may be able to concentrate their personal deductions in a particular year. If their itemized deductions are below the standard deduction in the following year (because of the shifting process), they can take advantage of the standard deduction.

These are just a few examples in which the timing of transactions can alter the impact of income taxes. Because they often deal with the disposition of prop-

[3]Selling price here means *adjusted selling price* as defined by the Code (selling price less expenses of fix-up and sale).
[4]$75,000 for married taxpayers filing separately.

erty, it is wise to investigate thoroughly the tax consequences of a contemplated property disposition and the possible forms it may take.

Tax Shelters

The term **tax shelter** is a somewhat broad term that generally describes investments which, by their nature, create either tax-exempt income or a probable deductible tax loss, or which defer taxes to the future. We have already mentioned Individual Retirement Accounts, which permit qualified individual taxpayers to defer taxes on their contributions and interest income until the amounts are withdrawn (after age $59\frac{1}{2}$). It is also well known that certain affluent taxpayers often invest in state or municipal securities, the interest on which is exempt from federal income tax. Indeed, this was a very effective method of sheltering income in the past when top individual tax rates were first 70% and then 50%. It can still be a modest method of sheltering investment income. The attractiveness depends on the taxpayer's marginal (top) tax rate. Suppose a taxpayer in the 28% marginal rate bracket had $50,000 to invest in either 9% municipal bonds or 12% industrial bonds (interest taxable) of equal merit. The municipal bonds would provide $4,500 tax-free income, whereas the industrial bonds would provide only $4,320 after-tax income ($6,000 − $1,680). The differential ($180) is not great. However, many taxpayers with high income levels reach a 33% marginal tax rate (because of the phase out of lower tax bracket rates described earlier in this chapter). A taxpayer in this situation would have after-tax income of $4,020 ($6,000 − $1,980) with the industrial bond investment as compared with a $4,500 return on the municipal bond investment.

Prior to the Tax Reform Act of 1986, a number of tax shelters permitted the taxpayer a tax-free cash inflow on an investment that generated a loss for tax purposes. Sometimes, groups of taxpayers made a joint investment—typically limited partnerships—in such ventures as apartment and condominium properties and oil properties. Revenue from rents and royalties exceeded out-of-pocket (cash) operating costs, so a distributable amount of cash existed; however, because of large accelerated depreciation write-offs, a tax loss was allocable to the investors. Taxpayers could use these losses to offset income from wages, dividends, interest, capital gains, etc. The new law does not allow the offsetting of such losses against other types of income. The law provides that deductions from "passive" activities (exclusive of dividends, interest, etc.) can be offset only against other "passive" income, or be deductible in full when the taxpayer disposes of his entire interest in the activity. Under the law, an activity is passive if it involves the conduct of a trade or business and if the taxpayer does not "materially participate" in the activity. The taxpayer must be involved on a *regular, continuous,* and *substantial* basis. Thus, the new law eliminates the effectiveness of many tax shelters. However, working interest in oil and gas properties are exempted from the general rules and therefore allow some individuals a tax shelter.

Forms of Business Organization

Most large businesses operate as corporations to have wider access to capital, limit liability, or enjoy other advantages of incorporation explained in Chapter 15. For small businesses, with perhaps a single owner or a few owners, tax considerations may well influence the form of ownership.

Let us examine some general factors in determining the relative tax effects. First, all income of single proprietorships and partnerships is taxable to the owners as earned, whether or not it is distributed. Second, corporations must pay a tax on earnings, but may deduct reasonable salaries paid to owners. Furthermore, corporations may pay only a portion of the earnings as dividends (as long as accumulations are not deemed unreasonable). Other relevant factors are the amount of the business earnings and the amount of the owners' other separate income.

For example, consider the comparative tax effects of the corporate and sole proprietorship forms of organization for a married individual whose business is expected to generate $50,000 net income annually. Of this amount, $30,000 is withdrawn each year (as a salary, if the corporate form is used). The owner's other income, less all deductions and exemptions, is about $8,000 annually. A comparison of the total tax effect of the two forms of organization is shown in Exhibit 28–6.

The example assumes no distribution of dividends by the corporation. This policy might require justification if questioned by the IRS. Generally, the IRS may impose a penalty on unreasonable retention of earnings without a genuine business purpose. Of course, the owner will be taxed on the $17,000 earnings retained ($20,000 − $3,000 tax) if distributed in the future. However, it is almost always beneficial to defer taxes to the future.

Obviously, no general rule or formula can determine the most beneficial form of organization for tax purposes. The type of analysis we have illustrated may be modified in response to changes in the levels of business income, other income, reasonableness of salary levels, dividend policy, and other factors. The addition

EXHIBIT 28–6
Comparative Tax Results in Two Forms of Organization

		Corporation	Sole Proprietorship
Income from business		$50,000	$50,000
Less: Owner's salary		30,000	—
Taxable business income		$20,000	$50,000
Corporate tax on $20,000 at 15%		$ 3,000	
Salary	$30,000		
Other income less deductions and exemptions	8,000		8,000
	$38,000		$58,000
Tax on $38,000: $4,463 + (28% × $8,250)		6,773	
Tax on $58,000: $4,463 + (28% × $28,250)			$12,373
Total tax		$ 9,773	$12,373

of owners and increases in the size and scope of the business may be influential. Finally, depending on the nature of the ownership, small corporations can sometimes elect to be taxed as partnerships.

KEY POINTS TO REMEMBER

(1) The four main classes of *taxpayers* are individuals, partnerships, corporations, and estates or trusts.

(2) The tax format for individual taxpayers is:

	Total Income	
Less:	Exclusions	(Items of income excluded by law)
	Gross Income	(Income subject to tax, before deductions and exemptions)
Less:	Deductions from Gross Income	(Business expenses and expenses incurred in the production of income)
Equals:	Adjusted Gross Income	
Less:	Itemized Deductions or Standard Deduction	(Deductible personal expenses or, in lieu of these, a standard deduction stipulated by law)
	Personal Exemptions	(A stipulated amount for taxpayer, spouse, and each dependent)
Equals:	Taxable Income	

(3) The benefit of the 15% individual tax rate bracket is phased out between $43,150 and $89,560 taxable income for single taxpayers and between $71,900 and $149,250 for married taxpayers filing jointly in 1988. Also, personal exemptions are phased out beginning at taxable incomes of $89,560 and $149,250, respectively, for single taxpayers and married taxpayers filing jointly.

(4) Net gains on sales of capital assets are taxed at regular rates for individuals and corporations, with a maximum rate of 28% for individuals and 34% for corporations after 1986. If capital transactions result in a loss, individual taxpayers may carry them forward to offset capital gains and up to $3,000 ordinary income in any year. Loss carryforwards of corporations can be offset only against capital gains.

(5) The tax format for corporations is:

	Gross Income	(All business revenue, gains, dividends, etc.)
Less:	Regular Deductions	(Business expenses, with exceptions, such as a limitation on charitable contributions)
	Special Deductions	(80% of dividends received from domestic corporations: 100% of affiliate dividends and other stipulated deductions)
Equals	Taxable Income	

SELF TEST QUESTIONS

(Answers are at the end of this chapter.)
Note: The following questions are based on tax law effective in 1988.

1. Which of the following is not a deduction from gross income to determine adjusted gross income of a married couple filing a joint return?
   (a) Qualified contribution to Individual Retirement Account.
   (b) Trade and business deductions.
   (c) Deductions for state and local income taxes.
   (d) Net operating loss deduction.
2. A single taxpayer had $30,000 gross income and $24,000 adjusted gross income. Her medical expenses amounted to $2,400. The deduction for medical expenses is:
   (a) $600 (b) $150 (c) $2,400 (d) $-0-
3. Which of the following is not allowed as an itemized deduction?
   (a) Property tax on home.
   (b) State income taxes.
   (c) State sales taxes.
   (d) Mortgage interest on second home.
4. Which of the following is not phased out at certain income levels?
   (a) Benefit of 15% rate bracket for individuals.
   (b) Standard deduction.
   (c) Personal exemptions.
   (d) Deduction for IRA contribution made by person covered by employer sponsored retirement plan.
5. Which of the following statements relating to corporate taxation is not true?
   (a) Corporations are permitted a deduction for 80% of domestic corporation dividends received.
   (b) Corporate contributions are limited to 10% of adjusted gross income.
   (c) Corporate capital losses cannot be offset against ordinary income.
   (d) Corporations must file tax returns within $2\frac{1}{2}$ months after the close of their calendar or fiscal year.

QUESTIONS

Note: In all questions, exercises, and problems use applicable law and rates for 1988.

28–1 In addition to raising revenue, what other purposes are served by the federal income tax?

28–2 Name the major entities recognized for federal income tax purposes.

28–3 How is the net income from sole proprietorships and partnerships taxed? Must either of these business entities file a federal income tax return?

28–4 Describe the general format used to determine an individual's taxable income.

28–5 Which of the following items can be *excluded* from gross income?

(1) Interest on savings accounts.
(2) Interest on municipal bonds.
(3) Social Security payments (benefits).
(4) Gambling gains.
(5) Bonuses.
(6) Life insurance proceeds paid at death of insured.
(7) Royalties.
(8) Tuition portion of scholarship of a degree candidate, not requiring services.

28–6 Generally describe the deductions allowable in computing an individual's adjusted gross income, and name two examples.

28–7 Why is the concept of adjusted gross income important in the calculation of an individual's taxable income?

28–8 Rita Adams, who operates a real estate agency as a sole proprietorship, had the following expenditures for the current year:

(1) Interest on office building mortgage.
(2) Interest on home mortgage.
(3) Property taxes on home.
(4) Expenses of automobile used solely in business.
(5) License on business automobile.
(6) License on personal automobile.
(7) State gasoline tax, business automobile.
(8) State gasoline tax, personal automobile.
(9) Sales taxes on personal items.
(10) Church contributions by Adams family.
(11) Loss on sale of office building.
(12) Net capital loss of $800 on personal investments.
(13) Uninsured termite damage to home.

Indicate whether each of these items is (a) deductible in obtaining adjusted gross income, (b) deductible from adjusted gross income, or (c) nondeductible.

28–9 What is meant by a *personal exemption*? How much is each personal exemption?

28–10 What are the criteria for determining whether a person qualifies as a dependent of a taxpayer?

28–11 Lora Reed, who is single, and has no dependents, has adjusted gross income of $34,000 in 1988. Personal expenses qualifying as itemized deductions amount to $2,400. Calculate her tax, using the appropriate schedule in Exhibit 28–2 (page 1087).

28–12 James Lyon, a single taxpayer, has taxable income in 1988 of $62,400. Calculate Lyon's tax liability using the appropriate schedule in Exhibit 28–2 (page 1087). Note that part of the benefit of the 15% rate is phased out.

28–13 An individual has a net capital gain of $5,000 in 1988. What is the maximum rate at which this amount is taxed?

28–14 An individual has a net capital gain of $2,000 in 1988. He also has a capital loss carryforward from preceding years of $6,000. How much of the carryforward can be used in 1988?

28–15 What is meant by a tax credit? Give an example of a tax credit.

28–16 Describe the basic accounting methods taxpayers may use in computing their taxable income.

28–17 What limitations related to adjusted gross income are there for medical expense deductions? For miscellaneous expense deductions?

28–18 Explain the dividends received deduction. Why is it a special deduction for corporations?

28–19 What tax factors might be considered by the owner or owners of a small business in choosing the form of business organization?

28–20 What is the difference between *tax evasion* and *tax avoidance*?

EXERCISES

Adjusted gross income

28–21 Calculate the adjusted gross income for the joint return of Martin and Joan Bryant from the following data:

Share of partnership net income	$42,500
Interest on municipal bonds	2,000
Dividend income	500
Interest income	180
Lottery prize	1,000
Gift from relative	2,500
Net capital gain on sale of securities	4,000
Qualified contributions to Individual Retirement Account	2,250

Taxable income

28–22 According to the joint return of Ben and Julia Mason, they have two dependents and their adjusted gross income is $32,000. Using the relevant data from the items shown below, calculate their taxable income.

Real estate taxes	$1,600	State gasoline taxes	$ 120
Interest on home mortgage	3,200	Health insurance premiums	800
Charitable contributions	700	Other medical expenses	1,800
Gift to relative	200	Automobile licenses	24
State income taxes	800	Employee moving expense	350
State sales taxes	240	Union dues	160

Individual tax liability

28–23 Using the appropriate schedule in Exhibit 28–2 (page 1087), calculate the amount of tax due (or overpayment) for Susan Wright, a single taxpayer (with no dependents) who has given you the following information:

Gross income	$28,000
Deductions to determine adjusted gross income	1,650
Allowable itemized personal expenses	3,200
Tax withheld from salary	3,540
Payments of estimated tax	500

Individual tax; phase out of 15% rate

28–24 Using the appropriate schedule in Exhibit 28–2 (page 1087), calculate the amount of tax due (or overpayment) for Rod Travis, a single taxpayer with no dependents. The following information is given:

Gross income	$67,000
Deductions to determine adjusted gross income	3,600
Allowable itemized personal expenses	4,800
Tax withheld from salary	11,800
Payments of estimated tax	3,200

Individual tax; phase out of 15% rate and exemption

28–25 Using the appropriate schedule in Exhibit 28–2 (page 1087), calculate the amount of the tax liability for James Martin, a single taxpayer with no dependents, who has taxable income of $120,000. Note that phasing out of both the benefit of the 15% tax rate and the personal exemption must be calculated.

Corporate tax liability

28–26 The Reilly Corporation has pretax income of $84,000 during the year 1988. In arriving at this amount, the firm included $8,000 in dividends from nonaffiliated domestic corporations and deducted $15,000 of charitable contributions. Calculate the corporation's federal income tax for the year, using the rate schedule given on page 1093.

PROBLEMS

Joint tax return

28–27 Jason and Mary Lund, who have three school-age children, are filing a joint federal income tax return. Jason, whose annual salary is $38,000 as an accountant for the Ward Corporation, operates a tax service in his spare time. During the current year, he had $6,400 gross income and $1,800 business expenses in his tax service. He received $80 in dividends from his investments and $500 interest on municipal bonds. Mary had $300 in dividend income on her stocks. In addition, Jason sold for $65 per share 100 shares of stock purchased five years ago for $30 per share. Income taxes deducted from Jason's salary for the year amounted to $4,850, and his payments of estimated tax were $450. Personal expenses of the Lund family for the year included the following:

Mortgage payments (of which $1,800 was interest)	$3,200
Real estate taxes	1,600
State income taxes	1,200
State sales taxes	380
Charitable contributions	620
Medical and dental expenses	2,150
License fees for auto, pets, etc.	60
Interest on charge accounts	240

REQUIRED

Calculate the amount of tax due (or overpayment) shown on the Lunds' joint income tax return for the current year. Use the appropriate schedule in Exhibit 28–2 (page 1087). Round computations to the nearest dollar.

Types of deductions

28–28 The following items relate to the federal income taxes of individuals who itemize their deductions in computing their tax. Consider each item independently.

(1) Fee paid employment agency for obtaining employment.
(2) Payment of $100 repair bill for damage to pleasure automobile from skid on icy road (not compensated for by insurance).
(3) Labor union dues.

(4) Contribution to Empty Stocking Fund formed by neighbors for children of a needy family.
(5) State income tax paid.
(6) Federal cigarette tax.
(7) State gasoline tax for pleasure car.
(8) iState fishing license.
(9) Gambling losses in excess of gambling gains.
(10) Fee paid by unemployed student to take the CPA examination.
(11) Fee paid to Smith & Brown, CPAs, for preparation of personal tax return.
(12) Cost of cleaning uniform paid by train conductor.
(13) Fair market value of furniture given to the Salvation Army.
(14) Entertainment expenses of an outside salesperson, not reimbursed.
(15) Life insurance premiums paid.
(16) Trade and business expenses of sole proprietorship.
(17) Net capital loss of $1,200 on sale of securities.

REQUIRED

Indicate whether each of the above items is (a) nondeductible, (b) deductible in determining adjusted gross income, or (c) deductible from adjusted gross income. If answer (c) is given, indicate if there are limitations on the amount of the deduction.

Joint tax return

28–29 John and Ann Boyd are married and are both under 65 years of age. Their one child, Lisa, is 18 years old and a full-time student at a university; they contribute over one-half of her support, and Lisa earned $1,500 from part-time work during the year.

Ann Boyd operates a retail dress shop. Her records are kept on the accrual basis; however, all sales are for cash. The following information is available for the year's operations:

Cash receipts from sales	$52,800
Merchandise inventory, January 1	12,600
Merchandise purchases	36,400
Rent expense	4,200
Utilities and supplies expense	900
Salaries of part-time help	3,600
Insurance expense	600
Merchandise inventory, December 31	13,800

John Boyd's annual salary as a purchasing agent for a local firm was $31,500, and income tax withheld was $3,600. Quarterly payments of estimated tax totaled $1,200. The following information for the year was compiled from Boyd's checkbook and other sources:

Dividends received	$ 950
Interest income:	
Savings account	700
Municipal bonds	500
Real estate taxes on home	2,200
State sales taxes	340
Medical expenses	1,220
State income taxes paid	760
Contribution to United Fund	350

Accountant's services (preparing last year's income tax return)	150
Auto license on personal car	36
Safe deposit box rental (used for insurance policies)	30
Subscriptions to professional journals	80
Country club dues	350
Interest expense on home mortgage	1,500
Interest paid on personal loans	600

During the year, John sold the following corporate stock:

Security	Holding Period	Cost	Proceeds
Teledyne	four years	$2,150	$3,950
Coca Cola	two years	2,400	2,000
Litton	four months	800	1,800
Goodrich	three months	2,250	1,650

REQUIRED

Compute the amount of tax due (or any overpayment) reported in the Boyds' joint income tax return. Use the appropriate schedule in Exhibit 28–2 (page 1087). (Round computations to the nearest dollar.)

Corporate tax return

28–30 The following information for the current year is from the records of the Litho Corporation:

Sales	$400,000
Interest earned on corporate bonds	9,000
Dividends received on Alcoa stock (a domestic corporation)	18,000
Dividends received on Devlin, Ltd., stock (a Canadian company)	5,000
Cost of goods sold	260,000
Selling and administrative expenses (excluding charitable contributions)	58,500
Charitable contributions	5,000
Net capital gain on sale of property	10,000

In addition, the corporation had a net capital loss carryforward of $6,000 from prior years, and a $9,000 charitable contributions deduction carryforward.

REQUIRED

Prepare a schedule showing the computation of Litho Corporation's total income tax liability for the year, using the rate schedule given on page 1093.

Tax effects—form of business

28–31 George Wilson, who is married and has one dependent, is opening a business with an estimated annual income of $90,000 before tax and owner's salary. He must decide whether the business should be operated as a corporation (with all shares owned by his wife and himself) or as a sole proprietorship. Wilson has annual investment income of $18,000, which is fully taxable. He estimates that his annual total itemized deductions are approximately $14,000.

If the business is a corporation, Wilson expects an annual salary of $40,000 and one-half of the after-tax corporate income in dividends. If the business is a sole proprietorship, he would withdraw $50,000 from the business each year.

REQUIRED

Prepare an analysis showing the expected tax results (to the nearest dollar) of the two types of business organization. Use the corporate tax rate schedule on page 1093 and the appropriate schedule in Exhibit 28–2 (page 1087).

ALTERNATE PROBLEMS

Joint tax return

28–27A Lee and Amy Jensen, who have two young children, are filing a joint federal income tax return. Lee's annual salary as a credit manager for the West Company is $35,600, from which $2,700 was withheld for federal income tax. Amy works part-time as an interior decorator; her gross receipts for the year were $3,300 and her business expenses were $1,500. The couple paid $480 estimated tax during the year. The Jensens' dividend income during the year amounted to $460. Amy also received a small bequest of $1,500 from a relative who died during the year. During the year, Lee had a long-term capital gain of $1,800 and a short-term loss of $3,000 from the sale of securities.

The family's personal expenses for the year included the following:

Contributions to United Fund and church	$ 900
Flood damage to house (not insured)	4,600
State fishing and hunting licenses	48
Medical and dental expenses (not paid by insurance)	2,360
State sales taxes	350
Real estate taxes	1,700
Interest on home mortgage	3,600
State income taxes paid	1,860

REQUIRED

Calculate the amount of tax due (or overpayment) shown in the Jensens' joint income tax return for the current year. Use the appropriate schedule in Exhibit 28–2 (page 1087). Round computations to the nearest dollar.

Types of deductions

28–28A The following items relate to the federal income taxes of individuals who itemize their deductions in computing their tax. Consider each independently.

(1) Purchase of Christmas seals (stamps) from tuberculosis association.
(2) Sales taxes incurred in operating a business.
(3) Federal excise taxes on telephone calls.
(4) Dog license.
(5) Tuition for Dale Carnegie course taken by insurance salesperson to improve selling skills.
(6) Loss of elm trees due to Dutch elm disease.
(7) Cost of spike shoes bought by professional baseball player.
(8) Cost of piano and ballet lessons for daughter.
(9) Employee moving expenses.
(10) Fee paid to employment agency.
(11) Net capital loss of $800.
(12) Wagering losses of $500 (gains of $900 included in gross income).
(13) Advisor's fee for personal investment advice.
(14) Cost of professional magazine subscriptions paid by university professor.
(15) Transportation expenses driving to and from one's regular place of employment.

REQUIRED

Indicate whether each of the above items is (a) nondeductible, (b) deductible in determining adjusted gross income, or (c) deductible from adjusted gross income. If answer (c) is given, indicate if there are limitations on the amount of the deduction.

Joint tax return

28–29A Tom and Susan Carver are both under 65 years of age and have two dependent children. Tom furnished over one-half the support for his mother-in-law, who lives with them. Her total income consists of $600 interest on a savings account. Susan has no outside employment. Tom owns an office building from which rentals for the year totaled $21,000. During the year, he had the following items related to the building:

Heat	$1,900
Janitor service	1,800
Depreciation	2,450
Interest on mortgage	3,200
Real estate taxes	2,600
Insurance premiums on three-year policy (paid January 1)	900

Tom's annual salary as sales manager for an insurance firm was $36,000, from which $4,050 was withheld for federal income taxes during the year. He also paid $420 in estimated tax during the year. The following information for the year was compiled from his checkbook and other sources:

Dividends received	$1,480
Interest income:	
Savings account	720
Municipal bonds	950
Real estate taxes on home	1,900
State sales taxes	350
Medical expenses	3,800
State income taxes paid	2,600
Contributions to United Fund	500
Accountant's services (preparing last year's income tax return)	125
Athletic club dues	600
Auto license on personal car	36
Safe deposit box rental (used for jewelry)	25
Subscriptions to professional journals	120
Lottery winnings	400
Interest expense on mortgage	3,800

During the year, Tom sold the following corporate stock:

Security	Holding Period	Cost	Proceeds
LTV	two years	$2,800	$4,400
Kroger	three years	1,900	1,200
General Foods	three months	3,200	1,800
Eli Lilly	five months	3,100	4,300

REQUIRED

Compute the amount of tax due (or any overpayment) reported in the Carvers' joint income tax return. Use the appropriate schedule in Exhibit 28–2 (page 1087). (Round computations to the nearest dollar.)

Corporate tax return

28–30A The following information for the current year is from the records of the Riverhill Company:

Sales	$1,800,000
Cost of goods sold	1,050,000
Interest expense	12,000
Selling and administrative expenses (excluding contributions)	520,000
Dividends received from wholly owned affiliate	8,000
Dividends received from Consolidated Freight (a domestic corporation)	12,000
Net capital gain on sale of assets	20,000
Charitable contributions	32,000

In addition, the corporation had a net capital loss carryforward of $6,000.

REQUIRED

Prepare a schedule showing the computation of Riverhill Company's total income tax liability for the year using the rate schedule given on page 1093.

BUSINESS DECISION PROBLEM

At the beginning of the current year, Alice Burton received a $90,000 inheritance from a relative. She asks your advice about the income tax treatment of the inheritance and also about several possible investment opportunities. She may invest the $90,000 in a partnership owned by two acquaintances or purchase either 12% high-grade industrial bonds or 8% tax-exempt municipal bonds.

Alice's annual share of the partnership net income would be 25% of an expected $60,000 for the next several years. If she invests in the partnership, she expects to withdraw only one-half of her share of net income annually.

Alice is unmarried and under 65 years of age. Her annual salary is $45,000, and she estimates that her total itemized deductions will amount to $11,500 for the year.

REQUIRED

(a) How is the $90,000 inheritance handled for income tax purposes?

(b) Which of the three investment alternatives should Alice choose if she is basing her decision on receiving the largest after-tax income for the current year? (Ignore the problem of risk in determining the best alternative.) Show calculations of the after-tax income to support your choice.

ANSWERS TO SELF-TEST QUESTIONS

1. (c) 2. (a) 3. (c) 4. (b) 5. (b)

COMPREHENSIVE PROBLEM—PART 6

This comprehensive problem utilizes the actual financial section of the 1985 annual report of Whirlpool Corporation, a major U.S. corporation. This financial section, provided on pages 1110–1123, includes management's discussion and analysis of financial condition and results of operations, the consolidated financial statements, notes to the consolidated financial statements, report of the independent auditors, and the report by management on the financial statements. Although some items in the financial section relate to matters not covered in an introductory accounting course, they are included to illustrate the comprehensive nature of the financial data. Note the similarity of Whirlpool's statement of changes in financial position to the statement of cash flows prepared using the indirect method.

REQUIRED

(a) Using data available in the financial statements, estimate the amount of accumulated depreciation and amortization on property, plant, and equipment sold or retired during 1985.

(b) Note F to the consolidated financial statements analyzes the firm's long-term debt. What kind of leases does the firm have?

(c) Why do product warranty liabilities appear in both the Current Liabilities and the Other Liabilities sections of the balance sheet?

(d) Refer to Note P, Estimated Effects of Inflation, in which Whirlpool Corporation shows a $5,804,000 purchasing power loss from holding net monetary assets during 1985. Using the information on average consumer price indexes, compute the 1985 inflation rate. Using this inflation rate, estimate the average amount of net monetary assets the firm held in 1985.

(e) In computing cash provided by continuing operations (in statement of changes in financial position): (1) The equity in net earnings of affiliated companies totaling $21,323,000 is deducted from Whirlpool's earnings from continuing operations. Why? (2) Dividends of $3,997,000 received from affiliated foreign companies is added to Whirlpool's earnings from continuing operations. Why?

(f) Whirlpool Corporation has a complex capital structure because it has outstanding stock options (see Note H). Yet the firm, correctly, does not make a dual presentation of primary earnings per share and fully diluted earnings per share. Why do you suppose this is the case? (Hint: One of the basic principles discussed in Chapter 13 applies here.)

(g) Why does the firm have 1985 deferred taxes in both the Current Liabilities and the Other Liabilities sections of the balance sheet?

(h) The firm has an interest in Whirlpool Acceptance Corporation. Why wasn't this interest eliminated in preparing the consolidated balance sheet? If Note A had not stated the subsidiary is wholly owned, how else can you determine this fact? (See Note C. Also notice that the firm has included $25,000,000 long-term notes receivable in its investment in this company, as explained in Note C.)

(i) Note D to the consolidated financial statements states that Whirlpool Corporation has equity interests ranging from 20% to 40% in three Brazilian companies, and that in 1985, the firm increased its equity interest in Inglis, Limited, a Canadian company, to over 50%. The firm consolidated the financial statements of Inglis, Limited, with those of Whirlpool Corporation in 1985. The firm shows $25,308,000 minority interest in its 1985 consolidated balance sheet and $3,938,000 minority interest in net earnings of subsidiary in its 1985 consolidated statement of operations. Do these amounts relate to the investments in the Brazilian companies or to Inglis, Limited? Why?

(j) Refer to the list of ratios in the Chapter 20 Key Points to Remember. Using the formulas shown there, compute the following ratios and relationships for Whirlpool's 1985 and 1984 data, and comment on the results: rate of return on assets, rate of return on common stockholders' equity, rate of return on sales, dividend payout ratio, equity ratio, bond interest coverage, current ratio, quick ratio, inventory turnover, and average collection period. At December 31, 1983, Whirlpool's total assets, in thousands of dollars, were $1,466,503, and total stockholders' equity, also in thousands of dollars, was $977,648. In calculating inventory turnover, use ending inventory rather than average inventory.

Management's Discussion and Analysis of Financial Condition and Results of Operations

I. Liquidity

The Company has prepared its Consolidated Statement of Changes in Financial Position (set forth on page 11) on a cash flow basis for each of the three years ended December 31, 1985 to inform readers about the Company's liquidity. Liquidity, for this purpose, is defined as the ability of an enterprise to generate adequate amounts of cash to meet its needs, and for this purpose cash includes short-term investments.

The Consolidated Statement of Changes in Financial Position analyzes the Company's transactions from a cash flow perspective and classifies them into the following three fundamental business activities:

- Operating activities—transactions primarily related to the manufacture and sale of the Company's products and cash dividends paid.
- Investing activities—capital expenditures for the acquisition of properties and tooling used in the production of the Company's products, as well as investments in affiliated companies and subsidiaries.
- Financing activities—transactions associated with outside sources of financing such as short and long-term debt and equity capital.

Short-term liquidity

Indicators of the Company's short-term liquidity status are as follows:

- The Company has experienced a positive cash flow from its operating activities, after the payment of dividends to its stockholders, during each of the last three years as reflected in the Consolidated Statement of Changes in Financial Position.
- The Company's ability to meet its maturing short-term obligations, as measured by the so-called "quick" or "acid test" ratio (cash, short-term investments and receivables to current liabilities), has averaged 1.4 to 1 at the end of the last three years and was 1.3 to 1 at December 31, 1985.
- At December 31, 1985 the Company and its consolidated subsidiaries had line of credit agreements with banks permitting borrowings by the Company and its various subsidiaries up to $132,000,000. Borrowings against these lines amounted to $4,446,000 at December 31, 1985. Additional line of credit agreements are available, if desirable. These credit agreements are adequate to meet the Company's and its consolidated subsidiaries short-term borrowing needs.

In the Company's opinion, its current financial resources, anticipated cash flow from operations and short-term borrowing capabilities are adequate to meet 1986 operating requirements.

On January 10, 1985, the Company signed a definitive agreement to acquire a company comprising the KitchenAid Division of Hobart Corporation, a business unit of Dart and Kraft, Inc., for cash and at the same time agreed to sell two manufacturing operations of the Division to Emerson Electric Co., for cash. The transactions were delayed due to litigation, but on January 29, 1986, the U.S. Court of Appeals for the Sixth Circuit issued an opinion affirming the lower court's lifting of a preliminary injunction. The purchase was completed on January 31, 1986. The results of KitchenAid's operations for 1985 are not reflected in the Company's Consolidated Financial Statements. (See Note N of the Notes to Consolidated Financial Statements.) The funds needed for the purchase reduced the Company's cash and short-term investments, and may require the Company to obtain outside financing for working capital during peak operating months of the year. However, the Company will retain the ability to continue its current level of dividends.

Long-term liquidity

Indicators of the Company's long-term liquidity status are as follows:

- During 1985 and 1984, the Company's cash flow from its operating activities, after the payment of dividends to its stockholders, was not adequate to meet its investing and financing activities. Funds for these activities were obtained from the Company's cash and short-term investment portfolio. In 1983, cash flow from its operating activities, after stockholder dividend payments, was adequate to meet investing and financing activities as indicated in the Consolidated Statement of Changes in Financial Position.
- No additional long-term debt has been incurred by the Company during the last three years. However, as a result of Inglis Limited becoming a majority-owned subsidiary in January, 1985, and the acquisition of the assets and certain liabilities of Mastercraft Industries Corp. in December, 1985, the long-term debt of these companies are included in the Company's December 31, 1985 Consolidated Balance Sheet. During the last three years, the percentage of long-term debt to invested capital has declined from 5.5% at December 31, 1983 to 3.9% at December 31, 1985.

- The Company's ability to meet its interest commitments, as measured by the fixed-charge coverage ratio (earnings from operations before income taxes, minority interest and interest expense to interest expense), is 43.0 times, based on the Company's 1985 consolidated earnings from operations.
- At July 1, 1985 (the latest valuation date), in the aggregate, the net assets available for benefits under the Company's various pension plans exceeded the pension obligations of these plans. (See Note K of the Notes to Consolidated Financial Statements)

The Company is actively pursuing additional investment opportunities including acquisitions. If these investments are consumated, additional long-term capital funds, either by borrowing or equity financing, may be necessary. The capital structure of the Company at December 31, 1985 could support increased levels of long-term debt, if desirable.

II. Capital Expenditures

The Company's capital expenditures during the last three years were primarily for the acquisition of tooling and equipment used in the production of major home appliances. Capital expenditures during 1985 reflected continuing efforts by the Company relating to the development and more efficient production of new or improved versions of existing products.

The Company believes that its manufacturing facilities are generally adequate for current production and are capable of increased production.

Capital expenditures in the last three years have been financed primarily through internally generated funds. It is anticipated that presently planned expenditures will be similarly financed. However, outside financing might be necessary if the Company consumates additional investments as described in Section I—Long-term liquidity.

III. Results of Operations

Sales, in terms of dollars, increased 10.7% in 1985 compared to 1984 and increased 17.6% in 1984 from the 1983 levels. Dollar sales in both 1985 and 1984 reflected increased unit shipments and a somewhat greater proportion of sales of *Whirlpool* brand products. The Company's unit sales increased 9.9% in 1985 compared to 1984 and increased 17.1% in 1984 from the 1983 levels. The consolidation of Inglis Limited in 1985 resulted in an increase in unit shipments of 8.2% over 1984. Net sales of Inglis Limited included in the Company's 1985 operating results were $263,033,000.

The Company's equity in net earnings of affiliated companies decreased in 1985 compared to 1984 due to a decline in earnings reported by the Company's Brazilian affiliates and the consolidation of Inglis Limited. The equity in net earnings of affiliated companies increased in 1984 compared to 1983 reflecting record earnings by Whirlpool Acceptance Corporation and improved earnings of the Brazilian affiliates.

The Company's other income decreased in 1985 from 1984 and in 1984 from 1983 largely due to lower levels of interest income resulting primarily from decreased funds available for short-term investments.

Cost of products sold by the Company increased 11.0% in 1985 from 1984 reflecting the increase in unit shipments in 1985 referred to above and higher amounts of depreciation, tooling amortization and engineering costs associated with new product designs, offset in part by a favorable LIFO inventory calculation. Cost of products sold in 1984 increased 17.8% from 1983 reflecting the increase in unit shipments in 1984.

Selling and administrative expenses relative to dollar sales were at a higher rate in 1985 than in 1984 reflecting primarily an increased level of administrative expense. Such expenses relative to dollar sales were at a higher rate in 1984 than in 1983 reflecting primarily the increased expenditures associated with the advertising of *Whirlpool* brand products, offset in part by higher unit shipments in 1984.

Provision for plant closings in 1984 and 1983 reflected the decision to close the Company's manufacturing facilities in St. Paul, Minnesota and some of the manufacturing facilities in Evansville, Indiana and to relocate to other Company manufacturing operations the production of vacuum cleaners, room air conditioners, dehumidifiers, freezers and residential icemakers.

As a result of the foregoing principal factors, earnings from continuing operations for 1985 were $182,319,000 compared with $189,565,000 for 1984 or a decrease of 3.8%, while 1984 earnings from continuing operations increased 16.3% over 1983 earnings from continuing operations of $163,038,000.

IV. Effects of Inflation

For information regarding the effects of inflation on certain reported financial information of the Company, see Note P of the Notes to Consolidated Financial Statements.

8 Consolidated Balance Sheet

Assets

December 31 thousands of dollars	1985	1984
Current Assets		
Cash	$ 28,983	$ 22,535
Short-term investments—Note C	272,064	288,086
Receivables, less allowances for doubtful accounts (1985—$1,903,000; 1984—$1,480,000)	247,480	199,476
Inventories—Note B	386,183	359,726
Prepaid expenses	37,646	34,719
Deferred income taxes	–	7,890
Total Current Assets	972,356	912,432
Investments and Other Assets		
Whirlpool Acceptance Corporation—Note C	149,173	137,517
Affiliated foreign companies—Note D	98,420	118,060
Other assets	32,187	10,095
	279,780	265,672
Property, Plant and Equipment		
Land	13,306	9,834
Buildings	261,289	212,072
Machinery, equipment and tools	497,842	391,980
	772,437	613,886
Less allowances for depreciation and amortization	264,225	226,975
	508,212	386,911
	$1,760,348	$1,565,015

Liabilities and Stockholders' Equity

	1985	1984
Current Liabilities		
Notes payable	$ 4,446	$ –
Accounts payable	205,862	195,613
Payrolls and other compensation	91,620	84,899
Taxes and other accrued expenses	71,883	71,341
Income taxes	–	3,922
Product warranty	16,624	19,979
Current maturities of long-term debt	10,170	–
Deferred income taxes	20,779	–
Total Current Liabilities	421,384	375,754
Other Liabilities		
Long-term debt—Note F	49,315	52,751
Product warranty	15,015	14,432
Deferred income taxes	42,706	25,796
	107,036	92,979
Minority Interest in Consolidated Subsidiary	25,308	–
Stockholders' Equity		
Capital stock—Notes G and H	36,662	36,617
Additional paid-in capital	33,887	32,620
Retained earnings—Notes F and G	1,136,071	1,027,045
	1,206,620	1,096,282
	$1,760,348	$1,565,015

See notes to consolidated financial statements

Consolidated Statement of Stockholders' Equity

Year Ended December 31 thousands of dollars	1985	1984	1983
Common Stock			
Balance at beginning of year	$ 36,617	$ 36,535	$ 36,430
Par value of shares issued under stock option plans	45	82	105
Balance at end of year	36,662	36,617	36,535
Additional Paid-in Capital			
Balance at beginning of year	32,620	30,450	27,489
Stock option transactions	1,267	2,170	2,961
Balance at end of year	33,887	32,620	30,450
Retained Earnings			
Balance at beginning of year	1,027,045	910,663	811,155
Net earnings	182,319	189,565	167,038
	1,209,364	1,100,228	978,193
Cash dividends paid	(73,293)	(73,183)	(67,530)
Balance at end of year	1,136,071	1,027,045	910,663
Stockholders' equity at end of year	$1,206,620	$1,096,282	$ 977,648
Cash dividends per share of common stock	$ 2.00	$ 2.00	$ 1.85

Consolidated Statement of Operations

Year Ended December 31 thousands of dollars	1985	1984	1983
Income			
Net sales—Note J	$3,474,456	$3,137,482	$2,667,682
Equity in net earnings of affiliated companies—Notes C and D	21,323	27,411	17,495
Other	32,260	42,919	49,113
	3,528,039	3,207,812	2,734,290
Deductions from Income			
Cost of products sold	2,748,421	2,476,235	2,102,740
Selling and administrative expenses	450,196	388,591	309,384
Interest on long-term debt	5,194	4,892	5,287
Other interest expense	2,471	1,665	885
Provision for plant closings	—	4,564	23,156
Minority interest in net earnings of subsidiary	3,938	—	—
Income taxes—Note I	135,500	142,300	129,800
	3,345,720	3,018,247	2,571,252
Earnings from continuing operations	182,319	189,565	163,038
Gain from discontinued operations	—	—	4,000
Net earnings	$ 182,319	$ 189,565	$ 167,038
Per share of common stock:			
Earnings from continuing operations	$ 4.98	$ 5.18	$ 4.47
Gain from discontinued operations	—	—	0.11
Net earnings	$ 4.98	$ 5.18	$ 4.58
Average number of common shares outstanding	36,642,590	36,585,557	36,495,995

See notes to consolidated financial statements

Consolidated Statement of Changes in Financial Position

Year Ended December 31 thousands of dollars	1985	1984	1983
Operating Activities			
Earnings from continuing operations	$ 182,319	$ 189,565	$ 163,038
Non cash charges (credits):			
Depreciation of plant and equipment	41,057	33,444	33,064
Amortization of tooling	45,925	36,726	28,218
Increase in noncurrent deferred income taxes	14,505	4,091	3,376
Equity in net earnings of affiliated companies:			
Whirlpool Acceptance Corporation	(11,657)	(11,568)	(8,014)
Affiliated foreign companies	(9,666)	(15,843)	(9,481)
Minority interest in net earnings of subsidiary	3,938	—	—
Decrease in long-term product warranty	(887)	(316)	(1,655)
Dividends received from affiliated foreign companies	3,997	4,255	4,352
Changes in components of operating working capital other than cash and short-term investments	4,611	(135,172)	33,299
Cash provided by continuing operations	274,142	105,182	246,197
Cash dividends paid	(73,293)	(73,183)	(67,530)
Cash provided by continuing operations retained in the business	200,849	31,999	178,667
Gain from discontinued operations net of non cash items	—	—	4,000
Cash provided by operations retained in the business	200,849	31,999	182,667
Investing Activities			
Additions to properties	(131,084)	(86,947)	(38,182)
Additions to tooling	(55,686)	(50,147)	(45,310)
Disposals of properties	10,284	3,094	3,031
Increase in investment in and loans to affiliated foreign companies and unconsolidated subsidiary	(400)	(2,220)	(51,745)
Other	(24,647)	(1,923)	(465)
Cash used for investing activities	(201,533)	(138,143)	(132,671)
Financing Activities			
Repayment of long-term debt	(10,203)	(3,897)	(4,200)
Stock option transactions	1,313	2,252	3,066
Cash used for financing activities	(8,890)	(1,645)	(1,134)
Increase (decrease) in cash and short-term investments	(9,574)	(107,789)	48,862
Cash and short-term investments at beginning of year	310,621	418,410	369,548
Cash and short-term investments at end of year	$ 301,047	$ 310,621	$ 418,410
Changes in Components of Operating Working Capital Other Than Cash and Short-term Investments			
Receivables	$ (29,792)	$ (16,699)	$ (16,492)
Inventories	26,308	(95,246)	(36,210)
Prepaid expenses	(1,911)	(25,238)	(1,815)
Deferred income taxes	30,308	22,011	(16,950)
Accounts payable	(6,414)	10,377	76,261
Accrued liabilities	(19,908)	(8,099)	53,229
Income taxes	(3,922)	(22,278)	(24,724)
Current maturities of long-term debt	9,942	—	—
	$ 4,611	$(135,172)	$ 33,299

See notes to consolidated financial statements

 Notes to Consolidated Financial Statements

Note A
Summary of Principal Accounting Policies

Principles of Consolidation: The consolidated financial statements include all majority-owned subsidiaries except Whirlpool Acceptance Corporation (a wholly-owned finance company) and its subsidiaries. Investments in Whirlpool Acceptance Corporation and in affiliated foreign companies are accounted for by the equity method.

Inventories: Substantially all inventories are stated at the lower of last-in, first-out (LIFO) cost or market. The remaining inventories are stated at the lower of first-in, first out (FIFO) cost or market.

Property, Plant and Equipment: Properties are stated at cost. Depreciation of plant and equipment and amortization of tooling are computed by the straight-line method based upon the estimated average useful lives of the various classes of assets.

Pensions: The cost of pension plans represents normal cost and amortization of prior-service cost over periods ranging to forty years. The Companies fund such costs as accrued.

Investment Tax Credits: Investment tax credits are accounted for by the flow-through method as a direct reduction of the current federal income tax provision.

Note B
Inventories

Inventories at December 31, 1985 and 1984 consisted of:

thousands of dollars	1985	1984
Finished products	$265,155	$234,260
Work in process	29,313	31,515
Raw materials	91,715	93,951
Total	$386,183	$359,726

Replacement cost of the LIFO inventories exceeded the carrying amount by approximately $184,000,000 at December 31, 1985 and $200,400,000 at December 31, 1984. Such inventories represented approximately 83% and 97% of total inventories at December 31, 1985 and 1984, respectively.

Note C
Whirlpool Acceptance Corporation

Whirlpool Acceptance Corporation provides financing services principally for dealers and distributors marketing products of the Companies, RCA Corporation and The Toro Company and also finances retail sales by dealers of such products and the products of other manufacturers. In addition, Whirlpool Acceptance Corporation provides equipment lease financing services.

The Company's investment in Whirlpool Acceptance Corporation at December 31, 1985 and 1984 includes $25,000,000 of long-term notes receivable. The Company's short-term investments at December 31, 1985 and 1984 include $50,000,000 of commercial paper (payable on demand) of Whirlpool Acceptance Corporation.

Condensed financial statements of Whirlpool Acceptance Corporation and its consolidated subsidiaries follow:

Balance Sheet

December 31 thousands of dollars	1985	1984
Assets		
Cash and marketable securities	$ 11,952	$ 20,716
Receivables—net	568,814	423,491
Other assets	21,477	23,535
	$602,243	$467,742
Liabilities and Stockholder's Equity		
Notes payable and other liabilities	$369,570	$291,225
Long-term debt	108,500	64,000
Stockholder's equity	124,173	112,517
	$602,243	$467,742

Statement of Operations

Year Ended December 31 thousands of dollars	1985	1984	1983
Earned income	$ 88,105	$ 85,082	$ 60,969
Operating and other expenses	35,772	32,754	24,607
Interest expense	32,406	31,723	21,894
Federal income taxes	8,270	9,037	6,454
Net Earnings	$ 11,657	$ 11,568	$ 8,014

Note D
Affiliated Foreign Companies

The Company has equity interests, ranging from 20% to 40%, in three Brazilian companies (Brastemp S.A., Embraco S.A. and Consul S.A.) engaged in manufacturing major home appliances and related equipment.

In January, 1985, the Company increased its equity interest in Inglis Limited, a leading manufacturer of major home appliances located in Canada, to over 50%. As a result, the financial statements of Inglis Limited were consolidated with those of the Company for 1985. If Inglis Limited had been consolidated for 1984, total assets would have been $1,668,570,000 and net sales would have been $3,362,447,000. Since the investment in Inglis Limited was accounted for by the equity method, the impact on consolidated earnings for 1984 would not have been significant.

The Company's investment in affiliated foreign companies includes notes receivable of $13,000,000 at December 31, 1985 and $14,600,000 at December 31, 1984.

Certain aggregate financial information relative to the affiliated foreign companies, including Inglis Limited in 1984 and 1983, is summarized as follows:

thousands of dollars	1985	1984	1983
Current assets	$251,963	$335,513	$290,565
Other assets	193,106	181,755	198,303
	$445,069	$517,268	$488,868
Current liabilities	$153,765	$192,732	$176,659
Other liabilities	26,793	27,789	42,474
Stockholders' equity	264,511	296,747	269,735
	$445,069	$517,268	$488,868
Net sales	$408,091	$623,333	$828,710
Cost of products sold	$339,113	$482,624	$594,902
Net income	$ 33,035	$ 47,328	$ 29,138

The Company's foreign investments are in Brazilian companies which operate in a highly inflationary economy. Foreign currency exchange losses, resulting from translation of the financial statements of the affiliated foreign companies, included in results of operations for 1985, 1984 and 1983 amounted to approximately $20,200,000, $29,900,000 and $34,100,000, respectively.

Note E
Lines of Credit

At December 31, 1985 the Companies have several line of credit agreements which expire on various dates in 1986 permitting borrowings up to $132,000,000 at the prime interest rate. Borrowings against these lines at December 31, 1985, amounted to $4,446,000. The Companies do not have formal compensating balance arrangements with their credit line banks. Generally, the banks are compensated for their credit lines by Company operating balances to the extent available, plus a fee which is paid by the Companies to the banks. Balances maintained pursuant to this arrangement during 1985 included amounts used, on occasion, to support lines of credit also available to Whirlpool Acceptance Corporation.

Note F
Long-Term Debt

Long-term debt at December 31, 1985 and 1984 consisted of:

thousands of dollars	Interest Rate	1985	1984
Sinking fund debentures:			
Due November 1, 1986	5¾%	$ 8,448	$ 8,448
Due February 1, 1988	11	3,720	—
Due September 15, 2000	9⅝	41,903	41,903
Lease obligations and other debt, expiring at various times from 1986 through 1998	5½ to 15	5,414	2,400
		59,485	52,751
Less current maturities		10,170	—
Total		$49,315	$52,751

At December 31, 1985, the Company held debentures in the face amount of $8,399,000 which have been deducted from the sinking fund requirements due in 1986 through 1988.

The annual maturities and sinking fund requirements are $10,170,000 in 1986, $1,722,000 in 1987, $3,746,000 in 1988, $3,856,000 in 1989 and $3,647,000 in 1990.

The indenture for the 5¾% debentures contains restrictions relating to payment of cash dividends and purchase of the Company's stock. At December 31, 1985, approximately $796,300,000 of retained earnings was free of such restrictions.

Note G
Stockholders' Equity

The Company has 125,000,000 authorized shares of common stock, par value $1 per share, of which 36,662,484 and 36,616,392 shares were outstanding at December 31, 1985 and 1984, respectively.

The Company has 10,000,000 authorized shares of preferred stock, par value $1 per share, none of which were issued at December 31, 1985 or 1984.

Consolidated retained earnings at December 31, 1985 included $61,290,000 of equity in undistributed net earnings of the affiliated foreign companies.

Note H
Stock Options

The Company's stock option plan permits the grant of stock options to key salaried employees of the Company and its subsidiaries. The plan authorizes the grant of 1,750,000 shares as either incentive or non-statutory stock options and, further, authorizes the grant of stock appreciation rights with respect to options granted or outstanding. The stock appreciation rights allow option holders, in lieu of exercising options, to receive payments in cash or shares of common stock or a combination thereof in an amount equal to the excess of the market price of the common stock over the option price.

Options outstanding at December 31, 1985 have expiration dates ranging from June 22, 1989 to December 10, 1995. Stock appreciation rights are outstanding with respect to 295,714 shares under option at December 31, 1985.

A summary of certain information regarding employee stock options follows:

	1985		1984	
	Number of Shares	Average Option Price	Number of Shares	Average Option Price
Outstanding at January 1	791,680	$40.48	765,255	$37.34
Granted	168,650	47.73	149,200	42.75
Exercised	(42,055)	23.38	(85,145)	18.61
Surrendered under stock appreciation rights	(33,220)	22.49	(14,130)	21.65
Cancelled or expired	(17,140)	45.89	(23,500)	43.30
Outstanding at December 31	867,915	$43.29	791,680	$40.48
Exercisable at December 31	587,561	$41.83	490,480	$37.69
Available for future grant at December 31	504,740		156,450	

Note I
Income Taxes

The provisions for income taxes applicable to continuing operations follow:

thousands of dollars	1985	1984	1983
Current:			
Federal	$ 77,298	$101,112	$123,505
State and local	12,040	15,086	19,869
	89,338	116,198	143,374
Deferred (credit):			
Federal	39,362	22,310	(11,591)
State and local	6,800	3,792	(1,983)
	46,162	26,102	(13,574)
Total Income Tax Expense	$135,500	$142,300	$129,800

Deferred income taxes result from the tax effect of transactions which are recognized in different periods for financial and tax reporting purposes including installment sales ($16,735,000 in 1985), pension costs and other employee benefits ($9,645,000 in 1985), depreciation expense ($13,925,000 in 1985), insurance expense and other items.

A reconciliation of the total income tax expense to the amount computed by applying the statutory federal income tax rate to earnings from continuing operations before income taxes and minority interest in net earnings of subsidiary follows:

thousands of dollars	1985	1984	1983
46% of earnings, as defined above	$148,008	$152,658	$134,705
State and local taxes, net of federal tax benefit	10,174	10,194	9,658
Equity in earnings of affiliated companies	(9,809)	(12,609)	(8,047)
Investment tax credit	(10,971)	(5,111)	(5,232)
Other items	(1,902)	(2,832)	(1,284)
Total Income Tax Expense	$135,500	$142,300	$129,800

Note J
Business Segment and Sales Information

The Company operates predominantly in the business segment classified as Major Home Appliances.

Percentages of consolidated net sales from continuing operations to Sears, Roebuck and Co. were 40% in 1985, 41% in 1984 and 43% in 1983.

Note K
Pension Plans

The Companies have various pension plans covering substantially all employees. The approximate cost of the plans applicable to continuing operations was $36,800,000 in 1985, $35,500,000 in 1984 and $34,900,000 in 1983.

Accumulated plan benefit information and plan net assets, as of the latest valuation date, were as follows:

July 1 thousands of dollars	1985	1984
Actuarial present value of accumulated plan benefits:		
Vested	$440,000	$399,100
Non-vested	51,500	46,700
Total	$491,500	$445,800
Net assets available for benefits	$563,900	$449,100

The assumed rate of return used in determining the actuarial present value of accumulated plan benefits was 7.5% for 1985 and 1984.

Note L
Supplementary Expense Information

Certain classes of expenses incurred and charged directly to continuing operations were as follows:

thousands of dollars	1985	1984	1983
Maintenance and repairs	$ 97,244	$ 91,857	$ 76,142
Research and development costs	66,430	48,740	41,000

Note M
Contingencies

The Company is involved in various legal actions arising in the normal course of business. Management, after taking into consideration legal counsel's evaluation of such actions, is of the opinion that the outcome thereof will not have a material adverse effect on the financial statements of the Company.

Note N
Subsequent Business Activities

On January 10, 1985, the Company signed a definitive agreement to acquire a company comprising the KitchenAid Division of Hobart Corporation, a business unit of Dart & Kraft, Inc., for cash and at the same time agreed to sell two manufacturing operations of the Division to Emerson Electric Co., for cash. The transactions were delayed due to litigation, but on January 29, 1986, the U.S. Court of Appeals for the Sixth Circuit issued an opinion affirming the lower court's lifting of a preliminary injunction. The purchase from Dart & Kraft, Inc. was completed on January 31, 1986 at a purchase price of approximately $150,000,000, reduced by the proceeds to the Company from the concurrent sale of the KitchenAid dishwasher and compactor manufacturing facilities to Emerson Electric Co., subject to adjustment pending finalization of certain financial data and other matters. Had the transaction occurred on January 1, 1985, the Company's consolidated net sales for 1985 would have been approximately $3,660,000,000; net earnings and earnings per common share would not have been materially affected.

Note O
Quarterly Results of Operations
(Unaudited)

The following is a tabulation of the unaudited quarterly results of operations for the years ended December 31, 1985 and 1984:

Three Months Ended thousands of dollars	March 31	June 30	Sept. 30	Dec. 31
1985:				
Net sales	$790,174	$967,391	$890,477	$826,414
Cost of products sold	$628,095	$769,891	$709,893	$640,542
Net earnings	$ 38,922	$ 48,902	$ 44,734	$ 49,761
Per share of common stock:				
Net earnings	$ 1.06	$ 1.34	$ 1.22	$ 1.36
Dividends paid	$ 0.50	$ 0.50	$ 0.50	$ 0.50
Stock price:				
High	$ 49½	$ 48¾	$ 50¾	$ 50½
Low	44¼	40½	44	42½
1984:				
Net sales	$764,526	$868,175	$811,384	$693,397
Cost of products sold	$593,830	$686,594	$634,596	$561,215
Net earnings	$ 52,885	$ 46,650	$ 53,457	$ 36,573
Per share of common stock:				
Net earnings	$ 1.45	$ 1.27	$ 1.46	$ 1.00
Dividends paid	$ 0.50	$ 0.50	$ 0.50	$ 0.50
Stock price:				
High	$ 50	$ 42¼	$ 45⅞	$ 46⅞
Low	38¾	36½	38½	38⅜

Note P
Estimated Effects of Inflation
(Unaudited)

A summary of certain financial data for the year ended December 31, 1985 adjusted for changes in specific prices and stated in thousands of dollars follows:

Earnings from continuing operations as reported	$ 182,319
Adjustments for changing prices:	
Cost of products sold	(23,545)
Depreciation and amortization expense	(16,335)
Earnings from continuing operations as adjusted for changing prices	$ 142,439
Purchasing power loss from holding net monetary assets during the year	$ 5,804
Increase in general price level of inventories and property, plant and equipment held during the year	$ 41,965
Less effect of increase in specific prices	15,037
Excess of increase in general price level over increase in the specific prices	$ 26,928

At December 31, 1985, the current cost of inventory was $570,241,000 and the current cost of net property, plant and equipment was $611,316,000.

A comparison of selected historical financial data and other information adjusted for changing prices and stated in thousands, except for per share amounts, of average 1985 dollars follows:

	1985	1984	1983	1982	1981
Historical Information Adjusted for Changes in Specific Prices					
Earnings from continuing operations	$ 142,439	$ 176,846	$ 152,715	$ 112,535	$ 115,179
Earnings from continuing operations per share of common stock	3.89	4.83	4.18	3.10	3.18
Net assets at year-end	1,472,064	1,434,229	1,357,799	1,291,744	1,247,714
Excess of increase in the general price level over increase in specific prices	26,928	17,842	8,244	(512)	35,084
Other Information					
Net sales	$3,474,456	$3,249,427	$2,880,453	$2,531,354	$2,882,638
Loss from decline in purchasing power of net monetary assets held	5,804	8,586	9,230	7,612	12,805
Cash dividends per share of common stock	2.00	2.07	2.00	1.84	1.89
Market price per share of common stock at year-end	49.38	48.16	52.37	48.76	30.01
Average consumer price index	322.2	311.1	298.4	289.1	272.4

The following methods were used in the determination of estimated current cost amounts:

(1) The current cost of inventories has been estimated on the basis of standard costs adjusted to reflect current material, labor and overhead variances; however, it is estimated that the increases in overhead which would result by applying the current cost provisions for depreciation of plant and equipment and amortization of tooling are minor and therefore not included therein.

(2) The current cost of property, plant and equipment has been estimated on the basis of engineering studies, vendor quotes of current market prices, geographic construction costs, architectural estimates or by applying index numbers derived from published sources for the appropriate classifications of assets.

(3) The current cost of products sold are adjusted from historical cost amounts only for the effect of LIFO inventory liquidations.

(4) The current cost of depreciation and amortization has been estimated on a straight-line basis using the same estimates of useful life and salvage value utilized in preparing the historical cost financial statements. The estimated current cost of property, plant and equipment was used in determining the basis upon which the estimated current cost of depreciation and amortization was computed.

Calculations of cost of products sold and depreciation and amortization expense are based on current cost and do not give effect to efficiencies that could be derived by replacing existing assets with technologically improved assets.

Computations of supplementary information exclude any adjustments to or allocations of the amount of income tax expense included in the historical cost financial statements. The effective tax rate for 1985 of 42.1% on a historical cost basis rises to 48.1% on a current cost basis.

Report of Ernst & Whinney, Independent Auditors

The Stockholders and Board of Directors
Whirlpool Corporation
Benton Harbor, Michigan

We have examined the consolidated financial statements of Whirlpool Corporation and consolidated subsidiaries for each of the three years in the period ended December 31, 1985. Our examinations were made in accordance with generally accepted auditing standards and, accordingly, included such tests of the accounting records and such other auditing procedures as we considered necessary in the circumstances. We did not examine the financial statements of Whirlpool Acceptance Corporation, which were used as the basis for recording the Company's equity in net earnings of that corporation, or the financial statements of Inglis Limited, a consolidated subsidiary (see Note D), which statements reflect total assets and revenues constituting 6.2% and 7.1%, respectively, in 1985 of the related consolidated totals. These statements were examined by other independent auditors whose reports thereon have been furnished to us and our opinion expressed herein, insofar as it relates to the amounts included for Whirlpool Acceptance Corporation and Inglis Limited, is based on the reports of other independent auditors.

In our opinion, based upon our examinations and the reports of other independent auditors, the accompanying balance sheet and statements of operations, stockholders' equity, and changes in financial position present fairly the consolidated financial position of Whirlpool Corporation and consolidated subsidiaries at December 31, 1985 and 1984, and the consolidated results of their operations and changes in their financial position for each of the three years in the period ended December 31, 1985, in conformity with generally accepted accounting principles applied on a consistent basis.

Chicago, Illinois
January 23, 1986, except for
Note N, as to which the date
is January 31, 1986

Report by Management on the Financial Statements

The management of Whirlpool Corporation has prepared the accompanying financial statements. The financial statements have been examined by Ernst & Whinney, independent auditors, whose report, based upon their audit and the reports of other independent auditors, expresses the opinion that these financial statements present fairly the consolidated financial position and results of operations of Whirlpool Corporation and its consolidated subsidiaries (later referred to as "the Company") in accordance with generally accepted accounting principles. Their examination is conducted in accordance with generally accepted auditing standards and includes a review of internal controls and tests of transactions.

The financial statements were prepared from the Company's accounting records, books and accounts which, in reasonable detail, accurately and fairly reflect all material transactions or dispositions of assets. The Company maintains a system of internal controls designed to provide reasonable assurance that the Company's accounting records, books and accounts are accurate and that transactions are properly recorded in the Company's books and records, and the Company's assets are maintained and accounted for, in accordance with management's authorizations. The Company's accounting records, policies and internal controls are regularly reviewed by the Company's internal audit staff.

The Audit Committee of the Board of Directors of Whirlpool Corporation, which is comprised of three Directors who are not employed by the Company, considers and makes recommendations to the Board of Directors as to accounting and auditing matters concerning the Company, including recommending for appointment by the Board of Directors the firm of independent auditors who is engaged on an annual basis to audit the financial statements of Whirlpool Corporation and certain of its wholly owned subsidiaries. The Audit Committee meets with the independent auditors at least twice yearly to review the scope of the audit, the results of the audit and such recommendations as may be made by said auditors with respect to the Company's accounting methods and system of internal controls.

Sales and Income Information

Year Ended December 31 thousands of dollars	Percent	1985	1984	1983
Contribution to Net Sales by Class of Similar Products				
Major Home Appliances:				
Home laundry appliances	37.4%	$1,300,981	$1,136,664	$1,017,019
Home refrigeration and room air conditioning equipment	35.4	1,227,909	1,159,493	968,505
Other home appliances	19.9	690,792	581,771	476,104
	92.7	3,219,682	2,877,928	2,461,628
Other Products and Services	7.3	254,774	259,554	206,054
	100.0%	$3,474,456	$3,137,482	$2,667,682
Contributions to Earnings from Continuing Operations before Income Taxes and Minority Interest				
Major Home Appliances	75.4%	$ 242,484	$ 238,407	$ 209,374
Other Products and Services	8.0	25,691	23,128	16,856
Other Income	10.0	32,259	42,919	49,113
Equity in Net Earnings of Affiliated Companies	6.6	21,323	27,411	17,495
	100.0%	$ 321,757	$ 331,865	$ 292,838

GLOSSARY

Chapter numbers at the end of each entry indicate where elaborations on the term may be found.

Absorption Costing A product costing method in which all manufacturing costs are treated as product costs. (Ch. 25)

Accelerated Cost Recovery System (ACRS) A system of accelerated depreciation for tax purposes introduced in the 1981 Economic Recovery Tax Act; it prescribes depreciation rates by asset classifications for assets acquired after 1980. (Ch. 10)

Accelerated Depreciation Any depreciation method under which the amounts of depreciation expense taken in the early years of an asset's life are larger than those amounts taken later. (Ch. 10)

Account A record of the additions, deductions, and balances of individual assets, liabilities, owners' equity, revenue and expenses. The basic component of a formal accounting system. (Ch. 2)

Accounting The process of recording, classifying, reporting, and interpreting the financial data of an organization. (Ch. 1)

Accounting Cycle Steps in the processing of accounting transactions during the accounting year: (1) analyzing transactions, (2) recording in journals, (3) posting to general ledger, (4) adjusting accounts, (5) preparing financial statements, and (6) closing temporary accounts. (Ch. 3)

Accounting Entity Those people, assets, and activities devoted to a specific economic purpose and for which a separate accounting should be made. (Chs. 1, 13)

Accounting Equation An expression of the equivalency in dollar amounts of assets and equities in double-entry bookkeeping; often stated as Assets = Liabilities + Owners' Equity. (Ch. 1)

Accounting Period That time period, typically one year, to which accounting reports are related. (Ch. 13)

Accounting Principles *See* Generally Accepted Accounting Principles.

Accounting Transaction A business activity or event that requires accounting recognition. (Ch. 1)

Accrual Basis The accounting basis whereby revenue is recognized in the period earned whether actually received or not and expenses are recognized and matched with the related revenue of the period whether actually paid or not. (Ch. 1)

Accrue To accumulate or increase; also to recognize such accumulation or increase, usually during the adjustment step of the accounting cycle. (Ch. 3)

Accumulated Depreciation A contra account to the related asset account reflecting the cumulative amounts recorded as depreciation for a specific asset or group of assets. (Ch. 3)

Adjusted Gross Income An income tax term denoting the amount obtained by subtracting from gross income certain business expenses and expenses incurred in producing rents and royalties. (Ch. 28)

Adjusted Trial Balance A trial balance of the general ledger accounts taken after adjustments have been made. (Ch. 4)

Adjusting Entries Those entries resulting from an attempt to reflect in the accounts various changes that may be appropriate although no source document is normally available; usually made to align recorded costs or revenue with the accounting period or to reflect unrecorded revenue and costs. (Ch.3)

After-tax Cash Flow The net amount of any receipt or expenditure after incorporating the effects of income taxes. (Ch. 27)

AICPA The American Institute of Certified Public Accountants, the national professional organization of CPAs in the United States. (Ch. 1)

Allowance for Uncollectible Accounts A contra asset account with a normal credit balance shown on the balance sheet as a deduction from accounts receivable to reflect the expected realizable amount of accounts receivable. (Ch. 8)

Allowance Method An accounting procedure whereby in the

period in which credit sales occur, the related amount of uncollectible accounts expense is estimated and recorded in the contra asset account Allowance for Uncollectible Accounts. (Ch. 8)

Amortization The periodic writing off or charging to expense of some amount of cost (usually associated with intangible assets). (Ch. 11)

APB The Accounting Principles Board, a committee of the AICPA responsible for formulating accounting principles until it was replaced in 1973 by the FASB. (Chs. 1, 13)

Appropriation of Retained Earnings Segregation or restriction of a portion of retained earnings that reduces the amount that would otherwise be available for dividends. No transfer of funds is necessarily involved, and the aggregate amount of retained earnings remains unchanged. (Ch. 16)

Articles of Co-partnership The formal written agreement among partners setting forth important aspects of the partnership such as name, nature, duration, and location of the business, capital contributions, duties, and profit and loss ratios. (Ch. 14)

Articles of Incorporation A document prepared by persons organizing a corporation in the United States that sets forth the structure and purposes of the corporation and specifics regarding stock to be issued. (Ch. 15)

Assets Those economic resources of an entity that can usefully be expressed in monetary terms; some examples are cash, accounts receivable, inventories, and plant and equipment. (Ch. 1)

Average Collection Period Trade accounts receivable divided by year's sales multiplied by 365. (Ch. 20)

Average Rate of Return A method of capital outlay analysis that focuses on the ratio of expected average annual net income to the related average investment. (Ch. 27)

Balance Sheet A financial report showing the financial position of an entity in terms of assets, liabilities, and owners' equity at a specific date. (Ch. 1)

Balance Sheet Equation Assets = Liabilities + Owners' Equity. (Ch. 1)

Bank Reconciliation A procedure or analysis explaining the various items—such as deposits in transit, checks outstanding, bank charges, and errors—that lead to differences between the balance shown on a bank statement and the related Cash account in the general ledger. (Ch. 7)

Betterment A capital expenditure that improves the quality of services rendered by a plant asset but does not necessarily extend its useful life. (Ch. 10)

Bond A form of interest-bearing note payable, usually issued by the borrower for relatively long periods to a group of lenders. Bonds may incorporate a wide variety of special provisions relating to security for the debt involved, methods of paying the periodic interest payments, and maturity and retirement provisions. (Ch. 17)

Bond Discount Excess of the face value of a bond over its issue price. Bond discount arises when the coupon rate of the bond is below the market rate of interest for that type of bond. (Chs. 7, 17)

Bond Interest Coverage Income before interest expense and income taxes divided by bond interest. Sometimes called *times interest earned.* (Ch. 20)

Bond Premium The excess of the issue price of a bond over its face value. Bond premium arises when the coupon interest rate of the bond is greater than the market rate for that type of bond. (Chs. 7, 17)

Bond Sinking Fund A fund accumulated through required periodic contributions (and investment income thereon) to be used for the retirement of a specific bond issue. (Ch. 17)

Book Value per Share The dollar amount of net assets represented by one share of stock; computed by dividing the amount of stockholders' equity associated with a class of stock by the outstanding number of shares of that class of stock. (Ch. 15)

Branch Accounting The procedures for maintaining the financial records of various outlets of a single firm and coordinating the data with the home office records. (App. B)

Break-even Point That level of business volume at which total revenue equals total costs. (Ch. 24)

Budgeting A process of formal financial planning. (Ch. 26)

Byproducts Those products having relatively little sales value compared with other products derived from a process. An example would be the wood shavings generated in a shaping department of a furniture factory. (Ch. 23)

Calendar Year Firms are said to be on a calendar year when their accounting year ends on December 31. (Ch. 3)

Capital Budgeting Planning long-term investments in plant and equipment. (Ch. 27)

Capital Expenditure An expenditure that increases the book value of long-term assets. (Ch. 10)

Capital Gains and Losses Gains

and losses from the sale or exhange of certain assets qualifying as "capital assets." Specific tax treatment of capital gains and losses depends on the length of time for which the assets are held (short term for one year or less, long term otherwise) and the net result of combining long- and short-term gains and losses. (Ch. 28)

Capital Lease A lease that transfers to the lessee substantially all of the benefits and risks related to ownership of the property. The lessee records the leased property as an asset and establishes a liability for the lease obligation. (Ch. 11)

Capital Ratios The quantitative relationship among the balances of partners' capital accounts. This factor is often reflected in the distribution of partnership profits and may be calculated using either beginning or average balances. (Ch. 14)

Capitalization of Interest A process adding interest to an asset's initial cost if a period of time is required to prepare the asset for use. (Ch. 10)

Cash Basis The accounting basis in which revenue is recognized only when money is received and expenses are recognized when money is paid. (Chs. 1, 19)

Cash Discount An amount—often 1 or 2% of the purchase price—that a buyer may deduct for paying within the discount period. (Ch. 5)

Cash Flow *See* After-tax Cash Flow.

Cash Flow Statement Also called Statement of Cash Flows. A statement showing a firm's cash inflows and outflows, classified into operating, investing, and financing categories. (Ch. 19)

Cash Over and Short An account which contains the amounts by which actual daily cash collections differ from the amounts recorded as being collected. (Ch. 7)

Cash Payback Period A method of capital outlay analysis that considers the time in years that it will take the related net future cash inflows to equal the original investment. (Ch. 27)

Certificate of Deposit An investment security available at financial institutions generally offering a fixed rate of return for a specified period. (Ch. 7)

Chart of Accounts A list of all the account titles and numbers found in the general ledger. (Ch. 3)

Check Register A special journal used in place of a cash disbursements journal when the voucher system of controlling expenditures is used; a record of all checks written in payment of vouchers. (Ch. 6)

Check Truncation Canceled checks are not returned by a bank to its depositors when monthly bank statements are mailed. (Ch. 7)

Closing Procedures The final step in the accounting cycle in which the balances in all temporary accounts are transferred to the owner's capital or the Retained Earnings account, leaving the temporary accounts with zero balances. (Chs. 4, 5, 21, App. B)

Collection Bases Those procedures in which revenue recognition is delayed until related amounts of cash are collected. The cost recovery method and the installment method are examples. (Ch. 13)

Common-size Statements A form of financial statement analysis in which only the relative percentages of financial statement items, rather than their dollar amounts, are shown. (Ch. 20)

Common Stock Basic ownership class of corporate capital stock, carrying the right to vote, share in earnings, participate in future stock issues, and share in any liquidation proceeds after prior claims have been settled. (Ch. 15)

Comparative Financial Statements A form of horizontal financial analysis involving comparison of two or more periods' statements showing dollar and percentage changes. (Ch. 20)

Compensating Balance A minimum amount that a financial institution requires a firm to maintain in its account as part of a borrowing arrangement. (Ch. 7)

Complex Capital Structure A corporate capital structure containing one or more potentially dilutive securities. Complex capital structures normally require a dual earnings per share presentation. (Ch. 16)

Compound Journal Entry An entry containing more than one debit and/or credit entry. (Ch. 3)

Conceptual Framework A cohesive set of interrelated objectives and fundamentals for external financial reporting developed by the FASB. (Ch. 13)

Conservatism An accounting principle dictating that judgmental determinations in accounting should tend toward understatement rather than overstatement of assets and income. (Ch. 13)

Consistency An accounting principle dictating that, unless otherwise disclosed, accounting reports should be prepared on a basis consistent with the preceding period. (Ch. 13)

Consolidated Statements Financial statements prepared with intercompany (reciprocal) accounts eliminated to portray the financial position and operating results of two or more affiliated companies as a single economic entity. (Ch. 18)

Consolidation A union of firms

such that the existing firms exchange their properties for the securities of a new firm and the old firms dissolve. (Ch. 18)

Constant Dollar Accounting An accounting process that adjusts financial data for changes in the general purchasing power of the dollar. (Ch. 13)

Consumer Price Index A price-level index of consumer goods and services published monthly by the Bureau of Labor Statistics of the Departmen t of Labor. (Ch. 13)

Contingent Liability A potential obligation, the eventual occurence of which usually depends on some future event beyond the control of the firm. Contingent liabilities may originate with such things as lawsuits, credit guarantees, and contested income tax assessments. (Ch. 12)

Contribution Margin The excess of revenue over variable costs; thus, the amount contributed toward the absorption of fixed cost and eventually the generation of profit. (Ch. 24)

Contribution Margin Ratio That portion of the sales price that is contribution margin. (Ch. 24)

Control Account A general ledger account, the balance of which reflects the aggregate balance of many related subsidiary accounts. Most firms maintain such records for credit customers and for creditors. (Ch. 6, 11)

Controller Usually the highest ranking accounting officer in a firm. (Ch. 1)

Convertible Bond A bond incorporating the holder's right to convert the bond to capital stock under prescribed terms. (Ch. 17)

Corporation A legal entity created by the granting of a charter from an appropriate governmental authority and owned by stockholders who have limited liability for corporate debt. (Ch. 15)

Cost Behavior Analysis Study of the ways in which specific costs respond to changes in the volume of business activity. (Ch. 24)

Cost Center Sometimes called an *expense center.* A division of a business with which specific costs can be identified. (Ch. 25)

Cost Method A method of accounting by a parent company for investments in subsidiary companies in which the parent company maintains the investment in subsidiary account at its cost, not recognizing periodically its share of subsidiary income or loss. *See also* Equity Method. (Ch. 18)

Cost of Capital *See* Weighted Average Cost of Capital.

Cost of Goods Manufactured See Manufacturing Costs.

Costs of Goods Sold The cost of merchandise sold to customers during the accounting period. It is calculated by adding the beginning inventory and net cost of purchases and deducting the ending inventory. (Ch. 5)

CPA Certified Public Accountant, a professional accountant who has passed the Uniform CPA Examination, satisfied other requirements regarding education, professional experience, and character, and been licensed to practice public accounting by a state, district, or territory. (Ch. 1)

Credit (Entry) An entry on the right-hand side (or in the credit column) of any account. (Ch. 2)

Credit Memorandum A form used by a seller to notify a customer of a reduction in the amount considered owed by the customer. (Ch. 5)

Cumulative Preferred Stock A type of preferred stock upon which any dividends in arrears must be paid before dividends can be paid on common stock. (Ch. 15)

Current Assets Assets that will either be used up or converted to cash within the normal operating cycle of the business or one year, whichever is longer. (Ch. 5)

Current Cost Accounting A system of accounting that reflects assets and expenses at their current replacement cost amounts. (Ch. 13)

Current Liabilities Obligations that will require within the coming year or the operating cycle, whichever is longer, (1) the use of existing current assets or (2) the creation of other current liabilities. (Chs. 5, 12)

Current Ratio Current assets divided by current liabilities. (Ch. 20)

Debit (Entry) An entry on the left-hand side (or in the debit column) of any account. (Ch. 2)

Declaration of Estimated Tax Income tax procedures requiring taxpayers with minimum amounts of income not subject to income tax withholding to submit quarterly estimates and payments of related income taxes owed. (Ch. 28)

Deferred Tax Accounts Accounts used in interperiod income tax allocation procedure, in which are recorded differences between the amounts of income taxes actually paid and amounts recognized in the accounts. Excess payments are Deferred Tax Charges; an excess of amounts recognized over taxes paid are Deferred Tax Credits. (Ch. 17)

Deficit A negative (or debit) balance in a corporation's Retained Earnings account. (Ch. 16)

Departmental Contribution The excess of departmental revenue over variable departmental expenses; contributed to the absorption of the firm's pool of fixed costs and expenses. (Ch. 25)

Depletion The allocation of the

cost of natural resources to the units extracted from the ground or, in the case of timberland, the board feet of timber cut. (Ch. 11)

Depreciation The decline in economic potential of limited-life assets originating from wear, deterioration, and obsolescence. (Ch. 10)

Depreciation Expense That portion of the original utility and cost of a tangible constructed asset that is recognized as having expired and thus is an expense. (Chs. 3, 10)

Differential Analysis A concept of limiting consideration in a decision situation to only those factors that differ among alternatives. (Ch. 25)

Differential Costs Costs that differ between two courses of action. (Ch. 25)

Direct Expenses (Costs) Costs that can be readily identified with a particular department, product, or activity. (Ch. 25)

Direct Labor All labor of workers applying their skills directly to the manufacture of products. The labor of workers indirectly supporting the manufacturing process is accounted for as indirect labor, part of factory overhead. (Ch. 21)

Direct Material All important materials or parts physically making up the product. Incidental amounts of materials are accounted for as indirect materials, part of factory overhead. (Ch. 21)

Direct Write-off Method An accounting procedure in which uncollectible accounts are charged to expense in the period they are determined to be uncollectible. (Ch. 8)

Discontinued Operations Operating segments of a company that have been sold, abandoned, or disposed of during the operating period. Related operating income (or loss) and related gains or losses on disposal are reported separately on the income statement. (Ch. 16)

Discount Period The number of days beyond the related sales invoice date during which payment entitles the buyer to deduct any cash discount offered (often 1 or 2%). (Ch. 5)

Discounts Lost An account reflecting the amount of cash discounts available but not taken. *See* Net Price Method of Recording Purchases. (Ch. 5)

Dividend A distribution to a corporation's stockholders usually in cash; sometimes in the corporation's stock (called a *stock dividend*); and much less frequently in property (called a *dividend in kind*). (Chs. 15, 16)

Dividend Payout Ratio Common stock dividends divided by common stock earnings. (Ch. 20)

Dividend Yield Common stock dividends per share divided by the market price per share. (Ch. 20)

Double Declining-balance Depreciation Method A depreciation method that allocates depreciation expense to each year in an accelerated pattern by applying a constant percentage to the declining book value of the asset. (Ch. 10)

Double-entry Accounting System A method of accounting that recognizes the duality of a transaction (source and disposition) such that any change in one account also causes a change in another account. For example, the receipt of cash would result in an increase in the Cash account but would also require the recognition of an increase in a liability, owners' equity, or revenue account or a decrease in an expense account or in some other asset account. (Ch. 2)

Earnings per Share Net income less any preferred dividend requirements divided by the number of common shares outstanding. (Chs. 16, 20)

Effective Interest Amortization A method of allocating bond premium or discount to various periods that results in a constant effective rate of interest and varying periodic amortization allocations. (Ch. 17, App. A)

Effective Tax Rate The amount of tax liability divided by related taxable income. (Ch. 28)

Electronic Data Processing (EDP) The processing of data utilizing computer hardware and software. (Ch. 6)

Electronic Funds Transfer (EFT) A system for transferring funds among parties electronically, without the need for paper checks. (Ch. 7)

Equity Method A method of accounting by parent companies for investments in subsidiaries in which the parent's share of subsidiary income or loss is periodically recorded in the parent company's accounts. *See also* Cost Method. (Ch. 18)

Equity Ratio Stockholders' equity divided by total assets. (Ch. 20)

Equivalent Units The smaller number of full measures of work accomplished that is the equivalent of a larger number of partially accomplished work units. For example, 1,000 units 60% processed is equivalent to 600 units fully processed. (Ch. 23)

Excess Present Value Index Ratio of the total present value of net future cash flows to the related cash investment. (Ch. 27)

Expenses Expired costs incurred by a firm in the process of earning revenue. (Ch. 1)

Extraordinary Item A transaction or event that is unusual in nature and occurs infrequently. Gains and losses on such items are shown separately, net of tax effects, in the income statement. (Ch. 16)

Extraordinary Repair An expenditure that extends a plant asset's expected useful life beyond the original estimate. (Ch. 10)

Factory Overhead All manufacturing costs not considered direct material or direct labor, including indirect materials, indirect labor, factory depreciation, taxes, and insurance. (Ch. 21)

Fair Labor Standards Act An act establishing minimum wage, overtime pay, and equal pay standards for employees and setting the necessary recordkeeping requirements for employers. (Ch. 12)

FASB The Financial Accounting Standards Board, a nongovernmental group organized in 1973 to replace the Accounting Principles Board and to promulgate authoritative rules for the general practice of financial accounting. (Ch. 1)

Federal Unemployment Taxes (FUTA) A federal tax levied against employers to help finance administration of the various unemployment compensation programs operated by the states. (Ch. 12)

FICA Federal Insurance Contributions Act, under which the income of an individual is taxed to support a national social security program providing retirement income, medical care, and death benefits. Employers pay a matching amount of tax on their eligible employees. (Ch. 12)

FIFO (First-in, First-out) Inventory Pricing A valuation method that assumes that the oldest (earliest purchased) goods on hand are sold first, resulting in an ending inventory priced at the most recent acquisition prices. (Ch. 9)

Financial Accounting Those accounting activities leading primarily to publishable, general-purpose financial statements such as the income statment, balance sheet, and statement of changes in financial position. (Ch. 1)

Finished Goods Inventory Units of product for which production has been completed. (Ch. 21)

Finished Goods Ledger A record of the amounts acquired, sold, and on hand, and the related costs of a specific finished product. In aggregate, finished goods ledger cards are a perpetual inventory record of finished goods and a subsidiary ledger for the Finished Goods Inventory account. (Ch. 22)

Fiscal Year Firms are said to be on a fiscal year when their accounting year ends on a date other than December 31. (Ch. 3)

Fixed Assets Sometimes called long-term assets, long-lived assets, or plant and equipment. May include land, buildings, fixtures, and equipment. (Ch. 10)

Fixed Costs Costs whose total remains constant within the relevant range even though the volume of activity may vary (Ch. 24)

Flexible Budget A financial plan formulated so that the assumed operating volume can be varied to agree with actual volume of activities attained. (Chs. 24, 26)

F.O.B. (Free on Board) Term used in conjunction with the terms factory, shipping point, or destination to indicate the point in the delivery of merchandise at which the purchaser bears freight costs. (Ch. 5)

Foreign Currency Transaction A transaction whose terms are fixed in the amount of foreign currency to be paid or received. (App. C)

Foreign Exchange Gain or Loss A gain or loss arising from a change in exchange rates before a foreign currency transaction is settled. (App. C)

Full Disclosure An accounting principle stipulating the disclosure of all facts necessary to make financial statements useful to readers. (Ch. 13)

Functional Currency The currency of the primary economic environment in which a foreign entity operates. (App. C)

Funds Defined most narrowly as cash; also defined as the amount of working capital or current assets less current liabilities. (Ch. 19)

General Journal A record of original entry in which are recorded all transactions not recorded in the special journals maintained by the business. (Ch. 6)

General Ledger A grouping or binding of the accounts in which the activities of an entity are recorded. (Ch. 2)

Generally Accepted Accounting Principles A group of standards or guides to action in preparing financial accounting reports. Their content and usefulness have evolved over many decades. (Chs. 1, 13)

Going Concern An accounting principle dictating that, in the absence of evidence to the contrary, a business is assumed to have an indefinite life. (Chs. 1, 13)

Goodwill The value that derives from a firm's ability to earn more than a normal rate of return on its physical assets. Goodwill is recognized in the accounts only when it is acquired through specific purchase and payment (as opposed to gradual development). (Ch. 11)

Governmental Accounting A subdivision of accounting practice relating primarily to accounting for federal, state, or local governmental units. (Ch. 1)

Gross Profit The excess of sales price over the net delivered cost of the product sold (sometimes called gross margin). (Ch. 5)

Gross Profit Inventory Method A procedure for estimating the cost of ending inventories by multiplying the representative cost of goods sold percentage times sales and deducting that amount from goods available for sale. (Ch. 9)

Hardware A term that describes the computer and its associated equipment. (Ch. 6)

Historical Cost The money equivalent of the object given up (and/or obligations assumed) in an exchange transaction. (Chs. 1, 13)

Horizontal Analysis *See* Trend Analysis.

Income The increase in the net assets of a firm from its operating activities during a period of time; also known as net income, profits, or earnings. Income is measured by subtracting expenses incurred from revenue earned. (Ch. 1)

Income Statement A financial report showing the results of an entity's operations in terms of revenue, expenses, and net income for a period of time. (Chs. 1, 16)

Income Summary Account An account used only during closing procedures and to which all temporary revenue and expense accounts are closed. At this point, the balance in the Income Summary account summarizes the firm's net income for the period. In turn, the Income Summary account is closed to the owner's capital or the Retained Earnings account. (Ch. 4)

Indirect Expenses (Costs) Costs (expenses) that are not readily identified with products or activities; usually allocated by some arbitrary formula to various products and activities. (Ch. 25)

Individual Earnings Record A detailed record maintained by an employer for each employee showing gross earnings, overtime premiums, all withholdings, payroll tax data, and net earnings paid, by calendar quarter. (Ch. 12)

Information System The coordinated efforts to record, organize, and present analyses and reports related to specific areas of activity and concern. (Ch. 1)

Installment Accounts The accounts receivable or payable for which payments or collections are routinely scheduled over extended periods, such as 24 or 36 months. (Ch. 8)

Intangible Assets A term applied by convention to a group of long-term assets that generally do not have physical existence, including patents, copyrights, franchises, trademarks, and goodwill. (Ch. 11)

Interactive Processing A type of processing in which master file information in an electronic data-processing system is available at random, and transactions may be processed in any order. (Ch. 6)

Interim Financial Statements Financial statements prepared at dates other than the firm's accounting year-end. Most monthly and quarterly financial statements are interim statements. (Chs. 4, 13)

Internal Auditing A continuing appraisal of a firm's operations accomplished by the firm's own internal audit staff to determine whether management's financial and operating policies are being properly implemented. (Chs. 1, 7)

Internal Control A plan of organization and all of the coordinate methods and measures adopted within a business to safeguard its assets, check the accuracy and reliability of its accounting data, promote operating efficiency, and encourage adherence to prescribed managerial policies. (Ch. 7)

Internal Revenue Code The codification of numerous revenue acts passed by Congress since 1913. Interpretation and application of the Code is supplemented by extensive Internal Revenue Code Regulations. (Ch. 28)

Interperiod Income Tax Allocation Apportionment of income tax expense to the income statement over the periods affected by timing differences between the recognition of revenue and expense on accounting statements and on related income tax returns. (Ch. 17)

Inventory A significant current asset for merchandisers and manufacturers. *See also* Finished Goods Inventory, Materials Inventory, Merchandise Inventory, and Work-in-Process Inventory. (Chs. 5, 21)

Inventory Turnover Cost of goods sold divided by average inventory. (Ch. 20)

Investments A category on the balance sheet where assets consisting of securities of other companies, sinking funds, and other long-term holdings are reported. Temporary investments in marketable securities are properly shown as current assets. (Chs. 7, 18)

Invoice A document used in business transactions that sets forth the precise terms regarding date, customer, vendor, quantities, prices, and freight and credit terms of a transaction. (Ch. 5)

Invoice Register A special journal, sometimes called a purchases journal, in which all acquisitions on account are chronologically recorded. (Ch.6)

IRS The Internal Revenue Service of the federal government, primarily responsible for applying the current tax codes and regulations and collecting income taxes for the federal government. (Ch. 28)

Job Cost Sheets A record of the specific manufacturing costs applied to a given job. When fully recorded, job cost sheets are a subsidiary ledger to the Work in Process Inventory account. (Ch. 22)

Job Order Cost Accounting A method of cost accounting—sometimes called job lot or specific order costing—in which manufacturing costs are assigned to specific jobs or batches of specialized products. (Ch. 22)

Joint Costs Costs common to two or more products or activities. (Ch. 23)

Joint Products Two or more products having significant value and derived from common inputs such as materials or processing. (Ch. 23)

Journals Tabular records in which business transactions are analyzed in terms of debits and credits and recorded in chronological order before being posted to the general ledger accounts. (Ch. 3)

Lease A contract between a lessor (owner) and lessee (tenant) for the rental of property. (Ch. 11)

Leasehold Improvements Expenditures made by the lessee to alter or improve leased property. Such improvements typically revert to the lessor on termination of the lease. (Ch.11)

Liabilities Present obligations resulting from past transactions that require the firm to pay money, provide goods, or perform services in the future. (Ch. 12)

LIFO (Last-in, First-out) Inventory Pricing A valuation method that assumes that the most recently purchased goods are sold first, resulting in an ending inventory priced at the earliest related acquisition prices. (Ch. 9)

Long-term Assets Relatively long-lived assets employed in operating the firm. Some examples are land, buildings, equipment, natural resources, and intangible assets. (Chs. 5, 10, 11)

Long-term Liabilities Debt obligations of the firm not due within the firm's current operating cycle or one year, whichever is longer. Examples are mortgage notes payable and bonds payable. (Chs. 5, 17)

Lower of Cost or Market Rule An accounting procedure providing for inventories to be carried at their acquisition price or their replacement price at the balance sheet date, whichever is lower. A similar rule applies to stock investment portfolios. (Chs. 7, 9, 18)

Managerial Accounting The accounting procedures carried out by an organization's accounting staff primarily to furnish its management with accounting analyses and reports needed for decision making. (Chs. 1, 25)

Manufacturing Costs Those costs—comprising direct material, direct labor, and factory overhead—necessary to bring the product to completion. Selling and nonfactory administrative costs are specifically excluded. (Ch. 21)

Manufacturing Margin The excess of revenue over variable manufacturing costs; an amount often presented on variable costing income statements. (Ch. 25)

Manufacturing Summary Account An account (used only during closing procedures) to which all temporary manufacturing costs and expenses are closed, resulting in a balance equal to the cost of goods manufactured. In turn, the Manufacturing Summary account is closed to the Income Summary account. (Ch. 21)

Margin of Safety The amount by which the actual sales level exceeds the break-even sales level. (Ch. 24)

Marginal Cost The cost associated with completing one more unit of production or activity. (Ch. 25)

Marginal Tax Rate The tax rate applicable to additional increments of taxable income, especially relevant to considering the after-tax consequence of proposed transactions. (Ch. 28)

Mark-up Percentage The amount of gross profit expressed as a percentage of sales. (Ch. 5)

Master Budget A comprehensive plan comprising all operating budgets related to sales, production, operating expenses, and finance. May include pro forma financial statements for the budgeting period. (Ch. 26)

Matching Expenses with Revenue An accounting principle requiring that, to the extent feasible, all expenses related to given revenue be deducted from that revenue for the determination of periodic income. (Ch. 13)

Materiality The concept that accounting transactions so small or insignificant that they do not affect one's actions may be recorded as is most expedient. (Ch. 13)

Materials Inventory All factory materials acquired but not yet placed in production. (Ch. 21)

Measuring Unit The unit of

measure in an accounting transaction, typically the base money unit of the most relevant currency. (Chs. 1, 13)

Merchandise Inventory An asset account in which is recorded the purchase price of merchandise held for resale. Sometimes simply termed *inventory*. (Ch. 5)

Merchandising The business activity of buying and selling goods already made, in contrast to a manufacturer or a service-oriented business. (Ch. 5)

Merger A union of firms in which one company acquires the assets of another and the latter company dissolves. (Ch. 18)

Minority Interest That portion of capital stock in a subsidiary corporation not owned by the controlling (parent) company. (Ch. 18)

Monetary Assets Cash and other assets that represent the right to receive a fixed number of dollars in the future, regardless of price-level changes. (Ch. 13)

Monetary Liabilities Obligations to disburse a fixed number of dollars in the future, regardless of price-level changes. (Ch. 13)

Moving Average Inventory Pricing A pricing method under a perpetual inventory system that recomputes an average unit cost of goods on hand each time a purchase occurs and uses that average unit cost to determine the cost of goods sold for each sale. (Ch. 9)

Multiple-step Income Statement An income statement in which one or more intermediate amounts (such as gross profit on sales) are derived before the ordinary, continuing income is reported. (Ch. 16)

Natural Resources Assets such as timber, petroleum, natural gas, coal, and other mineral deposits mined by the extractive industries. (Ch. 11)

Net Assets Total assets less total liabilities. Net assets are equal to owners' equity. (Ch. 1)

Net Income The excess of revenue earned over related expenses incurred, usually the final figure on the income statement. (Ch. 1)

Net Present Value Analysis A method of capital outlay analysis that compares a required investment amount with the present value of resulting net future cash flows discounted at the minimum desired rate of return. (Ch. 27)

Net Price Method of Recording Purchase An accounting procedure whereby purchases are recorded at amounts that anticipate the taking of any cash discounts available. When discounts are not taken, the amounts paid in excess of the recorded purchase price are charged to a Discounts Lost account. (Ch. 5)

Net Realizable Value An asset measure computed by subtracting the expected completion and disposal costs from the asset's estimated selling price. (Ch. 9)

Normal Balance The debit or credit balance of an account corresponding to the side of the account on which increases are recorded (debits for assets and expenses; credits for liabilities, owners' equity, and revenue). (Ch. 2)

Objectivity An accounting principle requiring that, whenever possible, accounting entries be based on objective (verifiable) evidence. (Chs. 1, 13)

Organization Costs Expenditures incurred in launching a business (usually a corporation); may include attorney's fees, various registration fees paid to state governments, and other start-up costs. (Ch. 11)

Overapplied Overhead The excess of overhead applied to production over the amount of overhead incurred. Such amounts are shown on interim balance sheets as deferred credits but are closed to cost of goods sold on year-end financial statements. (Ch. 22)

Overhead Rate The amount of overhead costs for some period divided by the amount of some measure of production activity such as direct labor hours. May be calculated on an actual cost incurred basis or on an estimated or predetermined basis. (Ch. 22)

Owners' Equity The interest or claim of an entity's owners in the entity's assets; equal to the excess of assets over liabilities. (Ch. 1)

Parent Company A company holding all or a majority of the stock of another company, which is called a subsidiary. (Ch. 18)

Partnership A voluntary association of two or more persons for the purpose of conducting a business for a profit. (Ch. 14)

Par Value An amount specified in the corporate charter for each share of stock and imprinted on the face of each stock certificate. Usually determines the legal capital of the corporation. (Ch. 15)

Payroll Register A detailed list, prepared each pay period, showing each employee's earnings and deductions for the period. (Ch. 12)

Percentage Depletion A depletion deduction permitted for tax purposes that is a specified percentage of the gross revenue from mining activities, with certain limitations. (Ch. 11)

Percentage of Completion A method of revenue recognition that allocates the estimated gross profit on a long-term project among the several accounting periods involved, in proportion to the estimated percentage of the contract completed each period. (Ch. 13)

Performance Reports Documents portraying, for a given operating unit, planned amounts of cost, actual costs incurred, and any related variances. (Ch. 25)

Period Costs (Expenses) Costs (expenses) associated with the period in which they are incurred (rather than with the product being produced). (Ch. 21)

Periodic Inventory Method A method of accounting for inventories in which no record is made in the Inventory account for the purchase or sale of merchandise at the time of such transactions. (Chs. 5, 9)

Perpetual Inventory Method A method of accounting for inventories in which both purchases and sales of merchandise are reflected in the Inventory account at the time such transactions occur. (Ch. 9)

Personal Exemptions A prescribed amount that a taxpayer may deduct for himself or herself and each qualified dependent in computing taxable income. (Ch. 28)

Petty Cash Fund A special, relatively small cash fund established for making minor cash disbursements in the operation of a business. (Ch. 7)

Plant Assets A firm's property, plant, and equipment. (Ch. 10)

Pooling of Interests Uniting the ownership interests of two or more companies through the exchange of 90% or more of the firms' voting stocks. (Ch. 18)

Post-closing Trial Balance A list of account titles and their balances after closing entries have been recorded and posted; all temporary accounts should have zero balances. (Ch. 4)

Posting The formal transcribing of amounts from the journals to the ledger(s) used in an accounting system. (Ch. 3)

Posting References A series of abbreviations used in the posting step of the accounting cycle that indicate to where or from where some entry is posted; account numbers and one- or two-letter abbreviations of journal titles are typically used. (Ch. 3)

Predetermined Overhead Rates Estimated overhead rates determined in advance for applying overhead to production during an operating period (usually one year). The rate is calculated by dividing total estimated overhead costs by the estimated amount of the activity (such as direct labor hours) used to assign factory overhead. *See also* Factory Overhead. (Ch. 22)

Preemptive Right The right of a stockholder to maintain his or her proportionate ownership in a corporation by having the right to purchase an appropriate share of any new stock issue. (Ch. 15)

Preferred Dividend Coverage Operating income divided by the sum of the annual bond interest and preferred dividend requirements. (Ch. 20)

Preferred Stock A class of corporate capital stock typically receiving priority over common stock in dividend payments and distribution of assets should the corporation be liquidated. (Ch. 15)

Present Value The estimated current worth of amounts to be received (or paid) in the future from which appropriate amounts of discount (or interest) have been deducted. (Ch. 17, App. A, Ch. 27)

Present Value Factors Sometimes called discount factors. Multipliers found in present value tables formulated to show the present value of $1 (or a $1 annuity) discounted at various interest rates and for various periods. (Ch. 17, App. A, Ch. 27, App. E)

Price–Earnings Ratio The market price of a share of stock divided by the related earnings per share. (Ch. 20)

Price Index A series of measurements, stated as percentages, indicating the relationship between the weighted average price of a sample of goods and services at various points in time and the weighted average price of a similar sample of goods and services at a common, or base, date. (Ch. 13)

Prior Service Cost The cost of providing retirement benefits earned by employees prior to the adoption or amendment of a pension plan. (Ch. 17)

Process Cost Accounting A method of assigning costs to relatively homogeneous products in an often continuous, high-volume operation. (Ch. 23)

Product Costs The costs properly associated with the product being produced (as opposed to the period in which the costs are incurred). Product costs are period costs (expenses) when the related products are sold. (Ch. 21)

Production Cost Report A report that allocates a department's total production costs for a period to units transferred out and to units in ending work in process. (Ch. 23)

Production Report A report (usually for a department) showing the beginning inventory of units, units started, units finished and transferred out, and any ending inventory of units. (Ch. 23)

Productivity Ratio *See* Return on Assets.

Promissory Note A written promise to pay a certain sum of money on demand or at a determinable future time (Ch. 8)

Proprietorship A form of business organization in which one person owns the business; sometimes termed *sole proprietorship.* (Ch. 1)

Purchase Method A procedure that treats a business combination from the viewpoint of the acquiring company as a purchase transaction. (Ch. 18)

Purchase Order A document completed by the purchasing firm setting forth the quantities, descriptions, prices, and vendors for merchandise to be purchased. (Ch. 5)

Purchase Requisition A form used within a firm to initiate the procedures leading to the purchase of needed items. (Ch. 5)

Purchases The title of the account in which is recorded the acquisition price of merchandise held for resale by companies using the periodic inventory method. (Ch. 5)

Purchasing Power Gain or Loss on Monetary Items The gain or loss in general purchasing power that results from holding monetary assets or owing monetary liabilities during periods of inflation or deflation. (Ch. 13)

Quick Ratio The total of cash, marketable securities, and receivables divided by current liabilities. (Ch. 20)

Realized Revenue is realized when the goods or services are exchanged for cash or claims to cash. (Ch. 13)

Real Time Processing Updating computer records when the transactions occur. (Ch. 6)

Receivable An amount due from a customer, employee, or other party; usually further described as an account receivable or note receivable and representing an asset of the business. (Ch. 8)

Receiving Report A document used within a firm to record formally the quantities and descriptions of merchandise received. (Ch. 5)

Records of Original Entry Usually the various journals incorporated in the firm's accounting system. *See also* Journals. (Ch. 3)

Relevant Range The range of changes in the volume of activity within which the assumptions made regarding cost behavior patterns are valid. (Ch. 24)

Remeasurement Procedures A process of converting foreign currency financial statements to U.S. dollars which essentially produces the same U.S. dollar financial statements as if the foreign entity's records had been initially maintained in the U.S. dollar. (App. C)

Research and Development Costs Expenditures made in the search for new knowledge and in the translation of this knowledge into new or significantly improved products or processes. (Ch. 11)

Retail Inventory Estimation Method A procedure for estimating ending inventories by (1) maintaining detailed records of all goods acquired and on hand at both retail and cost prices (and any changes in these), (2) calculating a cost-to-retail percentage, (3) estimating ending inventory at retail prices by subtracting sales from the retail price of merchandise available for sale, and (4) reducing the estimated inventory at retail to cost by applying the cost-to-retail percentage. (Ch. 9)

Retained Earnings Statement A statement showing the changes in retained earnings for the accounting period, including net income or loss, dividends declared, appropriations, and corrections of any errors in financial statements of prior periods. (Ch. 16)

Return on Assets Operating income divided by average total assets. (Ch. 20)

Return on Sales Net income divided by net sales. (Ch. 20)

Return on Stockholders' Equity Net income less preferred dividends divided by average common stockholders' equity. (Ch. 20)

Revenue The amount of cash received or claims established against customers stemming from the provision of goods or services by the firm. (Chs. 1, 13)

Revenue Expenditure An expenditure related to plant assets that is expensed when incurred. (Ch. 10)

Revenue Recognition at Point of Sale An accounting principle requiring that, with few exceptions, revenue be recognized at the point of sale. (Ch. 13)

Reversing Entries A bookkeeping technique whereby adjusting entries involving subsequent receipts or payments are literally reversed on the first day of the following accounting period. This procedure permits the routine recording of subsequent related receipts and payments without having to recognize the portions that were accrued at an earlier date. (Ch. 4)

Running Balance Account An account form having columns for debit entries, credit entries, and for the account balance. Sometimes called the *three-column* account form. (Ch. 2)

Sales The title of the account in which revenue from the sale of goods held for resale is recorded for merchandising and manufacturing companies. (Ch. 5)

Sales Returns and Allowances A contra account to Sales in which is recorded the selling price of merchandise returned by customers and/or the amounts of sales price adjustments allowed customers. (Ch. 5)

S Corporations Corporations that qualify for income tax treatment as partnerships. (Ch. 28)

SEC Securities and Exchange Commission, the federal agency that regulates the sale and exchange of most securities. (Ch. 1)

Semivariable Costs Those costs, sometimes called *mixed costs,* whose total responds, but less than proportionately, to changes in the volume of activity. (Ch. 24)

Service Departments Departments or cost centers that provide special support activities to various production departments. Examples are purchasing, personnel, and maintenance departments. (Ch. 23)

Single-step Income Statement An income statement in which the ordinary, continuing income of the business is derived in one step by subtracting total expenses from total revenue. (Ch. 16)

Sinking Fund Cash and other assets accumulated and segregated for some specific purpose such as retiring debt. (Ch. 17)

Software A term that describes the programs, written procedures, and other documentation associated with use of computers. (Chs. 6, 11)

Source Document Any written document evidencing an accounting transaction, such as a bank check or deposit slip, sales invoice, or cash register tape. (Ch. 3)

Special Journals The records of original entry other than the general journal that are designed for recording specific types of transactions such as cash receipts, sales, purchases, and cash disbursements. (Ch. 6)

Specific Identification Inventory Pricing A method involving the physical identification of goods actually sold and goods remaining on hand and pricing the latter at the actual prices paid for them. (Ch. 9)

Standard Costs Those costs, usually expressed on a per-unit basis, that under ideal operating conditions should be incurred for direct material, direct labor, and factory overhead. (Ch. 26)

State Unemployment Tax A payroll tax levied on employers by states to finance state unemployment compensation programs. (Ch. 12)

Stated Value A nominal amount that may be assigned to each share of no-par stock and accounted for much as if it were par value. (Ch. 15)

Statement of Cash Flows A financial statement showing a firm's cash inflows and cash outflows for a specific period, classified into operating, investing, and financing categories. (Ch. 19)

Statement of Financial Position An alternate title for a balance sheet, a financial statement showing an entity's financial position in terms of assets, liabilities, and owners' equity at a specific date. (Ch. 1)

Statement of Owners' Equity A financial statement reflecting the beginning balance, additions to, deductions from, and the ending balance of owners' equity for a specified period. (Ch. 1)

Statement of Partnership Liquidation A statement summarizing the liquidation events of a partnership and the effect these events have on each partner's capital. (Ch. 14)

Stock Dividends Additional shares of its own stock issued by a corporation to its current stockholders in proportion to their ownership interests. (Ch. 16)

Stock Split Additional shares of its own stock issued by a corporation to its current stockholders in proportion to their current ownership interests without changing the balances in the related stockholders' equity accounts. A stock split increases the number of shares outstanding and reduces the per-share market value of the stock. (Ch. 16)

Stock Subscriptions Contracts for acquiring stock on a deferred payment plan, often used when shares are sold directly rather than through an investment banker. (Ch. 15)

Straight-line Depreciation Method Allocates uniform amounts of depreciation expense to each full period of an asset's useful life. (Ch. 10)

Subsidiary Company *See* Parent Company.

Subsidiary Ledger A group of accounts, not part of the general ledger, that explain or reflect the detail (such as individual customer balances) underlying the balance in a related control account (such as Accounts Receivable) in the general ledger. (Chs. 6, 11)

Sum-of-the-Years'-Digits Depreciation Method An accelerated depreciation method that allocates depreciation expense to each year in a fractional proportion, the denominator of which is the sum of the years' digits in the useful life of the asset. (Ch. 10)

Summary of Significant Accounting Policies A financial statement disclosure, usually the initial note to the statements, that identifies the major accounting policies and procedures used by the company. (Ch. 13)

T Account An abbreviated form of the formal account; use is usually limited to illustrations of accounting techniques. (Ch. 2)

Tax Allocation within a Period The apportionment of total income taxes among the various sources of income or loss shown on an income statement. (Ch. 16)

Tax Avoidance Arranging business affairs to minimize the impact of income taxes; in contrast to tax evasion, tax avoidance is legal and considered an aspect of sound management. (Ch. 28)

Tax Credit (or Income Tax Credit) An amount that may be deducted directly from what would otherwise be the tax liability disregarding the tax credit. (Ch. 28)

Tax Evasion A deliberate misstatement of factors determining taxable income. Tax evasion is illegal and subjects the taxpayer to legal prosecution. *See also* Tax Avoidance. (Ch. 28)

Tax Shelter An investment that by its nature or by qualifying for special tax treatment creates either tax-exempt income or anticipated deductible tax losses (which shelter other income from income taxation). (Ch. 28)

Taxable Income Gross income less deductions from gross income, excess itemized deductions, and personal exemptions. (Ch. 28)

Time Value of Money An expression of the ability of money to earn interest, the total potential for which is a function of the principal amount, the applicable interest rate, and the time period involved. (Ch. 17, App. A, Ch. 27)

Timing Difference A revenue or expense amount that is recognized in one accounting period for tax purposes and in a different accounting period for financial reporting purposes. (Ch. 17)

Trade Discounts The differences between suggested retail prices and the prices at which wholesale purchasers are able to buy merchandise. (Ch. 5)

Trade Receivables and Payables Assets and liabilities arising from the ordinary open account transactions between a business and its regular trade customers or suppliers. (Ch. 8)

Trading on the Equity The use of borrowed funds to generate a return in excess of the interest rate that must be paid for the funds. (Ch. 20)

Transaction Any event or activity of the firm leading to entries in two or more accounts. (Ch. 1)

Translation Procedures A process of converting foreign currency financial statements to U.S. dollars which retains, in the converted data, the financial results and relationships among assets and liabilities that were created by the entity's operations in its foreign environment. (App. C)

Transporation In An account for recording the freight charges on merchandise purchased and held for resale. (Ch. 5)

Transportation Out An account for recording the freight charges incurred in the delivery of merchandise sold to customers. (Ch. 5)

Treasury Stock Shares of outstanding stock that have been reacquired by the issuing corporation for purposes other than retiring the stock. Treasury stock is recorded at cost and the account is shown on the balance sheet as a deduction from total stockholders' equity. (Ch. 15)

Trend Analysis An approach to financial statement analysis involving comparison of the same item over two or more years. Often trend percentages are calculated by choosing a base year and stating the amounts of subsequent years as percentages of that base year. (Ch. 20)

Trial Balance A list of the account titles in the general ledger, their respective debit or credit balances, and the totals of all accounts having debit balances and all accounts having credit balances. (Ch. 2)

Unadjusted Trial Balance A trial balance of the general ledger accounts taken before the adjusting step of the accounting cycle. (Ch. 4)

Uncollectible Accounts Expense The expense stemming from the inability of a business to collect an amount previously recorded as a receivable. Sometimes called bad debts expense. Normally classified as a selling or administrative expense. (Ch. 8)

Underapplied Overhead The excess of actual overhead costs incurred over the amounts applied to production. On interim balance sheets such amounts appear as deferred charges but are closed to cost of goods sold on year-end statements. (Ch. 22)

Units-of-Production Depreciation Method A depreciation method that allocates depreciation expense to each operating period in proportion to the amount of the asset's expected total production capacity used each period. (Ch. 10)

Variable Costing A product costing method in which only variable manufacturing costs are associated with the product; fixed manufacturing costs are treated as period costs in the period incurred. (Ch. 25)

Variable Costs Those costs the total of which responds proportionately to changes in volume of activity. (Ch. 25)

Variances Favorable or unfavorable differences between standard costs and actual costs. Variances are usually isolated for price and usage factors for direct materials and rate and efficiency factors for direct labor. For factory overhead, variances may be isolated for factors related to spending, efficiency, and volume. (Ch. 26, App. D)

Vertical Analysis An approach to financial statement analysis highlighting the quantitative relationship between amounts in the same financial statement. (Ch. 20)

Voucher Register A special journal or record of original entry (in lieu of a purchases journal) for recording in numerical order all vouchers supporting the disbursement of funds. (Ch. 6)

Voucher System A system for controlling expenditures requiring the preparation and approval of individual vouchers for each contemplated expenditure. (Ch. 6)

Weighted Average Cost of Capital Expressed as a percentage, the cost to the firm of acquiring investment capital, weighted to reflect the specific cost rates associated with and proportions used from specific sources such as equity securities, debt, and internally generated funds. (Ch. 27)

Weighted Average Inventory Pricing A method that spreads the total dollar cost of all goods available for sale equally among all units. (Ch. 9)

Withdrawals (Owners') The amounts that proprietors or partners withdraw, usually in cash and for personal objectives, from the assets of the firm. (Chs. 1, 14)

Working Capital The excess of current assets over current liabilities. (Chs. 1, 19)

Work-in-Process Inventory All units of product that are in the process of being manufactured. (Ch. 21)

Worksheet An informal accounting document used to facilitate the preparation of financial statements. (Chs. 4, 5, 19, 21)

Yield See Dividend Yield.

Zero-base Budgeting A budgeting process that requires each budgetary unit to justify all of its expenditures as if the unit's operations were just starting. (Ch. 26)

INDEX

D

A 6
B 7
C 8
D 9
E 0
F 1
G 2
H 3
I 4
J 5